THE ALMANAC
OF
AMERICAN
EDUCATION
2007

THE ALMANAC
OF
AMERICAN
EDUCATION
2007

EDITED BY DEIRDRE A. GAQUIN AND MARY MEGHAN RYAN

BERNAN PRESS

ISBN: 978-1-59888-081-6
ISSN: 1548-6346

Cover photo: www.punchstock.com

Composed and printed by Automated Graphic Systems, Inc., White Plains, MD, on acid-free paper that meets the American National Standards Institute Z39-48 standard.

2008 2007   4 3 2 1

BERNAN PRESS
4611-F Assembly Drive
Lanham, MD 20706
800-274-4447
email: info@bernan.com
www.bernan.com

Contents

Tables

PART A—NATIONAL SCHOOL ENROLLMENT AND EDUCATIONAL ATTAINMENT STATISTICS

ENROLLMENT TABLES

HISTORICAL ENROLLMENT TABLES

Figures

PART B—EDUCATION STATISTICS BY STATE

PART C—EDUCATION STATISTICS BY COUNTY

Preface

This edition of *The Almanac of American Education* serves as a guide to understanding and comparing the quality of education at the national, state, and county levels. Compiled from sources such as the U.S. Census Bureau and the National Center for Education Statistics (NCES), *The Almanac* contains historical and current data, insightful analysis, and useful graphics that paint a compelling picture of the state of education in the United States.

The Almanac is organized into three sections: Part A—National School Enrollment and Educational Attainment; Part B—Region and State Education Statistics; and Part C—County Education Statistics. The data presented in Part A are no longer available in print form from the Census Bureau. The data in Parts B and C have been specially tabulated for this publication from the NCES, the Census Bureau, and other sources.

The Almanac's contents and coverage allows users to answer—and ask—important questions about education, including:

- What are the nationwide trends in earnings by educational attainment level?
- Is the earnings gap between high school graduates and college graduates growing or shrinking?
- Which states have the highest and lowest high school dropout rates?
- Which states have the largest county-to-county variation in student-teacher ratios?
- Is there a relationship between student poverty rates and county-level expenditures per student?

The data in this volume meet the publication standards of the federal statistical agencies and the few nongovernmental organizations from which they were obtained. Every effort has been made to select accurate, meaningful, and useful data. All statistical data are subject to error arising from sampling variability, reporting errors, incomplete coverage, imputation, and other causes. The responsibility of the editors and publisher of this volume is limited to reasonable care in the reproduction and presentation of data obtained from established sources.

Deirdre A. Gaquin and Mary Meghan Ryan have edited this edition of *The Almanac of American Education*. Ms. Gaquin has been a data use consultant to private organizations, government agencies, and universities for over 25 years. Prior to that, she was director of Data Access Services at Data Use & Access Laboratories, a pioneer in private sector distribution of federal statistical data. A former president of the Association of Public Data Users, Ms. Gaquin has served on numerous boards, panels, and task forces concerned with federal statistical data and has worked on four decennial censuses. She holds a Master of Urban Planning (MUP) degree from Hunter College. Ms. Gaquin is also an editor of Bernan's *The Who, What, and Where of America: Understanding the Census Results*; *County and City Extra: Annual Metro, City, and County Data Book*; and *Places, Towns and Townships*.

Mary Meghan Ryan is a research editor with Bernan. She received her bachelor's degree in economics from the University of Maryland and is a former economist with the American Economics Group. She has also worked as a research assistant for FRANDATA. Ms. Ryan is also an associate editor of *Business Statistics of the United States: Patterns of Economic Change* and of *Vital Statistics of the United States: Births, Life Expectancy, Deaths, and Selected Health Data*, both published by Bernan.

Special thanks go to Jo A. Wilson and Lateef Padgett, both of Bernan, who prepared the graphics and layout, as well as coordinated the production aspects of this volume. Many thanks also to Shana Hertz, who copyedited this edition. Finally, much appreciation is due to the federal agency personnel who prepared the original data and generously responded to our requests for assistance.

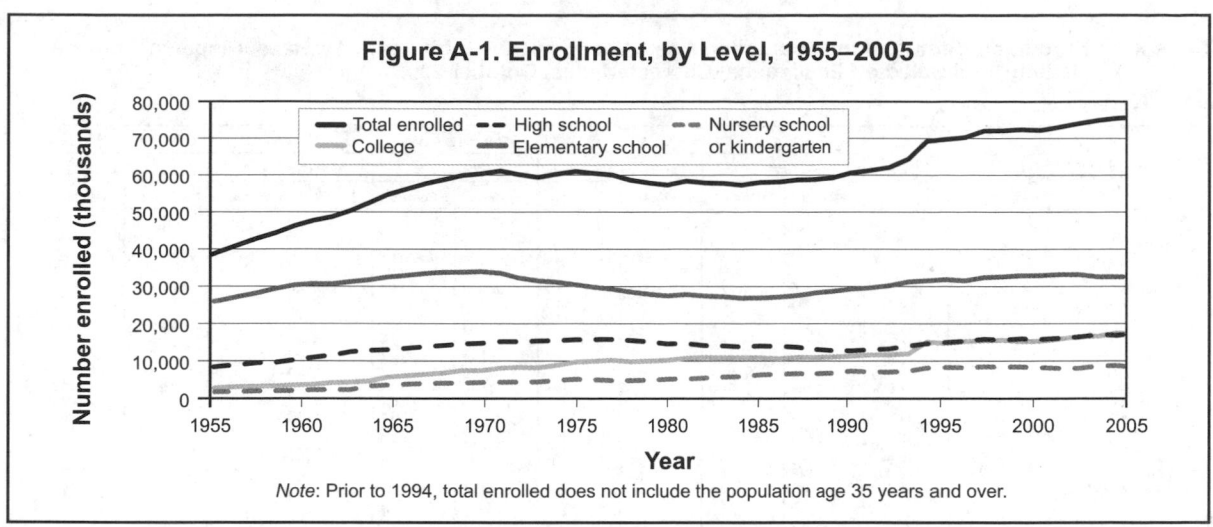

Figure A-1. Enrollment, by Level, 1955–2005

Note: Prior to 1994, total enrolled does not include the population age 35 years and over.

In 2005, almost 76 million people age 3 years and over were enrolled in school. This is the highest total enrollment ever measured for the nation, with the largest number ever of high school and college students. Elementary school enrollment peaked during the late 1960s and early 1970s, when the baby boomers were in school. After dropping below 27 million during the mid-1980s, elementary school enrollment steadily increased, with 21st century levels almost reaching the baby boom peak. This reflected both the children of the baby boomers and the increase in immigration. In 2005, 4.8 million foreign-born students were enrolled in school. (Table A-1 and A-10)

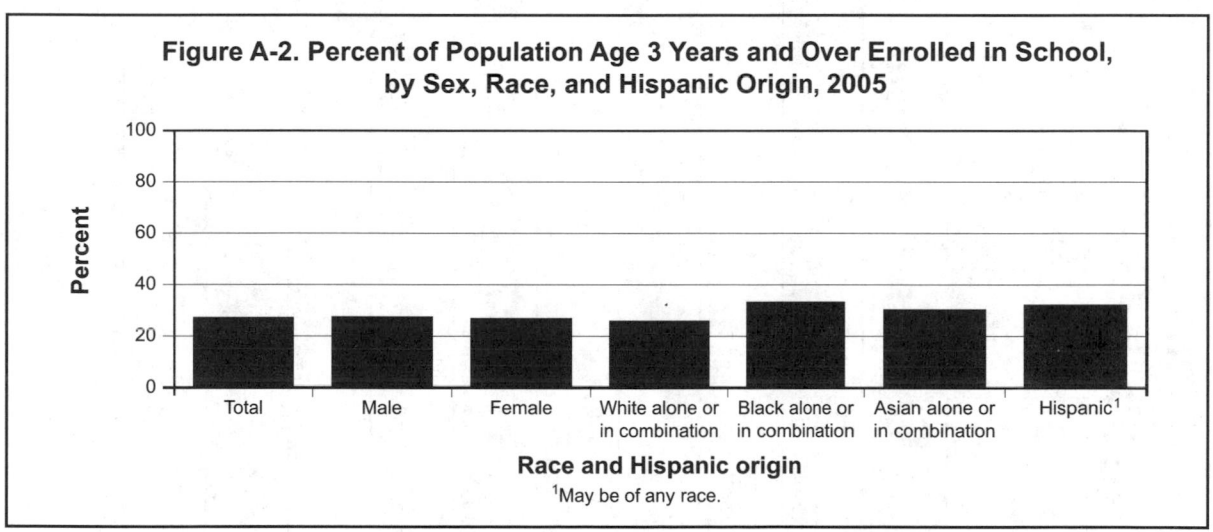

Figure A-2. Percent of Population Age 3 Years and Over Enrolled in School, by Sex, Race, and Hispanic Origin, 2005

[1] May be of any race.

Over 27 percent of people age 3 years and over were enrolled in school in 2005. While the enrollment rates for males and females were fairly similar, enrollment trends were significantly different for the race and ethnic groups. Almost 34 percent of Blacks age 3 years and over were enrolled in school, while only slightly more than 26 percent of Whites were enrolled in school. Hispanics had a rate of school enrollment of 32 percent. (Table A-1)

Table A-1. Enrollment Status of the Population Age 3 Years and Over, by Age, Sex, Race, Hispanic Origin, Nativity, and Selected Educational Characteristics, October 2005

(Numbers in thousands, percent.)

| Age, sex, race, Hispanic origin, and nativity | Total population | Enrolled in school | | | | | | | | | |
| | | Total | | Nursery or kindergarten | | Elementary | | High school | | College | |
		Number	Percent	Number	Percent	Number	Percent	Number	Percent	Number	Percent
ALL RACES											
Both Sexes											
3 years and over	279 862	75 780	27.1	8 515	3.0	32 438	11.6	17 354	6.2	17 472	6.2
3 and 4 years	8 179	4 383	53.6	4 383	53.6	-	-	-	-	-	-
5 and 6 years	7 844	7 486	95.4	4 097	52.2	3 389	43.2	-	-	-	-
7 to 9 years	11 795	11 628	98.6	35	0.3	11 593	98.3	-	-	-	-
10 to 13 years	16 536	16 308	98.6	-	-	15 998	96.7	310	1.9	-	-
14 and 15 years	8 549	8 375	98.0	-	-	1 361	15.9	6 998	81.9	16	0.2
16 and 17 years	8 906	8 472	95.1	-	-	35	0.4	8 272	92.9	165	1.9
18 and 19 years	7 559	5 109	67.6	-	-	10	0.1	1 372	18.1	3 727	49.3
20 and 21 years	8 357	4 069	48.7	-	-	5	0.1	119	1.4	3 945	47.2
22 to 24 years	11 938	3 254	27.3	-	-	16	0.1	75	0.6	3 162	26.5
25 to 29 years	19 681	2 340	11.9	-	-	13	0.1	36	0.2	2 291	11.6
30 to 34 years	19 460	1 344	6.9	-	-	1	-	34	0.2	1 309	6.7
35 to 44 years	42 947	1 762	4.1	-	-	11	-	95	0.2	1 657	3.9
45 to 54 years	42 392	913	2.2	-	-	3	-	28	0.1	883	2.1
55 years and over	65 719	336	0.5	-	-	3	-	15	-	318	0.5
Male											
3 years and over	136 661	37 386	27.4	4 354	3.2	16 626	12.2	8 868	6.5	7 539	5.5
3 and 4 years	4 158	2 196	52.8	2 196	52.8	-	-	-	-	-	-
5 and 6 years	4 059	3 850	94.8	2 145	52.8	1 705	42.0	-	-	-	-
7 to 9 years	5 995	5 886	98.2	13	0.2	5 872	98.0	-	-	-	-
10 to 13 years	8 481	8 343	98.4	-	-	8 206	96.8	137	1.6	-	-
14 and 15 years	4 352	4 245	97.5	-	-	782	18.0	3 463	79.6	1	-
16 and 17 years	4 470	4 252	95.1	-	-	26	0.6	4 166	93.2	61	1.4
18 and 19 years	3 880	2 580	66.5	-	-	5	0.1	899	23.2	1 675	43.2
20 and 21 years	4 304	1 949	45.3	-	-	3	0.1	69	1.6	1 878	43.6
22 to 24 years	5 892	1 487	25.2	-	-	13	0.2	54	0.9	1 420	24.1
25 to 29 years	9 848	944	9.6	-	-	5	-	15	0.2	923	9.4
30 to 34 years	9 646	565	5.9	-	-	-	-	4	-	562	5.8
35 to 44 years	21 157	627	3.0	-	-	8	-	46	0.2	573	2.7
45 to 54 years	20 738	336	1.6	-	-	-	-	6	-	330	1.6
55 years and over	29 680	126	0.4	-	-	-	-	10	-	115	0.4
Female											
3 years and over	143 201	38 394	26.8	4 161	2.9	15 813	11.0	8 486	5.9	9 934	6.9
3 and 4 years	4 021	2 187	54.4	2 187	54.4	-	-	-	-	-	-
5 and 6 years	3 785	3 636	96.1	1 953	51.6	1 683	44.5	-	-	-	-
7 to 9 years	5 800	5 743	99.0	22	0.4	5 721	98.6	-	-	-	-
10 to 13 years	8 055	7 965	98.9	-	-	7 791	96.7	173	2.2	-	-
14 and 15 years	4 197	4 130	98.4	-	-	579	13.8	3 535	84.2	15	0.4
16 and 17 years	4 436	4 220	95.1	-	-	10	0.2	4 106	92.6	104	2.4
18 and 19 years	3 679	2 530	68.8	-	-	5	0.1	472	12.8	2 052	55.8
20 and 21 years	4 053	2 120	52.3	-	-	2	0.1	50	1.2	2 067	51.0
22 to 24 years	6 046	1 767	29.2	-	-	3	0.1	22	0.4	1 742	28.8
25 to 29 years	9 833	1 396	14.2	-	-	8	0.1	20	0.2	1 368	13.9
30 to 34 years	9 814	778	7.9	-	-	1	-	31	0.3	747	7.6
35 to 44 years	21 790	1 135	5.2	-	-	3	-	49	0.2	1 083	5.0
45 to 54 years	21 654	577	2.7	-	-	3	-	22	0.1	552	2.6
55 years and over	36 039	211	0.6	-	-	3	-	5	-	203	0.6
WHITE ALONE OR IN COMBINATION											
Both Sexes											
3 years and over	229 917	60 035	26.1	6 821	3.0	25 682	11.2	13 741	6.0	13 791	6.0
3 and 4 years	6 445	3 475	53.9	3 475	53.9	-	-	-	-	-	-
5 and 6 years	6 239	5 948	95.3	3 326	53.3	2 622	42.0	-	-	-	-
7 to 9 years	9 414	9 279	98.6	20	0.2	9 259	98.4	-	-	-	-
10 to 13 years	13 089	12 917	98.7	-	-	12 693	97.0	224	1.7	-	-
14 and 15 years	6 765	6 653	98.3	-	-	1 041	15.4	5 597	82.7	16	0.2
16 and 17 years	7 059	6 731	95.3	-	-	16	0.2	6 605	93.6	109	1.6
18 and 19 years	6 078	4 117	67.7	-	-	10	0.2	1 064	17.5	3 043	50.1
20 and 21 years	6 758	3 333	49.3	-	-	5	0.1	84	1.2	3 244	48.0
22 to 24 years	9 509	2 494	26.2	-	-	13	0.1	48	0.5	2 433	25.6
25 to 29 years	15 693	1 774	11.3	-	-	9	0.1	25	0.2	1 740	11.1
30 to 34 years	15 521	966	6.2	-	-	1	-	11	0.1	954	6.1
35 to 44 years	35 048	1 376	3.9	-	-	11	-	53	0.2	1 313	3.7
45 to 54 years	35 279	703	2.0	-	-	2	-	18	0.1	682	1.9
55 years and over	57 019	267	0.5	-	-	-	-	11	-	256	0.4
Male											
3 years and over	113 225	29 660	26.2	3 464	3.1	13 205	11.7	7 014	6.2	5 978	5.3
3 and 4 years	3 308	1 740	52.6	1 740	52.6	-	-	-	-	-	-
5 and 6 years	3 211	3 041	94.7	1 714	53.4	1 327	41.3	-	-	-	-
7 to 9 years	4 795	4 709	98.2	10	0.2	4 699	98.0	-	-	-	-
10 to 13 years	6 712	6 617	98.6	-	-	6 524	97.2	93	1.4	-	-
14 and 15 years	3 450	3 390	98.3	-	-	619	17.9	2 771	80.3	1	-
16 and 17 years	3 536	3 367	95.2	-	-	9	0.3	3 315	93.8	42	1.2
18 and 19 years	3 149	2 068	65.7	-	-	5	0.2	692	22.0	1 371	43.5
20 and 21 years	3 475	1 567	45.1	-	-	3	0.1	45	1.3	1 519	43.7
22 to 24 years	4 770	1 172	24.6	-	-	9	0.2	34	0.7	1 128	23.7
25 to 29 years	7 986	711	8.9	-	-	1	-	15	0.2	696	8.7
30 to 34 years	7 837	424	5.4	-	-	-	-	-	-	424	5.4
35 to 44 years	17 531	510	2.9	-	-	8	-	36	0.2	466	2.7
45 to 54 years	17 496	247	1.4	-	-	-	-	5	-	242	1.4
55 years and over	25 969	95	0.4	-	-	-	-	7	-	88	0.3

- = Quantity zero or rounds to zero.

Table A-1. Enrollment Status of the Population Age 3 Years and Over, by Age, Sex, Race, Hispanic Origin, Nativity, and Selected Educational Characteristics, October 2005—*Continued*

(Numbers in thousands, percent.)

Age, sex, race, Hispanic origin, and nativity	Not enrolled in school					
	Total		High school graduate		Not a high school graduate	
	Number	Percent	Number	Percent	Number	Percent
ALL RACES						
Both Sexes						
3 years and over	204 082	72.9	168 638	60.3	35 444	12.7
3 and 4 years	3 796	46.4	-	-	3 796	46.4
5 and 6 years	359	4.6	-	-	359	4.6
7 to 9 years	167	1.4	-	-	167	1.4
10 to 13 years	228	1.4	-	-	228	1.4
14 and 15 years	174	2.0	31	0.4	143	1.7
16 and 17 years	434	4.9	130	1.5	303	3.4
18 and 19 years	2 450	32.4	1 789	23.7	661	8.7
20 and 21 years	4 288	51.3	3 280	39.2	1 008	12.1
22 to 24 years	8 685	72.7	7 200	60.3	1 485	12.4
25 to 29 years	17 341	88.1	14 892	75.7	2 449	12.4
30 to 34 years	18 116	93.1	15 666	80.5	2 450	12.6
35 to 44 years	41 185	95.9	36 316	84.6	4 869	11.3
45 to 54 years	41 479	97.8	36 996	87.3	4 483	10.6
55 years and over	65 383	99.5	52 339	79.6	13 044	19.8
Male						
3 years and over	99 275	72.6	81 414	59.6	17 861	13.1
3 and 4 years	1 962	47.2	-	-	1 962	47.2
5 and 6 years	209	5.2	-	-	209	5.2
7 to 9 years	109	1.8	-	-	109	1.8
10 to 13 years	138	1.6	-	-	138	1.6
14 and 15 years	107	2.5	25	0.6	82	1.9
16 and 17 years	218	4.9	61	1.4	156	3.5
18 and 19 years	1 301	33.5	909	23.4	392	10.1
20 and 21 years	2 355	54.7	1 736	40.3	619	14.4
22 to 24 years	4 405	74.8	3 564	60.5	841	14.3
25 to 29 years	8 904	90.4	7 530	76.5	1 374	14.0
30 to 34 years	9 080	94.1	7 736	80.2	1 344	13.9
35 to 44 years	20 530	97.0	17 902	84.6	2 628	12.4
45 to 54 years	20 402	98.4	18 063	87.1	2 339	11.3
55 years and over	29 554	99.6	23 887	80.5	5 667	19.1
Female						
3 years and over	104 807	73.2	87 224	60.9	17 584	12.3
3 and 4 years	1 835	45.6	-	-	1 835	45.6
5 and 6 years	149	3.9	-	-	149	3.9
7 to 9 years	57	1.0	-	-	57	1.0
10 to 13 years	90	1.1	-	-	90	1.1
14 and 15 years	67	1.6	6	0.1	61	1.4
16 and 17 years	216	4.9	69	1.6	147	3.3
18 and 19 years	1 149	31.2	880	23.9	269	7.3
20 and 21 years	1 933	47.7	1 544	38.1	389	9.6
22 to 24 years	4 279	70.8	3 636	60.1	644	10.6
25 to 29 years	8 436	85.8	7 362	74.9	1 074	10.9
30 to 34 years	9 036	92.1	7 929	80.8	1 106	11.3
35 to 44 years	20 655	94.8	18 414	84.5	2 241	10.3
45 to 54 years	21 076	97.3	18 932	87.4	2 144	9.9
55 years and over	35 828	99.4	28 452	78.9	7 377	20.5
WHITE ALONE OR IN COMBINATION						
Both Sexes						
3 years and over	169 882	73.9	141 276	61.4	28 607	12.4
3 and 4 years	2 970	46.1	-	-	2 970	46.1
5 and 6 years	291	4.7	-	-	291	4.7
7 to 9 years	135	1.4	-	-	135	1.4
10 to 13 years	171	1.3	-	-	171	1.3
14 and 15 years	112	1.7	15	0.2	97	1.4
16 and 17 years	328	4.7	96	1.4	232	3.3
18 and 19 years	1 961	32.3	1 424	23.4	537	8.8
20 and 21 years	3 425	50.7	2 623	38.8	802	11.9
22 to 24 years	7 015	73.8	5 814	61.1	1 200	12.6
25 to 29 years	13 919	88.7	11 868	75.6	2 051	13.1
30 to 34 years	14 555	93.8	12 445	80.2	2 110	13.6
35 to 44 years	33 672	96.1	29 591	84.4	4 080	11.6
45 to 54 years	34 576	98.0	31 057	88.0	3 519	10.0
55 years and over	56 752	99.5	46 342	81.3	10 410	18.3
Male						
3 years and over	83 565	73.8	68 763	60.7	14 802	13.1
3 and 4 years	1 568	47.4	-	-	1 568	47.4
5 and 6 years	170	5.3	-	-	170	5.3
7 to 9 years	86	1.8	-	-	86	1.8
10 to 13 years	95	1.4	-	-	95	1.4
14 and 15 years	59	1.7	13	0.4	47	1.4
16 and 17 years	169	4.8	52	1.5	118	3.3
18 and 19 years	1 081	34.3	760	24.1	321	10.2
20 and 21 years	1 907	54.9	1 408	40.5	499	14.4
22 to 24 years	3 599	75.4	2 900	60.8	698	14.6
25 to 29 years	7 275	91.1	6 069	76.0	1 206	15.1
30 to 34 years	7 413	94.6	6 233	79.5	1 180	15.1
35 to 44 years	17 021	97.1	14 739	84.1	2 282	13.0
45 to 54 years	17 249	98.6	15 353	87.7	1 896	10.8
55 years and over	25 874	99.6	21 238	81.8	4 636	17.9

- = Quantity zero or rounds to zero.

Table A-1. Enrollment Status of the Population Age 3 Years and Over, by Age, Sex, Race, Hispanic Origin, Nativity, and Selected Educational Characteristics, October 2005—*Continued*

(Numbers in thousands, percent.)

Age, sex, race, Hispanic origin, and nativity	Total population	Enrolled in school									
		Total		Nursery or kindergarten		Elementary		High school		College	
		Number	Percent	Number	Percent	Number	Percent	Number	Percent	Number	Percent
WHITE ALONE OR IN COMBINATION											
Female											
3 years and over	116 692	30 375	26.0	3 357	2.9	12 477	10.7	6 727	5.8	7 813	6.7
3 and 4 years	3 138	1 735	55.3	1 735	55.3	-	-	-	-	-	-
5 and 6 years	3 028	2 907	96.0	1 612	53.2	1 295	42.8	-	-	-	-
7 to 9 years	4 619	4 570	98.9	10	0.2	4 560	98.7	-	-	-	-
10 to 13 years	6 376	6 300	98.8	-	-	6 169	96.7	131	2.1	-	-
14 and 15 years	3 316	3 263	98.4	-	-	422	12.7	2 826	85.2	15	0.4
16 and 17 years	3 523	3 364	95.5	-	-	7	0.2	3 290	93.4	67	1.9
18 and 19 years	2 929	2 049	70.0	-	-	5	0.2	372	12.7	1 672	57.1
20 and 21 years	3 284	1 766	53.8	-	-	2	0.1	38	1.2	1 725	52.5
22 to 24 years	4 738	1 322	27.9	-	-	3	0.1	14	0.3	1 305	27.5
25 to 29 years	7 707	1 063	13.8	-	-	8	0.1	10	0.1	1 044	13.5
30 to 34 years	7 684	542	7.1	-	-	1	-	11	0.1	530	6.9
35 to 44 years	17 517	866	4.9	-	-	3	-	16	0.1	847	4.8
45 to 54 years	17 783	455	2.6	-	-	2	-	13	0.1	440	2.5
55 years and over	31 050	172	0.6	-	-	-	-	4	-	168	0.5
BLACK ALONE OR IN COMBINATION											
Both Sexes											
3 years and over	36 222	12 118	33.5	1 356	3.7	5 504	15.2	2 870	7.9	2 387	6.6
3 and 4 years	1 365	700	51.3	700	51.3	-	-	-	-	-	-
5 and 6 years	1 302	1 251	96.1	642	49.3	609	46.8	-	-	-	-
7 to 9 years	1 904	1 875	98.5	14	0.8	1 860	97.7	-	-	-	-
10 to 13 years	2 821	2 781	98.6	-	-	2 727	96.6	54	1.9	-	-
14 and 15 years	1 458	1 398	95.9	-	-	280	19.2	1 118	76.7	-	-
16 and 17 years	1 449	1 346	92.9	-	-	19	1.3	1 296	89.4	31	2.1
18 and 19 years	1 195	747	62.5	-	-	-	-	266	22.3	481	40.2
20 and 21 years	1 208	460	38.1	-	-	-	-	32	2.7	428	35.4
22 to 24 years	1 755	489	27.8	-	-	4	0.2	23	1.3	462	26.3
25 to 29 years	2 679	313	11.7	-	-	4	0.2	10	0.4	299	11.2
30 to 34 years	2 536	250	9.9	-	-	-	-	21	0.8	229	9.0
35 to 44 years	5 451	291	5.3	-	-	-	-	37	0.7	254	4.7
45 to 54 years	5 016	169	3.4	-	-	1	-	8	0.2	160	3.2
55 years and over	6 083	47	0.8	-	-	-	-	4	0.1	43	0.7
Male											
3 years and over	16 729	5 793	34.6	706	4.2	2 755	16.5	1 437	8.6	895	5.3
3 and 4 years	682	358	52.5	358	52.5	-	-	-	-	-	-
5 and 6 years	663	630	95.1	345	52.0	286	43.1	-	-	-	-
7 to 9 years	943	920	97.5	3	0.3	918	97.3	-	-	-	-
10 to 13 years	1 450	1 419	97.9	-	-	1 387	95.7	32	2.2	-	-
14 and 15 years	706	662	93.8	-	-	140	19.9	522	73.9	-	-
16 and 17 years	706	663	93.8	-	-	16	2.3	638	90.3	9	1.2
18 and 19 years	586	388	66.2	-	-	-	-	187	31.8	201	34.3
20 and 21 years	605	211	34.9	-	-	-	-	23	3.8	189	31.2
22 to 24 years	797	190	23.9	-	-	4	0.5	19	2.4	167	21.0
25 to 29 years	1 231	114	9.3	-	-	4	0.4	1	0.1	109	8.8
30 to 34 years	1 127	69	6.1	-	-	-	-	3	0.3	66	5.8
35 to 44 years	2 440	77	3.1	-	-	-	-	10	0.4	67	2.7
45 to 54 years	2 273	70	3.1	-	-	-	-	-	-	70	3.1
55 years and over	2 520	21	0.8	-	-	-	-	3	0.1	18	0.7
Female											
3 years and over	19 493	6 325	32.4	651	3.3	2 749	14.1	1 433	7.4	1 493	7.7
3 and 4 years	683	341	50.0	341	50.0	-	-	-	-	-	-
5 and 6 years	639	621	97.1	297	46.5	324	50.6	-	-	-	-
7 to 9 years	960	954	99.4	12	1.2	943	98.2	-	-	-	-
10 to 13 years	1 372	1 362	99.3	-	-	1 340	97.7	22	1.6	-	-
14 and 15 years	752	736	97.8	-	-	140	18.6	596	79.2	-	-
16 and 17 years	743	683	92.0	-	-	2	0.3	659	88.7	22	3.0
18 and 19 years	609	359	59.1	-	-	-	-	80	13.1	280	45.9
20 and 21 years	603	249	41.3	-	-	-	-	10	1.6	239	39.7
22 to 24 years	958	298	31.1	-	-	-	-	4	0.4	295	30.7
25 to 29 years	1 448	199	13.8	-	-	-	-	9	0.6	190	13.1
30 to 34 years	1 410	181	12.8	-	-	-	-	17	1.2	164	11.6
35 to 44 years	3 011	214	7.1	-	-	-	-	27	0.9	187	6.2
45 to 54 years	2 743	99	3.6	-	-	1	-	8	0.3	90	3.3
55 years and over	3 563	27	0.8	-	-	-	-	1	-	26	0.7
ASIAN ALONE OR IN COMBINATION											
Both Sexes											
3 years and over	13 009	3 964	30.5	379	2.9	1 495	11.5	792	6.1	1 297	10.0
3 and 4 years	423	230	54.4	230	54.4	-	-	-	-	-	-
5 and 6 years	352	336	95.5	148	41.9	189	53.6	-	-	-	-
7 to 9 years	582	579	99.6	1	0.1	579	99.4	-	-	-	-
10 to 13 years	732	714	97.5	-	-	680	92.9	34	4.6	-	-
14 and 15 years	367	363	98.7	-	-	45	12.2	318	86.5	-	-
16 and 17 years	420	413	98.2	-	-	-	-	388	92.3	25	5.9
18 and 19 years	286	246	86.2	-	-	-	-	42	14.7	204	71.5
20 and 21 years	381	294	77.1	-	-	-	-	2	0.5	292	76.7
22 to 24 years	632	281	44.4	-	-	-	-	4	0.6	277	43.8
25 to 29 years	1 150	240	20.9	-	-	-	-	-	-	240	20.9
30 to 34 years	1 298	122	9.4	-	-	-	-	-	-	122	9.4
35 to 44 years	2 262	93	4.1	-	-	-	-	4	0.2	88	3.9
45 to 54 years	1 824	33	1.8	-	-	-	-	1	0.1	32	1.8
55 years and over	2 299	19	0.8	-	-	3	0.1	-	-	17	0.7

- = Quantity zero or rounds to zero.

Table A-1. Enrollment Status of the Population Age 3 Years and Over, by Age, Sex, Race, Hispanic Origin, Nativity, and Selected Educational Characteristics, October 2005—*Continued*

(Numbers in thousands, percent.)

Age, sex, race, Hispanic origin, and nativity	Not enrolled in school					
	Total		High school graduate		Not a high school graduate	
	Number	Percent	Number	Percent	Number	Percent
WHITE ALONE OR IN COMBINATION						
Female						
3 years and over	86 317	74.0	72 513	62.1	13 805	11.8
3 and 4 years	1 402	44.7	-	-	1 402	44.7
5 and 6 years	121	4.0	-	-	121	4.0
7 to 9 years	49	1.1	-	-	49	1.1
10 to 13 years	77	1.2	-	-	77	1.2
14 and 15 years	53	1.6	2	0.1	51	1.5
16 and 17 years	159	4.5	44	1.3	115	3.3
18 and 19 years	880	30.0	665	22.7	216	7.4
20 and 21 years	1 518	46.2	1 216	37.0	302	9.2
22 to 24 years	3 416	72.1	2 914	61.5	502	10.6
25 to 29 years	6 644	86.2	5 799	75.2	845	11.0
30 to 34 years	7 142	92.9	6 212	80.8	930	12.1
35 to 44 years	16 651	95.1	14 853	84.8	1 798	10.3
45 to 54 years	17 327	97.4	15 704	88.3	1 623	9.1
55 years and over	30 878	99.4	25 104	80.8	5 774	18.6
BLACK ALONE OR IN COMBINATION						
Both Sexes						
3 years and over	24 105	66.5	18 771	51.8	5 334	14.7
3 and 4 years	666	48.7	-	-	666	48.7
5 and 6 years	51	3.9	-	-	51	3.9
7 to 9 years	29	1.5	-	-	29	1.5
10 to 13 years	40	1.4	-	-	40	1.4
14 and 15 years	60	4.1	13	0.9	47	3.3
16 and 17 years	103	7.1	31	2.2	72	5.0
18 and 19 years	448	37.5	336	28.1	112	9.4
20 and 21 years	748	61.9	567	46.9	181	15.0
22 to 24 years	1 266	72.2	1 029	58.7	237	13.5
25 to 29 years	2 366	88.3	2 053	76.7	312	11.7
30 to 34 years	2 286	90.1	2 020	79.7	266	10.5
35 to 44 years	5 160	94.7	4 546	83.4	614	11.3
45 to 54 years	4 847	96.6	4 177	83.3	670	13.4
55 years and over	6 035	99.2	3 998	65.7	2 037	33.5
Male						
3 years and over	10 936	65.4	8 477	50.7	2 460	14.7
3 and 4 years	324	47.5	-	-	324	47.5
5 and 6 years	32	4.9	-	-	32	4.9
7 to 9 years	23	2.5	-	-	23	2.5
10 to 13 years	31	2.1	-	-	31	2.1
14 and 15 years	44	6.2	8	1.2	35	5.0
16 and 17 years	43	6.2	10	1.4	34	4.8
18 and 19 years	198	33.8	136	23.2	62	10.7
20 and 21 years	394	65.1	289	47.7	105	17.4
22 to 24 years	606	76.1	484	60.7	122	15.4
25 to 29 years	1 117	90.7	990	80.5	126	10.3
30 to 34 years	1 058	93.9	933	82.8	125	11.1
35 to 44 years	2 364	96.9	2 075	85.0	289	11.8
45 to 54 years	2 203	96.9	1 884	82.9	319	14.0
55 years and over	2 499	99.2	1 668	66.2	831	33.0
Female						
3 years and over	13 168	67.6	10 294	52.8	2 874	14.7
3 and 4 years	341	50.0	-	-	341	50.0
5 and 6 years	18	2.9	-	-	18	2.9
7 to 9 years	6	0.6	-	-	6	0.6
10 to 13 years	9	0.7	-	-	9	0.7
14 and 15 years	16	2.2	4	0.6	12	1.6
16 and 17 years	60	8.0	22	2.9	38	5.1
18 and 19 years	249	40.9	200	32.8	49	8.1
20 and 21 years	354	58.7	278	46.1	76	12.6
22 to 24 years	660	68.9	545	56.9	114	11.9
25 to 29 years	1 249	86.2	1 063	73.4	186	12.8
30 to 34 years	1 229	87.2	1 087	77.1	141	10.0
35 to 44 years	2 796	92.9	2 471	82.1	325	10.8
45 to 54 years	2 644	96.4	2 293	83.6	351	12.8
55 years and over	3 536	99.2	2 330	65.4	1 206	33.8
ASIAN ALONE OR IN COMBINATION						
Both Sexes						
3 years and over	9 045	69.5	7 799	60.0	1 246	9.6
3 and 4 years	193	45.6	-	-	193	45.6
5 and 6 years	16	4.5	-	-	16	4.5
7 to 9 years	3	0.4	-	-	3	0.4
10 to 13 years	18	2.5	-	-	18	2.5
14 and 15 years	5	1.3	4	1.0	1	0.2
16 and 17 years	7	1.8	1	0.3	6	1.5
18 and 19 years	39	13.8	36	12.5	4	1.3
20 and 21 years	87	22.9	74	19.4	13	3.4
22 to 24 years	352	55.6	331	52.3	21	3.3
25 to 29 years	910	79.1	861	74.8	49	4.3
30 to 34 years	1 176	90.6	1 119	86.2	57	4.4
35 to 44 years	2 169	95.9	2 021	89.3	149	6.6
45 to 54 years	1 791	98.2	1 567	85.9	224	12.3
55 years and over	2 280	99.2	1 787	77.7	493	21.4

- = Quantity zero or rounds to zero.

Table A-1. Enrollment Status of the Population Age 3 Years and Over, by Age, Sex, Race, Hispanic Origin, Nativity, and Selected Educational Characteristics, October 2005—*Continued*

(Numbers in thousands, percent.)

Age, sex, race, Hispanic origin, and nativity	Total population	Enrolled in school									
		Total		Nursery or kindergarten		Elementary		High school		College	
		Number	Percent	Number	Percent	Number	Percent	Number	Percent	Number	Percent
ASIAN ALONE OR IN COMBINATION											
Male											
3 years and over	6 270	1 986	31.7	181	2.9	757	12.1	408	6.5	640	10.2
3 and 4 years	205	105	51.1	105	51.1	-	-	-	-	-	-
5 and 6 years	192	187	97.4	76	39.5	111	57.9	-	-	-	-
7 to 9 years	290	289	99.7	1	0.3	288	99.4	-	-	-	-
10 to 13 years	360	348	96.5	-	-	335	93.1	12	3.4	-	-
14 and 15 years	207	203	98.0	-	-	22	10.5	181	87.5	-	-
16 and 17 years	203	197	97.3	-	-	-	-	185	91.1	13	6.2
18 and 19 years	152	127	83.6	-	-	-	-	30	19.5	97	64.1
20 and 21 years	207	170	82.1	-	-	-	-	-	-	170	82.1
22 to 24 years	294	124	42.2	-	-	-	-	-	-	124	42.2
25 to 29 years	558	113	20.2	-	-	-	-	-	-	113	20.2
30 to 34 years	637	63	9.9	-	-	-	-	-	-	63	9.9
35 to 44 years	1 087	40	3.7	-	-	-	-	-	-	40	3.7
45 to 54 years	849	13	1.5	-	-	-	-	-	0.1	13	1.5
55 years and over	1 028	8	0.7	-	-	-	-	-	-	8	0.7
Female											
3 years and over	6 739	1 977	29.3	197	2.9	739	11.0	384	5.7	657	9.8
3 and 4 years	218	126	57.5	126	57.5	-	-	-	-	-	-
5 and 6 years	160	149	93.2	72	44.8	77	48.4	-	-	-	-
7 to 9 years	292	291	99.5	-	-	291	99.5	-	-	-	-
10 to 13 years	372	367	98.5	-	-	345	92.7	22	5.9	-	-
14 and 15 years	160	160	99.7	-	-	23	14.4	137	85.3	-	-
16 and 17 years	218	216	99.1	-	-	-	-	203	93.5	12	5.6
18 and 19 years	134	119	89.2	-	-	-	-	12	9.2	107	80.0
20 and 21 years	174	124	71.2	-	-	-	-	2	1.0	122	70.2
22 to 24 years	338	156	46.2	-	-	-	-	4	1.1	153	45.1
25 to 29 years	592	128	21.6	-	-	-	-	-	-	128	21.6
30 to 34 years	661	59	8.9	-	-	-	-	-	-	59	8.9
35 to 44 years	1 175	53	4.5	-	-	-	-	4	0.4	48	4.1
45 to 54 years	975	20	2.1	-	-	-	-	1	0.1	20	2.0
55 years and over	1 270	12	0.9	-	-	3	0.2	-	-	9	0.7
HISPANIC[1]											
Both Sexes											
3 years and over	39 884	12 809	32.1	1 601	4.0	6 330	15.9	2 937	7.4	1 942	4.9
3 and 4 years	1 799	773	43.0	773	43.0	-	-	-	-	-	-
5 and 6 years	1 633	1 532	93.8	822	50.3	711	43.5	-	-	-	-
7 to 9 years	2 389	2 326	97.4	6	0.3	2 320	97.1	-	-	-	-
10 to 13 years	3 135	3 068	97.9	-	-	3 010	96.0	59	1.9	-	-
14 and 15 years	1 472	1 431	97.3	-	-	253	17.2	1 175	79.8	3	0.2
16 and 17 years	1 466	1 357	92.6	-	-	4	0.2	1 325	90.4	28	1.9
18 and 19 years	1 253	681	54.3	-	-	3	0.3	272	21.7	406	32.4
20 and 21 years	1 492	447	30.0	-	-	2	0.1	25	1.7	420	28.1
22 to 24 years	2 152	419	19.5	-	-	13	0.6	17	0.8	389	18.1
25 to 29 years	3 992	310	7.8	-	-	5	0.1	16	0.4	288	7.2
30 to 34 years	3 765	158	4.2	-	-	-	-	8	0.2	150	4.0
35 to 44 years	6 364	228	3.6	-	-	10	0.1	27	0.4	192	3.0
45 to 54 years	4 301	60	1.4	-	-	-	-	8	0.2	52	1.2
55 years and over	4 671	19	0.4	-	-	-	-	5	0.1	13	0.3
Male											
3 years and over	20 464	6 351	31.0	820	4.0	3 240	15.8	1 488	7.3	804	3.9
3 and 4 years	917	394	43.0	394	43.0	-	-	-	-	-	-
5 and 6 years	847	783	92.4	421	49.7	362	42.7	-	-	-	-
7 to 9 years	1 210	1 162	96.0	5	0.4	1 157	95.6	-	-	-	-
10 to 13 years	1 616	1 571	97.2	-	-	1 540	95.3	31	1.9	-	-
14 and 15 years	740	723	97.8	-	-	158	21.3	566	76.5	-	-
16 and 17 years	728	674	92.5	-	-	4	0.5	660	90.7	10	1.4
18 and 19 years	663	343	51.8	-	-	3	0.5	166	25.1	173	26.2
20 and 21 years	790	199	25.2	-	-	-	-	16	2.0	183	23.2
22 to 24 years	1 160	203	17.5	-	-	9	0.8	11	0.9	183	15.8
25 to 29 years	2 191	123	5.6	-	-	-	-	13	0.6	111	5.1
30 to 34 years	2 009	52	2.6	-	-	-	-	-	-	52	2.6
35 to 44 years	3 325	89	2.7	-	-	6	0.2	22	0.7	60	1.8
45 to 54 years	2 159	24	1.1	-	-	-	-	-	-	24	1.1
55 years and over	2 109	11	0.5	-	-	-	-	3	0.1	8	0.4
Female											
3 years and over	19 420	6 458	33.3	782	4.0	3 090	15.9	1 449	7.5	1 137	5.9
3 and 4 years	882	379	43.0	379	43.0	-	-	-	-	-	-
5 and 6 years	786	750	95.3	401	51.0	349	44.4	-	-	-	-
7 to 9 years	1 178	1 164	98.8	1	0.1	1 163	98.7	-	-	-	-
10 to 13 years	1 518	1 497	98.6	-	-	1 470	96.8	27	1.8	-	-
14 and 15 years	732	708	96.7	-	-	95	13.0	610	83.3	3	0.5
16 and 17 years	737	683	92.6	-	-	-	-	665	90.1	18	2.4
18 and 19 years	591	338	57.2	-	-	-	-	105	17.8	232	39.3
20 and 21 years	703	248	35.3	-	-	2	0.3	9	1.3	237	33.7
22 to 24 years	992	216	21.8	-	-	3	0.3	7	0.7	206	20.8
25 to 29 years	1 801	187	10.4	-	-	5	0.3	4	0.2	178	9.9
30 to 34 years	1 756	107	6.1	-	-	-	-	8	0.5	98	5.6
35 to 44 years	3 039	139	4.6	-	-	3	0.1	4	0.1	132	4.3
45 to 54 years	2 143	36	1.7	-	-	-	-	8	0.4	28	1.3
55 years and over	2 561	7	0.3	-	-	-	-	2	0.1	5	0.2

[1] May be of any race.
- = Quantity zero or rounds to zero.

Table A-1. Enrollment Status of the Population Age 3 Years and Over, by Age, Sex, Race, Hispanic Origin, Nativity, and Selected Educational Characteristics, October 2005—*Continued*

(Numbers in thousands, percent.)

Age, sex, race, Hispanic origin, and nativity	Not enrolled in school					
	Total		High school graduate		Not a high school graduate	
	Number	Percent	Number	Percent	Number	Percent
ASIAN ALONE OR IN COMBINATION						
Male						
3 years and over	4 283	68.3	3 798	60.6	485	7.7
3 and 4 years	100	48.9	-	-	100	48.9
5 and 6 years	5	2.6	-	-	5	2.6
7 to 9 years	1	0.3	-	-	1	0.3
10 to 13 years	13	3.5	-	-	13	3.5
14 and 15 years	4	2.0	4	1.8	-	0.2
16 and 17 years	5	2.7	1	0.6	4	2.1
18 and 19 years	25	16.4	22	14.7	3	1.7
20 and 21 years	37	17.9	27	13.2	10	4.7
22 to 24 years	170	57.8	162	55.0	8	2.8
25 to 29 years	445	79.8	425	76.1	20	3.6
30 to 34 years	574	90.1	538	84.5	36	5.6
35 to 44 years	1 047	96.3	1 002	92.2	45	4.2
45 to 54 years	836	98.5	745	87.7	91	10.8
55 years and over	1 021	99.3	872	84.8	149	14.5
Female						
3 years and over	4 762	70.7	4 001	59.4	761	11.3
3 and 4 years	93	42.5	-	-	93	42.5
5 and 6 years	11	6.8	-	-	11	6.8
7 to 9 years	2	0.5	-	-	2	0.5
10 to 13 years	6	1.5	-	-	6	1.5
14 and 15 years	1	0.3	-	-	1	0.3
16 and 17 years	2	0.9	-	-	2	0.9
18 and 19 years	14	10.8	13	9.9	1	0.9
20 and 21 years	50	28.8	47	26.8	3	2.0
22 to 24 years	182	53.8	169	50.0	13	3.8
25 to 29 years	465	78.4	436	73.6	29	4.9
30 to 34 years	602	91.1	581	87.9	22	3.3
35 to 44 years	1 122	95.5	1 019	86.7	103	8.8
45 to 54 years	955	97.9	823	84.3	132	13.6
55 years and over	1 259	99.1	915	72.0	344	27.1
HISPANIC[1]						
Both Sexes						
3 years and over	27 074	67.9	14 985	37.6	12 089	30.3
3 and 4 years	1 026	57.0	-	-	1 026	57.0
5 and 6 years	101	6.2	-	-	101	6.2
7 to 9 years	63	2.6	-	-	63	2.6
10 to 13 years	66	2.1	-	-	66	2.1
14 and 15 years	40	2.7	2	0.1	38	2.6
16 and 17 years	109	7.4	16	1.1	93	6.3
18 and 19 years	573	45.7	346	27.6	227	18.1
20 and 21 years	1 045	70.0	599	40.2	446	29.9
22 to 24 years	1 733	80.5	1 070	49.7	663	30.8
25 to 29 years	3 682	92.2	2 307	57.8	1 375	34.4
30 to 34 years	3 606	95.8	2 199	58.4	1 407	37.4
35 to 44 years	6 136	96.4	3 746	58.9	2 390	37.6
45 to 54 years	4 242	98.6	2 584	60.1	1 658	38.5
55 years and over	4 652	99.6	2 116	45.3	2 536	54.3
Male						
3 years and over	14 112	69.0	7 708	37.7	6 404	31.3
3 and 4 years	523	57.0	-	-	523	57.0
5 and 6 years	64	7.6	-	-	64	7.6
7 to 9 years	48	4.0	-	-	48	4.0
10 to 13 years	45	2.8	-	-	45	2.8
14 and 15 years	16	2.2	-	-	16	2.2
16 and 17 years	54	7.5	10	1.3	45	6.2
18 and 19 years	320	48.2	176	26.6	144	21.7
20 and 21 years	590	74.8	316	40.0	274	34.7
22 to 24 years	957	82.5	537	46.3	420	36.2
25 to 29 years	2 067	94.4	1 262	57.6	805	36.7
30 to 34 years	1 957	97.4	1 182	58.9	775	38.6
35 to 44 years	3 237	97.3	1 928	58.0	1 309	39.4
45 to 54 years	2 135	98.9	1 284	59.5	851	39.4
55 years and over	2 098	99.5	1 012	48.0	1 086	51.5
Female						
3 years and over	12 962	66.7	7 278	37.5	5 684	29.3
3 and 4 years	503	57.0	-	-	503	57.0
5 and 6 years	37	4.7	-	-	37	4.7
7 to 9 years	15	1.2	-	-	15	1.2
10 to 13 years	21	1.4	-	-	21	1.4
14 and 15 years	24	3.3	2	0.3	22	3.0
16 and 17 years	55	7.4	7	0.9	48	6.5
18 and 19 years	253	42.8	170	28.8	83	14.0
20 and 21 years	455	64.7	283	40.3	172	24.4
22 to 24 years	776	78.2	533	53.7	243	24.5
25 to 29 years	1 614	89.6	1 044	58.0	570	31.7
30 to 34 years	1 649	93.9	1 017	57.9	632	36.0
35 to 44 years	2 899	95.4	1 818	59.8	1 082	35.6
45 to 54 years	2 107	98.3	1 300	60.7	807	37.7
55 years and over	2 554	99.7	1 104	43.1	1 450	56.6

[1]May be of any race.
- = Quantity zero or rounds to zero.

Table A-1. Enrollment Status of the Population Age 3 Years and Over, by Age, Sex, Race, Hispanic Origin, Nativity, and Selected Educational Characteristics, October 2005—*Continued*

(Numbers in thousands, percent.)

Age, sex, race, Hispanic origin, and nativity	Total population	Enrolled in school									
		Total		Nursery or kindergarten		Elementary		High school		College	
		Number	Percent	Number	Percent	Number	Percent	Number	Percent	Number	Percent
FOREIGN-BORN											
Both Sexes											
3 years and over	34 922	4 765	13.6	216	0.6	1 355	3.9	1 140	3.3	2 054	5.9
3 and 4 years	179	110	61.3	110	61.3	-	-	-	-	-	-
5 and 6 years	256	242	94.6	106	41.2	137	53.4	-	-	-	-
7 to 9 years	446	437	97.9	1	0.3	436	97.6	-	-	-	-
10 to 13 years	750	718	95.7	-	-	668	89.1	50	6.6	-	-
14 and 15 years	437	420	96.2	-	-	82	18.8	338	77.4	-	-
16 and 17 years	585	527	90.1	-	-	2	0.4	500	85.5	25	4.2
18 and 19 years	692	431	62.3	-	-	3	0.5	161	23.4	266	38.4
20 and 21 years	1 039	407	39.1	-	-	2	0.2	10	0.9	395	38.0
22 to 24 years	1 807	404	22.3	-	-	6	0.4	17	1.0	380	21.0
25 to 29 years	3 600	425	11.8	-	-	6	0.2	9	0.2	410	11.4
30 to 34 years	4 068	216	5.3	-	-	-	-	13	0.3	203	5.0
35 to 44 years	7 784	281	3.6	-	-	10	0.1	37	0.5	234	3.0
45 to 54 years	5 662	117	2.1	-	-	-	-	2	-	115	2.0
55 years and over	7 617	31	0.4	-	-	3	-	2	-	26	0.3
Male											
3 years and over	17 459	2 319	13.3	107	0.6	631	3.6	597	3.4	985	5.6
3 and 4 years	78	50	64.6	50	64.6	-	-	-	-	-	-
5 and 6 years	132	126	95.6	55	41.8	71	53.8	-	-	-	-
7 to 9 years	206	201	97.5	1	0.6	200	96.9	-	-	-	-
10 to 13 years	348	328	94.3	-	-	309	88.8	19	5.5	-	-
14 and 15 years	230	220	95.5	-	-	32	14.1	187	81.4	-	-
16 and 17 years	284	256	89.9	-	-	2	0.8	244	85.7	10	3.4
18 and 19 years	368	223	60.5	-	-	3	0.9	99	27.0	120	32.6
20 and 21 years	607	216	35.6	-	-	-	-	7	1.2	209	34.4
22 to 24 years	1 014	220	21.7	-	-	6	0.6	8	0.8	205	20.2
25 to 29 years	1 952	188	9.6	-	-	1	-	5	0.3	182	9.3
30 to 34 years	2 137	103	4.8	-	-	-	-	3	0.2	99	4.6
35 to 44 years	3 943	116	2.9	-	-	6	0.2	23	0.6	86	2.2
45 to 54 years	2 833	58	2.0	-	-	-	-	-	-	58	2.0
55 years and over	3 327	16	0.5	-	-	-	-	-	-	16	0.5
Female											
3 years and over	17 463	2 446	14.0	110	0.6	724	4.1	543	3.1	1 069	6.1
3 and 4 years	101	59	58.8	59	58.8	-	-	-	-	-	-
5 and 6 years	125	116	93.5	50	40.5	66	53.0	-	-	-	-
7 to 9 years	240	236	98.1	-	-	236	98.1	-	-	-	-
10 to 13 years	402	390	96.9	-	-	359	89.3	31	7.6	-	-
14 and 15 years	207	200	97.0	-	-	50	24.1	151	72.9	-	-
16 and 17 years	301	271	90.3	-	-	-	-	257	85.3	15	4.9
18 and 19 years	323	208	64.2	-	-	-	-	62	19.2	146	45.0
20 and 21 years	432	191	44.2	-	-	2	0.5	2	0.5	186	43.1
22 to 24 years	793	184	23.2	-	-	-	-	9	1.2	175	22.0
25 to 29 years	1 648	237	14.4	-	-	5	0.3	4	0.2	228	13.8
30 to 34 years	1 931	114	5.9	-	-	-	-	10	0.5	104	5.4
35 to 44 years	3 842	165	4.3	-	-	3	0.1	14	0.4	148	3.9
45 to 54 years	2 829	60	2.1	-	-	-	-	2	0.1	58	2.0
55 years and over	4 290	15	0.4	-	-	3	0.1	2	0.1	10	0.2
CHILDREN OF FOREIGN-BORN PARENTS											
Both Sexes											
3 years and over	63 311	16 924	26.7	1 903	3.0	7 343	11.6	3 637	5.7	4 041	6.4
3 and 4 years	2 035	997	49.0	997	49.0	-	-	-	-	-	-
5 and 6 years	1 835	1 737	94.6	901	49.1	836	45.6	-	-	-	-
7 to 9 years	2 705	2 654	98.1	6	0.2	2 649	97.9	-	-	-	-
10 to 13 years	3 706	3 650	98.5	-	-	3 543	95.6	107	2.9	-	-
14 and 15 years	1 763	1 719	97.5	-	-	276	15.7	1 436	81.5	7	0.4
16 and 17 years	1 828	1 716	93.8	-	-	2	0.1	1 657	90.6	56	3.1
18 and 19 years	1 592	1 053	66.1	-	-	3	0.2	305	19.2	744	46.7
20 and 21 years	2 011	946	47.0	-	-	2	0.1	31	1.5	913	45.4
22 to 24 years	2 959	825	27.9	-	-	9	0.3	25	0.8	791	26.7
25 to 29 years	5 260	660	12.5	-	-	9	0.2	16	0.3	635	12.1
30 to 34 years	5 457	339	6.2	-	-	-	-	13	0.2	326	6.0
35 to 44 years	10 013	384	3.8	-	-	10	0.1	38	0.4	336	3.4
45 to 54 years	7 694	182	2.4	-	-	-	-	6	0.1	176	2.3
55 years and over	14 453	63	0.4	-	-	3	-	2	-	58	0.4
Male											
3 years and over	31 396	8 390	26.7	1 028	3.3	3 659	11.7	1 822	5.8	1 881	6.0
3 and 4 years	1 081	522	48.3	522	48.3	-	-	-	-	-	-
5 and 6 years	989	934	94.5	500	50.6	434	43.9	-	-	-	-
7 to 9 years	1 329	1 292	97.2	6	0.4	1 286	96.8	-	-	-	-
10 to 13 years	1 857	1 829	98.5	-	-	1 776	95.6	54	2.9	-	-
14 and 15 years	864	839	97.1	-	-	141	16.3	699	80.8	-	-
16 and 17 years	876	826	94.3	-	-	2	0.3	804	91.7	21	2.3
18 and 19 years	842	530	63.0	-	-	3	0.4	189	22.5	338	40.1
20 and 21 years	1 097	491	44.7	-	-	-	-	22	2.0	469	42.7
22 to 24 years	1 580	429	27.1	-	-	9	0.6	15	1.0	404	25.6
25 to 29 years	2 770	272	9.8	-	-	1	-	13	0.5	258	9.3
30 to 34 years	2 821	164	5.8	-	-	-	-	3	0.1	160	5.7
35 to 44 years	5 015	154	3.1	-	-	6	0.1	23	0.5	124	2.5
45 to 54 years	3 875	78	2.0	-	-	-	-	-	-	78	2.0
55 years and over	6 400	30	0.5	-	-	-	-	-	-	30	0.5

- = Quantity zero or rounds to zero.

Table A-1. Enrollment Status of the Population Age 3 Years and Over, by Age, Sex, Race, Hispanic Origin, Nativity, and Selected Educational Characteristics, October 2005—*Continued*

(Numbers in thousands, percent.)

Age, sex, race, Hispanic origin, and nativity	Not enrolled in school					
	Total		High school graduate		Not a high school graduate	
	Number	Percent	Number	Percent	Number	Percent
FOREIGN-BORN						
Both Sexes						
3 years and over	30 157	86.4	20 112	57.6	10 045	28.8
3 and 4 years	69	38.7	-	-	69	38.7
5 and 6 years	14	5.4	-	-	14	5.4
7 to 9 years	10	2.1	-	-	10	2.1
10 to 13 years	32	4.3	-	-	32	4.3
14 and 15 years	17	3.8	5	1.1	12	2.7
16 and 17 years	58	9.9	19	3.2	39	6.7
18 and 19 years	261	37.7	134	19.3	127	18.4
20 and 21 years	632	60.9	342	32.9	290	28.0
22 to 24 years	1 404	77.7	853	47.2	551	30.5
25 to 29 years	3 175	88.2	2 073	57.6	1 102	30.6
30 to 34 years	3 852	94.7	2 562	63.0	1 290	31.7
35 to 44 years	7 503	96.4	5 203	66.8	2 301	29.6
45 to 54 years	5 544	97.9	3 955	69.8	1 590	28.1
55 years and over	7 586	99.6	4 967	65.2	2 619	34.4
Male						
3 years and over	15 140	86.7	9 976	57.1	5 164	29.6
3 and 4 years	27	35.4	-	-	27	35.4
5 and 6 years	6	4.4	-	-	6	4.4
7 to 9 years	5	2.5	-	-	5	2.5
10 to 13 years	20	5.7	-	-	20	5.7
14 and 15 years	10	4.5	5	2.1	5	2.4
16 and 17 years	29	10.1	8	2.7	21	7.4
18 and 19 years	145	39.5	72	19.6	73	19.9
20 and 21 years	391	64.4	192	31.6	199	32.8
22 to 24 years	795	78.3	454	44.7	341	33.6
25 to 29 years	1 764	90.4	1 095	56.1	669	34.3
30 to 34 years	2 034	95.2	1 316	61.6	718	33.6
35 to 44 years	3 827	97.1	2 595	65.8	1 232	31.2
45 to 54 years	2 776	98.0	1 964	69.3	812	28.7
55 years and over	3 311	99.5	2 276	68.4	1 034	31.1
Female						
3 years and over	15 017	86.0	10 136	58.0	4 881	28.0
3 and 4 years	42	41.2	-	-	42	41.2
5 and 6 years	8	6.5	*	-	8	6.5
7 to 9 years	4	1.9	-	-	4	1.9
10 to 13 years	13	3.1	-	-	13	3.1
14 and 15 years	6	3.0	-	-	6	3.0
16 and 17 years	29	9.7	11	3.8	18	6.0
18 and 19 years	116	35.8	61	19.0	54	16.8
20 and 21 years	241	55.8	150	34.8	91	21.1
22 to 24 years	609	76.8	399	50.3	210	26.5
25 to 29 years	1 411	85.6	978	59.4	433	26.3
30 to 34 years	1 818	94.1	1 246	64.5	572	29.6
35 to 44 years	3 677	95.7	2 608	67.9	1 069	27.8
45 to 54 years	2 769	97.9	1 991	70.4	778	27.5
55 years and over	4 275	99.6	2 691	62.7	1 584	36.9
CHILDREN OF FOREIGN-BORN PARENTS						
Both Sexes						
3 years and over	46 386	73.3	32 904	52.0	13 482	21.3
3 and 4 years	1 038	51.0	-	-	1 038	51.0
5 and 6 years	98	5.4	-	-	98	5.4
7 to 9 years	50	1.9	-	-	50	1.9
10 to 13 years	56	1.5	-	-	56	1.5
14 and 15 years	44	2.5	11	0.6	33	1.9
16 and 17 years	113	6.2	32	1.7	81	4.4
18 and 19 years	539	33.9	329	20.7	210	13.2
20 and 21 years	1 066	53.0	652	32.4	413	20.5
22 to 24 years	2 134	72.1	1 499	50.7	635	21.5
25 to 29 years	4 600	87.5	3 342	63.5	1 259	23.9
30 to 34 years	5 117	93.8	3 731	68.4	1 386	25.4
35 to 44 years	9 629	96.2	7 145	71.4	2 484	24.8
45 to 54 years	7 512	97.6	5 760	74.9	1 752	22.8
55 years and over	14 390	99.6	10 402	72.0	3 988	27.6
Male						
3 years and over	23 005	73.3	16 124	51.4	6 882	21.9
3 and 4 years	559	51.7	-	-	559	51.7
5 and 6 years	54	5.5	-	-	54	5.5
7 to 9 years	37	2.8	-	-	37	2.8
10 to 13 years	28	1.5	-	-	28	1.5
14 and 15 years	25	2.9	9	1.0	17	1.9
16 and 17 years	50	5.7	15	1.7	35	4.0
18 and 19 years	312	37.0	180	21.4	132	15.6
20 and 21 years	606	55.3	332	30.2	274	25.0
22 to 24 years	1 151	72.9	759	48.0	392	24.8
25 to 29 years	2 499	90.2	1 754	63.3	744	26.9
30 to 34 years	2 657	94.2	1 874	66.4	783	27.8
35 to 44 years	4 861	96.9	3 521	70.2	1 339	26.7
45 to 54 years	3 797	98.0	2 895	74.7	902	23.3
55 years and over	6 370	99.5	4 785	74.8	1 585	24.8

- = Quantity zero or rounds to zero.

Table A-1. Enrollment Status of the Population Age 3 Years and Over, by Age, Sex, Race, Hispanic Origin, Nativity, and Selected Educational Characteristics, October 2005—*Continued*

(Numbers in thousands, percent.)

Age, sex, race, Hispanic origin, and nativity	Total population	Enrolled in school									
		Total		Nursery or kindergarten		Elementary		High school		College	
		Number	Percent	Number	Percent	Number	Percent	Number	Percent	Number	Percent
CHILDREN OF FOREIGN-BORN PARENTS											
Female											
3 years and over	31 915	8 534	26.7	875	2.7	3 684	11.5	1 815	5.7	2 160	6.8
3 and 4 years	954	475	49.8	475	49.8	-	-	-	-	-	-
5 and 6 years	846	802	94.8	400	47.3	402	47.5	-	-	-	-
7 to 9 years	1 376	1 363	99.0	-	-	1 363	99.0	-	-	-	-
10 to 13 years	1 849	1 821	98.5	-	-	1 768	95.6	54	2.9	-	-
14 and 15 years	898	880	97.9	-	-	136	15.1	737	82.1	7	0.7
16 and 17 years	952	889	93.4	-	-	-	-	854	89.6	36	3.7
18 and 19 years	750	522	69.7	-	-	-	-	116	15.5	406	54.2
20 and 21 years	914	455	49.8	-	-	2	0.2	9	1.0	444	48.6
22 to 24 years	1 380	397	28.7	-	-	-	-	10	0.7	387	28.0
25 to 29 years	2 490	388	15.6	-	-	8	0.3	4	0.2	376	15.1
30 to 34 years	2 636	176	6.7	-	-	-	-	10	0.4	166	6.3
35 to 44 years	4 998	230	4.6	-	-	3	0.1	15	0.3	212	4.2
45 to 54 years	3 819	103	2.7	-	-	-	-	5	0.1	98	2.6
55 years and over	8 053	33	0.4	-	-	3	-	2	-	28	0.3

- = Quantity zero or rounds to zero.

Table A-1. Enrollment Status of the Population Age 3 Years and Over, by Age, Sex, Race, Hispanic Origin, Nativity, and Selected Educational Characteristics, October 2005—*Continued*

(Numbers in thousands, percent.)

Age, sex, race, Hispanic origin, and nativity	Not enrolled in school					
	Total		High school graduate		Not a high school graduate	
	Number	Percent	Number	Percent	Number	Percent
CHILDREN OF FOREIGN-BORN PARENTS						
Female						
3 years and over	23 381	73.3	16 780	52.6	6 601	20.7
3 and 4 years	479	50.2	-	-	479	50.2
5 and 6 years	44	5.2	-	-	44	5.2
7 to 9 years	13	1.0	-	-	13	1.0
10 to 13 years	28	1.5	-	-	28	1.5
14 and 15 years	18	2.1	2	0.2	16	1.8
16 and 17 years	63	6.6	17	1.8	46	4.8
18 and 19 years	228	30.3	149	19.9	78	10.5
20 and 21 years	459	50.2	321	35.1	139	15.2
22 to 24 years	983	71.3	740	53.7	243	17.6
25 to 29 years	2 102	84.4	1 587	63.8	514	20.7
30 to 34 years	2 460	93.3	1 857	70.5	603	22.9
35 to 44 years	4 768	95.4	3 624	72.5	1 145	22.9
45 to 54 years	3 715	97.3	2 865	75.0	850	22.3
55 years and over	8 020	99.6	5 617	69.7	2 403	29.8

- = Quantity zero or rounds to zero.

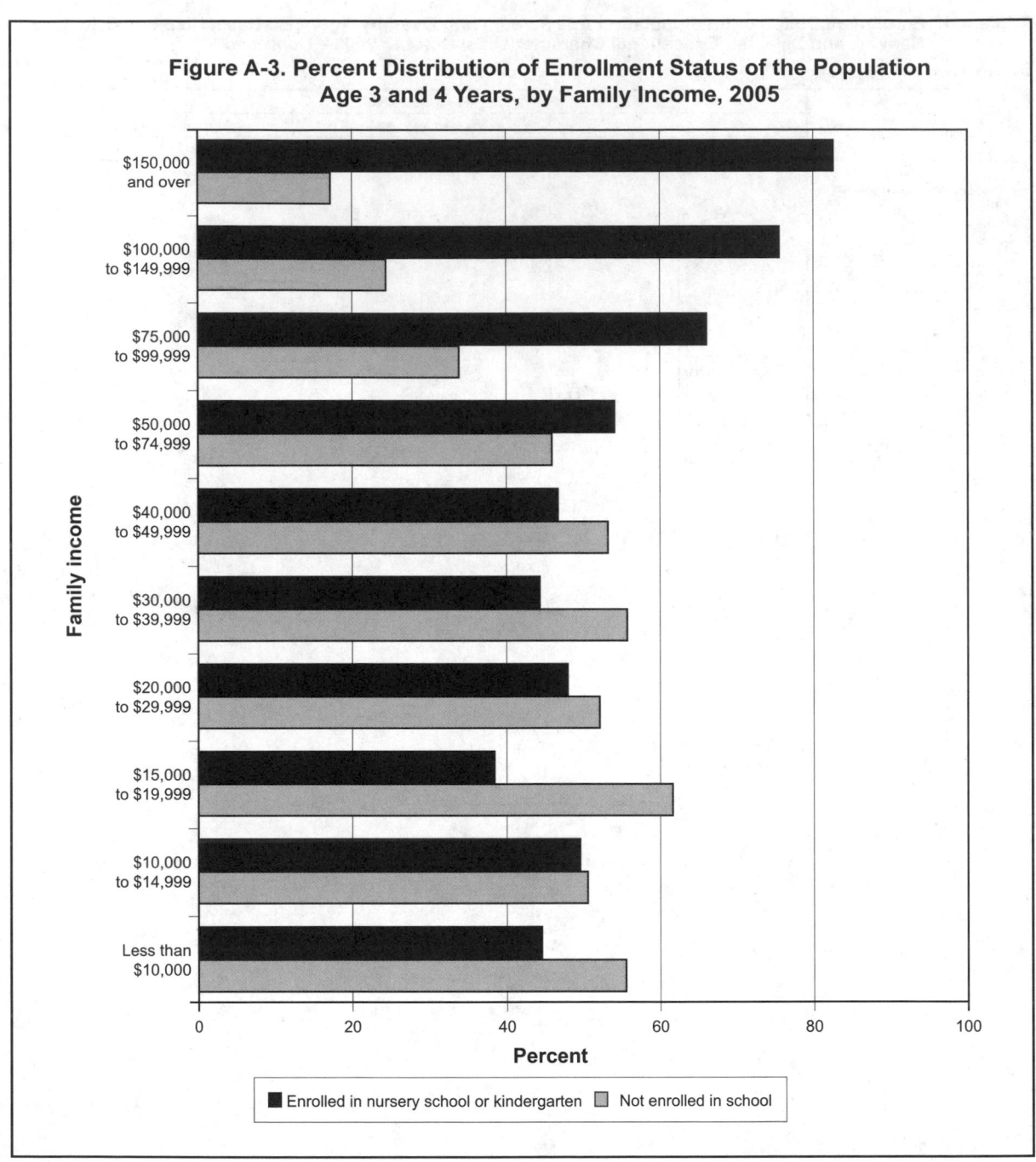

Figure A-3. Percent Distribution of Enrollment Status of the Population
Age 3 and 4 Years, by Family Income, 2005

In 2005, 54 percent of all 3- and 4-year-olds were enrolled in nursery school or kindergarten. As family income increased, school enrollment increased, as many of these programs were only available through private schools. Approximately 83 percent of children from families with incomes of over $150,000 were enrolled in nursery school or kindergarten, while only 46 percent of 3- and 4-year-olds from families with incomes of less than $30,000 attended school. (Table A-2)

Table A-2. Nursery and Primary School Enrollment of the Population Age 3 to 6 Years, by Mother's Labor Force Status and Education, Family Income, Race, and Hispanic Origin, October 2005

(Numbers in thousands.)

Characteristic	Population	Not enrolled	Nursery school	Kindergarten	Elementary school
ALL RACES					
3 to 6 Years					
Total	16 024	4 155	4 603	3 877	3 389
Labor force status of mother					
Children not living with mother	1 318	413	340	296	269
Mother employed part time	2 513	493	859	604	557
Mother employed full time	6 383	1 484	1 911	1 587	1 400
Mother unemployed	624	171	163	153	138
Mother not in the labor force	5 186	1 593	1 331	1 238	1 024
Education of mother					
Children not living with mother	1 318	413	340	296	269
Elementary: 0 to 8 years	663	269	89	156	149
High school: 9 to 11 years	1 336	434	307	324	271
High school graduate	3 925	1 176	985	934	830
Some college or associate's degree	4 274	1 038	1 241	1 056	940
Bachelor's degree or more	4 507	825	1 642	1 110	930
Family income	16 024	4 155	4 603	3 877	3 389
Less than $10,000	1 241	383	326	251	281
$10,000 to $14,999	744	213	206	175	150
$15,000 to $19,999	662	238	123	193	107
$20,000 to $29,999	1 632	530	441	316	345
$30,000 to $39,999	1 664	494	394	454	322
$40,000 to $49,999	1 212	362	311	285	254
$50,000 to $74,999	2 760	681	843	652	584
$75,000 to $99,999	1 537	287	510	403	338
$100,000 to $149,999	1 296	173	538	308	277
$150,000 and over	953	92	394	263	205
Not reported	2 323	702	519	576	526
3 to 4 Years					
Total	8 179	3 796	4 024	359	-
Labor force status of mother					
Children not living with mother	678	373	275	30	-
Mother employed part time	1 246	453	746	47	-
Mother employed full time	3 196	1 377	1 685	134	-
Mother unemployed	307	164	127	16	-
Mother not in the labor force	2 753	1 430	1 190	133	-
Education of mother					
Children not living with mother	678	373	275	30	-
Elementary: 0 to 8 years	020	241	76	12	-
High school: 9 to 11 years	718	408	262	47	-
High school graduate	2 016	1 073	842	101	-
Some college or associate's degree	2 140	943	1 097	100	-
Bachelor's degree or more	2 298	757	1 471	70	-
Family income	8 179	3 796	4 024	359	-
Less than $10,000	672	373	274	25	-
$10,000 to $14,999	370	187	162	21	-
$15,000 to $19,999	357	220	102	35	-
$20,000 to $29,999	889	463	386	40	-
$30,000 to $39,999	830	462	353	15	-
$40,000 to $49,999	645	343	286	15	-
$50,000 to $74,999	1 403	644	706	53	-
$75,000 to $99,999	758	257	468	33	-
$100,000 to $149,999	657	160	478	19	-
$150,000 and over	454	78	353	22	-
Not reported	1 143	609	455	79	-
5 Years					
Total	3 955	261	505	2 913	276
Labor force status of mother					
Children not living with mother	326	33	58	221	15
Mother employed part time	606	29	102	446	29
Mother employed full time	1 624	76	190	1 228	130
Mother unemployed	157	-	27	112	18
Mother not in the labor force	1 242	123	128	906	84
Education of mother					
Children not living with mother	326	33	58	221	15
Elementary: 0 to 8 years	175	25	10	125	15
High school: 9 to 11 years	319	17	39	241	22
High school graduate	1 008	77	127	723	80
Some college or associate's degree	1 011	68	122	738	83
Bachelor's degree or more	1 116	41	148	866	61
Family income	3 955	261	505	2 913	276
Less than $10,000	272	10	46	184	31
$10,000 to $14,999	200	18	34	134	14
$15,000 to $19,999	176	15	21	131	9
$20,000 to $29,999	357	45	41	240	31
$30,000 to $39,999	452	29	37	364	22
$40,000 to $49,999	270	6	22	216	26
$50,000 to $74,999	694	25	123	504	42
$75,000 to $99,999	365	13	36	306	11
$100,000 to $149,999	316	10	49	249	8
$150,000 and over	259	9	41	194	16
Not reported	595	81	55	392	67

- = Quantity zero or rounds to zero.

Table A-2. Nursery and Primary School Enrollment of the Population Age 3 to 6 Years, by Mother's Labor Force Status and Education, Family Income, Race, and Hispanic Origin, October 2005—*Continued*

(Numbers in thousands.)

Characteristic	Population	Not enrolled	Nursery school	Kindergarten	Elementary school
ALL RACES					
6 Years					
Total	3 889	98	74	605	3 112
Labor force status of mother					
Children not living with mother	314	8	6	45	254
Mother employed part time	661	11	12	111	527
Mother employed full time	1 563	31	36	225	1 271
Mother unemployed	160	7	8	26	120
Mother not in the labor force	1 191	41	12	198	940
Education of mother					
Children not living with mother	314	8	6	45	254
Elementary: 0 to 8 years	159	3	3	20	134
High school: 9 to 11 years	299	8	5	37	249
High school graduate	901	26	15	110	749
Some college or associate's degree	1 123	26	21	218	857
Bachelor's degree or more	1 093	26	23	175	869
Family income	3 889	98	74	605	3 112
Less than $10,000	297	-	6	42	250
$10,000 to $14,999	175	8	10	20	136
$15,000 to $19,999	129	3	-	27	98
$20,000 to $29,999	386	22	14	36	314
$30,000 to $39,999	382	3	4	75	300
$40,000 to $49,999	297	12	3	54	228
$50,000 to $74,999	663	11	13	95	543
$75,000 to $99,999	413	17	5	65	327
$100,000 to $149,999	324	4	11	40	269
$150,000 and over	240	4	-	46	189
Not reported	585	12	9	105	459
WHITE ALONE OR IN COMBINATION					
3 to 6 Years					
Total	12 684	3 261	3 642	3 159	2 622
Labor force status of mother					
Children not living with mother	972	301	234	230	207
Mother employed part time	2 167	434	730	528	474
Mother employed full time	4 792	1 121	1 430	1 235	1 006
Mother unemployed	370	107	103	100	60
Mother not in the labor force	4 383	1 298	1 145	1 065	875
Education of mother					
Children not living with mother	972	301	234	230	207
Elementary: 0 to 8 years	590	234	82	139	136
High school: 9 to 11 years	1 002	331	228	243	199
High school graduate	3 024	903	737	752	632
Some college or associate's degree	3 405	850	991	853	712
Bachelor's degree or more	3 692	643	1 371	942	736
Family income	12 684	3 261	3 642	3 159	2 622
Less than $10,000	681	235	176	144	126
$10,000 to $14,999	475	133	141	122	80
$15,000 to $19,999	504	187	85	142	88
$20,000 to $29,999	1 263	447	297	262	257
$30,000 to $39,999	1 345	390	307	372	275
$40,000 to $49,999	1 031	298	254	260	219
$50,000 to $74,999	2 376	590	722	567	497
$75,000 to $99,999	1 339	260	427	352	300
$100,000 to $149,999	1 094	138	463	275	217
$150,000 and over	856	72	361	243	180
Not reported	1 720	510	409	420	381
3 to 4 Years					
Total	6 445	2 970	3 199	277	-
Labor force status of mother					
Children not living with mother	485	273	194	18	-
Mother employed part time	1 070	402	625	43	-
Mother employed full time	2 392	1 039	1 262	91	-
Mother unemployed	203	103	85	15	-
Mother not in the labor force	2 296	1 153	1 032	111	-
Education of mother					
Children not living with mother	485	273	194	18	-
Elementary: 0 to 8 years	285	207	68	10	-
High school: 9 to 11 years	556	314	196	46	-
High school graduate	1 517	821	623	73	-
Some college or associate's degree	1 724	764	881	78	-
Bachelor's degree or more	1 878	591	1 235	52	-
Family income	6 445	2 970	3 199	277	-
Less than $10,000	395	226	149	21	-
$10,000 to $14,999	234	119	100	15	-
$15,000 to $19,999	261	174	64	22	-
$20,000 to $29,999	678	396	256	26	-
$30,000 to $39,999	648	361	278	9	-
$40,000 to $49,999	529	280	233	15	-
$50,000 to $74,999	1 217	558	614	45	-
$75,000 to $99,999	643	234	388	20	-
$100,000 to $149,999	559	127	415	17	-
$150,000 and over	408	60	327	21	-
Not reported	874	434	375	65	-

- = Quantity zero or rounds to zero.

Table A-2. Nursery and Primary School Enrollment of the Population Age 3 to 6 Years, by Mother's Labor Force Status and Education, Family Income, Race, and Hispanic Origin, October 2005—*Continued*

(Numbers in thousands.)

Characteristic	Population	Not enrolled	Nursery school	Kindergarten	Elementary school
WHITE ALONE OR IN COMBINATION					
5 Years					
Total	3 159	209	386	2 378	186
Labor force status of mother					
Children not living with mother	238	24	33	168	13
Mother employed part time	528	21	94	386	27
Mother employed full time	1 243	54	136	976	76
Mother unemployed	89	-	15	72	2
Mother not in the labor force	1 062	109	108	776	68
Education of mother					
Children not living with mother	238	24	33	168	13
Elementary: 0 to 8 years	160	23	10	111	15
High school: 9 to 11 years	222	10	28	171	13
High school graduate	810	61	99	597	53
Some college or associate's degree	804	63	94	588	59
Bachelor's degree or more	924	27	122	742	33
Family income					
Less than $10,000	3 159	209	386	2 378	186
Less than $10,000	149	9	22	101	16
$10,000 to $14,999	144	10	31	94	9
$15,000 to $19,999	134	10	21	99	4
$20,000 to $29,999	286	33	31	201	21
$30,000 to $39,999	366	26	25	296	18
$40,000 to $49,999	239	6	21	193	19
$50,000 to $74,999	595	23	99	439	34
$75,000 to $99,999	317	10	34	269	3
$100,000 to $149,999	265	7	38	218	2
$150,000 and over	235	7	34	181	13
Not reported	429	67	29	286	47
6 Years					
Total	3 080	82	58	504	2 435
Labor force status of mother					
Children not living with mother	249	4	6	45	194
Mother employed part time	569	11	12	100	447
Mother employed full time	1 157	28	31	168	930
Mother unemployed	78	4	3	14	58
Mother not in the labor force	1 025	35	6	178	807
Education of mother					
Children not living with mother	249	4	6	45	194
Elementary: 0 to 8 years	145	3	3	18	121
High school: 9 to 11 years	223	7	5	26	185
High school graduate	696	21	15	81	579
Some college or associate's degree	877	22	16	187	652
Bachelor's degree or more	889	25	13	147	704
Family income					
Less than $10,000	3 080	82	58	504	2 435
Less than $10,000	138	-	6	22	110
$10,000 to $14,999	97	4	10	12	72
$15,000 to $19,999	110	3	-	21	85
$20,000 to $29,999	299	18	11	34	236
$30,000 to $39,999	330	3	4	66	257
$40,000 to $49,999	264	12	-	52	200
$50,000 to $74,999	564	8	9	83	463
$75,000 to $99,999	300	16	5	62	297
$100,000 to $149,999	270	4	11	40	215
$150,000 and over	212	4	-	41	167
Not reported	417	9	4	69	334
BLACK ALONE OR IN COMBINATION					
3 to 6 Years					
Total	2 667	716	763	578	609
Labor force status of mother					
Children not living with mother	324	104	93	64	63
Mother employed part time	276	53	103	63	57
Mother employed full time	1 283	295	384	280	325
Mother unemployed	233	59	58	46	69
Mother not in the labor force	550	205	125	125	95
Education of mother					
Children not living with mother	324	104	93	64	63
Elementary: 0 to 8 years	41	15	6	9	10
High school: 9 to 11 years	313	92	77	81	63
High school graduate	800	255	206	162	177
Some college or associate's degree	776	164	237	182	194
Bachelor's degree or more	413	87	145	80	102
Family income					
Less than $10,000	2 667	716	763	578	609
Less than $10,000	564	149	156	117	142
$10,000 to $14,999	236	70	56	50	59
$15,000 to $19,999	153	49	35	50	19
$20,000 to $29,999	318	75	119	59	65
$30,000 to $39,999	280	84	82	62	52
$40,000 to $49,999	133	33	50	18	32
$50,000 to $74,999	287	65	90	72	60
$75,000 to $99,999	119	23	37	29	30
$100,000 to $149,999	85	19	29	12	25
$150,000 and over	41	8	25	7	1
Not reported	452	142	84	101	125

- = Quantity zero or rounds to zero.

Table A-2. Nursery and Primary School Enrollment of the Population Age 3 to 6 Years, by Mother's Labor Force Status and Education, Family Income, Race, and Hispanic Origin, October 2005—*Continued*

(Numbers in thousands.)

Characteristic	Population	Not enrolled	Nursery school	Kindergarten	Elementary school
BLACK ALONE OR IN COMBINATION					
3 to 4 Years					
Total	1 365	666	649	51	-
Labor force status of mother					
Children not living with mother	182	95	75	12	-
Mother employed part time	147	47	99	-	-
Mother employed full time	640	274	337	30	-
Mother unemployed	99	57	41	1	-
Mother not in the labor force	298	193	97	8	-
Education of mother					
Children not living with mother	182	95	75	12	-
Elementary: 0 to 8 years	23	15	6	2	-
High school: 9 to 11 years	156	89	66	1	-
High school graduate	424	233	177	14	-
Some college or associate's degree	382	159	203	20	-
Bachelor's degree or more	199	75	122	2	-
Family income	1 365	666	649	51	-
Less than $10,000	285	148	132	5	-
$10,000 to $14,999	119	62	52	6	-
$15,000 to $19,999	92	44	35	13	-
$20,000 to $29,999	180	61	107	12	-
$30,000 to $39,999	156	81	72	3	-
$40,000 to $49,999	80	33	47	-	-
$50,000 to $74,999	135	62	65	8	-
$75,000 to $99,999	59	19	37	2	-
$100,000 to $149,999	37	16	22	-	-
$150,000 and over	34	8	25	2	-
Not reported	188	133	54	1	-
5 Years					
Total	651	38	99	444	71
Labor force status of mother					
Children not living with mother	78	5	18	52	3
Mother employed part time	66	6	3	57	-
Mother employed full time	307	18	43	203	44
Mother unemployed	58	-	12	33	13
Mother not in the labor force	142	9	22	99	12
Education of mother					
Children not living with mother	78	5	18	52	3
Elementary: 0 to 8 years	8	1	-	7	-
High school: 9 to 11 years	90	3	11	68	8
High school graduate	191	18	28	122	22
Some college or associate's degree	182	-	28	136	18
Bachelor's degree or more	102	11	13	59	19
Family income	651	38	99	444	71
Less than $10,000	133	1	24	94	15
$10,000 to $14,999	50	6	4	37	4
$15,000 to $19,999	42	5	-	32	5
$20,000 to $29,999	71	11	9	45	7
$30,000 to $39,999	67	3	10	51	4
$40,000 to $49,999	25	-	-	18	7
$50,000 to $74,999	81	2	20	56	3
$75,000 to $99,999	32	2	-	25	5
$100,000 to $149,999	26	3	8	12	3
$150,000 and over	3	-	-	3	-
Not reported	122	6	25	71	20
6 Years					
Total	651	13	16	84	539
Labor force status of mother					
Children not living with mother	65	4	-	1	60
Mother employed part time	63	-	-	6	57
Mother employed full time	336	3	4	47	281
Mother unemployed	77	3	5	12	57
Mother not in the labor force	111	3	6	18	83
Education of mother					
Children not living with mother	65	4	-	1	60
Elementary: 0 to 8 years	10	-	-	-	10
High school: 9 to 11 years	67	-	-	12	55
High school graduate	184	3	-	26	155
Some college or associate's degree	212	4	6	26	176
Bachelor's degree or more	113	1	10	19	83
Family income	651	13	16	84	539
Less than $10,000	145	-	-	18	127
$10,000 to $14,999	66	3	-	8	55
$15,000 to $19,999	19	-	-	5	14
$20,000 to $29,999	68	4	3	2	59
$30,000 to $39,999	57	-	-	9	48
$40,000 to $49,999	28	-	3	-	25
$50,000 to $74,999	71	1	5	8	58
$75,000 to $99,999	29	2	-	2	25
$100,000 to $149,999	22	-	-	-	22
$150,000 and over	4	-	-	3	1
Not reported	142	3	5	29	105

- = Quantity zero or rounds to zero.

Table A-2. Nursery and Primary School Enrollment of the Population Age 3 to 6 Years, by Mother's Labor Force Status and Education, Family Income, Race, and Hispanic Origin, October 2005—*Continued*

(Numbers in thousands.)

Characteristic	Population	Not enrolled	Nursery school	Kindergarten	Elementary school
ASIAN ALONE OR IN COMBINATION					
3 to 6 Years					
Total	775	209	220	158	189
Labor force status of mother					
Children not living with mother	22	5	9	6	1
Mother employed part time	107	18	38	15	35
Mother employed full time	358	85	102	88	84
Mother unemployed	27	8	3	8	9
Mother not in the labor force	261	93	67	41	59
Education of mother					
Children not living with mother	22	5	9	6	1
Elementary: 0 to 8 years	24	16	-	4	4
High school: 9 to 11 years	30	15	-	4	10
High school graduate	146	34	43	34	35
Some college or associate's degree	123	38	22	20	43
Bachelor's degree or more	430	101	144	91	95
Family income	775	209	220	158	189
Less than $10,000	22	7	-	1	14
$10,000 to $14,999	30	7	7	4	12
$15,000 to $19,999	3	3	-	-	-
$20,000 to $29,999	48	12	16	2	19
$30,000 to $39,999	63	22	12	23	5
$40,000 to $49,999	54	31	8	10	6
$50,000 to $74,999	93	27	35	7	24
$75,000 to $99,999	94	9	44	23	18
$100,000 to $149,999	130	19	47	27	38
$150,000 and over	81	16	22	18	24
Not reported	156	55	27	45	30
3 to 4 Years					
Total	423	193	197	33	-
Labor force status of mother					
Children not living with mother	8	3	5	-	-
Mother employed part time	49	14	31	4	-
Mother employed full time	189	82	93	14	-
Mother unemployed	10	8	3	-	-
Mother not in the labor force	167	86	66	14	-
Education of mother					
Children not living with mother	8	3	5	-	-
Elementary: 0 to 8 years	18	10	-	-	-
High school: 9 to 11 years	10	10	-	-	-
High school graduate	86	33	39	14	-
Some college or associate's degree	60	35	22	3	-
Bachelor's degree or more	243	97	131	16	-
Family income	423	193	197	33	-
Less than $10,000	7	7	-	-	-
$10,000 to $14,999	10	3	7	-	-
$15,000 to $19,999	3	3	-	-	-
$20,000 to $29,999	26	12	13	1	-
$30,000 to $39,999	36	22	10	4	-
$40,000 to $49,999	39	31	8	-	-
$50,000 to $74,999	52	25	20	-	-
$75,000 to $99,999	63	9	42	12	-
$100,000 to $149,999	68	19	47	3	-
$150,000 and over	30	15	15	-	-
Not reported	88	48	26	14	-
5 Years					
Total	165	13	22	112	18
Labor force status of mother					
Children not living with mother	12	2	5	5	-
Mother employed part time	26	4	7	11	4
Mother employed full time	81	3	9	62	7
Mother unemployed	11	-	-	8	3
Mother not in the labor force	35	4	1	25	5
Education of mother					
Children not living with mother	12	2	5	5	-
Elementary: 0 to 8 years	2	-	-	2	-
High school: 9 to 11 years	9	4	-	4	-
High school graduate	29	-	4	20	5
Some college or associate's degree	21	3	-	15	3
Bachelor's degree or more	93	4	14	66	10
Family income	165	13	22	112	18
Less than $10,000	1	-	-	1	-
$10,000 to $14,999	7	3	-	4	-
$15,000 to $19,999	-	-	-	-	-
$20,000 to $29,999	4	-	3	1	-
$30,000 to $39,999	22	-	2	20	-
$40,000 to $49,999	8	-	-	8	1
$50,000 to $74,999	20	-	7	7	5
$75,000 to $99,999	15	-	2	10	3
$100,000 to $149,999	27	-	-	24	3
$150,000 and over	24	2	7	12	3
Not reported	38	8	1	26	4

- = Quantity zero or rounds to zero.

Table A-2. Nursery and Primary School Enrollment of the Population Age 3 to 6 Years, by Mother's Labor Force Status and Education, Family Income, Race, and Hispanic Origin, October 2005—*Continued*

(Numbers in thousands.)

Characteristic	Population	Not enrolled	Nursery school	Kindergarten	Elementary school
ASIAN ALONE OR IN COMBINATION					
6 Years					
Total	187	3	-	13	171
Labor force status of mother					
Children not living with mother	1	-	-	-	1
Mother employed part time	32	-	-	-	32
Mother employed full time	88	-	-	11	77
Mother unemployed	6	-	-	-	6
Mother not in the labor force	60	3	-	2	55
Education of mother					
Children not living with mother	1	-	-	-	1
Elementary: 0 to 8 years	6	-	-	2	4
High school: 9 to 11 years	11	1	-	-	10
High school graduate	32	2	-	-	30
Some college or associate's degree	42	-	-	2	40
Bachelor's degree or more	94	-	-	9	85
Family income	187	3	-	13	171
Less than $10,000	14	-	-	-	14
$10,000 to $14,999	14	1	-	-	12
$15,000 to $19,999	-	-	-	-	-
$20,000 to $29,999	19	-	-	-	19
$30,000 to $39,999	5	-	-	-	5
$40,000 to $49,999	7	-	-	2	5
$50,000 to $74,999	21	2	-	-	19
$75,000 to $99,999	16	-	-	1	15
$100,000 to $149,999	35	-	-	-	35
$150,000 and over	27	-	-	6	21
Not reported	30	-	-	4	26
HISPANIC[1]					
3 to 6 Years					
Total	3 433	1 127	797	798	711
Labor force status of mother					
Children not living with mother	312	127	62	51	72
Mother employed part time	391	101	128	94	68
Mother employed full time	1 163	343	280	284	256
Mother unemployed	142	53	36	30	23
Mother not in the labor force	1 425	503	292	339	291
Education of mother					
Children not living with mother	312	127	62	51	72
Elementary: 0 to 8 years	509	199	71	123	116
High school: 9 to 11 years	643	187	155	164	137
High school graduate	964	368	217	181	198
Some college or associate's degree	604	165	159	166	114
Bachelor's degree or more	400	81	132	113	74
Family income	3 433	1 127	797	798	711
Less than $10,000	317	117	74	61	66
$10,000 to $14,999	243	70	70	57	46
$15,000 to $19,999	276	103	54	67	52
$20,000 to $29,999	617	243	129	119	126
$30,000 to $39,999	433	145	71	125	92
$40,000 to $49,999	241	77	61	44	59
$50,000 to $74,999	448	142	107	103	96
$75,000 to $99,999	196	39	50	60	47
$100,000 to $149,999	112	13	33	48	18
$150,000 and over	62	3	30	15	13
Not reported	486	177	116	99	94
3 to 4 Years					
Total	1 799	1 026	669	105	-
Labor force status of mother					
Children not living with mother	174	117	48	9	-
Mother employed part time	221	97	107	17	-
Mother employed full time	579	315	234	30	-
Mother unemployed	78	50	25	4	-
Mother not in the labor force	747	447	256	45	-
Education of mother					
Children not living with mother	174	117	48	9	-
Elementary: 0 to 8 years	241	180	58	3	-
High school: 9 to 11 years	346	177	135	34	-
High school graduate	521	321	172	27	-
Some college or associate's degree	317	156	145	16	-
Bachelor's degree or more	201	75	110	15	-
Family income	1 799	1 026	669	105	-
Less than $10,000	171	113	54	4	-
$10,000 to $14,999	127	63	54	9	-
$15,000 to $19,999	151	100	43	9	-
$20,000 to $29,999	335	211	109	16	-
$30,000 to $39,999	199	134	62	3	-
$40,000 to $49,999	146	75	61	10	-
$50,000 to $74,999	236	136	79	21	-
$75,000 to $99,999	82	31	44	7	-
$100,000 to $149,999	43	8	32	3	-
$150,000 and over	39	3	30	5	-
Not reported	270	152	100	18	-

[1]May be of any race.
- = Quantity zero or rounds to zero.

Table A-2. Nursery and Primary School Enrollment of the Population Age 3 to 6 Years, by Mother's Labor Force Status and Education, Family Income, Race, and Hispanic Origin, October 2005—*Continued*

(Numbers in thousands.)

Characteristic	Population	Not enrolled	Nursery school	Kindergarten	Elementary school
HISPANIC[1]					
5 Years					
Total	862	68	110	610	74
Labor force status of mother					
Children not living with mother	61	8	10	40	3
Mother employed part time	83	3	15	61	5
Mother employed full time	322	12	40	230	39
Mother unemployed	33	-	8	25	-
Mother not in the labor force	363	45	36	255	27
Education of mother					
Children not living with mother	61	8	10	40	3
Elementary: 0 to 8 years	142	16	10	102	13
High school: 9 to 11 years	147	3	16	116	12
High school graduate	240	33	40	140	28
Some college or associate's degree	156	6	12	126	13
Bachelor's degree or more	117	2	22	86	6
Family income	862	68	110	610	74
Less than $10,000	84	4	16	51	12
$10,000 to $14,999	68	5	14	43	5
$15,000 to $19,999	59	-	11	44	3
$20,000 to $29,999	143	17	14	95	16
$30,000 to $39,999	131	8	9	107	8
$40,000 to $49,999	35	2	-	27	6
$50,000 to $74,999	115	6	25	79	5
$75,000 to $99,999	59	3	6	50	-
$100,000 to $149,999	45	2	1	41	-
$150,000 and over	13	-	-	10	3
Not reported	111	21	14	61	16
6 Years					
Total	771	33	18	83	637
Labor force status of mother					
Children not living with mother	77	3	3	2	69
Mother employed part time	87	1	6	17	63
Mother employed full time	262	15	6	24	218
Mother unemployed	31	3	3	1	23
Mother not in the labor force	315	11	-	39	264
Education of mother					
Children not living with mother	77	3	3	2	69
Elementary: 0 to 8 years	120	0	3	1	103
High school: 9 to 11 years	149	7	3	14	125
High school graduate	203	14	5	14	170
Some college or associate's degree	132	3	3	24	102
Bachelor's degree or more	83	4	-	12	68
Family income	771	33	18	83	637
Less than $10,000	62	-	3	5	54
$10,000 to $14,999	49	1	3	5	41
$15,000 to $19,999	66	3	-	14	49
$20,000 to $29,999	139	15	6	8	111
$30,000 to $39,999	103	3	-	16	84
$40,000 to $49,999	60	-	-	7	53
$50,000 to $74,999	97	-	3	3	91
$75,000 to $99,999	55	5	-	3	47
$100,000 to $149,999	24	3	*	3	18
$150,000 and over	11	-	-	-	11
Not reported	105	4	3	20	78

[1]May be of any race.
- = Quantity zero or rounds to zero.

Table A-3. Current Grade for the Population Age 15 to 24 Years Enrolled in School and Highest Grade Completed for the Population Enrolled in School Last Year, by Sex, Family Income, Race, and Hispanic Origin (for Primary Family Members), October 2005

(Numbers in thousands.)

Family income, sex, race, and Hispanic origin	Total population	Enrolled, current grade						
		Less than 9th	9th	10th	11th	12th	First year of college (graduated this year)	Other college
ALL RACES								
Both Sexes	21 469	168	1 145	4 068	4 216	3 753	1 556	885
Less than $10,000	1 331	21	117	243	241	162	24	52
$10,000 to $14,999	1 037	20	95	176	161	164	15	27
$15,000 to $19,999	654	3	44	127	120	96	26	21
$20,000 to $29,999	1 996	15	133	411	338	374	93	66
$30,000 to $39,999	1 972	15	107	357	359	335	112	51
$40,000 to $49,999	1 649	11	69	314	310	272	91	80
$50,000 to $74,999	3 773	13	171	722	772	700	317	170
$75,000 to $99,999	2 279	14	104	490	481	415	227	98
$100,000 to $149,999	1 920	9	63	342	515	362	222	71
$150,000 and over	1 204	13	46	284	287	239	168	36
Not reported	3 654	35	197	601	632	636	262	213
Male	11 687	97	632	2 105	2 111	2 001	713	472
Less than $10,000	735	17	50	130	122	105	9	22
$10,000 to $14,999	542	7	58	72	76	94	6	9
$15,000 to $19,999	306	-	21	50	64	53	9	10
$20,000 to $29,999	1 110	7	79	231	175	198	31	41
$30,000 to $39,999	1 075	8	34	173	189	189	51	27
$40,000 to $49,999	876	9	40	173	149	117	40	40
$50,000 to $74,999	2 031	7	94	351	364	393	125	113
$75,000 to $99,999	1 252	7	58	288	232	180	120	57
$100,000 to $149,999	1 058	7	40	176	274	203	104	31
$150,000 and over	640	3	29	137	154	142	79	14
Not reported	2 063	23	128	323	313	327	140	109
Female	9 782	70	513	1 963	2 105	1 752	843	412
Less than $10,000	596	3	66	113	118	56	15	30
$10,000 to $14,999	495	13	37	104	85	71	9	18
$15,000 to $19,999	347	3	23	77	56	43	16	11
$20,000 to $29,999	887	7	54	181	164	175	61	24
$30,000 to $39,999	897	7	73	184	170	145	61	24
$40,000 to $49,999	773	2	29	140	161	155	51	40
$50,000 to $74,999	1 742	5	·77	371	408	308	192	57
$75,000 to $99,999	1 027	7	46	202	249	235	108	42
$100,000 to $149,999	863	1	23	167	241	158	118	41
$150,000 and over	564	9	16	147	134	97	89	22
Not reported	1 591	13	68	278	318	308	122	104
WHITE ALONE OR IN COMBINATION								
Both Sexes	16 845	103	874	3 272	3 347	2 990	1 321	630
Less than $10,000	745	14	54	144	113	111	16	21
$10,000 to $14,999	676	4	73	120	84	124	12	19
$15,000 to $19,999	465	2	33	86	82	54	15	16
$20,000 to $29,999	1 419	10	102	310	240	264	67	27
$30,000 to $39,999	1 520	12	88	283	277	252	80	39
$40,000 to $49,999	1 349	6	53	260	255	223	90	64
$50,000 to $74,999	3 161	5	151	612	624	602	274	116
$75,000 to $99,999	2 014	11	99	434	441	358	198	91
$100,000 to $149,999	1 720	7	52	319	462	321	194	62
$150,000 and over	1 111	10	43	263	265	218	158	34
Not reported	2 665	21	126	440	502	464	217	142
Male	9 165	58	484	1 703	1 648	1 594	596	335
Less than $10,000	414	10	18	83	64	74	6	2
$10,000 to $14,999	357	1	48	52	36	76	6	7
$15,000 to $19,999	218	-	14	31	43	31	3	7
$20,000 to $29,999	786	6	65	168	115	137	24	15
$30,000 to $39,999	837	8	29	135	138	138	36	20
$40,000 to $49,999	708	5	31	141	116	97	40	32
$50,000 to $74,999	1 717	2	85	299	303	334	100	79
$75,000 to $99,999	1 114	7	56	256	214	163	102	51
$100,000 to $149,999	953	5	35	170	237	183	92	30
$150,000 and over	584	3	26	129	134	131	74	14
Not reported	1 477	11	76	238	250	231	112	78
Female	7 680	44	389	1 569	1 699	1 396	724	295
Less than $10,000	331	3	36	62	49	36	10	19
$10,000 to $14,999	319	4	25	68	48	48	6	13
$15,000 to $19,999	248	2	18	56	39	22	12	9
$20,000 to $29,999	633	4	37	142	125	127	42	12
$30,000 to $39,999	683	4	59	148	139	114	44	19
$40,000 to $49,999	641	2	21	119	140	126	51	31
$50,000 to $74,999	1 444	2	67	312	322	268	174	37
$75,000 to $99,999	900	4	43	178	227	195	96	39
$100,000 to $149,999	767	1	17	149	225	138	102	32
$150,000 and over	527	7	16	134	131	86	83	20
Not reported	1 188	10	50	202	252	234	105	64

- = Quantity zero or rounds to zero.

Table A-3. Current Grade for the Population Age 15 to 24 Years Enrolled in School and Highest Grade Completed for the Population Enrolled in School Last Year, by Sex, Family Income, Race, and Hispanic Origin (for Primary Family Members), October 2005—*Continued*

(Numbers in thousands.)

Family income, sex, race, and Hispanic origin	Not enrolled (enrolled last year), highest grade completed						Not enrolled and not enrolled last year
	7th or 8th	9th	10th	11th	12th (graduated this year)	Some college	
ALL RACES							
Both Sexes	16	69	56	204	707	498	4 130
Less than $10,000	-	7	2	29	57	25	352
$10,000 to $14,999	-	4	1	30	27	14	303
$15,000 to $19,999	-	2	5	8	26	14	163
$20,000 to $29,999	8	8	7	24	69	28	423
$30,000 to $39,999	3	9	4	6	77	42	495
$40,000 to $49,999	-	10	5	19	72	56	342
$50,000 to $74,999	3	6	11	26	112	102	646
$75,000 to $99,999	1	-	-	19	73	65	292
$100,000 to $149,999	-	7	1	6	31	46	245
$150,000 and over	-	5	-	4	26	31	67
Not reported	-	10	19	33	139	77	802
Male	11	47	36	114	388	283	2 676
Less than $10,000	-	4	2	26	13	18	216
$10,000 to $14,999	-	4	-	15	9	-	191
$15,000 to $19,999	-	2	4	-	12	3	77
$20,000 to $29,999	8	2	7	8	32	19	271
$30,000 to $39,999	-	9	-	1	48	30	316
$40,000 to $49,999	-	10	-	12	41	29	218
$50,000 to $74,999	1	6	11	17	62	49	437
$75,000 to $99,999	1	-	-	13	58	33	206
$100,000 to $149,999	-	4	1	1	21	29	167
$150,000 and over	-	-	-	-	20	20	42
Not reported	-	6	10	20	73	53	537
Female	5	22	19	90	319	215	1 453
Less than $10,000	-	4	-	3	44	7	136
$10,000 to $14,999	-	-	1	15	18	14	112
$15,000 to $19,999	-	-	1	7	14	11	86
$20,000 to $29,999	-	6	-	16	37	9	152
$30,000 to $39,999	3	-	4	5	29	12	179
$40,000 to $49,999	-	-	5	8	31	27	124
$50,000 to $74,999	2	-	-	9	50	53	209
$75,000 to $99,999	-	-	-	6	15	32	86
$100,000 to $149,999	-	3	-	5	10	16	79
$150,000 and over	-	5	-	4	6	11	25
Not reported	-	4	9	13	65	23	265
WHITE ALONE OR IN COMBINATION							
Both Sexes	12	43	40	138	533	395	3 146
Less than $10,000	-	-	2	16	28	14	211
$10,000 to $14,999	-	1	-	17	23	10	187
$15,000 to $19,999	-	2	5	2	20	10	138
$20,000 to $29,999	6	5	4	16	47	19	302
$30,000 to $39,999	3	5	-	5	58	33	384
$40,000 to $49,999	-	10	5	18	58	35	273
$50,000 to $74,999	3	6	11	26	91	93	546
$75,000 to $99,999	1	-	-	13	69	50	250
$100,000 to $149,999	-	3	1	6	31	43	219
$150,000 and over	-	5	-	4	20	28	64
Not reported	-	6	11	16	88	61	573
Male	8	28	25	72	302	225	2 085
Less than $10,000	-	-	2	13	5	11	126
$10,000 to $14,999	-	1	-	8	6	-	117
$15,000 to $19,999	-	2	4	-	10	3	69
$20,000 to $29,999	6	2	4	8	24	10	201
$30,000 to $39,999	-	5	-	-	42	27	258
$40,000 to $49,999	-	10	-	10	29	15	183
$50,000 to $74,999	1	6	11	17	55	44	380
$75,000 to $99,999	1	-	-	7	55	24	178
$100,000 to $149,999	-	-	1	1	21	29	148
$150,000 and over	-	-	-	-	14	17	40
Not reported	-	2	3	7	42	43	385
Female	5	15	15	66	231	170	1 061
Less than $10,000	-	-	-	3	24	3	85
$10,000 to $14,999	-	-	-	9	17	10	70
$15,000 to $19,999	-	-	1	2	9	7	70
$20,000 to $29,999	-	3	-	7	23	9	100
$30,000 to $39,999	3	-	-	5	16	6	126
$40,000 to $49,999	-	-	5	8	29	20	91
$50,000 to $74,999	2	-	-	9	37	49	166
$75,000 to $99,999	-	-	-	6	14	26	72
$100,000 to $149,999	-	3	-	5	10	13	71
$150,000 and over	-	5	-	4	6	11	23
Not reported	-	4	9	9	46	17	187

- = Quantity zero or rounds to zero.

Table A-3. Current Grade for the Population Age 15 to 24 Years Enrolled in School and Highest Grade Completed for the Population Enrolled in School Last Year, by Sex, Family Income, Race, and Hispanic Origin (for Primary Family Members), October 2005—*Continued*

(Numbers in thousands.)

Family income, sex, race, and Hispanic origin	Total population	Enrolled, current grade						
		Less than 9th	9th	10th	11th	12th	First year of college (graduated this year)	Other college
BLACK ALONE OR IN COMBINATION								
Both Sexes	3 773	61	251	653	686	587	183	177
Less than $10,000	573	7	61	99	127	49	8	32
$10,000 to $14,999	344	15	22	51	76	42	3	5
$15,000 to $19,999	143	1	11	34	34	28	8	-
$20,000 to $29,999	503	3	25	91	85	93	21	32
$30,000 to $39,999	361	3	18	65	60	65	25	9
$40,000 to $49,999	238	4	11	37	40	40	3	11
$50,000 to $74,999	443	8	17	84	103	70	28	25
$75,000 to $99,999	199	3	5	45	26	34	25	6
$100,000 to $149,999	144	2	11	18	30	27	23	3
$150,000 and over	55	2	3	14	11	14	3	-
Not reported	771	12	67	117	94	126	37	53
Male	2 033	34	139	317	360	320	95	88
Less than $10,000	314	7	32	48	55	30	3	20
$10,000 to $14,999	176	6	10	18	40	19	-	1
$15,000 to $19,999	60	-	7	14	16	13	3	-
$20,000 to $29,999	277	-	10	52	48	59	4	24
$30,000 to $39,999	182	-	4	33	35	40	11	3
$40,000 to $49,999	121	4	6	17	24	17	-	3
$50,000 to $74,999	230	5	9	39	47	49	20	11
$75,000 to $99,999	108	-	2	27	13	5	15	4
$100,000 to $149,999	83	2	5	8	25	12	11	-
$150,000 and over	33	-	3	5	11	8	-	-
Not reported	450	9	51	56	45	68	27	22
Female	1 740	26	112	336	326	267	89	89
Less than $10,000	259	-	28	50	72	19	5	12
$10,000 to $14,999	167	9	12	33	35	22	3	4
$15,000 to $19,999	83	-	4	20	17	15	5	-
$20,000 to $29,999	226	3	16	38	38	33	17	9
$30,000 to $39,999	180	3	14	32	25	25	14	6
$40,000 to $49,999	117	-	5	20	16	23	3	8
$50,000 to $74,999	213	3	8	45	56	21	8	14
$75,000 to $99,999	91	3	3	18	13	30	10	2
$100,000 to $149,999	60	-	6	10	6	15	12	3
$150,000 and over	23	2	-	8	-	6	3	-
Not reported	321	3	15	61	48	57	10	31
ASIAN ALONE OR IN COMBINATION								
Both Sexes	834	21	15	154	212	180	59	70
Less than $10,000	20	-	-	5	6	-	-	-
$10,000 to $14,999	8	-	-	3	-	-	-	-
$15,000 to $19,999	33	-	-	8	3	13	3	1
$20,000 to $29,999	61	-	-	5	16	19	4	7
$30,000 to $39,999	64	3	3	6	16	14	1	3
$40,000 to $49,999	53	6	6	19	14	5	-	6
$50,000 to $74,999	199	2	2	33	48	39	16	25
$75,000 to $99,999	90	-	-	12	27	27	9	2
$100,000 to $149,999	93	-	-	14	33	25	8	6
$150,000 and over	47	2	-	11	12	8	9	2
Not reported	168	9	5	37	37	30	8	19
Male	449	11	7	77	96	101	29	42
Less than $10,000	9	-	-	3	3	-	-	-
$10,000 to $14,999	3	-	-	-	-	-	-	-
$15,000 to $19,999	26	-	-	8	3	8	3	-
$20,000 to $29,999	27	-	-	3	5	6	3	3
$30,000 to $39,999	40	3	3	1	9	11	-	3
$40,000 to $49,999	33	3	3	11	9	2	-	6
$50,000 to $74,999	90	-	-	14	11	18	5	21
$75,000 to $99,999	48	-	-	6	14	14	8	2
$100,000 to $149,999	51	-	-	6	20	18	2	-
$150,000 and over	27	-	-	6	9	4	5	-
Not reported	93	6	2	20	13	21	2	7
Female	385	10	8	77	116	80	29	28
Less than $10,000	11	-	-	2	3	-	-	-
$10,000 to $14,999	5	-	-	3	-	-	-	-
$15,000 to $19,999	7	-	-	-	-	5	-	1
$20,000 to $29,999	33	-	-	2	11	13	1	4
$30,000 to $39,999	24	-	-	6	7	3	1	-
$40,000 to $49,999	20	3	3	8	5	3	-	-
$50,000 to $74,999	109	2	2	19	37	22	10	4
$75,000 to $99,999	41	-	-	6	14	13	1	-
$100,000 to $149,999	41	-	-	8	13	7	6	6
$150,000 and over	20	2	-	5	2	5	3	2
Not reported	75	3	3	18	24	9	6	12

- = Quantity zero or rounds to zero.

Table A-3. Current Grade for the Population Age 15 to 24 Years Enrolled in School and Highest Grade Completed for the Population Enrolled in School Last Year, by Sex, Family Income, Race, and Hispanic Origin (for Primary Family Members), October 2005—*Continued*

(Numbers in thousands.)

Family income, sex, race, and Hispanic origin	Not enrolled (enrolled last year), highest grade completed						Not enrolled and not enrolled last year
	7th or 8th	9th	10th	11th	12th (graduated this year)	Some college	
BLACK ALONE OR IN COMBINATION							
Both Sexes	2	26	11	63	163	84	825
Less than $10,000	-	7	-	13	28	7	135
$10,000 to $14,999	-	3	-	13	4	3	106
$15,000 to $19,999	-	-	-	5	6	4	12
$20,000 to $29,999	2	3	3	8	24	10	101
$30,000 to $39,999	-	4	4	-	15	5	88
$40,000 to $49,999	-	-	-	-	14	21	57
$50,000 to $74,999	-	-	-	-	20	7	80
$75,000 to $99,999	-	-	-	6	4	9	35
$100,000 to $149,999	-	4	-	-	-	3	22
$150,000 and over	-	-	-	-	3	3	3
Not reported	-	4	4	17	45	12	186
Male	2	19	7	40	78	48	485
Less than $10,000	-	4	-	13	8	3	90
$10,000 to $14,999	-	3	-	8	3	-	68
$15,000 to $19,999	-	-	-	-	2	-	4
$20,000 to $29,999	2	-	3	-	8	10	57
$30,000 to $39,999	-	4	-	-	6	3	41
$40,000 to $49,999	-	-	-	-	11	13	24
$50,000 to $74,999	-	-	-	-	6	4	39
$75,000 to $99,999	-	-	-	6	3	6	28
$100,000 to $149,999	-	4	-	-	-	-	17
$150,000 and over	-	-	-	-	3	3	-
Not reported	-	4	4	13	28	6	118
Female	-	7	4	23	86	36	340
Less than $10,000	-	4	-	-	20	4	46
$10,000 to $14,999	-	-	-	6	1	3	38
$15,000 to $19,999	-	-	-	5	5	4	8
$20,000 to $29,999	-	3	-	8	16	-	45
$30,000 to $39,999	-	-	4	-	9	2	47
$40,000 to $49,999	-	-	-	-	3	7	32
$50,000 to $74,999	-	-	-	-	14	3	41
$75,000 to $99,999	-	-	-	-	2	3	8
$100,000 to $149,999	-	-	-	-	-	3	6
$150,000 and over	-	-	-	-	-	-	3
Not reported	-	-	-	4	17	6	68
ASIAN ALONE OR IN COMBINATION							
Both Sexes	-	-	5	3	18	18	94
Less than $10,000	-	-	-	-	-	4	6
$10,000 to $14,999	-	-	1	-	-	-	4
$15,000 to $19,999	-	-	-	-	-	-	3
$20,000 to $29,999	-	-	-	-	-	-	11
$30,000 to $39,999	-	-	-	-	4	-	17
$40,000 to $49,999	-	-	-	2	-	-	1
$50,000 to $74,999	-	-	-	-	6	3	26
$75,000 to $99,999	-	-	-	-	1	7	4
$100,000 to $149,999	-	-	-	1	-	-	6
$150,000 and over	-	-	-	-	3	-	-
Not reported	-	-	4	-	4	4	15
Male	-	-	4	2	12	11	63
Less than $10,000	-	-	-	-	-	4	-
$10,000 to $14,999	-	-	-	-	-	-	3
$15,000 to $19,999	-	-	-	-	-	-	3
$20,000 to $29,999	-	-	-	-	-	-	7
$30,000 to $39,999	-	-	-	-	-	-	13
$40,000 to $49,999	-	-	-	2	-	-	1
$50,000 to $74,999	-	-	-	-	4	-	17
$75,000 to $99,999	-	-	-	-	-	4	1
$100,000 to $149,999	-	-	-	1	-	-	4
$150,000 and over	-	-	-	-	3	-	-
Not reported	-	-	4	-	4	4	13
Female	-	-	1	-	6	6	31
Less than $10,000	-	-	-	-	-	-	6
$10,000 to $14,999	-	-	1	-	-	-	1
$15,000 to $19,999	-	-	-	-	-	-	-
$20,000 to $29,999	-	-	-	-	-	-	3
$30,000 to $39,999	-	-	-	-	4	-	4
$40,000 to $49,999	-	-	-	-	-	-	-
$50,000 to $74,999	-	-	-	-	1	3	10
$75,000 to $99,999	-	-	-	-	1	3	4
$100,000 to $149,999	-	-	-	-	-	-	2
$150,000 and over	-	-	-	-	-	-	-
Not reported	-	-	-	-	-	1	3

- = Quantity zero or rounds to zero.

Table A-3. Current Grade for the Population Age 15 to 24 Years Enrolled in School and Highest Grade Completed for the Population Enrolled in School Last Year, by Sex, Family Income, Race, and Hispanic Origin (for Primary Family Members), October 2005—*Continued*

(Numbers in thousands.)

Family income, sex, race, and Hispanic origin	Total population	Enrolled, current grade						
		Less than 9th	9th	10th	11th	12th	First year of college (graduated this year)	Other college
HISPANIC[1]								
Both Sexes	3 784	18	220	693	639	624	165	160
Less than $10,000	296	5	18	42	57	47	6	9
$10,000 to $14,999	358	2	47	64	42	64	5	13
$15,000 to $19,999	206	-	15	47	37	27	3	12
$20,000 to $29,999	562	4	32	114	80	114	38	18
$30,000 to $39,999	434	-	23	66	85	76	6	12
$40,000 to $49,999	351	-	8	61	69	50	16	24
$50,000 to $74,999	495	-	25	109	83	89	25	12
$75,000 to $99,999	218	-	13	41	47	35	25	10
$100,000 to $149,999	129	-	1	30	26	17	12	6
$150,000 and over	48	-	-	11	9	17	4	3
Not reported	687	7	38	108	102	86	26	41
Male	2 070	9	133	358	302	332	75	78
Less than $10,000	163	5	9	32	23	28	3	-
$10,000 to $14,999	184	-	29	29	21	39	2	3
$15,000 to $19,999	87	-	6	15	13	15	-	3
$20,000 to $29,999	305	-	25	54	46	54	13	11
$30,000 to $39,999	240	-	8	26	45	41	3	10
$40,000 to $49,999	200	-	6	36	26	26	10	17
$50,000 to $74,999	277	-	15	51	44	54	6	7
$75,000 to $99,999	127	-	11	37	22	8	14	1
$100,000 to $149,999	61	-	1	11	6	11	6	-
$150,000 and over	24	-	-	8	3	9	3	-
Not reported	402	5	21	58	53	46	15	26
Female	1 714	8	87	336	337	291	90	81
Less than $10,000	133	-	9	9	35	20	3	9
$10,000 to $14,999	174	2	18	35	22	25	3	9
$15,000 to $19,999	119	-	9	31	24	12	3	9
$20,000 to $29,999	257	4	7	60	35	59	25	8
$30,000 to $39,999	194	-	14	40	40	34	3	2
$40,000 to $49,999	151	-	2	25	42	24	5	7
$50,000 to $74,999	218	-	9	59	40	35	20	5
$75,000 to $99,999	92	-	2	4	25	28	11	9
$100,000 to $149,999	68	-	-	19	20	7	6	6
$150,000 and over	24	-	-	4	5	8	1	3
Not reported	285	3	16	50	49	39	11	15

[1]May be of any race.
- = Quantity zero or rounds to zero.

Table A-3. Current Grade for the Population Age 15 to 24 Years Enrolled in School and Highest Grade Completed for the Population Enrolled in School Last Year, by Sex, Family Income, Race, and Hispanic Origin (for Primary Family Members), October 2005—*Continued*

(Numbers in thousands.)

Family income, sex, race, and Hispanic origin	Not enrolled (enrolled last year), highest grade completed						Not enrolled and not enrolled last year
	7th or 8th	9th	10th	11th	12th (graduated this year)	Some college	
HISPANIC[1]							
Both Sexes	2	4	12	46	129	68	1 004
Less than $10,000	-	-	-	9	8	-	94
$10,000 to $14,999	-	1	-	12	12	3	92
$15,000 to $19,999	-	-	-	-	3	-	62
$20,000 to $29,999	-	-	1	3	8	9	141
$30,000 to $39,999	-	-	4	1	22	16	125
$40,000 to $49,999	-	-	5	4	17	12	85
$50,000 to $74,999	2	1	-	4	14	7	122
$75,000 to $99,999	-	-	-	1	14	11	20
$100,000 to $149,999	-	-	-	-	4	1	31
$150,000 and over	-	-	-	-	3	-	1
Not reported	-	1	3	11	23	9	230
Male	-	3	4	26	65	41	643
Less than $10,000	-	-	-	9	-	-	54
$10,000 to $14,999	-	1	-	8	-	-	51
$15,000 to $19,999	-	-	-	-	3	-	32
$20,000 to $29,999	-	-	1	-	3	6	91
$30,000 to $39,999	-	-	-	-	14	12	80
$40,000 to $49,999	-	-	-	1	10	5	62
$50,000 to $74,999	-	1	-	-	11	3	85
$75,000 to $99,999	-	-	-	1	10	8	14
$100,000 to $149,999	-	-	-	-	3	1	23
$150,000 and over	-	-	-	-	-	-	-
Not reported	-	-	3	7	10	7	151
Female	2	1	8	20	64	27	361
Less than $10,000	-	-	-	-	8	-	39
$10,000 to $14,999	-	-	-	4	12	3	42
$15,000 to $19,999	-	-	-	-	-	-	30
$20,000 to $29,999	-	-	-	3	5	3	50
$30,000 to $39,999	-	-	4	1	8	4	45
$40,000 to $49,999	-	-	5	3	7	7	23
$50,000 to $74,999	2	-	-	4	3	4	38
$75,000 to $99,999	-	-	-	-	4	3	5
$100,000 to $149,999	-	-	-	-	1	-	9
$150,000 and over	-	-	-	-	3	-	1
Not reported	-	1	-	5	13	3	80

[1]May be of any race.
- = Quantity zero or rounds to zero.

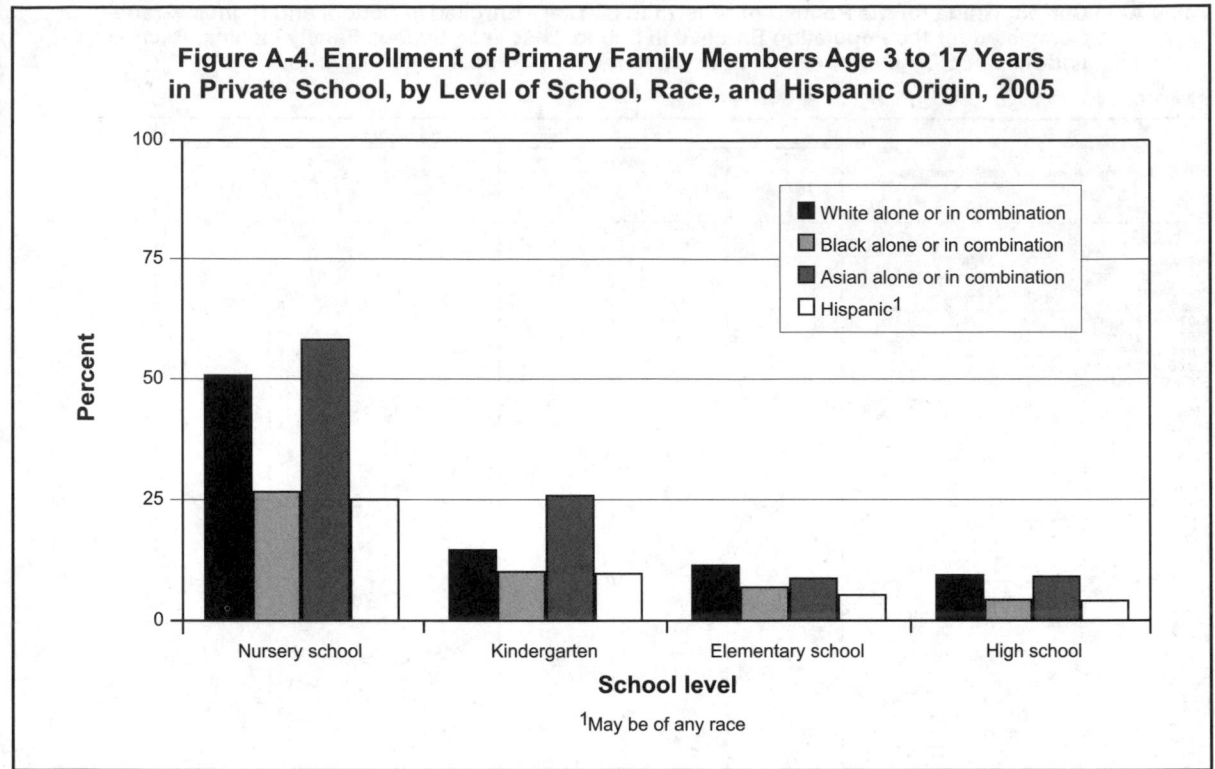

Figure A-4. Enrollment of Primary Family Members Age 3 to 17 Years in Private School, by Level of School, Race, and Hispanic Origin, 2005

Private school enrollment declined as grade level increased. Although close to half of all nursery school students were enrolled in private school in 2005, only 8.5 percent of high school students were enrolled in private schools that year. Whites and Asians had the highest rates of private school enrollment at all grade levels, while Hispanics had the lowest levels of private school enrollment at all levels. Private school enrollment was highest among children from higher-income families. (Table A-4)

Table A-4. Enrollment Status of Primary Family Members Age 3 to 17 Years, by Family Income, Level of Enrollment, Control of School, Sex, Race, and Hispanic Origin, October 2005

(Numbers in thousands.)

Control of school, sex, race, and Hispanic origin	Total enrollment	Family income										
		Less than $10,000	$10,000 to $14,999	$15,000 to $19,999	$20,000 to $29,999	$30,000 to $39,999	$40,000 to $49,999	$50,000 to $74,999	$75,000 to $99,999	$100,000 to $149,999	$150,000 and over	Not reported
ALL RACES												
Both Sexes	60 304	3 880	2 728	2 200	5 937	5 823	4 488	10 549	6 105	5 477	3 770	9 348
Nursery school												
Public	2 408	284	159	93	321	261	175	393	171	173	60	319
Private	2 110	39	39	24	108	117	123	444	334	360	329	192
Kindergarten												
Public	3 301	236	167	185	297	413	226	550	321	248	170	487
Private	552	20	8	8	16	29	55	94	78	59	94	91
Elementary												
Public	28 414	1 950	1 432	1 132	2 973	2 859	2 136	4 926	2 742	2 376	1 452	4 437
Private	3 324	130	49	35	171	251	215	602	407	437	535	493
High school												
Public	13 768	763	579	433	1 302	1 228	1 043	2 493	1 552	1 372	765	2 239
Private	1 284	35	26	9	73	76	66	238	152	204	241	163
Enrolled in college	163	-	6	-	18	5	15	36	18	20	8	38
Not enrolled												
3 to 14 years	4 537	400	230	269	588	540	402	706	313	206	108	774
15 to 17 years												
High school graduate	134	3	-	-	22	8	19	22	2	7	3	48
Not a high school graduate	311	20	34	12	48	37	13	44	14	17	5	67
Male	30 769	1 912	1 382	1 075	3 052	2 999	2 226	5 384	3 095	2 788	1 917	4 937
Nursery school												
Public	1 222	143	81	39	174	121	84	195	80	72	32	202
Private	1 089	25	19	11	65	57	58	222	189	167	159	116
Kindergarten												
Public	1 698	119	75	88	158	208	128	284	180	107	97	255
Private	278	8	-	4	10	18	31	43	41	28	51	45
Elementary												
Public	14 623	973	758	557	1 493	1 502	1 069	2 619	1 393	1 199	707	2 352
Private	1 644	50	28	21	80	141	84	306	197	229	275	233
High school												
Public	6 886	364	264	199	686	575	493	1 226	756	751	407	1 164
Private	611	23	16	4	38	38	25	84	89	97	124	72
Enrolled in college	53	-	2	-	4	3	6	4	7	3	1	21
Not enrolled												
3 to 14 years	2 417	194	117	150	309	317	225	300	150	121	50	415
15 to 17 years												
High school graduate	73	-	-	-	9	3	13	13	2	5	3	26
Not a high school graduate	176	13	21	2	27	17	9	28	11	9	1	36
Female	29 536	1 967	1 346	1 125	2 885	2 824	2 261	5 165	3 010	2 690	1 853	4 411
Nursery school												
Public	1 186	141	77	54	147	140	91	198	92	101	28	118
Private	1 021	14	19	13	43	60	65	222	146	193	170	76
Kindergarten												
Public	1 603	118	92	97	139	205	98	266	141	141	73	232
Private	274	12	8	4	6	11	24	51	37	31	43	46
Elementary												
Public	13 791	977	674	575	1 480	1 357	1 067	2 307	1 349	1 176	745	2 084
Private	1 680	80	21	14	91	110	131	296	209	208	260	259
High school												
Public	6 882	398	315	234	616	653	551	1 267	795	621	357	1 074
Private	673	12	10	5	36	37	40	154	64	106	117	91
Enrolled in college	110	-	3	-	14	2	9	32	11	16	6	17
Not enrolled												
3 to 14 years	2 120	207	113	119	279	223	177	346	163	85	49	360
15 to 17 years												
High school graduate	61	3	-	-	13	5	7	9	-	2	-	22
Not a high school graduate	136	7	13	10	21	19	4	16	3	8	5	31
WHITE ALONE OR IN COMBINATION												
Both Sexes	47 794	2 127	1 807	1 628	4 411	4 631	3 666	9 022	5 408	4 738	3 445	6 909
Nursery school												
Public	1 763	152	104	72	213	191	147	320	143	135	54	234
Private	1 810	21	29	10	73	107	97	396	280	323	306	168
Kindergarten												
Public	2 669	140	116	135	236	342	204	478	281	215	160	363
Private	455	7	3	8	16	17	52	86	67	59	84	56
Elementary												
Public	22 260	1 043	951	842	2 161	2 279	1 725	4 214	2 449	2 036	1 312	3 249
Private	2 862	75	29	25	151	221	177	528	382	393	502	380
High school												
Public	10 856	391	388	313	955	949	843	2 085	1 379	1 206	708	1 640
Private	1 126	35	18	2	62	69	64	211	125	180	222	139
Enrolled in college	119	-	5	-	7	1	15	24	12	16	5	34
Not enrolled												
3 to 14 years	3 552	247	147	215	494	423	323	615	280	159	86	563
15 to 17 years												
High school graduate	92	-	-	-	10	4	10	22	2	7	3	33
Not a high school graduate	229	17	19	7	34	29	9	42	7	10	5	52

- = Quantity zero or rounds to zero.

Table A-4. Enrollment Status of Primary Family Members Age 3 to 17 Years, by Family Income, Level of Enrollment, Control of School, Sex, Race, and Hispanic Origin, October 2005—*Continued*

(Numbers in thousands.)

Control of school, sex, race, and Hispanic origin	Total enrollment	Family income										
		Less than $10,000	$10,000 to $14,999	$15,000 to $19,999	$20,000 to $29,999	$30,000 to $39,999	$40,000 to $49,999	$50,000 to $74,999	$75,000 to $99,999	$100,000 to $149,999	$150,000 and over	Not reported
WHITE ALONE OR IN COMBINATION												
Male	24 383	1 106	878	804	2 254	2 358	1 838	4 630	2 748	2 375	1 761	3 630
Nursery school												
Public	864	74	49	34	114	80	74	152	67	58	28	134
Private	931	13	12	7	42	55	49	199	165	142	148	98
Kindergarten												
Public	1 369	72	44	69	127	172	117	257	153	91	89	178
Private	235	1	-	4	10	11	31	42	32	28	45	31
Elementary												
Public	11 470	534	492	418	1 077	1 201	878	2 230	1 255	1 005	650	1 730
Private	1 433	32	18	11	74	125	71	274	181	208	260	179
High school												
Public	5 412	214	178	133	501	424	387	1 027	678	655	378	838
Private	536	23	13	2	32	32	23	76	71	91	111	62
Enrolled in college	43	-	2	-	-	1	6	3	7	3	1	18
Not enrolled												
3 to 14 years	1 908	130	58	125	255	244	187	327	133	88	46	315
15 to 17 years												
High school graduate	60	-	-	-	5	-	9	13	2	5	3	22
Not a high school graduate	122	13	12	2	18	13	5	28	4	2	1	25
Female	23 412	1 021	930	824	2 157	2 273	1 828	4 392	2 660	2 363	1 684	3 279
Nursery school												
Public	898	78	55	38	99	111	72	168	75	77	25	100
Private	879	8	16	3	31	52	49	197	115	181	157	70
Kindergarten												
Public	1 300	67	73	65	109	170	87	221	128	124	71	186
Private	221	6	3	4	6	6	21	44	35	31	39	25
Elementary												
Public	10 790	509	459	424	1 085	1 078	847	1 983	1 194	1 031	662	1 519
Private	1 429	43	11	14	77	96	106	254	202	185	241	201
High school												
Public	5 444	177	209	180	454	525	456	1 058	701	550	330	801
Private	590	12	5	-	29	37	40	135	54	89	111	77
Enrolled in college	76	-	3	-	7	-	9	21	5	13	3	15
Not enrolled												
3 to 14 years	1 644	117	90	90	240	178	136	288	148	70	39	248
15 to 17 years												
High school graduate	32	-	-	-	5	4	1	9	-	2	-	11
Not a high school graduate	107	4	7	4	16	15	4	14	3	8	5	27
BLACK ALONE OR IN COMBINATION												
Both Sexes	10 035	1 740	858	504	1 324	1 042	638	1 124	454	422	149	1 779
Nursery school												
Public	551	136	50	21	87	68	24	57	20	16	6	67
Private	200	20	6	12	32	8	22	32	18	13	18	17
Kindergarten												
Public	528	100	47	50	63	56	15	62	29	12	6	86
Private	59	19	6	-	-	6	3	6	-	-	2	17
Elementary												
Public	4 997	873	449	246	707	525	333	543	199	199	56	867
Private	369	64	20	10	14	33	30	53	15	29	15	88
High school												
Public	2 290	364	182	96	290	235	149	275	117	114	29	440
Private	104	-	8	8	9	4	-	28	16	9	7	16
Enrolled in college	27	-	1	-	10	2	-	3	6	-	3	2
Not enrolled												
3 to 14 years	794	159	74	52	90	93	48	63	27	22	8	157
15 to 17 years												
High school graduate	36	3	-	-	12	4	9	-	-	-	-	8
Not a high school graduate	80	3	15	9	11	8	4	-	7	8	-	14
Male	5 053	794	460	237	670	563	296	561	209	249	79	936
Nursery school												
Public	316	72	31	4	49	40	11	33	8	7	6	55
Private	103	14	3	3	18	3	9	15	2	13	8	14
Kindergarten												
Public	265	45	28	20	32	27	7	22	25	9	3	47
Private	20	7	-	-	-	6	-	-	-	-	2	5
Elementary												
Public	2 526	423	239	117	349	279	155	296	82	109	28	450
Private	175	21	10	10	7	17	11	23	12	18	6	40
High school												
Public	1 122	145	84	51	151	118	70	143	50	65	21	224
Private	39	-	3	3	4	4	-	8	8	-	2	7
Enrolled in college	8	-	-	-	4	2	-	-	-	-	-	2
Not enrolled												
3 to 14 years	420	67	53	30	48	59	25	21	14	19	5	81
15 to 17 years												
High school graduate	10	-	-	-	4	3	4	-	-	-	-	-
Not a high school graduate	49	-	10	-	6	4	4	-	7	8	-	10

- = Quantity zero or rounds to zero.

Table A-4. Enrollment Status of Primary Family Members Age 3 to 17 Years, by Family Income, Level of Enrollment, Control of School, Sex, Race, and Hispanic Origin, October 2005—*Continued*

(Numbers in thousands.)

Control of school, sex, race, and Hispanic origin	Total enrollment	Family income										
		Less than $10,000	$10,000 to $14,999	$15,000 to $19,999	$20,000 to $29,999	$30,000 to $39,999	$40,000 to $49,999	$50,000 to $74,999	$75,000 to $99,999	$100,000 to $149,999	$150,000 and over	Not reported
BLACK ALONE OR IN COMBINATION												
Female	4 982	946	398	267	654	479	342	563	245	172	70	844
Nursery school												
Public	235	63	19	17	38	28	14	24	11	8	-	12
Private	97	6	3	9	14	5	13	17	16	-	10	3
Kindergarten												
Public	262	55	19	30	31	29	8	40	4	3	3	40
Private	39	12	6	-	-	-	3	6	-	-	-	12
Elementary												
Public	2 471	450	210	130	358	246	178	246	118	91	28	417
Private	194	43	10	-	7	15	19	30	3	10	9	48
High school												
Public	1 168	218	98	44	139	117	79	132	66	49	9	216
Private	66	-	5	5	5	-	-	21	8	8	4	9
Enrolled in college	19	-	1	-	6	-	-	3	6	-	3	-
Not enrolled												
3 to 14 years	374	92	22	23	42	34	24	43	14	3	3	76
15 to 17 years												
High school graduate	26	3	-	-	8	2	6	-	-	-	-	8
Not a high school graduate	31	3	6	9	5	4	-	-	-	-	-	4
ASIAN ALONE OR IN COMBINATION												
Both Sexes	2 838	76	53	62	196	207	187	466	308	401	244	637
Nursery school												
Public	91	-	-	-	15	8	4	17	9	19	2	17
Private	126	-	7	-	2	4	5	18	35	28	17	10
Kindergarten												
Public	118	1	4	-	2	18	9	5	17	26	10	25
Private	41	-	-	-	-	5	-	2	6	-	8	19
Elementary												
Public	1 356	50	28	36	107	98	78	212	137	175	105	331
Private	130	2	-	-	4	3	9	22	12	22	35	21
High school												
Public	659	18	6	23	52	44	51	146	62	84	32	141
Private	66	-	-	-	-	3	-	5	18	16	16	7
Enrolled in college	18	-	-	-	-	1	-	9	-	4	-	2
Not enrolled												
3 to 14 years	223	4	7	3	12	22	31	27	11	27	19	59
15 to 17 years												
High school graduate	5	-	-	-	-	-	1	1	-	-	-	4
Not a high school graduate	7	-	-	-	3	-	-	2	-	1	-	-
Male	1 435	34	28	33	100	102	91	210	158	220	115	345
Nursery school												
Public	40	-	-	-	6	8	-	6	4	3	-	13
Private	60	-	4	-	2	-	-	9	19	14	8	4
Kindergarten												
Public	62	1	-	-	1	9	6	1	2	13	8	22
Private	20	-	-	-	-	-	-	1	3	-	5	10
Elementary												
Public	693	22	17	17	56	41	38	113	76	102	39	172
Private	59	-	-	-	-	-	3	9	6	9	18	14
High school												
Public	338	7	-	15	23	26	30	57	30	54	14	82
Private	33	-	-	-	-	3	-	1	11	7	11	-
Enrolled in college	4	-	-	-	-	-	-	1	-	-	-	2
Not enrolled												
3 to 14 years	115	4	6	1	10	15	14	11	6	18	11	21
15 to 17 years												
High school graduate	5	-	-	-	-	-	1	1	-	-	-	4
Not a high school graduate	5	-	-	-	3	-	-	-	-	1	-	-
Female	1 403	42	25	29	96	105	96	256	150	182	130	293
Nursery school												
Public	51	-	-	-	8	-	4	11	5	16	2	4
Private	66	-	3	-	-	4	5	9	16	14	9	6
Kindergarten												
Public	56	-	4	-	1	9	4	4	15	14	2	3
Private	22	-	-	-	-	5	-	1	3	-	4	9
Elementary												
Public	663	28	11	19	51	57	39	99	61	73	65	159
Private	71	2	-	-	4	2	6	13	6	13	17	7
High school												
Public	320	11	6	8	29	18	21	89	31	30	18	58
Private	33	-	-	-	-	-	-	5	8	9	4	7
Enrolled in college	12	-	-	-	-	1	-	8	-	3	-	-
Not enrolled												
3 to 14 years	108	-	1	2	2	8	17	17	6	9	8	37
15 to 17 years												
High school graduate	-	-	-	-	-	-	-	-	-	-	-	-
Not a high school graduate	2	-	-	-	-	-	-	2	-	-	-	-

- = Quantity zero or rounds to zero.

Table A-4. Enrollment Status of Primary Family Members Age 3 to 17 Years, by Family Income, Level of Enrollment, Control of School, Sex, Race, and Hispanic Origin, October 2005—*Continued*

(Numbers in thousands.)

Control of school, sex, race, and Hispanic origin	Total enrollment	Family income										Not reported
		Less than $10,000	$10,000 to $14,999	$15,000 to $19,999	$20,000 to $29,999	$30,000 to $39,999	$40,000 to $49,999	$50,000 to $74,999	$75,000 to $99,999	$100,000 to $149,999	$150,000 and over	
HISPANIC[1]												
Both Sexes	11 523	967	964	834	1 937	1 451	886	1 608	615	402	177	1 682
Nursery school												
Public	588	71	62	53	107	58	49	71	21	9	4	83
Private	196	3	3	[1]1	17	14	12	36	29	24	26	29
Kindergarten												
Public	709	57	54	67	108	116	41	92	37	43	3	91
Private	76	4	-	-	8	5	3	13	19	5	13	7
Elementary												
Public	5 801	517	520	438	981	762	466	790	262	185	59	821
Private	325	16	3	3	44	37	18	74	36	25	28	41
High school												
Public	2 351	161	230	144	372	281	197	345	149	74	33	365
Private	101	3	6	-	11	2	7	24	14	18	9	8
Enrolled in college	29	-	6	-	4	-	1	3	2	3	-	11
Not enrolled												
3 to 14 years	1 258	130	70	128	269	163	87	151	44	13	3	200
15 to 17 years												
High school graduate	7	-	-	-	-	-	3	1	-	3	-	-
Not a high school graduate	82	4	9	-	17	14	3	10	1	-	-	24
Male	5 864	505	499	423	994	740	430	812	317	184	93	867
Nursery school												
Public	304	38	40	21	62	14	24	37	13	6	4	44
Private	84	3	3	-	7	2	2	17	12	2	11	23
Kindergarten												
Public	366	30	25	34	51	58	25	52	17	25	2	46
Private	45	1	-	-	5	2	3	11	12	5	4	4
Elementary												
Public	2 947	266	272	238	489	413	225	394	136	92	24	399
Private	171	9	3	-	25	20	4	38	22	8	21	23
High school												
Public	1 155	85	122	51	194	132	91	168	80	27	21	184
Private	52	3	6	-	8	-	2	14	4	7	3	5
Enrolled in college	10	-	2	-	-	-	-	-	2	-	-	5
Not enrolled												
3 to 14 years	682	67	20	79	143	93	51	77	16	8	2	124
15 to 17 years												
High school graduate	7	-	-	-	-	-	3	1	-	3	-	-
Not a high school graduate	40	4	6	-	10	4	-	4	1	-	-	10
Female	5 659	462	465	411	943	711	455	796	298	218	85	815
Nursery school												
Public	284	33	23	32	45	43	25	34	8	3	-	39
Private	111	-	-	1	10	11	9	19	17	22	15	6
Kindergarten												
Public	342	26	29	34	57	57	16	40	20	18	-	46
Private	30	3	-	-	3	3	-	2	7	-	9	3
Elementary												
Public	2 854	252	248	200	492	349	241	397	126	93	35	423
Private	154	8	-	3	19	18	14	36	15	17	7	18
High school												
Public	1 196	77	108	93	178	149	106	177	69	47	11	181
Private	48	-	-	-	3	2	5	9	9	11	6	4
Enrolled in college	19	-	3	-	4	-	1	3	-	3	-	5
Not enrolled												
3 to 14 years	576	63	51	48	126	70	35	74	28	4	1	76
15 to 17 years												
High school graduate	-	-	-	-	-	-	-	-	-	-	-	-
Not a high school graduate	43	-	3	-	7	9	3	7	-	-	-	14

[1]May be of any race.
- = Quantity zero or rounds to zero.

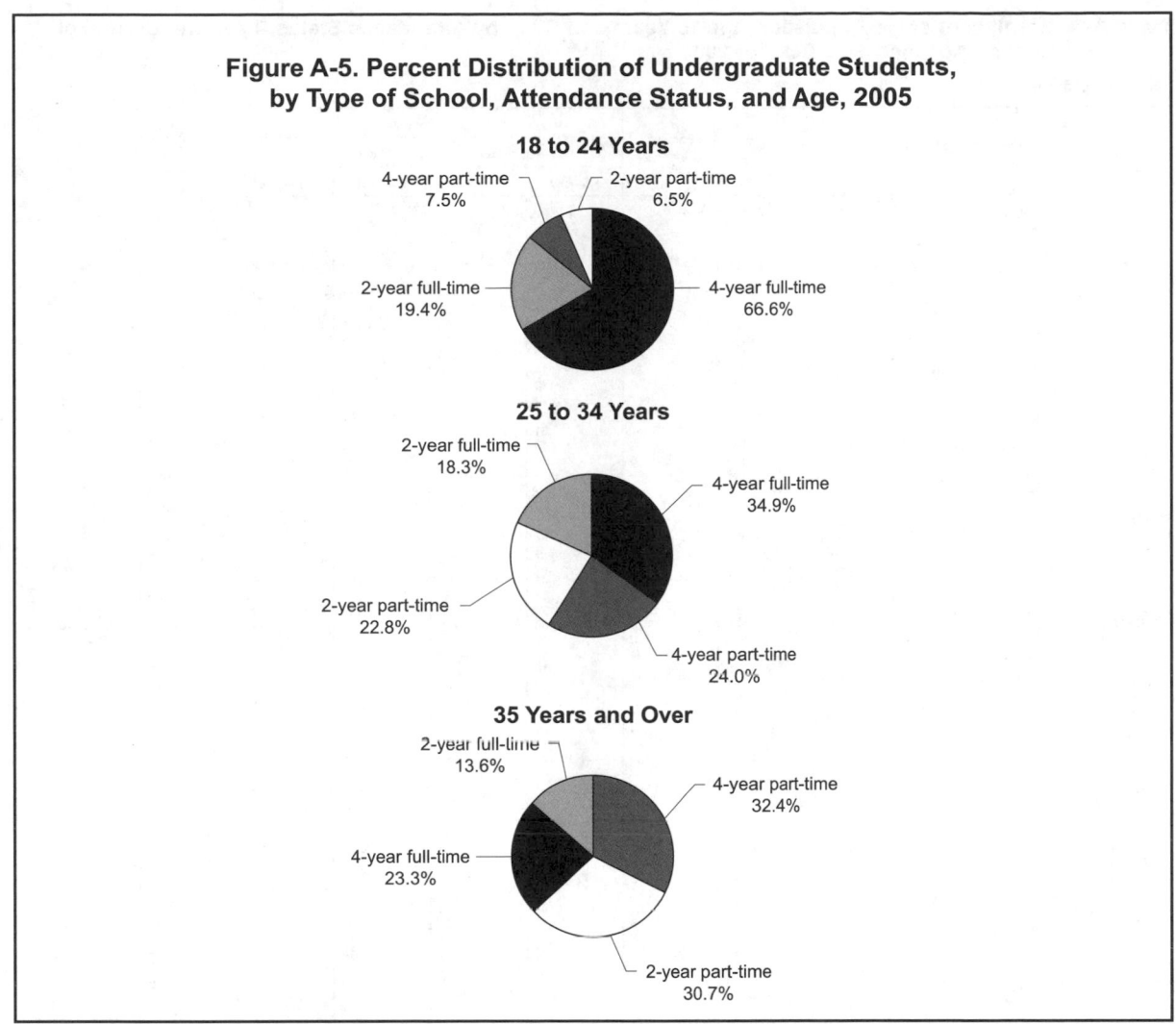

Figure A-5. Percent Distribution of Undergraduate Students, by Type of School, Attendance Status, and Age, 2005

18 to 24 Years

4-year part-time 7.5%
2-year part-time 6.5%
2-year full-time 19.4%
4-year full-time 66.6%

25 to 34 Years

2-year full-time 18.3%
4-year full-time 34.9%
2-year part-time 22.8%
4-year part-time 24.0%

35 Years and Over

2-year full-time 13.6%
4-year part-time 32.4%
4-year full-time 23.3%
2-year part-time 30.7%

In 2005, more than 17.4 million students were enrolled in colleges and universities; undergraduates accounted for 14.2 million members of this population. Undergraduate students attending four-year colleges were far more likely to be full-time students (81.5 percent) than students attending 2-year colleges (60.8 percent). Younger students were also more likely to be full-time students; 86 percent of students age 18 to 24 years were enrolled full time, while only 37 percent of students age 35 years and over were enrolled full time. Graduate students were more evenly divided between full-time and part-time status, with 48 percent of these students attending school full-time. (Table A-5)

Table A-5. Enrollment of the Population Age 15 Years and Over, by Attendance Status, Type and Control of School, Age, and Sex, October 2005

(Numbers in thousands.)

Age, control of school, sex, race, and Hispanic origin	Total enrollment	Enrolled below college	Undergraduate				Graduate	
			Two-year college		Four-year college		Full-time	Part-time
			Full-time	Part-time	Full-time	Part-time		
ALL RACES								
Both Sexes	31 800	14 327	2 632	1 695	8 018	1 823	1 587	1 717
Public								
15 years and over	26 631	13 196	2 345	1 545	5 941	1 461	969	1 174
15 to 17 years	11 637	11 476	34	28	93	6	1	-
18 and 19 years	4 266	1 307	917	190	1 740	112	-	-
20 and 21 years	3 141	122	561	210	1 978	194	76	-
22 to 24 years	2 571	83	312	205	1 278	289	287	115
25 to 29 years	1 777	39	214	278	397	276	307	266
30 to 34 years	978	34	120	169	148	154	143	209
35 to 39 years	762	47	74	159	113	154	54	160
40 to 44 years	554	45	48	112	69	109	37	134
45 to 49 years	391	21	31	93	66	56	17	107
50 to 54 years	289	8	19	60	23	69	19	92
55 to 59 years	159	4	10	12	25	33	18	57
60 to 64 years	45	-	4	15	2	5	1	17
65 years and over	60	8	-	14	7	4	8	18
Private								
15 years and over	5 169	1 132	287	149	2 077	362	618	544
15 to 17 years	1 035	1 015	-	-	17	-	3	-
18 and 19 years	843	75	80	10	660	15	-	3
20 and 21 years	928	2	44	18	786	56	21	-
22 to 24 years	683	8	61	25	326	91	136	35
25 to 29 years	563	10	20	32	140	36	213	112
30 to 34 years	366	1	38	9	61	48	104	104
35 to 39 years	243	10	12	20	26	21	53	102
40 to 44 years	204	4	14	18	34	28	20	86
45 to 49 years	146	1	16	3	19	33	37	37
50 to 54 years	87	-	2	7	6	16	21	35
55 to 59 years	50	5	-	3	1	13	8	20
60 to 64 years	13	-	-	-	2	4	1	6
65 years and over	9	-	-	3	-	3	-	3
Male	14 972	7 434	1 197	669	3 602	722	711	638
Public								
15 years and over	12 619	6 885	1 061	611	2 664	548	423	426
15 to 17 years	5 864	5 805	12	17	26	3	1	-
18 and 19 years	2 199	863	422	80	778	56	-	-
20 and 21 years	1 502	72	310	92	916	68	44	-
22 to 24 years	1 150	59	149	74	599	123	107	38
25 to 29 years	725	20	79	124	153	115	134	100
30 to 34 years	390	3	28	53	66	65	80	94
35 to 39 years	273	28	12	71	43	43	19	57
40 to 44 years	182	21	24	28	27	33	5	44
45 to 49 years	123	3	15	27	20	12	11	35
50 to 54 years	111	3	5	35	16	26	9	17
55 to 59 years	46	-	5	1	12	2	6	19
60 to 64 years	19	-	-	5	2	-	1	11
65 years and over	36	7	-	5	4	1	8	12
Private								
15 years and over	2 353	548	136	58	938	173	288	212
15 to 17 years	495	492	-	-	3	-	-	-
18 and 19 years	381	41	39	-	300	-	-	-
20 and 21 years	448	-	28	6	363	33	18	-
22 to 24 years	337	8	14	13	170	57	61	15
25 to 29 years	218	-	6	11	45	26	90	40
30 to 34 years	176	-	16	2	21	12	64	60
35 to 39 years	96	-	8	10	10	2	24	42
40 to 44 years	76	4	14	11	11	9	5	22
45 to 49 years	69	-	9	3	11	24	11	10
50 to 54 years	33	-	-	3	1	7	6	17
55 to 59 years	14	3	-	-	1	2	8	1
60 to 64 years	8	-	-	-	1	3	1	2
65 years and over	3	-	-	-	-	-	-	3

- = Quantity zero or rounds to zero.

Table A-5. Enrollment of the Population Age 15 Years and Over, by Attendance Status, Type and Control of School, Age, and Sex, October 2005—*Continued*

(Numbers in thousands.)

Age, control of school, sex, race, and Hispanic origin	Total enrollment	Enrolled below college	Undergraduate				Graduate	
			Two-year college		Four-year college		Full-time	Part-time
			Full-time	Part-time	Full-time	Part-time		
ALL RACES								
Female	16 827	6 894	1 436	1 026	4 416	1 101	875	1 079
Public								
15 years and over	14 012	6 310	1 284	934	3 277	913	546	748
15 to 17 years	5 773	5 671	22	11	67	3	-	-
18 and 19 years	2 067	444	495	111	962	56	-	-
20 and 21 years	1 640	50	250	118	1 062	126	33	-
22 to 24 years	1 421	25	163	131	679	166	180	77
25 to 29 years	1 052	19	136	153	245	161	173	166
30 to 34 years	588	31	92	116	82	89	64	115
35 to 39 years	489	19	62	88	71	111	35	103
40 to 44 years	372	23	24	84	42	76	33	90
45 to 49 years	268	18	17	66	46	43	7	72
50 to 54 years	178	6	14	25	7	42	9	75
55 to 59 years	114	4	5	11	13	31	12	38
60 to 64 years	27	-	4	10	-	5	-	6
65 years and over	24	1	-	10	3	4	-	6
Private								
15 years and over	2 816	583	152	92	1 139	189	330	331
15 to 17 years	540	523	-	-	14	-	3	-
18 and 19 years	462	34	40	10	360	15	-	3
20 and 21 years	480	2	16	13	423	23	4	-
22 to 24 years	346	-	46	13	157	35	75	20
25 to 29 years	344	10	14	22	94	10	123	71
30 to 34 years	190	1	22	7	40	37	40	44
35 to 39 years	147	10	4	11	15	19	28	60
40 to 44 years	128	-	-	7	23	20	14	64
45 to 49 years	78	1	6	-	8	8	26	27
50 to 54 years	54	-	2	4	5	9	15	18
55 to 59 years	36	3	-	3	-	11	-	20
60 to 64 years	5	-	-	-	-	1	-	4
65 years and over	6	-	-	3	-	3	-	-
WHITE ALONE OR IN COMBINATION								
Both Sexes	25 125	11 334	1 984	1 357	6 478	1 402	1 156	1 414
Public								
15 years and over	20 908	10 347	1 778	1 240	4 771	1 119	680	974
15 to 17 years	9 172	9 066	18	23	58	6	1	-
18 and 19 years	3 408	1 005	740	158	1 422	84	-	-
20 and 21 years	2 553	89	440	169	1 647	166	42	-
22 to 24 years	1 985	57	221	184	989	221	220	93
25 to 29 years	1 361	27	157	206	298	222	232	219
30 to 34 years	688	11	72	133	109	105	84	175
35 to 39 years	604	33	63	127	104	104	42	133
40 to 44 years	422	31	38	80	56	84	24	108
45 to 49 years	286	12	18	75	51	41	7	82
50 to 54 years	224	7	8	48	13	51	13	84
55 to 59 years	134	4	2	12	19	30	12	54
60 to 64 years	40	-	-	15	2	5	-	17
65 years and over	32	4	-	10	3	1	4	10
Private								
15 years and over	4 216	986	207	117	1 707	283	476	440
15 to 17 years	921	902	-	-	16	-	3	-
18 and 19 years	709	69	64	10	550	12	-	3
20 and 21 years	781	-	34	10	680	47	10	-
22 to 24 years	509	4	39	16	248	54	113	35
25 to 29 years	413	6	12	23	98	32	149	93
30 to 34 years	278	1	27	9	52	37	70	82
35 to 39 years	188	-	8	20	23	17	47	73
40 to 44 years	161	-	11	16	17	22	19	77
45 to 49 years	122	1	10	-	17	28	37	28
50 to 54 years	71	-	2	7	5	15	18	25
55 to 59 years	44	3	-	3	-	13	8	18
60 to 64 years	8	-	-	-	-	4	1	3
65 years and over	9	-	-	3	-	3	-	3

- = Quantity zero or rounds to zero.

Table A-5. Enrollment of the Population Age 15 Years and Over, by Attendance Status, Type and Control of School, Age, and Sex, October 2005—*Continued*

(Numbers in thousands.)

Age, control of school, sex, race, and Hispanic origin	Total enrollment	Enrolled below college	Undergraduate				Graduate	
			Two-year college		Four-year college			
			Full-time	Part-time	Full-time	Part-time	Full-time	Part-time
WHITE ALONE OR IN COMBINATION								
Male	11 858	5 881	932	501	2 911	582	518	534
Public								
15 years and over	9 908	5 394	828	463	2 131	434	304	354
15 to 17 years	4 621	4 581	8	12	16	3	1	-
18 and 19 years	1 740	656	348	63	630	42	-	-
20 and 21 years	1 193	49	244	60	764	58	19	-
22 to 24 years	900	39	115	72	465	98	82	28
25 to 29 years	554	15	58	82	110	98	113	78
30 to 34 years	287	-	12	48	47	43	57	79
35 to 39 years	229	25	12	57	42	27	12	54
40 to 44 years	148	19	21	14	23	33	5	33
45 to 49 years	87	3	9	21	14	11	3	26
50 to 54 years	76	3	-	27	8	18	3	17
55 to 59 years	37	-	-	1	9	2	6	19
60 to 64 years	18	-	-	5	2	-	-	11
65 years and over	17	4	-	-	-	1	4	8
Private								
15 years and over	1 950	486	104	38	780	148	213	180
15 to 17 years	441	439	-	-	3	-	-	-
18 and 19 years	328	41	30	-	258	-	-	-
20 and 21 years	374	-	21	1	313	33	6	-
22 to 24 years	271	4	14	8	138	40	52	15
25 to 29 years	157	-	6	6	23	26	63	33
30 to 34 years	137	-	10	2	20	12	41	52
35 to 39 years	82	-	6	9	10	2	19	36
40 to 44 years	51	-	11	10	5	2	5	19
45 to 49 years	61	-	6	-	11	22	11	10
50 to 54 years	24	-	-	3	-	6	6	9
55 to 59 years	13	3	-	-	-	2	8	1
60 to 64 years	7	-	-	-	-	3	1	2
65 years and over	3	-	-	-	-	-	-	3
Female	13 266	5 453	1 053	856	3 567	820	638	880
Public								
15 years and over	11 000	4 953	950	777	2 640	685	375	620
15 to 17 years	4 551	4 485	10	11	42	3	-	-
18 and 19 years	1 669	349	392	95	791	42	-	-
20 and 21 years	1 359	40	196	109	882	109	22	-
22 to 24 years	1 084	17	106	111	524	123	138	65
25 to 29 years	807	12	100	123	188	124	119	141
30 to 34 years	401	11	60	85	62	62	26	95
35 to 39 years	375	8	50	70	62	77	30	78
40 to 44 years	274	12	17	66	34	51	20	75
45 to 49 years	199	10	9	54	37	30	4	55
50 to 54 years	147	4	8	21	5	33	9	67
55 to 59 years	97	4	2	11	10	28	6	35
60 to 64 years	22	-	-	10	-	5	-	6
65 years and over	15	-	-	10	3	-	-	2
Private								
15 years and over	2 266	500	103	79	927	135	262	260
15 to 17 years	480	464	-	-	13	-	3	-
18 and 19 years	381	28	34	10	293	12	-	3
20 and 21 years	407	-	13	9	367	14	4	-
22 to 24 years	238	-	24	9	110	14	60	20
25 to 29 years	255	6	5	17	74	6	85	60
30 to 34 years	141	1	18	7	32	25	29	30
35 to 39 years	107	-	3	11	13	15	28	37
40 to 44 years	110	-	-	6	13	20	14	58
45 to 49 years	62	1	4	-	6	6	26	18
50 to 54 years	47	-	2	4	5	8	12	16
55 to 59 years	31	-	-	3	-	11	-	17
60 to 64 years	1	-	-	-	-	1	-	-
65 years and over	6	-	-	3	-	3	-	-

- = Quantity zero or rounds to zero.

Table A-5. Enrollment of the Population Age 15 Years and Over, by Attendance Status, Type and Control of School, Age, and Sex, October 2005—*Continued*

(Numbers in thousands.)

Age, control of school, sex, race, and Hispanic origin	Total enrollment	Enrolled below college	Undergraduate				Graduate	
			Two-year college		Four-year college			
			Full-time	Part-time	Full-time	Part-time	Full-time	Part-time
BLACK ALONE OR IN COMBINATION								
Both Sexes	4 821	2 433	465	260	981	354	139	187
Public								
15 years and over	4 186	2 320	399	235	724	287	112	109
15 to 17 years	1 969	1 939	15	-	15	-	-	-
18 and 19 years	645	261	122	30	208	26	-	-
20 and 21 years	369	30	72	32	196	21	19	-
22 to 24 years	360	23	59	19	171	51	28	9
25 to 29 years	238	11	42	55	55	43	23	9
30 to 34 years	206	21	36	30	34	46	15	25
35 to 39 years	123	10	12	21	8	44	7	21
40 to 44 years	103	13	9	22	12	25	8	14
45 to 49 years	90	8	13	18	13	12	7	18
50 to 54 years	43	1	7	4	5	14	4	7
55 to 59 years	16	-	8	-	3	3	-	2
60 to 64 years	4	-	4	-	-	-	-	-
65 years and over	21	4	-	5	4	4	-	4
Private								
15 years and over	635	114	66	25	257	67	27	78
15 to 17 years	85	84	-	-	1	-	-	-
18 and 19 years	102	6	11	-	83	2	-	-
20 and 21 years	91	2	5	5	75	5	-	-
22 to 24 years	129	4	22	8	58	30	7	-
25 to 29 years	76	4	8	9	22	4	13	15
30 to 34 years	44	-	8	-	9	12	5	11
35 to 39 years	41	10	4	-	3	3	-	22
40 to 44 years	24	4	3	-	5	6	-	6
45 to 49 years	21	-	6	3	2	4	-	6
50 to 54 years	15	-	1	-	-	1	3	11
55 to 59 years	2	-	-	-	-	-	-	2
60 to 64 years	4	-	-	-	-	-	-	4
65 years and over	-	-	-	-	-	-	-	-
Male	2 150	1 255	176	127	384	112	40	52
Public								
15 years and over	1 933	1 217	153	110	292	91	39	30
15 to 17 years	980	972	4	-	5	-	-	-
18 and 19 years	351	187	51	15	80	10	-	-
20 and 21 years	176	23	38	25	69	3	17	-
22 to 24 years	144	19	18	2	74	24	4	3
25 to 29 years	94	5	16	35	19	11	3	6
30 to 34 years	60	3	12	3	15	18	3	5
35 to 39 years	31	3	-	7	-	15	3	2
40 to 44 years	23	2	2	9	5	-	-	5
45 to 49 years	33	-	5	6	7	2	5	9
50 to 54 years	20	-	2	4	3	7	4	-
55 to 59 years	9	-	5	-	3	-	-	-
60 to 64 years	-	-	-	-	-	-	-	-
65 years and over	12	3	-	5	4	-	-	-
Private								
15 years and over	217	38	24	17	92	21	3	22
15 to 17 years	29	29	-	-	-	-	-	-
18 and 19 years	37	-	11	-	26	-	-	-
20 and 21 years	36	-	1	5	29	-	-	-
22 to 24 years	47	4	-	4	26	12	-	-
25 to 29 years	20	-	-	5	8	-	3	4
30 to 34 years	9	-	3	-	1	-	-	4
35 to 39 years	5	-	2	-	-	-	-	2
40 to 44 years	18	4	3	-	2	6	-	2
45 to 49 years	8	-	3	3	-	2	-	-
50 to 54 years	9	-	-	-	-	-	-	8
55 to 59 years	-	-	-	-	-	-	-	-
60 to 64 years	-	-	-	-	-	-	-	-
65 years and over	-	-	-	-	-	-	-	-

- = Quantity zero or rounds to zero.

Table A-5. Enrollment of the Population Age 15 Years and Over, by Attendance Status, Type and Control of School, Age, and Sex, October 2005—*Continued*

(Numbers in thousands.)

Age, control of school, sex, race, and Hispanic origin	Total enrollment	Enrolled below college	Undergraduate				Graduate	
			Two-year college		Four-year college		Full-time	Part-time
			Full-time	Part-time	Full-time	Part-time		
BLACK ALONE OR IN COMBINATION								
Female	2 671	1 179	288	133	597	242	97	135
Public								
15 years and over	2 254	1 103	246	125	432	196	73	80
15 to 17 years	989	967	11	-	10	-	-	-
18 and 19 years	294	74	71	15	119	15	-	-
20 and 21 years	193	7	33	7	126	18	2	-
22 to 24 years	216	4	41	17	96	27	24	7
25 to 29 years	144	6	26	21	37	32	20	3
30 to 34 years	146	17	24	27	19	27	12	20
35 to 39 years	92	7	12	14	8	28	4	18
40 to 44 years	79	11	7	13	7	25	8	9
45 to 49 years	57	8	8	12	7	10	2	10
50 to 54 years	23	1	6	-	2	7	-	7
55 to 59 years	8	-	3	-	-	3	-	2
60 to 64 years	4	-	4	-	-	-	-	-
65 years and over	9	1	-	-	-	4	-	4
Private								
15 years and over	418	76	43	8	165	46	24	56
15 to 17 years	55	55	-	-	-	-	-	-
18 and 19 years	65	6	-	-	57	2	-	-
20 and 21 years	56	2	3	-	46	4	-	-
22 to 24 years	82	-	22	4	32	17	6	-
25 to 29 years	55	3	8	4	14	4	10	11
30 to 34 years	35	-	4	-	8	12	5	7
35 to 39 years	36	10	1	-	3	3	-	19
40 to 44 years	7	-	-	-	3	-	-	4
45 to 49 years	13	-	2	-	2	2	-	6
50 to 54 years	7	-	1	-	-	1	3	2
55 to 59 years	2	-	-	-	-	-	-	2
60 to 64 years	4	-	-	-	-	-	-	4
65 years and over	-	-	-	-	-	-	-	-
ASIAN ALONE OR IN COMBINATION								
Both Sexes	1 897	600	178	73	570	70	288	119
Public								
15 years and over	1 543	550	161	62	449	58	174	88
15 to 17 years	523	498	2	5	18	-	-	-
18 and 19 years	207	41	50	2	108	6	-	-
20 and 21 years	230	2	48	11	143	11	16	-
22 to 24 years	229	4	28	2	123	15	39	17
25 to 29 years	166	-	16	15	41	9	50	35
30 to 34 years	78	-	10	4	8	3	44	9
35 to 39 years	35	4	3	10	2	4	6	6
40 to 44 years	28	-	1	10	1	-	4	12
45 to 49 years	11	-	-	-	-	3	3	5
50 to 54 years	19	1	3	4	3	6	2	1
55 to 59 years	9	-	-	-	3	-	6	-
60 to 64 years	1	-	-	-	-	-	1	-
65 years and over	7	-	-	-	-	-	3	4
Private								
15 years and over	355	50	17	11	121	12	114	30
15 to 17 years	46	46	-	-	-	-	-	-
18 and 19 years	39	1	7	-	32	-	-	-
20 and 21 years	64	-	5	4	39	4	11	-
22 to 24 years	52	-	4	1	23	7	17	1
25 to 29 years	74	-	-	-	15	-	54	5
30 to 34 years	43	-	-	4	1	-	26	13
35 to 39 years	12	-	-	1	-	-	5	7
40 to 44 years	18	-	1	2	12	-	1	3
45 to 49 years	3	-	-	-	-	-	-	3
50 to 54 years	-	-	-	-	-	-	-	-
55 to 59 years	3	3	-	-	-	-	-	-
60 to 64 years	-	-	-	-	-	-	-	-
65 years and over	-	-	-	-	-	-	-	-

- = Quantity zero or rounds to zero.

Table A-5. Enrollment of the Population Age 15 Years and Over, by Attendance Status, Type and Control of School, Age, and Sex, October 2005—*Continued*

(Numbers in thousands.)

Age, control of school, sex, race, and Hispanic origin	Total enrollment	Enrolled below college	Undergraduate				Graduate	
			Two-year college		Four-year college		Full-time	Part-time
			Full-time	Part-time	Full-time	Part-time		
ASIAN ALONE OR IN COMBINATION								
Male	934	294	74	39	305	24	145	53
Public								
15 years and over	743	269	68	36	235	19	77	39
15 to 17 years	252	239	2	5	5	-	-	-
18 and 19 years	107	29	20	2	52	4	-	-
20 and 21 years	130	-	22	8	88	5	7	-
22 to 24 years	103	-	15	1	57	2	21	7
25 to 29 years	70	-	2	8	24	5	16	15
30 to 34 years	37	-	2	-	4	3	19	9
35 to 39 years	13	-	-	7	2	-	5	-
40 to 44 years	10	-	1	5	-	-	-	5
45 to 49 years	3	-	-	-	-	-	3	-
50 to 54 years	9	-	3	1	3	-	2	-
55 to 59 years	-	-	-	-	-	-	-	-
60 to 64 years	1	-	-	-	-	-	1	-
65 years and over	7	-	-	-	-	-	3	4
Private								
15 years and over	191	25	6	3	70	5	68	14
15 to 17 years	25	25	-	-	-	-	-	-
18 and 19 years	20	1	-	-	20	-	-	-
20 and 21 years	39	-	5	-	22	-	11	-
22 to 24 years	22	-	-	1	8	4	9	-
25 to 29 years	43	-	-	-	14	-	23	5
30 to 34 years	26	-	-	-	1	-	19	6
35 to 39 years	9	-	-	1	-	-	5	4
40 to 44 years	7	-	1	1	5	-	-	-
45 to 49 years	-	-	-	-	-	-	-	-
50 to 54 years	-	-	-	-	-	-	-	-
55 to 59 years	-	-	-	-	-	-	-	-
60 to 64 years	-	-	-	-	-	-	-	-
65 years and over	-	-	-	-	-	-	-	-
Female	963	306	104	34	265	46	143	65
Public								
15 years and over	799	282	93	25	214	39	97	49
15 to 17 years	271	259	-	-	12	-	-	-
18 and 19 years	100	12	29	-	56	2	-	-
20 and 21 years	99	2	26	2	55	6	8	-
22 to 24 years	126	4	14	2	66	13	18	10
25 to 29 years	96	-	13	7	17	4	34	21
30 to 34 years	41	-	8	4	4	-	25	-
35 to 39 years	21	4	3	3	-	4	1	6
40 to 44 years	18	-	-	5	1	-	4	7
45 to 49 years	8	-	-	-	-	3	-	5
50 to 54 years	10	1	-	3	-	6	-	1
55 to 59 years	9	-	-	-	3	-	6	-
60 to 64 years	-	-	-	-	-	-	-	-
65 years and over	-	-	-	-	-	-	-	-
Private								
15 years and over	164	25	11	9	51	7	46	16
15 to 17 years	22	22	-	-	-	-	-	-
18 and 19 years	19	-	7	-	12	-	-	-
20 and 21 years	25	-	-	4	17	4	-	-
22 to 24 years	30	-	4	-	14	3	8	1
25 to 29 years	31	-	-	-	1	-	31	-
30 to 34 years	18	-	-	4	-	-	6	7
35 to 39 years	3	-	-	-	-	-	-	3
40 to 44 years	11	-	-	-	7	-	1	3
45 to 49 years	3	-	-	-	-	-	-	3
50 to 54 years	-	-	-	-	-	-	-	-
55 to 59 years	3	3	-	-	-	-	-	-
60 to 64 years	-	-	-	-	-	-	-	-
65 years and over	-	-	-	-	-	-	-	-

- = Quantity zero or rounds to zero.

Table A-5. Enrollment of the Population Age 15 Years and Over, by Attendance Status, Type and Control of School, Age, and Sex, October 2005—Continued

(Numbers in thousands.)

Age, control of school, sex, race, and Hispanic origin	Total enrollment	Enrolled below college	Undergraduate				Graduate	
			Two-year college		Four-year college		Full-time	Part-time
			Full-time	Part-time	Full-time	Part-time		
HISPANIC[1]								
Both Sexes	4 398	2 456	369	272	759	270	127	144
Public								
15 years and over	3 991	2 366	337	267	629	224	74	94
15 to 17 years	1 991	1 965	3	8	9	6	-	-
18 and 19 years	632	273	119	55	156	28	-	-
20 and 21 years	393	27	101	44	193	22	6	-
22 to 24 years	362	27	50	34	147	67	18	19
25 to 29 years	239	18	18	45	69	41	30	18
30 to 34 years	126	8	22	23	22	24	15	12
35 to 39 years	121	19	10	28	9	22	-	33
40 to 44 years	64	18	6	18	2	6	3	11
45 to 49 years	33	3	7	10	13	-	-	-
50 to 54 years	15	3	-	-	-	9	3	-
55 to 59 years	6	2	-	-	4	-	-	-
60 to 64 years	2	-	-	2	-	-	-	-
65 years and over	7	3	-	-	4	-	-	-
Private								
15 years and over	406	90	32	5	130	46	53	50
15 to 17 years	85	80	-	-	6	-	-	-
18 and 19 years	49	2	13	2	33	-	-	-
20 and 21 years	54	-	4	-	45	5	-	-
22 to 24 years	57	3	3	-	30	6	14	-
25 to 29 years	71	3	2	-	16	13	27	10
30 to 34 years	32	-	7	3	-	4	-	18
35 to 39 years	27	-	4	1	-	5	3	13
40 to 44 years	16	-	-	-	-	7	3	6
45 to 49 years	11	1	-	-	-	4	4	2
50 to 54 years	-	-	-	-	-	-	-	-
55 to 59 years	3	-	-	-	-	3	-	-
60 to 64 years	-	-	-	-	-	-	-	-
65 years and over	-	-	-	-	-	-	-	-
Male	2 071	1 267	167	108	321	110	51	47
Public								
15 years and over	1 868	1 227	147	108	249	86	24	28
15 to 17 years	990	982	-	2	2	3	-	-
18 and 19 years	320	167	53	24	64	11	-	-
20 and 21 years	160	16	48	19	74	-	4	-
22 to 24 years	171	17	30	16	65	35	1	6
25 to 29 years	89	13	5	17	17	24	14	-
30 to 34 years	26	-	-	5	9	4	5	3
35 to 39 years	52	15	1	12	5	-	-	18
40 to 44 years	30	13	6	5	2	3	-	-
45 to 49 years	13	-	4	6	3	-	-	-
50 to 54 years	6	-	-	-	-	6	-	-
55 to 59 years	4	-	-	-	4	-	-	-
60 to 64 years	-	-	-	-	-	-	-	-
65 years and over	7	3	-	-	4	-	-	-
Private								
15 years and over	203	40	20	-	72	25	26	20
15 to 17 years	37	35	-	-	2	-	-	-
18 and 19 years	23	2	7	-	14	-	-	-
20 and 21 years	39	-	-	-	35	5	-	-
22 to 24 years	32	3	-	-	17	5	6	-
25 to 29 years	34	-	2	-	4	11	16	1
30 to 34 years	25	-	7	-	-	-	-	18
35 to 39 years	4	-	4	-	-	-	-	-
40 to 44 years	3	-	-	-	-	-	3	-
45 to 49 years	5	-	-	-	-	4	2	-
50 to 54 years	-	-	-	-	-	-	-	-
55 to 59 years	-	-	-	-	-	-	-	-
60 to 64 years	-	-	-	-	-	-	-	-
65 years and over	-	-	-	-	-	-	-	-

[1]May be of any race.
- = Quantity zero or rounds to zero.

Table A-5. Enrollment of the Population Age 15 Years and Over, by Attendance Status, Type and Control of School, Age, and Sex, October 2005—*Continued*

(Numbers in thousands.)

Age, control of school, sex, race, and Hispanic origin	Total enrollment	Enrolled below college	Undergraduate				Graduate	
			Two-year college		Four-year college		Full-time	Part-time
			Full-time	Part-time	Full-time	Part-time		
HISPANIC[1]								
Female	2 327	1 189	202	165	439	160	77	96
Public								
15 years and over	2 123	1 139	189	159	380	139	50	66
15 to 17 years	1 001	983	3	6	7	3	-	-
18 and 19 years	312	105	66	31	92	17	-	-
20 and 21 years	233	11	54	25	119	22	2	-
22 to 24 years	191	10	20	18	82	32	17	13
25 to 29 years	149	6	13	28	52	17	15	18
30 to 34 years	100	8	22	18	13	20	10	9
35 to 39 years	69	3	9	15	5	22	-	16
40 to 44 years	33	4	-	12	-	3	3	11
45 to 49 years	20	3	3	4	11	-	-	-
50 to 54 years	9	3	-	-	-	3	3	-
55 to 59 years	2	2	-	-	-	-	-	-
60 to 64 years	2	-	-	2	-	-	-	-
65 years and over	-	-	-	-	-	-	-	-
Private								
15 years and over	204	50	12	5	59	21	27	30
15 to 17 years	49	45	-	-	3	-	-	-
18 and 19 years	26	-	5	2	19	-	-	-
20 and 21 years	14	-	4	-	11	-	-	-
22 to 24 years	25	-	3	-	13	-	8	-
25 to 29 years	37	3	-	-	13	2	12	8
30 to 34 years	7	-	-	3	-	4	-	-
35 to 39 years	23	-	-	1	-	5	3	13
40 to 44 years	14	-	-	-	-	7	1	6
45 to 49 years	6	1	-	-	-	-	3	2
50 to 54 years	-	-	-	-	-	-	-	-
55 to 59 years	3	-	-	-	-	3	-	-
60 to 64 years	-	-	-	-	-	-	-	-
65 years and over	-	-	-	-	-	-	-	-

[1]May be of any race.
- = Quantity zero or rounds to zero.

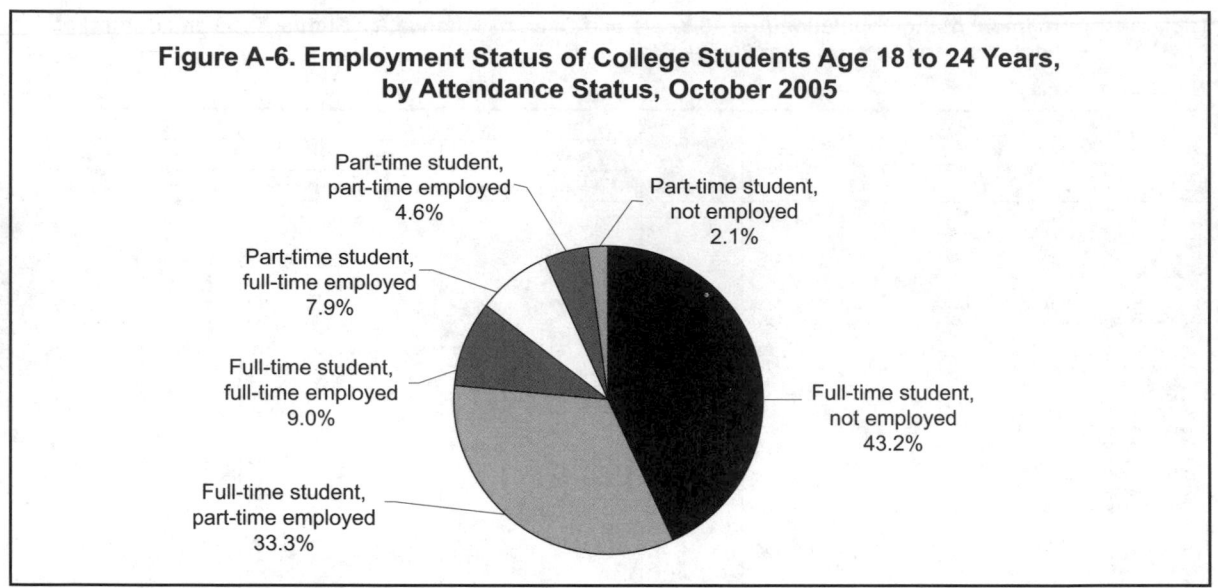

Figure A-6. Employment Status of College Students Age 18 to 24 Years, by Attendance Status, October 2005

Part-time student, part-time employed 4.6%

Part-time student, not employed 2.1%

Part-time student, full-time employed 7.9%

Full-time student, full-time employed 9.0%

Full-time student, not employed 43.2%

Full-time student, part-time employed 33.3%

In 2005, 26.4 percent of all high school students age 16 years and over were employed. While the vast majority were employed part time, 156,000 students between the ages of 16 and 19 were employed full time while attending high school full time. Nearly 55 percent of all college students between the ages of 18 and 24 years were employed in 2005; 16.9 percent of these students were employed full time. Close to 1 million students in this age range attended school full time and worked full time. Older students were more likely to be employed full time. Approximately 48 percent of college students age 25 to 34 years and 63 percent of students age 35 years and over were employed full time. (Table A-6)

Table A-6. Employment Status of High School and College Students Age 15 Years and Over, by Level of School, Attendance Status, Age, Sex, Race, and Hispanic Origin, October 2005

(Numbers in thousands.)

Attendance status, age, sex, race, and Hispanic origin	Total enrollment	Full-time students				Part-time students			
		Total enrollment	Full-time employed	Part-time employed	Not employed	Total enrollment	Full-time employed	Part-time employed	Not employed
ALL RACES									
Both Sexes									
15 years and over	31 533	26 297	2 121	6 993	17 183	5 235	3 520	1 010	705
Enrolled in high school	14 060	14 060	274	2 678	11 108	-	-	-	-
15 years	4 014	4 014	4	296	3 714	-	-	-	-
16 and 17 years	8 272	8 272	82	1 999	6 191	-	-	-	-
18 and 19 years	1 372	1 372	74	344	954	-	-	-	-
20 years and over	402	402	114	39	249	-	-	-	-
Enrolled in college	17 472	12 237	1 847	4 315	6 075	5 234	3 520	1 010	705
15 to 17 years	181	147	-	31	117	33	9	8	16
18 and 19 years	3 727	3 397	201	1 269	1 926	330	113	136	81
20 and 21 years	3 945	3 466	403	1 396	1 667	479	246	179	53
22 to 24 years	3 162	2 401	371	944	1 086	761	493	179	90
25 to 29 years	2 291	1 292	325	359	608	999	691	172	137
30 to 34 years	1 309	615	209	137	269	694	519	103	72
35 years and over	2 857	919	338	179	402	1 938	1 449	233	256
Male									
15 years and over	14 812	12 784	1 021	3 164	8 599	2 029	1 517	292	220
Enrolled in high school	7 273	7 273	155	1 344	5 775	-	-	-	-
15 years	2 005	2 005	3	163	1 839	-	-	-	-
16 and 17 years	4 166	4 166	39	942	3 185	-	-	-	-
18 and 19 years	899	899	49	218	632	-	-	-	-
20 years and over	203	203	64	21	119	-	-	-	-
Enrolled in college	7 539	5 511	865	1 821	2 826	2 029	1 516	291	220
15 to 17 years	62	42	-	12	30	20	5	8	0
18 and 19 years	1 675	1 540	105	549	886	136	64	43	29
20 and 21 years	1 878	1 679	202	573	904	199	107	68	23
22 to 24 years	1 420	1 101	167	431	504	320	219	67	34
25 to 29 years	923	507	126	132	249	416	319	51	46
30 to 34 years	562	275	106	63	106	286	248	18	20
35 years and over	1 019	367	159	61	147	652	554	36	62
Female									
15 years and over	16 720	13 514	1 101	3 829	8 584	3 207	2 003	718	485
Enrolled in high school	6 786	6 786	119	1 335	5 333	-	-	-	-
15 years	2 009	2 009	1	133	1 875	-	-	-	-
16 and 17 years	4 106	4 106	42	1 057	3 006	-	-	-	-
18 and 19 years	472	472	25	126	322	-	-	-	-
20 years and over	199	199	51	19	130	-	-	-	-
Enrolled in college	9 933	6 727	983	2 495	3 252	3 207	2 002	718	485
15 to 17 years	119	106	-	19	87	13	3	-	10
18 and 19 years	2 052	1 857	97	720	1 041	195	49	93	53
20 and 21 years	2 067	1 787	201	824	763	280	139	111	30
22 to 24 years	1 742	1 300	205	513	582	442	274	112	55
25 to 29 years	1 368	785	199	227	359	583	372	120	91
30 to 34 years	747	340	102	74	164	408	270	85	52
35 years and over	1 838	552	179	118	256	1 286	895	197	194
WHITE ALONE OR IN COMBINATION									
Both Sexes									
15 years and over	24 946	20 772	1 654	6 014	13 104	4 173	2 809	829	536
Enrolled in high school	11 155	11 155	211	2 382	8 563	-	-	-	-
15 years	3 236	3 236	4	261	2 971	-	-	-	-
16 and 17 years	6 605	6 605	59	1 789	4 757	-	-	-	-
18 and 19 years	1 064	1 064	66	309	689	-	-	-	-
20 years and over	250	250	82	23	146	-	-	-	-
Enrolled in college	13 790	9 618	1 443	3 634	4 541	4 173	2 809	830	535
15 to 17 years	125	96	-	30	67	29	9	8	11
18 and 19 years	3 043	2 776	172	1 103	1 501	267	95	115	58
20 and 21 years	3 244	2 852	338	1 195	1 319	392	208	152	32
22 to 24 years	2 433	1 830	297	744	789	604	399	139	65
25 to 29 years	1 740	946	246	298	401	795	569	139	87
30 to 34 years	954	414	136	104	174	540	389	83	69
35 years and over	2 251	704	254	160	290	1 546	1 140	194	213

- = Quantity zero or rounds to zero.

Table A-6. Employment Status of High School and College Students Age 15 Years and Over, by Level of School, Attendance Status, Age, Sex, Race, and Hispanic Origin, October 2005—*Continued*

(Numbers in thousands.)

Attendance status, age, sex, race, and Hispanic origin	Total enrollment	Full-time students Total enrollment	Full-time employed	Part-time employed	Not employed	Part-time students Total enrollment	Full-time employed	Part-time employed	Not employed
WHITE ALONE OR IN COMBINATION									
Male									
15 years and over	11 756	10 139	806	2 733	6 600	1 617	1 235	229	153
Enrolled in high school	5 779	5 779	128	1 206	4 444	-	-	-	-
15 years	1 629	1 629	3	152	1 474	-	-	-	-
16 and 17 years	3 315	3 315	25	845	2 446	-	-	-	-
18 and 19 years	692	692	44	194	453	-	-	-	-
20 years and over	143	143	56	15	71	-	-	-	-
Enrolled in college	5 977	4 360	676	1 526	2 156	1 616	1 234	229	154
15 to 17 years	43	28	-	12	16	15	5	8	2
18 and 19 years	1 371	1 266	92	480	693	105	51	34	20
20 and 21 years	1 519	1 368	170	465	733	151	85	54	12
22 to 24 years	1 128	867	127	351	388	261	181	59	21
25 to 29 years	696	373	103	112	158	323	258	34	31
30 to 34 years	424	187	66	53	68	236	203	14	20
35 years and over	796	271	118	53	100	525	451	26	48
Female									
15 years and over	13 189	10 633	848	3 281	6 504	2 556	1 574	600	383
Enrolled in high school	5 377	5 377	83	1 174	4 119	-	-	-	-
15 years	1 607	1 607	1	109	1 497	-	-	-	-
16 and 17 years	3 290	3 290	34	944	2 312	-	-	-	-
18 and 19 years	372	372	22	114	235	-	-	-	-
20 years and over	108	108	26	7	75	-	-	-	-
Enrolled in college	7 812	5 257	765	2 107	2 385	2 555	1 572	600	384
15 to 17 years	82	69	-	18	51	13	3	-	10
18 and 19 years	1 672	1 510	79	623	808	162	43	81	38
20 and 21 years	1 725	1 484	168	730	586	241	123	98	21
22 to 24 years	1 305	963	169	393	400	342	218	80	44
25 to 29 years	1 044	572	143	186	243	472	310	105	57
30 to 34 years	530	226	70	50	106	304	186	69	49
35 years and over	1 454	433	136	107	191	1 021	689	167	165
BLACK ALONE OR IN COMBINATION									
Both Sexes									
15 years and over	4 740	3 938	319	618	3 000	802	559	126	117
Enrolled in high school	2 352	2 352	54	214	2 084	-	-	-	-
15 years	655	655	-	33	622	-	-	-	-
16 and 17 years	1 296	1 296	19	142	1 135	-	-	-	-
18 and 19 years	266	266	7	27	232	-	-	-	-
20 years and over	135	135	28	12	95	-	-	-	-
Enrolled in college	2 388	1 586	266	404	916	802	559	126	117
15 to 17 years	31	31	-	1	30	-	-	-	-
18 and 19 years	481	423	23	107	294	57	11	21	26
20 and 21 years	428	366	43	118	205	62	30	14	18
22 to 24 years	462	345	48	111	186	117	80	26	12
25 to 29 years	299	163	44	35	84	136	89	18	28
30 to 34 years	229	106	39	18	49	124	104	16	3
35 years and over	458	152	69	14	68	306	245	31	30
Male									
15 years and over	2 096	1 805	136	244	1 425	291	218	31	42
Enrolled in high school	1 202	1 202	27	87	1 087	-	-	-	-
15 years	318	318	-	11	306	-	-	-	-
16 and 17 years	638	638	13	55	570	-	-	-	-
18 and 19 years	187	187	7	16	164	-	-	-	-
20 years and over	59	59	7	5	47	-	-	-	-
Enrolled in college	895	603	108	157	337	292	219	31	42
15 to 17 years	9	9	-	-	9	-	-	-	-
18 and 19 years	201	176	6	43	126	25	9	8	8
20 and 21 years	189	155	23	55	77	34	22	3	8
22 to 24 years	167	122	18	37	67	45	36	4	6
25 to 29 years	109	48	11	13	24	61	45	7	9
30 to 34 years	66	35	23	4	8	31	31	-	-
35 years and over	154	58	27	5	26	96	76	9	11

- = Quantity zero or rounds to zero.

Table A-6. Employment Status of High School and College Students Age 15 Years and Over, by Level of School, Attendance Status, Age, Sex, Race, and Hispanic Origin, October 2005—*Continued*

(Numbers in thousands.)

Attendance status, age, sex, race, and Hispanic origin	Total enrollment	Full-time students				Part-time students			
		Total enrollment	Full-time employed	Part-time employed	Not employed	Total enrollment	Full-time employed	Part-time employed	Not employed
BLACK ALONE OR IN COMBINATION									
Female									
15 years and over	2 644	2 133	183	374	1 576	511	341	95	75
Enrolled in high school	1 152	1 152	27	127	997	-	-	-	-
15 years	337	337	-	22	315	-	-	-	-
16 and 17 years	659	659	6	87	565	-	-	-	-
18 and 19 years	80	80	-	11	69	-	-	-	-
20 years and over	76	76	21	7	48	-	-	-	-
Enrolled in college	1 493	981	156	247	579	510	341	96	76
15 to 17 years	22	22	-	1	21	-	-	-	-
18 and 19 years	280	247	16	63	168	32	2	13	18
20 and 21 years	239	211	20	63	128	28	8	11	10
22 to 24 years	295	222	29	74	119	72	44	22	6
25 to 29 years	190	115	33	23	60	75	44	11	20
30 to 34 years	164	71	16	14	41	93	74	16	3
35 years and over	303	93	42	9	42	210	169	23	19
ASIAN ALONE OR IN COMBINATION									
Both Sexes									
15 years and over	1 888	1 627	139	361	1 127	262	152	60	49
Enrolled in high school	591	591	11	90	490	-	-	-	-
15 years	150	150	-	4	146	-	-	-	-
16 and 17 years	388	388	4	76	308	-	-	-	-
18 and 19 years	42	42	2	6	34	-	-	-	-
20 years and over	11	11	5	4	2	-	-	-	-
Enrolled in college	1 297	1 035	129	269	637	262	153	60	51
15 to 17 years	25	20	-	2	18	5	-	-	5
18 and 19 years	204	197	4	55	138	8	4	3	1
20 and 21 years	292	262	22	83	157	30	8	20	2
22 to 24 years	277	234	32	91	111	43	22	11	11
25 to 29 years	240	175	31	23	121	65	32	12	21
30 to 34 years	122	88	28	14	46	33	26	8	-
35 years and over	137	59	12	1	46	78	61	6	11
Male									
15 years and over	930	814	66	176	572	116	65	29	22
Enrolled in high school	290	290	1	46	242	-	-	-	-
15 years	75	75	-	1	74	-	-	-	-
16 and 17 years	185	185	1	39	145	-	-	-	-
18 and 19 years	30	30	-	6	23	-	-	-	-
Enrolled in college	640	524	66	130	328	116	65	28	23
15 to 17 years	13	8	-	2	5	5	-	-	5
18 and 19 years	97	92	3	22	67	5	4	1	1
20 and 21 years	170	156	7	49	100	13	-	11	2
22 to 24 years	124	110	24	45	42	15	3	4	7
25 to 29 years	113	80	9	7	64	33	18	8	7
30 to 34 years	63	45	12	4	29	18	15	3	-
35 years and over	60	33	11	1	21	27	25	1	1
Female									
15 years and over	958	813	74	184	555	145	86	31	28
Enrolled in high school	300	300	10	44	247	-	-	-	-
15 years	75	75	-	3	72	-	-	-	-
16 and 17 years	203	203	4	37	163	-	-	-	-
18 and 19 years	12	12	2	-	10	-	-	-	-
20 years and over	10	10	4	4	2	-	-	-	-
Enrolled in college	658	511	63	140	309	144	86	31	27
15 to 17 years	12	12	-	-	12	-	-	-	-
18 and 19 years	107	104	1	33	71	2	-	2	-
20 and 21 years	122	106	14	34	57	16	8	9	-
22 to 24 years	153	124	8	47	69	28	18	7	3
25 to 29 years	128	96	23	16	58	32	13	4	14
30 to 34 years	59	43	16	10	17	15	11	4	-
35 years and over	77	26	1	-	25	51	36	5	10

- = Quantity zero or rounds to zero.

Table A-6. Employment Status of High School and College Students Age 15 Years and Over, by Level of School, Attendance Status, Age, Sex, Race, and Hispanic Origin, October 2005—*Continued*

(Numbers in thousands.)

Attendance status, age, sex, race, and Hispanic origin	Total enrollment	Full-time students				Part-time students			
		Total enrollment	Full-time employed	Part-time employed	Not employed	Total enrollment	Full-time employed	Part-time employed	Not employed
HISPANIC[1]									
Both Sexes									
15 years and over	4 343	3 657	279	645	2 733	686	422	164	100
Enrolled in high school	2 402	2 402	83	278	2 041	-	-	-	-
15 years	698	698	-	31	668	-	-	-	-
16 and 17 years	1 325	1 325	13	202	1 111	-	-	-	-
18 and 19 years	272	272	25	32	214	-	-	-	-
20 years and over	107	107	45	13	48	-	-	-	-
Enrolled in college	1 941	1 256	195	367	692	687	422	165	99
15 to 17 years	31	18	-	1	17	14	2	3	8
18 and 19 years	406	321	25	86	209	85	28	37	20
20 and 21 years	420	349	34	129	186	71	37	24	10
22 to 24 years	389	263	30	85	148	126	83	36	7
25 to 29 years	288	162	46	36	79	127	79	24	24
30 to 34 years	150	66	26	14	26	84	57	15	12
35 years and over	257	77	34	16	27	180	136	26	18
Male									
15 years and over	2 038	1 773	146	296	1 331	266	187	51	28
Enrolled in high school	1 233	1 233	55	155	1 025	-	-	-	-
15 years	343	343	-	18	325	-	-	-	-
16 and 17 years	660	660	7	109	545	-	-	-	-
18 and 19 years	166	166	19	16	131	-	-	-	-
20 years and over	64	64	29	12	24	-	-	-	-
Enrolled in college	804	539	92	140	307	266	186	50	28
15 to 17 years	10	5	-	-	5	5	2	3	-
18 and 19 years	173	138	11	33	95	35	16	12	6
20 and 21 years	183	160	25	59	76	24	11	9	4
22 to 24 years	183	120	8	25	87	63	41	18	4
25 to 29 years	111	57	14	15	28	54	38	5	10
30 to 34 years	52	21	13	4	3	31	31	-	-
35 years and over	92	38	21	4	13	54	47	3	4
Female									
15 years and over	2 305	1 884	132	350	1 403	421	235	114	71
Enrolled in high school	1 167	1 167	29	122	1 016	-	-	-	-
15 years	355	355	-	12	343	-	-	-	-
16 and 17 years	665	665	6	93	566	-	-	-	-
18 and 19 years	105	105	6	16	83	-	-	-	-
20 years and over	42	42	17	1	24	-	-	-	-
Enrolled in college	1 137	717	104	227	385	420	236	114	72
15 to 17 years	21	13	-	1	12	8	-	-	8
18 and 19 years	232	183	15	54	114	50	12	24	14
20 and 21 years	237	189	9	70	110	47	25	15	7
22 to 24 years	206	143	23	60	61	63	43	18	3
25 to 29 years	178	105	32	21	51	73	40	19	14
30 to 34 years	98	45	12	9	23	53	27	15	12
35 years and over	165	39	13	12	14	126	89	23	14

[1]May be of any race.
- = Quantity zero or rounds to zero.

Table A-7. Employment Status and Enrollment in Vocational Courses for the Population Age 15 Years and Over, by Sex, Age, Educational Attainment, College Enrollment, Race, and Hispanic Origin, October 2005

(Numbers in thousands.)

Characteristic	Total population		Full-time employed		Part-time employed		Not employed	
	Total	Enrolled in vocational courses	Total	Enrolled in vocational courses	Total	Enrolled in vocational courses	Total	Enrolled in vocational courses
ALL RACES								
Both Sexes								
Total	231 257	4 259	118 430	2 561	25 853	598	86 974	1 101
15 to 19 years	20 764	311	1 683	62	4 603	103	14 478	146
20 to 24 years	20 295	663	9 855	285	4 229	122	6 212	256
25 to 34 years	39 140	1 015	27 380	681	3 719	109	8 040	226
35 to 44 years	42 947	908	30 775	638	4 007	95	8 165	174
45 to 64 years	72 914	1 228	45 783	869	6 762	139	20 369	220
65 years and over	35 197	134	2 954	26	2 534	30	29 710	78
Educational attainment	231 257	4 259	118 430	2 561	25 853	598	86 974	1 101
Not a high school graduate	45 079	263	11 516	132	4 899	16	28 665	115
High school graduate only	69 765	1 000	36 383	489	6 817	163	26 566	348
Some college or associate's degree	60 374	1 665	32 798	933	8 795	294	18 781	438
Bachelor's degree or more	56 038	1 331	37 734	1 007	5 342	124	12 962	200
College enrollment	231 257	4 259	118 430	2 561	25 853	598	86 974	1 101
Enrolled in college	17 472	1 095	5 367	435	5 325	234	6 780	426
Not enrolled in college	213 785	3 164	113 063	2 126	20 528	364	80 193	674
Male								
Total	111 791	2 016	68 633	1 423	8 717	161	34 440	432
15 to 19 years	10 526	162	999	40	2 178	44	7 350	78
20 to 24 years	10 197	336	5 589	166	1 788	43	2 821	127
25 to 34 years	19 494	508	16 254	401	1 039	22	2 200	84
35 to 44 years	21 157	401	18 096	348	778	20	2 283	33
45 to 64 years	35 416	543	25 793	441	1 733	23	7 891	80
65 years and over	15 002	65	1 903	26	1 202	9	11 896	30
Educational attainment	111 791	2 016	68 633	1 423	8 717	161	34 440	432
Not a high school graduate	22 792	126	7 969	89	2 317	9	12 505	29
I ligh school graduate only	33 749	482	21 947	305	2 108	44	9 693	134
Some college or associate's degree	27 693	754	17 784	470	2 780	90	7 129	194
Bachelor's degree or more	27 558	653	20 933	559	1 512	19	5 113	76
Colloge onrollment	111 791	2 016	68 633	1 423	8 717	161	34 440	432
Enrolled in college	7 539	487	2 382	228	2 113	76	3 044	183
Not enrolled in college	104 252	1 529	66 252	1 195	6 605	85	31 396	250
Female								
Total	119 466	2 243	49 797	1 138	17 136	437	52 533	668
15 to 19 years	10 238	149	684	22	2 425	59	7 128	68
20 to 24 years	10 099	327	4 266	119	2 441	79	3 391	129
25 to 34 years	19 647	507	11 126	279	2 680	86	5 840	141
35 to 44 years	21 790	507	12 679	291	3 229	75	5 882	141
45 to 64 years	37 498	685	19 990	428	5 029	117	12 479	141
65 years and over	20 195	69	1 051	-	1 331	21	17 813	48
Educational attainment	119 466	2 243	49 797	1 138	17 136	437	52 533	668
Not a high school graduate	22 288	137	3 546	44	2 582	7	16 159	86
High school graduate only	36 017	518	14 435	184	4 709	120	16 873	214
Some college or associate's degree	32 682	911	15 015	463	6 015	204	11 652	244
Bachelor's degree or more	28 480	678	16 801	448	3 831	106	7 849	124
College enrollment	119 466	2 243	49 797	1 138	17 136	437	52 533	668
Enrolled in college	9 934	609	2 986	208	3 212	158	3 736	243
Not enrolled in college	109 532	1 635	46 811	931	13 924	279	48 797	425

- = Quantity zero or rounds to zero.

Table A-7. Employment Status and Enrollment in Vocational Courses for the Population Age 15 Years and Over, by Sex, Age, Educational Attainment, College Enrollment, Race, and Hispanic Origin, October 2005—*Continued*

(Numbers in thousands.)

Characteristic	Total population		Full-time employed		Part-time employed		Not employed	
	Total	Enrolled in vocational courses	Total	Enrolled in vocational courses	Total	Enrolled in vocational courses	Total	Enrolled in vocational courses
WHITE ALONE OR IN COMBINATION								
Both Sexes								
Total	191 385	3 453	98 141	2 079	22 333	519	70 911	855
15 to 19 years	16 558	253	1 420	56	4 024	82	11 113	115
20 to 24 years	16 267	501	8 173	232	3 458	101	4 636	167
25 to 34 years	31 214	804	22 050	519	3 103	99	6 062	186
35 to 44 years	35 048	750	25 170	526	3 421	79	6 457	146
45 to 64 years	61 358	1 021	38 786	722	5 981	128	16 591	171
65 years and over	30 940	125	2 542	24	2 347	30	26 051	71
Educational attainment	191 385	3 453	98 141	2 079	22 333	519	70 911	855
Not a high school graduate	36 246	201	9 750	95	4 151	8	22 345	98
High school graduate only	57 884	818	29 974	402	5 875	151	22 035	266
Some college or associate's degree	50 610	1 344	27 388	768	7 573	243	15 649	334
Bachelor's degree or more	46 645	1 090	31 029	815	4 734	117	10 882	157
College enrollment	191 385	3 453	98 141	2 079	22 333	519	70 911	855
Enrolled in college	13 791	811	4 251	316	4 462	192	5 077	302
Not enrolled in college	177 594	2 642	93 890	1 763	17 870	327	65 834	553
Male								
Total	93 482	1 597	58 277	1 133	7 384	132	27 820	332
15 to 19 years	8 417	136	877	37	1 919	35	5 622	64
20 to 24 years	8 245	247	4 739	130	1 450	36	2 056	81
25 to 34 years	15 823	397	13 460	303	829	22	1 534	72
35 to 44 years	17 531	316	15 199	273	594	15	1 738	28
45 to 64 years	30 168	438	22 330	366	1 470	15	6 369	57
65 years and over	13 298	63	1 672	24	1 123	9	10 502	30
Educational attainment	93 482	1 597	58 277	1 133	7 384	132	27 820	332
Not a high school graduate	18 693	94	7 034	63	1 972	4	9 687	26
High school graduate only	28 051	388	18 461	252	1 752	40	7 838	95
Some college or associate's degree	23 469	594	15 226	382	2 320	69	5 922	143
Bachelor's degree or more	23 269	522	17 557	435	1 340	19	4 373	68
College enrollment	93 482	1 597	58 277	1 133	7 384	132	27 820	332
Enrolled in college	5 978	357	1 912	160	1 757	63	2 309	135
Not enrolled in college	87 504	1 240	56 365	974	5 628	69	25 512	198
Female								
Total	97 903	1 856	39 864	946	14 948	387	43 090	523
15 to 19 years	8 141	117	544	19	2 105	47	5 492	51
20 to 24 years	8 022	253	3 433	102	2 008	65	2 580	86
25 to 34 years	15 391	407	8 589	217	2 273	77	4 528	114
35 to 44 years	17 517	434	9 971	252	2 826	64	4 720	118
45 to 64 years	31 190	583	16 457	356	4 511	114	10 222	114
65 years and over	17 642	62	870	-	1 224	21	15 548	41
Educational attainment	97 903	1 856	39 864	946	14 948	387	43 090	523
Not a high school graduate	17 553	107	2 717	31	2 178	5	12 658	72
High school graduate only	29 833	431	11 514	149	4 123	110	14 196	171
Some college or associate's degree	27 141	750	12 162	386	5 253	174	9 726	191
Bachelor's degree or more	23 376	568	13 472	380	3 394	99	6 509	89
College enrollment	97 903	1 856	39 864	946	14 948	387	43 090	523
Enrolled in college	7 813	454	2 339	157	2 706	129	2 769	168
Not enrolled in college	90 090	1 402	37 525	789	12 242	258	40 322	355

- = Quantity zero or rounds to zero.

Table A-7. Employment Status and Enrollment in Vocational Courses for the Population Age 15 Years and Over, by Sex, Age, Educational Attainment, College Enrollment, Race, and Hispanic Origin, October 2005—*Continued*

(Numbers in thousands.)

Characteristic	Total population		Full-time employed		Part-time employed		Not employed	
	Total	Enrolled in vocational courses	Total	Enrolled in vocational courses	Total	Enrolled in vocational courses	Total	Enrolled in vocational courses
BLACK ALONE OR IN COMBINATION								
Both Sexes								
Total	28 117	566	13 939	348	2 445	53	11 732	165
15 to 19 years	3 389	40	225	3	431	15	2 734	22
20 to 24 years	2 963	122	1 289	44	518	17	1 156	62
25 to 34 years	5 215	137	3 530	105	435	4	1 250	29
35 to 44 years	5 451	115	3 834	88	399	6	1 219	20
45 to 64 years	8 094	143	4 808	106	523	11	2 763	25
65 years and over	3 004	9	255	2	140	-	2 610	7
Educational attainment	28 117	566	13 939	348	2 445	53	11 732	165
Not a high school graduate	6 951	54	1 277	35	590	5	5 084	14
High school graduate only	9 356	149	5 148	73	729	7	3 479	69
Some college or associate's degree	7 405	231	4 256	129	868	35	2 281	67
Bachelor's degree or more	4 405	133	3 259	111	257	7	889	16
College enrollment	28 117	566	13 939	348	2 445	53	11 732	165
Enrolled in college	2 387	225	824	102	530	32	1 033	90
Not enrolled in college	25 729	341	13 115	245	1 915	21	10 699	75
Male								
Total	12 661	283	6 734	199	930	21	4 997	63
15 to 19 years	1 668	19	110	3	174	9	1 385	7
20 to 24 years	1 402	66	641	29	212	4	549	33
25 to 34 years	2 358	63	1 744	57	151	-	463	6
35 to 44 years	2 440	63	1 852	57	148	-	441	6
45 to 64 years	3 635	70	2 263	50	187	8	1 185	12
65 years and over	1 158	2	124	2	59	-	974	-
Educational attainment	12 661	283	6 734	199	930	21	4 997	63
Not a high school graduate	3 284	30	668	22	275	5	2 340	3
High school graduate only	4 465	86	2 759	49	271	-	1 434	36
Some college or associate's degree	3 098	101	1 935	61	292	16	870	24
Bachelor's degree or more	1 814	66	1 371	66	91	-	352	-
College enrollment	12 661	283	6 734	199	930	21	4 997	63
Enrolled in college	895	96	327	58	188	10	380	29
Not enrolled in college	11 766	186	6 407	141	742	11	4 617	34
Female								
Total	15 456	284	7 206	149	1 515	32	6 735	103
15 to 19 years	1 721	21	115	-	257	6	1 349	15
20 to 24 years	1 561	56	648	14	306	13	607	29
25 to 34 years	2 858	75	1 786	47	284	4	787	24
35 to 44 years	3 011	52	1 982	31	251	6	777	15
45 to 64 years	4 459	72	2 545	56	336	3	1 578	13
65 years and over	1 847	7	130	-	80	-	1 636	7
Educational attainment	15 456	284	7 206	149	1 515	32	6 735	103
Not a high school graduate	3 667	24	608	12	315	-	2 743	12
High school graduate only	4 891	63	2 389	24	458	6	2 044	32
Some college or associate's degree	4 308	130	2 321	68	576	19	1 411	43
Bachelor's degree or more	2 591	67	1 888	45	166	7	537	16
College enrollment	15 456	284	7 206	149	1 515	32	6 735	103
Enrolled in college	1 493	129	497	45	342	22	653	62
Not enrolled in college	13 963	155	6 708	104	1 173	10	6 082	41

- = Quantity zero or rounds to zero.

Table A-7. Employment Status and Enrollment in Vocational Courses for the Population Age 15 Years and Over, by Sex, Age, Educational Attainment, College Enrollment, Race, and Hispanic Origin, October 2005—*Continued*

(Numbers in thousands.)

Characteristic	Total population		Full-time employed		Part-time employed		Not employed	
	Total	Enrolled in vocational courses	Total	Enrolled in vocational courses	Total	Enrolled in vocational courses	Total	Enrolled in vocational courses
ASIAN ALONE OR IN COMBINATION								
Total	10 713	219	5 807	120	1 017	23	3 889	76
15 to 19 years	867	16	32	-	152	6	683	11
20 to 24 years	1 013	39	377	8	254	4	382	27
25 to 34 years	2 448	63	1 639	50	165	3	644	10
35 to 44 years	2 262	39	1 645	21	180	10	436	8
45 to 64 years	2 986	61	1 958	41	224	-	804	20
65 years and over	1 137	-	156	-	42	-	939	-
Educational attainment	10 713	219	5 807	120	1 017	23	3 889	76
Not a high school graduate	1 627	3	394	2	157	-	1 076	1
High school graduate only	2 091	29	1 043	10	193	6	856	14
Some college or associate's degree	2 080	82	983	28	321	16	777	38
Bachelor's degree or more	4 914	104	3 387	80	346	-	1 181	23
College enrollment	10 713	219	5 807	120	1 017	23	3 889	76
Enrolled in college	1 297	60	280	14	331	9	687	36
Not enrolled in college	9 416	159	5 527	106	686	13	3 202	40
Male								
Total	5 099	126	3 323	81	367	8	1 410	37
15 to 19 years	438	5	16	-	76	-	346	5
20 to 24 years	501	23	180	5	123	3	198	15
25 to 34 years	1 195	41	967	35	54	-	174	6
35 to 44 years	1 087	19	969	14	33	5	85	-
45 to 64 years	1 388	38	1 084	27	64	-	240	10
65 years and over	490	-	107	-	15	-	367	-
Educational attainment	5 099	126	3 323	81	367	8	1 410	37
Not a high school graduate	664	3	205	2	61	-	398	1
High school graduate only	976	6	587	3	73	3	316	-
Some college or associate's degree	1 023	54	554	20	155	5	315	29
Bachelor's degree or more	2 435	64	1 977	56	78	-	380	8
College enrollment	5 099	126	3 323	81	367	8	1 410	37
Enrolled in college	640	30	130	8	159	3	351	19
Not enrolled in college	4 458	96	3 193	74	207	5	1 059	18
Female								
Total	5 614	93	2 484	39	650	14	2 480	39
15 to 19 years	429	11	16	-	75	6	338	5
20 to 24 years	512	16	196	3	131	1	184	12
25 to 34 years	1 253	22	672	15	111	3	470	4
35 to 44 years	1 175	20	676	7	147	5	351	8
45 to 64 years	1 598	24	874	14	160	-	564	10
65 years and over	648	-	49	-	26	-	572	-
Educational attainment	5 614	93	2 484	39	650	14	2 480	39
Not a high school graduate	963	-	189	-	96	-	678	-
High school graduate only	1 115	23	456	7	120	3	540	14
Some college or associate's degree	1 057	29	429	8	166	11	461	10
Bachelor's degree or more	2 479	41	1 410	24	268	-	801	16
College enrollment	5 614	93	2 484	39	650	14	2 480	39
Enrolled in college	657	30	150	7	171	6	336	17
Not enrolled in college	4 957	63	2 335	32	479	8	2 144	22

- = Quantity zero or rounds to zero.

Table A-7. Employment Status and Enrollment in Vocational Courses for the Population Age 15 Years and Over, by Sex, Age, Educational Attainment, College Enrollment, Race, and Hispanic Origin, October 2005—*Continued*

(Numbers in thousands.)

Characteristic	Total population		Full-time employed		Part-time employed		Not employed	
	Total	Enrolled in vocational courses	Total	Enrolled in vocational courses	Total	Enrolled in vocational courses	Total	Enrolled in vocational courses
HISPANIC[1]								
Both Sexes								
Total	30 192	556	16 395	313	2 712	61	11 085	182
15 to 19 years	3 455	32	384	8	480	9	2 591	14
20 to 24 years	3 645	99	1 882	52	587	14	1 176	33
25 to 34 years	7 756	215	5 284	116	622	18	1 851	81
35 to 44 years	6 364	135	4 500	85	514	12	1 351	37
45 to 64 years	6 709	68	4 081	47	454	7	2 174	13
65 years and over	2 263	8	264	5	56	-	1 942	4
Educational attainment	30 192	556	16 395	313	2 712	61	11 085	182
Not a high school graduate	13 226	129	5 663	68	1 035	4	6 528	57
High school graduate only	8 196	161	5 084	78	675	34	2 437	49
Some college or associate's degree ...	5 676	184	3 392	103	741	20	1 543	60
Bachelor's degree or more	3 094	82	2 256	64	262	3	577	15
College enrollment	30 192	556	16 395	313	2 712	61	11 085	182
Enrolled in college	1 942	150	618	54	532	28	792	67
Not enrolled in college	28 251	407	15 777	259	2 181	33	10 293	115
Male								
Total	15 493	276	10 621	209	1 016	7	3 855	60
15 to 19 years	1 750	9	249	3	245	5	1 255	-
20 to 24 years	1 950	48	1 257	33	257	-	436	15
25 to 34 years	4 200	119	3 578	80	216	2	406	38
35 to 44 years	3 325	60	2 906	56	143	-	276	3
45 to 64 years	3 306	32	2 446	31	126	-	733	1
65 years and over	962	8	185	5	29	-	748	4
Educational attainment	15 493	276	10 621	209	1 016	7	3 855	60
Not a high school graduate	6 960	57	4 141	47	457	-	2 362	10
High school graduate only	4 291	65	3 284	48	245	4	762	12
Some college or associate's degree ...	2 733	103	1 950	68	241	3	542	31
Bachelor's degree or more	1 509	52	1 246	45	73	-	190	7
College enrollment	15 493	276	10 621	209	1 016	7	3 855	60
Enrolled in college	804	55	279	29	191	5	335	21
Not enrolled in college	14 688	221	10 343	180	825	2	3 520	40
Female								
Total	14 700	280	5 774	104	1 696	54	7 230	121
15 to 19 years	1 705	23	135	5	234	4	1 336	14
20 to 24 years	1 695	51	625	19	330	14	739	18
25 to 34 years	3 557	95	1 706	36	406	17	1 445	43
35 to 44 years	3 039	75	1 593	29	371	12	1 075	34
45 to 64 years	3 404	36	1 635	16	328	7	1 440	12
65 years and over	1 300	-	79	-	27	-	1 194	-
Educational attainment	14 700	280	5 774	104	1 696	54	7 230	121
Not a high school graduate	6 267	73	1 522	21	578	4	4 167	47
High school graduate only	3 906	97	1 801	30	430	30	1 675	37
Some college or associate's degree ...	2 943	81	1 442	35	500	17	1 001	29
Bachelor's degree or more	1 585	30	1 009	18	189	3	387	8
College enrollment	14 700	280	5 774	104	1 696	54	7 230	121
Enrolled in college	1 137	94	339	25	341	23	457	46
Not enrolled in college	13 562	186	5 435	79	1 355	31	6 772	75

[1] May be of any race.
- = Quantity zero or rounds to zero.

Table A-8. Enrollment and Employment Status of Recent High School Graduates Age 16 to 24 Years, by Type of School, Educational Attainment Level for the Population Not Enrolled, Sex, Race, and Hispanic Origin, October 2005

(Numbers in thousands.)

Enrollment and employment status, sex, race, and Hispanic origin	Both sexes			Male			Female		
	Total	Graduated this year	Graduated earlier	Total	Graduated this year	Graduated earlier	Total	Graduated this year	Graduated earlier
ALL RACES	23 299	2 675	20 624	11 252	1 262	9 990	12 047	1 414	10 634
Enrolled in College	10 901	1 834	9 066	4 982	839	4 143	5 919	995	4 923
Enrolled in two-year college	2 657	639	2 017	1 234	309	926	1 422	331	1 092
Full-time	1 976	539	1 437	954	262	692	1 022	277	745
Part-time	680	100	580	280	46	234	400	54	346
Enrolled in four-year college	7 569	1 185	6 384	3 465	526	2 939	4 104	659	3 445
Full-time	6 815	1 128	5 687	3 131	500	2 630	3 684	627	3 057
Part-time	754	57	697	335	25	309	420	32	388
Enrolled in graduate school	675	10	665	283	4	278	392	5	387
Not Enrolled in College	12 399	841	11 558	6 270	423	5 847	6 129	418	5 710
Not employed	12 118	807	11 310	6 105	401	5 704	6 013	406	5 607
Enrolled in vocational school	281	34	247	165	22	144	115	12	104
WHITE ALONE OR IN COMBINATION	18 717	2 214	16 503	9 143	1 033	8 110	9 574	1 181	8 393
Enrolled in College	8 759	1 542	7 217	4 024	684	3 340	4 735	859	3 877
Enrolled in two-year college	2 098	511	1 587	981	235	746	1 118	276	841
Full-time	1 535	427	1 107	766	201	564	769	226	543
Part-time	564	84	480	215	34	182	348	50	298
Enrolled in four-year college	6 145	1 026	5 119	2 840	447	2 393	3 305	579	2 726
Full-time	5 558	981	4 577	2 567	430	2 137	2 991	552	2 439
Part-time	587	44	542	273	17	256	314	27	287
Enrolled in graduate school	516	6	510	203	2	201	313	4	309
Not Enrolled in College	9 958	671	9 287	5 119	349	4 770	4 839	322	4 517
Not employed	9 723	638	9 086	4 979	327	4 652	4 744	310	4 434
Enrolled in vocational school	235	34	201	140	22	118	95	12	83
BLACK ALONE OR IN COMBINATION	3 352	382	2 971	1 476	186	1 290	1 877	195	1 681
Enrolled in College	1 389	222	1 167	558	120	438	831	103	729
Enrolled in two-year college	397	102	294	174	60	113	223	42	181
Full-time	303	88	215	122	52	70	181	36	145
Part-time	93	14	79	51	8	43	42	7	36
Enrolled in four-year college	929	117	812	360	57	303	569	61	509
Full-time	800	106	694	315	51	263	485	55	431
Part-time	129	11	118	45	5	40	84	6	78
Enrolled in graduate school	63	3	61	24	3	22	39	-	39
Not Enrolled in College	1 963	159	1 804	918	67	851	1 045	93	953
Not employed	1 934	159	1 775	900	67	833	1 034	93	941
Enrolled in vocational school	29	-	29	18	-	18	11	-	11
ASIAN ALONE OR IN COMBINATION	1 228	90	1 139	613	48	565	615	41	574
Enrolled in College	787	76	711	400	40	360	387	35	351
Enrolled in two-year college	164	28	136	79	17	63	85	11	74
Full-time	140	23	117	63	12	51	77	11	66
Part-time	24	5	19	16	5	11	8	-	8
Enrolled in four-year college	523	46	476	266	24	242	257	23	234
Full-time	479	44	435	251	24	227	228	20	208
Part-time	44	2	41	15	-	15	29	2	26
Enrolled in graduate school	100	1	98	55	-	55	45	1	43
Not Enrolled in College	442	14	428	213	8	205	229	6	223
Not employed	426	14	412	206	8	198	221	6	215
Enrolled in vocational school	15	-	15	7	-	7	8	-	8
HISPANIC[1]	3 252	390	2 862	1 579	183	1 396	1 674	207	1 466
Enrolled in College	1 220	211	1 010	540	100	439	681	111	570
Enrolled in two-year college	425	100	326	194	51	143	231	49	182
Full-time	285	77	208	132	37	96	153	40	112
Part-time	140	22	118	62	14	48	79	9	70
Enrolled in four-year college	738	108	629	328	47	281	410	62	348
Full-time	607	93	514	269	40	229	338	54	284
Part-time	131	15	116	59	7	52	72	8	64
Enrolled in graduate school	58	3	55	18	3	15	40	-	40
Not Enrolled in College	2 032	179	1 852	1 039	83	956	993	97	896
Not employed	1 994	175	1 819	1 013	83	930	981	92	889
Enrolled in vocational school	38	5	34	26	-	26	12	5	7

[1]May be of any race.
- = Quantity zero or rounds to zero.

Table A-9. Enrollment Status for Children Age 5 to 24 Years in Families, by Control of School, Type of Family, Family Income, Race, and Hispanic Origin, October 2005

(Numbers in thousands.)

Family income, type of family, race, and Hispanic origin	Total	No dependents age 5 to 24 years[1]	Families with dependent children enrolled in kindergarten, elementary, or high school				Families with dependent children enrolled in college		
			None enrolled in elementary or high school	Public only	Public and private	Private only	None enrolled in college	One enrolled in college	Two or more enrolled in college
ALL RACES									
Total Families	77 842	39 414	6 852	28 028	780	2 768	32 392	5 183	852
Less than $10,000	3 758	1 423	395	1 809	34	97	2 148	169	18
$10,000 to $14,999	3 400	1 722	299	1 317	12	51	1 576	94	9
$15,000 to $19,999	2 795	1 459	220	1 071	18	27	1 223	110	3
$20,000 to $29,999	7 611	3 953	533	2 937	53	134	3 306	306	45
$30,000 to $39,999	7 701	3 998	633	2 807	70	193	3 262	403	38
$40,000 to $49,999	5 997	3 099	486	2 192	51	168	2 498	359	41
$50,000 to $74,999	13 521	6 729	1 226	4 925	133	509	5 595	1 039	158
$75,000 to $99,999	7 716	3 705	775	2 790	111	334	3 130	733	148
$100,000 to $149,999	6 930	3 377	664	2 410	111	368	2 702	713	138
$150,000 and over	4 408	2 086	422	1 329	92	479	1 785	431	106
Not reported	14 006	7 863	1 199	4 440	95	409	5 168	828	147
Married-Couple Families	58 542	32 734	4 134	18 891	574	2 208	21 341	3 790	677
Less than $10,000	1 177	657	83	408	6	22	448	59	13
$10,000 to $14,999	1 702	1 161	70	452	3	16	510	28	4
$15,000 to $19,999	1 532	1 017	92	410	-	12	471	40	3
$20,000 to $29,999	4 805	2 985	219	1 507	33	61	1 639	165	16
$30,000 to $39,999	5 506	3 252	320	1 751	48	136	2 008	223	23
$40,000 to $49,999	4 629	2 696	237	1 534	31	132	1 673	229	30
$50,000 to $74,999	11 308	5 957	804	4 024	95	427	4 470	771	110
$75,000 to $99,999	6 957	3 413	654	2 492	101	297	2 776	633	135
$100,000 to $149,999	6 407	3 195	588	2 174	104	346	2 420	657	134
$150,000 and over	4 169	2 018	378	1 235	88	450	1 661	400	91
Not reported	10 349	6 382	690	2 903	65	309	3 265	585	116
Female Family Householder[2]	14 125	4 398	1 824	7 273	180	449	8 575	1 007	143
Less than $10,000	2 223	600	238	1 283	28	74	1 536	81	5
$10,000 to $14,999	1 417	410	175	790	8	35	945	56	6
$15,000 to $19,999	957	289	77	563	18	11	628	41	-
$20,000 to $29,999	2 114	628	234	1 171	17	64	1 343	117	25
$30,000 to $39,999	1 557	453	205	825	22	52	942	149	12
$40,000 to $49,999	896	259	134	472	9	21	533	96	8
$50,000 to $74,999	1 423	454	279	595	31	63	739	189	40
$75,000 to $99,999	461	173	58	189	10	31	222	56	9
$100,000 to $149,999	298	89	44	148	6	10	175	31	3
$150,000 and over	143	35	30	58	2	18	82	16	10
Not reported	2 635	1 007	349	1 178	30	70	1 429	175	24
Male Family Householder[2]	5 175	2 281	894	1 864	25	112	2 476	386	32
Less than $10,000	358	166	74	117	-	1	164	29	-
$10,000 to $14,999	281	150	54	74	1	-	120	10	-
$15,000 to $19,999	306	153	50	98	-	4	124	29	-
$20,000 to $29,999	691	340	81	258	3	10	324	24	4
$30,000 to $39,999	638	293	109	231	-	5	311	31	3
$40,000 to $49,999	472	144	114	187	11	16	292	33	3
$50,000 to $74,999	791	318	143	306	6	19	387	79	7
$75,000 to $99,999	297	119	63	109	-	6	131	44	3
$100,000 to $149,999	225	92	32	88	-	12	107	24	1
$150,000 and over	95	33	14	36	2	10	42	14	6
Not reported	1 021	473	160	359	-	30	474	68	6
WHITE ALONE OR IN COMBINATION									
Total Families	64 568	34 100	5 362	22 134	612	2 361	25 618	4 176	674
Less than $10,000	2 269	953	224	1 012	14	66	1 207	97	13
$10,000 to $14,999	2 529	1 414	197	877	8	32	1 051	57	7
$15,000 to $19,999	2 206	1 234	171	771	2	27	908	61	3
$20,000 to $29,999	6 204	3 431	385	2 234	37	117	2 534	221	19
$30,000 to $39,999	6 407	3 531	456	2 209	55	155	2 560	289	27
$40,000 to $49,999	5 098	2 736	399	1 782	34	148	2 011	317	33
$50,000 to $74,999	11 670	5 963	967	4 185	107	448	4 761	818	128
$75,000 to $99,999	6 847	3 317	683	2 463	99	286	2 752	659	120
$100,000 to $149,999	6 116	3 005	592	2 093	96	330	2 361	631	119
$150,000 and over	3 982	1 906	376	1 182	92	427	1 597	385	95
Not reported	11 239	6 610	913	3 326	67	324	3 878	641	110
Married-Couple Families	51 124	29 186	3 496	16 027	490	1 927	18 160	3 225	554
Less than $10,000	878	492	69	297	-	20	329	48	10
$10,000 to $14,999	1 438	998	62	359	3	16	414	22	4
$15,000 to $19,999	1 337	901	78	346	-	12	408	24	3
$20,000 to $29,999	4 230	2 722	167	1 263	28	50	1 370	129	10
$30,000 to $39,999	4 810	2 963	239	1 456	38	113	1 674	155	18
$40,000 to $49,999	4 039	2 408	195	1 297	24	116	1 397	208	26
$50,000 to $74,999	9 961	5 361	676	3 469	80	375	3 873	646	81
$75,000 to $99,999	6 222	3 093	575	2 211	89	254	2 450	572	107
$100,000 to $149,999	5 714	2 863	529	1 911	93	319	2 140	593	118
$150,000 and over	3 779	1 843	342	1 105	87	402	1 498	357	82
Not reported	8 715	5 542	564	2 312	47	251	2 606	472	95

[1]Dependents are unmarried (or married with spouse absent) children, grandchildren, brothers/sisters or other relatives.
[2]No spouse present.
- = Quantity zero or rounds to zero.

Table A-9. Enrollment Status for Children Age 5 to 24 Years in Families, by Control of School, Type of Family, Family Income, Race, and Hispanic Origin, October 2005—*Continued*

(Numbers in thousands.)

Family income, type of family, race, and Hispanic origin	Total	No dependents age 5 to 24 years[1]	Families with dependent children enrolled in kindergarten, elementary, or high school				Families with dependent children enrolled in college		
			None enrolled in elementary or high school	Public only	Public and private	Private only	None enrolled in college	One enrolled in college	Two or more enrolled in college
WHITE ALONE OR IN COMBINATION									
Female Family Householder[2]	9 557	3 180	1 232	4 695	104	346	5 600	680	97
Less than $10,000	1 173	355	120	638	14	45	777	37	3
$10,000 to $14,999	890	303	100	466	3	16	555	28	3
$15,000 to $19,999	648	221	57	358	2	11	405	22	-
$20,000 to $29,999	1 449	443	164	775	6	61	926	71	9
$30,000 to $39,999	1 133	338	146	595	17	37	671	117	7
$40,000 to $49,999	693	214	111	345	3	21	399	76	4
$50,000 to $74,999	1 075	354	190	453	24	54	559	122	40
$75,000 to $99,999	374	127	49	162	10	26	191	47	9
$100,000 to $149,999	214	60	35	111	3	5	129	25	-
$150,000 and over	124	31	25	51	2	15	72	14	7
Not reported	1 784	734	235	741	20	54	914	121	15
Male Family Householder[2]	3 886	1 734	634	1 412	18	88	1 859	271	23
Less than $10,000	218	105	35	77	-	1	101	12	-
$10,000 to $14,999	201	113	35	51	1	-	81	7	-
$15,000 to $19,999	221	112	37	68	-	4	94	15	-
$20,000 to $29,999	525	267	54	196	3	7	238	21	-
$30,000 to $39,999	464	230	71	159	-	5	215	17	3
$40,000 to $49,999	365	114	92	141	8	11	215	33	3
$50,000 to $74,999	634	248	101	263	3	19	328	50	7
$75,000 to $99,999	251	96	59	89	-	6	111	40	3
$100,000 to $149,999	188	82	28	71	-	7	92	14	-
$150,000 and over	79	32	9	26	2	10	27	14	6
Not reported	740	334	114	273	-	19	357	48	1
BLACK ALONE OR IN COMBINATION									
Total Families	9 333	3 427	1 103	4 419	125	259	5 138	665	103
Less than $10,000	1 304	369	150	735	23	27	874	55	5
$10,000 to $14,999	724	225	83	393	4	19	473	24	2
$15,000 to $19,999	470	172	36	246	16	-	272	26	-
$20,000 to $29,999	1 116	380	119	596	11	10	651	69	16
$30,000 to $39,999	983	345	115	480	11	32	544	88	6
$40,000 to $49,999	619	216	64	311	14	15	380	20	3
$50,000 to $74,999	1 202	492	179	472	17	41	559	139	12
$75,000 to $99,999	460	187	59	193	-	21	210	48	15
$100,000 to $149,999	416	165	57	165	10	18	183	51	16
$150,000 and over	138	44	18	57	-	20	79	12	4
Not reported	1 901	831	222	771	19	57	913	132	24
Married-Couple Families	4 300	2 000	406	1 693	48	154	1 913	329	58
Less than $10,000	201	102	14	77	6	2	84	12	3
$10,000 to $14,999	174	98	2	74	-	-	74	2	-
$15,000 to $19,999	131	80	6	45	-	-	47	5	-
$20,000 to $29,999	369	159	33	166	4	7	189	18	3
$30,000 to $39,999	472	190	53	202	7	20	227	55	-
$40,000 to $49,999	367	163	25	162	7	10	197	7	-
$50,000 to $74,999	818	368	89	322	7	33	363	75	12
$75,000 to $99,999	366	144	47	157	-	18	172	35	15
$100,000 to $149,999	336	132	45	137	7	16	151	40	14
$150,000 and over	118	44	13	45	-	16	64	10	-
Not reported	948	521	80	307	9	32	346	70	11
Female Family Householder[2]	4 024	998	504	2 366	71	85	2 727	261	38
Less than $10,000	983	217	108	616	16	25	729	34	2
$10,000 to $14,999	480	95	65	297	4	19	362	21	2
$15,000 to $19,999	268	53	21	179	16	-	200	15	-
$20,000 to $29,999	606	158	64	378	7	-	390	49	9
$30,000 to $39,999	365	94	37	218	4	12	242	23	6
$40,000 to $49,999	165	35	15	112	3	-	115	11	3
$50,000 to $74,999	279	76	65	122	7	8	159	44	-
$75,000 to $99,999	54	23	9	19	-	3	22	9	-
$100,000 to $149,999	61	25	9	24	3	-	31	3	3
$150,000 and over	14	-	5	5	-	4	8	2	3
Not reported	751	223	106	396	10	15	468	50	10
Male Family Householder[2]	1 008	428	193	360	7	21	498	76	7
Less than $10,000	120	50	28	42	-	-	60	9	-
$10,000 to $14,999	70	32	16	22	-	-	37	2	-
$15,000 to $19,999	71	40	9	22	-	-	25	7	-
$20,000 to $29,999	141	64	22	52	-	3	72	3	3
$30,000 to $39,999	146	61	25	61	-	-	76	10	-
$40,000 to $49,999	88	18	25	37	4	5	68	3	-
$50,000 to $74,999	104	48	25	28	3	-	36	20	-
$75,000 to $99,999	41	21	4	17	-	-	17	4	-
$100,000 to $149,999	19	9	4	4	-	2	2	8	-
$150,000 and over	7	-	-	7	-	-	7	-	-
Not reported	202	87	35	69	-	11	99	12	3

[1]Dependents are unmarried (or married with spouse absent) children, grandchildren, brothers/sisters or other relatives.
[2]No spouse present.
- = Quantity zero or rounds to zero.

Table A-9. Enrollment Status for Children Age 5 to 24 Years in Families, by Control of School, Type of Family, Family Income, Race, and Hispanic Origin, October 2005—*Continued*

(Numbers in thousands.)

Family income, type of family, race, and Hispanic origin	Total	No dependents age 5 to 24 years[1]	Families with dependent children enrolled in kindergarten, elementary, or high school				Families with dependent children enrolled in college		
			None enrolled in elementary or high school	Public only	Public and private	Private only	None enrolled in college	One enrolled in college	Two or more enrolled in college
ASIAN ALONE OR IN COMBINATION									
Total Families	3 491	1 705	350	1 265	31	139	1 393	323	69
Less than $10,000	149	75	23	48	-	3	54	20	-
$10,000 to $14,999	89	50	13	25	-	-	26	13	-
$15,000 to $19,999	93	41	12	40	-	-	33	19	-
$20,000 to $29,999	224	110	26	86	3	-	86	18	11
$30,000 to $39,999	254	94	52	99	4	5	132	23	5
$40,000 to $49,999	230	126	23	75	-	6	77	23	4
$50,000 to $74,999	593	265	65	238	5	20	241	73	14
$75,000 to $99,999	403	201	38	130	8	26	163	25	14
$100,000 to $140,000	306	212	15	144	4	20	150	30	3
$150,000 and over	290	138	26	92	-	33	112	32	8
Not reported	772	394	55	290	7	25	320	47	10
Married-Couple Families	2 789	1 415	206	1 022	28	117	1 093	222	59
Less than $10,000	78	49	3	26	-	-	30	-	-
$10,000 to $14,999	50	41	2	7	-	-	7	2	-
$15,000 to $19,999	49	28	8	14	-	-	11	11	-
$20,000 to $29,999	148	78	13	58	-	-	53	14	4
$30,000 to $39,999	186	80	20	80	3	2	88	12	5
$40,000 to $49,999	180	103	14	57	-	6	60	13	4
$50,000 to $74,999	480	219	31	205	5	20	202	45	14
$75,000 to $99,999	369	178	37	122	8	24	153	25	13
$100,000 to $149,999	355	204	15	120	4	12	124	24	2
$150,000 and over	268	132	21	84	-	30	96	32	8
Not reported	625	303	42	249	7	24	270	43	8
Female Family Householder[2]	452	176	80	176	1	19	200	68	8
Less than $10,000	47	15	10	19	-	3	19	13	-
$10,000 to $14,999	31	5	8	19	-	-	19	7	-
$15,000 to $19,999	35	13	1	21	-	-	18	4	-
$20,000 to $29,999	49	24	9	17	-	-	16	3	7
$30,000 to $39,999	42	9	19	10	1	4	23	10	-
$40,000 to $49,999	34	12	9	13	-	-	13	10	-
$60,000 to $74,999	63	24	18	22	-	-	21	18	-
$75,000 to $99,999	28	18	1	8	-	2	10	-	-
$100,000 to $149,999	22	4	-	13	-	5	15	3	-
$150,000 and over	13	4	1	5	-	3	8	1	-
Not reported	86	47	7	31	-	2	39	-	-
Male Family Householder[2]	251	115	63	67	3	3	100	33	3
Less than $10,000	23	11	9	3	-	-	5	7	-
$10,000 to $14,999	8	4	3	-	-	-	-	3	-
$15,000 to $19,999	-	-	4	4	-	-	4	4	-
$20,000 to $29,999	26	9	4	11	3	-	17	1	-
$30,000 to $39,999	27	5	13	9	-	-	20	2	-
$40,000 to $49,999	15	11	-	5	-	-	5	-	-
$50,000 to $74,999	50	22	17	11	-	-	18	10	-
$75,000 to $99,999	6	5	1	-	-	-	1	-	-
$100,000 to $149,999	18	3	1	11	-	3	11	3	1
$150,000 and over	10	1	5	3	-	-	8	-	-
Not reported	61	44	7	10	-	-	10	4	2
HISPANIC[3]									
Total Families	10 049	3 514	1 015	5 177	84	258	5 775	672	87
Less than $10,000	754	227	69	443	8	7	497	26	3
$10,000 to $14,999	887	361	70	444	-	13	503	19	4
$15,000 to $19,999	648	195	80	370	-	3	422	32	-
$20,000 to $29,999	1 612	518	151	900	18	24	988	96	9
$30,000 to $39,999	1 311	485	105	692	10	20	743	80	3
$40,000 to $49,999	788	286	62	410	12	18	418	74	10
$50,000 to $74,999	1 309	401	152	690	7	59	749	131	28
$75,000 to $99,999	543	222	51	227	16	27	254	63	4
$100,000 to $149,999	330	105	34	165	3	22	190	24	11
$150,000 and over	170	78	18	46	8	21	75	14	3
Not reported	1 696	637	223	790	3	44	936	111	12
Married-Couple Families	6 823	2 607	526	3 447	56	186	3 688	464	63
Less than $10,000	268	111	23	133	-	1	146	9	3
$10,000 to $14,999	501	254	29	215	-	3	234	9	4
$15,000 to $19,999	382	142	42	198	-	-	231	8	-
$20,000 to $29,999	1 094	388	80	605	12	9	625	74	7
$30,000 to $39,999	963	364	57	512	10	20	550	46	3
$40,000 to $49,999	586	232	30	303	4	17	289	58	6
$50,000 to $74,999	1 066	316	85	608	7	49	633	98	18
$75,000 to $99,999	457	190	36	197	13	20	210	53	4
$100,000 to $149,999	290	85	25	154	3	22	171	24	11
$150,000 and over	150	72	14	40	8	16	64	10	3
Not reported	1 066	451	105	483	-	27	535	76	3

[1]Dependents are unmarried (or married with spouse absent) children, grandchildren, brothers/sisters or other relatives.
[2]No spouse present.
[3]May be of any race.
- = Quantity zero or rounds to zero.

Table A-9. Enrollment Status for Children Age 5 to 24 Years in Families, by Control of School, Type of Family, Family Income, Race, and Hispanic Origin, October 2005—*Continued*

(Numbers in thousands.)

Family income, type of family, race, and Hispanic origin	Total	No dependents age 5 to 24 years[1]	Families with dependent children enrolled in kindergarten, elementary, or high school				Families with dependent children enrolled in college		
			None enrolled in elementary or high school	Public only	Public and private	Private only	None enrolled in college	One enrolled in college	Two or more enrolled in college
HISPANIC[3]									
Female Family Householder[2]	2 269	505	296	1 390	24	54	1 590	154	20
Less than $10,000	431	88	37	293	8	6	332	11	-
$10,000 to $14,999	306	70	23	203	-	9	228	8	-
$15,000 to $19,999	187	28	17	139	-	3	145	15	-
$20,000 to $29,999	374	72	40	241	6	15	283	16	3
$30,000 to $39,999	239	63	37	139	-	-	141	35	-
$40,000 to $49,999	111	18	18	69	4	1	75	14	3
$50,000 to $74,999	111	28	37	41	-	6	58	20	5
$75,000 to $99,999	45	17	4	18	3	3	24	4	-
$100,000 to $149,999	. . .	. . .	. . .	. . .	. . .	. . .	. . .	. . .	. . .
$150,000 and over	19	5	4	6	-	4	9	4	-
Not reported	428	110	75	232	3	8	283	26	9
Male Family Householder[2]	957	402	193	341	5	18	497	54	5
Less than $10,000	55	28	9	17	-	-	20	7	-
$10,000 to $14,999	80	36	18	26	-	-	42	2	-
$15,000 to $19,999	79	25	21	33	-	-	46	9	-
$20,000 to $29,999	144	58	31	54	-	-	80	6	-
$30,000 to $39,999	109	58	11	40	-	-	51	-	-
$40,000 to $49,999	91	35	14	37	5	-	54	2	-
$50,000 to $74,999	132	56	30	41	-	4	58	13	5
$75,000 to $99,999	41	15	10	12	-	4	20	6	-
$100,000 to $149,999	22	15	5	3	-	-	8	-	-
$150,000 and over	1	-	-	-	-	1	1	-	-
Not reported	202	75	43	76	-	8	118	9	-

[1]Dependents are unmarried (or married with spouse absent) children, grandchildren, brothers/sisters or other relatives.
[2]No spouse present.
[3]May be of any race.
- = Quantity zero or rounds to zero.
. . . = Not available.

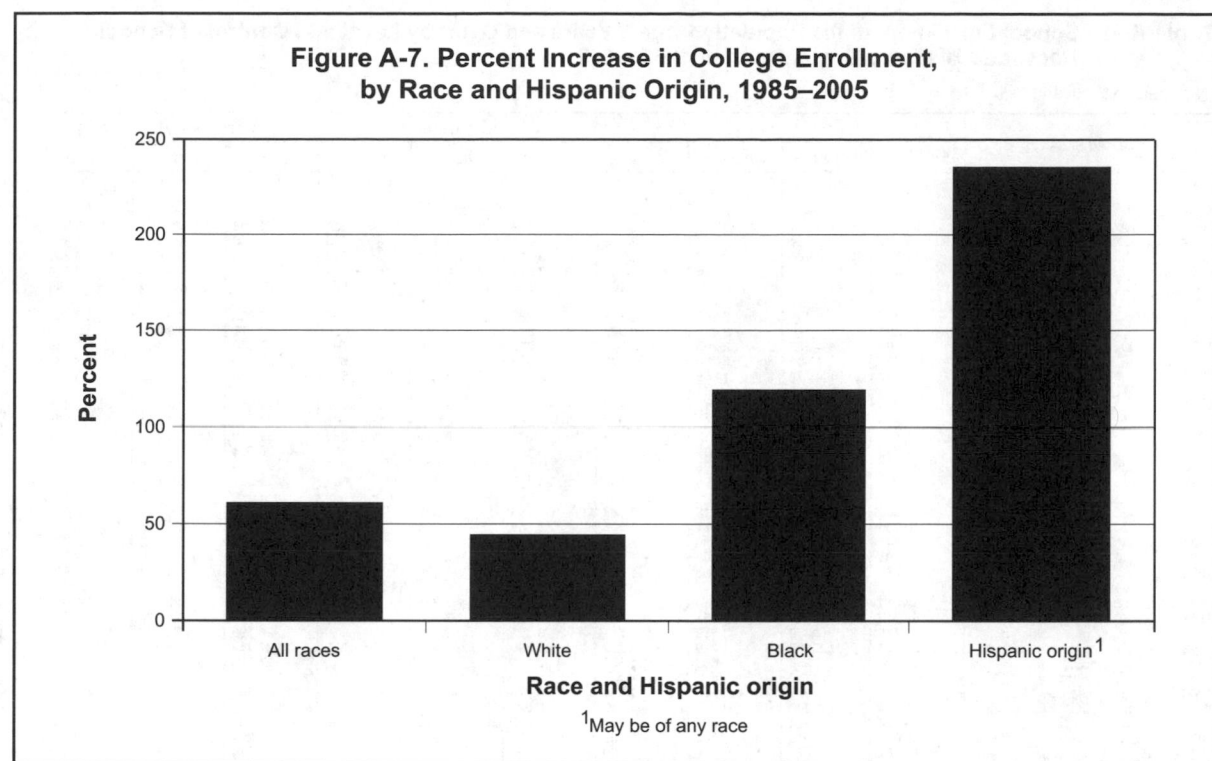

Figure A-7. Percent Increase in College Enrollment, by Race and Hispanic Origin, 1985–2005

Over the past 20 years, total college enrollment has gradually increased. For Blacks and Hispanics, this increase was substantial. In 1985, over 1 million Blacks were enrolled in college. By 2005, this number had jumped to nearly 2.3 million, an increase of 119 percent. For Hispanics, the increase was even more dramatic. From 1985 to 2005, enrollment for Hispanics more than tripled, with numbers rising from 579,000 to over 1.9 million. During this same time period, enrollment for Whites increased 44.4 percent, an increase of 4 million college students. (Table A-10)

Table A-10. School Enrollment of the Population Age 3 Years and Over, by Level and Control of School, Race, and Hispanic Origin, October 1955–2005

(Numbers in thousands.)

Year, race, and Hispanic origin	Total enrollment	Nursery school			Kindergarten			Elementary school		
		Total	Public	Private	Total	Public	Private	Total	Public	Private
All Races										
2005	75 780	4 603	2 480	2 123	3 912	3 301	552	32 438	28 414	3 324
2004	75 461	4 739	2 487	2 252	3 992	3 417	575	32 556	29 166	3 389
2003	74 911	4 928	2 567	2 361	3 719	3 098	622	32 565	29 204	3 361
2002	74 046	4 471	2 246	2 225	3 571	2 976	594	33 132	29 658	3 474
2001	73 124	4 289	2 161	2 128	3 737	3 145	591	33 166	29 800	3 366
2000	72 214	4 401	2 217	2 184	3 832	3 173	659	32 898	29 378	3 520
1999	72 395	4 578	2 269	2 309	3 825	3 167	658	32 873	29 264	3 609
1998	72 109	4 577	2 265	2 313	3 828	3 128	700	32 573	29 124	3 449
1997	72 031	4 500	2 254	2 246	3 933	3 271	663	32 369	29 308	3 061
1996	70 297	4 212	1 868	2 344	4 034	3 353	681	31 515	28 153	3 362
1995	69 769	4 399	2 012	2 387	3 877	3 174	704	31 815	28 384	3 431
1994[1]	69 272	4 259	1 940	2 319	3 863	3 278	585	31 512	28 131	3 381
1993r	64 414	3 032	1 258	1 774	4 275	3 589	686	31 219	28 278	2 941
1993	62 730	3 018	1 230	1 788	4 180	3 499	681	30 604	27 688	2 914
1992	62 082	2 899	1 098	1 801	4 130	3 507	623	30 165	27 066	3 102
1991	61 276	2 933	1 094	1 839	4 152	3 531	621	29 591	26 632	2 958
1990	60 588	3 401	1 212	2 188	3 899	3 332	567	29 265	26 591	2 674
1989	59 236	2 877	971	1 906	3 868	3 293	575	28 637	25 897	2 740
1988	58 847	2 639	838	1 770	3 958	3 420	538	28 223	25 443	2 778
1987	58 691	2 587	848	1 739	4 018	3 423	595	27 524	24 760	2 765
1986	58 153	2 554	835	1 719	3 961	3 328	633	27 121	24 163	2 958
1985	58 014	2 491	854	1 637	3 815	3 221	594	26 866	23 803	3 063
1984	57 313	2 354	761	1 593	3 484	2 953	531	26 838	24 120	2 718
1983	57 745	2 350	809	1 541	3 361	2 706	656	27 198	24 203	2 994
1982	57 905	2 153	729	1 423	3 299	2 746	553	27 412	24 381	3 031
1981	58 390	2 058	663	1 396	3 161	2 616	545	27 795	24 758	3 037
1980	57 348	1 987	633	1 354	3 176	2 690	486	27 449	24 398	3 051
1979	57 854	1 869	636	1 233	3 025	2 593	432	27 865	24 756	3 109
1978	58 616	1 824	587	1 237	2 989	2 493	496	28 490	25 252	3 238
1977	60 013	1 618	562	1 056	3 191	2 665	526	29 234	25 983	3 251
1976	60 482	1 526	476	1 050	3 490	2 962	528	29 774	26 698	3 075
1975	60 969	1 748	574	1 174	3 393	2 851	542	30 446	27 166	3 279
1974	60 259	1 607	423	1 184	3 252	2 726	526	31 126	27 956	3 169
1973	59 392	1 324	400	924	3 074	2 582	493	31 469	28 201	3 268
1972	60 142	1 283	402	881	3 135	2 636	499	32 242	28 693	3 549
1971	61 106	1 066	317	749	3 263	2 689	574	33 507	29 829	3 678
1970	60 357	1 096	333	763	3 183	2 647	536	33 950	30 001	3 949
1969	59 913	860	245	615	3 276	2 682	594	33 788	29 825	3 964
1968	58 791	816	262	554	3 268	2 709	559	33 761	29 527	4 234
1967	57 656	713	230	484	3 312	2 678	635	33 440	28 877	4 562
1966	56 167	688	215	473	3 115	2 527	588	32 916	28 208	4 706
1965	54 701	520	127	393	3 057	2 439	618	32 474	27 596	4 878
1964	52 490	471	91	380	2 830	2 349	481	31 734	26 811	4 923
1963	50 356	. . .	. . .	. . .	2 340	1 936	404	31 245	26 502	4 742
1962	48 704	. . .	. . .	. . .	2 319	1 914	405	30 661	26 148	4 513
1961	47 708	. . .	. . .	. . .	2 299	1 926	373	30 718	26 221	4 497
1960	46 260	. . .	. . .	. . .	2 092	1 691	401	30 349	25 814	4 535
1959	44 370	. . .	. . .	. . .	2 032	1 678	354	29 382	24 680	4 702
1958	42 900	. . .	. . .	. . .	1 991	1 569	422	28 184	23 800	4 385
1957	41 166	. . .	. . .	. . .	1 824	1 471	353	27 248	23 076	4 172
1956	39 353	. . .	. . .	. . .	1 758	1 566	192	26 169	22 474	3 695
1955	37 426	. . .	. . .	. . .	1 628	1 365	263	25 458	22 078	3 379

[1]Prior to 1994, total enrollment does not include the population age 35 years and over.
r = Revised, controlled to 1990 census–based population estimates; previous 1993 data controlled to 1980 census–based population estimates.
. . . = Not available.

Table A-10. School Enrollment of the Population Age 3 Years and Over, by Level and Control of School, Race, and Hispanic Origin, October 1955–2005—*Continued*

(Numbers in thousands.)

Year, race, and Hispanic origin	High school			College			
	Total	Public	Private	Total	Public	Private	Full-time
All Races							
2005	17 354	13 768	1 284	17 472	13 435	4 037	12 237
2004	16 791	15 498	1 293	17 383	13 652	3 731	11 990
2003	17 062	15 785	1 276	16 638	13 109	3 529	11 490
2002	16 374	15 064	1 310	16 497	12 834	3 664	11 141
2001	16 059	14 830	1 230	15 873	12 421	3 452	10 404
2000	15 770	14 431	1 339	15 314	12 008	3 305	10 159
1999	15 916	14 638	1 278	15 203	11 659	3 544	10 112
1998	15 584	14 299	1 285	15 547	11 984	3 563	10 184
1997	15 793	14 634	1 159	15 436	12 091	3 345	10 236
1996	15 309	14 113	1 197	15 226	12 014	3 212	9 839
1995	14 963	13 750	1 213	14 715	11 372	3 343	9 544
1994[1]	14 616	13 539	1 077	15 022	11 694	3 329	9 573
1993[r]	13 989	12 985	1 004	11 901	9 440	2 461	8 706
1993	13 522	12 542	977	11 409	9 031	2 374	8 308
1992	13 219	12 268	952	11 671	9 282	2 386	8 503
1991	13 010	12 069	945	11 589	9 078	2 511	8 461
1990	12 719	11 818	903	11 306	8 889	2 417	8 154
1989	12 786	11 980	806	11 066	8 576	2 490	7 905
1988	13 093	12 095	998	10 937	8 663	2 278	7 771
1987	13 647	12 577	1 070	10 915	8 556	2 361	7 560
1986	13 912	12 746	1 166	10 605	8 153	2 452	7 507
1985	13 979	12 764	1 215	10 863	8 379	2 483	7 720
1984	13 777	12 721	1 057	10 859	8 467	2 392	7 822
1983	14 010	12 792	1 218	10 825	8 185	2 640	7 711
1982	14 123	13 004	1 118	10 919	8 354	2 565	7 736
1981	14 642	13 523	1 119	10 734	8 159	2 576	7 569
1980	14 556	. . .	. . .	10 180	. . .	. . .	7 147
1979	15 116	13 994	1 122	9 978	7 699	2 280	7 010
1978	15 475	14 231	1 244	9 838	7 427	2 410	6 979
1977	15 753	14 505	1 248	10 217	7 925	2 292	7 196
1976	15 742	14 541	1 201	9 950	7 739	2 211	7 176
1975	15 683	14 500	1 180	9 697	7 704	1 994	7 105
1974	15 447	14 275	1 172	8 827	6 905	1 922	6 351
1973	15 347	14 162	1 184	8 179	6 224	1 955	6 089
1972	15 169	14 015	1 155	8 313	6 337	1 976	6 314
1971	15 183	14 057	1 126	8 087	6 271	1 816	6 204
1970	14 715	13 545	1 170	7 413	5 699	1 714	5 763
1969	14 553	13 400	1 153	7 435	5 439	1 995	5 810
1968	14 145	12 793	1 352	6 801	4 948	1 854	5 357
1967	13 790	12 498	1 292	6 401	4 540	1 861	4 976
1966	13 364	11 985	1 377	6 085	4 178	1 908	4 847
1965	12 975	11 517	1 457	5 675	3 840	1 835	4 414
1964	12 812	11 403	1 410	4 643	3 025	1 618	3 556
1963	12 438	11 186	1 251	4 336	2 897	1 439	3 260
1962	11 516	10 431	1 085	4 208	2 820	1 388	3 237
1961	10 959	9 817	1 141	3 731	2 376	1 354	2 902
1960	10 249	9 215	1 033	3 570	2 307	1 262	2 681
1959	9 616	8 571	1 045	3 340	2 120	1 220	2 464
1958	9 482	8 485	998	3 242	2 088	1 155	. . .
1957	8 956	8 059	897	3 138	2 054	1 084	. . .
1956	8 543	7 668	875	2 883	1 824	1 059	. . .
1955	7 961	7 181	780	2 379	1 515	864	. . .

[1] Prior to 1994, total enrollment does not include the population age 35 years and over.
r = Revised, controlled to 1990 census–based population estimates; previous 1993 data controlled to 1980 census–based population estimates.
. . . = Not available.

Table A-10. School Enrollment of the Population Age 3 Years and Over, by Level and Control of School, Race, and Hispanic Origin, October 1955–2005—*Continued*

(Numbers in thousands.)

Year, race, and Hispanic origin	Total enrollment	Nursery school			Kindergarten			Elementary school		
		Total	Public	Private	Total	Public	Private	Total	Public	Private
White										
2005	58 013	3 542	1 767	1 775	3 056	2 611	445	24 630	21 839	2 792
2004	57 585	3 566	1 703	1 863	3 043	2 571	472	24 773	21 889	2 883
2003	57 391	3 909	1 918	1 990	2 866	2 367	499	24 711	21 893	2 818
2002	57 501	3 473	1 613	1 860	2 760	2 240	520	25 625	22 703	2 922
2001	56 649	3 278	1 484	1 794	2 893	2 394	499	25 729	22 848	2 881
2000	56 344	3 392	1 539	1 853	2 998	2 453	545	25 562	22 538	3 024
1999	56 713	3 590	1 571	2 019	2 956	2 422	534	25 628	22 552	3 076
1998	56 515	3 549	1 598	1 951	2 933	2 356	577	25 489	22 547	2 942
1997	56 587	3 489	1 572	1 917	3 078	2 532	546	25 289	22 679	2 610
1996	55 378	3 284	1 314	1 970	3 163	2 596	567	24 692	21 785	2 907
1995	55 186	3 553	1 435	2 118	3 032	2 440	592	24 963	22 010	2 954
1994[1]	54 823	3 376	1 330	2 046	3 010	2 505	505	24 786	21 903	2 883
1993[r]	51 034	2 434	851	1 583	3 323	2 730	593	24 637	22 078	2 559
1993	49 985	2 447	843	1 604	3 273	2 681	592	24 249	21 714	2 535
1992	49 713	2 387	785	1 602	3 256	2 727	529	23 932	21 213	2 718
1991	49 156	2 447	810	1 637	3 274	2 766	508	23 547	20 948	2 599
1990	48 897	2 830	869	1 961	3 081	2 609	472	23 343	20 984	2 359
1989	47 923	2 393	712	1 681	3 118	2 611	506	22 867	20 468	2 399
1988	47 672	2 234	651	1 583	3 192	2 722	471	22 541	20 086	2 455
1987	47 471	2 204	630	1 574	3 120	2 591	529	22 037	19 538	2 498
1986	47 267	2 144	601	1 543	3 161	2 589	572	21 761	19 090	2 671
1985	47 452	2 087	617	1 470	3 060	2 545	515	21 593	18 817	2 776
1984	46 941	1 915	543	1 372	2 788	2 319	469	21 730	19 282	2 449
1983	47 423	1 932	563	1 369	2 769	2 181	588	22 054	19 340	2 714
1982	47 662	1 783	504	1 279	2 677	2 189	489	22 297	19 583	2 713
1981	48 169	1 685	447	1 238	2 597	2 130	467	22 663	19 924	2 739
1980	47 673	1 637	432	1 205	2 595	2 172	423	22 510	19 743	2 768
1979	48 225	1 537	428	1 110	2 437	2 069	368	22 959	20 174	2 785
1978	48 843	1 456	351	1 105	2 452	2 009	444	23 524	20 551	2 973
1977	50 151	1 314	372	942	2 611	2 153	458	24 262	21 312	2 950
1976	50 761	1 246	318	929	2 881	2 423	457	24 776	21 947	2 829
1975	51 430	1 432	392	1 040	2 845	2 363	483	25 412	22 351	3 059
1974	50 992	1 340	293	1 048	2 745	2 268	477	26 051	23 063	2 990
1973	50 617	1 087	242	845	2 584	2 139	445	26 531	23 506	3 025
1972	51 314	1 079	285	794	2 633	2 185	448	27 185	23 869	3 316
1971	52 081	888	225	664	2 735	2 207	527	28 187	24 720	3 466
1970	51 719	893	198	695	2 706	2 233	473	28 638	24 923	3 715
1969	51 465	676	136	539	2 803	2 289	515	28 572	24 803	3 768
1968	50 608	664	163	501	2 775	2 272	504	28 634	24 580	4 054
1967	49 721	564	134	429	2 840	2 254	587	28 415	24 044	4 371
1966	48 620	564	127	437	2 693	2 163	530	28 012	23 469	4 542
1965	47 451	451	93	358	2 648	2 086	562	27 679	22 976	4 703
1964	44 850	. . .	. . .	. . .	2 157	1 795	362	27 099	22 381	4 718
1963	43 815	. . .	. . .	. . .	2 064	1 699	365	26 709	22 181	4 527
1962	42 501	. . .	. . .	. . .	2 025	1 667	358	26 272	21 922	4 350
1961	42 498	. . .	. . .	. . .	1 968	1 618	350	26 294	22 014	4 281
1960	40 348	. . .	. . .	. . .	1 849	1 485	364	26 035	21 696	4 339
1959	38 857	. . .	. . .	. . .	1 758	1 434	324	25 395	20 854	4 541
1958	37 662	. . .	. . .	. . .	1 769	1 383	386	24 380	20 178	4 203
1957	36 132	. . .	. . .	. . .	1 595	1 258	337	23 610	19 595	4 015
1956	34 641	. . .	. . .	. . .	1 544	1 364	180	22 740	19 186	3 554
1955	32 929	. . .	. . .	. . .	1 484	1 244	240	22 185	18 947	3 238
Non-Hispanic White										
2005	46 338	2 810	1 211	1 599	2 308	1 936	372	18 858	16 335	2 523
2004	46 095	2 840	1 153	1 687	2 325	1 917	408	19 093	16 437	2 646
2003	46 440	3 184	1 382	1 802	2 245	1 804	440	19 252	16 735	2 517
2002	46 725	2 881	1 172	1 709	2 065	1 585	480	20 124	17 495	2 628
2001	46 110	2 725	1 054	1 671	2 203	1 781	422	20 298	17 693	2 605
2000	46 660	2 854	1 149	1 705	2 346	1 846	500	20 574	17 747	2 827
1999	47 292	3 044	1 146	1 898	2 307	1 839	468	20 779	17 960	2 819
1998	47 386	2 964	1 136	1 828	2 336	1 790	547	20 806	18 107	2 699
1997	47 776	2 956	1 143	1 813	2 456	1 970	486	20 839	18 426	2 413
1996	46 947	2 767	922	1 845	2 590	2 081	509	20 447	17 808	2 639
1995	48 019	3 104	1 129	1 975	2 551	2 047	504	21 256	18 518	2 738
1994[1]	47 679	3 024	1 090	1 934	2 522	2 059	462	21 170	18 555	2 615
1993	43 827	2 277	720	1 557	2 779	2 239	540	20 961	18 617	2 344

[1]Prior to 1994, total enrollment does not include the population age 35 years and over.
r = Revised, controlled to 1990 census–based population estimates; previous 1993 data controlled to 1980 census–based population estimates.
. . . = Not available.

Table A-10. School Enrollment of the Population Age 3 Years and Over, by Level and Control of School, Race, and Hispanic Origin, October 1955–2005—*Continued*

(Numbers in thousands.)

Year, race, and Hispanic origin	High school			College			
	Total	Public	Private	Total	Public	Private	Full-time
White							
2005	13 296	12 109	1 187	13 466	10 303	3 162	9 392
2004	12 823	11 684	1 138	13 381	10 478	2 904	9 257
2003	13 036	11 939	1 097	12 870	10 101	2 769	8 855
2002	12 862	11 730	1 132	12 781	9 774	3 007	8 613
2001	12 540	11 473	1 067	12 208	9 503	2 705	7 909
2000	12 392	11 259	1 133	11 999	9 364	2 636	7 945
1999	12 487	11 374	1 113	12 053	9 185	2 868	7 886
1998	12 142	11 013	1 130	12 401	9 518	2 883	8 012
1997	12 290	11 287	1 003	12 442	9 713	2 729	8 127
1996	12 052	10 999	1 053	12 188	9 567	2 622	7 849
1995	11 617	10 574	1 042	12 021	9 311	2 711	7 773
1994[1]	11 430	10 514	916	12 222	9 472	2 751	7 722
1993[r]	10 960	10 124	836	9 685	7 695	1 990	6 996
1993	10 651	9 834	819	9 366	7 428	1 940	6 739
1992	10 480	9 648	833	9 658	7 653	2 001	6 985
1991	10 309	9 467	841	9 579	7 464	2 118	6 919
1990	10 177	9 370	807	9 466	7 411	2 056	6 776
1989	10 172	9 443	730	9 374	7 219	2 158	6 658
1988	10 462	9 571	890	9 245	7 302	1 940	6 488
1987	10 967	10 019	947	9 143	7 113	2 034	6 275
1986	11 259	10 229	1 030	8 943	6 821	2 122	6 253
1985	11 378	10 258	1 120	9 334	7 131	2 203	6 597
1984	11 240	10 266	974	9 269	7 163	2 105	6 672
1983	11 425	10 339	1 086	9 242	6 949	2 293	6 532
1982	11 577	10 541	1 036	9 328	7 102	2 227	6 579
1981	12 062	11 035	1 027	9 162	6 906	2 256	6 452
1980	12 056	. . .	. . .	8 875	. . .	. . .	6 212
1979	12 583	11 549	1 033	8 709	6 672	2 037	6 058
1978	12 897	11 741	1 156	8 514	6 368	2 145	5 974
1977	13 152	11 980	1 172	8 812	6 743	2 069	6 165
1976	13 214	12 093	1 121	8 644	6 657	1 987	6 170
1975	13 224	12 112	1 112	8 516	6 724	1 792	6 183
1974	13 073	11 966	1 107	7 781	6 049	1 732	5 575
1973	13 091	11 967	1 124	7 324	5 550	1 773	5 408
1972	12 959	11 876	1 083	7 458	5 644	1 814	5 678
1971	12 998	11 937	1 061	7 273	5 624	1 650	5 560
1970	12 723	11 599	1 124	6 759	5 168	1 591	5 221
1969	12 588	11 502	1 085	6 827	4 967	1 860	5 307
1968	12 280	11 007	1 272	6 255	4 501	1 753	4 919
1967	11 997	10 769	1 228	5 905	4 155	1 750	4 604
1966	11 643	10 312	1 329	5 708	3 914	1 795	4 556
1965	11 356	9 961	1 395	5 317	3 568	1 749	4 111
1964	11 257	9 898	1 359	4 338	2 798	1 540	. . .
1963	10 994	9 782	1 212	4 050	2 680	1 370	. . .
1962	10 270	9 217	1 053	3 934	2 620	1 314	. . .
1961	9 737	8 635	1 102	3 498	2 205	1 293	. . .
1960	9 122	8 124	999	3 342	2 126	1 215	. . .
1959	8 586	7 572	1 014	3 118	1 960	1 158	. . .
1958	8 484	7 501	982	3 030	1 928	1 101	. . .
1957	7 995	7 121	874	2 932	1 924	1 006	. . .
1956	7 670	6 825	845	2 687	1 704	983	. . .
1955	7 036	6 303	733	2 224	1 429	795	. . .
Non-Hispanic White							
2005	10 647	9 566	1 081	11 715	8 852	2 863	8 247
2004	10 266	9 144	1 029	11 571	8 928	2 643	8 082
2003	10 463	9 473	990	11 295	8 742	2 553	7 810
2002	10 419	9 388	1 031	11 236	8 488	2 749	7 673
2001	10 281	9 331	950	10 602	8 133	2 469	6 980
2000	10 250	9 222	1 029	10 636	8 202	2 434	7 105
1999	10 344	9 314	1 030	10 818	8 158	2 660	7 162
1998	10 170	9 131	1 039	11 109	8 435	2 674	7 251
1997	10 280	9 358	922	11 245	8 688	2 558	7 378
1996	10 107	9 148	959	11 034	8 584	2 450	7 178
1995	10 084	9 094	991	11 024	8 439	2 585	7 194
1994[1]	9 786	8 951	835	11 178	8 568	2 610	7 152
1993	9 216	8 449	767	8 594	6 772	1 822	6 247

[1]Prior to 1994, total enrollment does not include the population age 35 years and over.
r = Revised, controlled to 1990 census–based population estimates; previous 1993 data controlled to 1980 census–based population estimates.
. . . = Not available.

Table A-10. School Enrollment of the Population Age 3 Years and Over, by Level and Control of School, Race, and Hispanic Origin, October 1955–2005—*Continued*

(Numbers in thousands.)

Year, race, and Hispanic origin	Total enrollment	Nursery school			Kindergarten			Elementary school		
		Total	Public	Private	Total	Public	Private	Total	Public	Private
Black[2]										
2005	11 384	719	542	177	538	486	52	5 106	4 747	359
2004	11 540	825	600	224	596	535	61	5 159	4 905	254
2003	11 408	697	484	212	558	495	63	5 245	4 942	302
2002	11 703	725	503	221	598	543	55	5 545	5 210	335
2001	11 630	787	537	250	605	536	69	5 478	5 160	318
2000	11 503	726	531	195	629	547	82	5 481	5 133	347
1999	11 282	729	569	160	632	558	74	5 388	5 002	386
1998	11 411	761	528	233	689	592	97	5 332	5 031	301
1997	11 270	796	582	214	632	571	61	5 332	5 049	284
1996	10 851	702	459	243	634	545	89	5 171	4 846	325
1995	10 753	663	478	185	653	564	89	5 185	4 845	340
1994[1]	10 702	721	513	208	662	603	59	5 086	4 709	378
1993[r]	9 786	433	320	113	721	649	72	5 009	4 733	276
1993	9 470	414	307	107	687	618	69	4 865	4 599	266
1992	9 150	374	250	124	688	625	63	4 730	4 494	234
1991	9 031	360	244	117	676	598	79	4 672	4 445	229
1990	8 854	431	283	148	636	574	62	4 627	4 428	199
1989	8 707	366	216	150	601	557	44	4 528	4 296	232
1988	8 609	286	168	118	591	547	44	4 538	4 289	250
1987	8 712	277	164	113	699	658	41	4 402	4 206	194
1986	8 556	315	200	115	647	600	47	4 326	4 134	193
1985	8 444	332	212	120	625	562	63	4 307	4 131	175
1984	8 226	340	179	161	563	513	51	4 123	3 947	177
1983	8 199	326	215	111	476	427	48	4 153	3 964	189
1982	8 262	305	192	113	508	463	45	4 194	3 974	220
1981	8 350	284	182	102	474	412	62	4 291	4 087	204
1980	8 251	294	180	115	490	440	50	4 259	4 058	202
1979	8 317	278	185	95	497	443	54	4 296	4 053	243
1978	8 416	312	210	102	451	414	38	4 356	4 154	202
1977	8 564	250	171	78	496	447	50	4 387	4 166	221
1976	8 518	226	146	80	542	482	60	4 430	4 256	175
1975	8 400	276	171	105	468	426	42	4 509	4 344	165
1974	8 215	227	121	106	463	416	47	4 585	4 455	131
1973	7 834	210	146	64	423	391	32	4 473	4 277	196
1972	7 959	185	113	72	448	402	46	4 573	4 382	191
1971	8 179	151	90	61	464	422	42	4 877	4 712	165
1970	7 829	178	129	49	426	374	53	4 868	4 668	200
1969	7 680	170	102	68	425	361	64	4 785	4 633	151
1968	7 448	132	89	43	448	397	51	4 716	4 569	146
1967	7 196	140	92	47	418	375	44	4 618	4 444	173
1966	7 547	125	88	37	420	364	56	4 904	4 739	165
1965	7 252	72	37	35	407	353	54	4 796	4 620	176
1964	6 807	. . .	. . .	. . .	312	275	37	4 634	4 430	205
1963	6 541	. . .	. . .	. . .	276	237	39	4 536	4 321	215
1962	6 203	. . .	. . .	. . .	294	247	47	4 389	4 226	163
1961	6 210	. . .	. . .	. . .	331	308	23	4 424	4 207	216
1960	5 910	. . .	. . .	. . .	243	206	37	4 313	4 118	195
1959	5 513	. . .	. . .	. . .	274	244	30	3 987	3 826	161
1958	5 238	. . .	. . .	. . .	222	186	36	3 804	3 621	182
1957	5 034	. . .	. . .	. . .	229	213	16	3 638	3 483	155
1956	4 712	. . .	. . .	. . .	214	202	12	3 429	3 287	142
1955	4 498	. . .	. . .	. . .	144	121	23	3 273	3 131	142
Asian[3]										
2005	3 377	185	80	105	138	99	39	1 228	1 137	91
2004	3 409	165	72	93	164	152	12	1 239	1 153	86
2003	3 312	138	56	82	122	93	29	1 258	1 122	136
2002	3 787	217	85	132	157	137	20	1 431	1 237	195
2001	3 803	161	91	70	181	161	20	1 409	1 263	146
2000	3 442	222	91	132	152	124	28	1 350	1 257	93
1999	3 621	205	96	109	195	148	47	1 461	1 343	118
1998	3 386	196	77	118	145	120	25	1 380	1 190	189
1997	3 261	168	59	108	161	110	51	1 329	1 186	144
1996	3 258	183	63	120	177	158	19	1 255	1 144	111
1995	1 863	76	28	47	75	62	13	697	622	74
1994[1]	2 057	76	27	50	74	60	14	785	707	78
1993	2 321	100	38	62	139	125	14	1 012	930	82

[1] Prior to 1994, total enrollment does not include the population age 35 years and over.
[2] Data shown for 1955 to 1966 for the Black population are for Black and Other races.
[3] Data from before 2003 consist of respondents who identified themselves as "Asian or Pacific Islanders."
[r] = Revised, controlled to 1990 census–based population estimates; previous 1993 data controlled to 1980 census–based population estimates.
. . . = Not available.

Table A-10. School Enrollment of the Population Age 3 Years and Over, by Level and Control of School, Race, and Hispanic Origin, October 1955–2005—*Continued*

(Numbers in thousands.)

Year, race, and Hispanic origin	High school			College			
	Total	Public	Private	Total	Public	Private	Full-time
Black[2]							
2005	2 723	2 592	131	2 298	1 800	498	1 526
2004	2 660	2 584	76	2 301	1 831	470	1 504
2003	2 765	2 691	74	2 144	1 773	371	1 416
2002	2 558	2 451	107	2 278	1 868	410	1 468
2001	2 531	2 412	119	2 230	1 766	463	1 475
2000	2 502	2 350	152	2 164	1 721	443	1 351
1999	2 536	2 427	109	1 998	1 587	411	1 372
1998	2 614	2 515	99	2 016	1 595	421	1 284
1997	2 605	2 516	89	1 903	1 546	357	1 280
1996	2 443	2 338	105	1 901	1 519	381	1 179
1995	2 481	2 370	111	1 772	1 353	419	1 117
1994[1]	2 434	2 313	121	1 800	1 439	361	1 147
1993[r]	2 317	2 197	120	1 305	1 006	299	951
1993	2 244	2 128	115	1 261	973	288	914
1992	2 152	2 072	72	1 217	980	237	904
1991	2 100	2 044	56	1 220	1 004	217	900
1990	1 975	1 909	65	1 188	963	227	869
1989	2 069	2 027	42	1 139	932	208	833
1988	2 079	2 016	62	1 114	894	220	801
1987	2 140	2 056	84	1 193	977	218	852
1986	2 130	2 040	91	1 138	896	242	859
1985	2 131	2 068	63	1 049	860	190	767
1984	2 061	2 002	59	1 138	918	220	810
1983	2 143	2 057	86	1 102	858	245	806
1982	2 128	2 073	55	1 127	865	263	800
1981	2 168	2 102	65	1 133	898	235	815
1980	2 200	. . .	. . .	1 007	. . .	. . .	723
1979	2 245	2 171	74	1 002	814	188	748
1978	2 276	2 211	65	1 020	822	199	753
1977	2 327	2 269	59	1 103	916	187	803
1976	2 258	2 187	71	1 062	887	175	817
1975	2 100	2 140	60	948	782	166	742
1974	2 125	2 072	54	814	659	155	589
1973	2 044	1 988	56	685	537	147	536
1972	2 025	1 971	54	727	582	145	525
1971	2 006	1 951	55	680	532	148	534
1970	1 834	1 794	41	522	422	100	427
1969	1 808	1 751	57	492	372	120	401
1968	1 718	1 656	62	434	359	75	338
1967	1 651	1 605	46	370	280	90	271
1966	1 721	1 673	48	282	. . .	. . .	210
1965	1 619	1 556	62	358	272	86	218
1964	1 556	1 505	51	306	227	78	. . .
1963	1 444	1 404	39	286	217	69	. . .
1962	1 246	1 214	32	274	200	74	. . .
1961	1 222	1 182	39	233	171	61	. . .
1960	1 127	1 092	34	227	180	46	. . .
1959	1 030	999	31	222	160	62	. . .
1958	998	981	17	212	160	53	. . .
1957	961	939	22	206	132	74	. . .
1956	873	843	30	196	120	76	. . .
1955	926	878	48	155	86	69	. . .
Asian[3]							
2005	642	596	46	1 184	904	279	948
2004	650	619	31	1 191	928	263	881
2003	632	585	47	1 162	833	328	901
2002	723	664	59	1 258	1 040	218	951
2001	771	736	35	1 280	1 026	254	921
2000	668	622	46	1 049	831	218	792
1999	719	666	53	1 041	779	261	787
1998	650	599	51	1 016	783	233	821
1997	656	600	57	947	712	235	721
1996	644	606	38	999	816	183	710
1995	399	375	24	617	470	147	456
1994[1]	399	365	34	723	548	174	530
1993	428	390	37	641	519	122	542

[1] Prior to 1994, total enrollment does not include the population age 35 years and over.
[2] Data shown for 1955 to 1966 for the Black population are for Black and Other races.
[3] Data from before 2003 consist of respondents who identified themselves as "Asian or Pacific Islanders."
r = Revised, controlled to 1990 census–based population estimates; previous 1993 data controlled to 1980 census–based population estimates.
. . . = Not available.

Table A-10. School Enrollment of the Population Age 3 Years and Over, by Level and Control of School, Race, and Hispanic Origin, October 1955–2005—_Continued_

(Numbers in thousands.)

Year, race, and Hispanic origin	Total enrollment	Nursery school			Kindergarten			Elementary school		
		Total	Public	Private	Total	Public	Private	Total	Public	Private
Hispanic[4]										
2005	12 809	797	601	196	804	725	79	6 330	5 991	339
2004	12 509	787	591	196	769	699	70	6 184	5 895	290
2003	11 929	768	561	206	694	633	61	5 974	5 651	322
2002	11 544	637	476	161	727	688	39	5 909	5 585	324
2001	11 163	593	452	141	728	641	87	5 779	5 478	301
2000	10 163	574	419	154	687	639	48	5 224	5 012	213
1999	9 936	585	458	127	666	594	73	5 088	4 829	259
1998	9 528	618	492	126	639	608	31	4 831	4 568	262
1997	9 220	548	436	112	648	589	59	4 644	4 427	217
1996	8 818	533	403	130	602	539	63	4 443	4 162	281
1995	8 563	510	350	160	558	465	93	4 434	4 165	269
1994[1]	8 183	400	278	122	559	516	43	4 162	3 848	314
1993[r]	7 651	231	169	62	639	576	63	4 027	3 779	248
1993	6 689	194	142	52	538	484	53	3 534	3 317	217
1992	6 598	209	139	70	554	493	60	3 525	3 271	252
1991	6 306	215	146	69	552	525	27	3 461	3 240	221
1990	6 072	242	153	88	475	446	29	3 301	3 107	197
1989	5 722	181	95	86	404	382	21	3 219	3 031	188
1988	5 588	151	111	40	461	445	16	3 160	2 954	207
1987	5 619	226	138	88	439	399	39	3 048	2 861	187
1986	5 513	179	114	65	465	421	44	2 995	2 787	208
1985	5 070	168	105	63	364	315	49	2 803	2 607	196
1984	4 284	117	78	39	293	267	26	2 384	2 218	166
1983	4 618	108	60	48	335	285	50	2 548	2 323	225
1982	4 478	83	46	37	329	291	37	2 501	2 276	225
1981	4 551	131	68	63	306	282	24	2 474	2 239	235
1980	4 263	146	70	75	263	234	30	2 363	2 134	228
1979	3 608	89	50	39	226	210	16	1 934	1 745	189
1978	3 455	87	47	39	231	198	33	1 893	1 704	188
1977	3 516	75	30	46	220	206	14	1 874	1 654	220
1976	3 623	68	38	30	262	242	20	1 934	1 768	165
1975	3 741	85	47	39	235	218	17	2 062	1 858	204
1974	3 620	85	37	48	225	207	18	2 040	1 780	260
1973	3 171	68	41	27	171	165	6	1 884	1 712	172
1972	3 257	61	43	18	241	227	14	1 879	1 705	173
White Alone or in Combination										
2005	60 035	3 642	1 819	1 823	3 179	2 715	463	25 682	22 794	2 888
2004	59 427	3 682	1 762	1 920	3 169	2 670	498	25 691	22 682	3 009
2003	59 184	4 039	1 989	2 050	3 002	2 477	525	25 581	22 686	2 895
Black Alone or in Combination										
2005	12 118	763	563	200	593	531	62	5 504	5 122	382
2004	12 303	864	622	242	676	606	70	5 540	5 251	289
2003	12 144	787	526	262	637	559	78	5 604	5 276	327
Asian Alone or in Combination										
2005	3 964	220	94	126	159	118	41	1 495	1 362	133
2004	3 943	208	82	127	191	169	21	1 497	1 350	148
2003	3 817	164	73	90	148	111	38	1 507	1 346	161

[1]Prior to 1994, total enrollment does not include the population age 35 years and over.
[4]May be of any race.
r = Revised, controlled to 1990 census–based population estimates; previous 1993 data controlled to 1980 census–based population estimates.

Table A-10. School Enrollment of the Population Age 3 Years and Over, by Level and Control of School, Race, and Hispanic Origin, October 1955–2005—*Continued*

(Numbers in thousands.)

Year, race, and Hispanic origin	High school			College			
	Total	Public	Private	Total	Public	Private	Full-time
Hispanic[4]							
2005	2 937	2 824	113	1 942	1 625	316	1 255
2004	2 793	2 685	108	1 975	1 676	299	1 276
2003	2 779	2 667	112	1 714	1 480	235	1 139
2002	2 614	2 513	101	1 656	1 374	283	1 004
2001	2 363	2 246	117	1 700	1 445	255	1 005
2000	2 253	2 144	108	1 426	1 219	207	873
1999	2 290	2 200	91	1 307	1 093	214	765
1998	2 077	1 978	98	1 363	1 137	226	801
1997	2 119	2 035	84	1 260	1 079	181	797
1996	2 018	1 922	96	1 223	1 031	192	708
1995	1 854	1 772	83	1 207	1 037	170	709
1994[1]	1 874	1 781	92	1 187	1 019	169	640
1993[r]	1 722	1 653	69	1 029	872	157	686
1993	1 556	1 496	60	867	731	134	573
1992	1 494	1 435	59	813	710	104	487
1991	1 357	1 299	61	721	607	115	481
1990	1 437	1 374	64	617	515	100	380
1989	1 278	1 231	48	642	557	82	416
1988	1 163	1 113	49	654	592	60	414
1987	1 239	1 160	80	668	551	115	414
1986	1 197	1 116	81	677	540	137	418
1985	1 156	1 090	167	579	464	116	381
1984	966	909	57	524	433	91	356
1983	1 104	1 027	77	523	441	82	335
1982	1 072	995	77	493	398	96	312
1981	1 130	1 056	74	510	398	112	343
1980	1 048	. . .	. . .	443	. . .	. . .	294
1979	920	875	45	440	365	75	314
1978	868	825	43	377	315	62	231
1977	928	836	92	418	357	60	287
1976	932	867	65	427	354	73	297
1975	948	886	61	411	358	53	207
1974	916	858	59	354	297	57	247
1973	758	707	51	290	247	43	201
1972	834	784	50	242	213	29	178
White Alone or in Combination							
2005	13 741	12 516	1 225	13 791	10 561	3 230	9 618
2004	13 218	12 047	1 170	13 668	10 711	2 957	9 468
2003	13 398	12 267	1 131	13 164	10 366	2 798	9 048
Black Alone or in Combination							
2005	2 870	2 729	141	2 387	1 866	521	1 585
2004	2 811	2 762	85	2 412	1 922	490	1 591
2003	2 889	2 800	89	2 227	1 846	381	1 482
Asian Alone or in Combination							
2005	792	726	67	1 297	993	305	1 036
2004	786	743	43	1 260	980	281	936
2003	736	674	62	1 262	925	337	965

[1] Prior to 1994, total enrollment does not include the population age 35 years and over.
[4] May be of any race.
r = Revised, controlled to 1990 census–based population estimates; previous 1993 data controlled to 1980 census–based population estimates.
. . . = Not available.

Table A-11. Population Age 6 to 17 Years Enrolled Below Modal Grade, by Sex, Race, and Hispanic Origin, 1971–2005

(Percent, numbers in thousands.)

Year, sex, race, and Hispanic origin	Percent below modal grade				Dropout rate, 15 to 17 years	Total population in age group			
	6 to 8 years	9 to 11 years	12 to 14 years	15 to 17 years		6 to 8 years	9 to 11 years	12 to 14 years	15 to 17 years
ALL RACES									
Both Sexes									
2005	20.4	25.0	27.9	29.4	2.8	11 784	11 998	12 689	13 204
2004	21.2	25.0	27.8	30.6	3.5	11 799	12 034	12 870	12 766
2003	21.3	28.1	28.8	30.6	3.2	11 866	12 124	12 951	12 753
2002	18.0	25.5	27.1	30.1	3.3	12 029	12 421	12 592	12 187
2001	18.6	23.7	25.9	29.7	3.8	11 972	12 738	12 357	12 031
2000	19.2	24.0	27.8	30.2	4.3	12 079	12 713	12 003	11 933
1999	17.4	25.3	26.5	30.8	4.0	12 159	12 537	11 921	12 048
1998	19.0	23.8	26.7	31.9	3.8	12 165	11 960	11 600	11 314
1997	18.6	24.2	28.5	32.1	3.6	12 325	11 866	11 650	11 953
1996	17.9	23.3	28.8	31.0	4.8	12 191	11 845	11 653	11 617
1995	17.5	25.6	30.8	32.8	4.1	11 728	11 812	11 582	11 401
1994	18.9	26.2	31.3	30.9	3.8	11 601	11 528	11 462	10 560
1993ʳ	18.7	28.1	31.0	32.3	3.8	11 363	11 283	10 981	10 247
1993	18.7	28.0	30.8	32.0	3.7	11 363	11 283	10 981	10 247
1992	19.4	28.4	30.9	30.5	3.6	11 260	11 183	10 723	10 114
1991	21.2	26.9	29.6	30.0	4.6	11 120	11 099	10 440	9 923
1990	21.5	27.6	31.0	30.1	4.7	11 015	10 914	10 152	9 912
1989	21.4	29.0	31.8	28.0	4.5	11 007	10 673	9 928	10 020
1988	20.4	28.4	28.7	26.2	5.1	10 906	10 350	9 869	10 379
1987	20.9	26.7	27.6	24.8	5.1	10 702	10 053	9 795	10 944
1986	19.2	26.5	27.3	25.8	4.9	10 389	9 959	9 908	11 149
1985	17.9	24.9	25.7	25.5	5.1	10 076	9 673	10 442	11 024
1984	16.6	23.9	27.0	24.6	5.3	9 707	9 594	10 858	10 711
1983	15.4	24.4	24.8	23.7	5.2	9 605	9 730	11 123	10 768
1982	16.6	22.8	23.9	23.0	5.4	9 492	10 169	10 989	11 131
1981	14.4	23.3	23.0	23.8	6.1	9 519	10 657	10 712	11 757
1980	14.3	20.3	22.6	22.5	6.6	9 350	10 681	10 537	11 835
1979	13.0	20.2	20.3	21.6	6.5	9 804	10 545	10 886	12 190
1978	12.4	19.5	19.2	21.8	6.5	10 246	10 448	11 391	12 346
1977	10.7	18.9	18.9	21.2	6.4	10 449	10 537	11 826	12 472
1976	10.6	18.1	19.8	22.2	6.3	10 334	10 872	12 137	12 550
1975	11.1	17.4	21.3	22.5	6.4	10 256	11 343	12 372	12 531
1974	10.3	17.8	21.7	21.6	7.1	10 343	11 789	12 415	12 566
1973	10.7	18.4	21.5	21.3	7.1	10 614	11 946	12 542	12 309
1972	10.7	19.6	21.9	22.3	6.6	11 119	12 152	12 451	12 283
1971	11.1	19.7	22.0	22.5	5.7	11 938	12 648	12 429	11 906
Male									
2005	22.6	28.2	30.2	32.9	3.0	6 014	6 126	6 523	6 645
2004	23.3	27.7	31.2	35.3	3.5	6 075	6 120	6 685	6 395
2003	23.9	32.0	31.8	35.1	3.4	6 198	6 331	6 426	6 569
2002	20.3	29.2	31.0	35.6	3.5	6 156	6 349	6 436	6 210
2001	22.1	26.1	28.7	34.0	4.3	6 147	6 540	6 311	6 182
2000	22.1	27.2	31.3	34.3	4.5	6 181	6 504	6 148	6 136
1999	18.8	28.9	30.2	36.2	3.9	6 211	6 471	6 048	6 195
1998	21.4	26.6	30.4	37.4	4.1	6 234	6 125	5 897	5 791
1997	21.9	27.7	33.4	37.8	3.7	6 295	6 112	5 932	6 126
1996	20.7	26.0	33.9	36.9	4.5	6 268	6 043	5 934	5 985
1995	20.2	28.0	35.2	38.5	3.5	5 999	6 027	5 930	5 840
1994	21.1	28.0	35.6	35.7	3.9	5 894	6 026	5 874	5 640
1993ʳ	21.2	32.1	35.4	40.3	3.3	5 837	5 736	5 629	5 262
1993	21.1	32.0	35.0	38.7	3.1	5 837	5 736	5 629	5 262
1992	21.6	32.6	37.0	35.2	2.7	5 738	5 742	5 502	5 166
1991	24.0	30.7	34.7	35.5	4.3	5 674	5 704	5 343	5 085
1990	23.9	32.0	36.2	35.3	4.6	5 629	5 603	5 200	5 078
1989	25.1	32.9	36.7	33.4	4.3	5 632	5 472	5 088	5 151
1988	23.5	33.2	33.7	30.6	4.8	5 580	5 298	5 065	5 286
1987	23.7	31.8	31.8	29.2	4.6	5 496	5 147	5 036	5 535
1986	22.9	30.4	32.2	30.2	4.9	5 311	5 113	5 066	5 697
1985	20.6	28.3	29.0	30.2	4.9	5 159	4 946	5 340	5 623
1984	18.8	27.7	31.1	30.2	5.5	4 963	4 905	5 521	5 469
1983	17.8	28.7	30.3	28.5	5.3	4 913	4 974	5 690	5 463
1982	19.2	26.4	28.0	27.9	5.2	4 852	5 198	5 566	5 688
1981	17.2	27.9	25.6	28.1	6.2	4 866	5 447	5 510	5 914
1980	16.4	23.4	27.3	26.8	6.4	4 774	5 453	5 282	6 067
1979	15.5	23.4	24.1	27.4	5.9	5 004	5 379	5 555	6 174
1978	14.7	22.9	22.9	26.2	6.7	5 227	5 326	5 797	6 265
1977	12.5	22.4	22.6	25.3	6.1	5 327	5 371	6 044	6 297
1976	12.5	20.9	23.4	27.5	5.7	5 265	5 540	6 185	6 356
1975	12.6	21.2	25.8	26.8	5.7	5 223	5 782	6 336	6 309
1974	12.2	21.2	25.9	26.3	7.0	5 267	6 011	6 329	6 352
1973	12.8	20.8	25.2	26.4	6.8	5 403	6 082	6 397	6 215
1972	12.5	23.3	26.8	26.8	6.2	5 662	6 188	6 322	6 232
1971	13.5	22.8	26.1	27.2	5.0	6 088	6 440	6 293	6 019

ʳ = Revised, controlled to 1990 census–based population estimates; previous 1993 data controlled to 1980 census–based population estimates.

Table A-11. Population Age 6 to 17 Years Enrolled Below Modal Grade, by Sex, Race, and Hispanic Origin, 1971–2005—*Continued*

(Percent, numbers in thousands.)

Year, sex, race, and Hispanic origin	Percent below modal grade				Dropout rate, 15 to 17 years	Total population in age group			
	6 to 8 years	9 to 11 years	12 to 14 years	15 to 17 years		6 to 8 years	9 to 11 years	12 to 14 years	15 to 17 years
ALL RACES									
Female									
2005	18.0	21.8	25.4	25.8	2.6	5 769	5 872	6 167	6 559
2004	19.0	27.2	24.1	25.8	3.5	5 724	5 914	6 185	6 371
2003	18.5	23.8	25.8	25.8	3.0	5 668	5 793	6 524	6 184
2002	15.6	21.7	23.0	24.4	3.1	5 872	6 072	6 156	5 977
2001	14.9	21.3	23.0	25.2	3.3	5 825	6 197	6 046	5 849
2000	16.1	20.6	24.2	25.8	4.2	5 897	6 209	5 855	5 797
1999	16.1	21.6	22.7	25.1	4.2	5 948	6 066	5 872	5 852
1998	16.5	20.9	22.8	26.2	3.5	5 931	5 835	5 703	5 523
1997	15.1	20.4	23.3	26.1	3.5	6 030	5 754	5 718	5 827
1996	14.9	20.4	23.4	24.7	5.3	5 923	5 802	5 719	5 632
1995	14.6	23.1	26.0	26.7	4.4	5 728	5 786	5 653	5 552
1994	16.5	24.2	26.7	24.8	3.6	5 705	5 644	5 666	5 384
1993r	16.3	24.0	26.4	26.4	4.4	5 526	5 545	5 353	4 984
1993	16.1	23.9	26.2	24.9	4.3	5 526	5 545	5 353	4 984
1992	17.1	23.5	24.6	25.6	4.5	5 523	5 441	5 220	4 947
1991	18.2	22.8	24.6	24.2	5.1	5 445	5 395	5 098	4 838
1990	19.1	23.2	25.7	24.7	4.7	5 387	5 312	4 951	4 834
1989	18.1	22.6	26.6	22.3	4.6	5 375	5 201	4 840	4 869
1988	17.3	23.6	23.4	21.7	5.4	5 327	5 052	4 803	5 093
1987	17.8	21.5	23.2	20.2	5.6	5 206	4 906	4 759	5 408
1986	15.2	22.4	22.1	21.1	4.9	5 078	4 846	4 842	5 452
1985	15.1	21.4	22.1	20.6	5.5	4 917	4 727	5 102	5 401
1984	14.2	19.8	22.9	18.7	5.1	4 744	4 689	5 337	5 242
1983	12.9	19.9	19.1	18.6	5.2	4 692	4 756	5 433	5 305
1982	13.8	19.0	19.7	17.9	5.7	4 640	4 971	5 423	5 443
1981	11.6	18.4	20.1	19.6	6.1	4 653	5 210	5 202	5 843
1980	12.1	17.0	17.8	18.0	6.7	4 576	5 228	5 255	5 768
1979	10.4	16.9	16.4	15.6	7.1	4 800	5 166	5 331	6 016
1978	10.1	16.0	15.3	17.2	6.4	5 019	5 122	5 594	6 081
1977	8.9	15.2	15.0	17.1	6.6	5 122	5 166	5 782	6 175
1976	8.6	15.1	16.0	16.8	7.0	5 069	5 332	5 952	6 194
1975	9.4	13.5	16.7	18.2	7.2	5 033	5 561	6 036	6 222
1974	8.3	14.4	17.4	16.8	7.1	5 076	5 778	6 086	6 214
1973	8.7	15.8	16.5	16.1	7.4	5 211	5 864	6 145	6 094
1972	8.9	15.7	17.0	17.7	7.1	5 457	5 964	6 129	6 051
1971	8.7	12.3	17.8	17.6	6.5	5 850	6 208	6 136	5 887
WHITE ALONE									
Both Sexes									
2005	21.0	23.5	27.6	28.5	2.6	8 929	9 194	9 680	10 131
2004	21.9	25.2	27.2	29.3	3.8	9 051	9 173	9 853	9 784
2003	21.5	27.6	28.3	29.4	3.2	9 102	9 112	9 875	9 889
2002	18.1	25.7	26.2	29.6	3.1	9 230	9 682	9 832	9 520
2001	19.2	22.7	25.2	28.9	3.8	9 330	9 826	9 651	9 480
2000	19.4	23.7	26.3	29.7	4.5	9 404	9 937	9 368	9 449
1999	18.3	24.6	25.8	30.0	4.2	9 539	9 768	9 323	9 428
1998	19.5	23.5	25.8	30.5	3.8	9 481	9 413	9 130	8 926
1997	18.8	24.0	27.9	30.3	3.5	9 555	9 390	9 167	9 352
1996	18.1	22.6	27.6	30.1	4.9	9 458	9 420	9 184	9 135
1995	17.7	24.9	29.2	31.0	3.9	9 221	9 340	9 130	8 933
1994	19.4	25.8	30.1	29.6	3.7	9 087	9 261	9 121	8 668
1993r	18.8	27.3	29.4	31.2	3.9	9 018	8 967	8 728	8 160
1993	18.7	27.2	29.2	29.7	3.6	9 074	9 017	8 783	8 159
1992	19.5	27.5	29.6	28.1	3.5	8 956	8 996	8 520	8 031
1991	21.3	25.7	27.7	27.2	4.7	8 874	8 840	8 328	7 903
1990	21.9	26.8	28.4	27.3	4.6	8 860	8 752	8 140	7 909
1989	22.4	26.8	29.9	25.7	4.6	8 858	8 527	7 994	8 026
1988	21.0	27.6	27.2	23.9	5.4	8 758	8 323	7 929	8 353
1987	21.1	25.9	26.0	22.7	5.1	8 606	8 117	7 846	8 887
1986	19.1	25.1	25.3	23.7	5.0	8 395	8 000	8 054	9 037
1985	18.0	23.3	23.3	23.0	5.3	8 136	7 840	8 429	9 045
1984	16.3	22.1	24.7	22.7	5.6	7 915	7 781	8 827	8 853
1983	15.5	22.4	23.1	21.1	5.4	7 821	7 906	9 152	8 831
1982	16.4	21.8	22.1	21.1	5.6	7 729	8 294	9 035	9 184
1981	14.7	22.2	21.0	21.6	6.1	7 782	8 741	8 813	9 762
1980	14.1	19.0	21.1	19.3	6.7	7 635	8 823	8 739	10 132
1979	12.9	18.4	18.5	19.4	6.5	8 041	8 747	9 026	10 239
1978	12.4	18.0	17.9	19.3	6.8	8 460	8 686	9 522	10 358
1977	10.6	17.7	17.5	19.3	6.6	8 675	8 771	9 918	10 510
1976	10.5	17.2	18.7	19.7	6.3	8 612	9 066	10 187	10 622
1975	11.0	16.0	20.0	20.4	6.3	8 566	9 486	10 466	10 583
1974	10.2	16.5	19.7	19.4	6.9	8 656	9 912	10 508	10 678
1973	10.6	17.3	19.9	19.1	7.0	8 929	10 117	10 704	10 481
1972	10.3	18.2	20.1	20.0	6.6	9 359	10 313	10 606	10 506
1971	10.5	18.3	20.4	19.9	5.5	9 988	10 692	10 682	10 231

r = Revised, controlled to 1990 census–based population estimates; previous 1993 data controlled to 1980 census–based population estimates.

Table A-11. Population Age 6 to 17 Years Enrolled Below Modal Grade, by Sex, Race, and Hispanic Origin, 1971–2005—*Continued*

(Percent, numbers in thousands.)

Year, sex, race, and Hispanic origin	Percent below modal grade				Dropout rate, 15 to 17 years	Total population in age group			
	6 to 8 years	9 to 11 years	12 to 14 years	15 to 17 years		6 to 8 years	9 to 11 years	12 to 14 years	15 to 17 years
WHITE ALONE									
Male									
2005	23.7	27.0	30.5	31.9	2.7	4 576	4 715	4 995	5 116
2004	24.4	27.5	30.9	33.8	3.8	4 706	4 647	5 168	4 905
2003	24.4	31.6	31.2	34.0	3.4	4 785	4 795	4 961	5 026
2002	21.7	29.5	30.4	34.7	3.2	4 737	4 965	5 044	4 875
2001	22.7	25.3	28.3	32.8	4.4	4 789	5 040	4 949	4 862
2000	22.5	27.6	29.6	34.0	4.4	4 815	5 094	4 798	4 861
1999	19.9	28.2	29.7	35.8	4.2	4 883	5 009	4 777	4 851
1998	21.9	26.4	30.2	36.2	4.4	4 851	4 823	4 686	4 571
1997	22.3	27.8	32.7	37.0	3.8	4 897	4 819	4 702	4 821
1996	20.8	25.9	32.3	36.5	4.5	4 849	4 836	4 706	4 694
1995	20.5	28.0	33.4	36.5	3.8	4 727	4 797	4 680	4 592
1994	22.0	27.9	34.4	35.2	4.0	4 659	4 758	4 679	4 457
1993r	21.4	31.8	33.8	37.6	3.2	4 625	4 601	4 476	4 178
1993	21.4	31.6	33.6	36.1	3.1	4 662	4 614	4 485	4 178
1992	21.5	31.8	35.8	32.4	2.8	4 602	4 607	4 359	4 115
1991	24.4	29.1	32.5	32.5	4.2	4 556	4 568	4 270	4 047
1990	24.6	31.3	33.3	32.6	4.8	4 555	4 482	4 186	4 054
1989	26.0	32.1	35.0	30.8	4.6	4 544	4 378	4 112	4 107
1988	24.7	32.8	32.2	28.8	5.1	4 493	4 272	4 062	4 281
1987	24.6	30.5	30.4	26.6	4.5	4 415	4 167	4 069	4 504
1986	22.9	28.9	30.1	27.9	5.2	4 307	4 108	4 125	4 624
1985	21.1	26.5	26.7	28.0	4.9	4 175	4 024	4 307	4 634
1984	18.1	25.8	28.7	28.1	5.8	4 061	3 994	4 501	4 542
1983	18.1	26.3	28.0	26.3	5.6	4 002	4 054	4 697	4 481
1982	19.3	26.2	26.2	26.1	5.3	3 956	4 260	4 591	4 711
1981	17.3	26.9	24.2	25.4	6.3	3 990	4 480	4 556	4 937
1980	16.3	21.9	25.7	23.9	6.7	3 907	4 517	4 399	5 066
1979	15.4	20.8	22.3	24.8	6.2	4 114	4 475	4 616	5 201
1978	14.7	21.2	22.0	23.1	7.2	4 328	4 441	4 843	5 287
1977	12.5	21.1	21.2	23.5	6.3	4 436	4 484	5 079	5 325
1976	12.6	20.2	22.1	24.8	5.6	4 402	4 632	5 200	5 398
1975	12.9	19.7	24.7	24.7	5.4	4 376	4 848	5 385	5 332
1974	12.1	19.5	23.7	23.8	7.0	4 422	5 066	5 383	5 402
1973	12.5	19.6	23.1	24.0	6.6	4 559	5 165	5 469	5 319
1972	12.2	21.9	24.6	24.3	6.1	4 778	5 266	5 410	5 340
1971	12.6	21.6	23.9	24.4	4.6	5 106	5 461	5 455	5 185
Female									
2005	18.1	19.8	24.5	24.9	2.5	4 353	4 479	4 685	5 015
2004	19.3	23.0	23.0	24.8	3.8	4 345	4 527	4 686	4 878
2003	18.3	23.1	25.3	24.7	3.0	4 317	4 317	4 914	4 863
2002	14.4	21.7	21.9	24.3	3.0	4 493	4 717	4 788	4 645
2001	15.5	20.0	21.8	24.9	3.1	4 541	4 786	4 701	4 618
2000	16.1	19.7	22.9	25.2	4.5	4 587	4 843	4 570	4 588
1999	16.7	20.7	21.8	23.9	4.1	4 655	4 579	4 546	4 578
1998	16.9	20.5	21.2	24.4	3.2	4 629	4 589	4 444	4 355
1997	15.1	20.0	22.7	23.2	3.3	4 658	4 571	4 464	4 530
1996	15.3	19.2	22.7	23.2	5.3	4 609	4 583	4 477	4 441
1995	14.7	21.6	24.8	25.0	4.1	4 494	4 543	4 449	4 342
1994	16.7	23.5	25.7	23.6	3.4	4 427	4 504	4 443	4 212
1993r	15.9	22.6	24.8	24.4	4.3	4 393	4 366	4 252	3 982
1993	15.8	22.5	24.6	23.1	4.2	4 412	4 404	4 298	3 982
1992	17.3	22.9	23.2	23.6	4.3	4 354	4 389	4 161	3 916
1991	18.1	22.1	22.6	21.5	5.2	4 318	4 272	4 058	3 856
1990	19.0	22.2	23.2	21.8	4.5	4 305	4 270	3 954	3 855
1989	18.6	21.3	24.5	20.3	4.7	4 314	4 149	3 882	3 919
1988	17.1	22.2	21.9	18.8	5.6	4 265	4 051	3 867	4 072
1987	17.3	21.0	21.3	18.7	5.8	4 191	3 950	3 777	4 383
1986	15.0	21.1	20.2	19.3	4.8	4 088	3 892	3 929	4 413
1985	14.8	19.9	19.7	17.6	5.7	3 961	3 816	4 122	4 411
1984	14.3	18.3	20.5	17.0	5.4	3 854	3 787	4 326	4 311
1983	12.7	18.3	17.9	15.8	5.2	3 819	3 852	4 455	4 350
1982	13.4	17.2	17.8	15.8	6.0	3 773	4 034	4 444	4 473
1981	11.9	17.3	17.6	17.6	5.9	3 792	4 261	4 257	4 825
1980	11.7	16.0	16.5	14.7	6.6	3 728	4 306	4 340	5 066
1979	10.3	15.8	14.5	13.8	6.9	3 927	4 272	4 410	5 038
1978	10.0	14.7	13.7	15.2	6.4	4 132	4 245	4 679	5 071
1977	8.5	14.1	13.7	14.9	6.8	4 239	4 287	4 839	5 185
1976	8.4	14.1	15.1	14.5	6.9	4 210	4 434	4 987	5 224
1975	9.1	12.2	15.1	16.0	7.1	4 190	4 638	5 081	5 251
1974	8.2	13.4	15.5	15.0	6.7	4 234	4 846	5 125	5 276
1973	8.5	14.8	16.5	14.0	7.4	4 370	4 952	5 235	5 162
1972	8.3	14.2	15.4	15.5	7.2	4 581	5 047	5 196	5 166
1971	8.4	14.9	16.6	15.2	6.3	4 882	5 231	5 227	5 046

r = Revised, controlled to 1990 census–based population estimates; previous 1993 data controlled to 1980 census–based population estimates.

Table A-11. Population Age 6 to 17 Years Enrolled Below Modal Grade, by Sex, Race, and Hispanic Origin, 1971–2005—*Continued*

(Percent, numbers in thousands.)

Year, sex, race, and Hispanic origin	Percent below modal grade				Dropout rate, 15 to 17 years	Total population in age group			
	6 to 8 years	9 to 11 years	12 to 14 years	15 to 17 years		6 to 8 years	9 to 11 years	12 to 14 years	15 to 17 years
NON-HISPANIC WHITE ALONE									
Both Sexes									
2005	22.1	23.0	26.0	28.0	2.1	6 728	7 052	7 584	8 150
2004	22.3	24.7	26.7	28.6	3.3	6 878	7 090	7 768	7 892
2003	21.8	27.1	27.3	28.7	2.8	7 006	7 102	7 889	7 980
2002	18.9	24.9	25.8	28.1	2.5	7 118	7 627	7 913	7 803
2001	19.9	23.1	25.3	28.1	3.1	7 325	7 726	7 773	7 829
2000	19.4	23.7	26.1	28.8	3.5	7 418	8 045	7 727	7 852
1999	18.9	24.2	25.3	28.9	3.6	7 717	7 938	7 669	7 879
1998	20.5	23.7	26.0	28.9	3.0	7 755	7 794	7 697	7 859
1997	19.7	24.6	27.3	28.4	3.2	7 729	7 775	7 789	7 866
1996	18.8	22.7	26.2	28.6	4.2	7 803	7 792	7 731	7 716
1995	18.2	24.5	28.0	29.2	3.4	7 853	8 000	7 872	7 795
1994	19.8	25.6	30.0	28.0	3.1	7 779	7 864	7 845	7 490
1993	18.8	27.2	28.8	29.5	3.0	7 736	7 802	7 600	7 022
Male									
2005	25.1	26.5	28.0	31.4	2.2	3 450	3 618	3 902	4 136
2004	24.5	27.4	30.2	33.7	3.4	3 548	3 605	4 054	3 994
2003	24.6	31.7	30.7	33.4	2.9	3 668	3 725	3 960	4 101
2002	22.7	29.0	30.7	33.6	2.4	3 667	3 969	4 005	4 038
2001	23.1	26.2	28.5	31.6	3.7	3 808	3 971	3 920	4 020
2000	22.5	27.7	30.0	33.4	3.4	3 795	4 135	3 970	4 034
1999	20.3	27.7	29.7	35.1	3.5	3 955	4 076	3 913	4 058
1998	23.1	26.5	30.8	34.3	3.6	4 016	4 003	3 894	3 981
1997	24.1	29.0	32.5	35.3	3.8	3 977	3 971	3 996	4 020
1996	22.5	25.9	30.8	35.1	4.1	3 964	4 035	3 957	3 959
1995	22.1	27.3	31.9	34.9	3.1	4 038	4 094	4 017	4 010
1994	22.8	28.0	34.3	33.6	2.9	3 993	4 010	4 030	3 866
1993	22.0	31.5	33.2	35.6	2.4	3 952	4 021	3 889	3 578
Female									
2005	18.9	19.2	23.9	24.6	2.0	3 277	3 434	3 682	4 014
2004	20.0	21.9	22.8	23.4	3.3	3 330	3 485	3 714	3 898
2003	18.6	22.2	24.0	23.7	2.6	3 337	3 377	3 929	3 878
2002	14.8	20.4	20.9	22.2	2.6	3 451	3 658	3 908	3 765
2001	16.4	19.8	22.0	24.4	2.6	3 517	3 755	3 853	3 809
2000	16.2	19.6	21.9	23.9	3.7	3 623	3 910	3 757	3 818
1999	17.4	20.5	20.8	22.3	3.0	3 701	3 004	3 757	3 040
1998	17.6	20.8	21.2	23.5	2.5	3 740	3 791	3 803	3 878
1997	15.0	19.9	21.8	21.3	2.6	3 752	3 804	3 793	3 846
1996	15.0	19.3	21.3	21.7	4.3	3 839	3 757	3 773	3 757
1995	14.1	21.5	23.8	23.1	3.8	3 815	3 906	3 854	3 784
1994	16.6	23.1	25.5	22.1	3.2	3 786	3 854	3 814	3 624
1993	15.4	22.6	24.2	23.1	3.6	3 784	3 782	3 710	3 444
BLACK ALONE									
Both Sexes									
2005	20.4	35.1	33.5	36.3	4.2	1 806	1 826	2 011	2 085
2004	19.4	26.9	33.9	38.8	2.3	1 775	1 906	2 034	1 992
2003	22.7	34.2	33.9	37.4	3.7	1 760	2 043	2 110	1 950
2002	19.6	28.6	32.8	36.2	3.9	2 017	2 048	2 036	1 943
2001	17.3	29.7	31.1	35.6	4.0	1 937	2 144	1 998	1 823
2000	19.6	26.9	37.8	34.6	4.7	1 976	2 082	1 961	1 852
1999	16.1	30.2	31.7	34.8	3.5	1 948	2 108	1 912	1 911
1998	18.3	26.6	31.4	38.4	3.6	2 019	1 934	1 840	1 801
1997	18.4	26.1	33.5	40.0	3.8	2 061	1 908	1 845	1 938
1996	18.4	29.2	36.8	36.9	4.8	2 054	1 847	1 839	1 858
1995	16.8	31.1	38.3	41.3	4.1	1 909	1 890	1 822	1 851
1994	18.4	35.1	36.1	37.7	3.3	1 912	1 795	1 835	1 809
1993ʳ	20.0	33.6	34.8	45.1	3.6	1 767	1 763	1 747	1 641
1993	19.9	33.4	38.8	43.3	3.6	1 709	1 710	1 695	1 642
1992	20.6	28.7	38.0	40.6	4.2	1 761	1 635	1 686	1 621
1991	21.0	34.3	40.7	43.4	5.3	1 674	1 701	1 643	1 574
1990	21.9	33.1	46.1	42.9	5.2	1 645	1 712	1 574	1 571
1989	19.6	34.0	41.3	39.3	3.9	1 642	1 682	1 554	1 618
1988	18.6	33.1	37.6	38.4	4.7	1 680	1 629	1 545	1 637
1987	19.8	33.1	35.6	35.3	5.1	1 679	1 554	1 552	1 654
1986	12.7	34.6	38.5	38.3	4.6	1 611	1 542	1 530	1 692
1985	18.0	33.9	37.9	37.7	4.6	1 568	1 498	1 635	1 627
1984	17.9	32.3	38.1	34.6	4.1	1 445	1 442	1 652	1 536
1983	15.3	34.9	34.4	35.8	4.7	1 429	1 450	1 601	1 617
1982	17.2	27.1	32.5	32.6	4.6	1 765	1 874	1 953	1 947
1981	13.9	26.2	33.7	36.1	6.3	1 437	1 594	1 615	1 679
1980	14.9	27.8	30.5	37.6	5.1	1 460	1 606	1 568	1 728
1979	12.5	29.5	29.2	34.3	6.4	1 515	1 576	1 636	1 722
1978	12.6	27.8	26.6	35.4	5.7	1 557	1 523	1 664	1 764
1977	11.3	24.9	26.3	32.2	5.4	1 552	1 558	1 698	1 754
1976	10.5	23.2	26.1	35.6	6.7	1 493	1 633	1 724	1 726
1975	11.9	26.1	29.2	34.9	8.0	1 489	1 656	1 720	1 760
1974	11.6	26.2	33.2	34.4	8.2	1 509	1 684	1 750	1 682
1973	12.0	25.8	31.7	35.4	8.2	1 525	1 650	1 671	1 671
1972	13.2	30.5	33.1	37.3	6.6	1 585	1 638	1 691	1 636
1971	14.2	27.9	34.7	40.2	7.0	1 794	1 787	1 638	1 533

ʳ = Revised, controlled to 1990 census–based population estimates; previous 1993 data controlled to 1980 census–based population estimates.

Table A-11. Population Age 6 to 17 Years Enrolled Below Modal Grade, by Sex, Race, and Hispanic Origin, 1971–2005—*Continued*

(Percent, numbers in thousands.)

Year, sex, race, and Hispanic origin	Percent below modal grade				Dropout rate, 15 to 17 years	Total population in age group			
	6 to 8 years	9 to 11 years	12 to 14 years	15 to 17 years		6 to 8 years	9 to 11 years	12 to 14 years	15 to 17 years
BLACK ALONE									
Male									
2005	22.0	37.1	34.7	40.0	5.2	912	913	1 011	1 041
2004	20.5	30.7	37.5	45.2	2.0	885	992	1 012	1 009
2003	23.6	36.8	38.7	43.4	3.9	927	1 059	975	1 047
2002	17.5	32.5	37.0	44.7	5.0	1 044	1 036	1 012	973
2001	21.1	31.1	33.3	42.8	3.5	978	1 108	1 010	924
2000	20.8	27.5	43.3	37.0	6.4	1 003	1 057	994	941
1999	15.9	34.2	36.3	37.6	3.0	964	1 085	969	992
1998	20.9	29.3	33.3	41.9	3.0	1 027	973	926	928
1997	21.3	29.3	39.4	43.8	3.1	1 019	994	934	979
1996	21.3	30.4	45.1	43.2	4.5	1 054	925	931	943
1995	18.8	31.2	45.0	47.5	2.9	982	944	922	952
1994	19.4	30.3	39.9	39.8	3.2	951	928	928	898
1993r	21.8	36.5	44.3	53.0	2.5	903	884	891	832
1993	21.6	36.5	44.2	51.8	2.5	864	857	867	832
1992	24.5	28.7	44.5	47.0	2.8	864	862	860	813
1991	22.9	39.6	46.2	50.6	5.4	846	878	839	798
1990	23.2	37.3	52.7	49.1	4.3	828	877	791	795
1989	21.7	38.8	44.8	46.7	2.8	831	858	785	828
1988	18.9	37.2	43.7	41.4	4.1	851	828	780	828
1987	21.6	41.1	39.7	42.3	4.9	861	779	802	818
1986	15.0	39.0	45.2	45.9	4.0	806	792	770	855
1985	19.5	38.2	41.4	40.3	5.4	778	775	830	816
1984	24.1	38.1	42.5	42.8	4.2	729	727	832	769
1983	16.8	42.0	43.1	40.6	4.4	721	723	808	799
1982	18.8	27.5	36.2	36.9	4.8	898	937	975	977
1981	17.7	34.2	33.3	42.4	5.4	723	811	814	832
1980	16.8	31.8	36.2	43.3	4.9	736	807	770	876
1979	14.7	37.3	33.8	43.6	4.0	762	796	828	853
1978	15.4	33.0	30.3	43.1	4.1	774	767	847	870
1977	12.1	29.8	31.1	35.3	4.8	776	782	858	868
1976	11.5	26.1	30.9	43.3	5.7	755	816	870	855
1975	12.8	30.7	32.5	40.2	7.6	743	849	845	879
1974	13.5	31.0	40.9	41.1	7.2	747	858	861	849
1973	14.1	29.5	38.0	42.0	8.5	752	831	837	824
1972	14.5	36.8	41.3	43.8	6.6	787	828	836	818
1971	18.1	30.9	38.5	47.6	7.4	890	900	810	757
Female									
2005	18.8	33.1	32.2	32.7	3.3	893	913	999	1 044
2004	18.3	27.8	30.4	32.1	2.6	890	914	1 022	983
2003	21.7	31.5	39.8	30.3	3.4	833	983	1 135	903
2002	22.0	24.7	28.7	27.8	2.8	973	1 012	1 024	970
2001	13.3	28.2	29.0	27.9	4.5	959	1 036	988	900
2000	18.2	26.4	32.0	32.3	2.9	974	1 025	968	911
1999	16.3	25.8	27.0	31.6	4.0	984	1 022	944	919
1998	15.6	23.8	29.6	34.6	4.3	992	960	914	873
1997	15.9	22.8	27.4	36.0	4.5	1 041	915	911	959
1996	13.4	28.1	28.4	30.3	4.9	1 000	922	909	915
1995	14.8	23.6	30.9	34.6	5.3	928	946	901	898
1994	17.5	29.1	32.3	35.4	3.6	961	867	908	911
1993r	18.0	30.8	33.1	36.6	4.7	864	879	856	809
1993	18.1	30.3	33.2	34.6	4.7	844	854	828	809
1992	16.7	28.7	31.2	34.2	5.6	897	773	826	808
1991	19.0	28.6	35.0	36.0	5.2	828	823	804	776
1990	20.7	28.7	39.3	36.6	6.1	817	835	783	776
1989	17.5	29.0	37.7	31.5	5.1	811	824	769	790
1988	18.2	28.8	31.4	35.2	5.3	829	801	765	809
1987	18.0	25.2	31.3	28.5	5.3	818	775	750	836
1986	...	...	...	...	...	...	...	...	...
1985	16.6	29.3	34.2	35.1	3.8	790	723	805	811
1984	11.5	26.4	33.5	26.3	4.0	716	715	820	767
1983	13.8	27.8	25.5	31.2	5.0	708	727	793	818
1982	15.5	26.7	28.7	28.1	4.3	867	937	978	970
1981	10.1	17.9	34.2	29.9	7.1	714	783	801	847
1980	12.8	23.8	25.1	31.7	5.3	724	799	798	852
1979	10.4	21.5	24.5	25.2	8.7	753	780	808	869
1978	9.8	22.6	22.6	27.9	7.2	783	756	817	894
1977	10.6	20.0	21.3	29.1	6.0	776	776	840	886
1976	9.5	20.3	21.2	28.1	7.7	738	817	854	871
1975	11.0	21.3	25.9	29.6	8.3	746	807	875	881
1974	9.7	21.3	25.8	27.5	9.2	762	826	889	833
1973	10.0	22.1	25.4	28.9	7.9	773	819	834	847
1972	11.9	24.1	25.1	30.9	6.6	798	810	855	818
1971	10.4	24.9	31.0	33.1	6.7	904	887	828	776

r = Revised, controlled to 1990 census–based population estimates; previous 1993 data controlled to 1980 census–based population estimates.
. . . = Not available.

Table A-11. Population Age 6 to 17 Years Enrolled Below Modal Grade, by Sex, Race, and Hispanic Origin, 1971–2005—*Continued*

(Percent, numbers in thousands.)

Year, sex, race, and Hispanic origin	Percent below modal grade				Dropout rate, 15 to 17 years	Total population in age group			
	6 to 8 years	9 to 11 years	12 to 14 years	15 to 17 years		6 to 8 years	9 to 11 years	12 to 14 years	15 to 17 years
ASIAN[1]									
Both Sexes									
2005	12.7	11.8	16.2	18.7	1.2	502	429	486	457
2004	12.1	11.2	20.8	23.1	1.7	417	468	490	491
2003	7.5	13.6	19.7	24.5	1.6	486	453	459	458
2002	11.1	12.3	20.4	18.6	2.7	602	490	530	553
2001	11.9	17.9	20.3	21.0	2.8	503	565	523	565
2000	10.7	15.5	17.5	22.2	0.6	524	490	490	475
1999	7.5	16.5	17.9	25.5	3.2	533	496	560	555
Male									
2005	12.2	13.2	13.2	17.5	1.6	261	202	265	228
2004	10.8	16.0	20.9	22.8	2.4	220	216	282	231
2003	7.3	15.9	20.3	19.3	-	226	223	261	231
2002	9.6	12.4	23.3	18.9	1.7	274	239	267	287
2001	15.2	16.6	19.0	22.2	4.9	265	294	256	313
2000	14.7	14.2	16.1	30.3	1.0	286	243	267	261
1999	8.4	16.4	17.6	30.3	2.2	277	269	246	276
Female									
2005	13.3	10.7	19.7	20.0	0.9	241	227	221	229
2004	13.5	7.1	20.8	23.3	1.1	196	253	208	260
2003	7.6	11.3	18.8	29.9	3.2	259	230	198	227
2002	12.4	12.2	17.5	18.2	3.7	327	251	263	266
2001	8.3	19.3	21.4	19.6	0.2	238	270	268	252
2000	5.9	16.7	19.2	12.3	0.1	239	247	224	215
1999	6.6	16.7	18.5	20.6	4.0	256	227	314	278
HISPANIC[2]									
Both Sexes									
2005	17.5	25.6	32.3	30.3	4.9	2 390	2 317	2 322	2 202
2004	20.7	27.5	29.3	32.2	6.1	2 382	2 250	2 283	2 072
2003	20.2	28.7	31.3	32.7	5.2	2 280	2 221	2 167	2 063
2002	15.5	28.4	27.9	35.6	5.9	2 258	2 204	2 079	1 841
2001	16.7	22.1	25.0	34.6	6.9	2 143	2 198	2 011	1 733
2000	19.4	23.2	27.3	34.4	8.8	2 067	1 965	1 744	1 671
1999	15.7	25.9	27.9	36.5	7.3	1 902	1 922	1 734	1 653
1998	15.4	23.2	24.6	33.8	7.6	1 903	1 740	1 542	1 424
1997	15.2	21.5	31.0	41.4	5.5	1 900	1 606	1 444	1 575
1996	14.9	22.9	35.5	39.0	8.4	1 711	1 680	1 550	1 478
1995	14.4	26.1	38.5	43.6	7.4	1 597	1 628	1 496	1 373
1994	16.8	28.4	32.3	39.9	8.8	1 526	1 593	1 442	1 347
1993r	18.9	29.2	33.2	42.2	8.2	1 390	1 255	1 204	1 225
1993	18.9	29.2	32.7	30.3	7.9	1 455	1 295	1 243	1 226
1992	16.2	25.3	34.3	39.9	8.1	1 272	1 371	1 141	1 110
1991	21.8	30.7	35.8	38.4	11.3	1 290	1 356	1 088	1 023
1990	21.5	34.8	37.7	39.8	9.0	1 270	1 230	1 095	1 062
1989	21.9	33.8	39.9	39.5	10.6	1 257	1 154	1 079	1 001
1988	23.2	37.0	45.0	36.8	13.7	1 248	1 107	1 052	953
1987	16.9	31.2	38.9	37.3	9.1	1 181	1 054	1 063	981
1986	19.1	33.3	42.5	35.5	11.0	1 067	1 119	1 025	1 018
1985	18.7	32.4	35.8	35.7	11.3	1 035	1 047	957	946
1984	20.2	32.7	34.7	38.5	10.7	901	829	806	816
1983	20.2	32.7	39.5	38.0	8.3	903	909	949	860
1982	21.9	32.6	37.3	37.0	10.9	923	875	924	883
1981	17.9	34.7	34.9	34.9	13.3	882	939	866	963
1980	20.8	26.1	34.8	35.8	12.6	881	949	863	889
1979	18.2	33.6	33.0	30.3	10.9	729	712	697	755
1978	19.8	29.1	33.6	37.8	12.3	723	684	666	751
1977	13.0	24.1	25.1	35.2	11.0	676	693	662	773

[1]Data from before 2003 consist of respondents who identified themselves as "Asian or Pacific Islanders."
[2]May be of any race.
r = Revised, controlled to 1990 census–based population estimates; previous 1993 data controlled to 1980 census–based population estimates.
 - = Quantity zero or rounds to zero.

Table A-11. Population Age 6 to 17 Years Enrolled Below Modal Grade, by Sex, Race, and Hispanic Origin, 1971–2005—*Continued*

(Percent, numbers in thousands.)

Year, sex, race, and Hispanic origin	Percent below modal grade				Dropout rate, 15 to 17 years	Total population in age group			
	6 to 8 years	9 to 11 years	12 to 14 years	15 to 17 years		6 to 8 years	9 to 11 years	12 to 14 years	15 to 17 years
HISPANIC[2]									
Male									
2005	19.6	28.4	38.0	35.0	4.7	1 219	1 192	1 202	1 087
2004	24.3	28.2	33.6	33.8	6.4	1 247	1 142	1 202	1 001
2003	23.0	31.2	32.3	35.9	6.2	1 205	1 178	1 081	1 020
2002	17.4	31.6	28.7	38.5	7.4	1 140	1 090	1 137	911
2001	21.2	23.4	27.8	40.8	7.7	1 065	1 128	1 093	895
2000	23.1	26.7	27.7	36.9	9.0	1 048	993	875	872
1999	17.9	29.5	29.7	38.9	7.6	973	990	893	854
1998	16.8	26.6	26.9	44.9	8.1	933	887	841	792
1997	15.3	22.3	33.7	45.8	3.7	969	863	735	836
1996	13.5	25.8	40.5	45.1	6.8	914	808	798	764
1995	11.4	31.1	42.4	47.6	7.5	794	839	776	697
1994	16.4	27.5	36.3	45.1	11.4	778	845	721	676
1993ʳ	19.1	35.1	37.2	50.4	7.6	722	612	618	658
1993	19.1	34.3	36.9	46.0	7.3	778	637	648	658
1992	15.6	27.2	42.5	46.2	6.8	636	687	602	576
1991	22.7	31.5	43.9	42.6	10.7	651	691	544	521
1990	22.2	36.4	40.2	43.8	9.0	676	616	590	564
1989	23.7	36.1	40.0	45.2	7.8	642	584	560	511
1988	26.9	42.0	53.8	40.5	12.4	676	566	470	523
1987	19.8	31.7	44.8	38.7	6.4	600	524	569	517
1986	22.2	38.0	49.3	37.8	10.8	544	555	535	471
1985	16.7	36.8	38.4	43.4	7.8	521	527	502	449
1984	18.3	35.7	33.1	42.8	10.0	443	420	423	432
1983	22.2	38.8	45.7	41.8	8.2	445	479	479	428
1982	23.1	36.4	39.1	43.4	10.1	428	426	466	477
1981	19.9	39.8	38.0	40.0	14.3	438	480	439	495
1980	22.5	29.9	40.5	40.7	13.5	418	481	415	445
1979	19.0	34.6	36.4	31.3	8.8	368	358	349	386
1978	23.5	29.9	33.9	37.3	13.6	388	335	339	413
1977	11.5	31.4	23.3	38.4	6.7	365	325	330	406
Female									
2005	15.4	22.7	26.0	25.7	5.1	1 171	1 126	1 119	1 115
2004	16.9	26.9	24.5	30.7	5.7	1 135	1 108	1 080	1 070
2003	17.1	25.7	30.3	29.7	4.3	1 075	1 043	1 086	1 042
2002	13.6	25.3	27.0	32.7	4.5	1 118	1 115	942	930
2001	12.2	20.8	21.6	28.0	6.0	1 078	1 070	918	838
2000	15.7	19.7	26.9	31.8	8.6	1 020	974	869	800
1999	13.5	22.0	26.1	33.8	6.9	930	932	841	800
1998	14.1	19.7	21.8	31.1	7.0	970	853	701	632
1997	15.0	20.4	28.8	36.1	7.4	939	803	710	739
1996	16.6	20.3	30.4	32.4	10.4	798	871	753	712
1995	17.5	20.6	34.5	39.5	7.2	802	789	721	677
1994	17.2	29.2	28.5	34.9	6.1	748	747	722	671
1993ʳ	18.9	24.2	29.0	32.3	8.7	667	643	586	567
1993	18.7	24.3	28.3	29.3	8.6	678	658	597	567
1992	16.8	23.4	25.0	33.1	9.6	636	684	539	534
1991	20.8	29.8	27.6	34.1	12.0	639	665	544	502
1990	20.7	33.2	34.9	35.3	9.0	594	614	505	498
1989	20.0	31.4	39.7	33.5	13.5	615	570	519	490
1988	18.7	31.8	37.8	32.3	15.3	572	541	582	430
1987	13.8	30.8	32.2	35.8	12.1	581	530	494	464
1986	15.9	28.7	35.1	33.5	11.2	523	564	490	547
1985	20.8	27.9	33.0	28.8	14.5	514	520	455	497
1984	22.1	29.6	36.6	33.6	11.5	458	409	383	384
1983	18.1	25.8	33.2	34.3	8.3	458	430	470	432
1982	20.8	29.0	35.6	29.6	11.8	495	449	458	406
1981	16.0	29.4	31.6	29.5	12.2	444	459	427	468
1980	19.2	22.2	29.5	30.9	11.7	463	468	448	444
1979	17.5	32.5	29.6	29.3	13.0	361	354	348	369
1978	15.5	28.4	33.3	38.5	10.7	335	349	327	338
1977	14.8	17.7	26.8	31.6	15.8	311	368	332	367

[2]May be of any race.

ʳ = Revised, controlled to 1990 census–based population estimates; previous 1993 data controlled to 1980 census–based population estimates.

Table A-11. Population Age 6 to 17 Years Enrolled Below Modal Grade, by Sex, Race, and Hispanic Origin, 1971–2005—*Continued*

(Percent, numbers in thousands.)

Year, sex, race, and Hispanic origin	Percent below modal grade				Dropout rate, 15 to 17 years	Total population in age group			
	6 to 8 years	9 to 11 years	12 to 14 years	15 to 17 years		6 to 8 years	9 to 11 years	12 to 14 years	15 to 17 years
WHITE ALONE OR IN COMBINATION									
Both Sexes									
2005	20.7	23.6	27.4	28.3	2.6	9 314	9 588	10 026	10 479
2004	21.9	25.2	26.9	29.1	3.9	9 422	9 506	10 175	10 079
2003	21.7	27.4	28.1	29.4	3.2	9 226	9 298	10 009	9 701
Male									
2005	23.3	27.0	30.4	31.8	2.7	4 751	4 925	5 151	5 268
2004	24.4	27.6	30.7	33.6	3.9	4 876	4 823	5 318	5 043
2003	24.5	31.6	31.0	33.8	3.4	4 830	4 858	5 005	4 941
Female									
2005	18.0	20.0	24.3	24.8	2.6	4 563	4 663	4 875	5 211
2004	19.2	22.7	22.8	24.7	3.9	4 545	4 683	4 857	5 037
2003	18.6	22.7	25.2	24.8	3.0	4 396	4 439	5 003	4 760
BLACK ALONE OR IN COMBINATION									
Both Sexes									
2005	19.9	34.3	32.8	35.5	4.4	1 970	1 982	2 137	2 194
2004	19.8	26.6	33.0	37.7	2.5	1 950	2 022	2 174	2 107
2003	23.2	33.5	33.4	36.8	3.8	1 884	2 141	2 189	1 937
Male									
2005	21.4	36.3	34.5	39.0	5.0	981	999	1 061	1 082
2004	20.6	30.0	37.1	43.9	1.9	966	1 042	1 065	1 056
2003	24.2	36.6	38.5	42.9	4.0	995	1 098	1 015	1 034
Female									
2005	18.5	32.4	31.1	32.1	3.7	990	983	1 076	1 112
2004	19.1	23.0	29.0	31.4	3.0	984	981	1 109	1 050
2003	22.0	30.4	29.0	29.8	3.4	889	1 043	1 174	903
ASIAN ALONE OR IN COMBINATION									
Both Sexes									
2005	13.0	12.0	16.3	18.0	1.2	600	531	576	581
2004	13.8	12.3	20.3	23.9	2.6	494	576	585	599
2003	8.8	14.9	18.4	23.5	2.4	570	546	546	526
Male									
2005	12.4	12.7	14.3	15.9	1.6	318	254	307	286
2004	12.3	16.2	19.3	21.4	3.6	254	278	324	286
2003	9.3	19.8	19.4	19.2	1.8	257	267	296	269
Female									
2005	13.6	11.3	18.5	20.0	0.9	282	276	269	295
2004	15.4	8.7	21.6	26.1	1.6	241	298	261	313
2003	8.4	10.3	17.2	28.0	3.1	314	279	251	257

Table A-12. High School Dropout Rates, by Sex, Grade, Race, and Hispanic Origin, October 1970–2005

(Numbers in thousands, percent.)

Year, grade, race, and Hispanic origin	Both sexes			Male			Female		
	Total students	Dropouts	Dropout rate	Total students	Dropouts	Dropout rate	Total students	Dropouts	Dropout rate
ALL RACES									
Grades 10–12									
2005	11 896	414	3.5	5 843	233	4.0	5 651	181	3.2
2004	11 166	486	4.4	5 624	266	4.7	5 542	220	4.0
2003	11 378	429	3.8	5 705	225	4.0	5 674	203	3.6
2002	10 989	367	3.3	5 504	193	3.5	5 484	174	3.2
2001	10 777	507	4.7	5 534	293	5.3	5 243	214	4.1
2000	10 773	488	4.5	5 417	280	5.2	5 356	208	3.9
1999	11 067	520	4.7	5 659	243	4.3	5 411	277	5.1
1998	10 791	479	4.4	5 486	237	4.3	5 305	243	4.6
1997	10 645	454	4.3	5 330	251	4.7	5 313	203	3.8
1996	10 249	485	4.7	5 175	240	4.6	5 072	244	4.8
1995	10 106	544	5.4	5 161	297	5.8	4 946	247	5.0
1994	9 922	497	5.0	5 048	249	4.9	4 873	247	5.1
1993ʳ	9 430	404	4.3	4 787	211	4.4	4 640	192	4.1
1993	9 021	382	4.2	4 570	199	4.4	4 452	183	4.1
1992	8 939	384	4.3	4 580	175	3.8	4 357	207	4.8
1991	8 612	348	4.0	4 380	167	3.8	4 231	180	4.3
1990	8 679	347	4.0	4 356	177	4.1	4 323	170	3.9
1989	8 974	404	4.5	4 519	203	4.5	4 453	199	4.5
1988	9 590	461	4.8	4 960	256	5.2	4 628	206	4.5
1987	9 802	403	4.1	4 921	215	4.4	4 879	187	3.8
1986	9 829	421	4.3	4 910	213	4.3	4 917	208	4.2
1985	9 704	504	5.2	4 831	259	5.4	4 874	245	5.0
1984	10 041	507	5.0	4 986	268	5.4	5 054	238	4.7
1983	10 331	535	5.2	5 130	294	5.7	5 200	241	4.6
1982	10 611	577	5.4	5 310	305	5.7	5 301	271	5.1
1981	10 868	639	5.9	5 379	322	6.0	5 487	316	5.8
1980	10 891	658	6.0	5 445	362	6.6	5 448	296	5.4
1979	11 136	744	6.7	5 479	369	6.7	5 658	377	6.7
1978	11 116	743	6.7	5 558	415	7.5	5 558	328	5.9
1977	11 300	734	6.5	5 657	392	6.9	5 643	342	6.1
1976	10 996	644	5.9	5 534	360	6.5	5 463	285	5.2
1975	11 033	639	5.8	5 485	296	5.4	5 548	343	6.2
1974	11 026	742	6.7	5 421	402	7.4	5 605	340	6.1
1973	10 851	683	6.3	5 407	370	6.8	5 444	313	5.7
1972	10 664	659	6.2	5 305	317	6.0	5 358	341	6.4
1971	10 451	562	5.4	5 193	297	5.7	5 258	266	5.1
1970	10 281	588	5.7	5 145	288	5.6	5 138	302	5.9
Grade 10									
2005	4 483	72	1.6	2 240	46	2.1	2 240	23	1.0
2004	4 028	99	2.5	2 096	56	2.7	1 931	42	2.2
2003	4 107	64	1.6	2 111	26	1.2	1 995	37	1.9
2002	3 896	55	1.4	1 963	36	1.8	1 934	19	1.0
2001	3 900	90	2.3	1 988	50	2.5	1 913	41	2.1
2000	3 957	77	1.9	2 036	48	2.4	1 920	28	1.5
1999	3 910	104	2.7	2 036	54	2.7	1 875	50	2.7
1998	3 883	90	2.3	1 971	36	1.8	1 911	54	2.8
1997	3 738	79	2.1	1 894	44	2.3	1 843	35	1.9
1996	3 691	94	2.5	1 906	50	2.6	1 784	43	2.4
1995	3 552	88	2.5	1 823	40	2.2	1 728	47	2.7
1994	3 474	76	2.2	1 793	45	2.5	1 681	31	1.8
1993ʳ	3 265	86	2.6	1 696	52	3.1	1 567	33	2.1
1993	3 139	81	2.6	1 627	50	3.1	1 513	31	2.0
1992	3 197	81	2.5	1 657	37	2.2	1 539	43	2.8
1991	3 132	105	3.4	1 571	46	2.9	1 561	59	3.8
1990	3 215	90	2.8	1 660	43	2.6	1 555	47	3.0
1989	3 071	99	3.2	1 567	56	3.6	1 504	43	2.9
1988	3 308	112	3.4	1 716	63	3.7	1 592	49	3.1
1987	3 492	106	3.0	1 818	45	2.5	1 674	61	3.6
1986	3 555	119	3.3	1 820	56	3.1	1 734	63	3.6
1985	3 491	143	4.1	1 797	74	4.1	1 695	69	4.1
1984	3 415	135	4.0	1 735	76	4.4	1 680	59	3.5
1983	3 468	129	3.7	1 755	70	4.0	1 713	59	3.4
1982	3 540	144	4.1	1 792	69	3.9	1 747	74	4.2
1981	3 735	144	3.9	1 816	65	3.6	1 918	78	4.1
1980	3 817	166	4.3	1 957	95	4.9	1 861	71	3.8
1979	3 920	217	5.5	1 985	102	5.1	1 934	114	5.9
1978	3 878	185	4.8	1 943	96	4.9	1 935	89	4.6
1977	3 970	177	4.5	2 021	96	4.8	1 949	81	4.2
1976	3 914	145	3.7	1 960	79	4.0	1 955	67	3.4
1975	3 983	183	4.6	2 017	87	4.3	1 967	97	4.9
1974	3 901	223	5.7	1 951	122	6.3	1 949	101	5.2
1973	3 899	210	5.4	1 930	112	5.8	1 969	98	5.0
1972	3 868	203	5.2	1 940	106	5.5	1 928	97	5.0
1971	3 762	174	4.6	1 925	95	4.9	1 838	79	4.3
1970	3 686	186	5.0	1 865	90	4.8	1 822	97	5.3

ʳ = Revised, controlled to 1990 census–based population estimates; previous 1993 data controlled to 1980 census–based population estimates.

Table A-12. High School Dropout Rates, by Sex, Grade, Race, and Hispanic Origin, October 1970–2005
—Continued

(Numbers in thousands, percent.)

Year, grade, race, and Hispanic origin	Both sexes			Male			Female		
	Total students	Dropouts	Dropout rate	Total students	Dropouts	Dropout rate	Total students	Dropouts	Dropout rate
ALL RACES									
Grade 11									
2005	4 080	72	1.8	2 184	46	2.1	1 896	26	1.4
2004	4 010	141	3.5	2 012	76	3.8	1 998	65	3.3
2003	4 327	117	2.7	2 158	68	3.2	2 169	49	2.3
2002	4 137	99	2.4	2 111	54	2.6	2 026	45	2.2
2001	4 114	139	3.4	2 134	72	3.4	1 979	67	3.4
2000	3 833	170	4.4	1 933	78	4.0	1 901	93	4.9
1999	4 036	150	3.7	2 052	69	3.4	1 984	81	4.0
1998	3 735	110	2.9	1 902	55	2.9	1 833	55	3.0
1997	3 882	142	3.7	1 957	71	3.6	1 925	71	3.7
1996	3 606	138	3.8	1 828	76	4.2	1 778	62	3.5
1995	3 568	159	4.5	1 846	89	4.8	1 724	71	4.1
1994	3 587	132	3.7	1 864	61	3.3	1 722	70	4.1
1993r	3 375	106	3.1	1 725	43	2.5	1 650	63	3.8
1993	3 218	100	3.1	1 643	40	2.4	1 575	60	3.8
1992	3 213	120	3.7	1 642	52	3.2	1 570	67	4.3
1991	3 083	101	3.3	1 598	42	2.6	1 484	58	3.9
1990	2 976	98	3.3	1 462	57	3.9	1 514	41	2.7
1989	3 302	125	3.8	1 683	67	4.0	1 618	57	3.5
1988	3 447	161	4.7	1 819	89	4.9	1 627	72	4.4
1987	3 566	122	3.4	1 766	71	4.0	1 800	51	2.8
1986	3 433	116	3.4	1 700	51	3.0	1 733	65	3.8
1985	3 274	139	4.2	1 618	70	4.3	1 656	69	4.2
1984	3 328	163	4.9	1 682	87	5.2	1 646	76	4.6
1983	3 601	162	4.5	1 825	87	4.8	1 775	75	4.2
1982	3 694	218	5.9	1 872	122	6.5	1 822	96	5.3
1981	3 787	262	6.9	1 937	144	7.4	1 850	118	6.4
1980	3 670	225	6.1	1 832	120	6.6	1 839	105	5.7
1979	3 718	229	6.2	1 840	102	5.5	1 879	128	6.8
1978	3 708	230	6.2	1 905	113	5.9	1 803	117	6.5
1977	3 832	244	6.4	1 964	133	6.8	1 867	110	5.9
1976	3 786	227	6.0	1 955	123	6.3	1 831	104	5.7
1975	3 596	230	6.4	1 828	103	5.6	1 767	126	7.1
1974	3 721	237	6.4	1 819	123	6.8	1 902	114	6.0
1973	3 631	237	6.5	1 877	126	6.7	1 754	111	6.3
1972	3 581	241	6.7	1 825	107	5.9	1 756	134	7.6
1971	3 585	185	5.2	1 772	82	4.6	1 811	103	5.7
1970	3 456	198	5.7	1 750	96	5.5	1 706	102	6.0
Grade 12									
2005	2 031	270	9.2	1 415	138	9.8	1 516	132	8.7
2004	3 130	247	7.9	1 516	133	8.8	1 614	114	7.1
2003	2 945	248	8.4	1 435	131	9.1	1 510	117	7.7
2002	2 956	214	7.2	1 432	104	7.3	1 524	110	7.2
2001	2 762	277	10.0	1 411	171	12.1	1 351	106	7.8
2000	2 983	241	8.1	1 447	154	10.6	1 535	87	5.7
1999	3 121	266	8.5	1 571	120	7.6	1 552	146	9.4
1998	3 173	279	8.8	1 613	146	9.0	1 560	133	8.5
1997	3 025	233	7.7	1 479	136	9.2	1 545	97	6.3
1996	2 952	253	8.6	1 441	114	7.9	1 510	139	9.2
1995	2 986	297	9.9	1 492	168	11.3	1 494	129	8.6
1994	2 861	289	10.1	1 391	143	10.3	1 470	146	9.9
1993r	2 790	212	7.6	1 366	116	8.5	1 423	96	6.7
1993	2 664	201	7.5	1 300	109	8.4	1 364	92	6.7
1992	2 529	183	7.2	1 281	86	6.7	1 248	97	7.8
1991	2 397	142	5.9	1 211	79	6.5	1 186	63	5.3
1990	2 488	159	6.4	1 234	77	6.2	1 254	82	6.5
1989	2 601	180	6.9	1 269	80	6.3	1 331	99	7.4
1988	2 835	188	6.6	1 425	104	7.3	1 409	85	6.0
1987	2 744	175	6.4	1 337	99	7.4	1 405	75	5.3
1986	2 841	186	6.5	1 390	106	7.6	1 450	80	5.5
1985	2 939	222	7.6	1 416	115	8.1	1 523	107	7.0
1984	3 298	209	6.3	1 569	105	6.7	1 728	103	6.0
1983	3 262	244	7.5	1 550	137	8.8	1 712	107	6.3
1982	3 377	215	6.4	1 646	114	6.9	1 732	101	5.8
1981	3 346	233	7.0	1 626	113	6.9	1 719	120	7.0
1980	3 404	267	7.8	1 656	147	8.9	1 748	120	6.9
1979	3 498	298	8.5	1 654	164	9.9	1 845	135	7.3
1978	3 530	328	9.3	1 710	206	12.0	1 820	122	6.7
1977	3 498	313	8.9	1 672	163	9.7	1 827	151	8.3
1976	3 296	272	8.3	1 619	158	9.8	1 677	114	6.8
1975	3 454	226	6.5	1 640	106	6.5	1 814	120	6.6
1974	3 404	282	8.3	1 651	157	9.5	1 754	125	7.1
1973	3 321	236	7.1	1 600	132	8.3	1 721	104	6.0
1972	3 215	215	6.7	1 540	104	6.8	1 674	110	6.6
1971	3 104	203	6.5	1 496	120	8.0	1 609	84	5.2
1970	3 139	204	6.5	1 530	102	6.7	1 610	103	6.4

r = Revised, controlled to 1990 census–based population estimates; previous 1993 data controlled to 1980 census–based population estimates.

Table A-12. High School Dropout Rates, by Sex, Grade, Race, and Hispanic Origin, October 1970–2005
—Continued

(Numbers in thousands, percent.)

Year, grade, race, and Hispanic origin	Both sexes			Male			Female		
	Total students	Dropouts	Dropout rate	Total students	Dropouts	Dropout rate	Total students	Dropouts	Dropout rate
WHITE									
Grades 10–12									
2005	8 855	271	3.1	4 472	151	3.4	4 382	120	2.7
2004	8 585	359	4.2	4 344	211	4.9	4 241	148	3.5
2003	8 781	321	3.7	4 434	172	3.9	4 347	148	3.4
2002	8 636	259	3.0	4 371	133	3.0	4 265	126	3.0
2001	8 490	388	4.6	4 363	230	5.3	4 126	158	3.8
2000	8 540	371	4.3	4 368	204	4.7	4 172	167	4.0
1999	8 665	380	4.4	4 426	180	4.1	4 238	198	4.7
1998	8 487	371	4.4	4 306	188	4.4	4 181	183	4.4
1997	8 402	355	4.2	4 220	208	4.9	4 180	145	3.5
1996	8 005	361	4.5	4 077	198	4.8	3 928	163	4.1
1995	7 926	402	5.1	4 079	220	5.4	3 849	183	4.8
1994	7 862	371	4.7	4 014	184	4.6	3 848	188	4.9
1993	7 442	306	4.1	3 790	157	4.1	3 654	150	4.1
1993	7 152	290	4.1	3 623	147	4.1	3 530	143	4.1
1992	7 077	292	4.1	3 646	140	3.8	3 430	151	4.4
1991	6 856	254	3.7	3 514	127	3.6	3 343	128	3.8
1990	6 984	266	3.8	3 522	144	4.1	3 462	122	3.5
1989	7 243	286	3.9	3 653	149	4.1	3 589	136	3.8
1988	7 727	362	4.7	4 016	203	5.1	3 712	161	4.3
1987	7 979	299	3.7	4 023	163	4.1	3 953	135	3.4
1986	8 011	333	4.2	4 007	168	4.2	4 007	166	4.1
1985	7 967	384	4.8	3 963	195	4.9	4 003	188	4.7
1984	8 221	410	5.0	4 119	220	5.3	4 101	190	4.6
1983	8 531	410	4.8	4 264	232	5.4	4 264	177	4.2
1982	8 769	444	5.1	4 381	231	5.3	4 390	214	4.9
1981	9 067	478	5.3	4 532	254	5.6	4 536	224	4.9
1980	9 177	517	5.6	4 624	294	6.4	4 554	224	4.9
1979	9 437	588	6.2	4 694	311	6.6	4 742	277	5.8
1978	9 360	574	6.1	4 747	329	6.9	4 611	244	5.3
1977	9 536	594	6.2	4 766	327	6.9	4 770	267	5.6
1976	9 362	532	5.7	4 708	297	6.3	4 654	235	5.0
1975	9 440	507	5.4	4 709	234	5.0	4 732	274	5.8
1974	9 403	566	6.0	4 650	326	7.0	4 754	241	5.1
1973	9 359	537	5.7	4 708	288	6.1	4 649	248	5.3
1972	9 173	520	5.7	4 588	247	5.4	4 583	272	5.9
1971	9 140	470	5.1	4 577	244	5.3	4 562	226	5.0
1970	8 959	449	5.0	4 496	212	4.7	4 462	237	5.3
NON-HISPANIC WHITE									
Grades 10–12									
2005	7 228	196	2.7	3 652	103	2.8	3 575	93	2.6
2004	7 015	245	3.5	3 582	130	3.6	3 434	115	3.4
2003	7 139	214	3.0	3 665	116	3.2	3 474	98	2.8
2002	7 124	173	2.4	3 620	84	2.3	3 504	89	2.6
2001	7 070	272	3.8	3 647	173	4.7	3 423	98	2.9
2000	7 159	276	3.9	3 648	150	4.1	3 511	126	3.6
1999	7 265	274	3.8	3 744	130	3.5	3 523	145	4.1
1998	7 174	266	3.7	3 605	130	3.6	3 570	137	3.8
1997	7 090	242	3.4	3 533	140	4.0	3 558	103	2.9
1996	6 850	267	3.9	3 511	145	4.1	3 337	121	3.6
1995	6 905	296	4.3	3 564	164	4.6	3 341	131	3.9
1994	6 839	274	4.0	3 496	137	3.9	3 343	137	4.1
1993	6 277	237	3.8	3 229	128	4.0	3 047	108	3.5

ʳ = Revised, controlled to 1990 census–based population estimates; previous 1993 data controlled to 1980 census–based population estimates.

Table A-12. High School Dropout Rates, by Sex, Grade, Race, and Hispanic Origin, October 1970–2005
—Continued

(Numbers in thousands, percent.)

Year, grade, race, and Hispanic origin	Both sexes			Male			Female		
	Total students	Dropouts	Dropout rate	Total students	Dropouts	Dropout rate	Total students	Dropouts	Dropout rate
BLACK									
Grades 10–12									
2005	1 763	122	6.9	943	71	7.5	821	51	6.2
2004	1 716	90	5.2	833	40	4.8	883	50	5.7
2003	1 698	76	4.5	812	33	4.1	886	43	4.9
2002	1 664	73	4.4	782	40	5.1	882	33	3.8
2001	1 655	95	5.7	828	51	6.2	827	45	5.4
2000	1 706	96	5.6	819	62	7.6	888	34	3.8
1999	1 794	107	6.0	925	48	5.2	870	59	6.8
1998	1 759	88	5.0	918	42	4.6	841	46	5.5
1997	1 678	80	4.8	813	33	4.1	866	49	5.7
1996	1 704	107	6.3	803	37	4.6	901	70	7.8
1995	1 598	97	6.1	797	63	7.9	802	35	4.4
1994	1 559	96	6.1	763	50	6.5	795	45	5.7
1993ʳ	1 499	80	5.3	740	43	5.8	758	37	4.9
1993	1 447	78	5.4	724	41	5.7	722	36	5.0
1992	1 422	70	4.9	702	23	3.3	720	48	6.7
1991	1 366	85	6.2	685	38	5.5	683	48	7.0
1990	1 303	66	5.1	636	26	4.1	666	40	6.0
1989	1 384	106	7.7	684	47	6.9	701	60	8.6
1988	1 468	93	6.3	751	50	6.7	717	43	6.0
1987	1 463	93	6.4	730	45	6.2	732	47	6.4
1986	1 449	68	4.7	711	34	4.8	737	34	4.6
1985	1 422	110	7.7	703	58	8.3	719	52	7.2
1984	1 524	88	5.8	711	44	6.2	813	43	5.3
1983	1 498	103	6.9	687	48	7.0	810	55	6.8
1982	1 553	121	7.8	786	71	9.0	767	50	6.5
1981	1 516	146	9.6	704	66	9.4	815	83	10.2
1980	1 496	124	8.3	714	57	8.0	781	66	8.5
1979	1 479	142	9.6	679	51	7.5	802	92	11.5
1978	1 542	160	10.4	706	78	11.0	835	81	9.7
1977	1 588	133	8.4	746	62	8.3	789	71	9.0
1976	1 449	105	7.2	729	62	8.5	721	45	6.2
1975	1 416	123	8.7	673	56	8.3	743	67	9.0
1974	1 441	167	11.6	679	73	10.8	761	93	12.2
1973	1 372	138	10.1	650	78	12.0	725	61	8.4
1972	1 373	133	9.7	644	65	10.1	756	68	0.0
1971	1 195	87	7.3	552	51	9.2	643	37	5.8
1970	1 192	133	11.2	587	74	12.6	606	60	9.9
ASIAN[1]									
Grades 10–12									
2005	424	6	1.4	218	5	2.3	206	1	0.5
2004	452	4	0.9	233	-	-	219	4	1.9
2003	457	11	2.4	237	3	1.4	221	7	3.4
2002	515	12	2.3	266	8	3.0	249	4	1.6
2001	470	10	2.1	274	9	3.3	197	1	0.5
2000	399	13	3.3	178	12	6.7	221	1	0.5
1999	523	25	4.8	269	13	4.8	253	12	4.7

[1] Data from before 2003 consist of respondents who identified themselves as "Asian or Pacific Islanders."
ʳ = Revised, controlled to 1990 census–based population estimates; previous 1993 data controlled to 1980 census–based population estimates.
- = Quantity zero or rounds to zero.

Table A-12. High School Dropout Rates, by Sex, Grade, Race, and Hispanic Origin, October 1970–2005
—*Continued*

(Numbers in thousands, percent.)

Year, grade, race, and Hispanic origin	Both sexes			Male			Female		
	Total students	Dropouts	Dropout rate	Total students	Dropouts	Dropout rate	Total students	Dropouts	Dropout rate
HISPANIC[2]									
Grades 10–12									
2005	1 814	86	4.7	910	51	5.6	903	35	3.9
2004	1 723	138	8.0	842	97	11.5	881	40	4.6
2003	1 792	116	6.5	846	65	7.7	945	51	5.4
2002	1 614	86	5.3	801	50	6.2	814	36	4.4
2001	1 487	121	8.1	755	57	7.5	732	64	8.7
2000	1 465	100	6.8	761	54	7.1	704	46	6.5
1999	1 482	105	7.1	729	50	6.9	751	55	7.3
1998	1 368	115	8.4	731	63	8.6	637	52	8.2
1997	1 377	119	8.6	710	74	10.4	668	45	6.7
1996	1 195	100	8.4	588	54	9.2	608	46	7.6
1995	1 251	145	11.6	644	70	10.9	608	76	12.5
1994	1 179	109	9.2	607	51	8.4	572	58	10.1
1993r	1 061	69	6.5	488	25	5.1	573	44	7.5
1993	943	60	6.4	436	21	4.8	508	39	7.7
1992	917	72	7.9	468	27	5.8	441	38	8.6
1991	809	59	7.3	396	41	10.4	417	20	4.8
1990	811	65	8.0	379	33	8.7	428	31	7.2
1989	762	59	7.7	394	30	7.6	366	28	7.7
1988	730	77	10.5	398	49	12.3	333	28	8.4
1987	769	43	5.6	380	19	5.0	389	24	6.2
1986	764	91	11.9	376	44	11.7	388	48	12.4
1985	729	71	9.7	333	31	9.3	396	39	9.8
1984	706	77	10.9	311	38	12.2	396	40	10.1
1983	691	68	9.8	351	48	13.7	340	21	6.2
1982	692	65	9.4	370	35	9.5	321	29	9.0
1981	717	77	10.7	350	37	10.6	367	40	10.9
1980	646	74	11.5	295	50	16.9	350	24	6.9
1979	593	58	9.8	295	30	10.2	298	27	9.1
1978	567	70	12.3	295	46	15.6	271	23	8.5
1977	627	50	8.0	341	35	10.3	287	15	5.2
1976	638	46	7.2	300	22	7.3	336	23	6.8
1975	614	67	10.9	317	32	10.1	294	34	11.6
1974	547	53	9.7	271	34	12.5	278	20	7.2
1973	499	50	10.0	240	19	7.9	259	31	12.0
1972	498	55	11.0	253	28	11.1	247	27	10.9
WHITE ALONE OR IN COMBINATION									
Grades 10–12									
2005	9 158	281	3.1	4 610	155	3.4	4 548	126	2.8
2004	8 821	382	4.3	4 464	222	5.0	4 357	160	3.7
2003	9 045	335	3.7	4 573	183	4.0	4 471	151	3.4
BLACK ALONE OR IN COMBINATION									
Grades 10–12									
2005	1 870	129	6.9	979	71	7.3	890	58	6.5
2004	1 797	99	5.5	869	40	4.6	928	59	6.3
2003	1 808	79	4.4	853	36	4.2	955	43	4.5
ASIAN ALONE OR IN COMBINATION									
Grades 10–12									
2005	525	8	1.5	270	6	2.2	256	2	0.8
2004	516	8	1.6	273	3	1.2	243	5	2.1
2003	533	17	3.1	278	8	3.0	254	8	3.3

[2]May be of any race.
r = Revised, controlled to 1990 census–based population estimates; previous 1993 data controlled to 1980 census–based population estimates.

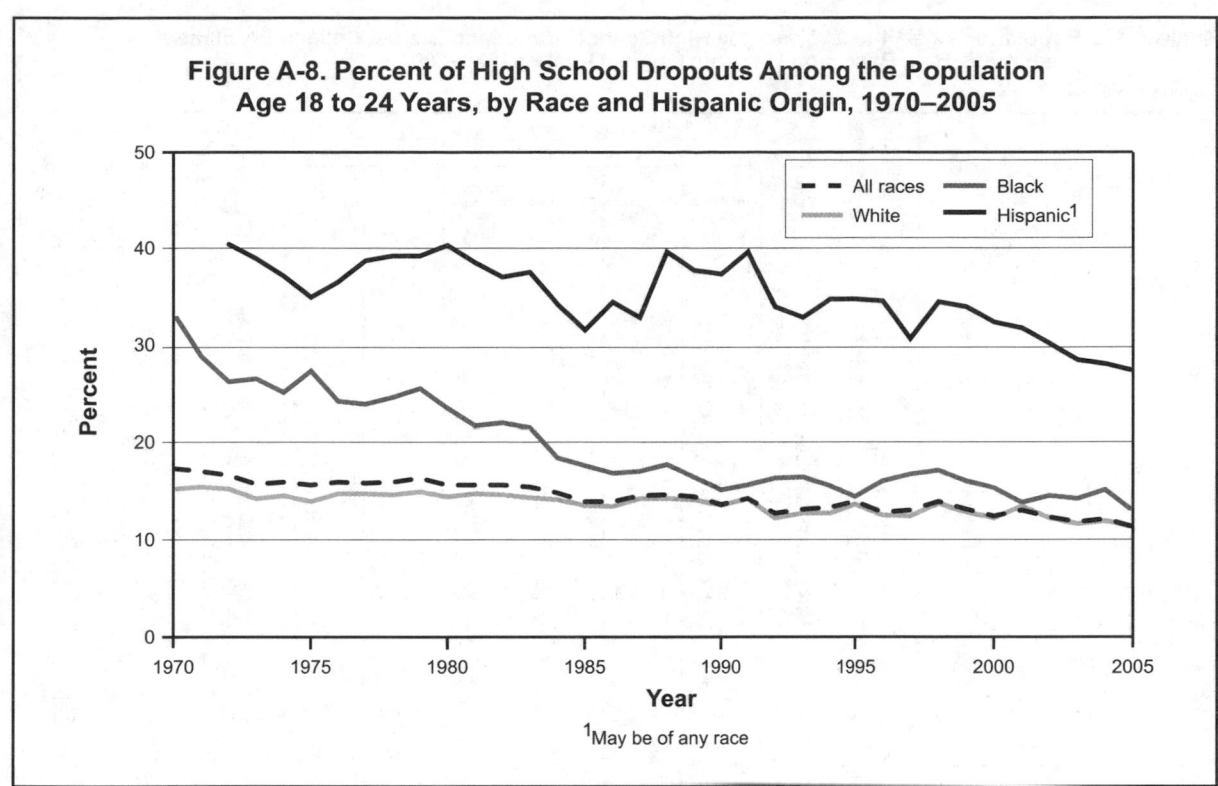

Figure A-8. Percent of High School Dropouts Among the Population Age 18 to 24 Years, by Race and Hispanic Origin, 1970–2005

The number of high school dropouts declined steadily between 1970 and 2005. In 1970, over 17 percent of the population between the ages of 18 and 24 years had dropped out of high school. By 2005, only 11.3 percent of the population had dropped out. While the proportion of dropouts has declined for all races, it declined most dramatically for Blacks. In 1970, approximately 1 out of every 3 Blacks between the ages of 18 and 24 years was a high school dropout. In 2005, fewer than 1 out of every 7 Blacks was a dropout.

The high school dropout rate for grades 10 to 12 was 3.5 percent in 2005, lower than the 2004 level, but slightly higher than the low of 3.3 percent in 2002. The dropout rate for men was higher than the rate for women in most years from 1970 to 2005. (Tables A-12 and A-13)

Table A-13. Population Age 14 to 24 Years, by High School Graduation Status, College Enrollment, Attainment, Sex, Race, and Hispanic Origin, October 1970–2005

(Numbers in thousands, percent.)

Year, sex, race, and Hispanic origin	Population, age 18 to 24 years								High school graduates, age 14 to 24 years		
		High school graduates		Percent:			High school dropouts			Percent:	
	Total	Total students	Enrolled in college	High school graduates	Enrolled in college	High school graduates enrolled in college	Number	Percent	All graduates	Enrolled in college	Enrolled or completed some college
ALL RACES											
Both Sexes											
2005	27 855	23 103	10 834	82.9	38.9	49.3	3 154	11.3	23 445	47.0	69.8
2004	27 948	23 086	10 611	82.6	38.0	46.0	3 836	12.1	23 379	46.2	69.0
2003	27 404	22 603	10 364	82.5	37.8	45.9	3 228	11.8	22 898	45.9	68.8
2002	27 367	22 319	10 033	81.6	36.7	45.0	3 375	12.3	22 639	45.2	67.6
2001	26 965	21 836	9 629	81.0	35.7	44.1	3 519	13.0	22 136	44.1	66.7
2000	26 658	21 822	9 452	81.9	35.5	43.3	3 315	12.4	22 080	43.5	66.7
1999	26 041	21 127	9 259	81.1	35.6	43.8	3 413	13.1	21 390	44.0	67.2
1998	25 507	20 567	9 322	80.6	36.6	45.3	3 544	13.9	20 775	45.5	68.0
1997	24 973	20 338	9 204	81.4	36.9	45.2	3 236	13.0	20 577	45.6	67.3
1996	24 671	20 131	8 767	81.6	35.5	43.5	3 147	12.8	20 465	44.0	67.2
1995	24 900	20 125	8 539	80.8	34.3	42.4	3 471	13.9	20 359	42.7	67.1
1994	25 254	20 581	8 729	81.5	34.6	42.4	3 365	13.3	20 779	42.7	66.9
1993r	25 522	20 844	8 630	81.7	33.8	41.4	3 349	13.1	21 060	41.6	65.3
1993	24 100	19 772	8 193	82.0	34.0	41.4	3 070	12.7	19 979	41.6	65.4
1992	24 278	19 921	8 343	82.1	34.4	41.9	3 083	12.7	20 194	42.3	65.6
1991	24 572	19 883	8 172	80.9	33.3	41.1	3 486	14.2	20 065	41.4	60.7
1990	24 852	20 311	7 964	82.3	32.0	39.1	3 379	13.6	20 571	39.6	58.9
1989	25 261	20 461	7 804	81.0	30.9	38.1	3 644	14.4	20 749	38.5	57.9
1988	25 733	20 900	7 791	81.2	30.3	37.3	3 749	14.6	21 204	37.6	57.4
1987	25 950	21 118	7 693	81.4	29.6	36.4	3 751	14.5	21 477	36.9	56.2
1986	26 512	21 768	7 477	82.1	28.2	34.3	3 687	13.9	22 086	34.8	55.0
1985	27 122	22 349	7 537	82.4	27.8	33.7	3 687	13.9	22 722	34.3	54.3
1984	28 031	22 870	7 591	81.6	27.1	33.2	4 142	14.8	23 252	33.7	53.0
1983	28 580	22 988	7 477	80.4	26.2	32.5	4 410	15.4	23 359	33.1	52.8
1982	28 846	23 291	7 678	80.7	26.6	33.0	4 500	15.6	23 708	33.5	52.7
1981	28 965	23 343	7 575	80.6	26.2	32.5	4 520	15.6	23 705	32.9	51.7
1980	28 957	23 413	7 400	80.9	25.6	31.6	4 515	15.6	23 856	32.1	51.1
1979	27 974	22 421	6 991	80.1	25.0	31.2	4 560	16.3	22 911	31.9	51.6
1978	27 647	22 309	6 995	80.7	25.3	31.4	4 388	15.9	22 759	31.9	51.4
1977	27 331	22 008	7 142	80.5	26.1	32.5	4 313	15.8	22 499	33.0	52.0
1976	26 919	21 677	7 181	80.5	26.7	33.1	4 276	15.9	22 158	33.7	53.4
1975	26 387	21 326	6 935	80.8	26.3	32.5	4 110	15.6	21 824	33.1	52.5
1974	25 670	20 725	6 316	80.7	24.6	30.5	4 070	15.9	21 267	31.2	51.3
1973	25 237	20 377	6 055	80.7	24.0	29.7	3 973	15.7	20 895	30.4	50.7
1972	24 579	19 618	6 257	79.8	25.5	31.9	4 068	16.6	20 107	32.6	52.9
1971	23 668	18 691	6 210	79.0	26.2	33.2	4 025	17.0	19 130	33.9	53.1
1970	22 552	17 768	5 805	78.8	25.7	32.7	3 908	17.3	18 218	33.5	52.3
Male											
2005	14 077	11 182	4 973	79.4	35.3	43.2	1 852	13.2	11 330	44.4	65.9
2004	14 018	11 258	4 865	80.3	34.7	43.2	1 942	13.9	11 364	43.5	65.0
2003	13 681	10 919	4 697	79.8	34.3	43.0	1 875	13.7	11 040	43.1	65.0
2002	13 744	10 823	4 629	78.7	33.7	42.8	1 925	14.0	10 975	42.9	64.6
2001	13 434	10 461	4 437	77.9	33.0	42.4	2 028	15.1	10 587	42.4	63.9
2000	13 338	10 622	4 343	79.6	32.6	40.9	1 837	13.8	10 736	41.0	63.1
1999	12 905	10 201	4 396	79.1	34.0	43.1	1 818	14.9	10 331	43.3	64.5
1998	12 764	9 915	4 403	77.7	34.5	44.4	2 018	15.8	10 006	44.5	64.9
1997	12 513	9 933	4 374	79.4	35.0	44.0	1 765	14.1	10 025	44.2	64.9
1996	12 285	9 815	4 187	80.0	34.1	42.6	1 628	13.2	9 960	43.0	65.6
1995	12 351	9 789	4 089	79.3	33.1	41.8	1 791	14.5	9 884	42.1	64.2
1994	12 557	9 970	4 152	79.4	33.1	41.6	1 804	14.4	10 051	41.9	64.9
1993r	12 712	10 142	4 237	79.8	33.3	41.8	1 745	13.7	10 229	42.0	63.9
1993	11 898	9 541	3 994	80.2	33.6	41.9	1 575	13.2	9 625	42.0	64.1
1992	11 965	9 576	3 912	80.0	32.7	40.9	1 617	13.5	9 706	41.3	64.1
1991	12 036	9 493	3 954	78.9	32.9	41.7	1 810	15.0	9 564	41.9	59.2
1990	12 134	9 778	3 922	80.6	32.3	40.1	1 689	13.9	9 894	40.5	58.0
1989	12 325	9 700	3 717	78.7	30.2	38.3	1 941	15.7	9 810	38.6	57.2
1988	12 491	9 832	3 770	78.7	30.2	38.3	1 950	15.6	9 947	38.5	56.5
1987	12 626	10 030	3 867	79.4	30.6	38.6	1 948	15.4	10 207	39.0	56.0
1986	12 921	10 338	3 702	80.0	28.7	35.8	1 924	14.9	10 465	36.2	54.4
1985	13 199	10 614	3 749	80.4	28.4	35.3	2 015	15.3	10 784	36.0	54.6
1984	13 744	10 914	3 929	79.4	28.6	36.0	2 184	15.9	11 052	36.4	53.6
1983	14 003	10 906	3 820	77.9	27.3	35.0	2 379	17.0	10 959	35.5	52.7
1982	14 083	11 120	3 837	79.0	27.2	34.5	2 329	16.5	11 295	35.0	53.0
1981	14 127	11 052	3 833	78.2	27.1	34.7	2 424	17.2	11 203	35.1	52.1
1980	14 107	11 125	3 717	78.9	26.3	33.4	2 390	16.9	11 309	33.7	51.4
1979	13 571	10 657	3 508	78.5	25.8	32.9	2 320	17.1	10 838	33.6	52.4
1978	13 385	10 614	3 621	79.3	27.1	34.1	2 200	16.4	10 789	34.5	52.6
1977	13 218	10 440	3 712	79.0	28.1	35.6	2 170	16.4	10 626	36.0	54.2
1976	13 012	10 312	3 673	79.2	28.2	35.6	2 109	16.2	10 492	36.0	55.7
1975	12 724	10 214	3 693	80.3	29.0	36.2	1 928	15.2	10 415	36.7	56.1
1974	12 315	9 835	3 411	79.9	27.7	34.7	1 958	15.9	10 073	35.3	55.6
1973	12 111	9 716	3 360	80.2	27.7	34.6	1 853	15.3	9 908	35.1	55.4
1972	11 712	9 247	3 534	79.0	30.2	38.2	1 898	16.2	9 461	38.8	59.0
1971	11 092	8 669	3 599	78.2	32.4	41.5	1 865	16.8	8 855	42.1	60.1
1970	10 385	8 087	3 331	77.9	32.1	41.2	1 746	16.8	8 279	41.8	59.2

r = Revised, controlled to 1990 census–based population estimates; previous 1993 data controlled to 1980 census–based population estimates.

Table A-13. Population Age 14 to 24 Years, by High School Graduation Status, College Enrollment, Attainment, Sex, Race, and Hispanic Origin, October 1970–2005—*Continued*

(Numbers in thousands, percent.)

Year, sex, race, and Hispanic origin	Population, age 18 to 24 years								High school graduates, age 14 to 24 years		
	Total	High school graduates		Percent:			High school dropouts		All graduates	Percent:	
		Total students	Enrolled in college	High school graduates	Enrolled in college	High school graduates enrolled in college	Number	Percent		Enrolled in college	Enrolled or completed some college
ALL RACES											
Female											
2005	13 778	11 921	5 861	86.5	42.5	55.8	1 302	9.5	12 115	49.4	73.4
2004	13 930	11 828	5 746	84.9	41.2	48.6	1 444	10.4	12 015	48.8	72.8
2003	13 724	11 684	5 667	85.1	41.3	48.5	1 354	9.9	11 858	48.5	72.2
2002	13 623	11 496	5 404	84.4	39.7	47.0	1 450	10.6	11 664	47.3	70.3
2001	13 531	11 375	5 192	84.1	38.4	45.7	1 491	11.0	11 549	45.7	69.4
2000	13 319	11 200	5 109	84.1	38.4	45.6	1 478	11.1	11 344	45.8	70.1
1999	13 136	10 926	4 863	83.2	37.0	44.5	1 594	12.1	11 058	44.6	69.8
1998	12 743	10 651	4 919	83.6	38.6	46.2	1 526	12.0	10 768	46.4	70.7
1997	12 460	10 403	4 829	83.5	38.8	46.4	1 471	11.8	10 549	46.8	69.6
1996	12 386	10 317	4 582	83.3	37.0	44.4	1 519	12.3	10 507	44.9	68.6
1995	12 548	10 338	4 452	82.4	35.5	43.1	1 679	13.4	10 477	43.4	69.8
1994	12 696	10 611	4 576	83.6	36.0	43.1	1 561	12.3	10 729	43.4	68.7
1993r	12 810	10 702	4 393	83.5	34.3	41.0	1 604	12.5	10 831	41.3	66.6
1993	12 202	10 232	4 199	83.9	34.4	41.0	1 494	12.2	10 355	41.2	66.7
1992	12 313	10 344	4 429	84.0	36.0	42.8	1 466	11.9	10 486	43.3	66.9
1991	12 536	10 391	4 218	82.9	33.6	40.6	1 676	13.4	10 502	41.0	62.1
1990	12 718	10 533	4 042	82.8	31.8	38.4	1 690	13.3	10 676	38.7	59.8
1989	12 936	10 758	4 085	83.2	31.6	38.0	1 702	13.2	10 936	38.4	58.6
1988	13 242	11 068	4 021	83.6	30.4	36.3	1 799	13.5	11 257	36.8	58.2
1987	13 324	11 086	3 826	83.2	28.7	34.5	1 803	13.5	11 268	35.0	56.4
1986	13 591	11 430	3 775	84.1	27.8	33.0	1 751	12.9	11 623	33.5	55.5
1985	13 923	11 736	3 788	84.3	27.2	32.3	1 804	13.0	11 937	32.8	54.0
1984	14 287	11 956	3 662	83.7	25.6	30.6	1 958	13.7	12 199	31.3	52.4
1983	14 577	12 082	3 657	82.9	25.1	30.3	2 031	13.9	12 294	31.0	52.8
1982	14 763	12 171	3 841	82.4	26.0	31.6	2 171	14.7	12 411	32.1	52.4
1981	14 838	12 290	3 741	82.8	25.2	30.4	2 097	14.1	12 503	31.0	51.3
1980	14 851	12 287	3 682	82.7	24.8	30.0	2 124	14.3	12 547	30.6	50.8
1979	14 403	11 763	3 482	81.7	24.2	29.6	2 240	15.6	12 074	30.4	50.8
1978	14 262	11 694	3 373	82.0	23.7	28.8	2 188	15.3	11 969	29.6	50.3
1977	14 113	11 569	3 431	82.0	24.0	29.7	2 142	15.2	11 875	30.3	50.0
1976	13 907	11 365	3 508	81.7	25.2	30.9	2 168	15.6	11 666	31.6	51.4
1975	13 663	11 113	3 243	81.3	23.7	29.2	2 181	16.0	11 407	29.9	49.2
1974	13 355	10 889	2 905	81.5	21.8	26.7	2 112	15.8	11 194	27.4	47.5
1973	13 126	10 663	2 696	81.2	20.5	25.3	2 119	16.1	10 986	26.1	46.5
1972	12 867	10 371	2 724	80.6	21.2	26.3	2 170	16.9	10 644	27.0	47.4
1971	12 576	10 020	2 610	79.7	20.8	26.0	2 159	17.2	10 272	26.9	47.1
1970	12 167	9 680	2 474	79.6	20.3	25.6	2 163	17.8	9 908	26.3	46.6
WHITE											
Both Sexes											
2005	21 777	18 130	8 498	83.3	39.0	50.4	2 466	11.3	18 352	46.9	70.0
2004	21 896	18 213	8 351	82.6	38.0	45.9	2 599	11.9	18 414	46.1	69.1
2003	21 502	17 901	8 150	83.3	37.9	45.5	2 489	11.6	18 123	45.5	69.1
2002	21 704	17 793	7 921	82.0	36.5	44.5	2 641	12.2	17 995	44.6	67.5
2001	21 372	17 348	7 548	81.2	35.3	43.5	2 865	13.4	17 547	43.5	67.0
2000	21 257	17 512	7 566	82.4	35.6	43.2	2 598	12.2	17 714	43.4	66.9
1999	20 866	17 052	7 447	81.7	35.7	43.7	2 680	12.8	17 220	43.8	67.5
1998	20 465	16 701	7 541	81.6	36.9	45.2	2 810	13.7	16 855	45.3	68.3
1997	20 020	16 557	7 495	82.7	37.4	45.3	2 476	12.4	16 733	45.6	67.7
1996	19 676	16 199	7 123	82.3	36.2	44.0	2 458	12.5	16 436	44.3	68.4
1995	19 866	16 269	7 011	81.9	35.3	43.1	2 711	13.6	16 439	43.4	68.3
1994	20 171	16 670	7 118	82.6	35.3	42.7	2 553	12.7	16 814	42.9	67.6
1993r	20 493	16 989	7 074	82.9	34.5	41.6	2 595	12.7	17 161	41.8	66.5
1993	19 430	16 196	6 763	83.4	34.8	41.8	2 369	12.2	16 361	41.9	66.7
1992	19 671	16 379	6 916	83.3	35.2	42.2	2 398	12.2	16 586	42.7	67.0
1991	19 980	16 324	6 813	81.7	34.1	41.7	2 845	14.2	16 467	42.0	62.3
1990	20 393	16 823	6 635	82.5	32.5	39.4	2 751	13.5	17 022	39.8	60.1
1989	20 825	17 089	6 631	82.1	31.8	38.8	2 926	14.1	17 329	39.1	58.9
1988	21 261	17 491	6 659	82.3	31.3	38.1	3 012	14.2	17 720	38.4	58.5
1987	21 493	17 689	6 483	82.3	30.2	36.6	3 042	14.2	17 982	37.1	56.8
1986	22 020	18 291	6 307	83.1	28.6	34.5	2 961	13.4	18 554	34.9	55.5
1985	22 632	18 916	6 500	83.6	28.7	34.4	3 050	13.5	19 229	35.0	55.3
1984	23 347	19 373	6 256	83.0	28.0	33.7	3 281	14.1	19 686	34.2	53.8
1983	23 899	19 643	6 463	82.2	27.0	32.9	3 428	14.3	19 948	33.5	53.4
1982	24 206	19 944	6 694	82.4	27.2	33.1	3 523	14.6	20 292	33.6	53.1
1981	24 486	20 123	6 549	82.2	26.7	32.5	3 590	14.7	20 439	33.0	52.1
1980	24 482	20 214	6 423	82.6	26.2	31.8	3 525	14.4	20 583	32.3	51.4
1979	23 895	19 616	6 120	82.1	25.6	31.2	3 571	14.9	20 033	31.8	51.7
1978	23 650	19 526	6 077	82.6	25.7	31.1	3 464	14.6	19 911	31.7	51.3
1977	23 430	19 291	6 209	82.3	26.5	32.2	3 445	14.7	19 712	32.6	52.1
1976	23 119	19 045	6 276	82.4	27.1	33.0	3 407	14.7	19 462	33.5	53.5
1975	22 703	18 883	6 116	83.2	26.9	32.4	3 149	13.9	19 298	33.0	52.7
1974	22 141	18 318	5 589	82.7	25.2	30.5	3 212	14.5	18 794	31.2	51.7
1973	21 766	18 023	5 438	82.8	25.0	30.2	3 085	14.2	18 470	30.8	51.6
1972	21 315	17 410	5 624	81.7	26.4	32.3	3 241	15.2	17 838	33.0	53.9
1971	20 533	16 593	5 594	81.3	27.2	33.5	3 156	15.4	17 087	34.2	54.1
1970	19 608	15 960	5 305	81.4	27.1	33.2	2 974	15.2	16 334	33.9	53.4

r = Revised, controlled to 1990 census–based population estimates; previous 1993 data controlled to 1980 census–based population estimates.

Table A-13. Population Age 14 to 24 Years, by High School Graduation Status, College Enrollment, Attainment, Sex, Race, and Hispanic Origin, October 1970–2005—*Continued*

(Numbers in thousands, percent.)

Year, sex, race, and Hispanic origin	Population, age 18 to 24 years								High school graduates, age 14 to 24 years		
	Total	High school graduates		Percent:			High school dropouts		All graduates	Percent:	
		Total students	Enrolled in college	High school graduates	Enrolled in college	High school graduates enrolled in college	Number	Percent		Enrolled in college	Enrolled or completed some college
WHITE											
Male											
2005	11 116	8 885	3 924	79.9	35.3	44.1	1 469	13.2	8 986	44.1	65.9
2004	11 107	9 001	3 855	81.0	34.7	42.8	1 524	13.7	9 067	43.1	64.4
2003	10 885	8 763	3 726	80.5	34.2	42.5	1 452	13.3	8 862	42.6	65.1
2002	10 986	8 717	3 701	79.4	33.7	42.5	1 506	13.7	8 833	42.5	64.6
2001	10 817	8 490	3 521	78.5	32.6	41.5	1 659	15.3	8 582	41.5	64.0
2000	10 739	8 603	3 522	80.1	32.8	40.9	1 450	13.5	8 690	41.1	63.5
1999	10 532	8 382	3 585	79.6	34.0	42.7	1 462	13.9	8 457	42.8	64.8
1998	10 400	8 194	3 634	78.8	34.9	44.3	1 628	15.7	8 256	44.4	65.5
1997	10 173	8 204	3 633	80.6	35.7	44.3	1 406	13.8	8 274	44.5	65.3
1996	9 897	8 000	3 419	80.8	34.5	42.7	1 275	12.9	8 104	43.0	66.0
1995	9 980	8 001	3 398	80.2	34.0	42.5	1 430	14.3	8 067	42.7	65.3
1994	10 123	8 168	3 406	80.7	33.6	41.7	1 377	13.6	8 227	41.9	65.4
1993r	10 294	8 338	3 498	81.0	34.0	42.0	1 388	13.5	8 411	42.1	65.1
1993	9 641	7 857	3 313	81.5	34.4	42.2	1 379	12.9	7 926	42.3	65.4
1992	9 744	7 911	3 291	81.2	33.8	41.6	1 300	13.3	8 016	42.1	65.8
1991	9 896	7 843	3 270	79.3	33.0	41.7	1 520	15.4	7 899	41.9	59.9
1990	10 053	8 157	3 292	81.1	32.7	40.3	1 430	14.2	8 246	40.7	58.8
1989	10 240	8 177	3 223	79.9	31.5	39.4	1 572	15.4	8 271	39.7	58.5
1988	10 380	8 268	3 260	79.7	31.4	39.4	1 594	15.4	8 365	39.6	57.8
1987	10 549	8 498	3 289	80.6	31.2	38.7	1 593	15.1	8 647	39.2	56.4
1986	10 814	8 780	3 168	81.2	29.3	36.1	1 575	14.6	8 886	36.4	55.1
1985	11 108	9 077	3 254	81.7	29.3	35.8	1 637	14.7	9 229	36.6	55.5
1984	11 521	9 348	3 406	81.1	29.6	36.4	1 744	15.1	9 459	36.8	54.2
1983	11 787	9 411	3 335	79.8	28.3	35.4	1 865	15.8	9 534	35.9	53.5
1982	11 874	9 611	3 308	80.9	27.9	34.4	1 810	15.2	9 761	34.9	53.2
1981	12 040	9 619	3 340	79.9	27.7	34.7	1 960	16.3	9 754	35.1	52.8
1980	12 011	9 686	3 275	80.6	27.3	33.8	1 883	15.7	9 838	34.1	51.8
1979	11 721	9 457	3 104	80.7	26.5	32.8	1 830	15.6	9 615	33.4	52.7
1978	11 572	9 438	3 195	81.6	27.6	33.9	1 722	14.9	9 582	34.3	52.5
1977	11 445	9 263	3 286	80.9	28.7	35.5	1 779	15.5	9 422	35.8	54.5
1976	11 279	9 186	3 250	81.4	28.8	35.4	1 691	15.0	9 340	35.7	55.9
1975	11 050	9 139	3 326	82.7	30.1	36.4	1 490	13.5	9 310	36.9	56.6
1974	10 722	8 768	3 035	81.8	28.3	34.6	1 579	14.7	8 980	35.2	55.9
1973	10 511	8 637	3 032	82.2	28.8	35.1	1 453	13.8	8 817	35.6	56.5
1972	10 212	8 278	3 195	81.1	31.3	38.6	1 506	14.7	8 462	39.2	60.1
1971	9 653	7 807	3 284	80.9	34.0	42.1	1 429	14.8	7 978	42.6	61.4
1970	9 053	7 324	3 096	80.9	34.2	42.3	1 297	14.3	7 496	42.9	60.9
Female											
2005	10 661	9 245	4 574	86.7	42.9	57.3	997	9.4	9 366	49.7	73.9
2004	10 789	9 212	4 496	85.4	41.7	48.8	1 075	10.0	9 347	49.0	73.5
2003	10 617	9 138	4 424	86.1	41.7	48.4	1 037	9.8	9 260	48.3	72.9
2002	10 718	9 075	4 220	84.7	39.4	46.5	1 135	10.6	9 162	46.6	70.4
2001	10 555	8 859	4 027	83.9	38.1	45.5	1 206	11.4	8 965	45.5	69.8
2000	10 517	8 909	4 044	84.7	38.5	45.4	1 148	10.9	9 024	45.6	70.2
1999	10 334	8 671	3 862	83.9	37.4	44.5	1 218	11.8	8 763	44.7	70.1
1998	10 065	8 507	3 907	84.5	38.8	45.9	1 181	11.7	8 599	46.2	71.0
1997	9 847	8 352	3 863	84.8	39.2	46.3	1 072	10.9	8 458	46.6	70.1
1996	9 778	8 200	3 705	83.9	37.9	45.2	1 182	12.1	8 333	45.6	70.7
1995	9 886	8 271	3 615	83.7	36.6	43.7	1 281	13.0	8 376	44.0	71.3
1994	10 048	8 503	3 714	84.6	37.0	43.7	1 175	11.7	8 588	43.9	69.7
1993r	10 199	8 651	3 576	84.8	35.1	41.3	1 207	11.8	8 750	41.5	67.9
1993	9 790	8 339	3 450	85.2	35.2	41.4	1 125	11.5	8 435	41.6	68.0
1992	9 928	8 468	3 625	85.3	36.5	42.8	1 098	11.1	8 569	43.2	68.1
1991	10 119	8 481	3 544	83.8	35.0	41.8	1 324	13.1	8 568	42.1	64.5
1990	10 340	8 666	3 344	83.8	32.3	38.6	1 322	12.8	8 775	38.9	61.4
1989	10 586	8 913	3 409	84.2	32.2	38.2	1 354	12.8	9 059	38.6	59.2
1988	10 881	9 223	3 399	84.8	31.2	36.9	1 418	13.0	9 355	37.3	59.1
1987	10 944	9 189	3 192	84.0	29.2	34.7	1 449	13.2	9 334	36.2	57.2
1986	11 205	9 509	3 139	84.9	28.0	33.0	1 388	12.4	9 667	33.6	55.8
1985	11 524	9 840	3 247	85.4	28.2	33.0	1 413	12.3	10 001	33.6	55.2
1984	11 826	10 026	3 120	84.8	26.4	31.1	1 535	13.0	10 089	31.8	53.4
1983	12 112	10 233	3 129	84.5	25.8	30.6	1 563	12.9	10 233	31.3	53.4
1982	12 332	10 333	3 285	83.8	26.6	31.8	1 713	13.0	10 530	32.3	52.9
1981	12 446	10 504	3 208	84.4	25.8	30.5	1 629	13.1	10 687	31.1	51.6
1980	12 471	10 528	3 147	84.4	25.2	29.9	1 642	13.2	10 749	30.6	50.9
1979	12 174	10 157	3 015	83.4	24.8	29.7	1 741	14.3	10 417	30.3	50.8
1978	12 078	10 088	2 882	83.5	23.9	28.6	1 742	14.4	10 327	29.3	50.3
1977	11 985	10 029	2 923	83.7	24.4	29.1	1 666	13.9	10 292	29.7	50.0
1976	11 840	9 860	3 026	83.3	25.6	30.7	1 717	14.5	10 118	31.4	51.3
1975	11 653	9 743	2 790	83.6	23.9	28.6	1 658	14.2	9 986	29.4	49.1
1974	11 419	9 551	2 555	83.6	22.4	26.8	1 633	14.3	9 811	27.5	47.8
1973	11 255	9 387	2 406	83.4	21.4	25.6	1 632	14.5	9 653	26.4	47.1
1972	11 103	9 132	2 428	82.2	21.9	26.6	1 735	15.6	9 377	27.4	48.3
1971	10 880	8 887	2 310	81.7	21.2	26.0	1 726	15.9	9 107	26.8	47.7
1970	10 555	8 634	2 209	81.8	20.9	25.6	1 675	15.9	8 837	26.3	47.2

r = Revised, controlled to 1990 census–based population estimates; previous 1993 data controlled to 1980 census–based population estimates.

Table A-13. Population Age 14 to 24 Years, by High School Graduation Status, College Enrollment, Attainment, Sex, Race, and Hispanic Origin, October 1970–2005—*Continued*

(Numbers in thousands, percent.)

Year, sex, race, and Hispanic origin	Population, age 18 to 24 years								High school graduates, age 14 to 24 years		
	Total	High school graduates		Percent:			High school dropouts		All graduates	Percent:	
		Total students	Enrolled in college	High school graduates	Enrolled in college	High school graduates enrolled in college	Number	Percent		Enrolled in college	Enrolled or completed some college
NON-HISPANIC WHITE											
Both Sexes											
2005	17 293	15 187	7 393	87.8	42.8	54.9	1 216	7.0	15 368	48.7	72.6
2004	17 326	15 224	7 228	87.9	41.7	47.5	1 313	7.6	15 382	47.7	71.8
2003	17 158	15 070	7 129	87.8	41.6	47.3	1 267	7.4	15 255	47.3	71.5
2002	17 131	14 910	7 004	87.0	40.9	47.0	1 289	7.5	15 089	47.1	70.4
2001	16 721	14 480	6 565	86.6	39.3	45.3	1 390	8.3	14 646	45.3	69.7
2000	17 327	15 187	6 709	87.7	38.7	44.2	1 316	7.6	15 344	44.3	69.0
1999	17 080	14 812	6 735	86.7	39.4	45.5	1 404	8.2	14 952	45.6	70.2
1998	16 634	14 402	6 757	86.6	40.6	46.9	1 491	9.0	14 542	47.0	70.6
1997	16 575	14 414	6 728	87.0	40.6	46.7	1 432	8.6	14 527	46.9	70.0
1996	16 339	14 288	6 447	87.5	39.5	45.1	1 303	8.0	14 501	45.5	70.7
1995	16 867	14 523	6 393	86.1	37.9	44.0	1 647	9.8	14 672	44.3	70.2
1994	17 114	14 916	6 521	87.2	38.1	43.7	1 505	8.8	15 049	44.0	69.2
1993	16 895	14 665	6 221	86.8	36.8	42.4	1 524	9.0	14 801	42.6	68.1
Male											
2005	8 700	7 443	3 429	85.5	39.4	48.7	685	7.9	7 526	46.0	68.6
2004	8 644	7 527	3 322	87.1	38.4	44.1	691	8.0	7 576	44.4	66.7
2003	8 538	7 325	3 291	85.8	38.5	44.9	721	8.4	7 401	45.0	68.5
2002	8 453	7 244	3 287	85.7	38.9	45.4	668	7.9	7 352	45.5	67.9
2001	8 343	7 112	3 094	85.3	37.1	43.4	741	8.9	7 191	43.4	67.1
2000	8 670	7 493	3 136	86.4	36.2	41.9	677	7.8	7 556	42.0	65.4
1999	8 580	7 301	3 284	85.1	38.3	45.0	753	8.8	7 369	45.0	67.7
1998	8 380	7 094	3 300	84.7	39.4	46.5	826	9.9	7 151	46.6	68.2
1997	8 326	7 112	3 276	85.4	39.3	46.1	797	9.6	7 154	46.3	68.1
1996	8 168	7 050	3 130	86.3	38.3	44.4	651	8.0	7 143	44.7	68.6
1995	8 399	7 089	3 105	84.4	37.0	43.8	883	10.5	7 147	44.0	67.3
1994	8 457	7 261	3 126	85.9	37.0	43.1	777	9.2	7 317	40.0	67.0
1993	8 403	7 138	3 071	84.9	36.6	43.0	811	9.7	7 191	43.2	67.1
Female											
2005	8 593	7 744	3 964	90.1	46.1	61.4	531	6.2	7 842	51.4	76.4
2004	8 628	7 697	3 900	89.2	45.0	50.7	622	7.2	7 805	50.9	76.8
2003	8 620	7 745	3 838	89.9	44.5	49.6	546	6.3	7 854	49.5	74.4
2002	8 678	7 666	3 717	88.3	42.8	48.5	621	7.2	7 736	48.6	72.8
2001	8 378	7 368	3 471	87.9	41.4	47.2	648	7.7	7 455	47.2	72.3
2000	8 657	7 693	3 573	88.9	41.3	46.4	638	7.4	7 789	40.0	72.5
1999	8 500	7 510	3 451	88.4	40.6	46.0	651	7.7	7 583	46.2	72.5
1998	8 254	7 308	3 457	88.5	41.9	47.3	665	8.1	7 391	47.5	73.0
1997	8 249	7 302	3 452	88.5	41.9	47.3	636	7.7	7 373	47.5	71.9
1996	8 171	7 238	3 317	88.6	40.6	45.8	652	8.0	7 358	46.3	72.8
1995	8 467	7 433	3 288	87.8	38.8	44.2	764	9.0	7 525	44.6	73.1
1994	8 657	7 655	3 395	88.4	39.2	44.4	728	8.4	7 732	44.6	71.3
1993	8 492	7 527	3 150	88.6	37.1	41.9	714	8.4	7 610	42.0	69.1

Table A-13. Population Age 14 to 24 Years, by High School Graduation Status, College Enrollment, Attainment, Sex, Race, and Hispanic Origin, October 1970–2005—*Continued*

(Numbers in thousands, percent.)

Year, sex, race, and Hispanic origin	Population, age 18 to 24 years								High school graduates, age 14 to 24 years		
		High school graduates		Percent:			High school dropouts			Percent:	
	Total	Total students	Enrolled in college	High school graduates	Enrolled in college	High school graduates enrolled in college	Number	Percent	All graduates	Enrolled in college	Enrolled or completed some college
BLACK											
Both Sexes											
2005	3 964	3 137	1 297	79.1	32.7	40.0	512	12.9	3 212	41.3	63.5
2004	3 940	3 050	1 238	77.4	31.4	40.6	596	15.1	3 112	41.1	63.2
2003	3 837	2 948	1 225	76.8	31.9	41.6	545	14.2	2 997	41.8	62.5
2002	3 924	3 040	1 226	77.5	31.3	40.3	571	14.5	3 117	41.1	61.2
2001	3 916	3 016	1 206	77.0	30.8	40.0	540	13.8	3 095	40.0	59.0
2000	4 013	3 090	1 216	77.0	30.3	39.4	615	15.3	3 129	39.5	61.0
1999	3 827	2 911	1 145	76.1	29.9	39.4	613	16.0	2 985	39.9	60.4
1998	3 745	2 747	1 116	73.4	29.8	40.6	642	17.1	2 790	40.8	61.8
1997	3 650	2 725	1 085	74.7	29.7	39.8	611	16.7	2 762	40.2	60.0
1996	3 637	2 738	983	75.3	27.0	35.9	581	16.0	2 805	36.6	54.6
1995	3 625	2 788	988	76.9	27.3	35.4	522	14.4	2 828	35.8	58.0
1994	3 661	2 818	1 001	77.0	27.3	35.5	568	15.5	2 859	36.3	59.2
1993r	3 666	2 747	897	74.9	24.5	32.7	600	16.4	2 771	32.8	54.0
1993	3 516	2 629	861	74.8	24.5	32.8	578	16.4	2 653	32.9	53.9
1992	3 521	2 625	886	74.6	25.2	33.8	575	16.3	2 668	34.3	53.3
1991	3 504	2 630	828	75.1	23.6	31.5	545	15.6	2 658	31.8	46.0
1990	3 520	2 710	894	77.0	25.4	33.0	530	15.1	2 759	33.7	48.0
1989	3 559	2 708	835	76.1	23.5	30.8	583	16.4	2 750	31.5	49.2
1988	3 568	2 680	752	75.1	21.1	28.1	631	17.7	2 741	28.6	46.3
1987	3 603	2 739	823	76.0	22.8	30.0	611	17.0	2 790	30.6	48.1
1986	3 653	2 795	812	76.5	22.2	29.1	617	16.8	2 837	29.3	47.8
1985	3 716	2 810	734	75.6	19.8	26.1	655	17.6	2 848	26.5	43.8
1984	3 862	2 885	786	74.7	20.4	27.2	712	18.4	2 950	28.0	45.2
1983	3 865	2 740	741	70.9	19.2	27.0	832	21.5	2 790	27.7	45.0
1982	3 872	2 744	767	70.9	19.8	28.0	851	22.0	2 793	28.2	45.5
1981	3 778	2 678	750	70.9	19.9	28.0	821	21.7	2 718	28.7	44.8
1980	3 721	2 592	715	69.7	19.2	27.6	876	23.5	2 656	28.1	45.9
1979	3 510	2 356	696	67.1	19.8	29.5	895	25.5	2 415	30.6	48.4
1978	3 452	2 340	694	67.8	20.1	29.7	850	24.6	2 396	30.6	47.8
1977	3 387	2 286	721	67.5	21.3	31.5	808	23.9	2 342	32.4	46.9
1976	3 315	2 239	749	67.5	22.6	33.5	803	24.2	2 291	34.2	50.4
1975	3 213	2 081	665	64.8	20.7	32.0	877	27.3	2 149	32.6	48.1
1974	3 105	2 083	555	67.1	17.9	26.6	780	25.1	2 145	27.5	44.8
1973	3 114	2 079	498	66.8	16.0	24.0	826	26.5	2 139	25.0	41.6
1972	2 986	1 992	540	66.7	18.1	27.1	782	26.2	2 044	28.0	42.0
1971	2 866	1 789	522	62.4	18.2	29.2	825	28.8	1 833	30.0	42.3
1970	2 692	1 602	416	59.5	15.5	26.0	897	33.3	1 635	26.7	39.4
Male											
2005	1 897	1 393	530	73.4	27.9	35.0	280	14.8	1 420	37.9	58.4
2004	1 852	1 341	479	72.4	25.9	35.7	331	17.9	1 363	36.1	60.9
2003	1 801	1 331	499	73.9	27.7	37.5	300	16.7	1 346	37.8	57.1
2002	1 843	1 354	475	73.5	25.8	35.1	311	16.9	1 372	35.6	56.1
2001	1 818	1 287	470	70.8	25.8	36.4	308	16.9	1 310	36.4	53.1
2000	1 885	1 389	470	73.7	24.9	33.8	329	17.4	1 409	34.1	53.5
1999	1 747	1 292	501	73.9	28.7	38.8	285	16.3	1 336	40.2	57.7
1998	1 724	1 163	445	67.5	25.8	38.2	354	20.5	1 186	38.5	57.5
1997	1 701	1 214	425	71.4	25.0	35.0	297	17.5	1 232	35.1	56.3
1996	1 682	1 199	422	71.3	25.1	35.2	292	17.4	1 225	35.8	53.7
1995	1 660	1 247	430	75.1	25.9	34.4	235	14.2	1 262	35.1	56.2
1994	1 733	1 277	440	73.7	25.4	34.5	303	17.5	1 293	35.3	57.9
1993r	1 703	1 240	387	72.8	22.7	31.2	266	15.6	1 247	31.4	50.1
1993	1 659	1 207	379	72.8	22.8	31.4	258	15.6	1 214	31.5	50.0
1992	1 676	1 211	356	72.3	21.2	29.4	259	15.5	1 226	29.7	49.4
1991	1 635	1 174	378	71.8	23.1	32.2	252	15.4	1 188	32.4	47.0
1990	1 634	1 240	426	75.9	26.1	34.4	223	13.6	1 260	35.1	48.8
1989	1 654	1 195	324	72.2	19.6	27.1	307	18.6	1 207	27.5	45.8
1988	1 653	1 189	297	71.9	18.0	25.0	312	18.9	1 205	25.1	42.5
1987	1 666	1 188	377	71.3	22.6	31.7	312	18.7	1 209	32.3	48.0
1986	1 687	1 220	349	72.3	20.7	28.6	300	17.8	1 239	29.1	44.4
1985	1 720	1 244	345	72.3	20.1	27.7	323	18.8	1 258	28.2	43.6
1984	1 811	1 272	367	70.2	20.3	28.9	362	20.2	1 295	29.6	45.2
1983	1 807	1 202	331	66.5	18.3	27.5	435	24.1	1 228	27.9	43.6
1982	1 786	1 171	331	65.6	18.5	28.3	458	25.6	1 188	28.6	44.5
1981	1 730	1 154	325	66.7	18.8	28.2	419	24.2	1 165	28.5	42.3
1980	1 690	1 115	293	66.0	17.3	26.3	440	26.0	1 141	26.9	44.1
1979	1 577	973	304	61.7	19.3	31.2	457	29.0	988	32.0	46.7
1978	1 554	956	305	61.5	19.6	31.9	451	29.0	981	32.4	49.3
1977	1 528	970	309	63.5	20.2	31.9	369	24.1	991	33.0	47.6
1976	1 503	936	331	62.3	22.0	35.4	393	26.1	952	35.9	50.3
1975	1 451	897	294	61.8	20.3	32.8	404	27.8	923	33.4	50.5
1974	1 396	919	280	65.8	20.1	30.5	346	24.8	941	31.1	47.3
1973	1 434	952	266	66.4	18.5	27.9	371	25.9	962	28.4	44.2
1972	1 373	870	287	63.4	20.9	33.0	373	27.2	897	34.0	47.4
1971	1 318	769	262	58.3	19.9	34.1	416	31.6	783	34.9	45.8
1970	1 220	668	192	54.8	15.7	28.7	436	35.7	684	29.5	41.4

r = Revised, controlled to 1990 census–based population estimates; previous 1993 data controlled to 1980 census–based population estimates.

Table A-13. Population Age 14 to 24 Years, by High School Graduation Status, College Enrollment, Attainment, Sex, Race, and Hispanic Origin, October 1970–2005—*Continued*

(Numbers in thousands, percent.)

Year, sex, race, and Hispanic origin	Population, age 18 to 24 years								High school graduates, age 14 to 24 years		
		High school graduates		Percent:			High school dropouts			Percent:	
	Total	Total students	Enrolled in college	High school graduates	Enrolled in college	High school graduates enrolled in college	Number	Percent	All graduates	Enrolled in college	Enrolled or completed some college
BLACK											
Female											
2005	2 067	1 745	767	84.4	37.1	44.9	232	11.2	1 793	44.0	67.5
2004	2 088	1 709	759	81.8	36.3	44.4	266	12.7	1 749	44.9	65.0
2003	2 035	1 618	726	79.5	35.7	44.9	245	12.0	1 652	45.1	66.8
2002	2 081	1 686	751	81.0	36.1	44.5	260	12.5	1 745	45.5	65.2
2001	2 098	1 729	736	82.4	35.1	42.7	232	11.0	1 785	42.7	63.3
2000	2 128	1 700	747	79.9	35.1	43.9	287	13.5	1 720	43.9	67.1
1999	2 080	1 619	644	77.9	31.0	39.8	327	15.7	1 650	39.6	62.6
1998	2 021	1 584	671	78.4	33.2	42.4	288	14.3	1 604	42.4	65.0
1997	1 949	1 511	659	77.5	33.8	43.6	314	16.1	1 529	43.1	63.0
1996	1 956	1 539	561	78.7	28.7	36.4	288	14.7	1 580	37.3	55.3
1995	1 965	1 541	558	78.4	28.4	36.2	287	14.6	1 566	36.3	59.5
1994	1 928	1 542	561	80.0	29.1	36.4	265	13.7	1 567	37.1	60.3
1993r	1 965	1 508	511	76.7	26.0	33.9	337	17.2	1 526	34.1	57.2
1993	1 857	1 425	484	76.7	26.1	34.0	319	17.2	1 441	34.1	57.1
1992	1 845	1 417	531	76.8	28.8	37.5	315	17.1	1 446	38.2	56.6
1991	1 869	1 455	450	77.8	24.1	30.9	296	15.8	1 468	31.4	45.2
1990	1 886	1 468	467	77.8	24.8	31.8	306	16.2	1 498	32.4	47.3
1989	1 905	1 511	511	79.3	26.8	33.8	277	14.5	1 541	34.7	51.8
1988	1 915	1 492	455	77.9	23.8	30.5	318	16.6	1 538	31.3	49.2
1987	1 937	1 550	445	80.0	23.0	28.7	298	15.4	1 579	29.4	48.9
1986	1 966	1 574	462	80.1	23.5	29.4	306	15.6	1 598	29.3	50.4
1985	1 996	1 565	389	78.4	19.5	24.9	332	16.6	1 592	25.1	44.0
1984	2 052	1 613	419	78.6	20.4	26.0	349	17.0	1 655	26.8	45.1
1983	2 058	1 539	411	74.8	20.0	26.7	398	19.3	1 561	27.5	46.3
1982	2 086	1 572	436	75.4	20.9	27.7	393	18.8	1 604	27.9	46.3
1981	2 040	1 520	424	74.5	20.7	27.8	402	19.6	1 554	28.8	46.6
1980	2 031	1 475	422	72.6	20.8	28.6	436	21.5	1 511	29.1	47.4
1979	1 934	1 383	392	71.5	20.3	28.3	439	22.7	1 426	29.7	49.8
1978	1 897	1 384	390	73.0	20.6	28.2	398	21.0	1 415	29.3	46.7
1977	1 859	1 317	413	70.8	22.2	31.4	409	23.0	1 354	31.9	46.2
1976	1 813	1 302	417	71.8	23.0	32.0	410	22.6	1 338	32.9	50.3
1975	1 761	1 182	372	67.1	21.1	31.5	473	26.9	1 224	32.0	46.4
1974	1 709	1 167	277	68.3	16.2	23.7	434	25.4	1 207	24.8	42.9
1973	1 681	1 125	231	66.9	13.7	20.5	456	27.1	1 177	22.2	39.4
1972	1 613	1 123	253	69.6	15.7	22.5	408	25.3	1 150	23.2	37.9
1971	1 547	1 019	259	65.9	16.7	25.4	409	26.4	1 049	26.4	39.8
1970	1 471	935	225	63.6	15.3	24.1	461	31.3	955	24.7	39.3
ASIAN[1]											
Both Sexes											
2005	1 145	1 072	693	93.6	60.5	74.9	34	3.0	1 098	65.1	87.0
2004	1 152	1 066	695	92.5	60.3	65.2	49	4.3	1 090	65.7	89.1
2003	1 144	1 030	693	90.1	60.6	67.3	56	4.9	1 046	67.7	88.2
2002	1 339	1 230	803	91.8	60.0	65.3	57	4.2	1 265	65.7	86.9
2001	1 312	1 197	794	91.2	60.5	66.5	47	3.6	1 218	66.5	87.6
2000	1 143	1 038	639	90.8	55.9	61.6	52	4.6	1 053	61.8	83.9
1999	1 130	1 019	626	90.2	55.4	61.4	58	5.1	1 035	62.0	85.5
Male											
2005	590	552	366	93.5	62.0	68.9	17	2.9	565	66.4	88.2
2004	586	549	373	93.7	63.6	67.9	15	2.5	561	68.4	88.2
2003	543	483	337	88.9	62.0	69.8	43	7.8	486	69.9	90.0
2002	707	637	417	90.0	59.0	65.5	38	5.4	652	65.3	86.7
2001	661	583	417	88.1	63.1	72.0	35	5.3	594	72.0	88.9
2000	571	521	337	91.1	58.9	64.7	34	6.0	527	64.7	85.6
1999	505	443	284	87.8	56.2	64.0	39	7.7	454	64.9	82.5
Female											
2005	555	521	327	93.8	58.9	81.4	17	3.0	533	63.7	85.8
2004	567	517	323	91.3	56.9	62.4	35	6.1	529	62.8	90.0
2003	601	547	356	91.2	59.3	65.1	13	2.2	561	65.9	86.7
2002	632	593	386	93.8	61.0	65.1	19	2.9	613	66.1	87.2
2001	651	614	377	94.3	57.9	61.3	12	1.8	625	61.3	86.3
2000	572	517	302	90.4	52.9	58.5	18	3.1	526	58.9	82.3
1999	626	576	342	92.1	54.7	59.4	19	3.1	582	59.7	87.8

[1]Data from before 2003 consist of respondents who identified themselves as "Asian or Pacific Islanders."
r = Revised, controlled to 1990 census–based population estimates; previous 1993 data controlled to 1980 census–based population estimates.

Table A-13. Population Age 14 to 24 Years, by High School Graduation Status, College Enrollment, Attainment, Sex, Race, and Hispanic Origin, October 1970–2005—*Continued*

(Numbers in thousands, percent.)

Year, sex, race, and Hispanic origin	Population, age 18 to 24 years								High school graduates, age 14 to 24 years		
	Total	High school graduates		Percent:			High school dropouts		All graduates	Percent:	
		Total students	Enrolled in college	High school graduates	Enrolled in college	High school graduates enrolled in college	Number	Percent		Enrolled in college	Enrolled or completed some college
HISPANIC[2]											
Both Sexes											
2005	4 898	3 230	1 215	66.0	24.8	32.4	1 335	27.3	3 280	38.0	57.3
2004	4 941	3 244	1 221	65.6	24.7	37.7	1 386	28.0	3 287	37.9	55.9
2003	4 754	3 096	1 115	65.1	23.5	36.0	1 353	28.4	3 135	36.0	56.5
2002	4 918	3 078	979	62.6	19.9	31.8	1 479	30.1	3 109	32.0	53.1
2001	4 892	3 031	1 035	62.0	21.1	34.2	1 548	31.7	3 068	34.2	52.8
2000	4 134	2 462	899	59.6	21.7	36.5	1 335	32.3	2 509	36.8	53.1
1999	3 953	2 325	739	58.8	18.7	31.8	1 340	33.9	2 359	31.7	49.6
1998	4 014	2 403	820	59.8	20.4	34.1	1 383	34.4	2 419	34.3	53.2
1997	3 606	2 236	806	62.0	22.4	36.0	1 103	30.6	2 302	37.1	54.3
1996	3 510	2 019	706	57.5	20.1	35.0	1 210	34.5	2 046	34.5	52.5
1995	3 603	2 112	745	58.6	20.7	35.3	1 250	34.7	2 142	35.7	55.8
1994	3 523	1 995	662	56.6	18.8	33.2	1 224	34.7	2 009	33.4	54.3
1993ʳ	3 363	2 049	728	60.9	21.6	35.5	1 103	32.8	2 081	35.8	55.6
1993	2 772	1 682	602	60.7	21.7	35.8	907	32.7	1 712	36.0	55.8
1992	2 754	1 579	586	57.3	21.3	37.1	936	33.9	1 603	37.6	55.0
1991	2 874	1 498	516	52.1	18.0	34.4	1 139	39.6	1 519	34.6	47.6
1990	2 749	1 498	435	54.5	15.8	29.0	1 025	37.3	1 523	29.4	44.7
1989	2 818	1 576	453	55.9	16.1	28.7	1 062	37.7	1 600	29.4	43.6
1988	2 642	1 458	450	55.2	17.0	30.9	1 046	39.6	1 481	31.3	47.0
1987	2 592	1 597	455	61.6	17.6	28.5	849	32.8	1 612	28.7	44.0
1986	2 514	1 507	458	59.9	18.2	30.4	864	34.4	1 535	30.9	45.6
1985	2 221	1 396	375	62.9	16.9	26.9	700	31.5	1 419	27.6	46.7
1984	2 018	1 212	362	60.1	17.9	29.9	691	34.2	1 223	30.0	46.0
1983	2 025	1 110	349	54.8	17.2	31.4	759	37.5	1 134	32.3	48.4
1982	2 001	1 153	337	57.6	16.8	29.2	740	37.0	1 173	30.0	47.3
1981	2 052	1 144	342	55.8	16.7	29.9	790	38.5	1 166	30.5	45.8
1980	2 033	1 099	327	54.1	16.1	29.8	820	40.3	1 117	30.1	47.3
1979	1 754	968	292	55.2	16.6	30.2	687	39.2	1 001	31.2	45.7
1978	1 672	935	254	55.9	15.2	27.2	656	39.2	965	28.0	43.2
1977	1 609	880	277	54.7	17.2	31.5	622	38.7	900	32.4	43.8
1976	1 551	862	309	55.6	19.9	35.8	566	36.5	891	36.3	48.9
1975	1 446	832	295	57.5	20.4	35.5	505	34.9	849	36.5	50.8
1974	1 506	842	272	55.9	18.1	32.3	558	37.1	858	33.1	47.8
1973	1 285	709	206	55.2	16.0	29.1	500	38.9	732	30.3	43.0
1972	1 338	694	179	51.9	13.4	25.8	541	40.4	709	27.2	36.7
Male											
2005	2 613	1 569	540	60.1	20.7	26.2	838	32.1	1 589	34.6	52.4
2004	2 648	1 597	574	60.3	21.7	36.0	888	33.5	1 614	35.9	53.0
2003	2 541	1 548	465	60.9	18.3	30.0	805	31.7	1 571	30.0	48.7
2002	2 707	1 562	439	57.7	16.2	28.1	914	33.8	1 572	28.1	48.4
2001	2 596	1 455	449	56.1	17.3	31.0	962	37.1	1 468	31.0	48.1
2000	2 171	1 172	401	54.0	18.5	34.2	800	36.8	1 197	34.5	50.8
1999	2 045	1 122	322	54.9	15.8	28.7	746	36.4	1 131	28.7	45.7
1998	2 109	1 146	346	54.3	16.4	30.2	838	39.7	1 153	30.0	47.2
1997	1 937	1 140	371	58.9	19.2	32.5	643	33.2	1 168	33.0	49.2
1996	1 815	994	300	54.8	16.5	30.2	657	36.2	1 005	30.6	48.8
1995	1 907	1 106	356	58.0	18.7	32.2	653	34.2	1 022	36.2	52.3
1994	1 896	1 021	312	53.8	16.5	30.6	685	36.1	1 026	30.7	52.7
1993ʳ	1 710	1 005	338	58.8	19.8	33.6	591	34.6	1 023	33.7	51.2
1993	1 354	786	266	58.1	19.6	33.8	470	34.7	803	33.9	51.1
1992	1 384	720	247	52.0	17.8	34.3	531	38.4	736	34.8	52.2
1991	1 503	719	211	47.8	14.0	29.3	668	44.4	728	29.7	42.2
1990	1 403	753	214	53.7	15.3	28.4	559	39.8	770	29.4	46.5
1989	1 439	756	211	52.5	14.7	27.9	580	40.3	767	28.2	42.7
1988	1 375	724	228	52.7	16.6	31.5	553	40.2	736	32.2	48.3
1987	1 337	795	247	59.5	18.5	31.1	461	34.5	803	31.1	45.1
1986	1 339	769	233	57.4	17.4	30.3	499	37.3	776	30.5	44.4
1985	1 132	659	168	58.2	14.8	25.5	405	35.8	675	26.4	44.9
1984	956	549	154	57.4	16.1	28.1	338	35.4	554	28.2	45.7
1983	968	476	152	49.2	15.7	31.9	396	40.9	489	33.1	47.4
1982	944	519	141	55.0	14.9	27.2	347	36.8	525	28.0	44.8
1981	988	498	164	50.4	16.6	32.9	428	43.3	506	33.6	48.6
1980	1 012	518	160	51.2	15.8	30.9	431	42.6	521	31.1	49.5
1979	837	454	153	54.2	18.3	33.7	328	39.2	469	34.3	49.5
1978	781	420	126	53.8	16.1	30.0	313	40.1	438	30.4	46.3
1977	754	396	139	52.5	18.4	35.1	295	39.1	404	35.9	46.5
1976	701	378	150	53.9	21.4	39.7	253	36.1	403	39.8	51.8
1975	678	383	145	56.5	21.4	37.9	221	32.6	390	37.9	55.4
1974	720	390	141	54.2	19.6	36.2	279	38.8	401	36.7	51.4
1973	625	348	105	55.7	16.8	30.2	228	36.5	361	32.1	45.4
1972	609	301	92	49.4	15.1	30.6	253	41.5	309	32.0	44.3

[2] May be of any race.
ʳ = Revised, controlled to 1990 census–based population estimates; previous 1993 data controlled to 1980 census–based population estimates.

Table A-13. Population Age 14 to 24 Years, by High School Graduation Status, College Enrollment, Attainment, Sex, Race, and Hispanic Origin, October 1970–2005—*Continued*

(Numbers in thousands, percent.)

Year, sex, race, and Hispanic origin	Population, age 18 to 24 years								High school graduates, age 14 to 24 years		
		High school graduates		Percent:			High school dropouts			Percent:	
	Total	Total students	Enrolled in college	High school graduates	Enrolled in college	High school graduates enrolled in college	Number	Percent	All graduates	Enrolled in college	Enrolled or completed some college
HISPANIC[2]											
Female											
2005	2 285	1 661	675	72.7	29.5	39.3	498	21.8	1 691	41.2	62.0
2004	2 293	1 647	647	71.8	28.2	39.3	498	21.7	1 673	39.8	58.6
2003	2 213	1 548	651	69.9	29.4	42.1	548	24.7	1 563	41.9	64.4
2002	2 211	1 516	540	68.6	24.4	35.6	565	25.6	1 537	35.9	57.9
2001	2 296	1 576	585	68.6	25.5	37.1	586	25.5	1 600	37.1	57.0
2000	1 963	1 290	498	65.7	25.4	38.6	535	27.3	1 312	38.9	55.2
1999	1 908	1 203	417	63.0	21.8	34.7	593	31.1	1 228	34.4	53.3
1998	1 906	1 257	474	66.0	24.9	37.7	545	28.6	1 266	38.2	58.7
1997	1 669	1 097	436	65.7	26.1	39.7	460	27.6	1 135	41.4	59.6
1996	1 694	1 026	406	60.6	24.0	39.6	554	32.7	1 043	40.4	56.0
1995	1 696	1 011	389	59.6	22.9	38.4	598	35.4	1 022	38.6	59.6
1994	1 628	973	350	59.8	21.5	36.0	539	33.1	983	36.2	55.9
1993r	1 652	1 045	390	63.3	23.6	37.3	510	30.9	1 059	37.8	60.1
1993	1 418	895	336	63.1	23.7	37.5	439	31.0	907	38.0	60.4
1992	1 369	860	339	62.8	24.8	39.4	405	29.6	867	39.9	57.4
1991	1 372	780	305	56.9	22.2	39.1	473	34.5	791	39.2	52.5
1990	1 346	745	221	55.3	16.4	29.7	465	34.5	753	29.5	43.0
1989	1 377	823	244	59.8	17.7	29.6	482	35.0	836	30.5	44.5
1988	1 267	736	224	58.1	17.7	30.4	492	38.8	747	30.5	45.8
1987	1 256	801	208	63.8	16.6	26.0	387	30.8	808	26.4	43.2
1986	1 175	739	226	62.9	19.2	30.6	365	31.1	759	31.4	46.8
1985	1 091	734	205	67.3	18.8	27.9	295	27.0	743	28.4	48.0
1984	1 061	661	207	62.3	19.5	31.3	353	33.2	667	31.5	46.6
1983	1 057	634	198	60.0	18.7	31.2	363	34.3	644	31.8	49.7
1982	1 056	634	196	60.0	18.6	30.9	393	37.2	648	31.8	49.2
1981	1 064	646	178	60.7	16.7	27.6	362	34.0	662	28.2	43.4
1980	1 021	579	165	56.7	16.2	28.5	389	38.1	595	29.1	45.4
1979	917	516	140	56.3	15.3	27.1	358	39.0	534	28.1	42.3
1978	891	516	128	57.9	14.4	24.8	343	38.5	528	25.8	40.0
1977	855	483	139	56.5	16.3	28.8	326	38.1	495	29.7	41.6
1976	850	483	160	56.8	18.8	33.1	313	36.8	489	33.5	46.5
1975	769	449	150	58.4	19.5	33.4	283	36.8	460	34.8	46.7
1974	786	451	129	57.4	16.4	28.6	280	35.6	459	29.2	43.4
1973	658	362	102	55.0	15.5	28.2	272	41.3	372	28.8	41.1
1972	728	394	88	54.1	12.1	22.3	288	39.6	402	23.6	31.1
WHITE ALONE OR IN COMBINATION											
Both Sexes											
2005	22 345	18 583	8 721	83.2	39.0	50.1	2 539	11.4	18 818	47.0	70.0
2004	22 411	18 663	8 544	83.3	38.1	45.8	2 639	11.8	18 868	46.0	69.0
2003	22 029	18 335	8 358	83.2	37.9	45.6	2 558	11.6	18 565	45.6	69.0
Male											
2005	11 394	9 086	4 018	79.7	35.3	43.5	1 519	13.3	9 193	44.2	60.0
2004	11 371	9 227	3 956	81.1	34.8	42.9	1 548	13.6	9 296	43.1	64.4
2003	11 147	8 967	3 815	80.4	34.2	42.5	1 493	13.4	9 070	42.6	65.1
Female											
2005	10 952	9 497	4 702	86.7	42.9	57.1	1 020	9.3	9 625	49.7	73.9
2004	11 040	9 436	4 588	85.5	41.6	48.6	1 091	9.9	9 572	48.8	73.5
2003	10 882	9 367	4 543	86.1	41.7	48.5	1 065	9.8	9 495	48.5	72.7
BLACK ALONE OR IN COMBINATION											
Both Sexes											
2005	4 158	3 303	1 371	79.4	33.0	31.7	530	12.7	3 378	41.5	63.5
2004	4 115	3 190	1 318	77.5	32.0	41.3	620	15.1	3 253	41.8	63.5
2003	4 016	3 091	1 285	77.0	32.0	41.6	563	14.0	3 141	41.9	62.0
Male											
2005	1 988	1 466	557	73.7	28.0	42.5	290	14.6	1 492	37.9	58.2
2004	1 951	1 418	521	72.7	26.7	36.7	347	17.8	1 442	37.0	61.3
2003	1 868	1 382	525	74.0	28.1	38.0	311	16.6	1 397	38.3	57.4
Female											
2005	2 170	1 837	814	84.7	37.5	21.2	240	11.1	1 885	44.3	67.7
2004	2 164	1 772	797	81.9	36.8	45.0	272	12.6	1 811	45.5	65.3
2003	2 148	1 708	760	79.5	35.4	44.5	252	11.7	1 744	44.7	65.7

[2]May be of any race.
r = Revised, controlled to 1990 census–based population estimates; previous 1993 data controlled to 1980 census–based population estimates.

Table A-13. Population Age 14 to 24 Years, by High School Graduation Status, College Enrollment, Attainment, Sex, Race, and Hispanic Origin, October 1970–2005—*Continued*

(Numbers in thousands, percent.)

Year, sex, race, and Hispanic origin	Population, age 18 to 24 years								High school graduates, age 14 to 24 years		
	Total	High school graduates		Percent:			High school dropouts		All graduates	Percent:	
		Total students	Enrolled in college	High school graduates	Enrolled in college	High school graduates enrolled in college	Number	Percent		Enrolled in college	Enrolled or completed some college
ASIAN ALONE OR IN COMBINATION											
Both Sexes											
2005	1 299	1 214	773	93.5	59.5	63.7	38	2.9	1 243	64.2	86.0
2004	1 263	1 167	750	92.5	59.4	64.3	53	4.2	1 191	64.6	87.6
2003	1 280	1 162	774	90.8	60.5	66.6	56	4.4	1 184	66.9	87.8
Male											
2005	653	603	392	92.4	59.9	65.0	20	3.1	621	65.1	86.3
2004	634	588	398	92.8	62.7	67.7	18	2.9	601	68.0	87.8
2003	609	545	370	89.5	60.8	67.9	43	7.1	551	67.7	88.7
Female											
2005	645	610	381	94.6	59.1	62.5	17	2.7	622	63.3	85.8
2004	628	579	352	92.1	56.0	60.8	35	5.5	591	61.2	87.5
2003	671	617	404	92.0	60.2	65.5	13	1.9	633	66.3	87.0

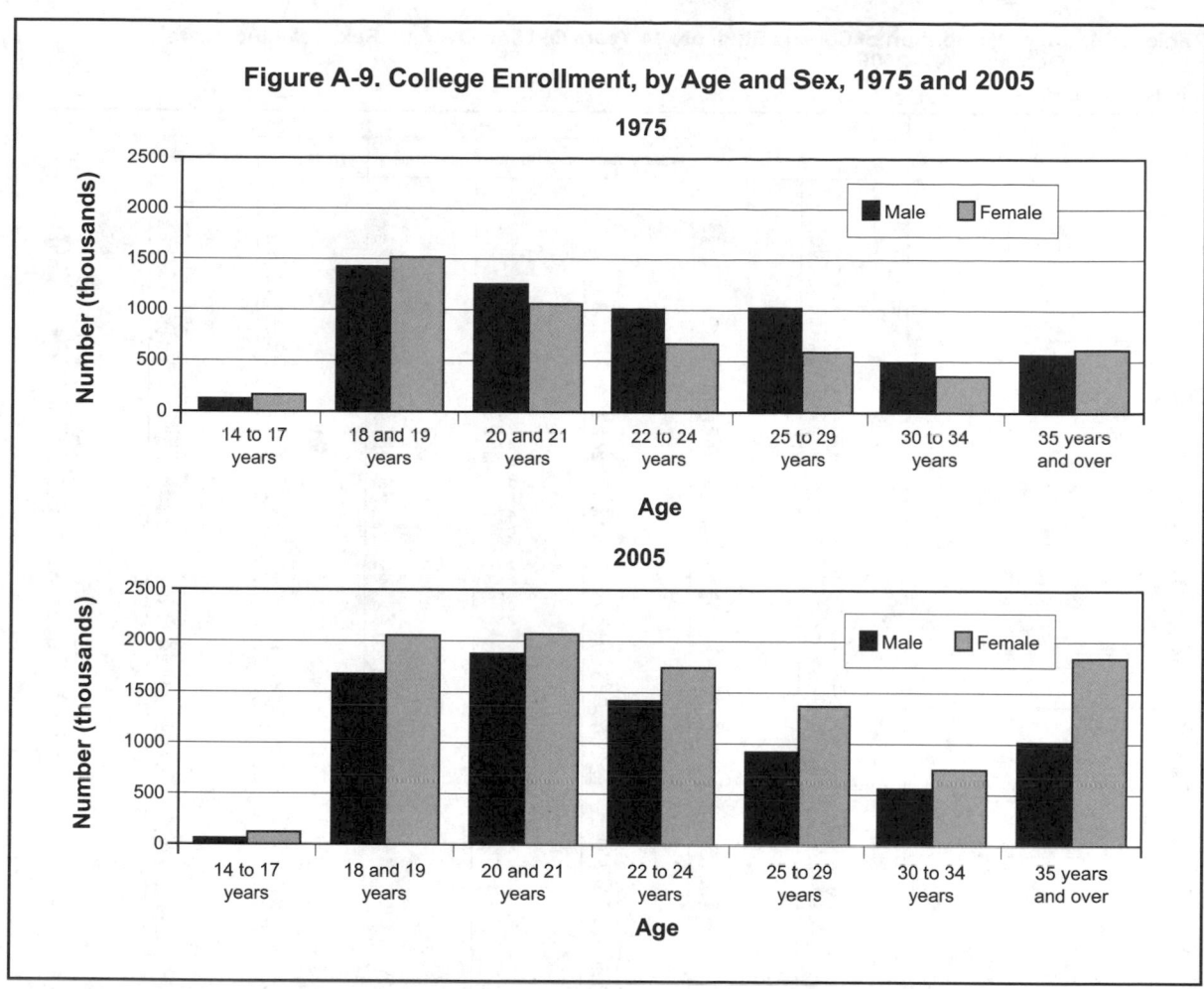

Figure A-9. College Enrollment, by Age and Sex, 1975 and 2005

In 2005, the number of female college students continued its trend of exceeding the number of male students, just as it had in every year since 1979. In 2005, women made up nearly 57 percent of all college students. In contrast, fewer than 46 percent of all college students were women in 1975. The greatest disparity was among Black college students; over 62 percent were women. Asians were the only race or ethnic group to have a higher enrollment rate for males than for females. However, even among Asians, the ratio was fairly even. Approximately 51 percent of Asian college students were male and 49 percent were female. Women also accounted for 59 percent of all graduate students in 2005. (Tables A-14 and A-15)

Table A-14. Age Distribution of College Students 14 Years Old and Over, by Sex, Selected Years, October 1947–2005

(Numbers in thousands.)

Year, race, and Hispanic origin	Total enrollment	Both sexes						
		14 to 17 years	18 and 19 years	20 and 21 years	22 to 24 years	25 to 29 years	30 to 34 years	35 years and over
All Races								
2005	17 472	181	3 727	3 945	3 162	2 291	1 309	2 857
2004	17 383	198	3 685	3 777	3 149	2 403	1 287	2 884
2003	16 638	150	3 512	3 533	3 320	2 164	1 330	2 630
2002	16 497	195	3 581	3 525	2 927	2 093	1 308	2 867
2001	15 873	138	3 478	3 421	2 731	2 084	1 337	2 685
2000	15 314	149	3 599	3 169	2 683	1 962	1 244	2 507
1999	15 203	151	3 520	3 120	2 620	1 940	1 155	2 697
1998	15 546	123	3 670	3 092	2 561	2 148	1 266	2 685
1997	15 436	171	3 362	3 143	2 699	2 154	1 116	2 791
1996	15 226	237	3 309	2 907	2 551	2 215	1 228	2 778
1995	14 715	158	3 101	2 940	2 498	2 143	1 206	2 669
1994[1]	15 022	150	3 051	3 028	2 650	2 026	1 393	2 725
1993r	14 394	130	3 070	2 892	2 668	1 914	1 226	2 493
1993	13 898	123	2 926	2 734	2 533	1 867	1 227	2 488
1992	14 035	205	2 892	2 938	2 512	1 829	1 296	2 364
1991	14 057	132	2 929	2 939	2 304	1 983	1 302	2 468
1990	13 621	178	3 019	2 767	2 178	1 927	1 235	2 319
1989	13 180	183	3 066	2 570	2 168	1 889	1 192	2 112
1988	13 116	182	3 046	2 681	2 064	1 735	1 228	2 179
1987	12 719	239	3 045	2 642	2 006	1 826	1 159	1 802
1986	12 651	201	2 967	2 374	2 136	1 860	1 245	1 867
1985	12 524	262	2 907	2 616	2 014	1 884	1 180	1 661
1984	12 304	253	2 867	2 597	2 127	1 857	1 158	1 445
1983	12 320	260	2 940	2 495	2 042	1 921	1 167	1 495
1982	12 308	254	2 929	2 689	2 060	1 859	1 129	1 389
1981	12 127	232	3 044	2 545	1 986	1 717	1 211	1 393
1980	11 387	249	2 933	2 423	1 870	1 641	1 062	1 207
1979	11 380	311	2 844	2 353	1 794	1 679	996	1 402
1978	11 141	274	2 899	2 298	1 798	1 619	950	1 303
1977	11 546	274	2 913	2 430	1 799	1 809	992	1 329
1976	11 139	281	2 937	2 398	1 846	1 686	803	1 189
1975	10 880	293	2 943	2 313	1 679	1 616	853	1 183
1974	9 852	309	2 597	2 192	1 527	1 482	720	1 025
1973	8 966	295	2 517	2 073	1 465	1 278	551	787
1972	9 096	295	2 680	2 116	1 461	1 229	531	783
1971	8 087	284	2 726	1 997	1 487	1 067	527	. . .
1970	7 413	260	2 594	1 857	1 354	939	410	. . .
1969	7 435	242	2 601	1 945	1 294	918	435	. . .
1968	6 801	281	2 501	1 826	1 029	790	373	. . .
1967	6 401	239	2 286	1 816	998	707	356	. . .
1966	6 085	254	2 440	1 472	987	679	254	. . .
1965	5 675	264	2 215	1 326	940	614	316	. . .
1964	4 643	291	1 616	1 287	670	523	256	. . .
1963	4 336	180	1 504	1 212	717	482	241	. . .
1962	4 208	233	1 612	996	630	486	251	. . .
1961	3 731	213	1 470	892	507	437	212	. . .
1960	3 570	222	1 299	790	509	491	259	. . .
1959	3 340	210	1 175	739	489	503	224	. . .
1958	3 242	167	1 114	[2]1 221	. . .	534	206	. . .
1957	3 138	176	989	[2]1 236	. . .	553	184	. . .
1956	2 883	167	934	[2]1 105	. . .	494	183	. . .
1955	2 379	147	745	[2]931	. . .	406	150	. . .
1950	2 175	180	733	[2]939	. . .	324	. . .	. . .
1947	2 311	188	620	[2]1 088	. . .	321	94	. . .

[1]Prior to 1994, total enrollment does not include the population age 35 years and over.
[2]Includes students age 20 to 24 years.
r = Revised, controlled to 1990 census–based population estimates; previous 1993 data controlled to 1980 census–based population estimates.
. . . = Not available.

Table A-14. Age Distribution of College Students 14 Years Old and Over, by Sex, Selected Years, October 1947–2005—*Continued*

(Numbers in thousands.)

Year, race, and Hispanic origin	Male							
	Total enrollment	14 to 17 years	18 and 19 years	20 and 21 years	22 to 24 years	25 to 29 years	30 to 34 years	35 years and over
All Races								
2005	7 539	62	1 675	1 878	1 420	923	562	1 019
2004	7 575	75	1 610	1 811	1 444	1 068	533	1 033
2003	7 318	61	1 568	1 551	1 578	982	607	970
2002	7 240	80	1 635	1 640	1 354	918	542	1 071
2001	6 875	54	1 570	1 579	1 287	917	559	908
2000	6 682	61	1 570	1 472	1 300	844	517	918
1999	6 956	78	1 648	1 525	1 224	911	547	1 023
1998	6 905	48	1 667	1 517	1 219	979	521	953
1997	6 843	59	1 561	1 521	1 292	1 052	457	899
1996	6 820	97	1 489	1 379	1 319	1 038	485	1 013
1995	6 703	68	1 431	1 423	1 235	1 008	553	985
1994¹	6 764	65	1 416	1 414	1 322	972	617	958
1993ʳ	6 599	55	1 407	1 405	1 425	892	534	880
1003	6 324	52	1 337	1 312	1 345	872	534	873
1992	6 192	97	1 325	1 344	1 243	845	547	789
1991	6 439	49	1 326	1 390	1 238	1 018	587	832
1990	6 192	86	1 443	1 364	1 115	910	502	772
1989	5 950	73	1 422	1 228	1 067	926	517	716
1988	5 950	58	1 365	1 295	1 110	835	560	727
1987	6 030	116	1 483	1 350	1 034	921	500	625
1986	5 957	82	1 421	1 161	1 120	968	577	628
1985	5 906	131	1 349	1 313	1 087	942	522	561
1984	5 989	91	1 373	1 337	1 219	965	527	476
1983	6 010	108	1 340	1 310	1 170	1 055	521	506
1982	5 899	112	1 376	1 346	1 115	968	492	490
1981	5 825	96	1 450	1 239	1 144	909	533	453
1980	5 430	96	1 369	1 246	989	853	472	405
1979	5 480	129	1 341	1 192	975	893	463	487
1978	5 580	106	1 391	1 202	1 028	922	474	457
1977	5 889	112	1 396	1 280	1 036	1 035	511	520
1976	5 785	105	1 391	1 209	1 073	1 067	451	489
1975	5 911	128	1 426	1 256	1 011	1 025	496	569
1974	5 402	145	1 262	1 206	943	951	420	476
1973	5 048	121	1 293	1 130	937	867	329	371
1972	5 218	141	1 366	1 170	998	848	330	365
1971	4 050	120	1 444	1 090	1 065	787	334	. . .
1970	4 401	130	1 346	1 083	902	684	256	. . .
1969	4 448	120	1 397	1 112	883	671	265	. . .
1968	4 124	134	1 357	1 093	702	603	236	. . .
1967	3 841	96	1 198	1 066	710	524	239	. . .
1966	3 749	105	1 355	899	722	494	174	. . .
1965	3 503	113	1 218	804	699	458	211	. . .
1964	2 888	165	866	769	510	396	182	. . .
1963	2 742	99	796	734	574	365	174	. . .
1962	2 742	125	891	617	508	406	195	. . .
1961	2 356	84	834	554	393	337	154	. . .
1960	2 339	99	734	503	411	399	193	. . .
1959	2 187	92	651	501	355	422	166	. . .
1958	2 129	73	621	²850	. . .	439	146	. . .
1957	2 028	77	538	²827	. . .	459	127	. . .
1956	1 932	77	512	²781	. . .	429	133	. . .
1955	1 579	57	432	²647	. . .	337	107	. . .
1950	1 474	74	395	²692	. . .	314	. . .	. . .
1947	1 687	87	343	²872	. . .	301	84	. . .

¹Prior to 1994, total enrollment does not include the population age 35 years and over.
²Includes students age 20 to 24 years.
ʳ = Revised, controlled to 1990 census–based population estimates; previous 1993 data controlled to 1980 census–based population estimates.
. . . = Not available.

Table A-14. Age Distribution of College Students 14 Years Old and Over, by Sex, Selected Years, October 1947–2005—*Continued*

(Numbers in thousands.)

Year, race, and Hispanic origin	Female							
	Total enrollment	14 to 17 years	18 and 19 years	20 and 21 years	22 to 24 years	25 to 29 years	30 to 34 years	35 years and over
All Races								
2005	9 934	119	2 052	2 067	1 742	1 368	747	1 838
2004	9 808	123	2 074	1 966	1 705	1 335	753	1 850
2003	9 319	89	1 944	1 982	1 742	1 181	723	1 660
2002	9 258	116	1 946	1 885	1 573	1 175	766	1 797
2001	8 998	84	1 907	1 841	1 444	1 167	778	1 776
2000	8 631	88	2 029	1 697	1 383	1 118	728	1 589
1999	8 247	73	1 872	1 595	1 396	1 029	608	1 674
1998	8 641	74	2 003	1 574	1 342	1 170	745	1 732
1997	8 593	112	1 801	1 622	1 406	1 102	658	1 892
1996	8 406	140	1 821	1 528	1 233	1 177	743	1 765
1995	8 013	90	1 671	1 518	1 263	1 135	653	1 684
1994[1]	8 258	85	1 635	1 613	1 328	1 054	776	1 766
1993r	7 795	75	1 663	1 487	1 243	1 022	692	1 613
1993	7 574	71	1 588	1 422	1 189	995	693	1 616
1992	7 844	107	1 566	1 594	1 269	984	748	1 575
1991	7 618	83	1 603	1 549	1 066	965	715	1 636
1990	7 429	91	1 576	1 403	1 063	1 017	732	1 546
1989	7 231	110	1 643	1 342	1 100	964	675	1 396
1988	7 166	124	1 682	1 386	953	900	668	1 452
1987	6 689	123	1 562	1 292	972	905	659	1 176
1986	6 694	120	1 546	1 213	1 016	892	667	1 240
1985	6 618	129	1 559	1 303	926	941	658	1 100
1984	6 315	161	1 494	1 260	908	892	630	970
1983	6 310	153	1 600	1 185	872	865	645	989
1982	6 410	141	1 553	1 343	945	891	637	900
1981	6 303	136	1 594	1 305	842	808	677	940
1980	5 957	153	1 565	1 178	882	788	590	802
1979	5 900	183	1 503	1 161	818	786	533	914
1978	5 559	168	1 507	1 096	770	697	476	845
1977	5 657	162	1 517	1 151	763	774	481	809
1976	5 354	176	1 546	1 189	773	619	352	700
1975	4 969	164	1 517	1 058	668	590	357	614
1974	4 449	165	1 335	986	584	531	300	548
1973	3 918	174	1 224	944	528	411	222	416
1972	3 877	153	1 314	946	464	381	200	418
1971	3 236	154	1 281	906	423	280	192	. . .
1970	3 013	130	1 248	774	452	255	154	. . .
1969	2 987	122	1 204	833	411	247	171	. . .
1968	2 677	147	1 144	733	328	187	138	. . .
1967	2 560	143	1 088	749	280	183	117	. . .
1966	2 337	149	1 085	573	265	185	80	. . .
1965	2 172	151	997	522	241	156	105	. . .
1964	1 755	126	750	518	160	127	74	. . .
1963	1 594	81	708	478	143	117	67	. . .
1962	1 466	108	721	379	122	80	56	. . .
1961	1 375	129	636	338	114	100	58	. . .
1960	1 231	123	565	287	98	92	66	. . .
1959	1 153	118	524	238	134	81	58	. . .
1958	1 113	94	493	[2]371	. . .	95	60	. . .
1957	1 110	99	451	[2]409	. . .	94	57	. . .
1956	951	90	422	[2]324	. . .	65	50	. . .
1955	800	90	313	[2]285	. . .	69	43	. . .
1950	701	106	338	[2]247	. . .	10	. . .	. . .
1947	624	101	277	[2]216	. . .	20	10	. . .

[1]Prior to 1994, total enrollment does not include the population age 35 years and over.
[2]Includes students age 20 to 24 years.
r = Revised, controlled to 1990 census–based population estimates; previous 1993 data controlled to 1980 census–based population estimates.
. . . = Not available.

Table A-14. Age Distribution of College Students 14 Years Old and Over, by Sex, Selected Years, October 1947–2005—*Continued*

(Numbers in thousands.)

Year, race, and Hispanic origin	Both sexes							
	Total enrollment	14 to 17 years	18 and 19 years	20 and 21 years	22 to 24 years	25 to 29 years	30 to 34 years	35 years and over
White								
2005	13 466	116	2 972	3 176	2 350	1 708	939	2 205
2004	13 381	134	2 946	3 016	2 389	1 776	974	2 146
2003	12 870	100	2 833	2 796	2 521	1 585	960	2 075
2002	12 781	109	2 891	2 810	2 220	1 582	933	2 236
2001	12 208	88	2 755	2 774	2 019	1 514	956	2 103
2000	11 999	117	2 914	2 590	2 062	1 433	906	1 978
1999	12 053	87	2 849	2 519	2 074	1 474	870	2 173
1998	12 401	93	2 994	2 537	2 010	1 604	964	2 199
1997	12 442	127	2 792	2 602	2 101	1 666	856	2 289
1996	12 189	167	2 731	2 362	2 030	1 704	940	2 254
1995	12 021	116	2 577	2 437	1 997	1 745	941	2 208
1994[1]	12 222	101	2 568	2 459	2 091	1 592	1 143	2 267
1993[r]	11 735	103	2 566	2 356	2 152	1 507	1 003	2 049
1993	11 434	98	2 456	2 243	2 064	1 490	1 015	2 068
1992	11 710	158	2 419	2 466	2 031	1 512	1 070	2 053
1991	11 686	104	2 487	2 449	1 877	1 598	1 063	2 107
1990	11 488	132	2 548	2 341	1 746	1 638	1 060	2 023
1989	11 243	147	2 648	2 170	1 813	1 611	986	1 868
1988	11 140	137	2 639	2 270	1 750	1 425	1 023	1 896
1987	10 731	194	2 564	2 254	1 665	1 483	985	1 584
1986	10 707	173	2 549	2 015	1 743	1 580	1 037	1 609
1985	10 781	229	2 539	2 257	1 704	1 590	1 014	1 448
1984	10 520	209	2 541	2 206	1 779	1 566	967	1 252
1983	10 565	214	2 597	2 161	1 705	1 603	961	1 324
1982	10 551	216	2 549	2 348	1 697	1 581	938	1 222
1981	10 353	197	2 639	2 239	1 671	1 390	1 027	1 190
1980	9 925	212	2 578	2 131	1 625	1 413	915	1 051
1979	9 956	256	2 498	2 079	1 543	1 474	859	1 247
1978	9 661	229	2 553	1 993	1 531	1 399	808	1 148
1977	9 962	227	2 579	2 099	1 531	1 550	827	1 149
1976	9 679	237	2 577	2 108	1 591	1 458	673	1 035
1975	9 546	252	2 613	2 042	1 461	1 410	737	1 031
1974	8 689	271	2 308	1 940	1 341	1 308	613	908
1973	8 014	253	2 281	1 865	1 292	1 152	481	690
1972	7 458	259	2 411	1 917	1 296	1 119	456	. . .
1971	7 273	251	2 485	1 758	1 361	966	463	. . .
1970	6 759	230	2 361	1 684	1 260	853	371	. . .
1969	6 827	222	2 377	1 762	1 208	855	404	. . .
1968	6 255	251	2 284	1 691	954	741	333	. . .
1967	5 905	220	2 105	1 688	915	646	329	. . .
1966	5 708	233	2 293	[2]2 313	. . .	[3]860	. . .	. . .
1965	5 317	233	2 074	[2]2 139	. . .	[3]871	. . .	. . .
1964	4 337	257	1 519	[2]1 850	. . .	[3]711	. . .	. . .
1963	4 050	171	1 391	[2]1 817	. . .	[3]671	. . .	. . .
1962	3 934	217	1 509	[2]1 517	. . .	[3]691	. . .	. . .
1961	3 498	204	1 388	[2]1 296	. . .	[3]610	. . .	. . .
1960	3 342	214	1 211	[2]1 209	. . .	[3]709	. . .	. . .
1959	3 118	193	1 101	[2]1 134	. . .	[3]690	. . .	. . .
1958	3 030	155	1 044	[2]1 136	. . .	[3]695	. . .	. . .
1957	2 932	161	921	[2]1 165	. . .	[3]685	. . .	. . .
1956	2 687	152	869	[2]1 025	. . .	[3]641	. . .	. . .
1955	2 224	125	715	[2]880	. . .	[3]504	. . .	. . .
Non-Hispanic White								
2005	11 715	93	2 618	2 769	2 006	1 445	806	1 977
2004	11 571	111	2 596	2 618	2 014	1 513	814	1 905
2003	11 295	90	2 486	2 419	2 225	1 371	832	1 872
2002	11 236	97	2 549	2 525	1 931	1 317	812	2 007
2001	10 602	74	2 383	2 450	1 732	1 283	827	1 854
2000	10 636	92	2 580	2 333	1 796	1 275	770	1 790
1999	10 818	80	2 574	2 324	1 837	1 283	755	1 965
1998	11 109	84	2 715	2 281	1 760	1 408	840	2 020
1997	11 246	81	2 491	2 361	1 876	1 504	779	2 153
1996	11 034	147	2 504	2 156	1 788	1 514	834	2 091
1995	11 024	103	2 372	2 226	1 796	1 618	859	2 051
1994[1]	11 178	93	2 362	2 255	1 904	1 444	1 018	2 101
1993	10 554	83	2 270	2 026	1 924	1 367	923	1 960

[1]Prior to 1994, total enrollment does not include the population age 35 years and over.
[2]Includes students age 20 to 24 years.
[3]Includes students age 25 to 34 years.
r = Revised, controlled to 1990 census–based population estimates; previous 1993 data controlled to 1980 census–based population estimates.
. . . = Not available.

Table A-14. Age Distribution of College Students 14 Years Old and Over, by Sex, Selected Years, October 1947–2005—*Continued*

(Numbers in thousands.)

Year, race, and Hispanic origin	Male							
	Total enrollment	14 to 17 years	18 and 19 years	20 and 21 years	22 to 24 years	25 to 29 years	30 to 34 years	35 years and over
White								
2005	5 843	38	1 343	1 488	1 092	685	420	777
2004	5 944	49	1 308	1 437	1 110	837	421	782
2003	5 714	48	1 258	1 236	1 232	723	435	783
2002	5 719	57	1 329	1 306	1 066	712	394	855
2001	5 383	36	1 273	1 305	943	693	401	731
2000	5 311	47	1 289	1 225	1 008	662	367	713
1999	5 562	32	1 335	1 226	1 026	715	414	804
1998	5 602	30	1 376	1 256	1 002	746	396	795
1997	5 552	48	1 314	1 289	1 030	802	345	725
1996	5 453	70	1 223	1 117	1 079	797	357	811
1995	5 535	44	1 195	1 201	1 002	857	432	804
1994[1]	5 524	44	1 212	1 140	1 054	749	512	815
1993[r]	5 403	44	1 157	1 196	1 145	705	451	705
1993	5 222	41	1 103	1 120	1 090	699	457	711
1992	5 210	82	1 102	1 162	1 027	689	471	678
1991	5 304	41	1 112	1 146	1 012	809	480	703
1990	5 235	63	1 218	1 151	923	782	434	665
1989	5 136	63	1 253	1 070	900	789	438	623
1988	5 078	50	1 194	1 114	952	685	470	613
1987	5 104	97	1 260	1 156	873	740	436	541
1986	5 074	69	1 254	982	932	835	475	528
1985	5 103	120	1 176	1 137	941	812	449	468
1984	5 111	73	1 224	1 143	1 039	796	434	402
1983	5 162	87	1 197	1 149	989	875	421	444
1982	5 077	95	1 189	1 188	931	831	415	428
1981	5 010	86	1 259	1 104	977	745	448	391
1980	4 804	79	1 232	1 114	878	735	400	366
1979	4 823	110	1 192	1 058	854	788	398	423
1978	4 913	90	1 239	1 056	900	810	413	405
1977	5 156	91	1 272	1 124	890	907	433	439
1976	5 084	89	1 244	1 073	933	936	382	427
1975	5 263	111	1 283	1 134	909	911	426	489
1974	4 782	128	1 143	1 067	825	855	350	414
1973	4 218	111	1 177	1 017	838	789	286	. . .
1972	4 395	120	1 242	1 062	891	784	296	. . .
1971	4 407	117	1 328	964	992	712	293	. . .
1970	4 066	117	1 251	995	850	622	231	. . .
1969	4 146	110	1 298	1 021	827	637	252	. . .
1968	3 843	117	1 262	1 021	666	564	213	. . .
1967	3 560	88	1 097	998	666	494	217	. . .
1966	3 536	93	1 281	[2]1 541	. . .	[3]621	. . .	. . .
1965	3 326	104	1 152	[2]1 441	. . .	[3]629	. . .	. . .
1964	2 720	147	823	[2]1 226	. . .	[3]524	. . .	. . .
1963	2 593	94	746	[2]1 246	. . .	[3]507	. . .	. . .
1962	2 586	120	836	[2]1 066	. . .	[3]564	. . .	. . .
1961	2 208	79	786	[2]883	. . .	[3]460	. . .	. . .
1960	2 214	97	691	[2]859	. . .	[3]567	. . .	. . .
1959	2 067	88	620	[2]798	. . .	[3]561	. . .	. . .
1958	1 999	68	577	[2]802	. . .	[3]552	. . .	. . .
1957	1 938	68	510	[2]797	. . .	[3]563	. . .	. . .
1956	1 808	68	474	[2]733	. . .	[3]533	. . .	. . .
1955	1 495	47	418	[2]621	. . .	[3]409	. . .	. . .
Non-Hispanic White								
2005	5 114	30	1 193	1 308	928	590	373	692
2004	5 146	44	1 150	1 242	930	710	372	698
2003	5 067	41	1 115	1 082	1 094	639	386	710
2002	5 060	57	1 179	1 162	947	596	350	770
2001	4 691	30	1 131	1 170	794	587	348	632
2000	4 716	35	1 138	1 109	890	603	296	646
1999	5 033	30	1 214	1 141	929	627	368	722
1998	5 084	30	1 280	1 123	897	668	348	738
1997	5 024	33	1 184	1 161	930	732	314	669
1996	4 961	61	1 136	1 039	955	727	303	740
1995	5 068	36	1 111	1 103	892	799	380	749
1994[1]	5 053	41	1 132	1 039	955	689	457	741
1993	4 838	36	1 038	1 016	1 017	663	399	670

[1]Prior to 1994, total enrollment does not include the population age 35 years and over.
[2]Includes students age 20 to 24 years.
[3]Includes students age 25 to 34 years.
r = Revised, controlled to 1990 census–based population estimates; previous 1993 data controlled to 1980 census–based population estimates.
. . . = Not available.

Table A-14. Age Distribution of College Students 14 Years Old and Over, by Sex, Selected Years, October 1947–2005—*Continued*

(Numbers in thousands.)

Year, race, and Hispanic origin	Female							
	Total enrollment	14 to 17 years	18 and 19 years	20 and 21 years	22 to 24 years	25 to 29 years	30 to 34 years	35 years and over
White								
2005	7 624	79	1 629	1 688	1 258	1 024	519	1 428
2004	7 438	86	1 638	1 579	1 279	939	553	1 364
2003	7 155	53	1 575	1 560	1 289	862	525	1 291
2002	7 062	52	1 562	1 504	1 154	870	539	1 381
2001	6 826	52	1 481	1 468	1 077	820	555	1 372
2000	6 689	70	1 625	1 365	1 054	770	539	1 266
1999	6 491	55	1 513	1 296	1 053	760	455	1 358
1998	6 799	63	1 618	1 281	1 008	858	567	1 405
1997	6 890	79	1 479	1 313	1 071	864	511	1 573
1996	6 735	97	1 508	1 246	951	906	583	1 443
1995	6 486	72	1 383	1 237	995	887	508	1 404
1994[1]	6 698	57	1 357	1 320	1 037	844	631	1 453
1993r	6 331	59	1 409	1 160	1 007	802	552	1 344
1993	6 212	57	1 353	1 123	974	791	558	1 357
1992	6 499	76	1 317	1 303	1 005	823	599	1 376
1991	6 382	63	1 375	1 304	865	789	583	1 404
1990	6 253	69	1 331	1 190	823	856	627	1 358
1989	6 107	84	1 395	1 101	913	822	548	1 245
1988	6 063	87	1 445	1 156	798	740	554	1 283
1987	5 627	97	1 304	1 097	791	743	550	1 044
1986	5 632	105	1 295	1 033	811	745	562	1 081
1985	5 679	110	1 363	1 120	764	778	565	979
1984	5 410	136	1 317	1 063	740	770	533	851
1983	5 404	127	1 400	1 012	717	728	540	880
1982	5 472	120	1 360	1 159	766	749	523	795
1981	5 342	111	1 380	1 134	694	646	578	799
1980	5 121	133	1 346	1 017	747	678	514	686
1979	5 131	146	1 306	1 021	688	686	461	823
1978	4 748	139	1 314	937	631	590	395	742
1977	4 806	135	1 307	975	641	643	394	711
1976	4 593	147	1 334	1 034	658	521	291	608
1975	4 284	141	1 330	908	552	500	311	542
1974	3 907	143	1 166	873	516	453	263	493
1973	3 107	142	1 104	848	454	363	196	. . .
1972	3 061	138	1 169	855	404	334	160	. . .
1971	2 867	134	1 157	794	359	262	170	. . .
1970	2 693	113	1 110	689	410	231	140	. . .
1969	2 681	112	1 079	741	380	218	151	. . .
1968	2 412	134	1 022	670	288	177	120	. . .
1967	2 346	133	1 009	690	250	152	112	. . .
1966	2 172	140	1 012	[2]772	. . .	[3]248	. . .	. . .
1965	1 991	129	922	[2]698	. . .	[3]242	. . .	. . .
1964	1 617	110	696	[2]624	. . .	[3]187	. . .	. . .
1963	1 457	77	645	[2]571	. . .	[3]164	. . .	. . .
1962	1 348	97	673	[2]451	. . .	[3]127	. . .	. . .
1961	1 290	125	602	[2]413	. . .	[3]150	. . .	. . .
1960	1 128	117	520	[2]350	. . .	[3]142	. . .	. . .
1959	1 051	105	481	[2]336	. . .	[3]129	. . .	. . .
1958	1 031	87	467	[2]334	. . .	[3]143	. . .	. . .
1957	994	93	411	[2]368	. . .	[3]122	. . .	. . .
1956	879	84	395	[2]292	. . .	[3]108	. . .	. . .
1955	729	78	297	[2]259	. . .	[3]95	. . .	. . .
Non-Hispanic White								
2005	6 601	63	1 425	1 461	1 078	855	433	1 285
2004	6 425	67	1 446	1 375	1 085	803	442	1 207
2003	6 228	49	1 371	1 337	1 130	732	446	1 163
2002	6 177	40	1 370	1 364	984	721	462	1 237
2001	5 912	44	1 252	1 280	938	695	479	1 222
2000	5 921	57	1 443	1 224	906	672	474	1 145
1999	5 785	49	1 360	1 183	908	656	387	1 241
1998	6 025	54	1 435	1 158	863	740	493	1 282
1997	6 222	48	1 307	1 200	946	771	465	1 485
1996	6 073	86	1 367	1 117	833	787	531	1 352
1995	5 956	67	1 261	1 123	904	819	479	1 302
1994[1]	6 124	53	1 229	1 216	950	755	561	1 361
1993	5 715	48	1 232	1 010	907	704	524	1 290

[1]Prior to 1994, total enrollment does not include the population age 35 years and over.
[2]Includes students age 20 to 24 years.
[3]Includes students age 25 to 34 years.
r = Revised, controlled to 1990 census–based population estimates; previous 1993 data controlled to 1980 census–based population estimates.
. . . = Not available.

Table A-14. Age Distribution of College Students 14 Years Old and Over, by Sex, Selected Years, October 1947–2005—*Continued*

(Numbers in thousands.)

Year, race, and Hispanic origin	Both sexes							
	Total enrollment	14 to 17 years	18 and 19 years	20 and 21 years	22 to 24 years	25 to 29 years	30 to 34 years	35 years and over
Black								
2005	2 217	28	431	393	435	282	217	430
2004	2 301	40	440	398	400	352	170	501
2003	2 144	28	374	415	435	289	214	388
2002	2 278	56	430	418	379	301	241	454
2001	2 230	33	444	383	379	283	279	429
2000	2 164	19	454	375	387	325	242	361
1999	1 998	45	430	389	325	254	199	354
1998	2 016	22	461	354	300	328	211	340
1997	1 903	24	381	321	383	258	165	372
1996	1 901	45	345	346	292	337	182	354
1995	1 772	24	344	339	305	233	193	334
1994[1]	1 800	36	310	347	344	256	184	323
1993r	1 599	13	322	311	264	253	143	293
1993	1 545	13	311	297	253	245	141	284
1992	1 424	28	291	316	279	170	132	208
1991	1 477	18	303	302	223	216	157	257
1990	1 393	35	349	287	258	150	108	207
1989	1 287	32	302	290	243	156	119	146
1988	1 321	33	281	273	198	188	142	206
1987	1 351	32	341	264	218	220	121	155
1986	1 359	19	308	242	262	187	143	198
1985	1 263	21	259	274	201	183	112	213
1984	1 332	40	265	274	247	182	131	193
1983	1 273	31	258	242	241	179	151	171
1982	1 294	22	274	242	251	196	142	167
1981	1 335	31	306	232	212	219	132	203
1980	1 163	30	283	225	180	176	113	156
1979	1 156	43	279	224	193	150	112	155
1978	1 175	38	270	238	186	167	121	155
1977	1 284	37	269	262	190	210	136	180
1976	1 217	34	302	252	195	171	109	154
1975	1 099	34	260	237	168	151	97	152
1974	930	34	233	190	132	136	88	117
1973	781	37	194	164	140	89	60	97
1972	727	32	229	168	143	87	68	...
1971	680	29	204	199	119	79	50	...
1970	522	21	191	152	73	54	31	...
1969	492	19	193	149	65	39	26	...
1968	434	20	182	112	58	33	29	...
1967	370	16	141	105	51	42	15	...
1966	282	17	112	[2]112	...	[3]41	...	...
1965	274	30	111	[2]99	...	[3]34	...	...
1964	234	30	78	[2]79	...	[3]47	...	...
1963	286	9	113	[2]112	...	[3]52	...	...
1962	274	16	103	[2]109	...	[3]46	...	...
1961	233	9	82	[2]103	...	[3]39	...	...
1960	227	8	88	[2]90	...	[3]41	...	...
1959	222	17	74	[2]94	...	[3]37	...	...
1958	212	12	70	[2]85	...	[3]45	...	...
1957	206	15	68	[2]71	...	[3]52	...	...
1956	196	15	65	[2]80	...	[3]36	...	...
1955	155	21	31	[2]51	...	[3]52	...	...
Asian[4]								
2005	1 184	22	188	272	234	226	114	129
2004	1 191	20	182	245	269	217	113	146
2003	1 162	16	209	219	264	228	108	116
2002	1 258	28	236	269	299	182	105	140
2001	1 280	17	247	245	302	265	90	115
2000	1 049	12	212	200	227	188	81	130
1999	1 041	16	223	192	211	187	71	142

[1]Prior to 1994, total enrollment does not include the population age 35 years and over.
[2]Includes students age 20 to 24 years.
[3]Includes students age 25 to 34 years.
[4]Data from before 2003 consists of respondents who identified themselves as "Asian or Pacific Islanders."
r = Revised, controlled to 1990 census–based population estimates; previous 1993 data controlled to 1980 census–based population estimates.
. . . = Not available.

Table A-14. Age Distribution of College Students 14 Years Old and Over, by Sex, Selected Years, October 1947–2005—*Continued*

(Numbers in thousands.)

Year, race, and Hispanic origin	Male							
	Total enrollment	14 to 17 years	18 and 19 years	20 and 21 years	22 to 24 years	25 to 29 years	30 to 34 years	35 years and over
Black								
2005	832	6	182	178	153	99	64	150
2004	776	13	165	169	146	92	41	151
2003	798	10	166	153	180	100	84	105
2002	802	14	179	175	121	97	83	133
2001	781	7	179	137	153	88	90	126
2000	815	10	163	137	169	110	92	133
1999	833	34	210	193	98	93	79	123
1998	770	12	194	162	88	140	67	105
1997	723	7	142	137	146	110	65	117
1996	764	17	145	155	122	142	64	120
1995	710	13	145	142	143	65	80	122
1994[1]	745	16	132	161	147	118	72	99
1993r	652	4	151	109	127	118	36	107
1993	636	4	148	107	124	116	36	102
1992	527	8	123	114	119	73	37	54
1991	629	7	137	138	103	99	55	90
1990	587	16	164	151	111	52	26	65
1989	480	8	126	104	94	65	37	47
1988	494	6	108	90	99	75	48	68
1987	587	13	154	124	99	99	37	62
1986	580	12	120	111	118	81	64	74
1985	552	10	121	140	84	64	40	93
1984	618	16	112	129	126	99	62	74
1983	560	12	93	112	126	91	64	62
1982	544	9	124	92	115	91	51	62
1981	566	7	133	92	100	115	57	62
1980	476	14	98	101	79	92	53	39
1979	498	12	110	110	84	71	47	64
1978	504	13	114	106	85	82	52	52
1977	571	18	90	115	104	101	62	81
1976	551	11	121	113	97	90	57	62
1975	523	14	111	107	76	82	53	80
1974	485	13	102	100	78	70	60	62
1973	358	7	96	93	77	49	36	. . .
1972	384	18	102	91	94	49	30	. . .
1071	363	11	94	106	62	58	31	. . .
1970	253	10	73	81	38	33	19	. . .
1969	236	10	86	75	41	15	10	. . .
1968	221	12	83	61	26	27	13	. . .
1967	199	7	78	57	32	15	11	. . .
1966	154	10	47	[2]72	. . .	[3]25	. . .	. . .
1965	126	8	52	[2]47	. . .	[3]19	. . .	. . .
1964	120	16	35	[2]36	. . .	[3]33	. . .	. . .
1963	149	5	50	[2]62	. . .	[3]32	. . .	. . .
1962	156	5	55	[2]59	. . .	[3]37	. . .	. . .
1961	148	5	48	[2]64	. . .	[3]31	. . .	. . .
1960	125	2	43	[2]55	. . .	[3]25	. . .	. . .
1959	120	4	31	[2]58	. . .	[3]27	. . .	. . .
1958	130	5	44	[2]48	. . .	[3]33	. . .	. . .
1957	90	9	28	[2]30	. . .	[3]23	. . .	. . .
1956	124	9	38	[2]48	. . .	[3]29	. . .	. . .
1955	84	9	15	[2]25	. . .	[3]35	. . .	. . .
Asian[4]								
2005	605	10	90	163	113	110	61	58
2004	636	11	92	135	145	116	65	71
2003	606	3	103	104	130	141	67	59
2002	649	8	121	137	160	101	56	67
2001	664	10	113	127	177	134	63	40
2000	517	4	108	109	120	66	51	60
1999	506	11	93	95	96	97	47	67

[1]Prior to 1994, total enrollment does not include the population age 35 years and over.
[2]Includes students age 20 to 24 years.
[3]Includes students age 25 to 34 years.
[4]Data from before 2003 consists of respondents who identified themselves as "Asian or Pacific Islanders."
r = Revised, controlled to 1990 census–based population estimates; previous 1993 data controlled to 1980 census–based population estimates.
. . . = Not available.

Table A-14. Age Distribution of College Students 14 Years Old and Over, by Sex, Selected Years, October 1947–2005—*Continued*

(Numbers in thousands.)

Year, race, and Hispanic origin	Female							
	Total enrollment	14 to 17 years	18 and 19 years	20 and 21 years	22 to 24 years	25 to 29 years	30 to 34 years	35 years and over
Black								
2005	1 385	22	249	215	282	183	153	281
2004	1 525	27	275	229	254	259	130	350
2003	1 346	19	209	262	255	188	130	283
2002	1 476	42	251	243	257	204	158	321
2001	1 449	26	265	245	226	195	190	302
2000	1 349	9	291	238	218	215	150	228
1999	1 164	10	221	196	227	161	120	229
1998	1 247	9	267	192	212	188	144	234
1997	1 180	17	238	184	237	149	100	255
1996	1 136	28	199	192	170	195	119	234
1995	1 062	11	199	197	162	168	113	212
1994[1]	1 054	21	178	186	197	138	112	224
1993[r]	947	9	172	202	137	135	107	186
1993	909	8	163	191	130	129	106	182
1992	897	21	168	202	161	97	95	154
1991	848	11	166	164	120	118	102	167
1990	807	19	185	136	146	98	82	141
1989	807	24	176	186	149	91	82	99
1988	827	27	173	183	99	113	94	138
1987	764	19	186	140	119	121	84	93
1986	779	7	187	131	144	106	79	124
1985	712	11	138	134	117	119	72	121
1984	714	24	153	145	121	83	69	119
1983	714	19	164	131	116	88	87	109
1982	750	12	150	150	136	105	92	105
1981	769	24	172	140	112	105	75	141
1980	686	16	185	124	101	84	60	116
1979	659	31	169	114	109	79	66	91
1978	671	25	155	133	102	85	68	103
1977	712	19	179	147	87	108	74	98
1976	665	23	181	139	97	81	52	92
1975	577	20	150	130	92	69	44	72
1974	448	22	131	91	55	66	28	55
1973	325	30	97	71	63	40	24	. . .
1972	343	14	127	77	49	38	38	. . .
1971	317	18	109	93	57	21	19	. . .
1970	269	11	118	71	36	22	11	. . .
1969	256	9	108	74	24	25	17	. . .
1968	213	8	100	51	32	7	15	. . .
1967	171	9	63	48	19	27	4	. . .
1966	128	7	65	[2]40	. . .	[3]16	. . .	. . .
1965	148	22	59	[2]52	. . .	[3]15	. . .	. . .
1964	114	14	43	[2]43	. . .	[3]14	. . .	. . .
1963	137	4	63	[2]50	. . .	[3]20	. . .	. . .
1962	118	11	48	[2]50	. . .	[3]9	. . .	. . .
1961	85	4	34	[2]39	. . .	[3]8	. . .	. . .
1960	102	6	45	[2]35	. . .	[3]16	. . .	. . .
1959	102	13	43	[2]36	. . .	[3]10	. . .	. . .
1958	82	7	26	[2]37	. . .	[3]12	. . .	. . .
1957	116	6	40	[2]41	. . .	[3]29	. . .	. . .
1956	72	6	27	[2]32	. . .	[3]7	. . .	. . .
1955	71	12	16	[2]26	. . .	[3]17	. . .	. . .
Asian[4]								
2005	579	12	98	109	120	116	53	71
2004	556	9	89	110	124	101	48	75
2003	556	13	107	115	134	88	42	57
2002	609	19	115	132	139	82	49	73
2001	616	6	134	118	125	131	27	75
2000	532	8	104	91	107	122	30	69
1999	534	5	130	97	115	89	24	74

[1]Prior to 1994, total enrollment does not include the population age 35 years and over.
[2]Includes students age 20 to 24 years.
[3]Includes students age 25 to 34 years.
[4]Data from before 2003 consists of respondents who identified themselves as "Asian or Pacific Islanders."
r = Revised, controlled to 1990 census–based population estimates; previous 1993 data controlled to 1980 census–based population estimates.
. . . = Not available.

Table A-14. Age Distribution of College Students 14 Years Old and Over, by Sex, Selected Years, October 1947–2005—*Continued*

(Numbers in thousands.)

Year, race, and Hispanic origin	Both sexes							
	Total enrollment	14 to 17 years	18 and 19 years	20 and 21 years	22 to 24 years	25 to 29 years	30 to 34 years	35 years and over
Hispanic[5]								
2005	1 942	31	406	420	389	288	150	257
2004	1 975	23	384	431	407	280	179	271
2003	1 714	12	379	407	329	224	156	207
2002	1 656	15	360	303	316	274	140	249
2001	1 700	14	387	342	306	255	136	260
2000	1 426	24	349	268	282	167	142	194
1999	1 307	7	297	197	247	207	127	225
1998	1 363	9	288	263	269	206	130	198
1997	1 260	49	316	254	236	174	80	151
1996	1 223	22	240	213	253	198	112	184
1995	1 207	20	264	245	236	153	97	193
1994[1]	1 187	9	225	230	207	180	132	205
1993[r]	1 169	17	222	299	207	178	106	139
1993	995	15	195	241	166	149	100	129
1992	918	17	230	200	156	124	90	102
1991	830	10	188	203	125	124	72	109
1990	748	13	148	188	99	109	59	130
1989	754	17	177	134	142	112	58	114
1988	747	13	203	110	137	118	73	93
1987	739	8	152	155	148	137	67	73
1986	794	16	171	146	141	164	67	89
1985	580	16	127	128	120	111	78	. . .
1984	524	5	136	133	93	100	57	. . .
1983	521	17	134	124	91	114	41	. . .
1982	494	16	143	104	90	94	47	. . .
1981	510	15	129	123	90	103	50	. . .
1980	443	10	137	94	84	69	49	. . .
1979	439	18	124	95	73	73	56	. . .
1978	377	15	109	68	77	78	30	. . .
1977	417	14	123	95	59	81	45	. . .
1976	426	13	143	80	83	73	31	. . .
1975	411	13	118	101	76	68	35	. . .
1974	354	11	112	96	64	39	32	. . .
1973	289	15	82	69	55	45	23	. . .
1972	242	14	70	60	49	34	15	. . .
White Alone or in Combination								
2005	13 791	125	3 043	3 244	2 433	1 740	954	2 251
2004	13 688	135	3 012	3 106	2 425	1 807	989	2 192
2003	13 164	106	2 905	2 808	2 584	1 613	989	2 099
Black Alone or in Combination								
2005	2 387	31	481	428	462	299	229	458
2004	2 412	40	466	436	416	371	170	512
2003	2 227	30	400	440	445	303	214	395
Asian Alone or in Combination								
2005	1 297	25	204	292	277	240	122	137
2004	1 260	20	203	266	281	222	116	152
2003	1 262	19	236	248	290	232	117	121

[1]Prior to 1994, total enrollment does not include the population age 35 years and over.
[5]May be of any race.
r = Revised, controlled to 1990 census–based population estimates; previous 1993 data controlled to 1980 census–based population estimates.
. . . = Not available.

Table A-14. Age Distribution of College Students 14 Years Old and Over, by Sex, Selected Years, October 1947–2005—*Continued*

(Numbers in thousands.)

Year, race, and Hispanic origin	Male							
	Total enrollment	14 to 17 years	18 and 19 years	20 and 21 years	22 to 24 years	25 to 29 years	30 to 34 years	35 years and over
Hispanic[5]								
2005	804	10	173	183	183	111	52	92
2004	852	5	171	212	191	131	53	89
2003	703	7	153	167	145	93	61	77
2002	705	3	156	151	132	118	49	97
2001	731	6	149	145	156	116	57	102
2000	619	12	160	118	123	61	75	70
1999	568	2	143	84	96	94	54	95
1998	550	...	97	139	110	86	54	64
1997	555	15	133	132	106	78	31	60
1996	529	8	98	78	124	79	54	90
1995	568	14	121	111	124	71	55	73
1994[1]	529	3	89	115	108	73	55	86
1993[r]	539	7	81	154	103	71	67	56
1993	442	6	69	118	79	57	63	51
1992	388	9	93	80	74	57	35	40
1991	347	5	68	79	64	64	30	37
1990	364	12	70	80	64	39	30	67
1989	353	5	75	66	70	63	31	42
1988	355	9	75	76	77	48	29	43
1987	390	3	76	100	71	77	42	21
1986	377	4	92	67	74	80	26	34
1985	279	10	44	53	71	72	29	...
1984	231	2	42	63	49	49	26	...
1983	253	10	41	61	50	74	17	...
1982	216	6	52	47	42	49	20	...
1981	258	6	57	68	39	55	33	...
1980	222	2	68	52	34	36	30	...
1979	225	8	67	43	43	39	25	...
1978	196	7	53	30	43	49	14	...
1977	224	6	54	45	40	56	23	...
1976	223	3	69	39	42	50	20	...
1975	218	3	53	52	40	45	25	...
1974	195	6	55	44	42	24	24	...
1973	168	11	39	37	29	32	20	...
1972	126	7	28	35	29	20	7	...
White Alone or in Combination								
2005	5 978	43	1 371	1 519	1 128	696	424	796
2004	6 068	49	1 331	1 494	1 131	847	425	792
2003	5 837	48	1 283	1 274	1 257	730	446	798
Black Alone or in Combination								
2005	895	9	201	189	167	109	66	154
2004	827	13	175	187	159	100	41	153
2003	826	10	175	165	186	100	84	107
Asian Alone or in Combination								
2005	640	13	97	170	124	113	63	60
2004	662	11	97	147	153	117	65	72
2003	649	3	112	115	143	142	72	61

[1]Prior to 1994, total enrollment does not include the population age 35 years and over.
[5]May be of any race.
r = Revised, controlled to 1990 census–based population estimates; previous 1993 data controlled to 1980 census–based population estimates.
... = Not available.

Table A-14. Age Distribution of College Students 14 Years Old and Over, by Sex, Selected Years, October 1947–2005—*Continued*

(Numbers in thousands.)

Year, race, and Hispanic origin	Total enrollment	Female						
		14 to 17 years	18 and 19 years	20 and 21 years	22 to 24 years	25 to 29 years	30 to 34 years	35 years and over
Hispanic[5]								
2005	1 137	21	232	237	206	178	98	165
2004	1 123	19	213	219	216	150	126	182
2003	1 011	5	226	240	185	131	95	130
2002	951	12	204	152	184	156	92	152
2001	969	8	238	197	150	139	80	157
2000	807	13	188	150	160	106	67	124
1999	739	5	154	113	151	113	73	130
1998	814	9	191	124	159	120	77	134
1997	704	34	183	123	130	96	49	91
1996	693	15	142	136	128	119	59	95
1995	639	6	143	134	112	82	42	120
1994[1]	659	6	136	119	99	106	78	119
1993[r]	630	10	141	145	104	107	40	83
1993	553	9	126	123	87	93	38	78
1992	530	7	137	120	82	67	55	62
1991	483	5	120	124	61	59	42	72
1990	384	1	78	108	35	70	29	63
1989	401	11	103	69	72	49	27	71
1988	391	4	129	35	60	70	43	51
1987	349	5	76	56	76	60	25	51
1986	417	12	79	80	67	84	41	54
1985	299	6	82	75	48	39	49	. . .
1984	292	3	94	70	43	51	31	. . .
1983	270	7	93	64	41	40	25	. . .
1982	278	10	91	57	48	45	27	. . .
1981	252	9	72	55	51	48	17	. . .
1980	221	8	63	42	50	33	20	. . .
1979	215	10	58	52	30	34	31	. . .
1978	181	8	56	38	34	29	16	. . .
1977	194	8	70	50	19	25	22	. . .
1976	203	9	74	45	41	23	11	. . .
1975	193	10	65	49	36	23	10	. . .
1974	157	5	56	51	22	15	8	. . .
1973	123	5	44	33	25	13	3	. . .
1972	117	7	43	25	20	14	8	. . .
White Alone or in Combination								
2005	7 813	82	1 672	1 725	1 305	1 044	530	1 454
2004	7 600	86	1 682	1 612	1 295	960	564	1 401
2003	7 328	57	1 622	1 594	1 327	883	543	1 302
Black Alone or in Combination								
2005	1 493	22	280	239	295	190	164	303
2004	1 584	27	290	249	258	271	130	359
2003	1 401	20	225	275	260	203	130	288
Asian Alone or in Combination								
2005	657	12	107	122	153	128	59	77
2004	598	9	106	118	128	105	51	80
2003	613	16	124	133	147	89	44	60

[1]Prior to 1994, total enrollment does not include the population age 35 years and over.
[5]May be of any race.
r = Revised, controlled to 1990 census–based population estimates; previous 1993 data controlled to 1980 census–based population estimates.
. . . = Not available.

Table A-15. College Enrollment of Students Age 14 Years and Over, by Type of College, Attendance Status, Age, and Sex, October 1970–2005

(Numbers in thousands.)

Year and type of college	Both sexes								Male			Female		
	Total enroll-ment	14 to 19 years	20 and 21 years	22 to 24 years	25 to 34 years	35 years and over	Public	Private	Total enroll-ment	Full-time	Part-time	Total enroll-ment	Full-time	Part-time
All Undergraduates														
2005	14 169	3 901	3 847	2 588	2 142	1 690	11 292	2 876	6 189	4 799	1 391	7 979	5 852	2 127
2004	14 004	3 863	3 700	2 431	2 257	1 753	11 384	2 620	6 156	4 714	1 442	7 848	5 704	3 102
2003	13 370	3 633	3 449	2 687	2 094	1 506	10 980	2 389	5 902	4 476	1 425	7 468	5 391	2 077
2002	13 426	3 743	3 457	2 355	2 106	1 764	10 830	2 595	5 929	4 462	1 467	7 497	5 273	2 223
2001	12 552	3 568	3 329	2 136	1 979	1 540	10 188	2 364	5 522	4 057	1 464	7 030	4 949	2 082
2000	12 401	3 710	3 093	2 113	1 988	1 498	10 044	2 357	5 520	4 059	1 461	6 881	4 832	2 049
1999	12 046	3 625	3 043	2 000	1 885	1 493	9 689	2 357	5 554	4 143	1 411	6 492	4 548	1 945
1998	12 509	3 749	3 019	2 025	2 101	1 616	10 100	2 410	5 621	4 051	1 570	6 888	4 765	2 123
1997	12 409	3 504	3 080	2 137	1 970	1 718	10 074	2 335	5 539	4 165	1 375	6 870	4 752	2 118
1996	12 305	3 526	2 856	2 017	2 226	1 680	10 121	2 183	5 533	4 032	1 502	6 772	4 502	2 269
1995	11 966	3 251	2 881	2 033	2 151	1 651	9 570	2 396	5 413	3 911	1 501	6 554	4 433	2 121
1994	12 410	3 192	3 006	2 099	2 281	1 832	9 983	2 427	5 526	3 969	1 557	6 883	4 480	2 404
1993r	11 959	3 197	2 879	2 131	2 118	1 634	9 706	2 253	5 442	4 020	1 422	6 517	4 346	2 171
1993	11 507	3 045	2 721	2 020	2 088	1 633	9 330	2 176	5 194	3 812	1 382	6 313	4 182	2 130
1992	11 643	3 097	2 902	2 004	2 090	1 550	9 519	2 124	5 091	3 724	1 365	6 553	4 338	2 214
1991	11 374	3 061	2 902	1 757	2 120	1 534	9 257	2 117	5 120	3 724	1 395	6 254	4 145	2 109
1990	11 108	3 194	2 740	1 681	2 067	1 425	9 031	2 076	5 030	3 628	1 402	6 077	3 967	2 109
1989	10 661	3 250	2 529	1 658	1 921	1 304	8 633	2 027	4 730	3 436	1 295	5 931	3 880	2 051
1988	10 605	3 229	2 645	1 600	1 865	1 266	8 617	1 988	4 763	3 441	1 322	5 842	3 816	2 026
1987	10 304	3 283	2 585	1 512	1 848	1 076	8 306	1 998	4 878	3 476	1 403	5 426	3 445	1 981
1986	10 036	3 158	2 298	1 583	1 932	1 065	7 955	2 081	4 663	3 350	1 312	5 373	3 474	1 899
1985	10 097	3 169	2 586	1 475	1 884	984	8 042	2 055	4 667	3 454	1 213	5 430	3 578	1 852
1984	9 910	3 120	2 564	1 547	1 826	852	7 944	1 966	4 725	3 573	1 152	5 185	3 419	1 766
1983	9 925	3 200	2 464	1 475	1 873	914	7 808	2 117	4 759	3 472	1 287	5 166	3 424	1 742
1982	9 952	3 183	2 657	1 526	1 745	843	7 908	2 044	4 703	3 485	1 218	5 249	3 480	1 769
1981	9 969	3 276	2 511	1 458	1 808	916	7 789	2 180	4 724	3 452	1 273	5 245	3 490	1 755
1980	9 279	3 182	2 393	1 316	1 598	791	. . .	. . .	4 353	3 247	1 105	4 927	3 210	1 717
1979	9 193	3 156	2 308	1 297	1 526	905	7 331	1 861	4 387	3 219	1 168	4 805	3 163	1 642
1978	8 947	3 173	2 246	1 233	1 505	790	7 008	1 939	4 445	3 269	1 176	4 502	3 031	1 471
1977[1]	8 408	3 184	2 376	1 206	1 640	. . .	6 683	1 724	4 372	3 304	1 068	4 027	3 002	1 025
1976	8 988	3 216	2 358	1 224	1 472	718	7 196	1 787	4 569	3 353	1 213	4 419	3 166	1 253
1975[1]	8 108	3 237	2 255	1 072	1 546	. . .	6 598	1 510	4 393	3 394	999	3 715	2 902	813
1974[1]	7 338	2 906	2 131	1 028	1 272	. . .	5 843	1 494	4 030	3 128	902	3 307	2 561	746
1973[1]	6 794	2 812	2 031	924	1 028	. . .	5 279	1 516	3 791	3 035	756	3 004	2 423	581
1972[1]	6 992	2 974	2 065	944	1 011	. . .	5 460	1 532	3 982	3 231	751	3 010	2 445	565
1971[1]	6 895	3 008	1 936	1 019	931	. . .	5 472	1 423	4 017	3 240	777	2 878	2 348	530
1970[1]	6 274	2 854	1 803	866	750	. . .	4 910	1 363	3 627	3 045	582	2 646	2 164	482
Two-Year College Students														
2005	4 327	1 259	833	603	882	751	3 890	437	1 866	1 197	669	2 462	1 436	1 026
2004	4 340	1 243	802	568	898	829	3 939	401	1 756	1 141	615	2 584	1 461	1 123
2003	4 384	1 178	746	843	834	784	3 999	385	1 782	1 055	726	2 603	1 507	1 095
2002	4 378	1 227	777	656	880	838	3 948	431	1 884	1 102	783	2 494	1 363	1 131
2001	4 159	1 200	776	605	832	746	3 749	410	1 802	1 057	745	2 357	1 252	1 105
2000	3 881	1 232	710	525	673	741	3 590	291	1 655	969	686	2 226	1 224	1 002
1999	3 794	1 187	715	460	683	749	3 482	312	1 637	949	688	2 157	1 157	1 000
1998	4 234	1 301	701	619	839	774	3 865	369	1 845	1 049	796	2 389	1 287	1 103
1997	4 078	1 178	760	528	806	807	3 780	298	1 663	983	680	2 415	1 307	1 108
1996	4 174	1 223	669	515	922	845	3 890	284	1 752	974	778	2 423	1 235	1 187
1995	3 882	1 028	608	593	892	761	3 553	330	1 626	898	728	2 256	1 124	1 132
1994	4 208	1 063	623	621	1 011	890	3 846	362	1 704	937	766	2 504	1 234	1 270
1993r	4 345	1 131	745	648	978	843	4 024	321	1 825	1 061	764	2 520	1 317	1 203
1993	4 196	1 077	696	614	965	844	3 884	311	1 748	1 006	742	2 448	1 268	1 179
1992	4 239	1 084	789	581	988	797	3 937	302	1 688	936	751	2 551	1 268	1 283
1991	4 277	1 120	732	560	1 084	781	4 025	252	1 798	973	825	2 479	1 239	1 239
1990	3 965	1 059	689	475	967	775	3 689	276	1 624	849	775	2 340	1 103	1 237
1989	3 627	1 048	557	467	880	676	3 382	245	1 464	777	688	2 163	949	1 214
1988	3 837	1 134	665	497	879	662	3 609	228	1 542	847	695	2 295	1 054	1 241
1987	3 648	1 111	624	457	851	605	3 405	243	1 522	780	742	2 127	937	1 190
1986	3 391	1 023	506	427	875	559	3 089	302	1 466	752	714	1 924	856	1 068
1985	3 289	959	558	403	851	518	3 009	281	1 336	702	634	1 954	914	1 040
1984	3 172	994	525	442	795	417	2 875	298	1 436	834	601	1 738	829	909
1983	3 416	1 050	595	405	882	485	3 136	280	1 498	807	691	1 919	897	1 022
1982	3 448	1 088	604	494	826	437	3 164	283	1 477	854	623	1 971	961	1 011
1981	3 347	1 144	566	414	768	455	3 091	255	1 475	837	638	1 872	909	963
1980	3 107	1 079	450	417	721	441	. . .	. . .	1 331	768	563	1 777	798	979
1979	2 897	933	403	407	664	490	2 710	187	1 251	684	567	1 646	725	921
1978	2 904	966	427	391	670	451	2 686	218	1 368	698	669	1 537	701	835
1977[1]	2 510	933	455	380	741	. . .	2 362	148	1 253	681	572	1 256	691	565
1976	2 854	907	444	367	718	419	2 688	165	1 400	760	640	1 454	743	711
1975[1]	2 561	1 024	431	354	752	. . .	2 437	123	1 412	850	562	1 148	717	431
1974[1]	2 072	834	369	305	565	. . .	1 917	154	1 172	709	463	899	528	371
1973[1]	1 797	816	278	254	449	. . .	1 669	128	1 012	629	383	785	471	314
1972[1]	1 910	883	334	267	426	. . .	1 816	94	1 125	770	355	785	484	301
1971[1]	1 830	928	307	263	331	. . .	1 726	105	1 087	726	361	743	473	270
1970[1]	1 692	895	281	234	283	. . .	1 559	133	1 001	726	275	691	452	239

[1] Data for 1970–1975 and 1977 do not include students age 35 years and over.
r = Revised, controlled to 1990 census–based population estimates; previous 1993 data controlled to 1980 census–based population estimates.
. . . = Not available.

Table A-15. College Enrollment of Students Age 14 Years and Over, by Type of College, Attendance Status, Age, and Sex, October 1970–2005—*Continued*

(Numbers in thousands.)

Year and type of college	Full-time						Part-time					
	Total enrollment	14 to 19 years	20 and 21 years	22 to 24 years	25 to 34 years	35 years and over	Total enrollment	14 to 19 years	20 and 21 years	22 to 24 years	25 to 34 years	35 years and over
All Undergraduates												
2005	10 651	3 540	3 369	1 977	1 139	625	3 518	360	479	611	1 003	1 065
2004	10 418	3 533	3 251	1 836	1 150	648	3 586	330	449	595	1 107	1 105
2003	9 868	3 299	2 992	1 948	1 081	547	3 502	334	457	739	1 013	959
2002	9 735	3 356	3 058	1 737	1 073	511	3 690	387	399	619	1 033	1 253
2001	9 006	3 190	2 840	1 524	976	476	3 546	378	489	612	1 003	1 064
2000	8 891	3 368	2 658	1 479	930	457	3 510	342	435	633	1 058	1 041
1999	8 691	3 280	2 625	1 485	888	412	3 355	345	418	514	997	1 081
1998	8 816	3 327	2 619	1 461	956	452	3 693	421	400	563	1 145	1 164
1997	8 917	3 144	2 704	1 576	960	532	3 492	360	376	560	1 010	1 186
1996	8 534	3 131	2 460	1 516	990	437	3 771	394	396	501	1 236	1 243
1995	8 344	2 902	2 462	1 444	1 004	533	3 622	349	419	589	1 147	1 118
1994	8 449	2 843	2 585	1 455	981	586	3 961	350	421	644	1 300	1 245
1993r	8 366	2 866	2 513	1 513	941	533	3 593	332	366	619	1 176	1 102
1993	7 994	2 732	2 380	1 429	927	527	3 513	314	342	590	1 161	1 106
1992	8 063	2 838	2 506	1 427	834	458	3 580	259	396	578	1 255	1 092
1991	7 869	2 809	2 534	1 248	878	400	3 505	252	368	509	1 242	1 134
1990	7 597	2 912	2 333	1 165	824	363	3 511	282	408	515	1 244	1 062
1989	7 314	2 989	2 209	1 122	655	341	3 346	260	321	536	1 266	963
1988	7 257	2 925	2 275	1 079	691	285	3 348	303	371	521	1 173	981
1987	6 920	2 892	2 179	1 005	610	235	3 384	391	406	507	1 238	841
1986	6 825	2 880	1 973	1 055	680	237	3 212	278	324	528	1 254	828
1985	7 033	2 900	2 237	1 017	701	178	3 065	269	349	457	1 184	806
1984	6 992	2 846	2 221	1 067	689	170	2 918	274	344	480	1 139	683
1983	6 896	2 895	2 124	993	718	166	3 029	305	340	482	1 153	748
1982	6 965	2 880	2 286	979	662	159	2 987	302	372	547	1 083	684
1981	6 942	2 983	2 157	986	613	202	3 027	293	353	471	1 195	715
1980	6 457	2 897	2 107	810	500	142	2 822	283	287	505	1 098	649
1979	6 383	2 892	1 994	815	523	158	2 810	264	314	482	1 003	748
1978	6 300	2 872	1 918	820	559	132	2 647	302	328	412	947	658
1977[1]	6 304	2 855	2 075	775	598	. . .	2 104	329	301	431	1 042	. . .
1976	6 519	2 963	2 033	821	563	138	2 466	253	325	403	909	577
1975[1]	6 296	2 987	1 958	696	655	. . .	1 812	250	297	376	891	. . .
1974[1]	5 689	2 661	1 842	697	488	. . .	1 649	245	289	331	784	. . .
1973[1]	5 460	2 629	1 801	630	398	. . .	1 334	183	230	294	630	. . .
1972[1]	5 678	2 797	1 845	624	412	. . .	1 314	177	220	320	599	. . .
1971[1]	5 588	2 801	1 729	700	357	. . .	1 307	207	207	319	574	. . .
1970[1]	5 208	2 685	1 628	591	301	. . .	1 066	169	175	275	449	. . .
Two-Year College Students												
2005	2 632	1 031	605	373	393	231	1 695	228	228	230	489	520
2004	2 602	1 027	553	327	425	269	1 738	216	249	241	472	560
2003	2 563	973	516	386	429	258	1 822	205	230	457	404	526
2002	2 464	975	571	344	374	200	1 914	252	206	312	506	638
2001	2 310	951	529	301	307	222	1 850	250	247	304	524	525
2000	2 193	993	507	278	230	184	1 688	239	202	247	444	557
1999	2 105	955	498	261	230	161	1 688	231	217	199	453	588
1998	2 336	1 024	495	331	302	184	1 899	277	206	288	537	591
1997	2 290	947	522	283	327	212	1 788	231	238	245	479	595
1996	2 209	995	457	271	315	171	1 965	227	212	244	607	674
1995	2 022	810	397	298	321	195	1 860	218	211	295	571	565
1994	2 172	848	407	319	341	256	2 036	215	216	302	669	634
1993r	2 378	891	515	348	365	259	1 967	240	230	300	613	585
1993	2 274	850	483	325	360	256	1 922	227	213	288	605	588
1992	2 205	897	528	287	304	188	2 034	187	261	294	683	609
1991	2 212	915	476	269	361	191	2 065	205	256	291	723	589
1990	1 953	847	408	227	310	160	2 012	212	281	247	657	615
1989	1 725	860	368	160	210	128	1 902	188	189	307	669	548
1988	1 901	926	410	209	227	128	1 936	207	256	288	651	534
1987	1 716	839	368	192	212	105	1 932	272	256	264	639	500
1986	1 608	814	296	170	223	105	1 783	209	210	257	652	454
1985	1 615	779	341	174	244	78	1 674	180	217	229	607	440
1984	1 663	812	330	190	247	84	1 509	182	195	252	548	333
1983	1 703	855	374	159	250	65	1 713	195	221	245	631	420
1982	1 814	883	381	214	260	77	1 634	205	223	280	566	356
1981	1 745	927	357	170	188	102	1 601	217	209	243	579	353
1980	1 566	884	287	160	167	67	1 542	195	163	256	554	374
1979	1 408	749	251	156	185	68	1 489	184	152	251	480	423
1978	1 400	776	243	157	167	57	1 505	190	184	234	503	394
1977[1]	1 372	718	283	162	208	. . .	1 138	216	172	218	533	. . .
1976	1 503	764	261	177	228	74	1 351	143	183	190	490	346
1975[1]	1 567	865	274	155	274	. . .	994	159	157	199	478	. . .
1974[1]	1 237	702	233	151	152	. . .	835	132	136	154	413	. . .
1973[1]	1 100	702	164	121	111	. . .	697	114	113	133	338	. . .
1972[1]	1 255	772	223	134	126	. . .	655	111	111	133	300	. . .
1971[1]	1 199	797	209	124	70	. . .	631	131	98	139	261	. . .
1970[1]	1 177	786	197	114	80	. . .	515	109	84	120	203	. . .

[1]Data for 1970–1975 and 1977 do not include students age 35 years and over.
r = Revised, controlled to 1990 census–based population estimates; previous 1993 data controlled to 1980 census–based population estimates.
. . . = Not available.

Table A-15. College Enrollment of Students Age 14 Years and Over, by Type of College, Attendance Status, Age, and Sex, October 1970–2005—*Continued*

(Numbers in thousands.)

Year and type of college	Both sexes								Male			Female		
	Total enrollment	14 to 19 years	20 and 21 years	22 to 24 years	25 to 34 years	35 years and over	Public	Private	Total enrollment	Full-time	Part-time	Total enrollment	Full-time	Part-time
Graduate Students														
2005	3 304	7	98	574	1 458	1 167	2 143	1 161	1 349	711	638	1 955	875	1 079
2004	3 378	20	77	718	1 433	1 131	2 267	1 111	1 419	726	693	1 959	845	1 114
2003	3 268	29	84	632	1 399	1 123	2 129	1 139	1 416	774	643	1 852	849	1 003
2002	3 072	33	68	572	1 296	1 104	2 003	1 068	1 311	632	679	1 761	774	987
2001	3 321	48	91	595	1 442	1 145	2 233	1 088	1 353	614	739	1 968	784	1 184
2000	2 913	38	77	571	1 218	1 009	1 965	948	1 162	546	616	1 750	722	1 028
1999	3 157	45	77	620	1 211	1 205	1 970	1 188	1 403	699	703	1 755	722	1 033
1998	3 037	45	73	536	1 313	1 070	1 884	1 153	1 284	614	669	1 753	758	995
1997	3 027	30	63	562	1 299	1 073	2 016	1 010	1 304	651	653	1 723	668	1 055
1996	2 922	21	52	534	1 217	1 098	1 893	1 029	1 288	650	638	1 634	655	979
1995	2 749	8	60	465	1 198	1 018	1 802	947	1 290	646	644	1 459	554	905
1994	2 613	9	21	551	1 138	893	1 710	902	1 238	619	619	1 375	505	870
1993r	2 435	3	14	537	1 022	859	1 611	824	1 156	601	555	1 278	458	820
1993	2 391	3	13	514	1 006	856	1 580	812	1 130	579	551	1 261	446	815
1992	2 392	-	36	508	1 035	814	1 546	846	1 102	606	496	1 291	521	770
1991	2 683	-	37	547	1 165	934	1 824	859	1 320	688	631	1 364	491	872
1990	2 514	2	27	497	1 095	893	1 722	792	1 162	569	593	1 352	531	820
1989	2 520	-	40	509	1 161	809	1 662	857	1 219	626	594	1 300	515	786
1988	2 511	-	36	464	1 098	913	1 716	795	1 187	522	666	1 324	435	889
1987	2 415	1	57	494	1 137	725	1 655	760	1 152	579	573	1 263	462	801
1986	2 365	-	44	530	1 057	732	1 624	741	1 184	596	589	1 181	479	702
1985	2 427	-	31	540	1 179	678	1 652	775	1 239	607	632	1 188	395	793
1984	2 395	-	32	580	1 190	594	1 648	747	1 263	654	610	1 132	440	692
1983	2 442	-	32	568	1 214	629	1 614	829	1 279	665	614	1 163	438	725
1982	2 393	1	31	534	1 244	584	1 587	806	1 216	626	590	1 178	421	756
1981	2 205	-	34	528	1 120	523	1 478	726	1 127	546	581	1 078	347	731
1980	2 173	2	31	554	1 104	481	. . .	. . .	1 106	526	581	1 066	372	694
1979	2 214	-	45	497	1 149	523	1 537	678	1 105	503	602	1 109	355	754
1978	2 217	-	51	565	1 064	536	1 454	762	1 149	516	633	1 068	366	702
1977[1]	1 810	2	53	593	1 161	. . .	1 241	568	995	548	447	813	338	475
1976	2 152	-	40	622	1 017	472	1 516	634	1 216	576	638	937	292	644
1975[1]	1 590	-	59	607	923	. . .	1 105	484	949	542	407	640	267	373
1974[1]	1 490	-	61	499	930	. . .	1 061	428	897	457	440	593	205	388
1973[1]	1 385	-	42	541	801	. . .	945	439	887	467	420	498	163	335
1972[1]	1 320	1	52	517	749	. . .	877	443	872	481	391	450	155	295
1971[1]	1 192	1	60	468	663	. . .	799	393	833	480	353	359	136	223
1970[1]	1 140	-	54	488	599	. . .	789	351	774	432	342	366	123	243

[1]Data for 1970–1975 and 1977 do not include students age 35 years and over.
r = Revised, controlled to 1990 census–based population estimates; previous 1993 data controlled to 1980 census–based population estimates.
- = Quantity zero or rounds to zero.
. . . = Not available.

Table A-15. College Enrollment of Students Age 14 Years and Over, by Type of College, Attendance Status, Age, and Sex, October 1970–2005—*Continued*

(Numbers in thousands.)

Year and type of college	Full-time						Part-time					
	Total enrollment	14 to 19 years	20 and 21 years	22 to 24 years	25 to 34 years	35 years and over	Total enrollment	14 to 19 years	20 and 21 years	22 to 24 years	25 to 34 years	35 years and over
Graduate Students												
2005	1 587	4	98	423	767	294	1 717	3	-	150	691	873
2004	1 571	20	76	548	675	252	1 807	-	1	170	757	878
2003	1 622	26	76	479	738	304	1 646	3	8	153	662	820
2002	1 406	31	61	432	631	251	1 666	2	6	140	666	852
2001	1 398	38	77	455	630	197	1 923	10	14	139	812	947
2000	1 268	32	67	414	544	211	1 645	6	10	156	674	798
1999	1 421	38	71	487	539	287	1 736	8	6	133	672	918
1998	1 372	45	58	429	579	262	1 665	-	15	107	734	808
1997	1 319	26	57	401	605	229	1 708	3	6	160	694	844
1996	1 305	18	42	420	570	254	1 617	3	9	114	647	844
1995	1 199	8	43	352	571	225	1 550	-	17	112	627	793
1994	1 124	9	19	377	544	175	1 489	-	2	174	594	718
1993r	1 059	3	11	376	482	186	1 376	-	3	161	540	673
1993	1 025	3	10	358	469	184	1 366	-	3	156	536	672
1992	1 126	-	33	387	478	228	1 266	-	3	120	557	586
1991	1 180	-	29	423	539	188	1 504	-	8	124	626	746
1990	1 100	2	25	376	518	180	1 413	-	2	121	577	714
1989	1 140	-	33	375	525	208	1 380	-	7	135	637	601
1988	956	-	31	304	465	157	1 555	-	5	160	634	756
1987	1 041	1	52	343	477	167	1 374	-	5	151	660	558
1986	1 074	-	40	412	465	157	1 291	-	4	120	593	575
1985	1 002	-	27	385	449	141	1 424	-	4	155	728	537
1984	1 093	-	27	427	544	95	1 302	-	6	153	644	498
1983	1 103	-	32	420	530	121	1 339	-	-	148	685	507
1982	1 047	-	28	381	522	116	1 346	1	4	153	721	467
1981	893	-	28	355	447	64	1 312	-	6	173	673	459
1980	898	2	24	403	403	66	1 275	-	6	152	702	415
1979	858	-	32	358	397	72	1 356	-	14	140	752	451
1978	882	-	38	396	376	71	1 335	-	14	169	688	465
1977[1]	886	2	43	382	459	. . .	922	-	10	211	702	. . .
1976	869	-	35	405	355	73	1 202	-	5	217	662	308
1975[1]	809	-	43	382	386	. . .	780	-	16	225	537	. . .
1974[1]	662	-	41	289	330	. . .	828	-	20	210	600	. . .
1973[1]	630	-	33	350	248	. . .	755	-	9	191	553	. . .
1972[1]	636	1	44	332	262	. . .	686	-	8	185	487	. . .
1971[1]	616	1	57	299	261	. . .	576	-	3	169	402	. . .
1970[1]	555	-	42	304	212	. . .	585	-	12	184	387	. . .

[1]Data for 1970–1975 and 1977 do not include students age 35 years and over.
r – Revised, controlled to 1990 census–based population estimates; previous 1993 data controlled to 1980 census–based population estimates.
- = Quantity zero or rounds to zero.
. . . = Not available.

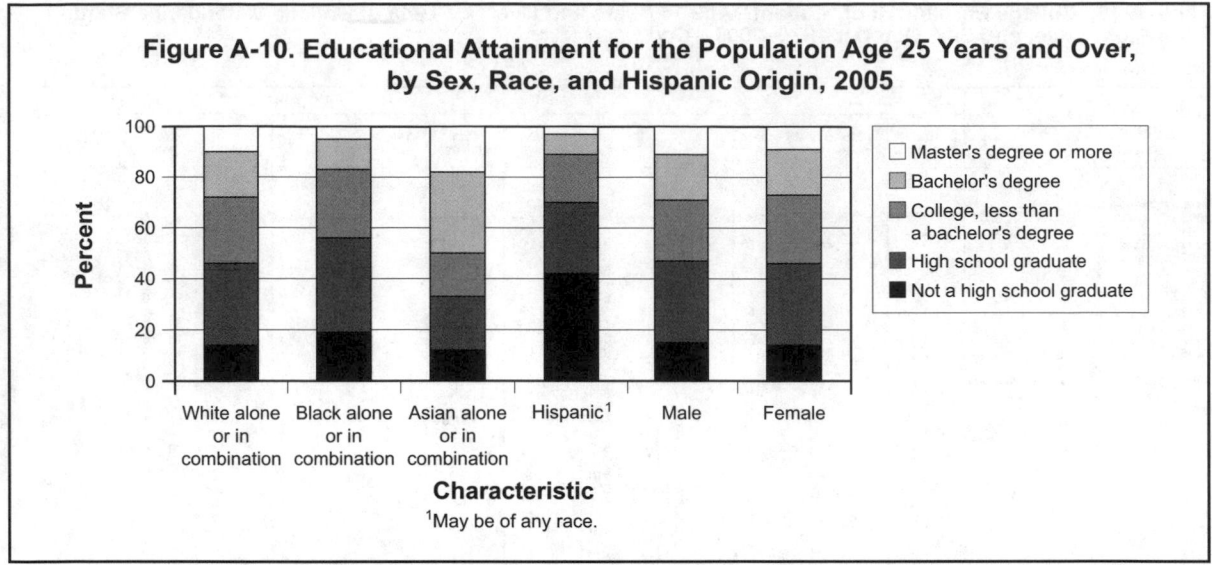

Figure A-10. Educational Attainment for the Population Age 25 Years and Over, by Sex, Race, and Hispanic Origin, 2005

¹May be of any race.

More than 85 percent of Americans over 25 years of age were high school graduates and nearly 28 percent held a bachelor's degree or more in 2005. This marked an increase of 10 percentage points from the 1980 college attainment levels. For people age 25 to 34 years old, nearly 87 percent had a high school diploma and more than 30 percent had a bachelor's degree or more. Women over 25 years of age had slightly higher rates of high school attainment, while men had higher rates of college attainment. Among race and ethnic groups, Asians had the highest high school graduation rate (87.9 percent), followed by Whites (85.7 percent), Blacks (81.3 percent), and Hispanics (58.5 percent). (Tables A-17, A-18, and A-27)

Table A-16. Educational Attainment of the Population Age 15 Years and Over, by Single Years of Age, Sex, Race, and Hispanic Origin, 2005

(Numbers in thousands.)

Age, sex, race, and Hispanic origin	Total	None	Elementary			High school				Some college, no degree	Associate's degree		Bachelor's degree	Master's degree	Professional degree	Doctorate degree
			1st to 4th grade	5th and 6th grade	7th and 8th grade	9th grade	10th grade	11th grade	High school graduate		Occupational	Academic				
ALL RACES																
Both Sexes																
15 years and over	230 437	985	2 156	4 017	7 994	8 649	9 686	13 483	69 446	41 727	9 477	8 072	36 520	12 928	2 946	2 352
15 years	4 321	2	5	20	1 920	1 898	387	47	27	14	-	-	-	-	-	-
16 years	4 407	-	7	7	385	1 817	1 812	335	28	12	2	-	2	-	-	-
17 years	4 334	2	3	9	80	313	1 756	2 023	114	30	-	-	1	1	-	-
18 years	3 975	5	13	18	49	101	325	1 949	865	633	5	3	8	-	2	-
19 years	3 626	3	6	31	51	82	120	484	1 290	1 517	28	7	7	-	-	-
20 years	4 105	7	9	31	54	117	141	306	1 266	2 041	52	62	15	2	-	-
21 years	3 994	3	16	35	57	89	94	246	1 217	1 924	130	112	70	2	-	-
22 years	4 149	3	8	37	56	99	117	254	1 313	1 531	148	124	452	4	-	2
23 years	4 005	2	22	56	59	79	109	215	1 186	1 179	131	132	805	26	4	-
24 years	4 154	10	32	66	53	124	91	189	1 246	1 036	176	169	901	52	5	3
25 years	4 101	17	20	97	67	101	92	221	1 190	844	166	163	947	142	32	2
26 years	3 804	13	23	66	50	81	106	185	1 139	764	202	162	802	159	41	11
27 years	3 865	13	14	60	87	73	80	204	1 154	739	178	152	864	191	42	14
28 years	3 814	14	30	68	50	97	70	199	1 174	698	148	167	870	172	35	21
29 years	3 918	14	28	75	67	80	96	140	1 059	760	170	151	918	252	73	34
30 years	3 774	10	31	71	68	74	46	159	1 089	704	178	124	864	259	68	28
31 years	3 744	14	26	101	62	102	67	164	981	691	204	162	848	249	43	31
32 years	3 793	18	44	64	60	119	76	144	1 078	646	182	168	841	274	47	31
33 years	4 068	11	26	72	58	90	70	142	1 130	725	207	176	925	321	63	49
34 years	4 430	10	36	72	60	80	80	180	1 276	785	228	220	955	343	65	40
35 years	4 307	13	31	99	77	62	63	160	1 303	680	248	186	905	324	87	70
36 years	4 031	20	20	60	61	87	68	143	1 155	714	215	170	883	299	65	72
37 years	4 007	11	36	86	66	62	61	153	1 244	686	206	172	787	318	72	47
38 years	4 162	25	38	67	53	82	95	167	1 312	679	187	164	897	282	69	45
39 years	4 144	17	22	88	49	78	78	152	1 362	697	238	173	826	240	87	38
40 years	4 728	8	46	85	77	81	89	170	1 464	811	277	220	934	323	93	51
41 years	4 438	15	33	74	71	67	73	152	1 430	776	275	207	852	298	79	34
42 years	4 513	17	34	63	93	57	93	180	1 530	732	269	216	875	251	53	50
43 years	4 404	13	24	59	54	74	93	147	1 401	777	238	202	880	309	67	66
44 years	4 616	13	44	92	69	66	103	153	1 542	736	231	221	901	329	79	37
45 years	4 772	22	40	87	59	77	82	156	1 596	822	229	251	914	309	70	59
46 years	4 291	18	40	66	57	69	101	169	1 452	694	250	176	802	269	78	51
47 years	4 569	19	24	54	61	71	108	132	1 464	886	269	225	795	313	83	64
48 years	4 325	12	38	62	67	61	71	127	1 357	806	221	194	836	337	73	62
49 years	4 278	10	24	73	54	88	90	162	1 412	723	242	183	800	285	78	53
50 years	4 435	15	46	77	76	59	79	118	1 546	744	209	211	764	352	77	62
51 years	4 020	17	35	75	68	53	65	123	1 289	723	206	163	757	355	50	40
52 years	3 943	17	30	40	62	53	71	130	1 247	704	193	182	739	355	67	52
53 years	3 561	19	17	55	75	56	67	105	1 047	596	199	183	711	303	70	58
54 years	3 766	10	21	76	69	53	67	120	1 077	673	188	180	696	398	57	80
55 years	3 569	18	34	57	61	57	91	95	1 068	660	163	148	629	367	58	60
56 years	3 460	15	32	44	96	56	81	78	1 133	627	166	149	566	284	69	64
57 years	3 567	14	29	58	79	54	83	119	1 008	619	208	151	644	352	65	83
58 years	3 379	30	42	64	77	34	93	120	1 013	577	162	150	553	331	69	63
59 years	2 797	16	35	29	63	52	78	67	945	487	120	117	467	212	44	64
60 years	2 812	14	34	58	68	53	58	110	916	497	110	140	437	223	53	41
61 years	2 638	12	20	49	61	63	63	102	909	448	89	94	416	231	34	47
62 years	2 722	11	32	43	98	49	103	105	887	388	114	92	412	263	45	80
63 years	2 326	8	22	37	88	50	69	109	876	341	72	56	376	146	23	53
64 years	2 267	10	33	46	74	49	65	114	844	347	96	93	324	124	19	30
65 years	2 390	8	36	74	105	64	112	110	836	355	85	72	323	162	33	14
66 years	2 078	10	40	49	80	58	66	81	821	301	53	73	259	121	43	25
67 years	1 976	13	28	64	84	59	79	111	729	315	55	67	205	101	23	45
68 years	1 847	24	42	47	79	45	59	79	694	277	59	42	236	111	33	19
69 years	1 839	13	42	36	104	52	86	86	692	237	66	44	221	115	17	27
70 years	1 665	16	43	29	99	40	66	84	648	221	53	34	223	60	19	30
71 years	1 694	12	36	51	86	50	75	68	659	237	64	24	187	82	36	28
72 years	1 678	11	32	47	106	35	65	95	613	263	48	34	191	98	12	28
73 years	1 587	16	42	39	107	49	67	108	560	198	50	36	208	59	26	19
74 years	1 636	23	33	33	107	61	89	56	590	215	54	35	223	83	12	23
75 years and over	16 820	207	425	567	1 558	646	782	882	5 950	2 185	464	287	1 771	704	239	153

- = Quantity zero or rounds to zero.

Table A-16. Educational Attainment of the Population Age 15 Years and Over, by Single Years of Age, Sex, Race, and Hispanic Origin, 2005—*Continued*

(Numbers in thousands.)

Age, sex, race, and Hispanic origin	Total	None	Elementary			High school				College						
			1st to 4th grade	5th and 6th grade	7th and 8th grade	9th grade	10th grade	11th grade	High school graduate	Some college, no degree	Associate's degree		Bachelor's degree	Master's degree	Professional degree	Doctorate degree
											Occupational	Academic				
ALL RACES																
Male																
15 years and over	111 694	443	1 155	2 113	4 051	4 368	4 800	6 766	33 844	19 471	4 222	3 254	17 559	6 154	1 904	1 592
15 years	2 209	2	5	14	1 040	911	188	26	16	7	-	-	-	-	-	-
16 years	2 247	-	-	1	233	941	911	145	16	1	-	-	-	-	-	-
17 years	2 272	2	1	9	48	187	960	989	58	15	-	-	1	-	-	-
18 years	1 973	2	10	14	38	50	195	995	421	240	4	1	2	-	2	-
19 years	1 802	3	2	27	31	38	74	302	634	676	9	4	1	-	-	-
20 years	2 136	4	5	19	31	66	56	199	731	971	23	23	7	2	-	-
21 years	2 003	3	9	17	37	57	44	127	698	882	57	46	27	1	-	-
22 years	2 093	2	8	25	33	50	59	143	743	740	69	49	169	2	-	2
23 years	2 025	1	9	26	31	52	45	124	689	594	60	65	322	6	-	-
24 years	2 035	7	18	55	32	79	51	82	687	470	83	65	389	11	3	3
25 years	2 074	17	13	59	55	55	41	109	664	437	77	66	414	48	16	2
26 years	1 902	12	16	39	28	43	56	123	598	356	90	67	370	84	14	5
27 years	1 959	4	6	25	54	37	45	118	653	375	87	87	383	59	23	2
28 years	1 917	8	23	39	21	54	22	113	654	340	77	72	402	67	16	9
29 years	1 975	7	17	42	22	32	49	70	644	343	85	74	423	99	55	14
30 years	1 855	8	17	36	43	43	19	92	611	326	74	44	390	106	31	15
31 years	1 865	4	17	57	33	59	38	99	506	345	97	79	387	104	23	16
32 years	1 879	8	21	22	33	61	42	70	607	328	86	81	378	105	23	14
33 years	2 021	6	18	48	27	48	35	79	578	344	97	79	447	146	39	30
34 years	2 231	3	15	46	38	42	38	95	701	388	100	97	451	152	40	25
35 years	2 133	10	28	55	40	28	33	85	699	327	124	82	400	132	53	38
36 years	2 070	11	5	34	39	45	43	81	652	337	98	57	430	160	35	42
37 years	1 994	4	20	46	42	36	36	73	666	336	100	68	374	135	38	18
38 years	2 003	11	24	28	27	40	48	91	683	294	82	58	428	124	37	27
39 years	2 064	13	14	47	24	48	39	107	702	331	101	67	398	101	52	21
40 years	2 393	8	22	56	44	56	47	98	783	357	138	91	443	161	53	36
41 years	2 137	6	22	33	36	26	36	83	758	324	126	94	386	140	54	13
42 years	2 231	8	18	34	62	35	43	94	850	325	114	81	395	119	23	30
43 years	2 183	5	17	27	32	47	46	92	706	355	104	79	434	156	42	42
44 years	2 260	4	26	52	43	26	48	79	789	366	99	77	429	165	38	19
45 years	2 282	10	21	51	36	42	31	90	822	351	100	81	408	151	45	43
46 years	2 069	10	26	24	29	41	62	78	757	323	130	56	337	116	49	29
47 years	2 220	11	13	26	27	42	48	73	714	461	117	73	363	151	49	51
48 years	2 227	10	26	36	27	27	41	73	704	411	99	69	426	181	56	42
49 years	2 137	5	19	36	26	37	60	91	740	326	124	60	381	145	56	31
50 years	2 202	7	37	48	44	29	45	56	761	351	94	93	373	174	50	42
51 years	1 879	-	20	34	38	26	31	59	612	331	87	66	368	147	37	24
52 years	2 004	9	22	22	38	28	29	57	631	335	86	88	403	177	48	32
53 years	1 678	6	9	21	30	22	36	43	476	276	79	76	394	133	48	30
54 years	1 856	3	7	48	36	20	21	34	514	335	85	75	370	212	38	59
55 years	1 676	8	20	37	23	27	50	39	464	304	77	72	309	165	35	47
56 years	1 675	12	10	21	51	29	35	34	501	300	80	65	299	141	50	46
57 years	1 676	4	17	24	40	31	40	51	420	304	75	65	330	162	48	64
58 years	1 633	23	21	36	44	22	44	65	445	266	81	46	274	171	46	49
59 years	1 349	3	14	13	27	22	41	33	427	231	58	46	254	102	31	47
60 years	1 285	7	25	31	23	27	26	46	351	234	45	52	241	112	39	25
61 years	1 277	7	8	36	25	28	30	56	403	210	42	43	212	117	24	35
62 years	1 329	2	20	20	62	28	44	49	379	186	46	47	212	138	33	62
63 years	1 093	5	14	25	45	23	31	46	369	142	23	23	198	88	21	41
64 years	1 059	6	20	27	22	31	25	39	369	138	45	34	186	76	15	26
65 years	1 138	-	21	33	55	30	61	51	343	169	32	23	178	106	25	10
66 years	1 038	1	15	17	43	29	28	37	368	158	23	39	154	68	36	22
67 years	957	3	20	27	47	28	49	55	314	154	22	27	106	50	13	43
68 years	859	9	16	23	35	28	28	30	302	136	22	18	106	69	26	13
69 years	823	3	24	22	47	29	28	30	266	105	28	16	129	66	10	18
70 years	723	3	17	15	65	22	30	21	245	99	15	4	116	45	13	14
71 years	736	5	9	26	39	21	30	32	222	123	25	12	94	48	28	23
72 years	760	-	22	26	38	20	23	35	229	126	28	16	111	47	12	27
73 years	714	3	28	18	52	22	30	39	229	73	13	21	113	36	20	17
74 years	718	7	15	17	39	20	31	19	211	105	31	19	129	40	10	23
75 years and over	6 681	77	174	239	598	244	304	319	2 062	877	149	77	905	332	187	136

- = Quantity zero or rounds to zero.

Table A-16. Educational Attainment of the Population Age 15 Years and Over, by Single Years of Age, Sex, Race, and Hispanic Origin, 2005—*Continued*

(Numbers in thousands.)

Age, sex, race, and Hispanic origin	Total	None	Elementary			High school				College						
			1st to 4th grade	5th and 6th grade	7th and 8th grade	9th grade	10th grade	11th grade	High school graduate	Some college, no degree	Associate's degree		Bachelor's degree	Master's degree	Professional degree	Doctorate degree
											Occupational	Academic				
ALL RACES																
Female																
15 years and over	118 742	543	1 001	1 904	3 943	4 281	4 886	6 717	35 602	22 256	5 256	4 818	18 961	6 774	1 041	760
15 years	2 111	-	-	6	880	986	198	22	11	7	-	-	-	-	-	-
16 years	2 160	-	7	6	152	877	902	189	12	11	2	-	2	-	-	-
17 years	2 062	-	1	-	31	127	796	1 034	56	15	-	-	-	1	-	-
18 years	2 002	3	3	4	11	51	130	954	444	393	1	1	6	-	-	-
19 years	1 824	-	4	4	20	44	46	182	656	842	19	3	5	-	-	-
20 years	1 969	2	4	13	23	51	85	106	535	1 071	30	40	8	-	-	-
21 years	1 991	1	7	18	21	32	51	119	519	1 042	73	66	43	1	-	-
22 years	2 056	1	-	12	23	50	58	111	571	791	79	75	283	3	-	-
23 years	1 980	2	13	30	27	27	64	91	496	585	71	67	483	20	4	-
24 years	2 119	3	14	11	21	45	40	107	560	566	93	105	513	40	2	-
25 years	2 027	-	7	39	12	46	51	111	526	407	89	97	533	94	16	-
26 years	1 903	1	8	27	22	37	50	62	541	407	112	95	432	75	27	6
27 years	1 906	9	8	35	33	36	35	85	501	365	92	65	481	132	20	12
28 years	1 897	5	7	29	29	43	48	86	520	358	71	96	468	105	20	12
29 years	1 943	7	11	33	45	48	48	71	415	417	86	77	494	153	19	20
30 years	1 919	2	14	35	25	31	27	67	478	378	104	80	474	154	36	13
31 years	1 879	10	9	44	29	43	29	65	475	345	108	84	461	144	20	14
32 years	1 914	10	23	42	27	59	33	75	471	318	95	87	464	169	24	17
33 years	2 047	6	9	24	31	42	35	63	552	381	110	97	479	176	23	19
34 years	2 199	7	21	26	22	38	43	85	574	397	128	123	504	191	25	15
35 years	2 174	3	4	44	37	34	30	75	605	352	124	104	505	192	35	31
36 years	1 961	9	14	26	22	42	25	61	503	377	117	113	453	139	31	30
37 years	2 013	7	16	40	24	26	26	79	578	350	106	104	412	183	34	29
38 years	2 159	13	15	39	26	42	47	76	629	385	105	106	470	158	32	18
39 years	2 080	4	7	40	26	30	39	45	660	366	137	106	428	139	35	18
40 years	2 335	-	24	29	33	25	42	72	681	454	139	129	491	162	40	15
41 years	2 301	10	12	41	35	40	36	69	672	452	150	113	466	159	24	21
42 years	2 282	8	16	29	30	23	51	86	680	408	156	134	480	132	30	20
43 years	2 221	8	7	32	22	27	47	55	694	423	134	123	446	153	25	25
44 years	2 356	9	18	40	26	39	55	74	753	370	132	143	472	164	41	18
45 years	2 489	11	19	36	23	35	51	65	774	471	129	169	506	158	26	16
46 years	2 223	8	14	42	28	28	39	91	694	370	121	120	465	152	28	21
47 years	2 349	8	11	28	34	29	60	58	751	425	151	152	432	162	33	14
48 years	2 098	1	13	27	40	34	30	54	654	395	121	125	410	156	17	20
49 years	2 141	6	5	37	28	51	30	70	673	397	118	123	419	140	23	22
50 years	2 233	8	9	29	32	30	35	62	785	393	116	119	391	178	27	20
51 years	2 141	17	16	41	31	27	34	64	677	392	119	97	389	208	13	16
52 years	1 939	8	8	17	25	26	42	73	617	369	107	94	336	178	19	20
53 years	1 883	13	8	34	45	34	31	62	571	320	120	108	317	170	22	28
54 years	1 909	7	14	29	33	33	46	86	563	338	104	105	326	186	19	21
55 years	1 893	10	13	21	38	31	41	56	605	356	86	76	320	202	24	14
56 years	1 786	3	21	23	45	27	46	44	632	328	86	84	266	143	19	18
57 years	1 891	9	12	34	38	23	44	67	588	315	133	86	315	190	18	19
58 years	1 745	7	21	28	33	12	49	56	568	311	81	104	279	160	23	15
59 years	1 447	13	21	15	36	30	37	34	519	256	63	71	213	110	12	17
60 years	1 527	7	10	26	45	26	32	64	565	263	65	88	196	111	14	16
61 years	1 361	5	12	13	36	35	33	46	506	238	46	51	204	114	10	11
62 years	1 393	10	11	22	37	21	60	56	507	202	68	45	200	125	12	18
63 years	1 233	3	8	12	43	28	37	62	507	199	49	33	177	58	3	13
64 years	1 208	4	14	19	51	17	39	75	474	208	52	59	138	48	4	4
65 years	1 251	8	15	41	50	34	52	59	494	186	53	48	144	56	8	4
66 years	1 040	9	25	32	36	28	38	43	453	143	29	34	105	53	7	4
67 years	1 020	10	8	37	37	30	30	56	415	161	33	40	99	51	10	2
68 years	987	15	27	24	44	17	31	49	393	141	37	24	131	42	7	6
69 years	1 016	10	18	14	58	23	57	55	426	132	38	28	93	49	7	9
70 years	942	13	26	14	34	18	37	64	403	122	38	30	107	15	6	16
71 years	958	7	27	25	47	29	45	35	437	114	39	12	93	34	8	5
72 years	918	11	10	21	67	15	43	59	384	136	21	18	80	51	-	-
73 years	873	13	14	21	55	27	37	69	331	125	38	15	95	23	6	2
74 years	918	16	18	15	68	40	58	37	378	110	22	15	93	43	3	-
75 years and over	10 139	130	251	327	960	402	478	564	3 888	1 307	314	210	866	372	52	17

- = Quantity zero or rounds to zero.

Table A-16. Educational Attainment of the Population Age 15 Years and Over, by Single Years of Age, Sex, Race, and Hispanic Origin, 2005—*Continued*

(Numbers in thousands.)

Age, sex, race, and Hispanic origin	Total	None	Elementary			High school				College						
			1st to 4th grade	5th and 6th grade	7th and 8th grade	9th grade	10th grade	11th grade	High school graduate	Some college, no degree	Associate's degree Occupational	Associate's degree Academic	Bachelor's degree	Master's degree	Professional degree	Doctorate degree
WHITE ALONE OR IN COMBINATION																
Both Sexes																
15 years and over	190 739	717	1 764	3 394	6 666	7 023	7 701	10 255	57 498	34 611	8 082	6 842	30 638	11 025	2 525	1 998
15 years	3 419	2	5	11	1 562	1 503	276	33	18	8	-	-	-	-	-	-
16 years	3 498	-	5	4	273	1 475	1 479	239	19	2	-	-	2	-	-	-
17 years	3 453	2	3	9	65	219	1 437	1 605	89	22	-	-	-	1	-	-
18 years	3 148	4	7	13	38	75	215	1 585	682	516	5	3	4	-	2	-
19 years	2 922	3	6	31	46	65	81	378	1 036	1 242	24	3	7	-	-	-
20 years	3 285	7	6	31	45	89	104	210	1 022	1 670	45	47	9	-	-	-
21 years	3 198	-	14	35	45	72	75	173	982	1 527	112	104	56	2	-	-
22 years	3 312	3	8	34	50	83	94	173	1 026	1 227	115	107	389	-	-	2
23 years	3 277	1	20	51	54	68	84	163	946	953	107	121	687	19	2	-
24 years	3 357	6	32	63	48	106	73	131	986	799	138	144	783	38	5	3
25 years	3 307	11	19	94	63	87	79	167	908	675	134	133	789	117	28	2
26 years	2 963	13	22	66	45	67	80	122	865	592	150	130	644	128	29	11
27 years	3 108	12	14	53	74	68	69	151	908	603	141	136	677	158	33	12
28 years	3 069	14	24	60	44	84	62	164	938	562	125	129	690	128	27	18
29 years	3 153	8	26	67	57	76	71	113	860	610	150	112	725	190	55	33
30 years	2 998	7	27	66	63	62	41	124	850	548	153	105	672	205	61	15
31 years	2 937	14	24	94	58	98	56	122	755	510	158	134	683	176	36	20
32 years	3 004	12	38	63	55	104	63	107	849	518	144	127	639	223	39	22
33 years	3 273	11	24	68	52	84	54	104	910	565	176	150	747	241	45	42
34 years	3 584	10	33	66	44	77	65	139	1 022	629	195	179	778	270	43	36
35 years	3 450	7	26	92	70	52	55	132	1 042	520	211	149	743	244	65	42
36 years	3 244	11	18	54	55	81	58	127	882	582	186	135	706	240	54	54
37 years	3 222	6	29	83	58	50	46	110	981	554	175	132	654	246	63	33
38 years	3 360	19	35	62	45	54	73	122	1 062	544	169	132	718	226	58	41
39 years	3 377	13	21	86	45	67	56	117	1 110	581	198	136	649	185	77	35
40 years	3 877	8	38	73	72	71	62	117	1 170	653	244	199	758	281	87	45
41 years	3 529	8	32	72	63	56	50	92	1 122	621	235	169	694	224	66	24
42 years	3 620	14	30	59	81	53	73	136	1 192	600	221	178	710	198	41	36
43 years	3 752	13	21	55	47	64	64	96	1 202	650	206	169	780	275	58	53
44 years	3 843	13	42	87	60	47	67	119	1 236	622	200	182	783	284	68	32
45 years	3 950	17	37	78	45	66	69	117	1 288	655	199	208	787	277	60	47
46 years	3 538	11	36	58	47	54	80	121	1 185	572	212	165	655	229	63	48
47 years	3 741	12	18	50	52	57	84	108	1 202	691	229	200	651	268	66	53
48 years	3 564	9	34	57	58	46	60	82	1 069	671	194	174	712	284	65	50
49 years	3 642	8	18	70	45	70	75	129	1 184	618	215	162	668	255	77	45
50 years	3 663	10	37	67	58	54	57	68	1 258	637	181	171	639	305	68	52
51 years	3 419	8	29	65	50	41	52	85	1 087	628	177	140	661	315	45	35
52 years	3 286	15	26	34	52	41	50	96	999	605	174	152	630	309	61	43
53 years	2 975	17	14	41	64	48	50	73	845	495	180	163	599	271	62	54
54 years	3 181	9	20	67	48	38	46	86	890	572	159	155	597	366	55	72
55 years	3 026	12	26	50	44	40	63	74	889	578	147	125	544	337	49	48
56 years	2 879	13	20	37	84	33	66	54	941	526	136	124	473	257	57	57
57 years	3 071	13	24	41	63	42	59	92	845	533	180	138	580	325	58	76
58 years	2 950	20	34	49	68	30	75	96	900	508	127	134	492	305	58	53
59 years	2 386	9	31	21	52	40	64	38	795	424	102	104	417	193	38	58
60 years	2 366	11	29	49	52	26	42	77	768	440	89	123	380	196	50	35
61 years	2 297	10	19	32	52	49	49	81	794	408	84	80	357	209	31	42
62 years	2 360	10	27	38	80	43	91	73	769	342	100	71	360	242	43	72
63 years	2 019	3	14	32	82	41	62	79	753	301	64	47	333	140	23	44
64 years	1 949	8	22	39	59	38	52	76	735	314	85	87	284	110	15	25
65 years	2 044	3	26	51	84	56	95	74	727	324	73	68	280	153	19	12
66 years	1 777	7	32	36	69	54	56	67	712	262	47	62	211	103	38	21
67 years	1 704	10	22	39	72	48	63	73	655	282	46	61	183	86	21	43
68 years	1 574	19	30	30	60	35	46	63	621	236	50	40	195	102	31	16
69 years	1 572	9	29	28	81	39	63	57	631	206	58	40	196	96	13	25
70 years	1 426	10	31	22	79	32	52	61	586	198	41	30	190	50	15	27
71 years	1 477	8	23	38	71	32	52	41	607	221	62	23	171	73	27	27
72 years	1 482	10	27	27	90	26	57	75	559	241	45	30	173	85	12	26
73 years	1 408	13	32	27	91	42	52	90	510	183	48	33	190	52	26	19
74 years	1 426	21	25	26	89	53	73	41	519	184	44	30	211	80	9	22
75 years and over	15 056	131	320	392	1 347	549	683	734	5 504	2 053	421	257	1 644	650	229	142

- = Quantity zero or rounds to zero.

Table A-16. Educational Attainment of the Population Age 15 Years and Over, by Single Years of Age, Sex, Race, and Hispanic Origin, 2005—*Continued*

(Numbers in thousands.)

Age, sex, race, and Hispanic origin	Total	None	Elementary			High school				College						
			1st to 4th grade	5th and 6th grade	7th and 8th grade	9th grade	10th grade	11th grade	High school graduate	Some college, no degree	Associate's degree		Bachelor's degree	Master's degree	Profes- sional degree	Doctor- ate degree
											Occupa- tional	Academic				
WHITE ALONE OR IN COMBINATION																
Male																
15 years and over	93 394	350	969	1 835	3 420	3 568	3 842	5 281	28 035	16 360	3 670	2 768	15 034	5 249	1 655	1 361
15 years	1 747	2	5	5	843	716	140	19	14	3	-	-	-	-	-	-
16 years	1 816	-	-	1	163	786	751	104	11	-	-	-	-	-	-	-
17 years	1 775	2	1	9	38	126	788	754	46	11	-	-	-	-	-	-
18 years	1 568	1	4	11	27	41	140	805	329	203	4	1	-	-	2	-
19 years	1 476	3	2	27	27	30	49	236	514	576	9	3	1	-	-	-
20 years	1 710	4	5	19	28	51	45	136	602	778	22	16	7	-	-	-
21 years	1 609	-	9	17	31	49	29	97	570	692	52	40	23	1	-	-
22 years	1 671	2	8	25	32	40	51	101	575	591	53	44	148	-	-	2
23 years	1 714	1	9	25	29	44	33	105	580	497	53	62	270	6	-	-
24 years	1 679	4	18	52	29	68	39	63	545	373	71	58	342	11	3	3
25 years	1 725	11	13	58	51	46	37	91	509	370	68	57	358	39	16	2
26 years	1 496	12	16	39	28	37	48	83	451	293	67	49	295	62	13	5
27 years	1 622	4	6	24	47	34	38	91	536	318	72	81	309	43	19	-
28 years	1 552	8	17	35	21	46	19	102	522	269	62	58	321	52	11	9
29 years	1 625	5	15	38	18	31	34	63	526	290	80	51	345	74	43	14
30 years	1 498	7	13	33	40	39	17	80	491	249	63	42	312	75	29	8
31 years	1 507	4	17	53	32	57	32	78	401	257	80	66	327	67	23	13
32 years	1 508	8	19	21	33	57	34	55	484	265	73	57	289	81	18	13
33 years	1 626	6	16	47	26	43	29	66	480	254	79	74	347	105	28	27
34 years	1 842	3	13	41	29	39	32	82	565	332	95	79	370	110	29	21
35 years	1 732	7	23	53	38	23	28	73	572	260	103	67	338	88	38	18
36 years	1 686	6	5	34	39	42	35	77	500	270	84	49	360	126	27	32
37 years	1 617	4	18	44	39	27	27	58	513	282	86	52	321	100	33	13
38 years	1 649	7	22	27	22	25	38	73	568	244	75	46	351	93	33	25
39 years	1 700	11	14	47	20	40	29	86	580	276	93	56	300	85	46	18
40 years	1 971	8	17	52	43	50	29	69	617	298	123	86	356	142	50	32
41 years	1 720	4	20	33	33	22	24	55	599	276	110	75	316	103	44	7
42 years	1 810	8	14	33	54	33	36	78	667	276	97	66	315	99	16	19
43 years	1 885	5	16	25	29	45	32	68	599	299	94	68	390	144	39	32
44 years	1 914	4	26	51	41	18	30	65	666	303	79	60	387	138	30	17
45 years	1 909	9	20	47	25	36	30	69	659	287	87	66	366	137	40	32
46 years	1 755	7	26	21	24	31	51	64	656	268	114	54	276	99	37	28
47 years	1 821	7	11	24	26	32	38	68	573	353	98	66	318	127	37	43
48 years	1 836	8	21	35	25	19	36	39	555	341	91	63	368	145	55	35
49 years	1 861	3	14	36	23	29	50	73	632	288	114	47	336	135	55	27
50 years	1 835	5	32	41	34	28	33	42	604	297	86	82	319	150	46	38
51 years	1 630	-	19	30	25	19	21	44	522	294	80	58	328	136	35	21
52 years	1 698	7	20	20	29	23	23	44	513	294	79	76	343	157	44	25
53 years	1 414	6	9	18	27	21	27	29	383	236	71	68	332	119	40	30
54 years	1 586	3	7	43	27	12	14	27	415	286	68	67	330	195	38	54
55 years	1 455	8	17	31	18	24	35	27	393	274	67	62	279	158	25	38
56 years	1 408	12	7	21	45	18	29	21	404	261	71	52	254	127	44	41
57 years	1 446	3	14	19	34	26	22	39	347	265	61	58	304	151	43	59
58 years	1 424	13	16	24	37	20	35	57	398	231	64	37	251	158	39	42
59 years	1 172	3	14	8	21	14	35	17	371	204	48	43	232	95	27	41
60 years	1 110	6	22	25	22	9	21	36	306	207	38	45	211	104	37	20
61 years	1 120	7	7	27	24	22	22	43	348	195	41	41	183	104	24	32
62 years	1 158	2	18	18	52	25	40	33	334	161	40	38	190	124	31	53
63 years	966	2	7	20	44	20	29	38	318	127	19	17	190	84	21	33
64 years	917	4	13	22	18	24	24	30	317	130	40	34	162	65	11	25
65 years	958	-	14	21	46	27	50	35	282	153	26	20	157	103	14	10
66 years	893	-	14	13	37	27	24	34	323	132	20	31	130	61	31	17
67 years	824	3	17	18	44	22	34	39	282	131	21	24	97	41	11	41
68 years	743	9	13	16	26	21	19	25	270	122	19	18	90	63	25	10
69 years	712	3	14	21	37	23	23	14	249	96	27	14	113	56	7	17
70 years	621	2	17	10	49	16	22	14	227	90	15	2	97	35	11	11
71 years	654	5	5	16	34	15	21	21	208	116	24	11	89	46	21	22
72 years	677	-	20	14	33	12	19	27	210	121	25	13	103	41	12	26
73 years	635	2	21	14	46	19	24	29	207	69	13	18	105	32	20	17
74 years	644	6	10	16	36	18	28	14	187	93	27	17	125	39	6	22
75 years and over	6 063	55	131	167	527	211	271	277	1 912	830	135	64	860	317	179	126

- = Quantity zero or rounds to zero.

Table A-16. Educational Attainment of the Population Age 15 Years and Over, by Single Years of Age, Sex, Race, and Hispanic Origin, 2005—*Continued*

(Numbers in thousands.)

Age, sex, race, and Hispanic origin	Total	None	Elementary			High school				College						
			1st to 4th grade	5th and 6th grade	7th and 8th grade	9th grade	10th grade	11th grade	High school graduate	Some college, no degree	Associate's degree		Bachelor's degree	Master's degree	Professional degree	Doctorate degree
											Occupational	Academic				
WHITE ALONE OR IN COMBINATION																
Female																
15 years and over	97 345	367	796	1 559	3 246	3 456	3 859	4 973	29 463	18 251	4 412	4 075	15 604	5 776	870	637
15 years	1 672	-	-	-	5	719	787	136	14	4	5	-	-	-	-	-
16 years	1 683	-	5	4	110	689	728	135	8	2	-	-	2	-	-	-
17 years	1 678	-	1	-	27	93	650	851	43	11	-	-	-	1	-	-
18 years	1 580	3	3	1	11	34	76	780	354	312	1	1	4	-	-	-
19 years	1 446	-	4	4	20	35	32	142	522	666	15	-	5	-	-	-
20 years	1 575	2	1	13	19	39	59	74	420	891	23	31	2	-	-	-
21 years	1 588	-	5	18	14	23	46	76	412	835	60	65	33	1	-	-
22 years	1 640	1	-	9	19	42	43	72	451	636	62	64	241	-	-	-
23 years	1 563	-	11	26	25	24	51	59	366	456	54	59	417	13	2	-
24 years	1 677	2	14	11	19	38	34	68	441	426	67	87	441	27	2	-
25 years	1 582	-	6	36	12	41	43	77	398	305	66	76	432	77	12	-
26 years	1 467	1	6	26	17	30	32	40	414	299	83	81	348	65	16	6
27 years	1 486	7	8	29	27	34	30	61	371	284	69	55	368	116	14	12
28 years	1 516	5	7	26	23	37	43	62	416	293	63	71	369	76	16	9
29 years	1 528	3	11	29	39	46	38	50	334	321	70	61	380	115	12	19
30 years	1 500	-	14	33	23	23	24	45	359	299	90	63	360	129	32	7
31 years	1 430	10	7	40	26	41	24	44	354	253	78	68	356	109	13	7
32 years	1 496	4	19	42	22	47	29	53	364	254	70	70	350	142	21	9
33 years	1 647	6	8	21	27	41	25	38	430	311	97	76	400	136	17	15
34 years	1 742	6	19	25	14	38	33	57	457	297	99	99	408	160	13	15
35 years	1 719	-	4	39	32	29	27	59	470	256	108	83	405	156	27	25
36 years	1 558	5	12	21	16	39	22	50	383	313	102	86	347	114	27	23
37 years	1 604	3	11	39	19	23	19	52	467	271	90	80	333	147	30	21
38 years	1 711	12	13	35	22	29	35	49	494	300	94	86	367	134	25	16
39 years	1 676	2	7	39	25	27	28	31	530	305	106	80	350	100	31	17
40 years	1 906	-	22	21	29	21	34	48	552	355	121	113	403	138	37	13
41 years	1 809	4	12	39	30	34	27	37	523	345	125	95	378	121	22	17
42 years	1 811	6	16	26	26	20	38	59	525	324	123	112	395	100	24	17
43 years	1 867	8	5	30	19	19	32	27	603	351	112	102	390	131	19	20
44 years	1 929	9	16	37	19	29	37	54	571	320	121	122	396	146	38	15
45 years	2 041	8	17	31	20	30	39	48	629	367	112	142	421	140	20	15
46 years	1 783	4	11	37	23	23	29	58	529	304	98	111	379	130	26	20
47 years	1 920	5	7	26	27	25	46	41	629	337	131	134	334	140	28	11
48 years	1 728	1	13	22	33	27	23	43	514	330	103	111	344	138	10	15
49 years	1 780	6	4	34	22	41	24	56	553	330	102	115	333	120	23	18
50 years	1 827	6	5	27	24	26	24	26	654	340	95	89	320	156	22	14
51 years	1 788	8	11	36	26	22	30	41	566	333	98	81	333	179	10	15
52 years	1 588	7	5	14	23	18	27	52	486	311	95	75	288	152	17	18
53 years	1 561	11	5	22	37	28	23	43	462	260	109	95	267	152	22	24
54 years	1 595	6	13	24	21	27	32	59	475	286	91	88	267	171	18	18
55 years	1 571	4	9	18	26	17	29	47	496	304	80	64	266	179	23	10
56 years	1 471	1	13	16	39	15	37	33	537	265	65	72	220	130	13	16
57 years	1 625	9	10	22	29	16	37	53	498	268	119	80	275	174	16	18
58 years	1 526	7	18	25	31	10	41	39	501	277	63	96	241	147	20	10
59 years	1 214	6	17	13	31	26	30	21	424	220	54	61	185	98	11	17
60 years	1 256	4	7	24	30	17	21	41	462	233	51	77	169	93	13	15
61 years	1 176	3	12	5	28	27	27	38	446	213	43	39	175	104	7	10
62 years	1 202	8	9	20	28	18	50	40	435	181	60	33	170	118	12	18
63 years	1 053	2	8	12	38	21	33	42	435	174	45	30	143	57	3	11
64 years	1 032	4	9	17	42	14	28	47	418	184	45	53	122	45	4	-
65 years	1 086	3	12	31	38	28	45	40	444	171	46	48	122	51	5	3
66 years	884	7	19	23	32	26	32	34	389	131	27	31	81	42	7	4
67 years	880	7	5	22	28	26	29	34	373	151	25	37	86	45	10	2
68 years	830	10	18	14	35	15	27	38	351	114	31	22	105	39	6	6
69 years	861	6	15	7	44	16	40	43	383	110	32	26	83	41	5	9
70 years	805	8	14	11	30	15	31	46	360	108	26	28	93	15	4	16
71 years	823	3	19	21	37	17	31	20	399	105	39	12	82	27	5	5
72 years	806	10	7	13	57	13	38	48	348	120	20	17	71	43	-	-
73 years	773	11	12	13	45	22	28	61	303	114	35	15	85	20	6	2
74 years	783	15	15	9	52	35	45	27	332	91	17	14	86	41	3	-
75 years and over	8 993	77	189	225	820	339	412	456	3 592	1 223	286	193	783	333	50	15

- = Quantity zero or rounds to zero.

Table A-16. Educational Attainment of the Population Age 15 Years and Over, by Single Years of Age, Sex, Race, and Hispanic Origin, 2005—*Continued*

(Numbers in thousands.)

Age, sex, race, and Hispanic origin	Total	None	1st to 4th grade	5th and 6th grade	7th and 8th grade	9th grade	10th grade	11th grade	High school graduate	Some college, no degree	Occupa-tional	Academic	Bachelor's degree	Master's degree	Profes-sional degree	Doctor-ate degree
			Elementary			High school				College	Associate's degree					
BLACK ALONE OR IN COMBINATION																
Both Sexes																
15 years and over	27 987	129	221	336	1 014	1 294	1 579	2 654	9 482	5 376	1 035	852	2 883	876	148	107
15 years	737	-	-	5	311	315	84	11	7	3	-	-	-	-	-	-
16 years	728	-	-	2	104	293	253	62	7	6	2	-	-	-	-	-
17 years	675	-	-	-	8	81	250	315	15	6	-	-	-	-	-	-
18 years	639	-	-	-	11	20	83	290	149	81	-	-	4	-	-	-
19 years	538	-	-	-	5	16	38	83	220	172	3	3	-	-	-	-
20 years	634	-	-	-	5	26	36	81	199	262	3	15	5	2	-	-
21 years	603	3	-	-	9	15	10	60	191	286	15	3	11	-	-	-
22 years	615	-	-	-	6	12	22	69	233	196	21	12	43	3	-	-
23 years	522	2	2	3	4	8	20	44	206	157	18	7	50	-	-	-
24 years	609	4	-	2	3	15	17	47	232	166	30	21	70	3	-	-
25 years	581	7	-	3	2	11	8	49	236	121	23	24	82	11	2	2
26 years	620	-	1	1	4	10	24	56	232	142	38	26	76	9	-	-
27 years	523	1	-	5	10	6	8	49	199	116	28	13	80	6	3	-
28 years	470	-	1	2	6	7	8	29	191	96	17	30	65	15	2	-
29 years	508	-	-	6	4	-	21	24	157	128	15	30	101	17	6	-
30 years	474	1	4	2	3	9	3	26	187	123	18	14	70	13	-	-
31 years	530	-	2	5	2	3	6	23	177	144	41	22	75	26	3	-
32 years	516	4	-	1	3	10	11	31	179	113	28	25	86	19	3	5
33 years	495	-	-	-	-	3	10	31	182	117	22	19	76	25	3	4
34 years	584	-	2	3	13	3	11	31	200	139	22	33	90	26	12	-
35 years	557	3	2	4	5	8	8	26	204	113	31	26	83	28	8	9
36 years	529	7	-	3	4	3	7	14	224	105	27	25	81	24	2	1
37 years	510	2	4	2	2	10	12	34	217	102	18	26	57	22	2	3
38 years	538	6	-	-	4	23	16	40	202	100	15	14	90	25	2	2
39 years	506	1	-	1	1	8	20	31	200	83	20	17	90	18	5	-
40 years	616	-	2	7	-	4	22	45	241	117	22	16	110	25	2	2
41 years	607	2	2	1	6	8	9	45	239	121	28	26	76	35	2	5
42 years	592	-	-	-	5	2	17	38	261	106	36	25	90	15	2	5
43 years	464	-	1	3	5	8	24	48	163	95	21	25	53	13	2	3
44 years	553	-	-	3	7	15	26	27	264	86	25	21	57	19	2	2
45 years	595	3	-	2	11	7	10	30	250	134	29	26	66	20	5	3
46 years	564	2	3	4	4	13	8	41	216	99	32	7	103	24	8	2
47 years	578	4	4	2	-	7	21	20	209	148	31	21	83	20	6	2
48 years	530	-	-	2	4	15	9	44	223	106	16	13	69	21	5	3
49 years	428	2	4	2	4	13	10	31	159	82	18	10	66	20	1	6
50 years	538	2	4	1	9	2	20	45	216	76	23	29	68	31	7	4
51 years	411	2	3	4	8	7	12	33	155	76	21	13	44	31	2	-
52 years	465	2	2	1	5	9	14	27	199	84	14	19	50	31	2	5
53 years	400	2	3	5	11	4	12	23	147	88	10	15	54	21	-	4
54 years	431	-	-	5	18	7	19	27	155	82	22	17	55	20	-	2
55 years	367	-	5	5	5	13	23	20	133	60	11	17	42	23	3	7
56 years	401	6	9	2	6	10	13	19	145	78	25	14	48	19	6	2
57 years	366	-	3	6	13	10	24	24	132	65	18	11	33	24	3	2
58 years	315	7	7	12	5	3	16	23	99	49	27	12	34	13	4	4
59 years	268	4	2	5	6	10	11	26	107	55	13	11	13	4	-	3
60 years	325	-	5	5	12	22	15	23	111	49	18	15	29	18	1	2
61 years	236	1	-	9	6	14	14	18	90	33	2	10	24	12	-	3
62 years	260	2	2	-	15	5	11	29	99	40	11	19	13	12	-	3
63 years	214	3	5	2	6	4	6	27	100	35	4	7	9	3	-	1
64 years	219	-	2	6	9	7	8	33	92	23	6	4	20	7	-	1
65 years	224	5	8	8	18	6	14	25	80	27	10	-	11	4	6	-
66 years	205	-	3	6	8	4	10	9	80	31	5	11	23	10	3	1
67 years	201	2	3	9	10	10	14	28	61	24	5	4	16	13	-	-
68 years	186	4	3	9	14	10	11	16	52	35	9	1	19	2	2	-
69 years	200	2	11	6	17	11	21	25	46	23	7	4	12	13	3	-
70 years	168	2	7	4	15	5	10	24	48	15	8	3	22	3	1	-
71 years	163	2	4	6	8	17	21	26	41	16	-	1	10	7	5	-
72 years	133	-	3	12	14	8	8	18	34	18	3	-	6	6	-	-
73 years	126	1	9	3	12	6	11	18	39	11	1	1	9	4	-	-
74 years	134	2	3	5	15	4	14	12	40	19	7	1	7	3	1	-
75 years and over	1 267	22	81	122	176	81	83	133	318	94	32	20	55	36	7	8

- = Quantity zero or rounds to zero.

Table A-16. Educational Attainment of the Population Age 15 Years and Over, by Single Years of Age, Sex, Race, and Hispanic Origin, 2005—*Continued*

(Numbers in thousands.)

Age, sex, race, and Hispanic origin	Total	None	Elementary 1st to 4th grade	Elementary 5th and 6th grade	Elementary 7th and 8th grade	High school 9th grade	High school 10th grade	High school 11th grade	High school graduate	Some college, no degree	Associate's degree Occupational	Associate's degree Academic	Bachelor's degree	Master's degree	Professional degree	Doctorate degree
BLACK ALONE OR IN COMBINATION																
Male																
15 years and over	12 614	67	111	162	487	626	755	1 205	4 602	2 287	391	332	1 133	320	77	59
15 years	362	-	-	4	166	154	30	6	2	-	-	-	-	-	-	-
16 years	330	-	-	-	63	121	117	25	3	-	-	-	-	-	-	-
17 years	388	-	-	-	8	54	141	176	6	4	-	-	-	-	-	-
18 years	294	-	-	-	11	7	46	136	73	19	-	-	2	-	-	-
19 years	257	-	-	-	5	8	25	56	103	60	1	-	-	-	-	-
20 years	336	-	-	-	2	14	10	55	110	134	-	8	-	2	-	-
21 years	281	3	-	-	6	6	6	21	93	136	4	2	3	-	-	-
22 years	308	-	-	-	2	7	7	41	130	92	9	4	16	-	-	-
23 years	207	-	-	-	2	5	13	15	91	64	3	-	14	-	-	-
24 years	279	3	-	-	2	3	8	11	15	133	74	4	3	24	-	-
25 years	260	7	-	1	2	7	1	23	133	48	10	8	20	-	-	2
26 years	288	-	-	-	-	4	9	36	120	52	14	15	31	7	-	-
27 years	234	-	-	-	4	2	5	26	99	42	8	5	42	1	-	-
28 years	226	-	1	-	-	4	3	8	97	53	12	11	34	1	-	-
29 years	232	-	-	3	3	-	13	7	99	45	3	18	37	2	3	-
30 years	208	1	4	2	3	4	-	6	97	48	10	2	21	10	-	-
31 years	224	-	-	2	1	1	3	12	84	64	13	7	29	8	-	-
32 years	237	-	-	1	-	3	7	9	97	53	9	14	36	3	3	-
33 years	241	-	-	-	-	3	6	9	83	71	12	4	37	13	1	3
34 years	240	-	2	3	6	3	4	9	101	45	2	12	36	12	7	-
35 years	246	3	2	1	2	4	5	12	94	43	17	12	27	13	7	5
36 years	236	5	-	-	-	3	5	3	115	48	12	6	28	9	1	1
37 years	241	-	2	2	-	6	7	12	126	41	9	10	18	7	-	-
38 years	238	4	-	-	3	14	8	19	92	40	5	7	33	12	-	2
39 years	231	1	-	-	1	5	9	17	94	36	6	5	51	3	4	-
40 years	293	-	-	2	-	1	16	23	130	38	9	6	55	9	-	2
41 years	274	-	2	-	3	3	6	20	129	33	15	15	26	16	2	3
42 years	280	-	-	-	5	-	7	15	144	40	10	9	38	8	-	3
43 years	197	-	-	2	1	1	12	21	86	37	6	9	18	2	-	-
44 years	237	-	-	-	2	8	14	12	102	52	14	8	14	9	2	-
45 years	275	1	-	-	9	5	1	17	137	51	13	9	20	8	2	3
46 years	230	-	-	2	3	10	4	12	82	45	14	-	45	7	7	-
47 years	273	2	2	2	-	5	9	6	107	87	14	5	20	10	2	1
48 years	267	-	-	-	2	8	4	33	117	59	4	2	28	10	1	-
49 years	183	2	3	-	2	9	7	17	71	27	3	9	22	7	1	4
50 years	266	2	4	1	4	-	10	13	126	32	8	10	43	10	4	-
51 years	168	-	-	1	3	2	9	14	77	28	6	4	12	10	1	-
52 years	201	2	2	-	3	3	4	11	95	36	5	9	19	9	-	4
53 years	172	-	-	2	4	1	6	8	70	37	6	4	27	9	-	-
54 years	204	-	-	2	9	4	6	6	84	37	14	7	22	11	-	-
55 years	159	-	3	5	1	3	13	10	61	22	7	7	17	3	3	4
56 years	176	4	3	-	4	4	6	11	66	26	5	6	25	12	2	2
57 years	174	-	3	2	3	5	17	12	61	29	9	6	13	8	2	2
58 years	145	7	5	9	4	-	6	7	45	25	11	7	10	3	3	2
59 years	114	-	-	2	3	8	4	14	35	27	7	3	6	1	-	3
60 years	126	-	2	5	2	15	4	8	32	24	6	5	18	4	-	1
61 years	101	-	-	6	-	5	8	11	41	11	1	2	9	6	-	1
62 years	122	-	2	-	8	3	3	14	43	22	4	9	3	6	-	3
63 years	90	2	5	2	2	3	2	8	41	14	4	4	2	1	-	-
64 years	93	-	2	5	4	4	-	9	49	6	-	-	9	5	-	-
65 years	116	-	7	5	9	2	11	9	45	13	6	-	3	1	4	-
66 years	94	-	1	2	4	2	4	3	29	20	3	8	11	3	3	1
67 years	101	-	2	6	2	6	13	14	27	15	1	1	5	9	-	-
68 years	77	-	-	5	5	7	7	5	21	13	3	-	10	-	-	-
69 years	79	-	9	1	9	7	5	14	12	6	2	2	6	4	2	-
70 years	61	1	-	3	11	3	4	6	11	6	-	2	10	2	1	-
71 years	57	-	1	5	1	6	9	11	9	6	-	-	5	1	3	-
72 years	54	-	1	9	5	7	4	8	12	4	3	-	3	1	-	-
73 years	58	1	7	2	3	2	4	10	16	4	-	1	6	1	-	-
74 years	41	1	2	1	1	-	3	5	14	6	2	1	1	1	1	-
75 years and over	433	14	32	52	65	26	22	36	101	33	14	6	15	7	4	6

- = Quantity zero or rounds to zero.

Table A-16. Educational Attainment of the Population Age 15 Years and Over, by Single Years of Age, Sex, Race, and Hispanic Origin, 2005—*Continued*

(Numbers in thousands.)

Age, sex, race, and Hispanic origin	Total	None	Elementary			High school				College						
			1st to 4th grade	5th and 6th grade	7th and 8th grade	9th grade	10th grade	11th grade	High school graduate	Some college, no degree	Associate's degree		Bachelor's degree	Master's degree	Professional degree	Doctorate degree
											Occupational	Academic				
BLACK ALONE OR IN COMBINATION																
Female																
15 years and over	15 373	63	110	174	526	668	824	1 450	4 880	3 089	645	520	1 749	555	71	49
15 years	374	-	-	1	145	162	54	6	5	3	-	-	-	-	-	-
16 years	398	-	-	2	41	171	136	37	4	6	2	-	-	-	-	-
17 years	287	-	-	-	-	27	110	139	8	2	-	-	-	-	-	-
18 years	345	-	-	-	-	12	37	155	76	62	-	-	2	-	-	-
19 years	282	-	-	-	-	8	13	27	116	112	2	3	-	-	-	-
20 years	298	-	-	-	3	12	26	25	88	128	3	7	5	-	-	-
21 years	322	1	-	-	3	8	4	39	98	150	10	1	7	-	-	-
22 years	307	-	-	-	4	6	15	28	103	104	12	8	26	3	-	-
23 years	315	2	2	3	2	3	7	29	116	93	15	7	36	-	-	-
24 years	331	1	-	-	-	7	6	32	99	91	27	18	46	3	-	-
25 years	321	-	-	2	-	5	8	26	103	73	13	16	62	11	2	-
26 years	332	-	1	1	4	5	16	20	113	90	24	10	46	2	-	-
27 years	288	1	-	5	6	4	3	22	100	74	20	7	38	4	3	-
28 years	245	-	-	2	6	3	5	21	94	43	4	19	32	13	2	-
29 years	276	-	-	2	1	-	8	18	58	83	12	12	64	15	3	-
30 years	266	-	-	-	-	5	3	21	90	75	8	12	49	4	-	-
31 years	306	-	2	4	1	2	3	11	94	80	28	14	45	18	3	-
32 years	279	4	-	-	3	7	4	22	82	59	19	11	50	15	-	4
33 years	254	-	-	-	-	-	5	22	100	46	10	15	40	13	2	1
34 years	344	-	-	-	8	-	7	22	99	93	20	21	54	14	5	-
35 years	310	-	-	2	3	4	3	14	110	70	14	14	56	15	1	3
36 years	293	2	-	3	4	1	2	11	109	57	15	19	53	16	1	-
37 years	268	2	1	1	2	3	4	22	90	61	8	15	39	15	2	3
38 years	301	2	-	-	2	9	8	21	110	60	10	7	57	13	2	-
39 years	275	-	-	1	-	3	11	14	108	47	23	12	39	15	1	-
40 years	323	-	2	4	-	3	7	22	111	79	13	10	55	16	2	-
41 years	333	2	-	1	3	5	3	25	110	88	14	11	49	19	-	2
42 years	313	-	-	-	-	2	10	23	107	66	26	16	52	7	2	3
43 years	267	-	1	2	4	7	12	27	76	57	15	16	35	11	2	2
44 years	316	-	-	3	5	7	12	16	163	34	10	13	42	10	-	2
45 years	320	2	-	2	2	2	9	14	113	83	16	16	46	12	4	-
46 years	334	2	3	2	1	3	4	29	134	54	19	7	57	16	2	2
47 years	305	2	2	-	-	2	12	14	103	62	17	15	63	10	4	-
48 years	263	-	-	2	2	7	4	12	106	47	13	11	41	11	5	3
49 years	245	-	1	2	2	4	3	14	88	55	15	1	44	13	-	2
50 years	272	-	-	-	5	2	11	33	89	44	15	18	25	21	3	4
51 years	243	2	3	3	5	5	3	19	77	48	15	9	32	22	1	-
52 years	264	-	-	1	2	6	10	16	104	48	9	11	31	22	2	2
53 years	228	2	3	4	7	3	6	15	78	51	5	12	27	13	-	4
54 years	227	-	-	3	8	3	13	21	71	45	8	10	34	9	-	2
55 years	208	-	2	-	4	10	11	10	72	38	5	10	25	20	-	3
56 years	225	2	6	2	2	5	7	8	79	52	20	8	23	7	5	-
57 years	192	-	-	3	9	5	6	12	71	35	8	5	20	16	-	-
58 years	170	-	1	3	1	2	10	15	54	25	16	5	25	10	2	1
59 years	154	4	2	2	3	3	7	11	72	29	7	8	6	2	-	-
60 years	199	-	3	-	11	7	11	15	79	25	12	10	11	15	1	-
61 years	135	1	-	2	6	8	6	6	49	22	1	9	16	5	-	2
62 years	138	1	-	-	7	2	8	15	57	17	7	10	10	5	-	-
63 years	124	2	-	-	4	1	4	19	59	21	-	3	7	1	-	1
64 years	125	-	1	1	5	3	8	24	43	17	5	4	11	2	-	1
65 years	108	5	1	3	9	3	3	16	35	14	5	-	8	3	2	-
66 years	112	-	2	4	3	2	6	6	52	11	2	3	12	7	-	-
67 years	100	2	1	4	8	4	1	14	34	9	5	3	12	4	-	-
68 years	109	4	3	4	9	2	4	10	31	22	6	1	9	2	2	-
69 years	121	2	2	5	7	5	15	11	34	17	6	1	7	9	1	-
70 years	106	1	7	1	4	2	6	17	37	9	8	2	12	-	-	-
71 years	106	2	2	1	7	11	12	14	31	10	-	1	5	6	2	-
72 years	78	-	3	4	10	2	5	10	23	14	1	-	3	5	-	-
73 years	67	-	1	2	9	4	8	8	22	6	1	-	3	3	-	-
74 years	93	1	1	4	13	4	11	7	26	13	5	-	5	2	-	-
75 years and over	834	8	49	70	111	55	61	97	217	61	18	13	40	29	3	2

- = Quantity zero or rounds to zero.

Table A-16. Educational Attainment of the Population Age 15 Years and Over, by Single Years of Age, Sex, Race, and Hispanic Origin, 2005—*Continued*

(Numbers in thousands.)

Age, sex, race, and Hispanic origin	Total	None	Elementary			High school				College						
			1st to 4th grade	5th and 6th grade	7th and 8th grade	9th grade	10th grade	11th grade	High school graduate	Some college, no degree	Associate's degree		Bachelor's degree	Master's degree	Profes-sional degree	Doctor-ate degree
											Occupa-tional	Academic				
ASIAN ALONE OR IN COMBINATION																
Both Sexes																
15 years and over	10 466	126	122	217	272	279	323	445	2 038	1 547	295	336	2 937	1 015	269	244
15 years	191	-	-	4	58	95	26	2	2	4	-	-	-	-	-	-
16 years	191	-	3	-	17	53	81	33	1	3	-	-	-	-	-	-
17 years	200	-	-	-	6	11	67	105	7	2	-	-	1	-	-	-
18 years	166	2	-	-	-	6	18	75	26	39	-	-	-	-	-	-
19 years	161	-	-	-	-	-	-	21	32	107	-	1	-	-	-	-
20 years	179	-	-	-	3	-	1	12	36	122	4	-	1	-	-	-
21 years	173	-	2	-	3	3	4	7	36	108	2	5	3	-	-	-
22 years	178	-	-	-	-	1	-	1	40	100	4	7	23	-	-	-
23 years	206	-	-	-	-	-	4	6	39	73	6	4	64	7	2	-
24 years	190	-	-	-	1	-	-	8	31	63	11	7	57	10	-	-
25 years	207	-	-	-	-	-	1	6	39	45	9	8	83	14	2	-
26 years	213	1	-	-	1	2	2	3	35	30	8	7	91	20	14	-
27 years	221	-	1	-	4	-	-	2	32	27	8	3	108	27	5	2
28 years	239	-	-	4	1	2	-	1	36	25	6	7	119	30	6	2
29 years	238	5	-	-	6	3	4	2	29	20	7	12	88	45	17	1
30 years	280	2	-	1	-	3	1	6	43	31	4	1	126	41	6	14
31 years	242	-	-	1	2	-	4	8	31	27	4	12	94	46	4	9
32 years	263	2	3	-	4	5	1	4	51	13	8	13	114	36	5	4
33 years	252	-	-	1	4	2	6	-	28	30	4	4	100	54	14	5
34 years	242	-	2	1	3	1	4	9	40	20	9	10	81	48	10	4
35 years	268	3	3	2	2	2	-	-	47	41	4	9	75	51	11	19
36 years	231	2	2	3	1	2	2	-	37	21	1	6	96	31	10	16
37 years	250	2	3	-	6	1	3	6	37	24	10	14	72	50	7	14
38 years	237	-	2	3	4	3	6	4	41	26	3	14	89	32	9	2
39 years	236	2	1	-	3	2	1	5	38	30	7	20	86	36	5	1
40 years	220	-	6	6	4	4	4	6	41	41	9	4	63	17	9	6
41 years	254	4	-	-	2	1	5	12	52	25	8	8	83	39	10	6
42 years	263	3	1	5	5	-	2	4	75	23	10	10	73	36	7	9
43 years	167	-	2	-	1	-	5	3	27	23	10	11	48	20	7	10
44 years	155	-	1	1	2	2	3	1	21	19	5	11	53	24	9	3
45 years	174	1	1	7	1	-	2	2	39	27	-	11	57	10	5	10
46 years	158	5	-	5	5	1	10	4	37	21	5	3	39	16	8	1
47 years	217	2	2	2	8	2	2	-	45	39	9	4	58	25	10	8
48 years	190	2	-	2	4	-	2	-	55	23	9	4	49	28	2	9
49 years	192	-	2	-	6	5	5	-	63	18	8	9	63	11	-	2
50 years	193	3	4	8	6	2	-	4	58	21	6	5	54	15	2	5
51 years	159	7	3	5	2	3	1	3	34	18	9	10	48	11	3	5
52 years	165	1	3	3	5	3	3	5	44	10	4	8	51	19	4	4
53 years	170	-	-	8	-	3	4	8	50	11	7	5	55	11	8	-
54 years	123	1	2	3	3	6	2	6	26	11	4	6	41	8	1	3
55 years	160	6	2	1	11	3	3	1	46	17	5	5	41	6	6	6
56 years	151	-	1	5	3	9	-	6	40	13	5	11	41	6	6	5
57 years	122	1	2	8	4	1	-	-	31	18	9	2	34	4	5	3
58 years	97	-	2	2	4	-	-	-	16	15	4	4	25	13	6	7
59 years	129	3	2	-	4	2	1	1	42	8	5	2	34	15	6	3
60 years	112	1	1	4	3	3	1	10	34	8	4	2	29	9	1	5
61 years	94	-	1	5	-	1	1	1	21	7	2	4	35	11	2	2
62 years	84	-	2	5	4	-	-	-	13	3	4	2	37	9	2	4
63 years	72	-	-	2	-	5	-	1	17	3	4	1	27	4	-	9
64 years	88	2	8	-	4	4	3	3	18	9	5	2	18	5	2	4
65 years	105	-	2	13	3	2	2	9	22	3	-	4	31	5	8	2
66 years	79	3	4	5	2	-	-	4	22	5	-	-	20	7	2	4
67 years	63	1	-	15	-	-	2	8	14	6	4	1	6	3	2	2
68 years	75	-	6	4	3	-	-	-	19	8	-	-	23	6	1	3
69 years	63	2	-	2	6	2	2	4	11	9	-	1	14	6	1	2
70 years	61	4	4	2	4	3	3	-	11	7	2	-	10	7	-	4
71 years	47	2	9	6	4	1	2	1	10	1	1	1	6	1	2	1
72 years	54	1	-	6	1	1	-	-	18	3	-	4	12	7	-	1
73 years	50	2	1	8	3	-	1	-	13	4	1	2	9	6	-	-
74 years	62	-	4	2	4	2	2	3	25	5	3	3	5	-	1	2
75 years and over	446	47	21	47	23	12	14	10	116	37	11	9	72	18	5	4

- = Quantity zero or rounds to zero.

Table A-16. Educational Attainment of the Population Age 15 Years and Over, by Single Years of Age, Sex, Race, and Hispanic Origin, 2005—*Continued*

(Numbers in thousands.)

Age, sex, race, and Hispanic origin	Total	None	Elementary			High school				College						
			1st to 4th grade	5th and 6th grade	7th and 8th grade	9th grade	10th grade	11th grade	High school graduate	Some college, no degree	Associate's degree		Bachelor's degree	Master's degree	Professional degree	Doctorate degree
											Occupational	Academic				
ASIAN ALONE OR IN COMBINATION																
Male																
15 years and over	5 005	25	42	80	119	138	152	226	986	718	126	149	1 335	573	169	167
15 years	100	-	-	4	28	48	15	-	-	4	-	-	-	-	-	-
16 years	104	-	-	-	12	36	39	16	1	-	-	-	-	-	-	-
17 years	103	-	-	-	2	3	34	60	2	-	-	-	1	-	-	-
18 years	91	2	-	-	-	1	4	49	18	17	-	-	-	-	-	-
19 years	71	-	-	-	-	-	-	10	15	44	-	1	-	-	-	-
20 years	87	-	-	-	3	-	1	8	15	60	1	-	-	-	-	-
21 years	87	-	-	-	-	-	4	3	25	49	-	5	1	-	-	-
22 years	94	-	-	-	-	1	-	-	29	51	3	4	5	-	-	-
23 years	107	-	-	-	-	-	-	4	20	40	5	3	35	-	-	-
24 years	78	-	-	-	-	-	-	3	18	21	7	4	25	-	-	-
25 years	91	-	-	-	-	-	1	-	17	22	-	3	39	8	-	-
26 years	112	-	-	-	-	-	-	-	27	12	4	4	48	15	3	-
27 years	92	-	-	-	4	-	-	-	12	15	6	1	35	16	2	2
28 years	115	-	-	4	-	-	-	-	28	11	3	2	48	14	5	-
29 years	112	2	-	-	2	1	2	1	14	9	1	6	40	22	12	-
30 years	141	-	-	-	-	-	1	6	21	23	1	-	58	21	3	7
31 years	115	-	-	1	-	-	3	3	14	17	4	8	32	30	-	4
32 years	130	-	2	-	1	-	1	4	28	8	3	10	51	20	2	-
33 years	127	-	-	-	-	-	-	-	15	12	4	-	58	27	10	2
34 years	136	-	-	-	3	-	2	5	26	12	2	6	44	30	4	4
35 years	143	-	3	-	-	2	-	-	28	19	2	4	35	30	6	15
36 years	121	-	-	-	-	2	2	-	27	11	-	-	38	24	7	10
37 years	121	-	-	-	3	1	1	2	20	10	3	7	35	28	6	5
38 years	104	-	-	1	2	1	2	-	18	6	2	3	42	21	5	1
39 years	112	-	1	-	2	2	1	5	18	17	2	6	43	13	2	1
40 years	117	-	6	1	-	4	2	4	27	22	4	1	28	9	3	4
41 years	121	2	-	-	-	-	2	6	18	15	-	4	44	19	7	3
42 years	124	-	1	2	3	-	-	1	30	10	4	6	40	11	7	8
43 years	88	-	2	-	1	-	1	3	14	14	4	3	27	9	2	8
44 years	74	-	1	-	-	1	-	1	12	7	3	5	20	18	5	2
45 years	79	-	1	4	1	-	-	2	19	10	-	5	20	5	3	9
46 years	67	3	-	2	2	-	6	-	11	9	1	2	15	9	7	1
47 years	104	1	1	-	1	-	-	-	30	14	5	2	23	14	9	5
48 years	97	2	-	-	-	-	1	-	25	9	3	2	26	21	-	7
49 years	82	-	2	-	1	-	2	-	33	7	7	4	23	3	-	-
50 years	76	-	-	6	3	-	-	1	20	16	-	-	11	14	-	4
51 years	63	-	1	2	2	3	-	-	10	7	2	3	24	3	2	3
52 years	92	-	-	1	5	2	-	-	22	3	1	2	34	14	4	4
53 years	83	-	-	1	-	-	2	5	21	2	3	3	32	6	8	-
54 years	52	-	-	1	1	4	-	-	11	7	3	-	18	4	1	3
55 years	57	-	-	1	4	-	2	1	10	6	5	2	13	4	6	6
56 years	78	-	-	-	-	5	-	2	25	7	3	6	20	1	4	3
57 years	56	1	-	3	3	1	-	-	14	8	5	-	12	4	3	2
58 years	57	-	-	2	3	-	-	-	7	9	3	1	13	10	4	4
59 years	53	-	-	-	3	-	1	1	19	-	3	-	12	6	5	3
60 years	45	1	1	2	-	3	1	2	10	4	1	1	12	4	1	3
61 years	50	-	1	-	-	1	-	-	12	4	-	-	22	7	-	2
62 years	40	-	-	2	2	-	-	-	-	1	2	-	19	8	2	4
63 years	31	-	-	2	-	-	-	1	9	1	-	1	6	4	-	8
64 years	42	2	4	-	-	4	-	-	4	3	4	-	14	4	2	1
65 years	58	-	-	7	-	-	-	6	10	3	-	4	18	3	6	1
66 years	42	-	-	2	2	-	-	1	13	5	-	-	10	4	1	4
67 years	25	-	-	3	-	-	2	2	4	5	-	1	4	-	2	2
68 years	30	-	-	-	3	-	-	-	9	1	-	-	6	6	1	3
69 years	29	-	-	-	-	-	1	2	3	4	-	-	10	6	-	2
70 years	36	-	-	1	4	2	3	-	6	-	-	-	7	7	-	4
71 years	21	-	3	4	4	1	-	-	4	-	1	1	-	-	2	1
72 years	25	-	-	2	1	1	-	-	6	2	-	4	6	4	-	1
73 years	19	-	-	2	3	-	-	-	7	-	-	2	2	3	-	-
74 years	25	-	2	-	-	2	-	-	8	1	3	1	4	-	1	2
75 years and over	167	6	11	16	3	6	10	4	46	15	-	5	30	9	4	3

- = Quantity zero or rounds to zero.

Table A-16. Educational Attainment of the Population Age 15 Years and Over, by Single Years of Age, Sex, Race, and Hispanic Origin, 2005—*Continued*

(Numbers in thousands.)

Age, sex, race, and Hispanic origin	Total	None	Elementary			High school				College						
			1st to 4th grade	5th and 6th grade	7th and 8th grade	9th grade	10th grade	11th grade	High school graduate	Some college, no degree	Associate's degree		Bachelor's degree	Master's degree	Profes-sional degree	Doctor-ate degree
											Occupa-tional	Academic				
ASIAN ALONE OR IN COMBINATION																
Female																
15 years and over	5 461	101	80	137	154	141	172	219	1 051	829	170	186	1 602	442	101	77
15 years	91	-	-	-	30	47	11	2	2	-	-	-	-	-	-	-
16 years	87	-	3	-	5	17	42	17	-	3	-	-	-	-	-	-
17 years	97	-	-	-	4	8	33	45	5	2	-	-	-	-	-	-
18 years	75	-	-	-	-	4	14	26	9	22	-	-	-	-	-	-
19 years	90	-	-	-	-	-	-	10	17	63	-	-	-	-	-	-
20 years	92	-	-	-	-	-	-	4	21	62	4	-	1	-	-	-
21 years	86	-	2	-	3	3	-	4	11	59	2	-	3	-	-	-
22 years	84	-	-	-	-	-	-	1	11	49	1	3	18	-	-	-
23 years	98	-	-	-	-	-	4	2	18	33	1	2	28	7	2	-
24 years	112	-	-	-	1	-	-	5	14	43	5	3	32	10	-	-
25 years	116	-	-	-	-	-	-	6	22	22	9	5	44	6	2	-
26 years	101	1	-	-	1	2	2	3	8	18	4	3	43	6	11	-
27 years	129	-	1	-	-	-	-	2	21	12	2	3	73	12	3	-
28 years	124	-	-	-	1	2	-	-	8	14	3	5	72	15	1	2
29 years	126	3	-	-	5	2	1	1	15	11	5	6	49	23	5	1
30 years	139	2	-	1	-	3	-	-	22	8	3	1	68	20	3	6
31 years	128	-	-	-	2	-	2	5	17	11	-	3	62	16	4	6
32 years	132	2	1	-	3	5	-	-	23	5	5	3	64	16	3	4
33 years	126	-	-	1	4	2	6	-	13	18	-	4	42	27	5	3
34 years	105	-	2	1	-	1	2	4	14	8	7	4	38	18	7	-
35 years	125	3	-	2	2	-	-	-	19	22	2	6	40	21	5	4
36 years	110	2	2	3	1	-	-	-	10	10	-	6	58	6	3	7
37 years	129	2	3	-	3	-	2	4	16	13	8	7	38	22	2	9
38 years	133	-	2	2	2	3	3	4	23	20	-	11	46	11	5	2
39 years	124	2	-	-	1	-	-	-	20	13	5	14	42	23	3	-
40 years	104	-	1	5	4	-	2	2	14	19	4	3	35	7	6	2
41 years	133	2	-	-	2	1	3	6	33	10	8	4	39	20	3	2
42 years	139	3	-	3	2	-	2	3	44	12	6	4	33	25	-	1
43 years	79	-	-	-	-	-	3	-	13	10	6	8	21	11	4	2
44 years	81	-	-	1	2	1	3	-	9	12	2	6	33	6	3	1
45 years	95	1	-	3	-	-	2	1	19	16	-	6	37	5	2	1
46 years	90	2	-	3	3	1	4	3	26	12	4	1	24	7	-	-
47 years	112	-	2	2	8	2	2	-	15	25	5	2	35	11	1	3
48 years	93	-	-	2	4	-	1	-	30	14	6	2	23	7	2	2
49 years	110	-	-	-	4	5	2	-	30	11	2	6	40	7	-	2
50 years	117	3	4	2	3	2	-	3	38	5	6	5	43	1	2	1
51 years	96	7	2	3	-	-	1	3	24	10	7	6	24	8	1	1
52 years	72	1	3	2	-	1	3	5	22	7	3	6	16	4	-	-
53 years	87	-	-	7	-	3	2	2	29	9	5	2	23	5	-	-
54 years	71	1	2	2	2	1	1	6	15	4	2	6	24	4	-	-
55 years	103	6	2	1	8	3	2	-	36	12	-	3	28	2	-	-
56 years	73	-	1	5	3	4	-	3	15	7	1	5	21	5	2	2
57 years	67	-	2	5	-	-	-	-	17	10	5	2	22	-	2	1
58 years	40	-	2	-	1	-	-	-	8	6	1	2	11	3	1	3
59 years	75	3	2	-	1	1	-	-	23	7	3	2	22	9	1	-
60 years	67	-	-	2	3	1	-	8	24	5	3	1	16	5	-	1
61 years	45	-	-	5	-	-	-	1	9	3	2	4	14	4	2	-
62 years	44	-	2	2	2	-	-	-	13	2	2	2	18	-	-	-
63 years	41	-	-	-	-	5	-	-	8	2	4	-	21	-	-	1
64 years	46	-	4	-	4	-	3	3	13	7	1	2	5	1	-	3
65 years	47	-	2	6	3	2	2	3	12	-	-	-	12	2	1	1
66 years	36	3	4	3	-	-	-	3	9	-	-	-	10	4	-	-
67 years	37	1	-	12	-	-	-	6	9	1	3	-	2	3	-	-
68 years	45	-	6	3	-	-	-	-	10	7	-	-	17	-	-	-
69 years	34	2	-	2	6	2	2	2	8	5	-	-	3	-	1	-
70 years	25	4	4	-	-	-	-	-	5	6	2	-	2	-	-	-
71 years	26	2	6	2	-	-	2	1	6	1	-	-	6	1	-	-
72 years	29	1	-	4	-	-	-	-	12	2	-	-	6	3	-	-
73 years	31	2	1	6	-	-	1	-	5	4	1	-	8	3	-	-
74 years	37	-	2	2	4	-	2	3	16	4	-	2	2	-	-	-
75 years and over	279	41	10	31	20	6	4	7	70	22	11	4	42	10	1	1

- = Quantity zero or rounds to zero.

Table A-16. Educational Attainment of the Population Age 15 Years and Over, by Single Years of Age, Sex, Race, and Hispanic Origin, 2005—*Continued*

(Numbers in thousands.)

| Age, sex, race, and Hispanic origin | Total | None | Elementary | | | High school | | | | College | | | | | | |
			1st to 4th grade	5th and 6th grade	7th and 8th grade	9th grade	10th grade	11th grade	High school graduate	Some college, no degree	Occupa-tional	Academic	Bachelor's degree	Master's degree	Profes-sional degree	Doctor-ate degree
HISPANIC[1]																
Both Sexes																
15 years and over	29 605	498	1 395	2 719	2 033	2 360	1 633	2 651	7 879	4 182	783	623	2 043	557	152	95
15 years	718	-	3	4	314	299	84	10	2	1	-	-	-	-	-	-
16 years	683	-	3	3	73	267	259	74	4	1	-	-	-	-	-	-
17 years	686	2	1	8	26	56	228	333	27	5	-	-	-	-	-	-
18 years	658	2	10	17	22	28	61	268	155	93	3	-	-	-	-	-
19 years	633	-	4	31	23	30	44	126	203	163	7	-	1	-	-	-
20 years	695	1	9	30	26	58	20	91	256	182	10	6	4	-	-	-
21 years	727	-	11	35	23	52	27	66	250	222	11	19	11	1	-	-
22 years	745	-	7	35	29	53	26	76	283	172	22	15	27	-	-	-
23 years	707	1	16	55	34	41	29	73	211	153	11	24	55	3	-	-
24 years	802	6	32	66	29	59	33	65	260	180	13	14	43	2	-	-
25 years	879	7	18	90	55	63	32	82	277	126	18	38	61	11	-	-
26 years	716	8	20	57	25	49	23	46	209	136	27	26	77	8	3	-
27 years	758	10	14	56	50	54	31	64	227	117	30	22	71	7	5	1
28 years	820	5	27	63	31	67	28	91	259	114	19	24	73	10	4	6
29 years	776	9	22	70	44	55	35	51	235	115	28	10	77	16	8	3
30 years	760	7	26	65	46	48	25	75	224	107	28	26	57	14	7	3
31 years	726	6	17	97	33	60	35	57	194	107	21	16	67	11	2	1
32 years	779	12	40	58	43	78	29	46	220	105	24	23	78	20	4	1
33 years	684	8	26	69	40	63	30	39	195	81	25	18	65	21	1	1
34 years	740	6	29	69	33	62	26	73	231	106	31	11	47	12	5	-
35 years	796	2	29	90	51	34	26	64	250	103	25	15	70	26	9	5
36 years	652	9	18	55	36	72	15	52	148	105	24	17	77	20	1	3
37 years	667	4	32	82	45	41	14	49	199	82	25	14	63	12	4	-
38 years	595	15	34	61	34	29	28	35	173	89	15	9	58	13	3	-
39 years	587	8	19	82	30	34	21	35	157	95	19	16	54	12	1	4
40 years	659	7	38	70	44	31	16	36	200	89	27	15	57	24	8	*
41 years	627	7	25	70	34	35	18	39	185	76	32	22	57	16	7	2
42 years	559	9	32	50	36	34	27	41	162	71	18	15	45	13	2	3
43 years	534	12	12	53	25	26	19	31	143	90	20	19	53	22	8	2
44 years	564	5	36	74	29	28	17	39	143	77	22	16	60	10	7	2
45 years	533	6	31	71	25	36	12	31	142	76	17	17	43	19	2	4
46 years	457	11	33	54	19	14	21	22	137	63	16	11	44	8	3	-
47 years	447	9	17	47	25	37	16	31	123	62	11	12	40	11	2	4
48 years	486	4	37	56	28	25	20	18	119	85	10	12	41	23	6	4
49 years	448	5	18	59	29	32	18	32	116	48	10	12	53	11	4	-
50 years	429	10	33	55	34	17	12	23	121	50	12	11	36	9	3	3
51 years	355	8	27	52	32	8	11	22	102	38	9	3	23	18	2	2
52 years	370	8	28	33	21	18	14	24	109	50	7	5	35	16	2	1
53 years	307	7	14	30	22	25	11	17	73	38	11	7	36	11	4	1
54 years	330	7	20	62	19	15	12	20	84	32	4	3	23	17	-	11
55 years	288	9	20	36	17	20	13	10	69	44	10	4	24	8	1	3
56 years	311	3	23	27	20	20	10	11	96	44	10	7	29	6	4	1
57 years	274	11	21	33	18	10	7	9	66	55	7	5	16	12	-	4
58 years	258	10	28	28	11	14	9	12	63	34	9	6	25	7	1	1
59 years	215	5	26	18	16	1	12	8	65	32	2	8	18	4	1	1
60 years	254	9	25	32	19	6	3	15	71	34	8	12	18	1	2	-
61 years	175	6	14	25	18	10	6	12	40	21	1	5	7	7	-	1
62 years	196	6	22	19	27	12	11	10	40	26	5	3	5	6	4	-
63 years	176	3	13	16	11	13	8	10	51	20	8	3	9	8	-	1
64 years	168	6	14	23	14	5	6	9	46	20	10	4	7	2	1	-
65 years	170	6	16	37	21	7	3	6	38	16	2	5	7	4	1	-
66 years	157	7	18	16	14	19	14	5	44	3	-	4	5	2	1	2
67 years	157	8	21	22	10	3	6	8	39	16	6	5	5	7	-	1
68 years	140	16	20	14	15	11	5	9	29	8	-	-	8	1	-	5
69 years	128	6	18	14	13	7	6	7	31	10	4	-	9	2	1	2
70 years	127	7	18	11	14	4	8	5	30	8	6	-	10	2	2	-
71 years	123	6	13	22	15	6	-	2	31	12	2	-	5	2	5	1
72 years	96	8	17	15	13	-	7	3	11	9	2	2	6	-	1	-
73 years	124	6	16	15	16	4	8	5	17	15	4	-	6	6	5	-
74 years	97	15	13	9	10	6	8	1	17	4	6	-	3	2	2	-
75 years and over	877	98	153	106	102	48	29	27	176	48	18	8	38	19	3	4

[1] May be of any race.
- = Quantity zero or rounds to zero.

Table A-16. Educational Attainment of the Population Age 15 Years and Over, by Single Years of Age, Sex, Race, and Hispanic Origin, 2005—*Continued*

(Numbers in thousands.)

Age, sex, race, and Hispanic origin	Total	None	Elementary 1st to 4th grade	Elementary 5th and 6th grade	Elementary 7th and 8th grade	High school 9th grade	High school 10th grade	High school 11th grade	High school graduate	Some college, no degree	Associate's degree Occupational	Associate's degree Academic	Bachelor's degree	Master's degree	Professional degree	Doctorate degree
HISPANIC[1]																
Male																
15 years and over	15 224	237	759	1 483	1 079	1 227	809	1 378	4 147	2 049	363	272	1 024	252	84	62
15 years	366	-	3	1	175	137	38	8	2	1	-	-	-	-	-	-
16 years	352	-	-	1	46	133	132	37	3	1	-	-	-	-	-	-
17 years	358	2	1	8	15	26	124	160	20	2	-	-	-	-	-	-
18 years	328	-	10	14	16	11	37	121	79	38	3	-	-	-	-	-
19 years	324	-	-	27	12	18	28	67	100	71	-	-	1	-	-	-
20 years	393	1	5	19	16	32	9	60	150	93	3	3	3	-	-	-
21 years	397	-	9	17	17	41	9	36	150	102	2	9	6	-	-	-
22 years	394	-	7	23	19	24	18	37	164	76	5	5	16	-	-	-
23 years	355	1	9	26	19	26	10	48	122	68	5	5	15	2	-	-
24 years	446	4	18	55	21	39	21	29	143	83	12	4	15	2	-	-
25 years	510	7	11	59	47	33	21	38	169	69	4	26	25	2	-	-
26 years	383	8	14	31	14	23	14	30	110	72	12	10	40	6	-	-
27 years	413	4	6	22	31	28	13	40	125	71	23	13	35	-	1	-
28 years	455	3	22	34	14	36	9	55	136	69	11	13	42	4	1	5
29 years	416	5	11	39	16	23	15	24	145	60	12	6	43	7	8	3
30 years	421	7	13	31	28	30	10	46	134	56	12	13	28	7	5	1
31 years	412	-	13	56	16	41	21	41	109	55	7	8	39	5	-	-
32 years	396	8	17	22	26	42	12	22	120	54	11	11	41	7	2	-
33 years	349	6	18	46	22	35	15	21	94	41	9	11	24	8	-	1
34 years	377	2	10	44	22	26	12	44	131	51	12	3	15	4	1	-
35 years	411	2	25	50	30	11	12	31	140	46	12	4	27	13	3	3
36 years	347	4	5	34	25	39	12	29	77	50	12	9	40	10	-	-
37 years	348	1	19	46	29	23	6	27	107	37	15	3	30	3	1	-
38 years	323	6	23	27	22	17	16	16	98	49	7	3	33	6	1	-
39 years	308	8	11	41	14	17	11	26	79	46	8	11	29	4	1	3
40 years	356	7	17	51	27	20	6	22	107	44	14	5	26	10	1	-
41 years	287	3	14	33	15	16	5	22	83	26	13	13	32	9	4	-
42 years	298	5	16	25	21	23	11	24	95	33	10	8	23	3	-	3
43 years	274	5	7	22	9	15	3	22	74	47	9	10	34	14	2	1
44 years	309	4	19	41	17	14	6	23	86	43	7	12	27	4	6	-
45 years	255	3	13	46	6	12	3	16	70	31	13	3	23	10	2	3
46 years	223	7	24	18	11	1	11	13	72	25	7	4	22	3	2	-
47 years	234	6	13	24	7	25	7	19	67	26	5	6	17	6	1	4
48 years	268	2	24	33	12	13	14	7	61	40	7	6	25	15	5	4
49 years	227	3	14	34	13	13	11	14	63	23	4	3	25	4	3	-
50 years	230	5	27	30	22	11	6	14	59	27	4	3	18	4	-	-
51 years	183	-	19	27	19	4	2	9	52	17	3	2	12	13	2	2
52 years	171	1	22	20	11	8	10	5	35	31	3	2	17	4	-	1
53 years	136	2	6	11	7	13	4	4	30	19	5	6	20	5	2	1
54 years	158	3	7	42	6	6	5	4	42	15	-	-	14	8	-	6
55 years	138	5	11	23	8	10	6	4	23	22	5	2	12	4	1	1
56 years	154	3	9	13	8	10	1	4	49	18	6	3	23	1	4	1
57 years	145	3	11	16	11	8	-	2	35	35	3	-	11	5	-	3
58 years	133	8	13	17	6	12	6	8	22	13	8	3	13	3	1	1
59 years	98	2	11	8	8	1	7	6	30	11	-	1	8	4	1	1
60 years	104	5	17	13	8	2	2	6	22	15	-	2	9	1	1	-
61 years	83	6	3	22	9	2	3	4	14	12	-	4	2	1	-	1
62 years	89	2	15	9	10	7	-	-	18	18	2	2	2	4	2	-
63 years	78	2	5	10	3	10	3	1	17	7	6	-	5	7	-	1
64 years	81	4	6	9	4	4	6	6	25	9	2	1	5	-	-	-
65 years	80	-	8	16	15	6	3	4	19	5	2	-	-	1	1	-
66 years	63	-	10	9	1	10	2	2	16	2	-	1	3	2	1	2
67 years	63	3	15	10	3	1	-	-	13	7	4	-	4	2	-	1
68 years	62	6	9	6	9	6	2	3	9	8	-	-	3	1	-	-
69 years	54	-	7	[1]6	6	1	5	1	13	7	1	-	3	2	1	2
70 years	58	2	7	4	10	2	3	1	13	5	4	-	5	2	2	-
71 years	52	4	2	12	5	1	-	2	12	5	-	-	2	1	5	1
72 years	34	-	11	6	1	-	5	-	2	6	1	-	1	-	1	-
73 years	56	1	11	6	7	1	4	1	8	8	-	-	5	-	5	-
74 years	44	6	6	5	1	4	2	1	6	2	4	-	3	-	1	-
75 years and over	363	40	52	34	28	25	18	12	79	26	14	1	23	5	2	4

[1]May be of any race.
- = Quantity zero or rounds to zero.

Table A-16. Educational Attainment of the Population Age 15 Years and Over, by Single Years of Age, Sex, Race, and Hispanic Origin, 2005—*Continued*

(Numbers in thousands.)

Age, sex, race, and Hispanic origin	Total	None	Elementary			High school				Some college, no degree	Associate's degree		Bachelor's degree	Master's degree	Professional degree	Doctorate degree
			1st to 4th grade	5th and 6th grade	7th and 8th grade	9th grade	10th grade	11th grade	High school graduate		Occupational	Academic				
HISPANIC[1]																
Female																
15 years and over	14 381	261	636	1 236	954	1 133	824	1 273	3 733	2 133	420	351	1 019	305	68	33
15 years	352	-	-	-	3	139	162	46	2	-	-	-	-	-	-	-
16 years	331	-	3	2	27	134	126	37	1	-	-	-	-	-	-	-
17 years	328	-	-	-	11	30	104	173	7	3	-	-	-	-	-	-
18 years	330	2	-	3	6	17	24	147	76	55	-	-	-	-	-	-
19 years	309	-	4	4	11	12	15	59	103	92	7	-	-	-	-	-
20 years	302	-	4	12	10	25	11	31	107	89	8	3	1	-	-	-
21 years	330	-	2	18	7	11	18	29	101	120	9	10	5	1	-	-
22 years	352	-	-	12	10	28	8	39	119	96	17	10	11	-	-	-
23 years	352	-	7	30	15	15	18	26	90	85	6	19	40	1	-	-
24 years	356	2	14	11	8	20	12	35	117	96	2	9	28	-	-	-
25 years	369	-	7	32	8	31	11	45	108	57	14	12	37	8	-	-
26 years	333	-	6	26	10	26	10	16	99	65	15	17	37	3	3	-
27 years	344	6	8	34	19	26	18	23	102	45	8	8	36	7	4	1
28 years	365	2	5	29	17	31	19	36	123	45	9	10	31	6	2	2
29 years	360	4	11	30	28	32	19	27	90	54	16	5	34	10	-	-
30 years	338	-	13	34	19	18	15	28	90	51	16	13	30	7	2	1
31 years	314	6	3	41	17	20	14	17	85	51	14	8	28	6	2	1
32 years	383	4	22	36	17	36	16	24	100	51	13	12	37	12	2	1
33 years	334	3	9	22	18	29	16	18	101	41	16	7	41	13	1	1
34 years	363	4	19	24	11	36	13	28	100	56	19	8	33	7	4	-
35 years	386	-	4	40	21	23	14	33	110	57	12	11	42	13	5	1
36 years	305	5	12	21	11	33	2	23	71	55	12	8	37	10	1	3
37 years	319	3	13	36	16	18	9	22	92	45	10	11	33	9	3	-
38 years	272	9	11	34	12	12	12	19	75	40	9	6	25	7	1	-
39 years	279	1	7	40	16	18	11	10	78	49	11	5	25	7	-	2
40 years	303	-	21	19	17	11	10	14	93	45	13	10	31	14	5	-
41 years	340	5	12	37	19	19	13	17	103	50	19	9	25	7	3	2
42 years	260	4	16	26	15	11	16	17	67	38	9	8	21	10	2	-
43 years	261	7	5	31	16	11	16	9	69	43	12	9	19	8	6	1
44 years	255	1	17	33	11	15	10	16	56	33	15	4	33	7	1	1
45 years	278	3	18	25	19	24	9	15	72	45	4	14	20	9	-	1
46 years	234	4	9	36	8	13	10	9	65	38	8	7	22	5	1	-
47 years	213	3	5	22	18	12	9	12	56	36	6	5	23	5	2	-
48 years	218	1	13	23	15	13	5	11	58	45	3	6	16	8	1	-
49 years	221	2	4	25	17	19	7	18	53	25	6	9	28	7	1	-
50 years	199	6	6	25	13	6	6	9	61	23	8	8	18	5	3	3
51 years	172	8	8	25	12	4	8	13	50	21	6	1	10	5	-	-
52 years	199	7	5	13	9	10	4	19	74	19	4	4	18	11	2	-
53 years	171	5	8	19	15	12	7	13	43	18	6	1	16	6	3	-
54 years	172	4	13	20	13	9	7	16	42	17	4	3	10	9	-	5
55 years	151	4	10	13	9	9	8	6	47	22	4	2	11	4	-	1
56 years	158	-	14	14	11	10	9	7	47	26	4	4	6	5	-	-
57 years	129	7	10	17	6	2	7	7	32	20	4	5	5	6	-	-
58 years	125	2	15	11	5	3	3	4	41	21	2	3	12	3	-	-
59 years	117	3	15	10	8	-	5	2	35	20	2	7	10	-	-	-
60 years	150	4	8	19	11	4	1	9	48	18	8	9	9	-	1	-
61 years	92	-	11	4	9	8	3	8	26	10	1	2	4	6	-	-
62 years	108	4	7	10	17	5	11	10	22	8	3	2	3	3	3	-
63 years	98	2	8	6	8	3	5	10	34	13	2	3	4	1	-	-
64 years	87	2	8	13	9	1	-	3	21	11	7	3	3	2	1	-
65 years	90	6	8	21	7	1	-	2	19	11	-	5	7	3	-	-
66 years	94	7	9	8	13	9	12	3	28	1	-	3	2	-	-	-
67 years	94	5	6	12	7	2	6	8	26	9	2	5	1	4	-	-
68 years	77	10	10	8	6	4	3	6	20	-	-	-	5	-	-	5
69 years	73	6	10	8	7	5	1	6	18	3	2	-	6	-	-	-
70 years	69	5	11	7	5	3	6	4	18	3	3	-	4	-	-	-
71 years	70	2	11	10	9	5	-	-	19	7	1	-	4	1	-	-
72 years	62	8	7	9	12	-	3	3	9	3	1	2	4	-	-	-
73 years	68	5	6	9	9	4	3	5	9	8	4	-	1	6	-	-
74 years	52	9	7	4	9	1	6	-	10	1	2	-	-	2	1	-
75 years and over	514	58	101	72	74	23	12	15	97	22	5	7	15	14	1	-

[1]May be of any race.
- = Quantity zero or rounds to zero.

Table A-17. Educational Attainment of the Population Age 15 Years and Over, by Age, Sex, Race, and Hispanic Origin, 2005

(Numbers in thousands.)

Age, sex, race, and Hispanic origin	Total population	None	Elementary			High school			
			1st to 4th grade	5th and 6th grade	7th and 8th grade	9th grade	10th grade	11th grade	High school graduate
ALL RACES									
Both Sexes									
15 years and over	230 437	985	2 156	4 017	7 994	8 649	9 686	13 483	69 446
15 to 17 years	13 061	4	15	37	2 385	4 029	3 955	2 405	169
18 and 19 years	7 601	9	19	49	100	182	445	2 433	2 155
20 to 24 years	20 408	26	87	225	280	509	553	1 209	6 229
25 to 29 years	19 501	71	115	366	322	432	444	949	5 715
30 to 34 years	19 809	64	164	380	308	467	340	790	5 554
35 to 39 years	20 651	84	147	400	306	370	365	775	6 376
40 to 44 years	22 699	66	182	374	364	345	451	802	7 367
45 to 49 years	22 235	81	166	342	298	366	452	745	7 282
50 to 54 years	19 726	78	150	323	351	273	350	596	6 207
55 to 59 years	16 771	93	172	253	377	254	427	479	5 167
60 to 64 years	12 765	55	142	232	389	264	357	539	4 431
65 to 69 years	10 130	68	188	271	452	278	402	467	3 773
70 to 74 years	8 260	79	185	199	505	234	363	410	3 071
75 years and over	16 820	207	425	567	1 558	646	782	882	5 950
15 to 17 years	13 061	4	15	37	2 385	4 029	3 955	2 405	169
18 years and over	217 375	981	2 142	3 980	5 608	4 620	5 731	11 078	69 277
15 to 24 years	41 070	39	121	311	2 765	4 720	4 953	6 047	8 553
25 years and over	189 367	947	2 036	3 706	5 229	3 929	4 734	7 436	60 893
15 to 64 years	195 227	631	1 358	2 980	5 478	7 491	8 139	11 723	56 653
65 years and over	35 209	354	798	1 037	2 515	1 158	1 547	1 759	12 793
Male									
15 years and over	111 694	443	1 155	2 113	4 051	4 368	4 800	6 766	33 844
15 to 17 years	6 728	4	6	24	1 321	2 039	2 059	1 160	90
18 and 19 years	3 775	6	11	41	69	88	269	1 297	1 055
20 to 24 years	10 292	17	49	142	165	304	255	675	3 547
25 to 29 years	9 826	49	74	204	181	221	213	534	3 212
30 to 34 years	9 851	29	88	209	174	253	172	434	3 003
35 to 39 years	10 265	49	92	210	172	196	199	439	3 401
40 to 44 years	11 204	31	105	202	217	190	220	446	3 887
45 to 49 years	10 935	46	105	173	145	189	243	405	3 737
50 to 54 years	9 620	25	94	172	185	125	162	249	2 993
55 to 59 years	8 009	51	83	131	185	131	210	221	2 256
60 to 64 years	6 042	26	87	140	177	137	156	236	1 871
65 to 69 years	4 815	16	96	123	227	144	193	204	1 593
70 to 74 years	3 651	18	90	102	234	105	144	146	1 136
75 years and over	6 681	77	174	239	598	244	304	319	2 062
15 to 17 years	6 728	4	6	24	1 321	2 039	2 059	1 160	90
18 years and over	104 966	439	1 149	2 089	2 730	2 329	2 741	5 606	33 754
15 to 24 years	20 795	27	66	207	1 555	2 431	2 584	3 132	4 692
25 years and over	90 899	416	1 089	1 906	2 496	1 937	2 216	3 634	29 151
15 to 64 years	96 548	332	795	1 649	2 992	3 874	4 158	6 097	29 053
65 years and over	15 147	111	361	464	1 059	494	641	669	4 791
Female									
15 years and over	118 742	543	1 001	1 904	3 943	4 281	4 886	6 717	35 602
15 to 17 years	6 333	-	9	12	1 064	1 990	1 896	1 245	79
18 and 19 years	3 826	3	8	8	31	95	176	1 136	1 100
20 to 24 years	10 115	9	38	84	115	204	297	534	2 681
25 to 29 years	9 676	22	41	162	141	210	232	416	2 503
30 to 34 years	9 958	35	76	171	133	214	168	355	2 551
35 to 39 years	10 387	36	55	190	134	174	166	337	2 975
40 to 44 years	11 495	35	76	172	147	155	232	356	3 480
45 to 49 years	11 299	35	61	169	153	178	210	340	3 546
50 to 54 years	10 106	53	55	151	165	148	187	348	3 214
55 to 59 years	8 762	42	89	121	191	122	217	258	2 911
60 to 64 years	6 722	29	55	92	212	127	201	303	2 560
65 to 69 years	5 315	52	92	148	225	133	208	262	2 180
70 to 74 years	4 609	61	95	97	271	129	220	264	1 934
75 years and over	10 139	130	251	327	960	402	478	564	3 888
15 to 17 years	6 333	-	9	12	1 064	1 990	1 896	1 245	79
18 years and over	112 409	542	992	1 892	2 879	2 291	2 990	5 472	35 523
15 to 24 years	20 275	12	55	104	1 210	2 289	2 369	2 915	3 860
25 years and over	98 467	530	947	1 800	2 733	1 992	2 517	3 802	31 742
15 to 64 years	98 679	299	564	1 332	2 486	3 616	3 981	5 627	27 600
65 years and over	20 063	244	438	572	1 456	664	906	1 090	8 002

- = Quantity zero or rounds to zero.

Table A-17. Educational Attainment of the Population Age 15 Years and Over, by Age, Sex, Race, and Hispanic Origin, 2005—*Continued*

(Numbers in thousands.)

Age, sex, race, and Hispanic origin	College						
	Some college, no degree	Associate's degree		Bachelor's degree	Master's degree	Professional degree	Doctorate degree
		Occupational	Academic				
ALL RACES							
Both Sexes							
15 years and over	41 727	9 477	8 072	36 520	12 928	2 946	2 352
15 to 17 years	56	2	-	3	1	-	-
18 and 19 years	2 150	33	10	15	-	2	-
20 to 24 years	7 711	637	600	2 243	86	10	5
25 to 29 years	3 805	864	796	4 401	916	224	80
30 to 34 years	3 551	999	849	4 433	1 447	285	178
35 to 39 years	3 456	1 094	865	4 298	1 462	381	273
40 to 44 years	3 832	1 290	1 066	4 441	1 510	371	238
45 to 49 years	3 930	1 212	1 029	4 147	1 512	382	289
50 to 54 years	3 439	996	919	3 668	1 764	320	292
55 to 59 years	2 971	820	715	2 860	1 546	304	335
60 to 64 years	2 021	481	474	1 964	987	175	252
65 to 69 years	1 485	317	298	1 244	610	149	130
70 to 74 years	1 134	268	162	1 032	383	104	128
75 years and over	2 185	464	287	1 771	704	239	153
15 to 17 years	56	2	-	3	1	-	-
18 years and over	41 670	9 475	8 072	36 517	12 926	2 946	2 352
15 to 24 years	9 918	672	609	2 260	88	11	5
25 years and over	31 809	8 805	7 462	34 260	12 840	2 934	2 347
15 to 64 years	36 923	8 428	7 325	32 473	11 231	2 453	1 941
65 years and over	4 804	1 049	747	4 047	1 697	492	411
Male							
15 years and over	19 471	4 222	3 254	17 559	6 154	1 904	1 592
15 to 17 years	23	-	-	1	-	-	-
18 and 19 years	916	13	5	3	-	2	-
20 to 24 years	3 657	292	247	913	22	3	5
25 to 29 years	1 851	415	366	1 993	358	123	31
30 to 34 years	1 731	455	380	2 052	612	166	101
35 to 39 years	1 625	505	333	2 030	652	215	147
40 to 44 years	1 726	579	423	2 087	740	210	140
45 to 49 years	1 872	570	340	1 915	745	255	196
50 to 54 years	1 627	431	396	1 908	844	221	187
55 to 59 years	1 405	371	294	1 466	742	209	252
60 to 64 years	911	201	198	1 049	531	132	189
65 to 69 years	722	128	124	672	359	109	106
70 to 74 years	526	111	72	563	216	82	105
75 years and over	877	149	77	905	332	187	136
15 to 17 years	23	-	-	I	-	-	-
18 years and over	19 448	4 222	3 254	17 558	6 154	1 904	1 592
15 to 24 years	4 596	305	252	918	22	5	5
25 years and over	14 875	3 917	3 002	16 641	6 132	1 899	1 587
15 to 64 years	17 345	3 833	2 982	15 419	5 246	1 527	1 246
65 years and over	2 126	389	272	2 140	907	377	346
Female							
15 years and over	22 256	5 256	4 818	18 961	6 774	1 041	760
15 to 17 years	33	2	-	2	1	-	-
18 and 19 years	1 234	20	4	11	-	-	-
20 to 24 years	4 054	345	353	1 329	64	6	-
25 to 29 years	1 954	449	430	2 408	558	101	49
30 to 34 years	1 820	545	470	2 381	835	129	78
35 to 39 years	1 830	589	533	2 268	810	165	126
40 to 44 years	2 106	711	643	2 354	769	161	99
45 to 49 years	2 058	641	690	2 232	768	127	93
50 to 54 years	1 812	565	523	1 760	920	99	105
55 to 59 years	1 565	449	421	1 393	804	95	83
60 to 64 years	1 110	280	276	915	455	43	63
65 to 69 years	763	189	174	572	251	40	25
70 to 74 years	608	157	91	469	167	23	23
75 years and over	1 307	314	210	866	372	52	17
15 to 17 years	33	2	-	2	1	-	-
18 years and over	22 222	5 254	4 818	18 959	6 773	1 041	760
15 to 24 years	5 322	367	357	1 342	66	6	-
25 years and over	16 934	4 888	4 461	17 619	6 709	1 035	760
15 to 64 years	19 577	4 595	4 343	17 054	5 985	926	695
65 years and over	2 678	661	475	1 907	790	115	65

- = Quantity zero or rounds to zero.

Table A-17. Educational Attainment of the Population Age 15 Years and Over, by Age, Sex, Race, and Hispanic Origin, 2005—Continued

(Numbers in thousands.)

Age, sex, race, and Hispanic origin	Total population	None	Elementary			High school			
			1st to 4th grade	5th and 6th grade	7th and 8th grade	9th grade	10th grade	11th grade	High school graduate
WHITE ALONE OR IN COMBINATION									
Both Sexes									
15 years and over	190 739	717	1 764	3 394	6 666	7 023	7 701	10 255	57 498
15 to 17 years	10 370	4	12	25	1 899	3 197	3 192	1 878	127
18 and 19 years	6 070	7	13	43	85	141	296	1 963	1 718
20 to 24 years	16 427	16	80	214	243	418	430	850	4 962
25 to 29 years	15 600	57	106	340	282	381	361	718	4 478
30 to 34 years	15 795	55	146	357	272	426	278	596	4 386
35 to 39 years	16 652	56	130	378	272	305	288	608	5 077
40 to 44 years	18 622	55	162	346	322	291	317	560	5 922
45 to 49 years	18 434	58	143	313	248	293	368	558	5 928
50 to 54 years	16 523	58	126	275	273	223	255	408	5 079
55 to 59 years	14 311	67	135	198	311	186	328	353	4 370
60 to 64 years	10 990	42	111	189	325	197	296	387	3 819
65 to 69 years	8 671	48	140	184	367	232	323	334	3 346
70 to 74 years	7 219	61	139	139	421	185	286	308	2 781
75 years and over	15 056	131	320	392	1 347	549	683	734	5 504
15 to 17 years	10 370	4	12	25	1 899	3 197	3 192	1 878	127
18 years and over	180 369	712	1 752	3 369	4 767	3 827	4 509	8 377	57 371
15 to 24 years	32 867	28	105	282	2 227	3 755	3 918	4 691	6 807
25 years and over	157 873	689	1 659	3 113	4 439	3 268	3 783	5 564	50 691
15 to 64 years	159 794	476	1 165	2 678	4 531	6 058	6 409	8 879	45 866
65 years and over	30 946	241	600	716	2 135	966	1 292	1 376	11 632
Male									
15 years and over	93 394	350	969	1 835	3 420	3 568	3 842	5 281	28 035
15 to 17 years	5 338	4	6	15	1 043	1 628	1 679	877	71
18 and 19 years	3 043	4	6	38	54	71	189	1 041	843
20 to 24 years	8 383	11	49	137	147	252	197	502	2 872
25 to 29 years	8 021	40	67	194	164	194	176	429	2 545
30 to 34 years	7 980	28	78	196	160	236	143	360	2 421
35 to 39 years	8 384	35	82	205	158	158	156	367	2 734
40 to 44 years	9 301	28	92	194	200	168	151	335	3 148
45 to 49 years	9 182	34	92	163	123	146	206	313	3 074
50 to 54 years	8 164	21	87	152	141	102	119	187	2 435
55 to 59 years	6 905	40	69	103	154	102	155	161	1 914
60 to 64 years	5 271	20	66	112	160	100	137	179	1 623
65 to 69 years	4 130	15	72	88	189	119	150	146	1 406
70 to 74 years	3 230	14	73	71	199	81	113	106	1 038
75 years and over	6 063	55	131	167	527	211	271	277	1 912
15 to 17 years	5 338	4	6	15	1 043	1 628	1 679	877	71
18 years and over	88 056	345	963	1 820	2 377	1 940	2 163	4 404	27 964
15 to 24 years	16 765	19	61	190	1 244	1 951	2 064	2 420	3 786
25 years and over	76 629	331	908	1 645	2 176	1 617	1 778	2 861	24 249
15 to 64 years	79 972	266	693	1 509	2 505	3 156	3 307	4 752	23 678
65 years and over	13 422	84	276	326	915	411	535	529	4 357
Female									
15 years and over	97 345	367	796	1 559	3 246	3 456	3 859	4 973	29 463
15 to 17 years	5 032	-	6	9	856	1 569	1 513	1 000	56
18 and 19 years	3 026	3	8	5	31	69	108	922	875
20 to 24 years	8 043	5	31	77	96	166	233	348	2 090
25 to 29 years	7 579	17	39	146	118	187	185	289	1 934
30 to 34 years	7 815	27	67	161	112	190	135	236	1 965
35 to 39 years	8 268	21	47	173	113	147	131	240	2 344
40 to 44 years	9 321	27	71	152	122	123	167	225	2 774
45 to 49 years	9 252	24	51	150	125	147	162	245	2 854
50 to 54 years	8 360	37	39	123	131	120	136	221	2 644
55 to 59 years	7 406	27	67	95	157	84	173	192	2 457
60 to 64 years	5 719	22	45	77	166	98	159	207	2 196
65 to 69 years	4 541	33	69	97	177	112	172	188	1 939
70 to 74 years	3 989	47	66	68	222	104	173	202	1 743
75 years and over	8 993	77	189	225	820	339	412	456	3 592
15 to 17 years	5 032	-	6	9	856	1 569	1 513	1 000	56
18 years and over	92 313	367	790	1 550	2 390	1 887	2 346	3 973	29 407
15 to 24 years	16 102	9	45	91	983	1 805	1 854	2 271	3 022
25 years and over	81 244	358	751	1 468	2 263	1 651	2 005	2 703	26 442
15 to 64 years	79 822	211	472	1 169	2 027	2 901	3 102	4 127	22 188
65 years and over	17 523	157	324	390	1 219	555	757	846	7 275

- = Quantity zero or rounds to zero.

Table A-17. Educational Attainment of the Population Age 15 Years and Over, by Age, Sex, Race, and Hispanic Origin, 2005—*Continued*

(Numbers in thousands.)

Age, sex, race, and Hispanic origin	Some college, no degree	Associate's degree Occupational	Associate's degree Academic	Bachelor's degree	Master's degree	Professional degree	Doctorate degree
		College					
WHITE ALONE OR IN COMBINATION							
Both Sexes							
15 years and over	34 611	8 082	6 842	30 638	11 025	2 525	1 998
15 to 17 years	33	-	-	2	1	-	-
18 and 19 years	1 757	29	5	10	-	2	-
20 to 24 years	6 175	518	524	1 924	60	8	5
25 to 29 years	3 042	700	640	3 525	720	172	76
30 to 34 years	2 770	825	695	3 519	1 114	224	134
35 to 39 years	2 781	939	684	3 470	1 142	317	207
40 to 44 years	3 146	1 105	898	3 725	1 263	320	190
45 to 49 years	3 206	1 049	909	3 474	1 313	331	242
50 to 54 years	2 937	871	781	3 126	1 565	291	257
55 to 59 years	2 570	691	627	2 506	1 418	260	292
60 to 64 years	1 806	421	407	1 714	897	162	217
65 to 69 years	1 310	274	270	1 064	540	121	117
70 to 74 years	1 027	240	146	935	341	89	120
75 years and over	2 053	421	257	1 644	650	229	142
15 to 17 years	33	-	-	2	1	-	-
18 years and over	34 578	8 082	6 842	30 636	11 023	2 525	1 998
15 to 24 years	7 965	546	529	1 936	61	9	5
25 years and over	26 645	7 535	6 313	28 702	10 964	2 516	1 993
15 to 64 years	30 221	7 147	6 169	26 995	9 494	2 086	1 618
65 years and over	4 389	935	673	3 643	1 531	439	380
Male							
15 years and over	16 360	3 670	2 768	15 034	5 249	1 655	1 361
15 to 17 years	14	-	-	-	-	-	-
18 and 19 years	779	12	4	1	-	2	-
20 to 24 years	2 931	251	219	790	18	3	5
25 to 29 years	1 530	249	296	1 628	270	101	29
30 to 34 years	1 356	391	318	1 644	438	128	82
35 to 39 years	1 335	440	270	1 669	492	177	105
40 to 44 years	1 451	503	354	1 763	626	180	108
45 to 49 years	1 538	504	296	1 664	643	223	164
50 to 54 years	1 407	383	352	1 652	757	202	167
55 to 59 years	1 235	311	253	1 320	690	178	220
60 to 64 years	820	177	175	936	481	123	163
65 to 69 years	633	112	106	587	323	88	94
70 to 74 years	489	103	61	519	194	70	97
75 years and over	830	135	64	860	317	179	126
15 to 17 years	14	-	-	-	-	-	-
18 years and over	16 345	3 670	2 768	15 034	5 249	1 655	1 361
15 to 24 years	3 725	263	223	791	18	5	5
25 years and over	12 635	3 406	2 545	14 243	5 231	1 650	1 356
15 to 64 years	14 408	3 320	2 537	13 068	4 415	1 318	1 043
65 years and over	1 952	350	231	1 966	834	338	318
Female							
15 years and over	18 251	4 412	4 075	15 604	5 776	870	637
15 to 17 years	18	-	-	2	1	-	-
18 and 19 years	978	16	1	9	-	-	-
20 to 24 years	3 244	266	305	1 134	42	4	-
25 to 29 years	1 502	352	345	1 897	450	71	46
30 to 34 years	1 413	435	377	1 875	676	96	52
35 to 39 years	1 445	499	414	1 801	650	140	102
40 to 44 years	1 695	602	543	1 962	636	140	82
45 to 49 years	1 668	545	613	1 810	670	108	79
50 to 54 years	1 530	488	428	1 474	809	89	90
55 to 59 years	1 335	380	373	1 186	728	82	71
60 to 64 years	985	244	232	778	417	39	54
65 to 69 years	677	161	164	477	217	33	23
70 to 74 years	538	138	85	416	147	18	23
75 years and over	1 223	286	193	783	333	50	15
15 to 17 years	18	-	-	2	1	-	-
18 years and over	18 233	4 412	4 075	15 602	5 775	870	637
15 to 24 years	4 240	283	306	1 145	44	4	-
25 years and over	14 011	4 129	3 768	14 459	5 733	866	637
15 to 64 years	15 814	3 827	3 632	13 927	5 080	769	576
65 years and over	2 437	585	442	1 676	697	101	62

- = Quantity zero or rounds to zero.

Table A-17. Educational Attainment of the Population Age 15 Years and Over, by Age, Sex, Race, and Hispanic Origin, 2005—*Continued*

(Numbers in thousands.)

Age, sex, race, and Hispanic origin	Total population	None	Elementary			High school			
			1st to 4th grade	5th and 6th grade	7th and 8th grade	9th grade	10th grade	11th grade	High school graduate
BLACK ALONE OR IN COMBINATION									
Both Sexes									
15 years and over	27 987	129	221	336	1 014	1 294	1 579	2 654	9 482
15 to 17 years	2 140	-	-	8	423	689	587	388	29
18 and 19 years	1 177	-	-	-	15	35	121	373	368
20 to 24 years	2 983	9	2	5	26	76	105	302	1 061
25 to 29 years	2 702	8	3	17	24	34	70	207	1 016
30 to 34 years	2 599	5	8	12	21	28	42	143	926
35 to 39 years	2 640	19	6	11	16	51	63	143	1 048
40 to 44 years	2 832	3	5	14	24	37	98	203	1 159
45 to 49 years	2 695	11	11	11	23	55	58	166	1 057
50 to 54 years	2 244	8	12	17	51	30	77	156	872
55 to 59 years	1 716	17	25	29	34	45	88	111	615
60 to 64 years	1 253	6	15	22	48	52	54	130	493
65 to 69 years	1 016	13	28	38	67	41	69	103	319
70 to 74 years	723	7	26	30	64	41	65	97	202
75 years and over	1 267	22	81	122	176	81	83	133	318
15 to 17 years	2 140	-	-	8	423	689	587	388	29
18 years and over	25 847	129	221	328	590	605	992	2 266	9 453
15 to 24 years	6 300	9	2	13	465	800	814	1 063	1 458
25 years and over	21 687	120	219	323	549	494	766	1 591	8 024
15 to 64 years	24 982	86	86	145	707	1 132	1 363	2 322	8 643
65 years and over	3 005	43	135	191	307	162	217	333	839
Male									
15 years and over	12 614	67	111	162	487	626	755	1 205	4 602
15 to 17 years	1 080	-	-	4	238	329	287	206	12
18 and 19 years	550	-	-	-	15	15	71	191	176
20 to 24 years	1 410	6	-	2	14	40	47	148	556
25 to 29 years	1 240	7	1	4	8	17	30	101	547
30 to 34 years	1 150	1	6	8	9	15	20	44	461
35 to 39 years	1 193	14	5	3	5	31	36	62	521
40 to 44 years	1 280	-	2	4	12	13	55	90	591
45 to 49 years	1 229	5	4	4	15	36	26	84	514
50 to 54 years	1 010	4	6	6	23	11	35	53	452
55 to 59 years	767	11	14	18	16	20	47	55	268
60 to 64 years	533	2	11	18	15	31	17	50	206
65 to 69 years	466	-	19	19	30	24	39	45	134
70 to 74 years	272	3	11	19	21	18	23	40	62
75 years and over	433	14	32	52	65	26	22	36	101
15 to 17 years	1 080	-	-	4	238	329	287	206	12
18 years and over	11 533	67	111	157	249	297	468	998	4 590
15 to 24 years	3 041	6	-	6	267	383	405	546	744
25 years and over	9 573	61	111	156	220	243	350	659	3 858
15 to 64 years	11 442	49	49	71	371	558	671	1 084	4 304
65 years and over	1 171	18	62	90	116	69	84	121	298
Female									
15 years and over	15 373	63	110	174	526	668	824	1 450	4 880
15 to 17 years	1 059	-	-	3	185	360	300	182	17
18 and 19 years	627	-	-	-	-	20	50	182	193
20 to 24 years	1 573	4	2	3	12	36	58	154	505
25 to 29 years	1 461	1	1	13	16	17	40	107	469
30 to 34 years	1 449	4	2	4	12	13	22	98	464
35 to 39 years	1 447	6	1	8	11	20	28	82	528
40 to 44 years	1 552	2	3	9	12	23	43	113	568
45 to 49 years	1 467	6	6	8	7	19	32	83	543
50 to 54 years	1 233	4	6	11	28	19	42	103	419
55 to 59 years	949	6	11	11	19	25	41	56	347
60 to 64 years	721	4	4	4	33	21	37	79	287
65 to 69 years	549	13	10	19	37	16	30	58	185
70 to 74 years	450	5	14	11	43	23	42	57	139
75 years and over	834	8	49	70	111	55	61	97	217
15 to 17 years	1 059	-	-	3	185	360	300	182	17
18 years and over	14 314	63	110	171	341	308	525	1 268	4 863
15 to 24 years	3 259	4	2	7	197	417	408	517	714
25 years and over	12 114	59	108	167	329	251	416	932	4 166
15 to 64 years	13 539	37	38	74	335	574	692	1 238	4 339
65 years and over	1 834	25	73	100	191	94	133	212	541

- = Quantity zero or rounds to zero.

Table A-17. Educational Attainment of the Population Age 15 Years and Over, by Age, Sex, Race, and Hispanic Origin, 2005—*Continued*

(Numbers in thousands.)

Age, sex, race, and Hispanic origin	Some college, no degree	Associate's degree		Bachelor's degree	Master's degree	Professional degree	Doctorate degree
		Occupational	Academic				
BLACK ALONE OR IN COMBINATION							
Both Sexes							
15 years and over	5 376	1 035	852	2 883	876	148	107
15 to 17 years	14	2	-	-	-	-	-
18 and 19 years	254	3	3	4	-	-	-
20 to 24 years	1 066	87	57	179	8	-	-
25 to 29 years	604	120	123	404	58	13	2
30 to 34 years	636	131	113	397	110	21	9
35 to 39 years	504	119	107	400	117	19	15
40 to 44 years	526	132	113	385	108	11	16
45 to 49 years	569	127	76	387	104	26	15
50 to 54 years	406	91	93	271	135	11	15
55 to 59 years	307	94	64	170	83	16	17
60 to 64 years	179	40	56	96	51	2	10
65 to 69 years	140	37	21	82	43	14	1
70 to 74 years	79	20	6	54	24	8	-
75 years and over	94	32	20	55	36	7	8
15 to 17 years	14	2	-	-	-	-	-
18 years and over	5 362	1 033	852	2 883	876	148	107
15 to 24 years	1 334	92	60	183	8	-	-
25 years and over	4 042	944	792	2 700	868	148	107
15 to 64 years	5 064	946	806	2 692	773	119	99
65 years and over	312	89	46	191	103	29	9
Male							
15 years and over	2 287	391	332	1 133	320	77	59
15 to 17 years	4	-	-	-	-	-	-
18 and 19 years	79	1	-	2	-	-	-
20 to 24 years	500	20	17	57	2	-	-
25 to 29 years	240	47	58	164	12	3	2
30 to 34 years	282	46	39	159	45	11	3
35 to 39 years	209	49	40	157	43	11	9
40 to 44 years	201	54	47	152	45	5	7
45 to 49 years	260	48	26	135	42	13	8
50 to 54 years	170	38	33	122	48	5	4
55 to 59 years	129	39	29	71	28	10	12
60 to 64 years	77	15	20	41	23	-	6
65 to 69 years	67	14	12	34	18	10	1
70 to 74 years	27	5	4	24	7	6	-
75 years and over	33	14	6	15	7	4	6
15 to 17 years	4	-	-	-	-	-	-
18 years and over	2 283	391	332	1 133	320	77	59
15 to 24 years	583	21	17	59	2	-	-
25 years and over	1 704	369	315	1 074	318	77	59
15 to 64 years	2 161	357	310	1 060	288	57	52
65 years and over	126	33	22	74	32	19	7
Female							
15 years and over	3 089	645	520	1 749	555	71	49
15 to 17 years	10	2	-	-	-	-	-
18 and 19 years	175	2	3	2	-	-	-
20 to 24 years	566	67	40	121	6	-	-
25 to 29 years	364	73	65	240	46	10	-
30 to 34 years	353	85	73	238	64	11	5
35 to 39 years	295	70	67	244	74	7	6
40 to 44 years	325	78	66	233	63	6	9
45 to 49 years	300	79	51	252	62	13	7
50 to 54 years	235	52	60	149	87	7	11
55 to 59 years	178	56	35	98	55	7	5
60 to 64 years	102	25	36	55	28	2	4
65 to 69 years	73	23	9	47	25	4	-
70 to 74 years	52	15	2	30	16	2	-
75 years and over	61	18	13	40	29	3	2
15 to 17 years	10	2	-	-	-	-	-
18 years and over	3 079	643	520	1 749	555	71	49
15 to 24 years	751	70	43	123	6	-	-
25 years and over	2 339	574	477	1 626	550	71	49
15 to 64 years	2 903	589	496	1 632	485	62	47
65 years and over	186	56	24	117	71	9	2

- = Quantity zero or rounds to zero.

Table A-17. Educational Attainment of the Population Age 15 Years and Over, by Age, Sex, Race, and Hispanic Origin, 2005—*Continued*

(Numbers in thousands.)

Age, sex, race, and Hispanic origin	Total population	None	Elementary			High school			
			1st to 4th grade	5th and 6th grade	7th and 8th grade	9th grade	10th grade	11th grade	High school graduate
ASIAN ALONE OR IN COMBINATION									
Both Sexes									
15 years and over	10 466	126	122	217	272	279	323	445	2 038
15 to 17 years	582	-	3	4	81	159	174	140	10
18 and 19 years	327	2	-	-	-	6	18	96	59
20 to 24 years	925	-	2	-	7	4	10	34	182
25 to 29 years	1 117	6	1	4	12	7	6	14	171
30 to 34 years	1 279	4	5	4	13	12	16	26	193
35 to 39 years	1 222	9	10	8	16	10	13	14	200
40 to 44 years	1 059	7	10	12	15	7	19	26	216
45 to 49 years	931	10	6	16	24	8	21	6	238
50 to 54 years	810	12	11	26	16	16	10	26	212
55 to 59 years	658	10	10	16	25	14	5	8	175
60 to 64 years	451	3	12	15	10	12	5	15	103
65 to 69 years	384	7	13	39	14	5	5	25	87
70 to 74 years	274	9	19	25	16	7	8	4	76
75 years and over	446	47	21	47	23	12	14	10	116
15 to 17 years	582	-	3	4	81	159	174	140	10
18 years and over	9 884	126	119	213	191	120	149	305	2 027
15 to 24 years	1 834	2	5	5	88	169	202	270	251
25 years and over	8 632	124	117	213	184	110	121	176	1 787
15 to 64 years	9 362	62	69	106	219	256	297	406	1 758
65 years and over	1 104	63	53	111	53	23	27	40	279
Male									
15 years and over	5 005	25	42	80	119	138	152	226	986
15 to 17 years	307	-	-	4	43	87	88	76	4
18 and 19 years	162	2	-	-	-	1	4	59	33
20 to 24 years	454	-	-	-	3	1	5	19	107
25 to 29 years	521	2	-	4	6	1	3	1	97
30 to 34 years	649	-	2	1	4	-	7	17	104
35 to 39 years	602	-	3	1	6	8	6	7	111
40 to 44 years	525	2	9	3	5	5	6	15	103
45 to 49 years	430	7	4	6	5	-	10	2	119
50 to 54 years	367	-	1	10	11	9	3	7	83
55 to 59 years	301	1	-	5	13	6	3	5	74
60 to 64 years	207	3	5	6	2	7	1	3	35
65 to 69 years	185	-	-	13	5	-	2	11	38
70 to 74 years	127	1	5	10	12	6	4	-	32
75 years and over	167	6	11	16	3	6	10	4	46
15 to 17 years	307	-	-	4	43	87	88	76	4
18 years and over	4 697	25	42	76	76	51	63	150	983
15 to 24 years	924	2	-	4	45	90	98	154	144
25 years and over	4 081	23	42	76	73	48	54	72	842
15 to 64 years	4 525	17	26	42	98	126	136	210	871
65 years and over	479	8	16	38	20	12	15	16	116
Female									
15 years and over	5 461	101	80	137	154	141	172	219	1 051
15 to 17 years	274	-	3	-	38	72	86	64	6
18 and 19 years	165	-	-	-	-	4	14	37	26
20 to 24 years	471	-	2	-	5	3	4	15	75
25 to 29 years	596	4	1	-	6	6	3	13	74
30 to 34 years	630	4	2	3	8	11	9	9	89
35 to 39 years	621	9	7	6	9	3	6	8	89
40 to 44 years	535	5	1	9	10	2	13	11	113
45 to 49 years	501	3	2	10	19	8	11	4	119
50 to 54 years	443	11	10	16	5	7	7	19	129
55 to 59 years	357	9	10	11	12	8	2	3	101
60 to 64 years	243	-	6	9	8	6	4	12	68
65 to 69 years	199	7	13	26	9	5	4	14	49
70 to 74 years	146	9	14	15	4	1	4	4	45
75 years and over	279	41	10	31	20	6	4	7	70
15 to 17 years	274	-	3	-	38	72	86	64	6
18 years and over	5 187	101	77	137	115	69	86	155	1 045
15 to 24 years	910	-	5	-	43	79	104	116	107
25 years and over	4 551	101	75	137	111	63	68	104	944
15 to 64 years	4 836	45	43	65	121	130	160	195	888
65 years and over	625	56	37	72	33	11	11	24	163

- = Quantity zero or rounds to zero.

Table A-17. Educational Attainment of the Population Age 15 Years and Over, by Age, Sex, Race, and Hispanic Origin, 2005—*Continued*

(Numbers in thousands.)

Age, sex, race, and Hispanic origin	Some college, no degree	Associate's degree		Bachelor's degree	Master's degree	Professional degree	Doctorate degree
		Occupational	Academic				
ASIAN ALONE OR IN COMBINATION							
Both Sexes							
15 years and over	1 547	295	336	2 937	1 015	269	244
15 to 17 years	9	-	-	1	-	-	-
18 and 19 years	146	-	1	-	-	-	-
20 to 24 years	467	29	23	149	17	2	-
25 to 29 years	147	37	37	489	137	43	5
30 to 34 years	121	30	40	515	226	39	35
35 to 39 years	141	24	64	418	199	44	53
40 to 44 years	131	41	44	320	135	42	34
45 to 49 years	127	31	32	266	89	25	30
50 to 54 years	69	31	34	249	63	18	17
55 to 59 years	72	28	24	175	44	29	23
60 to 64 years	30	19	11	147	38	7	23
65 to 69 years	31	5	6	93	27	13	12
70 to 74 years	19	7	10	42	21	3	8
75 years and over	37	11	9	72	18	5	4
15 to 17 years	9	-	-	1	-	-	-
18 years and over	1 538	295	336	2 936	1 015	269	244
15 to 24 years	622	29	24	150	17	2	-
25 years and over	925	266	312	2 787	998	267	244
15 to 64 years	1 460	272	311	2 729	949	248	220
65 years and over	87	23	25	208	67	21	24
Male							
15 years and over	718	126	149	1 335	573	169	167
15 to 17 years	4	-	-	1	-	-	-
18 and 19 years	61	-	1	-	-	-	-
20 to 24 years	220	16	15	66	-	-	-
25 to 29 years	70	15	15	209	75	22	2
30 to 34 years	72	14	24	241	128	17	16
35 to 39 years	63	9	20	193	116	26	31
40 to 44 years	67	15	19	159	66	25	25
45 to 49 years	48	15	15	107	52	19	22
50 to 54 years	35	9	10	119	41	14	14
55 to 59 years	29	19	10	70	25	22	17
60 to 64 years	11	8	3	72	28	5	18
65 to 69 years	18	1	5	49	19	11	11
70 to 74 years	3	4	7	18	14	3	8
75 years and over	15	-	5	30	9	4	3
15 to 17 years	4	-	-	1	-	-	-
18 years and over	714	126	149	1 334	573	169	167
15 to 24 years	286	16	17	67	-	-	-
25 years and over	432	110	133	1 268	573	169	167
15 to 64 years	682	120	131	1 238	532	151	146
65 years and over	36	6	18	97	42	18	21
Female							
15 years and over	829	170	186	1 602	442	101	77
15 to 17 years	5	-	-	-	-	-	-
18 and 19 years	85	-	-	-	-	-	-
20 to 24 years	246	13	8	82	17	2	-
25 to 29 years	77	23	23	280	61	21	3
30 to 34 years	50	16	16	274	98	22	19
35 to 39 years	78	15	44	225	83	18	22
40 to 44 years	64	26	25	161	69	16	9
45 to 49 years	78	17	17	159	37	6	8
50 to 54 years	35	22	25	130	22	4	3
55 to 59 years	42	10	14	105	19	7	6
60 to 64 years	18	11	9	74	10	2	5
65 to 69 years	13	4	1	44	8	3	1
70 to 74 years	16	3	2	24	7	-	-
75 years and over	22	11	4	42	10	1	1
15 to 17 years	5	-	-	-	-	-	-
18 years and over	825	170	186	1 602	442	101	77
15 to 24 years	335	13	8	82	17	2	-
25 years and over	494	157	179	1 519	425	98	77
15 to 64 years	778	152	180	1 491	417	97	74
65 years and over	51	18	7	111	25	4	2

- = Quantity zero or rounds to zero.

Table A-17. Educational Attainment of the Population Age 15 Years and Over, by Age, Sex, Race, and Hispanic Origin, 2005—*Continued*

(Numbers in thousands.)

Age, sex, race, and Hispanic origin	Total population	None	Elementary			High school			
			1st to 4th grade	5th and 6th grade	7th and 8th grade	9th grade	10th grade	11th grade	High school graduate
HISPANIC[1]									
Both Sexes									
15 years and over	29 605	498	1 395	2 719	2 033	2 360	1 633	2 651	7 879
15 to 17 years	2 087	2	7	14	414	622	571	417	33
18 and 19 years	1 291	2	14	47	45	59	105	394	359
20 to 24 years	3 676	9	76	222	142	263	135	370	1 261
25 to 29 years	3 949	40	100	335	205	288	149	333	1 207
30 to 34 years	3 688	40	138	358	196	311	145	290	1 063
35 to 39 years	3 299	39	130	369	196	210	104	236	926
40 to 44 years	2 944	41	143	318	168	155	97	186	833
45 to 49 years	2 371	35	137	286	126	145	87	134	637
50 to 54 years	1 791	40	121	232	128	82	60	105	489
55 to 59 years	1 347	37	118	142	82	65	52	50	360
60 to 64 years	969	30	88	115	88	46	35	57	249
65 to 69 years	751	44	93	103	74	46	33	34	181
70 to 74 years	566	42	78	73	68	20	31	17	106
75 years and over	877	98	153	106	102	48	29	27	176
15 to 17 years	2 087	2	7	14	414	622	571	417	33
18 years and over	27 518	496	1 389	2 705	1 619	1 738	1 062	2 234	7 846
15 to 24 years	7 054	13	97	283	600	944	810	1 181	1 652
25 years and over	22 551	486	1 299	2 436	1 433	1 416	823	1 470	6 227
15 to 64 years	27 411	314	1 072	2 438	1 789	2 246	1 539	2 572	7 417
65 years and over	2 194	184	324	281	244	115	94	79	463
Male									
15 years and over	15 224	237	759	1 483	1 079	1 227	809	1 378	4 147
15 to 17 years	1 076	2	4	10	236	295	294	205	25
18 and 19 years	652	-	10	41	28	29	65	187	179
20 to 24 years	1 984	6	48	140	91	163	66	209	727
25 to 29 years	2 178	27	63	184	123	144	73	188	684
30 to 34 years	1 956	23	71	201	113	173	71	175	588
35 to 39 years	1 738	22	84	198	120	107	57	129	500
40 to 44 years	1 525	24	72	172	89	88	31	113	446
45 to 49 years	1 206	21	88	154	49	65	46	69	334
50 to 54 years	878	10	82	130	66	41	27	35	219
55 to 59 years	668	21	55	77	42	41	21	24	158
60 to 64 years	433	17	46	63	35	24	14	17	97
65 to 69 years	322	10	49	47	34	25	11	9	70
70 to 74 years	245	13	36	33	25	8	13	5	41
75 years and over	363	40	52	34	28	25	18	12	79
15 to 17 years	1 076	2	4	10	236	295	294	205	25
18 years and over	14 148	235	755	1 474	842	932	515	1 173	4 122
15 to 24 years	3 712	8	62	190	355	487	426	601	931
25 years and over	11 512	228	698	1 293	723	740	383	777	3 215
15 to 64 years	14 294	174	622	1 369	992	1 169	766	1 351	3 957
65 years and over	930	63	138	114	87	58	43	27	190
Female									
15 years and over	14 381	261	636	1 236	954	1 133	824	1 273	3 733
15 to 17 years	1 012	-	3	5	178	327	276	213	8
18 and 19 years	639	2	4	6	16	30	39	207	180
20 to 24 years	1 691	2	28	82	50	100	69	161	533
25 to 29 years	1 771	12	37	151	82	144	76	146	522
30 to 34 years	1 732	18	67	157	82	137	74	115	476
35 to 39 years	1 561	17	46	172	76	104	47	107	426
40 to 44 years	1 419	17	71	146	79	67	66	73	387
45 to 49 years	1 165	13	48	132	77	80	41	64	303
50 to 54 years	913	29	40	102	62	41	33	70	270
55 to 59 years	679	16	63	65	40	25	31	26	202
60 to 64 years	535	13	42	52	53	22	21	40	152
65 to 69 years	429	34	43	56	40	21	22	25	111
70 to 74 years	321	29	41	39	44	12	18	12	65
75 years and over	514	58	101	72	74	23	12	15	97
15 to 17 years	1 012	-	3	5	178	327	276	213	8
18 years and over	13 370	261	633	1 231	777	806	548	1 061	3 725
15 to 24 years	3 342	4	35	93	244	457	385	580	721
25 years and over	11 039	257	601	1 143	710	676	440	693	3 012
15 to 64 years	13 118	140	450	1 069	797	1 076	773	1 221	3 460
65 years and over	1 264	121	186	167	158	57	51	52	273

[1]May be of any race.
- = Quantity zero or rounds to zero.

Table A-17. Educational Attainment of the Population Age 15 Years and Over, by Age, Sex, Race, and Hispanic Origin, 2005—*Continued*

(Numbers in thousands.)

Age, sex, race, and Hispanic origin	Some college, no degree	Associate's degree		Bachelor's degree	Master's degree	Professional degree	Doctorate degree
		Occupational	Academic				
HISPANIC[1]							
Both Sexes							
15 years and over	4 182	783	623	2 043	557	152	95
15 to 17 years	7	-	-	-	-	-	-
18 and 19 years	255	10	-	1	-	-	-
20 to 24 years	909	67	77	140	6	-	-
25 to 29 years	608	123	120	359	53	19	10
30 to 34 years	506	128	94	315	78	19	6
35 to 39 years	473	108	71	322	83	18	12
40 to 44 years	402	120	87	270	86	30	8
45 to 49 years	334	64	64	221	71	18	12
50 to 54 years	208	43	29	163	71	11	19
55 to 59 years	209	38	31	112	36	7	10
60 to 64 years	121	31	28	46	26	7	3
65 to 69 years	53	12	14	34	16	3	10
70 to 74 years	48	21	2	30	12	15	2
75 years and over	48	18	8	38	19	3	4
15 to 17 years	7	-	-	-	-	-	-
18 years and over	4 175	783	623	2 043	557	152	95
15 to 24 years	1 171	77	77	142	6	-	-
25 years and over	3 011	706	546	1 901	551	152	95
15 to 64 years	4 032	732	600	1 940	510	131	80
65 years and over	150	51	24	102	47	21	15
Male							
15 years and over	2 049	363	272	1 024	252	84	62
15 to 17 years	4	-	-	-	-	-	-
18 and 19 years	108	3	-	1	-	-	-
20 to 24 years	423	26	26	55	4	-	-
25 to 29 years	341	61	68	185	19	10	8
30 to 34 years	257	51	45	140	32	8	2
35 to 39 years	227	55	30	160	36	7	6
40 to 44 years	193	53	47	141	40	13	4
45 to 49 years	145	36	23	112	38	13	10
50 to 54 years	110	15	12	81	35	4	11
55 to 59 years	98	23	10	67	18	7	8
60 to 64 years	61	10	9	23	13	2	3
65 to 69 years	29	7	1	12	9	3	5
70 to 74 years	26	9	-	17	3	14	2
75 years and over	26	14	1	23	5	2	4
15 to 17 years	4	-	-	-	-	-	-
18 years and over	2 045	363	272	1 024	252	84	62
15 to 24 years	535	28	26	57	4	-	-
25 years and over	1 514	334	246	967	248	84	62
15 to 64 years	1 968	332	270	972	235	65	51
65 years and over	81	30	2	52	17	19	10
Female							
15 years and over	2 133	420	351	1 019	305	68	33
15 to 17 years	3	-	-	-	-	-	-
18 and 19 years	147	7	-	-	-	-	-
20 to 24 years	486	41	51	85	2	-	-
25 to 29 years	267	62	52	175	34	9	2
30 to 34 years	250	78	49	169	46	12	4
35 to 39 years	245	53	41	163	47	11	6
40 to 44 years	209	67	40	129	46	18	4
45 to 49 years	189	28	41	109	33	5	2
50 to 54 years	99	28	17	72	36	7	8
55 to 59 years	110	15	21	45	19	-	2
60 to 64 years	60	22	19	23	12	5	-
65 to 69 years	24	4	12	22	7	-	5
70 to 74 years	22	11	2	14	10	1	-
75 years and over	22	5	7	15	14	1	-
15 to 17 years	3	-	-	-	-	-	-
18 years and over	2 130	420	351	1 019	305	68	33
15 to 24 years	636	48	51	85	2	-	-
25 years and over	1 497	372	300	934	303	68	33
15 to 64 years	2 064	400	330	969	275	66	28
65 years and over	68	20	21	50	31	2	5

[1]May be of any race.
- = Quantity zero or rounds to zero.

Table A-18. Percent of High School and College Graduates Among the Population Age 15 Years and Over, by Age, Sex, Race, and Hispanic Origin, 2005

(Percent, except where noted.)

Age, sex, race, and Hispanic origin	Total population (thousands)	High school			College		
		Total population	Not a high school graduate	High school graduate or more	Total population	Less than a bachelor's degree	Bachelor's degree or more
ALL RACES							
Both Sexes							
15 years and over	230 437	100.0	20.4	79.6	100.0	76.2	23.8
15 to 17 years	13 061	100.0	98.2	1.8	100.0	100.0	-
18 and 19 years	7 601	100.0	42.6	57.4	100.0	99.8	0.2
20 to 24 years	20 408	100.0	14.1	85.9	100.0	88.5	11.5
25 to 29 years	19 501	100.0	13.8	86.2	100.0	71.2	28.8
30 to 34 years	19 809	100.0	12.7	87.3	100.0	68.0	32.0
35 to 39 years	20 651	100.0	11.9	88.1	100.0	68.9	31.1
40 to 44 years	22 699	100.0	11.4	88.6	100.0	71.1	28.9
45 to 49 years	22 235	100.0	11.0	89.0	100.0	71.5	28.5
50 to 54 years	19 726	100.0	10.8	89.2	100.0	69.4	30.6
55 to 59 years	16 771	100.0	12.2	87.8	100.0	69.9	30.1
60 to 64 years	12 765	100.0	15.5	84.5	100.0	73.5	26.5
65 to 69 years	10 130	100.0	21.0	79.0	100.0	78.9	21.1
70 to 74 years	8 260	100.0	23.9	76.1	100.0	80.1	19.9
75 years and over	16 820	100.0	30.1	69.9	100.0	83.0	17.0
15 to 17 years	13 061	100.0	98.2	1.8	100.0	100.0	-
18 years and over	217 375	100.0	15.7	84.3	100.0	74.8	25.2
15 to 24 years	41 070	100.0	46.2	53.8	100.0	94.2	5.8
25 years and over	189 367	100.0	14.8	85.2	100.0	72.3	27.7
15 to 64 years	195 227	100.0	19.4	80.6	100.0	75.4	24.6
65 years and over	35 209	100.0	26.0	74.0	100.0	81.1	18.9
Male							
15 years and over	111 694	100.0	21.2	78.8	100.0	75.6	24.4
15 to 17 years	6 728	100.0	98.3	1.7	100.0	100.0	-
18 and 19 years	3 775	100.0	47.2	52.8	100.0	99.9	0.1
20 to 24 years	10 292	100.0	15.6	84.4	100.0	90.8	9.2
25 to 29 years	9 826	100.0	15.0	85.0	100.0	74.5	25.5
30 to 34 years	9 851	100.0	13.8	86.2	100.0	70.3	29.7
35 to 39 years	10 265	100.0	13.2	86.8	100.0	70.3	29.7
40 to 44 years	11 204	100.0	12.6	87.4	100.0	71.6	28.4
45 to 49 years	10 935	100.0	11.9	88.1	100.0	71.6	28.4
50 to 54 years	9 620	100.0	10.5	89.5	100.0	67.2	32.8
55 to 59 years	8 009	100.0	12.6	87.4	100.0	66.7	33.3
60 to 64 years	6 042	100.0	15.9	84.1	100.0	68.5	31.5
65 to 69 years	4 815	100.0	20.8	79.2	100.0	74.1	25.9
70 to 74 years	3 651	100.0	23.0	77.0	100.0	73.6	26.4
75 years and over	6 681	100.0	29.3	70.7	100.0	76.7	23.3
15 to 17 years	6 728	100.0	98.3	1.7	100.0	100.0	-
18 years and over	104 966	100.0	16.3	83.7	100.0	74.1	25.9
15 to 24 years	20 795	100.0	48.1	51.9	100.0	95.4	4.6
25 years and over	90 899	100.0	15.1	84.9	100.0	71.1	28.9
15 to 64 years	96 548	100.0	20.6	79.4	100.0	75.7	24.3
65 years and over	15 147	100.0	25.1	74.9	100.0	75.1	24.9
Female							
15 years and over	118 742	100.0	19.6	80.4	100.0	76.8	23.2
15 to 17 years	6 333	100.0	98.2	1.8	100.0	99.9	0.1
18 and 19 years	3 826	100.0	38.1	61.9	100.0	99.7	0.3
20 to 24 years	10 115	100.0	12.7	87.3	100.0	86.2	13.8
25 to 29 years	9 676	100.0	12.6	87.4	100.0	67.8	32.2
30 to 34 years	9 958	100.0	11.6	88.4	100.0	65.6	34.4
35 to 39 years	10 387	100.0	10.5	89.5	100.0	67.6	32.4
40 to 44 years	11 495	100.0	10.2	89.8	100.0	70.6	29.4
45 to 49 years	11 299	100.0	10.1	89.9	100.0	71.5	28.5
50 to 54 years	10 106	100.0	11.0	89.0	100.0	71.5	28.5
55 to 59 years	8 762	100.0	11.9	88.1	100.0	72.9	27.1
60 to 64 years	6 722	100.0	15.2	84.8	100.0	78.0	22.0
65 to 69 years	5 315	100.0	21.1	78.9	100.0	83.3	16.7
70 to 74 years	4 609	100.0	24.7	75.3	100.0	85.2	14.8
75 years and over	10 139	100.0	30.7	69.3	100.0	87.1	12.9
15 to 17 years	6 333	100.0	98.2	1.8	100.0	99.9	0.1
18 years and over	112 409	100.0	15.2	84.8	100.0	75.5	24.5
15 to 24 years	20 275	100.0	44.2	55.8	100.0	93.0	7.0
25 years and over	98 467	100.0	14.5	85.5	100.0	73.5	26.5
15 to 64 years	98 679	100.0	18.1	81.9	100.0	75.0	25.0
65 years and over	20 063	100.0	26.8	73.2	100.0	85.7	14.3

- = Quantity zero or rounds to zero.

Table A-18. Percent of High School and College Graduates Among the Population Age 15 Years and Over, by Age, Sex, Race, and Hispanic Origin, 2005—*Continued*

(Percent, except where noted.)

Age, sex, race, and Hispanic origin	Total population (thousands)	High school			College		
		Total population	Not a high school graduate	High school graduate or more	Total population	Less than a bachelor's degree	Bachelor's degree or more
WHITE ALONE OR IN COMBINATION							
Both Sexes							
15 years and over	190 739	100.0	19.7	80.3	100.0	75.8	24.2
15 to 17 years	10 370	100.0	98.4	1.6	100.0	100.0	-
18 and 19 years	6 070	100.0	42.0	58.0	100.0	99.8	0.2
20 to 24 years	16 427	100.0	13.7	86.3	100.0	87.8	12.2
25 to 29 years	15 600	100.0	14.4	85.6	100.0	71.2	28.8
30 to 34 years	15 795	100.0	13.5	86.5	100.0	68.4	31.6
35 to 39 years	16 652	100.0	12.2	87.8	100.0	69.2	30.8
40 to 44 years	18 622	100.0	11.0	89.0	100.0	70.5	29.5
45 to 49 years	18 434	100.0	10.7	89.3	100.0	70.9	29.1
50 to 54 years	16 523	100.0	9.8	90.2	100.0	68.3	31.7
55 to 59 years	14 311	100.0	11.0	89.0	100.0	68.7	31.3
60 to 64 years	10 990	100.0	14.1	85.9	100.0	72.8	27.2
65 to 69 years	8 671	100.0	18.8	81.2	100.0	78.7	21.3
70 to 74 years	7 219	100.0	21.3	78.7	100.0	79.4	20.6
75 years and over	15 056	100.0	27.6	72.4	100.0	82.3	17.7
15 to 17 years	10 370	100.0	98.4	1.6	100.0	100.0	-
18 years and over	180 369	100.0	15.1	84.9	100.0	74.4	25.6
15 to 24 years	32 867	100.0	45.7	54.3	100.0	93.9	6.1
25 years and over	157 873	100.0	14.3	85.7	100.0	72.0	28.0
15 to 64 years	159 794	100.0	18.9	81.1	100.0	74.8	25.2
65 years and over	30 946	100.0	23.7	76.3	100.0	80.6	19.4
Male							
15 years and over	93 394	100.0	20.6	79.4	100.0	75.1	24.9
15 to 17 years	5 338	100.0	98.4	1.6	100.0	100.0	-
18 and 19 years	3 043	100.0	46.1	53.9	100.0	99.9	0.1
20 to 24 years	8 383	100.0	15.4	84.6	100.0	90.3	9.7
25 to 29 years	8 021	100.0	15.8	84.2	100.0	74.7	25.3
30 to 34 years	7 980	100.0	15.1	84.0	100.0	71.3	28.7
35 to 39 years	8 384	100.0	13.9	86.1	100.0	70.9	29.1
40 to 44 years	9 301	100.0	12.5	87.5	100.0	71.2	28.8
45 to 49 years	9 182	100.0	11.7	88.3	100.0	70.7	29.3
50 to 54 years	8 164	100.0	9.9	90.1	100.0	66.0	34.0
55 to 59 years	6 905	100.0	11.4	88.6	100.0	65.1	34.9
60 to 64 years	5 271	100.0	14.7	85.3	100.0	67.7	32.3
65 to 69 years	4 130	100.0	18.9	81.1	100.0	73.6	26.4
70 to 74 years	3 230	100.0	20.4	79.6	100.0	72.7	27.3
75 years and over	6 063	100.0	27.0	73.0	100.0	75.5	24.5
15 to 17 years	5 338	100.0	98.4	1.6	100.0	100.0	-
18 years and over	88 056	100.0	15.9	84.1	100.0	73.5	26.5
15 to 24 years	16 765	100.0	47.4	52.6	100.0	95.1	4.9
25 years and over	76 629	100.0	14.8	85.2	100.0	70.7	29.3
15 to 64 years	79 972	100.0	20.2	79.8	100.0	75.2	24.8
65 years and over	13 422	100.0	22.9	77.1	100.0	74.3	25.7
Female							
15 years and over	97 345	100.0	18.8	81.2	100.0	76.5	23.5
15 to 17 years	5 032	100.0	98.5	1.5	100.0	99.9	0.1
18 and 19 years	3 026	100.0	37.9	62.1	100.0	99.7	0.3
20 to 24 years	8 043	100.0	11.9	88.1	100.0	85.3	14.7
25 to 29 years	7 579	100.0	13.0	87.0	100.0	67.5	32.5
30 to 34 years	7 815	100.0	11.9	88.1	100.0	65.5	34.5
35 to 39 years	8 268	100.0	10.6	89.4	100.0	67.4	32.6
40 to 44 years	9 321	100.0	9.5	90.5	100.0	69.7	30.3
45 to 49 years	9 252	100.0	9.8	90.2	100.0	71.2	28.8
50 to 54 years	8 360	100.0	9.7	90.3	100.0	70.6	29.4
55 to 59 years	7 406	100.0	10.7	89.3	100.0	72.1	27.9
60 to 64 years	5 719	100.0	13.5	86.5	100.0	77.5	22.5
65 to 69 years	4 541	100.0	18.7	81.3	100.0	83.5	16.5
70 to 74 years	3 989	100.0	22.1	77.9	100.0	84.9	15.1
75 years and over	8 993	100.0	28.0	72.0	100.0	86.9	13.1
15 to 17 years	5 032	100.0	98.5	1.5	100.0	99.9	0.1
18 years and over	92 313	100.0	14.4	85.6	100.0	75.2	24.8
15 to 24 years	16 102	100.0	43.8	56.2	100.0	92.6	7.4
25 years and over	81 244	100.0	13.8	86.2	100.0	73.3	26.7
15 to 64 years	79 822	100.0	17.6	82.4	100.0	74.5	25.5
65 years and over	17 523	100.0	24.2	75.8	100.0	85.5	14.5

- = Quantity zero or rounds to zero.

Table A-18. Percent of High School and College Graduates Among the Population Age 15 Years and Over, by Age, Sex, Race, and Hispanic Origin, 2005—*Continued*

(Percent, except where noted.)

Age, sex, race, and Hispanic origin	Total population (thousands)	High school			College		
		Total population	Not a high school graduate	High school graduate or more	Total population	Less than a bachelor's degree	Bachelor's degree or more
BLACK ALONE OR IN COMBINATION							
Both Sexes							
15 years and over	27 987	100.0	25.8	74.2	100.0	85.7	14.3
15 to 17 years	2 140	100.0	97.9	2.1	100.0	100.0	-
18 and 19 years	1 177	100.0	46.3	53.7	100.0	99.6	0.4
20 to 24 years	2 983	100.0	17.6	82.4	100.0	93.8	6.2
25 to 29 years	2 702	100.0	13.4	86.6	100.0	82.4	17.6
30 to 34 years	2 599	100.0	9.9	90.1	100.0	79.4	20.6
35 to 39 years	2 640	100.0	11.8	88.2	100.0	79.1	20.9
40 to 44 years	2 832	100.0	13.5	86.5	100.0	81.7	18.3
45 to 49 years	2 695	100.0	12.4	87.6	100.0	80.3	19.7
50 to 54 years	2 244	100.0	15.6	84.4	100.0	80.7	19.3
55 to 59 years	1 716	100.0	20.4	79.6	100.0	83.3	16.7
60 to 64 years	1 253	100.0	26.0	74.0	100.0	87.3	12.7
65 to 69 years	1 016	100.0	35.4	64.6	100.0	86.3	13.7
70 to 74 years	723	100.0	45.7	54.3	100.0	88.2	11.8
75 years and over	1 267	100.0	55.1	44.9	100.0	91.6	8.4
15 to 17 years	2 140	100.0	97.9	2.1	100.0	100.0	-
18 years and over	25 847	100.0	19.9	80.1	100.0	84.5	15.5
15 to 24 years	6 300	100.0	50.2	49.8	100.0	97.0	3.0
25 years and over	21 687	100.0	18.7	81.3	100.0	82.4	17.6
15 to 64 years	24 982	100.0	23.4	76.6	100.0	85.3	14.7
65 years and over	3 005	100.0	46.2	53.8	100.0	89.0	11.0
Male							
15 years and over	12 614	100.0	27.1	72.9	100.0	87.4	12.6
15 to 17 years	1 080	100.0	98.5	1.5	100.0	100.0	-
18 and 19 years	550	100.0	53.1	46.9	100.0	99.6	0.4
20 to 24 years	1 410	100.0	18.2	81.8	100.0	95.8	4.2
25 to 29 years	1 240	100.0	13.6	86.4	100.0	85.4	14.6
30 to 34 years	1 150	100.0	8.9	91.1	100.0	81.0	19.0
35 to 39 years	1 193	100.0	13.0	87.0	100.0	81.6	18.4
40 to 44 years	1 280	100.0	13.8	86.2	100.0	83.7	16.3
45 to 49 years	1 229	100.0	14.2	85.8	100.0	83.9	16.1
50 to 54 years	1 010	100.0	13.6	86.4	100.0	82.3	17.7
55 to 59 years	767	100.0	23.7	76.3	100.0	84.2	15.8
60 to 64 years	533	100.0	27.0	73.0	100.0	86.8	13.2
65 to 69 years	466	100.0	37.9	62.1	100.0	86.6	13.4
70 to 74 years	272	100.0	50.0	50.0	100.0	86.2	13.8
75 years and over	433	100.0	56.9	43.1	100.0	92.6	7.4
15 to 17 years	1 080	100.0	98.5	1.5	100.0	100.0	-
18 years and over	11 533	100.0	20.4	79.6	100.0	86.2	13.8
15 to 24 years	3 041	100.0	53.1	46.9	100.0	98.0	2.0
25 years and over	9 573	100.0	18.8	81.2	100.0	84.0	16.0
15 to 64 years	11 442	100.0	24.9	75.1	100.0	87.3	12.7
65 years and over	1 171	100.0	47.8	52.2	100.0	88.7	11.3
Female							
15 years and over	15 373	100.0	24.8	75.2	100.0	84.2	15.8
15 to 17 years	1 059	100.0	97.3	2.7	100.0	100.0	-
18 and 19 years	627	100.0	40.3	59.7	100.0	99.7	0.3
20 to 24 years	1 573	100.0	17.1	82.9	100.0	91.9	8.1
25 to 29 years	1 461	100.0	13.3	86.7	100.0	79.7	20.3
30 to 34 years	1 449	100.0	10.7	89.3	100.0	78.1	21.9
35 to 39 years	1 447	100.0	10.8	89.2	100.0	77.1	22.9
40 to 44 years	1 552	100.0	13.3	86.7	100.0	80.0	20.0
45 to 49 years	1 467	100.0	10.9	89.1	100.0	77.2	22.8
50 to 54 years	1 233	100.0	17.2	82.8	100.0	79.4	20.6
55 to 59 years	949	100.0	17.7	82.3	100.0	82.6	17.4
60 to 64 years	721	100.0	25.3	74.7	100.0	87.7	12.3
65 to 69 years	549	100.0	33.3	66.7	100.0	86.1	13.9
70 to 74 years	450	100.0	43.1	56.9	100.0	89.4	10.6
75 years and over	834	100.0	54.1	45.9	100.0	91.1	8.9
15 to 17 years	1 059	100.0	97.3	2.7	100.0	100.0	-
18 years and over	14 314	100.0	19.5	80.5	100.0	83.1	16.9
15 to 24 years	3 259	100.0	47.6	52.4	100.0	96.0	4.0
25 years and over	12 114	100.0	18.7	81.3	100.0	81.1	18.9
15 to 64 years	13 539	100.0	22.1	77.9	100.0	83.6	16.4
65 years and over	1 834	100.0	45.2	54.8	100.0	89.2	10.8

- = Quantity zero or rounds to zero.

Table A-18. Percent of High School and College Graduates Among the Population Age 15 Years and Over, by Age, Sex, Race, and Hispanic Origin, 2005—*Continued*

(Percent, except where noted.)

Age, sex, race, and Hispanic origin	Total population (thousands)	High school			College		
		Total population	Not a high school graduate	High school graduate or more	Total population	Less than a bachelor's degree	Bachelor's degree or more
ASIAN ALONE OR IN COMBINATION							
Both Sexes							
15 years and over	10 466	100.0	17.1	82.9	100.0	57.3	42.7
15 to 17 years	582	100.0	96.5	3.5	100.0	99.8	0.2
18 and 19 years	327	100.0	37.0	63.0	100.0	100.0	-
20 to 24 years	925	100.0	6.2	93.8	100.0	81.9	18.1
25 to 29 years	1 117	100.0	4.5	95.5	100.0	39.7	60.3
30 to 34 years	1 279	100.0	6.2	93.8	100.0	36.2	63.8
35 to 39 years	1 222	100.0	6.6	93.4	100.0	41.6	58.4
40 to 44 years	1 059	100.0	9.1	90.9	100.0	49.9	50.1
45 to 49 years	931	100.0	9.9	90.1	100.0	55.9	44.1
50 to 54 years	810	100.0	14.5	85.5	100.0	57.3	42.7
55 to 59 years	658	100.0	13.3	86.7	100.0	58.8	41.2
60 to 64 years	451	100.0	16.1	83.9	100.0	52.4	47.6
65 to 69 years	384	100.0	28.3	71.7	100.0	62.0	38.0
70 to 74 years	274	100.0	31.9	68.1	100.0	72.9	27.1
75 years and over	446	100.0	38.9	61.1	100.0	77.7	22.3
15 to 17 years	582	100.0	96.5	3.5	100.0	99.8	0.2
18 years and over	9 884	100.0	12.4	87.6	100.0	54.8	45.2
15 to 24 years	1 834	100.0	40.3	59.7	100.0	90.8	9.2
25 years and over	8 632	100.0	12.1	87.9	100.0	50.2	49.8
15 to 64 years	9 362	100.0	15.1	84.9	100.0	55.7	44.3
65 years and over	1 104	100.0	33.5	66.5	100.0	71.1	28.9
Male							
15 years and over	5 005	100.0	15.6	84.4	100.0	55.2	44.8
15 to 17 years	307	100.0	97.0	3.0	100.0	99.6	0.4
18 and 19 years	162	100.0	40.8	59.2	100.0	100.0	-
20 to 24 years	454	100.0	6.3	93.7	100.0	85.3	14.7
25 to 29 years	521	100.0	3.3	96.7	100.0	41.0	59.0
30 to 34 years	649	100.0	5.0	95.0	100.0	38.0	62.0
35 to 39 years	602	100.0	5.4	94.6	100.0	39.1	60.9
40 to 44 years	525	100.0	8.7	91.3	100.0	47.6	52.4
45 to 49 years	430	100.0	7.8	92.2	100.0	53.4	46.6
50 to 54 years	367	100.0	11.4	88.6	100.0	48.7	51.3
55 to 59 years	301	100.0	11.0	89.0	100.0	55.1	44.9
60 to 64 years	207	100.0	13.0	87.0	100.0	40.6	59.4
65 to 69 years	185	100.0	17.1	82.9	100.0	51.5	48.5
70 to 74 years	127	100.0	29.8	70.2	100.0	66.0	34.0
75 years and over	167	100.0	33.2	66.8	100.0	73.0	27.0
15 to 17 years	307	100.0	97.0	3.0	100.0	99.6	0.4
18 years and over	4 697	100.0	10.3	89.7	100.0	52.2	47.8
15 to 24 years	924	100.0	42.6	57.4	100.0	92.6	7.4
25 years and over	4 081	100.0	9.5	90.5	100.0	46.7	53.3
15 to 64 years	4 525	100.0	14.5	85.5	100.0	54.3	45.7
65 years and over	479	100.0	26.1	73.9	100.0	62.9	37.1
Female							
15 years and over	5 461	100.0	18.4	81.6	100.0	59.3	40.7
15 to 17 years	274	100.0	96.0	4.0	100.0	100.0	-
18 and 19 years	165	100.0	33.2	66.8	100.0	100.0	-
20 to 24 years	471	100.0	6.1	93.9	100.0	78.6	21.4
25 to 29 years	596	100.0	5.6	94.4	100.0	38.5	61.5
30 to 34 years	630	100.0	7.4	92.6	100.0	34.4	65.6
35 to 39 years	621	100.0	7.7	92.3	100.0	44.1	55.9
40 to 44 years	535	100.0	9.5	90.5	100.0	52.1	47.9
45 to 49 years	501	100.0	11.7	88.3	100.0	58.0	42.0
50 to 54 years	443	100.0	17.0	83.0	100.0	64.4	35.6
55 to 59 years	357	100.0	15.3	84.7	100.0	61.9	38.1
60 to 64 years	243	100.0	18.7	81.3	100.0	62.4	37.6
65 to 69 years	199	100.0	38.7	61.3	100.0	71.8	28.2
70 to 74 years	146	100.0	33.8	66.2	100.0	78.9	21.1
75 years and over	279	100.0	42.3	57.7	100.0	80.6	19.4
15 to 17 years	274	100.0	96.0	4.0	100.0	100.0	-
18 years and over	5 187	100.0	14.3	85.7	100.0	57.2	42.8
15 to 24 years	910	100.0	38.1	61.9	100.0	88.9	11.1
25 years and over	4 551	100.0	14.4	85.6	100.0	53.4	46.6
15 to 64 years	4 836	100.0	15.7	84.3	100.0	57.0	43.0
65 years and over	625	100.0	39.1	60.9	100.0	77.4	22.6

- = Quantity zero or rounds to zero.

Table A-18. Percent of High School and College Graduates Among the Population Age 15 Years and Over, by Age, Sex, Race, and Hispanic Origin, 2005—*Continued*

(Percent, except where noted.)

Age, sex, race, and Hispanic origin	Total population (thousands)	High school			College		
		Total population	Not a high school graduate	High school graduate or more	Total population	Less than a bachelor's degree	Bachelor's degree or more
HISPANIC[1]							
Both Sexes							
15 years and over	29 605	100.0	44.9	55.1	100.0	90.4	9.6
15 to 17 years	2 087	100.0	98.1	1.9	100.0	100.0	-
18 and 19 years	1 291	100.0	51.6	48.4	100.0	99.9	0.1
20 to 24 years	3 676	100.0	33.1	66.9	100.0	96.0	4.0
25 to 29 years	3 949	100.0	36.7	63.3	100.0	88.8	11.2
30 to 34 years	3 688	100.0	40.1	59.9	100.0	88.7	11.3
35 to 39 years	3 299	100.0	39.0	61.0	100.0	86.8	13.2
40 to 44 years	2 944	100.0	37.6	62.4	100.0	86.6	13.4
45 to 49 years	2 371	100.0	40.1	59.9	100.0	86.4	13.6
50 to 54 years	1 791	100.0	42.9	57.1	100.0	85.8	14.2
55 to 59 years	1 347	100.0	40.5	59.5	100.0	87.7	12.3
60 to 64 years	969	100.0	47.3	52.7	100.0	91.6	8.4
65 to 69 years	751	100.0	56.9	43.1	100.0	91.5	8.5
70 to 74 years	566	100.0	58.3	41.7	100.0	89.5	10.5
75 years and over	877	100.0	64.3	35.7	100.0	92.8	7.2
15 to 17 years	2 087	100.0	98.1	1.9	100.0	100.0	-
18 years and over	27 518	100.0	40.9	59.1	100.0	89.7	10.3
15 to 24 years	7 054	100.0	55.7	44.3	100.0	97.9	2.1
25 years and over	22 551	100.0	41.5	58.5	100.0	88.0	12.0
15 to 64 years	27 411	100.0	43.7	56.3	100.0	90.3	9.7
65 years and over	2 194	100.0	60.2	39.8	100.0	91.5	8.5
Male							
15 years and over	15 224	100.0	45.8	54.2	100.0	90.7	9.3
15 to 17 years	1 076	100.0	97.3	2.7	100.0	100.0	-
18 and 19 years	652	100.0	55.3	44.7	100.0	99.8	0.2
20 to 24 years	1 984	100.0	36.4	63.6	100.0	97.0	3.0
25 to 29 years	2 178	100.0	36.8	63.2	100.0	89.8	10.2
30 to 34 years	1 956	100.0	42.3	57.7	100.0	90.4	9.6
35 to 39 years	1 738	100.0	41.2	58.8	100.0	88.0	12.0
40 to 44 years	1 525	100.0	38.5	61.5	100.0	87.0	13.0
45 to 49 years	1 206	100.0	41.0	59.0	100.0	85.6	14.4
50 to 54 years	878	100.0	44.5	55.5	100.0	85.0	15.0
55 to 59 years	668	100.0	41.8	58.2	100.0	85.1	14.9
60 to 64 years	433	100.0	49.8	50.2	100.0	90.4	9.6
65 to 69 years	322	100.0	57.5	42.5	100.0	90.8	9.2
70 to 74 years	245	100.0	54.6	45.4	100.0	85.7	14.3
75 years and over	363	100.0	57.7	42.3	100.0	90.8	9.2
15 to 17 years	1 076	100.0	97.3	2.7	100.0	100.0	-
18 years and over	14 148	100.0	41.9	58.1	100.0	90.0	10.0
15 to 24 years	3 712	100.0	57.4	42.6	100.0	98.4	1.6
25 years and over	11 512	100.0	42.1	57.9	100.0	88.2	11.8
15 to 64 years	14 294	100.0	45.1	54.9	100.0	90.7	9.3
65 years and over	930	100.0	56.8	43.2	100.0	89.5	10.5
Female							
15 years and over	14 381	100.0	43.9	56.1	100.0	90.1	9.9
15 to 17 years	1 012	100.0	98.9	1.1	100.0	100.0	-
18 and 19 years	639	100.0	47.7	52.3	100.0	100.0	-
20 to 24 years	1 691	100.0	29.1	70.9	100.0	94.8	5.2
25 to 29 years	1 771	100.0	36.6	63.4	100.0	87.6	12.4
30 to 34 years	1 732	100.0	37.6	62.4	100.0	86.7	13.3
35 to 39 years	1 561	100.0	36.4	63.6	100.0	85.5	14.5
40 to 44 years	1 419	100.0	36.6	63.4	100.0	86.1	13.9
45 to 49 years	1 165	100.0	39.1	60.9	100.0	87.3	12.7
50 to 54 years	913	100.0	41.2	58.8	100.0	86.6	13.4
55 to 59 years	679	100.0	39.1	60.9	100.0	90.4	9.6
60 to 64 years	535	100.0	45.3	54.7	100.0	92.5	7.5
65 to 69 years	429	100.0	56.5	43.5	100.0	92.0	8.0
70 to 74 years	321	100.0	61.0	39.0	100.0	92.4	7.6
75 years and over	514	100.0	68.9	31.1	100.0	94.2	5.8
15 to 17 years	1 012	100.0	98.9	1.1	100.0	100.0	-
18 years and over	13 370	100.0	39.8	60.2	100.0	89.3	10.7
15 to 24 years	3 342	100.0	53.8	46.2	100.0	97.4	2.6
25 years and over	11 039	100.0	40.9	59.1	100.0	87.9	12.1
15 to 64 years	13 118	100.0	42.1	57.9	100.0	89.8	10.2
65 years and over	1 264	100.0	62.7	37.3	100.0	93.0	7.0

[1]May be of any race.
- = Quantity zero or rounds to zero.

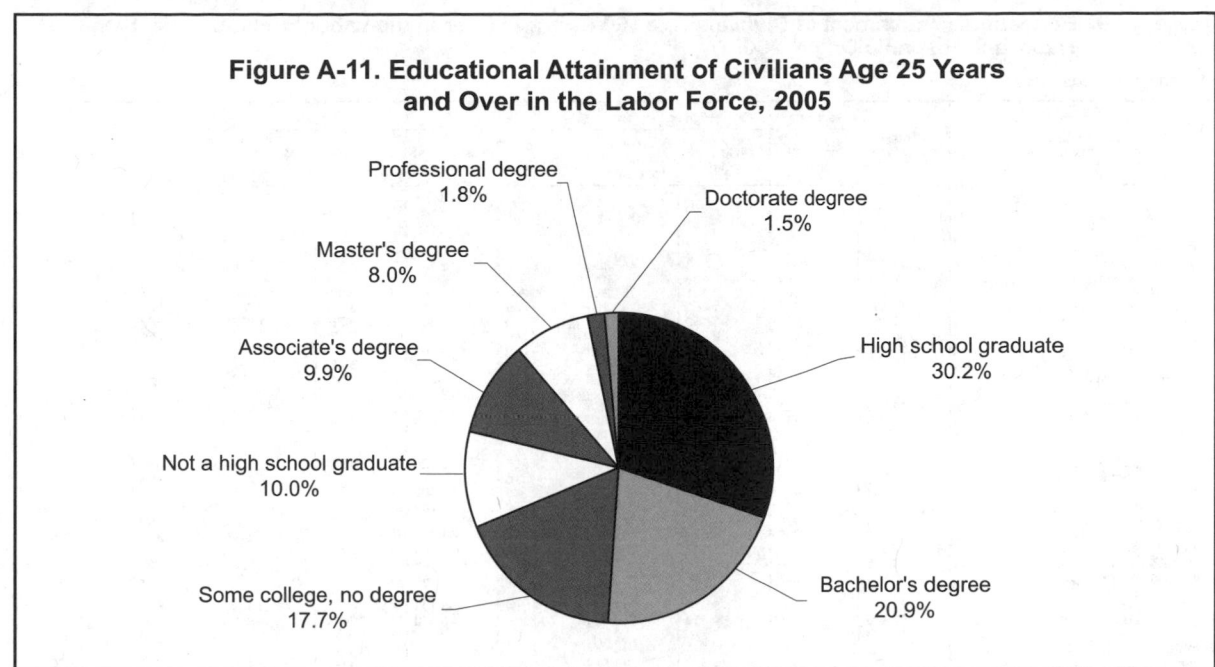

Figure A-11. Educational Attainment of Civilians Age 25 Years and Over in the Labor Force, 2005

Professional degree
1.8%

Doctorate degree
1.5%

Master's degree
8.0%

Associate's degree
9.9%

Not a high school graduate
10.0%

High school graduate
30.2%

Some college, no degree
17.7%

Bachelor's degree
20.9%

Nearly one-third of civilians over 25 years of age in the labor force held a bachelor's degree or more, a proportion higher than that of the general population in 2005. Only 10 percent of this group had not graduated from high school, compared with 14.8 percent of all people over 25 years of age. (Table A-19)

The civilian labor force has aged from 1995 to 2005. In 1995, about 53 percent of civilians in the labor force were between the ages of 25 and 44 years. By 2005, that number had declined to less than 46 percent. The percentage of civilians in the labor force over the age of 55 years increased from less than 12 percent in 1995 to over 16 percent in 2005.

Table A-19. Educational Attainment of Civilians Age 16 Years and Over in the Labor Force, by Age, Sex, Race, and Hispanic Origin, 2005

(Numbers in thousands.)

Age, sex, race, and Hispanic origin	Total population	Elementary — None to 8th grade	High school — 9th to 11th grade	High school graduate	College — Some college, no degree	Associate's degree	Bachelor's degree	Master's degree	Professional degree	Doctorate degree
ALL RACES										
Both Sexes										
16 years and over	147 477	5 314	13 313	44 382	28 622	13 405	28 112	10 078	2 314	1 938
16 and 17 years	2 685	93	2 489	87	13	2	2	-	-	-
18 to 24 years	19 083	502	2 931	6 321	6 363	1 009	1 865	80	7	5
25 to 29 years	15 654	594	1 289	4 461	3 053	1 457	3 751	787	189	73
30 to 34 years	16 137	610	1 158	4 381	2 940	1 561	3 785	1 273	262	167
35 to 44 years	35 896	1 345	2 228	11 253	6 056	3 737	7 520	2 622	664	470
45 to 54 years	34 162	1 110	1 793	10 610	6 030	3 568	6 844	3 015	637	554
55 to 64 years	18 623	705	1 014	5 543	3 288	1 736	3 496	1 922	402	516
65 years and over	5 236	353	410	1 726	879	334	848	380	153	152
18 years and over	144 792	5 221	10 824	44 295	28 609	13 403	28 110	10 078	2 314	1 938
25 years and over	125 709	4 719	7 892	37 974	22 247	12 394	26 245	9 998	2 307	1 933
Male										
16 years and over	78 859	3 655	7 733	24 809	14 265	6 129	14 463	4 959	1 537	1 308
16 and 17 years	1 340	68	1 222	45	6	-	-	-	-	-
18 to 24 years	10 039	411	1 752	3 693	2 915	460	780	19	5	5
25 to 29 years	8 589	442	825	2 807	1 592	709	1 747	327	110	28
30 to 34 years	8 878	438	743	2 622	1 587	766	1 912	564	152	95
35 to 44 years	19 336	901	1 375	6 415	3 020	1 719	3 915	1 312	402	278
45 to 54 years	17 916	710	1 020	5 717	3 018	1 569	3 562	1 501	442	376
55 to 64 years	9 836	460	573	2 687	1 664	766	1 991	995	301	398
65 years and over	2 925	225	222	823	463	141	556	242	124	128
18 years and over	77 518	3 587	6 511	24 765	14 260	6 129	14 463	4 959	1 537	1 308
25 years and over	67 480	3 176	4 759	21 072	11 345	5 670	13 683	4 940	1 532	1 303
Female										
16 years and over	68 618	1 659	5 580	19 573	14 357	7 275	13 649	5 119	777	630
16 and 17 years	1 345	25	1 267	42	7	2	2	-	-	-
18 to 24 years	9 044	92	1 179	2 628	3 448	549	1 085	61	2	-
25 to 29 years	7 065	152	463	1 653	1 461	748	2 004	460	79	45
30 to 34 years	7 259	172	415	1 759	1 353	796	1 873	709	110	72
35 to 44 years	16 560	445	853	4 838	3 036	2 018	3 606	1 310	262	191
45 to 54 years	16 247	400	773	4 893	3 012	1 999	3 282	1 514	195	178
55 to 64 years	8 787	245	442	2 856	1 624	970	1 505	927	101	118
65 years and over	2 311	128	188	903	415	194	292	138	29	25
18 years and over	67 274	1 634	4 312	19 531	14 350	7 273	13 647	5 119	777	630
25 years and over	58 229	1 542	3 133	16 902	10 902	6 724	12 562	5 058	775	630
WHITE ALONE OR IN COMBINATION										
Both Sexes										
16 years and over	122 754	4 642	10 691	36 518	23 785	11 387	23 528	8 588	1 979	1 637
16 and 17 years	2 291	78	2 130	70	12	-	2	-	-	-
18 to 24 years	15 824	455	2 401	5 161	5 258	869	1 613	56	7	5
25 to 29 years	12 688	538	1 025	3 542	2 470	1 180	3 060	645	155	71
30 to 34 years	12 932	556	955	3 475	2 291	1 291	3 030	1 002	207	125
35 to 44 years	29 417	1 229	1 712	9 141	4 948	3 143	6 208	2 114	557	366
45 to 54 years	28 805	948	1 361	8 779	5 086	3 120	5 811	2 660	564	476
55 to 64 years	16 152	568	781	4 765	2 909	1 495	3 068	1 761	354	450
65 years and over	4 644	270	326	1 584	813	289	736	349	135	142
18 years and over	120 462	4 564	8 561	36 447	23 773	11 387	23 526	8 588	1 979	1 637
25 years and over	104 638	4 109	6 161	31 287	18 515	10 518	21 913	8 532	1 972	1 632
Male										
16 years and over	66 750	3 254	6 386	20 713	12 099	5 298	12 366	4 199	1 333	1 104
16 and 17 years	1 124	54	1 032	34	4	-	-	-	-	-
18 to 24 years	8 463	379	1 462	3 076	2 430	412	680	15	5	5
25 to 29 years	7 165	409	690	2 302	1 350	592	1 446	255	94	28
30 to 34 years	7 291	405	652	2 156	1 261	653	1 550	413	124	77
35 to 44 years	16 125	847	1 102	5 301	2 537	1 467	3 282	1 046	336	205
45 to 54 years	15 320	613	809	4 761	2 580	1 397	3 110	1 328	396	326
55 to 64 years	8 636	373	458	2 320	1 503	658	1 797	913	268	345
65 years and over	2 626	173	181	763	433	120	499	228	110	118
18 years and over	65 626	3 199	5 354	20 678	12 095	5 298	12 366	4 199	1 333	1 104
25 years and over	57 163	2 821	3 892	17 603	9 665	4 887	11 686	4 184	1 328	1 099
Female										
16 years and over	56 003	1 389	4 305	15 805	11 685	6 089	11 162	4 389	646	533
16 and 17 years	1 167	24	1 098	36	7	-	2	-	-	-
18 to 24 years	7 361	77	939	2 085	2 827	458	933	41	2	-
25 to 29 years	5 522	129	335	1 241	1 119	589	1 614	391	61	43
30 to 34 years	5 641	151	303	1 319	1 030	638	1 480	589	84	48
35 to 44 years	13 293	382	609	3 840	2 410	1 676	2 925	1 068	221	161
45 to 54 years	13 485	335	553	4 018	2 505	1 723	2 701	1 332	167	150
55 to 64 years	7 516	195	322	2 445	1 406	837	1 271	847	87	106
65 years and over	2 019	97	145	821	380	169	236	121	25	25
18 years and over	54 836	1 365	3 207	15 769	11 678	6 089	11 160	4 389	646	533
25 years and over	47 476	1 288	2 268	13 684	8 851	5 632	10 227	4 348	644	533

- = Quantity zero or rounds to zero.

Table A-19. Educational Attainment of Civilians Age 16 Years and Over in the Labor Force, by Age, Sex, Race, and Hispanic Origin, 2005—*Continued*

(Numbers in thousands.)

Age, sex, race, and Hispanic origin	Total population	Elementary None to 8th grade	High school 9th to 11th grade	High school High school graduate	College Some college, no degree	College Associate's degree	College Bachelor's degree	College Master's degree	College Professional degree	College Doctorate degree
BLACK ALONE OR IN COMBINATION										
Both Sexes										
16 years and over	17 167	334	2 102	6 281	3 729	1 461	2 351	693	123	92
16 and 17 years	303	12	279	10	1	2	-	-	-	-
18 to 24 years	2 507	26	443	972	791	113	153	8	-	-
25 to 29 years	2 100	34	226	748	455	215	355	51	13	2
30 to 34 years	2 110	26	138	734	534	202	347	99	21	9
35 to 44 years	4 391	42	419	1 707	864	410	683	210	27	29
45 to 54 years	3 709	73	330	1 410	748	307	565	215	34	29
55 to 64 years	1 641	78	190	587	284	175	195	95	18	21
65 years and over	406	43	78	113	52	37	53	17	10	3
18 years and over	16 864	322	1 823	6 272	3 727	1 459	2 351	693	123	92
25 years and over	14 357	296	1 380	5 300	2 936	1 346	2 198	686	123	92
Male										
16 years and over	7 985	211	1 078	3 189	1 609	572	952	263	59	51
16 and 17 years	169	11	149	7	1	-	-	-	-	-
18 to 24 years	1 171	16	233	495	341	33	50	2	-	-
25 to 29 years	968	19	115	404	184	88	144	9	3	2
30 to 34 years	944	18	55	360	250	72	137	38	11	3
35 to 44 years	2 033	23	220	866	350	176	283	85	14	16
45 to 54 years	1 739	42	170	733	344	115	225	83	15	11
55 to 64 years	765	54	96	278	116	71	85	40	10	15
65 years and over	197	28	38	45	24	17	28	6	7	3
18 years and over	7 816	201	929	3 182	1 608	572	952	263	59	51
25 years and over	6 645	185	695	2 686	1 267	539	901	261	59	51
Female										
16 years and over	9 182	123	1 024	3 093	2 119	889	1 399	430	64	41
16 and 17 years	134	1	129	2	-	2	-	-	-	-
18 to 24 years	1 336	10	210	477	450	80	103	6	-	-
25 to 29 years	1 132	16	111	344	271	127	211	42	10	-
30 to 34 years	1 166	8	83	375	284	131	210	60	11	5
35 to 44 years	2 358	19	198	841	515	234	400	125	13	13
45 to 54 years	1 970	30	159	676	404	192	340	131	19	18
55 to 64 years	877	23	94	310	168	103	110	55	8	5
65 years and over	209	15	39	68	28	20	25	11	3	-
18 years and over	9 047	122	894	3 090	2 119	887	1 399	430	64	41
25 years and over	7 712	111	685	2 614	1 669	807	1 296	425	64	41
ASIAN ALONE OR IN COMBINATION										
Both Sexes										
16 years and over	6 748	250	368	1 316	952	478	2 176	789	214	204
16 and 17 years	92	2	84	6	-	-	-	-	-	-
18 to 24 years	679	4	48	166	304	33	108	15	-	-
25 to 29 years	796	11	13	135	113	61	346	89	26	2
30 to 34 years	1 010	17	47	147	98	58	402	175	32	35
35 to 44 years	1 853	62	73	315	201	145	612	290	80	75
45 to 54 years	1 408	72	71	344	151	115	432	137	42	44
55 to 64 years	751	49	28	181	77	60	222	67	26	41
65 years and over	159	34	4	22	8	5	55	16	8	7
18 years and over	6 656	248	284	1 310	952	478	2 176	789	214	204
25 years and over	5 977	244	235	1 143	648	445	2 069	775	214	204
Male										
16 years and over	3 636	129	179	752	471	226	1 099	488	146	148
16 and 17 years	44	2	40	2	-	-	-	-	-	-
18 to 24 years	354	4	34	112	134	20	50	-	-	-
25 to 29 years	417	7	3	84	53	27	164	62	16	-
30 to 34 years	581	8	21	91	62	37	218	111	17	15
35 to 44 years	1 029	23	41	182	110	61	328	177	51	56
45 to 54 years	726	39	27	182	70	46	206	88	33	34
55 to 64 years	395	26	10	87	37	33	105	42	20	35
65 years and over	89	20	1	12	4	3	27	7	7	7
18 years and over	3 592	127	138	749	471	226	1 099	488	146	148
25 years and over	3 238	123	104	638	337	206	1 049	488	146	148
Female										
16 years and over	3 112	121	189	564	481	252	1 078	301	68	56
16 and 17 years	48	-	44	4	-	-	-	-	-	-
18 to 24 years	325	-	14	55	170	13	58	15	-	-
25 to 29 years	380	4	10	51	60	34	182	27	9	2
30 to 34 years	428	9	26	56	35	22	183	63	15	19
35 to 44 years	823	39	32	132	91	85	284	113	29	19
45 to 54 years	682	33	44	162	81	69	226	49	9	9
55 to 64 years	356	23	17	94	39	28	117	25	6	7
65 years and over	70	14	2	10	5	2	28	9	1	-
18 years and over	3 064	121	145	561	481	252	1 078	301	68	56
25 years and over	2 739	121	131	506	311	239	1 020	287	68	56

- = Quantity zero or rounds to zero.

Table A-19. Educational Attainment of Civilians Age 16 Years and Over in the Labor Force, by Age, Sex, Race, and Hispanic Origin, 2005—Continued

(Numbers in thousands.)

Age, sex, race, and Hispanic origin	Total population	Elementary — None to 8th grade	High school — 9th to 11th grade	High school — High school graduate	College — Some college, no degree	College — Associate's degree	College — Bachelor's degree	College — Master's degree	College — Professional degree	College — Doctorate degree
HISPANIC[1]										
Both Sexes										
16 years and over	19 491	3 719	3 473	5 796	3 120	1 104	1 643	450	113	73
16 and 17 years	286	28	237	18	2	-	-	-	-	-
18 to 24 years	3 389	394	782	1 204	769	124	113	3	-	-
25 to 29 years	3 112	488	552	979	511	209	302	43	18	10
30 to 34 years	2 884	522	565	824	436	181	267	68	18	4
35 to 44 years	4 961	1 048	737	1 441	729	314	498	143	35	16
45 to 54 years	3 170	792	403	871	431	163	323	132	25	29
55 to 64 years	1 377	359	155	373	216	94	114	46	10	11
65 years and over	313	87	44	85	26	20	27	15	6	3
18 years and over	19 206	3 691	3 236	5 778	3 118	1 104	1 643	450	113	73
25 years and over	15 817	3 297	2 455	4 574	2 349	980	1 530	447	113	73
Male										
16 years and over	11 760	2 617	2 211	3 504	1 651	545	897	218	65	50
16 and 17 years	156	25	115	13	1	-	-	-	-	-
18 to 24 years	2 056	332	523	737	362	45	54	2	-	-
25 to 29 years	2 008	371	378	637	303	122	163	16	10	8
30 to 34 years	1 806	381	390	533	245	87	132	31	6	1
35 to 44 years	2 989	703	471	880	387	173	276	70	20	9
45 to 54 years	1 793	522	223	475	218	70	176	72	15	20
55 to 64 years	778	232	86	188	117	40	75	23	8	9
65 years and over	175	51	25	40	18	8	21	4	5	3
18 years and over	11 604	2 592	2 096	3 491	1 650	545	897	218	65	50
25 years and over	9 549	2 259	1 573	2 754	1 288	501	842	217	65	50
Female										
16 years and over	7 732	1 102	1 262	2 292	1 469	559	747	231	47	22
16 and 17 years	130	3	121	5	1	-	-	-	-	-
18 to 24 years	1 333	62	259	467	406	80	59	1	-	-
25 to 29 years	1 105	118	174	342	209	87	138	27	8	2
30 to 34 years	1 078	141	175	291	191	93	135	36	11	3
35 to 44 years	1 972	345	265	561	342	140	222	73	15	7
45 to 54 years	1 377	270	180	396	213	93	148	60	10	8
55 to 64 years	598	127	69	185	99	54	39	23	2	1
65 years and over	138	36	19	45	8	12	6	11	1	-
18 years and over	7 601	1 099	1 141	2 287	1 468	559	747	231	47	22
25 years and over	6 268	1 037	882	1 820	1 062	479	688	230	47	22

[1]May be of any race.
- = Quantity zero or rounds to zero.

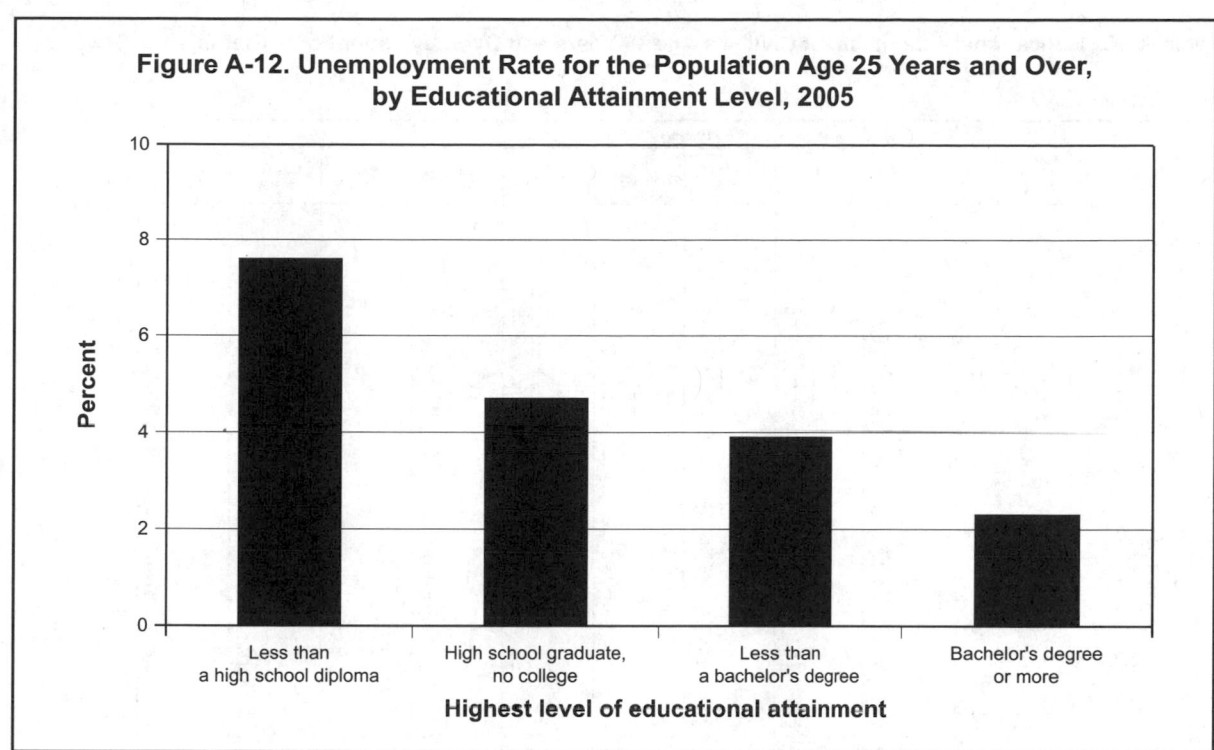

Figure A-12. Unemployment Rate for the Population Age 25 Years and Over, by Educational Attainment Level, 2005

The more education a person obtained, the less likely he or she was to be unemployed. The unemployment rate declined successively for each level of educational attainment. For people with less than a high school diploma, the unemployment rate was 7.6 percent. In comparison, the unemployment rate for people with a bachelor's degree or more was only 2.3 percent. The overall unemployment rate in 2005 was 5.1 percent. Although there were substantially more men than women over 25 years of age who were unemployed, women had a higher unemployment rate due to the fact that there were far more men than women in the labor force. In 2005, the labor force participation rate was 75.4 percent for men, but only 59.4 percent for women. (Table A-20)

Table A-20. Educational Attainment of Civilians Age 16 Years and Over, by Labor Force Status, Age, Sex, Race, and Hispanic Origin, 2005

(Numbers in thousands.)

Labor force status, age, sex, race, and Hispanic origin	Total population	Elementary — None to 8th grade	High school — 9th to 11th grade	High school graduate	College — Some college, no degree	Associate's degree	Bachelor's degree	Master's degree	Professional degree	Doctorate degree
ALL RACES										
Both Sexes										
Employed										
16 years and over	139 302	4 897	11 415	41 491	27 205	12 897	27 327	9 873	2 289	1 910
16 and 17 years	2 135	63	1 977	80	13	-	2	-	-	-
18 to 24 years	17 007	460	2 305	5 483	5 939	952	1 781	76	7	5
25 to 29 years	14 604	550	1 078	4 088	2 863	1 370	3 638	764	181	72
30 to 34 years	15 330	549	1 050	4 073	2 781	1 514	3 688	1 250	260	166
35 to 44 years	34 399	1 252	2 012	10 671	5 814	3 601	7 369	2 564	658	458
45 to 54 years	32 846	1 038	1 661	10 123	5 792	3 454	6 642	2 955	635	545
55 to 64 years	17 936	651	940	5 307	3 156	1 693	3 392	1 885	398	513
65 years and over	5 046	334	393	1 665	846	314	815	378	150	151
18 years and over	137 167	4 834	9 437	41 410	27 192	12 897	27 325	9 873	2 289	1 910
25 years and over	120 160	4 374	7 133	35 928	21 253	11 945	25 544	9 797	2 282	1 905
Unemployed										
16 years and over	8 175	417	1 898	2 891	1 418	508	785	205	25	28
16 and 17 years	550	30	512	6	-	2	-	-	-	-
18 to 24 years	2 076	42	627	839	424	57	84	4	-	-
25 to 29 years	1 051	45	211	373	190	88	113	22	8	1
30 to 34 years	807	62	108	308	159	48	98	23	2	1
35 to 44 years	1 497	93	216	582	243	136	151	58	6	12
45 to 54 years	1 317	72	132	487	238	114	202	60	3	9
55 to 64 years	687	54	75	236	132	43	104	37	4	3
65 years and over	190	20	17	60	32	20	33	2	3	2
18 years and over	7 625	387	1 386	2 885	1 418	506	785	205	25	28
25 years and over	5 549	345	760	2 046	994	449	701	201	25	28
Not in the Labor Force										
16 years and over	77 759	7 888	16 162	24 782	12 846	4 055	8 234	2 774	614	404
16 and 17 years	6 055	401	5 566	56	29	-	1	1	-	-
18 to 24 years	8 766	292	2 395	1 980	3 435	265	389	6	4	-
25 to 29 years	3 662	276	537	1 185	691	195	613	125	35	6
30 to 34 years	3 536	305	437	1 143	585	262	608	165	21	11
35 to 44 years	7 160	577	878	2 431	1 147	544	1 154	313	80	36
45 to 54 years	7 707	679	990	2 870	1 332	576	942	237	57	25
55 to 64 years	10 899	1 008	1 306	4 051	1 702	752	1 328	609	77	67
65 years and over	29 974	4 351	4 054	11 068	3 925	1 462	3 199	1 317	339	258
18 years and over	71 705	7 487	10 596	24 727	12 817	4 055	8 233	2 772	614	404
25 years and over	62 939	7 195	8 201	22 747	9 382	3 791	7 844	2 766	609	404
Male										
Employed										
16 years and over	74 168	3 392	6 658	23 016	13 525	5 892	13 998	4 876	1 523	1 290
16 and 17 years	1 014	47	921	41	6	-	-	-	-	-
18 to 24 years	8 817	378	1 388	3 160	2 690	437	737	17	5	5
25 to 29 years	7 997	417	719	2 577	1 487	664	1 679	321	106	28
30 to 34 years	8 418	398	679	2 431	1 501	741	1 863	559	151	95
35 to 44 years	18 477	835	1 263	6 049	2 891	1 655	3 824	1 290	401	269
45 to 54 years	17 184	673	949	5 424	2 901	1 513	3 443	1 469	440	372
55 to 64 years	9 450	431	533	2 546	1 601	749	1 917	979	298	395
65 years and over	2 812	214	207	788	447	132	534	240	123	126
18 years and over	73 154	3 345	5 737	22 975	13 519	5 892	13 998	4 876	1 523	1 290
25 years and over	64 337	2 967	4 349	19 815	10 828	5 455	13 260	4 859	1 518	1 285
Unemployed										
16 years and over	4 690	263	1 075	1 793	741	237	466	83	14	18
16 and 17 years	326	21	301	4	-	-	-	-	-	-
18 to 24 years	1 222	33	364	533	224	22	43	2	-	-
25 to 29 years	592	26	107	230	105	45	69	5	5	-
30 to 34 years	460	40	64	191	86	25	48	5	1	-
35 to 44 years	859	66	112	366	129	64	91	22	1	9
45 to 54 years	732	37	72	293	117	56	119	31	3	4
55 to 64 years	386	30	40	141	63	17	74	16	3	3
65 years and over	113	11	15	35	17	8	22	2	1	2
18 years and over	4 365	242	774	1 789	741	237	466	83	14	18
25 years and over	3 143	209	410	1 256	516	215	423	81	14	18
Not in the Labor Force										
16 years and over	29 844	3 043	7 065	8 779	4 990	1 267	2 954	1 120	351	274
16 and 17 years	3 177	227	2 909	29	10	-	1	-	-	-
18 to 24 years	3 893	88	1 132	830	1 611	93	136	3	-	-
25 to 29 years	1 078	63	142	345	200	64	222	28	12	2
30 to 34 years	855	63	115	352	123	44	111	39	2	6
35 to 44 years	1 861	176	312	816	258	90	143	44	18	3
45 to 54 years	2 556	237	352	1 003	474	161	234	64	26	5
55 to 64 years	4 202	420	520	1 435	652	295	524	277	40	40
65 years and over	12 222	1 769	1 582	3 968	1 662	520	1 583	665	253	218
18 years and over	26 667	2 816	4 155	8 750	4 980	1 267	2 953	1 120	351	274
25 years and over	22 774	2 728	3 023	7 919	3 369	1 174	2 818	1 117	351	274

- = Quantity zero or rounds to zero.

Table A-20. Educational Attainment of Civilians Age 16 Years and Over, by Labor Force Status, Age, Sex, Race, and Hispanic Origin, 2005—*Continued*

(Numbers in thousands.)

Labor force status, age, sex, race, and Hispanic origin	Total population	Elementary None to 8th grade	High school 9th to 11th grade	High school graduate	Some college, no degree	Associate's degree	Bachelor's degree	Master's degree	Professional degree	Doctorate degree
ALL RACES										
Female										
Employed										
16 years and over	65 134	1 505	4 757	18 475	13 680	7 005	13 329	4 997	766	620
16 and 17 years	1 121	16	1 056	40	7	-	2	-	-	-
18 to 24 years	8 190	83	917	2 323	3 249	514	1 044	59	2	-
25 to 29 years	6 607	133	359	1 511	1 376	705	1 959	443	75	44
30 to 34 years	6 913	151	371	1 642	1 280	773	1 824	691	109	71
35 to 44 years	15 922	418	749	4 622	2 923	1 946	3 545	1 274	257	189
45 to 54 years	15 662	365	712	4 699	2 891	1 941	3 199	1 486	195	174
55 to 64 years	8 486	220	407	2 761	1 555	944	1 475	906	100	118
65 years and over	2 234	120	186	877	399	182	281	138	27	25
18 years and over	64 013	1 489	3 700	18 435	13 673	7 005	13 327	4 997	766	620
25 years and over	55 824	1 407	2 784	16 112	10 424	6 490	12 284	4 938	764	620
Unemployed										
16 years and over	3 484	154	823	1 098	677	270	320	122	11	9
16 and 17 years	224	9	211	2	-	2	-	-	-	-
18 to 24 years	855	9	263	306	199	35	42	2	-	-
25 to 29 years	458	19	104	142	85	43	44	17	3	1
30 to 34 years	347	22	44	117	73	23	49	18	-	1
35 to 44 years	638	27	104	216	114	72	61	36	5	3
45 to 54 years	585	35	61	194	121	58	83	28	-	5
55 to 64 years	301	25	34	95	69	26	30	21	-	-
65 years and over	77	9	2	25	16	12	11	-	2	-
18 years and over	3 261	145	612	1 096	677	269	320	122	11	9
25 years and over	2 406	136	349	790	478	234	278	120	11	9
Not in the Labor Force										
16 years and over	47 015	4 844	9 098	16 004	7 856	2 789	5 280	1 653	263	130
16 and 17 years	2 877	174	2 657	26	19	-	-	1	-	-
18 to 24 years	4 873	204	1 263	1 150	1 824	172	254	3	4	-
25 to 29 years	2 585	214	395	840	490	131	391	97	23	4
30 to 34 years	2 682	242	322	791	462	218	496	126	19	6
35 to 44 years	5 200	400	566	1 615	888	454	1 011	269	62	33
45 to 54 years	5 151	442	637	1 867	858	415	709	172	31	20
55 to 64 years	6 697	588	786	2 615	1 050	457	803	332	37	27
65 years and over	17 752	2 582	2 472	7 100	2 263	942	1 615	652	86	40
18 years and over	45 038	4 671	6 441	15 977	7 837	2 789	5 280	1 652	263	130
25 years and over	40 165	4 467	5 178	14 828	6 013	2 617	5 026	1 648	258	130
WHITE ALONE OR IN COMBINATION										
Both Sexes										
Employed										
16 years and over	116 792	4 302	9 379	34 432	22 791	10 978	22 915	8 419	1 954	1 622
16 and 17 years	1 890	52	1 760	64	12	-	2	-	-	-
18 to 24 years	14 360	423	1 946	4 597	4 963	820	1 545	55	7	5
25 to 29 years	11 990	501	900	3 290	2 351	1 123	2 979	629	147	70
30 to 34 years	12 335	504	871	3 249	2 187	1 252	2 959	981	206	125
35 to 44 years	28 321	1 143	1 572	8 728	4 786	3 029	6 089	2 066	550	358
45 to 54 years	27 796	895	1 274	8 405	4 906	3 020	5 649	2 613	561	474
55 to 64 years	15 594	527	736	4 570	2 795	1 461	2 980	1 727	351	448
65 years and over	4 506	256	319	1 529	792	274	712	349	132	142
18 years and over	114 902	4 249	7 619	34 368	22 779	10 978	22 913	8 419	1 954	1 622
25 years and over	100 542	3 827	5 673	29 771	17 817	10 159	21 368	8 364	1 947	1 617
Unemployed										
16 years and over	5 961	341	1 312	2 085	994	409	613	168	25	15
16 and 17 years	401	26	369	6	-	-	-	-	-	-
18 to 24 years	1 464	33	455	564	295	50	68	1	-	-
25 to 29 years	697	37	126	252	118	58	81	17	8	1
30 to 34 years	598	52	84	225	104	38	71	21	1	-
35 to 44 years	1 096	86	139	414	162	114	119	48	6	9
45 to 54 years	1 009	53	87	374	180	100	161	48	3	2
55 to 64 years	558	41	44	196	114	34	89	34	3	3
65 years and over	139	13	8	55	21	15	24	-	3	-
18 years and over	5 560	315	942	2 079	994	409	613	168	25	15
25 years and over	4 096	282	488	1 515	699	359	545	168	25	15
Not in the Labor Force										
16 years and over	63 883	6 316	12 467	20 769	10 641	3 459	6 974	2 376	530	351
16 and 17 years	4 660	283	4 325	38	13	-	-	1	-	-
18 to 24 years	6 537	246	1 693	1 445	2 626	201	319	4	2	-
25 to 29 years	2 773	245	435	888	526	155	433	72	17	3
30 to 34 years	2 745	273	343	886	455	204	453	108	14	9
35 to 44 years	5 649	491	654	1 824	927	455	943	256	73	25
45 to 54 years	6 081	545	744	2 222	1 052	478	767	199	53	21
55 to 64 years	9 137	811	966	3 419	1 465	648	1 151	553	67	56
65 years and over	26 301	3 422	3 307	10 047	3 576	1 319	2 907	1 182	304	237
18 years and over	59 223	6 033	8 142	20 731	10 628	3 459	6 974	2 374	530	351
25 years and over	52 686	5 787	6 450	19 285	8 002	3 258	6 655	2 370	528	351

- = Quantity zero or rounds to zero.

Table A-20. Educational Attainment of Civilians Age 16 Years and Over, by Labor Force Status, Age, Sex, Race, and Hispanic Origin, 2005—*Continued*

(Numbers in thousands.)

Labor force status, age, sex, race, and Hispanic origin	Total population	Elementary	High school		College					
		None to 8th grade	9th to 11th grade	High school graduate	Some college, no degree	Associate's degree	Bachelor's degree	Master's degree	Professional degree	Doctorate degree
WHITE ALONE OR IN COMBINATION										
Male										
Employed										
16 years and over	63 195	3 032	5 613	19 356	11 557	5 103	11 991	4 131	1 318	1 094
16 and 17 years	884	37	813	30	4	-	-	-	-	-
18 to 24 years	7 559	352	1 188	2 696	2 259	390	650	15	5	5
25 to 29 years	6 752	389	621	2 135	1 286	561	1 394	250	89	28
30 to 34 years	6 918	370	598	2 001	1 198	632	1 509	410	122	77
35 to 44 years	15 466	786	1 026	5 028	2 442	1 412	3 212	1 025	335	199
45 to 54 years	14 757	583	760	4 537	2 492	1 348	3 014	1 305	393	325
55 to 64 years	8 316	351	434	2 199	1 452	644	1 732	898	265	342
65 years and over	2 542	164	174	730	424	114	481	228	109	118
18 years and over	62 311	2 995	4 800	19 326	11 552	5 103	11 991	4 131	1 318	1 094
25 years and over	54 751	2 643	3 612	16 630	9 293	4 712	11 342	4 116	1 313	1 089
Unemployed										
16 years and over	3 555	222	772	1 357	542	196	375	68	14	10
16 and 17 years	240	18	219	4	-	-	-	-	-	-
18 to 24 years	904	27	274	380	171	21	31	-	-	-
25 to 29 years	413	20	69	167	65	30	52	5	5	-
30 to 34 years	373	35	55	155	62	21	40	4	1	-
35 to 44 years	659	61	76	273	95	55	71	21	1	6
45 to 54 years	563	30	48	224	89	49	96	23	3	1
55 to 64 years	319	22	24	121	51	14	65	16	3	3
65 years and over	84	9	8	33	9	6	18	-	1	-
18 years and over	3 315	204	554	1 353	542	196	375	68	14	10
25 years and over	2 411	178	280	973	371	174	344	68	14	10
Not in the Labor Force										
16 years and over	24 278	2 461	5 421	7 122	4 101	1 071	2 557	990	308	247
16 and 17 years	2 466	159	2 277	23	7	-	-	-	-	-
18 to 24 years	2 844	66	785	568	1 241	71	110	3	-	-
25 to 29 years	729	54	109	198	143	47	159	13	7	-
30 to 34 years	587	57	85	240	76	30	70	21	2	5
35 to 44 years	1 364	146	230	546	202	74	110	37	16	3
45 to 54 years	1 961	199	264	742	359	132	184	54	23	3
55 to 64 years	3 528	350	376	1 211	552	256	458	256	33	36
65 years and over	10 797	1 428	1 295	3 593	1 519	461	1 467	606	227	200
18 years and over	21 811	2 301	3 144	7 099	4 094	1 071	2 557	990	308	247
25 years and over	18 967	2 235	2 359	6 531	2 853	1 000	2 448	987	308	247
Female										
Employed										
16 years and over	53 597	1 270	3 766	15 076	11 234	5 876	10 923	4 289	636	528
16 and 17 years	1 006	16	947	34	7	-	2	-	-	-
18 to 24 years	6 801	70	758	1 901	2 704	429	896	40	2	-
25 to 29 years	5 238	113	279	1 156	1 066	562	1 585	379	58	42
30 to 34 years	5 417	134	274	1 249	988	621	1 450	571	84	48
35 to 44 years	12 856	357	547	3 700	2 344	1 616	2 877	1 041	215	159
45 to 54 years	13 039	311	514	3 868	2 414	1 672	2 636	1 307	167	149
55 to 64 years	7 277	176	302	2 370	1 343	816	1 248	829	87	106
65 years and over	1 964	92	145	799	368	160	231	121	23	25
18 years and over	52 592	1 254	2 819	15 042	11 227	5 876	10 921	4 289	636	528
25 years and over	45 791	1 183	2 060	13 141	8 523	5 447	10 026	4 248	634	528
Unemployed										
16 years and over	2 406	119	539	729	451	213	239	100	10	5
16 and 17 years	161	8	151	2	-	-	-	-	-	-
18 to 24 years	560	6	180	184	124	28	37	1	-	-
25 to 29 years	284	16	57	85	54	27	29	12	3	1
30 to 34 years	224	17	29	70	42	18	31	18	-	-
35 to 44 years	437	25	63	140	66	59	48	27	5	3
45 to 54 years	446	24	39	150	91	51	65	25	-	1
55 to 64 years	239	19	20	75	63	21	23	18	-	-
65 years and over	55	4	-	22	12	9	5	-	2	-
18 years and over	2 244	111	388	726	451	213	239	100	10	5
25 years and over	1 684	105	208	543	328	185	201	100	10	5
Not in the Labor Force										
16 years and over	39 605	3 855	7 046	13 647	6 540	2 388	4 416	1 385	222	104
16 and 17 years	2 194	123	2 048	15	6	-	1	-	-	-
18 to 24 years	3 692	180	908	877	1 384	130	209	1	2	-
25 to 29 years	2 044	191	326	690	383	108	274	59	11	3
30 to 34 years	2 158	216	258	646	379	173	383	87	12	4
35 to 44 years	4 284	345	424	1 278	725	381	833	219	58	23
45 to 54 years	4 120	346	479	1 480	693	346	583	145	29	18
55 to 64 years	5 608	461	590	2 208	913	392	693	297	34	19
65 years and over	15 505	1 993	2 013	6 454	2 057	858	1 440	576	76	37
18 years and over	37 411	3 732	4 999	13 632	6 534	2 388	4 416	1 384	222	104
25 years and over	33 719	3 552	4 091	12 755	5 149	2 258	4 207	1 383	220	104

- = Quantity zero or rounds to zero.

Table A-20. Educational Attainment of Civilians Age 16 Years and Over, by Labor Force Status, Age, Sex, Race, and Hispanic Origin, 2005—*Continued*

(Numbers in thousands.)

Labor force status, age, sex, race, and Hispanic origin	Total population	Elementary None to 8th grade	High school 9th to 11th grade	High school High school graduate	College Some college, no degree	College Associate's degree	College Bachelor's degree	College Master's degree	College Professional degree	College Doctorate degree
BLACK ALONE OR IN COMBINATION										
Both Sexes										
Employed										
16 years and over	15 325	281	1 572	5 591	3 383	1 376	2 248	669	123	83
16 and 17 years	175	8	156	10	1	-	-	-	-	-
18 to 24 years	1 980	19	287	732	694	108	136	4	-	-
25 to 29 years	1 797	27	143	638	394	191	341	46	13	2
30 to 34 years	1 932	19	118	660	487	191	330	99	21	8
35 to 44 years	4 054	38	345	1 565	795	389	663	206	27	26
45 to 54 years	3 468	62	289	1 321	695	295	542	206	34	24
55 to 64 years	1 553	69	164	557	272	169	190	92	18	21
65 years and over	367	39	68	108	44	33	46	16	10	3
18 years and over	15 151	274	1 415	5 582	3 382	1 376	2 248	669	123	83
25 years and over	13 170	254	1 128	4 850	2 688	1 268	2 112	664	123	83
Unemployed										
16 years and over	1 841	53	530	690	345	85	103	25	-	10
16 and 17 years	128	4	123	-	-	2	-	-	-	-
18 to 24 years	526	7	156	240	97	6	17	3	-	-
25 to 29 years	303	7	83	110	61	24	14	5	-	-
30 to 34 years	178	7	20	75	47	12	17	-	-	1
35 to 44 years	337	4	74	142	69	21	20	4	-	3
45 to 54 years	241	11	40	88	52	12	23	9	-	6
55 to 64 years	89	8	26	30	11	5	5	3	-	-
65 years and over	39	4	9	5	8	4	7	2	-	-
18 years and over	1 713	49	408	690	345	83	103	25	-	10
25 years and over	1 187	42	252	450	248	78	86	21	-	10
Not in the Labor Force										
16 years and over	9 940	1 049	3 014	3 149	1 589	419	512	170	23	15
16 and 17 years	1 099	102	974	12	10	-	-	-	-	-
18 to 24 years	1 634	32	569	450	517	37	29	-	-	-
25 to 29 years	567	17	85	253	135	25	45	6	-	-
30 to 34 years	478	19	74	190	99	41	48	5	-	-
35 to 44 years	1 022	56	177	481	139	59	92	14	2	2
45 to 54 years	1 213	71	211	516	226	79	89	20	2	1
55 to 64 years	1 328	119	289	521	202	79	71	40	-	7
65 years and over	2 599	632	634	726	261	98	137	85	19	6
18 years and over	8 842	947	2 040	3 136	1 570	419	512	170	23	15
25 years and over	7 208	915	1 471	2 687	1 062	383	482	170	23	15
Male										
Employed										
16 years and over	7 048	178	805	2 821	1 445	537	903	254	59	45
16 and 17 years	92	7	76	7	1	-	-	-	-	-
18 to 24 years	900	12	153	364	300	31	41	-	-	-
25 to 29 years	814	13	77	340	150	77	136	9	3	2
30 to 34 years	879	14	50	330	231	68	134	38	11	3
35 to 44 years	1 868	19	187	789	320	168	274	85	14	13
45 to 54 years	1 602	37	149	675	318	110	211	78	15	8
55 to 64 years	715	50	82	264	107	68	79	40	10	15
65 years and over	177	27	31	44	18	16	27	5	7	3
18 years and over	6 956	171	728	2 814	1 444	537	903	254	59	45
25 years and over	6 055	159	576	2 449	1 144	506	862	254	59	45
Unemployed										
16 years and over	937	33	273	368	165	35	49	9	-	6
16 and 17 years	76	3	73	-	-	-	-	-	-	-
18 to 24 years	271	4	81	131	41	2	10	2	-	-
25 to 29 years	153	6	38	56	34	11	8	-	-	-
30 to 34 years	65	4	5	30	19	4	3	-	-	-
35 to 44 years	165	4	34	78	30	8	8	-	-	3
45 to 54 years	136	6	21	58	25	5	13	5	-	3
55 to 64 years	50	5	15	13	9	3	5	-	-	-
65 years and over	21	1	7	2	6	2	2	2	-	-
18 years and over	861	30	200	368	165	35	49	9	-	6
25 years and over	590	26	120	237	123	32	39	7	-	6
Not in the Labor Force										
16 years and over	4 147	444	1 317	1 373	634	144	166	45	16	8
16 and 17 years	548	61	483	3	2	-	-	-	-	-
18 to 24 years	777	21	278	229	234	5	9	-	-	-
25 to 29 years	247	2	32	134	45	14	18	2	-	-
30 to 34 years	195	6	24	101	30	13	20	1	-	-
35 to 44 years	387	21	66	228	36	12	17	2	2	-
45 to 54 years	484	25	74	229	94	29	28	3	-	1
55 to 64 years	535	51	124	196	90	32	28	11	-	3
65 years and over	974	258	235	253	102	38	45	26	13	4
18 years and over	3 599	384	835	1 370	632	144	166	45	16	8
25 years and over	2 822	363	556	1 141	398	138	157	45	16	8

- = Quantity zero or rounds to zero.

Table A-20. Educational Attainment of Civilians Age 16 Years and Over, by Labor Force Status, Age, Sex, Race, and Hispanic Origin, 2005—Continued

(Numbers in thousands.)

Labor force status, age, sex, race, and Hispanic origin	Total population	Elementary — None to 8th grade	High school — 9th to 11th grade	High school graduate	College — Some college, no degree	Associate's degree	Bachelor's degree	Master's degree	Professional degree	Doctorate degree
BLACK ALONE OR IN COMBINATION										
Female										
Employed										
16 years and over	8 278	103	767	2 770	1 938	839	1 345	414	63	38
16 and 17 years	83	-	80	2	-	-	-	-	-	-
18 to 24 years	1 080	7	135	368	394	77	95	4	-	-
25 to 29 years	982	14	66	291	245	114	205	37	10	-
30 to 34 years	1 054	5	68	330	256	123	196	60	11	4
35 to 44 years	2 186	19	158	777	475	221	388	121	13	13
45 to 54 years	1 865	25	140	646	377	185	331	128	19	15
55 to 64 years	838	20	83	293	166	101	110	52	8	5
65 years and over	190	12	37	64	26	17	20	11	3	-
18 years and over	8 195	103	687	2 768	1 938	839	1 345	414	63	38
25 years and over	7 115	95	552	2 400	1 545	762	1 250	410	63	38
Unemployed										
16 years and over	904	20	257	322	181	50	54	16	-	4
16 and 17 years	52	1	50	-	-	2	-	-	-	-
18 to 24 years	255	3	75	109	56	3	8	1	-	-
25 to 29 years	150	1	45	53	27	13	6	5	-	-
30 to 34 years	112	3	15	45	28	8	14	-	-	1
35 to 44 years	173	-	40	65	39	13	11	4	-	-
45 to 54 years	105	6	19	30	27	7	9	3	-	3
55 to 64 years	39	3	11	17	2	2	-	3	-	-
65 years and over	19	3	2	3	2	3	6	-	-	-
18 years and over	852	19	207	322	181	49	54	16	-	4
25 years and over	597	16	132	213	125	45	46	14	-	4
Not in the Labor Force										
16 years and over	5 793	605	1 697	1 776	955	276	345	125	7	7
16 and 17 years	550	42	491	10	8	-	-	-	-	-
18 to 24 years	857	11	291	221	283	31	20	-	-	-
25 to 29 years	320	16	53	120	91	11	27	4	-	-
30 to 34 years	283	14	51	89	70	28	28	4	-	-
35 to 44 years	635	34	111	252	102	47	75	12	-	2
45 to 54 years	729	46	137	287	132	50	60	17	1	-
55 to 64 years	794	68	165	325	112	48	43	29	-	4
65 years and over	1 625	375	399	473	158	60	92	60	6	2
18 years and over	5 243	563	1 206	1 766	947	276	345	125	7	7
25 years and over	4 386	552	915	1 546	664	244	325	125	7	7
ASIAN ALONE OR IN COMBINATION										
Both Sexes										
Employed										
16 years and over	6 457	231	337	1 235	896	468	2 095	779	214	201
16 and 17 years	74	2	66	6	-	-	-	-	-	-
18 to 24 years	624	2	44	148	283	33	100	15	-	-
25 to 29 years	749	11	13	124	103	57	326	88	26	2
30 to 34 years	982	16	44	142	90	58	392	173	32	35
35 to 44 years	1 805	59	73	297	193	144	598	286	80	75
45 to 54 years	1 355	66	69	326	148	113	414	134	42	43
55 to 64 years	716	44	23	171	73	58	213	67	26	41
65 years and over	152	31	4	22	8	4	53	16	8	6
18 years and over	6 383	230	271	1 229	896	468	2 095	779	214	201
25 years and over	5 759	228	227	1 081	614	434	1 996	764	214	201
Unemployed										
16 years and over	291	19	31	80	56	10	81	10	-	3
16 and 17 years	18	-	18	-	-	-	-	-	-	-
18 to 24 years	54	2	4	18	21	-	8	-	-	-
25 to 29 years	48	-	-	12	11	4	20	1	-	-
30 to 34 years	28	1	3	5	8	-	10	1	-	-
35 to 44 years	48	3	-	17	8	1	14	5	-	-
45 to 54 years	52	6	1	18	3	2	18	3	-	1
55 to 64 years	35	5	5	10	4	2	9	-	-	1
65 years and over	8	2	-	-	-	1	2	-	-	2
18 years and over	273	19	13	80	56	10	81	10	-	3
25 years and over	218	17	8	62	34	10	73	10	-	3
Not in the Labor Force										
16 years and over	3 485	425	557	709	582	149	742	225	55	41
16 and 17 years	299	24	266	2	5	-	1	-	-	-
18 to 24 years	570	7	119	74	306	19	41	2	2	-
25 to 29 years	311	13	14	34	30	13	139	47	18	3
30 to 34 years	261	8	7	43	24	10	110	51	7	1
35 to 44 years	410	25	17	96	69	26	117	43	5	12
45 to 54 years	331	49	18	106	45	14	81	15	-	3
55 to 64 years	358	52	31	97	25	23	100	15	10	5
65 years and over	945	247	86	257	79	44	153	51	13	17
18 years and over	3 186	401	291	707	578	149	741	225	55	41
25 years and over	2 617	394	172	633	272	130	700	223	53	41

- = Quantity zero or rounds to zero.

Table A-20. Educational Attainment of Civilians Age 16 Years and Over, by Labor Force Status, Age, Sex, Race, and Hispanic Origin, 2005—*Continued*

(Numbers in thousands.)

Labor force status, age, sex, race, and Hispanic origin	Total population	Elementary None to 8th grade	High school 9th to 11th grade	High school graduate	Some college, no degree	Associate's degree	Bachelor's degree	Master's degree	Professional degree	Doctorate degree
ASIAN ALONE OR IN COMBINATION										
Male										
Employed										
16 years and over	3 469	122	163	694	444	220	1 052	482	146	146
16 and 17 years	35	2	31	2	-	-	-	-	-	-
18 to 24 years	317	2	31	98	122	20	44	-	-	-
25 to 29 years	387	7	3	72	48	25	153	62	16	-
30 to 34 years	566	8	19	87	58	37	214	110	17	15
35 to 44 years	1 001	22	41	171	107	60	316	176	51	56
45 to 54 years	699	39	27	171	69	44	197	85	33	34
55 to 64 years	381	24	9	80	37	33	102	42	20	34
65 years and over	83	20	1	12	3	2	25	7	7	6
18 years and over	3 434	121	131	692	444	220	1 052	482	146	146
25 years and over	3 117	119	100	594	322	200	1 008	482	146	146
Unemployed										
16 years and over	167	6	16	57	27	6	47	6	-	2
16 and 17 years	9	-	9	-	-	-	-	-	-	-
18 to 24 years	37	2	3	13	12	-	6	-	-	-
25 to 29 years	30	-	-	12	6	2	10	-	-	-
30 to 34 years	16	-	3	4	4	-	5	1	-	-
35 to 44 years	29	1	-	11	3	1	12	1	-	-
45 to 54 years	27	-	-	11	1	2	9	3	-	-
55 to 64 years	14	2	1	6	-	-	3	-	-	1
65 years and over	6	-	-	-	-	1	2	-	-	2
18 years and over	158	6	7	57	27	6	47	6	-	2
25 years and over	121	4	4	44	14	6	41	6	-	2
Not in the Labor Force										
16 years and over	1 230	104	274	224	236	45	221	84	23	19
16 and 17 years	163	13	148	1	-	-	1	-	-	*
18 to 24 years	258	-	56	28	145	12	16	-	-	-
25 to 29 years	97	5	2	11	13	3	43	13	6	2
30 to 34 years	60	-	3	11	10	-	20	17	-	1
35 to 44 years	80	8	6	27	20	-	15	4	-	-
45 to 54 years	69	6	4	20	13	2	10	5	*	2
55 to 64 years	113	10	14	23	3	7	37	11	7	1
65 years and over	390	63	42	104	33	21	70	34	10	14
18 years and over	1 067	92	126	223	236	45	219	84	23	19
25 years and over	809	91	69	195	91	33	203	84	23	19
Female										
Employed										
16 years and over	2 988	109	175	541	452	248	1 044	297	68	55
16 and 17 years	39	-	35	4	-	-	-	-	-	-
18 to 24 years	308	-	13	50	161	13	56	15	-	-
25 to 29 years	362	4	10	51	55	32	173	26	9	2
30 to 34 years	416	8	26	54	32	22	178	63	14	19
35 to 44 years	804	37	32	126	86	85	281	110	29	19
45 to 54 years	657	27	43	155	79	69	217	49	9	9
55 to 64 years	335	21	14	91	35	26	111	25	6	7
65 years and over	68	12	2	10	5	2	28	9	1	-
18 years and over	2 949	109	140	537	452	248	1 044	297	68	55
25 years and over	2 642	109	127	487	291	235	988	282	68	55
Unemployed										
16 years and over	124	13	15	23	29	4	34	5	-	1
16 and 17 years	9	-	9	-	-	-	-	-	-	-
18 to 24 years	17	-	1	5	9	-	3	-	-	-
25 to 29 years	18	-	-	-	5	2	9	1	-	-
30 to 34 years	12	1	-	2	4	-	6	-	-	-
35 to 44 years	19	2	-	7	5	-	2	3	-	-
45 to 54 years	25	6	1	7	2	-	8	-	-	1
55 to 64 years	21	2	3	3	4	2	6	-	-	-
65 years and over	2	2	-	-	-	-	-	-	-	-
18 years and over	114	13	6	23	29	4	34	5	-	1
25 years and over	97	13	5	19	20	4	32	5	-	1
Not in the Labor Force										
16 years and over	2 255	320	284	485	346	104	522	141	32	21
16 and 17 years	136	12	118	1	5	-	-	-	-	-
18 to 24 years	311	7	63	45	161	7	24	2	2	-
25 to 29 years	215	8	12	23	17	11	97	34	12	1
30 to 34 years	202	8	4	33	14	10	90	35	7	-
35 to 44 years	330	17	11	70	49	25	102	39	5	12
45 to 54 years	262	43	14	86	32	12	63	10	-	2
55 to 64 years	245	43	17	75	21	16	62	4	3	4
65 years and over	555	184	44	153	46	23	83	16	3	2
18 years and over	2 119	309	165	484	342	104	522	141	32	21
25 years and over	1 808	302	103	439	181	97	497	139	30	21

- = Quantity zero or rounds to zero.

Table A-20. Educational Attainment of Civilians Age 16 Years and Over, by Labor Force Status, Age, Sex, Race, and Hispanic Origin, 2005—*Continued*

(Numbers in thousands.)

Labor force status, age, sex, race, and Hispanic origin	Total population	Elementary	High school		College					
		None to 8th grade	9th to 11th grade	High school graduate	Some college, no degree	Associate's degree	Bachelor's degree	Master's degree	Professional degree	Doctorate degree
HISPANIC[1]										
Both Sexes										
Employed										
16 years and over	18 241	3 447	3 128	5 420	2 967	1 060	1 601	440	113	66
16 and 17 years	224	19	186	15	2	-	-	-	-	-
18 to 24 years	3 029	372	669	1 060	707	112	106	3	-	-
25 to 29 years	2 955	459	504	934	496	202	290	43	18	10
30 to 34 years	2 705	469	521	769	421	178	261	63	18	4
35 to 44 years	4 721	981	688	1 373	699	307	486	137	35	14
45 to 54 years	3 012	746	373	826	413	153	319	132	25	25
55 to 64 years	1 300	324	143	360	205	88	113	46	10	11
65 years and over	296	76	43	81	25	20	27	15	6	3
18 years and over	18 017	3 427	2 941	5 404	2 965	1 060	1 601	440	113	66
25 years and over	14 988	3 055	2 273	4 344	2 258	948	1 495	437	113	66
Unemployed										
16 years and over	1 250	272	346	377	153	44	43	10	-	6
16 and 17 years	62	9	50	3	-	-	-	-	-	-
18 to 24 years	360	22	113	144	62	12	7	-	-	-
25 to 29 years	158	30	48	46	16	7	12	-	-	-
30 to 34 years	180	54	44	54	15	2	6	4	-	-
35 to 44 years	239	66	48	68	30	7	12	6	-	2
45 to 54 years	158	46	30	45	18	9	5	-	-	4
55 to 64 years	77	34	11	13	11	6	1	-	-	-
65 years and over	18	12	1	4	2	-	-	-	-	-
18 years and over	1 188	263	295	374	153	44	43	10	-	6
25 years and over	829	242	182	230	91	32	36	10	-	6
Not in the Labor Force										
16 years and over	9 323	2 606	2 776	2 057	1 036	294	388	104	39	22
16 and 17 years	1 084	88	980	12	4	-	-	-	-	-
18 to 24 years	1 552	161	543	403	384	29	27	3	-	-
25 to 29 years	825	191	219	219	93	33	57	10	2	-
30 to 34 years	793	210	181	238	67	37	47	9	2	2
35 to 44 years	1 267	357	250	318	139	69	90	26	13	4
45 to 54 years	984	312	210	255	111	37	46	7	4	2
55 to 64 years	938	341	150	234	114	34	44	16	4	2
65 years and over	1 881	945	244	378	124	55	76	32	15	13
18 years and over	8 239	2 518	1 796	2 044	1 032	294	388	104	39	22
25 years and over	6 687	2 357	1 253	1 641	648	265	361	101	39	22
Male										
Employed										
16 years and over	11 025	2 439	2 013	3 279	1 565	526	877	214	65	47
16 and 17 years	115	17	85	12	1	-	-	-	-	-
18 to 24 years	1 844	314	446	658	329	43	51	2	-	-
25 to 29 years	1 918	355	353	608	293	119	155	16	10	8
30 to 34 years	1 689	345	366	492	233	86	130	30	6	1
35 to 44 years	2 843	657	451	832	368	169	272	67	20	7
45 to 54 years	1 717	495	209	458	213	63	174	72	15	19
55 to 64 years	733	212	79	180	110	37	75	23	8	9
65 years and over	166	44	24	40	18	8	21	4	5	3
18 years and over	10 911	2 422	1 928	3 267	1 564	526	877	214	65	47
25 years and over	9 066	2 108	1 481	2 609	1 234	482	826	212	65	47
Unemployed										
16 years and over	734	179	198	225	86	20	19	4	-	3
16 and 17 years	41	9	30	2	-	-	-	-	-	-
18 to 24 years	211	18	77	79	33	2	3	-	-	-
25 to 29 years	89	15	24	29	10	3	9	-	-	-
30 to 34 years	117	35	24	41	12	1	2	2	-	-
35 to 44 years	146	46	21	48	19	4	4	3	-	2
45 to 54 years	76	28	14	18	6	7	2	-	-	1
55 to 64 years	45	20	7	8	7	3	-	-	-	-
65 years and over	9	7	1	1	-	-	-	-	-	-
18 years and over	694	170	168	223	86	20	19	4	-	3
25 years and over	482	151	91	144	53	18	17	4	-	3
Not in the Labor Force										
16 years and over	3 031	762	1 018	616	377	81	117	32	18	11
16 and 17 years	554	47	496	9	2	-	-	-	-	-
18 to 24 years	557	31	196	157	160	10	1	2	-	-
25 to 29 years	158	27	27	39	35	6	21	3	-	-
30 to 34 years	142	27	29	54	11	4	14	-	1	1
35 to 44 years	259	77	52	66	28	9	21	6	-	1
45 to 54 years	285	78	62	77	36	16	12	-	2	1
55 to 64 years	322	123	54	65	42	11	16	8	1	1
65 years and over	755	350	102	150	63	25	31	12	14	7
18 years and over	2 477	714	522	607	375	81	117	32	18	11
25 years and over	1 920	683	325	450	215	72	115	30	18	11

[1] May be of any race.
- = Quantity zero or rounds to zero.

Table A-20. Educational Attainment of Civilians Age 16 Years and Over, by Labor Force Status, Age, Sex, Race, and Hispanic Origin, 2005—*Continued*

(Numbers in thousands.)

Labor force status, age, sex, race, and Hispanic origin	Total population	Elementary: None to 8th grade	High school: 9th to 11th grade	High school graduate	College: Some college, no degree	Associate's degree	Bachelor's degree	Master's degree	Professional degree	Doctorate degree
HISPANIC[1]										
Female										
Employed										
16 years and over	7 216	1 008	1 115	2 140	1 402	534	724	225	47	19
16 and 17 years	109	2	101	4	1	-	-	-	-	-
18 to 24 years	1 185	58	222	402	377	69	55	1	-	-
25 to 29 years	1 037	103	150	326	203	82	135	27	8	2
30 to 34 years	1 016	123	155	278	189	92	131	33	11	3
35 to 44 years	1 879	325	238	540	331	138	214	70	15	7
45 to 54 years	1 295	251	164	368	200	90	145	60	10	5
55 to 64 years	567	112	64	180	95	51	38	23	2	1
65 years and over	129	32	19	42	7	12	6	11	1	-
18 years and over	7 107	1 006	1 013	2 137	1 401	534	724	225	47	19
25 years and over	5 922	947	791	1 734	1 024	466	669	224	47	19
Unemployed										
16 years and over	516	94	147	151	67	24	23	6	-	3
16 and 17 years	21	-	20	1	-	-	-	-	-	-
18 to 24 years	148	3	37	64	29	11	4	-	-	-
25 to 29 years	68	15	24	16	6	4	3	-	-	-
30 to 34 years	63	18	20	14	3	1	4	3	-	-
35 to 44 years	93	20	28	21	11	2	8	3	-	-
45 to 54 years	82	19	16	27	13	3	2	-	-	3
55 to 64 years	31	15	4	5	4	3	1	-	-	-
65 years and over	8	4	-	3	2	-	-	-	-	-
18 years and over	495	93	127	150	67	24	23	6	-	3
25 years and over	346	90	91	86	38	13	19	6	-	3
Not in the Labor Force										
16 years and over	6 291	1 844	1 758	1 441	659	213	271	73	21	11
16 and 17 years	530	41	484	3	2	-	-	-	-	-
18 to 24 years	994	130	347	247	224	20	26	1	-	-
25 to 29 years	666	164	192	180	58	27	36	7	2	-
30 to 34 years	652	183	151	184	57	33	33	9	-	1
35 to 44 years	1 008	280	198	252	112	60	70	10	13	3
45 to 54 years	699	234	148	178	74	21	34	7	2	2
55 to 64 years	616	217	96	169	72	22	29	8	3	-
65 years and over	1 126	595	142	228	60	30	44	20	1	5
18 years and over	5 762	1 804	1 274	1 438	657	213	271	73	21	11
25 years and over	4 767	1 674	927	1 191	433	193	246	71	21	11

[1] May be of any race.
- = Quantity zero or rounds to zero.

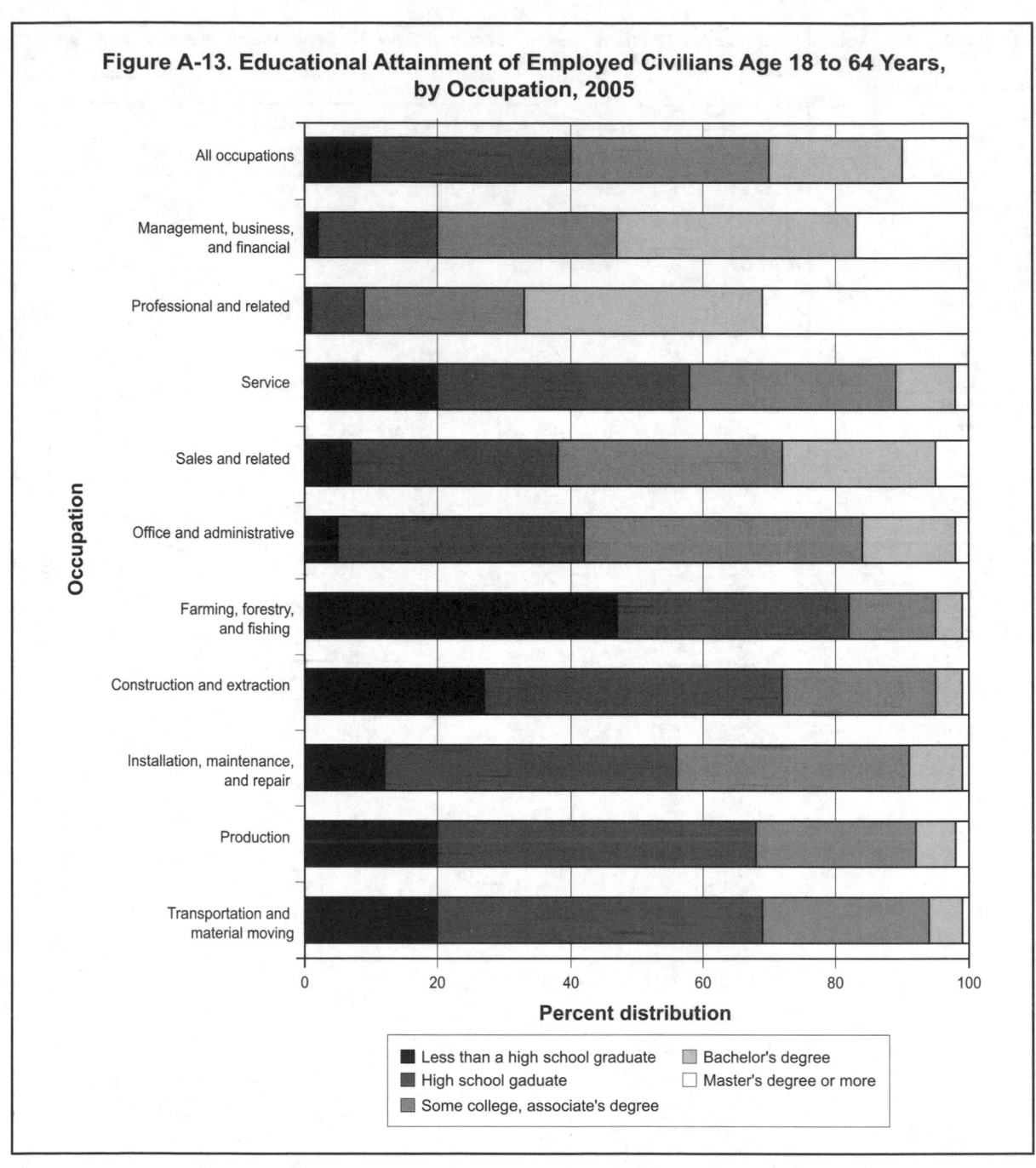

Figure A-13. Educational Attainment of Employed Civilians Age 18 to 64 Years, by Occupation, 2005

For persons between 18 and 64 years of age, professional and related occupations provided the most jobs, while farming, forestry, and fishing occupations employed the least number of people. More than 66 percent of those employed in professional and related occupations held a bachelor's degree or more. In contrast, only 5.7 percent of those employed in farming, forestry, and fishing occupations had reached this level of educational attainment. Nearly 47 percent of farming, forestry, and fishing employees did not have a high school diploma. Service occupations employed the most people without a high school diploma. (Table A-21)

Table A-21. Educational Attainment of Employed Civilians Age 18 to 64 Years, by Occupation, Age, Race, and Hispanic Origin, 2005

(Numbers in thousands.)

Occupation, age, race, and Hispanic origin	Total population	Elementary		High school	College					
		None to 8th grade	9th to 11th grade	High school graduate	Some college, no degree	Associate's degree	Bachelor's degree	Master's degree	Professional degree	Doctorate degree
ALL RACES										
18 to 64 Years										
Total	132 121	4 500	9 045	39 745	26 345	12 583	26 510	9 495	2 139	1 759
Management, business, and financial	18 920	97	329	3 361	3 379	1 713	6 827	2 773	192	249
Professional and related	27 493	55	243	2 322	3 384	3 222	9 849	5 260	1 739	1 418
Service	20 884	1 434	2 667	8 032	4 641	1 873	1 895	265	64	14
Sales and related	14 762	179	942	4 604	3 759	1 200	3 407	572	59	41
Office and administrative	18 369	141	706	6 718	5 630	2 102	2 634	368	52	18
Farming, forestry, and fishing	857	265	136	299	76	32	36	13	-	-
Construction and extraction	8 459	918	1 340	3 796	1 312	594	439	54	6	1
Installation, maintenance, and repair	5 013	156	459	2 200	1 036	729	370	58	2	3
Production	9 314	753	1 140	4 482	1 607	657	566	80	17	3
Transportation and material moving	8 051	502	1 074	3 931	1 522	461	487	53	8	11
18 to 24 Years										
Total	17 007	460	2 305	5 483	5 939	952	1 781	76	7	5
Management, business, and financial	737	-	29	143	248	50	242	25	-	-
Professional and related	2 031	2	86	208	704	217	764	39	7	5
Service	4 479	141	805	1 447	1 622	209	252	3	-	-
Sales and related	2 817	14	403	908	1 185	116	191	-	-	-
Office and administrative	2 865	13	226	890	1 302	171	256	8	-	-
Farming, forestry, and fishing	154	31	27	58	31	5	2	-	-	-
Construction and extraction	1 204	144	250	599	149	43	18	1	-	-
Installation, maintenance, and repair	548	16	69	251	138	61	13	-	-	-
Production	987	55	184	460	200	57	32	-	-	-
Transportation and material moving	1 185	45	226	518	360	24	12	-	-	-
25 to 34 Years										
Total	29 934	1 099	2 128	8 161	5 644	2 883	7 325	2 014	441	238
Management, business, and financial	3 746	32	71	550	671	512	1 641	440	12	18
Professional and related	6 847	7	56	449	692	730	3 033	1 291	379	210
Service	4 791	349	565	1 692	1 028	505	579	54	19	-
Sales and related	3 168	27	155	891	757	280	921	120	13	5
Office and administrative	3 935	29	158	1 277	1 180	470	740	64	14	2
Farming, forestry, and fishing	208	72	29	74	14	5	13	2	-	-
Construction and extraction	2 340	247	446	998	369	174	93	8	3	-
Installation, maintenance, and repair	1 103	37	122	440	225	170	96	11	-	-
Production	2 030	186	259	938	371	138	121	17	-	-
Transportation and material moving	1 768	113	267	851	337	100	88	8	1	3
35 to 44 Years										
Total	34 399	1 252	2 012	10 671	5 814	3 601	7 369	2 564	658	458
Management, business, and financial	5 514	17	73	1 058	902	515	2 049	805	53	42
Professional and related	7 352	18	55	665	806	895	2 597	1 383	542	390
Service	5 085	388	546	2 137	912	551	441	87	17	5
Sales and related	3 487	50	185	1 074	674	315	1 003	154	20	11
Office and administrative	4 436	45	145	1 632	1 227	588	701	77	14	7
Farming, forestry, and fishing	249	91	31	86	14	11	10	5	-	-
Construction and extraction	2 282	268	364	1 033	305	166	133	13	-	-
Installation, maintenance, and repair	1 376	45	118	626	218	244	114	11	-	-
Production	2 563	207	272	1 284	430	186	155	19	9	-
Transportation and material moving	2 057	122	222	1 075	326	130	166	11	2	2
45 to 64 Years										
Total	50 781	1 689	2 601	15 430	8 948	5 147	10 035	4 840	1 033	1 058
Management, business, and financial	8 924	48	156	1 610	1 558	837	2 895	1 504	127	189
Professional and related	11 263	28	46	1 000	1 182	1 380	3 455	2 548	810	813
Service	6 529	557	751	2 755	1 079	607	623	120	28	8
Sales and related	5 290	87	199	1 731	1 143	489	1 292	297	26	25
Office and administrative	7 133	54	177	2 919	1 921	873	937	219	24	9
Farming, forestry, and fishing	246	71	49	81	17	12	10	7	-	-
Construction and extraction	2 634	259	280	1 166	488	211	194	32	3	1
Installation, maintenance, and repair	1 986	58	150	882	455	254	147	36	2	3
Production	3 734	305	433	1 800	605	276	259	44	8	3
Transportation and material moving	3 042	222	359	1 486	500	207	222	34	5	6

- = Quantity zero or rounds to zero.

Table A-21. Educational Attainment of Employed Civilians Age 18 to 64 Years, by Occupation, Age, Race, and Hispanic Origin, 2005—*Continued*

(Numbers in thousands.)

Occupation, age, race, and Hispanic origin	Total population	Elementary None to 8th grade	High school 9th to 11th grade	High school graduate	College Some college, no degree	Associate's degree	Bachelor's degree	Master's degree	Professional degree	Doctorate degree
WHITE ALONE OR IN COMBINATION										
18 to 64 Years										
Total	110 397	3 993	7 300	32 838	21 988	10 704	22 201	8 070	1 823	1 480
Management, business, and financial	16 535	77	292	3 000	2 969	1 501	5 937	2 365	171	223
Professional and related	23 080	50	205	1 903	2 835	2 769	8 208	4 453	1 474	1 184
Service	16 340	1 227	1 980	6 032	3 737	1 556	1 525	222	53	8
Sales and related	12 592	153	770	3 892	3 206	1 030	2 949	505	53	35
Office and administrative	15 094	126	542	5 668	4 599	1 729	2 052	321	40	16
Farming, forestry, and fishing	775	249	120	260	70	31	33	13	-	-
Construction and extraction	7 667	852	1 187	3 467	1 184	537	390	44	4	1
Installation, maintenance, and repair	4 405	131	407	1 955	904	637	322	45	2	1
Production	7 459	672	914	3 538	1 304	543	410	59	16	3
Transportation and material moving	6 450	455	884	3 123	1 180	372	375	45	8	8
18 to 24 Years										
Total	14 360	423	1 946	4 597	4 963	820	1 545	55	7	5
Management, business, and financial	604	-	21	110	208	47	202	17	-	-
Professional and related	1 768	2	76	181	605	190	676	27	7	5
Service	3 751	127	664	1 181	1 377	184	216	3	-	-
Sales and related	2 275	10	327	729	952	93	165	-	-	-
Office and administrative	2 369	13	192	730	1 073	141	214	7	-	-
Farming, forestry, and fishing	149	31	26	54	31	5	2	-	-	-
Construction and extraction	1 129	130	229	570	143	40	16	1	-	-
Installation, maintenance, and repair	490	16	68	226	119	50	12	-	-	-
Production	830	54	149	381	163	52	32	-	-	-
Transportation and material moving	994	40	195	436	293	19	11	-	-	-
25 to 34 Years										
Total	24 325	1 005	1 771	6 540	4 538	2 375	5 938	1 610	353	195
Management, business, and financial	3 151	26	66	464	568	256	1 395	351	10	16
Professional and related	5 459	7	47	343	578	606	2 383	1 027	298	170
Service	3 739	310	432	1 248	787	406	491	47	19	-
Sales and related	2 616	26	132	723	608	225	783	101	11	5
Office and administrative	3 039	28	117	994	903	383	550	53	11	1
Farming, forestry, and fishing	182	64	25	64	11	5	12	2	-	-
Construction and extraction	2 163	233	408	925	339	160	87	8	3	-
Installation, maintenance, and repair	957	28	106	393	192	147	82	8	-	-
Production	1 651	177	221	744	299	111	89	8	-	-
Transportation and material moving	1 368	106	218	641	253	78	65	3	1	3
35 to 44 Years										
Total	28 321	1 143	1 572	8 728	4 786	3 029	6 089	2 066	550	358
Management, business, and financial	4 769	16	71	959	779	447	1 759	659	43	36
Professional and related	6 027	14	49	541	650	768	2 147	1 106	454	300
Service	3 867	338	376	1 542	726	464	339	63	16	4
Sales and related	2 973	46	136	908	593	265	871	128	16	11
Office and administrative	3 588	41	97	1 388	986	461	537	62	10	7
Farming, forestry, and fishing	232	90	30	74	14	11	9	5	-	-
Construction and extraction	2 065	262	307	940	272	152	119	13	-	-
Installation, maintenance, and repair	1 203	43	104	556	190	211	91	7	-	-
Production	2 024	183	212	1 006	346	148	106	14	9	-
Transportation and material moving	1 571	111	191	813	229	104	111	9	2	-
45 to 64 Years										
Total	43 390	1 422	2 010	12 974	7 701	4 481	8 629	4 339	912	922
Management, business, and financial	8 011	35	133	1 467	1 415	751	2 582	1 338	118	171
Professional and related	9 825	27	33	839	1 002	1 206	3 002	2 292	716	709
Service	4 981	453	509	2 061	847	503	479	108	18	4
Sales and related	4 728	71	176	1 532	1 052	447	1 131	275	26	19
Office and administrative	6 097	45	136	2 557	1 636	744	751	199	19	8
Farming, forestry, and fishing	212	65	39	67	14	11	10	7	-	-
Construction and extraction	2 310	227	243	1 032	430	186	168	22	1	1
Installation, maintenance, and repair	1 756	44	128	780	404	229	137	29	2	1
Production	2 954	258	332	1 406	495	233	183	36	7	3
Transportation and material moving	2 517	198	280	1 233	405	171	188	32	5	5

- = Quantity zero or rounds to zero.

Table A-21. Educational Attainment of Employed Civilians Age 18 to 64 Years, by Occupation, Age, Race, and Hispanic Origin, 2005—*Continued*

(Numbers in thousands.)

Occupation, age, race, and Hispanic origin	Total population	Elementary: None to 8th grade	High school: 9th to 11th grade	High school graduate	Some college, no degree	Associate's degree	Bachelor's degree	Master's degree	Professional degree	Doctorate degree
BLACK ALONE OR IN COMBINATION										
18 to 64 Years										
Total	14 783	235	1 347	5 474	3 338	1 343	2 202	653	113	79
Management, business, and financial	1 402	7	27	256	304	135	455	192	11	15
Professional and related	2 462	1	30	351	416	336	813	367	92	57
Service	3 416	95	546	1 596	708	247	196	27	-	1
Sales and related	1 425	14	132	520	421	90	226	15	4	2
Office and administrative	2 462	9	129	884	795	281	335	24	5	-
Farming, forestry, and fishing	53	9	11	27	4	-	2	-	-	-
Construction and extraction	572	27	121	261	96	33	23	8	2	-
Installation, maintenance, and repair	390	11	28	169	89	60	27	6	-	-
Production	1 252	27	150	712	215	86	56	6	-	-
Transportation and material moving	1 350	35	173	697	289	74	70	8	-	4
18 to 24 Years										
Total	1 980	19	287	732	694	108	136	4	-	-
Management, business, and financial	83	-	5	25	27	2	19	4	-	-
Professional and related	168	-	4	18	65	26	56	-	-	-
Service	562	7	118	222	178	19	18	-	-	-
Sales and related	434	4	66	162	182	13	8	-	-	-
Office and administrative	386	-	27	138	156	33	32	-	-	-
Farming, forestry, and fishing	2	-	-	2	-	-	-	-	-	-
Construction and extraction	42	3	13	23	-	3	-	-	-	-
Installation, maintenance, and repair	30	-	-	16	9	5	-	-	-	-
Production	121	-	27	60	27	4	2	-	-	-
Transportation and material moving	152	5	26	66	51	3	1	-	-	-
25 to 34 Years										
Total	3 729	46	261	1 298	881	382	672	145	34	10
Management, business, and financial	332	1	4	67	84	38	103	33	2	-
Professional and related	678	-	12	82	82	94	277	92	29	10
Service	820	26	100	346	199	87	57	5	-	-
Sales and related	378	-	16	137	114	35	73	3	-	-
Office and administrative	688	-	33	242	223	61	121	5	3	-
Farming, forestry, and fishing	14	5	1	4	2	-	2	-	-	-
Construction and extraction	118	4	23	56	20	10	5	-	-	-
Installation, maintenance, and repair	88	2	8	29	27	14	8	-	-	-
Production	263	3	22	152	52	21	10	4	-	-
Transportation and material moving	350	5	43	183	79	21	15	3	-	-
35 to 44 Years										
Total	4 054	38	345	1 565	795	389	663	206	27	26
Management, business, and financial	427	-	2	70	91	43	154	60	5	2
Professional and related	694	-	5	117	123	84	216	110	18	21
Service	904	17	140	479	135	67	51	15	-	-
Sales and related	324	2	40	113	59	24	76	6	4	-
Office and administrative	656	2	36	215	209	92	90	13	-	-
Farming, forestry, and fishing	13	1	1	10	-	-	-	-	-	-
Construction and extraction	167	4	52	74	26	5	6	-	-	-
Installation, maintenance, and repair	108	-	8	47	14	24	15	1	-	-
Production	363	7	34	216	58	28	19	-	-	-
Transportation and material moving	398	5	27	226	80	20	36	2	-	2
45 to 64 Years										
Total	5 020	131	454	1 879	968	464	732	298	52	44
Management, business, and financial	560	5	16	95	103	51	179	94	4	13
Professional and related	922	1	9	133	146	132	265	165	44	26
Service	1 130	45	188	550	196	74	69	7	-	1
Sales and related	289	8	10	109	66	18	69	6	-	2
Office and administrative	732	7	33	289	207	95	92	7	2	-
Farming, forestry, and fishing	24	3	8	11	2	-	-	-	-	-
Construction and extraction	245	16	33	109	51	15	12	8	2	-
Installation, maintenance, and repair	164	9	13	76	39	18	4	5	-	-
Production	505	17	67	283	78	32	25	2	-	-
Transportation and material moving	450	20	77	222	79	29	18	3	-	1

- = Quantity zero or rounds to zero.

Table A-21. Educational Attainment of Employed Civilians Age 18 to 64 Years, by Occupation, Age, Race, and Hispanic Origin, 2005—*Continued*

(Numbers in thousands.)

| Occupation, age, race, and Hispanic origin | Total population | Elementary | | High school | College | | | | | |
		None to 8th grade	9th to 11th grade	High school graduate	Some college, no degree	Associate's degree	Bachelor's degree	Master's degree	Professional degree	Doctorate degree
ASIAN ALONE OR IN COMBINATION										
18 to 64 Years										
Total	6 231	198	267	1 207	888	464	2 043	763	206	195
Management, business, and financial	919	7	8	88	92	66	422	215	11	9
Professional and related	1 859	4	4	46	118	101	809	426	177	174
Service	964	88	109	340	172	67	155	17	11	4
Sales and related	718	12	31	189	119	72	233	57	2	3
Office and administrative	756	6	24	150	211	81	255	25	3	2
Farming, forestry, and fishing	12	4	1	3	1	1	1	-	-	-
Construction and extraction	109	15	5	33	18	13	23	2	-	-
Installation, maintenance, and repair	185	11	14	72	31	32	17	7	-	2
Production	515	42	65	201	80	22	90	14	1	-
Transportation and material moving	194	8	6	86	46	9	38	1	-	-
18 to 24 Years										
Total	624	2	44	148	283	33	100	15	-	-
Management, business, and financial	38	-	-	7	14	1	13	3	-	-
Professional and related	92	-	1	6	38	4	34	10	-	-
Service	144	-	21	38	62	8	15	-	-	-
Sales and related	117	-	10	29	51	7	19	-	-	-
Office and administrative	130	-	4	28	79	1	15	2	-	-
Farming, forestry, and fishing	1	-	-	1	-	-	-	-	-	-
Construction and extraction	10	2	2	2	2	-	2	-	-	-
Installation, maintenance, and repair	27	-	-	14	7	6	1	-	-	-
Production	33	-	4	16	11	1	-	-	-	-
Transportation and material moving	33	-	2	9	17	5	-	-	-	-
25 to 34 Years										
Total	1 730	27	58	265	193	115	718	261	58	36
Management, business, and financial	261	-	1	14	25	15	149	55	-	2
Professional and related	698	-	-	15	29	29	365	172	57	33
Service	211	13	27	88	38	12	33	-	-	-
Sales and related	173	-	3	31	30	20	69	20	1	-
Office and administrative	178	2	5	34	39	23	67	7	-	2
Farming, forestry, and fishing	-	-	-	-	-	-	-	-	-	-
Construction and extraction	19	2	2	7	6	2	1	-	-	-
Installation, maintenance, and repair	45	7	4	14	3	7	6	3	-	-
Production	105	2	12	41	19	7	20	4	-	-
Transportation and material moving	38	-	3	22	4	1	7	1	-	-
35 to 44 Years										
Total	1 805	59	73	297	193	144	598	286	80	75
Management, business, and financial	304	2	-	24	24	22	137	86	6	4
Professional and related	598	4	1	4	24	31	230	161	73	70
Service	263	32	24	88	44	17	47	9	1	2
Sales and related	174	2	9	46	17	23	55	20	1	-
Office and administrative	181	2	8	25	32	30	82	3	-	-
Farming, forestry, and fishing	1	-	-	-	-	-	1	-	-	-
Construction and extraction	28	-	2	9	5	6	6	-	-	-
Installation, maintenance, and repair	56	2	6	19	14	9	5	2	-	-
Production	138	14	23	53	21	5	19	5	-	-
Transportation and material moving	61	1	1	30	13	1	16	-	-	-
45 to 64 Years										
Total	2 071	111	93	496	220	171	627	201	68	84
Management, business, and financial	316	5	7	43	29	28	123	71	6	4
Professional and related	470	-	2	21	28	37	179	83	48	72
Service	346	44	38	127	28	30	60	8	10	3
Sales and related	254	10	9	83	21	22	89	17	1	3
Office and administrative	267	2	6	63	61	27	91	14	3	1
Farming, forestry, and fishing	10	4	-	2	1	1	1	-	-	-
Construction and extraction	52	11	-	16	4	4	14	2	-	-
Installation, maintenance, and repair	56	2	4	25	7	10	5	1	-	2
Production	238	25	26	91	29	9	51	5	1	-
Transportation and material moving	62	7	1	25	12	3	15	-	-	-

- = Quantity zero or rounds to zero.

Table A-21. Educational Attainment of Employed Civilians Age 18 to 64 Years, by Occupation, Age, Race, and Hispanic Origin, 2005—*Continued*

(Numbers in thousands.)

Occupation, age, race, and Hispanic origin	Total population	Elementary None to 8th grade	High school 9th to 11th grade	High school graduate	College Some college, no degree	Associate's degree	Bachelor's degree	Master's degree	Professional degree	Doctorate degree
HISPANIC[1]										
18 to 64 Years										
Total	17 722	3 351	2 898	5 323	2 940	1 041	1 574	425	106	64
Management, business, and financial	1 269	37	82	302	283	109	332	111	5	8
Professional and related	1 758	24	71	248	329	227	527	207	77	47
Service	4 319	1 108	837	1 382	556	187	196	43	6	3
Sales and related	1 582	107	220	522	445	105	153	27	1	3
Office and administrative	2 151	77	189	804	687	202	159	21	12	-
Farming, forestry, and fishing	401	237	63	82	8	2	6	3	-	-
Construction and extraction	2 238	739	549	673	160	45	72	1	-	-
Installation, maintenance, and repair	621	90	127	208	103	54	34	2	-	1
Production	1 862	558	431	586	178	52	48	7	2	-
Transportation and material moving	1 521	374	328	515	193	59	48	2	1	1
18 to 24 Years										
Total	3 029	372	669	1 060	707	112	106	3	-	-
Management, business, and financial	82	-	12	31	25	4	10	2	-	-
Professional and related	212	-	26	42	71	33	40	-	-	-
Service	782	116	179	302	145	24	17	-	-	-
Sales and related	404	9	86	134	150	15	9	-	-	-
Office and administrative	467	8	65	162	191	25	15	1	-	-
Farming, forestry, and fishing	66	25	16	20	4	2	-	-	-	-
Construction and extraction	442	122	126	153	30	-	11	-	-	-
Installation, maintenance, and repair	68	12	20	24	10	3	-	-	-	-
Production	253	45	86	82	29	7	4	-	-	-
Transportation and material moving	254	35	53	112	52	-	-	-	-	-
25 to 34 Years										
Total	5 659	927	1 025	1 703	917	380	550	106	35	14
Management, business, and financial	427	16	36	100	92	44	111	25	1	2
Professional and related	560	3	21	78	90	85	202	47	24	11
Service	1 310	292	292	406	166	63	77	12	2	-
Sales and related	471	20	58	166	127	37	52	10	-	2
Office and administrative	706	19	49	268	224	74	59	6	6	-
Farming, forestry, and fishing	134	69	21	39	-	-	5	-	-	-
Construction and extraction	808	216	249	239	60	27	16	-	-	-
Installation, maintenance, and repair	203	22	41	76	32	15	15	2	-	-
Production	586	170	139	184	66	16	8	3	-	-
Transportation and material moving	455	100	122	147	59	19	6	-	1	-
35 to 44 Years										
Total	4 721	981	688	1 373	699	307	486	137	35	14
Management, business, and financial	372	8	18	99	81	33	95	35	3	-
Professional and related	481	9	15	60	93	62	130	75	25	12
Service	1 123	309	191	357	138	53	62	11	-	1
Sales and related	382	38	50	116	83	33	55	5	-	1
Office and administrative	506	27	46	181	139	50	54	5	4	-
Farming, forestry, and fishing	126	88	18	14	3	-	1	1	-	-
Construction and extraction	598	222	122	167	42	11	33	1	-	-
Installation, maintenance, and repair	180	25	33	65	23	29	6	-	-	-
Production	524	155	114	173	46	11	23	2	2	-
Transportation and material moving	430	100	83	141	50	25	28	2	-	-
45 to 64 Years										
Total	4 312	1 070	516	1 186	618	241	431	178	36	35
Management, business, and financial	388	13	17	74	85	29	115	49	1	6
Professional and related	505	13	9	68	74	47	156	85	28	25
Service	1 104	391	175	317	107	48	40	20	4	2
Sales and related	326	40	27	106	84	19	36	12	1	-
Office and administrative	472	23	29	193	133	53	31	9	2	-
Farming, forestry, and fishing	76	54	9	10	-	-	-	2	-	-
Construction and extraction	391	178	53	114	27	7	12	-	-	-
Installation, maintenance, and repair	169	32	34	43	39	7	13	-	-	1
Production	499	188	93	148	36	18	14	1	-	-
Transportation and material moving	383	139	70	114	31	14	13	-	-	1

[1]May be of any race.
- = Quantity zero or rounds to zero.

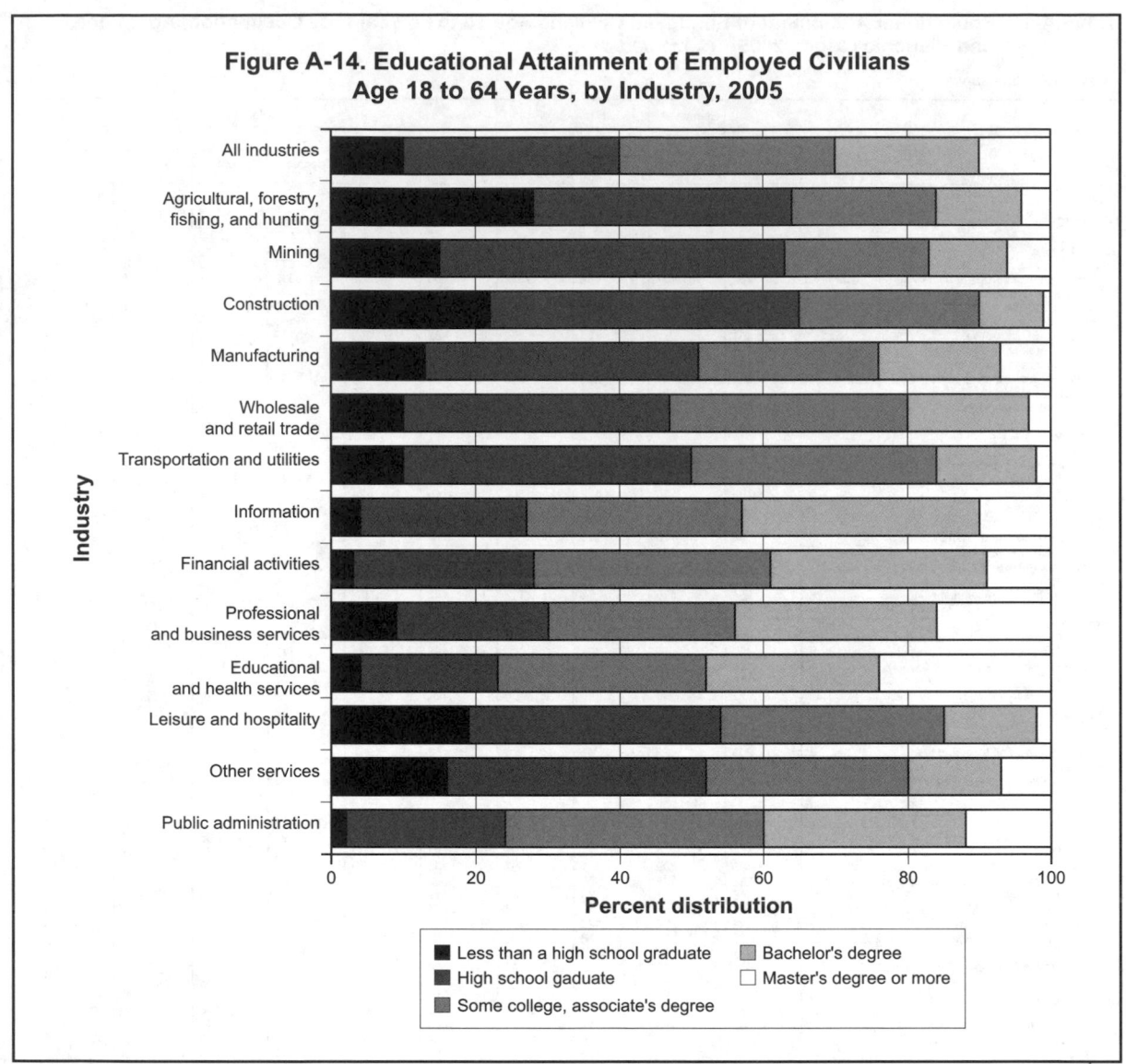

Figure A-14. Educational Attainment of Employed Civilians
Age 18 to 64 Years, by Industry, 2005

The educational and health services industry was the largest employer in the United States and employed more than 28 million people in 2005. Approximately 47 percent of people in the education and health services industry held a bachelor's degree or more, and about 23 percent of workers in this field had a master's degree or more. Mining was the smallest industry in terms of employment, with fewer than 600,000 workers. In mining, 16 percent of workers held a bachelor's degree or more, and 5.5 percent of workers had an advanced degree. Wholesale and retail trade employed the most people between the ages of 18 and 24 years. (Table A-22)

Table A-22. Educational Attainment of Employed Civilians Age 18 to 64 Years, by Industry, Age, Race, and Hispanic Origin, 2005

(Numbers in thousands.)

Industry, age, race, and Hispanic origin	Total population	Elementary: None to 8th grade	High school: 9th to 11th grade	High school graduate	College: Some college, no degree	Associate's degree	Bachelor's degree	Master's degree	Professional degree	Doctorate degree
ALL RACES										
18 to 64 Years										
Total	132 121	4 500	9 045	39 745	26 345	12 583	26 510	9 495	2 139	1 759
Agricultural, forestry, fishing, and hunting	1 753	304	184	635	233	125	212	49	7	3
Mining	598	41	51	289	84	37	63	27	3	3
Construction	10 260	901	1 379	4 403	1 733	777	899	150	10	7
Manufacturing	15 769	773	1 313	5 962	2 656	1 341	2 670	833	69	151
Wholesale and retail trade	19 388	467	1 504	7 106	4 928	1 559	3 181	531	69	43
Transportation and utilities	6 919	141	520	2 767	1 608	715	968	165	17	18
Information	3 118	18	97	716	672	271	1 027	277	20	20
Financial activities	9 630	82	233	2 398	2 208	929	2 913	746	81	40
Professional and business services	13 497	472	693	2 762	2 372	1 197	3 812	1 248	672	270
Educational and health services	28 048	283	936	5 465	4 774	3 435	6 823	4 347	975	1 010
Leisure and hospitality	10 410	608	1 416	3 598	2 528	655	1 330	220	39	16
Other services	6 373	383	621	2 262	1 107	684	855	356	43	61
Public administration	6 358	27	97	1 381	1 444	859	1 756	545	134	116
18 to 24 Years										
Total	17 007	460	2 305	5 483	5 939	952	1 781	76	7	5
Agricultural, forestry, fishing, and hunting	180	32	29	65	44	7	5	-	-	-
Mining	39	-	1	31	6	-	-	-	-	-
Construction	1 313	146	250	634	208	49	25	1	-	-
Manufacturing	1 233	66	181	508	269	81	127	-	-	-
Wholesale and retail trade	3 895	35	550	1 337	1 555	191	224	1	2	-
Transportation and utilities	465	5	66	195	149	26	24	-	-	-
Information	379	4	36	113	121	16	86	3	-	-
Financial activities	1 015	2	69	306	385	57	190	4	-	-
Professional and business services	1 331	34	151	383	410	86	244	16	5	2
Educational and health services	2 707	5	180	548	1 164	222	558	27	-	3
Leisure and hospitality	3 296	83	655	1 004	1 247	132	175	-	-	-
Other services	874	49	128	293	265	66	62	10	-	-
Public administration	279	-	8	66	116	17	59	12	-	-
25 to 34 Years										
Total	29 934	1 099	2 128	8 161	5 644	2 883	7 325	2 014	441	238
Agricultural, forestry, fishing, and hunting	314	84	36	101	33	17	37	6	-	-
Mining	143	6	15	78	16	7	11	9	-	1
Construction	2 801	241	478	1 134	449	231	241	25	3	-
Manufacturing	3 330	183	288	1 200	571	248	655	147	18	20
Wholesale and retail trade	4 261	102	296	1 434	1 114	360	812	106	23	13
Transportation and utilities	1 318	36	121	543	272	135	180	26	2	3
Information	870	3	24	160	211	73	333	59	3	4
Financial activities	2 230	15	54	523	455	218	802	149	13	1
Professional and business services	3 462	145	179	611	545	303	1 179	305	152	43
Educational and health services	6 113	22	169	936	952	754	1 997	969	179	137
Leisure and hospitality	2 461	177	297	786	519	209	407	47	17	2
Other services	1 285	84	153	429	204	141	227	40	8	-
Public administration	1 345	1	17	227	305	187	443	126	24	14
35 to 44 Years										
Total	34 399	1 252	2 012	10 671	5 814	3 601	7 369	2 564	658	458
Agricultural, forestry, fishing, and hunting	445	98	39	173	56	28	45	7	-	-
Mining	142	17	10	67	15	14	19	-	-	-
Construction	2 833	262	343	1 263	440	231	265	25	2	3
Manufacturing	4 607	226	336	1 739	718	386	828	310	18	47
Wholesale and retail trade	4 677	116	295	1 790	876	425	976	159	27	12
Transportation and utilities	1 969	30	129	782	436	235	305	47	2	3
Information	813	5	20	187	144	77	296	69	10	5
Financial activities	2 558	33	51	559	538	261	854	228	21	15
Professional and business services	3 678	140	182	736	561	324	1 093	364	206	72
Educational and health services	7 096	61	217	1 495	1 018	959	1 689	1 075	309	273
Leisure and hospitality	2 187	161	231	838	390	181	321	58	5	2
Other services	1 635	102	141	637	250	200	200	79	16	10
Public administration	1 760	2	18	406	372	281	480	144	40	17
45 to 64 Years										
Total	50 781	1 689	2 601	15 430	8 948	5 147	10 035	4 840	1 033	1 058
Agricultural, forestry, fishing, and hunting	813	91	80	296	101	73	125	36	7	3
Mining	275	18	24	113	48	16	33	18	3	2
Construction	3 313	253	308	1 372	636	265	368	99	5	5
Manufacturing	6 598	297	508	2 515	1 097	627	1 059	376	34	84
Wholesale and retail trade	6 555	213	363	2 545	1 383	583	1 169	265	17	18
Transportation and utilities	3 168	71	204	1 247	751	319	460	92	12	11
Information	1 057	6	17	257	195	105	312	146	7	12
Financial activities	3 827	31	59	1 009	831	393	1 067	365	47	25
Professional and business services	5 026	153	181	1 033	855	484	1 295	562	308	154
Educational and health services	12 132	194	370	2 487	1 640	1 501	2 580	2 276	487	597
Leisure and hospitality	2 466	187	233	971	372	133	426	115	17	12
Other services	2 578	149	199	902	389	276	366	227	19	50
Public administration	2 973	24	54	683	650	373	773	263	70	85

- = Quantity zero or rounds to zero.

Table A-22. Educational Attainment of Employed Civilians Age 18 to 64 Years, by Industry, Age, Race, and Hispanic Origin, 2005—*Continued*

(Numbers in thousands.)

Industry, age, race, and Hispanic origin	Total population	Elementary — None to 8th grade	High school — 9th to 11th grade	High school graduate	Some college, no degree	Associate's degree	Bachelor's degree	Master's degree	Professional degree	Doctorate degree
WHITE ALONE OR IN COMBINATION										
18 to 64 Years										
Total	110 397	3 993	7 300	32 838	21 988	10 704	22 201	8 070	1 823	1 480
Agricultural, forestry, fishing, and hunting	1 671	287	167	602	225	124	207	49	7	2
Mining	551	36	50	272	73	36	57	23	-	3
Construction	9 423	839	1 239	4 052	1 611	727	809	132	8	5
Manufacturing	13 086	673	1 053	4 854	2 224	1 158	2 261	687	64	113
Wholesale and retail trade	16 425	411	1 223	6 023	4 196	1 354	2 694	433	59	32
Transportation and utilities	5 531	130	423	2 203	1 280	575	753	139	15	14
Information	2 611	13	85	613	539	228	859	241	18	15
Financial activities	8 139	72	199	2 058	1 825	797	2 441	632	77	37
Professional and business services	11 437	437	560	2 319	2 033	1 008	3 264	985	618	213
Educational and health services	22 662	238	610	4 111	3 764	2 854	5 641	3 798	775	870
Leisure and hospitality	8 491	508	1 118	2 792	2 169	548	1 117	197	31	12
Other services	5 328	330	507	1 827	933	611	717	313	33	57
Public administration	5 042	20	65	1 113	1 115	684	1 381	443	116	106
18 to 24 Years										
Total	14 360	423	1 946	4 597	4 963	820	1 545	55	7	5
Agricultural, forestry, fishing, and hunting	175	32	27	61	44	7	5	-	-	-
Mining	33	-	1	31	-	-	-	-	-	-
Construction	1 232	133	227	600	204	45	23	1	-	-
Manufacturing	1 008	62	149	421	198	68	109	-	-	-
Wholesale and retail trade	3 277	33	460	1 141	1 280	165	195	1	2	-
Transportation and utilities	386	2	59	158	126	23	18	-	-	-
Information	325	4	35	95	99	12	78	3	-	-
Financial activities	838	2	64	264	302	47	155	3	-	-
Professional and business services	1 136	30	131	309	351	77	220	11	5	2
Educational and health services	2 223	4	137	418	971	181	487	23	-	3
Leisure and hospitality	2 791	76	544	808	1 087	119	158	-	-	-
Other services	726	46	102	239	218	63	51	6	-	-
Public administration	209	-	8	51	83	13	47	6	-	-
25 to 34 Years										
Total	24 325	1 005	1 771	6 540	4 538	2 375	5 938	1 610	353	195
Agricultural, forestry, fishing, and hunting	292	76	32	94	31	17	35	6	-	-
Mining	131	6	15	74	15	7	7	5	-	1
Construction	2 601	225	438	1 060	411	220	223	21	3	-
Manufacturing	2 701	170	245	950	466	202	522	112	18	15
Wholesale and retail trade	3 452	97	243	1 136	908	296	663	80	18	12
Transportation and utilities	1 028	33	99	395	217	112	147	21	2	3
Information	657	1	18	124	160	60	245	44	1	4
Financial activities	1 823	14	43	431	354	186	660	122	12	1
Professional and business services	2 788	142	148	505	437	233	953	204	134	32
Educational and health services	4 726	18	111	648	700	596	1 607	810	121	116
Leisure and hospitality	2 012	153	235	615	425	176	349	43	17	-
Other services	1 077	69	131	332	173	129	198	40	6	-
Public administration	1 036	1	12	177	240	141	330	102	22	11
35 to 44 Years										
Total	28 321	1 143	1 572	8 728	4 786	3 029	6 089	2 066	550	358
Agricultural, forestry, fishing, and hunting	429	98	37	160	55	28	44	7	-	-
Mining	138	17	10	66	15	14	16	-	-	-
Construction	2 613	256	304	1 169	406	220	234	22	2	-
Manufacturing	3 796	194	254	1 423	599	335	713	236	15	27
Wholesale and retail trade	3 954	104	225	1 521	751	373	825	123	24	8
Transportation and utilities	1 501	30	107	615	319	173	222	33	2	1
Information	704	3	18	168	110	66	266	59	10	3
Financial activities	2 101	33	44	465	430	214	708	173	20	13
Professional and business services	3 054	128	156	596	486	276	901	275	186	49
Educational and health services	5 582	52	126	1 081	788	787	1 366	912	239	230
Leisure and hospitality	1 742	140	172	636	322	149	268	49	3	2
Other services	1 330	87	110	506	217	173	148	67	12	10
Public administration	1 380	2	9	322	288	220	377	110	37	15
45 to 64 Years										
Total	43 390	1 422	2 010	12 974	7 701	4 481	8 629	4 339	912	922
Agricultural, forestry, fishing, and hunting	774	82	70	287	95	72	122	36	7	2
Mining	250	13	24	101	43	15	33	18	-	2
Construction	2 977	225	270	1 222	591	243	329	89	3	5
Manufacturing	5 581	247	404	2 059	961	553	916	339	31	71
Wholesale and retail trade	5 742	176	295	2 225	1 257	520	1 011	228	16	12
Transportation and utilities	2 616	65	159	1 035	618	267	367	86	10	10
Information	925	5	13	227	169	90	271	134	7	9
Financial activities	3 377	23	47	899	739	350	919	333	45	23
Professional and business services	4 459	138	125	908	759	422	1 190	495	293	130
Educational and health services	10 131	164	236	1 964	1 304	1 291	2 182	2 052	415	522
Leisure and hospitality	1 946	139	166	733	335	104	342	105	11	10
Other services	2 196	128	164	750	325	245	320	200	15	47
Public administration	2 418	17	36	562	505	310	626	225	57	80

- = Quantity zero or rounds to zero.

Table A-22. Educational Attainment of Employed Civilians Age 18 to 64 Years, by Industry, Age, Race, and Hispanic Origin, 2005—*Continued*

(Numbers in thousands.)

Industry, age, race, and Hispanic origin	Total population	Elementary — None to 8th grade	High school — 9th to 11th grade	High school graduate	College — Some college, no degree	Associate's degree	Bachelor's degree	Master's degree	Professional degree	Doctorate degree
BLACK ALONE OR IN COMBINATION										
18 to 64 Years										
Total	14 783	235	1 347	5 474	3 338	1 343	2 202	653	113	79
Agricultural, forestry, fishing, and hunting	44	8	11	19	4	-	3	-	-	-
Mining	27	-	-	13	7	1	2	2	2	-
Construction	568	26	105	283	82	26	37	6	3	-
Manufacturing	1 740	33	172	891	319	126	146	49	-	4
Wholesale and retail trade	1 925	37	225	776	524	121	211	21	6	3
Transportation and utilities	1 080	9	85	495	255	100	122	12	-	2
Information	349	-	6	84	114	38	91	16	-	-
Financial activities	972	8	29	255	271	95	266	45	2	1
Professional and business services	1 202	20	109	382	277	136	206	41	21	10
Educational and health services	4 017	19	271	1 229	836	463	711	376	59	53
Leisure and hospitality	1 208	46	240	543	242	57	71	8	-	-
Other services	649	24	69	273	126	53	79	19	5	2
Public administration	1 003	2	25	231	282	128	256	59	15	4
18 to 24 Years										
Total	1 980	19	287	732	694	108	136	4	-	-
Agricultural, forestry, fishing, and hunting	2	-	-	2	-	-	-	-	-	-
Mining	6	-	-	-	6	-	-	-	-	-
Construction	48	2	13	29	-	4	-	-	-	-
Manufacturing	164	4	21	69	54	9	7	-	-	-
Wholesale and retail trade	476	2	82	157	194	18	23	-	-	-
Transportation and utilities	61	3	2	33	16	-	6	-	-	-
Information	42	-	-	17	17	5	4	-	-	-
Financial activities	116	-	5	32	50	9	21	-	-	-
Professional and business services	151	3	17	65	47	8	11	-	-	-
Educational and health services	382	-	38	118	144	38	44	-	-	-
Leisure and hospitality	382	6	92	157	112	11	5	-	-	-
Other services	90	-	17	40	24	2	5	2	-	-
Public administration	59	-	-	14	29	4	9	3	-	-
25 to 34 Years										
Total	3 729	46	261	1 298	881	382	672	145	34	10
Agricultural, forestry, fishing, and hunting	11	5	1	2	1	-	1	-	-	-
Mining	7	-	-	4	-	-	2	2	-	-
Construction	117	4	22	58	20	6	8	-	-	-
Manufacturing	384	1	25	201	74	25	43	15	-	-
Wholesale and retail trade	560	3	43	235	162	45	65	3	2	2
Transportation and utilities	235	-	22	134	41	19	20	-	-	-
Information	146	-	1	34	44	14	44	8	-	-
Financial activities	261	1	11	69	79	27	67	6	2	-
Professional and business services	352	4	23	85	91	51	82	10	7	-
Educational and health services	981	2	44	266	219	125	211	90	20	6
Leisure and hospitality	313	19	55	109	74	24	31	-	-	-
Other services	134	7	11	59	25	12	19	-	2	-
Public administration	228	-	4	43	51	36	80	10	2	3
35 to 44 Years										
Total	4 054	38	345	1 565	795	389	663	206	27	26
Agricultural, forestry, fishing, and hunting	11	-	1	10	-	-	-	-	-	-
Mining	-	-	-	-	-	-	-	-	-	-
Construction	152	4	33	74	24	1	13	1	1	-
Manufacturing	510	8	56	265	89	35	35	20	-	2
Wholesale and retail trade	432	7	54	188	83	26	60	10	4	-
Transportation and utilities	366	-	21	142	98	45	52	5	-	2
Information	78	-	2	11	32	10	20	3	-	-
Financial activities	306	-	4	74	82	31	89	26	-	-
Professional and business services	331	5	23	118	60	36	74	9	4	2
Educational and health services	1 121	5	81	382	191	127	202	101	14	18
Leisure and hospitality	266	5	47	140	36	13	21	4	-	-
Other services	185	4	16	89	24	17	31	5	1	-
Public administration	295	-	8	71	75	48	66	23	3	2
45 to 64 Years										
Total	5 020	131	454	1 879	968	464	732	298	52	44
Agricultural, forestry, fishing, and hunting	20	3	9	5	3	-	1	-	-	-
Mining	14	-	-	9	1	1	-	-	2	-
Construction	252	16	36	123	39	14	18	5	2	-
Manufacturing	682	21	70	356	102	57	62	13	-	2
Wholesale and retail trade	456	25	47	196	84	33	63	8	-	1
Transportation and utilities	418	6	40	187	99	36	43	6	-	-
Information	82	-	3	21	21	10	22	5	-	-
Financial activities	288	7	9	80	60	29	88	14	-	1
Professional and business services	368	9	46	114	79	41	40	22	10	7
Educational and health services	1 533	12	109	463	282	173	254	185	25	30
Leisure and hospitality	247	16	47	137	19	10	15	4	-	-
Other services	240	14	25	86	52	22	24	12	2	2
Public administration	421	2	14	103	126	40	101	24	11	-

- = Quantity zero or rounds to zero.

Table A-22. Educational Attainment of Employed Civilians Age 18 to 64 Years, by Industry, Age, Race, and Hispanic Origin, 2005—*Continued*

(Numbers in thousands.)

Industry, age, race, and Hispanic origin	Total population	Elementary None to 8th grade	High school 9th to 11th grade	High school graduate	College Some college, no degree	Associate's degree	Bachelor's degree	Master's degree	Professional degree	Doctorate degree
ASIAN ALONE OR IN COMBINATION										
18 to 64 Years										
Total	6 231	198	267	1 207	888	464	2 043	763	206	195
Agricultural, forestry, fishing, and hunting	19	7	1	5	3	1	1	-	-	-
Mining	8	-	-	-	-	-	5	2	-	-
Construction	158	15	10	37	18	11	51	13	-	2
Manufacturing	828	49	66	178	98	50	252	94	6	34
Wholesale and retail trade	980	21	41	279	196	77	283	73	3	7
Transportation and utilities	262	2	6	61	58	28	88	16	2	2
Information	158	5	3	19	20	4	78	23	2	4
Financial activities	493	-	1	68	103	33	212	72	3	2
Professional and business services	816	11	11	47	64	51	332	221	34	44
Educational and health services	1 244	10	40	91	151	110	451	162	140	90
Leisure and hospitality	644	50	51	234	107	49	125	18	8	2
Other services	376	23	36	164	40	23	58	25	5	1
Public administration	245	4	3	23	30	27	105	44	2	7
18 to 24 Years										
Total	624	2	44	148	283	33	100	15	-	-
Agricultural, forestry, fishing, and hunting	-	-	-	-	-	-	-	-	-	-
Mining	3	-	-	3	-	-	-	-	-	-
Construction	11	2	2	4	-	-	4	-	-	-
Manufacturing	46	-	4	15	15	3	9	-	-	-
Wholesale and retail trade	149	-	5	38	86	10	11	-	-	-
Transportation and utilities	19	-	3	4	9	2	-	-	-	-
Information	13	-	-	4	5	-	4	-	-	-
Financial activities	54	-	1	9	29	3	11	2	-	-
Professional and business services	51	-	-	11	19	3	13	4	-	-
Educational and health services	104	-	5	10	50	7	28	4	-	-
Leisure and hospitality	105	-	14	37	41	2	11	-	-	-
Other services	53	-	9	15	21	2	3	2	-	-
Public administration	16	-	-	-	7	-	6	3	-	-
25 to 34 Years										
Total	1 730	27	58	265	193	115	718	261	58	36
Agricultural, forestry, fishing, and hunting	-	-	-	-	-	-	-	-	-	-
Mining	5	-	-	-	-	-	3	2	-	-
Construction	38	2	4	5	9	3	9	4	-	-
Manufacturing	217	5	13	41	30	15	89	19	-	5
Wholesale and retail trade	226	2	5	53	35	19	87	23	3	-
Transportation and utilities	41	2	2	11	8	3	12	5	-	-
Information	74	2	2	3	11	-	45	9	2	-
Financial activities	153	-	-	20	25	4	83	21	-	-
Professional and business services	316	-	8	15	16	15	145	93	14	11
Educational and health services	380	-	10	15	22	34	176	68	39	17
Leisure and hospitality	137	7	7	56	22	12	28	3	-	2
Other services	81	6	8	42	6	2	15	-	-	-
Public administration	63	-	-	4	8	7	27	14	1	2
35 to 44 Years										
Total	1 805	59	73	297	193	144	598	286	80	75
Agricultural, forestry, fishing, and hunting	1	-	-	-	-	-	1	-	-	-
Mining	3	-	-	-	-	-	3	-	-	-
Construction	43	-	4	10	4	4	17	3	-	2
Manufacturing	259	18	23	38	19	13	73	53	3	18
Wholesale and retail trade	274	2	14	72	41	24	92	25	-	4
Transportation and utilities	87	-	-	26	14	11	28	9	-	-
Information	30	2	-	5	1	1	12	8	-	2
Financial activities	139	-	-	13	20	12	63	30	1	2
Professional and business services	270	7	-	10	15	12	113	79	15	19
Educational and health services	356	3	7	21	33	37	116	55	55	28
Leisure and hospitality	160	15	11	51	30	16	30	6	3	-
Other services	116	12	14	43	8	9	19	7	4	-
Public administration	67	-	1	9	6	7	33	11	-	-
45 to 64 Years										
Total	2 071	111	93	496	220	171	627	201	68	84
Agricultural, forestry, fishing, and hunting	15	7	-	2	3	1	1	-	-	-
Mining	-	-	-	-	-	-	-	-	-	-
Construction	65	11	1	18	4	5	20	6	-	-
Manufacturing	306	26	26	84	33	18	82	23	3	11
Wholesale and retail trade	330	17	16	116	35	25	93	24	-	3
Transportation and utilities	116	-	3	21	28	11	48	2	2	2
Information	41	1	1	7	2	4	17	6	-	3
Financial activities	146	-	-	26	28	14	55	19	2	-
Professional and business services	179	4	3	11	15	20	62	45	6	14
Educational and health services	404	6	18	45	45	32	132	35	46	45
Leisure and hospitality	243	28	19	90	14	19	57	9	6	-
Other services	127	6	4	64	4	9	21	16	2	1
Public administration	99	4	2	11	9	13	40	16	1	4

- = Quantity zero or rounds to zero.

Table A-22. Educational Attainment of Employed Civilians Age 18 to 64 Years, by Industry, Age, Race, and Hispanic Origin, 2005—*Continued*

(Numbers in thousands.)

Industry, age, race, and Hispanic origin	Total population	Elementary		High school		College					
		None to 8th grade	9th to 11th grade	High school graduate	Some college, no degree	Associate's degree	Bachelor's degree	Master's degree	Professional degree	Doctorate degree
HISPANIC[1]										
18 to 64 Years										
Total	17 722	3 351	2 898	5 323	2 940	1 041	1 574	425	106	64
Agricultural, forestry, fishing, and hunting	438	250	71	89	16	1	7	3	-	1
Mining	82	19	8	40	9	2	3	-	-	1
Construction	2 387	735	565	723	206	69	85	2	-	-
Manufacturing	2 188	571	422	707	227	76	141	37	3	4
Wholesale and retail trade	2 524	327	413	877	586	139	148	28	3	3
Transportation and utilities	883	86	175	292	180	79	59	10	1	1
Information	305	8	19	95	81	20	62	19	-	2
Financial activities	941	47	78	316	236	92	143	27	2	1
Professional and business services	1 845	400	300	446	298	108	220	50	18	6
Educational and health services	2 460	171	228	647	512	254	380	171	64	33
Leisure and hospitality	2 053	466	396	690	295	79	98	23	5	1
Other services	1 065	265	207	285	146	51	84	21	3	2
Public administration	552	10	15	118	147	69	145	34	7	7
18 to 24 Years										
Total	3 029	372	669	1 060	707	112	106	3	-	-
Agricultural, forestry, fishing, and hunting	59	25	11	18	5	-	-	-	-	-
Mining	9	-	1	8	-	-	-	-	-	-
Construction	468	122	133	162	38	4	9	-	-	-
Manufacturing	250	52	71	84	35	4	4	-	-	-
Wholesale and retail trade	602	31	131	222	188	21	10	-	-	-
Transportation and utilities	101	1	27	41	27	5	-	-	-	-
Information	76	4	4	37	16	1	14	-	-	-
Financial activities	153	-	19	62	54	7	10	-	-	-
Professional and business services	287	32	68	90	67	11	16	2	-	-
Educational and health services	282	2	33	77	114	31	24	1	-	-
Leisure and hospitality	561	64	128	207	128	21	13	-	-	-
Other services	158	39	41	47	25	5	2	-	-	-
Public administration	23	-	2	6	8	3	3	-	-	-
25 to 34 Years										
Total	5 659	927	1 025	1 703	917	380	550	106	35	14
Agricultural, forestry, fishing, and hunting	153	73	27	45	4	-	5	-	-	-
Mining	30	6	5	12	2	-	2	-	-	1
Construction	864	210	265	254	81	35	18	-	-	-
Manufacturing	702	165	147	237	73	31	38	10	1	-
Wholesale and retail trade	779	80	130	284	194	39	42	8	-	1
Transportation and utilities	241	27	52	76	41	31	9	4	1	-
Information	100	1	10	25	29	6	17	10	-	2
Financial activities	319	9	19	115	75	38	55	8	1	-
Professional and business services	646	132	106	157	101	40	97	6	5	1
Educational and health services	711	13	54	180	143	95	157	40	19	9
Leisure and hospitality	634	148	129	211	74	28	33	8	4	-
Other services	297	64	76	71	43	15	26	3	-	-
Public administration	186	1	4	36	56	24	51	9	5	-
35 to 44 Years										
Total	4 721	981	688	1 373	699	307	486	137	35	14
Agricultural, forestry, fishing, and hunting	127	89	19	12	3	-	1	1	-	-
Mining	18	3	-	13	3	-	-	-	-	-
Construction	642	221	118	185	58	19	40	1	-	-
Manufacturing	644	175	107	216	60	23	45	15	-	1
Wholesale and retail trade	607	94	88	200	104	48	66	5	3	1
Transportation and utilities	289	27	57	87	54	32	31	1	-	-
Information	66	1	3	16	16	6	17	7	-	-
Financial activities	222	21	20	64	56	19	33	8	-	-
Professional and business services	498	119	81	112	73	33	48	21	11	1
Educational and health services	641	37	57	166	131	63	99	61	18	10
Leisure and hospitality	500	130	91	168	55	22	31	2	1	-
Other services	304	63	45	94	48	21	28	4	-	1
Public administration	163	-	3	42	37	22	48	11	1	-
45 to 64 Years										
Total	4 312	1 070	516	1 186	618	241	431	178	36	35
Agricultural, forestry, fishing, and hunting	99	62	14	14	3	1	1	2	-	1
Mining	25	10	2	6	4	2	1	-	-	-
Construction	412	181	50	121	29	12	18	2	-	-
Manufacturing	592	179	96	171	58	19	53	12	2	2
Wholesale and retail trade	535	122	64	171	101	32	30	15	-	1
Transportation and utilities	252	30	38	89	58	12	19	5	-	1
Information	64	1	2	17	20	7	14	2	-	-
Financial activities	247	17	19	75	51	27	45	10	1	1
Professional and business services	415	116	45	87	56	25	58	21	3	4
Educational and health services	827	119	85	223	123	65	100	69	27	15
Leisure and hospitality	359	123	49	105	39	8	21	13	-	1
Other services	306	100	46	74	30	11	28	14	3	1
Public administration	180	9	6	34	45	20	43	15	1	7

[1]May be of any race.
- = Quantity zero or rounds to zero.

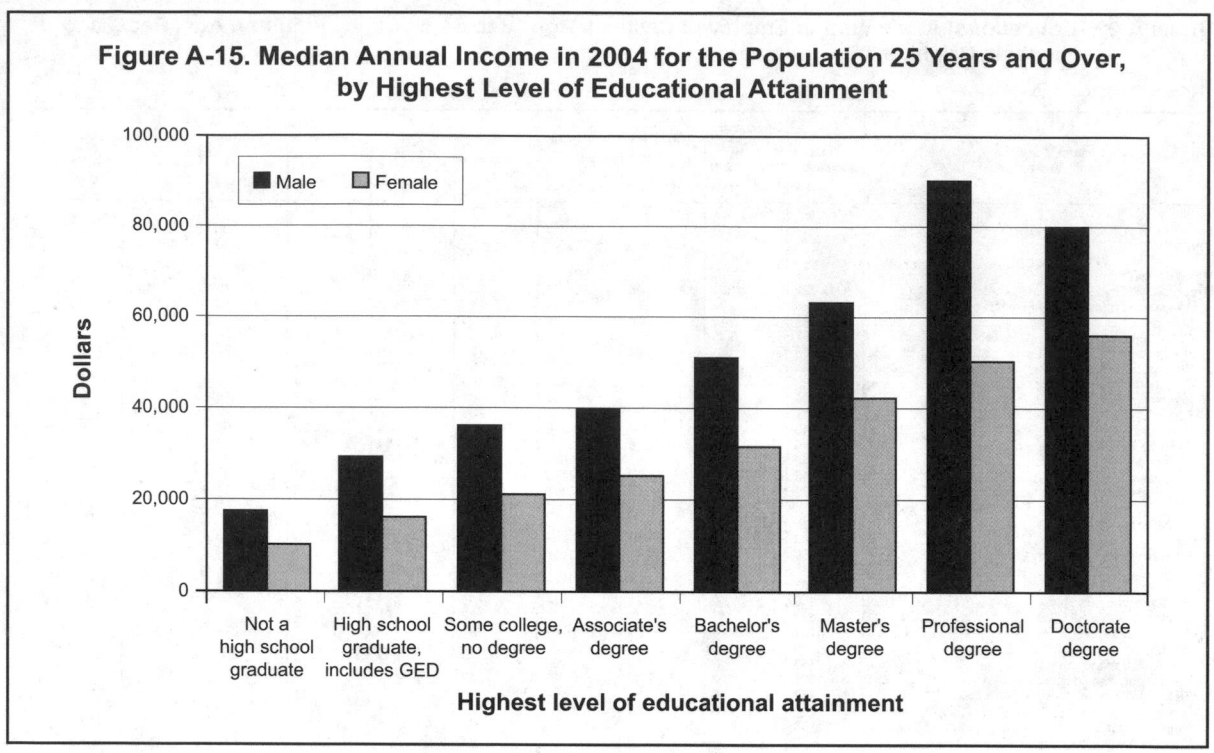

Figure A-15. Median Annual Income in 2004 for the Population 25 Years and Over, by Highest Level of Educational Attainment

The median income in 2004 for people age 25 years and over was $26,494. Men earned more than women at all levels of educational attainment. Men with some college and no degrees even earned significantly more than women with bachelor's degrees. For those who did not finish high school, the median income was $13,442. For high school graduates, median earnings rose to $21,826, while those with a bachelor's degree had a median income of $40,545. Those with a professional degree had the highest median income at $74,668.

Among people age 25 years and over with a bachelor's degrees, Whites had the highest median income ($40,959), followed by Asians ($38,344), Blacks ($37,058), and Hispanics ($35,933). Workers between the ages of 45 and 54 years had the highest median income for all education levels at $32,867, as well as the highest incomes for high school graduates ($27,098) and people with bachelor's degrees ($48,293). (Table A-23)

Table A-23. Income in 2004 by Educational Attainment for the Population Age 18 Years and Over, by Sex, Age, Race, and Hispanic Origin

(Numbers in thousands, dollars.)

| Characteristic | Total population | High school | | College | | | | | | |
| | | Not a high school graduate | High school graduate, includes GED | Some college, no degree | Associate's degree | Bachelor's degree or more | | | | |
						Total	Bachelor's degree	Master's degree	Professional degree	Doctorate degree
BOTH SEXES, 18 YEARS AND OVER										
All Workers										
All races										
Number with income	200 076	28 522	63 299	38 608	16 827	52 819	35 029	12 602	2 876	2 311
Median income ($)	24 108	12 437	20 733	22 279	30 026	42 956	38 880	50 693	74 207	72 073
Standard error	90	73	81	124	234	307	311	249	1 896	1 932
Mean income ($)	34 626	16 485	26 156	29 444	35 103	58 208	49 656	65 190	104 299	92 378
Standard error	125	155	150	213	269	366	350	884	2 529	2 469
White alone or in combination										
Number with income	167 694	23 059	53 020	32 353	14 405	44 855	29 624	10 792	2 473	1 966
Median income ($)	24 734	12 976	21 076	22 541	30 491	43 716	39 538	50 648	75 289	72 446
Standard error	98	110	89	182	194	321	339	280	1 939	2 054
Mean income ($)	35 576	16 869	26 890	30 208	35 671	59 301	50 767	65 785	105 069	94 715
Standard error	141	162	174	240	294	408	391	979	2 763	2 812
Black alone or in combination										
Number with income	22 787	4 149	8 222	4 812	1 763	3 840	2 737	849	145	107
Median income ($)	20 586	10 307	18 646	21 604	26 240	40 091	35 968	49 508	70 392	67 204
Standard error	154	194	314	288	525	520	509	1 394	5 953	10 960
Mean income ($)	26 291	14 619	21 730	25 530	29 974	47 929	41 669	56 242	94 927	78 120
Standard error	250	584	229	537	644	883	816	1 693	11 384	8 718
Asian alone or in combination										
Number with income	8 497	943	1 676	1 262	563	4 052	2 610	953	252	235
Median income ($)	26 906	12 157	19 826	18 300	28 864	42 379	37 053	52 476	62 556	69 603
Standard error	350	527	692	1 192	1 528	1 095	890	2 749	10 830	6 885
Mean income ($)	39 511	15 691	25 917	24 554	37 554	55 609	45 032	66 383	102 433	78 991
Standard error	738	619	838	1 097	2 367	1 356	1 263	3 663	8 245	4 751
Hispanic[1]										
Number with income	23 180	8 862	6 706	3 723	1 285	2 602	1 857	519	134	90
Median income ($)	18 953	14 913	19 838	22 223	26 738	36 966	34 916	49 033	43 318	47 558
Standard error	198	179	312	405	586	629	980	2 598	3 953	4 920
Mean income ($)	25 364	17 314	24 258	27 616	30 377	49 940	43 860	55 467	83 066	93 462
Standard error	294	252	536	696	756	1 623	1 020	2 991	9 519	22 418
Year-Round, Full-Time Workers										
All races										
Number with income	102 382	9 693	31 578	18 644	9 991	32 475	21 302	7 745	1 878	1 548
Median income ($)	37 238	21 772	30 757	35 799	38 822	56 062	50 750	62 672	[2]100 000	83 562
Standard error	79	112	91	170	491	231	185	668	16 196	1 791
Mean income ($)	49 660	26 436	36 383	42 644	45 239	74 890	64 379	82 708	132 558	110 426
Standard error	210	400	249	319	369	532	503	1 317	3 300	3 362
White alone or in combination										
Number with income	85 029	8 072	25 936	15 477	8 444	27 097	17 676	6 541	1 588	1 291
Median income ($)	38 686	21 864	31 567	36 781	40 337	57 143	51 655	62 846	[2]100 000	85 889
Standard error	176	125	101	186	249	251	212	761	24 222	2 071
Mean income ($)	51 205	26 493	37 802	44 146	46 239	76 975	66 557	83 652	134 985	114 389
Standard error	240	397	295	373	406	603	575	1 478	3 619	3 906
Black alone or in combination										
Number with income	11 920	1 137	4 517	2 504	1 123	2 637	1 879	571	107	78
Median income ($)	30 599	21 204	26 131	31 023	32 110	45 848	41 416	52 468	75 691	75 684
Standard error	146	313	201	239	584	685	350	1 770	3 892	6 991
Mean income ($)	36 813	26 752	28 891	34 537	37 175	56 730	49 668	65 756	108 647	88 787
Standard error	381	2 005	306	468	781	1 155	1 032	2 109	14 797	11 278
Asian alone or in combination										
Number with income	4 892	340	961	550	365	2 676	1 687	635	173	178
Median income ($)	41 357	22 202	27 212	32 537	36 492	55 943	49 512	72 296	95 752	80 214
Standard error	372	768	585	1 027	817	933	1 006	2 046	9 239	2 582
Mean income ($)	55 886	25 302	34 490	38 790	47 916	72 057	58 541	87 818	127 523	89 713
Standard error	1 150	1 176	1 252	2 054	3 295	1 868	1 760	5 061	10 647	5 292
Hispanic[1]										
Number with income	13 590	4 682	4 210	2 123	808	1 765	1 269	354	79	61
Median income ($)	26 042	20 307	25 570	31 666	33 460	46 854	42 219	56 006	80 295	(B)
Standard error	172	162	264	400	1 204	979	1 083	2 402	18 399	(B)
Mean income ($)	33 377	23 156	30 434	37 047	37 963	60 990	53 058	65 226	116 434	(B)
Standard error	398	422	636	648	922	2 040	1 865	3 405	13 936	(B)

[1]May be of any race.
[2]Median income over $100,000.
(B) = Base is too small to show the derived measure.

Table A-23. Income in 2004 by Educational Attainment for the Population Age 18 Years and Over, by Sex, Age, Race, and Hispanic Origin—*Continued*

(Numbers in thousands, dollars.)

Characteristic	Total population	High school		Some college, no degree	Associate's degree	College				
		Not a high school graduate	High school graduate, includes GED			Bachelor's degree or more				
						Total	Bachelor's degree	Master's degree	Professional degree	Doctorate degree
BOTH SEXES, 25 YEARS AND OVER										
All Workers										
All races										
Number with income	177 364	24 498	56 359	30 195	15 643	50 666	32 969	12 522	2 867	2 306
Median income ($)	26 494	13 442	21 826	27 137	30 984	45 029	40 545	50 796	74 668	72 120
Standard error	70	107	89	150	187	242	157	248	1 856	1 934
Mean income ($)	37 156	17 503	27 426	33 913	36 309	59 676	51 296	65 423	104 585	92 431
Standard error	138	159	159	261	284	380	368	889	2 535	2 474
White alone or in combination										
Number with income	148 966	19 768	47 346	25 451	13 392	43 007	27 845	10 737	2 463	1 961
Median income ($)	27 010	13 969	22 184	27 439	31 475	45 510	40 959	50 763	75 466	72 498
Standard error	79	115	100	206	206	212	182	280	1 749	2 058
Mean income ($)	38 129	17 885	28 152	34 722	36 892	60 820	52 487	65 995	105 405	94 784
Standard error	155	159	184	293	310	423	412	983	2 771	2 819
Black alone or in combination										
Number with income	19 736	3 546	7 153	3 737	1 633	3 665	2 570	841	145	107
Median income ($)	22 303	11 158	20 189	25 993	27 139	40 752	37 058	49 462	70 392	67 204
Standard error	165	197	235	403	613	354	539	1 403	5 953	10 960
Mean income ($)	28 395	15 785	22 955	29 229	30 987	49 210	43 062	56 396	94 927	78 120
Standard error	282	676	250	662	680	914	852	1 703	11 384	8 718
Asian alone or in combination										
Number with income	7 637	864	1 505	829	521	3 917	2 490	938	252	235
Median income ($)	30 219	12 771	20 911	25 633	30 316	44 533	38 344	53 954	62 556	69 603
Standard error	430	632	625	785	1 356	1 573	1 441	3 160	10 830	6 885
Mean income ($)	42 325	16 439	27 169	30 870	39 079	56 716	46 127	66 913	102 433	78 991
Standard error	810	662	918	1 566	2 535	1 397	1 315	3 716	8 245	4 751
Hispanic[1]										
Number with income	19 564	7 654	5 480	2 793	1 146	2 488	1 747	515	134	90
Median income ($)	20 743	15 469	21 395	27 145	28 703	38 104	35 933	49 613	43 318	47 558
Standard error	140	147	247	536	990	1 114	644	2 422	3 953	4 920
Mean income ($)	27 389	18 079	26 113	32 230	32 248	51 166	45 130	55 831	83 066	93 462
Standard error	334	286	586	890	812	1 688	1 708	3 007	9 519	22 418
Year-Round, Full-Time Workers										
All races										
Number with income	94 583	8 606	28 453	16 597	9 398	31 528	20 399	7 711	1 873	1 543
Median income ($)	39 781	22 301	31 756	37 815	40 423	56 955	51 557	62 830	[2]100 000	83 633
Standard error	162	118	93	297	226	232	185	708	17 226	1 805
Mean income ($)	51 711	27 098	37 770	44 983	46 405	76 135	65 769	82 883	132 876	110 563
Standard error	223	390	257	349	385	545	522	1 322	3 305	3 371
White alone or in combination										
Number with income	78 432	7 122	23 336	13 785	7 919	26 268	16 879	6 518	1 583	1 286
Median income ($)	40 789	22 449	32 836	39 649	41 376	58 784	52 693	63 002	[2]100 000	85 957
Standard error	84	178	254	326	249	535	439	798	24 184	2 070
Mean income ($)	53 406	27 161	39 320	46 648	47 514	78 358	68 142	83 818	135 370	114 567
Standard error	254	359	304	407	423	619	597	1 482	3 626	3 919
Black alone or in combination										
Number with income	10 970	1 038	4 057	2 233	1 068	2 573	1 819	567	107	78
Median income ($)	31 316	21 505	26 669	31 778	32 460	46 228	41 672	52 376	75 691	75 684
Standard error	148	321	207	234	1 067	676	345	1 563	3 892	6 991
Mean income ($)	38 031	27 462	29 693	36 037	37 843	57 253	50 195	65 760	108 647	88 787
Standard error	408	2 190	327	497	810	1 179	1 059	2 125	14 797	11 278
Asian alone or in combination										
Number with income	4 664	327	886	477	346	2 625	1 642	630	173	178
Median income ($)	42 123	22 393	28 158	34 311	36 816	56 434	50 017	72 595	95 752	80 214
Standard error	403	1 021	1 267	1 439	1 674	998	893	2 071	9 239	2 582
Mean income ($)	57 264	25 599	35 530	40 533	49 004	72 696	59 115	88 139	127 523	89 713
Standard error	1 200	1 212	1 345	2 343	3 453	1 900	1 803	5 101	10 647	5 292
Hispanic[1]										
Number with income	12 019	4 147	3 579	1 827	746	1 718	1 223	354	79	61
Median income ($)	27 278	20 751	26 930	35 098	35 262	47 383	43 031	56 006	80 295	(B)
Standard error	181	170	274	802	928	1 205	1 494	2 402	18 399	(B)
Mean income ($)	34 967	23 832	31 812	39 497	39 269	61 718	53 782	65 226	116 434	(B)
Standard error	427	471	612	720	969	2 087	1 923	3 405	13 936	(B)

[1]May be of any race.
[2]Median income over $100,000.
(B) = Base is too small to show the derived measure.

Table A-23. Income in 2004 by Educational Attainment for the Population Age 18 Years and Over, by Sex, Age, Race, and Hispanic Origin—*Continued*

(Numbers in thousands, dollars.)

Characteristic	Total population	High school — Not a high school graduate	High school graduate, includes GED	Some college, no degree	Associate's degree	College — Bachelor's degree or more — Total	Bachelor's degree	Master's degree	Professional degree	Doctorate degree
BOTH SEXES, 25 TO 64 YEARS										
All Workers										
All races										
Number with income	143 180	15 819	43 889	25 474	13 858	44 137	28 999	10 855	2 380	1 901
Median income ($)	30 447	15 884	25 109	29 701	32 273	47 250	41 943	52 188	80 665	76 424
Standard error	66	119	105	261	183	195	163	241	1 434	1 054
Mean income ($)	40 305	19 376	29 642	35 168	37 724	62 185	53 446	68 471	111 926	97 301
Standard error	161	203	190	275	300	420	407	988	2 870	2 850
White alone or in combination										
Number with income	118 737	12 774	35 958	21 126	11 795	37 082	24 241	9 226	2 027	1 585
Median income ($)	31 148	16 247	25 872	30 348	33 141	48 176	42 798	52 279	81 684	76 936
Standard error	75	129	123	162	397	315	382	315	1 267	1 380
Mean income ($)	41 583	19 865	30 773	36 195	38 379	63 636	54 938	69 221	113 235	100 667
Standard error	183	227	224	309	327	472	459	1 100	3 149	3 304
Black alone or in combination										
Number with income	16 903	2 253	6 363	3 440	1 497	3 346	2 385	745	116	98
Median income ($)	25 057	12 902	21 154	26 718	27 973	41 339	37 826	50 596	73 943	74 989
Standard error	219	475	229	404	782	348	802	677	3 483	8 013
Mean income ($)	30 062	16 838	23 784	29 854	31 801	50 339	43 959	58 320	104 822	79 727
Standard error	297	596	269	703	713	976	899	1 795	13 772	9 388
Asian alone or in combination										
Number with income	6 657	551	1 252	742	472	3 637	2 315	874	234	213
Median income ($)	32 325	16 600	23 603	26 514	32 212	46 002	40 098	56 962	63 704	75 208
Standard error	495	642	1 253	739	1 454	838	1 055	3 974	10 638	4 540
Mean income ($)	45 112	19 509	28 769	30 844	41 501	58 007	47 243	68 979	102 997	80 392
Standard error	895	914	1 038	1 228	2 751	1 480	1 392	3 952	8 720	4 915
Hispanic[1]										
Number with income	17 583	6 500	5 055	2 661	1 072	2 304	1 647	468	113	75
Median income ($)	21 767	16 506	21 984	27 914	29 829	39 669	36 524	50 411	44 707	52 004
Standard error	138	147	247	727	846	1 076	637	1 812	6 637	7 924
Mean income ($)	28 682	19 240	26 845	32 877	33 174	52 425	45 986	57 235	89 982	106 598
Standard error	306	329	628	931	848	1 796	1 783	3 245	10 837	26 532
Year-Round, Full-Time Workers										
All races										
Number with income	92 071	8 236	27 637	16 192	9 242	30 762	20 008	7 517	1 771	1 465
Median income ($)	39 608	22 167	31 695	37 513	40 385	56 706	51 465	62 568	[2]100 000	82 888
Standard error	164	120	94	242	228	231	186	647	17 170	1 775
Mean income ($)	51 319	26 478	37 467	44 460	46 166	75 574	65 484	82 706	130 837	109 940
Standard error	222	339	250	329	375	548	526	1 336	3 361	3 443
White alone or in combination										
Number with income	76 270	6 841	22 614	13 412	7 785	25 616	16 559	6 344	1 498	1 213
Median income ($)	40 703	22 304	32 702	39 351	41 325	58 171	52 459	62 631	[2]100 000	85 413
Standard error	84	135	243	331	250	543	348	716	24 810	2 336
Mean income ($)	52 984	26 811	38 985	46 075	47 228	77 699	67 799	83 579	132 972	113 781
Standard error	253	369	296	384	409	622	602	1 498	3 668	4 021
Black alone or in combination										
Number with income	10 725	974	3 984	2 203	1 048	2 514	1 782	556	98	76
Median income ($)	31 270	21 353	26 622	31 738	32 468	46 218	41 590	52 380	75 533	76 007
Standard error	149	323	209	235	1 174	682	352	1 571	3 488	6 825
Mean income ($)	37 727	24 779	29 616	35 917	37 836	57 140	50 055	65 681	111 689	89 831
Standard error	374	1 240	331	488	816	1 199	1 074	2 139	16 073	11 501
Asian alone or in combination										
Number with income	4 572	307	871	475	345	2 570	1 612	617	166	174
Median income ($)	42 092	22 741	28 301	34 260	36 807	56 334	50 018	72 675	86 770	80 450
Standard error	386	1 214	1 319	1 446	1 626	992	902	2 053	9 952	2 497
Mean income ($)	57 114	25 393	35 524	39 432	48 971	72 604	59 187	88 394	125 263	90 518
Standard error	1 204	1 215	1 356	1 565	3 462	1 930	1 829	5 200	11 028	5 387
Hispanic[1]										
Number with income	11 828	4 064	3 525	1 811	737	1 688	1 205	348	75	59
Median income ($)	27 231	20 723	26 842	34 922	35 348	47 175	42 509	55 767	80 896	(B)
Standard error	181	172	275	873	877	1 123	1 379	2 342	14 752	(B)
Mean income ($)	34 866	23 771	31 657	39 408	39 478	61 382	53 391	64 800	119 630	(B)
Standard error	431	479	617	726	972	2 110	1 926	3 442	14 518	(B)

[1]May be of any race.
[2]Median income over $100,000.
(B) = Base is too small to show the derived measure.

Table A-23. Income in 2004 by Educational Attainment for the Population Age 18 Years and Over, by Sex, Age, Race, and Hispanic Origin—*Continued*

(Numbers in thousands, dollars.)

Characteristic	Total population	High school — Not a high school graduate	High school graduate, includes GED	Some college, no degree	Associate's degree	College — Bachelor's degree or more — Total	Bachelor's degree	Master's degree	Professional degree	Doctorate degree
BOTH SEXES, 25 TO 34 YEARS										
All Workers										
All races										
Number with income	35 761	4 219	10 048	6 808	3 318	11 367	8 382	2 251	489	244
Median income ($)	26 676	16 109	22 193	25 729	28 867	38 883	36 673	41 897	51 583	51 899
Standard error	116	188	166	237	592	434	230	336	1 685	2 580
Mean income ($)	32 041	18 198	25 835	28 784	31 828	44 679	41 980	46 726	73 252	61 142
Standard error	207	415	367	355	499	447	466	867	4 788	3 190
White alone or in combination										
Number with income	28 792	3 535	7 968	5 420	2 727	9 139	6 782	1 771	384	200
Median income ($)	27 183	16 356	23 214	26 034	30 064	39 363	36 948	41 946	51 788	52 297
Standard error	133	196	357	276	462	461	249	342	2 627	3 193
Mean income ($)	32 755	18 719	27 079	29 596	32 592	45 057	42 431	46 831	75 219	60 344
Standard error	242	481	451	422	566	515	541	930	5 828	3 089
Black alone or in combination										
Number with income	4 746	507	1 694	1 124	449	970	764	160	34	10
Median income ($)	22 414	12 453	19 706	23 821	25 684	35 607	32 450	42 784	(B)	(B)
Standard error	385	1 332	490	1 241	744	764	1 002	1 668	(B)	(B)
Mean income ($)	25 825	14 956	20 685	25 053	28 003	40 373	36 703	49 980	(B)	(B)
Standard error	371	744	413	581	1 237	1 172	1 036	4 312	(B)	(B)
Asian alone or in combination										
Number with income	2 043	108	297	229	128	1 279	850	321	73	34
Median income ($)	30 817	14 608	22 337	26 325	26 530	39 071	37 259	40 066	(B)	(B)
Standard error	553	1 709	1 246	815	1 501	1 594	1 583	4 734	(B)	(B)
Mean income ($)	37 607	16 860	23 917	28 671	30 971	44 811	42 710	44 547	(B)	(B)
Standard error	925	1 543	1 153	1 996	2 228	1 323	1 371	2 724	(B)	(B)
Hispanic[1]										
Number with income	6 470	2 297	1 963	1 016	418	774	611	114	33	14
Median income ($)	20 968	16 374	20 791	26 376	27 160	35 439	34 582	39 728	(B)	(B)
Standard error	188	208	326	727	1 205	897	1 172	3 406	(B)	(B)
Mean income ($)	25 617	18 378	25 452	29 673	29 750	39 965	39 203	41 164	(B)	(B)
Standard error	542	731	1 195	867	1 112	2 070	2 493	3 319	(B)	(B)
Year-Round, Full-Time Workers										
All races										
Number with income	23 376	2 430	6 493	4 262	2 218	7 971	5 911	1 535	334	190
Median income ($)	33 712	20 939	27 683	32 303	34 657	45 242	42 177	49 718	70 596	59 650
Standard error	291	188	309	228	739	343	217	629	4 117	2 506
Mean income ($)	40 102	23 879	31 889	37 297	38 647	53 644	50 598	57 393	81 117	69 744
Standard error	254	666	431	482	616	493	548	1 079	3 303	3 713
White alone or in combination										
Number with income	19 011	2 104	5 210	3 426	1 809	6 459	4 813	1 229	260	156
Median income ($)	35 040	21 041	29 388	34 008	35 688	45 230	42 374	49 137	71 763	59 778
Standard error	208	209	414	677	372	384	360	846	2 925	3 471
Mean income ($)	40 751	24 193	33 293	38 466	39 666	53 681	50 999	56 304	81 874	68 575
Standard error	292	755	524	574	712	557	638	1 147	3 620	3 505
Black alone or in combination										
Number with income	2 925	224	1 035	671	305	688	534	119	26	8
Median income ($)	29 062	20 453	25 140	30 513	30 374	40 287	37 266	47 406	(B)	(B)
Standard error	504	449	505	332	715	744	1 320	2 184	(B)	(B)
Mean income ($)	32 335	21 528	25 546	31 498	33 756	46 264	42 195	58 189	(B)	(B)
Standard error	472	1 311	476	667	1 389	1 375	1 106	5 377	(B)	(B)
Asian alone or in combination										
Number with income	1 333	59	214	142	91	825	564	187	46	26
Median income ($)	40 552	(B)	26 815	31 655	32 499	50 894	49 129	52 284	(B)	(B)
Standard error	678	(B)	951	1 776	3 249	617	1 724	3 500	(B)	(B)
Mean income ($)	48 682	(B)	29 156	36 868	37 388	58 895	54 534	63 694	(B)	(B)
Standard error	1 172	(B)	1 285	2 623	2 368	1 636	1 580	3 518	(B)	(B)
Hispanic[1]										
Number with income	4 416	1 492	1 388	692	298	544	433	81	18	11
Median income ($)	25 248	19 760	24 863	32 388	31 597	40 584	39 078	50 881	(B)	(B)
Standard error	295	492	672	1 161	1 148	968	1 338	1 625	(B)	(B)
Mean income ($)	30 402	22 287	28 308	36 561	34 295	48 003	46 859	51 083	(B)	(B)
Standard error	589	1 087	630	1 068	1 092	2 776	3 353	3 800	(B)	(B)

[1]May be of any race.
(B) = Base is too small to show the derived measure.

Table A-23. Income in 2004 by Educational Attainment for the Population Age 18 Years and Over, by Sex, Age, Race, and Hispanic Origin—*Continued*

(Numbers in thousands, dollars.)

Characteristic	Total population	High school		College							
		Not a high school graduate	High school graduate, includes GED	Some college, no degree	Associate's degree	Bachelor's degree or more					
						Total	Bachelor's degree	Master's degree	Professional degree	Doctorate degree
BOTH SEXES, 35 TO 44 YEARS											
All Workers											
All races											
Number with income	40 348	4 220	12 579	6 916	4 134	12 498	8 384	2 893	721	498
Median income ($)	31 628	17 338	26 088	31 046	33 971	50 372	45 531	55 736	86 692	72 262
Standard error	124	258	192	263	696	302	455	942	3 589	3 764
Mean income ($)	42 547	21 026	30 929	37 155	38 653	65 780	57 900	72 679	112 451	90 732
Standard error	329	332	382	575	562	865	842	2 341	4 843	4 812
White alone or in combination											
Number with income	33 033	3 443	10 175	5 648	3 497	10 268	6 930	2 341	610	385
Median income ($)	32 199	17 617	26 940	31 651	34 388	50 868	46 354	55 366	88 163	71 536
Standard error	141	365	225	324	714	336	518	1 175	3 798	3 789
Mean income ($)	43 653	21 596	32 287	38 431	38 885	66 811	59 200	73 006	112 917	93 014
Standard error	374	384	459	684	622	968	930	2 673	5 333	5 785
Black alone or in combination											
Number with income	4 950	574	1 938	972	440	1 024	744	221	27	30
Median income ($)	26 487	15 258	21 700	29 097	31 157	41 553	39 894	46 975	(B)	(B)
Standard error	326	883	393	1 193	855	613	932	2 710	(B)	(B)
Mean income ($)	31 654	17 631	24 318	31 629	35 970	51 567	47 472	55 726	(B)	(B)
Standard error	509	685	478	867	1 372	1 788	1 949	2 812	(B)	(B)
Asian alone or in combination											
Number with income	2 076	146	353	241	150	1 185	692	324	83	85
Median income ($)	37 414	20 491	25 730	25 096	34 960	52 634	45 850	66 880	86 664	76 607
Standard error	1 368	2 157	1 441	1 663	1 695	1 909	1 818	3 507	16 995	9 700
Mean income ($)	52 810	21 759	29 546	29 703	44 311	69 351	56 625	82 189	114 366	79 587
Standard error	2 114	1 393	1 797	1 833	5 249	3 466	3 901	8 248	14 974	7 238
Hispanic[1]											
Number with income	5 385	1 929	1 548	809	354	744	531	157	36	19
Median income ($)	23 164	17 496	23 883	28 816	30 582	37 697	35 014	50 668	(B)	(B)
Standard error	466	434	907	1 246	1 063	1 839	1 969	4 819	(B)	(B)
Mean income ($)	30 378	21 046	28 340	33 726	35 635	52 657	44 867	63 504	(B)	(B)
Standard error	605	509	1 109	1 190	1 510	2 907	2 746	6 874	(B)	(B)
Year-Round, Full-Time Workers											
All races											
Number with income	27 755	2 530	8 610	4 704	2 873	9 035	6 005	2 081	551	397
Median income ($)	40 570	22 390	32 216	39 117	41 164	61 177	55 634	68 169	[2]100 000	80 542
Standard error	138	274	170	586	343	396	455	1 401	36 913	2 428
Mean income ($)	53 000	26 801	38 102	45 790	46 693	80 295	71 104	89 258	131 413	101 352
Standard error	437	438	489	695	690	1 109	1 063	3 117	5 658	5 660
White alone or in combination											
Number with income	22 584	2 108	6 972	3 804	2 381	7 317	4 896	1 655	456	310
Median income ($)	41 419	22 427	33 831	40 614	41 904	62 278	57 153	67 655	[2]100 000	80 145
Standard error	154	332	481	310	372	701	673	1 351	43 422	3 062
Mean income ($)	54 539	27 143	39 820	47 795	47 628	82 209	73 326	90 342	133 911	102 925
Standard error	498	500	588	838	775	1 252	1 175	3 622	6 276	6 783
Black alone or in combination											
Number with income	3 518	294	1 331	713	350	828	601	178	24	24
Median income ($)	32 024	21 292	26 858	32 489	34 126	46 545	42 437	51 255	(B)	(B)
Standard error	293	643	410	1 025	1 801	1 136	1 964	2 885	(B)	(B)
Mean income ($)	38 243	24 265	29 507	36 761	39 330	58 059	53 921	62 144	(B)	(B)
Standard error	629	980	554	838	1 450	2 077	2 265	3 114	(B)	(B)
Asian alone or in combination											
Number with income	1 477	106	239	149	113	869	494	243	64	67
Median income ($)	49 206	25 371	31 968	33 468	40 857	65 264	54 962	78 692	(B)	(B)
Standard error	1 718	1 606	2 252	2 426	4 016	1 895	1 868	2 457	(B)	(B)
Mean income ($)	66 457	26 328	37 333	39 205	53 422	85 773	70 625	102 010	(B)	(B)
Standard error	2 820	1 464	2 324	2 125	6 610	4 483	5 201	10 459	(B)	(B)
Hispanic[1]											
Number with income	3 835	1 302	1 143	576	246	566	410	116	25	14
Median income ($)	28 206	21 384	27 459	34 733	35 887	45 844	40 835	60 649	(B)	(B)
Standard error	629	293	760	1 774	1 391	1 670	2 083	4 668	(B)	(B)
Mean income ($)	36 464	25 219	33 476	40 148	42 713	61 864	51 986	75 756	(B)	(B)
Standard error	795	671	1 436	1 439	1 785	3 601	3 349	8 524	(B)	(B)

[1]May be of any race.
[2]Median income over $100,000.
(B) = Base is too small to show the derived measure.

Table A-23. Income in 2004 by Educational Attainment for the Population Age 18 Years and Over, by Sex, Age, Race, and Hispanic Origin—*Continued*

(Numbers in thousands, dollars.)

Characteristic	Total population	High school		College						
		Not a high school graduate	High school graduate, includes GED	Some college, no degree	Associate's degree	Bachelor's degree or more				
						Total	Bachelor's degree	Master's degree	Professional degree	Doctorate degree
BOTH SEXES, 45 TO 54 YEARS										
All Workers										
All races										
Number with income	39 391	3 893	12 398	7 008	4 012	12 078	7 581	3 230	694	572
Median income ($)	32 867	15 803	27 098	32 243	35 699	53 470	48 293	60 425	95 739	83 189
Standard error	309	266	210	250	373	730	723	1 003	8 703	3 513
Mean income ($)	45 116	20 019	32 279	38 767	40 867	71 477	59 733	79 381	131 314	109 846
Standard error	341	453	381	512	586	907	850	2 090	5 928	5 593
White alone or in combination										
Number with income	33 033	3 069	10 189	5 880	3 499	10 395	6 445	2 844	614	491
Median income ($)	34 890	16 364	28 509	33 527	36 182	55 146	50 105	60 065	99 765	86 512
Standard error	276	293	407	426	546	577	1 412	22 469	4 191
Mean income ($)	46 833	20 673	33 466	39 973	41 485	73 337	61 706	79 629	133 598	114 128
Standard error	387	544	444	585	604	1 007	946	2 279	6 443	6 383
Black alone or in combination										
Number with income	4 519	595	1 737	899	363	924	623	234	37	30
Median income ($)	26 540	12 064	23 127	28 939	30 448	50 439	42 980	59 322	(B)	(B)
Standard error	405	456	672	1 288	2 205	1 171	1 912	5 156	(B)	(B)
Mean income ($)	32 698	16 840	25 813	31 749	31 782	57 137	48 542	65 441	(B)	(B)
Standard error	557	783	548	922	1 341	1 923	1 796	3 478	(B)	(B)
Asian alone or in combination										
Number with income	1 559	171	377	180	121	709	472	147	42	46
Median income ($)	32 607	16 784	23 815	29 771	32 406	48 602	39 273	73 086	(B)	(B)
Standard error	1 477	1 352	1 620	3 222	2 591	1 701	2 068	6 452	(B)	(B)
Mean income ($)	46 160	20 265	32 229	34 366	48 979	62 345	46 222	94 082	(B)	(B)
Standard error	1 868	2 013	2 594	3 266	7 517	3 355	2 179	12 102	(B)	(B)
Hispanic[1]										
Number with income	3 689	1 430	1 014	512	180	551	357	135	28	29
Median income ($)	22 969	16 770	23 857	30 957	29 617	50 171	41 977	56 248	(B)	(B)
Standard error	613	322	1 003	880	2 205	2 451	2 449	3 614	(B)	(B)
Mean income ($)	31 943	19 498	28 442	33 994	34 613	67 901	56 702	66 917	(B)	(B)
Standard error	925	491	1 140	1 319	2 592	5 063	5 443	6 654	(B)	(B)
Year-Round, Full-Time Workers										
All races										
Number with income	26 925	2 063	8 422	4 764	2 804	8 870	5 425	2 457	552	435
Median income ($)	41 983	23 373	33 319	40 911	43 171	63 284	57 154	68 426	[2]100 000	92 036
Standard error	155	504	440	299	1 174	701	614	1 275	39 142	3 099
Mean income ($)	56 016	27 822	39 776	47 825	49 523	84 447	71 842	91 529	146 644	122 613
Standard error	451	758	482	650	707	1 130	1 058	2 583	6 840	6 631
White alone or in combination										
Number with income	22 578	1 657	6 923	4 013	2 445	7 538	4 529	2 150	490	367
Median income ($)	44 218	24 327	35 332	41 802	45 486	65 796	60 663	69 037	[2]100 000	93 871
Standard error	441	592	256	321	745	539	490	1 201	40 041	7 871
Mean income ($)	58 241	28 679	41 326	49 347	50 183	87 624	75 441	92 234	149 530	128 216
Standard error	515	906	563	743	712	1 279	1 227	2 828	7 394	7 672
Black alone or in combination										
Number with income	3 020	274	1 162	600	244	737	500	179	32	25
Median income ($)	32 169	21 116	27 799	32 689	37 095	51 858	48 344	62 220	(B)	(B)
Standard error	283	913	595	1 323	1 002	585	2 322	3 384	(B)	(B)
Mean income ($)	40 404	23 756	31 337	38 559	38 951	62 874	53 368	72 026	(B)	(B)
Standard error	717	1 209	621	1 051	1 561	2 243	2 031	4 050	(B)	(B)
Asian alone or in combination										
Number with income	1 153	100	276	121	92	563	363	127	31	40
Median income ($)	41 045	21 785	26 894	39 439	37 032	52 203	46 320	77 338	(B)	(B)
Standard error	809	759	1 061	2 613	4 489	2 485	1 951	3 793	(B)	(B)
Mean income ($)	55 845	26 394	38 760	44 087	58 335	71 628	54 560	104 351	(B)	(B)
Standard error	2 364	3 066	3 363	4 220	9 454	3 969	2 463	13 616	(B)	(B)
Hispanic[1]										
Number with income	2 512	886	703	367	118	436	267	121	21	26
Median income ($)	30 255	21 587	30 217	36 098	35 241	55 747	51 116	57 099	(B)	(B)
Standard error	456	512	886	1 181	2 384	2 211	2 159	3 532	(B)	(B)
Mean income ($)	38 942	24 389	34 778	40 877	42 198	72 652	61 271	63 018	(B)	(B)
Standard error	1 082	622	1 494	1 504	3 179	4 880	4 026	4 320	(B)	(B)

[1]May be of any race.
[2]Median income over $100,000.
(B) = Base is too small to show the derived measure.

Table A-23. Income in 2004 by Educational Attainment for the Population Age 18 Years and Over, by Sex, Age, Race, and Hispanic Origin—*Continued*

(Numbers in thousands, dollars.)

Characteristic	Total population	Not a high school graduate	High school graduate, includes GED	Some college, no degree	Associate's degree	Total	Bachelor's degree	Master's degree	Professional degree	Doctorate degree
BOTH SEXES, 55 TO 64 YEARS										
All Workers										
All races										
Number with income	27 677	3 486	8 863	4 741	2 394	8 192	4 650	2 480	475	586
Median income ($)	28 543	13 664	22 890	28 309	32 010	50 805	42 489	55 182	82 778	80 576
Standard error	300	276	352	627	535	371	834	1 113	5 367	1 818
Mean income ($)	40 868	18 085	28 442	36 113	39 024	67 296	55 835	69 091	122 646	105 702
Standard error	390	423	361	788	772	1 061	1 195	1 713	6 900	5 949
White alone or in combination										
Number with income	23 878	2 726	7 624	4 177	2 071	7 278	4 081	2 269	418	508
Median income ($)	29 849	14 026	23 572	29 000	32 784	51 337	45 097	54 649	82 471	81 376
Standard error	288	307	368	746	970	385	896	1 148	4 968	3 387
Mean income ($)	42 101	18 255	29 014	36 418	39 898	68 632	57 798	69 753	118 725	109 392
Standard error	428	364	403	771	850	1 153	1 337	1 846	6 948	6 722
Black alone or in combination										
Number with income	2 686	576	993	444	243	428	252	129	18	27
Median income ($)	21 733	12 472	18 919	26 087	25 869	44 485	36 556	59 002	(B)	(B)
Standard error	497	636	996	1 395	1 640	2 244	2 926	3 692	(B)	(B)
Mean income ($)	30 181	17 704	24 481	34 289	31 304	55 301	44 262	60 237	(B)	(B)
Standard error	1 137	1 967	814	4 486	1 870	3 797	2 869	3 669	(B)	(B)
Asian alone or in combination										
Number with income	978	125	225	91	72	462	299	81	35	46
Median income ($)	29 748	13 223	22 001	26 119	(B)	40 917	33 331	70 521	(B)	(B)
Standard error	1 673	1 590	2 708	3 519	(B)	3 954	2 290	5 343	(B)	(B)
Mean income ($)	42 776	18 144	28 153	32 369	(B)	58 790	40 060	67 343	(B)	(B)
Standard error	2 002	2 003	1 974	2 991	(B)	3 749	2 445	7 292	(B)	(B)
Hispanic[1]										
Number with income	2 038	842	529	312	119	234	147	60	14	12
Median income ($)	19 614	13 674	21 455	26 903	35 651	49 286	50 507	(B)	(B)	(B)
Standard error	667	668	1 303	1 647	2 313	2 710	4 859	(B)	(B)	(B)
Mean income ($)	28 027	17 018	24 577	39 258	35 687	56 433	52 200	(B)	(B)	(B)
Standard error	1 275	623	982	6 311	2 564	5 598	3 663	(B)	(B)	(B)
Year-Round, Full-Time Workers										
All races										
Number with income	14 014	1 211	4 110	2 461	1 346	4 885	2 666	1 443	334	441
Median income ($)	42 406	24 664	34 491	40 558	43 596	63 283	56 313	66 449	[2]100 000	95 581
Standard error	300	663	631	465	1 479	941	889	1 614	46 554	3 051
Mean income ($)	57 678	28 728	40 220	47 809	50 438	86 508	72 888	85 161	153 472	122 534
Standard error	647	1 005	571	759	1 063	1 606	1 854	2 608	8 894	7 497
White alone or in combination										
Number with income	12 095	971	3 507	2 167	1 149	4 300	2 320	1 309	291	379
Median income ($)	44 315	24 993	35 406	41 307	45 796	64 827	59 937	66 244	[2]100 000	97 015
Standard error	523	725	352	474	1 013	1 010	1 540	1 825	49 578	7 643
Mean income ($)	59 496	28 576	41 160	49 030	52 022	88 703	76 062	86 419	149 346	127 327
Standard error	719	693	640	832	1 193	1 762	2 093	2 852	8 994	8 547
Black alone or in combination										
Number with income	1 261	180	455	218	148	259	146	78	15	18
Median income ($)	32 201	24 133	29 299	32 755	35 316	52 243	41 495	61 317	(B)	(B)
Standard error	943	1 479	1 755	2 066	2 471	2 286	1 751	2 574	(B)	(B)
Mean income ($)	42 377	31 228	34 790	39 479	40 872	66 756	51 524	70 669	(B)	(B)
Standard error	1 671	5 983	1 358	1 888	2 507	5 847	4 088	4 742	(B)	(B)
Asian alone or in combination										
Number with income	606	41	142	61	48	312	190	58	23	39
Median income ($)	40 106	(B)	30 161	(B)	(B)	57 289	41 945	(B)	(B)	(B)
Standard error	2 153	(B)	2 490	(B)	(B)	3 979	4 023	(B)	(B)	(B)
Mean income ($)	55 299	(B)	35 787	(B)	(B)	73 948	52 121	(B)	(B)	(B)
Standard error	2 720	(B)	2 557	(B)	(B)	4 726	3 169	(B)	(B)	(B)
Hispanic[1]										
Number with income	1 064	384	289	176	74	140	94	28	9	7
Median income ($)	30 808	20 766	30 529	40 341	41 237	62 153	62 167	(B)	(B)	(B)
Standard error	621	731	1 243	2 521	975	2 706	2 282	(B)	(B)	(B)
Mean income ($)	38 007	23 203	32 942	45 112	45 255	76 303	67 148	(B)	(B)	(B)
Standard error	1 432	780	1 275	2 357	3 106	8 536	4 162	(B)	(B)	(B)

[1]May be of any race.
[2]Median income over $100,000.
(B) = Base is too small to show the derived measure.

Table A-23. Income in 2004 by Educational Attainment for the Population Age 18 Years and Over, by Sex, Age, Race, and Hispanic Origin—*Continued*

(Numbers in thousands, dollars.)

Characteristic	Total population	High school		Some college, no degree	Associate's degree	College				
		Not a high school graduate	High school graduate, includes GED			Bachelor's degree or more				
						Total	Bachelor's degree	Master's degree	Professional degree	Doctorate degree
BOTH SEXES, 65 YEARS AND OVER										
All Workers										
All races										
Number with income	34 184	8 679	12 469	4 721	1 784	6 529	3 969	1 667	486	404
Median income ($)	15 200	10 934	14 495	18 041	17 419	28 833	25 240	31 816	35 103	49 925
Standard error	98	92	109	292	420	476	545	972	1 517	2 835
Mean income ($)	23 966	14 089	19 626	27 146	25 317	42 715	35 590	45 582	68 668	69 563
Standard error	222	250	251	764	826	747	654	1 689	4 683	4 193
White alone or in combination										
Number with income	30 228	6 994	11 387	4 324	1 596	5 925	3 603	1 510	436	375
Median income ($)	15 753	11 331	14 721	18 300	17 644	29 077	25 351	32 628	34 814	51 099
Standard error	102	101	115	308	470	500	581	1 133	1 721	3 222
Mean income ($)	24 564	14 269	19 877	27 525	25 908	43 199	35 999	46 286	69 000	69 922
Standard error	238	159	270	822	905	802	698	1 828	5 106	4 410
Black alone or in combination										
Number with income	2 832	1 292	789	296	135	318	185	95	28	8
Median income ($)	11 590	9 531	12 285	14 577	17 238	27 695	25 854	27 102	(B)	(B)
Standard error	203	190	421	1 327	1 400	1 836	2 935	2 702	(B)	(B)
Mean income ($)	18 451	13 949	16 274	21 965	21 984	37 353	31 502	41 434	(B)	(B)
Standard error	804	1 535	574	1 686	2 042	2 233	2 185	4 977	(B)	(B)
Asian alone or in combination										
Number with income	980	312	252	87	48	279	175	64	18	22
Median income ($)	12 094	8 460	12 699	13 844	(B)	25 085	19 774	(B)	(B)	(B)
Standard error	486	449	639	1 961	(B)	3 775	3 559	(B)	(B)	(B)
Mean income ($)	23 394	11 015	19 224	31 091	(B)	39 939	31 385	(B)	(B)	(B)
Standard error	1 499	731	1 735	10 608	(B)	3 300	3 043	(B)	(B)	(B)
Hispanic[1]										
Number with income	1 980	1 154	424	142	74	183	100	46	21	15
Median income ($)	10 407	9 225	11 557	14 135	13 241	22 255	18 779	(B)	(B)	(B)
Standard error	259	189	550	1 314	3 456	3 030	3 463	(B)	(B)	(B)
Mean income ($)	15 910	11 540	17 405	20 193	18 884	35 386	31 100	(B)	(B)	(B)
Standard error	498	312	1 037	1 597	1 949	3 609	4 967	(B)	(B)	(B)
Year-Round, Full-Time Workers										
All races										
Number with income	2 511	370	815	404	155	765	391	194	101	78
Median income ($)	44 706	30 309	35 486	47 267	44 497	72 883	64 126	73 040	[2]100 000	88 222
Standard error	938	1 773	1 298	1 994	2 905	1 383	4 326	4 064	64 519	6 681
Mean income ($)	66 086	40 901	48 019	65 926	60 623	98 714	80 323	89 756	168 299	122 229
Standard error	2 080	4 941	2 920	5 486	6 611	4 261	3 893	9 108	16 184	16 263
White alone or in combination										
Number with income	2 161	281	721	373	133	651	320	173	85	72
Median income ($)	46 266	32 510	36 514	48 056	46 785	74 928	70 470	73 621	[2]100 000	(B)
Standard error	824	2 576	1 344	2 040	4 210	1 643	2 769	3 749	61 605	(B)
Mean income ($)	68 287	35 687	49 812	67 221	64 138	104 270	85 845	92 564	177 617	(B)
Standard error	2 241	1 383	3 279	5 884	7 579	4 883	4 569	10 081	18 812	(B)
Black alone or in combination										
Number with income	245	64	73	29	19	59	37	10	9	1
Median income ($)	34 095	(B)	(B)	(B)	(B)	(B)	(B)	(B)	(B)	(B)
Standard error	1 732	(B)	(B)	(B)	(B)	(B)	(B)	(B)	(B)	(B)
Mean income ($)	51 342	(B)	(B)	(B)	(B)	(B)	(B)	(B)	(B)	(B)
Standard error	8 019	(B)	(B)	(B)	(B)	(B)	(B)	(B)	(B)	(B)
Asian alone or in combination										
Number with income	92	19	15	1	1	54	29	13	7	4
Median income ($)	44 645	(B)	(B)	(B)	(B)	(B)	(B)	(B)	(B)	(B)
Standard error	4 692	(B)	(B)	(B)	(B)	(B)	(B)	(B)	(B)	(B)
Mean income ($)	64 738	(B)	(B)	(B)	(B)	(B)	(B)	(B)	(B)	(B)
Standard error	11 065	(B)	(B)	(B)	(B)	(B)	(B)	(B)	(B)	(B)
Hispanic[1]										
Number with income	190	82	54	15	8	30	17	5	4	2
Median income ($)	32 187	22 259	(B)	(B)	(B)	(B)	(B)	(B)	(B)	(B)
Standard error	1 776	1 558	(B)	(B)	(B)	(B)	(B)	(B)	(B)	(B)
Mean income ($)	41 194	26 836	(B)	(B)	(B)	(B)	(B)	(B)	(B)	(B)
Standard error	3 108	1 989	(B)	(B)	(B)	(B)	(B)	(B)	(B)	(B)

[1]May be of any race.
[2]Median income over $100,000.
(B) = Base is too small to show the derived measure.

Table A-23. Income in 2004 by Educational Attainment for the Population Age 18 Years and Over, by Sex, Age, Race, and Hispanic Origin—*Continued*

(Numbers in thousands, dollars.)

Characteristic	Total population	High school — Not a high school graduate	High school graduate, includes GED	Some college, no degree	Associate's degree	Bachelor's degree or more — Total	Bachelor's degree	Master's degree	Professional degree	Doctorate degree
MALE, 18 YEARS AND OVER										
All Workers										
All races										
Number with income	99 136	15 095	31 702	18 330	7 312	26 695	17 159	6 077	1 881	1 577
Median income ($)	31 145	16 370	26 703	29 817	37 149	55 133	49 772	63 052	89 945	79 993
Standard error	86	121	135	317	290	387	431	998	3 321	1 496
Mean income ($)	43 868	20 525	32 728	37 369	44 049	74 710	63 510	82 873	126 105	103 793
Standard error	219	272	254	383	486	626	596	1 562	3 575	3 387
White alone or in combination										
Number with income	84 162	12 651	26 640	15 585	6 323	22 960	14 775	5 196	1 637	1 351
Median income ($)	31 938	16 789	27 634	30 558	38 718	56 214	50 760	63 434	90 977	80 392
Standard error	96	129	230	231	733	346	289	1 088	3 930	1 721
Mean income ($)	45 299	20 893	33 970	38 594	45 221	76 465	65 276	84 497	126 822	106 905
Standard error	244	273	294	424	526	692	650	1 762	3 858	3 858
Black alone or in combination										
Number with income	10 069	1 862	3 961	2 042	683	1 519	1 072	314	74	58
Median income ($)	23 700	12 641	21 837	26 295	30 493	44 533	40 178	57 163	75 410	(B)
Standard error	454	283	292	664	1 003	1 531	1 126	3 801	10 099	(B)
Mean income ($)	30 486	18 697	25 288	30 432	34 645	56 681	47 915	69 552	118 573	(B)
Standard error	475	1 252	378	1 122	1 109	1 785	1 507	3 620	21 125	(B)
Asian alone or in combination										
Number with income	4 278	382	890	598	265	2 141	1 256	558	163	161
Median income ($)	33 357	15 018	24 965	23 274	30 841	51 595	43 567	65 265	95 559	81 073
Standard error	982	974	1 179	1 444	1 573	586	1 924	4 476	11 558	2 821
Mean income ($)	49 068	18 812	30 090	30 335	43 403	68 305	55 377	74 571	124 370	90 347
Standard error	1 209	1 056	1 319	2 079	4 412	2 083	2 336	4 224	11 523	6 082
Hispanic[1]										
Number with income	12 994	5 332	3 809	1 002	608	1 262	974	245	82	59
Median income ($)	21 822	17 411	22 229	26 422	33 442	45 390	42 022	52 312	54 106	(B)
Standard error	154	194	272	677	1 208	1 524	1 689	2 316	14 324	(B)
Mean income ($)	29 716	20 661	28 593	32 746	36 906	60 900	53 900	62 411	99 634	(B)
Standard error	473	382	897	1 267	1 119	2 690	2 623	4 789	12 637	(B)
Year-Round, Full-Time Workers										
All races										
Number with income	60 022	6 701	19 065	10 282	5 212	18 761	12 101	4 252	1 313	1 094
Median income ($)	41 687	23 513	34 632	41 401	44 430	66 067	59 337	75 351	[2]100 000	91 916
Standard error	99	309	336	196	775	368	728	691	24 211	2 311
Mean income ($)	56 501	28 733	40 545	49 493	51 038	87 993	74 685	97 655	151 908	120 895
Standard error	319	559	356	524	602	813	764	2 077	4 407	4 501
White alone or in combination										
Number with income	51 012	5 790	15 937	8 800	4 508	15 975	10 335	3 594	1 129	915
Median income ($)	42 515	23 743	35 932	42 224	45 854	67 362	60 880	75 364	[2]100 000	95 178
Standard error	205	332	170	214	402	590	315	776	25 239	2 836
Mean income ($)	58 151	28 579	42 117	51 185	52 275	90 360	76 991	99 679	153 684	126 562
Standard error	357	534	414	597	650	909	846	2 373	4 752	5 243
Black alone or in combination										
Number with income	5 821	645	2 445	1 131	487	1 111	791	225	50	44
Median income ($)	31 715	22 478	27 422	35 560	36 303	50 960	45 904	65 707	(B)	(B)
Standard error	215	699	436	624	1 006	756	1 618	5 112	(B)	(B)
Mean income ($)	39 935	31 649	31 277	38 490	39 683	65 375	55 242	80 414	(B)	(B)
Standard error	669	3 481	474	771	1 238	2 261	1 828	4 402	(B)	(B)
Asian alone or in combination										
Number with income	2 849	171	573	294	189	1 622	932	430	128	131
Median income ($)	46 594	22 203	30 641	35 085	36 811	62 298	52 283	76 652	97 738	84 256
Standard error	787	1 311	917	1 585	2 214	1 282	1 337	1 786	39 371	6 057
Mean income ($)	63 055	25 764	37 724	43 727	54 158	80 490	66 244	88 896	140 074	96 045
Standard error	1 665	1 441	1 817	3 625	5 908	2 559	2 979	5 040	13 628	6 652
Hispanic[1]										
Number with income	8 862	3 429	2 705	1 217	465	1 045	758	194	49	42
Median income ($)	26 926	21 240	26 856	35 613	36 661	51 590	48 753	57 253	(B)	(B)
Standard error	221	184	347	1 156	819	724	1 700	3 459	(B)	(B)
Mean income ($)	35 339	24 634	33 034	40 089	41 068	68 346	58 521	69 817	(B)	(B)
Standard error	555	550	949	962	1 210	3 047	2 538	5 652	(B)	(B)

[1]May be of any race.
[2]Median income over $100,000.
(B) = Base is too small to show the derived measure.

Table A-23. Income in 2004 by Educational Attainment for the Population Age 18 Years and Over, by Sex, Age, Race, and Hispanic Origin—*Continued*

(Numbers in thousands, dollars.)

Characteristic	Total population	High school		Some college, no degree	Associate's degree	College				
		Not a high school graduate	High school graduate, includes GED			Bachelor's degree or more				
						Total	Bachelor's degree	Master's degree	Professional degree	Doctorate degree
MALE, 25 YEARS AND OVER										
All Workers										
All races										
Number with income	87 570	12 774	27 798	14 404	6 782	25 809	16 302	6 058	1 876	1 572
Median income ($)	34 823	17 552	29 331	36 162	39 764	56 433	51 081	63 259	90 209	80 033
Standard error	199	173	241	254	552	320	257	1 049	3 251	1 483
Mean income ($)	47 444	22 005	34 704	43 532	45 792	76 376	65 489	83 031	126 405	103 907
Standard error	240	279	268	464	512	644	621	1 566	3 581	3 397
White alone or in combination										
Number with income	74 415	10 668	23 377	12 327	5 851	22 190	14 030	5 181	1 632	1 346
Median income ($)	35 884	18 196	30 455	37 185	40 914	57 551	52 026	63 603	91 254	80 449
Standard error	115	213	135	282	337	510	288	1 123	3 929	1 713
Mean income ($)	48 968	22 355	36 004	44 895	47 085	78 177	67 316	84 649	127 170	107 049
, Standard error	268	263	309	509	554	712	677	1 767	3 866	3 871
Black alone or in combination										
Number with income	8 726	1 596	3 435	1 579	649	1 463	1 018	312	74	58
Median income ($)	26 287	14 935	23 668	30 789	31 073	45 702	40 962	57 576	75 410	(B)
Standard error	261	554	649	445	919	1 000	711	3 821	10 099	(B)
Mean income ($)	33 068	20 433	26 913	34 949	35 426	58 220	49 564	69 962	118 573	(B)
Standard error	536	1 450	414	1 400	1 148	1 834	1 557	3 628	21 125	(B)
Asian alone or in combination										
Number with income	3 850	343	784	397	238	2 085	1 200	558	163	161
Median income ($)	36 930	16 072	26 000	29 505	32 058	52 127	45 853	65 265	95 559	81 073
Standard error	672	707	553	1 842	897	1 744	4 476	11 558	2 821	
Mean income ($)	52 860	20 143	32 063	38 859	46 021	69 534	56 909	74 571	124 370	90 347
Standard error	1 321	1 134	1 468	2 950	4 860	2 129	2 428	4 224	11 523	6 082
Hispanic[1]										
Number with income	10 910	4 517	3 066	1 457	558	1 310	925	243	82	59
Median income ($)	24 252	18 723	25 477	31 528	35 203	46 473	44 050	52 481	54 106	(B)
Standard error	334	346	376	587	1 073	1 253	1 926	2 359	14 324	(B)
Mean income ($)	32 320	21 836	31 141	38 008	38 657	62 189	55 267	62 740	99 634	(B)
Standard error	539	441	988	1 569	1 165	2 782	2 743	4 815	12 637	(B)
Year-Round, Full-Time Workers										
All races										
Number with income	55 453	5 891	17 051	9 256	4 906	18 347	11 705	4 243	1 308	1 090
Median income ($)	44 187	24 956	36 424	43 828	45 996	66 906	60 523	75 416	[2]100 000	91 988
Standard error	279	271	158	568	397	365	301	649	24 165	2 328
Mean income ($)	58 989	29 579	42 258	52 154	52 459	89 179	76 017	97 775	152 437	121 133
Standard error	337	545	361	566	628	828	785	2 080	4 415	4 519
White alone or in combination										
Number with income	47 084	5 061	14 245	7 949	4 227	15 599	9 976	3 588	1 124	910
Median income ($)	45 800	25 135	37 583	45 657	47 149	69 377	61 699	75 427	[2]100 000	95 267
Standard error	161	255	300	325	413	879	315	740	25 184	2 839
Mean income ($)	60 758	29 346	43 920	53 923	53 843	91 682	78 487	99 806	154 308	126 877
Standard error	377	479	419	644	679	927	870	2 377	4 763	5 267
Black alone or in combination										
Number with income	5 342	590	2 177	1 004	472	1 096	776	225	50	44
Median income ($)	32 876	23 792	29 204	36 857	36 697	51 113	46 166	65 707	(B)	(B)
Standard error	719	985	853	617	1 119	767	1 365	5 112	(B)	(B)
Mean income ($)	41 567	33 045	32 482	40 349	40 318	65 860	55 729	80 414	(B)	(B)
Standard error	720	3 789	513	810	1 256	2 286	1 854	4 402	(B)	(B)
Asian alone or in combination										
Number with income	2 720	162	520	258	179	1 600	910	430	128	131
Median income ($)	48 562	22 491	31 548	36 330	37 047	62 882	52 983	76 652	97 738	84 256
Standard error	1 401	1 644	754	1 695	2 813	1 419	1 647	1 786	39 371	6 057
Mean income ($)	64 793	26 311	39 322	45 842	55 404	81 087	66 950	88 896	140 074	96 045
Standard error	1 733	1 498	1 976	4 097	6 212	2 589	3 044	5 040	13 628	6 652
Hispanic[1]										
Number with income	7 790	2 995	2 274	1 069	434	1 015	728	194	49	42
Median income ($)	29 320	21 826	29 778	38 968	37 433	51 954	50 004	57 253	(B)	(B)
Standard error	487	194	627	1 190	1 507	913	1 460	3 459	(B)	(B)
Mean income ($)	37 218	25 584	34 700	42 615	42 405	69 267	59 409	69 817	(B)	(B)
Standard error	595	622	908	1 052	1 251	3 123	2 620	5 652	(B)	(B)

[1]May be of any race.
[2]Median income over $100,000.
(B) = Base is too small to show the derived measure.

Table A-23. Income in 2004 by Educational Attainment for the Population Age 18 Years and Over, by Sex, Age, Race, and Hispanic Origin—*Continued*

(Numbers in thousands, dollars.)

| Characteristic | Total population | High school | | Some college, no degree | Associate's degree | College | | | | |
| | | Not a high school graduate | High school graduate, includes GED | | | Bachelor's degree or more | | | | |
						Total	Bachelor's degree	Master's degree	Professional degree	Doctorate degree
MALE, 25 TO 64 YEARS										
All Workers										
All races										
Number with income	72 736	9 142	23 082	12 301	6 127	22 082	14 189	5 161	1 501	1 229
Median income ($)	37 322	20 189	31 229	38 326	41 092	60 518	53 775	67 907	[2]100 000	85 740
Standard error	109	147	122	437	311	272	695	1 244	24 887	2 882
Mean income ($)	50 448	23 494	36 442	45 052	47 087	80 185	68 559	87 588	137 956	112 710
Standard error	275	318	309	498	527	721	692	1 758	4 161	4 085
White alone or in combination										
Number with income	61 208	7 710	19 074	10 392	5 276	18 754	12 076	4 352	1 294	1 030
Median income ($)	39 504	20 489	32 245	40 219	42 161	61 651	56 007	68 817	[2]100 000	88 432
Standard error	255	157	134	216	344	287	403	1 371	26 470	2 519
Mean income ($)	52 309	23 948	38 126	46 754	48 439	82 559	70 870	89 771	139 432	117 630
Standard error	309	343	363	549	567	805	761	2 007	4 504	4 747
Black alone or in combination										
Number with income	7 612	1 071	3 151	1 456	594	1 337	948	282	54	51
Median income ($)	27 464	16 903	24 796	31 160	31 516	46 300	41 153	58 469	(B)	(B)
Standard error	376	489	554	467	1 103	888	718	2 968	(B)	(B)
Mean income ($)	34 216	20 779	27 424	35 409	35 920	58 924	50 235	70 795	(B)	(B)
Standard error	544	1 156	438	1 490	1 186	1 961	1 640	3 774	(B)	(B)
Asian alone or in combination										
Number with income	3 407	230	674	361	214	1 925	1 115	519	149	141
Median income ($)	40 489	20 310	27 020	30 407	34 685	53 987	46 899	70 543	95 535	82 238
Standard error	574	1 664	664	1 422	1 845	1 805	1 483	3 548	11 305	3 353
Mean income ($)	55 604	23 172	33 363	37 568	49 051	71 393	58 435	77 714	125 613	93 075
Standard error	1 433	1 406	1 617	2 103	5 334	2 262	2 585	4 475	12 410	6 362
Hispanic[1]										
Number with income	10 055	4 049	2 888	1 378	525	1 212	873	226	63	49
Median income ($)	25 371	20 071	26 012	32 019	35 842	47 497	45 114	53 491	(B)	(B)
Standard error	228	249	370	748	818	1 874	1 986	2 612	(B)	(B)
Mean income ($)	33 370	22 717	31 811	38 778	39 816	63 708	55 812	64 377	(B)	(B)
Standard error	578	485	1 042	1 650	1 198	2 965	2 861	5 117	(B)	(B)
Year-Round, Full-Time Workers										
All races										
Number with income	53 915	5 652	16 626	9 006	4 828	17 800	11 433	4 114	1 227	1 025
Median income ($)	43 852	24 613	36 303	43 434	45 949	66 598	60 416	75 336	[2]100 000	91 779
Standard error	288	314	157	601	398	368	301	738	25 123	2 305
Mean income ($)	58 426	28 763	41 969	51 451	52 116	88 459	75 745	97 516	149 637	120 640
Standard error	336	467	362	528	604	835	795	2 105	4 522	4 643
White alone or in combination										
Number with income	45 745	4 875	13 864	7 717	4 162	15 124	9 741	3 472	1 057	852
Median income ($)	45 628	24 841	37 416	45 503	47 076	68 465	61 559	75 306	[2]100 000	94 423
Standard error	164	312	229	332	399	981	314	870	26 054	2 761
Mean income ($)	60 182	28 929	43 623	53 176	53 444	90 865	78 171	99 479	151 004	126 216
Standard error	376	491	420	600	648	934	881	2 408	4 841	5 438
Black alone or in combination										
Number with income	5 206	552	2 144	987	459	1 061	754	220	43	42
Median income ($)	32 464	23 275	28 919	36 695	36 772	51 076	46 267	65 367	(B)	(B)
Standard error	552	911	894	634	1 125	757	1 278	4 448	(B)	(B)
Mean income ($)	40 891	28 584	32 328	40 063	40 226	65 667	55 621	79 909	(B)	(B)
Standard error	636	2 098	517	778	1 264	2 343	1 888	4 449	(B)	(B)
Asian alone or in combination										
Number with income	2 663	149	511	257	178	1 566	896	421	120	126
Median income ($)	48 668	23 753	31 556	36 257	37 029	63 085	53 002	76 913	96 541	85 416
Standard error	1 387	1 683	758	1 699	2 789	1 470	1 660	2 016	19 325	6 209
Mean income ($)	64 558	26 043	39 199	44 026	55 371	80 943	66 946	89 507	137 731	97 365
Standard error	1 732	1 383	1 992	2 591	6 221	2 629	3 082	5 121	14 357	6 811
Hispanic[1]										
Number with income	7 675	2 948	2 242	1 056	431	996	714	194	46	40
Median income ($)	29 139	21 810	29 523	38 656	37 519	51 941	49 853	57 253	(B)	(B)
Standard error	486	194	703	1 240	1 575	902	1 603	3 459	(B)	(B)
Mean income ($)	37 107	25 505	34 546	42 538	42 669	69 031	58 866	69 817	(B)	(B)
Standard error	600	630	917	1 063	1 240	3 160	2 621	5 652	(B)	(B)

[1]May be of any race.
[2]Median income over $100,000.
(B) = Base is too small to show the derived measure.

Table A-23. Income in 2004 by Educational Attainment for the Population Age 18 Years and Over, by Sex, Age, Race, and Hispanic Origin—*Continued*

(Numbers in thousands, dollars.)

Characteristic	Total population	High school		Some college, no degree	Associate's degree	College				
		Not a high school graduate	High school graduate, includes GED			Bachelor's degree or more				
						Total	Bachelor's degree	Master's degree	Professional degree	Doctorate degree
MALE, 25 TO 34 YEARS										
All Workers										
All races										
Number with income	18 725	2 610	5 852	3 409	1 579	5 273	3 927	947	276	122
Median income ($)	30 991	19 189	26 714	31 024	34 669	45 610	42 277	50 784	56 470	57 388
Standard error	155	427	232	328	1 006	461	421	503	6 144	2 591
Mean income ($)	37 356	21 635	30 194	34 992	38 766	54 190	50 894	57 205	85 521	65 955
Standard error	316	634	450	554	846	780	790	1 400	7 948	4 428
White alone or in combination										
Number with income	15 425	2 298	4 767	2 791	1 333	4 234	3 206	695	225	106
Median income ($)	31 717	19 645	28 391	31 995	35 879	45 890	42 815	51 208	57 047	57 843
Standard error	177	453	470	412	585	499	762	634	8 351	2 629
Mean income ($)	38 206	22 051	31 792	36 334	39 934	54 891	51 644	57 912	87 214	64 404
Standard error	361	706	535	642	952	902	914	1 442	9 406	3 337
Black alone or in combination										
Number with income	2 099	220	860	468	173	377	302	55	13	5
Median income ($)	25 397	16 929	21 281	28 453	27 118	36 577	33 607	(B)	(B)	(B)
Standard error	352	932	456	1 448	1 719	1 496	1 429	(B)	(B)	(B)
Mean income ($)	28 552	18 276	22 372	29 093	32 607	46 127	41 712	(B)	(B)	(B)
Standard error	635	1 397	626	1 015	2 162	2 339	1 933	(B)	(B)	(B)
Asian alone or in combination										
Number with income	1 081	44	177	126	67	665	419	195	37	13
Median income ($)	33 952	(B)	25 568	26 272	(B)	46 585	44 025	50 353	(B)	(B)
Standard error	1 687	(B)	1 371	993	(B)	1 592	2 598	2 338	(B)	(B)
Mean income ($)	43 775	(B)	26 685	30 967	(B)	53 293	50 429	53 466	(B)	(B)
Standard error	1 413	(B)	1 527	3 037	(B)	2 027	2 095	3 608	(B)	(B)
Hispanic[1]										
Number with income	3 930	1 545	1 215	562	221	385	311	48	16	8
Median income ($)	22 278	18 333	23 230	30 207	32 077	41 095	39 157	(B)	(B)	(B)
Standard error	212	638	930	1 174	1 452	1 401	1 918	(B)	(B)	(B)
Mean income ($)	28 933	21 181	29 755	32 713	33 997	48 985	47 853	(B)	(B)	(B)
Standard error	845	1 057	1 872	1 231	1 517	3 867	4 620	(B)	(B)	(B)
Year-Round, Full-Time Workers										
All races										
Number with income	14 109	1 798	4 321	2 504	1 256	4 228	3 177	746	202	101
Median income ($)	36 028	21 660	30 461	36 630	37 752	50 762	48 175	53 998	69 239	61 100
Standard error	171	217	217	332	1 041	306	871	1 669	6 262	6 732
Mean income ($)	42 632	25 326	33 535	41 308	42 890	59 993	57 003	64 584	84 486	70 902
Standard error	338	883	347	671	959	784	906	1 570	4 574	5 072
White alone or in combination										
Number with income	11 803	1 611	3 577	2 105	1 068	3 440	2 618	568	162	89
Median income ($)	36 563	21 818	31 435	37 198	39 742	50 796	48 280	54 273	72 437	60 981
Standard error	180	234	235	363	1 085	368	902	1 705	4 185	6 780
Mean income ($)	43 157	25 593	34 925	42 343	44 029	60 175	57 564	63 623	85 754	68 103
Standard error	376	970	393	766	1 090	883	1 048	1 569	4 820	3 689
Black alone or in combination										
Number with income	1 435	123	588	316	126	281	231	41	6	2
Median income ($)	29 075	20 634	25 060	31 945	31 589	40 401	36 849	(B)	(B)	(B)
Standard error	1 058	613	671	529	1 277	1 727	2 020	(B)	(B)	(B)
Mean income ($)	33 347	23 254	25 662	35 021	36 651	50 452	45 738	(B)	(B)	(B)
Standard error	763	2 116	690	1 112	2 016	2 730	2 029	(B)	(B)	(B)
Asian alone or in combination										
Number with income	804	30	140	74	56	502	325	135	31	9
Median income ($)	42 812	(B)	28 479	30 064	(B)	52 234	51 562	60 003	(B)	(B)
Standard error	2 001	(B)	1 799	1 541	(B)	1 689	1 409	5 781	(B)	(B)
Mean income ($)	52 213	(B)	30 438	40 691	(B)	63 183	59 019	66 222	(B)	(B)
Standard error	1 686	(B)	1 679	4 486	(B)	2 342	2 327	4 248	(B)	(B)
Hispanic[1]										
Number with income	3 008	1 151	941	423	184	307	248	46	6	5
Median income ($)	25 639	20 501	26 134	35 788	34 357	47 093	43 217	(B)	(B)	(B)
Standard error	370	253	504	1 373	1 850	2 564	2 641	(B)	(B)	(B)
Mean income ($)	31 632	23 520	30 212	37 834	36 446	54 935	53 651	(B)	(B)	(B)
Standard error	821	1 394	832	1 435	1 428	4 706	5 655	(B)	(B)	(B)

[1]May be of any race.
(B) = Base is too small to show the derived measure.

Table A-23. Income in 2004 by Educational Attainment for the Population Age 18 Years and Over, by Sex, Age, Race, and Hispanic Origin—*Continued*

(Numbers in thousands, dollars.)

| Characteristic | Total population | High school | | College | | | | | | |
| | | Not a high school graduate | High school graduate, includes GED | Some college, no degree | Associate's degree | Bachelor's degree or more | | | | |
						Total	Bachelor's degree	Master's degree	Professional degree	Doctorate degree
MALE, 35 TO 44 YEARS										
All Workers										
All races										
Number with income	20 611	2 546	6 876	3 250	1 811	6 126	4 047	1 378	415	284
Median income ($)	40 534	21 385	32 470	41 241	42 444	67 036	60 670	77 126	[2]100 000	81 449
Standard error	175	262	401	355	837	838	619	1 446	45 237	2 625
Mean income ($)	53 815	25 192	37 928	49 196	49 300	87 333	75 891	100 620	141 467	106 703
Standard error	568	476	641	1 087	1 030	1 521	1 394	4 499	7 400	7 428
White alone or in combination										
Number with income	17 122	2 175	5 629	2 721	1 547	5 048	3 382	1 105	349	210
Median income ($)	41 429	21 594	35 057	42 137	44 411	70 089	62 320	77 065	[2]100 000	81 265
Standard error	197	268	437	404	1 108	1 143	1 089	1 670	46 302	4 255
Mean income ($)	55 607	25 736	39 998	51 432	50 598	89 667	78 067	103 620	144 358	111 925
Standard error	643	535	766	1 273	1 138	1 711	1 485	5 348	8 116	9 630
Black alone or in combination										
Number with income	2 237	281	967	388	181	418	299	87	14	16
Median income ($)	30 551	18 205	25 313	35 399	35 979	49 130	42 459	61 913	(B)	(B)
Standard error	431	1 553	919	1 975	2 734	2 574	2 677	9 377	(B)	(B)
Mean income ($)	35 362	21 504	27 466	36 737	39 353	59 956	54 913	70 548	(B)	(B)
Standard error	779	1 144	760	1 318	2 184	2 875	3 137	5 339	(B)	(B)
Asian alone or in combination										
Number with income	1 079	66	202	116	62	631	344	179	51	56
Median income ($)	47 824	(B)	29 892	32 202	(B)	66 328	54 999	81 529	(B)	(B)
Standard error	2 294	(B)	2 781	2 129	(B)	3 241	2 244	3 449	(B)	(B)
Mean income ($)	66 497	(B)	33 301	38 850	(B)	87 924	74 571	97 412	(B)	(B)
Standard error	3 435	(B)	2 045	2 984	(B)	5 460	7 368	10 548	(B)	(B)
Hispanic[1]										
Number with income	3 007	1 212	908	410	182	384	281	73	19	9
Median income ($)	26 931	21 327	27 318	32 353	37 492	46 034	43 066	(B)	(B)	(B)
Standard error	401	350	942	2 609	2 824	2 555	3 373	(B)	(B)	(B)
Mean income ($)	35 205	25 027	33 295	40 137	43 736	62 506	51 617	(B)	(B)	(B)
Standard error	868	711	1 781	1 935	2 184	4 081	2 500	(B)	(B)	(B)
Year-Round, Full-Time Workers										
All races										
Number with income	16 534	1 739	5 277	2 629	1 535	5 352	3 528	1 200	374	247
Median income ($)	45 604	25 140	37 261	45 315	46 216	72 138	64 585	81 630	[2]100 000	85 094
Standard error	273	436	258	684	683	807	1 301	1 032	44 994	3 689
Mean income ($)	60 515	29 302	43 314	53 584	52 913	93 208	80 719	108 870	146 951	113 960
Standard error	664	566	748	1 158	1 137	1 675	1 508	5 072	7 684	8 207
White alone or in combination										
Number with income	13 815	1 513	4 370	2 209	1 303	4 417	2 964	958	312	182
Median income ($)	46 661	25 131	39 512	46 627	47 324	74 182	66 495	81 286	[2]100 000	85 832
Standard error	288	485	643	607	936	1 337	758	1 084	46 124	5 266
Mean income ($)	62 075	29 426	45 303	55 871	54 466	95 206	82 444	112 034	149 723	120 788
Standard error	746	628	886	1 352	1 260	1 879	1 585	6 065	8 429	10 712
Black alone or in combination										
Number with income	1 704	164	704	313	161	361	256	77	12	14
Median income ($)	35 645	24 308	30 882	37 367	36 346	54 984	50 276	75 983	(B)	(B)
Standard error	462	1 655	582	1 975	3 025	2 370	2 692	11 974	(B)	(B)
Mean income ($)	41 239	28 302	32 388	40 477	40 704	65 278	59 909	76 869	(B)	(B)
Standard error	919	1 521	865	1 287	2 318	3 157	3 466	5 495	(B)	(B)
Asian alone or in combination										
Number with income	899	50	150	92	55	550	291	162	47	49
Median income ($)	55 249	(B)	36 030	35 975	(B)	75 513	60 911	84 738	(B)	(B)
Standard error	2 159	(B)	1 281	3 327	(B)	2 805	3 102	4 282	(B)	(B)
Mean income ($)	75 276	(B)	39 305	43 370	(B)	96 453	83 096	105 517	(B)	(B)
Standard error	4 004	(B)	2 351	3 017	(B)	6 111	8 526	11 433	(B)	(B)
Hispanic[1]										
Number with income	2 480	932	732	336	153	325	241	57	18	7
Median income ($)	30 469	22 900	30 664	38 439	44 015	50 497	45 883	(B)	(B)	(B)
Standard error	338	734	475	2 014	2 942	2 751	3 001	(B)	(B)	(B)
Mean income ($)	38 973	27 527	37 225	43 597	48 148	66 623	53 818	(B)	(B)	(B)
Standard error	1 038	857	2 152	2 197	2 314	4 633	2 686	(B)	(B)	(B)

[1]May be of any race.
[2]Median income over $100,000.
(B) = Base is too small to show the derived measure.

Table A-23. Income in 2004 by Educational Attainment for the Population Age 18 Years and Over, by Sex, Age, Race, and Hispanic Origin—*Continued*

(Numbers in thousands, dollars.)

Characteristic	Total population	High school — Not a high school graduate	High school graduate, includes GED	Some college, no degree	Associate's degree	College — Bachelor's degree or more — Total	Bachelor's degree	Master's degree	Professional degree	Doctorate degree
MALE, 45 TO 54 YEARS										
All Workers										
All races										
Number with income	19 799	2 156	6 370	3 394	1 700	6 177	3 747	1 575	472	382
Median income ($)	41 865	20 512	33 909	42 207	46 127	69 693	61 736	73 898	[2]100 000	96 851
Standard error	213	373	669	531	774	1 122	628	1 657	39 938	5 946
Mean income ($)	56 917	23 945	39 989	49 143	50 720	91 860	76 685	99 513	156 688	128 995
Standard error	581	718	654	914	1 028	1 494	1 377	3 543	8 011	7 765
White alone or in combination										
Number with income	16 819	1 776	5 257	2 873	1 498	5 413	3 269	1 392	421	329
Median income ($)	44 457	20 875	35 896	44 529	47 428	71 342	64 372	74 254	[2]100 000	[2]100 000
Standard error	588	422	341	1 002	823	621	1 098	1 667	40 947	49 690
Mean income ($)	59 406	24 645	41 640	51 041	51 731	94 635	79 366	101 086	159 340	136 008
Standard error	655	849	761	1 038	1 010	1 637	1 468	3 938	8 613	8 767
Black alone or in combination										
Number with income	2 063	274	875	414	143	355	236	89	17	11
Median income ($)	30 343	17 489	26 892	35 002	37 247	51 787	50 140	65 072	(B)	(B)
Standard error	501	1 725	665	2 191	1 500	2 543	2 040	4 541	(B)	(B)
Mean income ($)	37 148	20 448	30 373	37 066	35 455	67 466	55 641	76 089	(B)	(B)
Standard error	979	1 161	899	1 539	2 192	4 188	3 752	7 145	(B)	(B)
Asian alone or in combination										
Number with income	759	70	187	77	47	376	215	91	33	36
Median income ($)	41 210	(B)	27 475	37 743	(B)	53 660	42 431	77 281	(B)	(B)
Standard error	1 003	(B)	2 237	2 524	(B)	4 560	2 794	8 081	(B)	(B)
Mean income ($)	57 900	(B)	41 545	44 778	(B)	73 957	56 357	93 887	(B)	(B)
Standard error	2 815	(B)	4 773	6 664	(B)	4 132	3 814	9 174	(B)	(B)
Hispanic[1]										
Number with income	1 989	837	525	249	74	302	191	73	17	21
Median income ($)	27 396	20 939	27 955	36 320	35 171	56 181	51 736	(B)	(B)	(B)
Standard error	722	620	1 759	2 690	2 549	3 040	2 986	(B)	(B)	(B)
Mean income ($)	37 862	22 837	34 078	40 574	42 583	82 575	72 965	(B)	(B)	(B)
Standard error	1 533	581	2 003	2 029	3 627	8 402	9 660	(B)	(B)	(B)
Year-Round, Full-Time Workers										
All races										
Number with income	15 245	1 321	4 844	2 553	1 384	5 142	3 080	1 348	394	318
Median income ($)	49 344	26 622	39 372	48 548	50 245	75 343	67 132	77 522	[2]100 000	97 601
Standard error	471	459	550	914	576	749	1 080	1 828	40 323	13 804
Mean income ($)	65 306	30 532	45 738	56 488	55 651	99 648	83 893	107 603	168 265	133 305
Standard error	695	1 082	767	1 101	1 133	1 671	1 517	3 951	8 891	8 606
White alone or in combination										
Number with income	13 095	1 100	4 046	2 206	1 232	4 509	2 679	1 197	358	273
Median income ($)	50 869	27 301	40 769	50 229	50 956	76 832	70 558	77 464	[2]100 000	[2]100 000
Standard error	222	584	305	678	518	632	1 063	1 852	41 321	55 708
Mean income ($)	67 745	31 327	47 313	58 127	56 239	102 821	87 326	109 000	169 534	140 173
Standard error	782	1 277	882	1 234	1 082	1 851	1 685	4 373	9 421	9 766
Black alone or in combination										
Number with income	1 445	153	612	271	107	299	205	67	15	11
Median income ($)	36 406	24 025	31 024	40 207	40 131	56 149	51 384	(B)	(B)	(B)
Standard error	686	1 338	419	2 101	1 323	3 283	2 426	(B)	(B)	(B)
Mean income ($)	44 517	26 869	35 561	44 113	40 782	73 584	60 133	(B)	(B)	(B)
Standard error	1 248	1 548	976	1 724	2 348	4 783	4 134	(B)	(B)	(B)
Asian alone or in combination										
Number with income	610	48	147	57	36	319	178	85	22	32
Median income ($)	47 464	(B)	35 097	(B)	(B)	62 891	49 273	80 666	(B)	(B)
Standard error	2 079	(B)	3 039	(B)	(B)	5 225	2 356	6 197	(B)	(B)
Mean income ($)	65 709	(B)	48 095	(B)	(B)	80 515	63 174	99 581	(B)	(B)
Standard error	3 286	(B)	5 818	(B)	(B)	4 514	4 193	9 311	(B)	(B)
Hispanic[1]										
Number with income	1 528	600	409	196	58	264	157	73	13	19
Median income ($)	31 492	25 028	31 773	41 652	(B)	60 740	55 474	(B)	(B)	(B)
Standard error	425	774	832	2 145	(B)	5 101	2 640	(B)	(B)	(B)
Mean income ($)	42 637	26 307	38 734	45 790	(B)	83 253	70 610	(B)	(B)	(B)
Standard error	1 639	644	2 441	2 261	(B)	7 586	6 238	(B)	(B)	(B)

[1]May be of any race.
[2]Median income over $100,000.
(B) = Base is too small to show the derived measure.

Table A-23. Income in 2004 by Educational Attainment for the Population Age 18 Years and Over, by Sex, Age, Race, and Hispanic Origin—*Continued*

(Numbers in thousands, dollars.)

Characteristic	Total population	High school		College						
		Not a high school graduate	High school graduate, includes GED	Some college, no degree	Associate's degree	Bachelor's degree or more				
						Total	Bachelor's degree	Master's degree	Professional degree	Doctorate degree
MALE, 55 TO 64 YEARS										
All Workers										
All races										
Number with income	13 600	1 828	3 983	2 246	1 035	4 505	2 466	1 260	338	440
Median income ($)	39 288	17 898	31 394	40 864	42 161	62 374	54 418	65 358	[2]100 000	89 797
Standard error	592	705	355	498	1 114	793	1 465	1 593	48 410	4 505
Mean income ($)	53 954	23 248	37 383	48 142	49 950	84 884	72 312	81 262	150 284	115 457
Standard error	696	742	662	1 494	1 345	1 701	2 078	2 411	8 999	7 594
White alone or in combination										
Number with income	11 841	1 459	3 419	2 006	898	4 057	2 217	1 159	297	383
Median income ($)	40 964	18 808	32 037	41 622	44 249	63 839	56 865	65 105	[2]100 000	91 147
Standard error	295	798	378	513	1 548	1 176	1 379	1 697	53 041	4 267
Mean income ($)	55 828	23 422	38 475	48 766	51 855	86 476	75 164	82 080	145 040	119 749
Standard error	753	581	744	1 403	1 494	1 821	2 279	2 563	9 051	8 573
Black alone or in combination										
Number with income	1 211	294	448	185	96	186	109	49	9	17
Median income ($)	26 083	15 627	26 212	28 858	28 578	46 310	37 759	(B)	(B)	(B)
Standard error	854	961	1 195	2 283	2 711	1 716	4 450	(B)	(B)	(B)
Mean income ($)	36 923	22 267	31 278	44 842	36 117	66 192	49 272	(B)	(B)	(B)
Standard error	2 355	3 766	1 418	10 432	3 209	8 126	5 441	(B)	(B)	(B)
Asian alone or in combination										
Number with income	486	49	107	40	36	251	135	53	26	35
Median income ($)	36 727	(B)	24 018	(B)	(B)	54 261	37 122	(B)	(B)	(B)
Standard error	1 568	(B)	3 981	(B)	(B)	4 216	2 778	(B)	(B)	(B)
Mean income ($)	54 134	(B)	30 207	(B)	(B)	73 956	45 490	(B)	(B)	(B)
Standard error	3 437	(B)	3 129	(B)	(B)	6 002	3 445	(B)	(B)	(B)
Hispanic[1]										
Number with income	1 038	454	239	156	47	140	89	30	9	10
Median income ($)	26 380	17 441	30 765	34 382	(B)	57 391	60 383	(B)	(B)	(B)
Standard error	789	821	1 303	5 000	(B)	4 876	3 517	(B)	(B)	(B)
Mean income ($)	36 077	21 553	31 648	54 162	(B)	66 729	60 110	(B)	(B)	(B)
Standard error	2 361	986	1 582	12 341	(B)	8 742	4 352	(D)	(B)	(B)
Year-Round, Full-Time Workers										
All races										
Number with income	8 026	794	2 183	1 319	652	3 077	1 645	818	255	357
Median income ($)	50 978	27 669	41 251	50 509	52 462	75 171	63 945	75 883	[2]100 000	97 753
Standard error	298	788	376	537	2 254	1 137	1 482	2 402	47 229	12 078
Mean income ($)	68 821	32 420	47 045	56 707	60 514	100 622	86 018	94 282	176 486	128 116
Standard error	1 010	1 483	920	1 116	1 777	2 297	2 870	3 188	10 985	8 994
White alone or in combination										
Number with income	7 030	650	1 869	1 194	557	2 757	1 479	747	224	306
Median income ($)	52 010	28 193	41 858	51 167	56 179	76 046	66 704	75 672	[2]100 000	[2]100 000
Standard error	320	894	381	559	1 246	800	2 489	2 391	50 895	33 604
Mean income ($)	70 955	31 981	48 355	58 139	62 907	102 648	89 506	95 402	170 522	134 006
Standard error	1 102	945	1 028	1 200	2 001	2 472	3 149	3 449	11 058	10 285
Black alone or in combination										
Number with income	619	111	238	86	64	118	61	34	8	13
Median income ($)	36 681	28 340	35 554	41 471	(B)	56 505	(B)	(B)	(B)	(B)
Standard error	1 380	2 423	2 166	5 218	(B)	4 389	(B)	(B)	(B)	(B)
Mean income ($)	48 950	37 248	40 276	44 271	(B)	83 048	(B)	(B)	(B)	(B)
Standard error	3 165	9 561	2 163	2 942	(B)	12 148	(B)	(B)	(B)	(B)
Asian alone or in combination										
Number with income	349	20	73	33	30	192	101	38	18	34
Median income ($)	46 136	(B)	(B)	(B)	(B)	66 047	46 432	(B)	(B)	(B)
Standard error	3 754	(B)	(B)	(B)	(B)	4 384	5 448	(B)	(B)	(B)
Mean income ($)	63 387	(B)	(B)	(B)	(B)	83 680	52 676	(B)	(B)	(B)
Standard error	4 185	(B)	(B)	(B)	(B)	6 865	4 165	(B)	(B)	(B)
Hispanic[1]										
Number with income	657	263	159	100	36	98	67	17	7	7
Median income ($)	34 308	22 434	35 368	50 273	(B)	64 879	(B)	(B)	(B)	(B)
Standard error	1 802	1 260	1 917	5 512	(B)	4 743	(B)	(B)	(B)	(B)
Mean income ($)	42 262	25 205	37 073	52 487	(B)	82 748	(B)	(B)	(B)	(B)
Standard error	2 151	1 021	1 872	3 442	(B)	11 658	(B)	(B)	(B)	(B)

[1]May be of any race.
[2]Median income over $100,000.
(B) = Base is too small to show the derived measure.

Table A-23. Income in 2004 by Educational Attainment for the Population Age 18 Years and Over, by Sex, Age, Race, and Hispanic Origin—*Continued*

(Numbers in thousands, dollars.)

| Characteristic | Total population | High school | | Some college, no degree | Associate's degree | College | | | | |
| | | Not a high school graduate | High school graduate, includes GED | | | Bachelor's degree or more | | | | |
						Total	Bachelor's degree	Master's degree	Professional degree	Doctorate degree
MALE, 65 YEARS AND OVER										
All Workers										
All races										
Number with income	14 834	3 632	4 716	2 103	654	3 726	2 112	897	374	343
Median income ($)	21 130	13 832	19 996	23 870	24 181	37 144	34 299	40 316	40 777	50 202
Standard error	196	210	269	552	933	659	723	1 605	4 878	3 882
Mean income ($)	32 718	18 258	26 200	34 642	33 672	53 806	44 864	56 814	80 059	72 358
Standard error	424	563	420	1 249	1 877	1 196	1 031	2 913	5 870	4 849
White alone or in combination										
Number with income	13 206	2 958	4 302	1 934	575	3 436	1 953	828	337	316
Median income ($)	21 811	14 394	20 436	24 070	24 370	37 427	34 599	41 490	37 459	51 168
Standard error	197	223	289	563	1 036	685	769	1 564	3 147	4 161
Mean income ($)	33 483	18 202	26 594	34 910	34 659	54 263	45 353	57 737	80 135	72 587
Standard error	445	302	448	1 331	2 093	1 270	1 090	3 106	6 373	5 128
Black alone or in combination										
Number with income	1 113	525	283	123	55	126	70	29	19	7
Median income ($)	14 995	11 748	15 760	19 559	(B)	37 879	(B)	(B)	(B)	(B)
Standard error	544	329	920	3 660	(B)	4 209	(B)	(B)	(B)	(B)
Mean income ($)	25 222	19 726	21 232	29 512	(B)	50 753	(B)	(B)	(B)	(B)
Standard error	1 934	3 724	1 150	3 402	(B)	4 499	(B)	(B)	(B)	(B)
Asian alone or in combination										
Number with income	443	112	110	36	23	159	85	39	14	19
Median income ($)	16 227	10 165	14 464	(B)	(B)	30 421	26 592	(B)	(B)	(B)
Standard error	972	1 045	967	(B)	(B)	2 194	2 989	(B)	(B)	(B)
Mean income ($)	31 770	13 948	24 141	(B)	(B)	47 082	37 061	(B)	(B)	(B)
Standard error	2 938	1 712	3 236	(B)	(B)	4 840	4 361	(B)	(B)	(B)
Hispanic[1]										
Number with income	854	467	177	78	32	97	51	16	19	10
Median income ($)	13 557	11 066	15 140	18 687	(B)	30 322	(B)	(B)	(B)	(B)
Standard error	661	503	2 111	2 546	(B)	3 622	(B)	(B)	(B)	(B)
Mean income ($)	19 970	14 210	20 235	24 513	(B)	43 368	(B)	(B)	(B)	(B)
Standard error	918	589	1 662	2 250	(B)	5 693	(B)	(B)	(B)	(B)
Year-Round, Full-Time Workers										
All races										
Number with income	1 537	238	425	249	77	546	272	129	80	64
Median income ($)	51 459	35 977	45 086	52 047	51 496	83 929	71 201	81 826	[2]100 000	(B)
Standard error	871	1 604	2 051	2 493	5 917	3 757	997	8 336	87 896	(B)
Mean income ($)	78 733	48 892	53 574	77 518	73 752	112 620	87 439	106 047	194 974	(B)
Standard error	3 016	7 556	3 084	8 646	12 511	5 656	4 914	13 183	19 021	(B)
White alone or in combination										
Number with income	1 339	185	380	232	65	475	234	115	66	58
Median income ($)	52 906	39 413	45 000	51 866	(B)	85 491	71 945	83 468	(B)	(B)
Standard error	1 628	2 216	2 203	2 427	(B)	3 871	2 840	8 215	(B)	(B)
Mean income ($)	80 436	40 294	54 725	78 769	(B)	117 683	91 617	109 632	(B)	(B)
Standard error	3 166	1 781	3 410	9 234	(B)	6 366	5 524	14 537	(B)	(B)
Black alone or in combination										
Number with income	136	37	33	16	12	35	22	4	6	1
Median income ($)	42 518	(B)	(B)	(B)	(B)	(B)	(B)	(B)	(B)	(B)
Standard error	1 856	(B)	(B)	(B)	(B)	(B)	(B)	(B)	(B)	(B)
Mean income ($)	67 452	(B)	(B)	(B)	(B)	(B)	(B)	(B)	(B)	(B)
Standard error	14 168	(B)	(B)	(B)	(B)	(B)	(B)	(B)	(B)	(B)
Asian alone or in combination										
Number with income	56	12	8	(B)	(B)	34	14	8	7	4
Median income ($)	(B)	(B)	(B)	(B)	(B)	(B)	(B)	(B)	(B)	(B)
Standard error	(B)	(B)	(B)	(B)	(B)	(B)	(B)	(B)	(B)	(B)
Mean income ($)	(B)	(B)	(B)	(B)	(B)	(B)	(B)	(B)	(B)	(B)
Standard error	(B)	(B)	(B)	(B)	(B)	(B)	(B)	(B)	(B)	(B)
Hispanic[1]										
Number with income	114	47	32	12	2	19	14	(B)	3	2
Median income ($)	40 006	(B)	(B)	(B)	(B)	(B)	(B)	(B)	(B)	(B)
Standard error	3 923	(B)	(B)	(B)	(B)	(B)	(B)	(B)	(B)	(B)
Mean income ($)	44 636	(B)	(B)	(B)	(B)	(B)	(B)	(B)	(B)	(B)
Standard error	4 414	(B)	(B)	(B)	(B)	(B)	(B)	(B)	(B)	(B)

[1]May be of any race.
[2]Median income over $100,000.
(B) = Base is too small to show the derived measure.

Table A-23. Income in 2004 by Educational Attainment for the Population Age 18 Years and Over, by Sex, Age, Race, and Hispanic Origin—*Continued*

(Numbers in thousands, dollars.)

| Characteristic | Total population | High school | | Some college, no degree | Associate's degree | College | | | | |
| | | Not a high school graduate | High school graduate, includes GED | | | Bachelor's degree or more | | | | |
						Total	Bachelor's degree	Master's degree	Professional degree	Doctorate degree
FEMALE, 18 YEARS AND OVER										
All Workers										
All races										
Number with income	100 940	13 426	31 597	20 277	9 514	26 124	17 870	6 524	995	733
Median income ($)	18 345	9 647	15 519	17 887	24 187	34 694	30 741	42 117	50 174	55 996
Standard error	103	81	102	194	330	331	190	298	1 977	1 896
Mean income ($)	25 549	11 943	19 562	22 280	28 227	41 345	36 352	48 720	63 096	67 838
Standard error	116	106	148	196	271	336	344	833	2 130	2 444
White alone or in combination										
Number with income	83 532	10 407	26 379	16 767	8 082	21 894	14 848	5 595	835	614
Median income ($)	18 372	9 836	15 482	17 650	24 080	34 252	30 363	41 984	48 276	56 031
Standard error	112	94	115	209	392	358	219	315	2 697	2 091
Mean income ($)	25 779	11 978	19 740	22 412	28 199	41 301	36 330	48 410	62 466	67 898
Standard error	130	119	171	226	293	370	394	863	2 377	2 613
Black alone or in combination										
Number with income	12 718	2 287	4 260	2 770	1 079	2 320	1 665	535	71	48
Median income ($)	17 872	8 783	15 896	19 850	23 894	37 042	33 782	45 617	(B)	(B)
Standard error	300	179	251	465	677	579	1 167	2 323	(B)	(B)
Mean income ($)	22 970	11 299	18 423	21 916	27 018	42 197	37 647	48 429	(B)	(B)
Standard error	238	258	254	415	764	848	906	1 504	(B)	(B)
Asian alone or in combination										
Number with income	4 218	560	785	663	297	1 911	1 353	394	88	74
Median income ($)	21 012	10 640	15 999	14 809	26 755	34 586	30 977	41 558	46 733	51 243
Standard error	445	705	660	1 414	1 588	1 699	736	3 282	5 586	6 526
Mean income ($)	29 010	13 561	21 188	19 344	32 326	41 386	35 427	54 781	62 006	54 206
Standard error	802	733	941	846	2 065	1 594	1 015	6 461	7 614	5 931
Hispanic[1]										
Number with income	10 186	3 530	2 896	1 841	677	1 239	882	274	52	31
Median income ($)	14 852	10 223	15 883	19 005	21 732	31 254	28 191	44 459	(D)	(D)
Standard error	240	187	289	796	976	749	1 634	4 164	(B)	(B)
Mean income ($)	19 814	12 258	18 556	22 371	24 515	37 900	32 767	49 255	(B)	(B)
Standard error	275	223	347	537	946	1 597	1 687	3 651	(B)	(B)
Year-Round, Full-Time Workers										
All races										
Number with income	42 360	2 992	12 512	8 361	4 779	13 713	9 201	3 493	565	453
Median income ($)	32 129	18 754	26 164	30 725	34 540	46 758	42 043	52 678	76 162	73 901
Standard error	84	283	124	144	468	246	188	760	1 113	2 398
Mean Income ($)	39 966	21 293	30 041	34 221	38 914	56 065	50 826	64 516	87 611	85 151
Standard error	222	303	309	269	382	547	552	1 387	3 019	3 340
White alone or in combination										
Number with income	34 016	2 282	9 998	6 677	3 936	11 121	7 340	2 946	459	375
Median income ($)	32 724	18 316	26 595	31 043	35 173	47 077	42 400	52 822	76 579	74 189
Standard error	215	323	144	176	347	263	316	858	1 705	2 637
Mean income ($)	40 788	21 201	30 925	34 869	39 326	57 747	51 866	64 097	88 988	84 693
Standard error	256	340	377	315	420	619	661	1 445	3 476	3 579
Black alone or in combination										
Number with income	6 098	492	2 071	1 373	635	1 525	1 087	346	57	34
Median income ($)	29 218	19 172	24 560	29 195	31 087	42 121	40 435	50 985	(B)	(B)
Standard error	378	695	537	667	547	401	392	562	(B)	(B)
Mean income ($)	33 833	20 334	26 075	31 281	35 251	50 431	45 612	56 218	(B)	(B)
Standard error	376	675	348	549	993	1 088	1 167	1 722	(B)	(B)
Asian alone or in combination										
Number with income	2 042	168	387	256	176	1 054	755	205	45	47
Median income ($)	36 528	22 202	24 459	31 151	36 002	50 160	45 000	63 147	(B)	(B)
Standard error	508	1 181	1 381	851	1 578	973	2 094	2 537	(B)	(B)
Mean income ($)	45 886	24 832	29 713	33 119	41 212	59 083	49 025	85 566	(B)	(B)
Standard error	1 441	1 865	1 510	1 346	2 395	2 571	1 273	11 556	(B)	(B)
Hispanic[1]										
Number with income	4 727	1 252	1 505	906	343	719	511	159	29	19
Median income ($)	24 331	16 900	22 413	29 417	28 652	40 955	37 276	53 101	(B)	(B)
Standard error	399	221	484	934	1 131	746	1 195	3 020	(B)	(B)
Mean income ($)	29 698	19 111	25 759	32 961	33 757	50 308	44 956	59 617	(B)	(B)
Standard error	466	444	479	769	1 377	2 251	2 639	3 006	(B)	(B)

[1]May be of any race.
(B) = Base is too small to show the derived measure.

Table A-23. Income in 2004 by Educational Attainment for the Population Age 18 Years and Over, by Sex, Age, Race, and Hispanic Origin—*Continued*

(Numbers in thousands, dollars.)

Characteristic	Total population	High school — Not a high school graduate	High school graduate, includes GED	College — Some college, no degree	Associate's degree	Bachelor's degree or more — Total	Bachelor's degree	Master's degree	Professional degree	Doctorate degree
FEMALE, 25 YEARS AND OVER										
All Workers										
All races										
Number with income	89 794	11 724	28 560	15 791	8 861	24 856	16 667	6 464	991	733
Median income ($)	20 147	10 198	16 164	21 159	25 199	35 725	31 584	42 242	50 311	55 996
Standard error	82	92	109	164	266	202	201	330	1 861	1 896
Mean income ($)	27 122	12 597	20 342	25 139	29 051	42 337	37 415	48 918	63 287	67 838
Standard error	128	116	162	241	284	351	365	840	2 136	2 444
White alone or in combination										
Number with income	74 551	9 100	23 969	13 124	7 540	20 816	13 815	5 555	831	614
Median income ($)	20 092	10 388	16 077	20 878	25 152	35 475	31 239	42 111	48 751	56 031
Standard error	92	100	124	187	313	228	232	317	2 586	2 091
Mean income ($)	27 311	12 645	20 494	25 167	28 982	42 317	37 427	48 598	62 691	67 898
Standard error	143	130	186	277	306	387	419	868	2 385	2 613
Black alone or in combination										
Number with income	11 010	1 949	3 718	2 157	983	2 201	1 552	529	71	48
Median income ($)	20 089	9 346	16 721	22 498	24 653	38 207	35 424	45 340	(B)	(B)
Standard error	253	181	261	541	808	889	701	2 320	(B)	(B)
Mean income ($)	24 692	11 979	19 298	25 040	28 052	43 220	38 796	48 404	(B)	(B)
Standard error	265	280	273	489	818	879	953	1 513	(B)	(B)
Asian alone or in combination										
Number with income	3 787	520	720	431	282	1 832	1 289	379	88	74
Median income ($)	22 460	10 995	16 503	20 798	27 442	35 451	31 548	42 215	46 733	51 243
Standard error	631	699	655	2 004	1 946	1 223	731	3 447	5 586	6 526
Mean income ($)	31 614	13 993	21 837	23 515	33 209	42 126	36 085	55 636	62 006	54 206
Standard error	882	778	1 009	1 139	2 150	1 655	1 051	6 704	7 614	5 931
Hispanic[1]										
Number with income	8 653	3 137	2 413	1 336	588	1 177	822	271	52	31
Median income ($)	15 848	10 557	16 802	22 526	23 714	31 977	30 106	44 945	(B)	(B)
Standard error	210	190	321	729	1 238	870	1 314	4 040	(B)	(B)
Mean income ($)	21 173	12 670	19 727	25 932	26 162	38 899	33 729	49 645	(B)	(B)
Standard error	315	244	392	673	1 049	1 669	1 795	3 670	(B)	(B)
Year-Round, Full-Time Workers										
All races										
Number with income	39 129	2 714	11 401	7 340	4 491	13 181	8 694	3 467	565	453
Median income ($)	33 560	19 210	26 903	31 720	35 434	47 646	43 306	52 766	76 162	73 901
Standard error	199	291	126	147	265	357	559	789	1 113	2 398
Mean income ($)	41 397	21 715	31 057	35 940	39 792	57 980	51 971	64 661	87 611	85 151
Standard error	237	325	336	295	394	565	578	1 397	3 019	3 340
White alone or in combination										
Number with income	31 347	2 060	9 090	5 836	3 692	10 668	6 903	2 930	459	375
Median income ($)	34 720	18 932	27 437	32 202	35 950	48 294	44 434	53 040	76 579	74 189
Standard error	216	331	181	183	303	443	563	929	1 705	2 637
Mean income ($)	42 364	21 793	32 111	36 738	40 266	58 876	53 192	64 241	88 988	84 693
Standard error	274	367	410	347	432	640	695	1 452	3 476	3 579
Black alone or in combination										
Number with income	5 628	447	1 880	1 228	595	1 476	1 043	341	57	34
Median income ($)	30 178	19 093	25 171	30 363	31 476	42 342	40 743	50 877	(B)	(B)
Standard error	212	736	350	273	530	760	384	559	(B)	(B)
Mean income ($)	34 675	20 087	26 463	32 511	35 881	50 862	46 077	56 107	(B)	(B)
Standard error	400	699	364	590	1 047	1 117	1 207	1 742	(B)	(B)
Asian alone or in combination										
Number with income	1 944	165	366	219	167	1 025	731	200	45	47
Median income ($)	36 951	22 290	24 774	32 002	36 508	50 303	45 136	63 765	(B)	(B)
Standard error	501	1 340	1 335	1 416	2 482	917	2 124	2 564	(B)	(B)
Mean income ($)	46 730	24 901	30 145	34 289	42 158	59 597	49 354	86 515	(B)	(B)
Standard error	1 507	1 897	1 588	1 518	2 479	2 639	1 301	11 857	(B)	(B)
Hispanic[1]										
Number with income	4 229	1 151	1 304	757	312	703	494	159	29	19
Median income ($)	25 491	16 954	24 355	31 351	29 794	41 212	37 728	53 101	(B)	(B)
Standard error	281	240	775	530	1 242	737	1 418	3 020	(B)	(B)
Mean income ($)	30 820	19 278	26 777	35 096	34 905	50 811	45 489	59 617	(B)	(B)
Standard error	513	478	525	867	1 482	2 297	2 720	3 006	(B)	(B)

[1]May be of any race.
(B) = Base is too small to show the derived measure.

Table A-23. Income in 2004 by Educational Attainment for the Population Age 18 Years and Over, by Sex, Age, Race, and Hispanic Origin—*Continued*

(Numbers in thousands, dollars.)

Characteristic	Total population	High school — Not a high school graduate	High school graduate, includes GED	Some college, no degree	Associate's degree	College — Bachelor's degree or more — Total	Bachelor's degree	Master's degree	Professional degree	Doctorate degree
FEMALE, 25 TO 64 YEARS										
All Workers										
All races										
Number with income	70 444	6 677	20 807	13 173	7 731	22 054	14 810	5 693	879	671
Median income ($)	23 536	11 206	19 027	22 630	26 818	37 384	33 495	45 226	52 415	56 593
Standard error	144	144	218	252	270	442	546	2 006	2 067	
Mean income ($)	29 833	13 737	22 099	25 937	30 304	44 163	38 967	51 140	67 450	69 107
Standard error	151	178	190	222	307	386	400	936	2 335	2 623
White alone or in combination										
Number with income	57 529	5 064	16 883	10 734	6 519	18 327	12 165	4 873	733	555
Median income ($)	23 777	11 179	19 315	22 439	26 862	37 311	33 127	45 157	51 590	56 533
Standard error	162	161	244	240	303	245	477	610	1 384	2 216
Mean income ($)	30 171	13 648	22 465	25 973	30 236	44 272	39 123	50 868	66 969	69 201
Standard error	171	202	224	254	332	429	463	969	2 622	2 832
Black alone or in combination										
Number with income	9 291	1 182	3 211	1 984	902	2 009	1 437	463	61	46
Median income ($)	22 179	10 596	17 921	23 776	25 920	39 974	36 271	48 295	(B)	(B)
Standard error	222	404	501	688	857	681	617	2 070	(B)	(B)
Mean income ($)	26 659	13 268	20 213	25 777	29 088	44 623	39 819	50 708	(B)	(B)
Standard error	300	401	299	513	871	938	1 007	1 606	(B)	(B)
Asian alone or in combination										
Number with income	3 250	320	578	380	257	1 711	1 199	354	85	71
Median income ($)	26 183	14 741	20 070	22 385	30 226	36 033	32 038	42 960	50 524	(B)
Standard error	536	911	1 192	1 788	2 401	744	1 215	3 597	7 210	(B)
Mean income ($)	34 114	16 875	23 417	24 466	35 209	42 946	36 841	56 188	63 414	(B)
Standard error	1 000	1 172	1 173	1 199	2 279	1 747	1 082	7 129	7 879	(B)
Hispanic[1]										
Number with income	7 528	2 450	2 166	1 272	546	1 091	774	241	50	25
Median income ($)	17 191	11 496	17 491	23 489	24 057	33 114	30 893	46 435	(B)	(B)
Standard error	210	212	476	898	1 143	1 284	749	3 424	(B)	(B)
Mean income ($)	22 421	13 496	20 223	26 486	26 784	39 891	34 901	50 533	(B)	(B)
Standard error	351	296	409	694	1 105	1 770	1 887	3 994	(B)	(B)
Year-Round, Full-Time Workers										
All races										
Number with income	38 156	2 583	11 010	7 186	4 413	12 962	8 575	3 402	544	439
Median income ($)	33 541	18 989	26 836	31 638	35 426	47 492	43 110	52 831	76 125	71 966
Standard error	201	294	127	149	263	327	555	806	2 019	2 445
Mean income ($)	41 277	21 478	30 670	35 698	39 656	57 878	51 804	64 799	88 431	84 969
Standard error	236	333	297	296	395	571	580	1 420	3 121	3 434
White alone or in combination										
Number with income	30 525	1 965	8 749	5 694	3 623	10 492	6 817	2 872	440	361
Median income ($)	34 685	18 680	27 352	32 093	35 920	48 106	44 224	53 096	76 491	71 809
Standard error	218	333	147	185	301	445	559	941	2 617	2 653
Mean income ($)	42 198	21 556	31 635	36 453	40 088	58 720	52 976	64 360	89 700	84 454
Standard error	272	375	360	348	433	647	696	1 477	3 608	3 700
Black alone or in combination										
Number with income	5 519	421	1 840	1 216	588	1 452	1 027	336	54	34
Median income ($)	30 206	18 991	25 153	30 380	31 511	42 331	40 665	50 901	(B)	(B)
Standard error	203	732	365	274	527	748	394	570	(B)	(B)
Mean income ($)	34 742	19 785	26 457	32 549	35 970	50 911	45 970	56 357	(B)	(B)
Standard error	406	703	369	594	1 058	1 133	1 222	1 763	(B)	(B)
Asian alone or in combination										
Number with income	1 908	158	359	218	166	1 004	715	195	45	47
Median income ($)	36 899	22 287	25 009	32 004	36 511	50 230	45 064	62 479	(B)	(B)
Standard error	497	1 304	1 267	1 414	2 478	972	2 119	2 433	(B)	(B)
Mean income ($)	46 726	24 782	30 297	34 029	42 103	59 606	49 466	85 995	(B)	(B)
Standard error	1 528	1 964	1 605	1 399	2 486	2 685	1 317	12 140	(B)	(B)
Hispanic[1]										
Number with income	4 153	1 116	1 283	754	305	692	490	153	28	19
Median income ($)	25 482	16 854	24 231	31 305	29 892	41 063	37 545	52 317	(B)	(B)
Standard error	285	244	802	529	1 232	732	1 357	2 848	(B)	(B)
Mean income ($)	30 724	19 192	26 609	35 025	34 972	50 376	45 419	58 439	(B)	(B)
Standard error	517	490	516	869	1 509	2 318	2 738	2 984	(B)	(B)

[1]May be of any race.
(B) = Base is too small to show the derived measure.

Table A-23. Income in 2004 by Educational Attainment for the Population Age 18 Years and Over, by Sex, Age, Race, and Hispanic Origin—*Continued*

(Numbers in thousands, dollars.)

Characteristic	Total population	High school		Some college, no degree	Associate's degree	College				
		Not a high school graduate	High school graduate, includes GED			Bachelor's degree or more				
						Total	Bachelor's degree	Master's degree	Professional degree	Doctorate degree
FEMALE, 25 TO 34 YEARS										
All Workers										
All races										
Number with income	17 035	1 609	4 195	3 398	1 738	6 094	4 454	1 303	213	121
Median income ($)	22 066	10 761	16 609	21 010	24 156	33 576	31 749	37 521	44 634	45 667
Standard error	157	338	250	286	920	559	271	956	2 851	3 582
Mean income ($)	26 199	12 624	19 754	22 554	25 521	36 449	34 121	39 113	57 393	56 312
Standard error	252	293	599	411	507	458	497	1 037	3 511	4 543
White alone or in combination										
Number with income	13 367	1 236	3 201	2 628	1 394	4 905	3 576	1 076	158	94
Median income ($)	22 188	10 835	16 541	20 797	24 379	33 741	31 772	38 256	45 400	45 481
Standard error	182	357	302	341	1 079	579	290	1 198	3 466	3 577
Mean income ($)	26 465	12 527	20 060	22 441	25 573	36 569	34 169	39 675	58 158	55 758
Standard error	302	333	772	497	555	524	575	1 152	4 053	5 343
Black alone or in combination										
Number with income	2 646	287	833	656	276	592	462	105	20	5
Median income ($)	21 245	9 270	16 822	21 378	23 655	35 107	31 669	41 158	(B)	(B)
Standard error	365	817	478	555	1 423	1 524	1 478	1 210	(B)	(B)
Mean income ($)	23 662	12 405	18 945	22 173	25 116	36 714	33 427	43 531	(B)	(B)
Standard error	429	709	526	650	1 450	1 175	1 119	3 028	(B)	(B)
Asian alone or in combination										
Number with income	961	63	119	103	61	613	431	126	35	20
Median income ($)	26 216	(B)	20 727	26 409	(B)	31 949	32 291	20 560	(B)	(B)
Standard error	972	(B)	2 031	2 030	(B)	1 661	1 957	4 697	(B)	(B)
Mean income ($)	30 670	(B)	19 829	25 864	(B)	35 608	35 206	30 744	(B)	(B)
Standard error	1 099	(B)	1 653	2 388	(B)	1 546	1 670	3 666	(B)	(B)
Hispanic[1]										
Number with income	2 540	752	748	453	196	388	300	65	17	5
Median income ($)	17 067	11 121	16 474	23 258	21 807	31 323	31 084	(B)	(B)	(B)
Standard error	356	435	482	910	2 009	804	805	(B)	(B)	(B)
Mean income ($)	20 485	12 626	18 461	25 906	24 955	31 016	30 226	(B)	(B)	(B)
Standard error	420	429	666	1 167	1 535	1 303	1 441	(B)	(B)	(B)
Year-Round, Full-Time Workers										
All races										
Number with income	9 267	632	2 172	1 757	961	3 742	2 733	788	131	88
Median income ($)	31 335	18 148	25 048	29 282	30 917	40 765	38 958	44 356	71 389	54 853
Standard error	150	591	357	680	361	235	555	1 299	6 498	5 528
Mean income ($)	36 249	19 765	28 616	31 582	33 102	46 469	43 152	50 584	75 919	68 422
Standard error	376	471	1 085	643	617	533	501	1 431	4 509	5 446
White alone or in combination										
Number with income	7 208	493	1 632	1 320	741	3 019	2 194	660	97	66
Median income ($)	31 674	17 399	25 092	29 399	31 377	40 687	38 666	43 867	71 338	(B)
Standard error	179	477	381	747	447	276	596	1 460	11 024	(B)
Mean income ($)	36 812	19 619	29 718	32 282	33 381	46 282	43 165	50 003	75 423	(B)
Standard error	459	525	1 430	818	662	606	574	1 604	5 276	(B)
Black alone or in combination										
Number with income	1 489	101	446	355	179	406	303	78	19	5
Median income ($)	29 056	20 239	25 298	28 188	29 366	40 256	37 473	44 076	(B)	(B)
Standard error	524	865	964	1 217	1 295	1 004	1 718	2 462	(B)	(B)
Mean income ($)	31 360	19 425	25 394	28 362	31 719	43 360	39 493	50 164	(B)	(B)
Standard error	561	1 301	627	726	1 872	1 329	1 152	3 337	(B)	(B)
Asian alone or in combination										
Number with income	529	29	74	68	34	322	238	52	15	16
Median income ($)	37 183	(B)	24 393	(B)	(B)	46 491	42 257	(B)	(B)	(B)
Standard error	1 133	(B)	2 007	(B)	(B)	3 259	2 646	(B)	(B)	(B)
Mean income ($)	43 311	(B)	26 733	(B)	(B)	52 219	48 415	(B)	(B)	(B)
Standard error	1 423	(B)	1 884	(B)	(B)	1 971	1 870	(B)	(B)	(B)
Hispanic[1]										
Number with income	1 407	340	447	268	114	237	184	34	12	5
Median income ($)	24 292	16 769	21 527	30 369	26 922	36 436	35 781	(B)	(B)	(B)
Standard error	713	434	491	1 404	1 135	990	1 168	(B)	(B)	(B)
Mean income ($)	27 772	18 114	24 300	34 553	30 828	39 013	37 744	(B)	(B)	(B)
Standard error	570	593	827	1 554	1 610	1 595	1 722	(B)	(B)	(B)

[1]May be of any race.
(B) = Base is too small to show the derived measure.

Table A-23. Income in 2004 by Educational Attainment for the Population Age 18 Years and Over, by Sex, Age, Race, and Hispanic Origin—*Continued*

(Numbers in thousands, dollars.)

Characteristic	Total population	High school		Some college, no degree	Associate's degree	College				
		Not a high school graduate	High school graduate, includes GED			Bachelor's degree or more				
						Total	Bachelor's degree	Master's degree	Professional degree	Doctorate degree
FEMALE, 35 TO 44 YEARS										
All Workers										
All races										
Number with income	19 737	1 673	5 703	3 665	2 322	6 372	4 337	1 515	305	213
Median income ($)	24 402	11 981	20 321	23 675	27 175	37 787	34 443	43 259	57 241	55 771
Standard error	266	239	206	635	522	554	763	1 358	5 999	4 173
Mean income ($)	30 780	14 689	22 493	26 476	30 350	45 058	41 108	47 266	73 050	69 481
Standard error	289	358	289	408	520	754	890	1 457	4 296	4 846
White alone or in combination										
Number with income	15 910	1 268	4 545	2 927	1 950	5 219	3 548	1 235	260	174
Median income ($)	24 318	11 801	20 431	23 547	26 695	37 409	33 822	42 714	54 272	58 258
Standard error	304	251	237	747	547	557	884	1 630	4 874	7 110
Mean income ($)	30 789	14 494	22 737	26 343	29 594	44 701	41 213	45 607	70 776	70 192
Standard error	316	412	331	460	553	807	1 032	1 067	4 753	4 593
Black alone or in combination										
Number with income	2 713	292	971	583	259	606	445	133	13	14
Median income ($)	23 937	11 895	20 033	25 163	29 622	39 137	37 043	42 350	(B)	(B)
Standard error	673	751	731	1 248	1 450	1 139	1 008	2 180	(B)	(B)
Mean income ($)	28 596	13 897	21 183	28 232	33 606	45 776	42 461	45 971	(B)	(B)
Standard error	662	677	557	1 117	1 742	2 236	2 444	2 614	(B)	(B)
Asian alone or in combination										
Number with income	996	79	150	124	87	553	347	144	32	29
Median income ($)	28 865	19 608	19 566	20 966	34 778	41 159	32 086	50 104	(B)	(B)
Standard error	1 682	2 455	2 244	3 714	2 255	2 720	2 806	5 519	(B)	(B)
Mean income ($)	37 985	19 138	24 507	21 168	38 027	48 158	38 829	63 194	(B)	(D)
Standard error	2 226	1 712	3 124	1 756	3 801	3 751	2 093	12 809	(B)	(B)
Hispanic[1]										
Number with income	2 200	717	630	398	172	360	249	83	16	10
Median income ($)	18 036	12 093	19 704	24 862	25 413	31 984	29 943	48 692	(B)	(B)
Standard error	748	287	1 186	2 087	1 183	1 446	1 994	5 466	(B)	(B)
Mean income ($)	23 845	14 317	21 305	27 132	27 073	42 147	37 251	48 993	(B)	(B)
Standard error	774	538	787	1 251	1 772	4 036	5 058	4 807	(B)	(B)
Year-Round, Full-Time Workers										
All races										
Number with income	11 220	790	3 332	2 075	1 338	3 683	2 476	880	176	149
Median income ($)	34 033	18 830	26 474	32 356	35 563	50 161	46 141	55 051	80 538	70 602
Standard error	347	460	233	381	582	511	565	1 286	5 422	5 541
Mean income ($)	41 927	21 298	29 847	35 918	39 557	61 533	57 404	62 503	98 474	80 517
Standard error	436	587	391	479	636	1 133	1 368	2 164	5 922	5 970
White alone or in combination										
Number with income	8 769	594	2 601	1 595	1 078	2 900	1 931	696	144	128
Median income ($)	35 017	18 163	26 942	33 296	35 822	50 740	46 780	55 579	80 611	70 920
Standard error	320	580	279	632	745	477	677	1 140	6 500	4 522
Mean income ($)	42 666	21 326	30 608	36 608	39 364	62 413	59 336	60 469	99 629	77 516
Standard error	483	696	453	562	686	1 231	1 658	1 265	6 818	5 206
Black alone or in combination										
Number with income	1 813	130	626	400	189	467	344	101	11	9
Median income ($)	30 474	19 158	24 967	30 833	32 244	42 007	40 945	43 870	(B)	(B)
Standard error	409	807	781	638	1 549	1 382	920	2 546	(B)	(B)
Mean income ($)	35 426	19 182	26 264	33 850	38 163	52 476	49 467	50 994	(B)	(B)
Standard error	855	849	628	1 071	1 815	2 719	2 960	2 930	(B)	(B)
Asian alone or in combination										
Number with income	578	55	88	57	58	318	203	81	16	17
Median income ($)	40 771	(B)	26 559	(B)	(B)	55 459	47 820	65 537	(B)	(B)
Standard error	1 344	(B)	3 824	(B)	(B)	2 594	2 518	2 520	(B)	(B)
Mean income ($)	52 756	(B)	33 968	(B)	(B)	67 340	52 771	95 000	(B)	(B)
Standard error	3 522	(B)	4 814	(B)	(B)	5 976	2 673	21 453	(B)	(B)
Hispanic[1]										
Number with income	1 354	369	411	239	93	241	169	58	6	7
Median income ($)	25 554	16 941	24 231	31 747	28 657	41 453	36 698	(B)	(B)	(B)
Standard error	500	533	1 187	1 121	961	1 546	2 532	(B)	(B)	(B)
Mean income ($)	31 871	19 396	26 793	35 301	33 751	55 459	49 369	(B)	(B)	(B)
Standard error	1 193	858	1 003	1 489	2 410	5 663	7 166	(B)	(B)	(B)

[1]May be of any race.
(B) = Base is too small to show the derived measure.

Table A-23. Income in 2004 by Educational Attainment for the Population Age 18 Years and Over, by Sex, Age, Race, and Hispanic Origin—*Continued*

(Numbers in thousands, dollars.)

Characteristic	Total population	High school		Some college, no degree	Associate's degree	College				
		Not a high school graduate	High school graduate, includes GED			Bachelor's degree or more				
						Total	Bachelor's degree	Master's degree	Professional degree	Doctorate degree
FEMALE, 45 TO 54 YEARS										
All Workers										
All races										
Number with income	19 592	1 736	6 028	3 614	2 311	5 901	3 834	1 654	221	190
Median income ($)	26 232	11 841	21 050	26 144	30 121	42 392	36 735	51 546	61 788	61 400
Standard error	190	309	254	367	641	577	478	497	4 177	5 858
Mean income ($)	33 191	15 143	24 131	29 025	33 621	50 139	43 167	60 205	77 259	71 491
Standard error	326	453	330	427	630	900	912	2 168	5 377	5 082
White alone or in combination										
Number with income	16 214	1 292	4 932	3 006	2 001	4 982	3 176	1 452	192	161
Median income ($)	26 622	12 008	21 419	26 167	30 421	42 281	36 462	51 043	60 127	56 208
Standard error	212	388	287	423	661	566	565	614	6 128	4 595
Mean income ($)	33 790	15 211	24 752	29 398	33 814	50 196	43 524	59 060	77 267	69 407
Standard error	368	509	386	483	678	999	1 071	2 221	6 068	5 777
Black alone or in combination										
Number with income	2 456	321	861	485	219	568	386	144	19	18
Median income ($)	23 944	10 473	19 889	26 033	26 156	47 915	40 570	53 728	(B)	(B)
Standard error	648	578	793	849	2 402	3 017	1 383	4 612	(B)	(B)
Mean income ($)	28 960	13 760	21 181	27 211	29 384	50 671	44 190	58 816	(B)	(B)
Standard error	596	1 018	565	1 031	1 665	1 623	1 709	3 308	(B)	(B)
Asian alone or in combination										
Number with income	799	101	190	102	73	332	256	56	8	10
Median income ($)	26 250	15 686	18 246	25 485	(B)	39 844	35 655	(B)	(B)	(B)
Standard error	1 073	977	1 773	3 411	(B)	2 673	2 397	(B)	(B)	(B)
Mean income ($)	35 003	18 877	23 040	26 435	(B)	49 195	37 701	(B)	(B)	(B)
Standard error	2 379	3 051	1 763	2 305	(B)	5 281	2 219	(B)	(B)	(B)
Hispanic[1]										
Number with income	1 700	593	489	263	105	248	166	62	11	8
Median income ($)	18 244	12 353	20 091	25 404	22 925	41 140	35 364	(B)	(B)	(B)
Standard error	740	672	1 115	2 119	2 592	2 567	4 288	(B)	(B)	(B)
Mean income ($)	25 017	14 785	22 395	27 763	29 001	50 009	37 991	(B)	(B)	(B)
Standard error	860	800	874	1 572	3 459	4 236	2 803	(B)	(B)	(B)
Year-Round, Full-Time Workers										
All races										
Number with income	11 679	742	3 578	2 211	1 419	3 727	2 344	1 108	157	117
Median income ($)	35 599	19 219	28 019	32 852	37 828	52 188	47 903	60 167	68 198	76 536
Standard error	235	619	382	621	697	361	935	1 747	4 820	3 463
Mean income ($)	43 890	23 005	31 705	37 823	43 546	63 477	56 006	71 984	92 454	93 511
Standard error	478	822	415	491	817	1 290	1 336	2 984	6 786	6 939
White alone or in combination										
Number with income	9 483	557	2 877	1 806	1 212	3 029	1 850	953	131	93
Median income ($)	36 458	19 719	29 413	34 291	38 618	53 229	49 502	59 709	68 891	72 489
Standard error	263	610	446	829	799	848	1 003	1 820	7 288	3 822
Mean income ($)	45 115	23 448	32 907	38 619	44 025	65 005	58 227	71 177	95 254	93 367
Standard error	547	902	491	556	879	1 479	1 650	3 085	7 888	8 376
Black alone or in combination										
Number with income	1 574	120	549	328	136	437	295	111	16	14
Median income ($)	30 783	16 372	25 107	30 984	35 480	51 269	42 764	57 591	(B)	(B)
Standard error	392	1 221	646	422	1 277	638	2 299	5 426	(B)	(B)
Mean income ($)	36 628	19 801	26 630	33 973	37 506	55 544	48 664	63 902	(B)	(B)
Standard error	744	1 828	658	1 206	2 077	1 770	1 827	3 489	(B)	(B)
Asian alone or in combination										
Number with income	543	52	128	64	55	243	184	41	8	8
Median income ($)	35 654	(B)	21 998	(B)	(B)	48 480	41 327	(B)	(B)	(B)
Standard error	1 094	(B)	1 211	(B)	(B)	2 070	3 919	(B)	(B)	(B)
Mean income ($)	44 770	(B)	27 999	(B)	(B)	59 934	46 197	(B)	(B)	(B)
Standard error	3 311	(B)	2 243	(B)	(B)	6 912	2 428	(B)	(B)	(B)
Hispanic[1]										
Number with income	983	285	294	170	60	172	109	48	7	6
Median income ($)	26 637	16 905	27 155	31 624	(B)	50 256	42 139	(B)	(B)	(B)
Standard error	685	389	1 047	1 252	(B)	3 226	2 652	(B)	(B)	(B)
Mean income ($)	33 201	20 360	29 280	35 210	(B)	56 383	47 812	(B)	(B)	(B)
Standard error	1 038	1 329	993	1 785	(B)	3 720	3 430	(B)	(B)	(B)

[1]May be of any race.
(B) = Base is too small to show the derived measure.

Table A-23. Income in 2004 by Educational Attainment for the Population Age 18 Years and Over, by Sex, Age, Race, and Hispanic Origin—*Continued*

(Numbers in thousands, dollars.)

| Characteristic | Total population | High school | | Some college, no degree | Associate's degree | College | | | | |
| | | Not a high school graduate | High school graduate, includes GED | | | Bachelor's degree or more | | | | |
						Total	Bachelor's degree	Master's degree	Professional degree	Doctorate degree
FEMALE, 55 TO 64 YEARS										
All Workers										
All races										
Number with income	14 077	1 657	4 880	2 494	1 359	3 686	2 183	1 219	137	145
Median income ($)	20 802	10 029	16 935	21 014	25 590	39 096	31 458	47 975	46 629	61 477
Standard error	230	279	358	453	1 058	1 024	681	1 464	4 848	4 703
Mean income ($)	28 226	12 386	21 145	25 280	30 702	45 799	37 223	56 514	54 814	76 157
Standard error	326	276	328	556	810	975	772	2 370	4 644	5 964
White alone or in combination										
Number with income	12 036	1 266	4 204	2 171	1 173	3 220	1 864	1 109	120	125
Median income ($)	21 052	9 973	17 218	20 456	26 004	39 434	31 410	47 138	45 580	62 094
Standard error	255	329	446	529	1 270	1 054	750	1 246	4 389	4 449
Mean income ($)	28 597	12 303	21 320	25 008	30 743	46 147	37 151	56 866	53 880	77 677
Standard error	365	320	362	604	861	1 083	833	2 590	4 559	6 572
Black alone or in combination										
Number with income	1 474	281	545	258	147	241	143	80	8	9
Median income ($)	18 423	10 315	15 584	24 478	23 359	41 194	35 828	54 610	(B)	(B)
Standard error	1 146	739	616	1 286	2 723	2 533	3 327	4 907	(B)	(B)
Mean income ($)	24 640	12 934	18 892	26 698	28 150	46 906	40 451	53 394	(B)	(B)
Standard error	695	678	812	1 553	2 217	2 241	2 837	3 445	(B)	(B)
Asian alone or in combination										
Number with income	492	76	117	50	36	211	164	28	8	10
Median income ($)	21 831	11 487	20 920	(B)	(B)	30 215	24 312	(B)	(B)	(B)
Standard error	1 291	1 001	3 471	(B)	(B)	4 985	2 482	(R)	(R)	(R)
Mean income ($)	31 557	13 640	26 286	(B)	(B)	40 763	35 585	(B)	(B)	(B)
Standard error	1 892	1 445	2 455	(B)	(B)	3 517	3 384	(B)	(B)	(B)
Hispanic[1]										
Number with income	999	387	289	156	72	94	58	29	5	1
Median income ($)	14 208	9 509	16 110	21 160	(B)	36 458	(B)	(B)	(B)	(B)
Standard error	903	506	1 242	1 868	(B)	6 860	(B)	(B)	(B)	(B)
Mean income ($)	19 666	11 691	18 716	24 379	(B)	41 194	(B)	(B)	(B)	(B)
Standard error	741	552	1 064	1 793	(B)	4 415	(B)	(D)	(B)	(B)
Year-Round, Full-Time Workers										
All races										
Number with income	5 988	417	1 927	1 141	694	1 808	1 021	625	78	83
Median income ($)	34 967	20 214	28 338	31 728	36 208	51 702	46 610	56 688	80 408	81 190
Standard error	496	535	607	392	525	529	700	1 355	7 324	1 132
Mean income ($)	42 743	21 699	32 490	37 520	40 970	62 497	51 735	73 218	78 723	98 619
Standard error	620	575	573	891	1 063	1 708	1 079	4 285	6 191	8 618
White alone or in combination										
Number with income	5 065	320	1 637	972	591	1 543	841	562	66	72
Median income ($)	35 435	19 792	28 967	32 044	36 688	51 982	47 328	56 072	(B)	(B)
Standard error	291	671	591	423	597	595	1 048	1 268	(B)	(B)
Mean income ($)	43 591	21 676	32 943	37 840	41 748	63 781	52 417	74 483	(B)	(B)
Standard error	708	677	638	987	1 161	1 953	1 167	4 751	(B)	(B)
Black alone or in combination										
Number with income	641	68	216	131	83	141	84	43	7	5
Median income ($)	30 420	(B)	25 453	30 632	32 470	50 167	40 666	(B)	(B)	(B)
Standard error	818	(B)	995	1 334	2 837	2 990	1 600	(B)	(B)	(B)
Mean income ($)	36 029	(B)	28 760	36 332	37 604	53 099	45 512	(B)	(B)	(B)
Standard error	1 128	(B)	1 422	2 404	3 169	2 777	3 633	(B)	(B)	(B)
Asian alone or in combination										
Number with income	257	21	69	28	18	119	89	20	4	5
Median income ($)	34 475	(B)	(B)	(B)	(B)	50 080	40 830	(B)	(B)	(B)
Standard error	1 751	(B)	(B)	(B)	(B)	5 588	5 314	(B)	(B)	(B)
Mean income ($)	44 310	(B)	(B)	(B)	(B)	58 267	51 493	(B)	(B)	(B)
Standard error	2 770	(B)	(B)	(B)	(B)	5 022	4 838	(B)	(B)	(B)
Hispanic[1]										
Number with income	406	120	130	76	37	41	27	11	2	(B)
Median income ($)	26 333	16 733	25 785	32 087	(B)	(B)	(B)	(B)	(B)	(B)
Standard error	888	738	982	2 056	(B)	(B)	(B)	(B)	(B)	(B)
Mean income ($)	31 128	18 841	27 916	35 409	(B)	(B)	(B)	(B)	(B)	(B)
Standard error	1 298	939	1 515	2 487	(B)	(B)	(B)	(B)	(B)	(B)

[1]May be of any race.
(B) = Base is too small to show the derived measure.

Table A-23. Income in 2004 by Educational Attainment for the Population Age 18 Years and Over, by Sex, Age, Race, and Hispanic Origin—*Continued*

(Numbers in thousands, dollars.)

| Characteristic | Total population | High school | | Some college, no degree | Associate's degree | College | | | | |
| | | Not a high school graduate | High school graduate, includes GED | | | Bachelor's degree or more | | | | |
						Total	Bachelor's degree	Master's degree	Professional degree	Doctorate degree
FEMALE, 65 YEARS AND OVER										
All Workers										
All races										
Number with income	19 350	5 047	7 753	2 618	1 129	2 802	1 857	770	112	61
Median income ($)	12 081	9 441	12 011	14 437	14 689	19 784	18 108	23 942	18 565	(B)
Standard error	73	88	113	266	421	449	530	989	3 378	(B)
Mean income ($)	17 256	11 088	15 626	21 124	20 471	27 964	25 045	32 506	30 710	(B)
Standard error	204	127	303	925	669	575	661	1 157	2 866	(B)
White alone or in combination										
Number with income	17 021	4 036	7 085	2 389	1 021	2 489	1 649	681	98	58
Median income ($)	12 371	9 755	12 135	14 625	14 820	19 739	18 110	24 029	16 467	(B)
Standard error	77	102	117	274	425	459	519	970	2 371	(B)
Mean income ($)	17 644	11 387	15 799	21 547	20 979	27 924	24 922	32 370	30 897	(B)
Standard error	227	144	327	1 006	727	611	699	1 224	3 239	(B)
Black alone or in combination										
Number with income	1 718	767	506	172	80	192	114	66	9	1
Median income ($)	9 920	8 500	10 694	12 091	15 185	23 129	21 370	(B)	(B)	(B)
Standard error	202	197	492	1 161	2 288	2 072	1 871	(B)	(B)	(B)
Mean income ($)	14 063	9 992	13 495	16 587	16 402	28 555	25 989	(B)	(B)	(B)
Standard error	380	339	572	1 373	1 345	1 874	2 212	(B)	(B)	(B)
Asian alone or in combination										
Number with income	536	199	141	50	24	120	89	24	3	2
Median income ($)	9 573	7 633	10 804	(B)	(B)	14 650	12 954	(B)	(B)	(B)
Standard error	413	469	988	(B)	(B)	2 866	2 425	(B)	(B)	(B)
Mean income ($)	16 482	9 355	15 382	(B)	(B)	30 483	25 952	(B)	(B)	(B)
Standard error	1 154	563	1 678	(B)	(B)	3 987	4 135	(B)	(B)	(B)
Hispanic[1]										
Number with income	1 125	686	247	63	41	85	48	30	2	5
Median income ($)	8 989	8 159	10 467	(B)	(B)	12 476	(B)	(B)	(B)	(B)
Standard error	224	260	622	(B)	(B)	3 459	(B)	(B)	(B)	(B)
Mean income ($)	12 827	9 722	15 370	(B)	(B)	26 302	(B)	(B)	(B)	(B)
Standard error	505	312	1 301	(B)	(B)	3 872	(B)	(B)	(B)	(B)
Year-Round, Full-Time Workers										
All races										
Number with income	973	131	390	154	77	219	118	65	21	13
Median income ($)	34 353	23 116	30 164	41 464	40 363	59 489	52 015	(B)	(B)	(B)
Standard error	1 351	862	916	1 625	5 725	4 940	5 158	(B)	(B)	(B)
Mean income ($)	46 102	26 379	41 968	47 201	47 514	64 024	64 016	(B)	(B)	(B)
Standard error	2 290	1 454	5 070	2 493	3 606	3 609	5 780	(B)	(B)	(B)
White alone or in combination										
Number with income	822	95	341	141	68	176	86	57	18	13
Median income ($)	36 019	23 263	30 647	42 268	(B)	61 775	58 158	(B)	(B)	(B)
Standard error	1 334	822	697	1 939	(B)	3 657	5 123	(B)	(B)	(B)
Mean income ($)	48 504	26 686	44 328	48 233	(B)	68 115	70 180	(B)	(B)	(B)
Standard error	2 677	1 726	5 784	2 536	(B)	4 313	7 638	(B)	(B)	(B)
Black alone or in combination										
Number with income	109	26	39	12	6	23	15	5	2	(B)
Median income ($)	26 895	(B)	(B)	(B)	(B)	(B)	(B)	(B)	(B)	(B)
Standard error	2 448	(B)	(B)	(B)	(B)	(B)	(B)	(B)	(B)	(B)
Mean income ($)	31 292	(B)	(B)	(B)	(B)	(B)	(B)	(B)	(B)	(B)
Standard error	1 884	(B)	(B)	(B)	(B)	(B)	(B)	(B)	(B)	(B)
Asian alone or in combination										
Number with income	35	6	6	(B)	(B)	20	15	4	(B)	(B)
Median income ($)	(B)	(B)	(B)	(B)	(B)	(B)	(B)	(B)	(B)	(B)
Standard error	(B)	(B)	(B)	(B)	(B)	(B)	(B)	(B)	(B)	(B)
Mean income ($)	(B)	(B)	(B)	(B)	(B)	(B)	(B)	(B)	(B)	(B)
Standard error	(B)	(B)	(B)	(B)	(B)	(B)	(B)	(B)	(B)	(B)
Hispanic[1]										
Number with income	76	35	21	2	6	10	3	5	(B)	(B)
Median income ($)	25 924	(B)	(B)	(B)	(B)	(B)	(B)	(B)	(B)	(B)
Standard error	1 967	(B)	(B)	(B)	(B)	(B)	(B)	(B)	(B)	(B)
Mean income ($)	36 024	(B)	(B)	(B)	(B)	(B)	(B)	(B)	(B)	(B)
Standard error	3 958	(B)	(B)	(B)	(B)	(B)	(B)	(B)	(B)	(B)

[1]May be of any race.
(B) = Base is too small to show the derived measure.

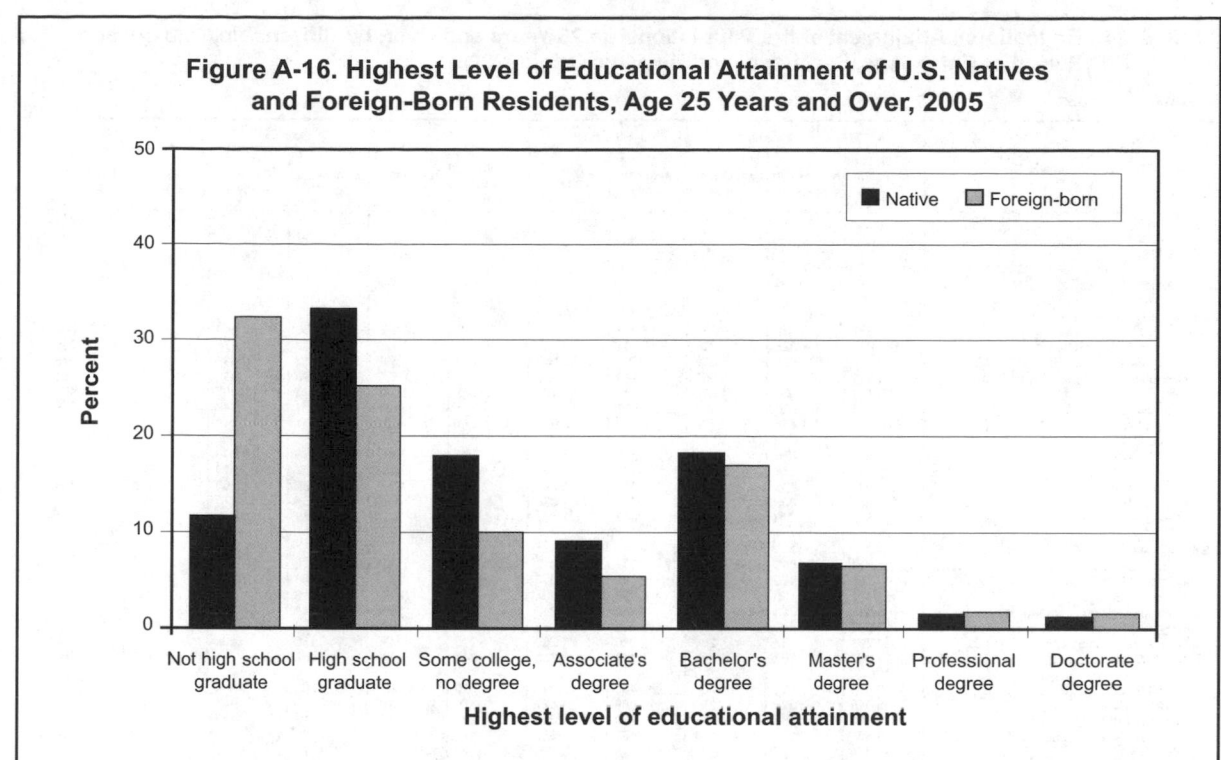

Figure A-16. Highest Level of Educational Attainment of U.S. Natives and Foreign-Born Residents, Age 25 Years and Over, 2005

In 2005, only 67.5 percent of foreign-born people in the United States were high school graduates. However, this percentage was significantly different among foreign-born people who were naturalized citizens and those who were not citizens. Among those that were not citizens, only 58.8 percent were high school graduates, whereas 79 percent of naturalized citizens were high school graduates. This was still significantly lower than the percentage for the native-born population (those who were U.S. citizens from birth). Nearly one-third (32.5 percent) of all immigrants who entered the country between 2000 and 2005 held a bachelor's degree or more, a sharp increase from those who arrived during the 1990s (26.5 percent). Among foreign-born persons who arrived from 2000 to 2005, 11.8 percent held master's degrees or more, compared with 9.5 percent of U.S. natives. The proportion of immigrants without a high school diploma remained steady from the 1970s to 2005, with between 31 and 32 percent of immigrants included in this category. Only 11.7 percent of U.S. natives were not high school graduates. (Table A-24)

Table A-24. Educational Attainment of the Population Age 25 Years and Over, by Citizenship, Nativity and Period of Entry, Age, Sex, Race, and Hispanic Origin, 2005

(Numbers in thousands.)

Characteristic	Total population	Elementary		High school		College					
		None to 4th grade	5th to 8th grade	9th to 11th grade	High school graduate	Some college, no degree	Associate's degree	Bachelor's degree	Master's degree	Professional degree	Doctorate degree
ALL RACES											
Both Sexes											
25 Years and Over											
Total	189 367	2 982	8 935	16 098	60 893	31 809	16 268	34 260	12 840	2 934	2 347
Born in the United States	160 885	1 028	4 888	12 851	53 697	28 962	14 720	29 432	10 978	2 444	1 885
Native parentage[1]	147 074	872	4 338	11 702	49 639	26 470	13 598	26 652	10 037	2 116	1 649
Foreign or mixed parentage[2]	13 811	156	550	1 149	4 059	2 491	1 122	2 780	940	328	236
Foreign-born	28 481	1 954	4 047	3 247	7 196	2 847	1 548	4 828	1 863	490	462
Naturalized citizen	12 377	500	1 147	967	3 258	1 576	917	2 534	949	301	229
Not a citizen	16 104	1 455	2 899	2 280	3 938	1 271	631	2 294	914	189	233
Period of entry:											
2000–2005	4 642	328	621	540	1 061	392	192	963	393	88	66
1990–1999	8 809	588	1 285	1 173	2 248	747	432	1 450	619	121	146
1980–1989	6 922	485	1 041	813	1 728	747	392	1 122	360	125	109
1970–1979	4 287	305	612	414	1 036	480	269	754	275	81	60
Before 1970	3 821	248	488	307	1 123	482	262	539	216	75	81
25 to 44 Years											
Total	82 661	893	2 819	6 531	25 012	14 644	7 824	17 573	5 335	1 261	770
Born in the United States	66 796	150	671	4 388	21 077	12 982	6 945	14 784	4 236	998	563
Native parentage[1]	61 477	126	589	4 055	19 835	11 868	6 466	13 343	3 876	842	477
Foreign or mixed parentage[2]	5 318	24	83	333	1 242	1 114	479	1 441	360	156	86
Foreign-born	15 865	743	2 147	2 143	3 935	1 661	879	2 789	1 099	263	206
Naturalized citizen	4 781	83	256	386	1 209	715	449	1 136	368	132	48
Not a citizen	11 084	661	1 891	1 757	2 726	947	430	1 653	731	131	158
Period of entry:											
2000–2005	3 673	194	480	469	813	310	152	784	344	71	56
1990–1999	6 496	322	950	938	1 667	595	340	1 030	461	87	107
1980–1989	3 960	188	572	560	1 018	500	227	619	175	68	30
1970–1979	1 461	31	131	157	357	217	123	306	100	29	11
Before 1970	274	7	14	19	80	40	37	49	17	8	3
45 to 64 Years											
Total	71 496	937	2 564	5 103	23 088	12 362	6 647	12 639	5 808	1 181	1 167
Born in the United States	62 646	301	1 367	4 327	20 852	11 442	6 118	11 035	5 210	1 021	973
Native parentage[1]	59 043	273	1 262	4 118	19 935	10 780	5 722	10 266	4 860	940	888
Foreign or mixed parentage[2]	3 603	27	105	209	917	662	396	769	350	81	85
Foreign-born	8 850	636	1 197	776	2 236	919	529	1 604	598	160	194
Naturalized citizen	4 896	131	403	364	1 280	629	360	1 058	435	111	125
Not a citizen	3 955	505	794	412	956	290	169	546	163	49	70
Period of entry:											
2000–2005	775	77	102	59	200	73	37	160	46	13	8
1990–1999	1 822	143	233	193	490	128	83	372	120	29	34
1980–1989	2 471	197	356	202	595	233	154	441	173	46	74
1970–1979	2 303	165	380	211	554	234	141	385	147	40	45
Before 1970	1 480	54	126	112	397	251	115	247	112	32	33
65 Years and Over											
Total	35 209	1 153	3 552	4 464	12 793	4 804	1 796	4 047	1 697	492	411
Born in the United States	31 444	578	2 850	4 137	11 768	4 537	1 656	3 613	1 531	424	349
Native parentage[1]	26 554	473	2 488	3 530	9 869	3 823	1 410	3 043	1 301	334	284
Foreign or mixed parentage[2]	4 890	105	363	607	1 899	715	246	569	230	91	65
Foreign-born	3 766	575	702	328	1 025	267	140	435	166	68	61
Naturalized citizen	2 700	286	488	216	770	232	108	340	146	58	56
Not a citizen	1 065	289	214	112	255	34	31	94	20	10	6
Period of entry:											
2000–2005	194	56	38	12	48	9	3	19	2	5	2
1990–1999	490	123	102	43	92	25	9	48	38	5	5
1980–1989	491	100	113	51	115	13	11	62	11	10	5
1970–1979	523	108	101	45	126	29	6	63	28	12	4
Before 1970	2 067	187	348	176	646	190	111	243	86	35	45

[1]Native parentage: Both parents born in the United States.
[2]Foreign parentage: One foreign-born parent.

Table A-24. Educational Attainment of the Population Age 25 Years and Over, by Citizenship, Nativity and Period of Entry, Age, Sex, Race, and Hispanic Origin, 2005—*Continued*

(Numbers in thousands.)

Characteristic	Total population	Elementary		High school		College					
		None to 4th grade	5th to 8th grade	9th to 11th grade	High school graduate	Some college, no degree	Associate's degree	Bachelor's degree	Master's degree	Professional degree	Doctorate degree
ALL RACES											
Male											
25 Years and Over											
Total	90 899	1 505	4 402	7 787	29 151	14 875	6 919	16 641	6 132	1 899	1 587
Born in the United States	76 659	548	2 361	6 138	25 619	13 436	6 246	14 354	5 092	1 606	1 259
Native parentage[1]	70 011	479	2 121	5 558	23 825	12 231	5 737	12 934	4 627	1 385	1 113
Foreign or mixed parentage[2]	6 648	68	240	580	1 794	1 206	509	1 420	465	221	146
Foreign-born	14 241	958	2 041	1 649	3 533	1 439	673	2 287	1 040	293	328
Naturalized citizen	5 886	193	500	430	1 508	747	405	1 214	531	186	173
Not a citizen	8 354	765	1 541	1 219	2 025	692	268	1 073	509	107	155
Period of entry:											
2000–2005	2 382	183	321	283	539	209	84	462	213	45	43
1990–1999	4 493	274	659	620	1 154	404	194	673	351	71	93
1980–1989	3 593	261	545	423	899	378	171	551	208	76	81
1970–1979	2 113	136	311	215	494	235	119	346	164	45	49
Before 1970	1 660	103	205	109	446	214	105	255	104	57	62
25 to 44 Years											
Total	41 146	517	1 569	3 518	13 504	6 934	3 456	8 162	2 363	705	418
Born in the United States	32 812	94	379	2 351	11 409	6 042	3 059	6 849	1 768	572	288
Native parentage[1]	30 072	79	343	2 166	10 696	5 456	2 815	6 159	1 623	481	253
Foreign or mixed parentage[2]	2 740	15	36	185	713	586	244	690	145	91	35
Foreign-born	8 333	423	1 190	1 166	2 094	892	397	1 314	595	133	130
Naturalized citizen	2 431	40	144	185	623	367	213	566	199	68	27
Not a citizen	5 903	383	1 046	982	1 471	525	184	748	397	65	103
Period of entry:											
2000–2005	1 901	119	263	247	433	171	64	355	178	31	40
1990–1999	3 393	164	513	509	887	322	156	479	246	53	64
1980–1989	2 167	121	332	319	559	271	102	303	106	33	20
1970–1979	742	16	70	82	180	107	61	152	61	10	4
Before 1970	131	3	12	10	35	21	14	25	4	6	2
45 to 64 Years											
Total	34 607	517	1 310	2 465	10 857	5 816	2 802	6 339	2 861	817	823
Born in the United States	30 272	189	711	2 111	9 814	5 394	2 583	5 583	2 509	707	670
Native parentage[1]	28 530	176	661	1 997	9 418	5 093	2 407	5 184	2 326	655	614
Foreign or mixed parentage[2]	1 742	13	50	114	396	302	176	399	183	53	56
Foreign-born	4 335	328	598	354	1 042	422	218	756	352	110	153
Naturalized citizen	2 313	53	180	159	587	271	145	485	252	77	104
Not a citizen	2 022	275	418	196	455	151	73	271	100	32	49
Period of entry:											
2000–2005	404	45	44	29	89	33	20	99	34	9	2
1990–1999	878	65	114	91	222	70	31	167	75	15	28
1980–1989	1 211	110	169	82	294	98	60	213	95	35	55
1970–1979	1 146	86	206	107	271	112	53	156	87	28	40
Before 1970	696	23	65	44	166	110	55	121	62	23	27
65 Years and Over											
Total	15 147	471	1 523	1 804	4 791	2 126	661	2 140	907	377	346
Born in the United States	13 575	265	1 270	1 676	4 395	2 000	603	1 923	815	327	301
Native parentage[1]	11 408	225	1 116	1 395	3 711	1 682	515	1 591	678	249	246
Foreign or mixed parentage[2]	2 166	40	154	281	684	318	88	332	136	78	55
Foreign-born	1 572	206	253	128	396	126	58	217	93	50	45
Naturalized citizen	1 142	99	177	86	297	109	47	164	81	41	42
Not a citizen	430	107	76	42	99	17	11	53	12	10	3
Period of entry:											
2000–2005	77	20	14	6	17	5	-	7	2	5	2
1990–1999	221	45	32	20	45	12	7	28	30	3	1
1980–1989	215	30	44	21	46	8	10	35	7	7	5
1970–1979	225	34	35	26	43	17	5	38	16	8	4
Before 1970	833	78	128	55	245	83	36	109	38	28	33

[1]Native parentage: Both parents born in the United States.
[2]Foreign parentage: One foreign-born parent.
- = Quantity zero or rounds to zero.

Table A-24. Educational Attainment of the Population Age 25 Years and Over, by Citizenship, Nativity and Period of Entry, Age, Sex, Race, and Hispanic Origin, 2005—*Continued*

(Numbers in thousands.)

Characteristic	Total population	Elementary		High school		College					
		None to 4th grade	5th to 8th grade	9th to 11th grade	High school graduate	Some college, no degree	Associate's degree	Bachelor's degree	Master's degree	Professional degree	Doctorate degree
ALL RACES											
Female											
25 Years and Over											
Total	98 467	1 477	4 533	8 311	31 742	16 934	9 349	17 619	6 709	1 035	760
Born in the United States	84 227	480	2 527	6 713	28 079	15 526	8 474	15 078	5 886	838	625
Native parentage[1]	77 063	393	2 217	6 144	25 814	14 240	7 861	13 718	5 410	731	535
Foreign or mixed parentage[2]	7 163	88	311	569	2 264	1 286	613	1 360	476	107	90
Foreign-born	14 241	997	2 005	1 598	3 663	1 408	875	2 541	823	197	134
Naturalized citizen	6 491	307	647	537	1 750	829	512	1 319	418	115	56
Not a citizen	7 750	690	1 358	1 061	1 913	579	363	1 221	405	82	78
Period of entry:											
2000–2005	2 260	144	299	257	521	183	108	501	179	43	23
1990–1999	4 316	314	626	553	1 094	343	238	776	268	50	52
1980–1989	3 330	224	496	390	829	369	221	571	152	49	28
1970–1979	2 174	169	301	199	542	245	151	407	111	36	11
Before 1970	2 162	145	283	198	677	268	157	285	112	19	19
25 to 44 Years											
Total	41 515	376	1 249	3 014	11 508	7 710	4 368	9 411	2 972	556	351
Born in the United States	33 983	55	292	2 036	9 668	6 940	3 886	7 936	2 468	426	275
Native parentage[1]	31 405	47	245	1 889	9 139	6 412	3 651	7 184	2 254	361	223
Foreign or mixed parentage[2]	2 578	9	47	148	529	528	235	751	214	65	52
Foreign-born	7 532	320	957	977	1 840	769	482	1 476	504	130	76
Naturalized citizen	2 350	43	112	202	585	347	236	570	169	64	21
Not a citizen	5 182	278	845	776	1 255	422	246	905	334	65	55
Period of entry:											
2000–2005	1 772	76	217	222	379	138	88	429	167	40	16
1990–1999	3 103	158	438	429	779	273	184	551	215	34	43
1980–1989	1 793	67	240	241	459	229	126	317	70	35	10
1970–1979	719	16	61	76	177	110	62	154	39	19	7
Before 1970	144	4	2	10	45	19	23	25	13	2	1
45 to 64 Years											
Total	36 890	420	1 255	2 638	12 231	6 546	3 846	6 300	2 947	364	344
Born in the United States	32 374	112	656	2 216	11 037	6 048	3 535	5 453	2 701	314	302
Native parentage[1]	30 513	98	600	2 121	10 516	5 687	3 315	5 082	2 534	286	274
Foreign or mixed parentage[2]	1 861	14	55	95	521	361	220	371	167	28	28
Foreign-born	4 516	308	599	422	1 194	498	311	848	246	50	41
Naturalized citizen	2 582	77	223	205	693	358	215	573	184	34	21
Not a citizen	1 933	230	376	216	501	139	96	275	63	17	20
Period of entry:											
2000–2005	371	32	58	30	111	40	17	61	13	4	6
1990–1999	944	77	119	101	268	58	52	205	45	13	6
1980–1989	1 260	88	187	119	301	136	94	227	79	12	18
1970–1979	1 157	79	174	104	283	123	88	228	60	12	5
Before 1970	784	31	61	67	231	141	60	126	50	9	6
65 Years and Over											
Total	20 063	681	2 029	2 660	8 002	2 678	1 135	1 907	790	115	65
Born in the United States	17 869	313	1 580	2 461	7 373	2 537	1 053	1 690	717	97	48
Native parentage[1]	15 145	248	1 371	2 135	6 159	2 140	895	1 452	623	84	38
Foreign or mixed parentage[2]	2 724	65	209	326	1 215	397	158	238	94	13	10
Foreign-born	2 193	368	449	199	629	141	82	217	73	17	17
Naturalized citizen	1 558	187	311	130	473	123	62	176	65	17	14
Not a citizen	635	182	138	69	157	18	20	41	8	-	3
Period of entry:											
2000–2005	117	37	24	6	31	4	3	12	-	-	-
1990–1999	268	79	70	23	47	12	2	20	8	3	4
1980–1989	276	69	69	30	68	5	1	27	4	3	-
1970–1979	298	74	66	20	83	12	1	25	12	4	-
Before 1970	1 234	109	220	121	400	107	74	133	49	7	13

[1]Native parentage: Both parents born in the United States.
[2]Foreign parentage: One foreign-born parent.
- = Quantity zero or rounds to zero.

Table A-24. Educational Attainment of the Population Age 25 Years and Over, by Citizenship, Nativity and Period of Entry, Age, Sex, Race, and Hispanic Origin, 2005—*Continued*

(Numbers in thousands.)

Characteristic	Total population	Elementary		High school		College					
		None to 4th grade	5th to 8th grade	9th to 11th grade	High school graduate	Some college, no degree	Associate's degree	Bachelor's degree	Master's degree	Professional degree	Doctorate degree
WHITE ALONE OR IN COMBINATION											
Both Sexes											
25 Years and Over											
Total	157 873	2 348	7 551	12 615	50 691	26 645	13 848	28 702	10 964	2 516	1 993
Born in the United States	138 847	737	4 090	10 003	45 751	24 844	12 935	26 448	10 049	2 255	1 737
Native parentage[1]	126 685	610	3 582	8 940	42 055	22 629	11 946	24 144	9 225	2 001	1 553
Foreign or mixed parentage[2]	12 162	127	507	1 063	3 696	2 215	989	2 303	824	254	184
Foreign-born	19 026	1 611	3 462	2 612	4 940	1 802	913	2 254	915	261	256
Naturalized citizen	7 382	370	881	695	2 092	936	474	1 128	521	153	132
Not a citizen	11 643	1 241	2 581	1 917	2 848	866	440	1 126	393	108	124
Period of entry:											
2000–2005	3 047	257	546	445	728	261	134	422	167	50	37
1990–1999	5 822	488	1 108	951	1 499	436	243	696	270	54	77
1980–1989	4 304	387	861	618	1 060	432	197	448	193	63	45
1970–1979	2 697	255	514	335	699	273	124	297	126	41	33
Before 1970	3 156	224	432	264	953	400	216	390	159	53	64
25 to 44 Years											
Total	66 669	767	2 568	5 129	19 863	11 738	6 485	14 239	4 239	1 033	606
Born in the United States	55 962	117	603	3 285	17 050	10 734	5 974	13 010	3 785	902	502
Native parentage[1]	51 701	103	523	2 991	16 008	9 807	5 583	11 923	3 518	804	441
Foreign or mixed parentage[2]	4 261	14	79	294	1 043	927	391	1 086	267	97	62
Foreign-born	10 707	650	1 965	1 844	2 813	1 004	511	1 230	454	132	104
Naturalized citizen	2 569	57	207	295	746	356	215	438	166	63	25
Not a citizen	8 137	593	1 758	1 549	2 066	648	296	792	288	69	79
Period of entry:											
2000–2005	2 505	165	440	402	613	211	109	349	145	41	29
1990–1999	4 410	281	859	797	1 185	341	100	405	178	33	54
1980–1989	2 640	170	535	483	697	286	114	236	74	34	12
1970–1979	933	28	117	144	251	131	69	117	50	17	8
Before 1970	219	7	14	18	67	34	32	32	8	7	1
45 to 64 Years											
Total	60 258	740	2 133	3 852	19 196	10 518	5 755	10 819	5 194	1 044	1 007
Born in the United States	54 662	228	1 141	3 312	17 846	9 917	5 458	10 059	4 841	956	904
Native parentage[1]	51 384	206	1 051	3 125	17 014	9 313	5 086	9 362	4 507	886	834
Foreign or mixed parentage[2]	3 278	22	90	186	832	604	372	697	334	70	70
Foreign-born	5 596	512	992	540	1 350	600	297	760	353	88	103
Naturalized citizen	2 803	80	299	249	738	407	179	475	258	55	62
Not a citizen	2 794	432	693	291	612	193	118	285	95	33	42
Period of entry:											
2000–2005	435	59	84	34	96	44	23	65	22	3	6
1990–1999	1 124	121	195	126	262	80	51	181	70	18	21
1980–1989	1 427	149	278	121	300	142	77	191	113	27	30
1970–1979	1 416	136	327	163	347	128	53	155	62	20	24
Before 1970	1 194	47	107	97	345	207	94	169	86	20	22
65 Years and Over											
Total	30 946	840	2 851	3 634	11 632	4 389	1 608	3 643	1 531	439	380
Born in the United States	28 223	392	2 346	3 406	10 855	4 192	1 503	3 379	1 423	397	331
Native parentage[1]	23 600	301	2 008	2 823	9 034	3 508	1 277	2 859	1 201	311	278
Foreign or mixed parentage[2]	4 623	91	338	583	1 821	684	225	520	222	86	52
Foreign-born	2 723	448	505	228	777	197	105	264	107	41	49
Naturalized citizen	2 010	233	375	151	608	172	79	214	97	36	46
Not a citizen	712	216	131	77	169	25	26	49	11	6	3
Period of entry:											
2000–2005	107	33	22	9	19	6	3	8	-	5	2
1990–1999	288	86	54	28	52	14	4	21	23	3	2
1980–1989	238	68	48	14	63	5	6	21	6	3	3
1970–1979	348	91	69	28	101	13	2	24	14	4	1
Before 1970	1 742	171	311	149	542	159	90	189	64	26	40

[1]Native parentage: Both parents born in the United States.
[2]Foreign parentage: One foreign-born parent.
- = Quantity zero or rounds to zero.

Table A-24. Educational Attainment of the Population Age 25 Years and Over, by Citizenship, Nativity and Period of Entry, Age, Sex, Race, and Hispanic Origin, 2005—*Continued*

(Numbers in thousands.)

Characteristic	Total population	Elementary		High school		College					
		None to 4th grade	5th to 8th grade	9th to 11th grade	High school graduate	Some college, no degree	Associate's degree	Bachelor's degree	Master's degree	Professional degree	Doctorate degree
WHITE ALONE OR IN COMBINATION											
Male											
25 Years and Over											
Total	76 629	1 239	3 820	6 256	24 249	12 635	5 951	14 243	5 231	1 650	1 356
Born in the United States	66 910	408	2 020	4 888	21 786	11 695	5 540	13 137	4 761	1 499	1 176
Native parentage[1]	61 080	353	1 798	4 350	20 165	10 618	5 098	11 952	4 354	1 334	1 059
Foreign or mixed parentage[2]	5 829	55	222	538	1 621	1 076	443	1 185	408	165	117
Foreign-born	9 719	830	1 801	1 368	2 463	940	411	1 106	470	151	180
Naturalized citizen	3 474	158	380	326	965	425	211	541	274	93	102
Not a citizen	6 245	672	1 421	1 043	1 498	515	199	566	195	58	78
Period of entry:											
2000–2005	1 635	148	300	243	394	156	62	198	85	25	25
1990–1999	3 044	241	592	511	788	253	111	342	135	24	47
1980–1989	2 320	223	468	334	570	218	93	233	103	42	35
1970–1979	1 364	123	263	184	335	134	61	150	71	19	26
Before 1970	1 357	96	177	96	377	179	84	183	77	41	47
25 to 44 Years											
Total	33 685	451	1 471	2 873	10 847	5 682	2 918	6 705	1 826	587	324
Born in the United States	27 876	75	358	1 846	9 315	5 120	2 664	6 112	1 606	522	258
Native parentage[1]	25 698	67	321	1 677	8 713	4 633	2 468	5 604	1 507	473	234
Foreign or mixed parentage[2]	2 178	8	36	168	603	487	196	508	99	48	25
Foreign-born	5 809	375	1 113	1 027	1 532	562	254	593	221	65	66
Naturalized citizen	1 330	31	121	152	401	165	111	216	86	31	16
Not a citizen	4 479	345	992	875	1 131	397	143	378	134	33	49
Period of entry:											
2000–2005	1 349	102	254	218	337	129	44	156	68	19	22
1990–1999	2 369	148	475	443	642	203	97	239	78	16	28
1980–1989	1 496	110	312	282	396	150	58	119	41	18	10
1970–1979	486	14	61	75	127	61	40	66	31	7	4
Before 1970	109	3	12	10	30	19	14	13	3	5	1
45 to 64 Years											
Total	29 522	428	1 108	1 907	9 045	5 000	2 451	5 571	2 571	726	714
Born in the United States	26 719	146	600	1 649	8 405	4 715	2 331	5 192	2 377	669	634
Native parentage[1]	25 122	137	558	1 545	8 043	4 434	2 167	4 830	2 199	625	584
Foreign or mixed parentage[2]	1 597	10	42	104	362	281	164	362	178	44	50
Foreign-born	2 803	282	508	258	640	285	120	379	194	57	79
Naturalized citizen	1 336	41	136	119	338	179	70	223	139	38	51
Not a citizen	1 467	241	372	139	302	106	50	156	55	19	28
Period of entry:											
2000–2005	239	34	35	20	49	25	18	38	17	1	2
1990–1999	544	60	97	58	121	40	12	89	39	9	19
1980–1989	718	91	136	48	151	65	29	97	59	21	21
1970–1979	738	76	183	91	175	64	19	67	31	10	21
Before 1970	565	21	56	41	145	91	43	87	48	16	17
65 Years and Over											
Total	13 422	360	1 241	1 476	4 357	1 952	581	1 966	834	338	318
Born in the United States	12 315	187	1 062	1 393	4 066	1 860	545	1 833	778	308	283
Native parentage[1]	10 260	149	919	1 128	3 410	1 551	463	1 518	647	235	241
Foreign or mixed parentage[2]	2 055	37	144	265	656	309	82	315	131	73	42
Foreign-born	1 108	173	179	83	291	92	36	133	56	29	35
Naturalized citizen	808	87	122	54	226	80	31	102	49	23	34
Not a citizen	300	87	57	29	65	12	6	32	6	6	1
Period of entry:											
2000–2005	47	12	11	4	8	2	-	3	-	5	1
1990–1999	131	34	20	10	25	9	2	14	17	-	-
1980–1989	106	23	21	4	23	3	6	17	4	3	3
1970–1979	140	33	19	19	32	9	2	16	9	1	1
Before 1970	683	72	109	46	203	69	27	83	26	20	29

[1]Native parentage: Both parents born in the United States.
[2]Foreign parentage: One foreign-born parent.
- = Quantity zero or rounds to zero.

Table A-24. Educational Attainment of the Population Age 25 Years and Over, by Citizenship, Nativity and Period of Entry, Age, Sex, Race, and Hispanic Origin, 2005—*Continued*

(Numbers in thousands.)

Characteristic	Total population	Elementary		High school		College					
		None to 4th grade	5th to 8th grade	9th to 11th grade	High school graduate	Some college, no degree	Associate's degree	Bachelor's degree	Master's degree	Professional degree	Doctorate degree
WHITE ALONE OR IN COMBINATION											
Female											
25 Years and Over											
Total	81 244	1 110	3 731	6 359	26 442	14 011	7 898	14 459	5 733	866	637
Born in the United States	71 937	329	2 070	5 115	23 965	13 149	7 395	13 311	5 288	756	561
Native parentage[1]	65 605	257	1 784	4 590	21 890	12 010	6 849	12 192	4 872	667	494
Foreign or mixed parentage[2]	6 332	72	286	525	2 074	1 139	546	1 118	416	89	67
Foreign-born	9 306	781	1 661	1 244	2 477	862	503	1 148	445	110	77
Naturalized citizen	3 908	212	501	370	1 127	511	262	587	247	60	30
Not a citizen	5 398	569	1 160	874	1 349	351	241	560	198	50	46
Period of entry:											
2000–2005	1 411	110	246	202	335	105	72	224	82	24	12
1990–1999	2 779	246	516	440	712	183	132	354	136	30	31
1980–1989	1 984	163	393	283	490	214	104	215	89	21	10
1970–1979	1 333	132	251	151	365	138	63	147	56	22	7
Before 1970	1 799	129	255	167	576	221	132	207	82	12	17
25 to 44 Years											
Total	32 984	317	1 097	2 256	9 016	6 056	3 567	7 534	2 413	447	282
Born in the United States	28 086	42	245	1 440	7 735	5 614	3 310	6 898	2 179	380	244
Native parentage[1]	26 003	36	202	1 314	7 295	5 174	3 115	6 319	2 010	331	207
Foreign or mixed parentage[2]	2 083	6	43	126	440	440	195	578	169	49	37
Foreign-born	4 898	275	851	816	1 281	441	257	636	234	67	38
Naturalized citizen	1 239	27	86	143	346	191	105	223	80	31	8
Not a citizen	3 659	248	766	673	935	251	152	414	154	36	30
Period of entry:											
2000–2005	1 156	64	186	184	276	82	64	193	77	23	7
1990–1999	2 041	133	384	354	543	138	91	256	99	18	26
1980–1989	1 144	60	223	201	301	136	56	118	33	15	2
1970–1979	447	14	56	70	124	70	29	51	19	9	4
Before 1970	110	4	2	8	37	15	17	19	5	2	-
45 to 64 Years											
Total	30 737	312	1 025	1 945	10 151	5 518	3 303	5 248	2 623	318	294
Born in the United States	27 943	82	541	1 663	9 441	5 203	3 127	4 867	2 464	287	270
Native parentage[1]	26 262	69	494	1 580	8 971	4 879	2 919	4 531	2 307	261	250
Foreign or mixed parentage[2]	1 682	12	48	82	470	324	208	335	156	27	20
Foreign-born	2 793	231	483	282	710	315	177	381	159	31	24
Naturalized citizen	1 467	39	163	129	400	228	108	252	120	17	10
Not a citizen	1 327	192	320	153	310	87	68	129	40	14	14
Period of entry:											
2000–2005	196	25	48	14	48	19	4	27	5	2	4
1990–1999	580	61	98	68	141	40	39	92	31	9	3
1980–1989	709	58	142	73	150	77	48	93	54	6	9
1970–1979	678	60	144	72	172	64	33	88	31	10	3
Before 1970	630	26	51	56	200	115	51	82	39	4	5
65 Years and Over											
Total	17 523	480	1 610	2 158	7 275	2 437	1 027	1 676	697	101	62
Born in the United States	15 908	205	1 284	2 013	6 789	2 332	958	1 546	645	89	47
Native parentage[1]	13 340	152	1 089	1 695	5 624	1 957	815	1 342	554	76	37
Foreign or mixed parentage[2]	2 568	53	195	317	1 165	375	143	205	91	13	10
Foreign-born	1 615	275	326	145	486	105	69	130	52	12	14
Naturalized citizen	1 202	146	252	97	382	92	49	113	47	12	11
Not a citizen	413	129	74	48	104	13	20	17	5	-	3
Period of entry:											
2000–2005	60	21	11	4	11	4	3	5	-	-	-
1990–1999	157	52	34	18	28	5	2	6	6	3	2
1980–1989	131	46	28	10	40	1	-	4	2	-	-
1970–1979	208	58	51	9	69	4	-	8	5	3	-
Before 1970	1 059	98	202	103	339	91	63	106	38	6	11

[1]Native parentage: Both parents born in the United States.
[2]Foreign parentage: One foreign-born parent.
- = Quantity zero or rounds to zero.

Table A-24. Educational Attainment of the Population Age 25 Years and Over, by Citizenship, Nativity and Period of Entry, Age, Sex, Race, and Hispanic Origin, 2005—*Continued*

(Numbers in thousands.)

Characteristic	Total population	Elementary		High school		College					
		None to 4th grade	5th to 8th grade	9th to 11th grade	High school graduate	Some college, no degree	Associate's degree	Bachelor's degree	Master's degree	Professional degree	Doctorate degree
BLACK ALONE OR IN COMBINATION											
Both Sexes											
25 Years and Over											
Total	21 687	339	872	2 851	8 024	4 042	1 735	2 700	868	148	107
Born in the United States	19 223	239	676	2 597	7 242	3 679	1 531	2 306	750	113	91
Native parentage[1]	18 778	239	672	2 575	7 122	3 578	1 491	2 206	715	100	81
Foreign or mixed parentage[2]	446	-	4	22	121	102	40	100	35	13	10
Foreign-born	2 464	101	196	255	782	363	204	394	118	35	16
Naturalized citizen	1 203	27	62	87	361	185	136	241	75	20	9
Not a citizen	1 261	74	134	167	421	178	68	154	43	14	8
Period of entry:											
2000–2005	387	27	33	43	112	64	12	71	17	5	4
1990–1999	774	32	68	105	240	113	72	105	25	12	2
1980–1989	704	32	49	55	252	91	54	124	35	8	4
1970–1979	398	8	30	27	113	67	49	61	32	5	6
Before 1970	200	2	16	24	66	29	17	32	9	5	-
25 to 44 Years											
Total	10 773	57	138	1 120	4 148	2 269	958	1 585	393	63	41
Born in the United States	9 339	22	55	984	3 671	2 020	837	1 337	331	47	36
Native parentage[1]	8 999	22	55	974	3 582	1 942	802	1 251	307	34	30
Foreign or mixed parentage[2]	340	-	-	10	89	79	35	86	24	13	5
Foreign-born	1 433	35	83	136	477	249	121	248	61	17	6
Naturalized citizen	561	6	5	29	174	110	77	125	26	6	1
Not a citizen	873	29	78	106	303	139	44	123	35	10	5
Period of entry:											
2000–2005	294	14	21	38	88	46	8	57	13	5	3
1990–1999	606	13	48	75	191	103	66	83	18	8	2
1980–1989	371	8	13	17	148	62	25	75	19	4	-
1970–1979	137	-	2	5	43	32	18	28	8	-	1
Before 1970	26	-	-	1	8	6	4	5	2	-	-
45 to 64 Years											
Total	7 909	105	236	1 020	3 037	1 461	642	924	373	56	57
Born in the United States	7 111	65	173	929	2 792	1 364	570	800	325	43	48
Native parentage[1]	7 036	65	170	924	2 771	1 346	569	787	315	43	44
Foreign or mixed parentage[2]	75	-	3	5	21	18	1	13	9	-	4
Foreign-born	798	39	63	90	244	97	72	124	48	12	9
Naturalized citizen	482	9	24	37	149	60	52	97	40	8	6
Not a citizen	316	30	38	53	95	37	19	27	8	4	3
Period of entry:											
2000–2005	77	6	6	5	20	18	4	14	3	-	1
1990–1999	146	11	14	28	47	8	6	22	6	4	-
1980–1989	281	15	23	35	97	23	25	43	14	3	4
1970–1979	222	6	16	16	65	33	29	30	22	2	3
Before 1970	71	2	4	6	15	14	8	15	3	4	-
65 Years and Over											
Total	3 005	178	498	712	839	312	136	191	103	29	9
Born in the United States	2 773	152	448	683	779	295	124	169	94	23	7
Native parentage[1]	2 743	152	446	677	768	290	120	168	93	23	7
Foreign or mixed parentage[2]	30	-	1	7	11	4	5	1	1	-	-
Foreign-born	232	26	50	29	60	18	11	22	8	5	2
Naturalized citizen	160	12	32	21	37	16	7	19	8	5	2
Not a citizen	72	14	18	8	23	2	4	3	-	-	-
Period of entry:											
2000–2005	16	7	6	-	3	-	-	-	-	-	-
1990–1999	22	8	6	3	2	1	-	-	2	-	-
1980–1989	52	9	14	3	7	5	4	7	2	1	-
1970–1979	39	3	12	7	5	2	2	3	1	3	2
Before 1970	103	-	12	16	43	9	5	13	4	2	-

[1]Native parentage: Both parents born in the United States.
[2]Foreign parentage: One foreign-born parent.
- = Quantity zero or rounds to zero.

Table A-24. Educational Attainment of the Population Age 25 Years and Over, by Citizenship, Nativity and Period of Entry, Age, Sex, Race, and Hispanic Origin, 2005—*Continued*

(Numbers in thousands.)

Characteristic	Total population	Elementary		High school		College					
		None to 4th grade	5th to 8th grade	9th to 11th grade	High school graduate	Some college, no degree	Associate's degree	Bachelor's degree	Master's degree	Professional degree	Doctorate degree
BLACK ALONE OR IN COMBINATION											
Male											
25 Years and Over											
Total	9 573	172	376	1 252	3 858	1 704	684	1 074	318	77	59
Born in the United States	8 348	119	286	1 123	3 499	1 517	597	858	254	50	46
Native parentage[1]	8 149	119	285	1 117	3 440	1 475	570	817	241	40	45
Foreign or mixed parentage[2]	198	-	1	6	58	42	26	41	13	10	2
Foreign-born	1 225	53	89	129	359	187	88	216	64	27	13
Naturalized citizen	605	13	27	35	159	110	64	135	38	17	8
Not a citizen	620	40	63	94	200	77	24	82	26	10	5
Period of entry:											
2000–2005	212	20	9	23	55	39	4	47	8	5	3
1990–1999	372	10	31	59	109	49	30	57	18	7	-
1980–1989	344	17	24	24	115	50	23	62	19	6	4
1970–1979	197	4	11	15	52	35	23	32	16	5	5
Before 1970	101	2	14	8	28	15	8	19	2	4	-
25 to 44 Years											
Total	4 863	35	54	513	2 120	932	381	631	145	30	22
Born in the United States	4 153	12	18	443	1 903	806	332	492	111	16	19
Native parentage[1]	3 986	12	18	442	1 855	770	307	456	102	7	17
Foreign or mixed parentage[2]	167	-	-	-	48	37	26	37	9	10	2
Foreign-born	710	23	36	71	217	125	48	139	34	13	3
Naturalized citizen	276	2	1	9	72	65	36	72	14	5	-
Not a citizen	434	21	35	62	145	60	12	67	21	8	3
Period of entry:											
2000–2005	165	13	3	20	45	31	4	36	5	5	3
1990–1999	294	4	25	40	87	43	27	48	12	6	-
1980–1989	182	6	6	9	62	36	9	39	12	2	-
1970–1979	61	-	2	2	18	13	8	12	5	-	-
Before 1970	9	-	-	-	4	2	-	3	-	-	-
45 to 64 Years											
Total	3 539	57	116	465	1 439	646	248	369	141	27	30
Born in the United States	3 137	38	86	423	1 320	593	218	301	115	19	23
Native parentage[1]	3 113	38	86	420	1 313	588	217	298	111	19	23
Foreign or mixed parentage[2]	23	-	-	4	7	5	1	4	4	-	-
Foreign-born	402	19	29	41	120	53	30	68	26	8	7
Naturalized citizen	246	4	8	15	73	35	22	56	21	7	6
Not a citizen	156	16	22	26	47	18	8	12	5	1	2
Period of entry:											
2000–2005	40	3	3	2	9	8	-	10	3	-	-
1990–1999	71	4	6	17	22	6	3	9	4	1	-
1980–1989	141	7	11	15	51	10	11	21	7	3	4
1970–1979	117	3	5	8	32	21	12	19	12	2	3
Before 1970	33	2	4	-	5	7	4	8	-	2	-
65 Years and Over											
Total	1 171	80	206	274	298	126	55	74	32	19	7
Born in the United States	1 058	69	183	257	276	117	46	64	28	14	5
Native parentage[1]	1 050	69	181	255	272	117	46	64	28	14	5
Foreign or mixed parentage[2]	8	-	1	2	4	-	-	-	-	-	-
Foreign-born	113	11	24	16	22	9	9	10	4	5	2
Naturalized citizen	82	8	18	11	14	9	5	6	4	5	2
Not a citizen	31	3	6	6	8	-	4	3	-	-	-
Period of entry:											
2000–2005	6	4	2	-	-	-	-	-	-	-	-
1990–1999	7	3	-	3	-	-	-	-	2	-	-
1980–1989	22	3	6	-	2	4	4	1	-	1	-
1970–1979	19	1	4	5	2	-	2	-	-	3	2
Before 1970	59	-	11	8	19	6	4	8	2	2	-

[1]Native parentage: Both parents born in the United States.
[2]Foreign parentage: One foreign-born parent.
- = Quantity zero or rounds to zero.

Table A-24. Educational Attainment of the Population Age 25 Years and Over, by Citizenship, Nativity and Period of Entry, Age, Sex, Race, and Hispanic Origin, 2005—*Continued*

(Numbers in thousands.)

Characteristic	Total population	Elementary		High school		College					
		None to 4th grade	5th to 8th grade	9th to 11th grade	High school graduate	Some college, no degree	Associate's degree	Bachelor's degree	Master's degree	Professional degree	Doctorate degree
BLACK ALONE OR IN COMBINATION											
Female											
25 Years and Over											
Total	12 114	167	496	1 599	4 166	2 339	1 051	1 626	550	71	49
Born in the United States	10 876	120	390	1 473	3 744	2 163	935	1 448	496	64	45
Native parentage[1]	10 629	120	387	1 458	3 681	2 103	921	1 389	474	60	36
Foreign or mixed parentage[2]	247	-	3	15	62	60	14	59	22	3	8
Foreign-born	1 238	47	107	126	423	176	117	178	54	8	4
Naturalized citizen	597	14	35	53	201	75	73	106	37	3	1
Not a citizen	641	34	71	73	221	101	44	72	17	5	3
Period of entry:											
2000–2005	176	7	23	20	57	25	9	25	9	-	1
1990–1999	402	21	37	46	130	64	42	48	7	5	2
1980–1989	360	15	26	31	137	41	30	63	15	1	-
1970–1979	201	4	19	13	60	33	27	29	16	-	1
Before 1970	100	-	1	15	38	14	9	14	7	1	-
25 to 44 Years											
Total	5 910	21	85	606	2 028	1 337	578	954	247	34	20
Born in the United States	5 187	9	38	541	1 768	1 214	504	844	220	30	17
Native parentage[1]	5 013	9	38	531	1 727	1 172	495	796	205	27	13
Foreign or mixed parentage[2]	174	-	-	10	41	42	9	49	15	3	4
Foreign-born	723	12	47	65	260	123	73	110	27	3	2
Naturalized citizen	285	4	4	21	103	44	41	53	13	1	1
Not a citizen	439	8	43	44	158	79	32	57	14	2	2
Period of entry:											
2000–2005	128	1	17	18	43	15	5	21	8	-	-
1990–1999	313	9	23	35	103	60	39	35	5	2	2
1980–1989	189	2	7	8	86	26	16	36	8	1	-
1970–1979	76	-	-	3	24	18	10	16	4	-	1
Before 1970	17	-	-	1	4	4	4	2	2	-	-
45 to 64 Years											
Total	4 370	48	120	555	1 597	815	393	554	232	28	27
Born in the United States	3 974	28	87	506	1 473	771	352	499	210	24	26
Native parentage[1]	3 923	28	84	505	1 458	757	352	490	205	24	22
Foreign or mixed parentage[2]	52	-	3	1	15	14	-	9	5	-	4
Foreign-born	396	20	33	49	125	44	41	56	22	4	1
Naturalized citizen	235	5	16	22	76	25	30	40	20	1	-
Not a citizen	161	15	17	27	49	20	11	15	2	3	1
Period of entry:											
2000–2005	37	2	2	3	11	10	4	4	1	-	1
1990–1999	75	7	8	11	25	2	3	13	2	3	-
1980–1989	140	8	11	20	46	13	14	22	6	-	-
1970–1979	105	3	11	8	33	12	17	10	11	-	-
Before 1970	39	-	-	6	10	7	4	7	3	1	-
65 Years and Over											
Total	1 834	98	292	438	541	186	80	117	71	9	2
Born in the United States	1 715	83	265	426	503	178	78	104	66	9	2
Native parentage[1]	1 693	83	265	422	496	173	74	104	65	9	2
Foreign or mixed parentage[2]	22	-	-	4	6	4	5	1	1	-	-
Foreign-born	119	15	27	12	38	8	2	13	4	-	-
Naturalized citizen	78	4	15	10	23	7	2	13	4	-	-
Not a citizen	41	11	12	2	15	2	-	-	-	-	-
Period of entry:											
2000–2005	10	3	4	-	3	-	-	-	-	-	-
1990–1999	15	5	6	-	2	1	-	-	-	-	-
1980–1989	30	6	8	3	5	2	-	5	2	-	-
1970–1979	20	1	8	1	3	2	-	3	1	-	-
Before 1970	44	-	1	8	24	3	2	5	1	-	-

[1] Native parentage: Both parents born in the United States.
[2] Foreign parentage: One foreign-born parent.
- = Quantity zero or rounds to zero.

Table A-24. Educational Attainment of the Population Age 25 Years and Over, by Citizenship, Nativity and Period of Entry, Age, Sex, Race, and Hispanic Origin, 2005—*Continued*

(Numbers in thousands.)

Characteristic	Total population	Elementary		High school		College					
		None to 4th grade	5th to 8th grade	9th to 11th grade	High school graduate	Some college, no degree	Associate's degree	Bachelor's degree	Master's degree	Professional degree	Doctorate degree
ASIAN ALONE OR IN COMBINATION											
Both Sexes											
25 Years and Over											
Total	8 632	241	397	407	1 787	925	578	2 787	998	267	244
Born in the United States	1 962	38	47	76	397	292	158	649	172	77	57
Native parentage[1]	722	8	14	21	166	110	61	241	81	11	10
Foreign or mixed parentage[2]	1 240	30	33	55	231	182	97	408	91	65	48
Foreign-born	6 670	203	350	332	1 390	634	421	2 138	826	190	187
Naturalized citizen	3 673	92	191	177	771	421	304	1 152	355	125	86
Not a citizen	2 997	112	159	154	618	213	117	986	471	65	101
Period of entry:											
2000–2005	1 146	34	36	48	201	65	44	457	202	34	25
1990–1999	2 099	60	99	98	475	189	112	628	322	51	64
1980–1989	1 860	60	123	129	403	206	137	551	137	55	59
1970–1979	1 134	34	59	47	212	124	98	388	115	34	21
Before 1970	431	16	31	11	99	50	29	113	49	16	17
25 to 44 Years											
Total	4 678	52	84	171	780	540	318	1 743	697	168	127
Born in the United States	1 136	10	4	34	185	170	81	448	119	53	31
Native parentage[1]	360	-	3	10	76	50	24	143	46	4	5
Foreign or mixed parentage[2]	776	10	2	24	109	121	57	305	73	48	26
Foreign-born	3 542	41	79	137	595	370	237	1 294	578	115	96
Naturalized citizen	1 593	15	44	60	270	219	152	572	173	64	22
Not a citizen	1 949	26	35	76	325	150	85	723	404	51	74
Period of entry:											
2000–2005	833	10	15	24	96	51	34	368	185	25	24
1990–1999	1 389	21	33	49	265	143	81	442	265	41	50
1980–1989	925	8	22	55	170	135	85	313	82	36	18
1970–1979	366	2	9	8	58	41	36	159	39	12	2
Before 1970	29	-	-	-	6	-	2	13	6	1	1
45 to 64 Years											
Total	2 850	73	149	147	728	298	212	836	235	78	93
Born in the United States	506	6	18	21	116	87	51	138	37	19	13
Native parentage[1]	281	1	8	9	60	54	28	84	28	7	4
Foreign or mixed parentage[2]	225	5	10	13	56	32	24	54	8	12	9
Foreign-born	2 343	67	131	126	612	211	160	698	198	59	80
Naturalized citizen	1 562	37	69	73	379	156	130	475	141	46	55
Not a citizen	781	30	62	52	233	55	31	223	58	12	25
Period of entry:											
2000–2005	244	7	13	20	80	10	10	78	15	9	1
1990–1999	533	11	25	37	174	38	26	159	44	7	11
1980–1989	742	29	53	40	189	68	51	204	51	17	39
1970–1979	636	17	31	29	135	70	60	195	64	17	18
Before 1970	189	3	10	-	33	26	13	62	24	8	11
65 Years and Over											
Total	1 104	116	164	90	279	87	48	208	67	21	24
Born in the United States	320	21	25	20	96	35	25	63	16	5	13
Native parentage[1]	80	7	3	2	30	6	9	14	7	-	-
Foreign or mixed parentage[2]	239	14	22	18	66	28	16	49	10	5	13
Foreign-born	785	95	139	70	183	53	23	145	50	16	11
Naturalized citizen	518	39	77	44	123	45	22	105	41	14	8
Not a citizen	267	56	62	26	61	8	1	41	9	2	2
Period of entry:											
2000–2005	69	17	8	4	25	3	-	10	2	-	-
1990–1999	178	28	42	12	36	9	5	28	13	3	3
1980–1989	193	22	48	33	44	3	1	34	4	2	2
1970–1979	131	15	19	10	19	13	2	35	12	5	1
Before 1970	213	13	21	11	60	24	15	39	19	6	5

[1] Native parentage: Both parents born in the United States.
[2] Foreign parentage: One foreign-born parent.
- = Quantity zero or rounds to zero.

Table A-24. Educational Attainment of the Population Age 25 Years and Over, by Citizenship, Nativity and Period of Entry, Age, Sex, Race, and Hispanic Origin, 2005—*Continued*

(Numbers in thousands.)

Characteristic	Total population	Elementary		High school		College					
		None to 4th grade	5th to 8th grade	9th to 11th grade	High school graduate	Some college, no degree	Associate's degree	Bachelor's degree	Master's degree	Professional degree	Doctorate degree
ASIAN ALONE OR IN COMBINATION											
Male											
25 Years and Over											
Total	4 081	65	149	174	842	432	243	1 268	573	169	167
Born in the United States	985	15	22	47	189	145	77	327	72	59	32
Native parentage[1]	352	1	9	12	81	58	30	123	27	8	4
Foreign or mixed parentage[2] ...	633	13	13	35	108	87	47	204	46	51	28
Foreign-born	3 096	50	127	127	653	287	166	941	500	110	135
Naturalized citizen	1 740	17	81	68	362	196	126	536	218	72	63
Not a citizen	1 356	33	46	58	291	91	39	406	282	38	72
Period of entry:											
2000–2005	496	9	10	14	80	13	18	207	114	15	15
1990–1999	1 004	18	32	38	231	95	49	261	198	37	44
1980–1989	898	15	48	61	204	105	50	259	89	25	43
1970–1979	516	4	30	13	101	55	35	163	75	21	18
Before 1970	183	3	7	1	37	18	14	52	25	10	15
25 to 44 Years											
Total	2 297	20	31	77	415	272	131	802	385	91	74
Born in the United States	600	7	1	25	107	88	43	231	49	38	12
Native parentage[1]	178	-	1	9	43	24	14	74	9	2	2
Foreign or mixed parentage[2] ...	422	7	-	17	64	64	29	157	39	36	10
Foreign-born	1 697	13	31	51	308	184	88	571	336	53	62
Naturalized citizen	789	5	21	25	139	120	62	279	97	30	12
Not a citizen	908	8	10	26	170	63	26	292	240	23	50
Period of entry:											
2000–2005	359	-	4	5	40	10	16	156	105	8	15
1990–1999	673	8	9	16	136	71	28	186	156	29	35
1980–1989	477	3	12	24	100	81	31	150	53	13	11
1970–1979	176	2	6	7	31	22	13	71	23	2	-
Before 1970	12	-	-	-	1	-	-	9	-	1	1
45 to 64 Years											
Total	1 305	22	59	54	311	124	88	368	146	60	72
Born in the United States	248	4	11	8	45	46	22	72	16	17	7
Native parentage[1]	138	1	6	2	24	33	10	40	14	6	2
Foreign or mixed parentage[2] ...	110	4	6	6	21	13	12	31	1	11	5
Foreign-born	1 057	17	48	47	266	78	66	297	130	43	65
Naturalized citizen	703	9	26	22	169	55	53	201	93	31	45
Not a citizen	354	9	22	25	97	23	13	96	37	12	20
Period of entry:											
2000–2005	113	5	5	7	31	-	2	47	8	8	-
1990–1999	247	2	11	15	75	22	16	62	31	6	8
1980–1989	338	8	19	20	85	23	19	92	31	11	30
1970–1979	275	2	13	5	61	25	21	70	46	15	17
Before 1970	84	-	-	-	14	8	8	26	14	4	11
65 Years and Over											
Total	479	24	59	43	116	36	24	97	42	18	21
Born in the United States	138	4	11	14	37	10	12	24	8	5	13
Native parentage[1]	37	1	3	1	14	1	5	8	3	-	-
Foreign or mixed parentage[2] ...	101	3	8	13	22	9	6	16	5	5	13
Foreign-born	342	20	48	29	79	26	12	73	34	13	8
Naturalized citizen	248	4	34	22	55	21	11	56	28	11	6
Not a citizen	93	16	14	7	24	5	1	17	6	2	2
Period of entry:											
2000–2005	24	4	-	2	9	3	-	4	2	-	-
1990–1999	84	8	12	7	20	3	5	14	11	3	1
1980–1989	83	4	17	17	20	1	-	17	4	1	2
1970–1979	64	-	12	2	9	8	1	22	7	4	1
Before 1970	86	3	7	1	22	11	6	17	10	5	4

[1]Native parentage: Both parents born in the United States.
[2]Foreign parentage: One foreign-born parent.
- = Quantity zero or rounds to zero.

Table A-24. Educational Attainment of the Population Age 25 Years and Over, by Citizenship, Nativity and Period of Entry, Age, Sex, Race, and Hispanic Origin, 2005—*Continued*

(Numbers in thousands.)

Characteristic	Total population	Elementary		High school		College					
		None to 4th grade	5th to 8th grade	9th to 11th grade	High school graduate	Some college, no degree	Associate's degree	Bachelor's degree	Master's degree	Professional degree	Doctorate degree
ASIAN ALONE OR IN COMBINATION											
Female											
25 Years and Over											
Total	4 551	176	248	234	944	494	335	1 519	425	98	77
Born in the United States	977	23	25	29	208	147	80	322	100	18	25
Native parentage[1]	370	6	5	9	84	52	31	118	54	3	5
Foreign or mixed parentage[2]	607	16	20	19	124	95	49	204	45	14	20
Foreign-born	3 574	153	223	205	736	347	255	1 197	326	81	52
Naturalized citizen	1 934	74	109	109	409	224	178	616	137	53	23
Not a citizen	1 641	79	113	96	327	122	77	581	188	28	29
Period of entry:											
2000–2005	651	24	27	34	121	52	26	250	88	19	10
1990–1999	1 096	42	68	60	244	94	63	368	124	14	20
1980–1989	962	45	75	68	198	101	87	292	49	30	17
1970–1979	618	30	29	34	111	69	63	225	40	13	3
Before 1970	248	12	24	10	62	32	16	62	24	5	2
25 to 44 Years											
Total	2 381	32	52	94	365	268	187	941	312	77	53
Born in the United States	536	4	4	9	78	82	38	218	71	15	19
Native parentage[1]	183	-	2	1	33	26	10	69	37	2	3
Foreign or mixed parentage[2]	353	4	2	8	45	56	28	149	34	13	15
Foreign-born	1 845	28	49	86	287	186	149	723	241	62	34
Naturalized citizen	805	10	24	36	131	99	90	293	77	35	10
Not a citizen	1 041	18	25	50	155	87	59	430	164	28	24
Period of entry:											
2000–2005	475	10	11	19	56	41	18	213	80	17	9
1990–1999	716	13	24	33	129	72	52	256	110	12	15
1980–1989	448	6	10	32	70	54	54	160	20	23	7
1970–1979	190	-	4	2	27	19	23	88	17	10	2
Before 1970	16	-	-	-	5	-	2	4	6	-	1
45 to 64 Years											
Total	1 545	52	90	93	416	174	124	468	89	18	21
Born in the United States	259	2	7	14	71	40	29	67	21	2	6
Native parentage[1]	144	-	2	7	36	21	17	44	14	1	2
Foreign or mixed parentage[2]	115	2	5	7	35	19	12	23	7	2	4
Foreign-born	1 286	50	83	79	346	134	95	401	68	15	15
Naturalized citizen	859	29	43	51	210	102	77	275	47	15	10
Not a citizen	426	21	40	27	136	32	18	127	21	-	5
Period of entry:											
2000–2005	131	2	8	13	49	10	8	31	8	2	1
1990–1999	285	9	14	22	99	16	11	98	12	2	3
1980–1989	404	21	34	21	104	45	32	112	20	6	10
1970–1979	361	15	18	23	74	45	39	125	18	2	2
Before 1970	105	3	10	-	20	18	5	36	10	4	-
65 Years and Over											
Total	625	92	105	47	163	51	25	111	25	4	2
Born in the United States	182	17	15	6	59	24	14	38	8	-	-
Native parentage[1]	43	6	-	1	16	5	4	6	4	-	-
Foreign or mixed parentage[2]	139	11	14	5	43	19	10	32	4	-	-
Foreign-born	443	75	91	41	104	27	11	72	17	3	2
Naturalized citizen	270	35	42	22	68	24	11	49	13	3	2
Not a citizen	174	40	48	19	36	3	-	24	3	-	-
Period of entry:											
2000–2005	45	13	8	2	16	1	-	7	-	-	-
1990–1999	94	19	30	5	16	6	-	14	2	-	1
1980–1989	110	18	31	16	24	2	1	17	-	1	-
1970–1979	67	15	8	9	11	5	1	13	5	1	-
Before 1970	127	10	14	10	38	14	9	22	9	1	1

[1]Native parentage: Both parents born in the United States.
[2]Foreign parentage: One foreign-born parent.
- = Quantity zero or rounds to zero.

Table A-24. Educational Attainment of the Population Age 25 Years and Over, by Citizenship, Nativity and Period of Entry, Age, Sex, Race, and Hispanic Origin, 2005—*Continued*

(Numbers in thousands.)

Characteristic	Total population	Elementary		High school		College					
		None to 4th grade	5th to 8th grade	9th to 11th grade	High school graduate	Some college, no degree	Associate's degree	Bachelor's degree	Master's degree	Professional degree	Doctorate degree
HISPANIC[3]											
Both Sexes											
25 Years and Over											
Total	22 551	1 784	3 869	3 709	6 227	3 011	1 252	1 901	551	152	95
Born in the United States	9 581	320	681	1 370	3 018	1 918	804	1 021	334	64	50
Native parentage[1]	6 678	216	460	990	2 238	1 292	555	635	234	32	27
Foreign or mixed parentage[2]	2 902	104	221	380	780	627	249	386	100	32	23
Foreign-born	12 971	1 464	3 188	2 339	3 209	1 092	448	880	217	88	45
Naturalized citizen	3 770	272	638	519	1 058	501	219	395	89	48	30
Not a citizen	9 201	1 192	2 550	1 820	2 151	591	229	486	128	40	15
Period of entry:											
2000–2005	2 217	233	520	416	524	175	78	185	59	26	2
1990–1999	4 272	446	1 103	907	1 118	259	120	241	56	12	11
1980–1989	3 399	372	844	601	812	335	124	221	51	22	16
1970–1979	1 879	231	485	291	442	192	63	134	28	10	3
Before 1970	1 203	183	237	124	313	131	63	99	23	18	12
25 to 44 Years											
Total	13 879	672	2 145	2 504	4 029	1 989	850	1 267	299	87	37
Born in the United States	5 466	29	181	724	1 802	1 255	544	705	167	39	21
Native parentage[1]	3 622	18	113	515	1 284	799	364	403	103	14	8
Foreign or mixed parentage[2]	1 845	11	68	208	518	455	180	302	64	24	13
Foreign-born	8 413	643	1 964	1 781	2 227	734	307	562	133	48	15
Naturalized citizen	1 691	58	192	265	523	258	127	205	36	21	5
Not a citizen	6 722	585	1 772	1 515	1 704	476	180	357	96	27	10
Period of entry:											
2000–2005	1 855	161	425	383	453	146	65	157	45	19	1
1990–1999	3 472	278	878	788	966	219	97	187	43	8	8
1980–1989	2 272	168	536	470	583	243	91	135	30	10	6
1970–1979	686	29	117	126	186	107	36	64	13	8	-
Before 1970	128	7	8	14	39	19	17	19	1	3	1
45 to 64 Years											
Total	6 478	605	1 199	917	1 735	872	328	532	204	44	43
Born in the United States	3 013	111	269	462	959	560	210	270	132	19	21
Native parentage[1]	2 350	90	198	354	787	428	152	202	108	15	16
Foreign or mixed parentage[2]	663	22	72	108	172	132	58	69	23	4	5
Foreign-born	3 465	493	930	455	776	312	118	262	73	25	22
Naturalized citizen	1 408	68	262	193	380	207	74	148	42	17	18
Not a citizen	2 057	426	667	262	397	105	43	114	30	7	5
Period of entry:											
2000–2005	292	54	72	24	64	28	13	22	14	2	-
1990–1999	654	107	189	103	132	32	20	52	11	4	3
1980–1989	986	153	270	118	206	88	33	79	21	8	9
1970–1979	1 004	135	316	149	217	82	27	61	12	2	2
Before 1970	529	43	82	61	157	83	25	48	14	8	8
65 Years and Over											
Total	2 194	508	525	288	463	150	74	102	47	21	15
Born in the United States	1 101	179	231	184	257	103	51	45	36	6	8
Native parentage[1]	707	108	149	121	167	64	39	30	24	2	4
Foreign or mixed parentage[2]	394	71	81	64	90	40	12	16	12	4	5
Foreign-born	1 092	328	295	103	206	46	23	57	11	15	7
Naturalized citizen	671	147	185	60	156	37	18	42	10	10	7
Not a citizen	422	181	110	43	50	10	6	15	2	5	-
Period of entry:											
2000–2005	70	18	23	9	6	1	-	6	-	5	1
1990–1999	146	60	35	17	20	8	2	3	2	-	-
1980–1989	141	51	38	12	24	4	-	7	-	3	2
1970–1979	189	66	52	16	38	4	-	8	3	-	1
Before 1970	546	133	147	49	117	29	22	33	7	7	3

[1]Native parentage: Both parents born in the United States.
[2]Foreign parentage: One foreign-born parent.
[3]May be of any race.
- = Quantity zero or rounds to zero.

Table A-24. Educational Attainment of the Population Age 25 Years and Over, by Citizenship, Nativity and Period of Entry, Age, Sex, Race, and Hispanic Origin, 2005—*Continued*

(Numbers in thousands.)

Characteristic	Total population	Elementary		High school		College					
		None to 4th grade	5th to 8th grade	9th to 11th grade	High school graduate	Some college, no degree	Associate's degree	Bachelor's degree	Master's degree	Professional degree	Doctorate degree
HISPANIC[3]											
Male											
25 Years and Over											
Total	11 512	926	2 017	1 900	3 215	1 514	580	967	248	84	62
Born in the United States	4 593	151	291	645	1 493	911	373	526	141	35	28
Native parentage[1]	3 181	101	194	464	1 101	601	253	328	103	19	17
Foreign or mixed parentage[2]	1 412	50	96	181	393	309	120	197	38	16	11
Foreign-born	6 919	775	1 726	1 255	1 722	603	207	441	107	49	34
Naturalized citizen	1 815	125	308	255	520	236	96	187	38	27	24
Not a citizen	5 103	650	1 418	1 000	1 202	366	111	255	69	22	9
Period of entry:											
2000–2005	1 252	136	292	233	301	108	39	96	32	14	1
1990–1999	2 284	221	598	491	610	150	59	115	27	5	6
1980–1989	1 871	220	463	328	460	176	56	111	28	15	13
1970–1979	959	117	258	150	212	104	27	71	14	3	3
Before 1970	553	81	116	52	139	65	26	48	5	12	9
25 to 44 Years											
Total	7 396	385	1 200	1 348	2 218	1 018	410	632	127	38	20
Born in the United States	2 725	17	90	351	970	596	266	345	62	18	10
Native parentage[1]	1 784	8	56	251	684	370	166	194	43	7	3
Foreign or mixed parentage[2]	941	8	34	100	286	226	100	151	19	11	6
Foreign-born	4 671	369	1 110	997	1 247	422	144	286	65	20	10
Naturalized citizen	863	29	111	139	274	121	59	98	18	9	4
Not a citizen	3 808	339	999	858	973	301	85	188	47	11	6
Period of entry:											
2000–2005	1 064	98	247	215	267	96	29	85	21	8	-
1990–1999	1 895	145	483	435	536	128	49	91	19	4	4
1980–1989	1 299	110	312	278	335	130	44	63	18	5	4
1970–1979	349	14	61	62	89	58	18	39	7	1	-
Before 1970	63	3	7	7	20	11	4	9	-	1	1
45 to 64 Years											
Total	3 186	340	616	424	808	414	138	283	104	27	32
Born in the United States	1 411	60	124	210	430	258	88	153	65	10	13
Native parentage[1]	1 116	51	92	153	363	198	68	120	52	10	10
Foreign or mixed parentage[2]	294	9	32	57	67	61	20	33	13	1	2
Foreign-born	1 775	281	492	215	378	156	50	131	39	16	19
Naturalized citizen	662	39	123	88	173	96	27	72	18	10	16
Not a citizen	1 114	242	369	127	205	60	23	59	21	6	3
Period of entry:											
2000–2005	152	31	35	14	29	12	10	8	11	1	-
1990–1999	330	56	98	51	65	18	8	23	8	1	2
1980–1989	508	93	132	47	112	43	12	44	10	7	7
1970–1979	538	81	181	81	106	43	9	28	6	1	2
Before 1970	248	20	45	23	66	39	10	28	4	6	8
65 Years and Over											
Total	930	200	201	127	190	81	33	52	17	19	10
Born in the United States	457	75	77	84	93	56	19	28	14	6	6
Native parentage[1]	281	42	46	59	53	33	18	14	8	2	4
Foreign or mixed parentage[2]	176	32	30	24	39	23	1	13	6	4	2
Foreign-born	473	126	124	43	97	25	14	24	3	13	4
Naturalized citizen	291	56	74	28	74	19	9	17	1	8	4
Not a citizen	182	70	50	15	23	6	4	8	1	5	-
Period of entry:											
2000–2005	36	7	9	4	5	-	-	3	-	5	1
1990–1999	59	21	17	5	9	4	2	1	-	-	-
1980–1989	63	17	19	4	12	3	-	3	-	3	2
1970–1979	72	22	16	7	16	3	-	5	1	-	1
Before 1970	243	58	64	22	54	15	12	12	1	5	-

[1]Native parentage: Both parents born in the United States.
[2]Foreign parentage: One foreign-born parent.
[3]May be of any race.
- = Quantity zero or rounds to zero.

Table A-24. Educational Attainment of the Population Age 25 Years and Over, by Citizenship, Nativity and Period of Entry, Age, Sex, Race, and Hispanic Origin, 2005—*Continued*

(Numbers in thousands.)

Characteristic	Total population	Elementary		High school		College					
		None to 4th grade	5th to 8th grade	9th to 11th grade	High school graduate	Some college, no degree	Associate's degree	Bachelor's degree	Master's degree	Professional degree	Doctorate degree
HISPANIC[3]											
Female											
25 Years and Over											
Total	11 039	858	1 853	1 809	3 012	1 497	672	934	303	68	33
Born in the United States	4 988	169	390	725	1 525	1 008	431	495	193	29	22
Native parentage[1]	3 497	115	266	526	1 137	690	302	306	132	13	10
Foreign or mixed parentage[2]	1 491	54	124	199	388	317	129	189	61	16	13
Foreign-born	6 052	689	1 462	1 084	1 487	489	241	439	110	39	11
Naturalized citizen	1 955	148	330	264	538	265	124	208	51	21	5
Not a citizen	4 097	541	1 132	820	949	224	117	231	59	18	6
Period of entry:											
2000–2005	966	97	228	183	223	67	39	89	27	12	1
1990–1999	1 988	224	505	416	508	109	60	126	28	7	4
1980–1989	1 528	152	381	272	352	160	68	110	23	7	3
1970–1979	920	114	227	141	230	88	36	63	14	7	-
Before 1970	650	102	122	72	174	66	38	51	18	6	3
25 to 44 Years											
Total	6 483	287	945	1 156	1 811	971	440	635	172	49	17
Born in the United States	2 741	13	91	372	832	659	278	360	104	21	12
Native parentage[1]	1 837	10	57	264	600	429	197	209	59	7	5
Foreign or mixed parentage[2]	904	3	34	109	232	230	80	151	45	13	7
Foreign-born	3 742	274	854	784	980	312	163	275	68	28	5
Naturalized citizen	828	28	81	127	249	137	68	106	18	12	1
Not a citizen	2 915	246	773	657	730	175	95	169	50	17	4
Period of entry:											
2000–2005	791	63	178	168	186	50	36	73	25	12	1
1990–1999	1 576	133	395	352	430	91	48	96	23	4	3
1980–1989	973	58	224	193	247	113	47	72	12	5	1
1970–1979	337	16	56	64	97	49	18	26	6	6	-
Before 1970	65	4	1	7	19	8	13	10	1	1	-
45 to 64 Years											
Total	3 292	265	583	493	927	458	190	249	100	17	11
Born in the United States	1 602	52	146	252	529	302	122	117	66	8	8
Native parentage[1]	1 233	39	106	201	424	231	83	82	56	6	5
Foreign or mixed parentage[2]	369	12	40	52	105	71	38	35	10	3	3
Foreign-born	1 690	213	438	240	399	156	68	131	34	8	3
Naturalized citizen	747	28	139	105	207	111	48	76	25	7	1
Not a citizen	943	184	299	135	192	45	21	55	9	1	2
Period of entry:											
2000–2005	141	23	36	10	36	15	3	13	2	1	-
1990–1999	325	52	91	52	67	14	12	29	3	2	1
1980–1989	478	60	138	71	93	45	21	35	11	2	2
1970–1979	466	54	135	68	111	39	18	33	6	1	-
Before 1970	281	23	37	38	92	43	15	20	11	2	-
65 Years and Over											
Total	1 264	307	324	161	273	68	42	50	31	2	5
Born in the United States	644	105	154	101	164	47	32	18	22	-	2
Native parentage[1]	426	66	103	61	113	31	21	15	16	-	-
Foreign or mixed parentage[2]	218	39	51	39	51	17	11	2	6	-	2
Foreign-born	619	203	171	60	109	21	10	33	9	2	3
Naturalized citizen	380	91	110	32	82	17	8	26	8	2	3
Not a citizen	239	111	60	28	27	4	2	7	1	-	-
Period of entry:											
2000–2005	35	11	14	4	1	1	-	3	-	-	-
1990–1999	87	40	19	12	11	3	-	1	2	-	-
1980–1989	77	34	19	8	12	1	-	3	-	-	-
1970–1979	117	44	36	9	22	1	-	4	1	-	-
Before 1970	303	74	83	27	63	14	10	21	6	2	3

[1]Native parentage: Both parents born in the United States.
[2]Foreign parentage: One foreign-born parent.
[3]May be of any race.
- = Quantity zero or rounds to zero.

Table A-25. Educational Attainment of the Population Age 18 Years and Over, by Marital Status, Age, Sex, Race, and Hispanic Origin, 2005

(Numbers in thousands.)

Age, sex, race, Hispanic origin, and marital status	Total population	Educational attainment								
		None to 8th grade	9th to 11th grade	High school graduate	Some college, no degree	Associate's degree	Bachelor's degree	Master's degree	Professional degree	Doctorate degree
ALL RACES										
Male										
18 Years and Over										
Total	104 966	6 406	10 676	33 754	19 448	7 475	17 558	6 154	1 904	1 592
Never married	29 761	1 551	4 282	9 792	7 181	1 648	4 033	873	237	165
Married, spouse present	59 370	3 422	4 447	18 278	9 682	4 750	11 507	4 623	1 443	1 219
Married, spouse absent, not separated	1 936	354	291	574	201	95	230	109	57	27
Separated	1 911	164	263	755	291	139	196	68	22	13
Widowed	2 727	474	417	876	328	103	325	123	41	40
Divorced	9 262	442	976	3 480	1 765	741	1 267	359	105	128
18 to 24 Years										
Total	14 067	499	2 889	4 602	4 572	557	917	22	5	5
Never married	12 592	406	2 625	3 958	4 277	477	826	15	5	3
Married, spouse present	1 219	76	198	536	254	71	78	5	-	2
Married, spouse absent, not separated	82	12	17	31	14	3	6	-	-	-
Separated	61	3	22	16	10	5	4	-	-	-
Widowed	8	-	-	4	4	-	-	-	-	-
Divorced	106	1	26	58	13	2	4	2	-	-
25 to 34 Years										
Total	19 677	1 010	1 827	6 216	3 582	1 615	4 045	971	279	132
Never married	8 583	418	814	2 779	1 600	613	1 875	346	110	27
Married, spouse present	9 342	485	742	2 792	1 659	850	1 991	577	156	90
Married, spouse absent, not separated	377	66	92	87	43	18	43	24	2	1
Separated	348	12	47	150	66	32	28	5	6	3
Widowed	26	-	11	7	-	2	1	4	-	-
Divorced	1 001	30	121	400	213	99	107	14	6	10
35 to 44 Years										
Total	21 469	1 077	1 690	7 288	3 352	1 841	4 117	1 392	426	287
Never married	4 315	267	436	1 679	670	285	667	218	53	40
Married, spouse present	13 653	598	000	4 106	2 066	1 277	3 027	1 072	327	230
Married, spouse absent, not separated	484	85	69	187	43	22	46	19	10	1
Separated	541	42	53	224	88	45	61	21	8	-
Widowed	103	9	23	41	13	4	8	3	1	-
Divorced	2 374	77	229	971	482	208	307	59	27	15
45 to 54 Years										
Total	20 555	946	1 373	6 729	3 500	1 737	3 823	1 588	476	383
Never married	2 693	209	225	975	430	181	433	169	38	33
Married, spouse present	13 846	520	754	4 196	2 371	1 252	2 831	1 246	373	303
Married, spouse absent, not separated	471	83	47	138	45	33	71	28	16	9
Separated	518	29	71	227	66	30	65	24	2	5
Widowed	180	11	20	70	28	15	28	3	5	-
Divorced	2 848	95	255	1 124	559	226	396	118	41	32
55 to 64 Years										
Total	14 051	880	1 092	4 127	2 316	1 064	2 516	1 273	341	441
Never married	908	134	90	233	140	47	145	71	5	44
Married, spouse present	10 455	526	701	3 075	1 747	804	1 965	1 021	284	332
Married, spouse absent, not separated	229	44	27	48	19	10	25	24	19	14
Separated	254	38	41	80	27	18	30	10	6	4
Widowed	341	36	56	94	51	16	44	33	9	3
Divorced	1 864	103	178	598	332	171	307	114	18	43
65 Years and Over										
Total	15 147	1 994	1 804	4 791	2 126	661	2 140	907	377	346
Never married	671	117	168	168	63	45	88	53	26	19
Married, spouse present	10 856	1 217	1 172	3 493	1 595	497	1 614	702	304	262
Married, spouse absent, not separated	294	65	38	82	37	10	38	14	9	1
Separated	189	41	29	59	34	8	9	8	-	1
Widowed	2 069	419	307	660	231	66	244	80	26	37
Divorced	1 069	137	166	329	165	35	147	51	13	27

- = Quantity zero or rounds to zero.

Table A-25. Educational Attainment of the Population Age 18 Years and Over, by Marital Status, Age, Sex, Race, and Hispanic Origin, 2005—*Continued*

(Numbers in thousands.)

Age, sex, race, Hispanic origin, and marital status	Total population	Educational attainment								
		None to 8th grade	9th to 11th grade	High school graduate	Some college, no degree	Associate's degree	Bachelor's degree	Master's degree	Professional degree	Doctorate degree
ALL RACES										
Female										
18 Years and Over										
Total	112 409	6 305	10 753	35 523	22 222	10 072	18 959	6 773	1 041	760
Never married	24 451	851	3 237	6 349	6 930	1 573	4 064	1 125	193	128
Married, spouse present	59 357	2 735	4 032	19 243	10 180	5 988	11 656	4 377	677	471
Married, spouse absent, not separated	1 630	173	208	529	274	110	205	95	15	22
Separated	2 858	264	470	946	543	258	249	97	18	13
Widowed	11 125	1 754	1 728	4 214	1 458	626	902	353	54	36
Divorced	12 989	528	1 079	4 243	2 837	1 516	1 884	727	84	90
18 to 24 Years										
Total	13 941	295	2 442	3 782	5 289	723	1 340	64	6	-
Never married	11 196	162	2 042	2 817	4 562	498	1 068	43	4	-
Married, spouse present	2 195	119	301	773	550	191	242	17	3	-
Married, spouse absent, not separated	166	7	32	48	58	10	10	2	-	-
Separated	181	5	46	61	50	10	9	-	-	-
Widowed	20	2	1	7	9	1	-	-	-	-
Divorced	183	1	20	75	60	14	11	2	-	-
25 to 34 Years										
Total	19 633	780	1 594	5 054	3 774	1 893	4 789	1 393	230	127
Never married	6 385	233	580	1 568	1 212	530	1 681	452	90	38
Married, spouse present	10 860	461	744	2 704	1 893	1 108	2 860	877	137	77
Married, spouse absent, not separated	277	12	35	96	68	11	39	7	1	6
Separated	615	40	108	196	160	46	53	10	2	2
Widowed	84	10	1	30	27	7	7	2	-	-
Divorced	1 412	23	126	460	414	191	149	45	-	4
35 to 44 Years										
Total	21 882	845	1 419	6 455	3 936	2 475	4 622	1 579	326	224
Never married	3 038	146	290	890	566	230	617	223	45	30
Married, spouse present	14 306	537	698	4 053	2 423	1 701	3 335	1 155	244	159
Married, spouse absent, not separated	343	25	50	92	57	25	65	23	1	5
Separated	813	53	119	286	159	89	71	24	5	7
Widowed	274	7	37	106	51	22	28	15	5	3
Divorced	3 108	78	224	1 029	679	407	506	139	26	20
45 to 54 Years										
Total	21 405	842	1 410	6 760	3 870	2 419	3 992	1 688	226	198
Never married	2 090	96	182	579	362	211	401	196	30	32
Married, spouse present	13 848	483	766	4 410	2 404	1 571	2 755	1 169	154	136
Married, spouse absent, not separated	292	25	27	101	32	25	36	32	10	5
Separated	677	64	95	211	101	68	82	50	4	3
Widowed	660	43	80	197	142	80	76	36	3	5
Divorced	3 837	131	261	1 262	830	464	642	205	25	16
55 to 64 Years										
Total	15 485	832	1 227	5 471	2 676	1 427	2 308	1 259	138	145
Never married	953	74	84	254	152	57	192	104	20	17
Married, spouse present	9 730	420	662	3 603	1 654	906	1 535	796	82	72
Married, spouse absent, not separated	220	28	22	61	30	15	33	22	3	6
Separated	372	61	59	114	58	38	28	10	3	-
Widowed	1 475	142	183	594	231	98	132	77	9	9
Divorced	2 734	108	218	845	551	313	387	251	21	41
65 Years and Over										
Total	20 063	2 710	2 660	8 002	2 678	1 135	1 907	790	115	65
Never married	789	140	59	240	76	46	105	107	6	11
Married, spouse present	8 417	714	861	3 701	1 256	512	928	362	56	26
Married, spouse absent, not separated	332	76	42	131	28	24	21	9	-	-
Separated	200	42	43	78	16	7	6	3	4	-
Widowed	8 611	1 550	1 425	3 280	999	419	659	223	37	19
Divorced	1 713	188	229	572	302	128	188	86	11	9

- = Quantity zero or rounds to zero.

Table A-25. Educational Attainment of the Population Age 18 Years and Over, by Marital Status, Age, Sex, Race, and Hispanic Origin, 2005—*Continued*

(Numbers in thousands.)

Age, sex, race, Hispanic origin, and marital status	Total population	Educational attainment								
		None to 8th grade	9th to 11th grade	High school graduate	Some college, no degree	Associate's degree	Bachelor's degree	Master's degree	Professional degree	Doctorate degree
WHITE ALONE OR IN COMBINATION										
Male										
18 Years and Over										
Total	88 056	5 504	8 507	27 964	16 345	6 437	15 034	5 249	1 655	1 361
Never married	23 293	1 326	3 229	7 375	5 664	1 347	3 287	726	196	142
Married, spouse present	51 798	2 980	3 806	15 949	8 528	4 196	10 053	3 970	1 278	1 038
Married, spouse absent, not separated	1 477	316	198	420	169	66	167	73	54	16
Separated	1 345	139	178	491	213	91	148	59	13	13
Widowed	2 320	380	325	782	276	88	289	113	32	35
Divorced	7 824	363	772	2 947	1 495	649	1 002	307	83	116
18 to 24 Years										
Total	11 427	445	2 251	3 715	3 711	487	791	18	5	5
Never married	10 132	356	2 015	3 162	3 451	418	709	13	5	3
Married, spouse present	1 079	74	178	463	222	64	72	5	-	2
Married, spouse absent, not separated	63	12	13	22	12	1	3	-	-	-
Separated	54	2	21	16	9	2	4	-	-	-
Widowed	8	-	-	4	4	-	-	-	-	-
Divorced	92	1	25	47	13	2	3	-	-	-
25 to 34 Years										
Total	16 000	928	1 538	4 966	2 896	1 352	3 272	708	229	111
Never married	6 549	379	652	2 006	1 223	471	1 457	254	88	20
Married, spouse present	8 035	447	674	2 435	1 412	746	1 682	433	129	77
Married, spouse absent, not separated	263	63	61	57	34	16	26	3	2	-
Separated	255	12	32	107	45	25	21	5	6	3
Widowed	23	-	11	7	-	1	-	4	-	-
Divorced	876	27	109	353	181	94	86	10	6	10
35 to 44 Years										
Total	17 685	994	1 335	5 882	2 787	1 566	3 433	1 118	358	213
Never married	3 236	238	295	1 148	518	227	550	186	43	32
Married, spouse present	11 622	552	747	3 596	1 753	1 115	2 557	851	282	168
Married, spouse absent, not separated	374	83	46	143	37	14	21	18	10	1
Separated	370	40	39	137	67	27	43	14	5	-
Widowed	85	8	20	34	8	4	8	1	1	-
Divorced	1 997	72	187	823	405	179	254	47	17	12
45 to 54 Years										
Total	17 345	812	1 073	5 509	2 945	1 535	3 316	1 400	425	330
Never married	2 108	175	146	736	309	154	371	156	30	29
Married, spouse present	11 982	442	629	3 550	2 068	1 113	2 481	1 097	342	262
Married, spouse absent, not separated	367	81	36	97	35	24	55	22	13	4
Separated	362	24	49	139	47	22	50	24	2	5
Widowed	146	7	13	59	23	14	23	-	5	-
Divorced	2 379	83	199	928	463	207	336	101	33	30
55 to 64 Years										
Total	12 176	724	834	3 536	2 055	917	2 256	1 171	301	383
Never married	719	93	58	184	108	38	123	71	5	40
Married, spouse present	9 252	452	572	2 677	1 589	709	1 776	940	252	287
Married, spouse absent, not separated	169	30	15	32	17	5	24	17	19	10
Separated	176	33	23	55	19	10	24	9	-	4
Widowed	276	30	39	78	41	14	34	31	7	3
Divorced	1 584	87	128	510	281	141	276	103	18	40
65 Years and Over										
Total	13 422	1 601	1 476	4 357	1 952	581	1 966	834	338	318
Never married	549	84	63	140	55	39	78	47	26	18
Married, spouse present	9 827	1 014	1 007	3 227	1 485	449	1 485	644	274	242
Married, spouse absent, not separated	241	46	26	68	34	6	37	13	9	1
Separated	128	29	15	36	26	5	7	8	-	1
Widowed	1 782	335	241	600	200	55	223	77	19	32
Divorced	896	92	124	286	152	27	136	45	10	23

- = Quantity zero or rounds to zero.

Table A-25. Educational Attainment of the Population Age 18 Years and Over, by Marital Status, Age, Sex, Race, and Hispanic Origin, 2005—*Continued*

(Numbers in thousands.)

Age, sex, race, Hispanic origin, and marital status	Total population	Educational attainment								
		None to 8th grade	9th to 11th grade	High school graduate	Some college, no degree	Associate's degree	Bachelor's degree	Master's degree	Professional degree	Doctorate degree
WHITE ALONE OR IN COMBINATION										
Female										
18 Years and Over										
Total	92 313	5 097	8 206	29 407	18 233	8 487	15 602	5 775	870	637
Never married	17 559	663	2 073	4 268	5 109	1 115	3 161	917	152	101
Married, spouse present	51 615	2 307	3 442	16 967	8 934	5 334	9 875	3 791	569	395
Married, spouse absent, not separated	1 130	126	138	385	188	60	135	67	10	21
Separated	2 022	212	353	611	406	177	159	79	15	10
Widowed	9 332	1 348	1 367	3 662	1 262	547	760	310	50	27
Divorced	10 655	441	832	3 514	2 333	1 254	1 511	611	74	84
18 to 24 Years										
Total	11 070	257	1 847	2 966	4 222	589	1 143	42	4	-
Never married	8 668	139	1 480	2 107	3 620	389	900	31	2	-
Married, spouse present	1 958	105	280	701	461	177	221	11	3	-
Married, spouse absent, not separated	125	5	25	33	48	8	7	-	-	-
Separated	151	5	42	51	39	6	9	-	-	-
Widowed	15	2	1	5	7	1	-	-	-	-
Divorced	152	1	18	69	47	10	7	-	-	-
25 to 34 Years										
Total	15 395	687	1 222	3 898	2 916	1 508	3 772	1 126	167	98
Never married	4 329	197	328	960	743	355	1 273	383	65	25
Married, spouse present	9 169	413	662	2 322	1 650	954	2 316	689	101	64
Married, spouse absent, not separated	186	11	30	64	45	3	22	6	-	6
Separated	477	37	94	138	127	34	37	9	1	-
Widowed	55	8	1	23	11	7	5	-	-	-
Divorced	1 178	21	107	392	340	155	120	39	-	3
35 to 44 Years										
Total	17 589	726	1 034	5 118	3 140	2 059	3 762	1 287	280	184
Never married	1 913	115	122	498	344	144	470	161	36	22
Married, spouse present	12 171	467	573	3 464	2 058	1 489	2 804	976	210	128
Married, spouse absent, not separated	200	20	26	61	30	11	33	12	1	5
Separated	559	48	92	177	113	61	40	16	5	7
Widowed	208	7	28	78	37	16	23	12	5	3
Divorced	2 537	69	193	840	557	338	391	108	22	19
45 to 54 Years										
Total	17 611	681	1 032	5 498	3 198	2 074	3 284	1 479	197	169
Never married	1 362	66	83	338	218	151	296	155	27	27
Married, spouse present	11 966	399	619	3 788	2 106	1 405	2 338	1 058	134	120
Married, spouse absent, not separated	204	20	20	72	17	12	30	22	6	5
Separated	475	53	63	129	76	53	49	44	4	3
Widowed	481	33	48	147	106	58	56	30	3	-
Divorced	3 124	110	200	1 024	674	395	514	170	23	14
55 to 64 Years										
Total	13 125	656	913	4 653	2 320	1 229	1 964	1 145	121	125
Never married	671	49	34	163	120	37	143	89	18	16
Married, spouse present	8 655	349	544	3 222	1 489	835	1 351	735	72	58
Married, spouse absent, not separated	155	20	11	39	26	6	27	19	3	5
Separated	234	44	35	69	37	22	18	7	1	-
Widowed	1 174	108	127	461	199	83	107	73	9	6
Divorced	2 236	87	162	699	447	246	317	221	17	39
65 Years and Over										
Total	17 523	2 090	2 158	7 275	2 437	1 027	1 676	697	101	62
Never married	617	97	25	201	63	39	79	98	3	11
Married, spouse present	7 695	575	764	3 471	1 170	473	845	322	48	25
Married, spouse absent, not separated	258	49	27	117	22	19	17	7	-	-
Separated	126	26	27	47	13	3	5	2	4	-
Widowed	7 399	1 191	1 162	2 948	902	382	569	195	34	18
Divorced	1 429	152	153	492	268	110	162	73	11	9

- = Quantity zero or rounds to zero.

Table A-25. Educational Attainment of the Population Age 18 Years and Over, by Marital Status, Age, Sex, Race, and Hispanic Origin, 2005—*Continued*

(Numbers in thousands.)

Age, sex, race, Hispanic origin, and marital status	Total population	Educational attainment								
		None to 8th grade	9th to 11th grade	High school graduate	Some college, no degree	Associate's degree	Bachelor's degree	Master's degree	Professional degree	Doctorate degree
BLACK ALONE OR IN COMBINATION										
Male										
18 Years and Over										
Total	11 533	584	1 763	4 590	2 283	723	1 133	320	77	59
Never married	4 871	172	884	2 056	1 111	212	358	49	20	10
Married, spouse present	4 462	235	482	1 665	830	361	596	220	36	37
Married, spouse absent, not separated	270	26	82	101	15	13	21	7	3	3
Separated	472	20	66	235	72	47	24	7	2	-
Widowed	311	72	78	75	41	12	22	6	5	-
Divorced	1 146	60	171	459	215	79	112	30	10	9
18 to 24 Years										
Total	1 960	37	512	732	580	38	59	2	-	-
Never married	1 844	37	494	667	557	33	54	2	-	-
Married, spouse present	95	-	14	52	22	2	5	-	-	-
Married, spouse absent, not separated	5	-	2	2	1	-	-	-	-	-
Separated	3	-	-	-	-	3	-	-	-	-
Widowed	-	-	-	-	-	-	-	-	-	-
Divorced	13	-	1	11	-	-	1	-	-	-
25 to 34 Years										
Total	2 390	44	227	1 008	522	190	322	58	14	5
Never married	1 412	26	133	644	293	109	183	17	7	1
Married, spouse present	742	19	46	261	186	68	118	36	7	3
Married, spouse absent, not separated	57	-	29	25	-	-	2	-	-	1
Separated	78	-	8	42	18	7	3	-	-	-
Widowed	3	-	-	-	-	2	1	-	-	-
Divorced	98	-	11	37	25	4	15	4	-	-
35 to 44 Years										
Total	2 473	45	287	1 112	410	191	308	88	16	17
Never married	871	25	127	466	122	38	66	17	7	3
Married, spouse present	1 004	11	97	410	216	106	182	58	4	11
Married, spouse absent, not separated	74	1	23	27	4	5	14	-	-	-
Separated	146	2	11	77	18	19	11	7	-	-
Widowed	17	-	3	7	5	-	-	2	-	-
Divorced	272	5	26	125	46	22	36	5	4	3
45 to 54 Years										
Total	2 239	68	245	966	440	145	257	90	17	12
Never married	485	19	73	210	106	19	40	10	6	1
Married, spouse present	1 146	33	92	470	216	93	162	69	4	8
Married, spouse absent, not separated	67	2	7	31	7	6	5	5	3	2
Separated	129	2	20	73	19	8	8	-	-	-
Widowed	27	4	5	8	5	-	4	-	-	-
Divorced	386	8	48	174	86	20	38	6	5	1
55 to 64 Years										
Total	1 300	105	220	474	206	103	113	51	10	18
Never married	165	40	30	47	28	6	9	-	-	4
Married, spouse present	765	38	105	309	115	63	78	38	6	12
Married, spouse absent, not separated	32	10	11	8	-	-	1	2	-	-
Separated	59	4	14	21	8	8	2	-	2	-
Widowed	43	4	12	10	6	1	4	2	2	-
Divorced	236	10	48	78	49	24	17	9	-	2
65 Years and Over										
Total	1 171	286	274	298	126	55	74	32	19	7
Never married	95	26	26	23	6	6	5	3	-	1
Married, spouse present	620	135	129	164	75	28	51	20	15	3
Married, spouse absent, not separated	35	12	10	7	3	2	-	1	-	-
Separated	58	11	14	21	9	3	-	-	-	-
Widowed	222	65	57	50	24	8	12	2	3	-
Divorced	141	37	37	34	10	8	5	6	1	3

- = Quantity zero or rounds to zero.

Table A-25. Educational Attainment of the Population Age 18 Years and Over, by Marital Status, Age, Sex, Race, and Hispanic Origin, 2005—*Continued*

(Numbers in thousands.)

Age, sex, race, Hispanic origin, and marital status	Total population	Educational attainment								
		None to 8th grade	9th to 11th grade	High school graduate	Some college, no degree	Associate's degree	Bachelor's degree	Master's degree	Professional degree	Doctorate degree
BLACK ALONE OR IN COMBINATION										
Female										
18 Years and Over										
Total	14 314	684	2 100	4 863	3 079	1 163	1 749	555	71	49
Never married	5 689	150	1 044	1 883	1 428	394	600	153	25	12
Married, spouse present	4 272	149	364	1 496	863	394	698	254	33	21
Married, spouse absent, not separated	333	24	54	105	64	42	31	9	4	-
Separated	735	36	111	306	132	65	67	16	-	2
Widowed	1 381	261	322	454	161	52	87	33	4	8
Divorced	1 903	65	204	619	431	216	266	90	6	5
18 to 24 Years										
Total	2 200	21	501	697	740	112	123	6	-	-
Never married	1 965	16	476	616	658	90	107	3	-	-
Married, spouse present	147	4	12	51	56	12	9	3	-	-
Married, spouse absent, not separated	30	2	7	10	5	4	2	-	-	-
Separated	23	-	3	8	9	3	-	-	-	-
Widowed	4	-	-	2	2	-	-	-	-	-
Divorced	30	-	2	10	10	4	5	-	-	-
25 to 34 Years										
Total	2 911	53	297	933	717	297	478	110	20	5
Never married	1 677	27	237	550	402	154	247	46	14	1
Married, spouse present	833	22	32	245	182	98	190	57	6	2
Married, spouse absent, not separated	58	1	4	28	17	5	4	-	-	-
Separated	128	1	11	52	37	12	12	-	-	2
Widowed	23	2	-	6	12	-	2	2	-	-
Divorced	192	-	13	53	68	29	23	5	-	-
35 to 44 Years										
Total	2 999	53	309	1 095	620	281	477	137	13	14
Never married	1 001	28	157	371	188	79	124	44	5	5
Married, spouse present	1 143	12	77	407	236	116	221	60	8	7
Married, spouse absent, not separated	100	2	17	23	24	11	19	3	-	-
Separated	234	5	27	104	45	21	25	6	-	-
Widowed	56	-	5	26	14	5	4	2	-	-
Divorced	464	6	26	163	113	49	83	22	-	2
45 to 54 Years										
Total	2 700	76	296	963	536	242	401	148	20	18
Never married	666	23	97	230	138	50	82	38	2	6
Married, spouse present	1 083	28	85	392	206	96	184	73	12	6
Married, spouse absent, not separated	54	5	5	16	8	11	3	2	4	-
Separated	173	5	31	74	21	13	23	5	-	-
Widowed	143	3	29	46	33	12	14	4	-	4
Divorced	582	12	50	205	130	60	94	26	2	2
55 to 64 Years										
Total	1 670	92	259	634	280	151	153	84	8	9
Never married	228	18	46	81	28	16	24	14	2	-
Married, spouse present	662	24	88	261	121	51	70	39	3	5
Married, spouse absent, not separated	41	3	11	13	4	7	2	2	-	-
Separated	108	8	24	42	15	12	5	3	-	-
Widowed	233	23	46	119	27	4	9	2	-	3
Divorced	397	16	44	119	84	61	44	24	4	2
65 Years and Over										
Total	1 834	390	438	541	186	80	117	71	9	2
Never married	151	38	32	35	14	6	16	9	2	-
Married, spouse present	404	59	70	140	63	22	24	23	3	-
Married, spouse absent, not separated	49	12	10	15	5	5	1	1	-	-
Separated	70	16	16	27	4	4	1	2	-	-
Widowed	921	234	242	255	74	31	58	23	4	1
Divorced	238	30	68	70	26	13	17	12	-	-

- = Quantity zero or rounds to zero.

Table A-25. Educational Attainment of the Population Age 18 Years and Over, by Marital Status, Age, Sex, Race, and Hispanic Origin, 2005—*Continued*

(Numbers in thousands.)

Age, sex, race, Hispanic origin, and marital status	Total population	Educational attainment								
		None to 8th grade	9th to 11th grade	High school graduate	Some college, no degree	Associate's degree	Bachelor's degree	Master's degree	Professional degree	Doctorate degree
ASIAN ALONE OR IN COMBINATION										
Male										
18 Years and Over										
Total	4 697	219	264	983	714	275	1 334	573	169	167
Never married	1 454	29	116	314	387	85	392	94	24	12
Married, spouse present	2 749	150	105	553	270	164	809	435	122	140
Married, spouse absent, not separated	161	11	7	45	9	13	40	27	-	8
Separated	64	3	10	24	5	1	15	-	7	-
Widowed	71	14	11	12	9	2	15	1	3	5
Divorced	190	13	13	35	35	10	64	16	12	3
18 to 24 Years										
Total	616	5	90	140	282	32	66	-	-	-
Never married	581	5	87	125	272	28	64	-	-	-
Married, spouse present	22	-	-	11	8	3	-	-	-	-
Married, spouse absent, not separated	10	-	2	4	1	1	2	-	-	-
Separated	3	-	1	-	1	-	-	-	-	-
Widowed	-	-	-	-	-	-	-	-	-	-
Divorced	-	-	-	-	-	-	-	-	-	-
25 to 34 Years										
Total	1 171	20	29	201	142	68	450	203	40	18
Never married	590	7	18	116	75	32	242	76	18	6
Married, spouse present	503	9	8	76	59	32	184	105	20	11
Married, spouse absent, not separated	54	2	2	5	7	2	14	21	-	-
Separated	8	-	-	1	-	1	6	-	-	-
Widowed	-	-	-	-	-	-	-	-	-	-
Divorced	16	2	2	4	1	1	5	-	2	-
35 to 44 Years										
Total	1 126	31	47	214	130	63	352	182	51	56
Never married	173	3	8	46	24	19	51	12	3	6
Married, spouse present	828	27	27	140	74	39	269	162	39	50
Married, spouse absent, not separated	30	-	-	14	-	2	12	1	-	-
Separated	17	-	3	5	3	-	2	-	3	-
Widowed	1	-	-	-	-	-	-	-	-	-
Divorced	78	-	9	9	28	2	18	7	5	-
45 to 54 Years										
Total	797	45	30	202	83	48	226	93	33	36
Never married	62	3	2	20	11	3	17	3	2	-
Married, spouse present	639	36	24	151	67	40	176	83	28	32
Married, spouse absent, not separated	29	-	1	9	1	2	11	-	-	4
Separated	19	3	2	12	-	-	2	-	-	-
Widowed	2	-	1	1	-	-	-	-	-	-
Divorced	47	3	-	9	3	2	20	6	3	1
55 to 64 Years										
Total	508	36	24	109	41	40	143	53	27	36
Never married	24	4	1	2	2	2	13	-	-	-
Married, spouse present	395	26	15	86	33	31	105	46	23	30
Married, spouse absent, not separated	23	2	1	8	-	3	-	5	-	4
Separated	16	-	4	4	-	-	4	-	4	-
Widowed	16	-	3	3	3	-	6	-	-	-
Divorced	34	3	-	7	1	4	15	2	-	2
65 Years and Over										
Total	479	82	43	116	36	24	97	42	18	21
Never married	24	7	-	6	3	1	5	2	1	-
Married, spouse present	363	51	31	90	28	20	75	38	12	17
Married, spouse absent, not separated	16	6	1	5	-	2	1	-	-	-
Separated	3	-	-	1	-	-	1	-	-	-
Widowed	53	14	7	8	5	1	9	1	3	5
Divorced	22	4	3	6	1	-	6	-	1	-

- = Quantity zero or rounds to zero.

Table A-25. Educational Attainment of the Population Age 18 Years and Over, by Marital Status, Age, Sex, Race, and Hispanic Origin, 2005—*Continued*

(Numbers in thousands.)

Age, sex, race, Hispanic origin, and marital status	Total population	Educational attainment								
		None to 8th grade	9th to 11th grade	High school graduate	Some college, no degree	Associate's degree	Bachelor's degree	Master's degree	Professional degree	Doctorate degree
ASIAN ALONE OR IN COMBINATION										
Female										
18 Years and Over										
Total	5 187	430	311	1 045	825	356	1 602	442	101	77
Never married	1 128	30	99	148	386	55	317	59	17	18
Married, spouse present	3 131	230	157	672	314	231	1 069	328	75	55
Married, spouse absent, not separated	155	23	9	32	22	8	38	21	1	1
Separated	97	13	3	35	13	10	19	2	2	-
Widowed	340	121	18	81	31	20	55	11	1	2
Divorced	336	13	25	78	60	31	103	20	5	1
18 to 24 Years										
Total	636	7	77	100	331	21	82	17	2	-
Never married	546	2	77	79	292	16	68	9	2	-
Married, spouse present	67	5	-	15	28	4	13	3	-	-
Married, spouse absent, not separated	13	-	-	4	6	-	1	2	-	-
Separated	3	-	-	-	1	1	-	-	-	-
Widowed	7	-	-	1	4	-	-	2	-	-
Divorced	-	-	-	-	-	-	-	-	-	-
25 to 34 Years										
Total	1 226	29	51	163	127	77	554	160	43	22
Never married	355	9	11	38	57	20	171	25	12	12
Married, spouse present	790	18	36	105	56	49	356	132	30	9
Married, spouse absent, not separated	27	-	-	3	5	4	12	2	1	-
Separated	8	-	1	5	-	-	2	-	-	-
Widowed	9	1	-	1	5	-	2	-	-	-
Divorced	37	1	4	11	4	4	12	-	-	1
35 to 44 Years										
Total	1 155	56	43	202	141	110	386	152	34	31
Never married	95	3	3	8	25	7	23	18	3	6
Married, spouse present	911	47	35	160	101	85	312	118	27	25
Married, spouse absent, not separated	38	3	3	5	2	2	15	8	-	-
Separated	23	-	-	10	2	4	5	2	-	-
Widowed	2	-	2	-	-	-	-	-	-	-
Divorced	86	2	-	19	11	13	31	6	4	-
45 to 54 Years										
Total	944	76	58	248	113	81	289	59	9	11
Never married	56	6	2	9	5	7	21	6	-	-
Married, spouse present	709	56	47	193	78	59	222	34	8	10
Married, spouse absent, not separated	31	-	2	11	6	-	3	8	-	-
Separated	29	4	1	12	4	-	8	-	-	-
Widowed	29	6	-	4	3	6	7	2	-	1
Divorced	90	3	5	19	16	7	29	9	-	-
55 to 64 Years										
Total	601	66	35	169	61	43	179	30	9	10
Never married	55	6	4	10	5	4	25	2	-	-
Married, spouse present	363	33	17	117	30	19	107	23	7	9
Married, spouse absent, not separated	26	6	-	9	1	2	5	2	-	1
Separated	29	9	-	3	5	5	4	-	2	-
Widowed	52	10	3	10	3	9	15	-	-	-
Divorced	76	1	10	19	18	4	22	2	-	-
65 Years and Over										
Total	625	198	47	163	51	25	111	25	4	2
Never married	21	4	2	4	2	-	9	-	-	-
Married, spouse present	291	71	21	81	21	16	59	17	3	1
Married, spouse absent, not separated	21	14	3	-	2	-	3	-	-	-
Separated	5	-	-	4	-	1	-	-	-	-
Widowed	247	104	13	65	19	5	31	8	1	1
Divorced	39	5	7	8	7	3	9	-	-	-

- = Quantity zero or rounds to zero.

Table A-25. Educational Attainment of the Population Age 18 Years and Over, by Marital Status, Age, Sex, Race, and Hispanic Origin, 2005—*Continued*

(Numbers in thousands.)

Age, sex, race, Hispanic origin, and marital status	Total population	Educational attainment								
		None to 8th grade	9th to 11th grade	High school graduate	Some college, no degree	Associate's degree	Bachelor's degree	Master's degree	Professional degree	Doctorate degree
HISPANIC[1]										
Male										
18 Years and Over										
Total	14 148	3 306	2 619	4 122	2 045	635	1 024	252	84	62
Never married	5 205	963	1 117	1 615	895	190	337	58	19	12
Married, spouse present	6 799	1 718	1 139	1 887	892	347	561	152	58	45
Married, spouse absent, not separated	658	262	122	177	51	19	18	7	2	-
Separated	380	92	79	109	44	14	29	9	3	1
Widowed	217	112	35	43	15	5	7	-	-	-
Divorced	889	159	128	292	147	60	73	27	1	3
18 to 24 Years										
Total	2 636	364	720	906	531	55	57	4	-	-
Never married	2 228	284	610	755	485	47	45	2	-	-
Married, spouse present	323	69	84	122	32	7	7	2	-	-
Married, spouse absent, not separated	40	7	12	13	6	1	2	-	-	-
Separated	17	1	10	3	-	-	4	-	-	-
Widowed	2	-	-	-	2	-	-	-	-	-
Divorced	25	1	4	14	6	-	-	-	-	-
25 to 34 Years										
Total	4 133	806	824	1 272	598	225	330	51	18	10
Never married	1 821	324	348	580	271	85	172	25	12	3
Married, spouse present	1 900	389	371	571	281	113	141	22	4	7
Married, spouse absent, not separated	172	60	49	41	14	6	2	-	1	-
Separated	88	10	25	25	15	8	4	-	-	-
Widowed	4	-	4	-	-	-	-	-	-	-
Divorced	149	22	27	54	17	13	12	4	-	-
35 to 44 Years										
Total	3 263	780	524	946	421	185	301	76	20	10
Never married	703	180	108	179	101	35	80	16	1	3
Married, spouse present	1 927	450	319	553	225	124	186	50	15	7
Married, spouse absent, not separated	228	80	37	77	21	5	4	3	1	-
Separated	110	29	14	36	15	1	11	-	3	-
Widowed	13	5	4	2	1	-	1	-	-	-
Divorced	282	35	44	99	58	20	19	7	-	-
45 to 54 Years										
Total	2 084	601	284	553	255	86	193	73	17	21
Never married	273	102	30	65	22	12	29	11	-	2
Married, spouse present	1 302	341	188	342	178	50	123	48	16	17
Married, spouse absent, not separated	159	81	17	36	7	8	9	1	-	-
Separated	91	21	15	31	6	2	8	8	-	-
Widowed	19	6	3	5	3	-	2	-	-	-
Divorced	240	50	31	75	39	16	21	5	1	3
55 to 64 Years										
Total	1 102	355	140	255	159	51	90	31	10	11
Never married	116	43	12	28	15	6	7	3	-	1
Married, spouse present	745	233	99	162	117	37	62	19	10	8
Married, spouse absent, not separated	41	23	4	8	3	1	1	3	-	-
Separated	45	15	13	8	4	-	2	1	-	1
Widowed	31	13	2	13	-	1	2	-	-	-
Divorced	125	29	11	36	20	7	17	5	-	-
65 Years and Over										
Total	930	401	127	190	81	33	52	17	19	10
Never married	63	29	8	8	1	4	4	-	5	3
Married, spouse present	602	235	78	138	59	16	42	12	14	7
Married, spouse absent, not separated	18	11	5	3	-	-	-	-	-	-
Separated	30	16	2	6	3	3	-	-	-	-
Widowed	150	88	22	23	10	5	2	-	-	-
Divorced	67	21	12	12	8	5	4	5	-	-

[1]May be of any race.
- = Quantity zero or rounds to zero.

Table A-25. Educational Attainment of the Population Age 18 Years and Over, by Marital Status, Age, Sex, Race, and Hispanic Origin, 2005—*Continued*

(Numbers in thousands.)

Age, sex, race, Hispanic origin, and marital status	Total population	Educational attainment								
		None to 8th grade	9th to 11th grade	High school graduate	Some college, no degree	Associate's degree	Bachelor's degree	Master's degree	Professional degree	Doctorate degree
HISPANIC[1]										
Female										
18 Years and Over										
Total	13 370	2 903	2 415	3 725	2 130	771	1 019	305	68	33
Never married	3 415	434	722	944	775	201	258	55	13	14
Married, spouse present	6 883	1 572	1 151	1 968	954	398	599	183	44	13
Married, spouse absent, not separated	288	82	60	74	39	9	13	10	-	-
Separated	672	165	181	186	78	22	33	7	1	-
Widowed	813	403	114	157	66	31	25	13	3	3
Divorced	1 299	248	187	397	218	110	91	38	7	4
18 to 24 Years										
Total	2 330	192	605	713	633	100	85	2	-	-
Never married	1 643	85	425	477	511	78	67	1	-	-
Married, spouse present	569	94	143	191	104	18	18	1	-	-
Married, spouse absent, not separated	46	7	15	10	14	-	-	-	-	-
Separated	43	5	18	19	1	1	-	-	-	-
Widowed	3	2	-	-	1	-	-	-	-	-
Divorced	26	-	5	17	2	1	-	-	-	-
25 to 34 Years										
Total	3 503	606	693	998	516	240	344	80	21	6
Never married	988	156	178	265	147	83	112	27	13	5
Married, spouse present	2 064	388	410	592	277	125	210	52	7	1
Married, spouse absent, not separated	80	8	22	24	18	1	7	-	-	-
Separated	194	33	61	52	33	5	9	-	1	-
Widowed	7	6	1	-	1	-	-	-	-	-
Divorced	171	15	20	64	41	25	5	-	-	-
35 to 44 Years										
Total	2 980	625	463	813	454	200	292	93	29	11
Never married	426	90	72	116	66	22	45	11	-	4
Married, spouse present	1 899	417	268	518	279	138	190	58	26	6
Married, spouse absent, not separated	57	17	11	14	4	1	5	5	-	-
Separated	199	40	48	59	26	7	17	2	-	-
Widowed	41	2	15	6	10	3	3	1	-	-
Divorced	358	59	48	101	70	29	33	16	3	-
45 to 54 Years										
Total	2 078	504	328	574	287	114	181	69	12	10
Never married	206	42	28	53	34	14	23	9	-	4
Married, spouse present	1 224	308	179	328	173	70	119	36	9	2
Married, spouse absent, not separated	47	14	9	17	1	-	1	5	-	-
Separated	124	37	35	26	15	3	6	3	-	-
Widowed	87	18	21	21	13	4	3	5	-	3
Divorced	390	85	57	129	52	23	29	11	2	2
55 to 64 Years										
Total	1 215	344	164	354	171	76	68	31	5	2
Never married	93	27	14	24	15	2	9	1	-	-
Married, spouse present	658	180	89	207	91	33	36	21	1	-
Married, spouse absent, not separated	36	18	2	8	2	5	-	-	-	-
Separated	60	26	3	19	4	5	1	1	-	-
Widowed	153	62	20	33	20	6	8	2	1	-
Divorced	214	31	36	62	39	23	13	6	2	1
65 Years and Over										
Total	1 264	632	161	273	68	42	50	31	2	5
Never married	59	34	5	10	2	1	2	5	-	-
Married, spouse present	469	185	63	132	29	14	26	15	1	4
Married, spouse absent, not separated	23	17	-	1	1	1	1	1	-	-
Separated	51	25	15	11	-	-	-	-	-	-
Widowed	521	313	57	96	21	17	11	5	1	-
Divorced	141	58	20	23	16	8	10	5	-	1

[1]May be of any race.
- = Quantity zero or rounds to zero.

Table A-26. Years of School Completed by the Population Age 25 Years and Over, by Sex and Age, Selected Years, 1940–2005

(Numbers in thousands, number of years.)

Age, sex, and year	Total population	Years of school completed						Median years
		Elementary		High school		College		
		0 to 4 years	5 to 8 years	1 to 3 years	4 years	1 to 3 years	4 years or more	
25 YEARS AND OVER								
Both Sexes								
2005	189 367	2 983	8 935	16 099	60 893	48 076	52 381	. . .
2004	186 876	2 858	8 888	15 999	59 811	47 571	51 749	. . .
2003	185 183	2 915	9 361	16 323	59 292	46 910	50 383	. . .
2002	182 142	2 902	9 668	16 378	58 456	46 042	48 696	. . .
2001	180 389	2 810	9 518	16 279	58 272	46 281	47 228	. . .
2000	175 230	2 742	9 438	15 674	58 086	44 445	44 845	. . .
1999	173 754	2 742	9 655	15 674	57 935	43 176	43 803	. . .
1998	172 211	2 834	9 948	16 776	58 174	42 506	41 973	. . .
1997	170 581	2 840	10 472	17 211	57 586	41 774	40 697	. . .
1996	168 323	3 027	10 595	17 102	56 559	41 372	39 668	. . .
1995	166 438	3 074	10 873	16 566	56 450	41 249	38 226	. . .
1994	164 512	3 156	11 359	16 925	56 515	40 014	36 544	. . .
1993	162 826	3 380	11 747	17 067	57 589	37 451	35 590	. . .
1992	160 827	3 449	11 989	17 672	57 860	35 520	34 337	. . .
1991	158 694	3 803	13 046	17 379	61 272	29 170	34 026	12.7
1990	156 538	3 833	13 758	17 461	60 119	28 075	33 291	12.7
1989	154 155	3 861	14 061	17 719	59 336	26 614	32 565	12.7
1988	151 635	3 714	14 550	17 847	58 940	25 799	30 787	12.7
1987	149 144	3 640	15 301	17 417	57 669	25 479	29 637	12.7
1986	146 606	3 894	15 672	17 484	56 338	24 729	28 489	12.6
1985	143 524	3 873	16 020	17 553	54 866	23 405	27 808	12.6
1984	140 794	3 884	16 258	17 433	54 073	22 281	26 862	12.6
1983	138 020	4 119	16 714	17 681	52 060	21 531	25 915	12.6
1982	135 526	4 119	17 232	18 006	51 426	20 692	24 050	12.6
1981	132 800	4 358	17 868	18 041	49 915	20 042	22 674	12.5
1980	130 409	4 390	18 426	18 086	47 934	19 379	22 193	12.5
1979	125 295	4 324	18 504	17 579	45 915	18 393	20 579	12.5
1978	123 019	4 445	19 309	18 175	44 381	17 379	19 332	12.4
1977	120 870	4 509	19 507	18 010	43 602	16 247	18 627	12.4
1976	118 848	4 601	19 912	18 204	43 157	15 477	17 496	12.4
1975	116 897	4 912	20 633	18 237	42 353	14 518	16 244	12.3
1974	115 005	5 106	21 200	18 274	41 460	13 665	15 300	12.3
1973	112 866	5 100	21 838	18 420	40 448	12 831	14 228	12.3
1972	111 133	5 124	22 503	18 855	39 171	12 117	13 364	12.2
1971	110 627	5 574	24 029	18 601	38 029	11 782	12 612	12.2
1970	109 310	5 747	24 519	18 682	37 134	11 164	12 062	12.2
1969	107 750	6 014	24 976	18 527	36 133	10 564	11 535	12.1
1968	106 469	6 248	25 467	18 724	34 603	10 254	11 171	12.1
1967	104 864	6 400	26 178	18 647	33 173	9 914	10 550	12.0
1966	103 876	6 705	26 478	18 859	32 391	9 235	10 212	12.0
1965	103 245	6 982	27 063	18 617	31 703	9 139	9 742	11.8
1964	102 421	7 295	27 551	18 419	30 728	9 085	9 345	11.7
1962	100 664	7 826	28 438	17 751	28 477	9 170	9 002	11.4
1960	99 465	8 303	31 218	19 140	24 440	8 747	7 617	10.6
1959	97 478	7 816	28 490	17 520	26 219	7 888	7 734	11.0
1957	95 630	8 561	29 316	16 951	24 832	6 985	7 172	10.6
1952	88 358	8 004	30 274	15 228	21 074	6 714	6 118	10.1
1950	87 484	9 491	31 617	14 817	17 625	6 246	5 272	9.3
1947	82 578	8 611	32 308	13 487	16 926	5 533	4 424	9.0
1940	74 776	10 105	34 413	11 182	10 552	4 075	3 407	8.6

. . . = Not available.

Table A-26. Years of School Completed by the Population Age 25 Years and Over, by Sex and Age, Selected Years, 1940–2005—*Continued*

(Numbers in thousands, number of years.)

Age, sex, and year	Total population	Years of school completed						Median years
		Elementary		High school		College		
		0 to 4 years	5 to 8 years	1 to 3 years	4 years	1 to 3 years	4 years or more	

25 YEARS AND OVER

Male

Age, sex, and year	Total population	0 to 4 years	5 to 8 years	1 to 3 years	4 years	1 to 3 years	4 years or more	Median years
2005	90 899	1 505	4 402	7 787	29 151	21 794	26 259	. . .
2004	89 558	1 496	4 308	7 766	27 889	21 763	26 336	. . .
2003	88 597	1 482	4 566	8 026	27 356	21 568	25 598	. . .
2002	86 996	1 457	4 743	7 894	26 947	21 127	24 828	. . .
2001	86 096	1 419	4 673	7 615	26 956	21 120	24 313	. . .
2000	83 611	1 341	4 577	7 298	26 651	20 493	23 252	. . .
1999	82 917	1 339	4 651	7 736	26 368	20 043	22 782	. . .
1998	82 376	1 431	4 727	8 017	26 575	19 792	21 832	. . .
1997	81 620	1 454	5 023	8 212	26 226	19 332	21 374	. . .
1996	80 339	1 537	5 067	7 930	25 649	19 301	20 854	. . .
1995	79 463	1 598	5 231	7 691	25 378	18 933	20 631	. . .
1994	78 539	1 669	5 427	7 789	25 404	18 544	19 705	. . .
1993	77 644	1 709	5 594	7 821	25 766	17 521	19 234	. . .
1992	76 579	1 737	5 726	8 085	25 774	16 631	18 627	. . .
1991	75 487	2 018	6 299	7 887	27 189	13 720	18 373	12.8
1990	74 421	2 004	6 557	8 000	26 426	13 271	18 164	12.8
1989	73 225	1 956	6 659	8 076	25 897	12 725	17 913	12.8
1988	71 911	1 852	6 849	8 247	25 638	12 057	17 268	12.7
1987	70 677	1 794	7 259	7 909	24 998	12 062	16 654	12.7
1986	69 503	1 978	7 446	7 872	24 260	11 856	16 091	12.7
1985	67 756	1 947	7 629	7 783	23 552	11 164	15 682	12.7
1984	66 350	1 945	7 688	7 837	22 990	10 678	15 211	12.7
1983	65 004	2 103	7 750	7 867	22 048	10 310	14 926	12.7
1982	63 764	2 074	7 987	7 960	21 749	10 020	13 974	12.6
1981	62 509	2 141	8 322	8 084	21 019	9 734	13 208	12.6
1980	61 389	2 212	8 627	8 046	20 080	9 593	12 832	12.6
1979	58 986	2 190	8 785	7 636	19 250	9 100	12 025	12.6
1978	57 922	2 230	9 195	7 821	18 620	8 657	11 398	12.5
1977	56 917	2 296	9 330	7 969	18 290	8 104	10 926	12.5
1976	55 902	2 371	9 463	7 923	18 048	7 699	10 397	12.5
1975	55 036	2 568	9 760	7 985	17 769	7 274	9 679	12.4
1974	54 167	2 637	10 186	7 966	17 488	6 756	9 135	12.4
1973	53 067	2 598	10 488	8 120	17 011	6 376	8 473	12.3
1972	52 351	2 634	10 854	8 413	16 424	5 972	8 055	12.3
1971	52 357	2 933	11 703	8 264	16 008	5 798	7 653	12.2
1970	51 784	3 031	11 925	8 355	15 571	5 580	7 321	12.2
1969	51 031	3 095	12 182	8 398	15 177	5 263	6 917	12.1
1968	50 510	3 261	12 407	8 564	14 613	4 945	6 721	12.1
1967	49 756	3 417	12 736	8 463	14 015	4 755	6 372	12.0
1966	49 410	3 614	12 992	8 611	13 672	4 342	6 180	11.8
1965	49 242	3 774	13 308	8 529	13 334	4 370	5 923	11.7
1964	48 975	3 959	13 467	8 537	12 902	4 394	5 714	11.5
1962	48 283	4 213	13 927	8 399	11 932	4 315	5 497	11.1
1960	47 997	4 522	15 562	8 988	10 175	4 127	4 626	10.3
1959	47 041	4 257	14 039	8 326	10 870	3 801	4 765	10.7
1957	46 208	4 610	14 634	8 003	10 230	3 347	4 359	10.3
1952	42 368	4 396	14 876	7 048	8 760	3 164	3 480	9.7
1950	42 627	5 074	15 852	6 974	7 511	2 888	3 008	9.0
1947	40 483	4 615	16 086	6 535	7 353	2 625	2 478	8.9
1940	37 463	5 550	17 639	5 333	4 507	1 824	2 021	8.6

. . . = Not available.

Table A-26. Years of School Completed by the Population Age 25 Years and Over, by Sex and Age, Selected Years, 1940–2005—*Continued*

(Numbers in thousands, number of years.)

Age, sex, and year	Total population	Years of school completed						Median years
		Elementary		High school		College		
		0 to 4 years	5 to 8 years	1 to 3 years	4 years	1 to 3 years	4 years or more	
25 YEARS AND OVER								
Female								
2005	98 467	1 477	4 532	8 311	31 742	26 283	26 122	. . .
2004	97 319	1 363	4 580	8 233	31 921	25 808	25 413	. . .
2003	96 586	1 433	4 795	8 297	31 936	25 342	24 784	. . .
2002	95 146	1 445	4 926	8 484	31 509	24 915	23 868	. . .
2001	94 293	1 392	4 845	8 664	31 316	25 161	22 915	. . .
2000	91 620	1 400	4 861	8 378	31 435	23 953	21 594	. . .
1999	90 837	1 404	5 004	8 707	31 566	23 133	21 021	. . .
1998	89 835	1 403	5 220	8 758	31 599	22 714	20 142	. . .
1997	88 061	1 387	5 450	8 999	31 360	22 442	19 323	. . .
1996	87 984	1 491	5 528	9 171	30 911	22 071	18 813	. . .
1995	86 975	1 476	5 642	8 874	31 072	22 317	17 594	. . .
1994	85 973	1 487	5 932	9 135	31 111	21 470	16 838	. . .
1993	85 181	1 672	6 154	9 246	31 823	19 930	16 357	. . .
1992	84 248	1 712	6 263	9 587	32 086	18 889	15 709	. . .
1991	83 207	1 784	6 747	9 491	34 083	15 449	15 652	12.7
1990	82 116	1 829	7 200	9 462	33 693	14 806	15 126	12.7
1989	80 930	1 904	7 402	9 643	33 440	13 888	14 652	12.6
1988	79 724	1 862	7 700	9 599	33 303	13 741	13 519	12.6
1987	78 467	1 846	8 042	9 508	32 671	13 417	12 983	12.6
1986	77 102	1 916	8 226	9 612	32 078	12 874	12 399	12.6
1985	75 768	1 926	8 390	9 770	31 314	12 242	12 126	12.6
1984	74 444	1 939	8 571	9 596	31 083	11 603	11 651	12.6
1983	73 016	2 015	8 964	9 814	30 012	11 220	10 990	12.5
1982	71 762	2 045	9 245	10 046	29 677	10 673	10 076	12.5
1981	70 390	2 217	9 545	9 957	28 096	10 300	9 466	12.5
1980	69 020	2 178	9 800	10 040	27 854	9 786	9 362	12.4
1979	66 309	2 133	9 720	9 945	26 665	9 293	8 554	12.4
1978	65 097	2 214	10 114	10 353	25 761	8 721	7 934	12.4
1977	63 953	2 213	10 236	10 349	25 312	8 142	7 701	12.4
1976	62 946	2 230	10 449	10 281	25 109	7 779	7 098	12.3
1975	61 861	2 344	10 871	10 252	24 584	7 243	6 565	12.3
1974	60 838	2 469	11 015	10 308	23 972	6 910	6 165	12.3
1973	59 799	2 502	11 350	10 300	23 437	6 454	5 755	12.2
1972	58 782	2 490	11 649	10 442	22 746	6 145	5 309	12.2
1971	58 270	2 641	12 327	10 339	22 021	5 984	4 959	12.2
1970	57 527	2 716	12 595	10 327	21 563	5 584	4 743	12.1
1969	56 719	2 919	12 796	10 131	20 955	5 301	4 619	12.1
1968	55 969	2 987	13 060	10 160	19 991	5 309	4 450	12.1
1967	55 107	2 985	13 439	10 185	19 157	5 162	4 178	12.0
1966	54 467	3 090	13 488	10 246	18 719	4 892	4 032	12.0
1965	54 004	3 207	13 753	10 085	18 369	4 767	3 820	12.0
1964	53 447	3 333	14 086	9 881	17 825	4 686	3 629	11.8
1962	52 381	3 613	14 511	9 352	16 545	4 855	3 505	11.6
1960	51 468	3 781	15 656	10 151	14 267	4 620	2 991	10.9
1959	50 437	3 559	14 451	9 194	15 349	4 087	2 969	11.2
1957	49 422	3 951	14 682	8 948	14 602	3 638	2 813	10.9
1952	45 990	3 608	15 398	8 180	12 314	3 550	2 638	10.4
1950	44 857	4 417	15 824	7 843	10 114	3 358	2 264	9.6
1947	42 095	3 996	16 222	6 952	9 573	2 908	1 946	8.9
1940	37 313	4 554	16 773	5 849	6 044	2 251	1 386	8.7

. . . = Not available.

Table A-26. Years of School Completed by the Population Age 25 Years and Over, by Sex and Age, Selected Years, 1940–2005—*Continued*

(Numbers in thousands, number of years.)

Age, sex, and year	Total population	Elementary		High school		College		Median years
		0 to 4 years	5 to 8 years	1 to 3 years	4 years	1 to 3 years	4 years or more	
25 TO 34 YEARS								
Both Sexes								
2005	39 310	414	1 375	3 422	11 269	10 865	11 965	. . .
2004	39 201	430	1 399	3 239	11 244	11 044	11 844	. . .
2003	39 242	370	1 370	3 336	11 392	10 986	11 791	. . .
2002	38 670	433	1 393	3 245	10 988	10 776	11 834	. . .
2001	38 865	380	1 317	3 202	11 294	11 146	11 526	. . .
2000	37 786	287	1 135	3 052	11 546	10 700	11 066	. . .
1999	38 474	280	1 142	3 296	11 826	10 893	11 040	. . .
1998	39 354	319	1 207	3 228	12 569	11 220	10 811	. . .
1997	40 256	334	1 163	3 624	12 710	11 524	10 892	. . .
1996	40 919	418	1 169	3 780	13 087	11 624	10 841	. . .
1995	41 388	394	1 264	3 667	14 061	11 659	10 342	. . .
1994	41 946	367	1 297	4 057	14 483	11 913	9 829	. . .
1993	41 864	382	1 223	3 894	15 036	11 361	9 968	. . .
1992	42 493	433	1 250	4 071	16 021	10 860	9 861	. . .
1991	42 905	465	1 322	4 178	17 503	9 283	10 153	12.9
1990	43 240	505	1 413	4 041	17 635	9 320	10 326	12.9
1989	43 240	446	1 352	4 013	17 901	9 072	10 454	12.9
1988	42 953	430	1 308	4 095	17 887	9 076	10 155	12.9
1987	42 635	390	1 360	3 995	17 539	9 157	10 196	12.9
1986	42 053	387	1 359	3 797	17 311	9 104	10 094	12.9
1985	40 858	362	1 328	3 703	16 748	8 980	9 737	12.9
1984	40 173	404	1 371	3 638	16 431	8 555	9 771	12.9
1983	39 342	376	1 324	3 664	15 804	8 567	9 605	12.9
1982	38 703	337	1 371	3 598	15 893	8 304	9 200	12.9
1981	37 828	337	1 428	3 665	15 419	8 198	8 782	12.9
1980	36 615	362	1 424	3 571	14 481	7 942	8 836	12.9
1979	34 053	370	1 381	3 452	13 338	7 415	8 096	12.9
1978	33 120	325	1 459	3 515	12 993	7 008	7 821	12.9
1977	32 284	269	1 383	3 715	12 845	6 398	7 676	12.8
1976	31 148	247	1 508	3 619	12 920	5 813	7 041	12.8
1975	30 092	313	1 644	3 743	12 544	5 403	6 443	12.7
1974	28 972	352	1 654	3 763	12 362	5 056	5 785	12.7
1973	27 793	333	1 850	3 915	12 194	4 454	5 047	12.6
1972	26 517	285	1 791	3 981	11 635	4 090	4 734	12.6
1971	25 545	327	2 011	3 986	11 232	3 822	4 169	12.6
1970	24 865	329	1 937	4 251	10 929	3 491	3 926	12.5
1969	24 072	359	2 086	4 140	10 592	3 202	3 693	12.5
1968	23 285	350	2 246	4 129	10 157	2 989	3 413	12.5
1967	22 388	319	2 293	4 017	9 645	2 946	3 169	12.5
1966	22 023	430	2 208	4 158	9 546	2 647	3 037	12.4
1965	21 980	543	2 437	4 058	9 500	2 561	2 880	12.4
1964	21 997	502	2 591	4 176	9 370	2 529	2 830	12.4
1962	22 130	597	2 936	4 371	8 815	2 552	2 859	12.4
1960	22 821	709	3 738	5 135	8 166	2 572	2 499	12.4
1959	22 922	761	3 348	4 741	8 979	2 398	2 480	12.3
1957	23 437	750	3 971	4 965	8 927	2 275	2 351	12.2
1952	23 138	844	4 362	4 898	8 620	2 220	2 052	12.2
1950	23 626	1 147	5 308	5 050	7 660	2 198	1 252	11.9
1947	22 627	1 015	5 523	4 997	7 630	1 908	1 378	11.9
1940	21 339	1 377	7 676	4 553	4 702	1 554	1 288	10.0

. . . = Not available.

Table A-26. Years of School Completed by the Population Age 25 Years and Over, by Sex and Age, Selected Years, 1940–2005—*Continued*

(Numbers in thousands, number of years.)

Age, sex, and year	Total population	Years of school completed						Median years
		Elementary		High school		College		
		0 to 4 years	5 to 8 years	1 to 3 years	4 years	1 to 3 years	4 years or more	
25 TO 34 YEARS								
Male								
2005	19 677	241	769	1 827	6 216	5 198	5 426	. . .
2004	19 598	280	793	1 723	6 020	5 286	5 495	. . .
2003	19 564	216	771	1 831	6 028	5 252	5 466	. . .
2002	19 234	280	809	1 782	5 751	5 131	5 480	. . .
2001	19 330	233	748	1 677	6 099	5 161	5 411	. . .
2000	18 563	155	593	1 637	5 989	4 870	5 318	. . .
1999	18 294	157	616	1 724	6 114	5 052	5 260	. . .
1998	19 526	190	654	1 735	6 592	5 233	5 125	. . .
1997	20 039	193	629	2 007	6 482	5 477	5 249	. . .
1996	20 390	225	601	2 055	6 701	5 536	5 274	. . .
1995	20 589	229	708	1 930	7 176	5 373	5 174	. . .
1994	20 873	230	716	2 134	7 408	5 510	4 873	. . .
1993	20 856	237	679	1 986	7 604	5 308	5 041	. . .
1992	21 125	231	682	2 057	8 113	5 116	4 927	. . .
1991	21 319	270	694	2 095	8 810	4 441	5 009	12.9
1990	21 462	295	759	2 153	8 649	4 392	5 215	12.9
1989	21 461	251	698	2 129	8 659	4 391	5 335	12.9
1988	21 277	237	651	2 227	8 569	4 273	5 319	12.9
1987	21 142	223	698	2 030	8 544	4 384	5 263	12.9
1986	20 956	227	715	1 887	8 359	4 488	5 279	12.9
1985	20 184	194	700	1 823	7 955	4 433	5 080	12.9
1984	19 876	231	721	1 739	7 798	4 238	5 150	12.9
1983	19 438	213	659	1 724	7 351	4 284	5 207	13.0
1982	19 090	182	659	1 654	7 380	4 162	5 053	13.0
1981	10 025	176	733	1 679	6 991	4 185	4 863	13.0
1980	18 051	198	699	1 639	6 393	4 166	4 957	13.0
1979	16 719	197	695	1 476	5 852	3 862	4 637	13.0
1978	16 263	154	717	1 526	5 701	3 698	4 471	13.1
1977	15 863	134	672	1 625	5 604	3 403	4 396	13.0
1976	15 266	134	724	1 566	5 672	3 085	4 087	12.9
1975	14 776	177	815	1 605	5 508	2 915	3 757	12.9
1974	14 222	211	859	1 617	5 491	2 672	3 372	12.8
1973	13 638	204	966	1 760	5 363	2 416	2 927	12.7
1972	13 030	157	927	1 796	5 150	2 191	2 809	12.7
1971	12 596	170	1 092	1 771	5 049	2 005	2 506	12.6
1970	12 236	189	1 063	1 896	4 833	1 842	2 412	12.6
1969	11 788	204	1 121	1 849	4 652	1 719	2 241	12.6
1968	11 381	193	1 192	1 880	4 473	1 505	2 136	12.5
1967	10 876	170	1 209	1 814	4 187	1 522	1 973	12.5
1966	10 701	241	1 162	1 839	4 191	1 374	1 894	12.5
1965	10 693	325	1 240	1 802	4 188	1 316	1 822	12.5
1964	10 729	297	1 344	1 962	4 008	1 306	1 812	12.4
1962	10 762	334	1 569	2 008	3 700	1 309	1 842	12.4
1960	11 184	420	2 026	2 441	3 356	1 316	1 624	12.2
1959	11 226	416	1 822	2 238	3 682	1 256	1 658	12.3
1957	11 368	423	2 097	2 446	3 542	1 181	1 556	12.2
1952	10 936	502	2 202	2 268	3 458	1 118	1 268	12.1
1950	11 454	631	2 705	2 426	3 250	1 117	1 037	11.5
1947	10 894	544	2 665	2 494	3 337	993	738	11.7
1940	10 521	779	3 932	2 220	2 049	692	744	9.7

. . . = Not available.

Table A-26. Years of School Completed by the Population Age 25 Years and Over, by Sex and Age, Selected Years, 1940–2005—*Continued*

(Numbers in thousands, number of years.)

Age, sex, and year	Total population	Years of school completed						Median years
		Elementary		High school		College		
		0 to 4 years	5 to 8 years	1 to 3 years	4 years	1 to 3 years	4 years or more	
25 TO 34 YEARS								
Female								
2005	19 633	173	607	1 594	5 053	5 667	6 539	. . .
2004	19 603	150	606	1 516	5 224	5 758	6 349	. . .
2003	19 679	153	598	1 503	5 364	5 734	6 325	. . .
2002	19 436	153	584	1 463	5 237	5 645	6 353	. . .
2001	19 536	147	569	1 525	5 195	5 985	6 115	. . .
2000	19 222	130	542	1 415	5 557	5 831	5 750	. . .
1999	19 551	122	525	1 572	5 712	5 842	5 779	. . .
1998	19 828	130	553	1 493	5 977	5 986	5 688	. . .
1997	20 217	149	533	1 615	6 227	6 047	5 643	. . .
1996	20 528	195	569	1 734	6 386	6 090	5 568	. . .
1995	20 800	165	556	1 738	6 885	6 286	5 170	. . .
1994	21 073	138	581	1 923	7 075	6 404	4 953	. . .
1993	21 007	143	543	1 907	7 432	6 054	4 928	. . .
1992	21 368	203	567	2 014	7 908	5 744	4 933	. . .
1991	21 586	195	629	2 085	8 693	4 841	5 143	12.9
1990	21 779	209	653	1 889	8 986	4 927	5 112	12.9
1989	21 777	195	654	1 885	9 242	4 681	5 119	12.9
1988	21 675	193	657	1 869	9 319	4 801	4 836	12.9
1987	21 494	168	662	1 965	8 995	4 772	4 932	12.9
1986	21 097	160	644	1 910	8 952	4 616	4 813	12.9
1985	20 673	168	627	1 880	8 794	4 547	4 657	12.9
1984	20 297	173	649	1 904	8 634	4 319	4 621	12.9
1983	19 903	161	665	1 941	8 452	4 285	4 398	12.9
1982	19 614	155	713	1 942	8 512	4 140	4 148	12.8
1981	19 203	161	698	1 986	8 427	4 013	3 918	12.8
1980	18 565	164	725	1 932	8 087	3 777	3 879	12.8
1979	17 334	173	685	1 977	7 486	3 553	3 460	12.8
1978	16 857	172	742	1 989	7 292	3 311	3 351	12.6
1977	16 421	136	710	2 088	7 212	2 995	3 280	12.7
1976	15 882	112	784	2 054	7 248	2 731	2 954	12.7
1975	15 316	135	833	2 139	7 037	2 489	2 686	12.6
1974	14 750	142	796	2 145	6 871	2 383	2 413	12.6
1973	14 155	129	884	2 154	6 830	2 037	2 121	12.6
1972	13 487	128	862	2 184	6 485	1 899	1 926	12.5
1971	12 950	156	919	2 212	6 183	1 816	1 663	12.5
1970	12 629	140	876	2 355	6 096	1 648	1 512	12.5
1969	12 285	155	965	2 291	5 941	1 481	1 451	12.4
1968	11 904	157	1 053	2 246	5 684	1 484	1 278	12.4
1967	11 512	149	1 084	2 200	5 458	1 426	1 195	12.4
1966	11 322	186	1 047	2 319	5 355	1 273	1 134	12.4
1965	11 284	218	1 197	2 256	5 310	1 244	1 060	12.4
1964	11 269	202	1 248	2 216	5 362	1 221	1 018	12.4
1962	11 368	263	1 367	2 363	5 115	1 243	1 017	12.3
1960	11 637	289	1 712	2 694	4 810	1 256	875	12.2
1959	11 696	345	1 526	2 503	5 297	1 142	822	12.3
1957	12 069	327	1 874	2 519	5 385	1 094	795	12.2
1952	12 202	342	2 160	2 630	5 162	1 102	784	12.2
1950	12 172	516	2 603	2 624	4 410	1 081	714	12.1
1947	11 733	471	2 858	2 503	4 293	915	640	12.0
1940	10 818	598	3 744	2 333	2 653	862	544	10.3

. . . = Not available.

Table A-26. Years of School Completed by the Population Age 25 Years and Over, by Sex and Age, Selected Years, 1940–2005—*Continued*

(Numbers in thousands, number of years.)

Age, sex, and year	Total population	Elementary 0 to 4 years	Elementary 5 to 8 years	High school 1 to 3 years	High school 4 years	College 1 to 3 years	College 4 years or more	Median years
35 TO 54 YEARS								
Both Sexes								
2005	85 311	954	2 757	5 892	27 232	23 129	25 347	. . .
2004	84 642	963	2 582	5 938	26 649	23 093	25 417	. . .
2003	84 308	957	2 620	6 112	26 346	23 039	25 234	. . .
2002	83 829	941	2 636	5 874	26 740	23 148	24 489	. . .
2001	83 286	886	2 612	5 899	26 356	23 271	24 262	. . .
2000	81 435	932	2 521	5 702	26 481	22 618	23 183	. . .
1999	79 976	872	2 535	6 052	26 367	21 561	22 589	. . .
1998	78 520	890	2 613	6 164	26 079	21 267	21 506	. . .
1997	76 973	867	2 686	6 045	26 054	20 684	20 635	. . .
1996	74 661	968	2 710	5 803	24 924	20 105	20 152	. . .
1995	73 028	927	2 561	5 664	24 070	19 926	19 878	. . .
1994	71 049	987	2 680	5 415	23 804	19 210	18 956	. . .
1993	68 845	942	2 486	5 538	23 927	17 984	17 970	. . .
1992	66 594	899	2 608	5 845	23 442	16 658	17 144	. . .
1991	64 351	995	3 057	5 522	24 815	13 348	16 614	12.9
1990	62 499	980	3 104	5 529	24 434	12 553	15 899	12.9
1989	60 494	999	3 315	5 800	23 334	11 627	15 417	12.9
1988	58 555	958	3 272	5 889	23 049	11 017	14 369	12.8
1987	56 650	842	3 398	5 656	22 820	10 523	13 409	12.8
1986	55 170	896	3 614	5 769	22 151	10 110	12 629	12.8
1985	53 697	899	3 639	5 978	21 600	9 217	12 363	12.8
1984	52 297	893	3 754	6 158	21 290	8 702	11 500	12.7
1983	50 956	973	4 044	6 313	20 788	8 045	10 795	12.7
1982	49 722	963	4 320	6 657	20 445	7 580	9 756	12.6
1981	48 680	1 038	4 531	6 770	20 032	7 116	9 181	12.6
1980	48 124	1 034	4 676	7 063	19 584	6 943	8 822	12.6
1979	47 437	1 030	4 895	7 132	19 488	6 655	8 237	12.5
1978	46 921	1 107	5 262	7 590	19 012	6 286	7 667	12.5
1977	46 409	1 192	5 445	7 781	18 781	6 013	7 190	12.5
1976	46 271	1 245	5 729	7 671	18 893	5 957	6 776	12.5
1975	46 193	1 296	5 942	7 765	19 010	5 673	6 506	12.4
1974	46 217	1 293	6 244	7 896	19 038	5 375	6 372	12.4
1973	45 910	1 344	6 519	8 001	18 651	5 318	6 076	12.4
1972	45 956	1 367	7 004	8 521	18 400	5 074	5 589	12.3
1971	46 294	1 439	7 588	8 393	18 334	5 082	5 460	12.3
1970	46 319	1 461	7 935	8 555	18 200	4 875	5 294	12.3
1969	46 255	1 644	8 313	8 586	17 773	4 749	5 190	12.3
1968	46 396	1 654	8 698	8 838	17 362	4 642	5 200	12.2
1967	46 321	1 771	9 036	9 138	16 906	4 525	4 947	12.2
1966	46 313	1 837	9 528	9 309	16 605	4 230	4 805	12.1
1965	46 296	1 827	9 812	9 266	16 359	4 384	4 647	12.1
1964	46 089	1 905	10 259	9 289	15 760	4 397	4 482	12.1
1962	45 287	2 181	10 795	8 938	14 668	4 452	4 253	12.0
1960	44 742	2 424	12 536	9 502	12 517	4 123	3 639	11.3
1959	43 989	2 303	11 657	8 719	13 244	3 715	3 709	11.8
1957	42 645	2 658	12 349	8 384	12 041	3 248	3 360	11.3
1952	39 014	2 606	13 274	7 348	9 374	3 148	2 802	10.5
1950	38 432	3 404	14 420	6 976	7 262	2 878	2 516	9.7
1947	36 717	3 203	15 184	6 311	6 715	2 622	2 221	9.0
1940	33 845	4 549	16 270	4 972	4 217	1 836	1 540	8.6

. . . = Not available.

Table A-26. Years of School Completed by the Population Age 25 Years and Over, by Sex and Age, Selected Years, 1940–2005—*Continued*

(Numbers in thousands, number of years.)

Age, sex, and year	Total population	Years of school completed						Median years
		Elementary		High school		College		
		0 to 4 years	5 to 8 years	1 to 3 years	4 years	1 to 3 years	4 years or more	
35 TO 54 YEARS								
Male								
2005	42 024	547	1 476	3 063	14 017	10 429	12 491	. . .
2004	41 612	577	1 323	3 157	13 238	10 636	12 682	. . .
2003	41 340	538	1 372	3 282	12 903	10 622	12 622	. . .
2002	41 154	513	1 333	3 063	13 133	10 739	12 373	. . .
2001	40 858	488	1 368	2 974	12 784	10 827	12 417	. . .
2000	40 024	479	1 288	2 845	12 845	10 716	11 854	. . .
1999	39 300	470	1 290	3 101	12 544	10 233	11 664	. . .
1998	38 654	486	1 333	3 284	12 239	10 098	11 214	. . .
1997	37 912	486	1 370	3 143	12 326	9 713	10 870	. . .
1996	36 596	520	1 319	2 877	11 749	9 514	10 526	. . .
1995	35 994	529	1 368	2 781	11 223	9 305	10 784	. . .
1994	34 998	545	1 383	2 621	11 009	9 073	10 369	. . .
1993	33 751	478	1 316	2 660	10 983	8 624	9 687	. . .
1992	32 619	472	1 368	2 750	10 670	7 968	9 389	. . .
1991	31 460	530	1 624	2 612	11 092	6 430	9 169	13.0
1990	30 623	527	1 658	2 573	10 790	6 169	8 905	13.0
1989	29 597	504	1 762	2 628	10 235	5 719	8 749	13.0
1988	28 645	498	1 725	2 654	10 100	5 327	8 340	12.9
1987	27 680	412	1 801	2 617	9 781	5 173	7 895	12.9
1986	26 925	475	1 919	2 699	9 393	5 013	7 426	12.9
1985	26 181	501	1 928	2 726	9 210	4 502	7 314	12.9
1984	25 460	506	2 014	2 831	8 926	4 257	6 929	12.8
1983	24 796	548	2 108	2 862	8 795	3 884	6 601	12.8
1982	24 164	530	2 302	2 989	8 609	3 757	5 977	12.7
1981	23 646	572	2 425	3 112	8 431	3 519	5 588	12.7
1980	23 373	590	2 492	3 202	8 278	3 442	5 370	12.7
1979	22 976	545	2 612	3 194	8 232	3 306	5 090	12.6
1978	22 719	609	2 779	3 377	8 001	3 136	4 817	12.6
1977	22 445	661	2 889	3 554	7 822	3 000	4 520	12.5
1976	22 403	730	3 004	3 473	7 904	2 969	4 323	12.5
1975	22 358	763	3 100	3 510	7 952	2 879	4 153	12.5
1974	22 367	733	3 286	3 532	8 004	2 730	4 081	12.6
1973	22 166	716	3 413	3 586	7 836	2 714	3 901	12.4
1972	22 200	749	3 674	3 917	7 663	2 564	3 631	12.4
1971	22 474	849	3 985	3 823	7 674	2 578	3 567	12.3
1970	22 475	834	4 208	3 876	7 612	2 555	3 390	12.3
1969	22 420	889	4 359	4 012	7 427	2 456	3 277	12.3
1968	22 521	931	4 487	4 160	7 324	2 364	3 257	12.2
1967	22 482	1 000	4 700	4 270	7 143	2 244	3 128	12.2
1966	22 508	1 085	4 886	4 455	6 990	2 029	3 063	12.1
1965	22 534	1 081	5 076	4 462	6 815	2 161	2 937	12.1
1964	22 457	1 158	5 226	4 416	6 657	2 212	2 789	12.2
1962	22 081	1 235	5 545	4 359	6 202	2 142	2 598	11.9
1960	21 919	1 397	6 415	4 579	5 364	1 957	2 206	11.1
1959	21 511	1 350	5 781	4 329	5 604	1 827	2 250	11.5
1957	20 873	1 491	6 293	3 987	5 195	1 558	1 972	11.0
1952	18 888	1 466	6 512	3 462	4 040	1 518	1 576	10.3
1950	18 896	1 834	7 338	3 339	3 151	1 271	1 403	9.6
1947	18 165	1 678	7 765	3 102	2 907	1 168	1 258	8.6
1940	17 127	2 480	8 458	2 388	1 798	819	917	8.5

. . . = Not available.

Table A-26. Years of School Completed by the Population Age 25 Years and Over, by Sex and Age, Selected Years, 1940–2005—*Continued*

(Numbers in thousands, number of years.)

Age, sex, and year	Total population	Years of school completed						Median years
		Elementary		High school		College		
		0 to 4 years	5 to 8 years	1 to 3 years	4 years	1 to 3 years	4 years or more	
35 TO 54 YEARS								
Female								
2005	43 287	407	1 280	2 829	13 215	12 700	12 856	. . .
2004	43 030	386	1 259	2 781	13 411	12 458	12 736	. . .
2003	42 968	419	1 248	2 830	13 443	12 417	12 611	. . .
2002	42 675	428	1 303	2 811	13 607	12 410	12 116	. . .
2001	42 428	398	1 244	2 926	13 572	12 444	11 844	. . .
2000	41 411	452	1 235	2 858	13 635	11 905	11 330	. . .
1999	40 676	402	1 248	2 950	13 825	11 326	10 925	. . .
1998	39 866	403	1 279	2 879	13 841	11 168	10 293	. . .
1997	39 061	381	1 319	2 902	13 726	10 969	9 766	. . .
1996	38 065	449	1 301	2 924	13 174	10 592	9 623	. . .
1995	37 034	396	1 192	2 881	12 846	10 623	9 096	. . .
1994	36 051	443	1 298	2 792	12 795	10 140	8 587	. . .
1993	35 093	462	1 169	2 877	12 944	9 358	8 283	. . .
1992	33 975	427	1 240	3 096	12 770	8 687	7 756	. . .
1991	32 891	464	1 431	2 910	13 723	6 919	7 443	12.8
1990	31 876	454	1 448	2 955	13 643	6 383	6 997	12.8
1989	30 898	498	1 552	3 171	13 099	5 908	6 669	12.8
1988	29 908	462	1 547	3 234	12 949	5 689	6 029	12.7
1987	28 969	430	1 598	3 039	13 038	5 349	5 513	12.7
1986	28 244	420	1 694	3 071	12 759	5 098	5 202	12.7
1985	27 516	398	1 710	3 252	12 391	4 715	5 049	12.7
1984	26 838	389	1 740	3 331	12 364	4 444	4 570	12.6
1983	26 161	427	1 935	3 450	11 993	4 161	4 193	12.6
1982	25 555	433	2 017	3 666	11 833	3 827	3 778	12.6
1981	25 034	467	2 105	3 681	11 599	3 005	3 595	12.6
1980	24 751	444	2 186	3 862	11 307	3 501	3 452	12.5
1979	24 461	486	2 282	3 935	11 258	3 353	3 147	12.5
1978	24 202	497	2 483	4 212	11 012	3 149	2 849	12.5
1977	23 964	534	2 557	4 227	10 959	3 014	2 678	12.4
1976	23 868	517	2 721	4 198	10 989	2 988	2 455	12.4
1975	23 835	533	2 842	4 256	11 058	2 793	2 352	12.4
1974	23 850	559	2 956	4 364	11 033	2 647	2 200	12.4
1973	23 744	628	3 106	4 415	10 815	2 603	2 174	12.3
1972	23 756	618	3 330	4 604	10 736	2 509	1 958	12.3
1971	23 821	590	3 604	4 570	10 660	2 505	1 894	12.3
1970	23 845	629	3 728	4 679	10 588	2 318	1 903	12.3
1969	23 834	755	3 953	4 575	10 349	2 293	1 913	12.3
1968	23 874	725	4 212	4 676	10 038	2 281	1 943	12.2
1967	23 839	773	4 334	4 868	9 762	2 282	1 819	12.2
1966	23 806	752	4 644	4 853	9 615	2 200	1 741	12.2
1965	23 765	746	4 735	4 803	9 545	2 223	1 712	12.2
1964	23 632	748	5 033	4 871	9 103	2 183	1 691	12.1
1962	23 206	946	5 250	4 579	8 466	2 310	1 655	12.1
1960	22 823	1 027	6 121	4 923	7 153	2 166	1 433	11.6
1959	22 478	953	5 876	4 390	7 640	1 888	1 459	12.0
1957	21 772	1 167	6 056	4 397	6 846	1 690	1 388	11.5
1952	20 126	1 140	6 762	3 886	5 334	1 630	1 226	10.7
1950	19 536	1 570	7 082	3 637	4 111	1 607	1 113	9.7
1947	18 552	1 525	7 419	3 209	3 808	1 454	963	9.3
1940	16 718	2 070	7 812	2 584	2 419	1 017	623	8.7

. . . = Not available.

Table A-26. Years of School Completed by the Population Age 25 Years and Over, by Sex and Age, Selected Years, 1940–2005—*Continued*

(Numbers in thousands, number of years.)

Age, sex, and year	Total population	Years of school completed						Median years
		Elementary		High school		College		
		0 to 4 years	5 to 8 years	1 to 3 years	4 years	1 to 3 years	4 years or more	
55 YEARS AND OVER								
Both Sexes								
2005	64 745	1 614	4 803	6 784	22 392	14 083	15 069	. . .
2004	63 034	1 465	4 907	6 821	21 918	13 434	14 488	. . .
2003	61 633	1 589	5 372	6 876	21 554	12 884	13 358	. . .
2002	59 644	1 528	5 639	7 258	20 728	12 117	12 374	. . .
2001	58 238	1 544	5 589	7 178	20 622	11 864	11 440	. . .
2000	56 008	1 524	5 780	6 921	20 059	11 126	10 598	. . .
1999	55 303	1 589	5 978	7 096	19 742	10 722	10 174	. . .
1998	54 337	1 624	6 126	7 385	19 526	10 022	9 654	. . .
1997	53 352	1 628	6 622	7 543	18 823	9 565	9 169	. . .
1996	52 742	1 642	6 716	7 520	18 549	9 642	8 677	. . .
1995	52 022	1 755	7 048	7 232	18 320	9 662	8 005	. . .
1994	51 516	1 802	7 382	7 454	18 228	8 890	7 761	. . .
1993	52 117	2 058	8 038	7 637	18 626	8 106	7 652	. . .
1992	51 740	2 118	8 133	7 756	18 397	8 005	7 332	. . .
1991	51 439	2 341	8 668	7 675	18 954	6 540	7 258	12.6
1990	50 798	2 349	9 239	7 893	18 050	6 202	7 064	12.3
1989	50 421	2 412	9 395	7 907	18 102	5 914	6 693	12.3
1988	50 128	2 325	9 969	7 860	18 004	5 705	6 263	12.3
1987	49 858	2 408	10 544	7 766	17 310	5 799	6 033	12.2
1986	49 383	2 611	10 699	7 917	16 876	5 515	5 767	12.2
1985	48 969	2 612	11 052	7 872	16 516	5 208	5 708	12.2
1984	48 324	2 584	11 131	7 636	16 353	5 026	5 593	12.2
1983	47 723	2 769	11 348	7 703	15 470	4 915	5 514	12.1
1982	47 102	2 818	11 541	7 751	15 091	4 807	5 095	12.1
1981	46 391	2 983	11 909	7 600	14 464	4 721	4 711	12.0
1980	45 670	2 994	12 326	7 451	13 869	4 494	4 535	12.0
1979	43 806	2 924	12 230	6 999	13 088	4 321	4 245	12.0
1978	42 977	3 013	12 593	7 069	12 376	4 086	3 843	11.6
1977	42 176	3 047	12 740	6 823	11 977	3 835	3 754	11.3
1976	41 429	3 107	12 674	6 915	11 346	3 709	3 677	11.1
1975	40 613	3 303	13 045	6 730	10 798	3 442	3 295	10.8
1974	39 817	3 461	13 302	6 615	10 060	3 233	3 145	10.4
1973	39 163	3 424	13 467	6 504	9 604	3 060	3 105	10.2
1972	38 659	3 471	13 706	6 351	9 136	2 952	3 042	10.0
1971	38 787	3 808	14 430	6 225	8 463	2 878	2 982	9.6
1970	38 126	3 957	14 647	5 877	8 005	2 797	2 843	9.2
1969	37 424	4 012	14 576	5 801	7 768	2 615	2 653	9.1
1968	36 789	4 244	14 522	5 760	7 085	2 624	2 558	8.9
1967	36 155	4 310	14 849	5 495	6 622	2 443	2 434	8.7
1966	35 540	4 438	14 742	5 392	6 240	2 358	2 370	8.6
1965	34 969	4 612	14 814	5 293	5 844	2 194	2 215	8.5
1964	34 335	4 888	14 701	4 954	5 598	2 159	2 033	8.3
1962	33 247	5 048	14 707	4 442	4 994	2 166	1 890	8.1
1960	31 902	5 169	14 944	4 503	3 757	2 051	1 479	8.5
1959	30 567	4 752	13 485	4 060	3 996	1 775	1 545	8.1
1957	29 548	5 153	12 996	3 602	3 864	1 462	1 461	8.0
1952	26 206	4 554	12 638	2 982	3 080	1 346	1 264	7.7
1950	25 427	4 940	11 947	2 791	2 704	1 170	1 005	8.3
1947	23 234	4 393	11 601	2 179	2 581	1 003	825	7.5
1940	19 592	4 178	10 467	1 656	1 633	685	579	8.2

. . . = Not available.

Table A-26. Years of School Completed by the Population Age 25 Years and Over, by Sex and Age, Selected Years, 1940–2005—*Continued*

(Numbers in thousands, number of years.)

Age, sex, and year	Total population	Years of school completed						Median years
		Elementary		High school		College		
		0 to 4 years	5 to 8 years	1 to 3 years	4 years	1 to 3 years	4 years or more	

55 YEARS AND OVER

Male

Age, sex, and year	Total population	0 to 4 years	5 to 8 years	1 to 3 years	4 years	1 to 3 years	4 years or more	Median years
2005	29 198	717	2 157	2 896	8 918	6 167	8 341	. . .
2004	28 347	639	2 192	2 885	8 631	5 841	8 159	. . .
2003	27 694	729	2 423	2 912	8 425	5 694	7 510	. . .
2002	26 608	664	2 601	3 048	8 063	5 257	6 975	. . .
2001	25 908	697	2 558	2 964	8 073	5 131	6 485	. . .
2000	25 023	706	2 696	2 817	7 816	4 906	6 079	. . .
1999	24 694	712	2 746	2 911	7 712	4 756	5 856	. . .
1998	24 197	755	2 740	3 000	7 745	4 461	5 496	. . .
1997	23 668	773	3 026	3 060	7 417	4 139	5 255	. . .
1996	23 352	795	3 058	2 998	7 198	4 254	5 055	. . .
1995	22 881	839	3 153	2 980	6 980	4 254	4 675	. . .
1994	22 669	894	3 327	3 037	6 987	3 962	4 462	. . .
1993	23 038	992	3 595	3 174	7 178	3 587	4 508	. . .
1992	22 836	1 033	3 676	3 277	6 991	3 549	4 312	. . .
1991	22 708	1 217	3 980	3 183	7 287	2 850	4 193	12.4
1990	22 337	1 182	4 141	3 274	6 986	2 707	4 046	12.4
1989	22 167	1 202	4 198	3 317	7 003	2 616	3 829	12.3
1988	21 989	1 117	4 471	3 366	6 968	2 455	3 609	12.3
1987	21 855	1 160	4 762	3 261	6 673	2 504	3 496	12.3
1986	21 622	1 275	4 813	3 286	6 509	2 355	3 385	12.2
1985	21 391	1 252	5 001	3 234	6 387	2 229	3 289	12.2
1984	21 014	1 209	4 951	3 270	6 265	2 185	3 132	12.2
1983	20 769	1 343	4 986	3 282	5 906	2 141	3 117	12.1
1982	20 508	1 362	5 026	3 313	5 759	2 102	2 946	12.1
1981	20 237	1 394	5 165	3 292	5 597	2 032	2 758	12.0
1980	19 967	1 424	5 436	3 206	5 409	1 986	2 506	11.9
1979	19 292	1 446	5 479	2 964	5 167	1 935	2 301	11.8
1978	18 939	1 467	5 701	2 919	4 919	1 824	2 110	11.4
1977	18 608	1 502	5 770	2 787	4 835	1 700	2 011	11.2
1976	18 233	1 507	5 733	2 884	4 473	1 646	1 989	11.0
1975	17 903	1 628	5 845	2 871	4 308	1 480	1 768	10.5
1974	17 579	1 693	6 042	2 817	3 903	1 356	1 682	10.1
1973	17 263	1 678	6 111	2 774	3 811	1 245	1 645	9.9
1972	17 120	1 728	6 252	2 698	3 612	1 215	1 614	9.6
1971	17 288	1 913	6 629	2 668	3 285	1 214	1 579	9.1
1970	17 074	2 011	6 655	2 583	3 127	1 182	1 516	9.0
1969	16 822	2 003	6 701	2 536	3 099	1 086	1 397	8.8
1968	16 609	2 137	6 728	2 523	2 816	1 078	1 328	8.7
1967	16 398	2 247	6 827	2 379	2 685	989	1 271	8.5
1966	16 201	2 288	6 944	2 317	2 491	939	1 223	8.3
1965	16 015	2 368	6 992	2 265	2 331	893	1 164	8.2
1964	15 789	2 504	6 897	2 159	2 237	876	1 113	8.1
1962	15 440	2 644	6 813	2 032	2 030	864	1 057	8.0
1960	14 895	2 704	7 121	1 969	1 453	853	796	8.4
1959	14 304	2 491	6 436	1 759	1 584	718	857	7.9
1957	13 967	2 696	6 244	1 570	1 493	608	831	7.7
1952	12 544	2 428	6 162	1 318	1 262	528	636	7.5
1950	12 277	2 609	5 808	1 209	1 111	500	569	8.2
1947	11 424	2 393	5 656	939	1 109	464	482	7.3
1940	9 815	2 293	5 249	724	660	313	361	8.1

. . . = Not available.

Table A-26. Years of School Completed by the Population Age 25 Years and Over, by Sex and Age, Selected Years, 1940–2005—*Continued*

(Numbers in thousands, number of years.)

Age, sex, and year	Total population	Years of school completed						Median years
		Elementary		High school		College		
		0 to 4 years	5 to 8 years	1 to 3 years	4 years	1 to 3 years	4 years or more	
55 YEARS AND OVER								
Female								
2005	35 547	897	2 645	3 887	13 474	7 916	6 728	. . .
2004	34 687	826	2 715	3 936	13 287	7 593	6 329	. . .
2003	33 939	860	2 949	3 964	13 129	7 190	5 848	. . .
2002	33 035	864	3 038	4 210	12 664	6 860	5 399	. . .
2001	32 329	847	3 032	4 213	12 549	6 733	4 956	. . .
2000	30 985	817	3 085	4 105	12 243	6 218	4 517	. . .
1999	30 609	879	3 232	4 186	12 031	5 965	4 319	. . .
1998	30 140	868	3 386	4 386	11 780	5 560	4 160	. . .
1997	29 684	855	3 596	4 483	11 407	5 427	3 916	. . .
1996	29 390	848	3 659	4 523	11 350	5 387	3 623	. . .
1995	29 142	915	3 894	4 255	11 340	5 410	3 330	. . .
1994	28 848	909	4 054	4 419	11 242	4 926	3 298	. . .
1993	29 080	1 066	4 442	4 462	11 447	4 519	3 149	. . .
1992	28 904	1 084	4 456	4 478	11 409	4 455	3 021	. . .
1991	28 729	1 125	4 687	4 495	11 667	3 690	3 066	12.3
1990	28 461	1 167	5 098	4 619	11 063	3 495	3 019	12.3
1989	28 255	1 211	5 195	4 587	11 099	3 300	2 863	12.3
1988	28 139	1 208	5 498	4 495	11 034	3 250	2 655	12.3
1987	28 004	1 248	5 782	4 504	10 637	3 294	2 539	12.2
1986	27 762	1 336	5 886	4 630	10 367	3 160	2 382	12.2
1985	27 578	1 360	6 052	4 638	10 129	2 979	2 420	12.2
1984	27 309	1 377	6 183	4 363	10 086	2 843	2 459	12.2
1983	26 954	1 428	6 364	4 423	9 567	2 774	2 398	12.1
1982	26 593	1 458	6 511	4 435	9 330	2 705	2 150	12.1
1981	26 152	1 589	6 742	4 308	8 868	2 690	1 954	12.0
1980	25 703	1 571	6 889	4 245	8 460	2 509	2 030	12.0
1979	24 514	1 474	6 750	4 034	7 920	2 389	1 944	12.0
1978	24 038	1 545	6 889	4 149	7 457	2 263	1 733	11.6
1977	23 568	1 546	6 972	4 034	7 141	2 135	1 742	11.0
1976	23 196	1 602	6 942	4 029	6 871	2 063	1 690	11.0
1975	22 710	1 675	7 198	3 858	6 490	1 962	1 527	10.9
1974	22 238	1 762	7 261	3 799	6 068	1 880	1 463	10.7
1973	21 900	1 746	7 359	3 729	5 790	1 814	1 461	10.5
1972	21 539	1 743	7 455	3 654	5 526	1 737	1 425	10.3
1971	21 500	1 896	7 805	3 556	5 179	1 665	1 402	9.9
1970	21 052	1 946	7 993	3 292	4 879	1 615	1 327	9.5
1969	20 601	2 009	7 878	3 264	4 669	1 526	1 255	9.4
1968	20 180	2 106	7 795	3 237	4 269	1 544	1 229	9.2
1967	19 756	2 063	8 021	3 117	3 937	1 454	1 164	8.9
1966	19 339	2 152	7 797	3 074	3 749	1 419	1 147	8.9
1965	18 955	2 243	7 821	3 026	3 514	1 300	1 048	8.7
1964	18 546	2 383	7 805	2 794	3 360	1 282	920	8.5
1962	17 807	2 404	7 894	2 410	2 964	1 302	833	8.3
1960	17 007	2 465	7 823	2 534	2 304	1 198	683	8.6
1959	16 263	2 261	7 049	2 301	2 412	1 057	688	8.3
1957	15 581	2 457	6 752	2 032	2 371	854	630	8.2
1952	13 662	2 126	6 476	1 664	1 818	818	628	7.9
1950	13 150	2 331	6 139	1 582	1 593	670	436	8.4
1947	11 810	2 000	5 945	1 240	1 472	539	343	7.6
1940	9 777	1 886	5 217	932	973	372	219	8.3

. . . = Not available.

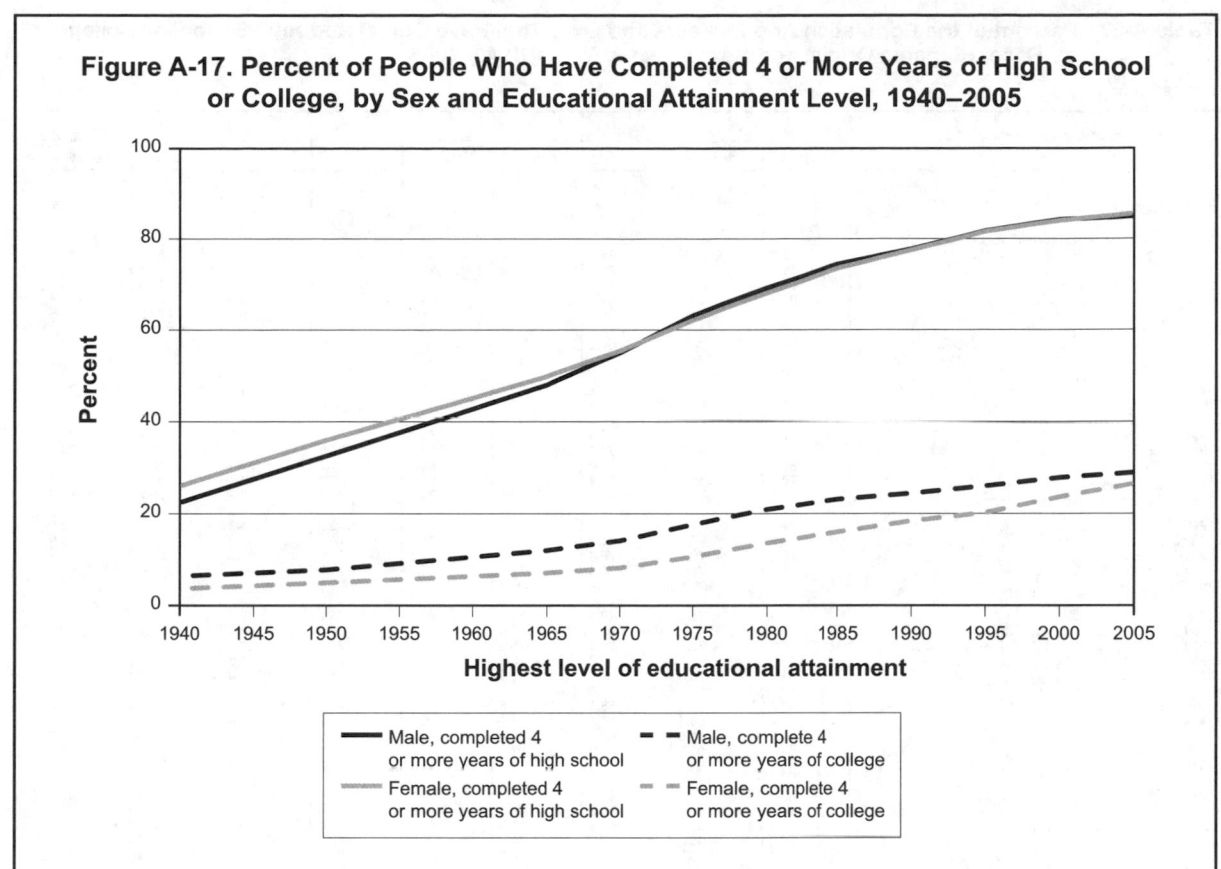

Figure A-17. Percent of People Who Have Completed 4 or More Years of High School or College, by Sex and Educational Attainment Level, 1940–2005

In 1940, only one in four Americans had completed high school. As recently as 1966, less than half of the U.S. population age 25 years and over had high school diplomas. By 2005, 85.2 percent of Americans in this age group were high school graduates. The high school graduation rate for women continued to exceed that of men, just as it had done in every year since 2001.

The percentage of college graduates, which constituted less than 5 percent of the population in 1940, had risen to 9.8 percent by 1966. By 2005, it included 27.7 percent of the population age 25 years and over. In recent years, women have narrowed the gap with men. In 1985, 23.1 percent of men and 16.0 percent of women age 25 years and over had graduated from college. Two decades later, in 2005, 28.9 percent of men and 26.5 percent of women were college graduates. (Table A-27)

Table A-27. Percent of the Population Age 25 Years and Over That Have Completed High School or College, by Race, Hispanic Origin, and Sex, Selected Years, 1940–2005

(Percent.)

Age, educational attainment level, and year	All races			White			Black[1]		
	Both sexes	Male	Female	Both sexes	Male	Female	Both sexes	Male	Female
25 YEARS AND OVER									
Completed 4 Years of High School or More									
2005	85.2	84.9	85.5	85.8	85.2	86.2	81.1	81.1	81.2
2004	85.2	84.8	85.4	85.8	85.3	86.3	80.6	80.4	80.8
2003[2]	84.6	84.1	85.0	85.1	84.5	85.7	80.0	79.6	80.3
2002	84.1	83.8	84.4	84.8	84.3	85.2	78.7	78.5	78.9
2001[3]	84.1	84.1	84.2	84.8	84.4	85.1	78.8	79.2	78.5
2000	84.1	84.2	84.0	84.9	84.8	85.0	78.5	78.7	78.3
1999	83.4	83.4	83.4	84.3	84.2	84.3	77.0	76.7	77.2
1998	82.8	82.8	82.9	83.7	83.6	83.8	76.0	75.2	76.7
1997	82.1	82.0	82.2	83.0	82.9	83.2	74.9	73.5	76.0
1996	81.7	81.9	81.6	82.8	82.7	82.8	74.3	74.3	74.2
1995	81.7	81.7	81.6	83.0	83.0	83.0	73.8	73.4	74.1
1994	80.9	81.0	80.7	82.0	82.1	81.9	72.9	71.7	73.8
1993	80.2	80.5	80.0	81.5	81.8	81.3	70.4	69.6	71.1
1992[4]	79.4	79.7	79.2	80.9	81.1	80.7	67.7	67.0	68.2
1991	78.4	78.5	78.3	79.9	79.8	79.9	66.7	66.7	66.7
1990	77.6	77.7	77.5	79.1	79.1	79.0	66.2	65.8	66.5
1989	76.9	77.2	76.6	78.4	78.6	78.2	64.6	64.2	65.0
1988	76.2	76.4	76.0	77.7	77.7	77.6	63.5	63.7	63.4
1987	75.6	76.0	75.3	77.0	77.3	76.7	63.4	63.0	63.7
1986	74.7	75.1	74.4	76.2	76.5	75.9	62.3	61.5	63.0
1985	73.9	74.4	73.5	75.5	76.0	75.1	59.8	58.4	60.8
1984	73.3	73.7	73.0	75.0	75.4	74.6	58.5	57.1	59.7
1983	72.1	72.7	71.5	73.8	74.4	73.3	56.8	56.5	57.1
1982	71.0	71.7	70.3	72.8	73.4	72.3	54.9	55.7	54.3
1981	69.7	70.3	69.1	71.6	72.1	71.2	52.9	53.2	52.6
1980	68.6	69.2	68.1	70.5	71.0	70.1	51.2	51.1	51.3
1979	67.7	68.4	67.1	69.7	70.3	69.2	49.4	49.2	49.5
1978	65.9	66.8	65.2	67.9	68.6	67.2	47.6	47.9	47.3
1977	64.9	65.6	64.4	67.0	67.5	66.5	45.5	45.6	45.4
1976	64.1	64.7	63.5	66.1	66.7	65.5	43.8	42.3	45.0
1975	62.5	63.1	62.1	64.5	65.0	64.1	42.5	41.6	43.3
1974	61.2	61.6	60.9	63.3	63.6	63.0	40.8	39.9	41.5
1973	59.8	60.0	59.6	61.9	62.1	61.7	39.2	38.2	40.1
1972	58.2	58.2	58.2	60.4	60.3	60.5	36.6	35.7	37.2
1971	56.4	56.3	56.6	58.6	58.4	58.8	34.7	33.8	35.4
1970	55.2	55.0	55.4	57.4	57.2	57.6	33.7	32.4	34.8
1969	54.0	53.6	54.4	56.3	55.7	56.7	32.3	31.9	32.6
1968	52.6	52.0	53.2	54.9	54.3	55.5	30.1	28.9	31.0
1967	51.1	50.5	51.7	53.4	52.8	53.8	29.5	27.1	31.5
1966	49.9	49.0	50.8	52.2	51.3	53.0	27.8	25.8	29.5
1965	49.0	48.0	49.9	51.3	50.2	52.2	27.2	25.8	28.4
1964	48.0	47.0	48.9	50.3	49.3	51.2	25.7	23.7	27.4
1962	46.3	45.0	47.5	48.7	47.4	49.9	24.8	23.2	26.2
1959	43.7	42.2	45.2	46.1	44.5	47.7	20.7	19.6	21.6
1957	41.6	39.7	43.3	43.2	41.1	45.1	18.4	16.9	19.7
1952	38.8	36.9	40.5	. . .	. . .	. . .	15.0	14.0	15.7
1950	34.3	32.6	36.0	. . .	. . .	. . .	13.7	12.5	14.7
1947	33.1	31.4	34.7	35.0	33.2	36.7	13.6	12.7	14.5
1940	24.5	22.7	26.3	26.1	24.2	28.1	7.7	6.9	8.4

[1]Includes Black and other races from 1940 to 1962; from 1963 to 2003, data are for the Black population only.
[2]Starting in 2003, respondents could choose more than one race. The race data in this table for 2003 onward represent respondents who indicated only one race.
[3]Starting in 2001, data are from the expanded Current Population Survey (CPS) sample and were calculated using population controls based on Census 2000.
[4]Beginning with the 1992 data, a new survey question has resulted in different educational attainment categories than those that were used in earlier years. Data shown as "completed 4 years of high school or more" are now designated as "high school graduate." Data shown as "completed 4 years of college or more" are now designated "bachelor's degree," "master's degree," "doctorate degree," and "professional degree." Due to the change in question format, median years of schooling cannot be derived.
. . . = Not available.

Table A-27. Percent of the Population Age 25 Years and Over That Have Completed High School or College, by Race, Hispanic Origin, and Sex, Selected Years, 1940–2005—*Continued*

(Percent.)

Age, educational attainment level, and year	Hispanic[5]			White alone or in combination			Black alone or in combination		
	Both sexes	Male	Female	Both sexes	Male	Female	Both sexes	Male	Female
25 YEARS AND OVER									
Completed 4 Years of High School or More									
2005	58.5	58.0	58.9	85.7	85.2	86.2	81.3	81.2	81.3
2004	58.4	57.3	59.5	85.8	85.3	86.2	80.6	80.3	80.9
2003[2]	57.0	56.3	57.8	85.1	84.5	85.7	80.0	79.5	80.3
2002	57.0	56.1	57.9	...	...	...	...	...	...
2001[3]	56.8	55.5	58.0	...	...	...	...	...	...
2000	57.0	56.6	57.5	...	...	...	...	...	...
1999	56.1	56.0	56.3	...	...	...	...	...	...
1998	55.5	55.7	55.3	...	...	...	...	...	...
1997	54.7	54.9	54.6	...	...	...	...	...	...
1996	53.1	53.0	53.3	...	...	...	...	...	...
1995	53.4	52.9	53.8	...	...	...	...	...	...
1994	53.3	53.4	53.2	...	...	...	...	...	...
1993	53.1	52.9	53.2	...	...	...	...	...	...
1992[4]	52.6	53.7	51.5	...	...	...	...	...	...
1991	51.3	51.4	51.2	...	...	...	...	...	...
1990	50.8	50.3	51.3	...	...	...	...	...	...
1989	50.9	51.0	50.7	...	...	...	...	...	...
1988	51.0	52.0	50.0	...	...	...	...	...	...
1987	50.9	51.8	50.0	...	...	...	...	...	...
1986	48.5	49.2	47.8	...	...	...	...	...	...
1985	47.9	48.5	47.4	...	...	...	...	...	...
1984	47.1	48.6	45.7	...	...	...	...	...	...
1983	46.2	48.6	44.2	...	...	...	...	...	...
1982	45.9	48.1	44.1	...	...	...	...	...	...
1981	44.5	45.5	43.6	...	...	...	...	...	...
1980	45.3	46.4	44.1	...	...	...	...	...	...
1979	42.0	42.3	41.7	...	...	...	...	...	...
1978	40.8	42.2	39.6	...	...	...	...	...	...
1977	39.6	42.3	37.2	...	...	...	...	...	...
1976	39.3	41.4	37.3	...	...	...	...	...	...
1975	37.9	39.5	36.7	...	...	...	...	...	...
1974	36.5	38.3	34.9	...	...	...	...	...	...
1973	...	...	...	...	...	...	...	...	...
1972	...	...	...	...	...	...	...	...	...
1971	...	...	...	...	...	...	...	...	...
1970	...	...	...	...	...	...	...	...	...
1969	...	...	...	...	...	...	...	...	...
1968	...	...	...	...	...	...	...	...	...
1967	...	...	...	...	...	...	...	...	...
1966	...	...	...	...	...	...	...	...	...
1965	...	...	...	...	...	...	...	...	...
1964	...	...	...	...	...	...	...	...	...
1962	...	...	...	...	...	...	...	...	...
1959	...	...	...	...	...	...	...	...	...
1957	...	...	...	...	...	...	...	...	...
1952	...	...	...	...	...	...	...	...	...
1950	...	...	...	...	...	...	...	...	...
1947	...	...	...	...	...	...	...	...	...
1940	...	...	...	...	...	...	...	...	...

[2]Starting in 2003, respondents could choose more than one race. The race data in this table for 2003 onward represent respondents who indicated only one race.
[3]Starting in 2001, data are from the expanded Current Population Survey (CPS) sample and were calculated using population controls based on Census 2000.
[4]Beginning with the 1992 data, a new survey question has resulted in different educational attainment categories than those that were used in earlier years. Data shown as "completed 4 years of high school or more" are now designated as "high school graduate." Data shown as "completed 4 years of college or more" are now designated "bachelor's degree," "master's degree," "doctorate degree," and "professional degree." Due to the change in question format, median years of schooling cannot be derived.
[5]May be of any race.
... = Not available.

Table A-27. Percent of the Population Age 25 Years and Over That Have Completed High School or College, by Race, Hispanic Origin, and Sex, Selected Years, 1940–2005—*Continued*

(Percent.)

Age, educational attainment level, and year	All races			White			Black[1]		
	Both sexes	Male	Female	Both sexes	Male	Female	Both sexes	Male	Female
25 YEARS AND OVER									
Completed 4 Years of College or More									
2005	27.7	28.9	26.5	28.1	29.4	26.8	17.6	16.0	18.8
2004	27.7	29.4	26.1	28.2	30.0	26.4	17.6	16.6	18.5
2003[2]	27.2	28.9	25.7	27.6	29.4	25.9	17.3	16.7	17.8
2002	26.7	28.5	25.1	27.2	29.1	25.4	17.0	16.4	17.5
2001[3]	26.2	28.2	24.3	26.6	28.7	24.6	15.7	15.3	16.1
2000	25.6	27.8	23.6	26.1	28.5	23.9	16.5	16.3	16.7
1999	25.2	27.5	23.1	25.9	28.5	23.5	15.4	14.2	16.4
1998	24.4	26.5	22.4	25.0	27.3	22.8	14.7	13.9	15.4
1997	23.9	26.2	21.7	24.6	27.0	22.3	13.3	12.5	13.9
1996	23.6	26.0	21.4	24.3	26.9	21.8	13.6	12.4	14.6
1995	23.0	26.0	20.2	24.0	27.2	21.0	13.2	13.6	12.9
1994	22.2	25.1	19.6	22.9	26.1	20.0	12.9	12.8	13.0
1993	21.9	24.8	19.2	22.6	25.7	19.7	12.2	11.9	12.4
1992[4]	21.4	24.3	18.6	22.1	25.2	19.1	11.9	11.9	12.0
1991	21.4	24.3	18.8	22.2	25.4	19.3	11.5	11.4	11.6
1990	21.3	24.4	18.4	22.0	25.3	19.0	11.3	11.9	10.8
1989	21.1	24.5	18.1	21.8	25.4	18.5	11.8	11.7	11.9
1988	20.3	24.0	17.0	20.9	25.0	17.3	11.2	11.1	11.4
1987	19.9	23.6	16.5	20.5	24.5	16.9	10.7	11.0	10.4
1986	19.4	23.2	16.1	20.1	24.1	16.4	10.9	11.2	10.7
1985	19.4	23.1	16.0	20.0	24.0	16.3	11.1	11.2	11.0
1984	19.1	22.9	15.7	19.8	23.9	16.0	10.4	10.4	10.4
1983	18.8	23.0	15.1	19.5	24.0	15.4	9.5	10.0	9.2
1982	17.7	21.9	14.0	18.5	23.0	14.4	8.8	9.1	8.5
1981	17.1	21.1	13.4	17.8	22.2	13.8	8.2	8.2	8.2
1980	17.0	20.9	13.6	17.8	22.1	14.0	7.9	7.7	8.1
1979	16.4	20.4	12.9	17.2	21.4	13.3	7.9	8.3	7.5
1978	15.7	19.7	12.2	16.4	20.7	12.6	7.2	7.3	7.1
1977	15.4	19.2	12.0	16.1	20.2	12.4	7.2	7.0	7.4
1976	14.7	18.6	11.3	15.4	19.6	11.6	6.6	6.3	6.8
1975	13.9	17.6	10.6	14.5	18.4	11.0	6.4	6.7	6.2
1974	13.3	16.9	10.1	14.0	17.7	10.6	5.5	5.7	5.3
1973	12.6	16.0	9.6	13.1	16.8	9.9	6.0	5.9	6.0
1972	12.0	15.4	9.0	12.6	16.2	9.4	5.1	5.5	4.8
1971	11.4	14.6	8.5	12.0	15.5	8.9	4.5	4.7	4.3
1970	11.0	14.1	8.2	11.6	15.0	8.6	4.5	4.6	4.4
1969	10.7	13.6	8.1	11.2	14.3	8.5	4.6	4.8	4.5
1968	10.5	13.3	8.0	11.0	14.1	8.3	4.3	3.7	4.8
1967	10.1	12.8	7.6	10.6	13.6	7.9	4.0	3.4	4.4
1966	9.8	12.5	7.4	10.4	13.3	7.7	3.8	3.9	3.7
1965	9.4	12.0	7.1	9.9	12.7	7.3	4.7	4.9	4.5
1964	9.1	11.7	6.8	9.6	12.3	7.1	3.9	4.5	3.4
1962	8.9	11.4	6.7	9.5	12.2	7.0	4.0	3.9	4.0
1959	8.1	10.3	6.0	8.6	11.0	6.2	3.3	3.8	2.9
1957	7.6	9.6	5.8	8.0	10.1	6.0	2.9	2.7	3.0
1952	7.0	8.3	5.8	...	...	...	2.4	2.0	2.7
1950	6.2	7.3	5.2	...	...	...	2.3	2.1	2.4
1947	5.4	6.2	4.7	5.7	6.6	4.9	2.5	2.4	2.6
1940	4.6	5.5	3.8	4.9	5.9	4.0	1.3	1.4	1.2

[1]Includes Black and other races from 1940 to 1962; from 1963 to 2003, data are for the Black population only.
[2]Starting in 2003, respondents could choose more than one race. The race data in this table for 2003 onward represent respondents who indicated only one race.
[3]Starting in 2001, data are from the expanded Current Population Survey (CPS) sample and were calculated using population controls based on Census 2000.
[4]Beginning with the 1992 data, a new survey question has resulted in different educational attainment categories than those that were used in earlier years. Data shown as "completed 4 years of high school or more" are now designated as "high school graduate." Data shown as "completed 4 years of college or more" are now designated "bachelor's degree," "master's degree," "doctorate degree," and "professional degree." Due to the change in question format, median years of schooling cannot be derived.
... = Not available.

Table A-27. Percent of the Population Age 25 Years and Over That Have Completed High School or College, by Race, Hispanic Origin, and Sex, Selected Years, 1940–2005—*Continued*

(Percent.)

Age, educational attainment level, and year	Hispanic[5]			White alone or in combination			Black alone or in combination		
	Both sexes	Male	Female	Both sexes	Male	Female	Both sexes	Male	Female
25 YEARS AND OVER									
Completed 4 Years of College or More									
2005	12.0	11.8	12.1	28.0	29.3	26.7	17.6	16.0	19.0
2004	12.1	11.8	12.3	28.0	29.9	26.3	17.7	16.5	18.6
2003[2]	11.4	11.2	11.6	27.5	29.3	25.8	17.5	16.8	18.0
2002	11.1	11.0	11.2	...	...	...	...	...	...
2001[3]	11.1	10.8	11.4	...	...	...	...	...	...
2000	10.6	10.7	10.6	...	...	...	...	...	...
1999	10.9	10.7	11.0	...	...	...	...	...	...
1998	11.0	11.1	10.9	...	...	...	...	...	...
1997	10.3	10.6	10.1	...	...	...	...	...	...
1996	9.3	10.3	8.3	...	...	...	...	...	...
1995	9.3	10.1	8.4	...	...	...	...	...	...
1994	9.1	9.6	8.6	...	...	...	...	...	...
1993	9.0	9.5	8.5	...	...	...	...	...	...
1992[4]	9.3	10.2	8.5	...	...	...	...	...	...
1991	9.7	10.0	9.4	...	...	...	...	...	...
1990	9.2	9.8	8.7	...	...	...	...	...	...
1989	9.9	11.0	8.8	...	...	...	...	...	...
1988	10.1	12.3	8.1	...	...	...	...	...	...
1987	8.6	9.7	7.5	...	...	...	...	...	...
1986	8.4	9.5	7.4	...	...	...	...	...	...
1985	8.5	9.7	7.3	...	...	...	...	...	...
1984	8.2	9.5	7.0	...	...	...	...	...	...
1983	7.9	9.2	6.8	...	...	...	...	...	...
1982	7.8	9.6	6.2	...	...	...	...	...	...
1981	7.7	9.7	5.9	...	...	...	...	...	...
1980	7.9	9.7	6.2	...	...	...	...	...	...
1979	6.7	8.2	5.3	...	...	...	...	...	...
1978	7.0	8.6	5.7	...	...	...	...	...	...
1977	6.2	8.1	4.4	...	...	...	...	...	...
1976	6.1	8.6	4.0	...	...	...	...	...	...
1975	6.3	8.3	4.6	...	...	...	...	...	...
1974	5.5	7.1	4.0	...	...	...	...	...	...
1973	...	...	...	...	...	...	...	...	...
1972	...	...	...	...	...	...	...	...	...
1971	...	...	...	...	...	...	...	...	...
1970	...	...	...	...	...	...	...	...	...
1969	...	...	...	...	...	...	...	...	...
1968	...	...	...	...	...	...	...	...	...
1967	...	...	...	...	...	...	...	...	...
1966	...	...	...	...	...	...	...	...	...
1965	...	...	...	...	...	...	...	...	...
1964	...	...	...	...	...	...	...	...	...
1962	...	...	...	...	...	...	...	...	...
1959	...	...	...	...	...	...	...	...	...
1957	...	...	...	...	...	...	...	...	...
1952	...	...	...	...	...	...	...	...	...
1950	...	...	...	...	...	...	...	...	...
1947	...	...	...	...	...	...	...	...	...
1940	...	...	...	...	...	...	...	...	...

[2]Starting in 2003, respondents could choose more than one race. The race data in this table for 2003 onward represent respondents who indicated only one race.

[3]Starting in 2001, data are from the expanded Current Population Survey (CPS) sample and were calculated using population controls based on Census 2000.

[4]Beginning with the 1992 data, a new survey question has resulted in different educational attainment categories than those that were used in earlier years. Data shown as "completed 4 years of high school or more" are now designated as "high school graduate." Data shown as "completed 4 years of college or more" are now designated "bachelor's degree," "master's degree," "doctorate degree," and "professional degree." Due to the change in question format, median years of schooling cannot be derived.

[5]May be of any race.

. . . = Not available.

Table A-27. Percent of the Population Age 25 Years and Over That Have Completed High School or College, by Race, Hispanic Origin, and Sex, Selected Years, 1940–2005—*Continued*

(Percent.)

Age, educational attainment level, and year	All races			White			Black[1]		
	Both sexes	Male	Female	Both sexes	Male	Female	Both sexes	Male	Female
25 TO 29 YEARS									
Completed 4 Years of High School or More									
2005	86.1	85.0	87.3	85.7	84.3	87.1	86.4	86.4	86.5
2004	86.6	85.2	88.0	85.9	83.7	88.1	87.9	90.1	86.1
2003[2]	86.5	84.9	88.2	85.7	83.8	87.6	87.6	86.4	88.5
2002	86.4	84.7	88.1	85.9	84.1	87.7	86.6	85.0	88.0
2001[3]	86.8	85.3	88.3	86.4	84.6	88.3	86.3	85.4	87.0
2000	88.1	86.7	89.4	88.3	86.6	90.0	85.9	86.6	85.3
1999	87.8	86.1	89.5	87.6	85.8	89.3	88.2	87.7	88.6
1998	88.1	86.6	89.6	88.1	86.3	90.0	87.6	87.6	87.6
1997	87.4	85.8	88.9	87.6	85.8	89.4	86.2	85.2	87.1
1996	87.3	86.5	88.1	87.5	86.3	88.8	85.6	87.2	84.2
1995	86.8	86.3	87.4	87.4	86.6	88.2	86.5	88.1	85.1
1994	86.1	84.5	87.6	86.5	84.7	88.3	84.1	82.9	85.0
1993	86.7	86.0	87.4	87.3	86.1	88.5	82.8	85.0	80.9
1992[4]	86.3	86.1	86.5	87.0	86.5	87.6	80.9	82.5	79.5
1991	85.4	84.9	85.8	85.8	85.1	86.6	81.7	83.5	80.1
1990	85.7	84.4	87.0	86.3	84.6	88.1	81.7	81.5	81.8
1989	85.5	84.4	86.5	86.0	84.8	87.1	82.2	80.6	83.6
1988	85.7	84.4	87.0	86.5	84.8	88.2	80.7	80.6	80.7
1987	86.0	85.5	86.4	86.3	85.6	87.0	83.3	84.8	82.1
1986	86.1	85.9	86.4	86.5	85.6	87.4	83.4	86.5	80.6
1985	86.1	85.9	86.4	86.8	86.4	87.3	80.6	80.8	80.4
1984	85.9	85.6	86.3	86.9	86.8	87.0	78.9	75.9	81.5
1983	86.0	86.0	86.0	86.9	86.9	86.9	79.4	78.9	79.8
1982	86.2	86.3	86.1	86.9	87.0	86.8	80.9	80.5	81.3
1981	86.3	86.5	86.1	87.6	87.6	87.6	77.3	78.4	76.4
1980	85.4	85.4	85.5	86.9	86.8	87.0	76.6	74.8	78.1
1979	85.6	86.3	84.9	87.0	87.7	86.4	74.8	73.9	75.4
1978	85.3	86.0	84.6	86.3	86.8	85.8	77.3	78.5	76.3
1977	85.4	86.6	84.2	86.8	87.6	86.0	74.4	77.5	72.0
1976	84.7	86.0	83.5	85.9	87.3	84.6	73.8	72.5	74.9
1975	83.1	84.5	81.8	84.4	85.7	83.2	71.0	72.2	70.1
1974	81.9	83.1	80.8	83.4	84.1	82.7	68.2	71.1	66.0
1973	80.2	80.6	79.8	82.0	82.4	81.6	64.2	63.1	64.9
1972	79.8	80.5	79.2	81.5	82.3	80.8	64.1	61.8	66.2
1971	77.2	78.1	76.4	79.5	80.8	78.3	57.5	54.1	60.7
1970	75.4	76.6	74.2	77.8	79.2	76.4	56.2	54.5	57.9
1969	74.7	75.6	73.8	77.0	77.5	76.6	55.8	59.8	52.3
1968	73.2	73.7	72.7	75.3	75.5	75.0	55.8	58.1	53.6
1967	72.5	72.1	72.9	74.8	74.3	75.3	53.4	51.7	55.0
1966	71.0	70.9	71.2	73.8	73.2	74.4	47.9	48.9	47.0
1965	70.3	70.5	70.1	72.8	72.7	72.8	50.3	50.3	50.4
1964	69.2	68.8	69.5	72.1	71.8	72.4	45.0	41.6	47.9
1962	65.9	65.8	66.1	69.2	69.2	69.3	41.6	38.9	43.8
1959	63.9	63.9	64.0	67.2	66.9	67.4	39.5	40.6	38.6
1957	60.2	57.9	62.4	63.3	60.7	65.7	31.6	27.4	35.2
1952	57.1	55.3	58.7	. . .	. . .	. . .	28.1	27.9	28.3
1950	52.8	50.6	55.0	. . .	. . .	. . .	23.6	21.3	25.5
1947	51.4	49.4	53.3	54.9	52.9	56.8	22.3	19.6	24.7
1940	38.1	36.0	40.1	41.2	38.9	43.4	12.3	10.6	13.6

[1]Includes Black and other races from 1940 to 1962; from 1963 to 2003, data are for the Black population only.
[2]Starting in 2003, respondents could choose more than one race. The race data in this table for 2003 onward represent respondents who indicated only one race.
[3]Starting in 2001, data are from the expanded Current Population Survey (CPS) sample and were calculated using population controls based on Census 2000.
[4]Beginning with the 1992 data, a new survey question has resulted in different educational attainment categories than those that were used in earlier years. Data shown as "completed 4 years of high school or more" are now designated as "high school graduate." Data shown as "completed 4 years of college or more" are now designated "bachelor's degree," "master's degree," "doctorate degree," and "professional degree." Due to the change in question format, median years of schooling cannot be derived.
. . . = Not available.

Table A-27. Percent of the Population Age 25 Years and Over That Have Completed High School or College, by Race, Hispanic Origin, and Sex, Selected Years, 1940–2005—*Continued*

(Percent.)

Age, educational attainment level, and year	Hispanic[5]			White alone or in combination			Black alone or in combination		
	Both sexes	Male	Female	Both sexes	Male	Female	Both sexes	Male	Female
25 TO 29 YEARS									
Completed 4 Years of High School or More									
2005	63.3	63.2	63.4	85.6	84.2	87.0	86.6	86.5	86.7
2004	62.4	60.1	65.2	85.9	83.9	87.9	87.8	89.9	86.2
2003[2]	61.7	59.6	64.2	85.7	83.9	87.6	87.4	86.4	88.5
2002	62.4	60.2	65.0	...	...	...	...	...	...
2001[3]	62.4	58.3	67.3	...	...	...	...	...	...
2000	62.8	59.2	66.4	...	...	...	...	...	...
1999	61.6	57.4	66.0	...	...	...	...	...	...
1998	62.8	59.9	66.3	...	...	...	...	...	...
1997	61.8	59.2	64.9	...	...	...	...	...	...
1996	61.1	59.7	62.9	...	...	...	...	...	...
1995	57.1	55.7	58.7	...	...	...	...	...	...
1994	60.3	58.0	63.0	...	...	...	...	...	...
1993	60.9	58.3	64.0	...	...	...	...	...	...
1992[4]	60.9	61.1	60.6	...	...	...	...	...	...
1991	56.7	56.4	57.1	...	...	...	...	...	...
1990	58.2	56.6	59.9	...	...	...	...	...	...
1989	61.0	61.0	61.0	...	...	...	...	...	...
1988	62.0	59.4	65.0	...	...	...	...	...	...
1987	59.8	58.6	61.0	...	...	...	...	...	...
1986	59.1	58.2	60.0	...	...	...	...	...	...
1985	60.9	58.6	63.1	...	...	...	...	...	...
1984	58.6	56.8	60.2	...	...	...	...	...	...
1983	58.3	57.8	58.9	...	...	...	...	...	...
1982	60.9	60.7	61.2	...	...	...	...	...	...
1981	59.8	59.1	60.4	...	...	...	...	...	...
1980	58.6	58.3	58.8	...	...	...	...	...	...
1979	57.0	55.5	58.5	...	...	...	...	...	...
1978	56.6	58.5	54.7	...	...	...	...	...	...
1977	58.1	62.1	54.8	...	...	...	...	...	...
1976	58.1	57.6	58.4	...	...	...	...	...	...
1975	51.7	51.1	52.1	...	...	...	...	...	...
1974	52.5	55.1	49.9	...	...	...	...	...	...
1973	...	...	...	...	...	...	...	...	...
1972	...	...	...	...	...	...	...	...	...
1971	...	...	...	...	...	...	...	...	...
1970	...	...	...	...	...	...	...	...	...
1969	...	...	...	...	...	...	...	...	...
1968	...	...	...	...	...	...	...	...	...
1967	...	...	...	...	...	...	...	...	...
1966	...	...	...	...	...	...	...	...	...
1965	...	...	...	...	...	...	...	...	...
1964	...	...	...	...	...	...	...	...	...
1962	...	...	...	...	...	...	...	...	...
1959	...	...	...	...	...	...	...	...	...
1957	...	...	...	...	...	...	...	...	...
1952	...	...	...	...	...	...	...	...	...
1950	...	...	...	...	...	...	...	...	...
1947	...	...	...	...	...	...	...	...	...
1940	...	...	...	...	...	...	...	...	...

[2]Starting in 2003, respondents could choose more than one race. The race data in this table for 2003 onward represent respondents who indicated only one race.
[3]Starting in 2001, data are from the expanded Current Population Survey (CPS) sample and were calculated using population controls based on Census 2000.
[4]Beginning with the 1992 data, a new survey question has resulted in different educational attainment categories than those that were used in earlier years. Data shown as "completed 4 years of high school or more" are now designated as "high school graduate." Data shown as "completed 4 years of college or more" are now designated "bachelor's degree," "master's degree," "doctorate degree," and "professional degree." Due to the change in question format, median years of schooling cannot be derived.
[5]May be of any race.
. . . = Not available.

Table A-27. Percent of the Population Age 25 Years and Over That Have Completed High School or College, by Race, Hispanic Origin, and Sex, Selected Years, 1940–2005—*Continued*

(Percent.)

Age, educational attainment level, and year	All races			White			Black[1]		
	Both sexes	Male	Female	Both sexes	Male	Female	Both sexes	Male	Female
25 TO 29 YEARS									
Completed 4 Years of College or More									
2005	28.8	25.5	32.2	28.9	25.3	32.7	17.3	14.2	20.0
2004	28.7	26.1	31.4	28.9	25.8	32.1	16.9	13.4	19.7
2003[2]	28.4	26.0	30.9	28.3	25.3	31.5	17.2	17.5	17.0
2002	29.3	26.9	31.8	29.7	26.5	33.1	17.5	17.4	17.7
2001[3]	28.4	25.5	31.3	28.5	25.1	32.1	16.8	15.6	17.9
2000	29.1	27.9	30.1	29.6	27.8	31.3	17.5	18.1	17.0
1999	28.2	26.8	29.5	29.3	27.6	30.9	15.0	13.1	16.5
1998	27.3	25.6	29.0	28.4	26.5	30.4	15.8	14.2	17.0
1997	27.8	26.3	29.3	28.9	27.2	30.7	14.4	12.1	16.4
1996	27.1	26.1	28.2	28.1	27.2	29.1	14.6	12.4	16.4
1995	24.7	24.5	24.9	26.0	25.4	26.6	15.3	17.2	13.6
1994	23.3	22.5	24.0	24.2	23.6	24.8	13.7	11.7	15.4
1993	23.7	23.4	23.9	24.7	24.4	25.1	13.2	12.6	13.8
1992[4]	23.6	23.2	24.0	25.0	24.2	25.7	11.3	12.0	10.6
1991	23.2	23.0	23.4	24.6	24.1	25.0	11.0	11.5	10.6
1990	23.2	23.7	22.8	24.2	24.2	24.3	13.4	15.1	11.9
1989	23.4	23.9	22.9	24.4	24.8	24.0	12.7	12.0	13.3
1988	22.5	23.2	21.9	23.5	24.0	22.9	12.2	12.6	11.9
1987	22.0	22.3	21.7	23.0	23.3	22.8	11.4	11.6	11.1
1986	22.4	22.9	21.9	23.5	24.1	22.9	11.8	10.1	13.3
1985	22.2	23.1	21.3	23.2	24.2	22.2	11.5	10.3	12.6
1984	21.9	23.2	20.7	23.1	24.3	21.9	11.6	12.9	10.5
1983	22.5	23.9	21.1	23.4	25.0	21.8	12.9	13.1	12.8
1982	21.7	23.3	20.2	22.7	24.5	20.9	12.6	11.8	13.2
1981	21.3	23.1	19.6	22.4	24.3	20.5	11.6	12.1	11.1
1980	22.5	24.0	21.0	23.7	25.5	22.0	11.6	10.5	12.5
1979	23.1	25.6	20.5	24.3	27.1	21.5	12.4	13.3	11.7
1978	23.3	26.0	20.6	24.5	27.6	21.4	11.8	10.7	12.6
1977	24.0	27.0	21.1	25.3	28.5	22.1	12.6	12.8	12.4
1976	23.7	27.5	20.1	24.6	28.7	20.6	13.0	12.0	13.6
1975	21.9	25.1	18.7	22.8	26.3	19.4	10.7	11.4	10.1
1974	20.7	23.9	17.6	22.0	25.3	18.8	7.9	8.8	7.2
1973	19.0	21.6	16.4	19.9	22.8	17.0	8.1	7.1	8.8
1972	19.0	22.0	16.0	19.9	23.1	16.7	8.3	7.1	9.4
1971	16.9	20.1	13.8	17.9	21.3	14.6	6.4	6.4	6.5
1970	16.4	20.0	12.9	17.3	21.3	13.3	7.3	6.7	8.0
1969	16.0	19.4	12.8	17.0	20.6	13.4	6.7	8.1	5.5
1968	14.7	18.0	11.6	15.6	19.1	12.3	5.3	5.3	5.3
1967	14.6	17.2	12.1	15.5	18.3	12.7	5.4	4.2	6.3
1966	14.0	16.8	11.3	14.7	17.9	11.8	5.9	5.4	6.4
1965	12.4	15.6	9.5	13.0	16.4	9.8	6.8	7.3	6.8
1964	12.8	16.6	9.2	13.6	17.5	9.9	5.5	7.5	3.9
1962	13.1	17.2	9.2	14.3	18.7	10.0	4.2	5.7	3.0
1959	11.1	14.8	7.6	11.9	15.9	8.1	4.6	5.6	3.7
1957	10.4	13.5	7.5	11.1	14.5	7.8	4.1	3.3	5.0
1952	10.1	13.8	6.7	. . .	. . .	. . .	4.6	3.2	5.8
1950	7.7	9.6	5.9	. . .	. . .	. . .	2.9	2.4	3.2
1947	5.6	5.8	5.4	5.9	6.2	5.7	2.8	2.6	2.9
1940	5.9	6.9	4.9	6.4	7.5	5.3	1.6	1.5	1.7

[1]Includes Black and other races from 1940 to 1962; from 1963 to 2003, data are for the Black population only.
[2]Starting in 2003, respondents could choose more than one race. The race data in this table for 2003 onward represent respondents who indicated only one race.
[3]Starting in 2001, data are from the expanded Current Population Survey (CPS) sample and were calculated using population controls based on Census 2000.
[4]Beginning with the 1992 data, a new survey question has resulted in different educational attainment categories than those that were used in earlier years. Data shown as "completed 4 years of high school or more" are now designated as "high school graduate." Data shown as "completed 4 years of college or more" are now designated "bachelor's degree," "master's degree," "doctorate degree," and "professional degree." Due to the change in question format, median years of schooling cannot be derived.
. . . = Not available.

Table A-27. Percent of the Population Age 25 Years and Over That Have Completed High School or College, by Race, Hispanic Origin, and Sex, Selected Years, 1940–2005—*Continued*

(Percent.)

Age, educational attainment level, and year	Hispanic[5]			White alone or in combination			Black alone or in combination		
	Both sexes	Male	Female	Both sexes	Male	Female	Both sexes	Male	Female
25 TO 29 YEARS									
Completed 4 Years of College or More									
2005	11.2	10.2	12.4	28.8	25.3	32.5	17.7	14.6	20.3
2004	10.9	9.6	12.4	28.7	25.7	31.8	16.8	13.4	19.5
2003[2]	10.0	8.4	12.0	28.2	25.2	31.4	17.3	17.4	17.3
2002	8.9	8.3	9.7	...	...	...	...	...	...
2001[3]	10.5	8.2	13.3	...	...	...	...	...	...
2000	9.7	8.3	11.0	...	...	...	...	...	...
1999	8.9	7.5	10.4	...	...	...	...	...	...
1998	10.4	9.5	11.3	...	...	...	...	...	...
1997	11.0	9.6	10.1	...	...	...	...	...	...
1996	10.0	10.2	9.8	...	...	...	...	...	...
1995	8.9	7.8	10.1	...	...	...	...	...	...
1994	8.0	6.6	9.8	...	...	...	...	...	...
1993	8.3	7.1	9.8	...	...	...	...	...	...
1992[4]	9.5	8.8	10.3	...	...	...	...	...	...
1991	9.2	8.1	10.4	...	...	...	...	...	...
1990	8.1	7.3	9.1	...	...	...	...	...	...
1989	10.1	9.6	10.6	...	...	...	...	...	...
1988	11.4	12.1	10.6	...	...	...	...	...	...
1987	8.7	9.2	8.2	...	...	...	...	...	...
1986	9.0	8.9	9.1	...	...	...	...	...	...
1985	11.1	10.9	11.2	...	...	...	...	...	...
1984	10.6	9.6	11.6	...	...	...	...	...	...
1983	10.4	9.6	11.1	...	...	...	...	...	...
1982	9.7	10.7	8.7	...	...	...	...	...	...
1981	7.5	8.6	6.5	...	...	...	...	...	...
1980	7.7	8.4	6.9	...	...	...	...	...	...
1979	7.3	7.9	6.8	...	...	...	...	...	...
1978	9.6	9.6	9.7	...	...	...	...	...	...
1977	6.7	7.2	6.4	...	...	...	...	...	...
1976	7.4	10.3	4.8	...	...	...	...	...	...
1975	8.8	10.0	7.3	...	...	...	...	...	...
1974	5.7	7.2	4.6	...	...	...	...	...	...
1973	...	...	...	...	...	...	...	...	...
1972	...	...	...	...	...	...	...	...	...
1971	...	...	...	...	...	...	...	...	...
1970	...	...	...	...	...	...	...	...	...
1969	...	...	...	...	...	...	...	...	...
1968	...	...	...	...	...	...	...	...	...
1967	...	...	...	...	...	...	...	...	...
1966	...	...	...	...	...	...	...	...	...
1965	...	...	...	...	...	...	...	...	...
1964	...	...	...	...	...	...	...	...	...
1962	...	...	...	...	...	...	...	...	...
1959	...	...	...	...	...	...	...	...	...
1957	...	...	...	...	...	...	...	...	...
1952	...	...	...	...	...	...	...	...	...
1950	...	...	...	...	...	...	...	...	...
1947	...	...	...	...	...	...	...	...	...
1940	...	...	...	...	...	...	...	...	...

[2]Starting in 2003, respondents could choose more than one race. The race data in this table for 2003 onward represent respondents who indicated only one race.
[3]Starting in 2001, data are from the expanded Current Population Survey (CPS) sample and were calculated using population controls based on Census 2000.
[4]Beginning with the 1992 data, a new survey question has resulted in different educational attainment categories than those that were used in earlier years. Data shown as "completed 4 years of high school or more" are now designated as "high school graduate." Data shown as "completed 4 years of college or more" are now designated "bachelor's degree," "master's degree," "doctorate degree," and "professional degree." Due to the change in question format, median years of schooling cannot be derived.
[5]May be of any race.
. . . = Not available.

Table A-28. Mean Earnings of Workers Age 18 Years and Over, by Educational Attainment, Race, Sex, and Hispanic Origin, Selected Years, 1975–2004

(Dollars, numbers in thousands.)

Sex, race, Hispanic origin, and year	Total population		Not a high school graduate		High school graduate		Some college/associate's degree		Bachelor's degree[1]		Advanced degree[1]	
	Mean earnings (dollars)	Number with earnings	Mean earnings (dollars)	Number with earnings	Mean earnings (dollars)	Number with earnings	Mean earnings (dollars)	Number with earnings	Mean earnings (dollars)	Number with earnings	Mean earnings (dollars)	Number with earnings
ALL RACES												
Both Sexes												
2004	37 899	150 095	19 182	16 372	28 631	45 571	32 010	44 387	51 568	29 004	78 224	14 713
2003[2]	37 046	148 660	18 734	16 282	27 915	45 064	31 498	44 048	51 206	28 672	74 602	14 592
2002	36 308	148 492	18 826	16 931	27 280	45 407	31 046	43 776	51 194	28 257	72 824	14 119
2001	35 805	147 829	18 793	17 293	26 795	45 641	30 782	43 214	50 623	27 980	72 869	13 700
2000[3]	34 514	147 966	17 738	17 425	25 692	45 977	29 939	43 874	49 595	27 488	71 194	13 200
1999	32 356	144 640	16 121	16 737	24 572	46 082	28 403	42 860	45 678	26 215	67 697	12 749
1998	30 928	142 053	16 053	16 742	23 594	45 987	27 566	41 412	43 782	25 818	63 473	12 095
1997	29 514	140 367	16 124	16 962	22 895	45 976	26 235	40 802	40 478	25 035	63 229	11 591
1996	28 106	138 703	15 011	17 075	22 154	45 908	25 181	40 410	38 112	24 028	61 317	11 281
1995	26 792	136 221	14 013	16 990	21 431	44 546	23 862	40 142	36 980	23 285	56 667	11 258
1994	25 852	135 096	13 697	16 479	20 248	44 614	22 226	40 135	37 224	22 712	56 105	11 155
1993	24 674	133 119	12 820	16 575	19 422	44 779	21 539	39 429	35 121	21 815	55 789	10 521
1992	23 227	130 860	12 809	16 612	18 737	45 340	20 867	37 339	32 629	21 091	48 652	10 479
1991	22 332	130 371	12 613	17 553	18 261	46 508	20 551	35 732	31 323	20 475	46 039	10 103
1990	21 793	130 080	12 582	18 698	17 820	51 977	20 694	28 993	31 112	18 128	41 458	12 285
1989	21 414	129 094	12 242	19 137	17 594	51 846	20 255	28 078	30 736	17 767	41 019	12 265
1988	20 060	127 564	11 889	19 635	16 750	51 297	19 066	27 217	28 344	17 308	37 724	12 109
1987	19 016	124 874	11 824	19 748	15 939	50 815	18 054	26 404	26 919	16 497	35 968	11 411
1986	18 149	122 757	11 203	19 665	15 120	50 104	17 073	26 113	26 511	15 788	34 787	11 087
1985	17 181	120 651	10 726	19 692	14 457	49 674	16 349	25 402	24 877	15 373	32 909	10 510
1984	16 083	118 183	10 384	20 206	13 893	48 452	14 936	24 463	23 072	14 653	30 192	10 410
1983	15 137	115 095	9 853	20 020	13 044	47 560	14 245	23 208	21 532	13 929	28 333	10 377
1982	14 351	113 451	9 387	20 789	12 560	46 584	13 503	22 602	20 272	13 425	26 915	10 051
1981	13 624	113 301	9 357	22 296	12 109	47 332	13 176	21 759	19 006	12 579	25 281	9 336
1980	12 665	111 919	8 845	23 028	11 314	46 795	12 409	21 384	18 075	12 175	23 308	8 535
1979	11 795	110 826	8 420	23 783	10 624	45 497	11 377	21 174	16 514	11 751	21 874	8 621
1978	10 812	106 436	7 759	23 787	9 834	43 510	10 357	20 121	15 291	11 001	20 173	8 017
1977	9 887	103 119	7 066	24 854	9 013	41 696	9 607	18 905	14 207	10 357	19 077	7 309
1976	9 180	100 510	6 720	25 035	8 393	40 570	8 813	17 786	13 033	10 132	17 911	6 985
1975	8 552	97 881	6 198	24 916	7 843	39 827	8 388	16 917	12 332	9 764	16 725	6 457
Male												
2004	46 008	79 765	22 537	10 188	34 050	25 209	39 509	21 473	63 753	14 860	97 855	8 032
2003[2]	44 726	78 869	21 447	10 173	33 266	24 292	38 451	21 534	63 084	14 849	91 831	8 019
2002	44 310	78 757	22 091	10 526	32 673	24 174	38 377	21 599	63 503	14 667	90 761	7 788
2001	43 648	78 342	21 508	10 572	32 363	24 239	37 429	21 390	63 354	14 507	90 130	7 631
2000[3]	42 772	78 319	21 007	10 535	31 446	24 439	37 372	21 526	62 609	14 375	88 077	7 442
1999	40 257	76 233	18 855	9 917	30 414	24 235	35 326	21 173	57 706	13 683	84 051	7 225
1998	38 134	75 213	19 155	10 085	28 742	24 155	34 179	20 545	55 057	13 486	77 217	6 942
1997	36 556	74 596	19 575	10 348	28 307	24 152	32 641	20 359	50 056	13 008	78 032	6 728
1996	34 705	73 955	17 826	10 583	27 642	23 966	31 426	20 208	46 702	12 552	74 406	6 636
1995	33 251	72 634	16 748	10 312	26 333	23 473	29 851	19 918	46 111	12 251	69 588	6 679
1994	32 087	72 246	16 633	9 981	25 038	23 418	27 636	19 859	46 278	12 324	67 032	6 663
1993	30 568	71 183	14 946	10 151	23 973	23 388	26 614	19 532	43 499	11 810	68 221	6 302
1992	28 448	70 409	14 934	10 335	22 978	23 610	25 660	18 768	40 039	11 353	58 324	6 344
1991	27 494	70 145	15 056	10 679	22 663	24 110	25 345	18 076	38 484	11 126	54 449	6 154
1990	27 164	70 218	14 991	11 412	22 378	26 753	26 120	14 844	38 901	9 807	49 768	7 402
1989	27 025	69 798	14 727	11 774	22 508	26 469	25 555	14 384	38 692	9 737	50 144	7 434
1988	25 344	69 006	14 551	11 993	21 481	26 080	23 827	14 019	35 906	9 466	45 677	7 449
1987	24 015	67 951	14 544	12 117	20 364	25 981	22 781	13 433	33 677	9 286	43 140	7 134
1986	23 057	67 189	13 703	12 208	19 453	25 562	21 784	13 502	33 376	8 908	41 836	7 009
1985	21 823	66 439	13 124	12 137	18 575	25 496	20 698	13 385	31 433	8 794	39 768	6 627
1984	20 452	65 005	12 775	12 325	18 016	24 827	18 863	12 818	29 203	8 387	35 804	6 648
1983	19 175	63 816	12 052	12 376	16 728	24 449	18 052	12 261	27 239	8 010	33 635	6 719
1982	18 244	63 489	11 513	12 868	16 160	24 059	17 108	12 103	25 758	7 865	32 109	6 594
1981	17 542	63 547	11 668	13 701	15 900	24 435	16 870	11 784	24 353	7 393	30 072	6 235
1980	16 382	62 825	11 042	14 273	15 002	24 023	15 871	11 663	23 340	7 132	27 846	5 733
1979	15 430	62 464	10 628	14 711	14 317	23 318	14 716	11 781	21 482	6 889	26 411	5 765
1978	14 154	60 586	9 894	14 550	13 188	22 650	13 382	11 352	19 861	6 611	24 274	5 422
1977	12 888	59 441	8 939	15 369	12 092	21 846	12 393	10 848	18 187	6 341	22 786	5 038
1976	11 923	58 419	8 522	15 634	11 189	21 499	11 376	10 282	16 714	6 135	21 202	4 868
1975	11 091	57 297	7 843	15 613	10 475	21 347	10 805	9 851	15 758	5 960	19 672	4 526

[1]For data prior to 1991, some college/associate's degree equals 1 to 3 years of college completed, a bachelor's degree equals 4 years of college completed, and an advanced degree equals 5 or more years of college completed.
[2]Starting in 2003, respondents could choose more than one race. The race data in this table from 2003 onward represent respondents who indicated only one race.
[3]Beginning in 2000, earnings data are from the expanded Current Population Survey (CPS) sample and were calculated using population controls based on Census 2000.

Table A-28. Mean Earnings of Workers Age 18 Years and Over, by Educational Attainment, Race, Sex, and Hispanic Origin, Selected Years, 1975–2004—*Continued*

(Dollars, numbers in thousands.)

Sex, race, Hispanic origin, and year	Total population		Not a high school graduate		High school graduate		Some college/associate's degree		Bachelor's degree[1]		Advanced degree[1]	
	Mean earnings (dollars)	Number with earnings	Mean earnings (dollars)	Number with earnings	Mean earnings (dollars)	Number with earnings	Mean earnings (dollars)	Number with earnings	Mean earnings (dollars)	Number with earnings	Mean earnings (dollars)	Number with earnings
ALL RACES												
Female												
2004	28 691	70 285	13 655	6 183	21 923	20 361	24 983	22 914	38 776	14 143	54 623	6 680
2003[2]	28 367	69 790	14 214	6 108	21 659	20 772	24 848	22 514	38 447	13 823	53 579	6 572
2002	27 271	69 735	13 459	6 404	21 141	21 233	23 905	22 176	37 909	13 589	50 756	6 330
2001	26 962	69 487	14 524	6 720	20 489	21 402	24 268	21 824	36 913	13 472	51 160	6 068
2000[3]	25 228	69 647	12 739	6 890	19 162	21 538	22 779	22 348	35 328	13 113	49 368	5 757
1999	23 551	68 409	12 145	6 819	18 092	21 847	21 644	22 687	32 546	12 533	46 307	5 523
1998	22 818	66 840	11 353	6 657	17 898	21 832	21 056	20 867	31 452	12 332	44 954	5 153
1997	21 528	65 771	10 725	6 614	16 906	21 824	19 856	20 442	30 119	12 027	42 744	4 863
1996	20 570	64 748	10 421	6 492	16 161	21 942	18 933	20 202	28 701	11 466	42 625	4 646
1995	19 414	63 587	9 790	6 678	15 970	21 073	17 962	20 224	26 841	11 034	37 813	4 578
1994	18 684	62 850	9 189	6 498	14 955	21 195	16 928	20 276	26 483	10 388	39 905	4 493
1993	17 900	61 937	9 462	6 425	14 446	21 391	16 555	19 897	25 232	10 005	37 212	4 218
1992	17 145	60 451	9 311	6 277	14 128	21 730	16 023	18 571	23 991	9 738	33 814	4 135
1991	16 320	60 226	8 818	6 875	13 523	22 398	15 643	17 657	22 802	9 348	32 929	3 948
1990	15 493	59 862	8 808	7 286	12 986	25 224	15 002	14 149	21 933	8 321	28 862	4 883
1989	14 809	59 296	8 268	7 363	12 468	25 377	14 688	13 694	21 089	8 030	26 977	4 831
1988	13 833	58 558	7 711	7 642	11 857	25 217	14 009	13 198	19 216	7 842	25 010	4 660
1987	13 049	56 923	7 504	7 631	11 309	24 834	13 158	12 971	18 217	7 211	24 004	4 277
1986	12 214	55 568	7 109	7 457	10 606	24 542	12 029	12 611	17 623	6 880	22 672	4 078
1985	11 493	54 212	6 874	7 555	10 115	24 178	11 504	12 017	16 114	6 579	21 202	3 883
1984	10 742	53 178	6 644	7 881	9 561	23 625	10 614	11 645	14 865	6 266	20 275	3 762
1983	10 111	51 279	6 292	7 644	9 147	23 111	9 981	10 947	13 808	5 919	18 593	3 658
1982	9 403	49 902	5 932	7 921	8 716	22 525	9 348	10 499	12 511	5 560	17 009	3 457
1981	8 619	49 754	5 673	8 595	8 063	22 897	8 811	9 975	11 384	5 186	15 647	3 101
1980	7 909	49 094	5 263	8 755	7 423	22 772	8 256	9 721	10 628	5 043	14 022	2 802
1979	7 099	48 362	4 840	9 072	6 741	22 179	7 190	9 393	9 474	4 862	12 717	2 856
1978	6 396	45 850	4 397	9 237	6 192	20 000	6 441	8 760	8 408	4 390	11 603	2 595
1977	5 804	43 678	4 032	9 485	5 624	19 850	5 856	8 057	7 923	4 016	10 848	2 271
1976	5 373	42 091	3 723	9 401	5 240	19 071	5 301	7 504	7 383	3 997	10 345	2 117
1975	4 968	40 584	3 438	9 303	4 802	18 480	5 019	7 066	6 963	3 804	9 818	1 931
WHITE												
Both Sexes												
2004	38 930	123 383	19 365	13 295	29 590	37 140	32 751	36 547	52 893	24 001	79 071	12 397
2003[2]	38 053	122 599	19 110	13 094	28 708	36 951	32 346	36 318	52 259	24 010	75 638	12 226
2002	37 376	122 699	19 264	13 740	28 145	37 380	31 878	36 023	52 479	23 638	73 870	11 916
2001	36 844	122 930	19 120	14 012	27 700	37 969	31 482	35 722	51 631	23 531	74 398	11 694
2000[3]	35 527	123 039	18 285	14 172	26 444	38 133	30 638	36 334	50 969	23 110	71 983	11 288
1999	33 326	120 916	16 623	13 585	25 270	38 428	29 105	35 634	46 894	22 322	68 910	10 949
1998	32 057	119 201	16 474	13 531	24 409	38 397	28 318	34 540	44 852	22 266	65 379	10 467
1997	30 515	117 985	16 596	13 782	23 618	38 409	26 906	34 274	41 439	21 528	65 058	9 994
1996	28 844	117 230	15 358	13 972	22 782	38 463	25 511	34 087	38 936	20 846	61 779	9 861
1995	27 556	115 636	14 234	13 869	22 154	37 802	24 349	33 850	37 711	20 203	57 054	9 914
1994	26 696	114 586	13 941	13 119	20 911	37 562	22 648	34 006	37 996	19 917	56 475	9 981
1993	25 440	113 342	13 171	13 480	19 918	37 826	21 924	33 728	35 846	18 922	56 964	9 386
1992	23 932	112 120	13 193	13 494	19 265	38 692	21 357	32 014	33 092	18 555	49 347	9 363
1991	22 998	111 830	12 914	14 041	18 766	39 764	21 013	30 973	31 837	18 033	46 498	9 019
1990	22 401	111 972	12 773	15 191	18 257	44 635	21 095	25 105	31 626	15 993	41 908	11 049
1989	22 035	111 243	12 654	15 628	18 011	44 726	20 678	24 212	31 266	15 723	41 610	10 952
1988	20 616	110 159	12 236	16 042	17 183	44 399	19 384	23 643	28 886	15 221	38 129	10 854
1987	19 599	108 407	12 502	16 165	16 339	44 235	18 265	23 083	27 741	14 624	36 175	10 300
1986	18 698	106 384	11 605	16 094	15 514	43 593	17 371	22 653	27 061	14 055	35 265	9 987
1985	17 709	104 818	11 115	16 149	14 815	43 347	16 701	22 131	25 376	13 670	33 401	9 522
1984	16 546	103 022	10 732	16 559	14 274	42 547	15 197	21 451	23 472	13 056	30 515	9 409
1983	15 556	101 035	10 239	16 568	13 357	42 007	14 486	20 452	21 914	12 577	28 532	9 430
1982	14 767	99 488	9 719	17 132	12 854	41 157	13 799	19 967	20 760	12 103	27 040	9 127
1981	14 027	99 510	9 737	18 298	12 355	42 080	13 424	19 102	19 389	11 450	25 564	8 582
1980	13 040	98 358	9 743	18 925	11 524	41 600	12 677	18 888	18 434	11 067	23 466	7 876
1979	12 155	97 544	8 827	19 504	10 431	40 458	11 574	18 835	16 758	10 807	22 085	7 940
1978	11 135	94 002	8 135	19 516	10 020	38 915	10 504	18 022	15 463	10 171	20 531	7 376
1977	10 191	91 254	7 415	20 492	9 173	37 521	9 771	16 968	14 462	9 534	19 337	6 739
1976	9 469	89 099	7 018	20 625	8 559	36 523	8 958	16 127	13 279	9 325	18 153	6 498
1975	8 815	86 894	6 438	20 696	8 005	35 799	8 525	15 423	12 597	8 955	16 920	6 021

[1] For data prior to 1991, some college/associate's degree equals 1 to 3 years of college completed, a bachelor's degree equals 4 years of college completed, and an advanced degree equals 5 or more years of college completed.

[2] Starting in 2003, respondents could choose more than one race. The race data in this table from 2003 onward represent respondents who indicated only one race.

[3] Beginning in 2000, earnings data are from the expanded Current Population Survey (CPS) sample and were calculated using population controls based on Census 2000.

Table A-28. Mean Earnings of Workers Age 18 Years and Over, by Educational Attainment, Race, Sex, and Hispanic Origin, Selected Years, 1975–2004—*Continued*

(Dollars, numbers in thousands.)

Sex, race, Hispanic origin, and year	Total population Mean earnings (dollars)	Number with earnings	Not a high school graduate Mean earnings (dollars)	Number with earnings	High school graduate Mean earnings (dollars)	Number with earnings	Some college/associate's degree Mean earnings (dollars)	Number with earnings	Bachelor's degree[1] Mean earnings (dollars)	Number with earnings	Advanced degree[1] Mean earnings (dollars)	Number with earnings
WHITE												
Male												
2004	47 404	66 677	22 598	8 591	35 360	20 781	40 639	17 990	65 652	12 555	100 084	6 758
2003[2]	46 114	66 199	21 791	8 500	34 224	20 238	39 594	18 060	65 264	12 665	94 017	6 734
2002	45 793	66 202	22 539	8 841	33 920	20 156	39 605	18 068	65 439	12 512	92 733	6 623
2001	45 071	66 216	22 006	8 833	33 545	20 465	38 501	17 957	65 046	12 396	92 304	6 562
2000[3]	44 181	66 222	21 561	8 859	32 528	20 553	38 476	18 179	64 831	12 271	89 812	6 359
1999	41 598	64 856	19 320	8 286	31 279	20 526	36 518	17 928	59 606	11 851	85 345	6 265
1998	39 638	64 181	19 632	8 430	29 782	20 388	35 277	17 407	56 620	11 874	79 734	6 083
1997	37 933	63 738	20 071	8 670	29 298	20 426	33 691	17 423	51 678	11 340	80 322	5 879
1996	35 821	63 532	18 246	8 899	28 591	20 329	32 238	17 418	48 014	11 065	75 481	5 821
1995	34 276	62 520	17 032	8 660	27 467	19 982	30 529	17 136	47 016	10 851	70 155	5 891
1994	33 292	62 029	16 835	8 133	26 125	19 833	28 240	17 091	47 575	10 992	67 629	5 979
1993	31 719	61 356	15 295	8 430	24 781	19 835	27 297	16 959	44 505	10 452	70 000	5 680
1992	29 515	60 919	15 414	8 487	23 844	20 259	26 387	16 335	40 893	10 118	59 329	5 720
1991	28 516	60 770	15 499	8 720	23 475	20 765	26 090	15 873	39 547	9 893	55 257	5 519
1990	28 105	60 676	15 319	9 476	23 135	23 088	26 841	13 003	39 780	8 770	50 385	6 731
1989	28 013	60 877	15 217	9 805	23 291	23 029	26 260	12 582	39 654	8 750	51 031	6 710
1988	26 184	60 221	14 943	10 008	22 216	22 707	24 462	12 277	36 637	8 467	46 181	6 762
1987	24 898	59 468	15 303	10 132	21 012	22 682	23 310	11 771	34 865	8 384	43 440	6 499
1986	23 892	58 932	14 168	10 239	20 128	22 392	22 303	11 846	34 273	8 041	42 480	6 413
1985	22 604	58 385	13 579	10 163	19 203	22 357	21 240	11 831	32 165	7 970	40 358	6 064
1984	21 174	57 362	13 248	10 280	18 681	21 989	19 344	11 387	29 781	7 624	36 219	6 081
1983	19 812	56 641	12 573	10 387	17 281	21 733	18 388	10 974	27 726	7 379	33 981	6 168
1982	18 859	56 364	11 952	10 816	16 662	21 436	17 571	10 822	26 404	7 242	32 266	6 047
1981	18 141	56 397	12 094	11 523	16 352	21 809	17 303	10 448	24 943	6 824	30 396	5 794
1980	16 945	55 772	11 539	11 937	15 382	21 453	16 313	10 400	23 803	6 618	27 991	5 363
1979	15 971	55 556	11 127	12 291	13 916	20 834	15 043	10 572	21 785	6 464	26 645	5 395
1978	14 627	54 113	10 358	12 141	13 534	20 328	13 589	10 350	20 085	6 205	24 635	5 088
1977	13 329	53 174	9 366	12 903	12 377	19 773	12 657	9 853	18 521	5 941	23 093	4 704
1976	12 342	52 312	8 867	13 117	11 497	19 446	11 616	9 394	16 995	5 765	21 490	4 589
1975	11 448	51 510	8 110	13 191	10 726	19 361	11 028	9 096	16 079	5 587	19 858	4 275
Female												
2004	28 966	56 705	13 459	4 703	22 260	16 358	25 104	18 556	38 898	11 445	53 895	5 641
2003[2]	28 591	56 400	14 149	4 593	22 028	16 712	25 177	18 258	37 739	11 344	53 102	5 492
2002	27 512	56 496	13 354	4 898	21 388	17 224	24 101	17 954	37 903	11 126	50 270	5 293
2001	27 240	56 714	14 197	5 178	20 866	17 503	24 387	17 764	36 698	11 135	51 499	5 131
2000[3]	25 441	56 816	12 823	5 313	19 330	17 579	22 790	18 155	35 273	10 838	48 982	4 929
1999	23 756	56 061	12 405	5 299	18 381	17 902	21 598	17 705	32 507	10 471	45 741	4 684
1998	23 213	55 020	11 255	5 102	18 327	18 009	21 246	17 132	31 406	10 393	45 462	4 384
1997	21 779	54 247	10 700	5 111	17 166	17 983	19 892	16 852	30 041	10 188	43 236	4 114
1996	20 590	53 697	10 290	5 073	16 270	18 134	18 482	16 669	28 667	9 781	42 049	4 041
1995	19 647	53 117	9 582	5 208	16 196	17 820	18 011	16 714	26 916	9 352	37 864	4 022
1994	18 912	52 557	9 220	4 987	15 078	17 729	16 998	16 915	26 198	8 925	39 816	4 002
1993	18 028	51 986	9 624	5 050	14 557	17 991	16 490	16 769	25 161	8 470	36 988	3 705
1992	17 289	51 200	9 428	5 007	14 233	18 434	16 116	15 679	23 738	8 437	33 675	3 643
1991	16 431	51 060	8 677	5 321	13 621	18 999	15 677	15 100	22 471	8 140	32 687	3 500
1990	15 559	50 905	8 725	5 715	13 031	21 547	14 922	12 102	21 725	7 223	28 694	4 318
1989	14 810	50 366	8 338	5 823	12 406	21 697	14 640	11 630	20 741	6 973	26 709	4 242
1988	13 902	49 938	7 747	6 034	11 915	21 692	13 898	11 366	19 169	6 754	24 824	4 092
1987	13 161	48 939	7 798	6 033	11 421	21 553	13 015	11 312	18 170	6 240	23 753	3 801
1986	12 247	47 452	7 123	5 855	10 641	21 201	11 964	10 807	17 418	6 014	22 320	3 574
1985	11 555	46 433	6 931	5 986	10 142	20 990	11 488	10 300	15 883	5 700	21 202	3 458
1984	10 732	45 660	6 614	6 279	9 561	20 558	10 504	10 064	14 617	5 432	20 092	3 328
1983	10 126	44 394	6 317	6 181	9 150	20 274	9 969	9 478	13 664	5 198	18 230	3 262
1982	9 419	43 124	5 896	6 316	8 714	19 721	9 336	9 145	12 352	4 861	16 779	3 080
1981	8 646	43 113	5 727	6 775	8 054	20 271	8 740	8 654	11 196	4 626	15 523	2 788
1980	7 926	42 586	6 675	6 988	7 415	20 147	8 221	8 488	10 447	4 449	13 809	2 513
1979	7 105	41 988	6 419	7 213	6 731	19 624	7 135	8 263	9 275	4 343	12 420	2 545
1978	6 398	39 889	4 476	7 375	6 176	18 587	6 342	7 672	8 231	3 966	11 404	2 288
1977	5 808	38 080	4 097	7 589	5 604	17 748	5 774	7 115	7 750	3 593	10 655	2 035
1976	5 383	36 787	3 788	7 508	5 214	17 077	5 250	6 733	7 262	3 560	10 131	1 909
1975	4 982	35 384	3 500	7 505	4 800	16 438	4 926	6 327	6 822	3 368	9 728	1 746

[1]For data prior to 1991, some college/associate's degree equals 1 to 3 years of college completed, a bachelor's degree equals 4 years of college completed, and an advanced degree equals 5 or more years of college completed.
[2]Starting in 2003, respondents could choose more than one race. The race data in this table from 2003 onward represent respondents who indicated only one race.
[3]Beginning in 2000, earnings data are from the expanded Current Population Survey (CPS) sample and were calculated using population controls based on Census 2000.

Table A-28. Mean Earnings of Workers Age 18 Years and Over, by Educational Attainment, Race, Sex, and Hispanic Origin, Selected Years, 1975–2004—*Continued*

(Dollars, numbers in thousands.)

Sex, race, Hispanic origin, and year	Total population		Not a high school graduate		High school graduate		Some college/associate's degree		Bachelor's degree[1]		Advanced degree[1]	
	Mean earnings (dollars)	Number with earnings	Mean earnings (dollars)	Number with earnings	Mean earnings (dollars)	Number with earnings	Mean earnings (dollars)	Number with earnings	Mean earnings (dollars)	Number with earnings	Mean earnings (dollars)	Number with earnings
BLACK												
Both Sexes												
2004	29 105	16 640	17 948	2 039	23 492	6 135	27 760	5 197	42 298	2 359	65 458	908
2003[2]	28 838	16 389	16 201	2 095	23 777	5 941	27 187	5 119	42 968	2 321	64 164	911
2002	28 179	16 352	16 516	2 148	22 823	5 822	27 626	5 255	42 285	2 275	59 944	851
2001	27 031	16 683	17 248	2 382	21 743	5 729	26 907	5 481	40 165	2 212	55 771	877
2000[3]	26 204	16 756	15 201	2 434	21 789	6 020	26 324	5 431	41 513	2 060	52 373	809
1999	24 979	16 936	13 569	2 393	20 991	6 112	25 176	5 417	37 422	2 140	52 437	873
1998	22 829	16 201	13 672	2 402	19 236	6 053	23 927	4 559	36 373	1 897	44 760	764
1997	21 909	15 873	13 185	2 437	18 980	5 964	22 899	4 902	32 062	1 846	42 791	724
1996	21 978	15 255	13 110	2 383	18 722	5 844	23 628	4 783	31 955	1 655	48 731	590
1995	20 537	14 847	12 956	2 389	17 072	5 453	21 824	4 727	29 666	1 684	46 654	595
1994	19 772	14 754	12 705	2 290	16 446	5 596	19 631	4 610	30 938	1 679	48 653	579
1993	18 614	14 315	11 065	2 352	16 122	5 521	18 867	4 279	29 953	1 638	41 221	525
1992	17 416	13 836	11 077	2 451	15 260	5 379	18 719	4 054	27 457	1 429	41 439	523
1991	16 809	13 865	11 248	2 860	15 060	5 512	17 850	3 581	25 630	1 383	38 002	528
1990	16 627	13 731	11 184	2 853	14 794	6 049	18 209	3 004	26 448	1 217	32 962	607
1989	16 072	13 600	10 066	2 883	14 613	5 894	17 385	3 008	25 357	1 121	32 740	694
1988	15 318	13 356	10 202	2 970	13 835	5 760	16 760	2 802	23 689	1 204	30 802	621
1987	14 136	13 023	9 976	3 015	12 862	5 699	15 491	2 617	20 805	1 097	29 163	596
1986	13 494	12 729	9 365	3 028	12 276	5 470	14 743	2 662	21 403	1 004	27 503	564
1985	12 926	12 427	9 116	3 009	11 791	5 223	13 805	2 615	20 533	1 046	26 246	535
1984	12 002	11 948	8 725	3 127	10 882	4 927	12 890	2 396	19 330	937	24 072	561
1983	11 299	11 296	7 867	3 035	10 557	4 692	12 426	2 206	17 207	828	23 506	535
1982	10 610	11 001	7 700	3 188	10 207	4 501	11 110	2 067	16 152	747	22 050	488
1981	10 117	11 088	7 520	3 514	9 994	4 388	11 456	2 078	14 587	708	19 463	398
1980	11 085	5 576	8 421	2 054	11 563	2 119	12 393	964	15 616	283	19 960	353
1979	8 720	10 856	6 424	3 776	8 723	4 267	9 895	1 826	13 473	622	18 182	366
1978	7 981	10 420	5 918	3 841	8 152	3 944	9 026	1 689	12 870	557	15 076	389
1977	7 271	10 014	5 406	3 946	7 553	3 604	8 321	1 578	11 088	532	14 749	354
1976	6 716	9 744	5 304	4 008	6 805	3 515	7 331	1 370	10 331	547	15 013	305
1975	6 190	9 368	4 989	3 922	6 281	3 495	7 212	1 193	9 473	517	12 333	241
Male												
2004	33 029	7 673	23 018	1 026	26 619	3 116	32 262	2 178	47 648	962	79 053	387
2003[2]	32 545	7 469	17 915	1 039	28 102	2 910	31 556	2 156	45 635	966	76 871	397
2002	31 790	7 483	19 294	1 072	25 582	2 832	32 764	2 283	47 018	974	75 050	321
2001	30 502	7 727	18 543	1 210	25 037	2 759	31 084	2 457	46 511	943	67 007	356
2000[3]	30 109	7 700	17 992	1 235	25 219	2 942	30 966	2 291	49 270	880	60 207	349
1999	28 821	7 806	16 391	1 199	25 849	2 934	28 442	2 338	42 530	971	59 587	365
1998	26 090	7 488	16 013	1 190	22 698	2 974	26 586	2 215	42 539	792	51 198	318
1997	25 080	7 370	15 423	1 304	22 440	2 862	27 215	2 108	35 792	818	49 940	278
1996	25 067	7 125	15 461	1 290	22 267	2 836	26 365	2 047	35 558	700	65 981	253
1995	23 876	7 090	14 877	1 280	19 514	2 812	26 846	2 047	36 026	659	57 186	293
1994	22 614	7 009	15 984	1 191	18 527	2 818	23 748	1 959	34 073	758	52 829	281
1993	21 108	6 833	13 074	1 305	18 668	2 775	21 734	1 804	35 147	721	47 372	228
1992	19 278	6 822	12 661	1 457	16 978	2 683	22 697	1 796	30 989	643	48 968	244
1991	18 607	6 830	15 714	1 624	17 352	2 731	20 548	1 570	26 075	650	43 927	255
1990	18 859	6 781	13 031	1 563	17 046	3 013	21 152	1 372	29 471	564	39 104	269
1989	18 108	6 654	11 827	1 614	16 658	2 848	20 253	1 352	27 493	515	38 166	326
1988	17 782	6 593	12 439	1 671	16 345	2 795	19 265	1 311	28 506	533	36 452	283
1987	16 171	6 505	11 899	1 711	14 800	2 769	18 081	1 250	23 345	482	34 073	294
1986	15 441	6 326	11 248	1 691	14 214	2 666	17 419	1 226	23 412	480	31 054	263
1985	14 932	6 237	10 802	1 716	13 721	2 572	16 415	1 230	23 818	477	31 947	243
1984	13 560	5 899	10 216	1 780	12 382	2 339	14 960	1 106	21 986	424	27 893	250
1983	12 789	5 707	9 094	1 768	11 956	2 312	15 113	996	20 370	363	25 466	268
1982	12 203	5 535	9 153	1 798	11 952	2 213	12 926	953	17 658	319	26 452	253
1981	11 937	5 651	9 266	1 925	11 905	2 191	13 740	1 002	16 624	327	21 082	205
1980	11 085	5 576	8 421	2 054	11 563	2 119	12 393	964	15 616	283	23 346	156
1979	10 403	5 581	7 938	2 138	10 662	2 087	11 971	931	16 161	259	21 092	166
1978	9 651	5 350	7 423	2 156	9 869	1 982	11 197	770	16 009	260	18 083	181
1977	8 710	5 220	6 648	2 230	9 332	1 770	10 023	799	12 978	234	16 385	188
1976	7 991	5 156	6 670	2 289	8 056	1 766	8 688	726	12 246	233	17 859	143
1975	7 541	4 864	6 364	2 247	7 847	1 684	8 505	599	11 318	213	13 720	121

[1] For data prior to 1991, some college/associate's degree equals 1 to 3 years of college completed, a bachelor's degree equals 4 years of college completed, and an advanced degree equals 5 or more years of college completed.
[2] Starting in 2003, respondents could choose more than one race. The race data in this table from 2003 onward represent respondents who indicated only one race.
[3] Beginning in 2000, earnings data are from the expanded Current Population Survey (CPS) sample and were calculated using population controls based on Census 2000.

Table A-28. Mean Earnings of Workers Age 18 Years and Over, by Educational Attainment, Race, Sex, and Hispanic Origin, Selected Years, 1975–2004—*Continued*

(Dollars, numbers in thousands.)

Sex, race, Hispanic origin, and year	Total population		Not a high school graduate		High school graduate		Some college/associate's degree		Bachelor's degree[1]		Advanced degree[1]	
	Mean earnings (dollars)	Number with earnings	Mean earnings (dollars)	Number with earnings	Mean earnings (dollars)	Number with earnings	Mean earnings (dollars)	Number with earnings	Mean earnings (dollars)	Number with earnings	Mean earnings (dollars)	Number with earnings
BLACK												
Female												
2004	25 747	8 967	12 807	1 012	20 265	3 019	24 508	3 017	38 612	1 396	55 337	520
2003[2]	25 735	8 919	14 513	1 056	19 623	3 030	24 007	2 963	41 066	1 355	54 346	514
2002	25 131	8 868	13 748	1 075	20 209	2 989	23 679	2 972	38 741	1 301	50 766	529
2001	24 036	8 956	15 912	1 172	18 683	2 970	23 511	3 023	35 448	1 269	48 080	521
2000[3]	22 884	9 056	12 321	1 198	18 510	3 078	22 937	3 140	35 719	1 179	46 416	459
1999	21 694	9 130	10 734	1 194	16 506	3 178	22 699	3 080	33 184	1 170	47 358	509
1998	20 026	8 713	11 372	1 212	15 892	3 078	20 371	2 870	31 952	1 105	40 214	448
1997	19 161	8 503	10 607	1 132	15 789	3 102	19 643	2 794	29 091	1 027	38 392	448
1996	19 271	8 129	10 337	1 094	15 379	3 008	21 581	2 736	29 311	954	35 785	337
1995	17 485	7 757	10 739	1 108	14 473	2 641	17 985	2 679	25 577	1 025	36 585	304
1994	17 200	7 745	9 150	1 099	14 333	2 777	16 589	2 651	28 356	921	44 618	297
1993	16 336	7 481	8 562	1 048	13 550	2 746	16 778	2 475	25 865	917	36 485	296
1992	15 605	7 014	8 756	995	13 550	2 696	15 553	2 256	24 572	786	34 902	281
1991	15 065	7 034	9 151	1 237	12 810	2 781	15 743	2 010	25 235	733	32 467	273
1990	14 449	6 950	8 946	1 290	12 560	3 036	15 734	1 632	23 837	653	28 074	338
1989	14 122	6 946	7 827	1 269	12 701	3 046	15 044	1 656	23 541	606	27 933	368
1988	12 916	6 763	7 325	1 299	11 469	2 965	14 557	1 491	19 862	671	26 072	338
1987	12 106	6 518	7 452	1 304	11 030	2 930	13 123	1 367	18 815	615	24 383	302
1986	11 571	6 403	6 984	1 337	10 434	2 804	12 459	1 436	19 562	524	24 400	301
1985	10 904	6 190	6 879	1 293	9 918	2 651	11 488	1 385	17 779	569	21 502	292
1984	10 482	6 049	6 754	1 347	9 527	2 588	11 115	1 290	17 134	513	21 000	311
1983	9 778	5 589	6 154	1 267	9 197	2 380	10 215	1 210	14 738	465	21 539	267
1982	9 024	5 546	6 047	1 390	8 737	2 378	9 574	1 114	13 284	428	19 198	235
1981	8 225	5 437	5 404	1 589	8 088	2 197	9 329	1 076	12 839	381	17 743	193
1980	7 684	. . .	4 685	. . .	7 508	. . .	8 544	. . .	12 389	. . .	17 278	. . .
1979	6 940	5 275	4 448	1 638	6 866	2 180	7 735	895	11 555	363	15 766	200
HISPANIC[4]												
Both Sexes												
2004	27 263	19 343	19 025	6 935	25 823	5 740	29 260	4 369	45 166	1 669	69 839	629
2003[2]	25 810	18 786	18 349	6 767	23 472	5 517	28 494	4 235	43 676	1 663	62 794	603
2002	25 824	18 409	18 981	6 748	24 163	5 499	27 757	4 024	40 949	1 568	67 679	569
2001	24 786	17 575	18 334	6 533	22 866	5 265	27 523	3 842	40 586	1 416	62 194	517
2000[3]	23 855	17 161	17 156	6 428	22 009	5 145	25 276	3 737	44 661	1 395	63 908	455
1999	22 096	15 122	16 106	5 601	20 704	4 539	24 577	3 392	36 212	1 117	55 352	472
1998	22 117	14 372	15 832	5 281	20 978	4 219	23 091	3 289	35 014	1 156	62 583	425
1997	20 766	13 972	15 069	5 238	19 558	4 082	22 001	3 075	33 465	1 140	58 571	437
1996	19 439	13 365	13 287	5 062	18 528	3 783	22 209	3 096	32 955	1 027	49 873	398
1995	18 262	12 434	13 068	4 784	18 333	3 594	19 923	2 856	30 602	866	45 612	334
1994	18 568	12 035	13 733	4 686	17 323	3 444	21 041	2 723	29 165	844	51 898	337
1993	17 102	11 644	11 852	4 425	16 591	3 367	19 043	2 728	30 359	799	45 034	325
1992	16 824	10 171	11 836	3 962	16 714	2 991	19 778	2 242	28 260	702	46 736	274
1991	16 300	10 006	11 335	3 906	16 142	3 045	19 123	2 080	26 623	665	40 154	311
1990	15 943	9 729	10 368	3 929	15 417	3 282	19 206	1 534	25 703	601	38 075	382
1989	15 714	9 570	11 500	3 985	14 901	3 188	18 707	1 513	28 157	535	39 273	349
1988	15 007	9 226	11 045	3 824	14 667	2 953	18 101	1 511	23 745	596	33 843	340
1987	14 695	8 817	10 961	3 457	13 958	2 982	16 899	1 400	23 105	644	34 413	335
1986	13 558	8 393	9 896	3 379	13 389	2 835	16 523	1 411	22 707	471	28 316	295
1985	13 120	7 840	9 956	3 223	13 044	2 661	15 318	1 226	20 878	458	28 357	273
1984	12 583	7 349	9 671	3 129	12 858	2 457	14 359	1 116	19 924	381	26 327	265
1983	11 901	6 222	9 473	2 674	12 077	2 030	13 371	976	17 972	320	24 352	222
1982	11 307	5 914	8 498	2 583	11 539	1 967	13 108	873	18 186	303	28 167	186
1981	10 872	5 930	8 645	2 648	11 046	1 966	12 971	834	16 114	320	24 082	161
1980	10 062	5 723	8 119	2 649	10 182	1 824	11 891	808	15 676	283	21 910	157
1979	9 248	5 545	7 683	2 533	9 338	1 812	10 181	768	14 940	240	18 273	190
1978	8 460	4 898	7 138	2 345	8 512	1 554	9 575	661	13 985	213	17 333	125
1977	7 761	4 752	6 547	2 306	8 079	1 461	8 172	656	12 572	210	16 660	118
1976	7 081	4 303	5 984	2 107	7 580	1 309	7 252	592	11 242	177	14 000	118
1975	6 567	4 078	5 462	2 028	6 759	1 293	7 154	474	10 573	173	15 756	111

[1]For data prior to 1991, some college/associate's degree equals 1 to 3 years of college completed, a bachelor's degree equals 4 years of college completed, and an advanced degree equals 5 or more years of college completed.
[2]Starting in 2003, respondents could choose more than one race. The race data in this table from 2003 onward represent respondents who indicated only one race.
[3]Beginning in 2000, earnings data are from the expanded Current Population Survey (CPS) sample and were calculated using population controls based on Census 2000.
[4]May be of any race.
. . . = Not available.

Table A-28. Mean Earnings of Workers Age 18 Years and Over, by Educational Attainment, Race, Sex, and Hispanic Origin, Selected Years, 1975–2004—*Continued*

(Dollars, numbers in thousands.)

Sex, race, Hispanic origin, and year	Total population		Not a high school graduate		High school graduate		Some college/associate's degree		Bachelor's degree[1]		Advanced degree[1]	
	Mean earnings (dollars)	Number with earnings	Mean earnings (dollars)	Number with earnings	Mean earnings (dollars)	Number with earnings	Mean earnings (dollars)	Number with earnings	Mean earnings (dollars)	Number with earnings	Mean earnings (dollars)	Number with earnings
HISPANIC[4]												
Male												
2004	30 828	11 562	21 606	4 633	29 694	3 439	34 447	2 241	53 567	915	84 152	331
2003[2]	28 806	11 195	20 637	4 556	26 652	3 234	34 157	2 193	49 298	867	71 446	344
2002	29 084	10 979	21 611	4 506	27 992	3 205	32 935	2 112	46 115	815	73 836	338
2001	27 964	10 258	20 614	4 289	26 745	2 985	32 595	1 962	45 445	748	75 746	272
2000[3]	27 253	9 996	19 501	4 236	25 629	2 940	30 155	1 873	55 050	722	81 447	223
1999	24 970	8 713	18 020	3 592	23 736	2 597	29 387	1 698	42 733	577	66 745	250
1998	25 534	8 288	17 756	3 428	24 739	2 413	26 483	1 652	40 889	569	83 754	226
1997	23 520	8 261	17 447	3 444	22 253	2 391	25 923	1 598	37 963	557	68 097	272
1996	21 870	7 975	14 986	3 382	21 593	2 116	26 682	1 687	38 130	531	49 307	259
1995	20 312	7 337	14 774	3 140	20 882	2 039	22 171	1 475	35 109	466	50 802	215
1994	21 288	7 117	16 355	3 111	19 667	1 937	24 517	1 410	33 797	450	60 858	210
1993	19 460	6 957	13 572	2 928	18 765	1 954	22 417	1 444	37 554	438	52 441	194
1992	18 842	6 034	13 313	2 633	19 357	1 665	23 033	1 193	33 430	380	53 645	164
1991	18 516	5 932	13 133	2 548	18 582	1 705	21 974	1 131	31 699	356	45 873	193
1990	18 320	5 745	13 182	2 562	18 100	1 812	22 376	852	31 485	314	47 479	205
1989	18 087	5 641	13 167	2 632	17 579	1 711	22 374	810	32 767	292	49 088	196
1988	17 357	5 477	12 836	2 517	17 446	1 621	21 631	811	26 935	333	40 916	194
1987	17 048	5 248	12 823	2 281	16 774	1 616	19 414	758	26 581	383	39 014	211
1986	15 624	5 037	11 262	2 262	15 948	1 546	19 675	778	27 427	274	32 538	176
1985	15 293	4 702	11 671	2 111	15 602	1 491	18 168	678	24 723	267	32 831	155
1984	14 957	4 344	11 441	2 022	15 763	1 319	17 261	611	23 835	223	30 727	168
1983	14 265	3 577	11 353	1 678	14 584	1 074	16 626	514	21 911	170	28 680	141
1982	13 484	3 480	10 108	1 622	13 883	1 083	15 560	495	22 565	153	34 474	125
1981	13 052	3 504	10 447	1 686	13 513	1 037	15 432	489	19 201	177	27 619	114
1980	12 310	3 401	9 825	1 707	13 108	961	14 331	451	19 224	167	24 642	114
1979	11 332	3 269	9 393	1 615	11 714	952	12 489	441	18 923	142	21 299	118
1978	10 470	3 015	9 000	1 400	10 040	915	11 545	400	16 000	127	20 702	92
1977	9 655	2 833	8 192	1 460	10 386	776	9 924	391	15 189	120	19 025	85
1976	8 787	2 571	7 440	1 321	9 640	712	8 843	342	13 650	114	16 184	81
1975	8 162	2 456	6 745	1 287	8 546	691	8 807	279	12 881	113	17 991	86
Female												
2004	21 967	7 781	13 830	2 302	20 037	2 300	23 796	2 127	34 949	753	53 887	297
2003[2]	21 391	7 591	13 632	2 210	18 967	2 283	22 411	2 042	37 550	795	51 294	258
2002	21 008	7 430	13 694	2 241	18 810	2 293	22 035	1 911	35 357	753	58 623	230
2001	20 330	7 316	13 976	2 243	17 786	2 279	22 229	1 879	35 142	668	47 176	245
2000[3]	19 115	7 164	12 622	2 191	17 180	2 204	20 372	1 864	33 489	672	47 057	232
1999	18 187	6 409	12 684	2 010	16 653	1 943	19 754	1 694	29 249	540	42 503	222
1998	17 461	6 804	12 273	1 854	15 952	1 806	20 460	1 639	29 317	587	38 422	200
1997	16 781	5 711	10 503	1 794	15 747	1 691	17 759	1 477	29 173	584	43 051	165
1996	15 841	5 390	9 867	1 680	14 635	1 667	16 856	1 409	27 407	495	50 960	139
1995	15 310	5 096	9 809	1 644	14 989	1 555	17 521	1 380	25 338	399	36 255	118
1994	14 631	4 918	8 559	1 576	14 313	1 508	17 309	1 313	23 867	393	37 269	127
1993	13 602	4 687	8 489	1 498	13 584	1 413	15 250	1 284	21 627	361	34 001	131
1992	13 880	4 137	8 913	1 330	13 396	1 326	16 076	1 049	22 160	322	34 551	110
1991	13 069	4 072	4 809	1 358	13 043	1 339	15 721	948	20 791	309	30 721	117
1990	12 516	3 984	5 093	1 367	12 109	1 470	15 245	682	19 378	287	27 184	177
1989	12 307	3 929	8 256	1 353	11 799	1 477	14 482	703	22 617	243	26 700	153
1988	11 573	3 749	7 597	1 307	11 284	1 332	14 012	700	19 707	263	24 444	146
1987	11 234	3 569	7 350	1 176	10 627	1 366	13 929	642	18 003	261	26 584	124
1986	10 457	3 356	7 130	1 117	10 319	1 289	12 648	633	16 142	197	22 071	119
1985	9 865	3 138	6 699	1 112	9 784	1 170	11 791	548	15 503	191	22 480	118
1984	9 150	3 005	6 438	1 107	9 492	1 138	10 848	505	14 404	158	18 706	97
1983	8 704	2 645	6 305	996	9 261	956	9 750	462	13 507	150	16 817	81
1982	8 195	2 434	5 781	961	8 668	884	9 896	378	13 719	150	15 244	61
1981	7 723	2 426	5 486	962	8 292	929	9 483	345	12 292	143	15 503	47
1980	6 770	2 322	5 028	942	6 923	863	8 808	357	10 568	116	14 668	43
1979	6 255	2 276	4 675	918	6 708	860	7 069	327	9 168	98	13 313	72
1978	5 501	1 983	4 135	847	5 834	739	6 686	268	9 684	86	10 908	43
1977	4 964	1 919	3 707	846	5 466	685	5 588	265	9 082	90	10 569	33
1976	4 548	1 732	3 537	786	5 124	597	5 075	250	6 884	63	9 218	37
1975	4 152	1 622	3 233	741	4 708	602	4 790	195	6 226	60	8 067	25

[1]For data prior to 1991, some college/associate's degree equals 1 to 3 years of college completed, a bachelor's degree equals 4 years of college completed, and an advanced degree equals 5 or more years of college completed.
[2]Starting in 2003, respondents could choose more than one race. The race data in this table from 2003 onward represent respondents who indicated only one race.
[3]Beginning in 2000, earnings data are from the expanded Current Population Survey (CPS) sample and were calculated using population controls based on Census 2000.
[4]May be of any race.

Table A-28. Mean Earnings of Workers Age 18 Years and Over, by Educational Attainment, Race, Sex, and Hispanic Origin, Selected Years, 1975–2004—*Continued*

(Dollars, numbers in thousands.)

Sex, race, Hispanic origin, and year	Total population		Not a high school graduate		High school graduate		Some college/associate's degree		Bachelor's degree[1]		Advanced degree[1]	
	Mean earnings (dollars)	Number with earnings	Mean earnings (dollars)	Number with earnings	Mean earnings (dollars)	Number with earnings	Mean earnings (dollars)	Number with earnings	Mean earnings (dollars)	Number with earnings	Mean earnings (dollars)	Number with earnings
WHITE ALONE OR IN COMBINATION												
Both Sexes												
2004	38 855	125 387	19 365	13 539	29 595	37 639	32 736	37 287	52 790	24 361	78 747	12 560
2003	37 958	124 456	18 734	16 282	27 915	45 064	31 498	44 048	51 206	28 672	74 601	14 592
2002	37 290	124 337	19 278	13 957	28 107	37 863	31 767	36 639	52 509	23 865	73 773	12 011
Male												
2004	47 275	67 758	22 576	8 751	35 348	21 073	40 627	18 361	65 498	12 728	99 534	6 842
2003	45 989	67 198	21 787	8 682	34 225	20 534	39 555	18 421	65 237	12 774	93 792	6 785
2002	45 682	67 082	22 601	8 977	33 846	20 430	39 439	18 377	65 548	12 621	92 575	6 675
Female												
2004	28 954	57 629	13 498	4 788	22 277	16 565	25 079	18 925	38 886	11 632	53 859	5 717
2003	28 532	57 257	14 086	4 684	22 029	16 926	25 093	18 616	37 750	11 476	53 021	5 552
2002	27 457	57 254	13 286	4 979	21 381	17 433	24 046	18 261	37 872	11 243	50 255	5 336
BLACK ALONE OR IN COMBINATION												
Both Sexes												
2004	29 031	17 109	17 821	2 085	23 458	6 298	27 801	5 369	42 131	2 414	64 545	941
2003	28 854	16 871	16 238	2 177	23 956	6 082	27 095	5 296	42 991	2 374	63 966	940
2002	28 255	16 833	17 114	2 217	22 762	5 940	27 582	5 441	42 099	2 348	60 458	884
Male												
2004	32 919	7 884	22 755	1 049	26 575	3 202	32 466	2 258	47 448	976	77 648	398
2003	32 574	7 689	17 982	1 088	28 323	2 981	31 591	2 233	45 705	982	76 954	402
2002	31 967	7 734	20 537	1 114	25 510	2 902	32 696	2 375	46 942	1 009	76 003	332
Female												
2004	25 707	9 224	12 818	1 035	20 236	3 096	24 415	3 111	38 522	1 438	54 931	543
2003	25 739	9 182	14 495	1 089	19 765	3 100	23 816	3 063	41 073	1 391	54 265	538
2002	25 099	9 098	13 656	1 103	20 137	3 038	23 621	3 066	38 447	1 339	51 101	552

[1]For data prior to 1991, some college/associate's degree equals 1 to 3 years of college completed, a bachelor's degree equals 4 years of college completed, and an advanced degree equals 5 or more years of college completed.

NOTES AND DEFINITIONS: NATIONAL SCHOOL ENROLLMENT AND EDUCATIONAL ATTAINMENT

ENROLLMENT SOURCE: U.S. Census Bureau. School enrollment—characteristics of students: October 2005. *2006 Current Population Survey (CPS) Report.* (Oct. 2006) <http://www.census.gov/population/www/socdemo/school.html>.

ATTAINMENT SOURCE: U.S. Census Bureau. Educational attainment in the United States: March 2005. *Annual Social and Economic Supplement to the Current Population Survey.* <http://www.census.gov/population/www/socdemo/education/cps2005.html>.

Tables in Part A are derived from the October 2005 Current Population Survey (CPS) and the March 2005 Current Population Survey. The Census Bureau disseminated comparable tables in the P-20 series of *Current Population Reports* (CPR) for most years between 1947 and 1994. Since then, these tables have not been available in printed form. However, they can be found on the Census Bureau Web site at <http://www.census.gov>. In the historical series, data prior to 1992 are not strictly comparable to data after 1992. Before 1992, the CPS did not ask questions about degrees received; educational attainment was gauged only by years of school completed. For information about the availability of earlier reports, or for answers to data questions not addressed in this section, contact the Education and Social Stratification Branch, Population Division, Census Bureau at (301) 763-2464.

Age. Age classification is based on the age of the person at his or her last birthday.

Citizenship status. There are five categories of citizenship status: 1) born in the United States; 2) born in Puerto Rico or another outlying area of the United States; 3) born abroad to U.S. citizen parents; 4) naturalized citizens; and 5) non-citizens. Place of birth was asked for every household member and for the parents of every household member in the CPS sample. People born in the United States or its outlying areas, or whose parents were born in the United States or its outlying areas, were not asked citizenship questions. Citizenship statuses (1), (2), and (3) were assigned during the editing phase of data preparation, based on the place of birth of the household member or the place of birth of his or her parents. People born outside the United States and its outlying areas, whose parents were born outside the United States and its outlying areas, were asked, "Are you a citizen of the United States?" 'Yes' answers were assigned to the "naturalized citizen" category (4), and 'No' answers were assigned to the "not a citizen" category (5) during the editing process. People for whom no birthplace was provided were also assigned a citizenship status during the editing process; for example, the citizenship status of a child might have been assigned based on the citizenship status of his or her mother.

Dropouts. See School, dropout rate, annual high school.

Earnings. See Income.

Educational attainment. Data on educational attainment are derived from a single question that asks, "What is the highest grade of school ... completed, or the highest degree ... received?"

The single educational attainment question now in use was introduced into the CPS in January 1992. It is similar to the question used in the 1990 Decennial Census of Population and Housing. Consequently, data on educational attainment from the 1992 CPS are not directly comparable to CPS data from earlier years. The new question replaces the previous two-part question used in the CPS, which asked respondents to report the highest grade they attended and whether or not they completed that grade.

The question concerning educational attainment applies only to progress in "regular" schools. Such schools include graded public, private, and parochial elementary and high schools (both junior and senior high schools), colleges, universities, and professional schools, and both day schools and night schools. Thus, regular schooling is that which may advance a person toward an elementary school certificate, a high school diploma, or a college, university, or professional school degree. Non-regular schooling was counted only if the credits obtained were regarded as transferable to a school within the regular school system.

Family. A family is a group of two people or more residing together (including the householder) related by birth, marriage, or adoption; all such people (including related subfamily members) are considered members of one family. Beginning with the 1980 Current Population Survey, unrelated subfamilies (formerly referred to as secondary families) are no longer included in the count of families, nor are members of unrelated subfamilies included in the count of family members. The number of families is equal to the number of family households; however, the count of family members differs from the count of family household members, as family household members include any non-relatives living in the household.

Family household. A family household is a household maintained by a householder within a family (as defined above). It includes any unrelated people (unrelated subfamily members and/or secondary individuals) residing in the household. The number of family households is equal to the number of families; however, the count of family household members differs from the count of family members. Family household members include all people living in the household, whereas family members include only the householder and his or her relatives. (See Family for more information.)

Hispanic origin. People of Hispanic origin were identified by a question that asked respondents to self-identify their origin or desent. Respondents were asked to select their origin (and the origin of other household members) from a "flash card" listing different ethnicities. People of Hispanic origin were those who indicated that their descent was of Mexican, Puerto Rican, Cuban, Central or South American, or some other Hispanic origin. It should be noted that people of Hispanic origin may be of any race.

People who were of non-Hispanic White origin were identified by crossing the responses to two self-identification questions: (1) origin or descent; and (2) race. Respondents were asked to select their race (and the race of other household members) from a "flash card" listing racial groups. Since March 1989, the population has been divided into five groups on the basis of race: White; Black; American Indian, Eskimo, or Aleut; Asian or Pacific Islander; and Other races. The last category

includes any race other than the four indicated races. Respondents who identified their race as White and did not select one of the Hispanic origin subgroups (Mexican, Puerto Rican, Cuban, Central or South American) were classified as non-Hispanic White.

Household. A household consists of all the people who occupy a housing unit. A house, apartment, group of rooms, or single room is regarded as a housing unit when it is occupied or intended for occupancy as separate living quarters (meaning that occupants do not live and eat with any other persons in the structure and have direct access to their dwelling from outside or through a common hall). A household includes related family members and all unrelated people—such as lodgers, foster children, wards, or employees—who share the housing unit. A person living alone in a housing unit, or a group of unrelated people sharing a dwelling (such as partners or roomers), are also counted as a household. The count of households excludes group quarters. There are two major categories of households: "family" and "nonfamily." (See Family household and Nonfamily household for more information.)

Householder. The householder is the person (or one of the people) in whose name the housing unit is owned or rented (maintained). If there is no such person, any adult member of the household—excluding roomers, boarders, and paid employees—can be counted as the householder. If a married couple jointly owns or rents the housing unit, the householder may be either the husband or the wife. The person designated as the householder is the "reference person" to whom the relationship of all other household members, if any, is recorded.

The number of householders is equal to the number of households. The number of family householders is also equal to the number of families.

Head versus householder. The Census Bureau discontinued the use of the terms "head of household" and "head of family" beginning with the 1980 CPS. Instead, the terms "householder" and "family householder" are used. Recent social changes have resulted in a greater sharing of household responsibilities among the adult members. This has made the term "head" increasingly inappropriate in the analysis of household and family data. Specifically, beginning in 1980, the Census Bureau discontinued its longtime practice of always classifying the husband as the reference person (head of household) when he was living with his wife.

INCOME. Definitions of income and the types of income are found below:

Income, Official definition of. For each person age 15 years and over in the sample, the CPS asks questions about the amount of money income received during the preceding calendar year from each of the following sources: earnings; unemployment compensation; workers' compensation; Social Security; Supplemental Security Income; public assistance or welfare payments; veterans' payments; survivor benefits; disability benefits; pension or retirement income; interest, dividends, rents, royalties, and estates and trusts; educational assistance; child support; alimony; financial assistance from outside the household; and other income.

Although the income statistics refer to receipts during the preceding calendar year, demographic characteristics such as age, labor force status, and family or household composition are as of the survey date. The income of the family/household does not include amounts received by members who were members of the family/household during all or part of the income year if these people no longer resided in the family/household at the time of interview. However, the CPS collects income data for people who are current residents, but who did not reside in the household during the income year.

Data on consumer income collected in the CPS by the Census Bureau cover money income (exclusive of certain money receipts, such as capital gains) received before payments for personal income taxes, Social Security, union dues, Medicare deductions, etc. Therefore, money income does not reflect the fact that some families receive part of their income in the form of noncash benefits, such as food stamps, health benefits, rent-free housing, and goods produced and consumed on the farm. Money income also does not reflect the fact that noncash benefits are also received by some nonfarm residents. These benefits often take the form of the use of business transportation and facilities, full or partial payments by business for retirement programs, medical and educational expenses, etc. Data users should consider these elements when comparing income levels.

Moreover, readers should be aware that respondents in household surveys tend to underreport their income for many different reasons. Based on an analysis of independently derived income estimates, the Census Bureau determined that respondents report income earned from wages or salaries much more accurately than income earned from other sources of income, and that the reported wage and salary income is nearly equal to independent estimates of aggregate income.

The Census Bureau collects data for the following income sources:

Alimony. Alimony includes all periodic payments received from ex-spouses. It excludes one-time property settlements.

Child support. Child support includes all periodic payments received from an absent parent for the support of his or her children, even if these payments are made through a state or local government office.

Disability benefits. Disability benefits include payments people received due to a health problem or disability (other than those received from Social Security). Respondents can report payments from 10 sources, including workers' compensation, companies or unions, federal government (civil service), military, state or local governments, railroad retirement, accident or disability insurance, Black Lung payments, state temporary sickness, or other disability payments.

Dividends. Dividends include income received from stock holdings and mutual fund shares. The CPS does not include capital gains from the sale of stock holdings as income.

Earnings. The Census Bureau classifies earnings from respondents' longest job (or self-employment) and other employment earnings into three types:

• Money wage, or salary income, is the total income people receive for work performed as an employee during the income year. This category includes wages, salary, armed forces pay, commissions, tips, piece-rate payments, and cash bonuses earned, before deductions are made for items such as taxes, bonds, pensions, and union dues.

• Net income from nonfarm self-employment is the net money income (gross receipts minus expenses) from a respondent's own business, professional enterprise, or partnership. Gross receipts include the value of all goods sold and all services rendered. Expenses include items such as the costs of goods purchased; rent, heat, power, and depreciation charges; wages and salaries paid; and business taxes (but not personal income taxes). In general, the Census Bureau considers inventory changes in determining net income from nonfarm self-employment; replies based on income tax returns or other official records reflect inventory changes. However, when respondents do not report values of inventory changes, interviewers will accept net income figures exclusive of inventory changes. The Census Bureau does not include the value of saleable merchandise consumed by the proprietors of retail stores as part of net income.

• Net income from farm self-employment is the net money income (gross receipts minus operating expenses) from the operation of a farm by a person acting on their own account as owner, renter, or sharecropper. Gross receipts include the value of all products sold, payments from government farm programs, money received from renting farm equipment to others, rent received from farm property if payment is based on the percentage of crops produced, and incidental receipts from the sale of items such as wood, sand, and gravel.

Operating expenses include items such as the cost of feed, fertilizer, seed, and other farming supplies; cash wages paid to farmhands; depreciation charges; cash rent; interest on farm mortgages; farm building repairs; and farm taxes (not state and federal personal income taxes). The Census Bureau does not include the value of fuel, food, or other farm products used for family living as part of net income, and only considers inventory changes in determining net income when they are accounted for in income tax returns or other official records. Otherwise, the Census Bureau does not take inventory changes into account.

Educational assistance. Educational assistance includes Pell Grants, other government educational assistance, scholarships or grants, and any financial assistance received from employers, friends, or relatives not residing in the student's household.

Financial assistance from outside the household. Financial assistance from outside the household includes periodic payments received from non-household members. This type of assistance excludes gifts and sporadic assistance.

Government transfers. Government transfers include payments received from the following sources: unemployment compensation, state workers' compensation, Social Security, Supplemental Security Income (SSI), public assistance, veterans' payments, government survivor benefits, government disability benefits, government pensions, and government educational assistance.

Interest income. Interest income includes payments received or credited to accounts from bonds, treasury notes, individual retirement accounts (IRAs), certificates of deposit, interest-bearing savings and checking accounts, and all other interest-paying investments.

Other income. Other income includes any other unclassified payments received regularly. Some examples are state programs such as foster child payments, military family allotments, and income received from foreign government pensions.

Pension or retirement income. Pension or retirement income includes payments received from eight sources, including companies or unions; federal government (civil service); military; state or local governments; railroad retirement; annuities or paid-up insurance policies; IRAs, Keogh, or 401(k) payments; or other retirement income.

Public assistance or welfare payments. Public assistance or welfare payments include cash payments to low-income persons, including payments given under programs such as Aid to Families with Dependent Children (AFDC, ADC) and Temporary Assistance to Needy Families (TANF), emergency assistance, and other general assistance.

Rents, royalties, and estates and trusts. Rents, royalties, and estates and trusts include net income received from the rental of a house, a store, or other property; receipts from boarders or lodgers;

net royalty income; and periodic payments from estate or trust funds.

Social Security. Social Security includes pensions, survivors' benefits, and permanent disability insurance payments made by the Social Security Administration prior to medical insurance deductions. The Census Bureau does not include Medicare reimbursements for health services as Social Security benefits.

Supplemental Security Income. Supplemental Security Income includes federal, state, and local welfare agency payments to low-income people age 65 years and over and to blind or disabled people of any age.

Survivor benefits. Survivor benefits include payments received from survivors' or widows' pensions, estates, trusts, annuities, or any other types of survivors' benefits. Respondents can report payments from 10 different sources, including private companies or unions, federal government (civil service), military, state or local governments, railroad retirement, workers' compensation, Black Lung payments, estates and trusts, annuities or paid-up insurance policies, and other survivor payments.

Unemployment compensation. Unemployment compensation includes payments made to the respondent from government unemployment agencies or private companies during periods of unemployment. It also accounts for any strike benefits the respondent received from union funds.

Veterans' payments. Veterans' payments include periodic payments from the Department of Veterans Affairs to disabled members of the armed forces or survivors of deceased veterans for education and on-the-job training. These payments also include means-tested assistance to veterans.

Workers' compensation. Workers' compensation includes periodic payments from public or private insurance companies for work-related injuries.

The Census Bureau does not count the following receipts as income: (1) capital gains (or losses) from the sale of property, including stocks, bonds, houses, or cars (unless the person was engaged in the business of selling such property, in which case the CPS counts the net proceeds as income from self-

employment); (2) withdrawals of bank deposits; (3) money borrowed; (4) tax refunds; (5) gifts; and (6) lump-sum inheritances or insurance payments.

The Census Bureau combines all sources of income into two major types:

Total money earnings. Total money earnings is the algebraic sum of money wages, salary, and net income from farm and nonfarm self-employment.

Income other than earnings. Income other than earnings is the algebraic sum of all sources of money income, except wages and salaries and income from self-employment.

Mean (average) income. Mean (average) income is the amount obtained by dividing the total aggregate income of a group by the number of units in that group. The means for households, families, and unrelated individuals are based respectively on all households, all families, and all unrelated individuals. The means (averages) for people are based on people age 15 years and over with income.

Median income. Median income is the amount that divides the income distribution into two equal groups. Half of all people have incomes above the median, and half of all people have incomes below the median. The medians for households, families, and unrelated individuals are respectively based on all households, all families, and all unrelated individuals. The medians for people are based on people age 15 years and over with income.

LABOR FORCE STATUS. Definitions of labor force characteristics are found below:

Current job (basic data). A worker's current job is the job held during the reference week (the week before the survey). A person holding two or more jobs is classified as being in the job at which he or she spent the most hours during the reference week. The unemployed are classified according to their most recent full-time job of two weeks or more, or by the job (either the full-time or part-time job) from which they were laid off. The occupation/industry classification system for the 1990 Decennial Census of Population was first used to code CPS data for the January 1992 file. The occupation/industry classification system for the 2000

Decennial Census of Population was first used to code CPS data for the January 2003 file.

Employed. Employed persons include all civilians who, during the survey week, did any work at all as paid employees or in their own business or profession, or on their own farm, or who worked 15 hours or more as unpaid workers on a farm or a business operated by a member of the family; and all people who had jobs but were not working due to illness, bad weather, vacation, labor-management dispute, or personal reasons, whether or not they were seeking other jobs. Each employed person is counted only once. People who held two or more jobs are counted as working in the job at which they worked the greatest number of hours during the survey week. If a person worked an equal number of hours at two or more jobs, he or she is counted as working at the job that they have held the longest.

Labor force. Workers are classified as being in the labor force if they are employed, unemployed, or in the armed forces during the survey week. The "civilian labor force" includes all civilians classified as employed or unemployed. The file includes labor force data for civilians age 15 years and over. However, the official definition of the civilian labor force consists of workers age 16 years and over.

Not in labor force. All civilians age 15 years and over who are not classified as employed or unemployed are considered not to be in the labor force. These people are further classified as being engaged in a major activity such as keeping house, going to school, unable to work because of long-term physical or mental illness, and "other," which is mostly composed of retired persons. Those who report doing unpaid work on a family-owned farm or in a family-owned business for less than 15 hours are also classified as not in the labor force.

For persons not in the labor force, questions about previous work experience, intentions to seek work again, current desire for a job, and reasons for not seeking work are only asked of households in the fourth and eighth months of the sample. These are the "outgoing" groups—those that were in the sample for three previous months and would not be in it for the subsequent month.

Finally, it should be noted that the unemployment rate represents the number of unemployed persons as a percentage of the civilian labor force age 16 years and over. This measure can be computed for groups within the labor force by sex, age, marital status, race, etc. The job loser, job leaver, reentrant, and new entrant rates are each calculated as a percentage of the civilian labor force age 16 years and over; the sum of the rates for the four groups thus equals the total unemployment rate.

Unemployed. Unemployed persons are civilians who, during the survey week, had no employment but were available for work and had engaged in any specific job-seeking activity within the past four previous weeks, such as registering at a public or private employment office, meeting with prospective employers, checking with friends or relatives, placing and answering advertisements, writing letters of application, or being on a union or professional register. Others in this category were waiting to be called back to a job from which they had been laid off or were within 30 days of starting a new wage or salary job. This category consists of job leavers, job losers, new job entrants, and job reentrants.

Work experience. A person with work experience is one who did any work for pay or profit or worked without pay on a family-operated farm or business at any time during the preceding calendar year, on a part time or full time basis. A full-time worker is a worker who worked 35 hours or more per week during a majority of the weeks in the preceding calendar year. A year-round worker is a worker who worked for 50 weeks or more during the preceding calendar year. A full-time, year-round worker is a person who worked full time (35 or more hours per week) for 50 or more weeks during the previous calendar year.

Level of school completed. The statistics on level of school completed indicate the number of persons enrolled at each of five levels: nursery school, kindergarten, elementary school (first to eighth grades), high school (ninth to twelfth grades), and college or professional school. The last group includes graduate students at colleges and universities. Those enrolled in elementary school, middle school, intermediate school, or junior high school through eighth grade are classified as being in elementary school. All persons enrolled in ninth through twelfth grade are classified as being in high school.

Metropolitan-nonmetropolitan residence. A metropolitan area (MA) consists of a large population nucleus and its adjacent communities, with a high degree of economic and social integration between the two. Some MAs are defined around two or more nuclei.

The MA classification is a statistical standard, developed for federal agencies to use in the production, analysis, and publication of data on MAs. The Federal Office of Management and Budget designate and design MAs based on a set of official published standards. These standards were developed by the interagency Federal Executive Committee on Metropolitan Areas, with the intention of producing definitions that keep the MA designation as consistent as possible throughout the nation.

Each MA must contain either a place with a minimum population of 50,000 or a Census Bureau–defined urbanized area with a total MA population of at least 100,000 (75,000 in New England). An MA comprises one or more central counties. It may also include outlying counties that have close economic and social relationships with the central county. An outlying county must have a specified level of commuting to the central county. It also must meet metropolitan character standards, including population density, urban population, and population growth. In New England, MAs are composed of cities and towns, rather than whole counties.

The territory, population, and housing units in MAs are referred to as "metropolitan." The metropolitan category is subdivided into "inside central city" and "outside central city." The territory, population, and housing units located outside MAs are referred to as "nonmetropolitan."

To meet the needs of various users, the standards provide a flexible structure of metropolitan definitions. MAs refer collectively to metropolitan statistical areas (MSAs), consolidated metropolitan statistical areas (CMSAs), and primary metropolitan statistical areas (PMSAs). Documentation of the MA standards and how they are applied is available through this address: Secretary, Federal Executive Committee on Metropolitan Areas, Population Division, U.S. Bureau of the Census, Washington, DC 20233.

Central city. In each MSA and CMSA, the largest place and, in some cases, additional places are designated as "central cities" under the official standards. However, a few PMSAs do not have central cities. An MA takes its title from its largest central cities. There are also central cities not included in an MA title. An MA central city does not include any part of that city that extends outside the MA boundary.

Consolidated and primary metropolitan statistical area. If an MA has more than 1 million people, primary metropolitan statistical areas (PMSAs) may be defined within it. PMSAs consist of a large urbanized county or cluster of counties with very strong internal economic and social links and close ties to other portions of the larger area. When PMSAs are established, the larger area to which they belong is designated as a consolidated metropolitan statistical area (CMSA).

Metropolitan statistical area. Metropolitan statistical areas (MSAs) are relatively freestanding MAs not closely associated with other MAs. These areas are typically surrounded by nonmetropolitan counties.

Modal grade. See School, Modal grade.

Nativity. There are two major categories of nativity, native born and foreign born. A person who is native is a citizens at birth. All people with the following citizenship status are native born: (1) born in the United States; (2) born in Puerto Rico or an outlying area of the U.S.; and (3) born abroad of American parents. (See Citizenship status for more information.) All other people are classified as foreign born.

Nonfamily household. A nonfamily household consists of a householder living alone (a one-person household) or a household shared exclusively by unrelated people.

Population coverage. The sample for the CPS includes the civilian noninstitutional population of the United States, along with members of the armed forces in the United States living off post or with their families on post. It excludes all other members of the armed forces. The information on the Hispanic population from the CPS was collected in the 50 states and the District of Columbia and does not include residents of outlying areas or of U.S. territories such as Guam, Puerto Rico, and the U.S. Virgin Islands.

Race. The race of individuals was identified through a question requiring self-identification of the person's race. Respondents were asked to select their race from a "flash card" listing racial groups. Since March 1989, the population has been divided into five groups on the basis of race: White; Black; American Indian, Eskimo, or Aleut; Asian or Pacific Islander; and Other races. The last category includes any other race except the four mentioned. In most of the published tables, Other races are included in the total population data line but are not shown individually.

Reference person. The reference person serves as the central point for determining relationships within the household. The household reference person is the person listed as the householder. (See Householder for more information.) The subfamily reference person is either the single parent or the husband or wife in a married-couple situation.

Rounding. Percentages are rounded to the nearest 10th of a percent; therefore, the percentages in a distribution do not always sum to exactly 100 percent.

School, Dropout rate, annual high school. The annual high school dropout rate is an estimate of the proportion of students who drop out of school in a single year. This section briefly explains how the annual dropout rate is calculated; for further explanation and details of its derivation, see *Current Population Report (Series P-20, No. 413): "School Enrollment—Social and Economic Characteristics of Students: October 1983."*

Annual dropout rates for a single grade (X) are estimated as the ratio between the number of people enrolled in grade (X) in the year preceding the survey who did not complete grade (X) and are not currently enrolled to the number enrolled in grade (X) at the start of the year preceding this survey. People reported as enrolled last year but not currently enrolled are presented by the highest grade completed in Table 8 of the *Current Population Report* on school enrollment. They are presumed to

have dropped out of the succeeding grade (except for those who graduated this year). Thus, individuals counted as 10th grade dropouts are those whose highest grade completed is the 9th grade, but who are not currently enrolled in school. (The dropout classification also includes those people who finished the 9th grade in the spring preceding the survey and were not enrolled on the survey date.) These estimates form the numerator of the annual grade-specific dropout rate.

People currently enrolled in high school are presumed to have been enrolled in and have successfully completed the preceding grade during the preceding year. For example, those who have successfully completed the 10th grade would be enrolled in the 11th grade. Along with the people who dropped out of that grade, they comprise the denominator of the estimate of the annual grade-specific dropout rate:

$$\text{Dropout from Grade n} = \frac{\text{Not enrolled and highest grade completed} = n-1}{(\text{Enrolled in } n+1 + \text{Not enrolled and highest grade completed} = n-1)}$$

It cannot be presumed that all 12th grade graduates will enroll in college. The estimate of the number of people enrolled in the 12th grade one year prior to the survey is constructed as the sum of the number of people reported to have graduated from high school "this year" (whether or not they are currently enrolled in college) and those not currently enrolled who were enrolled last year and whose highest grade completed is the 11th grade (dropouts). The annual dropout rate for all grades during one year can be obtained by summing the components of the rates for the individual grades—the sum of all people previously enrolled in the 10th, 11th, or 12th grade last year, but who are not currently enrolled and do not have a high school diploma.

In addition to the annual rate, two other estimates of dropouts are frequently used. The annual dropout rate is different from a "pool" (or status) measure, such as the proportion of high school dropouts within an age group. A third measure of dropouts is the "cohort measure," most commonly from a longitudinal study, in which the proportion of a specific group of people enrolled in a specific year is calculated. These people did not receive diplomas (and are no longer in school) some years later. For example, the proportion of a cohort enrolled in 9th grade in year X, who were not enrolled and had not received a diploma by year X equals 4.

School enrollment. The school enrollment statistics from the CPS are based on replies to inquiries concerning current regular school enrollment. Those counted as enrolled had attended a public, parochial, or other private school in the regular school system at ant time during the current or previous school year. Such schools include nursery schools, kindergartens, elementary schools, high schools, colleges, universities, and professional schools. Attendance could have been on either a full-time or part-time basis during the day or night. Regular schooling is that which advances a person toward an elementary or high school diploma or toward a college, university, or professional school degree. Children enrolled in nursery schools and kindergarten are included in the enrollment figures for regular schools and are shown separately.

Enrollment in schools not in the regular school system, such as trade schools, business colleges, and schools for the mentally handicapped is not included, as these schools do not advance students toward regular school degrees.

People enrolled in classes not requiring their physical presence in school, such as correspondence courses or other courses of independent study, and those enrolled in training courses given directly on the job, are also excluded from the count of those enrolled in school, unless such courses are being counted for credit at a regular school.

School enrollment in the year preceding current survey. All respondents were asked to state their school enrollment status as of October of the preceding year. Before 1988, this question was only asked of people not currently attending regular school and people who were enrolled in college. In the tabulations of previous year's secondary school enrollment, those currently enrolled in high school were assumed to have been enrolled the previous year.

Comparability of enrollment data in previous years. Changes in the edit and tabulation packages used to process the October CPS school enrollment supplement caused some minor revisions to the estimates. The current edit and tabulation package

began with 1987 data. The 1986 data published in the *Current Population Report (Series P-20 No. 429)* were reprocessed with the rewritten programs in order to clarify comparability. Time series tables usually show only the revised estimates for 1986. The previous edit and tabulation package was used from 1967 to 1986.

Major changes in the data caused by to the 1987 edit revisions were: (1) Among 14- and 15-year-olds, an edit improvement allowed people with unreported enrollment data, who were previously imputed as "not enrolled," to be enrolled; (2) Revisions in the tabulation of enrollment in the previous year simplified the calculation of an annual high school dropout rate; (3) Edit improvements caused increases in college enrollment estimates, most notably above the age of 24. This age group was largely ignored in earlier edits; (4) Type of college is fully allocated (discussed earlier in the section); (5) Tabulations of type of college (2-year and 4-year colleges) were made available by race; (6) Dependent family members became consistently defined; (7) New tabulations of employment status, vocational course enrollment, college retention and re-entry, and families with children enrolled in public and private school became available beginning in 1987.

In the series of reports on school enrollment for 1987 to 1992, race and Hispanic origin were erroneously tabulated for a small percentage of children age 3 to 14 years. Race and Hispanic origin of an adult in the household were attributed to the child, rather than using the child's reported characteristics. In the vast majority of cases, these characteristics were the same for family members, but for a small percentage of children, they were different. The correction made the following proportional changes in the numbers of children in each group: White (-0.5 percent), Black (+3.1 percent), and Hispanic (-4.6 percent).

Published data on enrollment from the October CPS for 1981 to 1993 used population controls based on the 1980 census. Beginning in 1994, estimates used 1990 census–based population controls, including adjustment for undercount. Time series tables show two sets of data for 1993; the data labeled "1993r" were processed using population controls based on the 1990 census with adjustments for undercount. The change in 1994 from a paper-and-pencil survey to a computer-assisted survey had some affect on the data. Most notably, the enrollment question for children age 3 to 5 years was different from the question for older children—it included a reference to nursery school. In 1994, reported nursery school enrollment was significantly higher than in earlier years.

Attendance, full time and part time. College students are classified according to their attendance status. A student is categorized as attending college full time if he or she was taking 12 or more hours of classes during the average school week, and part time if he or she was taking less than 12 hours of classes per average school week.

College enrollment. The college enrollment statistics are based on reports of school enrollment, including the grade in which the respondent was enrolled. Students enrolled in college at any time during the current term or school year were counted as enrolled, except those who had left for the remainder of the term. Thus, regular college enrollment includes those attending two-year or four-year colleges, universities, or professional schools (such as medical or law schools) in courses that advance students toward a recognized college or university degree (such as a B.A. or an M.A.). Attendance may be full time or part time during the day or night. The college student need not be working toward a degree, but he or she must be enrolled in a class for which credit would be applied toward a degree. (See school enrollment for more information.) Students are classified by year of college, based on the academic year (not calendar year). The undergraduate years are the first through fourth year, or freshman through senior years. Graduate or professional school years include the fifth year and higher.

Two-year and four-year colleges. College students were asked if their school was a two-year college (junior or community college) or a four-year college or university. Students enrolled in the first four years of college (undergraduates) were classified by the type of school that they attended. Graduate students are shown as a separate group.

Vocational school enrollment. Vocational school enrollment includes enrollment in business, vocational, technical, secretarial, trade, or correspon-

dence courses that are not counted as regular school enrollment. This category excludes recreation or adult education classes. Courses that counted as college enrollment are also excluded.

School, Modal grade. Enrolled people are classified according to their relative progress in school and whether the grade or year in which they were enrolled was below, at, or above the modal (or typical) grade for students of their age at the time of the survey. The modal grade is the year of school in which the largest proportion of students of a given age were enrolled.

School, Nursery. A nursery school is defined as a group or class that has been organized to provide educational experiences for children during the year or years preceding kindergarten. It includes instruction as an important and integral phase of its childcare program. Private homes, in which essentially custodial care is provided, are not considered nursery schools. Children attending nursery school are classified as attending for part of the day or for the full day. Part-day attendance refers to those who attend either in the morning or in the afternoon. Full-day attendance refers to those who attend in the morning and in the afternoon. Children enrolled in Head Start programs or similar local agency-sponsored programs that provide preschool education to young children are counted as being enrolled in under nursery school.

School, Public or private. A public school is defined as any educational institution operated by publicly elected or appointed school officials and supported by public funds. Private schools include educational institutions established and operated by religious bodies, as well as those that are under other private controls. In cases in which a school or college was both publicly and privately controlled or supported, enrollment was counted according to whether the school was primarily public or private.

Undocumented immigrants or illegal aliens. Since all residents of the United States living in households are represented in the sample of households interviewed by the CPS, undocumented immigrants or illegal aliens are probably included in CPS data. Because the CPS makes no attempt to ascertain the legal status of any person interviewed, these individuals cannot be identified from CPS data.

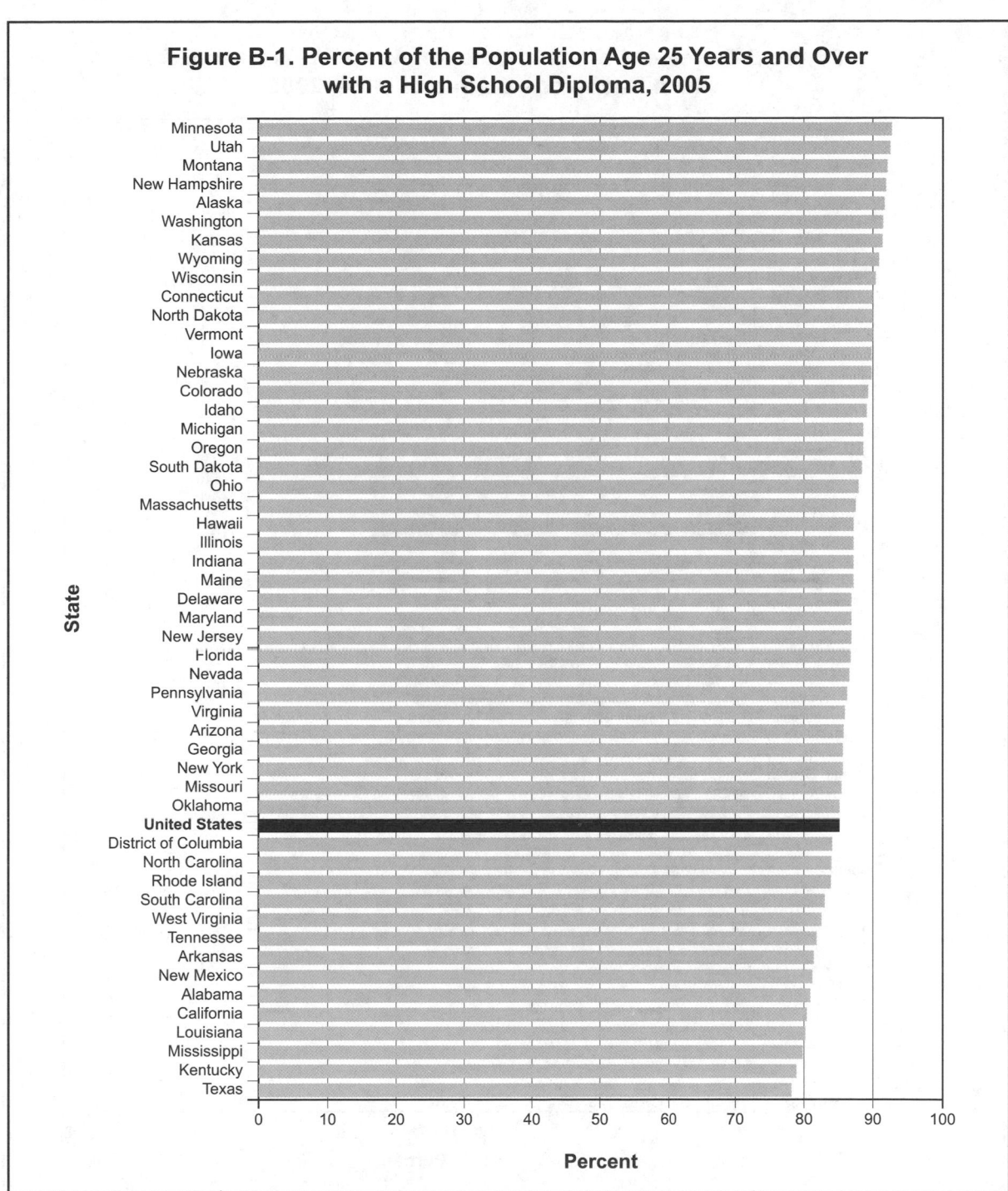

Figure B-1. Percent of the Population Age 25 Years and Over with a High School Diploma, 2005

In 2005, 85.2 percent of the U.S. population over 25 years of age had graduated from high school. Twelve states had high school attainment levels of 90 percent or more, and only three states had high school attainment levels below 80 percent. In 1975, less than two-thirds of people over 25 years of age had graduated from high school.

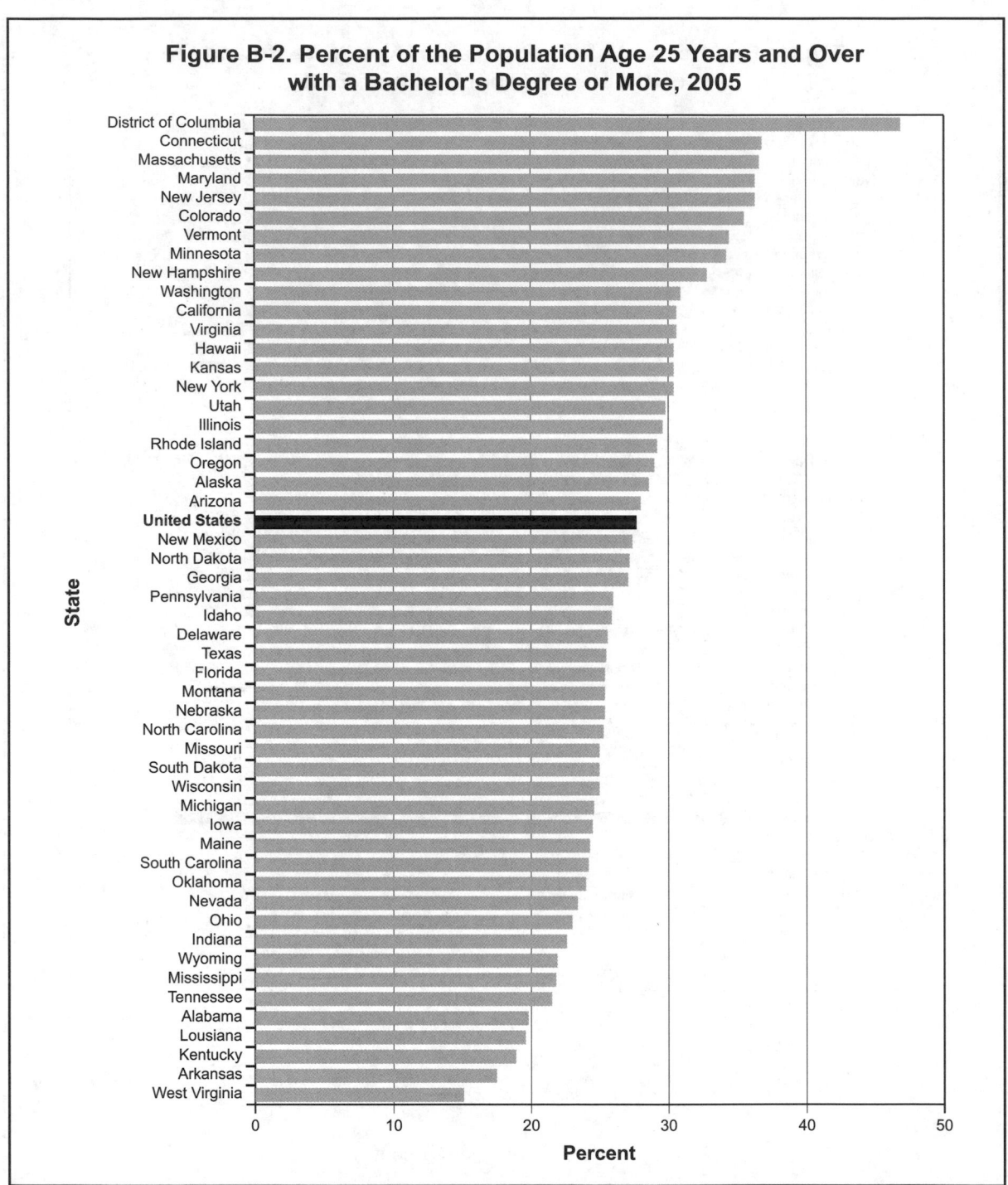

Figure B-2. Percent of the Population Age 25 Years and Over with a Bachelor's Degree or More, 2005

The percentage of the U.S. population with a bachelor's degree or more remained stable at 27.7 percent from 2004 to 2005. In the District of Columbia, approximately 47 percent of the residents held a bachelor's degree, by far the highest rate in the nation. Only five states had college attainment levels of less than 20 percent, with West Virginia ranking last at 15.1 percent.

Table B-1. Educational Attainment of the Population Age 18 Years and Over, by Region, Age, Sex, Race, and Hispanic Origin, 2005

(Numbers in thousands.)

Region, age, sex, race, and Hispanic origin	Total	Elementary	High school		College					
		None to 8th grade	9th to 11th grade	High school graduate	Some college, no degree	Associate's degree	Bachelor's degree	Master's degree	Professional degree	Doctorate degree
ALL RACES										
Northeast										
Both sexes										
18 years and over	41 059	2 035	3 717	14 069	6 325	3 067	7 496	3 063	793	491
18 to 24 years	4 936	100	858	1 485	1 780	222	471	20	-	-
25 to 34 years	6 736	240	431	1 922	1 014	568	1 749	585	165	61
35 to 44 years	8 461	284	515	2 867	1 111	782	1 862	715	218	107
45 to 54 years	8 183	293	495	2 795	1 033	757	1 682	818	168	142
55 to 64 years	5 702	277	429	2 034	763	422	941	595	127	114
65 years and over	7 041	841	990	2 965	624	317	791	330	115	67
18 to 24 years	4 936	100	858	1 485	1 780	222	471	20	-	-
25 years and over	36 123	1 935	2 860	12 585	4 545	2 845	7 025	3 043	793	491
Male										
18 years and over	19 593	989	1 777	6 771	3 035	1 289	3 547	1 357	489	341
18 to 24 years	2 518	60	452	847	861	94	197	6	-	-
25 to 34 years	3 331	123	232	1 037	498	259	810	230	108	33
35 to 44 years	4 147	180	271	1 548	513	291	848	311	120	65
45 to 54 years	3 987	152	239	1 428	456	328	815	367	103	99
55 to 64 years	2 713	139	191	831	388	193	506	291	85	89
65 years and over	2 898	335	393	1 079	318	124	369	153	73	55
18 to 24 years	2 518	60	452	847	861	94	197	6	-	-
25 years and over	17 075	929	1 325	5 923	2 173	1 195	3 349	1 351	489	341
Female										
18 years and over	21 466	1 046	1 940	7 299	3 291	1 779	3 950	1 706	304	151
18 to 24 years	2 418	39	406	637	918	129	274	14	-	-
25 to 34 years	3 406	117	199	885	516	310	939	355	57	28
35 to 44 years	4 314	104	244	1 319	598	490	1 014	404	98	42
45 to 54 years	4 195	141	256	1 368	577	429	867	451	65	43
55 to 64 years	2 989	138	238	1 203	375	229	434	304	42	26
65 years and over	4 144	506	597	1 886	307	193	423	178	42	13
18 to 24 years	2 418	39	406	637	918	129	274	14	-	-
25 years and over	19 048	1 007	1 534	6 661	2 372	1 650	3 676	1 092	304	151
Midwest										
Both sexes										
18 years and over	48 555	1 774	4 425	16 824	9 556	4 336	7 888	2 737	563	452
18 to 24 years	6 315	109	1 232	1 830	2 230	341	558	12	2	-
25 to 34 years	8 615	184	603	2 695	1 676	866	1 977	475	84	54
35 to 44 years	9 339	171	571	3 090	1 593	1 100	1 910	663	131	110
45 to 54 years	9 674	177	484	3 450	1 772	1 086	1 705	729	160	111
55 to 64 years	6 678	209	471	2 542	1 202	554	945	544	106	106
65 years and over	7 934	925	1 063	3 216	1 083	388	794	314	80	71
18 to 24 years	6 315	109	1 232	1 830	2 230	341	558	12	2	-
25 years and over	42 240	1 665	3 193	14 993	7 326	3 994	7 330	2 725	561	452
Male										
18 years and over	23 427	902	2 152	8 249	4 423	1 883	3 814	1 317	373	315
18 to 24 years	3 143	65	637	1 004	1 028	172	237	-	-	-
25 to 34 years	4 327	109	312	1 498	781	405	929	217	49	27
35 to 44 years	4 568	90	313	1 614	711	497	905	309	64	65
45 to 54 years	4 752	100	228	1 755	869	444	832	330	113	82
55 to 64 years	3 177	107	236	1 122	574	226	500	254	82	78
65 years and over	3 460	432	425	1 257	461	139	412	207	65	63
18 to 24 years	3 143	65	637	1 004	1 028	172	237	-	-	-
25 years and over	20 284	836	1 515	7 246	3 396	1 711	3 577	1 316	373	315
Female										
18 years and over	25 128	873	2 273	8 574	5 133	2 452	4 074	1 421	190	136
18 to 24 years	3 171	44	595	827	1 202	169	322	12	2	-
25 to 34 years	4 287	75	291	1 197	896	462	1 047	258	35	27
35 to 44 years	4 772	81	259	1 476	882	603	1 005	354	67	44
45 to 54 years	4 923	77	256	1 695	904	641	873	399	48	29
55 to 64 years	3 501	102	236	1 420	628	328	445	291	24	28
65 years and over	4 474	493	638	1 960	622	249	382	107	15	8
18 to 24 years	3 171	44	595	827	1 202	169	322	12	2	-
25 years and over	21 956	829	1 679	7 748	3 931	2 283	3 753	1 409	189	136

- = Quantity zero or rounds to zero.

Table B-1. Educational Attainment of the Population Age 18 Years and Over, by Region, Age, Sex, Race, and Hispanic Origin, 2005—*Continued*

(Numbers in thousands.)

Region, age, sex, race, and Hispanic origin	Total	Elementary None to 8th grade	High school 9th to 11th grade	High school graduate	Some college, no degree	Associate's degree	Bachelor's degree	Master's degree	Professional degree	Doctorate degree
ALL RACES										
South										
Both sexes										
18 years and over	78 319	5 112	8 873	25 544	14 878	6 003	12 140	4 034	944	792
18 to 24 years	10 170	300	2 071	3 254	3 344	394	756	41	4	5
25 to 34 years	14 321	638	1 437	4 273	2 721	1 264	3 006	752	155	75
35 to 44 years	15 474	680	1 256	5 254	2 667	1 446	2 800	951	238	182
45 to 54 years	14 735	668	1 278	4 924	2 613	1 376	2 541	940	212	182
55 to 64 years	10 855	781	1 075	3 527	1 753	884	1 681	797	148	209
65 years and over	12 764	2 044	1 756	4 311	1 780	638	1 356	553	187	138
18 to 24 years	10 170	300	2 071	3 254	3 344	394	756	41	4	5
25 years and over	68 149	4 812	6 801	22 290	11 534	5 608	11 384	3 993	940	787
Male										
18 years and over	37 680	2 621	4 486	12 465	6 837	2 487	5 800	1 859	618	507
18 to 24 years	5 119	193	1 161	1 778	1 527	162	282	11	-	5
25 to 34 years	7 070	384	785	2 320	1 324	560	1 299	297	71	30
35 to 44 years	7 661	394	693	2 793	1 162	595	1 338	442	155	89
45 to 54 years	7 179	359	642	2 393	1 255	560	1 259	457	142	112
55 to 64 years	5 105	403	506	1 546	768	373	867	390	97	154
65 years and over	5 546	889	698	1 633	801	237	754	261	155	117
18 to 24 years	5 119	193	1 161	1 778	1 527	162	282	11	-	5
25 years and over	32 561	2 428	3 325	10 687	5 310	2 326	5 517	1 848	618	502
Female										
18 years and over	40 638	2 491	4 387	13 079	8 041	3 515	6 341	2 174	326	285
18 to 24 years	5 051	107	910	1 476	1 817	233	474	29	4	-
25 to 34 years	7 250	254	652	1 953	1 397	704	1 707	455	84	45
35 to 44 years	7 813	287	562	2 460	1 506	851	1 462	509	83	93
45 to 54 years	7 556	309	636	2 531	1 358	816	1 282	483	70	71
55 to 64 years	5 750	378	568	1 981	984	511	814	407	51	55
65 years and over	7 218	1 155	1 058	2 678	979	401	602	292	32	21
18 to 24 years	5 051	107	910	1 476	1 817	233	474	29	4	-
25 years and over	35 588	2 384	3 477	11 603	6 224	3 283	5 867	2 145	321	285
West										
Both sexes										
18 years and over	49 443	3 790	4 413	12 840	10 911	4 141	8 992	3 092	646	617
18 to 24 years	6 588	285	1 169	1 814	2 508	322	472	13	5	-
25 to 34 years	9 639	727	951	2 379	1 945	810	2 103	550	105	68
35 to 44 years	10 076	787	767	2 532	1 916	988	2 167	643	165	112
45 to 54 years	9 369	650	526	2 319	1 951	938	1 887	789	162	146
55 to 64 years	6 301	446	345	1 496	1 275	631	1 257	597	98	157
65 years and over	7 470	894	655	2 300	1 317	453	1 106	500	110	134
18 to 24 years	6 588	285	1 169	1 814	2 508	322	472	13	5	-
25 years and over	42 855	3 504	3 244	11 026	8 404	3 820	8 520	3 079	641	617
Male										
18 years and over	24 266	1 894	2 261	6 269	5 153	1 816	4 398	1 620	425	430
18 to 24 years	3 287	180	638	973	1 156	129	201	4	5	-
25 to 34 years	4 948	395	498	1 359	979	392	1 007	226	51	41
35 to 44 years	5 093	414	413	1 332	966	456	1 025	331	87	67
45 to 54 years	4 638	336	264	1 153	920	405	917	434	119	90
55 to 64 years	3 056	232	159	628	586	272	643	339	78	120
65 years and over	3 243	338	287	822	546	161	606	286	85	111
18 to 24 years	3 287	180	638	973	1 156	129	201	4	5	-
25 years and over	20 979	1 714	1 622	5 295	3 997	1 687	4 197	1 617	420	430
Female										
18 years and over	25 177	1 895	2 153	6 571	5 758	2 325	4 594	1 472	221	188
18 to 24 years	3 301	105	531	841	1 351	192	271	9	-	-
25 to 34 years	4 690	333	453	1 019	965	418	1 096	324	54	27
35 to 44 years	4 983	373	354	1 199	950	531	1 142	311	78	45
45 to 54 years	4 731	314	262	1 166	1 031	533	970	356	43	56
55 to 64 years	3 245	214	186	868	689	359	615	258	20	37
65 years and over	4 227	556	368	1 478	771	292	501	213	25	23
18 to 24 years	3 301	105	531	841	1 351	192	271	9	-	-
25 years and over	21 876	1 790	1 622	5 730	4 407	2 133	4 323	1 463	221	188

- = Quantity zero or rounds to zero.

Table B-1. Educational Attainment of the Population Age 18 Years and Over, by Region, Age, Sex, Race, and Hispanic Origin, 2005—*Continued*

(Numbers in thousands.)

Region, age, sex, race, and Hispanic origin	Total	Elementary — None to 8th grade	High school — 9th to 11th grade	High school graduate	College — Some college, no degree	Associate's degree	Bachelor's degree	Master's degree	Professional degree	Doctorate degree
NON-HISPANIC WHITE ALONE OR IN COMBINATION										
Northeast										
Both sexes										
18 years and over	30 985	994	2 226	10 815	4 807	2 450	6 069	2 585	649	391
18 to 24 years	3 477	35	496	1 021	1 336	176	396	16	-	-
25 to 34 years	4 470	78	165	1 226	681	406	1 301	452	114	47
35 to 44 years	6 096	87	245	2 080	792	612	1 437	579	182	81
45 to 54 years	6 332	91	261	2 154	793	638	1 437	699	147	112
55 to 64 years	4 646	133	276	1 654	655	351	817	554	112	95
65 years and over	5 965	570	783	2 680	550	268	681	285	94	55
18 to 24 years	3 477	35	496	1 021	1 336	176	396	16	-	-
25 years and over	27 509	958	1 729	9 794	3 471	2 274	5 674	2 569	649	391
Male										
18 years and over	14 915	482	1 077	5 198	2 374	1 042	2 942	1 134	397	268
18 to 24 years	1 801	20	268	596	665	77	171	4	-	-
25 to 34 years	2 242	48	91	664	352	197	613	171	81	26
35 to 44 years	3 009	61	149	1 139	380	224	664	249	96	47
45 to 54 years	3 134	49	132	1 126	351	284	713	312	90	76
55 to 64 years	2 268	72	131	691	342	162	453	269	74	74
65 years and over	2 461	232	305	982	285	98	328	130	57	45
18 to 24 years	1 801	20	268	596	665	77	171	4	-	-
25 years and over	13 114	462	809	4 602	1 709	965	2 771	1 130	397	268
Female										
18 years and over	16 071	512	1 148	5 616	2 433	1 408	3 128	1 451	252	122
18 to 24 years	1 676	16	228	425	671	99	225	12	-	-
25 to 34 years	2 227	30	75	562	329	208	688	281	33	22
35 to 44 years	3 087	25	95	942	412	389	774	330	86	34
45 to 54 years	3 198	41	129	1 028	442	354	724	388	57	35
55 to 64 years	2 378	62	144	963	314	189	364	285	38	20
65 years and over	3 504	338	478	1 698	265	170	353	154	37	11
18 to 24 years	1 676	16	228	425	671	99	225	12	-	-
25 years and over	14 395	496	920	5 191	1 762	1 310	2 903	1 439	252	122
Midwest										
Both sexes										
18 years and over	40 431	1 064	3 193	14 218	7 984	3 849	6 914	2 346	484	378
18 to 24 years	4 907	44	843	1 397	1 820	295	502	7	2	-
25 to 34 years	6 563	44	351	2 045	1 200	740	1 653	355	70	46
35 to 44 years	7 669	54	388	2 523	1 328	983	1 670	543	102	78
45 to 54 years	8 254	71	335	2 965	1 519	982	1 495	646	142	98
55 to 64 years	5 851	113	388	2 286	1 048	495	832	503	94	91
65 years and over	7 188	738	888	3 001	1 011	355	763	292	74	65
18 to 24 years	4 907	44	843	1 397	1 820	295	502	7	2	-
25 years and over	35 524	1 021	2 350	12 821	6 165	3 555	6 413	2 340	482	378
Male										
18 years and over	19 511	540	1 563	6 931	3 731	1 677	3 349	1 117	334	269
18 to 24 years	2 441	26	438	764	847	151	216	-	-	-
25 to 34 years	3 281	26	198	1 150	606	342	757	136	42	23
35 to 44 years	3 751	35	216	1 311	592	451	787	257	53	49
45 to 54 years	4 101	44	156	1 527	756	408	744	292	104	72
55 to 64 years	2 784	59	194	1 005	501	204	445	235	73	67
65 years and over	3 153	351	361	1 174	430	121	400	196	61	57
18 to 24 years	2 441	26	438	764	847	151	216	-	-	-
25 years and over	17 070	515	1 126	6 167	2 884	1 526	3 133	1 117	334	269
Female										
18 years and over	20 920	524	1 630	7 287	4 253	2 172	3 565	1 230	150	109
18 to 24 years	2 466	18	405	633	973	144	286	7	2	-
25 to 34 years	3 282	18	153	895	654	398	895	219	27	22
35 to 44 years	3 918	19	172	1 212	736	531	883	286	49	29
45 to 54 years	4 152	27	179	1 438	763	575	751	354	38	27
55 to 64 years	3 067	54	194	1 282	547	291	387	268	21	23
65 years and over	4 035	387	527	1 828	581	233	363	96	13	8
18 to 24 years	2 466	18	405	633	973	144	286	7	2	-
25 years and over	18 454	506	1 225	6 655	3 280	2 028	3 280	1 223	148	109

- = Quantity zero or rounds to zero.

Table B-1. Educational Attainment of the Population Age 18 Years and Over, by Region, Age, Sex, Race, and Hispanic Origin, 2005—*Continued*

(Numbers in thousands.)

Region, age, sex, race, and Hispanic origin	Total	Elementary	High school		College					
		None to 8th grade	9th to 11th grade	High school graduate	Some college, no degree	Associate's degree	Bachelor's degree	Master's degree	Professional degree	Doctorate degree
NON-HISPANIC WHITE ALONE OR IN COMBINATION										
South										
Both sexes										
18 years and over	52 420	2 052	4 775	16 999	10 388	4 416	9 284	3 127	750	630
18 to 24 years	5 899	72	1 017	1 821	2 136	257	561	27	2	5
25 to 34 years	8 212	100	556	2 318	1 640	827	2 110	508	105	48
35 to 44 years	9 881	193	583	3 271	1 776	1 019	2 041	680	186	133
45 to 54 years	10 195	229	729	3 286	1 869	1 058	1 955	756	173	139
55 to 64 years	8 153	378	643	2 615	1 383	704	1 447	681	123	180
65 years and over	10 080	1 080	1 247	3 687	1 584	551	1 171	475	159	125
18 to 24 years	5 899	72	1 017	1 821	2 136	257	561	27	2	5
25 years and over	46 522	1 980	3 759	15 177	8 252	4 159	8 724	3 100	747	625
Male										
18 years and over	25 320	1 067	2 449	8 166	4 827	1 847	4 570	1 469	515	411
18 to 24 years	2 924	43	579	989	976	120	205	8	-	5
25 to 34 years	4 077	58	329	1 299	789	380	946	204	52	20
35 to 44 years	4 921	130	341	1 752	799	414	986	313	125	60
45 to 54 years	5 065	129	401	1 582	939	436	996	372	123	87
55 to 64 years	3 861	203	299	1 142	608	297	761	336	83	131
65 years and over	4 474	503	500	1 402	716	200	677	236	133	107
18 to 24 years	2 924	43	579	989	976	120	205	8	-	5
25 years and over	22 397	1 024	1 870	7 177	3 852	1 727	4 365	1 461	515	406
Female										
18 years and over	27 100	985	2 326	8 832	5 561	2 569	4 714	1 658	235	219
18 to 24 years	2 975	29	437	832	1 161	137	356	19	2	-
25 to 34 years	4 136	41	227	1 019	851	447	1 164	305	53	28
35 to 44 years	4 961	63	242	1 519	977	605	1 054	366	62	72
45 to 54 years	5 130	100	328	1 705	930	622	960	384	51	52
55 to 64 years	4 292	175	344	1 473	774	407	686	345	40	48
65 years and over	5 606	576	748	2 285	868	351	494	239	26	19
18 to 24 years	2 975	29	437	832	1 161	137	356	19	2	-
25 years and over	24 125	956	1 889	8 000	4 400	2 432	4 358	1 638	232	219
West										
Both sexes										
18 years and over	30 463	516	1 716	7 948	7 499	2 882	6 457	2 439	496	510
18 to 24 years	3 550	25	487	928	1 558	202	341	4	5	-
25 to 34 years	4 894	45	220	1 145	1 174	454	1 346	389	69	52
35 to 44 years	5 713	21	200	1 455	1 233	649	1 500	451	119	84
45 to 54 years	6 226	37	198	1 535	1 451	738	1 368	645	133	122
55 to 64 years	4 460	73	167	1 064	982	474	970	517	78	133
65 years and over	5 620	315	445	1 822	1 101	364	931	432	91	119
18 to 24 years	3 550	25	487	928	1 558	202	341	4	5	-
25 years and over	26 912	491	1 229	7 020	5 941	2 680	6 116	2 435	491	510
Male										
18 years and over	14 863	222	905	3 786	3 496	1 269	3 212	1 289	330	353
18 to 24 years	1 776	10	280	518	731	85	145	2	5	-
25 to 34 years	2 451	20	125	648	577	223	641	148	36	32
35 to 44 years	2 899	8	114	784	627	304	721	230	65	46
45 to 54 years	3 066	15	111	750	660	322	686	354	94	74
55 to 64 years	2 222	44	82	464	456	204	507	300	61	102
65 years and over	2 449	125	192	622	445	130	511	254	69	99
18 to 24 years	1 776	10	280	518	731	85	145	2	5	-
25 years and over	13 087	212	625	3 268	2 765	1 184	3 067	1 287	325	353
Female										
18 years and over	15 600	293	811	4 162	4 003	1 613	3 246	1 149	166	156
18 to 24 years	1 774	15	207	410	827	116	196	2	-	-
25 to 34 years	2 443	25	95	497	596	230	705	241	33	20
35 to 44 years	2 814	13	86	671	607	346	780	221	54	38
45 to 54 years	3 160	22	86	785	791	416	682	291	39	48
55 to 64 years	2 238	29	85	600	526	270	463	217	17	32
65 years and over	3 171	189	252	1 199	657	234	420	178	23	19
18 to 24 years	1 774	15	207	410	827	116	196	2	-	-
25 years and over	13 826	278	604	3 752	3 176	1 496	3 049	1 147	166	156

- = Quantity zero or rounds to zero.

Table B-1. Educational Attainment of the Population Age 18 Years and Over, by Region, Age, Sex, Race, and Hispanic Origin, 2005—*Continued*

(Numbers in thousands.)

Region, age, sex, race, and Hispanic origin	Total	Elementary None to 8th grade	High school 9th to 11th grade	High school graduate	Some college, no degree	Associate's degree	Bachelor's degree	Master's degree	Professional degree	Doctorate degree
BLACK ALONE OR IN COMBINATION										
Northeast										
Both sexes										
18 years and over	4 795	252	738	1 824	828	339	587	168	37	22
18 to 24 years	744	14	199	264	216	25	26	-	-	-
25 to 34 years	923	25	94	347	174	83	160	25	12	3
35 to 44 years	1 074	31	117	429	175	86	186	39	8	3
45 to 54 years	890	41	97	365	137	66	124	55	2	3
55 to 64 years	552	33	102	215	73	48	42	27	5	7
65 years and over	613	108	129	204	53	31	49	23	10	6
18 to 24 years	744	14	199	264	216	25	26	-	-	-
25 years and over	4 052	238	539	1 560	612	314	561	168	37	22
Male										
18 years and over	2 100	114	342	837	343	130	241	58	20	15
18 to 24 years	336	9	92	134	83	8	9	-	-	-
25 to 34 years	437	6	48	181	76	34	78	5	6	3
35 to 44 years	479	14	54	213	72	32	76	11	6	1
45 to 54 years	397	22	47	176	60	26	44	21	2	-
55 to 64 years	214	13	46	75	31	18	14	11	2	5
65 years and over	236	50	55	58	21	13	20	10	4	5
18 to 24 years	336	9	92	134	83	8	9	-	-	-
25 years and over	1 764	105	250	703	260	122	231	58	20	15
Female										
18 years and over	2 695	138	396	987	485	209	346	111	17	8
18 to 24 years	408	5	107	130	133	17	16	-	-	-
25 to 34 years	486	19	46	166	98	49	82	20	6	-
35 to 44 years	595	17	63	216	103	54	110	27	2	2
45 to 54 years	493	19	50	189	77	40	80	34	-	3
55 to 64 years	307	20	56	140	42	31	20	16	3	1
65 years and over	377	58	74	146	32	18	30	13	5	1
18 to 24 years	408	5	107	130	133	17	16	-	-	-
25 years and over	2 288	133	289	857	352	192	330	111	17	8
Midwest										
Both sexes										
18 years and over	4 586	157	708	1 697	1 041	321	461	166	20	16
18 to 24 years	752	10	205	267	222	27	20	2	-	-
25 to 34 years	1 000	11	114	350	297	77	117	29	5	-
35 to 44 years	890	6	94	362	177	78	119	40	8	8
45 to 54 years	888	5	90	357	176	77	121	53	6	3
55 to 64 years	520	26	59	185	116	37	65	27	-	5
65 years and over	536	99	146	176	53	25	20	15	2	1
18 to 24 years	752	10	205	267	222	27	20	2	-	-
25 years and over	3 834	147	503	1 430	819	293	441	164	20	16
Male										
18 years and over	2 039	77	303	826	427	131	185	72	9	10
18 to 24 years	349	6	104	135	88	11	5	-	-	-
25 to 34 years	434	5	36	175	105	34	55	20	4	-
35 to 44 years	409	4	43	189	78	30	47	12	1	5
45 to 54 years	395	-	42	173	82	27	44	23	2	2
55 to 64 years	230	10	28	82	53	15	29	9	-	2
65 years and over	222	51	49	71	22	14	5	7	2	1
18 to 24 years	349	6	104	135	88	11	5	-	-	-
25 years and over	1 690	71	198	691	340	121	180	72	9	10
Female										
18 years and over	2 547	80	405	871	614	189	276	94	11	7
18 to 24 years	404	4	100	132	134	16	15	2	-	-
25 to 34 years	566	5	78	175	192	42	62	10	1	-
35 to 44 years	481	2	51	172	99	47	72	28	7	3
45 to 54 years	493	5	48	183	95	50	77	29	4	1
55 to 64 years	290	16	31	103	63	22	36	18	-	2
65 years and over	314	47	97	106	30	11	15	8	-	-
18 to 24 years	404	4	100	132	134	16	15	2	-	-
25 years and over	2 144	76	305	739	480	173	261	92	11	7

- = Quantity zero or rounds to zero.

Table B-1. Educational Attainment of the Population Age 18 Years and Over, by Region, Age, Sex, Race, and Hispanic Origin, 2005—*Continued*

(Numbers in thousands.)

Region, age, sex, race, and Hispanic origin	Total	Elementary		High school		College					
		None to 8th grade	9th to 11th grade	High school graduate	Some college, no degree	Associate's degree	Bachelor's degree	Master's degree	Professional degree	Doctorate degree
BLACK ALONE OR IN COMBINATION										
South										
Both sexes										
18 years and over	13 971	785	2 164	5 170	2 819	978	1 494	437	68	57
18 to 24 years	2 287	34	539	778	743	72	116	6	-	-
25 to 34 years	2 840	41	289	1 063	621	266	446	96	15	3
35 to 44 years	2 939	49	332	1 252	545	244	385	106	12	15
45 to 54 years	2 711	90	316	1 075	544	213	330	103	20	20
55 to 64 years	1 624	133	296	631	231	124	119	68	7	16
65 years and over	1 570	439	392	372	136	59	99	57	14	2
18 to 24 years	2 287	34	539	778	743	72	116	6	-	-
25 years and over	11 684	752	1 625	4 392	2 076	906	1 378	431	68	57
Male										
18 years and over	6 203	354	1 003	2 560	1 178	350	550	147	32	30
18 to 24 years	1 113	22	286	409	346	13	35	2	-	-
25 to 34 years	1 222	23	129	545	258	90	145	27	4	2
35 to 44 years	1 324	19	164	640	202	96	144	42	9	8
45 to 54 years	1 227	41	141	547	232	80	134	37	6	8
55 to 64 years	730	79	132	288	92	48	53	26	2	11
65 years and over	587	169	152	131	48	22	39	13	11	1
18 to 24 years	1 113	22	286	409	346	13	35	2	-	-
25 years and over	5 090	332	717	2 151	832	336	515	145	32	30
Female										
18 years and over	7 768	432	1 161	2 610	1 641	628	944	289	36	27
18 to 24 years	1 174	12	253	370	397	59	81	4	-	-
25 to 34 years	1 618	17	160	518	363	176	301	70	11	2
35 to 44 years	1 615	30	168	612	343	147	241	64	3	7
45 to 54 years	1 484	49	176	528	312	133	195	66	14	12
55 to 64 years	894	54	165	343	138	76	65	42	5	5
65 years and over	983	269	240	241	88	37	60	44	3	-
18 to 24 years	1 174	12	253	370	397	59	81	4	-	-
25 years and over	6 594	420	908	2 241	1 244	569	863	286	36	27
West										
Both sexes										
18 years and over	2 494	75	254	763	674	248	341	105	23	12
18 to 24 years	377	-	70	120	140	26	22	-	-	-
25 to 34 years	538	20	27	182	147	62	77	17	2	4
35 to 44 years	569	12	53	164	134	64	96	40	2	5
45 to 54 years	450	8	37	132	118	32	84	27	9	3
55 to 64 years	274	4	22	78	66	44	40	13	6	-
65 years and over	287	30	46	86	71	20	22	7	4	-
18 to 24 years	377	-	70	120	140	26	22	-	-	-
25 years and over	2 117	75	184	643	535	222	320	105	23	12
Male										
18 years and over	1 191	40	116	368	335	111	158	44	16	4
18 to 24 years	163	-	29	54	63	6	10	-	-	-
25 to 34 years	296	9	14	107	83	32	45	6	-	-
35 to 44 years	260	8	26	69	59	32	42	22	-	2
45 to 54 years	220	5	15	70	66	13	34	9	7	2
55 to 64 years	125	3	14	28	29	22	17	5	6	-
65 years and over	126	15	18	38	35	6	10	2	3	-
18 to 24 years	163	-	29	54	63	6	10	-	-	-
25 years and over	1 029	40	87	313	272	105	148	44	16	4
Female										
18 years and over	1 303	35	138	395	339	137	183	61	7	8
18 to 24 years	214	-	40	66	76	20	12	-	-	-
25 to 34 years	241	11	12	75	64	30	32	11	2	4
35 to 44 years	308	4	27	95	75	32	54	18	2	2
45 to 54 years	230	3	22	63	52	19	50	19	2	1
55 to 64 years	149	2	7	49	36	23	23	8	-	-
65 years and over	161	15	28	48	36	14	13	6	1	-
18 to 24 years	214	-	40	66	76	20	12	-	-	-
25 years and over	1 089	35	97	329	263	117	172	61	7	8

- = Quantity zero or rounds to zero.

Table B-1. Educational Attainment of the Population Age 18 Years and Over, by Region, Age, Sex, Race, and Hispanic Origin, 2005—*Continued*

(Numbers in thousands.)

Region, age, sex, race, and Hispanic origin	Total	Elementary	High school		College					
		None to 8th grade	9th to 11th grade	High school graduate	Some college, no degree	Associate's degree	Bachelor's degree	Master's degree	Professional degree	Doctorate degree
ASIAN ALONE OR IN COMBINATION										
Northeast										
Both sexes										
18 years and over	1 937	167	132	405	199	107	552	223	87	65
18 to 24 years	196	4	38	41	84	4	24	2	-	-
25 to 34 years	482	10	19	68	33	24	199	86	30	13
35 to 44 years	498	23	22	113	43	28	157	68	24	20
45 to 54 years	351	38	30	99	24	27	64	40	14	15
55 to 64 years	226	31	11	66	12	15	59	12	10	10
65 years and over	183	61	12	19	4	9	50	15	8	5
18 to 24 years	196	4	38	41	84	4	24	2	-	-
25 years and over	1 740	162	94	365	115	103	528	221	87	65
Male										
18 years and over	936	66	54	211	99	44	232	126	60	45
18 to 24 years	108	4	21	23	48	4	7	-	-	-
25 to 34 years	212	5	9	36	12	3	84	41	14	7
35 to 44 years	262	8	11	60	23	10	79	41	17	12
45 to 54 years	180	19	12	54	10	8	27	25	12	12
55 to 64 years	103	12	1	27	4	10	21	10	9	8
65 years and over	72	17	-	11	1	8	13	9	7	5
18 to 24 years	108	4	21	23	48	4	7	-	-	-
25 years and over	828	62	33	188	50	40	224	126	60	45
Female										
18 years and over	1 000	101	78	194	100	63	320	98	27	20
18 to 24 years	88	-	17	18	35	-	16	2	-	-
25 to 34 years	271	5	10	32	21	20	114	45	16	6
35 to 44 years	237	15	11	53	20	17	78	27	7	8
45 to 54 years	172	18	18	45	14	19	37	15	3	3
55 to 64 years	123	18	9	39	0	5	38	2	-	2
65 years and over	110	44	12	7	2	2	36	6	1	-
18 to 24 years	88	-	17	18	35	-	16	2	-	-
25 years and over	912	101	61	176	65	63	304	96	27	20
Midwest										
Both sexes										
18 years and over	1 178	58	76	191	191	55	334	174	46	52
18 to 24 years	216	3	34	32	106	14	23	4	-	-
25 to 34 years	357	6	14	62	28	14	139	74	13	8
35 to 44 years	244	7	11	35	16	8	71	58	15	22
45 to 54 years	177	13	7	31	26	10	55	20	8	8
55 to 64 years	112	7	1	23	9	7	33	12	9	9
65 years and over	71	23	10	9	6	2	12	5	1	5
18 to 24 years	216	3	34	32	106	14	23	4	-	-
25 years and over	962	56	42	159	85	42	311	170	46	52
Male										
18 years and over	602	13	36	94	89	26	182	102	26	34
18 to 24 years	112	-	17	21	51	8	15	-	-	-
25 to 34 years	199	-	5	35	14	6	75	53	7	3
35 to 44 years	126	2	7	19	5	5	39	29	8	12
45 to 54 years	81	4	2	9	11	2	31	10	5	7
55 to 64 years	60	2	-	10	8	3	16	8	6	7
65 years and over	24	5	5	1	-	1	6	2	-	5
18 to 24 years	112	-	17	21	51	8	15	-	-	-
25 years and over	490	13	20	73	38	18	167	102	26	34
Female										
18 years and over	575	45	40	97	102	29	152	72	20	19
18 to 24 years	104	3	17	12	56	5	8	4	-	-
25 to 34 years	158	6	8	27	14	8	64	21	6	5
35 to 44 years	118	5	4	16	11	3	32	29	7	11
45 to 54 years	96	9	5	22	14	8	24	10	3	1
55 to 64 years	52	5	1	13	2	4	17	5	3	2
65 years and over	47	19	4	8	6	1	6	3	1	-
18 to 24 years	104	3	17	12	56	5	8	4	-	-
25 years and over	471	43	23	85	46	24	144	68	20	19

- = Quantity zero or rounds to zero.

Table B-1. Educational Attainment of the Population Age 18 Years and Over, by Region, Age, Sex, Race, and Hispanic Origin, 2005—*Continued*

(Numbers in thousands.)

Region, age, sex, race, and Hispanic origin	Total	Elementary		High school		College					
		None to 8th grade	9th to 11th grade	High school graduate	Some college, no degree	Associate's degree	Bachelor's degree	Master's degree	Professional degree	Doctorate degree
ASIAN ALONE OR IN COMBINATION										
South										
Both sexes										
18 years and over	1 999	109	123	471	340	72	518	246	60	61
18 to 24 years	268	2	38	52	135	3	34	4	2	-
25 to 34 years	532	8	19	105	69	11	191	98	18	13
35 to 44 years	498	18	14	99	69	32	123	95	23	25
45 to 54 years	340	13	19	122	34	20	95	24	8	6
55 to 64 years	198	12	19	53	20	4	53	19	7	11
65 years and over	163	56	14	40	14	2	22	6	3	6
18 to 24 years	268	2	38	52	135	3	34	4	2	-
25 years and over	1 732	107	85	419	205	69	484	242	58	61
Male										
18 years and over	943	36	61	219	146	24	234	146	35	41
18 to 24 years	120	-	23	34	46	-	17	-	-	-
25 to 34 years	262	3	11	55	44	5	78	57	6	4
35 to 44 years	242	3	6	48	30	10	62	51	16	17
45 to 54 years	147	7	5	40	10	7	47	17	7	6
55 to 64 years	89	2	8	23	5	2	21	15	4	9
65 years and over	84	21	9	19	11	-	10	6	3	5
18 to 24 years	120	-	23	34	46	-	17	-	-	-
25 years and over	823	36	38	185	100	24	218	146	35	41
Female										
18 years and over	1 057	73	62	252	194	48	283	100	25	19
18 to 24 years	148	2	15	18	88	3	17	4	2	-
25 to 34 years	270	5	8	51	25	6	113	42	11	9
35 to 44 years	256	16	9	51	39	22	60	44	7	8
45 to 54 years	194	6	14	81	24	13	48	7	1	-
55 to 64 years	110	11	11	30	15	2	33	4	3	1
65 years and over	79	35	5	21	3	2	12	-	-	1
18 to 24 years	148	2	15	18	88	3	17	4	2	-
25 years and over	909	72	47	234	106	45	266	97	23	19
West										
Both sexes										
18 years and over	4 771	315	243	960	808	396	1 532	372	76	66
18 to 24 years	572	3	57	116	288	32	68	7	-	-
25 to 34 years	1 025	25	29	129	139	96	475	104	22	6
35 to 44 years	1 041	38	43	169	144	104	387	113	23	19
45 to 54 years	872	58	32	199	113	71	301	68	12	17
55 to 64 years	573	51	27	136	61	57	176	39	9	16
65 years and over	688	140	54	212	65	35	124	41	9	8
18 to 24 years	572	3	57	116	288	32	68	7	-	-
25 years and over	4 199	312	186	844	520	364	1 464	365	76	66
Male										
18 years and over	2 216	105	112	458	380	181	686	200	47	48
18 to 24 years	276	1	29	63	137	20	27	-	-	-
25 to 34 years	498	12	5	76	71	53	213	52	12	4
35 to 44 years	496	18	24	87	72	38	172	61	10	15
45 to 54 years	390	15	11	99	51	30	122	41	10	11
55 to 64 years	257	19	15	49	25	25	85	20	8	11
65 years and over	299	40	29	85	24	15	68	25	7	6
18 to 24 years	276	1	29	63	137	20	27	-	-	-
25 years and over	1 940	104	83	395	243	161	659	200	47	48
Female										
18 years and over	2 555	210	131	502	429	216	847	172	29	19
18 to 24 years	296	2	28	53	152	13	41	7	-	-
25 to 34 years	527	13	25	53	67	43	262	51	10	2
35 to 44 years	544	20	19	82	71	67	216	52	13	4
45 to 54 years	482	43	21	100	61	41	179	27	2	7
55 to 64 years	317	32	13	86	36	33	92	19	2	4
65 years and over	389	100	26	127	40	20	56	16	2	1
18 to 24 years	296	2	28	53	152	13	41	7	-	-
25 years and over	2 259	209	103	449	277	203	805	165	29	19

- = Quantity zero or rounds to zero.

Table B-1. Educational Attainment of the Population Age 18 Years and Over, by Region, Age, Sex, Race, and Hispanic Origin, 2005—*Continued*

(Numbers in thousands.)

Region, age, sex, race, and Hispanic origin	Total	Elementary	High school		College					
		None to 8th grade	9th to 11th grade	High school graduate	Some college, no degree	Associate's degree	Bachelor's degree	Master's degree	Professional degree	Doctorate degree
HISPANIC[1]										
Northeast										
Both sexes										
18 years and over	3 861	675	682	1 213	603	187	353	98	26	24
18 to 24 years	655	51	151	214	189	23	26	[1]2	-	-
25 to 34 years	987	136	160	325	148	67	116	25	10	-
35 to 44 years	913	155	140	285	124	53	114	32	3	6
45 to 54 years	670	135	116	201	88	24	59	27	5	14
55 to 64 years	329	84	48	122	33	12	22	4	1	3
65 years and over	308	115	68	66	20	10	15	7	6	2
18 to 24 years	655	51	151	214	189	23	26	2	-	-
25 years and over	3 206	625	531	1 000	414	165	327	96	26	24
Male										
18 years and over	1 865	345	327	617	262	79	162	43	14	16
18 to 24 years	329	30	77	123	85	5	7	2	-	-
25 to 34 years	499	66	91	178	65	29	48	13	8	-
35 to 44 years	452	104	60	155	45	25	47	11	-	4
45 to 54 years	301	66	52	81	38	11	32	11	-	11
55 to 64 years	150	43	13	51	17	5	19	1	-	1
65 years and over	134	37	35	28	12	4	8	4	6	-
18 to 24 years	329	30	77	123	85	5	7	2	-	-
25 years and over	1 536	316	250	494	177	73	154	40	14	16
Female										
18 years and over	1 996	330	355	596	340	109	192	55	12	8
10 to 24 years	326	21	74	91	104	17	18	-	-	-
25 to 34 years	488	70	68	146	83	38	68	12	3	-
35 to 44 years	460	51	81	129	79	28	67	21	3	1
45 to 54 years	368	69	64	120	50	13	27	17	5	3
55 to 64 years	179	41	34	72	16	7	4	2	1	2
65 years and over	174	78	33	38	8	6	7	4	-	2
18 to 24 years	326	21	74	91	104	17	18	-	-	-
25 years and over	1 670	309	281	505	236	91	173	55	12	8
Midwest										
Both sexes										
18 years and over	2 310	495	427	692	344	99	180	53	15	6
18 to 24 years	458	53	148	137	103	5	13	-	-	-
25 to 34 years	722	125	123	251	95	39	69	16	2	1
35 to 44 years	508	106	71	158	63	27	52	23	7	3
45 to 54 years	315	88	46	78	43	11	34	10	4	1
55 to 64 years	185	62	21	49	27	12	11	2	-	1
65 years and over	122	61	18	20	13	5	1	1	2	-
18 to 24 years	458	53	148	137	103	5	13	-	-	-
25 years and over	1 852	442	279	556	241	94	166	53	15	6
Male										
18 years and over	1 260	271	240	387	183	45	97	28	5	5
18 to 24 years	257	34	79	83	56	1	3	-	-	-
25 to 34 years	425	78	70	147	56	23	41	9	-	1
35 to 44 years	272	49	44	87	35	10	31	11	2	1
45 to 54 years	156	52	25	37	17	5	13	5	2	1
55 to 64 years	97	33	13	25	12	3	8	2	-	1
65 years and over	53	25	8	8	7	3	-	1	1	-
18 to 24 years	257	34	79	83	56	1	3	-	-	-
25 years and over	1 003	237	161	304	127	44	94	28	5	5
Female										
18 years and over	1 050	224	187	305	161	54	83	25	10	2
18 to 24 years	202	19	69	53	47	3	10	-	-	-
25 to 34 years	297	48	52	104	39	16	28	7	2	-
35 to 44 years	236	57	26	70	28	16	20	12	5	2
45 to 54 years	159	36	21	41	26	6	21	6	2	-
55 to 64 years	88	28	8	24	15	9	3	-	-	-
65 years and over	69	36	10	12	6	3	1	-	1	-
18 to 24 years	202	19	69	53	47	3	10	-	-	-
25 years and over	849	205	118	252	114	51	73	25	10	2

[1]May be of any race.
- = Quantity zero or rounds to zero.

Table B-1. Educational Attainment of the Population Age 18 Years and Over, by Region, Age, Sex, Race, and Hispanic Origin, 2005—*Continued*

(Numbers in thousands.)

Region, age, sex, race, and Hispanic origin	Total	Elementary	High school		College					
		None to 8th grade	9th to 11th grade	High school graduate	Some college, no degree	Associate's degree	Bachelor's degree	Master's degree	Professional degree	Doctorate degree
HISPANIC[1]										
South										
Both sexes										
18 years and over	9 897	2 163	1 806	2 896	1 359	516	840	221	58	37
18 to 24 years	1 784	194	495	629	350	61	50	4	-	-
25 to 34 years	2 756	495	567	793	400	156	273	48	16	9
35 to 44 years	2 134	424	318	623	287	142	248	71	14	8
45 to 54 years	1 446	336	209	425	167	79	152	55	12	12
55 to 64 years	859	250	119	222	117	53	59	28	9	1
65 years and over	917	464	99	203	40	25	59	15	7	5
18 to 24 years	1 784	194	495	629	350	61	50	4	-	-
25 years and over	8 112	1 969	1 312	2 266	1 010	454	790	217	58	37
Male										
18 years and over	5 177	1 167	969	1 514	700	254	426	94	35	18
18 to 24 years	992	131	286	356	167	28	23	2	-	-
25 to 34 years	1 515	301	311	430	235	83	132	9	9	4
35 to 44 years	1 144	244	174	343	137	68	135	34	6	3
45 to 54 years	722	182	93	215	78	35	78	29	8	6
55 to 64 years	418	121	67	90	61	26	31	14	7	1
65 years and over	386	188	38	80	23	15	27	6	6	4
18 to 24 years	992	131	286	356	167	28	23	2	-	-
25 years and over	4 186	1 036	683	1 158	533	227	404	92	35	18
Female										
18 years and over	4 719	997	837	1 382	659	262	414	127	23	18
18 to 24 years	792	63	209	274	183	34	28	2	-	-
25 to 34 years	1 241	194	256	363	165	73	140	39	7	5
35 to 44 years	990	179	143	280	150	74	112	37	9	6
45 to 54 years	724	154	116	210	89	44	74	26	4	7
55 to 64 years	441	129	52	132	56	27	28	14	2	-
65 years and over	531	277	61	122	17	10	32	9	1	1
18 to 24 years	792	63	209	274	183	34	28	2	-	-
25 years and over	3 927	933	628	1 108	476	228	386	125	23	18
West										
Both sexes										
18 years and over	11 449	2 876	2 119	3 045	1 869	604	670	185	53	28
18 to 24 years	2 069	258	532	640	523	65	52	-	-	-
25 to 34 years	3 172	656	667	900	471	203	216	42	10	6
35 to 44 years	2 688	720	459	694	401	164	179	42	24	3
45 to 54 years	1 731	545	242	422	244	86	130	50	8	4
55 to 64 years	943	304	116	215	153	51	65	28	4	7
65 years and over	846	393	102	174	78	35	28	23	6	8
18 to 24 years	2 069	258	532	640	523	65	52	-	-	-
25 years and over	9 380	2 618	1 587	2 405	1 347	539	618	185	53	28
Male										
18 years and over	5 845	1 523	1 083	1 603	900	257	339	88	30	23
18 to 24 years	1 059	169	278	344	224	20	23	-	-	-
25 to 34 years	1 695	361	351	516	241	90	109	20	1	5
35 to 44 years	1 394	382	246	360	203	82	87	20	12	2
45 to 54 years	905	301	115	220	122	36	70	29	8	4
55 to 64 years	436	158	46	89	70	18	32	13	3	7
65 years and over	356	152	46	74	39	11	18	5	6	5
18 to 24 years	1 059	169	278	344	224	20	23	-	-	-
25 years and over	4 787	1 354	805	1 259	676	237	316	88	30	23
Female										
18 years and over	5 604	1 352	1 036	1 442	970	347	331	97	23	6
18 to 24 years	1 010	89	253	295	299	45	29	-	-	-
25 to 34 years	1 477	295	316	384	230	113	107	22	9	1
35 to 44 years	1 294	338	213	334	198	83	92	23	12	2
45 to 54 years	826	244	128	202	122	50	60	20	-	-
55 to 64 years	507	146	70	126	83	33	33	14	1	-
65 years and over	490	241	56	101	38	23	10	18	-	2
18 to 24 years	1 010	89	253	295	299	45	29	-	-	-
25 years and over	4 594	1 264	783	1 146	671	302	302	97	23	6

[1]May be of any race.
- = Quantity zero or rounds to zero.

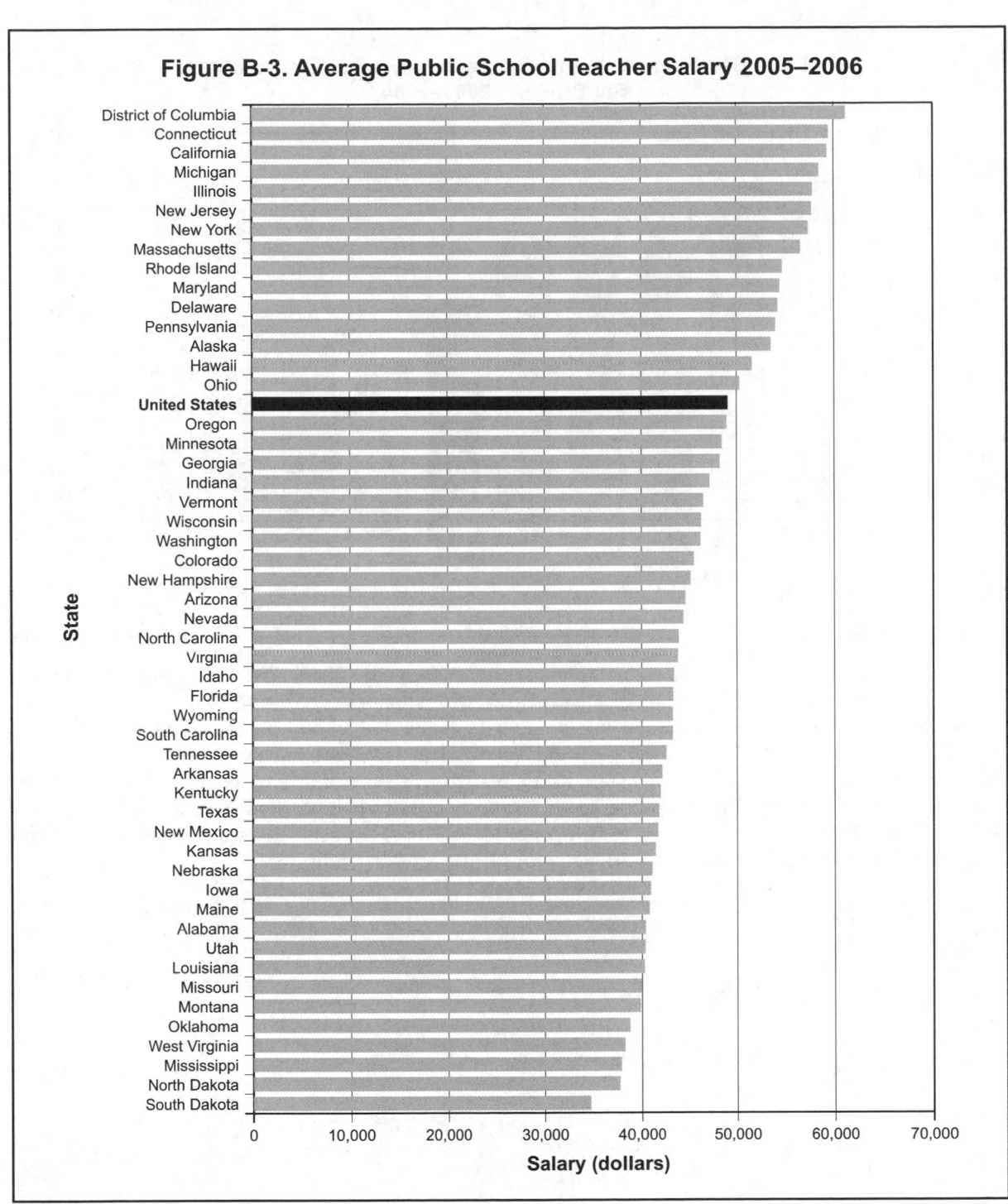

Figure B-3. Average Public School Teacher Salary 2005–2006

For the 2005–2006 school year, the average public school teacher's salary was $49,109, an increase of 2.8 percent from the previous school year. Salaries ranged from $34,709 in South Dakota to $61,195 in the District of Columbia. Teacher salaries were typically higher in the New England states; three of these six states ranked in the top ten nationally.

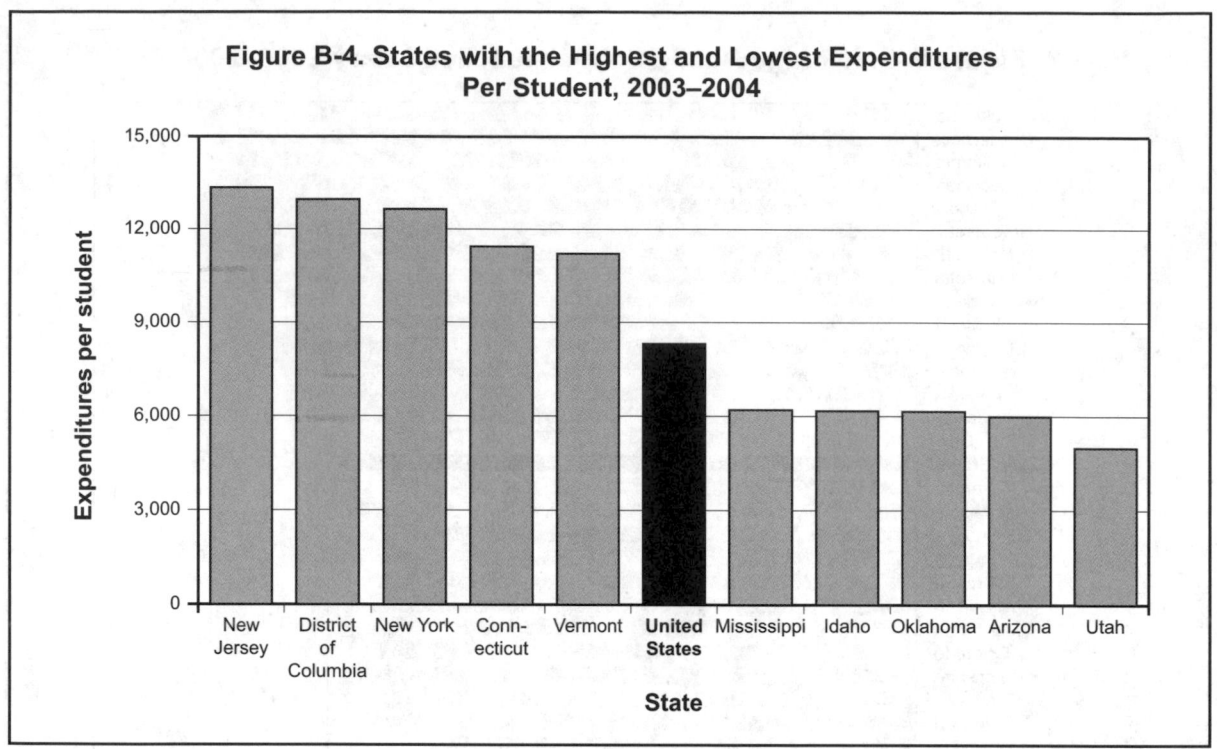

Figure B-4. States with the Highest and Lowest Expenditures Per Student, 2003–2004

Nationally, the average expenditure per student was $8,310 for the 2003–2004 school year. Instruction accounted for more than 66 percent of all expenses, with support services at 29.8 percent and non-instructional expenses at 4.1 percent. New Jersey had the highest expenditure per student at $13,338, followed by the District of Columbia at $12,959 and New York at $12,638. Utah had the lowest expenditure per student at $4,991 and was the only state with a per student expenditure of less than $5,900. Teacher salaries were also significantly below average in Utah. Nine states had per student expenditures of over $10,000, and 12 states spent less than $7,000 per student. New Hampshire was the only New England state that did not rank in the top ten nationally for per student expenditures.

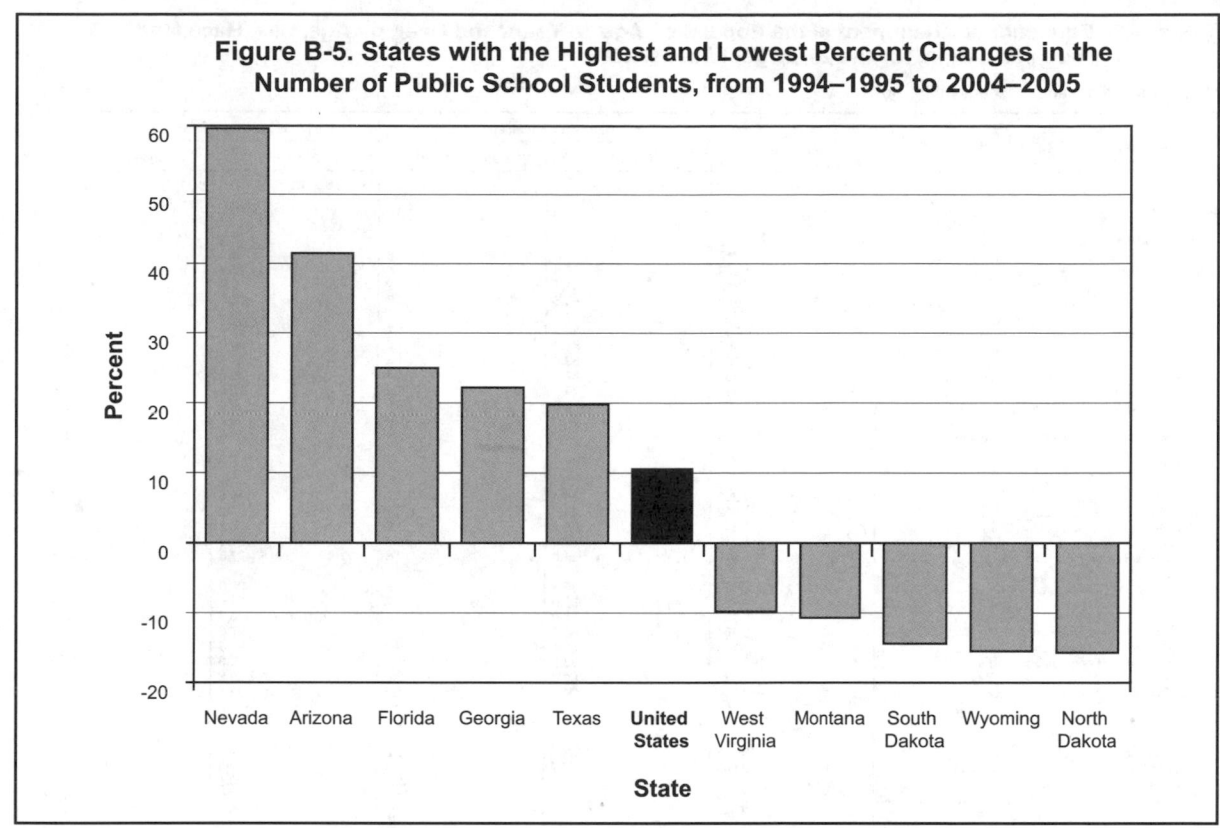

Figure B-5. States with the Highest and Lowest Percent Changes in the Number of Public School Students, from 1994–1995 to 2004–2005

There was a huge variation by state in the percent change in the number of students from the 1994–1995 school year to the 2004–2005 school year. In the past 10 years, the number of students in the United States increased by 10.6 percent. However, in Nevada, the number of students increased dramatically, rising 59.6 percent. Arizona had the next-highest increase at 41.5 percent. Nine states experienced increases of 18 percent or more. Other states that experienced rapid growth in the number of students, but are not represented in the figure above, include North Carolina, Colorado, California, and New Jersey. Fifteen states saw a decline in their student populations from the 1994–1995 school year to the 2004–2005 school year, including four of the seven states in the West North Central region.

Table B-2. Educational Attainment of the Population Age 18 Years and Over, by Age, Sex, Race, and Hispanic Origin, for the 25 Largest States, 2005

(Numbers in thousands, except where noted.)

State, age, sex, race, and Hispanic origin	Total population	High school graduates		Bachelor's degree or more	
		Percent	Margin of error[1]	Percent	Margin of error[1]
ALABAMA					
18 years and over	3 416	80.3	1.2	17.9	1.1
18 to 24 years	412	75.8	3.6	4.0	1.6
25 to 44 years	1 257	88.4	1.5	23.3	2.0
45 to 64 years	1 248	81.4	1.9	19.5	1.9
65 years and over	499	60.8	3.7	11.8	2.4
25 years and over	3 004	80.9	1.2	19.8	1.2
Male	1 407	79.7	1.8	20.9	1.8
Female	1 598	82.0	1.6	18.8	1.7
White alone or in combination	2 287	82.1	1.4	20.6	1.4
Black alone or in combination	691	76.3	2.9	15.1	2.5
Asian alone or in combination	26	(B)	(B)	(B)	(B)
Hispanic[2]	15	(B)	(B)	(B)	(B)
Non-Hispanic White alone or in combination	2 273	82.0	1.4	20.6	1.4
ARIZONA					
18 years and over	4 201	84.4	1.2	25.6	1.4
18 to 24 years	502	73.8	4.1	7.3	2.4
25 to 44 years	1 680	85.6	1.8	26.3	2.3
45 to 64 years	1 248	87.2	2.0	30.9	2.7
65 years and over	771	84.0	2.8	27.3	3.4
25 years and over	3 699	85.8	1.2	28.0	1.6
Male	1 792	85.6	1.7	29.6	2.3
Female	1 907	86.0	1.7	26.6	2.1
White alone or in combination	3 361	85.7	1.3	27.6	1.6
Black alone or in combination	133	89.1	6.0	17.3	7.3
Asian alone or in combination	116	93.9	5.0	62.0	10.0
Hispanic[2]	883	60.2	3.0	9.9	1.8
Non-Hispanic White alone or in combination	2 514	94.2	1.0	33.6	2.0
CALIFORNIA					
18 years and over	26 265	80.0	0.6	27.5	0.6
18 to 24 years	3 589	77.8	1.6	8.0	1.1
25 to 44 years	10 693	79.2	0.9	30.5	1.0
45 to 64 years	8 084	83.8	1.0	32.9	1.2
65 years and over	3 899	76.5	1.6	26.1	1.7
25 years and over	22 676	80.4	0.6	30.6	0.7
Male	11 131	80.4	0.9	32.3	1.0
Female	11 545	80.4	0.9	28.9	1.0
White alone or in combination	17 998	78.7	0.7	28.5	0.8
Black alone or in combination	1 519	86.6	2.2	21.9	2.7
Asian alone or in combination	2 911	88.6	1.5	50.2	2.3
Hispanic[2]	6 663	52.5	1.3	9.0	0.7
Non-Hispanic White alone or in combination	11 593	93.6	0.5	39.4	1.1
COLORADO					
18 years and over	3 356	88.2	0.8	32.1	1.2
18 to 24 years	409	80.8	2.9	7.8	2.0
25 to 44 years	1 428	88.4	1.3	38.0	1.9
45 to 64 years	1 120	92.7	1.1	36.6	2.1
65 years and over	398	82.7	2.8	23.3	3.1
25 years and over	2 946	89.3	0.8	35.5	1.3
Male	1 431	89.7	1.2	37.6	1.9
Female	1 515	88.9	1.2	33.5	1.8
White alone or in combination	2 741	89.7	0.9	36.3	1.4
Black alone or in combination	118	87.8	4.7	19.9	5.8
Asian alone or in combination	66	(B)	(B)	(B)	(B)
Hispanic[2]	486	62.9	2.8	10.6	1.8
Non-Hispanic White alone or in combination	2 286	95.2	0.7	41.3	1.5
FLORIDA					
18 years and over	13 408	86.0	0.6	23.4	0.7
18 to 24 years	1 441	79.4	2.2	6.8	1.4
25 to 44 years	4 749	90.0	0.9	27.6	1.3
45 to 64 years	4 374	88.1	1.0	27.3	1.4
65 years and over	2 844	79.3	1.6	19.1	1.5
25 years and over	11 967	86.8	0.6	25.4	0.8
Male	5 764	86.5	0.9	27.5	1.2
Female	6 203	87.1	0.9	23.5	1.1
White alone or in combination	10 171	88.3	0.7	27.0	0.9
Black alone or in combination	1 498	76.4	2.4	13.2	1.9
Asian alone or in combination	303	87.7	4.1	30.9	5.8
Hispanic[2]	2 093	72.9	1.7	21.2	1.6
Non-Hispanic White alone or in combination	8 144	92.1	0.6	28.4	1.0

[1]The margin of error, when added to or subtracted from the estimate, provides the 90-percent confidence interval.
[2]May be of any race.
(B) = Base is too small to show the derived measure.

Table B-2. Educational Attainment of the Population Age 18 Years and Over, by Age, Sex, Race, and Hispanic Origin, for the 25 Largest States, 2005—*Continued*

(Numbers in thousands, except where noted.)

State, age, sex, race, and Hispanic origin	Total population	High school graduates		Bachelor's degree or more	
		Percent	Margin of error[1]	Percent	Margin of error[1]
GEORGIA					
18 years and over	6 366	85.0	1.1	24.4	1.3
18 to 24 years	888	80.4	3.2	8.0	2.2
25 to 44 years	2 639	88.9	1.5	30.2	2.1
45 to 64 years	2 065	86.6	1.8	27.4	2.3
65 years and over	775	72.6	3.8	15.4	3.1
25 years and over	5 478	85.7	1.1	27.1	1.4
Male	2 568	84.4	1.7	27.7	2.1
Female	2 910	86.9	1.5	26.5	2.0
White alone or in combination	3 785	86.6	1.3	29.7	1.8
Black alone or in combination	1 521	82.5	2.5	17.8	2.5
Asian alone or in combination	153	92.0	5.6	50.7	10.3
Hispanic[2]	275	61.5	6.1	14.9	4.5
Non-Hispanic White alone or in combination	3 529	88.5	1.3	30.7	1.9
ILLINOIS					
18 years and over	9 351	86.2	0.7	26.9	0.9
18 to 24 years	1 283	80.0	2.1	10.1	1.6
25 to 44 years	3 568	90.0	0.9	33.1	1.5
45 to 64 years	2 954	90.1	1.0	30.3	1.6
65 years and over	1 546	75.2	2.1	20.2	1.9
25 years and over	8 068	87.2	0.7	29.6	1.0
Male	3 898	88.4	1.0	31.6	1.4
Female	4 170	86.1	1.0	27.7	1.3
White alone or in combination	6 609	88.1	0.7	29.4	1.1
Black alone or in combination	1 084	80.6	2.4	18.1	2.3
Asian alone or in combination	354	93.9	2.5	70.1	4.9
Hispanic[2]	842	60.0	2.8	12.4	1.9
Non-Hispanic White alone or in combination	5 799	92.0	0.7	31.8	1.1
INDIANA					
18 years and over	4 531	85.5	0.9	20.7	1.0
18 to 24 years	524	72.3	3.4	6.0	1.8
25 to 44 years	1 740	80.3	1.3	23.7	1.8
45 to 64 years	1 592	90.3	1.3	25.4	1.9
65 years and over	665	74.5	2.9	13.1	2.3
25 years and over	4 007	87.2	0.9	22.6	1.2
Male	1 921	87.7	1.3	22.7	1.7
Female	2 086	86.8	1.3	22.5	1.6
White alone or in combination	3 652	87.5	1.0	23.0	1.2
Black alone or in combination	297	84.7	3.9	11.4	3.4
Asian alone or in combination	50	(B)	(B)	(B)	(B)
Hispanic[2]	122	44.2	6.9	6.3	3.4
Non-Hispanic White alone or in combination	3 532	89.0	0.9	23.6	1.2
LOUISIANA					
18 years and over	3 273	78.9	1.3	18.0	1.2
18 to 24 years	465	70.7	3.9	7.7	2.3
25 to 44 years	1 209	83.6	2.0	23.6	2.3
45 to 64 years	1 045	82.8	2.2	18.6	2.2
65 years and over	554	68.0	3.7	13.1	2.7
25 years and over	2 808	80.2	1.4	19.6	1.4
Male	1 311	77.7	2.1	18.4	2.0
Female	1 497	82.4	1.8	20.7	1.9
White alone or in combination	1 955	84.7	1.5	23.8	1.8
Black alone or in combination	808	69.6	3.2	9.4	2.0
Asian alone or in combination	41	(B)	(B)	(B)	(B)
Hispanic[2]	48	(B)	(B)	(B)	(B)
Non-Hispanic White alone or in combination	1 907	85.2	1.5	23.9	1.8
MARYLAND					
18 years and over	4 161	86.4	1.0	34.3	1.4
18 to 24 years	455	82.5	3.3	17.9	3.3
25 to 44 years	1 665	87.1	1.5	37.6	2.2
45 to 64 years	1 402	92.0	1.3	39.3	2.4
65 years and over	639	75.1	3.2	26.3	3.2
25 years and over	3 706	86.9	1.0	36.3	1.5
Male	1 751	86.3	1.5	37.1	2.1
Female	1 956	87.5	1.4	35.6	2.0
White alone or in combination	2 532	86.6	1.2	38.5	1.8
Black alone or in combination	1 001	87.2	2.1	26.6	2.7
Asian alone or in combination	169	88.6	4.8	59.0	7.4
Hispanic[2]	223	48.5	5.4	16.2	4.0
Non-Hispanic White alone or in combination	2 322	90.3	1.1	40.6	1.9

[1]The margin of error, when added to or subtracted from the estimate, provides the 90-percent confidence interval.
[2]May be of any race.
(B) = Base is too small to show the derived measure.

Table B-2. Educational Attainment of the Population Age 18 Years and Over, by Age, Sex, Race, and Hispanic Origin, for the 25 Largest States, 2005—*Continued*

(Numbers in thousands, except where noted.)

State, age, sex, race, and Hispanic origin	Total population	High school graduates		Bachelor's degree or more	
		Percent	Margin of error[1]	Percent	Margin of error[1]
MASSACHUSETTS					
18 years and over	4 881	87.2	0.8	33.4	1.2
18 to 24 years	601	85.2	2.6	10.6	2.2
25 to 44 years	1 864	90.5	1.2	42.3	2.0
45 to 64 years	1 692	90.3	1.3	36.6	2.1
65 years and over	724	73.0	2.9	22.2	2.7
25 years and over	4 281	87.5	0.9	36.6	1.3
Male	2 031	87.7	1.3	38.5	1.9
Female	2 250	87.3	1.2	35.0	1.8
White alone or in combination	3 775	88.8	0.9	37.6	1.4
Black alone or in combination	264	73.8	5.1	16.7	4.3
Asian alone or in combination	246	83.6	4.4	46.0	6.0
Hispanic[2]	272	58.6	4.6	13.2	3.2
Non-Hispanic White alone or in combination	3 555	90.8	0.9	39.1	1.4
MICHIGAN					
18 years and over	7 429	87.1	0.7	22.7	0.9
18 to 24 years	920	76.7	2.6	9.8	1.8
25 to 44 years	2 772	92.7	0.9	29.7	1.6
45 to 64 years	2 507	90.9	1.1	24.8	1.6
65 years and over	1 230	74.3	2.3	12.4	1.7
25 years and over	6 509	88.6	0.7	24.6	1.0
Male	3 124	87.7	1.1	26.0	1.4
Female	3 384	89.3	1.0	23.2	1.3
White alone or in combination	5 512	88.8	0.8	24.3	1.1
Black alone or in combination	820	86.9	2.3	19.4	2.7
Asian alone or in combination	162	90.6	4.5	66.0	7.3
Hispanic[2]	180	65.2	5.7	19.4	4.7
Non-Hispanic White alone or in combination	5 355	89.4	0.8	24.4	1.1
MINNESOTA					
18 years and over	3 876	91.1	0.7	30.9	1.2
18 to 24 years	511	80.7	2.8	9.3	2.1
25 to 44 years	1 473	95.8	0.8	37.8	2.0
45 to 64 years	1 327	95.4	0.9	35.3	2.1
65 years and over	565	78.4	2.8	22.2	2.8
25 years and over	3 365	92.7	0.7	34.2	1.3
Male	1 662	92.7	1.0	36.0	1.9
Female	1 703	92.8	1.0	32.5	1.8
White alone or in combination	3 100	93.1	0.7	34.1	1.4
Black alone or in combination	130	92.9	3.8	26.8	6.6
Asian alone or in combination	132	86.0	5.1	44.2	7.4
Hispanic[2]	107	67.7	6.3	14.3	4.7
Non-Hispanic White alone or in combination	3 000	94.0	0.7	34.8	1.4
MISSOURI					
18 years and over	4 203	84.5	1.0	23.0	1.2
18 to 24 years	488	77.6	3.4	7.5	2.1
25 to 44 years	1 576	89.4	1.4	29.6	2.1
45 to 64 years	1 425	91.9	1.3	27.1	2.1
65 years and over	714	63.9	3.2	10.5	2.1
25 years and over	3 715	85.5	1.0	25.0	1.3
Male	1 735	85.3	1.5	26.9	1.9
Female	1 980	85.6	1.4	23.3	1.7
White alone or in combination	3 254	86.1	1.1	25.6	1.4
Black alone or in combination	390	78.9	3.9	13.8	3.3
Asian alone or in combination	54	(B)	(B)	(B)	(B)
Hispanic[2]	81	72.1	7.8	15.9	6.4
Non-Hispanic White alone or in combination	3 177	86.5	1.1	25.9	1.4
NEW JERSEY					
18 years and over	6 454	86.5	0.7	33.6	1.0
18 to 24 years	701	82.7	2.5	11.1	2.1
25 to 44 years	2 462	90.6	1.0	40.8	1.7
45 to 64 years	2 238	89.3	1.1	40.3	1.8
65 years and over	1 053	73.4	2.4	17.2	2.0
25 years and over	5 753	86.9	0.8	36.3	1.1
Male	2 754	86.4	1.1	38.0	1.6
Female	3 000	87.5	1.0	34.8	1.5
White alone or in combination	4 634	87.5	0.8	36.2	1.2
Black alone or in combination	750	81.3	2.6	21.8	2.8
Asian alone or in combination	357	93.4	2.4	70.3	4.5
Hispanic[2]	766	62.4	2.7	15.7	2.0
Non-Hispanic White alone or in combination	3 917	92.2	0.7	40.2	1.4

[1]The margin of error, when added to or subtracted from the estimate, provides the 90-percent confidence interval.
[2]May be of any race.
(B) = Base is too small to show the derived measure.

Table B-2. Educational Attainment of the Population Age 18 Years and Over, by Age, Sex, Race, and Hispanic Origin, for the 25 Largest States, 2005—*Continued*

(Numbers in thousands, except where noted.)

State, age, sex, race, and Hispanic origin	Total population	High school graduates		Bachelor's degree or more	
		Percent	Margin of error[1]	Percent	Margin of error[1]
NEW YORK					
18 years and over	14 455	84.8	0.6	28.0	0.7
18 to 24 years	1 812	78.2	1.8	10.8	1.4
25 to 44 years	5 469	89.0	0.8	33.9	1.2
45 to 64 years	4 691	87.9	0.9	31.2	1.3
65 years and over	2 483	74.3	1.7	21.3	1.6
25 years and over	12 643	85.7	0.6	30.4	0.8
Male	5 984	86.2	0.8	30.8	1.1
Female	6 659	85.2	0.8	30.1	1.1
White alone or in combination	9 753	87.0	0.6	31.5	0.9
Black alone or in combination	2 005	81.9	1.7	19.5	1.8
Asian alone or in combination	895	81.3	2.6	43.3	3.4
Hispanic[2]	1 647	65.1	2.0	15.1	1.5
Non-Hispanic White alone or in combination	8 363	90.8	0.6	34.3	1.0
NORTH CAROLINA					
18 years and over	6 290	82.8	1.0	22.6	1.1
18 to 24 years	863	75.3	3.1	5.5	1.6
25 to 44 years	2 375	88.5	1.4	26.5	1.9
45 to 64 years	2 113	86.8	1.5	27.6	2.0
65 years and over	939	66.3	3.2	17.3	2.6
25 years and over	5 427	84.0	1.0	25.3	1.2
Male	2 597	83.8	1.5	25.9	1.8
Female	2 830	84.2	1.4	24.8	1.7
White alone or in combination	4 098	85.0	1.2	28.1	1.5
Black alone or in combination	1 084	81.0	2.6	13.0	2.3
Asian alone or in combination	132	88.3	6.2	46.0	9.6
Hispanic[2]	287	46.2	5.4	7.6	2.8
Non-Hispanic White alone or in combination	3 831	87.9	1.1	29.5	1.5
OHIO					
18 years and over	8 463	86.8	0.7	21.2	0.8
18 to 24 years	1 130	70.8	2.3	9.5	1.6
25 to 44 years	3 000	91.8	0.9	26.7	1.5
45 to 64 years	2 963	90.4	1.0	22.6	1.4
65 years and over	1 369	74.0	2.2	15.9	1.9
25 years and over	7 333	87.9	0.7	23.0	0.9
Male	3 463	87.3	1.1	23.9	1.4
Female	3 870	88.4	1.0	22.2	1.3
White alone or in combination	6 476	88.6	0.7	23.8	1.0
Black alone or in combination	791	82.4	2.7	14.2	2.5
Asian alone or in combination	61	(B)	(B)	(B)	(B)
Hispanic[2]	159	70.8	5.9	17.6	5.0
Non-Hispanic White alone or in combination	6 329	89.1	0.7	24.0	1.0
PENNSYLVANIA					
18 years and over	9 331	85.6	0.7	23.9	0.8
18 to 24 years	1 122	80.3	2.2	8.6	1.5
25 to 44 years	3 274	91.0	0.9	32.4	1.5
45 to 64 years	3 159	89.2	1.0	27.0	1.4
65 years and over	1 777	72.5	1.9	12.2	1.4
25 years and over	8 209	86.3	0.7	26.0	0.9
Male	3 830	86.5	1.0	27.3	1.3
Female	4 379	86.2	0.9	24.8	1.2
White alone or in combination	7 296	86.9	0.7	26.0	0.9
Black alone or in combination	773	80.0	2.8	17.7	2.6
Asian alone or in combination	146	91.2	4.5	70.0	7.3
Hispanic[2]	269	62.4	4.7	16.1	3.6
Non-Hispanic White alone or in combination	7 038	87.8	0.7	26.4	1.0
SOUTH CAROLINA					
18 years and over	3 093	81.4	1.2	22.1	1.3
18 to 24 years	408	70.6	3.9	8.5	2.4
25 to 44 years	1 130	89.1	1.6	27.4	2.3
45 to 64 years	1 005	83.9	2.0	23.8	2.3
65 years and over	549	68.7	3.4	18.3	2.8
25 years and over	2 685	83.0	1.2	24.2	1.4
Male	1 256	82.0	1.9	24.0	2.1
Female	1 428	83.8	1.7	24.3	2.0
White alone or in combination	1 953	85.9	1.4	27.1	1.7
Black alone or in combination	702	74.9	3.0	15.3	2.5
Asian alone or in combination	21	(B)	(B)	(B)	(B)
Hispanic[2]	60	(B)	(B)	(B)	(B)
Non-Hispanic White alone or in combination	1 896	86.3	1.4	27.7	1.8

[1]The margin of error, when added to or subtracted from the estimate, provides the 90-percent confidence interval.
[2]May be of any race.
(B) = Base is too small to show the derived measure.

Table B-2. Educational Attainment of the Population Age 18 Years and Over, by Age, Sex, Race, and Hispanic Origin, for the 25 Largest States, 2005—*Continued*

(Numbers in thousands, except where noted.)

State, age, sex, race, and Hispanic origin	Total population	High school graduates		Bachelor's degree or more	
		Percent	Margin of error[1]	Percent	Margin of error[1]
TENNESSEE					
18 years and over	4 448	81.5	1.2	19.8	1.2
18 to 24 years	618	79.6	3.4	9.5	2.5
25 to 44 years	1 641	86.9	1.7	24.2	2.2
45 to 64 years	1 418	85.3	2.0	21.5	2.3
65 years and over	772	64.6	3.6	15.6	2.7
25 years and over	3 830	81.8	1.3	21.5	1.4
Male	1 836	80.9	1.9	22.2	2.0
Female	1 994	82.6	1.8	20.8	1.9
White alone or in combination	3 190	81.6	1.4	22.3	1.5
Black alone or in combination	581	83.0	3.5	16.5	3.4
Asian alone or in combination	41	(B)	(B)	(B)	(B)
Hispanic[2]	99	45.4	9.2	7.0	4.7
Non-Hispanic White alone or in combination	3 100	82.6	1.4	22.7	1.6
TEXAS					
18 years and over	16 025	77.4	0.7	22.8	0.7
18 to 24 years	2 275	72.2	2.0	6.2	1.1
25 to 44 years	6 578	80.0	1.1	25.7	1.2
45 to 64 years	4 991	81.0	1.2	27.6	1.4
65 years and over	2 181	66.4	2.2	20.4	1.9
25 years and over	13 750	78.2	0.8	25.5	0.8
Male	6 647	77.7	1.1	27.1	1.2
Female	7 103	78.7	1.1	24.0	1.1
White alone or in combination	11 756	77.1	0.8	25.2	0.9
Black alone or in combination	1 471	84.5	2.2	19.5	2.4
Asian alone or in combination	468	87.8	3.5	52.3	5.3
Hispanic[2]	4 465	54.4	1.4	9.9	0.8
Non-Hispanic White alone or in combination	7 371	90.7	0.7	34.5	1.2
VIRGINIA					
18 years and over	5 546	85.4	1.0	28.3	1.3
18 to 24 years	748	81.2	3.0	13.2	2.6
25 to 44 years	2 042	88.7	1.5	33.8	2.2
45 to 64 years	1 934	87.3	1.6	31.0	2.2
65 years and over	822	76.5	3.1	21.9	3.1
25 years and over	4 798	86.0	1.1	30.6	1.4
Male	2 295	85.9	1.5	31.3	2.1
Female	2 503	86.2	1.5	30.0	1.9
White alone or in combination	3 767	87.4	1.1	31.4	1.6
Black alone or in combination	807	78.2	3.3	19.2	3.1
Asian alone or in combination	232	89.9	4.5	57.1	7.3
Hispanic[2]	285	61.1	5.4	16.2	4.1
Non-Hispanic White alone or in combination	3 490	89.6	1.1	32.6	1.7
WASHINGTON					
18 years and over	4 606	89.7	0.9	28.0	1.4
18 to 24 years	572	77.2	3.7	8.0	2.4
25 to 44 years	1 772	91.8	1.4	30.2	2.3
45 to 64 years	1 570	94.1	1.3	35.2	2.5
65 years and over	693	85.0	2.9	23.0	3.4
25 years and over	4 035	91.5	0.9	30.9	1.5
Male	1 950	90.7	1.4	34.0	2.3
Female	2 085	92.3	1.2	28.0	2.1
White alone or in combination	3 576	92.2	0.9	30.7	1.6
Black alone or in combination	115	89.5	6.4	23.2	8.8
Asian alone or in combination	291	85.6	4.6	40.0	6.4
Hispanic[2]	203	61.9	6.3	12.6	4.3
Non-Hispanic White alone or in combination	3 391	94.0	0.9	31.7	1.7
WISCONSIN					
18 years and over	4 155	88.9	0.8	22.7	1.1
18 to 24 years	551	79.0	2.8	7.2	1.8
25 to 44 years	1 515	92.0	1.1	27.3	1.9
45 to 64 years	1 367	94.8	1.0	26.3	1.9
65 years and over	722	78.9	2.5	17.9	2.3
25 years and over	3 604	90.4	0.8	25.0	1.2
Male	1 751	90.3	1.1	26.3	1.7
Female	1 853	90.5	1.1	23.9	1.6
White alone or in combination	3 368	91.2	0.8	25.4	1.2
Black alone or in combination	151	82.0	5.4	14.1	4.9
Asian alone or in combination	60	(B)	(B)	(B)	(B)
Hispanic[2]	137	63.3	5.8	10.0	3.6
Non-Hispanic White alone or in combination	3 233	92.4	0.8	26.1	1.3

[1]The margin of error, when added to or subtracted from the estimate, provides the 90-percent confidence interval.
[2]May be of any race.
(B) = Base is too small to show the derived measure.

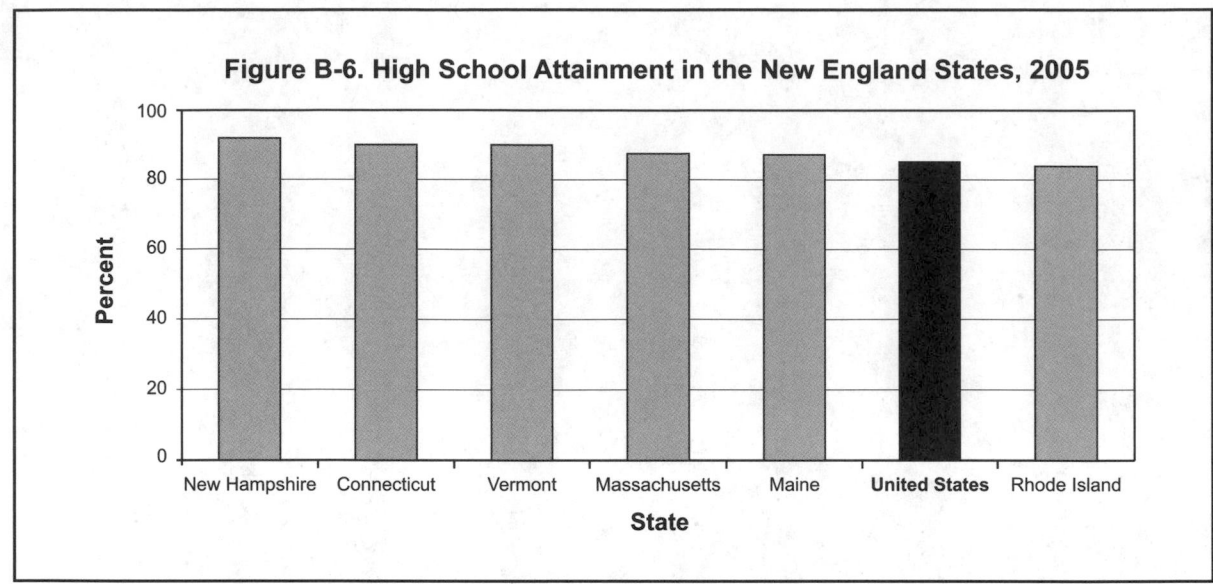

Figure B-6. High School Attainment in the New England States, 2005

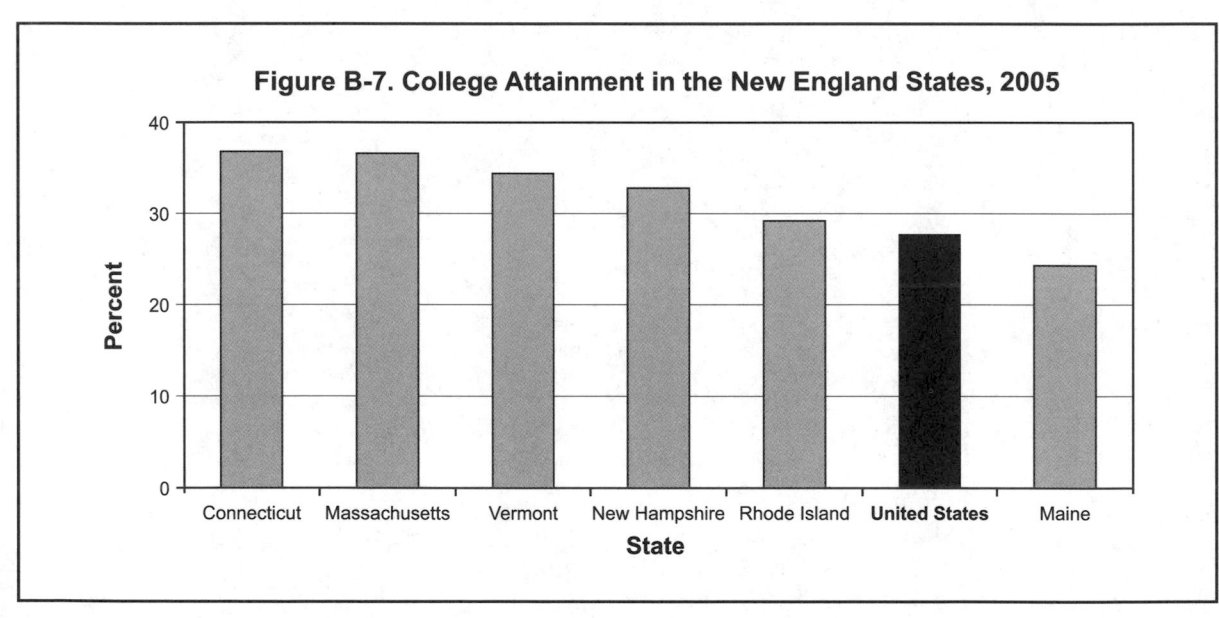

Figure B-7. College Attainment in the New England States, 2005

NEW ENGLAND STATES:

The six New England states are Connecticut, Maine, Massachusetts, New Hampshire, Rhode Island, and Vermont. In 2005, they accounted for 4.8 percent of the U.S. population and, with 2.2 million students, 4.5 percent of the nation's students. The New England states had 1,698 school districts, ranging from 493 in Massachusetts to 49 in Rhode Island. These states ranked above average on most educational measures.

While most of the nation's population growth occurred in the West and the South, the New England states had population growth of just 2.3 percent from 2000 to 2005, compared with the U.S. population increase of 5.3 percent. With the exception of New Hampshire, the New England states had below-average population growth. The population of Massachusetts, the nation's 13th most populous state, grew by less than 1 percent from 2000 to 2005; this ranked among the slowest growth rates in the United States. Nationally, 17.9 percent of the population was between 5 and 17 years of age, while in New England less than 17 percent of the population was school aged. At about 16 percent, each Maine and Vermont had among the smallest proportions of school-aged residents in the United States. Rhode Island and Massachusetts were also among the lowest 15 proportions in the nation.

Along with fewer students, these states had below average student-teacher ratios. Vermont and Maine had the lowest ratios in the nation, both below 12 students per teacher in 2004–2005. The other New England states were all below the national average of 15.8 students per teacher. With the exception of Maine, all the states in New England had an above average proportion of students in private schools.

At 16.5 percent, New Hampshire had the smallest proportion of students in the United States who were eligible for free or reduced-price meals. All of the New England states were below the national proportion of 37.4 percent (this includes only 45 states and the District of Columbia; Connecticut is one of the missing states.) In the United States, 17.6 percent of children under 18 years of age lived in households below the poverty level. Rhode Island, at 18.1 percent, was the only New England state that exceeded this level. New Hampshire had the lowest proportion in the nation, with just 5.5 percent of children living in poverty. Vermont was the

next lowest at only 7.4 percent. Connecticut, Massachusetts, and New Hampshire were among the five states with median incomes of more than $79,000 for a family of four. Maine's median income was $59,596, which made it the only state in New England with a median income below the national median of $65,093.

Massachusetts had the highest proportions of students who scored at the proficient level or better on the National Assessment of Educational Progress assessments, which are examinations of students' knowledge of and skills in such subjects as math, reading, science, and writing. In 2005, more than 40 percent of the Massachusetts's students were deemed proficient in math and reading at both the 4th and 8th grade levels. New Hampshire, Vermont, and Connecticut had high proportions of students scoring at or above the proficient level. Rhode Island was the only state in New England with proportions at or below the U.S. average. Almost 8 percent of the 1.5 million high school juniors who took the Preliminary Scholastic Assessment Test/National Merit Scholarship Qualifying Test (PSAT/NMSQT) resided in New England. Vermont, New Hampshire, and Massachusetts, had above average proportions of students who scored 65 or over, which may have qualified these students for National Merit Scholarships.

High school students in New England tended to choose the SAT over the ACT. Among the 2006 high school graduates in Massachusetts in 2006, 85 percent took the SAT, which ranked second in the nation behind New York. Connecticut and New Hampshire followed closely at 84 and 82 percent, respectively. The other states in New England were well above the national average of 49 percent. As with most states with high proportions of test takers, the average scores tended to be lower. The New England average scores were close to the national average of 1518.

More than 87 percent of people in all the New England states (except Rhode Island), were high school graduates. New Hampshire had the fourth-highest proportions of high school graduates in the nation, with 91.9 percent.

The six New England states had college attainment levels that ranked among the top in the nation. Connecticut and Massachusetts ranked first and second among the states (behind only by the District of Columbia), with 36.8 and 36.6 percent of their respective populations holding a bachelor's degrees.

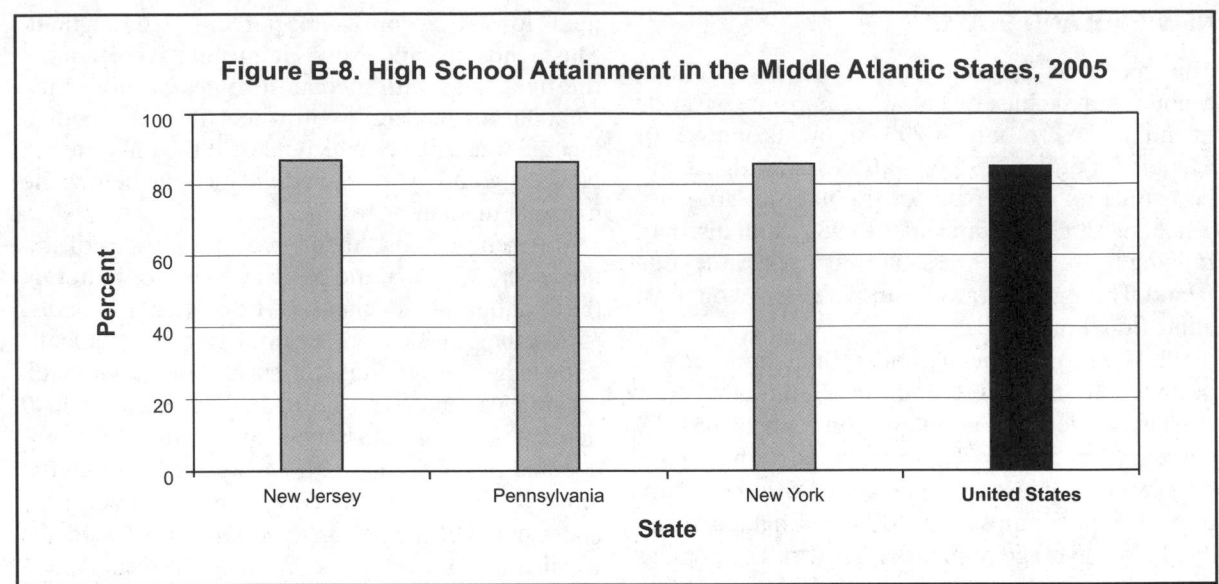

Figure B-8. High School Attainment in the Middle Atlantic States, 2005

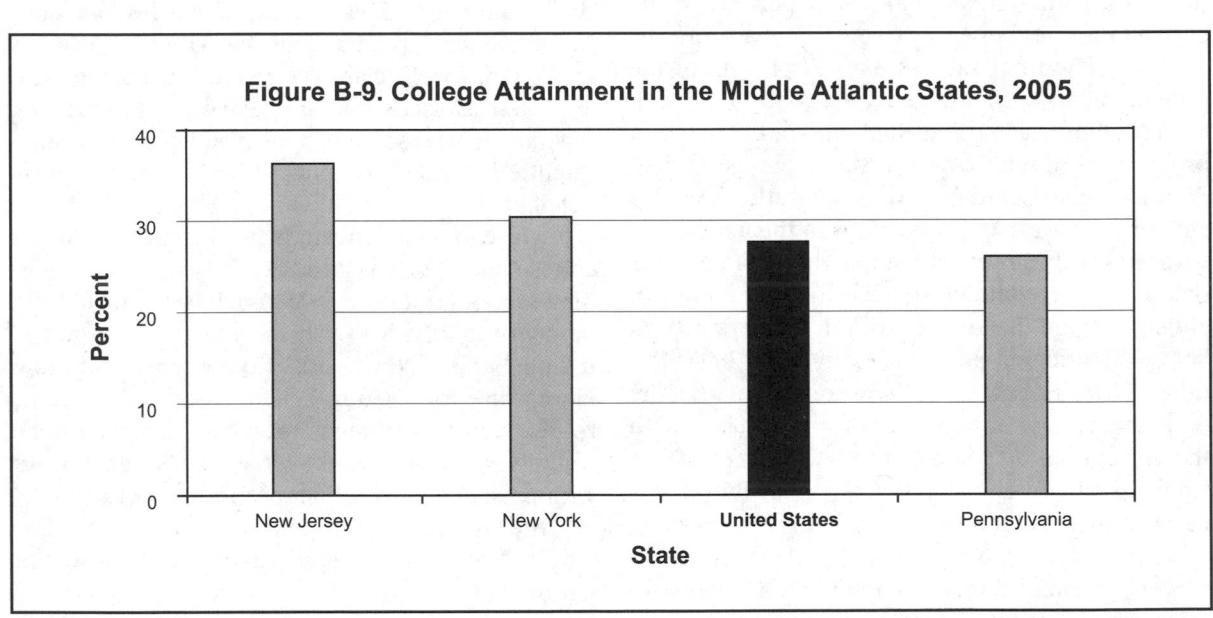

Figure B-9. College Attainment in the Middle Atlantic States, 2005

MIDDLE ATLANTIC STATES:

The Middle Atlantic region of the United States has just three states: New Jersey, New York, and Pennsylvania. These states are among the 10 largest in the nation, with a combined population of 40 million people or 13.6 percent of the U.S. population. From 2000 to 2005, the U.S. population increased by 5.3 percent, but the population of the Middle Atlantic states only increased by 1.8 percent. Pennsylvania and New York had two of the lowest rates of growth in the nation, at 1.2 and 1.5 percent, respectively, while New Jersey's population growth rate of 3.4 percent was also below average. Despite these low rates, New York and Pennsylvania retained their ranks as the third and sixth most populous states, respectively.

With nearly 7 million people between 5 and 17 years of age, the Middle Atlantic states accounted for 13.1 percent of the nation's school-age population. Both New York and Pennsylvania had below average proportions of school-age children, while New Jersey slightly exceeded the U.S. average at 18.1 percent. Together, New Jersey, New York, and Pennsylvania had just over 6 million students enrolled in public elementary and secondary schools. New Jersey's student membership in public schools increased by nearly 19 percent from 1995 to 2005 (the ninth-highest growth rate in the nation). New York was one of three states where the number of public school teachers exceeded 200,000, and New Jersey and Pennsylvania were among the five states with between 100,000 and 200,000 teachers. The three Middle Atlantic states had among the 10 highest proportions of students attending private schools, with a combined total of nearly one million children enrolled in private school during the 2003–2004 school year.

Together, the Middle Atlantic division had over 2,200 school districts, led by New York with 835. The number of schools ranged from 4,470 in New York to 2,440 in New Jersey. Minorities made up about 47 percent of New York's public school students, while in Pennsylvania, they totaled less than 25 percent of public school students. New Jersey's student-teacher ratio of 12.1 was one of the lowest in the nation, and New York's ratio of 13.0 was also very low. Pennsylvania's ratio of 15.1 students per teacher was closer to the national average of 15.8.

More than 20 percent of New York children under 18 years of age lived in poverty in 2005. New Jersey had the third-lowest proportion, with just 8.8 percent of students living in poverty. Both New York, at 18.2 percent, and Pennsylvania, at 28.3 percent, had lower proportions of students who qualified for free or reduced-price lunches. New Jersey had no data available. The median income of a family of four in the Middle Atlantic states exceeded the U.S. average. New Jersey had the highest median income in the country at $87,412. The U.S. median income was $65,093. The average public school teacher salary in New Jersey was $57,707, ranking the state sixth in the nation, followed by New York with $57,354. Pennsylvania was also among the top 15 states for public school teacher salaries.

The Middle Atlantic region ranked right in the middle of the states for high school attainment, for people 25 years and over, ranging from 86.9 percent in New Jersey to 85.7 percent in New York. New Jersey had the second-highest average freshman graduation rate, with 86.3 percent of its estimated freshmen from the 2000–2001 school year graduating 4 years later. Pennsylvania was also among the top ten. There were no data for New York.

With 88 percent of high school graduates taking the SAT, New York ranked first in the nation for level of SAT test takers; New Jersey and Pennsylvania both ranked among the top 10. States along the east coast, especially those in the Northeast, had higher proportions of students who took the SAT instead of the ACT. The scores in the Middle Atlantic states ranged from 1507 in New Jersey to 1476 in Pennsylvania; all below the national average of 1518.

College attainment levels were slightly below average in Pennsylvania, but were above average in New Jersey and New York. New Jersey tied with Maryland at 4th in the nation, with 36.3 percent of its population age 25 years and over holding bachelor's degrees or more. New York also ranked among the top 15 proportions for college attainment in the nation. All three Middle Atlantic states had high proportions of enrollment in private institutions of higher education. These states all exceeded 35 percent, while 25 percent of all students in the nation were enrolled in private colleges.

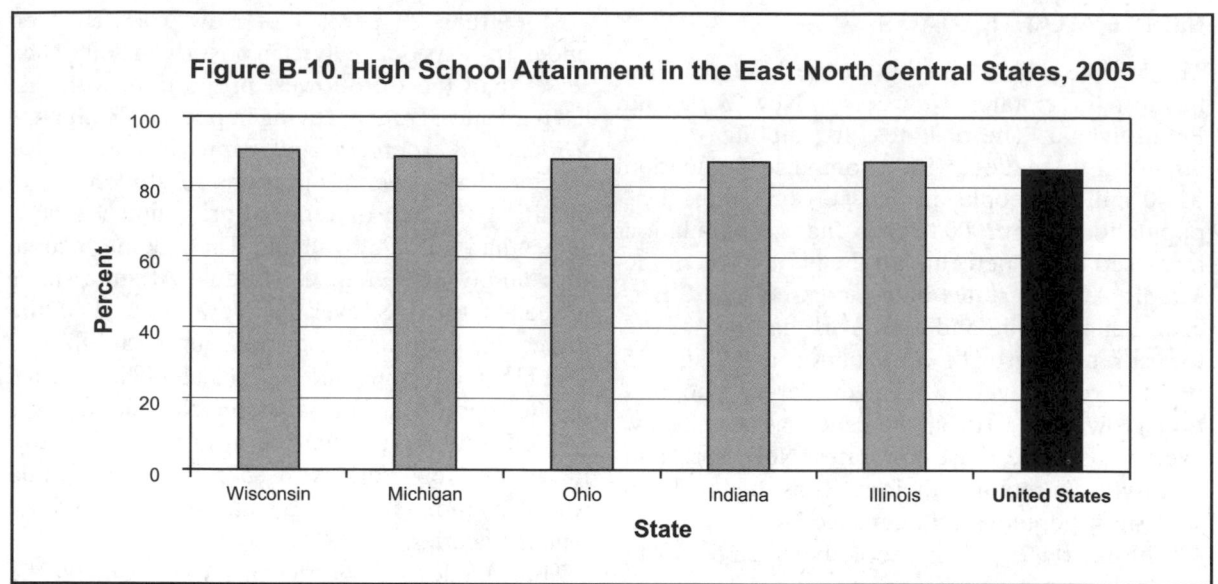

Figure B-10. High School Attainment in the East North Central States, 2005

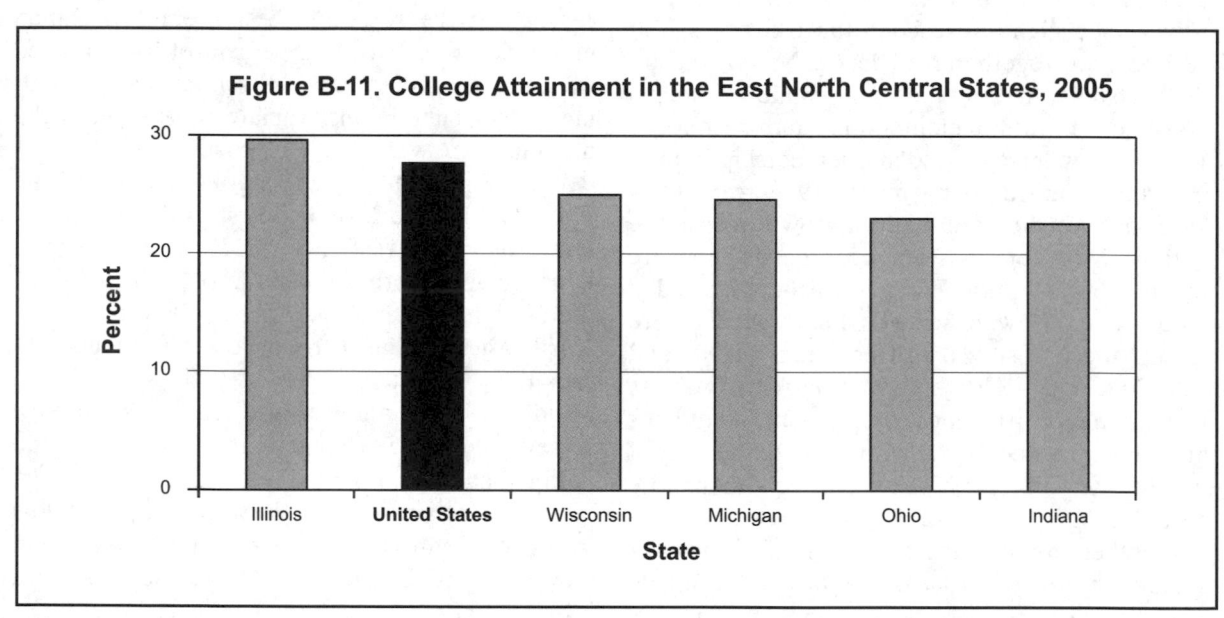

Figure B-11. College Attainment in the East North Central States, 2005

EAST NORTH CENTRAL STATES:

The East North Central region, bordering the Great Lakes, includes Illinois, Indiana, Michigan, Ohio, and Wisconsin, and combines with the West North Central region to form the Midwest region. This region contained three of the ten most populous states in 2005, and the region's total population exceeded 46 million people. This accounted for 15.6 percent of the U.S. population. The East North Central states had about 8.4 million residents between the ages of 5 and 17 years.

There were more than 7.5 million students enrolled in public schools in over 3,900 school districts in these five states, in over 16,000 schools. Wisconsin, Illinois, and Ohio had above average proportions of their students enrolled in private schools. Within all five states combined, nearly 1 million students were enrolled in private schools. Illinois had the largest proportion of minority students in the region, with Black and Hispanic students comprising more than 38 percent of the state's public school students. Indiana was one of only 13 states where non-Hispanic White students numbered more than 80 percent.

All of the East North Central states had below average growth in their numbers of students from 1995 to 2005, but none had decreasing numbers. Illinois' 9.5 percent increase was close to the national level of 10.6 percent. Michigan had a 25 percent increase in the number of teachers between 1995 and 2005, but still had the 8th highest student-teacher ratio in the country, at 17.4 students per teacher. Indiana and Illinois were slightly above the U.S. average ratio of 15.8, while Ohio and Wisconsin had lower ratios. All of the East North Central states surpassed the U.S. average expenditure of $8,310 per student, with Wisconsin ranking the highest in the division at $9,240. Illinois spent more than $18 billion a year on public schools, ranking the state 5th in the nation. Michigan and Ohio also ranked among the top 10, with expenditures exceeding $15 billion. Michigan spent about 62 percent on instruction and instruction-related expenses, giving it as the fourth-lowest proportion in the nation.

In the 45 states and District of Columbia that reported data on eligibility for free and reduced-price lunches, 37.4 percent of students met the eligibility requirements. Illinois and Indiana were very close to this total, and Michigan and Ohio had lower levels that were still over 30 percent. (Wisconsin did not report data.) Indiana was the only one of these five states with an above average proportion of children living in poverty—18.6 percent, while Wisconsin had only 13.6 percent of its children living below the poverty level. This was one of the 20 lowest in the nation. Michigan had the lowest rate among the East North Central states of low-income children (living at or below 200 percent of the poverty level) who lacked health insurance, but all five states had below average proportions of low-income children without health insurance.

Illinois had the eighth-highest median income of a family of four in the United States at $72,368, while Wisconsin and Michigan ranked 15th and 17th, respectively. Indiana had the lowest median income in the East North Central region, at $65,009, just slightly below the U.S. median of $65,093.

All five states had levels of high school attainment, for residents 25 years and over that surpassed the national average of 85.2 percent. They ranged from a high of 90.1 percent in Wisconsin, which ranked 9th in the nation, to 87.2 percent in Illinois and Indiana. Of the 46 states reporting dropout rates in 2001–2002 Wisconsin had the lowest reported dropout rate at 1.9 percent.

Illinois had the third-highest average SAT score in the nation, but only 9 percent of its graduating students took the test during the 2005–2006 school year. Of all the states in this part of the country, only Indiana graduates overwhelmingly chose the SAT over the ACT. Indiana also had the lowest average score in the region at 1493. In Illinois, all graduating seniors took the ACT, with an average score of 20.5, which was the lowest in the region and below the U.S. average score of 21.1. Wisconsin, Michigan, and Ohio each had more than 65 percent of their graduates take the ACT. The scores in those states ranged from a high of 22.2 in Wisconsin to 21.5 in both Michigan and Ohio.

Of the East North Central states, only Illinois exceeded the national average college attainment level of 27.7 percent—29.6 percent of Illinois's adults had bachelor's degrees, the 17th highest level in the nation. The other states in the East North Central region had proportions ranging from 25.0 percent in Wisconsin to 22.6 percent in Indiana.

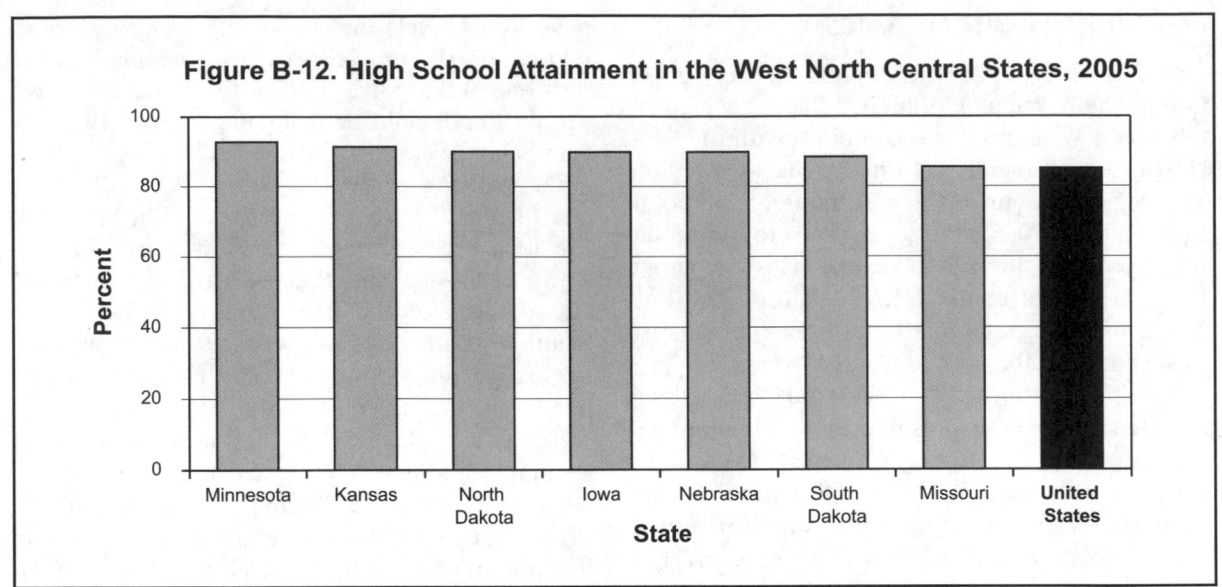

Figure B-12. High School Attainment in the West North Central States, 2005

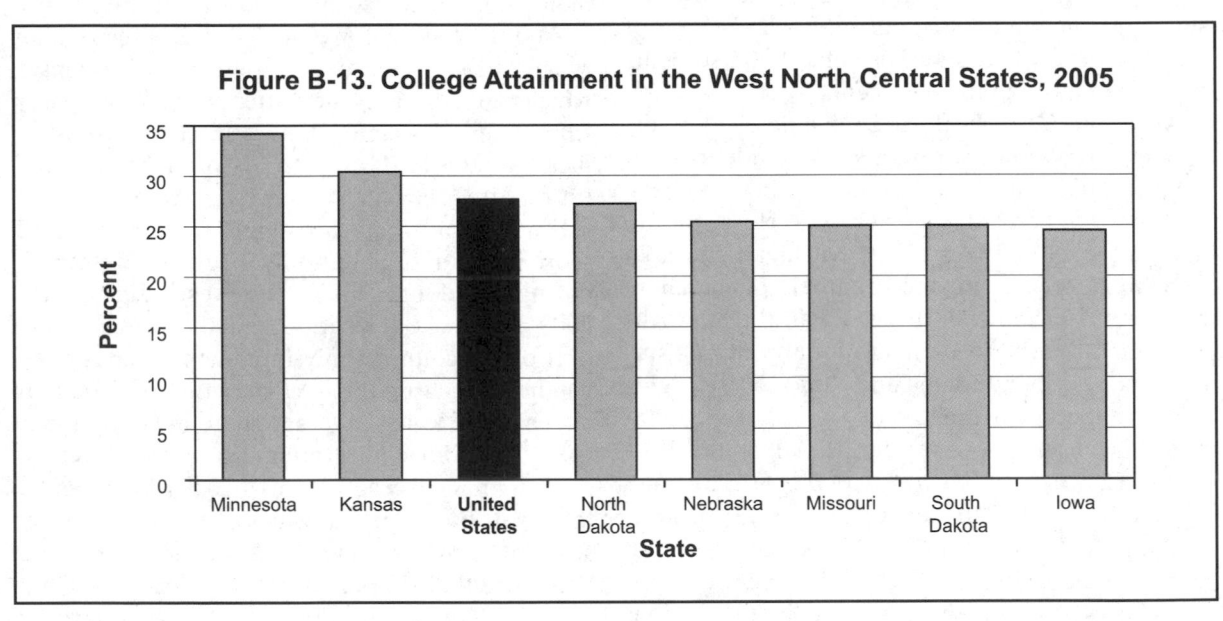

Figure B-13. College Attainment in the West North Central States, 2005

WEST NORTH CENTRAL STATES:

Iowa, Kansas, Minnesota, Missouri, Nebraska, North Dakota, and South Dakota are the seven states of the West North Central division. In 2005, there were more than 3.2 million public school students living in these states. Expenditures for public schools in this region reached over $25 billion during the 2003–2004 school year.

The combined population of the West North Central states totaled close to 20 million people. With the exception of Minnesota and Missouri, these states ranked among the lower half of states in the nation by population size. Both Dakotas were among the seven states and the District of Columbia with fewer than 1 million people. Missouri had the highest total population of the group, and ranked 18th in the nation. All seven states had lower than average population growth from 2000 to 2005, with North Dakota experiencing a slight population loss. Minnesota grew by 4.3 percent during this period, the highest rate in the division, but still lower than the U.S. average growth rate of 5.3 percent.

Student-teacher ratios were below the U.S. average in all of the West North Central states, except for Minnesota, which was slightly above average. North Dakota, South Dakota, Nebraska, Iowa, and Missouri all ranked among the lowest 15 states in the nation, with proportions of less than 14 students per teacher. (The national average was 15.8 students per teacher). Minnesota and Nebraska were the only states in the division with above average per student expenditures. South Dakota had the lowest expenditures among the West North Central states, with $7,068 spent per student.

Both Minnesota and North Dakota had low proportions of students who were eligible for free or reduced-price meals. Of the 45 states with data and District of Columbia, these two states were among only eight with fewer than 30 percent of eligible students. Only Kansas and Missouri slightly exceeded the U.S. average of 37.4 percent. The same two states—Kansas and Missouri—had rates of children in poverty slightly above the national average of 17.6 percent. The other West North Central states had lower levels of children living in poverty; Minnesota's rate, 10 percent, was tied with Hawaii for fourth lowest in the nation.

Minnesota was one of six states with a median income for a family of four exceeding $75,000 per year. North Dakota had the lowest median income of these seven states at $57,092. The U.S. average was $65,093. Average teacher salaries were below average in the West North Central states. Only Minnesota's exceeded $45,000, but the state's average salary remained slightly below the U.S. average of $49,109. North and South Dakota had the two lowest average teacher salaries in the nation, as well as the lowest proportion of teachers with master's degrees or higher (about 20 percent, compared with a national level of over 40 percent).

Minnesota had the highest high school attainment level in the nation, with 92.7 percent of its residents 25 years and over holding high school diplomas. Most of the other states in the division had high school attainment levels of close to or above 90 percent. Missouri had the lowest level among these states, but, at 85.5 percent, it was slightly above the national average. These states also had high average freshman graduation rates, with five of the seven highest proportions of estimated high school freshmen who graduated four years later. With the exception of Missouri, these states had lower than average proportions of 16- to 19-year olds who were neither high school graduates nor students.

All 7 states in the West North Central region were in the top 10 states when ranked by SAT scores, and surpassed the national average by more than 200 points. However, fewer than 10 percent of high school graduates in this region took the test in these states. High school students in this region were more likely to take the ACT. In each of these states, 65 percent or more of graduates took the ACT. In North Dakota, 80 percent of high school graduates took the ACT, while only 40 percent took the test nationally. As in most states with high proportions of test takers, the average scores tended to be lower. However, in the West North Central division, the averages in all seven states exceeded the national average of 21.1. Minnesota's test scores ranked among the top 10 states.

College attainment levels in the West North Central division ranged from 34.2 percent in Minnesota to 24.5 percent in Iowa. Kansas and Minnesota are among 14 states and the District of Columbia in which 30 percent or more of the population over 25 years of age were college graduates.

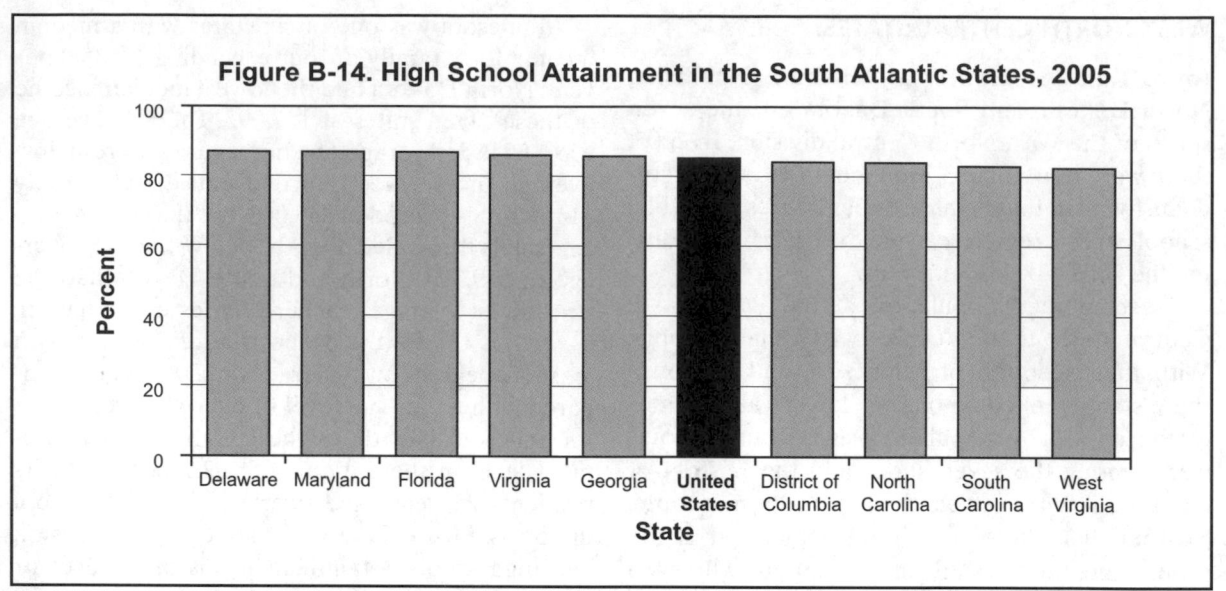

Figure B-14. High School Attainment in the South Atlantic States, 2005

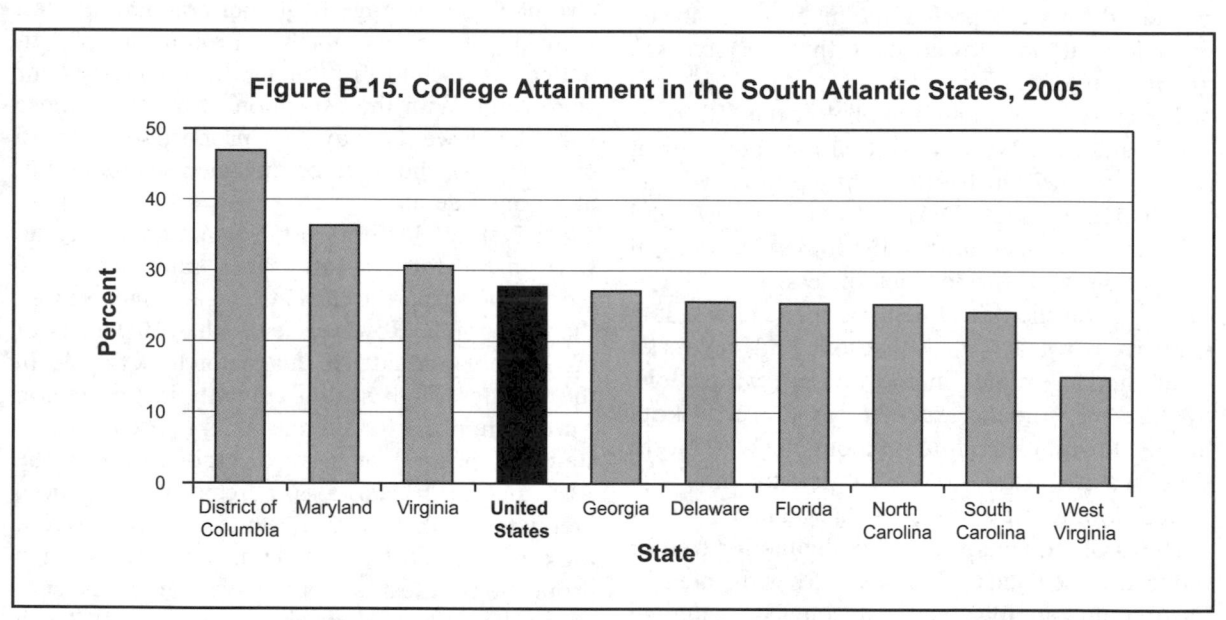

Figure B-15. College Attainment in the South Atlantic States, 2005

SOUTH ATLANTIC STATES:

The South Atlantic division of the United States includes Delaware, the District of Columbia, Florida, Georgia, Maryland, North Carolina, South Carolina, Virginia, and West Virginia. This was the largest division in the nation in 2005, with over 56 million total residents, and over 8.8 million students enrolled in public elementary and secondary schools. These eight states and the District of Columbia were home to 19 percent of the United State's population.

Georgia had the 10th highest proportion of school-age children in the nation and Maryland ranked 15th, but most of the South Atlantic states had a lower than average proportion of children between the ages of 5 and 17 years. The District of Columbia had the lowest proportion in the nation at 13.5 percent. However, it can be misleading to compare the District of Columbia with the 50 states, rather than with other cities. Unlike any of the states, it has an entirely urban population; thus, its characteristics are more similar to other large cities. For example, Seattle, San Francisco, and Boston had youth populations that were as low or lower than the District of Columbia's. West Virginia was the only state in which the proportion of school-age children was under 16 percent.

Virginia had among the lowest student-teacher ratios in the United States, with a ratio of 12.9, and West Virginia was slightly higher at 14.0 students per teacher. Of the South Atlantic states, only Florida exceeded the national average of 15.8 students per teacher. Florida had the 10th highest ratio in the nation. More than 47 percent of teachers in Delaware had fewer than 10 years of experience, the fifth-highest proportion in the nation. At the other extreme, nearly 49 percent of West Virginia public school teachers had 20 years or more of experience, the highest proportion in the nation.

Per student expenditures ranged from $12,959 in the District of Columbia, which was the second-highest in the nation, to $6,613 in North Carolina, which was among the ten lowest in the nation. Florida had the highest total expenditures in the division, with $17.6 billion, and was among the 11 states that had expenditures exceeding $10 billion per year. The District of Columbia spent 61.1 percent of its public school expenditures on instruction and instruction-related costs, which was one of the lowest proportions in the nation.

About two-thirds of the public school students in the District of Columbia qualified for free or reduced-price meals, which was the highest proportion in the nation when compared with states. Mississippi and Louisiana were the only states in which more than 60 percent of the students qualified. Virginia and Maryland had proportions of 32 percent or less, which was below the average for reporting states. More than 38 percent of children in the District of Columbia lived in poverty, while the bordering states of Maryland and Virginia had rates of about 13 percent. Georgia and West Virginia were among 11 states in which the child poverty level exceeded 20 percent.

Maryland had the fourth-highest median income for a family of four. With $72,680, Delaware also ranked among the top 10 states. West Virginia had the second-lowest median family income in the nation at $46,169.

Georgia and Delaware were among the 10 states with the highest dropout rates in the nation. Virginia's dropout rate was less than 3.0 percent and was among the lowest 10 of the 46 states with data. Georgia and South Carolina had low averaged freshman graduations rates, with only about 60 percent of students who began as public high school freshmen graduating. In Georgia more than 10 percent of teenagers between the ages of 16 and 19 years had not graduated from high school and were not enrolled in school. This was among the highest proportions in the nation and well above the U.S. average of 7.3 percent.

With the exception of West Virginia, most high school seniors in the South Atlantic states took the SAT. In the District of Columbia, 78 percent of graduates took the SAT. The other states in the division were all between 60 and 75 percent, except for West Virginia (20 percent). Only 15 states and the District of Columbia had SAT scores below the national average of 1518; Delaware, Georgia, Maryland, North Carolina, South Carolina, and Florida were six of those states. The proportion of ACT test takers ranged from 64 percent in West Virginia to 4 percent in Delaware.

The District of Columbia had the highest proportion of college graduates in the nation. Maryland tied with New Jersey for 4th, with 36.3 percent, and Virginia tied with California for 11th, with 30.6 percent.

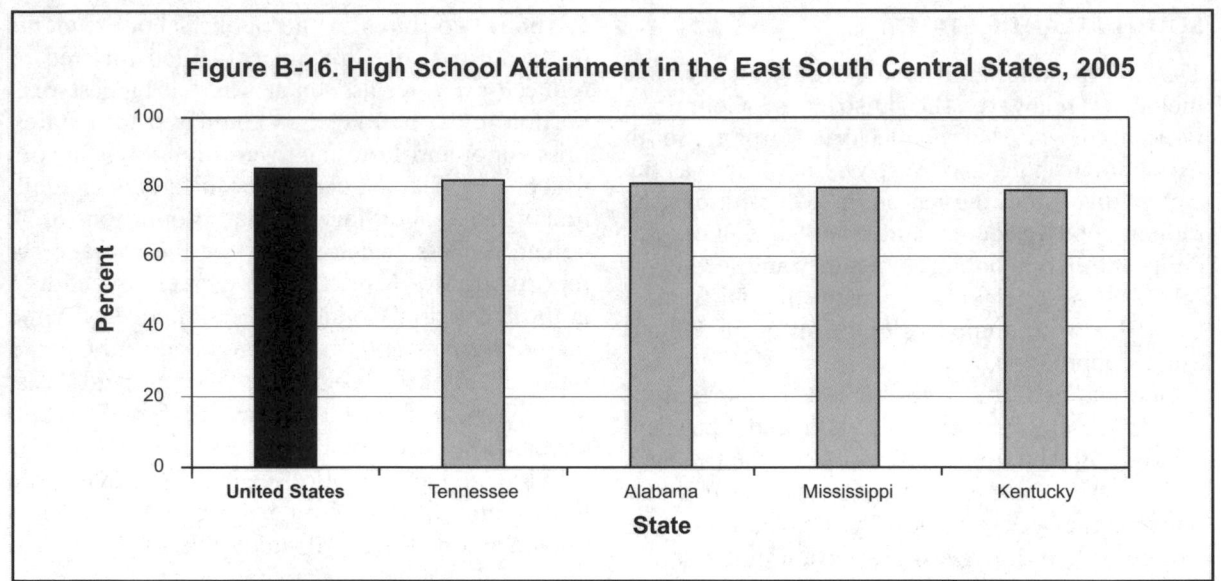

Figure B-16. High School Attainment in the East South Central States, 2005

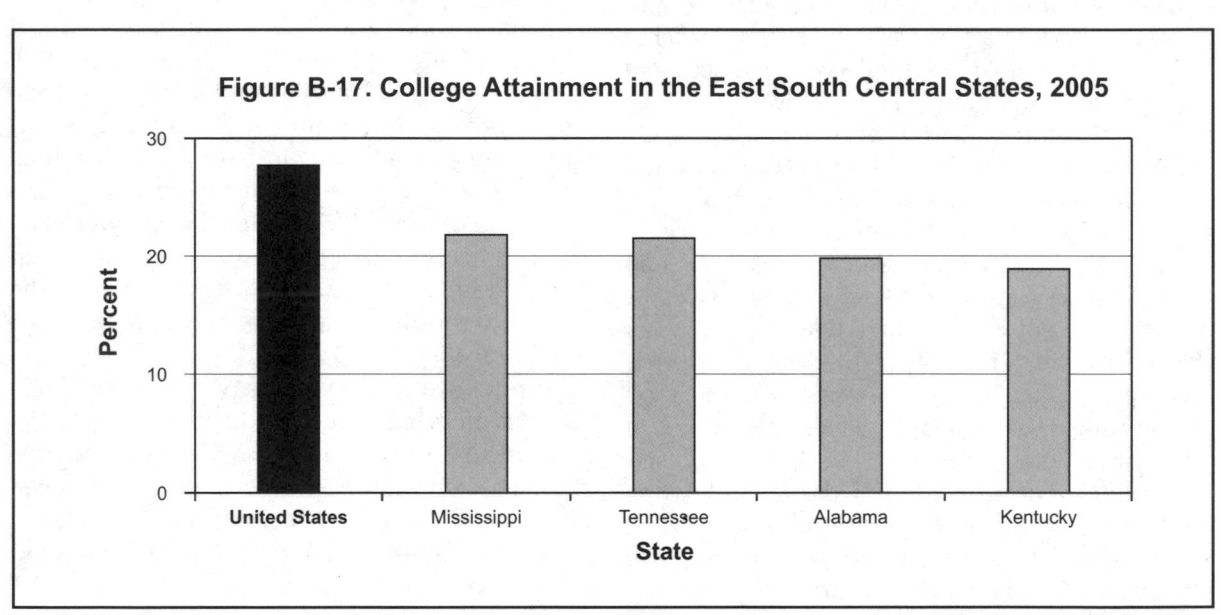

Figure B-17. College Attainment in the East South Central States, 2005

EAST SOUTH CENTRAL STATES:

The East South Central states fell below the U.S. averages for most educational measures. This region—comprising Alabama, Kentucky, Mississippi, and Tennessee—accounted for 17.6 million people, less than 6 percent of the country's population. In the 2004–2005 school year, these states totaled 630 school districts, 5,321 schools, and 2.8 million public school students.

These four states had over 3 million people between the ages of 5 and 17 years. Mississippi was one of four states tied for tenth in the nation with a school-age proportion of the population of 18.4 percent. With a high proportion of young people, it is not surprising that Mississippi's expenditures per student were the fifth lowest in the nation, coming in at just below $6,200. Alabama and Tennessee were also among the 10 states with the lowest per student expenditures. Tennessee directed nearly 70 percent of its expenditures toward instruction and instruction-related expenses, which ranked the state fourth in the nation for these expenditures.

Alabama and Mississippi ranked among the top 10 of the 45 states and the District of Columbia that reported student eligibility for free or reduced-price meals (neither Kentucky nor Tennessee reported data). In Mississippi nearly two-thirds of public school students were eligible, which was the highest proportion of any state and slightly below the proportion for the District of Columbia. All four of these states exceeded the national average for percentage of children living in poverty. Mississippi ranked second in the nation with more than 30 percent of its children living in poverty. Tennessee had the lowest proportion of children living in poverty. However, at 19.5 percent its rate was still higher than the national rate of 17.8 percent.

All four states ranked among the lowest 10 in the nation for their proportions of high school graduates age 25 years and over. They ranged from a high of 81.8 percent in Mississippi to 78.9 percent in Kentucky, and all fell short of the national average of 85.2 percent. Mississippi and Kentucky, together with Texas, were the only states in the nation with high school attainment levels of less than 80 percent.

The states of the East South Central division had average student-teacher ratios, except for Alabama, which was well below the U.S. average. The number of public school students in Tennessee increased by 6.8 percent from 1995 to 2005, but the number of teachers jumped 26.6 percent to over 60,000 during the same period. Alabama and Mississippi were among 15 states in which student membership declined during the 10-year period.

In Tennessee, nearly 45 percent of teachers had fewer than 10 years of experience, placing it among the top 15 percentages in this category. All four states had below average teacher salaries, despite the fact that more than half of the teachers in Kentucky and Alabama had master's degrees. At $37,924, Mississippi's salaries were the third lowest in the nation, surpassing only North Dakota and South Dakota. Tennessee had the highest average salary in the division at $42,537.

Alabama and Mississippi were among six states and the District of Columbia with fewer than 20 percent of their 8th graders achieving math proficiency on the 2005 National Assessment of Education Progress. Kentucky had the highest level of achievement among the East South Central states, with 23 percent of its students deemed proficient. The U.S. average was 28 percent. In 2006, high school graduates split mostly along regional lines between taking the SAT and the ACT. In the East South Central states, most graduates chose the ACT. Mississippi and Tennessee had the highest proportions of ACT test takers in the area, with 93 percent of their high school graduates taking the test. Mississippi tied with three other states for the lowest proportion of high school graduates taking the SAT, just 4 percent of graduates taking the test. All of the states in the East South Central region had 76 percent or more of their 2006 high school graduates taking the ACT, far surpassing the U.S. average of 40 percent. All four states had below average ACT scores, and, as with most states in which few graduating seniors took the SAT, each state had average SAT scores over 1600, which was much higher than the national average of 1518.

All states in this region had below average college attainment levels for residents age 25 years and over. They all ranked among the bottom seven states in the nation, and all are below 22 percent, well below the U.S. average of 27.7 percent. Over 900,000 students attended institutions of higher education in these four states. Mississippi was one of six states in which 60 percent or more of bachelor's degrees awarded were given to women.

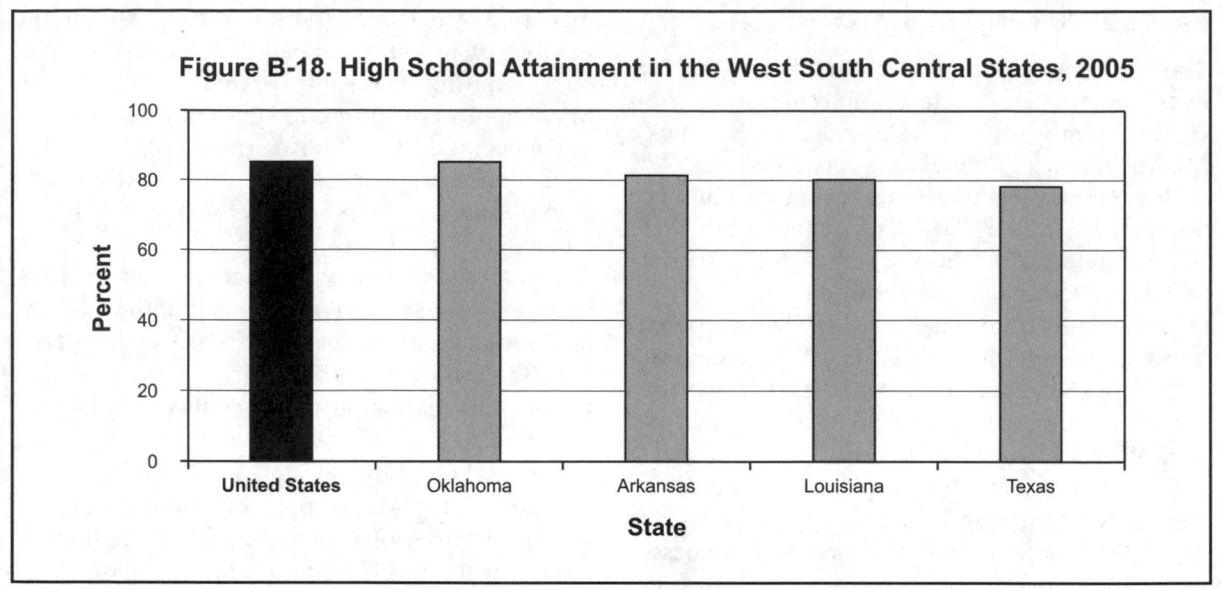

Figure B-18. High School Attainment in the West South Central States, 2005

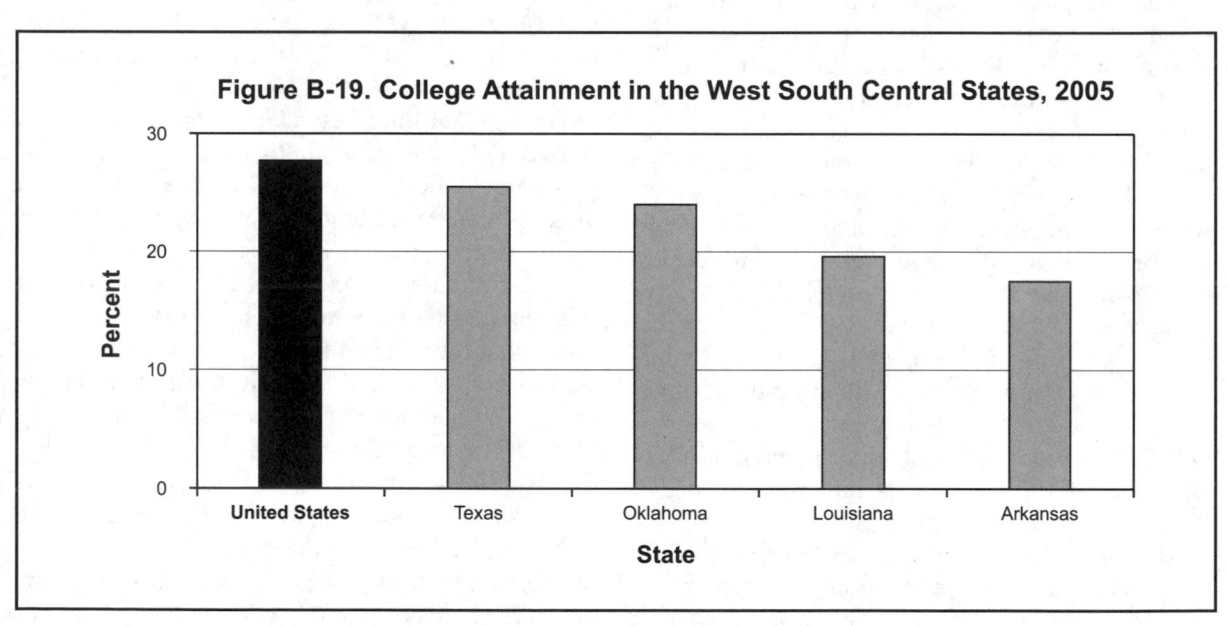

Figure B-19. College Attainment in the West South Central States, 2005

WEST SOUTH CENTRAL STATES:

Arkansas, Louisiana, Oklahoma, and Texas make make up the West South Central region of the United States. These four states added up to more than 33 million people in 2005, with more than 6 million of them between 5 and 17 years of age. More than two-thirds of the region's population lived in Texas.

With a population growth rate of more than 22 percent during the 1990s, Texas surpassed New York to become the second-largest state in the nation. Much of the nation's growth has taken place in the West and the South. From 2000 to 2005, Texas grew by nearly 10 percent. In 2005, 19.5 percent of Texas residents were between 5 and 17 years of age. This was the third-highest proportion of school-aged population in the nation. Louisiana, before Hurricane Katrina, also had a school-aged population proportion exceeding the U.S. average of 17.9 percent.

Nearly 13 percent of the nation's public school students attended schools in the West South Central states. Texas had more than 4.4 million students attending public schools. The number of Louisiana public school students decreased by more than 9 percent from 1995 to 2005. (The long-term effects of Hurricane Katrina on Louisiana school enrollment and other educational measures were not yet known.) The number of students in Texas grew by nearly 20 percent. The states of the West South Central region had below average student-teacher ratios. These ratios ranged from 15.6 in Oklahoma to 14.7 in Louisiana. The number of teachers in Texas grew by more than 25 percent from 1995 to 2005 and reached 294,547 during the 2004–2005 school year.

Texas had the third-highest level of public school expenditures in the United States, with over $30 billion per year. The other three states in the division had expenditures ranging from $5.3 billion in Louisiana to $3.1 billion in Arkansas. Per student expenditures in the West South Central states were below average. The amounts in this division ranged from $6,154 in Oklahoma to $7,271 in Louisiana.

There were more than 2,300 school districts in the West South Central states, ranging from 1,279 in Texas to 91 in Louisiana. Texas had more school districts than any other state. While Oklahoma had 603 districts, half as many as Texas, it had just 14.3 per-

cent as many public school students. Louisiana had one of the highest proportions of private school students, while Oklahoma, Texas, and Arkansas had among the lowest proportions of private school students in the nation. Texas and Louisiana were among the nine states and the District of Columbia in which minority public school students exceeded 50 percent of the student population. Nearly 45 percent of Texas's public school students were of Hispanic origin, which ranked the state third after New Mexico and California.

The West South Central states had high proportions of students who qualified for free or reduced-price meals. At 47.7 percent, Texas had the lowest eligibility level in the region. The other three states had among the 7 highest levels in the 46 states with reported data and the District of Columbia. In Louisiana, more than 61 percent of students were eligible. Arkansas had the lowest proportion of children living in poverty of the states in the region, but at 18.6 percent, it was still above the national proportion of 17.6 percent. Louisiana, and Texas had among the highest proportions of children living in poverty in the nation. Louisiana ranked third (24.7 percent) and Texas ranked sixth (22.0 percent).

The median income of a family of four in this region was below the U.S. level of $65,093. Arkansas was one of five states with median incomes of less than $50,000. Texas had the highest median income in the region at $54,544, which was still one of the lowest 10 median incomes in the nation.

Only Oklahoma met the U.S. average high school attainment level for people 25 years and over. Texas was one of only three states in which the proportion of high school graduates was less than 80 percent.

Most high school graduates in West South Central states opted for the ACT over the SAT. Only Texas had more high school graduates taking the SAT. Texas was one of 15 states and the District of Columbia with an average score below the U.S. average of 1518. Arkansas had one of the smallest proportions of SAT test takers, with just 5 percent of graduates taking the test.

Arkansas and Louisiana were among five states in the United States with a proportion of college graduates age 25 years and over. In Oklahoma, 24 percent of residents had bachelor's degrees, as did 25.5 percent in Texas.

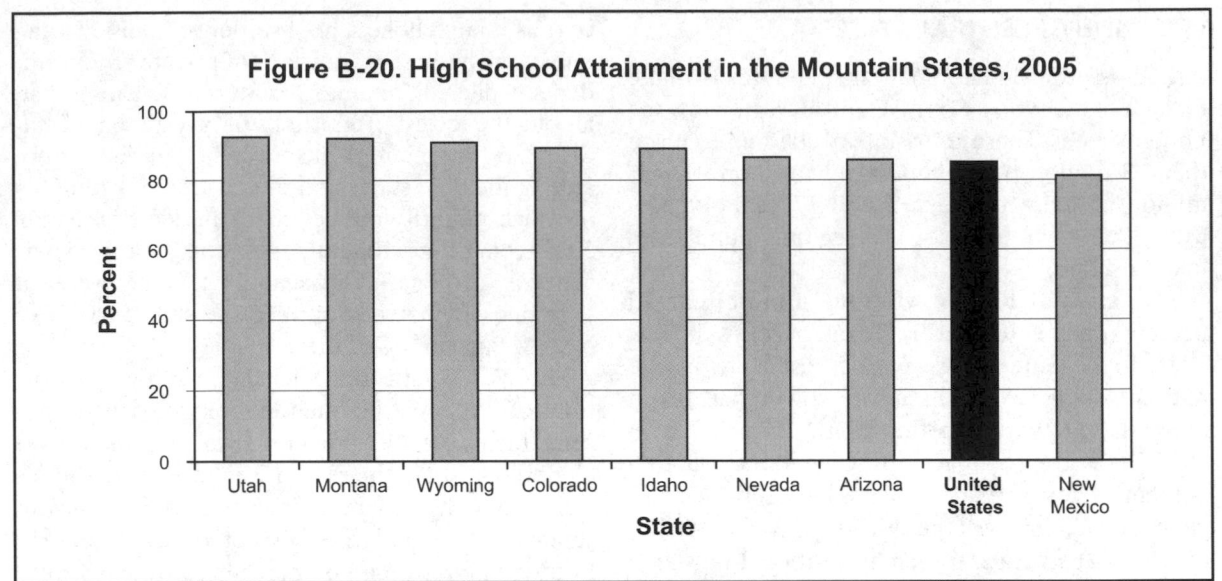

Figure B-20. High School Attainment in the Mountain States, 2005

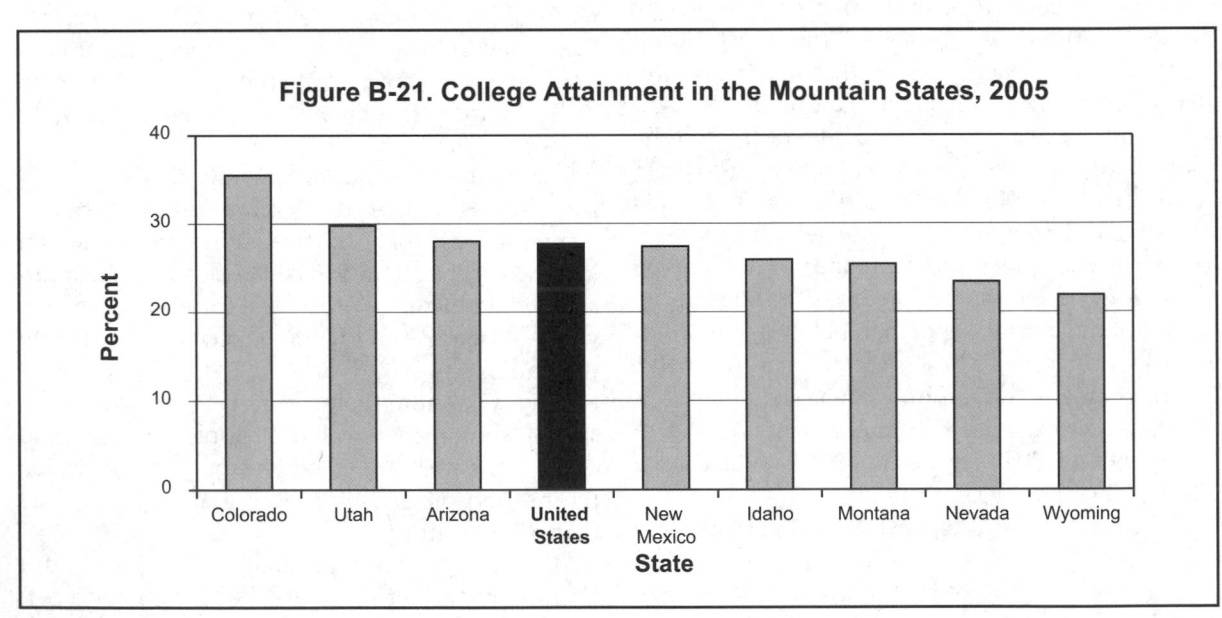

Figure B-21. College Attainment in the Mountain States, 2005

MOUNTAIN STATES:

The Mountain region includes Arizona, Colorado, Idaho, Montana, Nevada, New Mexico, Utah, and Wyoming. There were more than 20 million people residing in these 8 states in 2005, accounting for about 6.8 percent of the U.S. population. Nevada and Arizona ranked first and second, respectively, for their percentage increases in population from 2000 to 2005. Idaho, Utah, and Colorado also ranked among the top 10 fastest-growing states in the nation. There were more than 2 million new residents in these eight states from 2000 to 2005.

There were more than 3.5 million students in this region in 2005. Utah had the second-highest proportion of school-aged population in the nation. Utah and Alaska were the only states in which this proportion exceeded 20 percent of the population. Idaho and Arizona were also among the top six states for proportions of school-age population. Not surprisingly, Utah had the highest student-teacher ratio in the United States. Arizona, Nevada, Idaho, and Colorado also ranked among the top 10 highest ratios. New Mexico and Arizona had among the highest proportions of minority students. Hispanics made up more than 53 percent of New Mexico's public school students. New Mexico and Montana had proportions of American Indian students exceeding 11 percent. In Wyoming, 85.6 percent of public school students were non-Hispanic White.

Over 58 percent of New Mexico's students were eligible for free or reduced-price lunches, placing the state among the five highest proportions in the nation. Montana, Wyoming, and Colorado all had levels of eligibility below the U.S. average of 37.4 percent. New Mexico, Arizona, and Montana had above average proportions of children living in poverty. New Mexico had the fourth-highest proportion of children living in poverty in the nation, at 24.7 percent. In Idaho and Utah, fewer than 13 percent of children lived in poverty, which was well below the national total of 17.6 percent.

Colorado was the only Mountain state with a median income for a family of four that exceeded the national level. The other states in this division were all below the national median of $65,093. New Mexico and Montana were among five states with medians below $50,000. All eight states had

lower than average teacher salaries. Colorado had the highest average teacher salary in the division, at $45,616, which was still below the U.S. average of $49,109.

Average SAT scores ranged from 1487 in Nevada to 1667 in Utah and 1670 in Colorado. Except for Nevada, the Mountain states had above average SAT scores. However, the majority of high school graduates in the Mountain states did not take the SAT. In Nevada, 40 percent of high school graduates took the SAT, and in Utah, just 7 percent took the test. (Most students in this division take the ACT). In Colorado, 100 percent of its 2006 high school graduates took the ACT.

High school attainment levels for the population age 25 years and over tended to be high in the Mountain states. New Mexico was the only state in this division with a high school attainment level below the national average. Fewer than 82 percent of New Mexico's population had graduated from high school, placing the state among the 7 lowest proportions in the nation. Montana, Wyoming, and Utah had three of the highest proportions of high school graduates in the nation. They were among the 12 states that had more than 90 percent of their residents holding high school diplomas.

Arizona and Nevada had among the highest dropout rates among the 45 states that reported data and the District of Columbia. Arizona had the highest rate in the nation, and Nevada ranked seventh. Utah had the lowest rate of reporting Mountain states. (Colorado had no data). Nevada had the highest proportion in the nation of teenagers between the ages of 16 and 19 years who were not in high school, and have not graduated (10.7 percent). Arizona and New Mexico also had high proportions of these at-risk teenagers, with more than 9 percent each. Of the Mountain states, only Montana and Utah had dropout levels lower than the U.S. average of 7.3 percent.

Colorado had one of the highest levels of college attainment in the nation for the population 25 years and over. The state was among eight states in which college graduates accounted for one-third or more of the population age 25 years and over. Utah and Arizona were the only other states in the region that exceeded the national average of 27.7 percent. Wyoming ranked among the bottom 10 states on this measure.

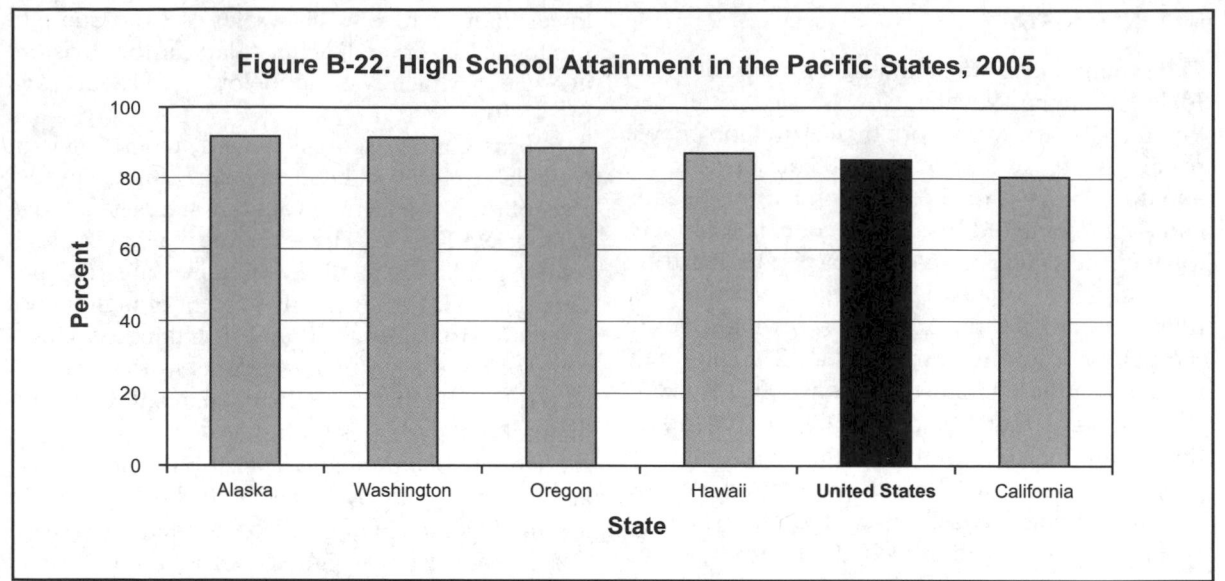

Figure B-22. High School Attainment in the Pacific States, 2005

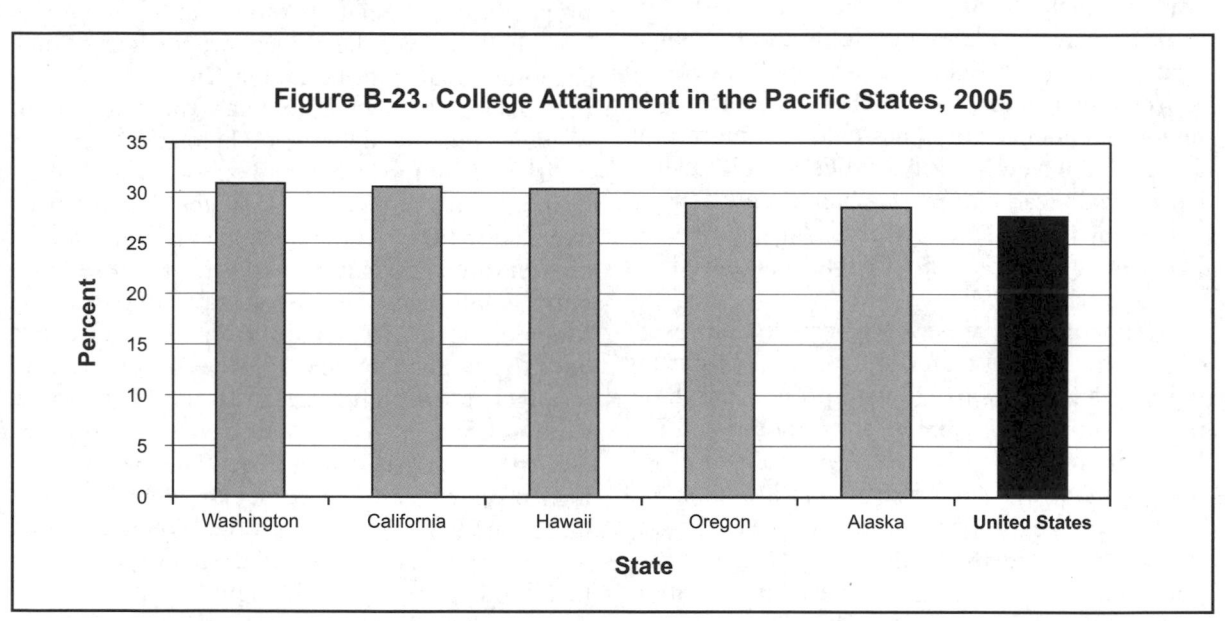

Figure B-23. College Attainment in the Pacific States, 2005

PACIFIC STATES:

The Pacific states are Alaska, California, Hawaii, Oregon, and Washington. The population of the Pacific region exceeded 47 million in 2005, with 75 percent of the population living in California, the nation's most populous state. The Pacific division represented more than 16 percent of the nation's population and over 8 million public school students. This was one of the larger divisions in the United States.

Alaska had the highest proportion of school-aged population in the nation. Only Alaska and Utah had more than 20 percent of their populations fall in this age group. California ranked 4th, with 19.4 percent. Hawaii, Oregon, and Washington all had levels of school-aged population below the U.S. average of 17.9 percent. From 2000 to 2005, all five states had growth rates that matched or exceeded the national rate of 5.3 percent. California and Washington both increased by 6.7 percent.

Alaska had the highest proportion of migrant students in the nation at 5 percent. Oregon ranked second, and California tied Washington for third; all had proportions of 3.7 percent or higher in this category. Nationally, 1.5 percent of public school students were migrants. In both California and Hawaii, minority students made up the majority of public school students. In California, about one-fourth of public school students were English-Language Learners, which was the highest proportion of these learners in the nation.

The number of school districts ranged from 1,140 in California to a single school district in Hawaii. Most of the states in this region had below average proportions of private school students, but Hawaii had one of the highest proportions in the nation. Alaska had one of the smallest proportions of private school students in the country, with fewer than 5 percent of its students attending private schools.

California had the highest public school expenditures in the nation. During the 2003–2004 school year, the state spent nearly $50 billion. Hawaii, with considerably fewer students, spent about $1.5 billion. In Alaska, 62.5 percent of expenditures went towards instruction and instruction-related costs; this was among the 10 lowest proportions in the nation for these types of expenditures. California was the only state in the division that exceeded the national average of 66.1 percent of expenditures going toward instruction and instruction-related expenses.

Alaska and Hawaii were the only Pacific states with above average per student expenditures. At $10,116, Alaska had the ninth-highest total in the United States. Washington had the lowest total in the Pacific region, with $7,391 spent per student.

Nearly half of California's public school students qualified for free or reduced-price meals. Oregon and Hawaii had eligibility that was also above the U.S. average of 37.4 percent. Alaska was well below this level at 28.6 percent. The proportion of children living in poverty ranged from 18.5 percent in California to 10 percent in Hawaii. Nationally, 17.6 percent of children live in poverty. All of the Pacific states, except for Oregon, had high median incomes for a family of four. Alaska had the highest median income in the region at $72,110, although Hawaii, Washington, and California each exceeded $67,000.

About 50 percent or more of the high school graduates in each of the Pacific states took the SAT. Washington had the highest average score in the division at 1570, while Hawaii the lowest at 1463. The proportion of students that took the ACT ranged from 25 percent in Alaska to 13 percent in Oregon. Washington and Oregon had among the highest average ACT scores in the nation. All of the states in this region matched or exceeded the national average score of 21.1.

Alaska and Washington were two of the twelve states with high school attainment levels of more than 90 percent for the population 25 years and over. California was the only state in the division with below average high school attainment levels. Almost 20 percent of people over 25 years of age in California had not graduated from high school. The state ranked among the five lowest high school attainment records in the United States.

All five states in the Pacific region had above average college attainment levels, for the population 25 years and over, with most of their levels at around 30 percent. More than 3 million students were enrolled in institutions of higher education in the Pacific states, and almost 80 percent of these students studied in California. California awarded more bachelor's, first professional, and doctoral degrees than any other state, and also awarded more than 10 percent of all degrees conferred in the United States.

Table B-3. Population, School, and Student Characteristics by State

FIPS code	State	Population, 2005		Median income of a family of four, 2003 (dollars)	Children under 18 years of age in poverty, 2005 (percent)	Poverty and health insurance, 2005		
		Total	Age 5 to 17 years (percent)			Total children under 19 years of age (thousands)	Low-income children under 19 years of age (percent)	Low-income children with no health insurance (percent)
		1	2	3	4	5	6	7
00	UNITED STATES	296 410 404	17.9	65 093	17.6	77 210	38.7	7.2
01	Alabama	4 557 808	17.4	55 448	24.7	1 127	44.1	3.7
02	Alaska	663 661	20.7	72 110	12.1	194	33.8	3.7
04	Arizona	5 939 292	18.9	58 206	21.6	1 680	49.6	13.5
05	Arkansas	2 779 154	17.6	48 353	18.6	708	45.7	6.9
06	California	36 132 147	19.4	67 814	18.5	10 097	41.0	8.9
08	Colorado	4 665 177	18.0	71 559	14.7	1 230	32.1	8.5
09	Connecticut	3 510 297	17.8	86 001	12.4	870	25.7	5.4
10	Delaware	843 524	16.7	72 680	14.2	205	33.9	7.3
11	District of Columbia	550 521	13.5	56 067	38.6	117	56.0	5.1
12	Florida	17 789 864	16.6	58 605	15.8	4 180	38.6	11.8
13	Georgia	9 072 576	18.4	62 294	21.2	2 467	41.7	7.3
15	Hawaii	1 275 194	16.4	71 320	10.0	315	27.4	2.1
16	Idaho	1 429 096	18.8	53 376	12.4	413	39.1	6.7
17	Illinois	12 763 371	18.4	72 368	15.6	3 424	34.6	6.0
18	Indiana	6 271 973	18.7	65 009	18.6	1 664	41.2	5.3
19	Iowa	2 966 334	16.5	64 341	14.5	722	31.3	2.6
20	Kansas	2 744 687	17.7	64 215	17.8	721	37.8	4.8
21	Kentucky	4 173 405	17.0	53 198	21.2	1 044	41.5	5.2
22	Louisiana	4 523 628	18.2	50 529	24.7	1 119	45.5	5.4
23	Maine	1 321 505	15.9	59 596	15.8	298	38.4	5.3
24	Maryland	5 600 388	18.2	82 363	13.3	1 443	29.5	4.4
25	Massachusetts	6 398 743	16.6	82 561	11.6	1 587	27.2	2.1
26	Michigan	10 120 860	18.5	68 602	16.3	2 656	35.9	3.0
27	Minnesota	5 132 799	17.4	76 733	10.0	1 289	23.7	3.0
28	Mississippi	2 921 088	18.4	46 570	30.7	801	54.1	9.0
29	Missouri	5 800 310	17.3	64 128	17.7	1 456	38.5	5.3
30	Montana	935 670	16.2	49 124	19.8	226	42.9	9.8
31	Nebraska	1 758 787	17.5	63 625	12.3	452	31.5	3.4
32	Nevada	2 414 807	18.5	63 005	13.4	679	36.4	8.1
33	New Hampshire	1 309 940	17.6	79 339	5.5	312	19.7	2.0
34	New Jersey	8 717 925	18.1	87 412	8.8	2 258	23.9	5.4
35	New Mexico	1 928 384	18.4	45 867	24.7	527	53.0	16.2
36	New York	19 254 630	17.1	69 354	20.5	4 793	41.1	5.1
37	North Carolina	8 683 242	17.7	56 712	18.3	2 296	40.5	8.7
38	North Dakota	636 677	15.7	57 092	13.3	152	35.1	6.2
39	Ohio	11 464 042	17.7	66 066	17.4	2 846	36.4	5.1
40	Oklahoma	3 547 884	17.2	50 216	20.8	880	45.5	7.2
41	Oregon	3 641 056	17.1	61 570	17.7	920	42.9	7.5
42	Pennsylvania	12 429 616	16.8	68 578	16.9	2 954	36.5	5.5
44	Rhode Island	1 076 189	16.8	71 098	18.1	263	32.4	3.6
45	South Carolina	4 255 083	17.5	56 433	19.4	1 050	43.7	6.5
46	South Dakota	775 933	17.5	59 272	16.0	198	36.5	5.4
47	Tennessee	5 962 959	16.8	55 401	19.5	1 490	43.0	7.0
48	Texas	22 859 968	19.5	54 554	22.0	6 731	47.6	13.4
49	Utah	2 469 585	20.5	62 032	11.8	800	35.1	7.5
50	Vermont	623 050	16.2	65 876	7.4	144	26.0	2.2
51	Virginia	7 567 465	17.3	71 697	12.5	1 907	31.8	5.6
53	Washington	6 287 759	17.3	69 130	14.9	1 593	34.9	5.4
54	West Virginia	1 816 856	15.4	46 169	21.4	406	44.7	4.0
55	Wisconsin	5 536 201	17.3	69 010	13.6	1 379	33.3	4.5
56	Wyoming	509 294	16.3	56 065	13.7	123	31.2	6.6

Table B-3. Population, School, and Student Characteristics by State—*Continued*

FIPS code	State	Educational attainment, 2005			Public schools and school districts, 2004–2005					
							Type of school			
		Population age 25 years and over (thousands)	High school graduates (percent)	Bachelor's degree or more (percent)	Number of school districts	Total schools	Regular schools	Special education schools	Vocational schools	Alternative schools
		8	9	10	11	12	13	14	15	16
00	**UNITED STATES**	189 367	85.2	27.7	18 041	93 295	86 487	1 635	326	4 847
01	Alabama	3 004	80.9	19.8	135	1 386	1 337	21	1	27
02	Alaska	393	91.7	28.6	55	497	471	4	1	21
04	Arizona	3 699	85.8	28.0	609	1 976	1 823	11	84	58
05	Arkansas	1 833	81.4	17.5	355	1 130	1 121	4	-	5
06	California	22 676	80.4	30.6	1 140	9 373	8 046	129	-	1 198
08	Colorado	2 946	89.3	35.5	200	1 679	1 598	8	4	69
09	Connecticut	2 377	90.0	36.8	197	1 095	1 011	31	17	36
10	Delaware	553	86.9	25.6	36	198	173	13	5	7
11	District of Columbia	379	84.1	46.9	43	214	189	14	2	9
12	Florida	11 967	86.8	25.4	74	3 498	3 200	111	19	168
13	Georgia	5 478	85.7	27.1	204	2 069	2 037	8	-	24
15	Hawaii	854	87.2	30.4	1	285	281	3	-	1
16	Idaho	859	89.1	25.9	123	662	593	5	-	64
17	Illinois	8 068	87.2	29.6	1 117	4 245	3 888	229	-	128
18	Indiana	4 007	87.2	22.6	361	1 913	1 855	26	-	32
19	Iowa	1 929	89.8	24.5	384	1 524	1 440	10	-	74
20	Kansas	1 698	91.4	30.4	309	1 400	1 400	-	-	-
21	Kentucky	2 656	78.9	18.9	196	1 368	1 224	8	-	136
22	Louisiana	2 808	80.2	19.6	91	1 510	1 362	36	-	112
23	Maine	889	87.2	24.3	331	655	652	3	-	-
24	Maryland	3 706	86.9	36.3	26	1 372	1 267	44	10	51
25	Massachusetts	4 281	87.5	36.6	493	1 872	1 806	1	39	26
26	Michigan	6 509	88.6	24.6	835	3 901	3 495	168	13	225
27	Minnesota	3 365	92.7	34.2	561	2 214	1 623	246	1	344
28	Mississippi	1 811	79.8	21.8	163	896	896	-	-	-
29	Missouri	3 715	85.5	25.0	532	2 257	2 183	13	-	61
30	Montana	609	92.1	25.4	531	852	847	2	-	3
31	Nebraska	1 118	89.8	25.4	567	1 203	1 163	40	-	-
32	Nevada	1 563	86.6	23.4	18	556	516	5	1	34
33	New Hampshire	853	91.9	32.8	263	477	477	-	-	-
34	New Jersey	5 753	86.9	36.3	676	2 440	2 311	75	54	-
35	New Mexico	1 211	81.2	27.4	89	834	757	16	2	59
36	New York	12 643	85.7	30.4	835	4 470	4 290	65	25	90
37	North Carolina	5 427	84.0	25.3	217	2 283	2 190	21	1	71
38	North Dakota	412	90.0	27.2	255	511	511	-	-	-
39	Ohio	7 333	87.9	23.0	1 139	3 862	3 838	13	8	3
40	Oklahoma	2 235	85.2	24.0	603	1 787	1 707	-	-	-
41	Oregon	2 379	88.6	29.0	223	1 208	1 173	2	-	33
42	Pennsylvania	8 209	86.3	26.0	731	3 189	3 149	12	16	12
44	Rhode Island	694	83.9	29.2	49	334	320	4	3	7
45	South Carolina	2 685	83.0	24.2	102	1 101	1 079	10	-	12
46	South Dakota	483	88.4	25.0	194	713	688	2	-	23
47	Tennessee	3 830	81.8	21.5	136	1 671	1 621	16	7	27
48	Texas	13 750	78.2	25.5	1 279	7 941	6 967	3	-	971
49	Utah	1 300	92.5	29.8	84	915	767	41	2	105
50	Vermont	423	90.0	34.4	365	361	316	43	-	2
51	Virginia	4 798	86.0	30.6	228	1 861	1 827	11	-	23
53	Washington	4 035	91.5	30.9	306	2 203	1 854	97	7	245
54	West Virginia	1 228	82.5	15.1	57	752	721	7	3	21
55	Wisconsin	3 604	90.4	25.0	461	2 206	2 000	4	1	201
56	Wyoming	330	90.9	21.9	62	376	347	-	-	29

- = Quantity zero or rounds to zero.

Table B-3. Population, School, and Student Characteristics by State—*Continued*

FIPS code	State	Public schools and students, 2004–2005									
		Total schools	Charter schools	Magnet schools	Title I status			Level of students			
					Title I eligible schools	Title I schoolwide schools	Students in Title I schoolwide schools (percent)	Number of students	Primary schools (percent)	Middle schools (percent)	High schools (percent)
		17	18	19	20	21	22	23	24	25	26
00	UNITED STATES	93 295	3 294	. . .	51 022	29 089	30.0	48 794 911	38.8	30.8	29.7
01	Alabama	1 386	. . .	37	695	567	34.6	730 140	38.9	32.5	28.5
02	Alaska	497	21	16	298	116	17.6	132 970	37.6	31.5	30.8
04	Arizona	1 976	492	20	1 140	626	35.4	1 043 298	38.7	30.1	30.7
05	Arkansas	1 130	17	10	825	532	40.4	463 115	39.7	31.0	29.1
06	California	9 373	494	465	5 287	3 071	35.1	6 441 557	38.8	30.7	29.7
08	Colorado	1 679	110	5	873	348	17.3	765 976	40.0	30.6	29.4
09	Connecticut	1 095	14	34	497	140	11.9	577 390	39.1	30.9	30.0
10	Delaware	198	13	2	97	60	26.8	119 091	37.4	32.8	29.8
11	District of Columbia	214	39	3	173	165	82.0	76 714	42.1	28.6	23.1
12	Florida	3 498	299	. . .	1 384	1 347	34.9	2 639 336	39.6	30.8	29.6
13	Georgia	2 069	49	59	1 150	954	37.6	1 553 437	40.7	31.3	28.0
15	Hawaii	285	27	. . .	196	176	59.4	183 185	39.1	31.2	29.6
16	Idaho	662	19	. . .	495	95	12.5	256 084	38.6	31.0	30.4
17	Illinois	4 245	26	356	2 392	1 015	25.9	2 097 503	39.9	30.8	29.3
18	Indiana	1 913	22	26	1 058	188	7.8	1 021 348	38.7	31.8	29.5
19	Iowa	1 524	2	. . .	684	129	8.0	478 319	37.1	30.6	32.2
20	Kansas	1 400	20	31	641	252	18.1	469 136	36.4	29.9	30.6
21	Kentucky	1 368	. . .	39	893	779	50.9	674 796	41.8	29.6	27.8
22	Louisiana	1 510	17	68	934	782	46.6	724 281	42.6	31.1	26.3
23	Maine	655	. . .	1	505	48	4.4	198 820	36.3	32.2	31.5
24	Maryland	1 372	1	. . .	384	313	16.3	865 561	37.7	31.3	31.0
25	Massachusetts	1 872	57	5	1 089	476	22.2	975 574	39.0	30.9	30.1
26	Michigan	3 901	239	. . .	1 141	1 141	27.3	1 750 919	36.9	30.5	30.0
27	Minnesota	2 214	123	66	953	241	8.4	838 503	36.2	30.4	33.4
28	Mississippi	896	1	6	687	639	65.1	495 376	39.4	32.0	26.1
29	Missouri	2 257	. . .	44	1 191	418	15.6	905 449	37.8	31.7	30.6
30	Montana	852	. . .	. . .	691	156	17.8	146 705	35.7	31.4	32.7
31	Nebraska	1 203	. . .	. . .	485	186	15.9	285 761	38.1	30.1	31.8
32	Nevada	556	19	1	124	123	18.6	400 083	39.9	32.1	27.8
33	New Hampshire	477	3	. . .	248	30	4.3	206 852	35.4	32.1	32.2
34	New Jersey	2 440	49	. . .	. . .	. . .	. . .	1 393 347	37.2	29.7	28.7
35	New Mexico	834	44	1	501	363	38.0	326 102	38.7	31.2	30.1
36	New York	4 470	58	33	3 186	1 241	29.4	2 836 337	36.5	30.2	29.6
37	North Carolina	2 283	97	139	1 144	902	29.5	1 385 754	39.7	31.5	28.9
38	North Dakota	511	. . .	. . .	351	63	10.3	100 513	35.7	31.0	33.2
39	Ohio	3 862	245	. . .	2 681	999	21.4	1 840 032	37.7	31.1	31.1
40	Oklahoma	1 787	12	. . .	1 289	960	44.4	629 476	41.8	29.6	27.8
41	Oregon	1 208	39	. . .	1 207	327	21.6	552 322	37.0	31.1	31.7
42	Pennsylvania	3 189	109	34	2 110	572	17.5	1 828 089	35.6	31.8	32.3
44	Rhode Island	334	11	. . .	147	62	18.4	156 498	36.3	32.1	31.6
45	South Carolina	1 101	22	60	555	507	36.6	703 736	40.0	31.7	28.3
46	South Dakota	713	. . .	. . .	344	129	14.9	122 798	37.2	31.1	31.7
47	Tennessee	1 671	7	31	899	729	37.3	941 091	38.9	30.8	28.7
48	Texas	7 941	295	. . .	5 263	4 843	59.8	4 405 215	42.4	29.8	27.7
49	Utah	915	27	8	227	179	14.7	503 607	41.0	29.6	29.4
50	Vermont	361	. . .	. . .	214	95	26.3	98 352	36.9	30.1	32.7
51	Virginia	1 861	4	172	779	779	28.0	1 204 739	38.3	31.4	30.3
53	Washington	2 203	. . .	. . .	1 224	510	20.8	1 020 005	37.3	30.9	31.8
54	West Virginia	752	. . .	. . .	412	354	33.3	280 129	39.3	31.2	29.5
55	Wisconsin	2 206	149	2	1 076	300	14.8	864 757	37.1	29.8	33.2
56	Wyoming	376	2	. . .	203	62	15.1	84 733	36.3	31.3	32.4

. . . = Not available.

Table B-3. Population, School, and Student Characteristics by State—*Continued*

		Characteristics of public school students, 2004–2005 (percent)								
						Race and Hispanic origin of students				
FIPS code	State	Students eligible for free or reduced-price meals	Students with IEP[1]	English-language learners	Migrant students	Non-Hispanic White	Non-Hispanic Black	Hispanic[2]	Asian or Pacific Islander	American Indian and Alaska Native
		27	28	29	30	31	32	33	34	35
00	**UNITED STATES**	37.4	13.7	. . .	1.5	56.9	17.0	18.7	4.4	1.2
01	Alabama	51.6	12.7	2.2	0.6	59.7	36.1	2.4	1.0	0.8
02	Alaska	28.6	13.5	16.9	5.0	58.3	4.6	4.1	6.7	26.3
04	Arizona	48.0	18.8	20.2	1.3	48.3	5.0	38.2	2.3	6.2
05	Arkansas	51.9	12.4	4.9	1.9	69.2	23.0	6.0	1.3	0.6
06	California	49.0	10.8	25.2	3.7	30.8	7.8	46.0	11.1	0.8
08	Colorado	31.5	10.8	12.0	2.5	63.5	5.9	26.2	3.2	1.2
09	Connecticut	. . .	11.6	5.2	. . .	67.5	13.8	15.0	3.4	0.4
10	Delaware	35.6	14.8	4.3	0.2	56.2	32.3	8.5	2.7	0.3
11	District of Columbia	65.8	19.6	8.0	0.8	4.6	84.5	9.5	1.4	0.0
12	Florida	47.4	15.2	8.1	1.1	50.5	24.1	23.0	2.1	0.3
13	Georgia	47.9	12.3	4.0	0.7	49.4	38.0	7.7	2.6	0.2
15	Hawaii	41.6	12.4	9.3	0.6	20.0	2.4	4.5	72.5	0.6
16	Idaho	38.6	11.2	9.0	3.2	83.5	1.0	12.4	1.5	1.6
17	Illinois	37.5	15.4	. . .	-	56.6	20.6	18.3	3.7	0.2
18	Indiana	35.8	17.1	5.3	. . .	81.0	12.4	5.2	1.1	0.3
19	Iowa	31.1	15.2	4.2	1.5	87.4	4.8	5.4	1.9	0.6
20	Kansas	38.6	13.0	7.0	1.9	74.2	8.5	11.4	2.3	1.4
21	Kentucky	. . .	15.8	1.9	1.7	81.8	9.9	1.7	0.8	0.2
22	Louisiana	61.6	14.2	1.9	0.7	48.3	47.7	1.9	1.4	0.7
23	Maine	32.3	16.9	1.9	. . .	95.5	1.9	0.8	1.3	0.5
24	Maryland	32.1	12.9	3.0	-	49.5	38.1	7.0	5.0	0.4
25	Massachusetts	27.7	16.6	5.9	0.2	74.2	8.9	11.8	4.8	0.3
26	Michigan	33.7	14.0	7.4	0.3	72.2	19.8	4.2	2.2	1.0
27	Minnesota	29.5	13.7	7.8	0.3	79.3	8.2	5.0	5.5	2.1
28	Mississippi	64.3	13.9	0.9	. . .	47.0	50.8	1.3	0.8	0.2
29	Missouri	39.1	. . .	. . .	0.2	77.3	17.9	2.9	1.5	0.4
30	Montana	33.7	13.3	7.0	. . .	84.5	0.8	2.3	1.1	11.3
31	Nebraska	34.8	16.5	7.4	2.4	78.5	7.4	10.8	1.7	1.6
32	Nevada	. . .	11.3	18.0	0.1	. . .	. . .	. . .	. . .	. . .
33	New Hampshire	16.5	14.7	1.5	0.1	93.8	1.6	2.6	1.8	0.3
34	New Jersey	. . .	. . .	. . .	. . .	57.1	17.7	17.7	7.2	0.2
35	New Mexico	58.1	19.6	19.4	0.7	31.9	2.5	53.3	1.2	11.1
36	New York	18.2	. . .	. . .	. . .	53.1	19.9	19.8	6.7	0.5
37	North Carolina	45.1	13.9	5.0	1.0	57.4	31.6	7.5	2.0	1.5
38	North Dakota	29.1	14.6	4.5	0.4	87.2	1.2	2.4	0.9	8.3
39	Ohio	31.3	14.2	2.0	0.2	77.3	16.7	2.2	1.3	0.1
40	Oklahoma	53.9	15.1	8.1	0.6	60.6	10.8	8.2	1.6	18.7
41	Oregon	41.9	14.2	12.5	3.9	72.8	3.2	14.0	4.4	2.2
42	Pennsylvania	28.3	14.5	. . .	0.5	75.5	16.0	6.0	2.3	0.1
44	Rhode Island	32.4	18.1	6.0	0.1	70.9	8.6	16.8	3.2	0.6
45	South Carolina	52.2	14.3	1.8	0.1	53.7	40.6	3.6	1.2	0.3
46	South Dakota	30.0	14.0	4.3	0.5	84.6	1.6	1.9	1.0	10.9
47	Tennessee	. . .	17.8	. . .	. . .	70.0	25.1	3.3	1.4	0.2
48	Texas	47.7	11.8	15.7	2.6	37.7	14.2	44.7	3.0	0.3
49	Utah	32.4	12.6	9.3	0.8	81.2	1.2	11.4	2.9	1.5
50	Vermont	25.2	13.2	2.5	0.7	95.2	1.4	0.9	1.5	0.5
51	Virginia	31.1	14.5	5.7	0.1	59.7	26.7	7.0	4.9	0.3
53	Washington	36.1	12.2	7.6	3.7	70.4	5.7	12.9	7.9	2.7
54	West Virginia	50.4	17.9	0.8	-	93.9	4.8	0.6	0.6	0.1
55	Wisconsin	. . .	14.9	6.7	0.1	78.3	10.5	6.3	3.4	1.5
56	Wyoming	32.0	. . .	4.5	0.3	85.6	1.4	8.6	1.0	3.4

[1]IEP = Individual Education Program. See notes and definitions at the end of this section.
[2]May be of any race.
- = Quantity zero or rounds to zero.
. . . = Not available.

Table B-3. Population, School, and Student Characteristics by State—*Continued*

		Public school outcomes					Private schools		
FIPS code	State	Dropouts, grades 9–12, 2001–2002 (percent)	9th grade membership, 2001–2002	12th grade membership, 2004–2005	High school graduates, 2002–2003	Averaged freshman graduation rates, 2003–2004	Number of schools, 2003–2004	Enrollment, 2003–2004	High school graduates, 2002–2003
		36	37	38	39	40	41	42	43
00	UNITED STATES	. . .	4 012 333	3 094 349	2 595 650	75.0	28 384	5 122 772	295 755
01	Alabama	3.7	61 038	42 672	39 218	65.0	408	73 105	4 671
02	Alaska	8.1	11 734	8 766	7 446	67.2	75	6 177	296
04	Arizona	10.5	72 859	71 035	45 961	66.8	292	46 366	2 402
05	Arkansas	5.3	35 894	28 640	27 253	76.8	189	27 500	1 351
06	California	. . .	499 505	409 576	343 480	73.9	3 377	623 105	31 946
08	Colorado	. . .	62 756	50 387	45 535	78.7	345	50 123	2 423
09	Connecticut	2.6	46 621	38 340	34 618	80.7	361	74 430	6 629
10	Delaware	6.2	10 602	7 390	7 077	72.9	121	25 576	1 298
11	District of Columbia	. . .	4 012	2 820	3 307	68.2	82	16 376	1 202
12	Florida	3.7	248 764	149 810	139 239	66.4	1 803	323 766	16 595
13	Georgia	6.5	128 734	83 872	77 020	61.2	665	120 697	7 079
15	Hawaii	5.1	16 036	10 794	10 501	72.6	133	37 228	2 780
16	Idaho	3.9	19 923	17 506	15 659	81.5	107	10 994	535
17	Illinois	6.4	165 529	132 658	124 763	80.3	1 346	270 490	15 173
18	Indiana	2.3	78 945	63 316	57 636	73.5	784	109 101	4 947
19	Iowa	2.4	39 818	36 434	34 403	85.8	266	45 309	2 689
20	Kansas	3.1	38 621	33 593	30 155	77.9	229	41 762	2 209
21	Kentucky	4.0	53 583	39 200	38 144	73.0	368	71 067	3 806
22	Louisiana	7.0	57 164	40 034	38 723	69.4	440	140 492	9 151
23	Maine	2.8	16 689	14 402	13 378	77.6	151	20 696	2 772
24	Maryland	3.9	73 300	57 432	53 545	79.5	727	149 253	8 084
25	Massachusetts	. . .	80 394	63 852	59 192	79.3	688	134 708	10 725
26	Michigan	. . .	145 651	111 055	100 206	72.5	983	160 049	9 502
27	Minnesota	3.8	69 032	71 636	59 096	84.7	568	93 935	4 602
28	Mississippi	3.9	38 498	25 801	25 285	62.7	240	49 729	3 544
29	Missouri	3.6	75 156	61 838	57 983	80.4	633	119 812	7 235
30	Montana	3.9	13 004	11 173	10 500	80.4	104	8 924	498
31	Nebraska	4.2	23 855	21 557	20 506	87.6	242	39 454	2 419
32	Nevada	6.4	32 086	21 385	17 318	57.4	111	18 219	676
33	New Hampshire	4.0	17 646	14 847	13 428	78.7	165	23 692	2 471
34	New Jersey	2.5	98 784	88 378	83 826	86.3	964	204 732	12 902
35	New Mexico	5.2	28 816	19 518	18 307	67.0	176	22 416	1 280
36	New York	7.1	245 540	166 975	. . .	. . .	1 959	458 079	28 050
37	North Carolina	5.7	114 236	79 257	73 055	71.4	661	102 642	5 086
38	North Dakota	2.0	8 906	8 143	7 888	86.1	52	6 209	490
39	Ohio	3.1	155 727	127 379	119 029	81.3	987	239 323	13 943
40	Oklahoma	4.4	49 034	37 938	36 799	77.0	168	27 603	1 532
41	Oregon	4.9	45 067	41 125	36 826	74.2	362	46 968	2 717
42	Pennsylvania	3.3	159 919	132 551	123 474	82.2	2 009	316 337	19 367
44	Rhode Island	4.3	13 538	10 533	9 278	75.9	139	28 119	1 943
45	South Carolina	3.3	64 279	38 736	35 962	60.6	345	58 005	2 963
46	South Dakota	2.8	10 629	9 389	9 001	83.7	95	10 817	506
47	Tennessee	3.8	74 322	55 490	50 203	66.1	551	87 055	5 457
48	Texas	3.8	366 895	247 655	244 165	76.7	1 282	220 206	10 682
49	Utah	3.7	35 029	35 671	30 423	83.0	108	15 907	1 070
50	Vermont	4.0	8 595	7 552	7 127	85.4	123	12 218	1 370
51	Virginia	2.9	100 599	77 965	75 101	79.3	604	104 304	6 000
53	Washington	7.1	86 396	74 121	61 394	74.6	556	78 746	3 800
54	West Virginia	3.7	23 328	18 319	17 339	76.9	166	14 397	815
55	Wisconsin	1.9	77 802	69 510	. . .	. . .	1 041	134 474	6 028
56	Wyoming	5.8	7 443	6 323	5 878	76.0	35	2 079	46

. . . = Not available.

Table B-3. Population, School, and Student Characteristics by State—*Continued*

FIPS code	State	Public and private school characteristics								Average public school teacher salary, 2005–2006[3]
		Public schools, 2004–2005					Private schools, 2003–2004			
		Student membership		Teachers		Student-teacher ratio	Total enrollment	Total teachers	Student-teacher ratio	
		Total	Percent change from 1994–1995 to 2004–2005	Total	Percent change from 1994–1995 to 2004–2005					
		44	45	46	47	48	49	50	51	52
00	UNITED STATES	48 794 911	10.6	3 090 513	21.1	15.8	5 122 772	425 238	12.0	49 109
01	Alabama	730 140	-0.9	51 594	20.6	14.2	73 105	6 379	11.5	40 347
02	Alaska	132 970	4.7	7 756	7.6	17.1	6 177	623	9.9	53 553
04	Arizona	1 043 298	41.5	48 935	28.3	21.3	46 366	3 625	12.8	44 672
05	Arkansas	463 115	3.5	31 234	19.3	14.8	27 500	2 376	11.6	42 093
06	California	6 441 557	19.1	305 969	36.0	21.1	623 105	47 625	13.1	59 345
08	Colorado	765 976	19.6	45 165	29.4	17.0	50 123	4 644	10.8	45 616
09	Connecticut	577 390	13.9	38 808	9.9	14.9	74 430	7 728	9.6	59 499
10	Delaware	119 091	11.5	7 856	22.4	15.2	25 576	2 245	11.4	54 264
11	District of Columbia	76 714	-4.6	5 387	-11.8	14.2	16 376	1 931	8.5	61 195
12	Florida	2 639 336	25.0	154 864	39.9	17.0	323 766	27 144	11.9	43 302
13	Georgia	1 553 437	22.2	104 987	34.7	14.8	120 697	11 533	10.5	48 300
15	Hawaii	183 185	-0.3	11 146	8.8	16.4	37 228	3 070	12.1	51 599
16	Idaho	256 084	6.5	14 269	13.4	17.9	10 994	923	11.9	43 390
17	Illinois	2 097 503	9.5	131 047	18.2	16.0	270 490	19 502	13.9	57 819
18	Indiana	1 021 348	5.4	60 563	9.1	16.9	109 101	7 998	13.6	47 255
19	Iowa	478 319	-4.4	34 697	9.4	13.8	45 309	3 414	13.3	40 877
20	Kansas	469 136	1.8	32 932	7.7	14.2	41 762	3 138	13.3	41 369
21	Kentucky	674 796	2.6	41 463	6.9	16.3	71 067	5 400	13.2	41 903
22	Louisiana	724 281	-9.2	49 192	3.3	14.7	140 492	10 005	14.0	40 253
23	Maine	198 820	-6.5	16 656	8.1	11.9	20 696	2 079	10.0	40 737
24	Maryland	865 561	9.4	55 101	18.3	15.7	149 253	13 668	10.9	54 486
25	Massachusetts	975 574	9.2	73 399	21.3	13.3	134 708	13 798	9.8	56 587
26	Michigan	1 750 919	8.4	100 634	25.0	17.4	160 049	11 771	13.6	58 482
27	Minnesota	838 503	2.0	52 152	11.1	16.1	93 935	7 149	13.1	48 489
28	Mississippi	495 376	-2.1	31 321	8.5	15.8	49 729	4 183	11.9	37 924
29	Missouri	905 449	3.1	65 481	15.7	13.8	119 812	9 320	12.9	39 922
30	Montana	146 705	-10.7	10 224	1.4	14.3	8 924	898	9.9	39 832
31	Nebraska	285 761	-0.5	21 077	6.6	13.6	39 454	2 874	13.7	41 026
32	Nevada	400 083	59.6	20 950	56.2	19.1	18 219	1 327	13.7	44 426
33	New Hampshire	206 852	9.3	15 298	26.3	13.5	23 692	2 447	9.7	45 263
34	New Jersey	1 393 347	18.7	114 875	34.7	12.1	204 732	17 969	11.4	57 707
35	New Mexico	326 102	-0.4	21 730	14.2	15.0	22 416	2 140	10.5	41 637
36	New York	2 836 337	2.5	218 612	19.9	13.0	458 079	38 898	11.8	57 354
37	North Carolina	1 385 754	19.8	92 550	29.3	15.0	102 642	9 897	10.4	43 922
38	North Dakota	100 513	-15.7	8 070	3.5	12.5	6 209	557	11.1	37 773
39	Ohio	1 840 032	1.4	118 060	8.2	15.6	239 323	16 857	14.2	50 314
40	Oklahoma	629 476	3.2	40 416	2.6	15.6	27 603	2 528	10.9	38 772
41	Oregon	552 322	5.8	27 431	4.7	20.1	46 968	3 672	12.8	48 981
42	Pennsylvania	1 828 089	3.6	121 167	17.7	15.1	316 337	24 349	13.0	54 027
44	Rhode Island	156 498	6.1	11 898	18.2	13.2	28 119	2 563	11.0	54 730
45	South Carolina	703 736	8.5	46 914	19.0	15.0	58 005	5 339	10.9	43 242
46	South Dakota	122 798	-14.4	9 064	-9.2	13.5	10 817	922	11.7	34 709
47	Tennessee	941 091	6.8	60 022	26.6	15.7	87 055	8 222	10.6	42 537
48	Texas	4 405 215	19.8	294 547	25.8	15.0	220 206	20 673	10.7	41 744
49	Utah	503 607	6.1	22 287	14.2	22.6	15 907	1 425	11.2	40 316
50	Vermont	98 352	-5.9	8 720	15.3	11.3	12 218	1 501	8.1	46 622
51	Virginia	1 204 739	13.6	93 732	29.3	12.9	104 304	10 339	10.1	43 823
53	Washington	1 020 005	8.7	53 125	14.4	19.2	78 746	6 398	12.3	46 326
54	West Virginia	280 129	-9.8	19 958	-5.1	14.0	14 397	1 360	10.6	38 284
55	Wisconsin	864 757	0.5	60 521	12.0	14.3	134 474	10 557	12.7	46 390
56	Wyoming	84 733	-15.5	6 657	-1.4	12.7	2 079	255	8.2	43 255

[3]National Education Association. Highlights Table 2: Summary of Selected Estimates Data for 2005–06. *Rankings & Estimates: Rankings of the States 2005 and Estimates of School Statistics, 2006*, page 67. Reprinted with permission of the National Education Association © 2006. All rights reserved. <http://www.nea.org>.

Table B-3. Population, School, and Student Characteristics by State—*Continued*

FIPS code	State	Staff employed by public elementary and secondary school systems and percent of total staff, 2004–2005								
		Total staff	Teachers		Instructional aides		Instructional coordinators		Guidance counselors	
			Number	Percent of total staff	Number	Percent of total staff	Number	Percent of total staff	Number	Percent of total staff
		53	54	55	56	57	58	59	60	61
00	UNITED STATES	6 053 465	3 090 513	51.1	707 028	11.7	47 688	0.8	101 842	1.7
01	Alabama	92 795	51 594	55.6	6 458	7.0	836	0.9	1 705	1.8
02	Alaska	17 632	7 756	44.0	2 200	12.5	173	1.0	270	1.5
04	Arizona	97 953	48 935	50.0	13 713	14.0	192	0.2	1 351	1.4
05	Arkansas	66 127	31 234	47.2	7 196	10.9	623	0.9	1 264	1.9
06	California	574 614	305 969	53.2	68 118	11.9	6 663	1.2	6 508	1.1
08	Colorado	91 337	45 165	49.4	10 269	11.2	1 425	1.6	1 409	1.5
09	Connecticut	83 879	38 808	46.3	12 689	15.1	369	0.4	1 352	1.6
10	Delaware	14 966	7 856	52.5	1 693	11.3	206	1.4	268	1.8
11	District of Columbia	12 162	5 387	44.3	1 339	11.0	105	0.9	99	0.8
12	Florida	311 853	154 864	49.7	31 517	10.1	677	0.2	5 942	1.9
13	Georgia	209 746	104 987	50.1	24 535	11.7	1 439	0.7	3 417	1.6
15	Hawaii	20 531	11 146	54.3	2 084	10.2	559	2.7	657	3.2
16	Idaho	25 533	14 269	55.9	2 736	10.7	264	1.0	590	2.3
17	Illinois	261 237	131 047	50.2	34 411	13.2	1 059	0.4	3 117	1.2
18	Indiana	133 375	60 563	45.4	19 355	14.5	1 720	1.3	1 827	1.4
19	Iowa	68 450	34 697	50.7	9 475	13.8	482	0.7	1 157	1.7
20	Kansas	64 114	32 932	51.4	7 108	11.1	110	0.2	1 112	1.7
21	Kentucky	95 920	41 463	43.2	13 634	14.2	887	0.9	1 425	1.5
22	Louisiana	101 381	49 192	48.5	11 149	11.0	1 446	1.4	3 317	3.3
23	Maine	34 899	16 656	47.7	5 974	17.1	320	0.9	650	1.9
24	Maryland	108 296	55 101	50.9	9 747	9.0	1 285	1.2	2 230	2.1
25	Massachusetts	137 613	73 399	53.3	19 652	14.3	908	0.7	2 117	1.5
26	Michigan	209 831	100 634	48.0	25 444	12.1	3 338	1.6	2 762	1.3
27	Minnesota	104 367	52 152	50.0	14 459	13.9	1 450	1.4	1 055	1.0
28	Mississippi	67 249	31 321	46.6	8 698	12.9	703	1.0	1 018	1.5
29	Missouri	125 868	65 481	52.0	11 575	9.2	981	0.8	2 562	2.0
30	Montana	18 762	10 224	54.5	1 917	10.2	188	1.0	433	2.3
31	Nebraska	40 998	21 077	51.4	4 720	11.5	456	1.1	767	1.9
32	Nevada	31 260	20 950	67.0	3 683	11.8	546	1.7	713	2.3
33	New Hampshire	31 408	15 298	48.7	6 429	20.5	201	0.6	823	2.6
34	New Jersey	213 418	114 875	53.8	25 878	12.1	2 701	1.3	2 382	1.1
35	New Mexico	46 531	21 730	46.7	5 400	11.6	907	1.9	772	1.7
36	New York	399 089	218 612	54.8	54 938	13.8	2 172	0.5	6 551	1.6
37	North Carolina	177 308	92 550	52.2	28 598	16.1	962	0.5	3 514	2.0
38	North Dakota	15 157	8 070	53.2	1 638	10.8	104	0.7	277	1.8
39	Ohio	239 988	118 060	49.2	17 321	7.2	601	0.3	3 828	1.6
40	Oklahoma	77 466	40 416	52.2	6 997	9.0	472	0.6	1 559	2.0
41	Oregon	56 637	27 431	48.4	9 585	16.9	495	0.9	1 221	2.2
42	Pennsylvania	237 122	121 167	51.1	26 510	11.2	1 457	0.6	4 409	1.9
44	Rhode Island	23 031	11 898	51.7	2 567	11.1	204	0.9	2 614	11.3
45	South Carolina	65 014	46 914	72.2	2 686	4.1	721	1.1	1 736	2.7
46	South Dakota	18 106	9 064	50.1	3 383	18.7	377	2.1	289	1.6
47	Tennessee	111 891	60 022	53.6	14 181	12.7	778	0.7	1 936	1.7
48	Texas	607 364	294 547	48.5	59 855	9.9	1 518	0.2	10 151	1.7
49	Utah	44 499	22 287	50.1	6 954	15.6	732	1.6	675	1.5
50	Vermont	18 899	8 720	46.1	4 339	23.0	296	1.6	426	2.3
51	Virginia	179 688	93 732	52.2	17 833	9.9	1 447	0.8	2 579	1.4
53	Washington	111 848	53 125	47.5	10 300	9.2	231	0.2	1 981	1.8
54	West Virginia	37 979	19 958	52.6	3 191	8.4	354	0.9	673	1.8
55	Wisconsin	104 018	60 521	58.2	10 951	10.5	1 395	1.3	1 963	1.9
56	Wyoming	14 256	6 657	46.7	1 946	13.7	153	1.1	389	2.7

Table B-3. Population, School, and Student Characteristics by State—*Continued*

FIPS code	State	Staff employed by public elementary and secondary school systems and percent of total staff, 2004–2005									
		Librarians		Support staff		School administrators		School district administrators		School and school district administrative support staff	
		Number	Percent of total staff	Number	Percent of total staff	Number	Percent of total staff	Number	Percent of total staff	Number	Percent of total staff
		62	63	64	65	66	67	68	69	70	71
00	**UNITED STATES**	54 145	0.9	1 397 236	23.1	165 693	2.7	64 092	1.1	425 228	7.0
01	Alabama	1 369	1.5	21 112	22.8	3 487	3.8	1 081	1.2	5 153	5.6
02	Alaska	146	0.8	3 635	20.6	707	4.0	445	2.5	2 300	13.0
04	Arizona	827	0.8	23 122	23.6	2 223	2.3	418	0.4	7 172	7.3
05	Arkansas	954	1.4	19 405	29.3	1 569	2.4	659	1.0	3 223	4.9
06	California	1 138	0.2	114 007	20.0	13 752	2.4	2 723	0.5	54 856	9.5
08	Colorado	842	0.9	22 039	24.1	2 442	2.7	1 010	1.1	6 736	7.4
09	Connecticut	789	0.9	21 468	25.6	2 258	2.7	1 383	1.6	4 763	5.7
10	Delaware	132	0.9	3 381	22.6	374	2.5	297	2.0	759	5.1
11	District of Columbia	41	0.3	3 581	29.4	398	3.3	130	1.1	1 082	8.9
12	Florida	2 800	0.9	76 484	24.5	7 242	2.3	1 892	0.6	30 435	9.8
13	Georgia	2 192	1.0	55 510	26.5	5 169	2.5	1 982	0.9	10 515	5.0
15	Hawaii	291	1.4	3 680	17.9	505	2.5	196	1.0	1 413	6.9
16	Idaho	171	0.7	5 333	20.9	716	2.8	115	0.5	1 339	5.2
17	Illinois	2 176	0.8	60 878	23.3	6 457	2.5	3 942	1.5	18 150	6.9
18	Indiana	996	0.7	36 911	27.7	3 023	2.3	1 045	0.8	7 935	5.9
19	Iowa	561	0.8	14 917	21.8	2 195	3.2	945	1.4	4 021	5.9
20	Kansas	924	1.4	16 023	25.0	1 717	2.7	1 260	2.0	2 928	4.6
21	Kentucky	1 115	1.2	26 310	27.4	2 208	2.3	836	0.9	8 042	8.4
22	Louisiana	1 259	1.2	26 028	25.7	2 731	2.7	301	0.3	5 958	5.9
23	Maine	266	0.8	7 407	21.2	947	2.7	610	1.7	2 069	5.9
24	Maryland	1 140	1.1	29 504	27.2	3 226	3.0	834	0.8	5 229	4.8
25	Massachusetts	949	0.7	25 176	18.3	3 892	2.8	1 603	1.2	9 917	7.2
26	Michigan	1 429	0.7	53 197	25.4	5 100	2.5	3 288	1.6	14 571	6.0
27	Minnesota	922	0.9	24 071	23.1	1 986	1.9	1 915	1.8	6 357	6.1
28	Mississippi	951	1.4	17 751	26.4	1 773	2.6	984	1.5	4 050	6.0
29	Missouri	1 622	1.3	30 358	24.1	3 066	2.4	1 316	1.0	8 907	7.1
30	Montana	362	1.9	3 726	19.9	503	2.7	140	0.7	1 269	6.8
31	Nebraska	549	1.3	9 771	23.8	1 014	2.5	573	1.4	2 071	5.1
32	Nevada	343	1.1	1 511	4.8	924	3.0	263	0.8	2 327	7.4
33	New Hampshire	302	1.0	6 062	19.3	543	1.7	521	1.7	1 229	3.9
34	New Jersey	1 553	0.7	45 432	21.3	4 013	1.9	1 488	0.7	15 096	7.1
35	New Mexico	296	0.6	12 265	26.4	1 014	2.2	580	1.2	3 567	7.7
36	New York	3 329	0.8	71 122	17.8	7 911	2.0	2 839	0.7	31 615	7.9
37	North Carolina	2 337	1.3	32 701	18.4	4 901	2.8	1 650	0.9	10 095	5.7
38	North Dakota	203	1.3	3 518	23.2	388	2.6	478	3.2	481	3.2
39	Ohio	1 642	0.7	55 278	23.0	4 792	2.0	7 991	3.3	30 475	12.7
40	Oklahoma	1 016	1.3	18 964	24.5	2 107	2.7	528	0.7	5 407	7.0
41	Oregon	431	0.8	10 719	18.9	1 592	2.8	639	1.1	4 524	8.0
42	Pennsylvania	2 225	0.9	58 667	24.7	4 686	2.0	1 709	0.7	16 292	6.9
44	Rhode Island	215	0.9	2 484	10.8	1 991	8.6	155	0.7	903	3.9
45	South Carolina	1 140	1.8	2 127	3.3	3 298	5.1	302	0.5	6 090	9.4
46	South Dakota	148	0.8	3 202	17.7	397	2.2	441	2.4	805	4.4
47	Tennessee	1 566	1.4	24 183	21.6	3 420	3.1	170	0.2	5 635	5.0
48	Texas	4 893	0.8	166 802	27.5	30 737	5.1	7 863	1.3	30 998	5.1
49	Utah	262	0.6	9 123	20.5	1 060	2.4	375	0.8	3 031	6.8
50	Vermont	220	1.2	3 255	17.2	432	2.3	148	0.8	1 063	5.6
51	Virginia	2 002	1.1	43 013	23.9	4 083	2.3	1 461	0.8	13 538	7.5
53	Washington	1 298	1.2	37 614	33.6	2 795	2.5	897	0.8	3 607	3.2
54	West Virginia	387	1.0	9 797	25.8	1 056	2.8	437	1.2	2 126	5.6
55	Wisconsin	1 292	1.2	20 392	19.6	2 473	2.4	926	0.9	4 105	3.9
56	Wyoming	132	0.9	3 340	23.4	332	2.3	308	2.2	999	7.0

Table B-3. Population, School, and Student Characteristics by State—*Continued*

FIPS code	State	Highest degree earned and years of experience for teachers in public elementary and secondary schools, 1999–2000						
		Highest degree earned			Years of experience (percent distribution)			
		Number of teachers	Bachelor's degree (percent)	Master's degree or more (percent)	Under 3 years	3 to 9 years	10 to 20 years	20 years or more
		72	73	74	75	76	77	78
00	UNITED STATES	3 002 258	52.0	41.9	12.9	28.8	28.5	29.8
01	Alabama	50 605	41.2	51.2	12.7	28.0	32.3	26.9
02	Alaska	8 340	59.0	36.9	15.6	31.0	34.4	18.9
04	Arizona	48 557	50.8	43.3	16.3	30.2	31.9	21.6
05	Arkansas	30 410	67.4	29.0	10.6	25.4	33.4	30.6
06	California	280 036	61.5	30.3	15.1	33.9	28.3	22.7
08	Colorado	42 352	45.8	50.0	15.6	27.7	27.1	29.6
09	Connecticut	42 178	16.7	65.3	11.5	26.7	26.6	35.2
10	Delaware	7 538	48.7	43.5	11.4	36.3	25.4	26.9
11	District of Columbia	5 712	41.8	46.4	14.6	20.6	23.2	41.6
12	Florida	128 634	61.0	33.6	11.6	30.3	28.8	29.4
13	Georgia	88 161	50.1	37.6	13.0	33.4	27.6	26.0
15	Hawaii	12 112	50.2	23.9	16.0	33.4	24.8	25.8
16	Idaho	14 451	70.3	26.7	13.0	27.3	31.6	28.1
17	Illinois	137 213	46.8	48.9	11.6	27.2	26.5	34.6
18	Indiana	61 184	31.8	63.6	11.1	24.5	23.4	41.1
19	Iowa	38 116	66.0	32.3	10.5	26.2	26.9	36.4
20	Kansas	34 134	60.9	36.8	15.7	25.9	31.3	27.1
21	Kentucky	42 879	27.5	54.0	10.1	31.3	33.5	25.1
22	Louisiana	50 806	63.7	29.3	10.3	30.6	31.0	28.2
23	Maine	17 536	66.3	29.2	10.5	20.3	32.8	36.4
24	Maryland	54 583	45.3	48.5	13.9	30.8	25.3	30.0
25	Massachusetts	78 260	38.6	54.8	11.9	24.9	24.9	38.3
26	Michigan	100 232	42.7	52.2	13.2	30.5	25.3	31.0
27	Minnesota	57 791	54.4	40.8	16.4	28.1	25.0	30.5
28	Mississippi	33 097	58.1	37.0	11.7	24.4	33.5	30.4
29	Missouri	64 094	49.2	46.6	15.1	31.4	26.6	26.9
30	Montana	11 937	70.4	25.7	10.9	25.9	33.4	29.8
31	Nebraska	23 119	59.2	38.8	10.6	25.2	30.5	33.6
32	Nevada	17 273	52.4	43.9	14.9	35.1	25.7	24.3
33	New Hampshire	14 985	51.9	44.4	15.1	22.4	31.5	31.0
34	New Jersey	98 310	58.4	34.7	11.7	25.1	26.0	37.1
35	New Mexico	21 188	56.1	39.1	12.5	38.6	26.5	22.4
36	New York	208 313	21.8	68.4	14.1	25.3	27.6	33.0
37	North Carolina	86 020	67.5	29.5	17.2	28.5	25.2	29.1
38	North Dakota	9 252	77.8	20.0	12.1	25.1	30.4	32.3
39	Ohio	123 370	50.4	45.7	12.0	26.4	29.0	32.6
40	Oklahoma	45 830	63.5	33.3	10.6	30.9	32.1	26.4
41	Oregon	28 584	50.0	46.5	14.0	28.2	32.7	25.1
42	Pennsylvania	126 915	49.5	45.2	9.7	25.2	27.5	37.6
44	Rhode Island	11 616	43.7	51.7	9.4	26.2	30.7	33.8
45	South Carolina	43 754	48.0	43.3	12.0	28.1	31.0	29.0
46	South Dakota	11 708	75.4	23.2	12.9	25.7	35.5	26.0
47	Tennessee	58 296	50.9	41.1	13.9	30.7	27.0	28.4
48	Texas	266 661	69.7	27.1	12.5	32.4	31.2	23.9
49	Utah	23 346	70.4	23.5	15.6	31.5	31.9	21.0
50	Vermont	9 186	49.3	46.1	16.5	24.2	29.1	30.2
51	Virginia	80 987	55.4	40.8	13.3	28.1	28.8	29.8
53	Washington	54 816	46.0	46.8	11.6	28.7	31.6	28.2
54	West Virginia	22 571	37.5	55.6	5.6	14.7	31.0	48.8
55	Wisconsin	67 362	56.5	39.6	12.8	28.7	26.4	32.2
56	Wyoming	7 848	69.8	28.2	10.4	23.5	33.5	32.6

Table B-3. Population, School, and Student Characteristics by State—*Continued*

FIPS code	State	National Assessment of Educational Progress: Percent of public school students at or above the proficient level					SAT Reasoning Test: Average scores, 2006[4]			
		Math, 2005		Reading, 2005		Writing, 2002				
		Grade 4	Grade 8	Grade 4	Grade 8	Grade 8	Critical reading	Math	Writing	Percent of high school graduates who took the SAT
		79	80	81	82	83	84	85	86	87
00	UNITED STATES	35	28	30	29	30	503	518	497	48
01	Alabama	21	15	22	22	20	565	561	565	9
02	Alaska	34	29	27	26	...	517	517	493	51
04	Arizona	28	26	24	23	20	521	528	507	32
05	Arkansas	34	22	30	26	19	574	568	567	5
06	California	28	22	21	21	23	501	518	501	49
08	Colorado	39	32	37	32	...	558	564	548	26
09	Connecticut	42	35	38	34	45	512	516	511	84
10	Delaware	36	30	34	30	35	495	500	484	73
11	District of Columbia	10	7	11	12	10	487	472	482	78
12	Florida	37	26	30	25	32	496	497	480	65
13	Georgia	30	23	26	25	25	494	496	487	70
15	Hawaii	27	18	23	18	18	482	509	472	60
16	Idaho	40	30	33	32	29	543	545	525	19
17	Illinois	32	29	29	31	...	591	609	586	9
18	Indiana	38	30	30	28	26	498	509	486	62
19	Iowa	37	34	33	34	...	602	613	591	4
20	Kansas	47	34	32	35	32	582	590	566	8
21	Kentucky	26	23	31	31	25	562	562	555	11
22	Louisiana	24	16	20	20	18	570	571	571	6
23	Maine	39	30	35	38	36	501	501	491	73
24	Maryland	38	30	32	30	35	503	509	499	70
25	Massachusetts	49	43	44	44	42	513	524	510	85
26	Michigan	38	29	32	28	24	568	583	555	10
27	Minnesota	47	43	38	37	...	591	600	574	10
28	Mississippi	19	14	18	18	13	556	541	562	4
29	Missouri	31	26	33	31	27	587	591	582	7
30	Montana	38	36	36	37	29	538	545	524	28
31	Nebraska	36	35	34	35	32	576	583	566	7
32	Nevada	26	21	21	22	16	498	508	481	40
33	New Hampshire	47	35	39	38	...	520	524	509	82
34	New Jersey	45	36	37	38	...	496	515	496	82
35	New Mexico	19	14	20	19	18	557	549	543	13
36	New York	36	31	33	33	30	493	510	483	88
37	North Carolina	40	32	29	27	34	495	513	485	71
38	North Dakota	40	35	35	37	24	610	617	588	4
39	Ohio	43	33	34	36	38	535	544	521	28
40	Oklahoma	29	21	25	25	27	576	574	563	7
41	Oregon	37	34	29	33	33	523	529	503	55
42	Pennsylvania	41	31	36	36	32	493	500	483	74
44	Rhode Island	31	24	30	29	29	495	502	490	69
45	South Carolina	36	30	26	25	20	487	498	480	62
46	South Dakota	41	36	33	35	...	590	604	578	4
47	Tennessee	28	21	27	26	24	573	569	572	15
48	Texas	40	31	29	26	31	491	506	487	52
49	Utah	37	30	34	29	23	560	557	550	7
50	Vermont	44	38	39	37	41	513	519	502	67
51	Virginia	39	33	37	36	32	512	513	500	73
53	Washington	42	36	36	34	34	527	532	511	54
54	West Virginia	25	18	26	22	21	519	510	515	20
55	Wisconsin	40	36	33	35	...	588	600	577	6
56	Wyoming	43	29	34	36	28	548	555	537	10

[4] "2006 College-Bound Seniors" Copyright (c) 2006–2007 The College Board, www.collegeboard.com. Reproduced with permission.
... = Not available.

Table B-3. Population, School, and Student Characteristics by State—*Continued*

FIPS code	State	ACT, 2006[5]		Preliminary SAT (PSAT)/ National Merit Scholarship Qualifying Test (NMSQT), 2006–2007[6]			
		Average composite score	Percent of high school graduates who took the ACT	Number of high school juniors who took the PSAT/NMSQT	Critical reading	Math	Writing skills
					Percent of test-takers achieving scores of 65 or above		
		88	89	90	91	92	93
00	**UNITED STATES**	21.1	40	1 553 731	7.5	8.2	6.3
01	Alabama..................................	20.2	79	13 348	8.5	6.8	7.5
02	Alaska....................................	21.1	25	2 453	11.2	8.1	7.0
04	Arizona...................................	21.6	18	16 254	8.9	8.9	7.0
05	Arkansas................................	20.6	75	7 005	8.5	6.0	7.1
06	California.................................	21.6	14	170 074	7.4	9.7	7.1
08	Colorado.................................	20.3	100	20 267	9.9	8.8	7.3
09	Connecticut.............................	23.1	12	33 556	7.6	7.9	6.7
10	Delaware................................	21.4	5	5 824	8.4	7.1	5.9
11	District of Columbia..................	18.4	30	4 620	11.5	9.2	10.7
12	Florida....................................	20.3	45	62 303	8.3	8.1	6.1
13	Georgia..................................	20.2	30	39 852	8.1	8.1	7.2
15	Hawaii....................................	21.9	17	6 555	5.2	9.9	5.9
16	Idaho.....................................	21.4	57	5 306	7.7	7.5	5.0
17	Illinois....................................	20.5	100	50 451	9.5	12.0	7.3
18	Indiana...................................	21.7	20	50 476	5.0	5.4	3.6
19	Iowa......................................	22.1	65	9 310	10.7	12.3	7.7
20	Kansas...................................	21.8	75	10 977	10.9	10.5	7.7
21	Kentucky................................	20.6	76	13 223	8.6	7.7	6.3
22	Louisiana................................	20.1	74	11 435	7.6	7.1	7.6
23	Maine....................................	22.3	10	10 963	6.5	4.7	4.3
24	Maryland.................................	21.4	12	50 942	7.5	7.7	6.5
25	Massachusetts.........................	23.0	13	51 916	9.0	10.3	8.2
26	Michigan.................................	21.5	67	36 632	8.2	8.5	5.9
27	Minnesota...............................	22.3	67	21 320	11.6	11.7	7.0
28	Mississippi..............................	18.8	93	6 395	6.6	4.6	6.8
29	Missouri.................................	21.6	70	15 171	12.7	11.8	10.1
30	Montana.................................	21.9	57	4 965	7.6	7.4	4.3
31	Nebraska................................	21.9	76	7 442	7.2	8.1	5.8
32	Nevada..................................	21.5	27	6 419	6.3	7.4	4.9
33	New Hampshire.......................	22.6	12	9 918	9.1	9.0	7.2
34	New Jersey.............................	21.8	8	72 401	6.9	9.0	7.0
35	New Mexico............................	20.1	60	4 902	10.4	7.8	7.4
36	New York................................	22.6	17	157 307	5.5	6.6	4.5
37	North Carolina.........................	20.5	14	49 993	6.4	6.9	4.8
38	North Dakota...........................	21.4	80	2 348	6.4	8.8	4.4
39	Ohio......................................	21.5	66	54 899	8.2	8.4	6.1
40	Oklahoma...............................	20.5	72	8 437	10.7	9.2	8.5
41	Oregon..................................	22.4	13	16 928	9.0	7.4	5.7
42	Pennsylvania...........................	21.8	9	80 239	6.7	7.0	6.1
44	Rhode Island...........................	21.2	8	10 621	5.3	4.6	3.6
45	South Carolina.........................	19.5	39	16 267	7.3	7.2	6.1
46	South Dakota...........................	21.8	75	3 156	7.1	6.9	4.3
47	Tennessee..............................	20.7	93	15 742	11.7	9.6	9.8
48	Texas....................................	20.3	29	157 871	5.4	6.7	5.0
49	Utah......................................	21.7	69	4 471	13.2	11.1	7.6
50	Vermont.................................	22.5	19	4 566	10.8	8.5	6.9
51	Virginia..................................	21.1	15	53 287	8.7	7.8	6.4
53	Washington.............................	22.9	15	28 850	11.0	9.2	7.3
54	West Virginia...........................	20.6	64	4 452	7.6	5.8	6.1
55	Wisconsin...............................	22.2	68	21 951	8.9	10.0	6.1
56	Wyoming................................	21.6	71	1 823	5.6	5.8	3.6

[5]*2006 ACT Composite Averages by State.* © 2006 by ACT, Inc. Reprinted with permission. All rights reserved. <http://www.act.org>.
[6] "PSAT/NMSQT 2006–2007 College-Bound Juniors State Summary Reports" Copyright (c) 2006–2007 The College Board, www.collegeboard.com. Reproduced with permission.

Table B-3. Population, School, and Student Characteristics by State—*Continued*

FIPS code	State	Revenues for public elementary and secondary schools, by source, 2003–2004 school year				Current expenditures for public elementary and secondary schools, by function, 2003–2004				
		Total revenue (thousands of dollars)	Percent from:			Total current expenditures (thousands of dollars)	Percent for:			Per student expenditures (dollars)
			Federal government	State government	Local government		Instruction	Support services	Non-instruction	
		94	95	96	97	98	99	100	101	102
00	UNITED STATES	462 015 502	9.1	47.1	43.9	403 376 186	66.1	29.8	4.1	8 310
01	Alabama	5 373 546	12.2	55.6	32.2	4 812 479	64.3	28.8	6.9	6 581
02	Alaska	1 550 365	18.5	56.7	24.8	1 354 846	62.5	34.3	3.3	10 116
04	Arizona	7 641 235	11.9	47.8	40.3	6 063 009	62.4	33.0	4.6	5 991
05	Arkansas	3 428 091	12.7	53.3	34.0	3 109 644	65.9	28.6	5.4	6 842
06	California	57 598 368	10.9	55.6	33.5	49 215 866	67.1	29.1	3.8	7 673
08	Colorado	6 545 403	6.8	43.3	49.9	5 666 191	62.3	34.2	3.5	7 478
09	Connecticut	7 396 816	5.1	36.3	58.6	6 600 767	67.1	29.2	3.7	11 436
10	Delaware	1 296 963	9.0	62.0	29.0	1 201 631	62.4	32.9	4.7	10 212
11	District of Columbia	1 224 730	15.2	-	84.8	1 011 536	61.1	35.9	3.0	12 959
12	Florida	21 042 496	10.6	43.7	45.8	17 578 884	65.4	29.7	4.9	6 793
13	Georgia	13 828 817	8.9	45.9	45.2	11 788 616	68.8	26.0	5.1	7 742
15	Hawaii	2 141 931	11.0	86.6	2.4	1 566 792	65.6	29.4	5.0	8 533
16	Idaho	1 752 753	10.4	58.1	31.6	1 555 006	65.8	29.7	4.4	6 168
17	Illinois	20 713 607	8.4	33.4	58.2	18 081 827	63.9	32.9	3.2	8 606
18	Indiana	10 086 811	6.8	51.0	42.3	8 524 980	63.8	32.0	4.1	8 431
19	Iowa	4 256 454	8.6	45.9	45.5	3 669 797	66.0	29.2	4.9	7 626
20	Kansas	4 545 376	9.1	51.1	39.8	3 658 421	64.0	31.4	4.6	7 776
21	Kentucky	5 077 772	12.2	57.3	30.6	4 551 648	65.7	28.6	5.7	6 861
22	Louisiana	5 786 338	13.5	48.7	37.7	5 290 964	65.2	28.8	6.0	7 271
23	Maine	2 183 576	8.7	42.2	49.1	1 969 497	70.2	26.5	3.2	9 746
24	Maryland	9 004 475	6.5	38.1	55.4	8 198 454	69.3	26.3	4.5	9 433
25	Massachusetts	11 716 904	6.7	40.4	52.9	10 799 765	69.4	27.8	2.8	11 015
26	Michigan	18 032 874	8.0	61.8	30.1	15 983 044	61.8	35.1	3.1	9 094
27	Minnesota	8 565 550	6.2	69.5	24.3	7 084 005	69.7	25.7	4.7	8 405
28	Mississippi	3 483 210	15.4	54.8	29.8	3 059 569	64.7	29.3	6.1	6 199
29	Missouri	7 937 576	8.6	34.3	57.1	6 832 454	65.1	30.4	4.5	7 542
30	Montana	1 267 696	15.4	44.6	40.0	1 160 838	65.0	30.9	4.1	7 825
31	Nebraska	2 663 032	9.0	32.8	58.2	2 413 404	67.2	25.8	6.9	8 452
32	Nevada	3 075 673	7.4	29.6	63.1	2 470 581	66.4	30.3	3.3	6 410
33	New Hampshire	2 116 169	5.7	45.8	48.5	1 900 240	68.0	28.9	3.1	9 161
34	New Jersey	20 476 709	4.5	43.4	52.1	18 416 695	62.6	34.3	3.2	13 338
35	New Mexico	2 918 985	17.6	69.2	13.2	2 446 115	60.9	34.6	4.6	7 572
36	New York	40 610 043	7.6	43.2	49.1	36 205 111	71.2	26.5	2.3	12 638
37	North Carolina	9 877 454	10.5	62.9	26.7	8 994 620	66.7	27.6	5.6	6 613
38	North Dakota	877 701	15.4	38.1	46.5	746 025	62.8	29.3	7.8	7 297
39	Ohio	18 913 893	7.2	44.9	47.9	16 662 985	63.6	33.1	3.3	9 029
40	Oklahoma	4 363 285	12.9	54.4	32.7	3 853 308	60.5	32.6	6.9	6 154
41	Oregon	5 116 226	9.1	52.0	38.9	4 199 485	63.3	33.2	3.6	7 618
42	Pennsylvania	19 966 277	8.3	35.8	56.0	17 680 332	65.5	30.6	4.0	9 708
44	Rhode Island	1 863 135	7.4	41.2	51.4	1 765 585	68.9	28.6	2.5	11 078
45	South Carolina	5 978 578	10.6	46.1	43.3	5 017 833	65.9	28.6	5.4	7 177
46	South Dakota	1 015 552	15.7	34.4	50.0	887 328	63.2	31.4	5.5	7 068
47	Tennessee	6 478 661	10.7	42.9	46.4	6 056 657	69.5	25.2	5.4	6 466
48	Texas	35 409 121	10.8	38.6	50.6	30 974 890	65.8	29.0	5.2	7 151
49	Utah	3 028 885	9.9	55.7	34.5	2 475 550	68.4	25.6	6.0	4 991
50	Vermont	1 208 241	7.8	66.3	25.9	1 111 029	67.7	29.5	2.8	11 211
51	Virginia	10 921 942	7.0	38.8	54.2	9 798 239	67.6	28.4	4.0	8 219
53	Washington	8 910 263	9.3	61.2	29.5	7 549 235	64.2	30.9	4.9	7 391
54	West Virginia	2 687 459	11.5	60.7	27.9	2 415 043	64.3	30.1	5.5	8 588
55	Wisconsin	9 087 054	6.5	52.2	41.3	8 131 276	66.4	30.4	3.2	9 240
56	Wyoming	971 434	9.7	52.2	38.1	814 092	64.5	32.3	3.2	9 308

- = Quantity zero or rounds to zero.

Table B-3. Population, School, and Student Characteristics, by State—*Continued*

FIPS code	State	Enrollment in degree-granting institutions of higher education, fall 2004									
		Total	Attendance status		Level of enrollment				Control of institution		
			Full-time	Part-time	Four-year	Two-year	First professional	Graduate	Public	Private, not-for-profit	Private, for-profit
		103	104	105	106	107	108	109	110	111	112
00	UNITED STATES	17 272 044	10 610 177	6 661 867	8 235 060	6 545 570	334 529	2 156 885	12 980 112	3 411 685	880 247
01	Alabama	255 826	172 737	83 089	139 033	79 339	4 436	33 018	226 989	23 181	5 656
02	Alaska	30 869	13 130	17 739	27 377	1 186	-	2 306	29 515	952	402
04	Arizona	490 925	303 699	187 226	192 819	217 597	3 178	77 331	317 974	9 981	162 970
05	Arkansas	138 399	91 811	46 588	79 007	46 629	1 836	10 927	123 973	13 377	1 049
06	California	2 374 045	1 204 395	1 169 650	679 920	1 427 506	33 845	232 774	1 987 283	273 906	112 856
08	Colorado	300 914	175 892	125 022	154 427	93 969	4 169	48 349	239 308	30 231	31 375
09	Connecticut	172 775	108 686	64 089	90 774	48 297	3 524	30 180	110 354	60 271	2 150
10	Delaware	49 804	31 936	17 868	27 996	13 911	1 167	6 730	38 243	11 561	-
11	District of Columbia	99 988	61 109	38 879	59 930	-	9 790	30 268	5 388	70 687	23 913
12	Florida	866 665	484 145	382 520	457 808	303 582	14 804	90 471	649 857	142 340	74 468
13	Georgia	434 283	291 726	142 557	234 213	143 053	7 998	49 019	335 979	61 190	37 114
15	Hawaii	67 225	40 323	26 902	30 956	27 069	604	8 596	50 569	13 963	2 693
16	Idaho	76 311	52 763	23 548	55 877	12 736	582	7 116	60 695	14 071	1 545
17	Illinois	801 401	449 611	351 790	298 037	369 212	17 859	116 293	563 593	202 733	35 075
18	Indiana	356 801	246 399	110 402	230 454	77 904	6 469	41 974	266 916	77 232	12 653
19	Iowa	217 646	145 423	72 223	110 724	83 184	7 124	16 614	149 776	54 094	13 776
20	Kansas	191 590	113 296	78 294	91 803	76 357	2 501	20 929	170 149	20 351	1 090
21	Kentucky	240 097	152 896	87 201	121 518	89 071	4 647	24 861	197 991	28 645	13 461
22	Louisiana	246 301	179 182	67 119	157 201	54 700	6 399	28 001	208 218	30 249	7 834
23	Maine	65 415	40 071	25 344	44 104	13 290	825	7 196	47 284	17 170	961
24	Maryland	312 493	165 614	146 879	130 334	122 006	4 322	55 831	256 582	50 625	5 286
25	Massachusetts	439 245	299 430	139 815	238 366	89 969	16 091	94 819	187 873	246 710	4 662
26	Michigan	620 980	359 526	261 454	314 782	214 301	12 583	79 314	500 873	111 565	8 542
27	Minnesota	349 021	225 006	124 015	164 791	115 948	7 819	60 463	241 245	66 786	40 990
28	Mississippi	152 115	116 423	35 692	65 345	70 104	2 525	14 141	137 543	12 688	1 884
29	Missouri	365 204	220 236	144 968	203 040	93 929	11 559	56 676	214 561	134 829	15 814
30	Montana	47 173	35 956	11 217	33 615	9 128	472	3 958	42 289	4 884	-
31	Nebraska	121 053	79 572	41 481	62 427	41 338	3 618	13 670	93 195	25 468	2 390
32	Nevada	105 961	50 229	55 732	76 669	18 894	923	9 475	96 773	505	8 683
33	New Hampshire	70 163	46 839	23 324	43 821	15 378	726	10 238	40 642	24 823	4 698
34	New Jersey	380 374	225 846	154 528	167 863	153 631	6 184	52 696	305 034	69 370	5 970
35	New Mexico	131 577	68 772	62 805	50 348	64 446	981	15 802	121 339	3 614	6 624
36	New York	1 141 525	799 394	342 131	609 027	305 593	30 479	196 426	623 192	471 654	46 679
37	North Carolina	472 709	299 649	173 060	215 536	202 250	7 610	47 313	389 143	80 539	3 027
38	North Dakota	49 533	37 878	11 655	34 010	10 764	402	4 327	43 275	5 536	722
39	Ohio	614 234	411 515	202 719	326 174	200 395	13 231	74 434	454 377	136 247	23 610
40	Oklahoma	207 625	136 151	71 474	114 090	68 677	4 519	20 339	179 281	22 095	6 249
41	Oregon	199 985	122 191	77 794	89 212	85 407	4 777	20 589	165 375	27 035	7 575
42	Pennsylvania	688 780	494 691	194 089	409 046	162 276	19 053	98 405	384 525	262 148	42 107
44	Rhode Island	80 377	57 431	22 946	52 831	16 843	1 515	9 188	39 920	39 907	550
45	South Carolina	208 910	140 632	68 278	103 533	80 880	3 392	21 105	172 386	34 589	1 935
46	South Dakota	48 708	32 920	15 788	37 315	5 887	626	4 880	37 598	7 879	3 231
47	Tennessee	278 055	201 225	76 830	154 060	85 858	5 913	32 224	199 904	62 656	15 495
48	Texas	1 229 197	686 665	542 532	495 259	587 408	20 367	126 163	1 071 926	122 989	34 282
49	Utah	194 324	118 707	75 617	138 646	38 263	1 443	15 972	145 182	40 963	8 179
50	Vermont	38 639	27 803	10 836	27 166	6 147	957	4 369	22 980	15 322	337
51	Virginia	425 181	257 092	168 089	202 472	158 012	9 039	55 658	343 391	61 153	20 637
53	Washington	343 524	214 259	129 265	122 495	188 449	4 867	27 713	293 145	40 855	9 524
54	West Virginia	97 884	73 069	24 815	67 215	18 173	1 928	10 568	83 274	12 125	2 485
55	Wisconsin	331 506	211 954	119 552	177 251	115 876	4 389	33 990	266 884	59 941	4 681
56	Wyoming	33 955	19 518	14 437	9 589	20 748	432	3 186	31 597	-	2 358

- = Quantity zero or rounds to zero.

Table B-3. Population, School, and Student Characteristics, by State—*Continued*

FIPS code	State	Race and ethnicity of students enrolled in institutions of higher education, fall 2004						
		Total	Non-Hispanic White	Non-Hispanic Black	Hispanic[2]	Asian or Pacific Islander	American Indian and Alaska Native	Nonresident alien
		113	114	115	116	117	118	119
00	UNITED STATES	17 272 044	11 422 770	2 164 683	1 809 593	1 108 693	176 138	590 167
01	Alabama	255 826	166 656	74 412	3 568	3 342	1 858	5 990
02	Alaska	30 869	22 316	1 094	1 044	1 344	4 155	916
04	Arizona	490 925	315 925	34 908	78 300	17 588	17 419	26 785
05	Arkansas	138 399	104 737	25 271	2 375	1 996	1 532	2 488
06	California	2 374 045	1 040 123	182 775	609 600	444 352	22 300	74 095
08	Colorado	300 914	231 068	14 002	33 308	11 490	4 350	6 696
09	Connecticut	172 775	126 513	17 903	13 673	7 440	722	6 524
10	Delaware	49 804	35 935	9 255	1 679	1 371	180	1 384
11	District of Columbia	99 988	48 634	33 207	4 444	6 627	376	6 700
12	Florida	866 665	492 832	156 587	154 246	29 044	3 668	30 288
13	Georgia	434 283	262 308	131 236	11 168	15 616	1 442	12 513
15	Hawaii	67 225	17 952	1 523	1 954	40 412	329	5 055
16	Idaho	76 311	67 429	596	3 202	1 397	1 068	2 619
17	Illinois	801 401	524 866	110 995	91 517	47 237	2 657	24 129
18	Indiana	356 801	295 973	29 117	9 947	7 115	1 316	13 333
19	Iowa	217 646	189 641	9 598	5 442	4 466	1 115	7 384
20	Kansas	191 590	156 552	11 177	8 082	6 737	3 083	5 959
21	Kentucky	240 097	208 553	21 041	2 661	2 799	699	4 344
22	Louisiana	246 301	150 456	75 586	5 919	5 037	1 543	7 760
23	Maine	65 415	60 277	1 106	772	1 013	862	1 385
24	Maryland	312 493	182 062	84 638	11 594	19 868	1 257	13 074
25	Massachusetts	439 245	319 010	33 961	26 054	31 650	1 914	26 656
20	Michigan	020 000	475 409	00 171	10 044	20 515	5 100	20 100
27	Minnesota	349 021	292 323	21 732	6 687	14 877	4 121	9 281
28	Mississippi	152 115	88 612	58 345	1 128	1 254	754	2 022
29	Missouri	365 204	290 291	43 938	9 939	8 993	2 237	9 806
30	Montana	47 173	40 219	287	717	503	4 602	845
31	Nebraska	121 053	104 754	5 076	3 949	2 790	999	3 485
32	Nevada	105 961	69 004	8 044	13 963	10 777	1 523	2 650
33	New Hampshire	70 163	63 040	1 552	1 734	1 784	380	1 673
34	New Jersey	380 374	228 670	53 986	49 132	32 232	1 124	15 230
35	New Mexico	131 577	57 086	3 721	53 672	2 527	11 503	3 068
36	New York	1 141 525	698 133	160 941	127 658	88 274	4 016	62 503
37	North Carolina	472 709	320 135	112 820	10 878	11 252	5 894	11 730
38	North Dakota	49 533	42 560	743	611	488	3 394	1 737
39	Ohio	614 234	497 895	71 307	11 649	12 994	2 323	18 066
40	Oklahoma	207 625	146 224	18 771	6 834	4 674	21 015	10 107
41	Oregon	199 985	163 889	4 509	10 230	12 606	3 271	5 480
42	Pennsylvania	688 780	546 202	69 837	19 496	28 457	1 867	22 921
44	Rhode Island	80 377	64 546	4 596	4 866	3 420	337	2 612
45	South Carolina	208 910	140 288	58 099	3 115	3 088	832	3 488
46	South Dakota	48 708	42 049	672	515	396	3 926	1 150
47	Tennessee	278 055	207 872	53 992	4 652	5 143	971	5 425
48	Texas	1 229 197	645 856	150 899	315 988	60 221	6 383	49 850
49	Utah	194 324	170 333	1 865	8 590	5 643	2 310	5 583
50	Vermont	38 639	35 301	706	772	828	244	788
51	Virginia	425 181	293 131	80 684	14 946	23 322	2 233	10 865
53	Washington	343 524	262 771	14 507	18 084	32 297	6 273	9 592
54	West Virginia	97 884	88 168	5 006	946	1 072	355	2 337
55	Wisconsin	331 506	285 736	16 759	9 126	9 191	3 501	7 193
56	Wyoming	33 955	30 700	329	1 509	298	617	502

[2]May be of any race.

Table B-3. Population, School, and Student Characteristics by State—*Continued*

FIPS code	State	Migration patterns of college freshmen, fall 2004		Degrees conferred by institutions of higher education, 2003–2004							
		Percent of out-of-state students enrolled	Percent of resident students enrolled in out-of-state institutions	Total degrees	Associate's degrees	Bachelor's degrees			Master's degrees	First professional degrees	Doctoral degrees
						Total	Public	Private			
		120	121	122	123	124	125	126	127	128	129
00	UNITED STATES	X	X	2 755 202	665 301	1 399 542	905 718	493 824	558 940	83 041	48 378
01	Alabama	20.3	10.0	40 896	8 914	21 386	17 643	3 743	9 059	1 016	521
02	Alaska	9.7	38.7	2 996	986	1 405	1 288	117	585	-	20
04	Arizona	27.7	9.5	59 408	14 018	26 225	17 350	8 875	17 464	770	931
05	Arkansas	15.4	11.1	18 952	4 887	10 784	8 537	2 247	2 597	465	219
06	California	10.5	7.9	299 861	89 534	142 418	104 322	38 096	53 293	8 703	5 913
08	Colorado	18.6	15.5	45 688	9 827	24 107	19 135	4 972	10 027	947	780
09	Connecticut	29.5	38.5	31 390	4 737	16 643	8 149	8 494	8 381	949	680
10	Delaware	39.0	28.4	8 644	1 159	5 101	3 811	1 290	1 940	243	201
11	District of Columbia	87.7	66.8	21 950	816	9 435	302	9 133	8 468	2 655	576
12	Florida	19.4	8.5	151 289	57 926	63 811	42 797	21 014	23 175	3 469	2 908
13	Georgia	16.1	13.2	66 783	12 927	36 162	23 638	12 524	14 442	2 118	1 134
15	Hawaii	28.2	31.1	11 322	3 654	5 499	3 314	2 185	1 897	145	127
16	Idaho	25.9	24.1	10 697	3 273	6 042	4 378	1 664	1 116	161	105
17	Illinois	11.8	19.2	127 927	28 738	59 537	31 678	27 859	32 732	4 422	2 498
18	Indiana	22.1	12.8	63 265	13 253	36 388	24 522	11 866	10 836	1 664	1 124
19	Iowa	27.7	11.6	37 349	11 076	20 174	11 122	9 052	3 967	1 526	606
20	Kansas	19.4	13.2	30 917	7 732	16 022	12 624	3 398	5 989	741	433
21	Kentucky	21.5	11.2	33 557	8 660	17 243	13 123	4 120	6 190	1 040	424
22	Louisiana	13.8	8.6	35 872	5 841	21 336	17 450	3 886	6 414	1 710	571
23	Maine	26.0	33.0	10 098	2 252	6 059	3 600	2 459	1 542	202	43
24	Maryland	21.4	31.2	48 224	9 023	23 999	18 295	5 704	12 999	1 140	1 063
25	Massachusetts	35.0	26.7	91 436	11 373	45 583	13 299	32 284	27 768	4 228	2 484
26	Michigan	8.9	9.3	101 481	21 836	51 166	38 615	12 551	24 204	2 716	1 559
27	Minnesota	17.3	19.7	55 637	14 189	27 324	17 330	9 994	11 433	1 659	1 032
28	Mississippi	14.6	7.1	24 440	8 224	11 663	9 774	1 889	3 668	528	357
29	Missouri	18.7	15.3	66 477	12 396	34 006	17 647	16 359	16 285	2 557	1 233
30	Montana	23.9	25.4	8 481	1 811	5 369	4 772	597	1 087	134	80
31	Nebraska	17.7	17.3	20 559	4 295	11 439	7 145	4 294	3 630	813	382
32	Nevada	13.9	17.0	10 094	2 872	5 136	4 714	422	1 796	169	121
33	New Hampshire	46.6	44.3	14 321	3 289	7 908	4 125	3 783	2 839	158	127
34	New Jersey	7.9	32.9	59 649	14 206	30 564	22 185	8 379	12 035	1 662	1 182
35	New Mexico	17.2	18.0	14 997	4 271	7 217	5 948	1 269	2 983	243	283
36	New York	18.3	15.8	238 262	55 634	106 995	43 882	63 113	63 270	8 373	3 990
37	North Carolina	20.0	9.3	70 805	17 517	38 774	26 441	12 333	11 378	1 888	1 248
38	North Dakota	41.8	28.6	8 530	2 172	5 033	4 226	807	1 054	181	90
39	Ohio	12.2	13.1	102 874	22 310	56 256	35 860	20 396	19 246	3 212	1 850
40	Oklahoma	14.9	9.4	33 232	8 701	17 424	13 767	3 657	5 607	1 098	402
41	Oregon	21.8	16.7	32 416	8 301	16 664	12 114	4 550	5 877	1 070	504
42	Pennsylvania	22.0	14.4	133 554	24 576	75 343	37 569	37 774	26 288	4 548	2 799
44	Rhode Island	58.1	29.8	15 532	3 540	9 251	3 137	6 114	2 171	321	249
45	South Carolina	18.7	10.8	31 947	8 039	17 891	12 972	4 919	4 765	820	432
46	South Dakota	26.4	25.0	8 671	2 508	4 752	3 349	1 403	1 116	204	91
47	Tennessee	18.4	14.1	44 297	8 733	24 983	15 756	9 227	8 304	1 431	846
48	Texas	7.5	8.0	163 224	39 302	85 539	66 182	19 357	30 549	5 082	2 752
49	Utah	29.0	7.8	34 255	9 401	19 909	12 008	7 901	4 167	416	362
50	Vermont	67.5	57.7	7 814	1 390	4 648	2 328	2 320	1 474	247	55
51	Virginia	23.7	18.4	65 298	14 034	35 660	27 027	8 633	11 948	2 407	1 249
53	Washington	13.0	19.9	61 296	23 676	27 240	20 456	6 784	8 481	1 170	729
54	West Virginia	24.6	13.2	15 875	3 323	9 101	7 442	1 659	2 829	453	169
55	Wisconsin	15.3	16.9	54 092	11 340	31 759	23 401	8 358	9 155	1 036	802
56	Wyoming	50.1	30.7	5 072	2 809	1 670	1 670	-	420	131	42

X = Not applicable.
- = Quantity zero or rounds to zero.

Table B-3. Population, School, and Student Characteristics by State—*Continued*

FIPS code	State	Enrollment, 2005								Dropouts, 2005	
		Total enrollment		K–12 enrollment		College and graduate school enrollment				Total population, 16 to 19 years	Not a high school graduate, not enrolled in school (percent)
		Number	Percent public	Number	Percent public	Number	Percent public	Percent female	Percent 25 years of age and over		
		130	131	132	133	134	135	136	137	138	139
00	**UNITED STATES**	75 919 435	83.9	53 095 435	90.4	18 038 591	76.0	56.6	48.4	15 271 218	7.3
01	Alabama	1 107 450	85.6	792 494	89.5	248 247	86.4	56.9	45.8	232 429	9.5
02	Alaska	186 843	88.6	138 785	93.2	36 642	86.6	58.3	62.0	43 073	9.3
04	Arizona	1 554 918	89.1	1 104 508	94.6	367 358	82.1	55.5	52.8	310 705	9.2
05	Arkansas	673 553	89.5	488 467	93.5	143 917	86.8	60.3	48.1	150 424	7.8
06	California	10 281 601	86.2	7 094 823	91.8	2 597 943	80.8	55.3	49.5	1 977 382	6.8
08	Colorado	1 203 115	86.2	826 826	92.5	299 920	79.6	52.7	51.9	232 813	8.2
09	Connecticut	888 842	81.2	624 087	91.5	199 884	62.0	56.4	49.6	172 386	4.0
10	Delaware	199 582	77.6	139 224	85.2	46 220	73.2	59.6	50.2	38 711	9.1
11	District of Columbia	120 339	66.4	76 800	85.7	36 225	30.8	59.6	67.8	15 492	8.3
12	Florida	4 228 051	82.3	2 949 422	89.4	999 175	76.0	57.4	49.4	881 425	8.5
13	Georgia	2 371 083	84.6	1 658 174	91.0	530 842	77.7	59.3	50.9	469 166	10.4
15	Hawaii	312 471	76.7	210 746	83.9	80 256	73.6	56.7	48.6	60 672	3.1
16	Idaho	366 744	87.2	264 407	94.2	84 552	76.8	55.7	47.2	82 517	8.5
17	Illinois	3 411 463	81.1	2 330 658	88.8	842 430	69.5	56.3	48.2	657 548	6.8
18	Indiana	1 589 614	83.9	1 144 004	89.5	345 414	80.3	56.8	47.1	315 023	8.7
19	Iowa	704 615	85.4	489 480	91.5	167 708	76.0	58.2	42.8	147 870	5.4
20	Kansas	713 998	85.8	484 298	90.4	182 051	82.5	54.5	47.1	142 491	6.2
21	Kentucky	989 574	84.8	703 589	88.5	226 405	82.4	58.2	46.7	203 911	9.0
22	Louisiana	1 180 592	80.8	830 574	83.9	265 864	81.4	59.2	42.3	253 623	8.4
23	Maine	296 233	86.0	210 771	92.5	70 992	73.9	62.4	55.0	66 758	6.7
24	Maryland	1 483 858	78.5	1 012 859	85.6	377 854	72.0	58.4	53.1	294 765	7.2
25	Massachusetts	1 575 699	75.7	1 066 448	89.3	398 142	50.9	56.5	51.9	290 427	4.9
26	Michigan	2 712 184	86.7	1 882 120	91.2	675 911	81.8	56.0	47.2	539 836	6.5
27	Minnesota	1 289 951	84.4	899 018	90.6	307 259	75.6	57.1	44.4	271 116	4.2
28	Mississippi	751 432	87.5	539 169	91.1	154 586	86.5	62.2	44.9	159 757	9.0
29	Missouri	1 396 175	81.9	985 891	87.6	317 850	73.2	58.1	45.2	295 484	7.8
30	Montana	209 317	89.5	148 288	94.4	49 185	84.6	55.1	46.7	48 819	7.2
31	Nebraska	445 741	82.4	305 557	88.0	110 586	79.3	56.5	45.4	89 930	5.1
32	Nevada	584 893	90.0	438 792	95.2	124 077	81.6	53.3	53.3	118 842	10.7
33	New Hampshire	318 118	79.5	230 214	90.9	69 487	62.3	63.1	49.6	65 296	5.8
34	New Jersey	2 275 052	78.9	1 579 347	88.2	510 201	64.6	56.4	44.0	450 907	5.5
35	New Mexico	521 618	90.2	356 881	93.4	136 199	88.5	59.6	53.7	118 147	9.6
36	New York	4 835 203	76.8	3 330 469	86.7	1 194 953	59.5	56.4	46.6	939 064	6.5
37	North Carolina	2 183 555	86.2	1 534 637	91.9	509 036	81.5	58.7	54.2	418 468	8.9
38	North Dakota	146 083	90.6	99 159	93.5	39 863	88.9	58.9	41.8	31 311	4.5
39	Ohio	2 843 379	82.5	2 007 521	88.0	660 980	77.2	57.7	46.8	585 410	6.4
40	Oklahoma	870 176	89.2	603 082	93.2	211 757	84.2	57.1	48.2	187 124	9.7
41	Oregon	877 043	86.0	611 580	91.6	219 232	82.3	56.1	51.9	180 746	6.8
42	Pennsylvania	2 922 181	77.4	2 062 959	86.3	683 197	63.9	56.2	44.6	602 152	6.5
44	Rhode Island	263 678	77.9	180 450	88.0	69 981	62.2	57.9	49.1	45 784	7.7
45	South Carolina	1 025 953	85.3	752 237	90.7	212 631	80.0	60.0	49.6	210 699	9.3
46	South Dakota	184 793	86.6	131 363	91.4	40 950	80.5	56.3	40.5	41 142	6.8
47	Tennessee	1 355 738	84.7	985 644	90.0	289 800	79.1	58.6	47.1	294 981	8.2
48	Texas	6 241 175	88.8	4 473 518	94.0	1 355 656	83.0	56.1	47.6	1 254 509	7.8
49	Utah	751 354	86.9	498 753	95.7	205 052	75.8	47.4	45.5	144 683	7.1
50	Vermont	144 829	82.2	100 286	91.6	36 339	66.4	60.2	48.7	30 804	4.9
51	Virginia	1 897 723	83.4	1 306 901	91.4	465 127	76.1	54.2	49.6	375 530	5.6
53	Washington	1 543 422	86.8	1 081 009	92.8	378 060	81.0	55.7	50.8	332 146	7.3
54	West Virginia	389 179	90.5	278 557	95.1	91 983	83.9	57.6	43.7	83 765	8.8
55	Wisconsin	1 381 255	83.4	967 996	88.1	342 287	79.5	57.7	47.0	288 467	5.6
56	Wyoming	117 997	93.0	82 593	97.1	28 325	87.9	59.2	50.1	26 688	8.0

NOTES AND DEFINITIONS: REGION AND STATE EDUCATION STATISTICS

This section provides details about each items source and relevant definitions. Internet references are provided when available. In some cases, the Internet reference will lead to a general Web page instead of to the precise data included in this volume. Additional data sources, such as the Census Bureau's online FERRET (Federal Electronic Research and Review Extraction Tool) and CD-ROM databases from the National Center for Education Statistics (NCES), were often used.

TABLES B-1 AND B-2
Source: Census Bureau. 2005. Tables 12 and 14a. Educational attainment in the United States: 2005. *Annual Social and Economic Supplement to the Current Population Survey.* <http://www.census.gov/population/www/socdemo/education/cps2005.html>.

The Census Bureau disseminated comparable tables in the P-20 series of the Current Population Reports for most years between 1947 and 1994. Since that time, these tables have been unavailable in printed form. They can be found on the Census Bureau Web site at <http://www.census.gov>.

GEOGRAPHIC DEFINITIONS
Data are presented for the four major regions and nine divisions of the United States. These groups of states are as follows:

NORTHEAST: Connecticut, Maine, Massachusetts, New Hampshire, New Jersey, New York, Pennsylvania, Rhode Island, and Vermont

New England—Connecticut, Maine, Massachusetts, New Hampshire, Rhode Island, and Vermont
Middle Atlantic—New Jersey, New York, and Pennsylvania

MIDWEST: Illinois, Indiana, Iowa, Kansas, Michigan, Minnesota, Missouri, Nebraska, North Dakota, Ohio, South Dakota, and Wisconsin

East North Central—Illinois, Indiana, Michigan, Ohio, and Wisconsin
West North Central—Iowa, Kansas, Minnesota, Missouri, Nebraska, North Dakota, and South Dakota

SOUTH: Alabama, Arkansas, Delaware, District of Columbia, Florida, Georgia, Kentucky, Louisiana, Maryland, Mississippi, North Carolina, Oklahoma, South Carolina, Tennessee, Texas, Virginia, and West Virginia

East South Central—Alabama, Kentucky, Mississippi, and Tennessee
South Atlantic—Delaware, District of Columbia, Florida, Georgia, Maryland, North Carolina, South Carolina, Virginia, and West Virginia
West South Central—Arkansas, Louisiana, Oklahoma, and Texas

WEST: Alaska, Arizona, California, Colorado, Hawaii, Idaho, Montana, Nevada, New Mexico, Oregon, Utah, Washington, and Wyoming

Mountain—Arizona, Colorado, Idaho, Montana, Nevada, New Mexico, Utah, and Wyoming
Pacific—Alaska, California, Hawaii, Oregon, and Washington

TABLE B-3

POPULATION, ITEMS 1–2
Source: U.S. Census Bureau. *Population Estimates Program.* <http://www.census.gov/popest/national/files/NST_EST2005_ALLDATA.csv>.

The population data for 2005 are U.S. Census Bureau estimates of the resident population as of July 1, 2005.

INCOME, POVERTY, AND HEALTH INSURANCE, ITEMS 3–7
Source: U.S. Census Bureau. August 2006. *Income, Poverty, and Health Insurance Coverage in the United States: 2005* (Current Population Reports, P60-231). < http://www.census.gov/prod/2006pubs/p60-231.pdf>.

Additional Internet sources:
• <http://www.census.gov/hhes/income/4person.html>
• <http://pubdb3.census.gov/macro/032006/pov/new46_100125_03.htm>
• <http://pubdb3.census.gov/macro/032006/health/h10_000.htm>

The data on income are derived from the responses of a national sample of persons age 15 years and over in about 50,000 households. Total money income has been defined by the Census Bureau for statistical purposes as the sum of the following: wage or salary income, nonfarm self-employment income, Social Security and railroad retirement income, public assistance income, and all other regularly received income, such as interest, dividends, veterans' payments, pensions, unemployment compensation, and alimony. Receipts not counted as income include various "lump sum" payments, such as capital gains or inheritances. The total represents the amount of income received before deductions for personal income taxes, Social Security, bond purchases, union dues, Medicare deductions, and the like.

Family income includes the income of all family members age 15 years and over. Median family income was usually higher than median household income, because many households consist of only one person. The median divides the income distribution into two equal parts—one part consisting of families with incomes above the median and the other part consisting of families with incomes below the median.

Poverty status is based on the definition prescribed by the U.S. Office of Management and Budget as the standard to be used by federal agencies for statistical purposes. A family is classified as below the poverty level (or "in poverty") if its total family income was less than the poverty threshold specified for the applicable family size, age of householder, and number of related children under 18 years old present in the family. The poverty threshold for a four-person family with two children under 18 years old was $19,971 in 2005. A child is defined as low income if his or her family's income was less than 200 percent of the poverty threshold.

Persons lacking health insurance coverage include those not covered by a private health plan or by Medicaid, Medicare, or a military health plan.

EDUCATIONAL ATTAINMENT, ITEMS 8–10
Source: U.S. Census Bureau. October 2006. Table 13. Educational attainment in the United States. *2005 Annual Social and Economic Supplement to the Current Population Survey*. <http://www.census.gov/population/www/socdemo/education/cps2005.html>.

The data on educational attainment are derived from the responses of a national sample of persons from about 50,000 households. Statistics for educational attainment only include persons age 25 years and over. Respondents were asked to state the highest grade of school attended or the highest degree received. Those who passed a high school equivalency examination are considered high school graduates. Schooling received in foreign schools is reported as the equivalent grade or years in the regular American school system.

SCHOOL DISTRICTS, ITEM 11
Source: U.S. Department of Education. National Center for Education Statistics. *Common Core of Data, 2004–2005* (Local Education Agency Universe, 2004–2005, version 1a). <http://nces.ed.gov/ccd/>.

A school district or Local Education Agency (LEA) is a local-level education agency that exists primarily to operate public schools or to contract for public school services. A public school is controlled and operated by publicly elected or appointed officials, and it derives its primary support from public funds.

The state numbers are from the Common Core of Data (CCD) state universe, which includes approximately 18,000 regular school districts with students in membership. Not included are special districts that typically offer research, administrative, or other support services to client agencies. The CCD data now include charter schools. Since charter schools are typically managed independently from the local school district, each one was considered a single district.

NUMBER AND TYPE OF SCHOOLS, ITEMS 12–22
Sources: U.S. Department of Education. National Center for Education Statistics. *Common Core of Data, 2004–2005*. <http://nces.ed.gov/ccd/>.—U.S. Department of Education. National Center for Education Statistics. *Overview of Public Elementary and Secondary Students, Staff, Schools, School Districts, Revenues, and Expenditures: School Year 2004–2005 and Fiscal Year 2004* (NCES Report 2007-309).

The state data are from the CCD state universe. There are approximately 93,000 schools represented, including all those that reported membership in 2004–2005.

Regular schools do not focus primarily on special, vocational, or alternative education, though they may offer these programs in addition to the regular curriculum. Special education schools focus primarily on special education, with materials and instructional approaches adapted to meet students' needs. Vocational education schools focus on vocational, technical, or career education. They provide education or training in at least one semi-skilled or technical occupation. Alternative education schools address students' needs that typically cannot be met in a regular school setting. These schools provide nontraditional educational experiences.

A charter school is a school that provides free public elementary and/or secondary education to eligible students under a specific charter granted by the state legislature or other appropriate authority; the school must have also been designated as charter schools by these authorities. Charter schools can be administered by regular school districts, State Education Agencies (SEAs), or chartering organizations.

A magnet school or program is a special school or program designed to attract students of different racial and ethnic backgrounds for the purpose of reducing, preventing, or eliminating racial isolation and/or to provide an academic or social focus on a particular theme.

A Title I eligible school is a school designated under appropriate state and federal regulations as being high poverty and eligible for participation in programs authorized by Title I of P.L. 107-110. A Title I school is one in which the percentage of children from low-income families is at least as high as the percentage of children from low-income families served by the LEA as a whole, or a school designated by the LEA as Title I eligible because 35 percent or more of the children are from low-income families. A Title I schoolwide school is a school in which all the students are designated under appropriate state and federal regulations as eligible for participation in Title I programs authorized by Title I of P.L. 107-110.

NUMBER AND GRADE LEVEL OF STUDENTS, ITEMS 23–26
Source: U.S. Department of Education. National Center for Education Statistics. *Common Core of Data State Nonfiscal Survey of Public*

Elementary/Secondary Education: School Year 2004–2005 (version 1d). <http://nces.ed.gov/ccd/>.

The primary grades include pre-kindergarten through grade 4. Middle school grades included grades 5 through 8. High school grades include grades 9 through 12. Ungraded students are included in the total but are not separately listed. Some states have no ungraded students.

STUDENTS WHO ARE ELIGIBLE FOR FREE OR REDUCED-PRICE MEALS, ITEM 27
Sources: U.S. Department of Education. National Center for Education Statistics. *Common Core of Data, 2004–2005.* <http://nces.ed.gov/ccd/>.—U.S. Department of Education. National Center for Education Statistics. *Overview of Public Elementary and Secondary Students, Staff, Schools, School Districts, Revenues, and Expenditures: School Year 2004–2005 and Fiscal Year 2004* (NCES Report 2007-309).

The Free and Reduced-Price Lunch Program is a program under the National School Lunch Act that provides cash subsidies for free or reduced-price meals to students based on family size and income criteria. Participation in the Free and Reduced-Price Lunch Program depends on income, and eligibility is often used to estimate student needs.

STUDENTS WITH INDIVIDUAL EDUCATION PROGRAMS, ITEM 28
Sources: U.S. Department of Education. National Center for Education Statistics. *Common Core of Data, 2004–2005.* <http://nces.ed.gov/ccd/>.—U.S. Department of Education. National Center for Education Statistics. *Overview of Public Elementary and Secondary Students, Staff, Schools, School Districts, Revenues, and Expenditures: School Year 2004–2005 and Fiscal Year 2004* (NCES Report 2007-309).

An Individualized Education Program (IEP) is a written instructional plan for students with disabilities who are designated as special education students under IDEA (Individuals with Disabilities Education Act). An IEP includes a statement of present levels of educational performance of a child; a statement of annual goals, including short-term instructional objectives; a statement of specific educational services to be provided and the extent to which the child will be able to participate in regular educational programs; a projected date for initiation and the anticipated duration of services; appropriate objectives, criteria, and evaluation procedures; and schedules for determining, on at least an annual basis, whether instructional objectives are being achieved.

STUDENTS WHO ARE ENGLISH-LANGUAGE LEARNERS, ITEM 29

Sources: U.S. Department of Education. National Center for Education Statistics. *Common Core of Data, 2004–2005.* <http://nces.ed.gov/ccd/>.—U.S. Department of Education. National Center for Education Statistics. *Overview of Public Elementary and Secondary Students, Staff, Schools, School Districts, Revenues, and Expenditures: School Year 2004–2005 and Fiscal Year 2004* (NCES Report 2007-309).

This category includes the number of students who are served in appropriate programs of language assistance (e.g., English as a Second Language, High Intensity Language Training, and bilingual education). This designation changed from Limited-English Proficient (LEP) to English-Language Learners (ELL) in the 2001–2002 school year

STUDENTS WHO ARE MIGRANTS, ITEM 30

Sources: U.S. Department of Education. National Center for Education Statistics. *Common Core of Data, 2004–2005.* <http://nces.ed.gov/ccd/>.— Build-a-Table from *Public Elementary/Secondary School Universe Survey.*

This column provides the total number of migrant students enrolled in school during the previous year and the cumulative, unduplicated numbers (within a school) of migrant students enrolled at any time during the previous regular school year.

RACE AND HISPANIC ORIGIN, ITEMS 31–35

Sources: U.S. Department of Education. National Center for Education Statistics. *Common Core of Data, 2004–2005.* <http://nces.ed.gov/ccd/>.— Build-a-Table from the *State Nonfiscal Survey of Public Elementary/Secondary Education.*

The racial and ethnic categories used in the CCD are those approved by the U.S. Office of Management and Budget at the time these data were collected. These categories are mutually exclusive.

DROPOUTS, ITEM 36

Sources: U.S. Department of Education. National Center for Education Statistics. *Common Core of Data, 2001–2002.* <http://nces.ed.gov/ccd/>.— U.S. Department of Education. National Center for Education Statistics. *Dropout Rates in the United States: 2002 and 2003.* (NCES Report 2006-062).

A dropout is a student who was enrolled in school at some time during the previous school year who was not enrolled at the beginning of the current school year and who had not graduated from high school or completed a state or district-approved educational program and who did not meet any of the following exclusionary conditions: transferal to another public school district, private school, or state- or district-approved educational program; temporary absent due to suspension or school-approved illness; or death.

Most of the states that reported on dropouts used an October through September cycle; however, the following states reported on a July through June cycle: Alabama, Alaska, Arizona, Florida, Illinois, Maryland, New Jersey, New York, Tennessee, and Vermont.

MEMBERSHIP AND GRADUATES, ITEMS 37–39

Sources: U.S. Department of Education. National Center for Education Statistics. *Common Core of Data, 2001–2002 and 2004–2005.* <http://nces.ed.gov/ccd/>.—Build-a-Table from the *State Nonfiscal Survey of Public Elementary/Secondary Education.*

The total numbers of students shown in columns 37 and 38 are those reported in the 2004–2005 State Nonfiscal Survey of Public Elementary/Secondary Education.

The number of graduates includes individuals who received a regular diploma, individuals who received a diploma from a program different than the regular school program, and individuals who received a certificate of attendance or other certificate of completion in lieu of a diploma during the previous school year and subsequent summer school session. Recipients of high school equivalency certificates are not included.

AVERAGED FRESHMAN GRADUATION RATE, ITEM 40

Sources: U.S. Department of Education. National Center for Education Statistics. *Common Core of Data, 1999–2000* through *2004–2005*. <http://nces.ed.gov/ccd/>.—U.S. Department of Education. National Center for Education Statistics. *Overview of Public Elementary and Secondary Students, Staff, Schools, School Districts, Revenues, and Expenditures: School Year 2004–2005 and Fiscal Year 2004* (NCES Report 2007-309).

The averaged freshman graduation rate provides an estimate of the percentage of high school students who graduate on time. The rate uses aggregate student enrollment data (to estimate the size of an incoming freshman class) and aggregate counts of the number of diplomas awarded 4 years later. The incoming freshman class size is estimated by summing the enrollment in 8th grade in one year, 9th grade in the next year, and 10th grade in the year after that, and then dividing by three. The averaging is intended to account for prior-year retentions in the 9th grade.

PRIVATE SCHOOLS, ITEMS 41–43

Sources: U.S. Department of Education. National Center for Education Statistics. *Private School Universe Survey, 2003–2004*. <http://nces.ed.gov/surveys/pss/>.—U.S. Department of Education. National Center for Education Statistics. *Characteristics of Private Schools in the United States: Results from the 2003–2004 Private School Universe Survey* (NCES Report 2006-319).

Since 1989, the Census Bureau has conducted the biennial Private School Universe Survey (PSS) for NCES. The PSS is designed to generate biennial data on the total number of private schools, students, and teachers and to build a universe of private schools in all of the states and the District of Columbia to serve as a sampling frame of private schools for NCES sample surveys. The target population for the PSS is every school in all of the states and the District of Columbia that are not primarily supported by public funds, provide instruction for one or more grades between kindergarten and grade 12 (or comparable ungraded levels), and have one or more teachers. Organizations or institutions that provide support for home schooling, but do not provide classroom instruction, are not included. Although the PSS has begun to collect limited data on the many private schools for which kindergarten is the highest grade, the data in this volume are for (traditional) schools that include at least one grade between grades 1 and 12.

A private school is controlled by an individual or agency other than a state, a subdivision of a state, or the federal government; is usually supported primarily by nonpublic funds; and the operation of its program does not rest with publicly elected or appointed officials. Private schools include both nonprofit and proprietary institutions.

PUBLIC AND PRIVATE SCHOOL CHARACTERISTICS, ITEMS 44–51

Sources: U.S. Department of Education. National Center for Education Statistics. *Common Core of Data, 1994–1995* and *2004–2005*. <http://nces.ed.gov/ccd/>.—Build-a-Table from the *State Nonfiscal Survey of Public Elementary/Secondary Education*.U.S. Department of Education. National Center for Education Statistics. *Private School Universe Survey, 2003–2004*. <http://nces.ed.gov/surveys/pss/>.—U.S. Department of Education. National Center for Education Statistics. *Characteristics of Private Schools in the United States: Results from the 2003–2004 Private School Universe Survey* (NCES Report 2006-319).

The public school numbers are from the CCD state universe. Teacher counts measure the number of full-time equivalent teachers, including teachers who are employed by agencies and not assigned to specific schools. The student-teacher ratio is calculated by dividing the number of students in all schools by the number of full-time equivalent teachers employed by all schools and agencies.

The private school numbers are derived from the PSS, as published in *Characteristics of Private Schools in the United States: Results From the 2003–2004 Private School Universe Survey*. These estimates measured full-time equivalent teachers. The student-teacher ratio is calculated by dividing the number of students enrolled in all schools by the number of full-time equivalent teachers employed by all schools.

TEACHER SALARIES, ITEM 52

Source: National Education Association. Rankings & estimates database. *Rankings & Estimates: Rankings of the States 2005 and Estimates of School Statistics,* 2006. (Washington, D.C.: NEA, 2006.) <http://www.nea.org/edstats/images/06rankings.pdf>. All rights reserved. Reprinted with permission.

The National Education Association (NEA) publishes average teacher salaries by state in its annual *Estimates of School Statistics.* The information is compiled from surveys conducted by the state departments of education. If a state does not provide a salary amount, the NEA develops an estimate. In this volume, estimates are used for Arizona, Arkansas, California, Colorado, Connecticut the District of Columbia, Idaho, Louisiana, Kentucky, Maryland, Massachusetts, Michigan, Minnesota, Mississippi, Montana, Nebraska, New Jersey, New York, Ohio, Oregon, Pennsylvania, Rhode Island, South Carolina, Utah, Vermont, and Virginia.

The average salary used is for public school teachers is defined as the arithmetic mean of the salaries of the group described. This figure is the average gross salary before deductions for Social Security, retirement, health insurance, and the like.

PUBLIC SCHOOL STAFF, ITEMS 53–71

Sources: U.S. Department of Education. National Center for Education Statistics. *Common Core of Data, 2004–2005.* <http://nces.ed.gov/ccd/>.—U.S. Department of Education. National Center for Education Statistics. *Overview of Public Elementary and Secondary Students, Staff, Schools, School Districts, Revenues, and Expenditures: School Year 2004–2005 and Fiscal Year 2004* (NCES Report 2007-309).

The number of teachers represents full-time equivalent teachers employed within the state. Instructional aides directly assist teachers in providing instruction. Instructional coordinators help teachers through curriculum development and in-service training. Support staff includes those involved with food, health, library, maintenance, transportation, security, and other services in public schools. School administrators are principals and assistant principals. School district administrators include the Local Education Agency (LEA) super-

intendents, deputies, assistant superintendents, and other persons with district-wide responsibilities.

CHARACTERISTICS OF TEACHERS, ITEMS 72–78

Source: U.S. Department of Education. National Center for Education Statistics. Table 67. Schools and staffing survey, 1999–2000. *Digest of Education Statistics, 2005.* <http://nces.ed.gov/surveys/sass/>.

The highest degree earned and years of experience are from the 1999–2000 Schools and Staffing Survey (SASS), as published in the *Digest of Education Statistics, 2005.*

SASS is a set of linked questionnaires that covers public school districts, public and private schools, principals, and teachers as its core components. Data for SASS are collected through a sample survey of schools, the school districts associated with sample schools, and the schools' principals and teachers. The 1999–2000 SASS estimates were based on a sample of approximately 13,500 schools (9,900 public and 3,600 private), 67,000 teachers (56,000 public and 11,000 private, and 5,500 public school districts.

NATIONAL ASSESSMENT OF EDUCATIONAL PROGRESS, ITEMS 79–83

Source: U.S. Department of Education. National Center for Education Statistics. *National Assessment of Educational Progress, 2002 and 2005.* <http://nces.ed.gov/nationsreportcard/>.

The National Assessment of Educational Progress (NAEP) is a congressionally mandated project of the National Center for Education Statistics (NCES) that has, for more than a quarter of a century, continually collected and reported information on what American students know and what they can do. It is the nation's only ongoing, comparable, and representative assessment of student achievement. Its assessments are based on a national probability sample of public and nonpublic school students enrolled in grades 4, 8, or 12. Results are only provided for group performance, as NAEP is forbidden by law to report results at an individual or school level. The assessment questions are written around a framework prepared for each content area—reading, writing, mathematics, science, and other; this framework represents the consensus of groups of curriculum experts, educators, and members of the general public on what such a test should cover.

In response to legislation passed by Congress in 1988, the NAEP program includes voluntary state-by-state assessments. To help ensure valid state-by-state results, NCES applies minimum school and student participation rate standards for its reporting activities. Results are not reported for jurisdictions that failed to meet these standards.

This volume includes the proportion of students in specific grades whose NAEP mathematics, science, and writing assessment results were designated as "proficient," or better for their grades. The achievement level results describe what students participating in the NAEP assessment should know and what they should be able to do. The National Assessment Governing Board (NAGB) adopted three achievement levels: basic, proficient, and advanced. The basic level denotes partial mastery of fundamental knowledge and skills, the proficient level shows solid academic performance and competency in challenging subject matter, and the advanced level signifies superior performance. Achievement levels are based on collective judgments gathered from a broadly representative panel of teachers, education specialists, and members of the general public about what students should know and be able to do relative to the body of content reflected in the NAEP assessment framework.

SAT REASONING TEST SCORES, ITEMS 84–87

Source: "2006 College-Bound Seniors" Copyright © 2006–2007 The College Board, <www.collegeboard.com>. Reproduced with permission.

The total number of high school graduates who took the SAT in 2006 is based on the projection of the number of high school graduates in 2006 by the Western Interstate Commission for Higher Education and the number of students in the class of 2006 who took the SAT Reasoning Test. Updated projections make it inappropriate to compare these percentages with those of previous years.

The SAT is an examination administered by the Educational Testing Service that is used to predict the facility with which an individual will progress in college-level academic classes.

The *Profile of College-Bound Seniors* presents data for 2006 high school graduates who participated in the SAT program during their high school years. Students are counted once no matter how often they tested, and only their most recent scores are included in the data. The class of 2006 was the first to take the new SAT, which includes writing as well as critical reading and math. Each test is scored on a scale of 200 to 800.

The College Board cautions that relationships between test scores and other factors such as educational background, gender, race/ethnic background, parental education, and household income are complex and interdependent. These factors do not directly affect test performance; rather, they are associated with educational experiences both on tests such as the SAT and in school work. Moreover, not all students in a high school, school district, or state take the SAT. Since the population of test takers is self-selected, using aggregate SAT scores to compare or evaluate teachers, schools, districts, states, or other educational units is not valid, and the College Board strongly discourages such uses.

Interpreting SAT scores for states requires unique considerations. The most significant factor to consider in interpreting SAT scores for any group or subgroup of test takers is the proportion of students taking the test. For example, it is important to recognize that some states have lower participation rates. Typically, test takers in these low-participation states have strong academic backgrounds and to the nation's most selective colleges and scholarship programs. For these states, it is expected that the SAT mean scores reported for students will be higher than the national average.

ACT ASSESSMENT COMPOSITE SCORES, ITEMS 88–89

Source: ACT, Inc. *2006 ACT Composite Averages by State*. <http://www.act.org/news/data/06/states.html>. © 2006 by ACT, Inc.

Totals for graduating seniors were obtained from: ACT, Inc. *Knocking at the College Door— December 2003, Projections of High School*

Graduates by State, Income and Race/Ethnicity, 1998–2018. (Boulder, CO: Western Interstate Commission for Higher Education, 2003).

Founded in 1959 as the American College Testing Program, ACT, Inc., is an independent, not-for-profit organization that provides over 100 assessment, research, information, and program management services in the broad areas of educational planning, career planning, and workforce development. The ACT Assessment is designed to assess high school students' general educational development and their ability to complete college-level work. The test covers four skill areas: English, mathematics, reading, and science reasoning. Data in this volume are based on all high school graduates in the class of 2006 who took the ACT Assessment during their sophomore, junior, or senior year. For students who took the test more than once, only their most recent scores are used. Students who tested on campus, used extended time testing, or failed to list a valid high school code not included.

College-bound students who take the ACT Assessment are not representative of college-bound students nationally. Students residing in the Midwest, the Mountain West, the Plains, and the South are overrepresented among ACT-tested students, compared with college-bound students nationally. ACT-tested students also tend to enroll in public college and universities more frequently than college-bound students nationally.

Caution should be used in comparing state and national norms. State norms may differ from national norms for non-educational reasons, such as the representativeness of the ACT-tested population and the demographic makeup of a state.

PSAT/NMSQT® (PRELIMINARY SAT/NATIONAL MERIT SCHOLARSHIP QUALIFYING TEST), ITEMS 90–93

Source: "PSAT/NMSQT 2006–2007 College-Bound Juniors State Summary Reports" Copyright © 2006–2007 The College Board, <www.collegeboard.com>. Reproduced with permission.

The PSAT/NMSQT (Preliminary SAT/National Merit Scholarship Qualifying Test) is a program co-sponsored by the College Board and the National Merit Scholarship Corporation. The test serves several functions: it helps assess skills necessary for college-level work, prepares students for the SAT, enters students in competitions for national scholarships (including the National Merit Scholarship Corporation scholarship programs), and helps students receive access to information and applications for educational and financial aid information from colleges, universities, and scholarship programs.

Verbal, math, and writing skills scores are each reported on a 20 to 80 scale. The average scores of juniors in each section are between 47 and 49. Unless students earn scores that are much lower than average, the PSAT/NMSQT shows that they are likely developing the kinds of critical reading, math problem-solving, and writing skills needed for academic success in college.

The sum of the verbal, math, and writing skills scores makes up the Selection Index, which is used by National Merit Scholarship Corporation to designate those who will be honored in its scholarship programs. The qualifying score varies from state to state, depending on the scores and the proportion of test takers in each state. Scores between 65 and 80 on each skill mark the approximate level of the achievement needed to qualify. In states with higher percentages of scores in this range, a student must achieve a higher Selection Index to be a designated a National Merit semifinalist.

REVENUES, ITEMS 94–97
Source: U.S. Department of Education. National Center for Education Statistics. *Common Core of Data, Fiscal Year 2004.* <http://nces.ed.gov/ccd/>.

These data are from the National Public Education Financial Survey (NPEFS) for fiscal year 2004 (school year 2003–2004). The state data include adjustments made by NCES. Values that were missing and not reported elsewhere in the survey were imputed based on corresponding proportions in reporting states. Other adjustments were made when a single value was reported that included two or more categories. NCES distributed portions of the single reported value to the missing items. In addition to these adjustments, the NPEFS may also include state-run education programs. Consequently, these numbers may differ from the state totals in Table C, which are dervied from a different survey.

Charter school systems' reporting requirements vary from state to state and data are not currently reported uniformly to the State Education Agencies (SEAs). Note that some charter school data may be missing from this volume, since some charter schools were not required to submit finance data to their SEAs. Only those charter schools that submit data to the SEAs, and whose SEAs maintain the data, are included in the CCD fiscal files.

Revenues from federal sources include direct grants-in-aid from the federal government, federal grants-in-aid through the state or an intermediate agency, and other revenue in lieu of taxes to compensate a school district for nontaxable federal institutions within a district's boundaries.

State revenues include revenues that can be used without restriction, revenues for categorical purposes, and revenues in lieu of taxation. Also included are revenues from payments made by a state for the benefit of the Local Education Agency (LEA) or contributions of equipment or supplies. Such revenues include the payment of a pension fund by the state on behalf of an LEA employee for services rendered and contributions of fixed assets (property, plant, or equipment), such as school buses and textbooks.

Revenues from local sources include local property and non-property tax revenues, taxes levied or assessed by an LEA, revenues from a local government to the LEA, tuition received, transportation fees, earnings on investments from LEA holdings, net revenues from food services (gross receipts less gross expenditures), net revenues from student activities (gross receipts less gross expenditures), and other revenues (textbook sales, donations, and property rentals). Intermediate revenues were included in local revenue totals. Intermediate revenues are derived from sources other than Local or State Education Agencies; these sources operate at an intermediate level between Local and State Education Agencies and possess independent fundraising capabilities (such as county or municipal agencies).

EXPENDITURES, ITEMS 98–102

Source: U.S. Department of Education. National Center for Education Statistics. *Common Core of Data, Fiscal Year 2003.* <http://nces.ed.gov/ccd/>.

Data are from the National Public Education Financial Survey data file for fiscal year 2004 (school year 2003–2004). The state data include adjustments made by NCES. Values that were missing and not reported elsewhere in the survey were imputed based on proportions in reporting states. Other adjustments were made when a single value was reported that included two or more categories. NCES distributed portions of the single reported value to the missing items. In addition to these adjustments, the NPEFS may include state-run education programs. Consequently, these numbers may differ from the state totals in Table C, which come from a different survey.

Current expenditures consist of expenditures for the categories of instruction, support services, and non-instructional services for salaries; employee benefits; purchased services and supplies; and payments by the state made for or on behalf of school systems. These expenditures do not include expenditures for debt service, capital outlay, and property (e.g., equipment), or direct costs (e.g., Head Start, adult education, community colleges, etc.) and community services expenditures.

Instructional expenses comprise current expenditures for activities that deal directly with the interaction between students and teachers. These expenditures include teacher salaries and benefits, supplies (such as textbooks), instructional staff support (i.e., salaries for librarians and instructional specialists), and purchased instructional services.

Support services expenditures consist of current expenditures for activities supporting instruction. These services include operation and maintenance of buildings, school administration, student support services (e. g., nurses, therapists, and guidance counselors), student transportation, school district administration, business services, research, and data processing.

Noninstructional expenditures are mostly for food service, but also consist of expenditures for enterprise operations, such as bookstores and interscholastic athletics.

Current expenditures per student are derived by dividing total current expenditures by the fall student membership count from the CCD. Student membership consists of the count of students enrolled on or about October 1 and is comparable across all states.

HIGHER EDUCATION, ITEMS 103–129

Sources: U.S. Department of Education. National Center for Education Statistics. Integrated Postsecondary Education Data System (IPEDS). *Enrollment in Postsecondary Institutions, Fall 2004, Graduation Rates, 1998 & 2001 Cohorts; and Financial Statistics, Fiscal Year 2004* [for migration data] <http://nces.ed.gov/pubs2006/2006155.pdf> — U.S. Department of Education. National Center for Education Statistics. *Digest of Education Statistics, 2005.* <http://nces.ed.gov/pubs2006/2006030.pdf>.

The Integrated Postsecondary Education Data System (IPEDS) surveys approximately 10,000 postsecondary institutions, including universities, colleges, and institutions offering technical and vocational education beyond the high school level. This survey, which began in 1986, replaced the Higher Education General Information Survey (HEGIS). IPEDS is made up of eight integrated components that obtain information on who provides postsecondary education (institutions), who participates in it and completes it (students), what programs are offered and which ones are completed, and the specific human and financial resources involved in the provision of institutionally based postsecondary education. These components are organized into the following categories: Institutional Characteristics, including instructional activity; Fall Enrollment, including age and residence; Enrollment in Occupationally Specific Programs; Completions; Finance; Staff; Salaries of Full-Time Instructional Faculty; and Academic Libraries.

Institutions of higher education include those with courses leading to an associate's degree or higher, or those with courses accepted for credit toward such degrees. A public institution is controlled and operated by publicly elected or appointed officials and derives its primary support from public funds. A private institution is controlled by an individual or agency other than a state, a subdivision of a state, or the federal government; it is usually primarily supported by non-public funds, and the operation of its program does not rest with publicly elected or appointed officials. Private institutions comprise both not-for-profit and proprietary institutions.

Full-time students include undergraduate students enrolled for 12 or more semester credits, 12 or more quarter credits, or 24 or more contact hours a week each term; graduate students enrolled for 9 or more semester credits or 9 or more quarter credits, or students involved in thesis or dissertation preparation who are considered full time students by the institution; and first-professional students (as defined by the institution).

Types of institutions include the following:

- Degree-granting institutions, which offer associate's, bachelor's, master's, doctoral and/or first-professional degrees.

- Level categories include four-year and higher (four-year) institutions, at least two but less than four-year (two-year) institutions, and less than two-year institutions.

A four-year institution is a postsecondary institution that offers programs of at least four years' duration or programs at or above the baccalaureate level. This category includes schools that only offer post-baccalaureate certificates and those that only offer graduate programs. Also included are freestanding medical, law, and other first-professional schools.

A two-year institution is a postsecondary institution that offers programs of at least two years' duration but less than four years' duration. This category includes occupational and vocational schools with programs of at least 1,800 hours and academic institutions with programs of less than four years' duration. It does not include bachelor's degree–granting institutions where the baccalaureate program can be completed in three years.

Control categories are public, private not-for-profit, and private for-profit.

Race/ethnicity categories are categories used to describe groups to which individuals belong, identify with, or belong to in the eyes of the community. A person may be counted in only one group.

The groups used to categorize U.S. citizens, resident aliens, and other eligible non-citizens were as follows: non-Hispanic Black; American Indian and Alaska Native; Asian or Pacific Islander; Hispanic; and non-Hispanic White.

A nonresident alien is a person who is not a citizen or national of the United States, and who is in this country on a visa or temporary basis; a nonresident alien does not have the right to remain in the United States indefinitely.

Migration refers to the movement of students from their home state of residence to another state to attend a postsecondary institution.

An associate's degree is a degree granted for the successful completion of a sub-baccalaureate program of studies, and usually requires at least two years (or the equivalent) of full-time college-level study. This category also includes degrees granted in a cooperative or work-study program.

A bachelor's degree is a degree granted for the successful completion of a baccalaureate program of studies, and usually requires at least four years (or the equivalent) of full-time college-level study. This category includes degrees granted in a cooperative or work-study program.

A master's degree is awarded for successful completion of a program generally requiring 1 or 2 years of full-time, college-level study beyond the bachelor's degree. One type of master's degree, including the master of arts degree (M.A.), and the master of science degree (M. S.), is awarded in the liberal arts and sciences for advanced scholarship in a subject field or discipline and demonstrated ability to perform scholarly research. A second type of master's degree is awarded for the completion of a professionally oriented program. These include master's degrees in education (M. Ed.), business administration (M. B. A.), fine arts (M. F. A.), music (M. M.), social work (M. S. W.), and public administration (M. P. W.) A third type of master's degree is awarded in professional fields for study beyond the first-professional degree, such as the master of laws (LL. M.) and the masters of science in various medical specializations.

A first-professional degree requires the completion of a program that meets all of the following criteria: (1) completion of the academic requirements to begin practice in the profession, (2) at least 2 years of college work prior to entering the program, and (3) a total of at least 6 academic years of college work to complete the degree program, including prior required college work plus the length of the professional program itself. First-professional degrees are awarded in the following 10 fields: chiropractic (D.C. or D.C.M.), dentistry (D.D.S. or D.M.D.), law (L.L.B. or J.D.), medicine (M.D.), optometry (O.D.), osteopathic medicine (D.O.), pharmacy (Pharm.D.), podiatry (D.P.M., D.P., or Pod.D.), theology (M.Div., M.H.L., B.D., or Ordination), and veterinary medicine (D.V.M.).

A doctoral degree carries the title of doctor. The doctor of philosophy degree (Ph. D.) is the highest academic degree and requires mastery within a field of knowledge and a demonstrated ability to perform scholarly research. Other doctoral degrees are awarded for fulfilling specialized requirements in a professional field, such as education (Ed. D.), musical arts (D. M. A.), business administration (D. B. A.), and engineering (D. Eng. or D. E. S.). Many doctoral degrees in academic and professional fields require a master's degree as a prerequisite. First-professional degrees, such as M. D. and D. D. S. degrees, are not included under this heading.

SCHOOL ENROLLMENT AND TYPE OF SCHOOL, ITEMS 130–137
Source: U.S. Census Bureau. *2005 American Community Survey* (generated using American FactFinder). <http://factfinder.census.gov>.

School enrollment is enrollment in a regular school, either public or private, including nursery schools, kindergarten, and elementary schools, as well as schooling that leads to a high school diploma or college degree. Schools supported and controlled primarily by the federal, state, or local government are defined as public schools (including tribal schools). Schools primarily supported and controlled by religious organizations or other private groups are considered private schools.

DROPOUTS, ITEMS 138–139
Source: U.S. Census Bureau. *2005 American Community Survey*. <http://www.census.gov/acs/www/>.

The "not enrolled, not high school graduate" category includes people of compulsory school attendance age or older who were not enrolled in school and were not high school graduates. These people may be referred to as "high school dropouts." However, there is no criterion regarding when they dropped out of school, thus, some may have never attended high school. This column includes only persons age 16 to 19 years.

PART C—COUNTY EDUCATION STATISTICS

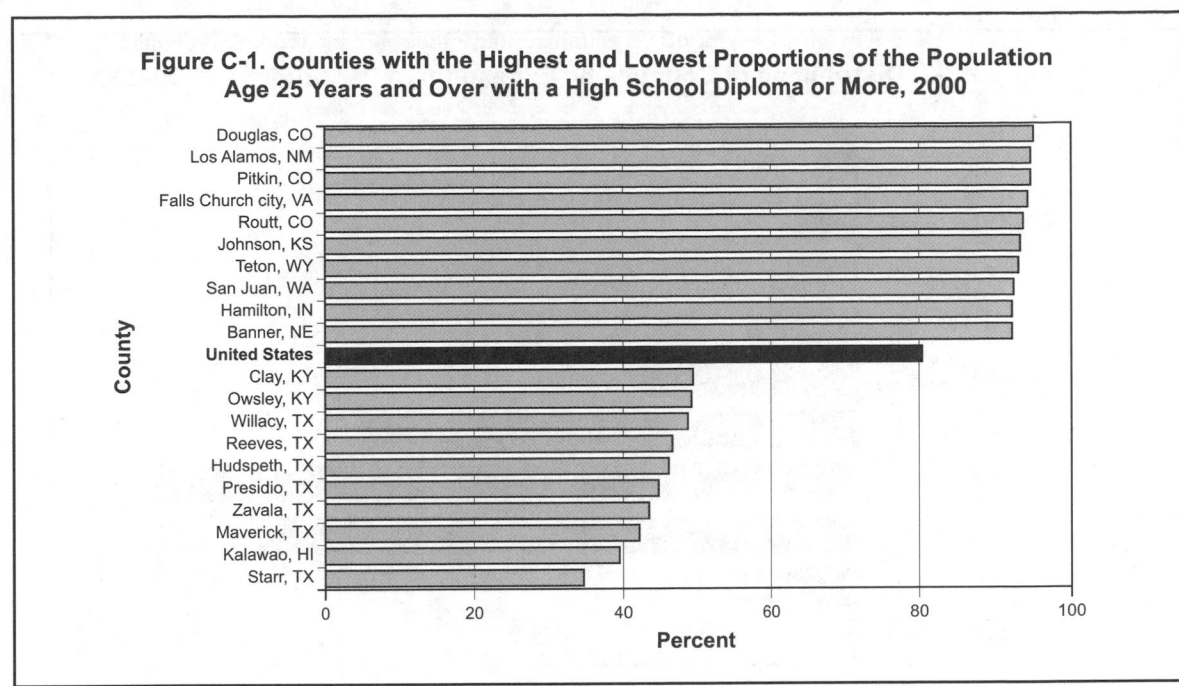

Figure C-1. Counties with the Highest and Lowest Proportions of the Population Age 25 Years and Over with a High School Diploma or More, 2000

In five counties—three of them which were in Colorado—more than 95 percent of the population age 25 years and over had graduated from high school. Just 11 counties had high school attainment levels of less than 50 percent; eight of these counties were in Texas. In 2000, 12 counties had college attainment levels that exceeded 50 percent. Half of these counties were located in the suburbs of Washington, DC. Just two counties, one in Alaska and one in Kentucky, had college attainment levels of less than 5 percent.

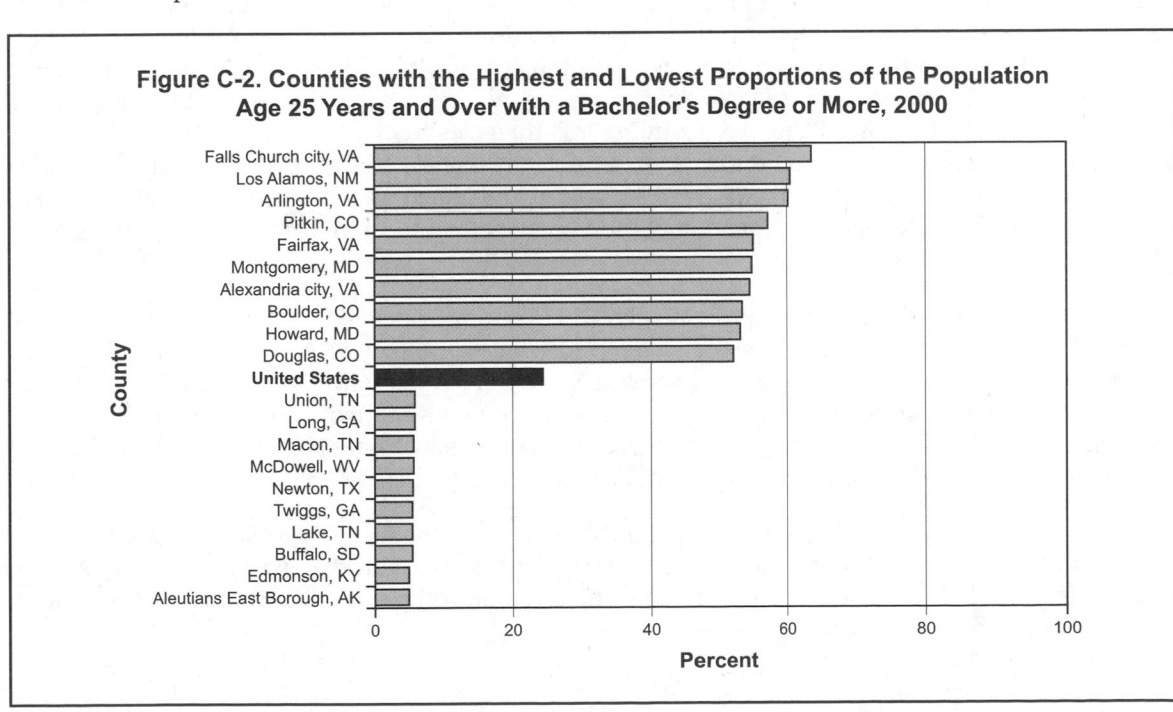

Figure C-2. Counties with the Highest and Lowest Proportions of the Population Age 25 Years and Over with a Bachelor's Degree or More, 2000

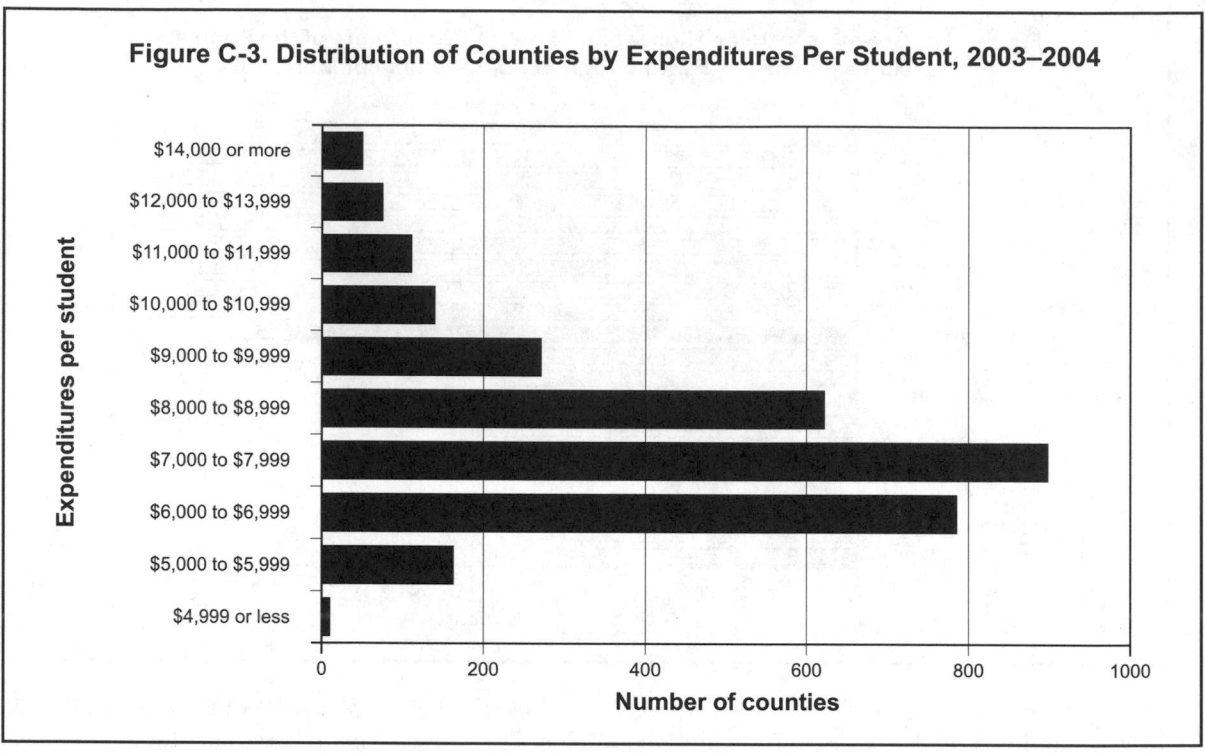

Figure C-3. Distribution of Counties by Expenditures Per Student, 2003–2004

Expenditures per student ranged from more than $30,000 in Michigans's remote Keweenaw County, to about $4,500 in Washington County and Tooele County, two of the fast-growing counties in Utah with high proportions of school-aged children. Utah was home to 8 of the 10 counties with per student expenditures of less than $5,000; it also had the highest proportion of school-aged population of all the states. At the other extreme, the 13 counties with expenditures above $20,000 per student all had small student populations. Keweenaw county, located at the northernmost point of Michigan's Upper Peninsula, had only 3 students. The median per student expenditure for the nation was $7,617 (with half of all counties spending more and half of all counties spending less than the median). Los Angeles County had the largest total enrollment (1,737,830 students), as well as the highest educational expenditure, with $14.1 billion spent in fiscal year 2004; this was followed closely by New York City with $13.7 billion spent for its 1,029,143 students. Keweenaw County had the lowest expenditures at $94,000, and all of its funding came from local sources.

In the United States, there were approximately 3,100 counties (including county equivalents), 18,041 Local Education Agencies (school districts), 97,935 public schools, and more than 48.7 million public school students. Some counties—even large counties, such as Miami-Dade County in Florida—had only one school district, while others had many. For example, Arizona's Maricopa County, had 258 school districts and Cook County in Illinois had 173. In recent years, many charter schools were established, and each one has been designated a separate school district.

Student-teacher ratios varied greatly from county to county, ranging from a handful of counties that exceeded 25 students per teacher to a low of 3.0 students per teacher in Keweenaw County, Michigan (the county with only 3 students). The median student-teacher ratio was 14.3. About 1,000 counties had student-teacher ratios between 14 and 16.

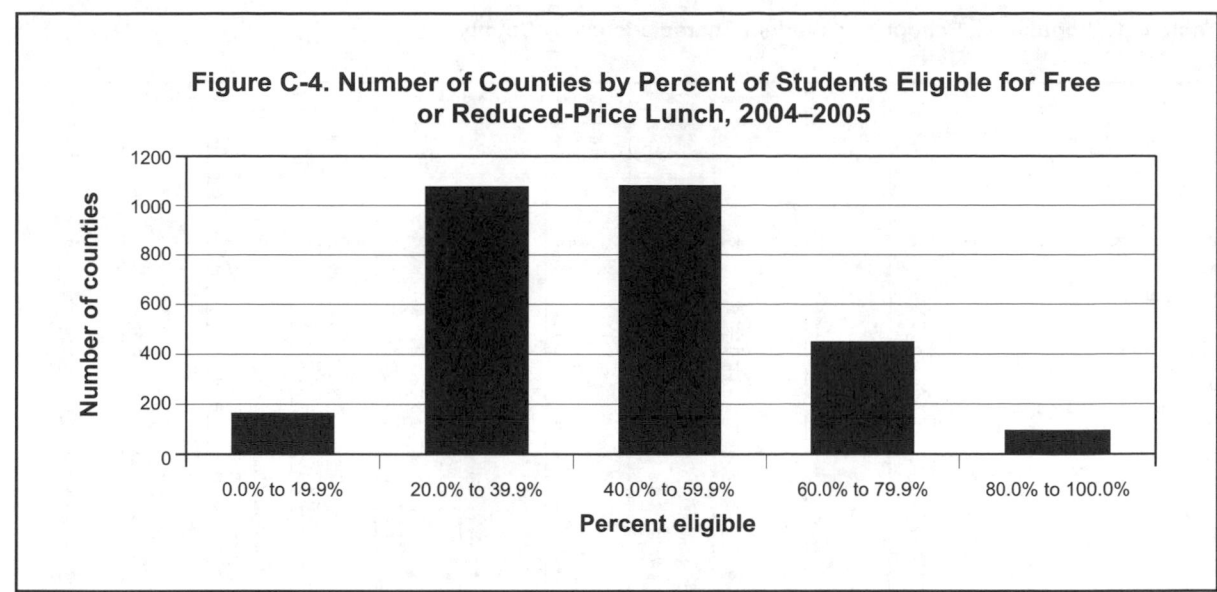

Figure C-4. Number of Counties by Percent of Students Eligible for Free or Reduced-Price Lunch, 2004–2005

There were more than 40 counties (most located in the South), in which 90 percent or more of students were eligible for free or reduced-price lunches during the 2004–2005 school year. Among the 14 counties with proportions exceeding 98 percent, 11 were in Mississippi. There were only 16 counties in which fewer than 10 percent of students were poor enough to qualify for these federal programs. There were nearly 1,000 counties, with a total of 13.7 million students, in which at least half of the students were classified in this lower-income category.

California and Texas were home to 40 of the 122 counties with proportions of English-Language Learners of 20 percent or more. Among counties with populations under 50,000, there were seven in which more than half of the students spoke another language at home—usually a Native American language.

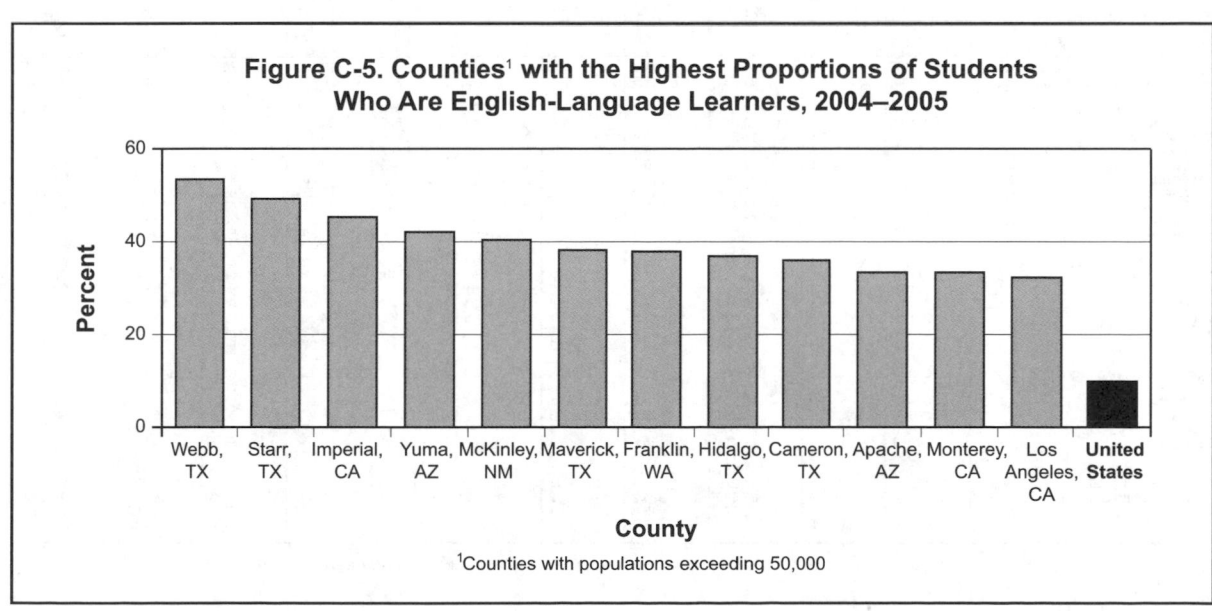

Figure C-5. Counties[1] with the Highest Proportions of Students Who Are English-Language Learners, 2004–2005

[1]Counties with populations exceeding 50,000

Table C-1. Population, School, and Student Characteristics by County

STATE County	State/ county code	County type[1]	Population, 2005		Number of schools and students, 2004–2005			Resident enrollment, 2000			
			Total	Percent 5 to 17 years	School districts	Schools	Students	Total	Percent public	K–12	Percent public
			1	2	3	4	5	6	7	8	9
UNITED STATES	00000		296 410 404	17.9	18 041	97 935	48 739 107	76 632 927	83.6	54 192 083	89.3
ALABAMA	01000		4 557 808	17.4	135	1 554	730 140	1 155 504	86.1	837 350	89.4
Autauga, AL	01001	2	48 612	19.3	1	14	9 200	11 887	83.4	9 502	86.9
Baldwin, AL	01003	4	162 586	16.6	1	47	24 443	32 637	83.9	25 805	89.1
Barbour, AL	01005	6	28 414	17.2	2	11	4 265	6 889	88.7	5 760	89.8
Bibb, AL	01007	1	21 516	17.7	1	10	3 559	4 908	87.3	4 142	89.7
Blount, AL	01009	1	55 725	17.5	2	18	9 118	11 833	90.5	9 431	95.3
Bullock, AL	01011	6	11 055	17.0	1	5	1 781	2 884	85.6	2 414	85.9
Butler, AL	01013	6	20 766	17.7	1	8	3 548	5 453	84.6	4 552	84.2
Calhoun, AL	01015	3	112 141	16.2	5	39	18 090	27 855	90.5	19 267	91.6
Chambers, AL	01017	6	35 460	17.6	2	14	5 317	8 386	85.8	6 548	86.7
Cherokee, AL	01019	8	24 522	15.8	1	8	4 225	4 661	93.6	3 836	97.1
Chilton, AL	01021	1	41 744	17.7	1	12	7 210	9 022	91.1	7 509	94.0
Choctaw, AL	01023	9	14 807	17.5	1	5	2 072	3 792	78.2	3 156	77.1
Clarke, AL	01025	7	27 269	19.2	2	12	5 196	6 977	85.5	5 962	88.0
Clay, AL	01027	9	13 964	16.1	1	4	2 064	3 083	92.1	2 567	92.5
Cleburne, AL	01029	8	14 460	16.9	1	7	2 503	3 139	92.4	2 432	95.1
Coffee, AL	01031	6	45 567	17.2	3	18	8 361	11 041	91.8	8 284	95.2
Colbert, AL	01033	3	54 660	16.6	4	27	8 481	12 414	91.7	9 836	92.8
Conecuh, AL	01035	9	13 257	17.8	1	6	1 847	3 355	87.0	2 810	87.7
Coosa, AL	01037	8	11 162	16.8	1	4	1 507	2 688	91.2	2 300	91.4
Covington, AL	01039	7	37 003	16.3	3	14	6 237	8 418	95.8	6 710	98.0
Crenshaw, AL	01041	8	13 727	16.7	1	4	2 485	3 118	90.0	2 599	91.3
Cullman, AL	01043	6	79 886	16.7	2	35	12 520	18 082	92.6	13 754	94.0
Dale, AL	01045	4	48 748	18.6	3	20	6 995	12 680	90.7	9 468	94.0
Dallas, AL	01047	4	44 366	19.4	2	27	8 690	13 032	84.9	10 258	87.3
DeKalb, AL	01049	6	67 271	17.2	2	18	11 044	14 045	94.4	11 435	96.4
Elmore, AL	01051	2	73 937	17.5	2	18	12 136	16 377	85.3	12 967	89.3
Escambia, AL	01053	6	38 082	16.6	2	17	5 890	8 744	91.0	6 955	93.7
Etowah, AL	01055	3	103 189	16.8	3	45	15 971	23 661	88.9	17 868	90.9
Fayette, AL	01057	9	18 228	16.5	1	6	2 602	4 234	94.6	3 301	97.6
Franklin, AL	01059	6	30 737	16.8	2	11	5 434	6 948	94.7	5 687	96.7
Geneva, AL	01061	3	25 735	16.2	2	12	3 961	5 693	93.5	4 715	96.2
Greene, AL	01063	3	9 661	19.7	1	5	1 612	2 616	90.6	2 181	92.4
Hale, AL	01065	3	18 316	19.1	1	10	3 166	4 564	91.3	3 799	91.4
Henry, AL	01067	3	16 610	16.2	1	7	2 713	3 715	90.5	3 026	93.2
Houston, AL	01069	3	94 249	17.7	2	31	14 870	22 033	84.3	17 275	86.2
Jackson, AL	01071	6	53 650	16.9	2	25	8 734	11 505	94.9	9 368	96.4
Jefferson, AL	01073	1	657 229	17.1	12	190	95 108	174 793	84.0	124 485	90.2
Lamar, AL	01075	9	14 962	15.9	1	5	2 403	3 521	95.3	2 890	97.1
Lauderdale, AL	01077	3	87 691	15.8	2	22	13 040	22 201	88.6	15 145	90.6
Lawrence, AL	01079	3	34 605	17.7	1	17	5 652	8 031	91.7	6 667	92.9
Lee, AL	01081	3	123 254	15.7	3	31	18 759	45 855	91.3	19 485	90.2
Limestone, AL	01083	2	70 469	17.2	2	20	10 938	16 015	89.3	12 113	92.6
Lowndes, AL	01085	2	13 076	19.7	1	9	2 311	3 714	88.0	3 192	88.4
Macon, AL	01087	6	22 810	17.3	1	8	3 276	8 743	65.6	4 702	90.0
Madison, AL	01089	2	298 192	17.8	3	86	47 065	78 591	82.6	51 678	87.1
Marengo, AL	01091	7	21 879	19.5	3	13	4 514	5 926	89.3	4 999	90.7
Marion, AL	01093	8	30 154	15.6	2	14	4 939	6 373	92.3	5 123	95.9
Marshall, AL	01095	4	85 634	17.2	5	33	15 253	18 171	93.7	14 556	96.6
Mobile, AL	01097	2	401 427	19.0	2	118	63 987	110 152	78.7	82 148	81.7
Monroe, AL	01099	7	23 733	19.5	1	12	4 297	6 146	86.7	5 059	87.7
Montgomery, AL	01101	2	221 619	18.0	2	69	32 066	65 349	79.2	43 518	81.4
Morgan, AL	01103	3	113 740	17.5	3	43	19 582	26 429	89.2	20 603	92.9
Perry, AL	01105	8	11 371	20.4	1	4	2 094	3 389	87.6	2 585	91.3
Pickens, AL	01107	8	20 178	18.5	1	10	3 242	5 436	89.9	4 382	90.8
Pike, AL	01109	6	29 639	16.3	2	11	4 521	9 104	86.6	5 330	83.5
Randolph, AL	01111	6	22 717	17.7	2	10	3 742	5 262	91.2	4 290	93.2
Russell, AL	01113	2	49 326	19.0	2	18	8 900	12 521	89.7	9 866	92.5
St. Clair, AL	01115	1	72 330	17.4	2	24	11 642	15 126	87.2	12 249	91.4
Shelby, AL	01117	1	171 465	17.9	2	50	34 901	37 311	78.8	26 646	83.3
Sumter, AL	01119	8	13 819	19.8	1	7	2 570	4 704	89.4	3 291	86.6
Talladega, AL	01121	4	80 457	17.2	4	36	13 224	19 125	89.8	15 320	92.7
Tallapoosa, AL	01123	6	40 717	16.9	2	11	6 848	9 775	94.2	7 677	97.0
Tuscaloosa, AL	01125	3	168 908	16.0	2	51	26 002	52 373	89.4	28 564	90.3
Walker, AL	01127	1	70 117	16.3	2	30	11 049	15 536	90.4	12 057	93.0
Washington, AL	01129	8	17 773	19.6	1	8	3 577	4 562	95.3	3 845	96.5
Wilcox, AL	01131	8	12 937	21.0	1	7	2 334	3 626	88.0	3 095	89.3
Winston, AL	01133	6	24 498	16.6	2	13	4 457	5 275	95.1	4 311	97.0
ALASKA	02000		663 661	20.7	55	520	132 937	185 760	89.9	142 653	93.2
Aleutians East, AK	02013	9	2 713	8.8	1	7	294	409	98.8	342	100.0
Aleutians West, AK	02016	7	5 382	10.2	3	7	572	925	88.4	698	96.7
Anchorage, AK	02020	2	275 043	20.5	1	97	49 545	74 625	87.4	55 296	92.0
Bethel, AK	02050	7	17 127	26.7	3	42	4 721	5 584	96.7	4 814	98.1
Bristol Bay, AK	02060	9	1 112	19.5	3	28	1 304	385	95.6	306	95.8
Denali, AK	02068	8	1 881	14.8	. . .	. . .	. . .	456	92.3	344	94.2
Dillingham, AK	02070	9	4 926	26.6	1	2	541	1 710	97.3	1 434	98.9
Fairbanks North Star, AK	02090	3	87 560	20.2	2	47	16 661	26 307	89.6	18 063	91.2
Haines, AK	02100	9	2 272	15.8	1	4	300	584	79.6	486	86.0
Juneau, AK	02110	5	30 987	18.7	2	13	5 351	8 777	90.9	6 210	93.1

[1]County type codes are from the Economic Research Service of the United States Department of Agriculture. See notes and definitions at the end of this section.
. . . = Not available.

Table C-1. Population, School, and Student Characteristics by County—*Continued*

STATE County	Characteristics of students, 2004–2005				Outcomes		Staff and students, 2004–2005		
	Percent with IEP[2]	Percent eligible for free or reduced-price lunch	Percent minority	Percent English-language learners	Number of graduates, 2003–2004	Percent dropouts, grades 9–12, 2001–2002	Number of teachers	Student-teacher ratio	Central administration staff
	10	11	12	13	14	15	16	17	18
UNITED STATES	13.7	40.3	42.3	9.9	...	...	2 862 014	17.0	...
ALABAMA	12.7	52.2	40.3	2.0	...	3.7	51 592	14.2	...
Autauga, AL	11.0	40.0	26.0	0.9	466	5.4	600	15.3	1
Baldwin, AL	16.0	35.8	19.2	1.7	1 326	3.1	1 743	14.0	137
Barbour, AL	13.2	69.9	67.8	0.9	215	6.1	290	14.7	19
Bibb, AL	14.7	61.5	28.8	0.4	148	2.4	226	15.7	18
Blount, AL	13.9	40.7	10.6	8.3	481	5.0	661	13.8	43
Bullock, AL	13.8	92.0	99.8	2.8	101	4.3	124	14.4	19
Butler, AL	15.9	74.6	60.4	0.2	225	5.8	247	14.4	31
Calhoun, AL	11.9	50.4	30.0	1.4	982	4.3	1 295	14.0	93
Chambers, AL	11.6	70.2	57.9	0.2	242	3.9	370	14.4	31
Cherokee, AL	12.9	40.0	7.9	0.0	240	5.0	345	12.3	20
Chilton, AL	15.9	50.7	19.7	4.5	401	2.4	538	13.4	33
Choctaw, AL	13.1	81.8	74.6	0.0	129	4.0	153	13.6	7
Clarke, AL	12.0	63.5	59.4	0.1	276	1.5	352	14.8	13
Clay, AL	15.4	57.5	26.6	2.7	119	1.3	157	13.1	2
Cleburne, AL	16.4	53.8	5.4	0.6	154	4.0	208	12.1	13
Coffee, AL	11.2	42.3	30.4	1.6	515	3.5	632	13.2	20
Colbert, AL	11.2	51.5	24.6	0.7	491	4.1	620	13.7	81
Conecuh, AL	17.5	85.0	80.2	0.0	87	6.4	137	13.5	21
Coosa, AL	14.3	66.4	51.3	0.1	87	4.3	107	14.2	10
Covington, AL	13.1	52.8	19.4	0.2	353	4.2	454	13.7	35
Crenshaw, AL	12.3	62.6	34.5	0.8	149	4.0	193	12.9	16
Cullman, AL	12.5	47.5	5.1	3.2	745	4.5	890	14.1	58
Dale, AL	11.5	53.0	35.7	0.2	488	5.3	476	14.7	48
Dallas, AL	11.2	84.3	86.3	0.0	482	4.9	926	15.5	31
DeKalb, AL	10.9	55.7	26.0	12.7	486	4.4	926	11.9	48
Elmore, AL	11.7	44.0	28.5	1.4	573	5.9	744	16.3	47
Escambia, AL	11.0	61.5	44.9	0.1	252	3.6	402	14.7	42
Etowah, AL	15.6	53.8	25.2	2.7	842	3.5	1 098	14.5	86
Fayette, AL	12.2	48.0	16.7	0.0	162	4.8	193	13.5	1
Franklin, AL	11.9	56.5	15.8	8.7	301	3.5	449	12.1	16
Geneva, AL	13.7	52.1	18.9	0.9	231	4.8	289	13.7	4
Greene, AL	11.0	92.9	99.9	0.0	68	11.0	110	14.7	21
Hale, AL	11.5	75.8	74.1	0.0	202	3.2	267	11.8	21
Henry, AL	11.6	66.5	46.9	0.4	152	6.1	181	15.0	13
Houston, AL	13.7	48.8	40.8	0.6	876	4.4	1 000	14.9	2
Jackson, AL	10.5	55.3	14.6	1.2	467	4.2	681	12.8	60
Jefferson, AL	13.0	50.2	56.2	1.7	...	2.6	6 589	14.4	...
Lamar, AL	10.7	49.2	19.5	0.0	163	2.5	207	11.6	18
Lauderdale, AL	11.0	43.0	16.3	1.4	831	1.7	919	14.2	31
Lawrence, AL	10.8	53.8	38.5	1.0	366	2.6	429	13.2	35
Lee, AL	9.3	44.5	38.5	1.2	969	1.3	1 301	14.4	112
Limestone, AL	11.0	36.4	19.9	4.7	543	4.3	849	12.9	45
Lowndes, AL	12.9	95.0	99.4	0.0	128	1.5	153	15.2	31
Macon, AL	12.2	80.6	97.2	0.1	181	0.5	232	14.1	30
Madison, AL	11.3	32.7	36.4	1.6	2 572	3.3	3 220	14.6	350
Marengo, AL	9.9	74.5	70.6	0.3	245	1.8	367	12.3	36
Marion, AL	11.0	45.3	7.0	0.7	284	3.5	383	12.9	30
Marshall, AL	11.2	48.0	12.3	7.6	713	4.1	1 061	14.4	119
Mobile, AL	14.6	67.6	54.6	1.6	3 178	4.0	4 228	15.1	23
Monroe, AL	11.2	65.2	56.8	0.1	281	3.1	322	13.3	24
Montgomery, AL	13.2	66.0	80.0	2.2	...	4.4	2 363	13.6	290
Morgan, AL	13.5	42.4	23.8	3.9	1 021	4.0	1 440	13.6	128
Perry, AL	14.5	97.6	99.1	0.0	109	3.3	151	13.9	4
Pickens, AL	10.8	70.3	65.7	0.1	190	4.5	259	12.5	25
Pike, AL	15.4	67.8	55.6	1.2	228	2.4	337	13.4	39
Randolph, AL	11.2	56.1	31.1	1.6	179	3.1	278	13.5	16
Russell, AL	11.7	68.9	56.3	0.0	493	5.6	593	15.0	66
St. Clair, AL	13.0	40.4	12.1	1.1	596	4.7	747	15.6	29
Shelby, AL	9.0	22.6	18.9	5.0	1 966	2.6	2 524	13.8	123
Sumter, AL	14.4	93.6	99.9	0.0	186	0.9	178	14.5	4
Talladega, AL	14.6	66.6	44.4	0.3	...	4.9	920	14.4	79
Tallapoosa, AL	14.0	52.7	40.1	0.5	336	7.1	525	13.0	44
Tuscaloosa, AL	14.7	48.7	45.5	0.7	1 234	4.1	1 712	15.2	151
Walker, AL	15.1	50.6	10.7	0.3	610	4.4	768	14.4	78
Washington, AL	9.8	57.1	40.9	0.1	238	1.0	277	12.9	2
Wilcox, AL	11.1	97.3	99.6	0.0	133	4.7	177	13.2	24
Winston, AL	13.1	56.8	2.2	1.2	288	3.1	373	12.0	25
ALASKA	13.5	...	41.7	16.2	...	8.1	7 756	17.1	...
Aleutians East, AK	17.7	...	87.8	0.0	19	...	34	8.6	...
Aleutians West, AK	11.7	...	67.3	20.8	28	...	51	11.3	...
Anchorage, AK	14.1	...	41.5	15.4	2 693	8.6	2 823	17.5	...
Bethel, AK	14.5	71.3	96.0	74.0	166	17.4	351	13.4	...
Bristol Bay, AK	16.6	...	66.8	52.3	57	7.3	63	20.6	...
Denali, AK	...	...	...	...	...	...	...	...	...
Dillingham, AK	18.3	64.5	95.5	0.7	21	1.4	40	13.5	...
Fairbanks North Star, AK	13.4	...	26.6	5.8	902	10.5	882	18.9	...
Haines, AK	13.3	37.1	26.4	1.0	21	11.0	21	14.3	...
Juneau, AK	13.6	14.4	38.8	17.3	...	8.9	310	17.2	...

[2]IEP = Individual Education Program. See notes and definitions at the end of this section.
. . . = Not available.

Table C-1. Population, School, and Student Characteristics by County—*Continued*

STATE County	Total revenue (thousands of dollars)	Percent of revenue from: Federal government	Percent of revenue from: State government	Percent of revenue from: Local government	Total expenditures (thousands of dollars)	Amount per student (dollars)	Percent for instruction	Total	Percent in armed forces	Percent high school graduates	Percent not enrolled, not employed, not in armed forces, not high school graduate
	19	20	21	22	23	24	25	26	27	28	29
UNITED STATES	473 000 583	8.8	45.8	45.4	402 127 507	8 350	66.0	15 930 458	0.6	10.5	5.5
ALABAMA	5 356 113	11.7	55.5	32.8	4 788 729	6 556	64.3	255 315	0.2	9.6	7.1
Autauga, AL	57 121	9.0	65.1	25.9	49 223	5 406	66.8	2 390	0.0	13.5	7.1
Baldwin, AL	178 731	8.0	46.8	45.2	162 575	6 764	66.2	7 374	0.0	10.2	6.1
Barbour, AL	30 748	16.8	59.6	23.6	28 855	6 666	64.3	1 664	0.0	10.7	11.4
Bibb, AL	24 608	16.3	68.1	15.6	22 766	6 451	65.6	1 144	0.0	15.1	8.0
Blount, AL	55 566	9.7	68.1	22.1	50 432	5 578	64.7	2 764	0.2	10.6	9.2
Bullock, AL	12 988	20.6	63.6	15.8	13 113	7 205	63.7	654	0.0	8.4	12.5
Butler, AL	24 869	22.7	60.9	16.5	22 714	6 386	66.2	1 406	0.0	6.0	9.5
Calhoun, AL	119 228	12.7	63.8	23.5	113 358	6 251	63.2	6 252	0.2	8.9	7.2
Chambers, AL	36 600	14.6	60.9	24.4	33 318	6 159	62.5	2 082	0.0	11.8	7.1
Cherokee, AL	28 599	10.2	63.8	26.0	26 246	6 243	64.3	1 136	0.0	12.5	10.7
Chilton, AL	44 068	11.7	66.8	21.5	41 269	5 811	64.7	2 150	0.0	16.6	7.3
Choctaw, AL	18 049	20.0	54.6	25.5	14 739	6 865	60.1	951	0.0	6.8	6.6
Clarke, AL	35 151	15.3	63.3	21.4	33 438	6 437	64.2	1 624	0.0	10.8	8.9
Clay, AL	15 345	11.5	69.0	19.4	13 895	6 848	65.2	655	0.5	9.9	4.9
Cleburne, AL	16 524	11.5	71.2	17.4	15 586	5 969	64.1	768	0.0	9.0	8.6
Coffee, AL	56 910	11.6	61.9	26.6	52 385	6 358	63.7	2 525	0.2	11.7	8.8
Colbert, AL	64 902	9.7	54.7	35.6	59 860	7 037	60.9	2 876	0.0	9.8	6.2
Conecuh, AL	14 721	25.1	58.0	16.9	13 218	7 133	63.8	751	0.0	8.0	8.3
Coosa, AL	12 062	16.4	65.1	18.5	10 735	6 635	59.8	668	0.0	15.7	6.3
Covington, AL	42 047	12.7	61.7	25.6	38 265	6 052	64.9	1 972	0.7	11.8	8.5
Crenshaw, AL	15 751	15.4	66.1	18.4	14 665	5 988	65.3	728	0.0	6.3	6.5
Cullman, AL	83 391	11.4	61.3	27.3	78 042	6 286	62.7	4 283	0.0	11.9	7.9
Dale, AL	47 432	13.8	63.5	22.7	44 161	6 225	62.4	2 775	6.0	16.6	5.7
Dallas, AL	58 808	20.4	62.7	16.8	55 068	6 280	64.1	3 125	0.0	6.6	10.1
DeKalb, AL	72 924	12.3	62.8	24.9	67 680	6 238	63.9	3 343	0.0	10.7	9.1
Elmore, AL	75 877	10.3	68.0	21.7	68 270	5 638	66.9	3 608	0.2	13.1	8.4
Escambia, AL	41 925	14.3	62.1	23.5	39 997	6 693	62.9	2 147	0.0	12.0	12.2
Etowah, AL	110 423	13.1	61.9	25.0	100 237	6 340	65.5	5 786	0.0	10.1	10.5
Fayette, AL	17 532	10.5	68.1	21.3	16 330	6 148	63.8	992	0.0	7.0	11.8
Franklin, AL	39 847	14.2	60.0	25.8	35 136	6 526	64.2	1 675	0.0	13.6	7.9
Geneva, AL	25 795	12.8	66.0	21.2	23 777	5 946	65.1	1 295	0.5	7.3	6.2
Greene, AL	14 362	23.8	54.3	21.9	12 618	7 717	63.1	694	0.0	9.1	16.9
Hale, AL	22 966	18.5	65.5	16.1	21 152	6 404	65.2	1 193	0.0	11.1	9.5
Henry, AL	19 190	12.6	66.8	20.6	17 520	6 569	62.6	893	0.0	8.4	8.0
Houston, AL	99 718	13.5	58.7	27.8	93 935	6 263	64.2	4 832	0.0	8.9	5.5
Jackson, AL	66 608	10.4	58.2	31.4	59 966	6 816	59.9	2 794	0.0	14.2	6.4
Jefferson, AL	858 704	9.5	48.0	42.5	739 198	6 912	64.6	36 688	0.0	10.2	6.4
Lamar, AL	19 169	11.4	70.6	18.1	16 018	6 480	62.0	917	0.0	13.8	6.3
Lauderdale, AL	95 624	10.0	56.6	33.4	90 318	6 944	65.0	4 930	0.0	7.1	5.7
Lawrence, AL	43 104	13.6	60.9	25.5	37 907	6 604	63.1	1 982	0.0	11.5	10.6
Lee, AL	142 938	9.3	51.6	39.1	123 282	6 751	66.6	10 016	0.0	5.0	2.9
Limestone, AL	79 656	7.9	55.2	36.9	73 003	6 797	65.8	3 229	0.3	12.0	7.9
Lowndes, AL	22 022	29.6	51.7	18.7	20 416	8 454	62.1	905	0.1	11.0	11.3
Macon, AL	27 403	19.6	62.5	17.9	24 468	6 471	62.3	2 192	0.5	5.7	5.1
Madison, AL	367 039	7.9	48.2	43.9	312 868	6 734	65.2	15 636	1.3	8.5	5.7
Marengo, AL	31 145	16.9	62.6	20.5	29 681	6 533	64.8	1 322	0.1	10.5	7.7
Marion, AL	33 963	11.6	65.7	22.7	30 630	6 162	65.2	1 508	0.0	10.4	7.4
Marshall, AL	115 741	9.4	55.0	35.5	98 740	6 463	62.6	4 270	0.1	7.8	9.3
Mobile, AL	459 717	14.9	56.2	28.9	416 592	6 431	63.0	23 622	0.1	9.1	7.2
Monroe, AL	29 571	16.0	63.2	20.8	27 311	6 164	66.3	1 505	0.0	8.8	10.6
Montgomery, AL	237 882	14.3	54.4	31.3	215 821	6 630	65.3	12 924	0.2	8.7	8.3
Morgan, AL	152 279	8.5	49.0	42.5	138 226	7 068	64.7	5 898	0.2	10.0	8.4
Perry, AL	16 476	27.1	59.3	13.6	15 187	7 005	64.7	852	0.0	10.8	9.6
Pickens, AL	23 099	15.9	66.3	17.8	21 837	6 583	62.6	1 254	0.0	7.4	7.1
Pike, AL	33 946	15.8	55.7	28.5	30 796	6 893	63.0	2 161	0.0	5.5	6.2
Randolph, AL	28 092	10.6	57.4	32.0	22 975	6 188	63.8	1 188	0.0	8.7	8.4
Russell, AL	63 087	14.5	59.2	26.3	57 676	6 435	62.6	2 663	0.6	9.4	6.8
St. Clair, AL	71 823	10.9	62.3	26.8	64 704	5 714	65.8	3 147	0.0	10.8	7.3
Shelby, AL	181 350	6.0	46.9	47.1	157 581	6 991	64.6	7 202	0.0	7.7	4.0
Sumter, AL	20 938	23.3	56.1	20.5	18 447	7 009	63.1	949	0.0	6.1	6.7
Talladega, AL	93 522	12.8	58.7	28.5	84 577	6 556	62.9	4 591	0.2	12.5	7.6
Tallapoosa, AL	47 623	11.4	58.9	29.6	44 371	6 395	65.8	2 056	0.0	10.9	7.3
Tuscaloosa, AL	199 818	10.5	52.2	37.3	167 641	6 370	64.3	12 685	0.0	7.2	4.4
Walker, AL	84 455	12.1	57.8	30.1	75 292	6 860	63.1	3 756	0.0	9.6	7.9
Washington, AL	23 557	14.2	57.9	27.9	22 263	6 227	65.7	1 212	0.0	17.2	6.3
Wilcox, AL	18 380	22.9	58.0	19.1	17 872	7 204	60.9	941	0.0	5.4	13.9
Winston, AL	32 604	11.0	61.8	27.2	28 487	6 360	63.3	1 145	0.0	11.7	7.7
ALASKA	1 477 152	19.4	54.8	25.8	1 346 690	10 114	62.4	38 321	2.3	15.1	5.2
Aleutians East, AK	6 317	26.5	53.0	20.5	6 861	22 349	66.7	116	0.0	24.1	3.4
Aleutians West, AK	12 624	15.3	57.1	27.7	9 078	15 898	58.8	156	0.0	13.5	1.3
Anchorage, AK	430 337	13.6	54.2	32.1	411 794	8 282	65.1	15 210	3.1	16.6	4.7
Bethel, AK	104 303	33.8	63.6	2.6	81 299	17 375	61.3	1 175	0.0	14.6	8.6
Bristol Bay, AK	26 173	31.3	59.9	8.8	18 019	20 360	58.4	75	0.0	18.7	9.3
Denali, AK	. . .	. . .	. . .	. . .	. . .	. . .	. . .	104	6.7	18.3	5.8
Dillingham, AK	7 757	23.2	57.4	19.5	6 496	12 516	59.3	310	0.0	16.1	8.7
Fairbanks North Star, AK	156 547	20.4	53.8	25.9	151 733	9 488	63.1	5 230	5.6	16.1	4.7
Haines, AK	4 072	10.2	44.9	44.9	3 637	11 088	61.8	125	0.0	10.4	4.0
Juneau, AK	50 825	8.2	48.4	43.4	48 738	8 902	65.2	1 692	0.4	13.2	1.2

. . . = Not available.

Table C-1. Population, School, and Student Characteristics by County—*Continued*

STATE County	High school graduates, 2000			College enrollment, 2000		College graduates, 2000 (percent)						
	Population 25 years and over	High school graduate or less (percent)	High school graduate or more (percent)	Number	Percent public	Bachelor's degree or more	+/- U.S. percentage with bachelor's degree or more	Non-Hispanic White	Black	American Indian and Alaska Native	Asian or Pacific Islander	Hispanic[3]
	30	31	32	33	34	35	36	37	38	39	40	41
UNITED STATES	182 211 639	48.2	80.4	17 483 262	74.6	24.4	X	27.0	14.3	11.5	43.1	10.4
ALABAMA	2 887 400	55.1	75.3	243 275	85.3	19.0	-5.4	21.2	11.5	13.0	47.2	14.6
Autauga, AL	27 589	55.1	78.7	1 695	82.4	18.0	-6.4	20.0	7.6	12.3	16.7	15.1
Baldwin, AL	96 010	47.6	82.0	4 708	78.8	23.1	-1.3	24.8	7.5	14.2	29.2	17.9
Barbour, AL	18 896	67.8	64.7	743	92.2	10.9	-13.5	16.5	3.8	0.0	0.0	9.7
Bibb, AL	13 540	72.5	63.2	500	87.4	7.1	-17.3	8.5	1.2	11.5	0.0	16.2
Blount, AL	33 702	65.6	70.4	1 600	89.0	9.6	-14.8	9.8	2.5	2.6	62.7	4.4
Bullock, AL	7 570	74.8	60.5	282	82.6	7.7	-16.7	15.8	4.4	0.0	0.0	8.3
Butler, AL	13 767	66.7	67.8	673	94.4	10.4	-14.0	13.3	4.8	0.0	91.3	0.0
Calhoun, AL	74 015	58.3	73.9	7 129	94.0	15.2	-9.2	16.4	8.9	13.2	31.7	9.5
Chambers, AL	24 497	67.9	64.2	1 122	91.0	9.5	-14.9	12.2	4.3	0.0	40.0	15.9
Cherokee, AL	16 825	71.3	63.5	571	83.0	9.7	-14.7	9.8	7.2	14.0	46.9	5.0
Chilton, AL	25 902	69.6	66.2	935	88.7	9.9	-14.5	10.6	5.4	0.0	17.2	4.3
Choctaw, AL	10 569	69.8	65.0	424	95.3	9.6	-14.8	13.1	4.4	0.0	40.0	13.4
Clarke, AL	17 702	66.8	70.8	559	84.8	12.1	-12.3	16.4	5.2	22.2	34.5	0.0
Clay, AL	9 767	71.8	66.0	357	92.4	7.8	-16.6	8.8	2.7	0.0	0.0	0.7
Cleburne, AL	9 533	72.9	62.9	501	87.8	9.2	-15.2	9.5	4.2	6.7	. . .	13.3
Coffee, AL	28 885	53.1	73.2	1 991	91.4	19.3	-5.1	21.5	8.5	13.8	21.7	26.5
Colbert, AL	37 384	60.6	73.3	1 904	97.5	14.1	-10.3	15.2	7.6	8.4	37.0	16.5
Conecuh, AL	9 230	70.4	67.7	385	95.8	9.2	-15.2	10.4	7.6	0.0	0.0	15.0
Coosa, AL	8 255	72.6	65.7	247	88.3	8.0	-16.4	10.4	3.1	0.0	. . .	0.0
Covington, AL	25 705	64.5	68.4	1 166	93.6	12.2	-12.2	12.9	5.8	8.6	20.8	14.4
Crenshaw, AL	9 268	68.9	60.1	425	87.3	11.2	-13.2	13.0	5.4	40.0	. . .	3.8
Cullman, AL	51 787	61.6	70.4	3 327	94.3	11.9	-12.5	12.1	8.6	4.3	16.2	4.2
Dale, AL	31 390	51.4	77.8	2 353	89.9	14.0	-10.4	15.1	7.9	12.1	18.8	15.8
Dallas, AL	28 742	63.2	70.3	1 870	77.9	13.9	-10.5	20.4	9.0	7.9	40.7	14.9
DeKalb, AL	42 740	70.2	63.8	1 696	91.2	8.3	-16.1	8.4	2.5	11.3	27.1	1.9
Elmore, AL	43 177	56.2	77.6	2 245	83.1	16.6	-7.8	18.9	6.5	12.6	34.2	12.7
Escambia, AL	25 510	66.2	68.5	1 296	87.9	10.6	-13.8	12.7	6.1	2.6	8.1	9.8
Etowah, AL	69 829	58.2	74.1	4 130	91.9	13.4	-11.0	14.3	7.4	8.0	33.8	7.8
Fayette, AL	12 579	68.9	66.1	663	93.2	9.2	-15.2	9.2	8.7	0.0	46.9	0.0
Franklin, AL	20 860	68.4	62.1	945	90.2	9.7	-14.7	9.9	9.3	24.7	0.0	6.2
Geneva, AL	17 588	66.4	65.6	625	89.6	8.7	-15.7	9.4	1.4	9.0	76.7	1.4
Greene, AL	6 204	70.1	64.8	225	83.6	10.5	-13.9	15.8	8.6	. . .	100.0	30.0
Hale, AL	10 591	70.7	65.2	467	94.0	8.1	-16.3	11.1	5.2	47.4	100.0	9.2
Henry, AL	10 967	62.4	66.7	488	93.6	14.1	-10.3	17.6	5.8	66.7	. . .	3.8
Houston, AL	58 671	53.8	76.5	3 113	90.0	18.4	-6.0	21.1	8.3	9.6	34.8	13.1
Jackson, AL	36 435	67.8	67.0	1 435	94.1	10.4	-14.0	10.7	5.2	9.7	19.0	5.7
Jefferson, AL	434 158	47.0	80.9	38 365	76.4	24.6	0.2	30.0	14.3	23.0	63.9	18.8
Lamar, AL	10 758	72.5	65.1	443	95.7	7.8	-16.6	8.1	5.3	0.0	31.8	7.1
Lauderdale, AL	58 894	57.8	76.4	5 618	93.6	18.5	-5.9	19.3	9.5	17.3	50.8	16.0
Lawrence, AL	22 894	73.8	65.6	997	94.1	7.5	-16.9	7.4	5.2	10.4	30.2	18.2
Lee, AL	62 170	45.3	81.4	24 433	95.0	27.9	3.5	31.9	12.2	25.9	64.7	23.8
Limestone, AL	43 456	58.0	74.5	2 898	90.6	16.9	-7.5	18.2	8.8	14.7	41.0	3.3
Lowndes, AL	8 183	69.1	64.3	348	86.8	11.0	-13.4	21.4	6.1	0.0	. . .	20.0
Macon, AL	13 055	55.0	70.0	3 440	20.5	18.8	-5.6	15.2	18.7	10.7	90.1	4.0
Madison, AL	180 389	36.5	85.4	21 212	84.2	34.3	9.9	36.8	23.9	21.4	52.9	26.5
Marengo, AL	14 326	65.4	71.9	707	90.1	12.1	-12.3	18.4	4.9	0.0	0.0	17.2
Marion, AL	21 611	69.7	63.2	932	86.1	8.0	-16.4	8.2	3.5	0.0	0.0	6.4
Marshall, AL	54 961	61.1	69.4	2 441	92.7	13.9	-10.5	14.4	5.4	12.2	32.8	2.9
Mobile, AL	250 122	55.2	76.7	20 709	76.9	18.6	-5.8	21.9	10.7	7.8	33.9	21.5
Monroe, AL	15 378	66.5	67.9	768	88.4	11.8	-12.6	15.6	5.0	11.1	25.0	11.6
Montgomery, AL	141 342	44.1	80.3	16 879	82.4	28.5	4.1	36.5	18.2	11.3	32.7	25.2
Morgan, AL	73 331	54.0	76.3	3 925	91.4	18.4	-6.0	19.6	7.4	23.7	54.3	10.9
Perry, AL	6 978	68.0	62.4	551	72.2	10.0	-14.4	16.4	6.4	0.0	0.0	3.4
Pickens, AL	13 536	68.1	69.7	641	90.0	9.8	-14.6	12.3	5.7	0.0	35.3	0.0
Pike, AL	17 703	60.9	69.1	3 315	95.7	18.4	-6.0	24.7	6.6	8.3	35.0	4.6
Randolph, AL	14 762	70.1	61.9	745	93.8	10.0	-14.4	10.8	6.2	0.0	48.1	6.7
Russell, AL	32 107	66.5	66.5	1 766	92.9	9.7	-14.7	11.1	6.4	22.8	36.5	11.2
St. Clair, AL	43 101	63.3	71.3	1 905	81.3	11.1	-13.3	11.5	6.0	6.1	34.9	12.9
Shelby, AL	94 185	36.2	86.8	7 321	85.8	36.8	12.4	37.8	24.9	19.7	72.3	22.0
Sumter, AL	8 731	66.4	64.8	1 075	96.0	12.4	-12.0	27.4	6.1	0.0	0.0	12.8
Talladega, AL	53 060	64.8	69.7	2 625	84.4	11.2	-13.2	13.0	6.4	21.8	34.1	12.9
Tallapoosa, AL	28 373	62.9	70.1	1 221	87.8	14.1	-10.3	16.4	6.3	16.7	38.6	34.3
Tuscaloosa, AL	99 039	49.6	78.8	21 141	91.4	24.0	-0.4	27.9	12.1	15.7	65.6	22.7
Walker, AL	47 919	67.5	67.2	2 581	87.8	9.1	-15.3	9.0	8.4	7.8	37.3	5.0
Washington, AL	11 240	71.3	72.3	441	88.0	8.6	-15.8	9.8	6.6	4.5	0.0	0.0
Wilcox, AL	7 979	70.7	59.5	328	88.4	10.1	-14.3	18.0	6.1	0.0	0.0	0.0
Winston, AL	17 078	71.7	62.6	709	90.8	8.3	-16.1	7.9	0.0	34.7	82.6	13.3
ALASKA	379 556	39.5	88.3	32 303	85.3	24.7	0.3	29.5	14.9	6.0	20.4	15.3
Aleutians East, AK	2 007	74.2	74.7	28	82.1	4.9	-19.5	17.5	0.0	1.4	1.3	0.0
Aleutians West, AK	4 251	55.9	78.5	161	51.6	11.0	-13.4	22.9	0.8	3.2	3.4	6.8
Anchorage, AK	159 931	33.9	90.3	15 169	81.9	28.9	4.5	33.0	15.5	10.6	23.1	16.3
Bethel, AK	8 026	67.6	71.0	375	85.9	13.1	-11.3	46.5	7.4	4.5	24.7	30.9
Bristol Bay, AK	782	45.1	88.9	54	92.6	21.1	-3.3	28.9	0.0	8.9	22.2	40.0
Denali, AK	1 316	38.7	91.7	88	89.8	22.7	-1.7	24.2	11.8	6.7	23.5	23.5
Dillingham, AK	2 655	57.3	76.6	176	87.5	16.4	-8.0	39.6	33.3	4.6	45.0	20.4
Fairbanks North Star, AK	47 974	33.7	91.8	6 952	91.7	27.0	2.6	30.0	12.5	9.8	24.6	15.5
Haines, AK	1 660	42.2	88.9	60	60.0	23.8	-0.6	26.3	0.0	8.5	20.0	31.3
Juneau, AK	19 899	28.8	93.2	1 890	93.0	36.0	11.6	41.5	23.0	7.9	32.1	19.9

[3]May be of any race.
X = Not applicable.
. . . = Not available.

Table C-1. Population, School, and Student Characteristics by County—Continued

STATE County	State/ county code	County type[1]	Population, 2005		Number of schools and students, 2004–2005			Resident enrollment, 2000			
			Total	Percent 5 to 17 years	School districts	Schools	Students	Total	Percent public	K–12	Percent public
			1	2	3	4	5	6	7	8	9
Kenai Peninsula, AK	02122	7	51 960	19.8	1	45	9 715	14 004	90.4	11 739	92.8
Ketchikan Gateway, AK	02130	7	13 262	19.6	1	10	2 325	3 744	88.8	3 051	92.3
Kodiak Island, AK	02150	7	13 051	22.9	1	15	2 701	3 975	86.4	3 150	90.3
Lake and Peninsula, AK	02164	9	1 570	25.7	...	...	645	645	92.7	555	94.8
Matanuska-Susitna, AK	02170	2	76 006	21.2	1	38	14 768	18 008	91.5	14 884	93.6
Nome, AK	02180	7	9 328	24.9	2	20	2 474	3 129	97.5	2 659	99.2
North Slope, AK	02185	7	6 924	25.0	1	10	1 938	2 623	97.6	2 148	99.0
Northwest Arctic, AK	02188	7	7 621	27.5	1	13	2 143	2 505	98.0	2 202	99.2
Prince of Wales-Outer Ketchikan, AK ..	02201	9	5 660	20.3	5	20	1 497	1 694	95.6	1 473	96.6
Sitka, AK	02220	7	8 986	18.3	1	1	369	2 617	86.1	1 864	95.5
Skagway-Hoonah-Angoon, AK	02232	9	3 126	17.0	4	9	498	908	89.4	732	91.4
Southeast Fairbanks, AK	02240	8	6 614	21.6	2	16	1 703	1 970	85.3	1 574	85.9
Valdez-Cordova, AK	02261	9	9 899	19.8	4	18	2 183	2 929	91.9	2 337	95.9
Wade Hampton, AK	02270	9	7 541	29.7	3	13	2 573	2 968	99.1	2 583	99.5
Wrangell-Petersburg, AK	02280	7	6 245	20.0	4	13	2 669	1 783	93.7	1 542	96.2
Yakutat , AK	02282	9	722	16.2	1	2	134	218	100.0	173	100.0
Yukon-Koyukuk, AK	02290	8	6 143	22.8	6	30	5 958	2 278	97.2	1 994	97.6
ARIZONA	04000		5 939 292	18.9	609	2 047	1 043 298	1 401 840	89.4	988 818	93.6
Apache, AZ	04001	6	69 343	25.7	14	41	13 677	25 885	95.4	21 435	97.0
Cochise, AZ	04003	4	126 106	18.4	29	75	22 703	32 791	91.2	23 733	94.3
Coconino, AZ	04005	3	123 866	19.2	24	66	22 514	42 187	93.3	25 217	93.8
Gila, AZ	04007	4	51 663	17.5	14	31	8 540	12 718	92.8	10 261	94.1
Graham, AZ	04009	6	33 073	21.2	12	30	7 285	10 949	93.8	7 879	94.6
Greenlee, AZ	04011	7	7 621	22.8	7	9	1 624	2 476	95.0	2 070	97.1
La Paz, AZ	04012	6	20 238	14.3	7	13	2 828	3 969	95.3	3 303	96.0
Maricopa, AZ	04013	1	3 635 528	19.2	258	1 023	652 081	833 554	88.2	584 324	93.4
Mohave, AZ	04015	4	187 200	16.6	24	82	27 342	32 934	91.7	25 729	94.2
Navajo, AZ	04017	4	108 432	24.1	24	87	28 687	32 682	95.1	26 882	96.5
Pima, AZ	04019	2	924 786	17.5	86	335	147 626	236 404	89.2	153 693	91.7
Pinal, AZ	04021	1	229 549	18.1	30	85	35 680	42 725	92.5	33 416	95.3
Santa Cruz, AZ	04023	4	42 009	22.7	11	25	10 447	12 026	94.1	10 092	97.2
Yavapai, AZ	04025	3	198 701	15.1	54	91	26 643	37 187	86.8	26 770	93.2
Yuma, AZ	04027	3	181 277	20.4	15	54	35 621	43 353	95.3	34 014	96.9
ARKANSAS	05000		2 779 154	17.6	355	1 158	463 115	675 109	89.3	503 693	92.6
Arkansas, AR	05001	6	20 073	17.3	5	12	3 538	5 072	88.9	3 938	93.0
Ashley, AR	05003	7	23 178	18.6	3	14	4 318	6 158	94.8	5 065	97.2
Baxter, AR	05005	7	40 330	13.7	3	10	5 047	7 019	92.6	5 533	96.7
Benton, AR	05007	2	186 938	18.8	8	50	30 554	36 954	86.6	29 280	92.0
Boone, AR	05009	7	35 793	16.6	8	20	6 145	7 417	91.1	6 016	93.0
Bradley, AR	05011	6	12 192	16.2	2	7	2 138	2 852	96.5	2 383	97.7
Calhoun, AR	05013	9	5 589	16.8	1	2	765	1 351	95.4	1 159	96.9
Carroll, AR	05015	6	26 999	16.6	3	9	3 716	5 062	91.2	4 297	92.2
Chicot, AR	05017	7	13 027	18.5	3	9	2 288	3 640	90.6	2 961	89.7
Clark, AR	05019	7	22 916	14.8	4	11	4 118	7 933	78.7	3 821	96.0
Clay, AR	05021	7	16 578	16.5	3	9	2 944	3 670	95.6	2 960	98.3
Cleburne, AR	05023	6	25 391	15.0	5	11	3 463	4 705	91.1	3 905	94.6
Cleveland, AR	05025	3	8 903	17.7	4	6	1 469	2 085	95.9	1 697	98.2
Columbia, AR	05027	7	24 695	16.7	7	11	4 019	7 482	95.4	4 889	97.0
Conway, AR	05029	6	20 739	17.6	4	10	3 300	4 962	91.2	3 877	93.4
Craighead, AR	05031	3	86 735	16.9	8	37	14 610	22 728	91.6	14 353	93.9
Crawford, AR	05033	2	57 630	19.3	5	25	11 003	13 483	92.9	10 961	96.2
Crittenden, AR	05035	1	51 862	21.4	6	24	11 174	14 577	92.1	11 592	95.2
Cross, AR	05037	6	19 237	19.1	3	10	3 962	5 275	94.9	4 316	97.7
Dallas, AR	05039	6	8 524	18.3	3	3	1 168	2 357	97.4	2 015	99.5
Desha, AR	05041	6	14 358	19.0	4	11	3 306	4 212	96.1	3 406	97.9
Drew, AR	05043	7	18 693	17.7	4	8	3 352	5 425	96.9	3 633	98.6
Faulkner, AR	05045	2	97 147	17.1	7	33	15 554	26 908	84.8	16 292	91.0
Franklin, AR	05047	2	18 218	17.5	6	9	3 345	4 051	94.6	3 379	96.5
Fulton, AR	05049	9	11 934	15.4	3	6	1 571	2 435	94.5	2 031	96.1
Garland, AR	05051	3	93 551	15.2	8	27	13 359	18 185	89.9	14 253	93.5
Grant, AR	05053	2	17 348	17.9	2	8	4 787	3 925	95.0	3 194	97.4
Greene, AR	05055	6	39 401	17.6	4	15	7 024	8 654	91.2	6 798	94.5
Hempstead, AR	05057	6	23 383	18.9	5	11	4 103	5 894	94.1	4 618	96.3
Hot Spring, AR	05059	6	31 264	17.4	6	17	5 512	7 183	93.2	5 578	96.6
Howard, AR	05061	7	14 552	18.3	4	10	3 090	3 353	93.0	2 847	95.5
Independence, AR	05063	7	34 737	16.6	8	20	5 863	8 165	87.9	6 268	95.4
Izard, AR	05065	9	13 430	14.7	5	8	1 880	2 658	93.1	2 093	94.8
Jackson, AR	05067	6	17 601	15.4	4	10	3 198	4 023	94.8	3 200	98.2
Jefferson, AR	05069	3	81 700	17.9	7	38	14 269	22 966	92.9	16 558	95.4
Johnson, AR	05071	6	24 042	17.3	4	10	4 019	5 363	93.9	4 256	97.9
Lafayette, AR	05073	8	8 027	17.3	2	7	1 387	2 064	97.1	1 706	98.2
Lawrence, AR	05075	6	17 153	16.3	9	13	3 293	4 345	89.3	3 181	96.8
Lee, AR	05077	6	11 545	17.1	1	4	1 557	3 184	89.4	2 646	88.1
Lincoln, AR	05079	3	14 262	14.7	3	4	1 802	2 933	93.8	2 397	94.9

[1]County type codes are from the Economic Research Service of the United States Department of Agriculture. See notes and definitions at the end of this section.

Table C-1. Population, School, and Student Characteristics by County—*Continued*

STATE County	Characteristics of students, 2004–2005				Outcomes		Staff and students, 2004–2005		
	Percent with IEP[2]	Percent eligible for free or reduced-price lunch	Percent minority	Percent English-language learners	Number of graduates, 2003–2004	Percent dropouts, grades 9–12, 2001–2002	Number of teachers	Student-teacher ratio	Central administration staff
	10	11	12	13	14	15	16	17	18
Kenai Peninsula, AK	14.5	35.9	17.0	8.8	625	7.2	532	18.2	. . .
Ketchikan Gateway, AK	15.0	28.3	41.0	2.4	134	8.6	139	16.8	. . .
Kodiak Island, AK	16.5	32.5	54.4	15.3	162	3.1	179	15.1	. . .
Lake and Peninsula, AK	. . .	72.9	90.9	. . .	. . .	. . .	. . .	. . .	. . .
Matanuska-Susitna, AK	13.5	32.7	16.1	3.7	1 016	6.3	825	17.9	. . .
Nome, AK	13.8	63.4	92.8	56.1	107	12.7	201	12.3	. . .
North Slope, AK	11.8	28.5	93.4	46.6	102	7.1	195	9.9	. . .
Northwest Arctic, AK	8.4	82.5	94.6	36.4	80	10.0	165	13.0	. . .
Prince of Wales-Outer Ketchikan, AK	14.8	. . .	50.6	0.0	66	4.7	107	13.9	. . .
Sitka, AK	2.4	29.7	54.8	7.9	60	4.7	16	23.2	. . .
Skagway-Hoonah-Angoon, AK	10.6	54.9	63.3	0.0	34	2.7	44	11.3	. . .
Southeast Fairbanks, AK	8.7	. . .	31.8	18.4	91	4.3	92	18.5	. . .
Valdez-Cordova, AK	14.4	35.1	33.4	2.4	137	4.0	130	15.8	. . .
Wade Hampton, AK	10.0	78.7	99.5	84.1	103	16.6	174	14.8	. . .
Wrangell-Petersburg, AK	16.6	. . .	37.8	2.0	187	2.7	186	14.4	. . .
Yakutat , AK	13.4	78.4	81.3	0.0	6	. . .	12	11.6	. . .
Yukon-Koyukuk, AK	6.9	. . .	55.3	2.8	224	3.4	175	34.1	. . .
ARIZONA	18.1	53.6	51.7	18.7	. . .	10.5	48 932	21.3	. . .
Apache, AZ	20.3	. . .	81.6	33.4	. . .	11.6	902	15.2	40
Cochise, AZ	17.0	62.0	55.9	16.5	. . .	6.2	1 171	19.4	59
Coconino, AZ	23.1	54.2	55.8	16.9	. . .	11.1	1 247	18.1	. . .
Gila, AZ	22.2	59.6	45.9	5.6	. . .	11.4	501	17.0	. . .
Graham, AZ	14.5	. . .	44.7	0.9	. . .	11.4	335	21.8	14
Greenlee, AZ	19.2	44.2	56.8	0.0	. . .	3.3	111	14.6	6
La Paz, AZ	24.9	80.8	64.7	14.3	. . .	11.0	172	16.5	13
Maricopa, AZ	17.4	48.6	49.3	18.9	. . .	10.0	29 858	21.8	. . .
Mohave, AZ	20.0	57.9	25.7	6.3	. . .	13.2	1 142	23.9	33
Navajo, AZ	15.9	. . .	60.2	20.6	. . .	11.0	1 232	23.3	56
Pima, AZ	20.5	58.7	57.1	16.0	. . .	10.1	7 098	20.8	65
Pinal, AZ	19.7	64.4	52.0	10.2	. . .	12.5	1 716	20.8	. . .
Santa Cruz, AZ	12.3	71.3	93.5	63.6	. . .	9.6	548	19.1	. . .
Yavapai, AZ	20.2	49.7	24.0	7.5	. . .	7.6	1 158	23.0	45
Yuma, AZ	15.3	79.1	79.9	42.1	. . .	9.0	1 741	20.5	. . .
ARKANSAS	12.2	51.0	30.8	4.0	. . .	5.3	31 234	14.8	. . .
Arkansas, AR	9.8	54.5	37.1	0.0	. . .	4.9	268	13.2	. . .
Ashley, AR	10.3	57.8	38.6	3.2	. . .	5.1	280	15.4	. . .
Baxter, AR	11.9	49.5	2.0	0.2	. . .	5.5	332	15.2	33
Benton, AR	10.8	39.5	23.7	13.3	. . .	4.7	1 849	16.5	126
Boone, AR	11.5	46.5	1.8	0.3	. . .	4.3	427	14.4	37
Bradley, AR	9.5	66.4	50.9	6.3	. . .	2.8	150	14.3	19
Calhoun, AR	12.9	55.7	31.4	1.6	. . .	6.0	52	14.7	4
Carroll, AR	12.3	54.7	21.2	10.4	. . .	6.5	267	13.9	26
Chicot, AR	9.7	83.5	83.0	2.2	. . .	4.8	176	13.0	29
Clark, AR	13.2	50.0	38.7	3.6	. . .	3.8	289	14.2	28
Clay, AR	16.4	48.2	0.8	0.0	. . .	5.2	216	13.6	24
Cleburne, AR	15.5	48.0	1.9	0.1	. . .	5.6	265	13.1	. . .
Cleveland, AR	11.0	47.3	17.2	0.1	. . .	1.4	114	12.9	. . .
Columbia, AR	10.5	54.8	51.6	0.5	. . .	4.4	269	14.9	. . .
Conway, AR	13.3	54.7	23.9	1.6	. . .	4.0	237	13.9	23
Craighead, AR	12.5	44.0	20.2	1.8	. . .	3.6	956	15.3	79
Crawford, AR	10.6	48.2	10.6	3.6	. . .	4.0	715	15.4	62
Crittenden, AR	12.7	71.0	67.4	0.1	. . .	6.6	714	15.6	. . .
Cross, AR	14.4	58.6	32.6	0.1	. . .	4.4	285	13.9	33
Dallas, AR	10.4	52.0	49.9	0.0	. . .	4.2	82	14.2	. . .
Desha, AR	12.8	69.2	61.7	2.1	. . .	4.7	254	13.0	. . .
Drew, AR	9.8	53.7	38.2	1.7	. . .	2.7	228	14.7	21
Faulkner, AR	14.0	36.3	17.6	0.7	. . .	4.1	979	15.9	98
Franklin, AR	11.6	41.5	4.2	0.4	. . .	5.6	232	14.4	. . .
Fulton, AR	14.0	55.7	2.3	0.0	. . .	1.4	122	12.9	16
Garland, AR	12.0	49.3	19.9	2.9	. . .	2.9	885	15.1	101
Grant, AR	12.6	38.4	4.0	0.7	. . .	4.3	295	16.2	35
Greene, AR	14.9	50.1	2.2	0.5	. . .	4.6	463	15.2	. . .
Hempstead, AR	11.0	62.1	52.6	6.4	. . .	4.8	290	14.1	. . .
Hot Spring, AR	13.6	51.8	15.1	0.6	. . .	4.6	401	13.7	45
Howard, AR	11.6	56.3	37.6	3.3	. . .	4.1	243	12.7	. . .
Independence, AR	15.9	50.4	8.7	2.3	. . .	4.0	431	13.6	. . .
Izard, AR	15.2	58.8	1.5	0.0	. . .	2.4	153	12.3	. . .
Jackson, AR	12.8	61.9	23.4	0.8	. . .	7.8	252	12.7	. . .
Jefferson, AR	10.4	60.6	68.6	0.3	. . .	5.8	920	15.5	65
Johnson, AR	10.6	59.4	14.7	7.1	. . .	5.9	265	15.2	. . .
Lafayette, AR	8.3	72.6	54.4	0.4	. . .	2.4	100	13.9	16
Lawrence, AR	16.5	60.7	1.1	0.0	. . .	2.1	244	13.5	. . .
Lee, AR	13.1	90.1	91.3	0.1	. . .	9.2	105	14.8	10
Lincoln, AR	12.3	50.3	29.9	3.3	. . .	6.6	114	15.8	. . .

[2]IEP = Individual Education Program. See notes and definitions at the end of this section.
. . . = Not available.

Table C-1. Population, School, and Student Characteristics by County—*Continued*

STATE County	Revenue, 2003–2004				Current expenditures, 2003–2004			Resident population, 16 to 19 years, 2000			
	Total revenue (thousands of dollars)	Percent of revenue from:			Total expenditures (thousands of dollars)	Amount per student (dollars)	Percent for instruction	Total	Percent in armed forces	Percent high school graduates	Percent not enrolled, not employed, not in armed forces, not high school graduate
		Federal government	State government	Local government							
	19	20	21	22	23	24	25	26	27	28	29
Kenai Peninsula, AK	91 423	8.7	51.9	39.4	89 865	9 317	60.0	3 224	0.9	12.4	2.8
Ketchikan Gateway, AK	22 062	10.8	53.6	35.5	21 439	8 982	65.0	866	2.5	14.3	7.0
Kodiak Island, AK	31 361	17.8	53.1	29.1	30 186	11 192	62.7	727	2.1	19.5	2.2
Lake and Peninsula, AK	11 123	32.0	55.2	12.8	10 484	24 157	56.5	149	0.0	16.1	8.1
Matanuska-Susitna, AK	133 170	10.4	62.4	27.2	130 065	9 050	57.5	3 925	0.2	11.4	5.0
Nome, AK	55 116	36.4	57.1	6.5	44 327	17 472	66.5	644	0.0	13.0	14.8
North Slope, AK	50 235	27.1	19.8	53.2	48 509	23 491	56.5	556	0.0	17.6	7.2
Northwest Arctic, AK	50 985	24.7	41.4	33.8	40 094	18 109	56.9	539	0.0	16.0	20.4
Prince of Wales-Outer Ketchikan, AK ..	23 976	41.8	50.1	8.1	21 353	12 400	68.1	361	0.0	11.1	4.2
Sitka, AK	15 316	15.8	46.9	37.3	14 425	9 465	66.7	501	5.8	19.8	3.0
Skagway-Hoonah-Angoon, AK	11 899	28.4	56.3	15.3	9 801	18 633	65.3	188	0.0	10.6	8.5
Southeast Fairbanks, AK	8 832	27.2	69.9	2.9	7 988	15 912	60.3	405	2.0	16.5	6.4
Valdez-Cordova, AK	28 175	16.8	56.1	27.1	26 328	11 775	66.3	611	0.8	12.9	5.9
Wade Hampton, AK	55 868	35.3	61.6	3.0	38 461	15 101	62.1	573	0.0	12.7	10.8
Wrangell-Petersburg, AK	14 009	22.0	54.7	23.3	12 825	10 599	63.0	345	0.0	13.0	3.5
Yakutat , AK	2 002	13.9	55.8	30.3	2 177	17 416	60.1	46	0.0	13.0	6.5
Yukon-Koyukuk, AK	72 645	23.1	68.9	8.0	60 708	7 654	58.1	468	0.0	9.8	10.0
ARIZONA	7 640 237	11.7	47.3	41.0	6 051 902	6 214	59.4	288 587	0.6	11.1	8.4
Apache, AZ	174 046	46.7	37.5	15.8	129 184	8 961	53.8	5 232	0.0	9.7	11.9
Cochise, AZ	156 552	17.2	54.9	27.9	135 949	6 499	59.2	7 562	10.4	19.8	6.1
Coconino, AZ	184 010	24.1	35.3	40.6	141 336	6 986	58.3	8 192	0.0	7.9	6.6
Gila, AZ	74 772	24.0	43.9	32.1	59 466	6 819	57.4	2 558	0.0	10.4	9.6
Graham, AZ	43 606	17.4	64.2	18.4	36 228	6 218	62.2	2 653	0.0	10.8	7.9
Greenlee, AZ	12 089	6.7	25.4	67.8	10 155	6 005	57.7	538	0.0	10.0	2.2
La Paz, AZ	25 243	33.3	37.0	29.7	22 275	8 001	54.9	923	0.0	10.9	8.2
Maricopa, AZ	4 714 170	8.2	46.2	45.6	3 670 068	6 054	60.7	168 713	0.2	11.3	8.4
Mohave, AZ	183 317	11.3	49.7	39.0	149 093	5 446	60.0	7 038	0.0	13.9	11.8
Navajo, AZ	211 704	35.3	42.5	22.2	173 156	7 717	56.5	7 191	0.0	10.3	10.5
Pima, AZ	1 073 204	11.2	50.0	38.8	901 595	6 303	57.9	49 172	0.7	10.0	6.8
Pinal, AZ	247 611	14.5	53.0	32.5	202 824	6 820	56.1	9 460	0.0	10.9	14.5
Santa Cruz, AZ	90 407	13.6	58.8	27.6	62 611	6 107	54.7	2 215	0.0	8.2	8.4
Yavapai, AZ	183 704	10.0	45.0	45.0	150 891	5 854	58.6	7 946	0.1	10.5	6.0
Yuma, AZ	265 802	14.3	60.8	24.9	207 071	6 000	56.9	9 194	3.3	11.4	9.6
ARKANSAS	3 391 263	12.5	53.1	34.5	3 063 259	6 743	66.1	156 258	0.2	13.2	5.4
Arkansas, AR	24 310	11.9	52.8	35.4	23 491	6 564	67.6	1 142	0.0	11.6	6.5
Ashley, AR	29 628	16.7	55.1	28.2	27 262	6 121	64.1	1 373	0.0	9.7	4.4
Baxter, AR	32 765	11.5	43.7	44.8	30 543	6 163	66.9	1 655	0.0	22.9	2.8
Benton, AR	239 677	5.8	39.4	54.8	177 692	6 156	68.0	8 071	0.0	13.8	4.4
Boone, AR	43 351	10.6	53.7	35.7	39 530	6 582	66.9	1 867	0.0	15.3	4.2
Bradley, AR	17 034	17.0	57.4	25.7	15 310	7 033	68.6	679	1.2	23.3	3.5
Calhoun, AR	4 917	10.7	46.8	42.4	4 644	6 559	63.1	273	0.0	13.9	0.0
Carroll, AR	24 503	10.7	47.6	41.7	22 876	6 369	66.4	1 457	0.0	21.4	6.2
Chicot, AR	19 349	19.8	50.6	29.6	18 071	7 700	62.6	916	0.0	12.1	6.6
Clark, AR	28 126	18.0	46.4	35.5	24 929	7 982	60.8	2 054	0.0	5.9	1.3
Clay, AR	17 547	10.7	57.6	31.7	17 247	6 360	67.2	777	0.0	18.5	1.3
Cleburne, AR	23 483	13.4	45.4	41.2	20 337	6 026	65.8	1 131	0.0	14.1	4.7
Cleveland, AR	10 829	9.4	59.7	30.9	9 794	6 618	64.7	453	0.0	19.9	3.5
Columbia, AR	29 930	14.7	55.5	29.9	27 814	6 604	67.0	1 800	0.0	7.9	5.2
Conway, AR	29 106	11.4	52.4	36.2	27 016	8 279	63.5	1 158	0.0	14.6	5.4
Craighead, AR	99 681	13.0	52.4	34.6	87 584	6 178	66.3	5 400	0.0	14.2	2.0
Crawford, AR	74 491	12.3	61.8	25.9	66 595	6 257	67.4	3 033	0.0	12.2	4.0
Crittenden, AR	75 055	14.2	62.9	22.9	69 012	6 285	66.9	3 230	0.0	9.2	7.5
Cross, AR	27 259	15.6	60.8	23.6	25 457	6 502	67.5	1 232	0.0	13.3	6.7
Dallas, AR	12 145	11.7	66.2	22.1	12 013	7 555	69.7	602	0.0	11.3	11.8
Desha, AR	23 947	16.6	53.0	30.4	22 818	7 430	63.8	963	0.1	9.9	4.0
Drew, AR	32 134	24.6	52.1	23.2	25 403	7 941	67.4	1 343	0.0	10.3	3.9
Faulkner, AR	103 089	8.7	57.6	33.7	92 068	6 095	68.0	6 320	0.2	9.6	1.2
Franklin, AR	28 906	20.1	52.3	27.6	24 834	7 029	69.3	1 195	0.0	16.5	6.1
Fulton, AR	10 534	12.5	61.0	26.5	10 046	6 403	65.7	552	0.0	10.5	3.8
Garland, AR	97 573	13.4	43.6	43.0	87 660	6 631	65.1	4 158	0.0	15.6	6.3
Grant, AR	29 371	8.1	65.0	26.9	27 788	5 975	66.7	885	0.0	16.9	2.0
Greene, AR	45 232	11.2	58.4	30.5	41 914	6 275	65.4	2 054	0.0	15.9	6.4
Hempstead, AR	28 339	16.9	63.8	19.3	29 396	7 495	66.6	1 363	0.0	13.4	10.4
Hot Spring, AR	38 016	12.1	56.2	31.7	34 420	6 317	65.2	1 662	0.0	16.3	5.1
Howard, AR	20 341	12.4	57.3	30.3	19 526	6 632	67.1	855	0.0	11.6	9.6
Independence, AR	40 793	11.5	52.2	36.3	39 281	6 906	63.7	2 132	0.7	15.1	3.0
Izard, AR	15 898	13.4	56.5	30.1	15 075	7 918	66.3	610	0.0	15.1	5.9
Jackson, AR	19 122	22.3	48.2	29.4	18 205	7 236	65.9	1 108	0.2	7.3	15.2
Jefferson, AR	102 726	13.9	57.3	28.9	96 568	6 798	67.3	5 609	0.0	12.9	6.0
Johnson, AR	28 497	14.3	59.6	26.2	25 462	6 159	66.7	1 393	0.4	12.3	8.0
Lafayette, AR	11 859	15.8	58.9	25.3	9 705	7 053	64.2	513	0.0	9.4	4.5
Lawrence, AR	26 235	13.0	57.3	29.7	23 034	7 136	67.6	1 107	0.0	13.2	4.2
Lee, AR	12 373	29.0	55.2	15.8	11 228	7 156	63.5	818	0.0	10.9	9.5
Lincoln, AR	14 712	15.6	61.4	23.0	12 880	6 320	65.0	804	0.0	18.0	6.6

Table C-1. Population, School, and Student Characteristics by County—*Continued*

STATE County	High school graduates, 2000			College enrollment, 2000		College graduates, 2000 (percent)						
	Population 25 years and over	High school graduate or less (percent)	High school graduate or more (percent)	Number	Percent public	Bachelor's degree or more	+/- U.S. percentage with bachelor's degree or more	Non-Hispanic White	Black	American Indian and Alaska Native	Asian or Pacific Islander	Hispanic[3]
	30	31	32	33	34	35	36	37	38	39	40	41
Kenai Peninsula, AK	31 388	43.3	88.5	1 623	86.9	20.3	-4.1	22.1	5.4	3.4	20.5	14.1
Ketchikan Gateway, AK	8 999	40.1	89.6	456	86.0	20.2	-4.2	22.9	0.0	4.3	23.5	28.1
Kodiak Island, AK	8 187	45.9	85.4	543	83.4	18.7	-5.7	24.7	16.2	5.4	9.8	10.6
Lake and Peninsula, AK	981	67.1	72.2	39	66.7	12.4	-12.0	40.2	. . .	2.0	0.0	0.0
Matanuska-Susitna, AK	35 721	43.2	88.1	2 100	88.7	18.3	-6.1	19.3	19.8	5.9	17.4	9.0
Nome, AK	4 916	63.3	74.8	278	91.4	14.7	-9.7	42.4	25.0	3.3	24.5	6.5
North Slope, AK	3 883	57.6	77.4	250	88.0	17.0	-7.4	48.0	39.5	3.3	24.7	13.8
Northwest Arctic, AK	3 498	68.4	72.0	121	89.3	12.7	-11.7	44.8	0.0	3.3	39.5	34.8
Prince of Wales-Outer Ketchikan, AK	3 797	57.0	84.1	109	90.8	14.2	-10.2	19.7	33.3	5.1	12.5	7.7
Sitka, AK	5 608	34.7	90.6	575	65.9	29.5	5.1	36.6	45.2	8.2	20.4	14.7
Skagway-Hoonah-Angoon, AK	2 273	46.1	84.4	104	75.0	21.6	-2.8	27.4	0.0	6.7	15.4	44.7
Southeast Fairbanks, AK	3 693	48.3	86.8	286	85.0	18.2	-6.2	20.6	11.9	4.4	0.0	20.6
Valdez Cordova, AK	6 441	41.4	00.5	416	78.1	21.2	-3.2	23.8	20.8	5.7	24.2	17.4
Wade Hampton, AK	3 082	74.9	66.3	119	94.1	9.1	-15.3	68.1	42.9	2.8	55.6	16.7
Wrangell-Petersburg, AK	4 359	50.6	85.8	140	83.6	16.3	-8.1	19.2	. . .	2.0	16.5	13.2
Yakutat , AK	522	49.0	84.3	27	100.0	17.6	-6.8	20.4	100.0	10.9	20.0	0.0
Yukon-Koyukuk, AK	3 707	65.0	74.3	164	91.5	14.2	-10.2	35.0	0.0	4.3	33.3	24.2
ARIZONA	3 256 184	43.3	81.0	331 099	84.5	23.5	-0.9	28.1	18.6	7.3	43.2	8.1
Apache, AZ	36 217	61.2	63.6	3 235	87.5	11.3	-13.1	25.4	8.3	6.7	51.1	7.9
Cochise, AZ	75 774	45.2	79.5	7 459	86.4	18.8	-5.6	23.7	18.9	6.9	18.1	5.8
Coconino, AZ	65 976	37.9	83.8	14 842	95.6	29.9	5.5	40.2	21.8	7.8	45.3	15.3
Gila, AZ	35 150	50.5	78.2	1 886	90.5	13.9	-10.5	16.6	9.3	1.9	41.6	6.3
Graham, AZ	19 302	54.5	75.6	2 540	94.2	11.8	-12.6	17.6	4.0	2.5	27.5	2.2
Greenlee, AZ	5 207	52.6	82.5	222	89.6	12.2	-12.2	16.0	6.9	0.0	0.0	7.3
La Paz, AZ	14 389	64.6	69.3	437	90.4	8.7	-15.7	9.8	16.9	6.5	16.9	3.8
Maricopa, AZ	1 934 957	40.6	82.5	197 913	81.2	25.9	1.5	30.2	19.9	11.2	45.7	8.1
Mohave, AZ	109 347	57.4	77.5	5 259	91.3	9.9	-14.5	10.3	6.2	6.0	22.8	6.0
Navajo, AZ	54 215	56.6	71.2	3 956	88.5	12.3	-12.1	19.9	6.4	4.2	25.9	4.8
Pima, AZ	546 200	39.9	83.4	69 727	90.0	26.7	2.3	32.5	16.8	9.4	42.2	10.9
Pinal, AZ	119 102	57.7	72.7	6 840	85.5	11.9	-12.5	15.6	7.4	2.0	22.6	3.9
Santa Cruz, AZ	22 445	62.2	60.7	1 314	88.0	15.2	-9.2	37.5	11.2	6.3	16.5	7.9
Yavapai, AZ	120 223	43.5	84.7	8 408	72.2	21.1	-3.3	22.3	39.5	9.7	42.4	7.7
Yuma, AZ	97 680	59.9	65.8	7 061	93.1	11.8	-12.6	16.6	12.6	6.2	23.4	4.7
ARKANSAS	1 731 200	58.8	75.3	128 063	85.2	16.7	-7.7	17.9	10.2	12.1	31.5	7.1
Arkansas, AR	13 888	67.4	72.4	743	90.8	12.2	-12.2	14.0	4.8	0.0	31.1	0.0
Ashley, AR	15 722	70.7	72.5	671	88.1	10.1	-14.3	11.8	4.6	12.3	44.4	3.2
Baxter, AR	28 861	60.0	77.5	911	94.7	12.8	-11.6	12.8	0.0	13.1	18.8	5.4
Benton, AR	99 436	52.4	80.4	5 637	71.6	20.3	-4.1	21.3	27.2	11.7	35.9	6.2
Boone, AR	23 070	58.2	76.8	988	89.4	12.7	-11.7	12.7	0.0	5.9	30.0	16.2
Bradley, AR	8 368	70.2	66.6	345	92.2	11.9	-12.5	14.9	6.0	. . .	0.0	5.1
Calhoun, AR	3 906	74.8	68.7	115	83.5	7.3	-17.1	8.4	3.1	0.0	0.0	7.1
Carroll, AR	17 207	62.3	71.8	398	91.2	13.8	-10.6	14.5	0.0	17.8	18.2	4.8
Chicot, AR	9 062	71.0	64.2	348	98.6	11.7	-12.7	15.9	7.2	0.0	27.5	7.5
Clark, AR	13 735	57.1	75.3	3 738	61.6	19.8	-4.6	23.1	8.7	35.6	56.8	7.3
Clay, AR	12 175	77.2	60.6	402	91.5	7.4	-17.0	7.3	0.0	3.8	100.0	0.0
Cleburne, AR	17 299	61.6	74.8	538	86.4	13.9	-10.5	14.0	20.0	14.3	55.6	4.7
Cleveland, AR	5 659	70.3	73.1	253	88.1	10.0	-14.4	11.1	2.7	0.0	10.0	0.0
Columbia, AR	16 039	61.7	74.1	2 082	95.3	16.8	-7.6	22.0	6.5	4.2	33.3	7.2
Conway, AR	13 480	68.2	73.2	712	89.9	11.5	-12.9	12.3	7.5	23.8	19.4	4.6
Craighead, AR	50 725	55.5	77.3	6 945	90.3	20.9	-3.5	21.5	14.4	8.6	22.0	11.6
Crawford, AR	33 765	64.5	71.5	1 655	88.1	9.7	-14.7	9.9	8.7	4.6	7.0	9.4
Crittenden, AR	30 251	64.0	69.2	1 928	86.6	12.8	-11.6	18.0	5.4	11.3	15.4	0.0
Cross, AR	12 412	69.8	68.3	645	92.6	9.9	-14.5	10.8	6.4	14.5	22.2	0.0
Dallas, AR	5 989	74.3	66.8	212	88.2	9.6	-14.8	14.8	1.6	0.0	. . .	0.0
Desha, AR	9 574	71.0	65.0	457	92.3	11.1	-13.3	14.1	6.9	0.0	45.9	0.0
Drew, AR	11 553	61.3	73.1	1 484	97.3	17.3	-7.1	20.6	8.2	0.0	13.0	9.1
Faulkner, AR	50 849	47.9	83.3	9 182	79.8	25.2	0.8	26.2	14.9	18.3	41.1	15.4
Franklin, AR	11 654	64.3	71.1	466	92.5	11.0	-13.4	11.2	0.0	13.8	9.1	0.0
Fulton, AR	8 243	66.9	72.2	276	88.8	10.5	-13.9	10.5	. . .	5.0	27.8	6.1
Garland, AR	62 694	54.5	78.3	2 731	87.6	18.0	-6.4	18.8	8.2	18.3	34.0	11.6
Grant, AR	10 824	65.1	77.2	539	89.2	11.0	-13.4	11.0	14.7	23.6	16.1	0.0
Greene, AR	24 510	68.5	72.1	1 233	80.5	10.9	-13.5	11.1	0.0	10.1	0.0	0.0
Hempstead, AR	14 869	69.2	69.2	932	92.4	11.0	-13.4	13.2	7.2	0.0	41.7	2.0
Hot Spring, AR	20 260	66.4	73.3	1 005	89.5	11.2	-13.2	11.7	7.2	15.4	22.0	4.1
Howard, AR	9 271	67.1	70.7	328	89.0	11.6	-12.8	13.1	6.8	6.3	5.7	8.2
Independence, AR	22 705	64.2	75.5	1 382	62.2	13.7	-10.7	13.8	11.1	23.8	11.4	3.1
Izard, AR	9 524	63.2	73.3	457	86.7	11.7	-12.7	11.8	0.0	7.5	62.5	30.4
Jackson, AR	12 204	72.3	66.0	545	89.2	10.3	-14.1	10.8	6.4	4.9	47.8	5.3
Jefferson, AR	53 132	60.0	74.8	4 998	93.1	15.7	-8.7	15.6	15.7	8.6	49.5	5.2
Johnson, AR	14 901	69.0	67.6	841	85.0	13.1	-11.3	13.5	10.0	7.6	0.0	8.3
Lafayette, AR	5 692	70.7	65.3	218	91.7	9.5	-14.9	13.0	2.9	0.0	6.7	0.0
Lawrence, AR	11 824	73.5	63.3	809	57.1	8.5	-15.9	8.6	0.0	2.4	11.5	0.0
Lee, AR	7 924	73.4	56.2	361	95.8	7.3	-17.1	8.1	6.8	23.2	0.0	0.0
Lincoln, AR	9 533	72.8	65.0	307	93.5	7.6	-16.8	9.5	4.0	0.0	0.0	1.5

[3]May be of any race.
. . . = Not available.

Table C-1. Population, School, and Student Characteristics by County—*Continued*

STATE County	State/ county code	County type[1]	Population, 2005		Number of schools and students, 2004–2005			Resident enrollment, 2000			
			Total	Percent 5 to 17 years	School districts	Schools	Students	Total	Percent public	K–12	Percent public
			1	2	3	4	5	6	7	8	9
Little River, AR	05081	6	13 227	17.6	2	7	2 262	3 128	92.9	2 481	94.9
Logan, AR	05083	6	22 944	17.8	4	10	3 499	5 033	92.9	4 293	95.1
Lonoke, AR	05085	2	60 658	19.2	3	9	3 550	14 008	93.0	11 362	96.9
Madison, AR	05087	2	14 962	18.0	3	6	2 497	3 198	95.4	2 875	96.3
Marion, AR	05089	9	16 735	15.2	3	6	1 928	3 301	92.2	2 770	93.4
Miller, AR	05091	3	43 162	18.3	4	16	6 463	9 869	89.4	7 692	92.2
Mississippi, AR	05093	4	47 911	20.8	6	24	9 034	13 939	92.7	11 331	93.9
Monroe, AR	05095	7	9 302	18.9	3	6	1 707	2 564	87.9	2 218	88.4
Montgomery, AR	05097	8	9 274	16.8	3	4	1 221	1 860	94.7	1 589	95.5
Nevada, AR	05099	7	9 550	16.8	3	5	1 524	2 425	96.9	1 927	99.0
Newton, AR	05101	9	8 452	16.1	5	10	1 378	1 944	94.8	1 656	94.5
Ouachita, AR	05103	7	27 102	17.5	6	18	5 324	7 398	93.4	5 915	94.7
Perry, AR	05105	2	10 468	17.7	3	4	1 743	2 325	91.9	1 958	94.7
Phillips, AR	05107	7	24 107	22.3	7	15	5 126	8 079	90.0	6 506	91.0
Pike, AR	05109	9	11 038	17.4	3	6	1 376	2 606	93.5	2 111	95.2
Poinsett, AR	05111	3	25 349	18.3	6	13	4 802	5 948	96.9	4 997	97.5
Polk, AR	05113	7	20 176	17.6	6	16	4 042	4 834	93.4	3 852	94.6
Pope, AR	05115	5	56 580	17.2	5	23	9 634	15 194	93.8	10 420	95.9
Prairie, AR	05117	8	9 113	15.6	3	6	1 339	2 040	93.6	1 761	95.6
Pulaski, AR	05119	2	366 463	17.4	9	129	62 522	94 618	80.0	66 912	81.2
Randolph, AR	05121	7	18 465	17.0	4	6	2 441	4 304	92.8	3 368	95.0
St. Francis, AR	05123	6	27 902	19.1	4	14	5 341	8 028	94.3	6 323	94.4
Saline, AR	05125	2	91 188	17.7	5	21	12 796	20 335	88.0	15 742	93.1
Scott, AR	05127	6	11 150	18.4	2	6	2 737	2 425	96.4	2 123	97.6
Searcy, AR	05129	9	7 969	15.5	5	11	1 795	1 770	96.8	1 471	97.5
Sebastian, AR	05131	2	118 750	18.1	6	39	18 068	27 690	88.4	21 523	90.9
Sevier, AR	05133	7	16 456	19.6	4	10	3 417	3 907	96.5	3 254	98.0
Sharp, AR	05135	7	17 397	15.7	5	11	3 598	3 404	92.6	2 774	94.9
Stone, AR	05137	9	11 716	15.5	3	6	1 716	2 284	94.0	1 962	95.5
Union, AR	05139	5	44 186	17.7	10	26	8 160	11 194	91.0	9 106	92.7
Van Buren, AR	05141	8	16 529	15.1	5	12	2 425	3 205	93.9	2 688	95.9
Washington, AR	05143	2	180 357	17.2	11	56	30 667	46 255	91.3	27 413	93.9
White, AR	05145	4	71 332	16.8	11	30	11 963	18 439	75.5	12 232	91.9
Woodruff, AR	05147	9	8 098	18.3	2	4	752	2 089	96.6	1 674	97.9
Yell, AR	05149	6	21 391	17.6	7	14	4 258	4 761	94.7	4 062	96.7
CALIFORNIA	06000		36 132 147	19.4	1 140	9 690	6 322 189	10 129 990	85.9	7 026 326	90.5
Alameda, CA	06001	1	1 448 905	17.7	29	381	215 801	417 264	83.1	264 846	87.2
Alpine, CA	06003	8	1 159	12.9	2	8	141	296	91.2	208	88.9
Amador, CA	06005	6	38 471	14.2	4	17	5 356	8 110	87.8	6 659	92.5
Butte, CA	06007	3	214 185	16.8	16	98	33 385	66 431	93.1	38 232	93.0
Calaveras, CA	06009	6	46 871	15.8	6	32	6 913	9 406	93.3	7 597	96.1
Colusa, CA	06011	6	21 095	21.1	5	21	4 478	5 596	94.4	4 635	96.1
Contra Costa, CA	06013	1	1 017 787	19.2	20	257	166 024	270 131	83.3	189 347	89.2
Del Norte, CA	06015	7	28 705	16.9	3	21	5 209	7 135	87.9	5 685	87.7
El Dorado, CA	06017	1	176 841	17.9	17	70	29 368	44 193	89.6	32 460	92.8
Fresno, CA	06019	2	877 584	22.2	37	330	193 866	263 942	93.0	197 351	96.1
Glenn, CA	06021	6	27 759	21.2	11	37	5 977	7 721	95.1	6 253	97.0
Humboldt, CA	06023	5	128 376	15.9	35	96	19 989	38 481	93.2	22 774	93.3
Imperial, CA	06025	3	155 823	21.2	18	62	35 720	47 441	94.6	36 443	96.2
Inyo, CA	06027	7	18 156	16.7	9	26	3 265	4 326	92.1	3 460	95.8
Kern, CA	06029	2	756 825	22.2	53	254	165 817	205 960	91.8	161 296	94.5
Kings, CA	06031	3	143 420	20.0	17	62	27 372	37 449	90.4	29 332	92.6
Lake, CA	06033	4	65 147	17.6	9	41	10 325	14 144	93.6	11 232	95.3
Lassen, CA	06035	6	34 751	15.2	12	37	5 933	8 900	91.9	6 518	94.0
Los Angeles, CA	06037	1	9 935 475	20.0	101	1 960	1 737 830	2 931 076	84.3	2 041 738	89.2
Madera, CA	06039	3	142 788	20.2	11	71	27 821	35 998	92.7	28 604	95.2
Marin, CA	06041	1	246 960	14.7	20	69	27 783	57 014	74.3	37 704	81.2
Mariposa, CA	06043	8	18 069	14.9	3	17	2 491	4 096	88.6	3 096	90.9
Mendocino, CA	06045	4	88 161	17.6	14	77	14 407	22 795	92.5	17 157	94.3
Merced, CA	06047	3	241 706	24.0	21	93	52 921	70 396	93.2	55 741	94.9
Modoc, CA	06049	6	9 534	17.6	4	17	1 672	2 336	97.4	2 005	97.6
Mono, CA	06051	7	12 509	16.1	4	22	2 235	2 917	89.6	2 210	92.3
Monterey, CA	06053	2	412 104	19.8	28	161	90 892	117 126	89.3	86 811	92.7
Napa, CA	06055	3	132 764	17.2	7	52	19 654	33 203	81.7	23 590	88.0
Nevada, CA	06057	4	98 394	15.7	12	67	19 300	23 203	90.9	17 457	94.3
Orange, CA	06059	1	2 988 072	19.4	32	602	513 744	847 671	85.2	569 481	90.1
Placer, CA	06061	1	317 028	17.5	19	101	58 163	69 856	87.1	50 421	91.7
Plumas, CA	06063	7	21 477	15.4	3	17	3 086	5 030	93.2	3 871	95.1
Riverside, CA	06065	1	1 946 419	21.1	26	438	380 964	465 645	89.0	356 146	93.0
Sacramento, CA	06067	1	1 363 482	19.9	19	380	235 906	366 459	87.8	253 944	90.7
San Benito, CA	06069	1	55 936	22.9	11	22	11 715	16 010	89.1	12 580	91.7
San Bernardino, CA	06071	1	1 963 535	22.8	38	519	423 780	555 363	89.0	420 751	93.3
San Diego, CA	06073	1	2 933 462	18.3	44	710	498 186	827 975	86.6	539 834	91.8
San Francisco, CA	06075	1	739 426	9.4	5	126	58 735	182 963	73.6	88 461	76.2
San Joaquin, CA	06077	2	664 116	21.7	18	208	135 262	176 188	87.5	133 856	92.3
San Luis Obispo, CA	06079	3	255 478	15.1	13	81	36 361	77 496	91.1	42 791	91.7

[1]County type codes are from the Economic Research Service of the United States Department of Agriculture. See notes and definitions at the end of this section.

Table C-1. Population, School, and Student Characteristics by County—*Continued*

STATE County	Characteristics of students, 2004–2005				Outcomes		Staff and students, 2004–2005		
	Percent with IEP[2]	Percent eligible for free or reduced-price lunch	Percent minority	Percent English-language learners	Number of graduates, 2003–2004	Percent dropouts, grades 9–12, 2001–2002	Number of teachers	Student-teacher ratio	Central administration staff
	10	11	12	13	14	15	16	17	18
Little River, AR	12.1	48.1	31.2	0.0	. . .	4.3	158	14.3	11
Logan, AR	12.7	54.8	5.8	1.1	. . .	5.2	254	13.8	23
Lonoke, AR	16.3	34.2	11.1	1.9	. . .	5.1	251	14.1	24
Madison, AR	13.4	52.9	7.0	3.4	. . .	5.5	162	15.4	. . .
Marion, AR	15.2	59.4	1.4	0.0	. . .	5.0	142	13.6	. . .
Miller, AR	14.6	58.3	35.1	0.6	. . .	4.9	439	14.7	. . .
Mississippi, AR	15.8	79.5	49.8	0.4	. . .	8.1	641	14.1	65
Monroe, AR	11.8	89.0	59.7	0.2	. . .	6.4	137	12.5	. . .
Montgomery, AR	11.5	62.6	6.5	2.2	. . .	3.2	91	13.4	. . .
Nevada, AR	12.9	65.0	44.2	1.5	. . .	2.0	117	13.0	. . .
Newton, AR	15.7	66.7	13.7	0.0	. . .	4.0	124	11.1	. . .
Ouachita, AR	11.5	59.9	56.7	0.3	. . .	5.5	379	14.0	44
Perry, AR	16.9	46.1	3.3	0.0	. . .	8.8	115	15.2	. . .
Phillips, AR	11.1	89.9	83.1	0.2	. . .	9.3	372	13.8	. . .
Pike, AR	13.9	53.4	14.1	1.0	. . .	3.3	113	12.2	13
Poinsett, AR	17.8	61.1	13.3	0.8	. . .	5.5	334	14.4	41
Polk, AR	11.0	59.5	9.0	3.0	. . .	6.4	289	14.0	. . .
Pope, AR	12.0	47.2	11.0	2.0	. . .	5.2	691	13.9	59
Prairie, AR	13.2	49.7	23.0	0.0	. . .	5.6	107	12.5	16
Pulaski, AR	10.3	52.8	61.8	2.0	. . .	8.4	4 137	15.1	462
Randolph, AR	14.5	58.5	2.6	0.1	. . .	4.2	154	15.9	. . .
St. Francis, AR	13.7	91.3	71.5	0.1	. . .	6.8	382	14.0	34
Saline, AR	12.8	27.0	6.8	1.9	. . .	4.0	779	16.4	. . .
Scott, AR	11.2	57.6	9.7	3.7	. . .	3.1	187	14.6	16
Searcy, AR	16.1	71.3	1.6	0.0	. . .	2.3	149	12.0	. . .
Sebastian, AR	12.6	48.2	32.3	11.0	. . .	4.8	1 102	16.4	106
Sevier, AR	9.4	64.1	45.4	9.8	. . .	6.9	216	15.8	28
Sharp, AR	13.9	56.5	2.3	0.1	. . .	3.6	245	14.7	. . .
Stone, AR	14.4	56.8	2.2	0.1	. . .	4.4	130	13.2	. . .
Union, AR	9.9	50.1	44.7	0.6	. . .	2.6	579	14.1	. . .
Van Buren, AR	17.0	60.8	4.3	0.3	. . .	6.7	214	11.3	. . .
Washington, AR	10.8	41.4	26.8	19.5	. . .	5.1	1 929	15.9	. . .
White, AR	13.8	46.1	8.8	1.0	. . .	4.3	804	14.9	. . .
Woodruff, AR	18.6	77.3	65.2	0.0	. . .	3.6	72	10.4	. . .
Yell, AR	11.5	60.3	25.4	11.1	. . .	7.3	320	13.3	. . .
CALIFORNIA	10.8	49.0	68.1	25.1	. . .	. . .	298 392	21.2	. . .
Alameda, CA	10.6	35.6	72.6	20.6	. . .	. . .	10 696	20.2	. . .
Alpine, CA	22.7	46.7	39.0	0.0	. . .	. . .	16	8.7	4
Amador, CA	11.9	25.0	23.0	2.2	. . .	. . .	270	19.8	. . .
Butte, CA	12.7	47.7	29.8	11.7	. . .	. . .	1 729	19.3	. . .
Calaveras, CA	10.9	31.1	14.3	1.4	. . .	. . .	339	20.4	. . .
Colusa, CA	12.7	66.5	66.9	38.8	. . .	. . .	252	17.8	32
Contra Costa, CA	12.3	29.5	52.2	15.2	. . .	. . .	8 026	20.7	. . .
Del Norte, CA	10.9	55.2	35.8	7.9	. . .	. . .	260	20.1	. . .
El Dorado, CA	11.4	21.2	19.3	4.9	. . .	. . .	1 388	21.2	. . .
Fresno, CA	9.9	65.8	74.4	26.9	. . .	. . .	9 472	20.5	. . .
Glenn, CA	10.4	59.6	52.6	16.1	. . .	. . .	332	18.0	. . .
Humboldt, CA	14.0	40.3	28.1	4.8	. . .	. . .	1 071	18.7	. . .
Imperial, CA	8.5	66.3	90.5	45.3	. . .	. . .	1 725	20.7	. . .
Inyo, CA	11.5	32.5	41.2	10.5	. . .	. . .	185	17.6	. . .
Kern, CA	9.7	62.1	65.7	20.6	. . .	. . .	7 920	20.9	. . .
Kings, CA	10.3	62.9	68.9	21.7	. . .	. . .	1 359	20.1	. . .
Lake, CA	12.3	59.0	30.4	8.5	. . .	. . .	523	19.8	. . .
Lassen, CA	13.2	38.1	24.8	2.2	. . .	. . .	308	19.3	. . .
Los Angeles, CA	10.7	60.5	83.4	32.3	. . .	. . .	80 160	21.7	. . .
Madera, CA	10.4	63.3	67.0	30.8	. . .	. . .	1 310	21.2	159
Marin, CA	14.0	18.3	29.4	10.4	. . .	. . .	1 511	18.4	. . .
Mariposa, CA	15.9	36.3	16.4	1.6	. . .	. . .	141	17.7	. . .
Mendocino, CA	13.7	58.2	39.7	18.2	. . .	. . .	841	17.1	. . .
Merced, CA	10.5	65.7	73.3	31.6	. . .	. . .	2 556	20.7	. . .
Modoc, CA	11.8	49.1	24.1	5.6	. . .	. . .	107	15.6	. . .
Mono, CA	17.1	42.2	41.9	21.6	. . .	. . .	150	14.9	. . .
Monterey, CA	10.1	61.5	78.9	33.4	. . .	. . .	4 331	21.0	. . .
Napa, CA	13.9	39.5	51.8	25.2	. . .	. . .	1 020	19.3	. . .
Nevada, CA	9.7	22.3	12.0	5.0	. . .	. . .	974	19.8	90
Orange, CA	9.9	39.0	62.8	29.1	. . .	. . .	22 336	23.0	. . .
Placer, CA	10.6	16.4	21.6	4.4	. . .	. . .	2 772	21.0	. . .
Plumas, CA	12.0	35.8	22.3	3.7	. . .	. . .	160	19.2	. . .
Riverside, CA	10.5	50.2	66.0	23.6	. . .	. . .	17 252	22.1	. . .
Sacramento, CA	11.0	45.3	57.1	19.2	. . .	. . .	11 439	20.6	. . .
San Benito, CA	12.0	41.0	63.7	22.2	. . .	. . .	538	21.8	60
San Bernardino, CA	10.8	52.3	70.7	19.9	. . .	. . .	18 922	22.4	. . .
San Diego, CA	11.6	41.7	62.0	23.5	. . .	. . .	24 289	20.5	. . .
San Francisco, CA	12.0	52.4	90.2	28.9	. . .	. . .	3 275	17.9	. . .
San Joaquin, CA	9.7	48.3	69.2	21.5	. . .	. . .	6 428	21.0	. . .
San Luis Obispo, CA	11.3	30.3	32.4	11.9	. . .	. . .	1 881	19.3	. . .

[2]IEP = Individual Education Program. See notes and definitions at the end of this section.
. . . = Not available.

Table C-1. Population, School, and Student Characteristics by County—*Continued*

STATE County	Revenue, 2003–2004				Current expenditures, 2003–2004			Resident population, 16 to 19 years, 2000			
	Total revenue (thousands of dollars)	Percent of revenue from:			Total expenditures (thousands of dollars)	Amount per student (dollars)	Percent for instruction	Total	Percent in armed forces	Percent high school graduates	Percent not enrolled, not employed, not in armed forces, not high school graduate
		Federal government	State government	Local government							
	19	20	21	22	23	24	25	26	27	28	29
Little River, AR	14 835	9.8	36.6	53.6	14 547	6 588	64.0	695	0.0	19.9	3.3
Logan, AR	25 179	16.3	57.9	25.8	22 169	6 325	64.8	1 234	0.1	17.8	5.2
Lonoke, AR	73 731	11.2	64.7	24.1	69 475	6 214	70.3	3 102	0.7	15.0	5.6
Madison, AR	18 005	12.8	62.7	24.5	16 429	6 137	66.0	813	0.0	15.0	4.4
Marion, AR	16 376	14.5	52.7	32.8	14 813	6 667	62.7	774	0.0	11.1	1.7
Miller, AR	46 783	11.1	58.8	30.1	43 122	6 694	66.3	2 225	0.0	14.7	8.6
Mississippi, AR	62 577	15.5	61.3	23.2	61 984	6 736	66.8	3 268	0.0	14.4	10.4
Monroe, AR	13 733	27.6	53.4	19.0	12 734	7 235	61.3	566	0.0	14.1	4.9
Montgomery, AR	10 260	21.9	49.8	28.4	9 057	6 103	67.3	459	0.0	10.5	6.8
Nevada, AR	12 919	11.2	62.0	26.8	11 756	6 331	65.8	480	0.0	12.3	2.1
Newton, AR	10 453	17.7	56.9	25.4	9 754	7 729	64.4	500	0.0	14.6	4.4
Ouachita, AR	37 577	16.2	61.8	22.0	35 270	7 322	65.0	1 647	0.0	11.8	6.1
Perry, AR	12 222	10.9	64.6	24.5	11 172	6 210	64.4	579	0.0	15.4	8.8
Phillips, AR	43 334	23.1	59.4	17.5	44 178	8 479	64.1	1 854	0.2	8.0	7.2
Pike, AR	15 718	11.0	58.5	30.6	14 752	6 414	65.5	609	0.0	8.5	3.0
Poinsett, AR	38 483	23.4	54.4	22.2	34 542	7 405	67.2	1 520	0.0	12.4	8.8
Polk, AR	23 784	15.1	59.9	24.9	23 172	6 345	64.8	1 142	0.4	14.1	4.0
Pope, AR	70 387	11.9	46.9	41.2	65 497	6 895	64.1	3 688	0.1	10.9	5.4
Prairie, AR	10 147	11.7	52.9	35.4	9 339	6 647	65.6	490	0.0	12.9	3.9
Pulaski, AR	464 992	10.9	46.7	42.5	420 672	7 905	63.9	19 002	1.3	13.3	5.9
Randolph, AR	18 728	12.4	61.8	25.7	17 604	6 346	67.0	1 000	0.0	19.5	9.6
St. Francis, AR	39 444	20.0	60.3	19.7	37 372	6 975	63.1	1 853	0.0	12.3	6.4
Saline, AR	80 490	7.1	60.9	32.0	72 840	5 809	70.1	4 127	0.0	14.4	4.6
Scott, AR	12 205	20.7	61.5	17.8	9 626	5 679	65.6	604	0.0	15.2	6.5
Searcy, AR	9 567	14.6	63.1	22.3	8 614	6 891	63.9	473	0.0	17.3	3.2
Sebastian, AR	140 126	13.9	47.1	38.9	125 402	6 629	67.4	6 418	0.3	12.8	6.6
Sevier, AR	24 621	13.2	62.5	24.3	23 200	7 156	64.6	968	0.0	14.7	6.1
Sharp, AR	21 507	10.7	61.4	27.9	19 165	5 910	65.8	870	0.0	16.7	9.3
Stone, AR	12 832	21.4	55.4	23.1	10 660	6 330	67.1	587	0.0	25.6	4.1
Union, AR	55 564	11.9	54.6	33.5	53 443	6 672	67.6	2 802	0.0	14.2	7.1
Van Buren, AR	16 872	13.2	57.9	28.8	16 885	7 086	64.0	730	0.0	20.1	5.3
Washington, AR	220 194	8.3	49.9	41.7	197 224	6 704	68.1	10 993	0.0	11.7	4.5
White, AR	86 357	12.1	57.4	30.5	76 299	6 458	64.0	4 613	0.0	10.0	5.4
Woodruff, AR	10 409	16.8	55.9	27.3	9 657	7 003	64.4	498	0.0	8.6	11.8
Yell, AR	27 969	14.4	63.9	21.7	26 306	6 475	66.7	1 328	0.0	16.9	6.8
CALIFORNIA	60 162 326	11.0	52.8	36.2	48 740 822	7 756	66.9	1 925 479	0.8	9.9	5.8
Alameda, CA	2 037 509	9.0	47.2	43.8	1 647 137	7 647	68.3	71 920	0.1	8.7	5.1
Alpine, CA	6 411	25.7	22.8	51.5	3 718	25 466	56.6	86	0.0	34.9	7.0
Amador, CA	49 669	7.0	43.6	49.4	34 251	7 124	66.6	2 350	0.0	10.5	8.1
Butte, CA	327 671	17.6	49.3	33.2	280 185	8 297	63.5	13 482	0.1	8.2	2.7
Calaveras, CA	67 563	7.5	29.2	63.3	57 193	8 358	62.6	2 061	0.0	12.8	5.1
Colusa, CA	47 936	14.2	55.6	30.2	39 212	8 944	63.1	1 480	0.0	8.6	11.8
Contra Costa, CA	1 594 074	6.8	44.2	49.0	1 201 955	7 296	68.1	48 997	0.0	9.1	3.9
Del Norte, CA	50 858	15.9	62.5	21.6	42 932	7 901	72.7	1 693	0.0	13.2	7.2
El Dorado, CA	254 754	8.8	46.9	44.3	218 585	7 519	64.9	8 592	0.0	11.7	2.2
Fresno, CA	1 718 431	13.6	62.4	24.0	1 463 392	7 672	65.5	54 287	0.0	9.1	6.9
Glenn, CA	61 037	17.6	57.3	25.2	51 428	8 482	62.7	1 596	0.0	10.8	4.2
Humboldt, CA	199 436	12.0	56.6	31.4	168 695	8 343	64.6	7 987	0.3	11.8	4.0
Imperial, CA	376 199	18.8	58.3	22.9	297 778	8 569	65.4	9 576	0.2	9.1	6.7
Inyo, CA	45 390	12.9	40.7	46.4	34 904	10 260	59.5	934	0.0	14.6	2.9
Kern, CA	1 510 739	15.5	61.3	23.2	1 242 260	7 801	62.6	42 920	0.5	11.6	7.2
Kings, CA	229 623	15.0	64.1	20.9	204 396	7 614	61.8	7 867	4.1	14.5	8.6
Lake, CA	100 857	15.1	50.9	34.0	82 698	7 940	62.1	2 895	0.0	11.8	7.1
Lassen, CA	53 960	14.9	52.8	32.3	44 689	8 858	63.7	1 735	0.0	16.4	4.8
Los Angeles, CA	17 085 449	12.8	61.8	25.4	14 086 621	8 089	67.5	539 900	0.1	8.0	7.1
Madera, CA	275 914	11.3	60.6	28.1	207 764	7 642	62.6	8 045	0.0	11.1	9.1
Marin, CA	336 127	5.8	18.5	75.7	267 322	9 378	66.1	9 466	0.1	8.2	3.6
Mariposa, CA	30 804	8.7	53.3	37.9	21 745	8 591	60.9	863	0.0	18.4	4.1
Mendocino, CA	169 920	12.5	49.2	38.4	137 880	9 393	64.9	5 310	0.3	14.3	6.8
Merced, CA	487 657	13.7	62.4	23.9	425 823	7 807	66.1	14 424	0.0	10.2	7.2
Modoc, CA	30 836	20.5	53.8	25.7	25 364	11 018	65.5	517	0.0	14.5	3.9
Mono, CA	28 445	10.2	23.6	66.2	23 458	10 505	62.2	680	5.3	30.6	4.3
Monterey, CA	736 712	11.7	47.1	41.2	603 613	8 181	66.7	25 375	3.6	11.9	7.6
Napa, CA	191 554	7.9	23.8	68.3	162 688	8 231	68.7	6 854	0.0	9.5	3.5
Nevada, CA	131 004	5.7	41.6	52.7	111 155	7 352	67.4	4 998	0.0	8.2	4.1
Orange, CA	4 399 600	8.7	45.5	45.8	3 724 741	7 226	67.9	151 675	0.1	8.0	4.9
Placer, CA	623 745	5.9	36.8	57.4	419 999	6 805	64.6	13 370	0.0	10.0	2.7
Plumas, CA	31 879	23.2	23.0	53.8	26 650	8 485	63.2	1 169	0.0	11.6	1.5
Riverside, CA	3 462 923	10.7	56.6	32.7	2 581 131	7 083	66.5	93 272	0.1	12.4	6.0
Sacramento, CA	2 259 831	10.5	54.6	34.8	1 851 156	7 874	66.3	67 282	0.4	11.8	5.6
San Benito, CA	104 426	7.5	49.3	43.3	90 210	7 727	68.6	2 807	0.0	14.9	4.5
San Bernardino, CA	3 578 570	10.2	66.3	23.5	2 843 942	6 844	66.7	109 876	1.8	12.9	6.7
San Diego, CA	4 870 842	9.2	46.0	44.7	3 907 804	7 855	67.0	158 984	5.9	14.7	4.6
San Francisco, CA	661 412	12.6	26.0	61.3	578 079	9 795	65.4	26 234	0.2	8.5	4.2
San Joaquin, CA	1 184 872	10.0	59.2	30.9	956 643	7 301	68.5	37 229	0.0	10.7	7.0
San Luis Obispo, CA	338 881	9.0	30.8	60.2	274 406	7 528	65.9	18 175	0.1	8.8	2.3

Table C-1. Population, School, and Student Characteristics by County—*Continued*

STATE County	High school graduates, 2000			College enrollment, 2000		College graduates, 2000 (percent)						
	Population 25 years and over	High school graduate or less (percent)	High school graduate or more (percent)	Number	Percent public	Bachelor's degree or more	+/- U.S. percentage with bachelor's degree or more	Non-Hispanic White	Black	American Indian and Alaska Native	Asian or Pacific Islander	Hispanic[3]
	30	31	32	33	34	35	36	37	38	39	40	41
Little River, AR	9 009	64.7	73.4	385	91.9	9.9	-14.5	11.7	3.4	8.4	0.0	5.0
Logan, AR	15 004	68.6	69.8	508	86.8	9.4	-15.0	9.1	4.0	24.5	68.9	12.3
Lonoke, AR	33 468	58.0	77.6	1 678	90.2	14.6	-9.8	15.2	6.5	2.2	3.7	13.3
Madison, AR	9 327	71.0	67.8	182	97.3	10.1	-14.3	10.3	0.0	9.4	7.1	2.6
Marion, AR	11 593	62.3	76.0	400	86.8	10.4	-14.0	10.3	...	10.9	6.8	8.2
Miller, AR	25 790	61.5	74.3	1 392	90.5	12.5	-11.9	14.2	6.0	0.0	50.4	9.6
Mississippi, AR	31 612	67.4	64.7	1 655	94.6	11.3	-13.1	13.5	5.5	1.8	44.8	7.0
Monroe, AR	6 602	74.4	63.8	208	94.2	8.4	-16.0	9.6	6.1	0.0	0.0	2.2
Montgomery, AR	6 464	69.4	69.8	185	88.1	8.8	-15.6	8.8	...	27.0	0.0	3.1
Nevada, AR	6 575	70.2	69.1	366	94.5	10.7	-13.7	13.3	5.1	0.0	...	1.2
Newton, AR	5 814	67.6	70.2	156	96.8	11.8	-12.6	11.7	0.0	32.7	...	6.9
Ouachita, AR	18 975	61.4	73.5	965	93.7	12.7	-11.7	15.6	7.2	23.4	41.5	12.0
Perry, AR	6 859	67.6	73.8	257	80.5	11.1	-13.3	10.7	44.3	4.4	62.5	4.8
Phillips, AR	15 420	64.3	62.2	923	87.6	12.4	-12.0	16.6	8.0	0.0	40.5	5.1
Pike, AR	7 653	70.3	68.8	357	94.4	10.1	-14.3	10.1	6.5	20.7	15.4	7.6
Poinsett, AR	16 674	77.5	62.0	678	93.4	6.3	-18.1	6.7	2.2	0.0	0.0	0.0
Polk, AR	13 505	63.6	72.6	711	88.2	10.9	-13.5	11.2	0.0	0.0	24.0	6.3
Pope, AR	34 297	56.1	77.4	3 951	94.0	19.0	-5.4	19.3	14.8	14.1	12.4	12.8
Prairie, AR	6 550	70.6	68.2	167	89.2	9.0	-15.4	9.7	3.6	0.0	0.0	3.8
Pulaski, AR	235 921	42.7	84.4	20 254	85.3	28.1	3.7	32.9	15.5	21.3	47.1	16.2
Randolph, AR	12 207	69.1	69.2	571	94.9	10.6	-13.8	10.6	0.0	0.0	0.0	12.0
St. Francis, AR	18 173	67.6	65.1	1 147	96.8	9.6	-14.8	13.0	6.4	16.7	22.0	0.3
Saline, AR	55 796	55.4	82.3	3 030	85.3	16.4	-8.0	16.4	11.9	13.9	24.0	9.6
Scott, AR	7 141	71.8	65.4	177	88.7	8.4	-16.0	8.6	...	0.0	28.6	0.0
Searcy, AR	5 792	72.6	68.0	208	92.3	8.4	-16.0	8.4	0.0	8.8	11.1	20.8
Sebastian, AR	74 601	54.6	76.6	4 352	90.1	16.6	-7.8	18.3	7.9	15.3	7.0	4.6
Sevier, AR	9 828	69.2	64.6	479	92.7	9.2	-15.2	10.9	4.8	2.8	0.0	1.8
Sharp, AR	12 294	65.4	72.9	391	81.6	10.3	-14.1	10.4	0.0	9.8	7.7	12.2
Stone, AR	8 119	70.4	68.0	263	84.0	9.8	-14.6	9.9	0.0	0.0	100.0	0.0
Union, AR	29 986	61.0	74.5	1 427	91.9	14.9	-9.5	18.5	5.7	2.2	43.7	8.6
Van Buren, AR	11 602	65.2	71.6	363	87.1	11.5	-12.9	11.5	38.5	23.2	0.0	12.1
Washington, AR	94 019	51.0	79.5	16 443	93.0	24.5	0.1	25.3	25.0	13.0	50.6	6.1
White, AR	42 366	62.8	72.9	5 349	39.5	15.5	-8.9	15.8	12.6	2.1	14.4	11.3
Woodruff, AR	5 716	76.1	60.6	229	90.4	8.0	-16.4	8.7	6.4	0.0	0.0	9.7
Yell, AR	13 659	71.6	64.1	439	88.2	10.9	-13.5	12.1	2.7	11.5	1.0	1.2
CALIFORNIA	21 298 900	43.3	76.8	2 556 598	80.3	26.6	2.2	33.8	17.2	11.4	40.9	7.7
Alameda, CA	953 716	36.7	82.4	126 921	81.5	34.9	10.5	42.7	18.8	16.7	45.3	12.7
Alpine, CA	797	37.6	88.3	67	95.5	28.2	3.8	34.1	...	3.0	0.0	8.7
Amador, CA	25 549	46.3	84.0	1 063	71.9	16.6	-7.8	18.0	0.5	14.4	32.9	7.8
Butte, CA	126 736	42.1	02.3	25 780	96.2	21.8	-2.6	23.2	14.6	10.5	25.6	11.7
Calaveras, CA	29 201	42.9	85.7	1 426	82.3	17.1	-7.3	17.9	25.2	7.4	54.7	5.5
Colusa, CA	10 912	60.1	64.0	722	89.6	10.6	-13.8	16.5	0.0	6.0	10.0	2.3
Contra Costa, CA	625 641	32.9	86.9	61 975	78.2	35.0	10.6	40.1	18.3	17.7	48.0	12.5
Del Norte, CA	18 459	55.8	71.6	1 127	92.0	11.0	-13.4	13.2	1.3	6.0	12.5	4.2
El Dorado, CA	105 034	33.1	89.1	9 288	88.8	26.5	2.1	27.6	50.6	11.9	35.5	10.7
Fresno, CA	455 540	53.6	67.5	54 663	86.9	17.5	-6.9	26.2	11.8	7.5	24.5	5.6
Glenn, CA	16 099	58.3	68.5	1 058	91.8	10.7	-13.7	12.8	11.0	6.7	9.6	2.8
Humboldt, CA	81 501	40.8	84.9	13 891	96.3	23.0	-1.4	24.2	11.4	12.4	28.9	15.4
Imperial, CA	83 632	62.9	59.0	8 705	93.1	10.3	-14.1	19.7	4.5	5.4	30.7	6.4
Inyo, CA	12 566	49.0	82.3	546	83.3	17.1	-7.3	20.0	0.0	4.1	20.9	3.0
Kern, CA	383 667	56.9	68.5	34 561	86.5	13.5	-10.9	18.6	7.4	6.9	28.0	3.7
Kings, CA	77 095	60.1	68.8	6 475	84.0	10.4	-14.0	16.7	3.3	4.0	21.1	3.3
Lake, CA	40 717	52.5	77.3	2 295	89.2	12.1	-12.3	12.9	5.8	1.8	31.2	5.0
Lassen, CA	22 963	51.2	79.6	2 013	89.2	10.7	-13.7	13.9	0.3	3.0	13.3	2.2
Los Angeles, CA	5 882 948	48.9	69.9	730 314	76.1	24.9	0.5	37.7	17.8	11.6	42.4	6.8
Madera, CA	74 830	59.9	65.4	5 995	84.4	12.0	-12.4	17.2	7.2	9.3	27.6	3.7
Marin, CA	183 694	21.2	91.2	14 513	72.1	51.3	26.9	56.0	16.8	26.2	54.7	18.1
Mariposa, CA	12 196	41.2	85.1	819	85.8	20.2	-4.2	20.8	51.6	7.8	25.4	19.6
Mendocino, CA	56 886	45.2	80.8	4 500	90.5	20.2	-4.2	22.6	14.7	4.9	35.5	7.1
Merced, CA	116 725	60.1	63.8	11 077	91.0	11.0	-13.4	16.6	11.1	7.4	13.2	3.5
Modoc, CA	6 464	52.3	77.1	192	97.9	12.4	-12.0	13.4	0.0	0.0	7.1	11.4
Mono, CA	8 674	32.7	87.9	601	83.2	28.9	4.5	32.8	58.3	12.2	46.8	4.9
Monterey, CA	244 128	50.1	68.4	24 295	82.3	22.5	-1.9	36.4	11.3	8.7	26.5	4.6
Napa, CA	83 938	40.1	80.4	7 765	71.5	26.4	2.0	30.5	11.3	12.1	40.0	7.4
Nevada, CA	65 148	33.5	90.3	4 524	88.7	26.1	1.7	26.8	37.2	14.1	23.8	15.0
Orange, CA	1 813 456	38.0	79.5	230 749	82.4	30.8	6.4	37.6	27.6	13.3	40.9	8.5
Placer, CA	165 894	30.8	90.5	14 728	85.1	30.3	5.9	31.1	39.4	20.3	45.4	15.7
Plumas, CA	14 786	39.7	88.0	922	90.5	17.5	-6.9	18.2	5.2	2.2	32.3	3.9
Riverside, CA	936 024	49.7	75.0	88 703	81.6	16.6	-7.8	20.7	15.1	9.5	36.7	5.8
Sacramento, CA	772 488	39.6	83.3	93 272	86.4	24.8	0.4	28.2	15.4	13.6	29.7	12.0
San Benito, CA	31 401	48.3	74.9	2 570	88.3	17.1	-7.3	25.5	16.3	15.5	27.3	5.6
San Bernardino, CA	983 273	50.8	74.2	108 262	79.3	15.9	-8.5	19.2	14.8	9.0	42.0	6.4
San Diego, CA	1 773 327	37.3	82.6	242 117	81.8	29.5	5.1	36.1	16.3	13.8	36.0	10.7
San Francisco, CA	595 805	32.7	81.2	85 159	74.0	45.0	20.6	63.2	18.1	28.0	31.6	20.3
San Joaquin, CA	333 572	54.0	71.2	33 087	75.1	14.5	-9.9	18.2	9.7	6.4	20.7	5.3
San Luis Obispo, CA	159 196	36.2	85.6	31 338	94.4	26.7	2.3	29.8	7.6	11.6	34.1	8.9

[3]May be of any race.
. . . = Not available.

Table C-1. Population, School, and Student Characteristics by County—*Continued*

STATE County	State/county code	County type[1]	Population, 2005 Total	Percent 5 to 17 years	Number of schools and students, 2004–2005 School districts	Schools	Students	Resident enrollment, 2000 Total	Percent public	K–12	Percent public
			1	2	3	4	5	6	7	8	9
San Mateo, CA	06081	1	699 610	16.4	25	174	88 273	184 928	77.1	121 187	81.6
Santa Barbara, CA	06083	2	400 762	17.7	25	123	67 551	127 198	86.6	74 970	92.2
Santa Clara, CA	06085	1	1 699 052	17.4	35	394	253 065	476 333	80.1	305 563	87.5
Santa Cruz, CA	06087	2	249 666	16.3	13	46	19 459	76 840	86.9	46 143	88.6
Shasta, CA	06089	3	179 904	17.9	27	103	29 455	45 010	88.2	33 592	91.8
Sierra, CA	06091	8	3 434	16.8	3	12	609	875	95.4	699	98.6
Siskiyou, CA	06093	7	45 259	16.3	32	68	7 497	11 200	92.9	8 563	95.0
Solano, CA	06095	2	411 593	20.5	9	115	73 968	116 471	87.1	85 648	90.9
Sonoma, CA	06097	2	466 477	17.5	43	184	72 949	125 553	86.4	86 107	89.9
Stanislaus, CA	06099	2	505 505	21.9	30	175	106 043	136 838	90.8	106 277	93.2
Sutter, CA	06101	3	88 876	19.9	14	44	17 435	22 869	92.2	17 600	94.8
Tehama, CA	06103	4	61 197	19.2	20	48	11 075	15 427	94.2	12 146	95.7
Trinity, CA	06105	8	13 622	15.6	11	20	1 829	3 112	94.8	2 548	95.1
Tulare, CA	06107	2	410 874	23.3	49	177	92 126	118 065	93.4	94 339	95.7
Tuolumne, CA	06109	4	59 380	13.9	13	43	7 669	13 347	89.5	9 741	90.2
Ventura, CA	06111	2	796 106	20.1	22	202	140 879	224 449	85.5	162 520	90.3
Yolo, CA	06113	1	184 932	17.6	7	62	29 429	64 875	92.0	32 000	92.9
Yuba, CA	06115	3	67 153	21.7	6	40	15 031	18 858	93.6	14 106	95.1
COLORADO	08000		4 665 177	18.0	200	1 693	765 976	1 166 004	86.1	804 108	91.2
Adams, CO	08001	1	399 426	20.4	10	319	175 341	90 893	89.3	69 858	93.6
Alamosa, CO	08003	7	15 282	19.0	3	8	2 588	5 251	91.8	3 079	91.9
Arapahoe, CO	08005	1	529 090	18.9	6	95	70 460	134 175	84.5	97 404	91.0
Archuleta, CO	08007	7	11 886	16.2	1	5	1 577	2 222	87.8	1 975	90.7
Baca, CO	08009	9	4 069	16.9	5	13	1 145	1 117	95.6	909	96.1
Bent, CO	08011	7	5 558	16.5	2	8	877	1 547	94.4	1 197	95.2
Boulder, CO	08013	2	280 440	15.9	[4]2	[4]54	[4]28 049	83 834	85.8	44 218	89.5
Broomfield, CO	08014	1	43 478	20.4	(4)	(4)	(4)	11 520	84.7	8 317	90.9
Chaffee, CO	08015	7	16 968	13.5	2	7	2 152	3 408	83.3	2 620	87.4
Cheyenne, CO	08017	9	1 953	20.5	2	5	372	606	96.9	508	97.2
Clear Creek, CO	08019	1	9 197	15.9	2	5	1 154	2 042	86.5	1 570	92.4
Conejos, CO	08021	9	8 512	22.1	4	13	2 140	2 611	98.0	2 119	98.8
Costilla, CO	08023	9	3 424	17.1	1	3	294	908	94.2	733	96.5
Crowley, CO	08025	8	5 401	13.1	1	3	579	1 362	89.3	930	88.1
Custer, CO	08027	8	3 860	15.3	1	3	527	687	87.3	579	87.7
Delta, CO	08029	6	29 947	16.8	1	14	5 141	5 975	87.7	5 042	89.1
Denver, CO	08031	1	557 917	15.2	2	1	334	130 485	80.6	83 908	88.2
Dolores, CO	08033	9	1 827	15.4	1	3	270	365	93.2	312	93.9
Douglas, CO	08035	1	249 416	21.1	1	63	44 761	51 934	80.4	37 565	90.0
Eagle, CO	08037	5	47 530	15.7	1	16	5 157	9 194	85.7	6 782	91.7
Elbert, CO	08039	1	22 788	20.5	5	18	3 985	5 926	87.9	4 876	92.2
El Paso, CO	08041	2	565 582	19.5	17	198	101 060	146 429	83.8	103 247	90.9
Fremont, CO	08043	4	47 766	14.8	3	18	6 218	10 309	87.4	7 865	90.2
Garfield, CO	08045	5	49 810	18.7	3	24	9 872	10 894	89.2	8 442	93.1
Gilpin, CO	08047	1	4 932	14.2	1	2	388	1 027	83.2	732	90.6
Grand, CO	08049	8	13 211	14.8	2	9	1 824	2 475	90.3	2 038	94.7
Gunnison, CO	08051	7	14 226	11.8	1	7	1 604	4 697	92.0	1 918	94.0
Hinsdale, CO	08053	9	765	14.2	1	1	83	138	78.3	111	82.0
Huerfano, CO	08055	6	7 771	14.2	2	7	974	1 747	83.3	1 349	84.7
Jackson, CO	08057	9	1 448	16.5	1	2	263	367	94.3	303	93.1
Jefferson, CO	08059	1	526 801	18.2	1	167	86 868	141 368	84.0	100 009	89.5
Kiowa, CO	08061	9	1 422	16.7	2	5	263	425	98.8	341	100.0
Kit Carson, CO	08063	7	7 642	19.2	5	13	1 562	2 120	93.8	1 743	96.2
Lake, CO	08065	7	7 738	19.6	2	7	1 341	2 047	95.7	1 521	98.9
La Plata, CO	08067	6	47 452	15.2	4	19	6 575	13 191	89.7	7 778	91.5
Larimer, CO	08069	2	271 927	16.5	4	85	41 221	80 102	89.3	44 334	90.9
Las Animas, CO	08071	7	15 446	17.2	6	16	3 319	3 954	91.0	2 816	89.6
Lincoln, CO	08073	8	5 618	16.4	4	8	942	1 595	88.7	1 323	88.9
Logan, CO	08075	7	20 719	17.7	4	15	3 317	5 725	90.8	4 078	91.6
Mesa, CO	08077	3	129 872	17.2	4	45	20 806	29 470	89.3	21 719	91.9
Mineral, CO	08079	9	932	13.5	1	2	158	178	96.6	138	98.6
Moffat, CO	08081	7	13 417	19.5	1	9	2 402	3 639	93.0	2 835	94.3
Montezuma, CO	08083	6	24 778	19.1	4	20	4 535	5 872	94.3	4 789	96.2
Montrose, CO	08085	7	37 482	18.2	2	18	6 198	7 732	91.9	6 780	93.4
Morgan, CO	08087	6	27 995	21.4	5	17	5 639	7 075	94.1	5 760	96.1
Otero, CO	08089	6	19 495	18.9	7	19	3 598	5 382	94.7	4 069	95.7
Ouray, CO	08091	9	4 260	16.3	2	6	595	779	94.4	664	97.6
Park, CO	08093	1	16 949	16.5	2	8	2 010	3 289	87.0	2 589	91.3
Phillips, CO	08095	9	4 586	20.0	3	4	948	1 133	94.4	905	96.7
Pitkin, CO	08097	7	14 914	10.9	1	5	1 604	2 799	81.6	1 922	91.7
Prowers, CO	08099	7	13 892	21.2	5	14	2 733	4 102	97.3	3 164	98.1
Pueblo, CO	08101	3	151 322	18.4	3	63	25 785	37 564	91.6	27 023	94.1
Rio Blanco, CO	08103	9	5 973	17.5	3	6	1 154	1 726	97.3	1 269	98.0
Rio Grande, CO	08105	7	12 227	18.8	3	12	2 371	3 385	93.7	2 585	95.4
Routt, CO	08107	7	21 313	15.1	4	12	2 854	4 656	88.0	3 316	91.5
Saguache, CO	08109	9	7 031	19.4	3	11	1 034	1 558	92.6	1 277	93.9
San Juan, CO	08111	9	577	11.4	1	3	54	111	93.7	88	95.5
San Miguel, CO	08113	9	7 213	11.9	3	5	853	1 155	81.6	873	89.9
Sedgwick, CO	08115	9	2 529	16.8	2	4	434	601	96.0	488	96.9
Summit, CO	08117	7	24 892	11.4	1	8	2 909	4 229	88.2	2 878	92.6

[1]County type codes are from the Economic Research Service of the United States Department of Agriculture. See notes and definitions at the end of this section.
[4]Broomfield County is included with Boulder County.

Table C-1. Population, School, and Student Characteristics by County—*Continued*

STATE County	Characteristics of students, 2004–2005				Outcomes		Staff and students, 2004–2005		
	Percent with IEP[2]	Percent eligible for free or reduced-price lunch	Percent minority	Percent English-language learners	Number of graduates, 2003–2004	Percent dropouts, grades 9–12, 2001–2002	Number of teachers	Student-teacher ratio	Central administration staff
	10	11	12	13	14	15	16	17	18
San Mateo, CA	11.3	29.2	64.1	22.5	. . .	. . .	4 534	19.5	. . .
Santa Barbara, CA	10.8	44.6	64.1	27.9	. . .	. . .	3 240	20.9	. . .
Santa Clara, CA	10.6	33.4	70.6	25.6	. . .	. . .	12 329	20.5	. . .
Santa Cruz, CA	12.8	40.3	54.0	10.1	. . .	. . .	922	21.1	. . .
Shasta, CA	10.9	43.8	19.6	2.6	. . .	. . .	1 466	20.1	. . .
Sierra, CA	12.0	34.6	15.2	2.3	. . .	. . .	47	13.0	. . .
Siskiyou, CA	10.3	48.1	25.6	4.9	. . .	. . .	458	16.4	. . .
Solano, CA	11.6	33.2	62.1	12.1	. . .	. . .	3 518	21.0	. . .
Sonoma, CA	13.0	29.3	39.1	21.0	. . .	. . .	3 622	20.1	. . .
Stanislaus, CA	12.3	50.5	58.0	23.0	. . .	. . .	5 021	21.1	. . .
Sutter, CA	11.6	49.2	49.9	18.7	. . .	. . .	859	20.3	. . .
Tehama, CA	9.4	53.8	31.8	13.0	. . .	. . .	567	19.5	. . .
Trinity, CA	17.6	54.4	17.7	0.9	. . .	. . .	125	14.6	21
Tulare, CA	7.7	67.2	73.1	28.8	. . .	. . .	4 397	21.0	. . .
Tuolumne, CA	12.0	35.6	15.4	1.0	. . .	. . .	406	18.9	50
Ventura, CA	10.7	36.7	56.5	21.6	. . .	. . .	6 343	22.2	. . .
Yolo, CA	11.0	39.3	53.0	21.9	. . .	. . .	1 467	20.1	. . .
Yuba, CA	12.3	62.3	48.5	16.3	. . .	. . .	808	18.6	93
COLORADO	10.8	31.5	36.5	11.8	. . .	. . .	45 165	17.0	. . .
Adams, CO	11.5	40.6	52.9	27.7	. . .	. . .	9 589	18.3	1 257
Alamosa, CO	12.0	59.3	55.4	9.9	. . .	. . .	177	14.6	25
Arapahoe, CO	11.2	25.9	40.3	5.6	4 827	. . .	4 141	17.0	390
Archuleta, CO	10.2	39.8	24.7	2.0	130	. . .	100	15.8	9
Baca, CO	9.1	43.3	23.3	4.2	96	. . .	85	13.5	14
Bent, CO	12.7	60.2	39.3	2.5	55	. . .	70	12.5	7
Boulder, CO	[4]11.8	18.0	25.9	[4]9.6	[4]1 979	. . .	[4]1 697	[4]16.5	[4]198
Broomfield, CO	([4])	11.8	20.7	([4])	([4])	. . .	([4])	([4])	([4])
Chaffee, CO	11.0	32.3	10.8	0.9	147	. . .	150	14.4	15
Cheyenne, CO	11.3	39.2	15.9	3.5	35	. . .	45	8.3	3
Clear Creek, CO	14.0	22.0	9.1	0.3	. . .	. . .	72	16.1	10
Conejos, CO	7.9	70.1	62.2	0.6	177	. . .	155	13.8	21
Costilla, CO	10.2	77.6	73.1	20.7	15	. . .	24	12.5	6
Crowley, CO	11.7	63.2	33.3	0.2	36	. . .	41	14.0	2
Custer, CO	11.4	26.9	5.7	0.0	44	. . .	38	13.7	6
Delta, OO	12.4	41.4	10.6	8.4	327	. . .	288	17.0	24
Denver, CO	10.2	61.1	80.3	0.0	. . .	. . .	21	15.9	7
Dolores, CO	11.1	34.8	10.7	0.0	25	. . .	25	10.7	4
Douglas, CO	8.8	3.5	12.9	2.7	2 146	. . .	2 460	18.2	231
Eagle, CO	9.5	25.4	45.3	31.3	281	. . .	364	14.2	29
Elbert, CO	10.3	11.2	9.7	0.4	273	. . .	258	15.4	27
El Paso, CO	9.8	27.4	31.0	4.1	. . .	. . .	6 158	16.4	. . .
Fremont, CO	15.7	37.5	12.2	0.4	429	. . .	385	16.2	43
Garfield, CO	8.5	33.2	34.3	23.7	519	. . .	612	16.1	57
Gilpin, CO	12.6	15.5	8.0	1.3	25	. . .	32	12.1	5
Grand, CO	11.2	20.2	10.4	6.6	136	. . .	138	13.2	10
Gunnison, CO	7.4	15.1	13.5	3.5	111	. . .	119	13.5	5
Hinsdale, CO	4.8	28.9	3.6	0.0	2	. . .	10	8.2	2
Huerfano, CO	9.2	57.2	49.3	0.6	55	. . .	71	13.7	8
Jackson, CO	19.0	44.9	16.7	3.4	23	. . .	21	12.8	2
Jefferson, CO	10.5	19.6	22.9	5.2	5 849	. . .	4 641	18.7	470
Kiowa, CO	10.6	39.9	10.6	2.3	28	. . .	29	9.0	5
Kit Carson, CO	9.2	46.4	23.9	13.1	114	. . .	124	12.6	16
Lake, CO	16.8	51.3	63.7	31.9	78	. . .	98	13.7	25
La Plata, CO	10.4	23.7	22.6	2.6	. . .	. . .	456	14.4	62
Larimer, CO	10.5	22.8	18.9	6.8	. . .	. . .	2 422	17.0	254
Las Animas, CO	10.4	39.9	46.4	1.1	158	. . .	215	15.5	27
Lincoln, CO	16.3	35.4	12.3	4.4	60	. . .	79	11.9	18
Logan, CO	13.8	37.8	17.7	3.5	229	. . .	234	14.2	26
Mesa, CO	12.0	40.2	20.0	2.8	. . .	. . .	1 213	17.2	143
Mineral, CO	5.7	21.5	6.3	0.0	12	. . .	18	8.8	3
Moffat, CO	12.1	25.6	14.9	5.0	150	. . .	146	16.5	18
Montezuma, CO	12.8	47.7	35.3	26.1	260	. . .	294	15.4	33
Montrose, CO	11.6	43.4	28.5	10.6	367	. . .	379	16.3	25
Morgan, CO	9.7	52.8	47.0	18.5	. . .	. . .	374	15.1	55
Otero, CO	11.5	55.2	51.1	4.1	239	. . .	285	12.6	36
Ouray, CO	9.7	18.5	10.3	3.2	23	. . .	50	11.8	9
Park, CO	11.7	22.9	9.0	0.7	137	. . .	125	16.1	19
Phillips, CO	12.7	34.8	23.4	6.3	. . .	. . .	74	12.8	13
Pitkin, CO	5.4	2.0	15.7	12.0	93	. . .	128	12.6	11
Prowers, CO	10.8	55.0	45.5	11.5	. . .	. . .	201	13.6	32
Pueblo, CO	11.3	53.1	52.0	4.0	. . .	. . .	1 533	16.8	133
Rio Blanco, CO	14.9	24.2	10.1	1.7	. . .	. . .	72	16.1	11
Rio Grande, CO	10.4	53.9	55.0	8.0	167	. . .	168	14.1	14
Routt, CO	14.7	10.9	6.6	1.4	. . .	. . .	202	14.1	21
Saguache, CO	9.7	73.1	67.8	24.1	69	. . .	96	10.8	16
San Juan, CO	14.8	68.5	33.3	14.8	6	. . .	7	8.3	3
San Miguel, CO	10.3	17.5	10.7	7.3	. . .	. . .	74	11.5	9
Sedgwick, CO	15.4	44.0	23.3	2.1	27	. . .	38	11.5	3
Summit, CO	8.9	21.1	22.2	18.6	135	. . .	211	13.8	16

2IEP = Individual Education Program. See notes and definitions at the end of this section.
4Broomfield County is included with Boulder County.
 . . . = Not available.

Table C-1. Population, School, and Student Characteristics by County—*Continued*

STATE County	Revenue, 2003–2004				Current expenditures, 2003–2004			Resident population, 16 to 19 years, 2000			
	Total revenue (thousands of dollars)	Percent of revenue from:			Total expenditures (thousands of dollars)	Amount per student (dollars)	Percent for instruction	Total	Percent in armed forces	Percent high school graduates	Percent not enrolled, not employed, not in armed forces, not high school graduate
		Federal government	State government	Local government							
	19	20	21	22	23	24	25	26	27	28	29
San Mateo, CA	930 157	6.8	18.6	74.6	764 160	8 637	66.6	32 251	0.0	7.4	4.4
Santa Barbara, CA	594 881	11.0	40.4	48.5	514 203	7 616	68.7	26 449	0.3	7.3	4.2
Santa Clara, CA	2 583 947	8.9	24.6	66.5	2 048 894	8 137	67.4	85 189	0.0	7.9	4.5
Santa Cruz, CA	420 958	11.3	46.0	42.8	326 507	8 351	64.7	15 913	0.0	8.1	4.6
Shasta, CA	326 747	14.0	50.4	35.6	248 824	8 381	63.4	9 897	0.0	10.3	4.1
Sierra, CA	9 962	21.6	48.1	30.4	8 819	13 505	55.7	206	0.0	19.9	0.0
Siskiyou, CA	80 380	20.3	46.2	33.6	67 375	9 971	61.8	2 597	0.0	9.5	3.6
Solano, CA	626 026	8.5	57.0	34.6	516 394	7 198	67.4	22 795	1.8	12.8	4.2
Sonoma, CA	728 534	5.8	34.6	59.6	586 238	8 053	68.0	25 183	0.5	11.3	4.5
Stanislaus, CA	1 066 419	12.2	55.4	32.4	819 084	7 823	70.1	28 694	0.0	12.5	6.4
Sutter, CA	166 485	10.9	61.3	27.8	126 039	7 425	64.0	4 725	0.0	11.7	5.8
Tehama, CA	111 456	14.2	54.3	31.5	94 564	8 645	66.8	3 288	0.0	12.3	3.2
Trinity, CA	32 772	26.9	51.2	21.9	25 927	12 647	59.4	628	0.0	10.4	2.5
Tulare, CA	893 480	17.1	61.7	21.2	713 927	7 912	66.4	25 935	0.0	10.0	7.5
Tuolumne, CA	80 666	10.4	49.2	40.4	65 159	8 657	62.1	2 911	0.0	10.3	4.6
Ventura, CA	1 298 455	9.0	52.1	38.9	1 039 674	7 168	66.7	43 659	0.8	9.5	4.6
Yolo, CA	291 532	9.2	52.1	38.7	214 265	7 308	65.0	14 269	0.0	6.5	3.0
Yuba, CA	165 949	15.3	62.1	22.5	117 167	7 924	64.2	3 927	3.6	13.0	6.7
COLORADO	6 527 456	6.7	43.4	49.9	5 613 532	7 422	62.6	243 396	0.9	12.4	5.9
Adams, CO	572 572	6.7	51.2	42.1	471 262	6 951	65.3	19 823	0.1	15.6	10.0
Alamosa, CO	27 436	24.2	47.5	28.3	25 077	8 991	63.2	1 396	0.0	10.7	6.9
Arapahoe, CO	870 873	4.9	45.0	50.1	744 630	7 279	65.6	26 415	0.3	12.8	4.3
Archuleta, CO	12 410	5.9	37.7	56.4	11 150	7 180	58.0	543	0.0	11.0	5.5
Baca, CO	10 752	9.5	65.0	25.5	9 146	8 292	55.1	277	0.0	7.6	1.4
Bent, CO	8 217	9.5	60.5	30.1	7 021	8 173	63.5	306	0.0	11.4	5.9
Boulder, CO	[4]433 174	45.4	[4]29.4	[4]65.2	[4]362 138	[4]7 301	[4]66.4	16 997	0.0	7.8	3.1
Broomfield, CO	([4])	([4])	([4])	([4])	([4])	([4])	([4])	2 052	0.0	12.4	2.0
Chaffee, CO	19 884	7.4	39.9	52.7	17 332	8 058	61.4	798	0.0	14.3	4.8
Cheyenne, CO	6 865	10.4	36.6	53.0	4 354	11 611	58.4	155	0.0	3.9	6.5
Clear Creek, CO	13 288	6.0	27.1	66.9	9 631	7 920	62.2	447	0.0	9.8	3.8
Conejos, CO	15 817	8.5	77.1	14.3	13 525	7 111	63.5	619	0.0	9.2	4.7
Costilla, CO	6 560	15.3	39.5	45.1	6 279	13 532	55.1	245	0.8	19.2	9.8
Crowley, CO	4 572	8.1	71.5	20.4	4 344	7 204	60.9	231	0.0	12.1	5.6
Custer, CO	4 184	4.5	29.7	65.8	3 677	7 458	62.3	127	0.0	5.5	6.3
Delta, CO	42 270	7.7	56.5	35.7	34 775	6 836	64.0	1 402	0.0	13.0	5.5
Denver, CO	683 682	10.1	32.7	57.2	567 118	7 866	61.3	26 299	0.0	13.3	12.6
Dolores, CO	3 313	4.7	49.3	46.0	2 870	10 250	57.0	88	0.0	12.5	1.1
Douglas, CO	361 758	1.8	38.8	59.4	311 994	7 442	62.7	7 620	0.0	7.7	2.0
Eagle, CO	52 978	3.6	10.6	85.8	44 793	8 840	58.9	1 872	0.0	9.4	13.5
Elbert, CO	33 726	2.7	59.6	37.6	27 372	6 745	58.8	1 308	0.0	7.0	4.4
El Paso, CO	811 573	7.7	51.4	41.0	718 567	7 247	62.4	30 763	6.7	18.6	5.0
Fremont, CO	48 396	8.3	56.6	35.1	41 800	6 627	63.4	2 245	0.0	9.4	6.4
Garfield, CO	80 712	4.8	38.4	56.8	63 374	6 541	63.3	2 408	0.3	14.4	6.3
Gilpin, CO	6 095	1.1	26.8	72.1	3 391	8 055	55.5	186	0.0	9.7	0.0
Grand, CO	18 871	2.9	17.9	79.2	15 289	8 269	66.3	627	0.0	20.1	1.0
Gunnison, CO	14 339	4.5	16.1	79.3	11 741	7 155	64.4	1 116	0.0	7.9	0.4
Hinsdale, CO	1 301	11.4	26.7	62.0	1 081	12 718	63.0	30	0.0	6.7	0.0
Huerfano, CO	10 574	16.3	43.1	40.6	7 610	7 695	58.2	348	0.0	11.8	4.9
Jackson, CO	2 801	2.1	44.4	53.5	2 645	9 480	58.1	99	0.0	11.1	3.0
Jefferson, CO	728 636	4.5	42.8	52.7	683 352	7 839	57.5	28 286	0.0	10.9	3.6
Kiowa, CO	3 583	10.5	55.4	34.1	2 802	10 301	59.6	119	0.0	7.6	0.0
Kit Carson, CO	16 993	4.0	50.6	45.4	13 130	8 433	62.0	464	0.0	8.0	3.0
Lake, CO	18 572	22.7	38.4	38.9	14 747	12 238	61.6	468	0.0	12.4	9.0
La Plata, CO	67 651	6.5	32.9	60.6	52 937	8 055	62.3	3 309	0.0	9.9	3.3
Larimer, CO	342 526	5.7	39.3	55.0	312 163	7 573	59.6	17 029	0.1	9.2	2.9
Las Animas, CO	27 706	6.2	67.8	26.0	22 688	6 748	62.3	875	0.0	9.6	8.6
Lincoln, CO	14 585	24.9	42.6	32.6	11 589	12 161	62.7	367	0.0	7.1	4.9
Logan, CO	27 585	8.7	60.3	31.0	24 144	7 035	63.4	1 477	0.0	11.8	3.0
Mesa, CO	156 725	8.1	52.6	39.3	142 169	6 813	63.6	7 200	0.0	13.8	6.9
Mineral, CO	2 172	2.4	57.1	40.5	1 766	9 977	67.3	31	0.0	0.0	0.0
Moffat, CO	18 968	6.4	22.4	71.3	18 438	7 355	65.2	830	0.0	15.4	12.7
Montezuma, CO	36 533	12.9	52.7	34.4	31 883	7 017	62.8	1 337	0.0	14.7	5.9
Montrose, CO	46 344	11.1	54.6	34.3	43 632	7 251	61.9	1 904	0.0	15.1	8.2
Morgan, CO	48 533	11.9	46.6	41.5	38 901	6 819	62.2	1 682	0.0	10.0	8.4
Otero, CO	37 064	10.9	64.8	24.3	30 688	8 494	62.0	1 281	0.0	11.5	5.3
Ouray, CO	7 117	3.8	38.7	57.6	5 316	9 294	61.5	161	0.0	1.2	0.0
Park, CO	17 955	3.1	37.8	59.0	15 086	7 370	58.4	710	0.0	10.4	1.3
Phillips, CO	12 525	20.0	38.4	41.5	10 090	10 689	60.2	240	0.0	10.4	0.0
Pitkin, CO	21 543	0.5	14.0	85.5	16 775	10 795	67.1	516	0.0	8.5	3.1
Prowers, CO	27 118	11.9	62.2	26.0	22 670	8 025	63.6	997	0.7	8.0	8.5
Pueblo, CO	204 895	11.4	57.3	31.3	180 744	7 022	62.4	8 387	0.0	9.9	8.6
Rio Blanco, CO	13 072	7.1	38.5	54.4	10 642	8 824	60.2	531	0.0	10.5	5.3
Rio Grande, CO	20 961	8.7	61.2	30.1	17 160	7 165	62.6	687	0.0	10.8	6.3
Routt, CO	35 253	5.6	11.9	82.5	28 476	10 006	60.0	979	0.0	14.6	1.3
Saguache, CO	11 844	12.9	60.9	26.1	9 181	8 702	64.4	392	0.0	9.9	8.9
San Juan, CO	1 188	16.6	30.4	53.0	851	12 894	53.5	31	0.0	0.0	0.0
San Miguel, CO	13 391	4.8	22.6	72.7	8 944	10 292	63.5	263	0.0	16.3	4.2
Sedgwick, CO	4 583	1.8	61.1	37.0	3 700	7 806	62.6	133	0.0	14.3	0.0
Summit, CO	40 186	1.4	6.1	92.5	26 682	9 432	64.6	912	0.0	32.9	3.0

[4]Broomfield County is included with Boulder County.

Table C-1. Population, School, and Student Characteristics by County—*Continued*

STATE County	Population 25 years and over	High school graduate or less (percent)	High school graduate or more (percent)	College enrollment, 2000 Number	Percent public	Bachelor's degree or more	+/- U.S. percentage with bachelor's degree or more	Non-Hispanic White	Black	American Indian and Alaska Native	Asian or Pacific Islander	Hispanic[3]
	30	31	32	33	34	35	36	37	38	39	40	41
San Mateo, CA	490 285	32.2	85.3	51 250	76.4	39.0	14.6	45.2	20.0	20.4	48.3	12.3
Santa Barbara, CA	246 729	39.8	79.2	46 317	81.7	29.4	5.0	38.9	16.9	12.3	37.1	7.0
Santa Clara, CA	1 113 058	32.5	83.4	141 601	72.5	40.5	16.1	47.1	29.7	16.3	50.9	11.0
Santa Cruz, CA	164 999	33.3	83.2	27 005	89.5	34.2	9.8	41.0	22.7	18.1	40.7	9.3
Shasta, CA	107 272	44.4	83.3	8 952	81.3	16.6	-7.8	17.2	12.7	5.4	17.3	10.8
Sierra, CA	2 540	43.5	85.2	124	96.0	17.2	-7.2	18.0	. . .	8.3	100.0	5.9
Siskiyou, CA	30 682	44.4	83.8	2 109	90.9	17.7	-6.7	19.2	5.0	7.2	10.5	6.7
Solano, CA	246 488	40.7	83.8	24 612	81.6	21.4	-3.0	23.9	14.7	8.2	31.1	9.8
Sonoma, CA	306 564	35.5	84.9	32 351	86.5	28.5	4.1	31.7	21.6	10.6	35.3	9.6
Stanislaus, CA	264 578	55.7	70.4	24 120	87.9	14.1	-10.3	17.2	14.7	7.4	21.0	5.1
Sutter, CA	49 071	50.6	73.0	4 072	87.7	15.3	-9.1	17.3	12.6	11.3	19.2	5.3
Tehama, CA	36 261	55.1	75.7	2 501	93.2	11.3	-13.1	12.5	10.0	6.9	38.5	2.4
Trinity, CA	9 433	48.6	81.0	441	92.5	15.5	-8.9	16.6	0.0	1.4	6.8	5.5
Tulare, CA	204 888	61.3	61.7	17 959	87.5	11.5	-12.9	17.5	6.7	4.6	18.4	3.6
Tuolumne, CA	38 977	45.4	84.3	2 825	91.3	16.1	-8.3	17.4	2.5	5.3	46.5	4.8
Ventura, CA	471 756	39.6	80.1	48 445	81.6	26.9	2.5	33.3	27.1	15.1	46.3	7.6
Yolo, CA	95 423	40.0	79.8	30 104	95.1	34.1	9.7	40.7	22.3	14.2	55.3	9.6
Yuba, CA	35 218	55.4	71.8	3 732	90.6	10.3	-14.1	11.6	14.6	4.5	10.2	3.7
COLORADO	2 776 632	36.3	86.9	282 832	80.2	32.7	8.3	37.0	20.5	14.1	41.9	10.4
Adams, CO	213 699	52.9	78.2	14 816	77.2	16.8	-7.6	20.2	16.2	6.2	22.7	6.5
Alamosa, CO	8 567	44.5	82.6	1 945	94.8	27.0	2.6	33.8	42.6	13.8	40.5	16.4
Arapahoe, CO	316 560	29.9	90.7	27 529	73.6	37.0	12.6	40.7	24.5	19.5	40.1	15.2
Archuleta, CO	6 821	39.5	87.3	141	82.3	29.0	4.6	32.2	0.0	14.1	33.3	9.7
Baca, CO	3 152	55.8	78.5	112	87.5	14.0	-10.4	14.6	. . .	13.2	71.4	3.4
Bent, CO	4 037	57.9	77.2	232	88.8	11.5	-12.9	15.8	2.5	0.0	21.9	1.3
Boulder, CO	172 247	22.0	92.8	34 400	88.8	53.2	28.8	56.2	42.5	29.6	66.0	18.2
Broomfield, CO	24 316	27.9	93.1	2 242	90.5	37.9	13.5	38.8	66.7	29.0	47.5	21.5
Chaffee, CO	11 837	41.4	88.5	507	82.4	24.3	-0.1	26.4	0.0	8.4	40.0	7.3
Cheyenne, CO	1 431	50.7	84.1	51	90.2	14.2	-10.2	14.6	. . .	0.0	. . .	8.3
Clear Creek, CO	6 702	28.1	93.4	300	71.0	38.8	14.4	39.7	0.0	20.4	32.6	14.5
Conejos, CO	4 979	61.8	72.1	320	95.3	14.4	-10.0	22.5	0.0	1.0	33.3	9.1
Costilla, CO	2 506	59.2	68.2	100	73.0	12.8	-11.6	23.0	0.0	16.7	16.3	7.3
Crowley, CO	3 897	57.0	77.5	370	95.9	11.9	-12.5	16.7	0.0	1.1	9.1	1.6
Custer, CO	2 548	37.8	90.3	63	79.4	26.7	2.3	27.4	0.0	0.0	. . .	22.6
Delta, CO	19 330	53.9	90.1	638	80.4	17.0	-6.8	19.0	0.0	15.4	23.6	3.9
Denver, CO	374 478	41.1	78.9	38 309	67.5	34.5	10.1	47.8	17.8	13.7	40.3	7.8
Dolores, CO	1 323	57.2	76.0	33	90.9	13.5	-10.9	13.8	. . .	0.0	57.1	15.0
Douglas, CO	112 436	16.2	97.0	8 719	69.8	51.9	27.5	52.4	57.0	36.9	59.0	37.6
Eagle, CO	27 178	29.9	86.6	1 625	80.1	42.6	18.2	51.0	14.3	23.5	47.8	6.7
Elbert, CO	12 814	34.9	92.5	655	67.5	26.6	2.2	26.7	25.9	31.3	66.7	17.4
El Paso, CO	320 420	31.6	91.3	33 737	70.2	31.8	7.4	34.9	19.0	13.3	33.7	14.1
Fremont, CO	33 214	56.2	80.5	1 820	82.7	13.5	-10.9	15.9	0.2	4.9	6.1	3.8
Garfield, CO	27 884	41.5	85.4	1 676	86.1	23.8	-0.6	26.2	0.0	9.5	34.3	6.5
Gilpin, CO	3 501	31.5	94.1	210	72.4	31.2	6.8	31.9	65.5	0.0	36.7	3.6
Grand, CO	8 571	31.7	92.3	301	76.7	34.5	10.1	35.1	0.0	9.8	72.7	17.6
Gunnison, CO	8 504	23.7	94.1	2 556	93.4	43.6	19.2	45.0	23.7	31.4	7.7	20.1
Hinsdale, CO	593	27.7	93.1	16	56.3	34.9	10.5	35.5	. . .	0.0	100.0	0.0
Huerfano, CO	5 647	54.5	77.8	255	78.0	16.1	-8.3	21.4	3.4	4.6	48.5	5.7
Jackson, CO	1 098	49.8	86.2	26	100.0	19.9	-4.5	20.2	0.0	0.0	100.0	13.2
Jefferson, CO	350 537	30.8	91.8	30 941	77.2	36.5	12.1	38.2	32.5	21.3	47.7	17.4
Kiowa, CO	1 085	49.2	86.3	49	89.8	16.1	-8.3	16.1	0.0	0.0	. . .	26.7
Kit Carson, CO	5 254	54.6	77.0	204	86.3	15.4	-9.0	16.9	12.1	0.0	0.0	4.8
Lake, CO	4 710	47.8	79.5	403	88.3	19.5	-4.9	26.8	. . .	0.0	77.8	2.2
La Plata, CO	27 973	31.7	91.4	4 732	93.1	36.4	12.0	39.7	21.1	14.3	32.4	14.3
Larimer, CO	156 426	29.0	92.3	31 384	93.1	39.5	15.1	40.8	39.4	16.9	61.9	17.4
Las Animas, CO	10 279	50.3	76.9	885	95.7	16.2	-8.2	21.2	0.0	4.1	33.3	7.9
Lincoln, CO	4 214	53.2	81.8	166	84.3	13.2	-11.2	14.5	10.3	13.9	0.0	4.1
Logan, CO	13 074	49.7	82.3	1 291	94.3	14.6	-9.8	15.8	20.3	0.0	5.9	2.6
Mesa, CO	76 358	45.3	85.0	5 836	88.6	22.0	-2.4	23.2	16.8	4.7	24.5	9.9
Mineral, CO	631	36.8	91.6	25	84.0	31.2	6.8	31.7	. . .	0.0	. . .	0.0
Moffat, CO	8 404	53.8	79.6	496	92.5	12.5	-11.9	13.1	48.0	12.2	33.3	3.1
Montezuma, CO	15 512	51.9	81.1	723	87.8	21.0	-3.4	23.7	0.0	5.4	12.5	8.4
Montrose, CO	22 089	52.7	80.7	498	86.3	18.7	-5.7	20.2	8.5	21.0	13.4	6.1
Morgan, CO	16 661	59.6	71.4	796	89.6	13.5	-10.9	16.8	21.1	12.1	18.8	2.4
Otero, CO	13 172	55.0	75.7	963	92.9	15.4	-9.0	20.7	68.8	0.8	41.2	4.3
Ouray, CO	2 741	28.2	93.4	56	66.1	36.8	12.4	37.6	0.0	10.0	0.0	19.7
Park, CO	10 371	33.4	93.3	432	67.8	30.3	5.9	30.6	34.5	27.3	51.9	18.9
Phillips, CO	2 999	50.6	81.6	116	90.5	19.9	-4.5	21.3	0.0	50.0	25.0	5.7
Pitkin, CO	11 322	14.6	96.3	659	66.6	57.1	32.7	60.1	82.7	23.5	38.3	13.9
Prowers, CO	8 545	56.9	72.0	599	96.7	11.9	-12.5	14.4	100.0	3.6	23.5	4.7
Pueblo, CO	92 080	49.7	81.3	8 081	90.3	18.3	-6.1	22.8	15.7	11.0	42.1	9.5
Rio Blanco, CO	3 857	43.6	88.4	385	91.0	19.5	-4.9	19.8	. . .	15.8	66.7	9.0
Rio Grande, CO	7 959	51.9	78.1	500	90.4	18.8	-5.6	26.6	. . .	4.5	16.7	5.4
Routt, CO	13 267	22.4	95.3	1 014	86.9	42.5	18.1	43.3	77.8	22.0	14.7	23.2
Saguache, CO	3 760	54.8	70.0	166	85.5	19.6	-4.8	29.2	0.0	8.7	50.0	4.5
San Juan, CO	428	22.4	92.1	14	78.6	43.7	19.3	45.8	. . .	0.0	50.0	20.0
San Miguel, CO	4 762	21.4	93.6	182	57.1	48.5	24.1	50.6	20.0	15.4	49.0	11.3
Sedgwick, CO	1 938	56.2	79.3	69	92.8	13.4	-11.0	14.8	0.0	0.0	0.0	2.4
Summit, CO	15 795	24.4	93.3	1 056	83.4	48.3	23.9	51.7	21.7	26.1	42.4	14.8

[3] May be of any race.
. . . = Not available.

Table C-1. Population, School, and Student Characteristics by County—*Continued*

STATE County	State/county code	County type[1]	Population, 2005 Total	Population, 2005 Percent 5 to 17 years	Number of schools and students, 2004–2005 School districts	Number of schools and students, 2004–2005 Schools	Number of schools and students, 2004–2005 Students	Resident enrollment, 2000 Total	Resident enrollment, 2000 Percent public	Resident enrollment, 2000 K–12	Resident enrollment, 2000 Percent public
			1	2	3	4	5	6	7	8	9
Teller, CO	08119	2	21 918	17.7	2	7	3 697	5 228	87.5	4 209	93.1
Washington, CO	08121	9	4 633	18.5	5	10	938	1 252	97.0	1 034	96.8
Weld, CO	08123	3	228 943	19.1	13	115	56 201	55 843	91.4	37 126	93.4
Yuma, CO	08125	7	9 789	19.8	4	11	1 869	2 574	93.2	2 159	96.9
CONNECTICUT	09000		3 510 297	17.8	197	1 103	577 390	910 869	80.3	639 968	89.5
Fairfield, CT	09001	2	902 775	18.8	31	234	147 053	233 796	75.9	167 739	86.3
Hartford, CT	09003	1	877 393	17.7	37	281	147 733	226 420	84.6	162 211	91.4
Litchfield, CT	09005	4	190 071	17.4	25	78	29 321	45 238	83.7	34 508	90.2
Middlesex, CT	09007	1	163 214	16.7	15	69	34 332	39 840	77.0	26 978	90.9
New Haven, CT	09009	2	846 766	17.5	31	254	134 036	225 396	76.5	154 863	89.0
New London, CT	09011	2	266 618	17.5	24	100	43 109	67 054	83.1	48 220	91.7
Tolland, CT	09013	1	147 634	15.7	16	45	23 389	43 189	90.5	24 004	94.5
Windham, CT	09015	4	115 826	17.2	18	42	18 417	29 936	88.9	21 445	90.6
DELAWARE	10000		843 524	16.7	36	222	119 107	209 979	78.2	143 780	82.7
Kent, DE	10001	3	143 968	17.9	10	48	22 730	35 984	86.8	25 303	92.2
New Castle, DE	10003	1	523 008	17.0	17	125	70 557	139 816	73.6	92 041	77.1
Sussex, DE	10005	4	176 548	14.7	9	49	25 820	34 179	88.0	26 436	92.8
DISTRICT OF COLUMBIA	11000		550 521	13.5	43	216	76 714	157 475	67.3	88 568	84.9
District of Columbia	11001	1	550 521	13.5	43	216	76 714	157 475	67.3	88 568	84.9
FLORIDA	12000		17 789 864	16.6	75	3 700	2 654 987	3 933 279	82.8	2 775 141	88.5
Alachua, FL	12001	3	223 852	13.8	2	70	30 418	90 184	91.8	32 792	89.3
Baker, FL	12003	1	24 569	18.5	1	7	4 775	5 495	91.4	4 509	94.7
Bay, FL	12005	3	161 558	17.0	1	45	27 147	36 970	90.0	27 420	92.6
Bradford, FL	12007	6	28 118	15.2	1	13	3 831	5 921	90.6	4 735	91.4
Brevard, FL	12009	2	531 250	15.8	1	110	74 824	112 005	82.0	80 722	88.6
Broward, FL	12011	1	1 777 638	17.8	1	275	274 591	410 814	79.3	290 350	87.1
Calhoun, FL	12013	6	13 290	16.3	1	7	2 313	2 907	97.7	2 364	98.0
Charlotte, FL	12015	3	157 536	12.0	1	23	17 507	22 784	87.6	17 899	92.5
Citrus, FL	12017	4	134 370	13.0	1	25	15 720	19 963	89.2	16 026	93.2
Clay, FL	12019	1	171 095	18.9	1	34	32 605	40 121	86.9	30 688	91.8
Collier, FL	12021	2	307 242	14.5	1	64	42 105	46 873	86.2	36 873	91.5
Columbia, FL	12023	6	64 040	17.6	1	15	9 957	13 898	90.6	11 213	92.4
DeSoto, FL	12027	6	35 406	15.7	1	14	4 942	6 014	93.5	5 087	95.5
Dixie, FL	12029	6	14 647	15.2	1	5	2 144	2 814	93.0	2 350	96.8
Duval, FL	12031	1	826 436	19.0	1	183	129 486	211 236	81.3	151 264	85.6
Escambia, FL	12033	2	296 772	16.8	1	78	43 953	78 198	81.3	53 184	87.2
Flagler, FL	12035	4	76 410	13.3	1	10	9 698	9 366	87.0	6 882	93.1
Franklin, FL	12037	6	10 177	14.9	1	7	1 371	1 962	94.4	1 583	95.5
Gadsden, FL	12039	2	46 428	18.0	1	22	6 710	11 903	88.7	9 547	89.5
Gilchrist, FL	12041	3	16 402	16.8	1	5	2 858	3 574	94.0	2 968	95.5
Glades, FL	12043	6	11 252	15.8	1	5	1 237	2 213	92.7	1 757	94.2
Gulf, FL	12045	6	13 975	15.2	1	8	2 177	3 072	94.6	2 321	97.0
Hamilton, FL	12047	6	13 983	16.0	1	7	2 017	2 853	91.8	2 466	92.6
Hardee, FL	12049	6	28 286	19.1	1	9	5 146	6 525	94.4	5 483	97.2
Hendry, FL	12051	4	39 561	20.9	1	14	7 604	9 811	93.4	8 191	95.8
Hernando, FL	12053	1	158 409	14.4	1	23	20 666	23 878	85.4	18 867	89.3
Highlands, FL	12055	4	95 496	14.2	1	18	12 049	15 766	88.8	12 420	93.7
Hillsborough, FL	12057	1	1 132 152	18.3	1	258	189 469	267 599	82.0	187 070	87.8
Holmes, FL	12059	6	19 264	16.0	1	9	3 389	4 161	92.6	3 444	93.2
Indian River, FL	12061	3	128 594	13.9	1	28	17 099	22 308	82.8	17 024	87.9
Jackson, FL	12063	6	48 985	15.6	2	24	7 814	11 144	90.5	8 562	93.0
Jefferson, FL	12065	2	14 490	14.6	1	6	1 379	3 050	78.3	2 422	80.6
Lafayette, FL	12067	8	7 953	14.4	1	2	1 058	1 406	92.0	1 052	98.3
Lake, FL	12069	1	277 035	14.5	1	57	36 117	40 624	85.9	32 367	89.6
Lee, FL	12071	2	544 758	14.8	1	98	71 210	81 283	84.3	62 918	88.9
Leon, FL	12073	2	245 756	15.1	3	61	35 031	93 932	89.9	38 023	87.6
Levy, FL	12075	8	37 998	16.9	1	16	6 284	7 753	93.1	6 303	95.9
Liberty, FL	12077	8	7 773	14.7	1	9	1 396	1 492	92.6	1 217	92.9
Madison, FL	12079	6	19 092	17.7	1	9	3 211	4 656	89.5	3 840	89.0
Manatee, FL	12081	2	306 779	15.5	1	75	41 351	52 553	85.4	40 225	90.5
Marion, FL	12083	2	303 442	15.4	1	65	41 205	54 173	85.6	42 621	88.9
Martin, FL	12085	2	139 728	13.9	1	33	17 917	24 414	82.2	18 261	89.0
Miami-Dade, FL	12086	1	2 376 014	17.7	1	384	368 933	643 727	80.6	443 852	87.6
Monroe, FL	12087	4	76 329	12.2	1	19	8 677	14 277	85.8	10 266	93.4
Nassau, FL	12089	1	64 746	17.3	1	19	10 748	14 083	88.6	10 897	94.1
Okaloosa, FL	12091	3	182 172	17.5	1	55	31 756	44 445	89.2	31 577	93.0
Okeechobee, FL	12093	4	39 836	17.6	1	19	7 348	8 521	94.2	6 898	97.1
Orange, FL	12095	1	1 023 023	18.3	2	206	177 235	248 040	82.6	167 077	88.3
Osceola, FL	12097	1	231 578	18.8	1	61	47 446	44 944	86.6	35 247	92.5
Palm Beach, FL	12099	1	1 268 548	15.7	2	232	175 715	254 671	79.6	183 941	86.0

[1]County type codes are from the Economic Research Service of the United States Department of Agriculture. See notes and definitions at the end of this section.

Table C-1. Population, School, and Student Characteristics by County—*Continued*

STATE County	Characteristics of students, 2004–2005				Outcomes		Staff and students, 2004–2005		
	Percent with IEP[2]	Percent eligible for free or reduced-price lunch	Percent minority	Percent English-language learners	Number of graduates, 2003–2004	Percent dropouts, grades 9–12, 2001–2002	Number of teachers	Student-teacher ratio	Central administration staff
	10	11	12	13	14	15	16	17	18
Teller, CO	11.4	19.3	9.3	0.4	257	. . .	235	15.7	23
Washington, CO	11.0	38.3	11.9	2.1	68	. . .	100	9.4	7
Weld, CO	10.3	39.1	42.5	17.2	3 106	. . .	3 358	16.7	286
Yuma, CO	12.7	50.8	27.6	15.4	133	. . .	144	13.0	17
CONNECTICUT	11.6	26.3	32.5	4.8	. . .	2.6	38 278	15.1	. . .
Fairfield, CT	9.9	26.6	35.1	6.4	. . .	2.8	9 695	15.2	. . .
Hartford, CT	13.1	27.2	40.1	5.4	. . .	2.5	9 628	15.3	947
Litchfield, CT	12.4	11.9	7.9	1.6	. . .	2.1	1 891	15.5	197
Middlesex, CT	11.4	13.6	14.9	3.2	. . .	1.1	2 674	12.8	184
New Haven, CT	11.4	34.7	39.1	4.9	. . .	2.5	8 678	15.4	765
New London, CT	12.4	20.1	23.4	3.5	. . .	4.3	2 869	15.0	301
Tolland, CT	10.4	10.6	9.9	1.0	. . .	2.2	1 606	14.6	123
Windham, CT	13.0	28.6	17.3	3.6	. . .	4.2	1 237	14.9	167
DELAWARE	14.7	35.6	43.8	4.1	. . .	6.2	7 855	15.2	. . .
Kent, DE	16.5	34.0	36.8	1.7	. . .	4.1	1 531	14.8	182
New Castle, DE	13.7	33.9	49.2	4.5	. . .	7.4	4 504	15.7	. . .
Sussex, DE	16.0	42.1	35.2	4.9	. . .	4.9	1 820	14.2	187
DISTRICT OF COLUMBIA	17.0	66.0	95.4	7.4	. . .	. . .	5 386	14.2	. . .
District of Columbia	17.0	66.0	95.4	7.4	3 307	. . .	5 386	14.2	. . .
FLORIDA	15.2	47.4	49.5	8.1	. . .	3.7	154 864	17.1	. . .
Alachua, FL	19.0	47.4	47.0	1.4	1 777	5.8	1 735	17.5	413
Baker, FL	11.5	45.2	15.2	0.1	215	4.7	263	18.2	48
Bay, FL	19.5	48.1	20.6	1.0	1 358	1.8	1 599	17.0	208
Bradford, FL	23.6	58.5	28.0	0.2	239	4.3	237	16.2	29
Brevard, FL	17.7	32.9	22.6	1.6	4 462	0.9	4 468	16.7	293
Broward, FL	11.4	41.1	65.2	10.0	14 192	1.6	15 271	18.0	1 138
Calhoun, FL	23.6	54.9	15.8	0.6	119	3.2	160	14.5	27
Charlotte, FL	18.8	26.4	15.6	0.9	1 166	4.2	1 005	17.4	153
Citrus, FL	18.3	45.5	9.8	0.7	984	4.8	951	16.5	157
Clay, FL	19.1	25.2	18.6	0.6	2 042	2.8	2 003	16.3	242
Collier, FL	14.8	45.8	51.2	14.8	2 275	4.4	2 479	17.0	339
Columbia, FL	19.1	56.1	26.8	0.3	540	1.7	612	16.3	103
DeSoto, FL	18.7	61.1	48.2	8.7	220	3.7	290	17.0	76
Dixie, FL	21.9	65.7	11.4	0.0	126	3.6	120	17.9	31
Duval, FL	15.6	45.1	53.1	2.6	6 225	6.7	7 345	17.6	1 387
Escambia, FL	16.9	63.0	42.8	0.7	2 267	2.8	2 740	16.0	378
Flagler, FL	15.6	32.0	22.2	2.6	466	2.3	680	14.3	119
Franklin, FL	17.8	61.5	16.6	0.5	77	2.8	79	17.4	19
Gadsden, FL	17.8	75.9	95.5	6.4	258	5.4	419	16.0	101
Gilchrist, FL	26.7	50.4	6.8	0.8	135	2.9	187	15.3	37
Glades, FL	17.7	70.1	51.5	4.8	52	8.2	76	16.3	15
Gulf, FL	19.6	48.5	17.2	0.0	132	0.5	138	15.8	23
Hamilton, FL	16.2	60.2	56.3	3.8	111	2.8	122	16.5	39
Hardee, FL	19.5	65.7	59.6	8.7	240	7.5	314	16.4	70
Hendry, FL	16.9	66.8	66.5	8.0	439	6.1	409	18.6	69
Hernando, FL	16.7	47.1	17.3	1.7	1 012	2.3	1 274	16.2	93
Highlands, FL	17.1	60.5	42.4	4.3	651	5.3	746	16.2	129
Hillsborough, FL	15.3	52.2	52.4	10.4	9 380	2.8	11 975	15.8	1 103
Holmes, FL	15.6	57.3	5.8	0.3	229	3.1	214	15.8	18
Indian River, FL	14.1	46.3	30.8	4.5	962	1.8	994	17.2	76
Jackson, FL	22.1	58.6	35.4	0.6	. . .	2.7	473	16.5	76
Jefferson, FL	27.4	72.5	73.0	0.4	82	4.2	92	15.0	21
Lafayette, FL	12.1	55.5	21.3	3.2	62	5.0	67	15.8	11
Lake, FL	16.1	41.7	30.9	5.1	1 877	5.5	2 169	16.7	288
Lee, FL	14.8	46.3	39.4	10.0	3 545	9.0	4 018	17.7	469
Leon, FL	17.8	37.5	46.9	1.1	2 063	3.6	2 072	16.9	209
Levy, FL	24.4	55.5	22.2	2.2	306	3.6	390	16.1	62
Liberty, FL	25.7	50.4	19.6	0.6	71	0.8	96	14.5	17
Madison, FL	23.0	63.7	60.1	0.2	198	6.8	161	19.9	27
Manatee, FL	19.0	44.5	36.5	6.6	2 118	3.7	2 407	17.2	272
Marion, FL	17.5	56.2	33.0	3.4	2 340	3.5	2 398	17.2	297
Martin, FL	16.7	36.0	27.7	9.8	1 021	0.6	1 022	17.5	130
Miami-Dade, FL	11.9	64.1	89.9	16.3	18 599	4.8	20 086	18.4	2 114
Monroe, FL	18.3	39.0	35.1	5.6	518	4.2	553	15.7	108
Nassau, FL	15.4	35.5	11.4	0.2	658	4.0	624	17.2	64
Okaloosa, FL	15.5	31.5	20.0	0.8	2 038	3.6	1 813	17.5	150
Okeechobee, FL	21.4	54.1	37.2	4.7	385	5.6	417	17.6	60
Orange, FL	15.3	49.6	60.5	15.3	. . .	3.4	10 304	17.2	2 018
Osceola, FL	15.1	55.8	60.9	16.7	2 378	5.6	2 485	19.1	328
Palm Beach, FL	14.8	39.1	54.4	11.5	9 313	3.1	10 056	17.5	843

[2]IEP = Individual Education Program. See notes and definitions at the end of this section.
. . . = Not available.

Table C-1. Population, School, and Student Characteristics by County—*Continued*

STATE County	Revenue, 2003–2004				Current expenditures, 2003–2004			Resident population, 16 to 19 years, 2000			
	Total revenue (thousands of dollars)	Percent of revenue from:			Total expenditures (thousands of dollars)	Amount per student (dollars)	Percent for instruction	Total	Percent in armed forces	Percent high school graduates	Percent not enrolled, not employed, not in armed forces, not high school graduate
		Federal government	State government	Local government							
	19	20	21	22	23	24	25	26	27	28	29
Teller, CO	30 047	3.2	46.5	50.3	24 804	6 641	66.7	1 130	0.0	14.1	4.9
Washington, CO	10 738	2.7	56.1	41.3	9 648	10 103	61.3	312	0.0	5.8	1.3
Weld, CO	264 533	6.4	49.2	44.4	219 970	6 623	65.7	12 913	0.0	9.0	6.2
Yuma, CO	17 338	5.3	48.0	46.6	13 778	7 340	60.9	601	0.0	7.8	1.8
CONNECTICUT	7 302 284	4.9	34.8	60.3	6 193 052	11 163	66.6	169 277	0.6	8.9	4.4
Fairfield, CT	1 931 590	4.1	22.5	73.5	1 708 749	11 700	66.9	39 493	0.0	7.5	3.6
Hartford, CT	1 836 314	5.1	37.4	57.5	1 588 650	11 043	67.4	42 608	0.1	8.6	5.5
Litchfield, CT	353 169	3.6	29.6	66.8	307 209	10 716	66.5	8 090	0.0	12.1	2.4
Middlesex, CT	326 556	3.1	29.8	67.2	259 554	11 062	65.8	7 196	0.0	6.9	3.1
New Haven, CT	1 781 500	6.3	42.6	51.1	1 456 038	11 040	65.9	42 794	0.1	8.7	5.4
New London, CT	548 246	4.5	39.4	56.1	444 330	10 993	65.3	13 209	6.6	17.1	3.4
Tolland, CT	277 642	2.8	40.5	56.8	239 917	10 271	66.6	9 564	0.1	4.4	1.6
Windham, CT	247 267	8.6	52.4	38.9	188 605	11 038	66.8	6 323	0.3	8.7	4.6
DELAWARE	1 382 955	7.8	62.0	30.2	1 190 694	10 110	63.0	44 154	0.3	11.5	5.6
Kent, DE	275 971	12.0	68.1	19.9	250 823	9 680	63.6	7 812	1.3	11.1	5.1
New Castle, DE	859 411	6.1	59.7	34.2	716 841	10 256	62.7	29 102	0.1	11.4	5.4
Sussex, DE	247 573	8.9	63.2	27.9	223 030	10 150	63.2	7 240	0.1	12.2	7.2
DISTRICT OF COLUMBIA	1 225 132	15.0	0.0	85.0	1 050 347	13 977	60.3	32 400	1.0	8.2	6.7
District of Columbia	1 225 132	15.0	0.0	85.0	1 050 347	13 977	60.3	32 400	1.0	8.2	6.7
FLORIDA	21 623 923	10.1	44.4	45.6	17 589 859	6 784	65.4	794 066	0.7	10.2	6.3
Alachua, FL	236 053	13.5	47.9	38.5	203 288	6 903	63.5	19 335	0.0	5.6	1.9
Baker, FL	31 416	11.2	70.4	18.4	29 011	6 299	60.2	1 315	0.0	11.6	14.1
Bay, FL	211 759	11.1	44.7	44.2	172 171	6 446	65.9	7 949	2.3	13.4	5.2
Bradford, FL	30 479	13.1	63.2	23.7	27 996	7 162	62.6	1 382	0.4	12.9	7.7
Brevard, FL	549 521	9.0	51.3	39.7	468 986	6 346	69.5	22 865	0.2	9.1	6.1
Broward, FL	2 231 773	9.0	48.3	42.7	1 839 583	6 742	65.1	73 499	0.0	9.3	5.4
Calhoun, FL	16 015	13.8	71.1	15.1	14 929	6 710	65.8	663	0.0	16.6	5.3
Charlotte, FL	151 485	8.7	24.4	66.9	122 439	6 691	63.9	4 880	0.0	13.7	4.9
Citrus, FL	123 534	9.6	39.8	50.7	109 754	7 073	63.8	4 639	0.0	12.1	7.1
Clay, FL	220 780	7.1	62.6	30.3	183 665	5 855	67.7	8 239	0.3	9.8	4.8
Collier, FL	417 070	8.6	13.8	77.6	322 505	8 031	63.4	10 207	0.1	11.1	8.9
Columbia, FL	70 033	13.7	64.3	22.0	62 524	6 387	62.5	3 592	0.1	12.0	10.2
DeSoto, FL	40 061	17.2	57.6	25.2	37 265	7 490	65.0	2 042	0.0	9.2	14.7
Dixie, FL	16 850	15.6	62.7	21.8	15 491	7 142	56.7	736	0.0	20.5	7.7
Duval, FL	946 951	10.6	47.7	41.7	821 556	6 341	67.6	42 483	2.0	12.2	6.5
Escambia, FL	337 547	13.1	52.4	34.5	285 339	6 485	63.2	19 846	15.0	23.7	4.4
Flagler, FL	89 259	6.1	41.6	52.4	56 091	6 550	58.9	1 749	0.0	13.0	4.5
Franklin, FL	14 895	13.6	16.0	70.4	11 196	8 312	61.8	517	0.0	19.3	4.6
Gadsden, FL	60 237	22.1	60.6	17.3	52 235	7 518	58.8	2 664	0.1	8.5	8.9
Gilchrist, FL	20 802	14.3	64.8	20.9	20 080	7 090	61.8	917	0.0	14.6	11.0
Glades, FL	14 464	15.0	56.7	28.3	8 962	8 856	59.2	491	0.0	19.1	5.3
Gulf, FL	19 372	13.5	30.2	56.3	16 153	7 513	60.8	559	0.0	13.4	4.5
Hamilton, FL	26 692	12.3	69.4	18.3	15 201	7 390	60.9	797	0.0	13.3	13.8
Hardee, FL	39 514	16.9	49.9	33.2	36 083	6 911	62.3	1 801	0.0	12.8	11.0
Hendry, FL	58 064	15.1	56.3	28.6	53 528	6 984	63.2	2 700	0.0	8.8	11.8
Hernando, FL	157 601	8.4	47.9	43.7	118 189	6 031	62.9	5 403	0.0	14.0	6.2
Highlands, FL	91 152	15.3	48.6	36.1	82 332	7 057	61.6	3 531	0.0	13.2	7.4
Hillsborough, FL	1 579 958	13.1	53.3	33.6	1 214 654	6 678	65.9	52 941	0.2	10.7	7.5
Holmes, FL	32 162	13.5	73.6	12.9	23 979	7 088	62.5	1 011	0.0	10.2	6.8
Indian River, FL	142 939	8.3	25.0	66.7	109 431	6 578	63.9	4 932	0.6	11.2	6.8
Jackson, FL	55 864	16.4	63.0	20.6	50 607	7 037	62.9	2 608	0.1	10.8	6.2
Jefferson, FL	23 227	14.8	70.8	14.4	12 440	8 355	62.2	691	0.0	8.1	8.4
Lafayette, FL	7 996	16.0	63.3	20.7	7 687	7 427	61.1	375	0.0	6.7	15.5
Lake, FL	266 930	8.1	46.9	45.0	211 456	6 221	64.1	8 260	0.0	11.0	6.6
Lee, FL	640 307	8.3	24.3	67.4	457 576	6 884	59.9	17 053	0.4	14.5	7.2
Leon, FL	282 053	10.3	48.0	41.8	214 699	6 669	64.8	21 304	0.1	5.4	1.9
Levy, FL	46 837	12.2	62.2	25.6	42 542	6 853	64.2	1 968	0.5	10.2	9.8
Liberty, FL	11 391	16.5	69.6	13.8	10 247	7 293	68.2	372	0.0	2.7	8.6
Madison, FL	25 012	17.0	65.0	18.0	22 427	6 911	62.6	1 005	0.0	6.6	10.6
Manatee, FL	347 193	9.3	34.6	56.1	272 642	6 771	66.0	10 524	0.6	11.6	6.8
Marion, FL	308 317	12.1	53.3	34.6	268 296	6 644	64.0	11 281	0.1	10.9	7.5
Martin, FL	167 817	8.5	20.6	70.9	122 615	6 895	64.3	4 579	0.0	6.1	9.2
Miami-Dade, FL	3 244 666	11.6	46.6	41.8	2 713 056	7 297	65.1	123 037	0.1	7.7	6.8
Monroe, FL	104 868	8.4	13.8	77.7	72 763	7 961	63.7	2 776	1.7	17.0	4.3
Nassau, FL	74 057	7.4	39.4	53.2	62 283	5 896	62.1	2 900	0.0	11.2	5.5
Okaloosa, FL	222 170	11.0	50.3	38.7	197 433	6 270	67.2	9 554	5.7	17.8	3.0
Okeechobee, FL	53 499	13.0	60.4	26.6	48 127	6 612	62.7	2 304	0.0	7.6	12.8
Orange, FL	1 380 847	8.7	41.3	49.9	1 071 215	6 453	67.5	49 260	0.1	10.1	6.2
Osceola, FL	345 418	8.5	51.6	39.9	267 279	6 087	65.0	9 337	0.0	10.1	6.2
Palm Beach, FL	1 573 522	7.6	30.4	62.0	1 248 312	7 332	68.9	49 015	0.0	8.5	6.9

Table C-1. Population, School, and Student Characteristics by County—*Continued*

STATE County	High school graduates, 2000			College enrollment, 2000		College graduates, 2000 (percent)						
	Population 25 years and over	High school graduate or less (percent)	High school graduate or more (percent)	Number	Percent public	Bachelor's degree or more	+/- U.S. percentage with bachelor's degree or more	Non-Hispanic White	Black	American Indian and Alaska Native	Asian or Pacific Islander	Hispanic[3]
	30	31	32	33	34	35	36	37	38	39	40	41
Teller, CO	14 240	29.5	94.0	635	72.0	31.7	7.3	32.3	31.4	9.5	31.0	15.8
Washington, CO	3 314	51.9	81.7	116	95.7	14.3	-10.1	14.3	0.0	27.8	75.0	7.6
Weld, CO	106 245	47.2	79.6	15 531	92.4	21.6	-2.8	25.7	23.4	13.0	48.4	6.5
Yuma, CO	6 340	54.3	79.5	225	76.9	15.5	-8.9	16.5	100.0	25.0	. . .	4.1
CONNECTICUT	2 295 617	44.5	84.0	204 212	61.8	31.4	7.0	34.2	13.7	15.7	57.2	11.3
Fairfield, CT	596 371	39.2	84.4	44 981	54.1	39.9	15.5	45.8	13.9	23.3	59.2	11.7
Hartford, CT	579 839	46.3	82.4	48 436	72.0	29.6	5.2	33.2	13.3	15.3	50.7	10.0
Litchfield, CT	127 305	45.5	85.9	7 392	68.9	27.5	3.1	27.5	20.4	15.0	42.4	24.1
Middlesex, CT	108 106	39.8	88.7	9 945	48.4	33.8	9.4	34.4	18.5	22.8	53.0	29.7
New Haven, CT	551 642	47.8	83.0	55 307	48.5	27.6	3.2	29.9	13.6	14.9	65.7	10.0
New London, CT	173 910	46.0	86.0	14 440	61.9	26.2	1.8	27.5	12.5	10.9	42.8	11.9
Tolland, CT	87 202	39.8	09.2	16 790	90.9	32.8	8.4	32.5	20.0	18.9	70.9	21.6
Windham, CT	71 242	56.1	79.6	6 921	88.2	19.0	-5.4	19.5	9.8	10.7	35.5	10.3
DELAWARE	514 658	48.8	82.6	51 407	74.4	25.0	0.6	26.9	14.4	13.2	61.0	13.5
Kent, DE	79 249	53.5	79.4	8 588	77.9	18.6	-5.8	19.4	15.6	9.4	33.9	11.8
New Castle, DE	324 810	44.2	85.5	37 364	72.9	29.5	5.1	32.1	16.0	26.3	67.3	14.3
Sussex, DE	110 599	59.1	76.5	5 455	79.6	16.6	-7.8	18.3	6.5	5.5	35.6	11.2
DISTRICT OF COLUMBIA	384 535	42.8	77.8	59 498	41.0	39.1	14.7	80.6	17.5	28.1	58.1	24.8
District of Columbia	384 535	42.8	77.8	59 498	41.0	39.1	14.7	80.6	17.5	28.1	58.1	24.8
FLORIDA	11 024 645	48.9	79.9	886 825	76.2	22.3	-2.1	24.7	12.4	14.9	40.3	17.5
Alachua, FL	123 524	32.2	88.1	53 371	96.2	38.7	14.3	42.2	14.3	35.3	78.6	47.0
Baker, FL	13 953	69.5	71.9	723	84.4	8.2	-16.2	8.9	5.6	0.0	0.0	5.1
Bay, FL	99 771	49.6	81.0	6 965	90.3	17.7	-6.7	18.5	9.5	9.8	22.5	19.0
Bradford, FL	17 883	66.0	74.2	795	89.9	8.4	-16.0	10.2	2.2	0.0	30.4	5.4
Brevard, FL	339 738	42.5	86.3	23 877	70.4	23.6	-0.8	24.3	12.1	10.3	37.0	22.9
Broward, FL	1 126 502	46.4	82.0	88 536	68.6	24.5	0.1	27.2	14.7	15.2	38.4	23.0
Calhoun, FL	8 884	69.4	69.1	397	98.0	7.7	-16.7	8.6	3.3	15.8	31.7	0.0
Charlotte, FL	113 071	53.5	82.1	3 279	79.6	17.6	-6.8	17.6	14.0	8.8	42.7	17.3
Citrus, FL	92 594	59.7	78.3	2 722	82.0	13.2	-11.2	13.1	9.1	15.0	42.1	11.0
Clay, FL	90 382	45.3	86.4	6 892	82.8	20.1	-4.3	20.2	17.6	11.4	31.0	17.9
Collier, FL	185 357	44.5	81.8	6 692	73.3	27.9	3.5	32.4	8.9	8.5	43.8	7.1
Columbia, FL	36 880	60.2	74.7	1 874	88.3	10.9	-13.5	11.2	6.0	33.6	50.8	16.1
DeSoto, FL	21 222	71.8	63.5	556	81.8	8.4	-16.0	10.7	2.8	0.0	33.6	2.3
Dixie, FL	9 643	73.5	65.9	358	70.4	6.8	-17.6	7.1	1.9	0.0	20.0	4.8
Duval, FL	499 602	46.3	82.7	43 351	79.1	21.9	-2.5	24.6	13.1	17.9	34.0	21.8
Escambia, FL	189 710	46.3	82.1	20 805	70.5	21.0	-3.4	23.9	9.8	9.3	23.2	22.8
Flagler, FL	38 616	46.1	85.9	1 784	79.7	21.2	-3.2	21.4	18.9	26.3	37.2	17.1
Franklin, FL	8 202	68.1	68.3	246	92.7	12.4	-12.0	14.0	3.7	18.5	63.2	7.2
Gadsden, FL	28 932	65.2	70.7	1 599	90.8	12.9	-11.5	20.8	6.8	18.8	43.5	4.3
Gilchrist, FL	8 866	63.7	72.4	431	88.9	9.4	-15.0	9.6	4.3	0.0	0.0	7.1
Glades, FL	7 403	67.0	69.8	285	87.7	9.8	-14.6	11.2	3.2	14.3	48.6	3.1
Gulf, FL	9 527	64.6	72.6	592	92.9	10.1	-14.3	11.1	0.6	8.2	23.5	6.4
Hamilton, FL	8 758	72.2	62.9	232	92.7	7.3	-17.1	9.3	3.9	0.0	16.0	3.0
Hardee, FL	16 509	73.5	58.0	627	78.1	8.4	-16.0	11.3	6.2	8.7	43.3	1.4
Hendry, FL	20 551	74.9	54.2	873	86.8	8.2	-16.2	12.4	3.8	9.4	36.5	2.7
Hernando, FL	99 082	59.3	78.5	3 490	79.0	12.7	-11.7	12.9	10.0	2.9	28.2	8.9
Highlands, FL	65 087	60.1	74.5	2 080	80.5	13.6	-10.8	14.2	5.1	22.9	48.5	9.2
Hillsborough, FL	653 841	45.9	80.8	60 920	76.1	25.1	0.7	28.5	14.6	21.1	42.7	15.7
Holmes, FL	12 659	72.6	65.2	524	91.8	8.8	-15.6	9.1	2.2	12.0	21.6	3.3
Indian River, FL	84 531	47.5	81.6	3 733	71.7	23.1	-1.3	24.8	7.6	19.2	44.9	9.1
Jackson, FL	31 771	63.5	69.1	2 115	81.7	12.8	-11.6	14.9	7.1	6.7	44.7	11.6
Jefferson, FL	8 911	59.1	73.2	392	75.5	16.9	-7.5	23.3	6.7	0.0	30.8	6.9
Lafayette, FL	4 745	71.9	68.2	226	80.1	7.2	-17.2	9.2	0.4	0.0	0.0	1.4
Lake, FL	155 572	54.5	79.8	5 504	81.6	16.6	-7.8	17.3	7.3	1.7	33.5	14.5
Lee, FL	327 672	50.2	82.3	12 539	79.1	21.1	-3.3	22.6	8.9	11.4	40.7	8.9
Leon, FL	137 537	29.8	89.1	50 886	95.7	41.7	17.3	46.2	27.3	28.0	65.5	38.2
Levy, FL	24 030	64.3	73.9	930	85.4	10.6	-13.8	10.6	8.0	12.8	57.1	14.0
Liberty, FL	4 828	74.9	65.6	218	96.8	7.4	-17.0	8.9	1.8	0.0	17.6	0.0
Madison, FL	12 254	66.7	67.5	597	93.1	10.2	-14.2	13.5	4.7	0.0	0.0	6.9
Manatee, FL	192 789	50.4	81.4	8 183	78.7	20.8	-3.6	22.3	10.9	10.9	32.6	8.3
Marion, FL	187 187	57.7	78.2	8 078	81.5	13.7	-10.7	14.0	10.5	16.5	34.9	9.5
Martin, FL	96 467	43.0	85.3	4 372	73.5	26.3	1.9	27.7	7.4	4.3	42.9	14.1
Miami-Dade, FL	1 491 789	54.5	67.9	160 435	69.4	21.7	-2.7	38.0	11.5	15.8	44.7	18.1
Monroe, FL	61 161	44.0	84.9	3 028	74.1	25.5	1.1	28.2	8.8	13.0	47.3	13.9
Nassau, FL	38 972	53.4	81.0	2 188	80.1	18.9	-5.5	19.8	8.4	12.7	26.1	10.8
Okaloosa, FL	112 429	39.1	88.0	9 816	89.6	24.2	-0.2	26.1	11.9	15.4	14.8	19.6
Okeechobee, FL	23 388	68.8	65.1	1 136	84.4	8.9	-15.5	9.6	6.4	21.1	51.3	5.0
Orange, FL	574 101	44.0	81.8	64 155	77.9	26.1	1.7	30.7	14.7	14.5	40.6	17.0
Osceola, FL	110 607	54.8	79.1	7 092	70.5	15.7	-8.7	16.3	11.6	6.3	40.0	12.5
Palm Beach, FL	817 899	43.3	83.6	50 064	72.1	27.7	3.3	31.3	11.4	16.5	47.3	15.3

[3]May be of any race.
. . . = Not available.

Table C-1. Population, School, and Student Characteristics by County—*Continued*

STATE County	State/ county code	County type[1]	Population, 2005		Number of schools and students, 2004–2005			Resident enrollment, 2000			
			Total	Percent 5 to 17 years	School districts	Schools	Students	Total	Percent public	K–12	Percent public
			1	2	3	4	5	6	7	8	9
Pasco, FL	12101	1	429 065	15.5	1	73	60 846	67 546	86.5	51 677	92.4
Pinellas, FL	12103	1	928 032	14.7	2	174	113 651	190 563	79.3	133 945	85.0
Polk, FL	12105	2	542 912	17.7	1	158	86 292	114 180	84.6	88 103	91.0
Putnam, FL	12107	4	73 568	17.9	1	23	12 456	16 240	92.0	13 307	94.4
St. Johns, FL	12109	1	161 525	16.1	2	47	25 148	30 609	77.5	22 042	86.6
St. Lucie, FL	12111	2	241 305	16.3	1	47	34 912	43 393	86.7	33 356	90.1
Santa Rosa, FL	12113	2	143 105	17.9	1	37	25 038	31 346	88.5	23 695	91.0
Sarasota, FL	12115	2	366 256	12.4	1	58	41 405	55 269	81.6	40 983	87.2
Seminole, FL	12117	1	401 619	18.2	1	76	66 692	99 337	81.4	69 909	86.8
Sumter, FL	12119	4	64 182	12.1	1	14	7 157	8 862	88.8	7 121	92.5
Suwannee, FL	12121	6	38 624	16.7	1	10	5 834	7 960	86.7	6 459	89.4
Taylor, FL	12123	6	19 622	16.9	1	9	3 501	4 676	92.4	3 760	94.5
Union, FL	12125	6	14 916	14.1	1	6	2 204	2 866	93.2	2 297	96.0
Volusia, FL	12127	2	490 055	15.0	1	90	65 281	101 190	78.4	68 193	89.9
Wakulla, FL	12129	2	28 212	16.8	1	11	4 884	5 852	94.7	4 542	97.7
Walton, FL	12131	6	50 324	15.7	1	18	6 557	8 374	91.9	6 868	95.6
Washington, FL	12133	6	22 299	16.9	1	8	3 490	4 640	94.6	3 819	97.6
GEORGIA	13000		9 072 576	18.4	205	2 492	1 553 541	2 211 688	85.6	1 598 291	91.3
Appling, GA	13001	7	17 954	18.5	1	8	3 443	4 329	93.0	3 615	94.3
Atkinson, GA	13003	9	8 030	21.3	1	3	1 696	1 770	96.0	1 561	96.9
Bacon, GA	13005	7	10 379	17.8	1	4	1 879	2 262	95.9	1 788	95.6
Baker, GA	13007	3	4 154	19.6	1	3	391	1 114	90.3	913	90.6
Baldwin, GA	13009	4	45 230	14.3	1	11	6 032	13 169	80.0	8 038	84.0
Banks, GA	13011	8	16 055	18.0	1	5	2 550	3 185	91.8	2 631	94.9
Barrow, GA	13013	1	59 954	19.4	1	17	10 156	11 251	88.4	9 130	93.2
Bartow, GA	13015	1	89 229	19.0	2	27	17 962	18 576	90.5	15 176	94.8
Ben Hill, GA	13017	7	17 316	19.2	1	6	3 314	4 520	91.9	3 554	96.7
Berrien, GA	13019	6	16 708	18.7	1	5	3 072	4 085	94.9	3 090	96.6
Bibb, GA	13021	3	154 918	18.9	1	47	25 148	42 862	78.9	30 324	86.2
Bleckley, GA	13023	6	12 141	18.8	1	5	2 481	3 502	93.5	2 406	97.5
Brantley, GA	13025	3	15 491	19.5	1	6	3 361	3 729	94.8	3 109	96.0
Brooks, GA	13027	3	16 327	18.5	1	5	2 445	4 275	93.1	3 509	94.7
Bryan, GA	13029	2	28 549	20.2	1	12	6 060	6 744	91.0	5 370	94.5
Bulloch, GA	13031	4	61 454	14.9	3	23	8 792	23 132	93.9	9 391	91.9
Burke, GA	13033	2	23 299	21.2	1	6	4 594	6 592	90.9	5 529	91.8
Butts, GA	13035	1	21 045	17.8	1	6	3 485	4 354	92.9	3 567	96.2
Calhoun, GA	13037	8	5 972	15.4	1	2	746	1 498	80.5	1 132	80.7
Camden, GA	13039	4	45 759	22.5	1	14	9 646	13 254	92.9	10 149	97.1
Candler, GA	13043	7	10 321	18.1	1	5	1 921	2 343	92.9	1 917	95.3
Carroll, GA	13045	1	105 453	17.6	3	30	17 877	24 665	92.9	16 383	94.4
Catoosa, GA	13047	2	60 813	18.2	1	17	10 230	13 012	90.1	10 040	93.7
Charlton, GA	13049	6	10 790	18.6	1	5	1 992	2 586	93.6	2 221	94.7
Chatham, GA	13051	1	238 410	17.5	1	55	34 595	64 990	77.4	44 375	82.8
Chattahoochee, GA	13053	2	14 679	20.4	1	3	533	4 158	90.9	3 027	95.5
Chattooga, GA	13055	6	26 570	16.3	2	14	4 286	5 264	91.5	4 234	95.5
Cherokee, GA	13057	1	184 211	19.3	1	39	31 065	36 937	84.1	27 510	92.5
Clarke, GA	13059	3	104 439	11.3	1	24	11 637	44 372	91.8	13 088	88.5
Clay, GA	13061	9	3 242	17.6	1	2	377	867	92.2	675	93.6
Clayton, GA	13063	1	267 966	20.9	1	62	51 405	68 358	88.8	51 453	94.3
Clinch, GA	13065	6	6 996	19.4	1	7	1 431	1 784	97.5	1 477	99.8
Cobb, GA	13067	1	663 818	18.1	3	120	111 493	165 032	82.3	114 905	90.4
Coffee, GA	13069	7	39 674	19.6	1	15	7 993	9 786	92.7	7 661	95.3
Colquitt, GA	13071	6	43 915	19.0	1	17	8 494	10 489	94.5	8 422	97.1
Columbia, GA	13073	2	103 812	19.9	1	29	20 570	26 407	86.9	20 242	91.0
Cook, GA	13075	6	16 366	19.6	2	5	3 252	4 164	95.4	3 266	98.1
Coweta, GA	13077	1	109 903	19.6	3	31	19 803	23 339	85.2	18 412	90.0
Crawford, GA	13079	3	12 874	19.1	1	5	2 067	3 288	90.5	2 663	91.7
Crisp, GA	13081	6	22 017	20.3	1	8	4 341	5 839	92.2	4 751	94.2
Dade, GA	13083	2	16 040	16.5	1	5	2 642	3 991	77.8	2 698	92.3
Dawson, GA	13085	1	19 731	17.4	1	7	3 133	3 395	92.2	2 804	95.6
Decatur, GA	13087	6	28 618	20.0	1	11	5 774	7 686	92.9	6 026	94.7
DeKalb, GA	13089	1	677 959	16.9	4	291	153 902	182 326	77.6	119 724	88.8
Dodge, GA	13091	7	19 574	18.4	2	7	3 555	4 906	96.1	3 963	98.4
Dooly, GA	13093	6	11 749	16.8	1	3	1 502	3 117	86.4	2 513	86.7
Dougherty, GA	13095	3	94 882	19.6	1	33	16 894	28 401	88.7	19 574	89.7
Douglas, GA	13097	1	112 760	19.8	1	33	20 997	25 409	84.8	19 159	91.4
Early, GA	13099	6	12 056	20.2	1	4	2 621	3 276	93.7	2 617	94.5
Echols, GA	13101	3	4 253	18.1	1	1	734	999	98.6	831	98.8
Effingham, GA	13103	2	46 924	19.7	1	17	9 778	10 636	93.0	8 498	96.6
Elbert, GA	13105	6	20 799	17.6	1	8	3 673	4 834	94.5	4 043	98.0
Emanuel, GA	13107	7	22 108	18.1	1	11	4 502	5 720	94.1	4 745	94.5
Evans, GA	13109	6	11 443	18.2	2	5	2 001	2 588	91.7	2 265	92.5
Fannin, GA	13111	8	21 887	14.6	1	5	3 177	3 861	93.6	3 128	96.0
Fayette, GA	13113	1	104 248	19.5	1	29	21 603	27 262	85.2	21 549	89.8
Floyd, GA	13115	3	94 198	17.4	3	34	15 779	23 133	81.5	16 375	93.0
Forsyth, GA	13117	1	140 393	19.1	1	29	23 612	23 873	82.1	17 633	91.0
Franklin, GA	13119	8	21 590	16.9	1	7	3 764	5 002	84.6	3 659	98.5
Fulton, GA	13121	1	915 623	17.4	4	98	76 269	219 663	76.6	145 409	86.9

[1]County type codes are from the Economic Research Service of the United States Department of Agriculture. See notes and definitions at the end of this section.

Table C-1. Population, School, and Student Characteristics by County—*Continued*

STATE County	Characteristics of students, 2004–2005				Outcomes		Staff and students, 2004–2005		
	Percent with IEP[2]	Percent eligible for free or reduced-price lunch	Percent minority	Percent English-language learners	Number of graduates, 2003–2004	Percent dropouts, grades 9–12, 2001–2002	Number of teachers	Student-teacher ratio	Central administration staff
	10	11	12	13	14	15	16	17	18
Pasco, FL	18.7	47.5	16.7	2.9	2 914	4.2	3 643	16.7	453
Pinellas, FL	17.1	43.6	30.6	2.8	...	6.3	6 768	16.8	...
Polk, FL	14.5	51.6	40.8	5.4	4 591	3.6	5 660	15.2	384
Putnam, FL	18.8	67.7	38.5	3.7	575	2.5	724	17.2	88
St. Johns, FL	17.4	21.2	14.8	0.4	1 509	2.5	1 556	16.2	245
St. Lucie, FL	13.4	50.2	47.2	5.3	1 577	1.6	1 758	19.9	269
Santa Rosa, FL	15.3	31.6	10.0	0.4	1 576	2.1	1 397	17.9	91
Sarasota, FL	16.5	39.5	21.6	4.9	2 281	3.6	2 685	15.4	164
Seminole, FL	13.4	29.5	34.0	3.1	3 861	1.5	3 915	17.0	229
Sumter, FL	15.8	55.5	27.6	4.3	323	2.8	422	17.0	55
Suwannee, FL	13.0	53.3	24.0	2.1	332	3.5	351	16.6	50
Taylor, FL	19.3	60.1	26.1	0.2	195	3.0	215	16.3	36
Union, FL	17.7	48.1	20.7	0.4	134	1.9	171	12.9	31
Volusia, FL	18.1	39.5	29.3	3.5	3 775	1.9	4 054	18.1	373
Wakulla, FL	19.2	36.3	12.1	0.1	249	5.7	280	17.4	40
Walton, FL	15.1	50.3	12.0	1.0	283	6.1	411	16.0	47
Washington, FL	15.1	57.0	21.4	0.0	198	2.8	246	14.2	74
GEORGIA	12.3	47.9	49.5	3.9	...	6.5	104 995	14.8	...
Appling, GA	16.6	59.7	33.3	2.1	165	7.4	241	14.3	14
Atkinson, GA	15.2	79.1	49.3	6.3	77	10.8	104	16.4	6
Bacon, GA	14.4	53.5	26.2	1.0	118	8.0	131	14.4	11
Baker, GA	17.1	98.7	79.2	0.0	...	...	32	12.2	2
Baldwin, GA	17.5	57.1	67.0	0.9	273	3.7	459	13.2	19
Banks, GA	14.5	54.7	9.2	2.4	116	8.6	162	15.7	10
Barrow, GA	15.9	39.5	25.8	5.2	433	6.6	671	15.1	29
Bartow, GA	13.5	42.2	19.9	3.1	796	7.0	1 214	14.8	45
Ben Hill, GA	14.5	68.9	51.7	3.6	162	10.0	235	14.1	15
Berrien, GA	12.8	55.5	19.9	0.0	158	8.4	190	16.2	15
Bibb, GA	11.0	68.5	75.4	1.1	985	10.3	1 586	15.9	112
Bleckley, GA	15.0	51.1	30.8	1.0	123	7.8	158	15.7	9
Brantley, GA	13.9	54.9	4.0	0.0	149	10.4	222	15.2	10
Brooks, GA	14.1	75.6	65.2	2.1	127	9.3	176	13.9	19
Bryan, GA	8.9	30.6	20.8	0.0	352	5.7	378	16.0	13
Bulloch, GA	15.5	54.2	41.5	1.5	...	7.0	679	12.9	65
Burke, GA	11.5	78.7	69.3	0.0	188	9.3	314	14.6	17
Butts, GA	13.3	48.8	60.1	0.0	101	3.6	222	15.6	17
Calhoun, GA	14.9	90.9	96.5	0.8	39	5.6	49	15.1	6
Camden, GA	13.5	39.4	31.8	0.6	501	6.8	642	15.0	31
Candler, GA	14.6	67.0	46.5	4.4	90	10.1	124	15.5	9
Carroll, GA	14.2	47.6	27.2	1.9	864	6.7	1 153	15.5	63
Catoosa, GA	13.1	37.1	5.2	0.6	452	7.0	681	15.0	27
Charlton, GA	14.3	59.6	34.0	0.0	100	6.5	131	15.2	9
Chatham, GA	11.6	58.0	71.9	0.9	1 406	16.8	2 480	14.0	176
Chattahoochee, GA	13.7	77.9	37.6	0.2	0	...	42	12.7	5
Chattooga, GA	19.1	50.6	12.4	1.6	209	6.8	291	14.7	14
Cherokee, GA	12.4	20.1	15.4	3.7	1 449	4.5	2 082	14.9	87
Clarke, GA	15.3	66.5	76.5	6.9	534	10.7	891	13.1	47
Clay, GA	14.1	92.8	98.4	0.0	...	...	29	13.0	2
Clayton, GA	10.0	67.2	90.4	5.2	2 212	8.2	3 361	15.3	156
Clinch, GA	21.8	60.9	40.6	0.0	89	7.4	110	13.0	6
Cobb, GA	13.1	33.2	47.5	7.0	...	3.8	7 685	14.5	399
Coffee, GA	12.3	69.1	44.5	3.7	356	9.3	561	14.2	38
Colquitt, GA	14.1	63.6	44.2	4.0	376	7.6	560	15.2	30
Columbia, GA	10.0	22.3	21.3	0.6	1 158	4.8	1 267	16.2	52
Cook, GA	13.2	60.5	43.8	1.9	...	7.7	208	15.6	26
Coweta, GA	14.6	30.4	27.7	1.1	...	5.5	1 283	15.4	78
Crawford, GA	17.8	61.7	29.9	0.0	120	5.6	134	15.4	10
Crisp, GA	11.8	70.1	61.1	0.7	225	9.8	316	13.8	22
Dade, GA	12.2	40.5	1.6	0.2	114	4.0	167	15.8	10
Dawson, GA	12.5	29.7	3.9	1.0	150	7.5	238	13.2	15
Decatur, GA	11.1	67.6	58.0	1.5	279	7.8	396	14.6	16
DeKalb, GA	9.5	60.8	88.6	4.0	...	6.6	10 559	14.6	890
Dodge, GA	11.7	62.4	38.6	0.3	...	5.9	241	14.7	26
Dooly, GA	10.1	85.0	89.8	3.3	63	12.1	106	14.2	13
Dougherty, GA	12.0	69.1	86.0	0.2	766	8.0	1 075	15.7	68
Douglas, GA	11.9	41.9	45.5	2.0	1 152	5.7	1 314	16.0	77
Early, GA	14.1	73.5	65.0	0.5	151	4.7	180	14.6	11
Echols, GA	9.8	59.8	32.0	4.8	40	5.3	47	15.5	6
Effingham, GA	15.2	31.3	18.1	0.4	509	5.8	621	15.8	35
Elbert, GA	12.0	56.7	44.1	1.9	205	7.1	268	13.7	11
Emanuel, GA	17.0	67.9	47.6	1.4	231	7.0	292	15.4	15
Evans, GA	18.8	72.2	55.2	4.3	...	6.0	142	14.1	13
Fannin, GA	15.0	44.4	1.9	0.2	167	4.9	203	15.7	12
Fayette, GA	10.9	11.1	27.0	1.8	1 526	2.0	1 483	14.6	61
Floyd, GA	15.6	52.2	29.1	4.0	...	7.3	1 143	13.8	85
Forsyth, GA	13.2	12.9	10.3	4.2	926	2.7	1 495	15.8	59
Franklin, GA	14.9	44.7	15.0	1.8	172	6.9	243	15.5	10
Fulton, GA	11.3	48.0	71.1	5.1	...	5.1	5 350	14.3	420

[2]IEP = Individual Education Program. See notes and definitions at the end of this section.
... = Not available.

Table C-1. Population, School, and Student Characteristics by County—*Continued*

STATE County	Revenue, 2003–2004				Current expenditures, 2003–2004			Resident population, 16 to 19 years, 2000			
	Total revenue (thousands of dollars)	Percent of revenue from:			Total expenditures (thousands of dollars)	Amount per student (dollars)	Percent for instruction	Total	Percent in armed forces	Percent high school graduates	Percent not enrolled, not employed, not in armed forces, not high school graduate
		Federal government	State government	Local government							
	19	20	21	22	23	24	25	26	27	28	29
Pasco, FL	448 929	8.8	58.5	32.7	369 692	6 428	64.9	14 076	0.1	11.7	5.8
Pinellas, FL	920 279	10.1	42.6	47.3	773 319	6 753	63.7	36 204	0.2	11.2	5.9
Polk, FL	644 591	11.4	52.8	35.9	574 225	6 825	66.3	25 278	0.0	9.9	8.1
Putnam, FL	88 453	13.8	57.8	28.4	81 391	6 649	62.6	3 725	0.0	10.2	9.1
St. Johns, FL	192 130	5.7	30.3	63.9	160 022	6 900	66.2	5 896	0.0	10.4	2.0
St. Lucie, FL	271 978	10.3	45.5	44.1	209 857	6 398	63.5	8 988	0.0	9.7	9.3
Santa Rosa, FL	171 486	9.7	58.6	31.6	144 966	5 934	61.8	6 309	0.2	9.1	3.6
Sarasota, FL	413 836	6.1	17.2	76.7	309 648	7 832	64.1	10 743	0.0	11.3	4.1
Seminole, FL	502 201	6.9	48.9	44.3	399 519	6 156	66.7	18 797	0.0	8.9	4.1
Sumter, FL	50 892	12.6	50.0	37.3	45 994	6 708	67.0	2 078	0.0	9.8	13.4
Suwannee, FL	42 098	13.6	63.7	22.7	40 330	6 886	63.9	1 987	0.0	10.9	9.5
Taylor, FL	28 956	18.0	51.6	30.5	26 066	7 316	61.8	1 093	0.0	6.0	11.2
Union, FL	16 083	12.2	69.9	18.0	14 931	6 877	61.1	665	0.3	10.2	16.1
Volusia, FL	537 578	9.0	42.7	48.3	423 770	6 612	65.7	22 260	0.1	9.9	6.0
Wakulla, FL	34 377	8.3	68.1	23.6	30 188	6 378	61.7	1 281	0.5	11.5	8.3
Walton, FL	59 078	10.4	17.9	71.7	46 620	7 139	64.5	1 863	0.5	10.6	4.5
Washington, FL	40 549	14.1	66.3	19.6	31 003	9 052	60.9	935	0.0	15.2	8.3
GEORGIA	14 136 215	8.5	44.8	46.7	11 772 664	7 733	68.9	471 799	1.7	11.2	7.3
Appling, GA	36 116	11.1	57.2	31.7	26 330	7 832	70.0	1 130	0.0	11.3	8.3
Atkinson, GA	13 478	13.2	68.9	17.9	11 508	6 789	67.7	502	0.0	18.1	16.9
Bacon, GA	15 665	14.7	61.4	23.9	13 805	7 327	67.9	523	0.0	17.4	6.1
Baker, GA	6 361	17.6	36.4	46.0	4 667	13 296	61.6	249	0.0	3.2	5.6
Baldwin, GA	54 669	14.7	63.5	21.8	45 210	7 602	69.2	3 752	0.0	6.6	6.7
Banks, GA	23 502	7.8	51.7	40.6	16 614	6 762	67.7	815	0.0	13.5	6.4
Barrow, GA	87 568	6.2	58.5	35.4	71 709	7 342	69.3	2 225	0.0	11.4	8.2
Bartow, GA	151 433	5.9	53.0	41.2	127 957	7 269	68.9	3 768	0.0	13.6	12.2
Ben Hill, GA	27 681	12.5	61.5	25.9	24 688	7 461	69.7	1 111	0.0	9.2	9.0
Berrien, GA	22 913	17.2	61.1	21.7	20 496	6 733	68.0	857	0.0	15.4	8.5
Bibb, GA	223 232	12.3	45.3	42.4	183 054	7 242	67.2	8 916	0.1	9.5	9.5
Bleckley, GA	22 329	9.0	72.7	18.4	16 353	6 724	67.3	984	0.0	12.2	4.5
Brantley, GA	23 786	12.7	67.3	20.0	22 058	6 624	67.3	812	0.0	12.8	4.7
Brooks, GA	20 962	15.7	62.0	22.3	19 184	7 601	68.7	1 120	2.0	12.4	10.4
Bryan, GA	43 468	7.4	53.8	38.8	35 297	6 119	69.6	1 355	0.0	9.8	8.3
Bulloch, GA	81 507	14.7	53.4	31.9	75 282	8 859	67.9	6 536	0.1	4.9	2.7
Burke, GA	39 388	14.3	34.4	51.3	37 188	7 985	62.7	1 541	0.8	8.0	10.6
Butts, GA	27 867	9.7	48.1	42.2	23 906	7 006	63.1	1 027	0.0	13.0	13.5
Calhoun, GA	7 793	14.4	49.8	35.8	6 509	9 181	61.5	333	0.0	10.8	6.0
Camden, GA	74 142	16.4	62.9	20.7	66 112	6 838	68.0	2 816	11.7	20.7	5.0
Candler, GA	15 849	15.1	59.6	25.3	13 499	6 991	67.5	491	0.0	5.7	8.8
Carroll, GA	150 673	9.1	54.5	36.5	127 475	7 327	69.1	5 999	0.0	8.7	8.0
Catoosa, GA	84 975	8.1	56.9	35.0	68 775	6 796	70.5	2 754	0.0	10.1	5.7
Charlton, GA	15 650	12.1	59.5	28.4	14 653	7 169	68.0	675	0.0	15.7	12.7
Chatham, GA	268 435	10.7	42.6	46.8	260 156	7 538	68.8	13 182	2.8	13.4	6.0
Chattahoochee, GA	6 064	16.0	63.8	20.2	4 645	9 558	60.6	1 303	67.8	71.1	3.1
Chattooga, GA	36 757	12.5	58.8	28.7	33 181	7 652	70.9	1 417	0.4	17.7	10.6
Cherokee, GA	291 191	4.0	46.4	49.6	215 649	7 258	70.8	7 243	0.1	9.8	5.6
Clarke, GA	131 082	10.7	36.8	52.5	106 787	9 284	63.5	10 245	1.1	5.6	4.7
Clay, GA	4 294	27.6	45.3	27.2	3 764	11 071	60.7	232	0.0	10.8	6.5
Clayton, GA	426 744	8.9	49.6	41.6	372 027	7 359	69.4	13 381	0.3	12.7	7.4
Clinch, GA	12 298	14.1	63.7	22.2	11 901	8 163	67.0	395	0.0	6.3	3.3
Cobb, GA	1 030 682	5.2	37.9	56.8	857 776	7 824	72.5	31 156	0.0	9.9	5.3
Coffee, GA	58 308	13.9	66.7	19.4	59 644	7 639	70.0	2 275	0.0	7.6	9.0
Colquitt, GA	71 473	14.2	63.2	22.7	62 939	7 476	68.4	2 754	2.9	10.8	10.7
Columbia, GA	145 619	5.1	54.4	40.5	132 007	6 580	71.3	5 336	0.0	8.8	3.3
Cook, GA	31 153	23.3	55.0	21.7	25 310	8 015	61.6	915	0.0	15.2	7.2
Coweta, GA	158 323	6.7	46.6	46.7	142 783	7 501	69.2	4 522	0.0	9.9	7.4
Crawford, GA	16 312	13.9	58.3	27.7	14 908	7 174	66.9	578	0.0	12.6	6.7
Crisp, GA	39 333	15.2	55.2	29.6	34 374	7 834	67.3	1 270	0.0	9.8	15.1
Dade, GA	22 414	11.2	58.6	30.1	19 407	7 357	70.1	1 042	0.0	8.1	8.5
Dawson, GA	31 097	5.0	34.9	60.2	24 549	8 121	68.7	752	0.0	19.4	10.0
Decatur, GA	47 132	14.2	57.2	28.6	41 677	7 294	70.7	1 605	0.0	8.8	9.3
DeKalb, GA	978 168	7.4	37.9	54.7	853 093	8 358	68.1	35 836	0.1	9.0	6.8
Dodge, GA	33 742	20.7	60.0	19.3	28 736	8 113	69.1	1 113	0.0	4.5	11.3
Dooly, GA	15 276	17.7	50.9	31.4	13 150	8 376	63.6	681	1.0	6.9	9.5
Dougherty, GA	149 198	13.6	49.1	37.3	133 740	7 940	65.4	6 697	10.6	12.7	7.0
Douglas, GA	169 037	5.9	46.1	48.0	137 150	6 963	67.4	4 929	0.0	11.8	4.3
Early, GA	23 235	16.7	56.1	27.1	19 340	7 134	70.9	679	0.0	17.4	9.4
Echols, GA	5 743	13.7	63.4	22.9	5 342	7 161	68.9	235	0.0	3.0	5.5
Effingham, GA	72 612	7.2	58.9	33.8	60 678	6 490	70.1	2 334	0.0	12.1	6.8
Elbert, GA	31 815	10.2	59.1	30.7	28 716	7 678	68.4	1 142	0.0	14.7	9.8
Emanuel, GA	35 172	16.8	64.2	18.9	32 343	7 060	69.8	1 569	0.0	9.4	10.5
Evans, GA	15 568	14.9	61.3	23.8	14 279	7 563	68.5	629	0.0	6.4	14.8
Fannin, GA	28 720	10.3	47.2	42.5	24 576	7 869	67.9	848	0.0	13.7	4.7
Fayette, GA	186 859	2.7	44.9	52.4	155 278	7 316	70.9	5 421	0.2	6.1	2.0
Floyd, GA	145 422	9.7	50.2	40.1	126 036	8 034	69.7	5 395	0.1	11.7	9.5
Forsyth, GA	210 193	3.0	36.4	60.6	157 885	7 155	68.5	3 849	0.0	7.3	4.3
Franklin, GA	29 959	9.3	54.0	36.7	25 900	7 082	71.7	1 120	0.0	11.3	5.1
Fulton, GA	1 534 684	7.7	25.6	66.7	1 259 941	10 046	68.6	44 610	0.2	7.9	8.0

Table C-1. Population, School, and Student Characteristics by County—*Continued*

STATE County	High school graduates, 2000			College enrollment, 2000		College graduates, 2000 (percent)						
	Population 25 years and over	High school graduate or less (percent)	High school graduate or more (percent)	Number	Percent public	Bachelor's degree or more	+/- U.S. percentage with bachelor's degree or more	Non-Hispanic White	Black	American Indian and Alaska Native	Asian or Pacific Islander	Hispanic[3]
	30	31	32	33	34	35	36	37	38	39	40	41
Pasco, FL	255 472	59.2	77.6	11 290	74.4	13.1	-11.3	12.7	13.0	5.9	45.2	14.2
Pinellas, FL	686 094	45.6	84.0	41 446	74.6	22.9	-1.5	23.8	10.5	18.1	33.6	20.0
Polk, FL	326 208	58.9	74.8	18 134	66.2	14.9	-9.5	16.0	8.9	13.0	40.0	8.6
Putnam, FL	47 761	67.0	70.4	1 984	84.9	9.4	-15.0	10.1	6.6	9.2	24.3	2.1
St. Johns, FL	86 199	37.3	87.2	6 425	59.5	33.1	8.7	34.2	12.6	50.0	58.7	25.9
St. Lucie, FL	136 448	55.0	77.7	7 060	83.1	15.1	-9.3	16.2	8.9	7.9	30.2	11.5
Santa Rosa, FL	78 166	43.8	85.4	5 600	91.2	22.9	-1.5	23.7	6.2	11.3	28.8	23.9
Sarasota, FL	256 802	43.0	87.1	10 210	75.7	27.4	3.0	28.2	10.5	24.4	35.0	19.5
Seminole, FL	243 216	35.7	88.7	22 095	79.8	31.0	6.6	32.8	18.5	26.6	47.6	23.3
Sumter, FL	41 509	61.6	77.3	1 221	70.7	12.2	-12.2	12.9	5.1	13.8	56.4	13.5
Suwannee, FL	23 492	65.6	73.2	953	81.4	10.5	-13.9	10.9	6.5	25.2	56.1	7.7
Taylor, FL	12 914	70.9	70.0	585	87.7	8.9	-15.5	10.0	3.1	0.0	57.6	5.0
Union, FL	9 363	66.4	72.5	429	78.3	7.5	-16.0	0.3	2.1	4.0	15.0	5.8
Volusia, FL	317 225	50.2	82.0	26 362	57.6	17.6	-6.8	18.1	14.7	16.9	35.8	11.7
Wakulla, FL	15 211	56.6	78.4	794	89.8	15.7	-8.7	17.4	4.5	0.0	10.0	16.1
Walton, FL	28 838	56.4	76.0	1 108	85.8	16.2	-8.2	17.4	2.6	12.6	25.8	12.6
Washington, FL	14 338	67.6	71.2	566	84.5	9.2	-15.2	9.5	6.1	8.6	0.0	8.0
GEORGIA	5 185 965	50.1	78.6	436 555	75.2	24.3	-0.1	27.7	15.5	18.1	43.8	13.6
Appling, GA	11 004	69.9	67.3	394	86.3	8.4	-16.0	9.6	3.8	0.0	32.7	0.0
Atkinson, GA	4 503	79.6	56.3	100	87.0	6.9	-17.5	9.0	3.4	0.0	20.0	0.5
Bacon, GA	6 525	76.3	67.7	317	98.1	6.6	-17.8	7.3	1.1	0.0	52.8	4.4
Baker, GA	2 543	74.4	66.0	103	97.1	10.7	-13.7	16.3	3.9	. . .	100.0	4.3
Baldwin, GA	28 445	62.8	72.6	4 231	73.8	16.2	-8.2	21.7	7.4	0.0	45.1	29.8
Banks, GA	9 401	72.9	65.4	328	81.7	8.6	-15.8	8.8	11.0	6.3	0.0	0.0
Barrow, GA	29 317	62.7	73.3	1 143	82.3	10.9	-13.5	11.6	5.8	21.5	16.6	2.0
Bartow, GA	48 709	62.4	71.8	2 093	80.0	14.1	-10.3	14.5	10.3	22.3	29.0	6.3
Ben Hill, GA	10 990	71.4	65.8	591	72.1	9.5	-14.9	12.8	2.6	19.4	0.0	0.0
Berrien, GA	10 451	68.6	66.0	604	94.2	9.4	-15.0	10.0	4.0	24.6	17.8	8.6
Bibb, GA	97 463	54.5	77.2	8 815	59.1	21.3	-3.1	29.1	10.1	19.2	47.3	25.8
Bleckley, GA	7 268	64.0	71.7	867	90.1	12.5	-11.9	14.5	5.6	. . .	0.0	0.0
Brantley, GA	9 282	74.9	72.5	379	89.2	6.2	-18.2	6.4	2.8	100.0	11.1	0.0
Brooks, GA	10 455	69.6	67.5	518	90.3	11.3	-13.1	15.1	4.3	0.0	0.0	4.4
Bryan, GA	14 333	53.8	79.0	825	86.8	19.3	-5.1	20.2	7.4	0.0	49.3	39.3
Bulloch, GA	28 740	51.7	77.9	12 889	96.8	25.4	1.0	29.6	11.5	0.0	70.4	15.8
Burke, GA	13 338	72.1	64.9	613	87.9	9.5	-14.9	14.0	4.5	0.0	60.0	0.0
Butts, GA	13 055	70.1	69.8	511	79.8	8.6	-15.8	9.5	5.6	0.0	43.8	25.0
Calhoun, GA	4 277	68.2	65.5	228	71.1	11.7	-12.7	18.6	6.4	. . .	. . .	8.3
Camden, GA	24 073	49.9	83.3	2 121	81.8	16.0	-8.4	17.1	10.0	30.5	22.7	16.2
Candler, GA	6 166	72.3	56.9	240	90.8	10.2	-14.2	13.6	3.0	0.0	. . .	3.6
Carroll, GA	53 464	63.2	71.1	6 435	94.8	16.5	-7.9	17.7	8.6	23.5	49.3	15.8
Catoosa, GA	35 231	58.8	76.0	2 014	88.1	13.8	-10.6	13.8	14.1	12.6	23.3	6.8
Charlton, GA	6 404	77.0	65.1	250	88.4	6.4	-18.0	8.0	1.7	5.9	28.3	0.0
Chatham, GA	147 849	46.7	80.2	15 613	69.0	25.0	0.6	32.1	12.6	12.9	36.2	23.4
Chattahoochee, GA	6 417	34.3	88.8	837	80.0	25.0	0.6	32.5	11.2	25.0	21.3	29.4
Chattooga, GA	17 054	74.2	60.4	619	74.5	7.7	-16.7	8.0	3.9	40.9	33.3	6.6
Cherokee, GA	91 141	42.9	84.4	5 781	71.0	27.0	2.6	27.6	21.7	22.7	39.9	14.5
Clarke, GA	51 845	40.6	81.0	29 695	94.7	30.8	15.4	52.9	11.3	14.8	76.4	21.3
Clay, GA	2 215	71.2	64.3	114	85.1	10.1	-14.3	15.8	4.3	85.7	0.0	60.0
Clayton, GA	141 554	51.8	80.1	11 042	74.8	16.6	-7.8	13.9	20.2	21.3	15.9	6.1
Clinch, GA	4 380	73.6	58.9	162	90.1	10.4	-14.0	12.8	3.0	0.0	61.5	41.7
Cobb, GA	395 349	32.0	88.8	35 713	73.6	39.8	15.4	42.7	31.9	32.0	54.0	19.3
Coffee, GA	22 798	68.1	64.8	1 299	91.1	10.0	-14.4	11.9	4.1	22.7	55.8	5.3
Colquitt, GA	26 127	70.9	64.9	1 159	89.6	11.4	-13.0	14.5	3.6	7.0	36.8	1.4
Columbia, GA	56 562	37.9	87.9	3 983	86.6	32.0	7.6	32.2	24.4	19.4	53.0	31.2
Cook, GA	9 876	71.4	64.6	530	93.6	8.1	-16.3	10.1	3.0	0.0	4.2	3.2
Coweta, GA	56 821	51.2	81.6	2 735	79.6	20.6	-3.8	22.7	11.1	11.3	44.2	12.2
Crawford, GA	8 050	72.4	67.3	410	85.9	6.8	-17.6	7.5	5.0	0.0	. . .	0.0
Crisp, GA	13 709	68.6	65.9	606	85.3	12.8	-11.6	17.7	3.9	0.0	48.8	7.9
Dade, GA	9 728	63.3	67.0	1 047	35.8	10.9	-13.5	10.8	0.0	0.0	36.1	12.5
Dawson, GA	10 752	53.7	79.5	358	81.3	18.1	-6.3	18.3	83.3	0.0	0.0	4.5
Decatur, GA	17 633	63.9	69.7	1 019	94.5	12.1	-12.3	14.0	8.2	14.1	37.1	13.0
DeKalb, GA	429 981	35.3	85.1	47 609	57.6	36.3	11.9	55.7	22.8	24.5	46.6	14.8
Dodge, GA	12 501	70.3	66.3	555	83.1	11.6	-12.8	13.7	5.5	0.0	49.3	0.9
Dooly, GA	7 309	69.4	68.5	384	82.3	9.6	-14.8	13.6	5.1	0.0	51.3	1.2
Dougherty, GA	58 024	54.6	73.7	6 215	89.0	17.8	-6.6	23.1	13.4	16.4	15.4	15.4
Douglas, GA	58 687	53.5	81.1	4 171	66.0	19.2	-5.2	17.6	25.6	18.3	50.2	16.9
Early, GA	7 872	65.0	68.4	393	94.7	12.6	-11.8	16.4	7.1	. . .	100.0	10.1
Echols, GA	2 167	75.2	60.5	97	95.9	8.4	-16.0	10.3	0.0	. . .	50.0	2.0
Effingham, GA	23 129	61.6	78.9	1 184	88.5	13.6	-10.8	13.8	11.0	14.3	28.3	16.5
Elbert, GA	13 617	72.0	67.2	492	75.8	9.8	-14.6	12.3	3.1	100.0	42.9	13.7
Emanuel, GA	13 465	73.7	61.4	658	94.1	10.1	-14.3	11.8	5.3	30.4	58.8	4.0
Evans, GA	6 540	73.5	65.7	205	82.9	9.0	-15.4	11.7	2.7	0.0	57.4	0.0
Fannin, GA	14 291	68.0	70.9	474	88.2	10.4	-14.0	10.4	66.7	14.3	20.5	8.0
Fayette, GA	59 016	31.6	92.4	3 663	79.5	36.2	11.8	35.5	42.5	25.5	46.0	26.5
Floyd, GA	58 651	61.8	71.5	4 971	50.4	15.8	-8.6	17.8	4.5	17.2	28.6	5.7
Forsyth, GA	65 027	37.8	85.7	2 978	77.2	34.6	10.2	35.0	25.3	27.9	64.0	18.1
Franklin, GA	13 448	70.4	67.0	1 013	36.0	10.3	-14.1	11.2	0.8	0.0	37.5	0.0
Fulton, GA	527 738	35.4	84.0	55 078	59.3	41.4	17.0	60.6	18.3	28.1	60.3	20.1

[3]May be of any race.
. . . = Not available.

Table C-1. Population, School, and Student Characteristics by County—*Continued*

STATE County	State/ county code	County type[1]	Population, 2005		Number of schools and students, 2004–2005			Resident enrollment, 2000			
			Total	Percent 5 to 17 years	School districts	Schools	Students	Total	Percent public	K–12	Percent public
	1		1	2	3	4	5	6	7	8	9
Gilmer, GA	13123	6	27 335	16.7	2	8	4 088	4 750	89.8	3 934	94.1
Glascock, GA	13125	9	2 705	16.3	1	1	598	564	91.3	474	94.5
Glynn, GA	13127	3	71 874	17.7	1	19	12 037	16 443	88.8	12 887	91.2
Gordon, GA	13129	6	50 279	17.8	2	16	9 557	10 354	92.3	8 291	95.4
Grady, GA	13131	6	24 466	18.3	1	8	4 461	6 185	92.5	4 966	94.0
Greene, GA	13133	6	15 693	16.5	1	7	2 242	3 385	85.6	2 693	87.1
Gwinnett, GA	13135	1	726 273	19.3	2	126	137 781	161 510	85.8	119 551	92.9
Habersham, GA	13137	6	39 603	16.3	1	13	6 272	8 166	85.7	6 134	95.9
Hall, GA	13139	3	165 771	18.6	2	41	28 345	33 309	89.6	26 158	95.1
Hancock, GA	13141	7	9 643	16.3	1	4	1 524	2 704	91.5	2 155	92.3
Haralson, GA	13143	1	28 338	18.1	2	13	5 503	5 956	93.3	4 784	95.1
Harris, GA	13145	2	27 779	17.4	1	7	4 521	6 252	86.8	4 797	87.0
Hart, GA	13147	6	24 036	16.8	1	6	3 560	4 886	92.8	3 969	97.3
Heard, GA	13149	1	11 346	20.6	1	6	2 181	2 767	93.9	2 286	94.4
Henry, GA	13151	1	167 848	20.2	1	44	32 416	32 860	84.7	25 449	90.0
Houston, GA	13153	3	126 163	19.3	1	36	23 998	32 495	89.5	24 077	92.6
Irwin, GA	13155	7	10 093	19.9	1	4	1 762	2 682	95.9	2 266	95.8
Jackson, GA	13157	6	52 292	18.1	3	20	9 346	9 885	91.2	8 057	94.7
Jasper, GA	13159	1	13 147	18.5	1	6	2 036	2 876	86.9	2 373	87.8
Jeff Davis, GA	13161	7	13 083	18.7	1	5	2 690	2 880	92.6	2 328	96.4
Jefferson, GA	13163	6	16 926	19.2	1	7	3 327	4 628	88.6	3 911	89.5
Jenkins, GA	13165	6	8 729	19.5	1	4	1 728	2 381	94.3	1 969	96.8
Johnson, GA	13167	9	9 538	20.0	1	4	1 260	2 318	94.4	1 858	95.3
Jones, GA	13169	3	26 836	18.0	1	10	5 234	6 342	89.0	5 160	92.6
Lamar, GA	13171	1	16 378	17.8	1	4	2 533	4 354	90.7	2 824	92.5
Lanier, GA	13173	3	7 553	18.6	1	4	1 522	1 834	93.5	1 530	93.9
Laurens, GA	13175	6	46 896	18.4	2	17	9 318	11 544	93.4	9 240	94.7
Lee, GA	13177	3	31 099	20.3	1	7	5 549	7 626	90.8	6 043	92.7
Liberty, GA	13179	3	57 544	23.6	1	15	11 424	17 177	91.7	13 082	95.6
Lincoln, GA	13181	8	8 207	16.8	1	3	1 399	1 953	96.5	1 648	97.9
Long, GA	13183	3	11 083	23.4	1	3	2 178	2 788	93.2	2 211	95.3
Lowndes, GA	13185	3	96 705	18.0	2	23	16 581	30 067	91.0	18 445	92.5
Lumpkin, GA	13187	6	24 324	16.7	1	6	3 671	6 383	92.1	3 764	94.1
McDuffie, GA	13189	2	21 743	18.9	2	9	4 223	5 669	90.7	4 565	92.2
McIntosh, GA	13191	3	11 068	19.4	1	4	1 921	2 737	88.2	2 355	90.4
Macon, GA	13193	6	13 745	18.7	1	4	2 135	3 765	87.8	3 040	87.3
Madison, GA	13195	3	27 289	18.5	1	8	4 596	5 893	89.5	4 759	92.3
Marion, GA	13197	2	7 244	19.8	1	3	1 700	1 824	93.4	1 526	95.0
Meriwether, GA	13199	1	22 919	18.4	2	11	3 834	5 667	88.3	4 659	89.4
Miller, GA	13201	8	6 228	17.4	1	4	1 127	1 707	88.3	1 328	91.3
Mitchell, GA	13205	6	23 791	18.5	3	10	4 386	6 545	88.2	5 285	88.8
Monroe, GA	13207	3	23 785	17.6	1	6	3 806	5 835	84.2	4 410	84.9
Montgomery, GA	13209	9	8 909	17.4	1	4	1 265	2 506	76.9	1 594	96.3
Morgan, GA	13211	6	17 492	18.4	1	6	3 223	3 886	86.7	3 111	93.4
Murray, GA	13213	3	40 812	19.5	1	10	7 581	8 373	94.9	7 119	97.3
Muscogee, GA	13215	2	185 271	19.1	1	62	33 069	50 950	89.1	36 797	91.0
Newton, GA	13217	1	86 713	19.1	1	20	15 773	16 015	84.2	12 419	90.4
Oconee, GA	13219	3	29 748	20.5	1	10	5 789	7 782	83.3	6 034	88.5
Oglethorpe, GA	13221	3	13 609	18.3	2	6	2 317	3 078	87.4	2 396	91.8
Paulding, GA	13223	1	112 411	21.1	1	28	21 732	21 260	88.8	16 957	94.3
Peach, GA	13225	6	24 794	17.4	2	7	4 055	7 642	84.6	4 930	91.3
Pickens, GA	13227	1	28 442	16.2	1	7	4 195	4 808	92.4	3 842	95.8
Pierce, GA	13229	6	17 119	17.8	1	4	3 407	3 931	96.2	3 108	97.7
Pike, GA	13231	1	16 128	18.8	1	4	3 000	3 534	85.7	2 842	88.8
Polk, GA	13233	6	40 479	18.1	1	13	7 112	9 338	92.5	7 361	95.2
Pulaski, GA	13235	6	9 737	15.9	1	5	1 686	2 205	89.5	1 688	89.4
Putnam, GA	13237	6	19 829	15.7	1	4	2 650	4 207	81.1	3 332	82.1
Quitman, GA	13239	9	2 467	16.7	1	1	310	609	92.3	535	91.4
Rabun, GA	13241	9	16 087	15.9	1	7	2 250	2 961	85.6	2 450	89.6
Randolph, GA	13243	6	7 310	19.1	1	4	1 591	2 230	79.6	1 647	87.5
Richmond, GA	13245	2	195 769	18.8	1	58	34 141	56 607	88.4	41 134	91.8
Rockdale, GA	13247	1	78 545	19.4	1	20	14 623	19 019	88.6	14 818	93.0
Schley, GA	13249	8	4 122	20.7	2	2	1 251	1 062	88.4	851	90.8
Screven, GA	13251	6	15 430	20.0	1	4	3 030	4 374	94.3	3 439	96.0
Seminole, GA	13253	6	9 226	18.2	1	3	1 737	2 359	90.6	1 800	93.9
Spalding, GA	13255	1	61 289	19.3	2	24	10 813	14 632	87.9	11 806	90.9
Stephens, GA	13257	7	25 060	16.9	1	7	4 324	6 355	76.6	4 381	93.8
Stewart, GA	13259	8	4 882	17.9	1	3	697	1 265	87.2	991	85.4
Sumter, GA	13261	6	32 912	19.9	1	10	5 631	9 860	87.0	6 896	85.5
Talbot, GA	13263	8	6 709	16.9	1	1	776	1 505	85.0	1 236	85.9
Taliaferro, GA	13265	8	1 826	16.3	1	1	275	463	86.6	379	92.9
Tattnall, GA	13267	6	23 211	15.7	1	8	3 366	4 802	84.1	3 912	86.4
Taylor, GA	13269	8	8 887	19.4	1	4	1 595	2 199	95.5	1 805	96.2
Telfair, GA	13271	7	13 205	13.3	1	4	1 695	2 480	95.0	2 006	97.0
Terrell, GA	13273	3	10 711	19.7	1	4	1 660	2 960	87.0	2 402	85.6
Thomas, GA	13275	4	44 692	18.3	2	18	8 619	11 646	87.0	9 084	91.6
Tift, GA	13277	4	40 793	19.1	1	13	7 708	10 744	90.5	7 675	92.4
Toombs, GA	13279	7	27 274	19.6	2	10	5 389	6 704	93.0	5 445	94.9
Towns, GA	13281	9	10 315	12.0	1	4	1 606	1 865	74.0	1 156	95.8
Treutlen, GA	13283	7	6 753	18.3	1	2	1 241	1 671	92.1	1 385	95.7

[1]County type codes are from the Economic Research Service of the United States Department of Agriculture. See notes and definitions at the end of this section.

Table C-1. Population, School, and Student Characteristics by County—*Continued*

STATE County	Characteristics of students, 2004–2005				Outcomes		Staff and students, 2004–2005		
	Percent with IEP[2]	Percent eligible for free or reduced-price lunch	Percent minority	Percent English-language learners	Number of graduates, 2003–2004	Percent dropouts, grades 9–12, 2001–2002	Number of teachers	Student-teacher ratio	Central administration staff
	10	11	12	13	14	15	16	17	18
Gilmer, GA	11.6	53.4	12.9	8.2	. . .	5.8	294	13.9	30
Glascock, GA	15.6	47.3	13.2	0.0	33	10.1	38	15.7	5
Glynn, GA	13.1	47.0	43.9	1.9	603	10.0	866	13.9	43
Gordon, GA	14.4	45.6	18.2	5.0	415	7.8	621	15.4	37
Grady, GA	11.1	57.7	46.3	2.6	245	6.7	317	14.1	26
Greene, GA	15.3	78.9	73.5	1.1	119	2.0	174	12.9	15
Gwinnett, GA	11.5	34.2	51.7	11.0	7 323	3.2	9 380	14.7	286
Habersham, GA	13.3	41.4	22.8	6.6	302	7.5	434	14.5	16
Hall, GA	10.2	50.0	42.3	16.6	1 209	7.7	1 866	15.2	53
Hancock, GA	13.8	89.3	98.7	0.1	92	12.0	105	14.5	8
Haralson, GA	16.1	39.9	6.2	0.0	261	7.9	354	15.5	18
Harris, GA	8.1	34.5	23.6	0.2	229	6.0	278	16.3	14
Hart, GA	12.9	47.1	29.7	1.2	205	5.8	238	14.9	8
Heard, GA	13.2	52.6	12.4	0.0	86	4.5	142	15.3	8
Henry, GA	11.8	27.1	39.2	1.5	1 424	4.0	1 999	16.2	56
Houston, GA	12.8	41.0	39.9	1.3	1 297	5.8	1 636	14.7	78
Irwin, GA	17.9	62.4	37.8	0.0	130	8.0	127	13.9	10
Jackson, GA	15.1	39.4	14.9	2.8	420	6.8	607	15.4	38
Jasper, GA	14.4	61.1	38.6	2.6	121	10.3	143	14.3	12
Jeff Davis, GA	13.9	59.3	26.3	3.6	115	7.9	182	14.8	19
Jefferson, GA	15.0	81.6	76.1	0.7	217	5.2	224	14.8	18
Jenkins, GA	14.2	77.1	55.2	1.7	99	12.1	122	14.2	9
Johnson, GA	17.9	71.8	52.3	0.0	76	5.5	96	13.1	10
Jones, GA	12.3	34.0	26.7	0.0	252	8.2	316	16.6	12
Lamar, GA	11.4	60.1	41.6	0.5	111	5.9	152	16.6	10
Lanier, GA	15.7	68.1	30.9	0.2	62	9.1	103	14.7	10
Laurens, GA	13.1	60.9	48.1	0.3	448	6.1	644	14.5	26
Lee, GA	9.0	31.7	17.6	0.5	315	2.8	340	16.3	16
Liberty, GA	12.2	57.0	67.5	0.9	521	4.3	745	15.3	45
Lincoln, GA	14.1	61.2	42.6	0.0	95	3.2	101	13.9	8
Long, GA	9.6	69.7	38.9	6.5	69	10.8	131	16.6	11
Lowndes, GA	15.2	49.1	50.6	1.1	878	8.1	1 090	15.2	57
Lumpkin, GA	13.7	39.8	8.2	2.5	196	4.7	231	15.9	12
McDuffie, GA	12.7	64.2	51.8	0.4	. . .	6.6	291	14.5	34
McIntosh, GA	8.9	75.1	53.9	0.1	96	13.4	115	16.7	10
Macon, GA	0.1	81.3	88.8	2.8	96	9.7	139	15.4	8
Madison, GA	16.3	45.0	12.3	1.0	259	6.4	318	14.4	16
Marion, GA	11.2	67.6	46.4	0.4	91	12.9	112	15.2	9
Meriwether, GA	25.0	80.6	61.6	0.4	. . .	9.4	293	13.1	24
Miller, GA	10.0	56.3	40.1	0.0	74	3.1	84	13.4	4
Mitchell, GA	14.0	73.8	67.7	1.6	. . .	10.5	306	14.3	32
Monroe, GA	15.8	49.1	36.4	0.7	206	5.4	249	15.3	12
Montgomery, GA	11.8	69.6	43.4	2.8	68	11.2	86	14.7	6
Morgan, GA	13.1	37.8	34.8	0.3	186	3.3	222	14.5	14
Murray, GA	11.1	55.7	15.2	3.7	277	11.7	471	16.1	22
Muscogee, GA	13.0	55.4	66.7	1.4	1 605	6.8	2 207	15.0	136
Newton, GA	13.8	47.3	46.3	2.3	584	5.0	1 031	15.3	23
Oconee, GA	11.3	17.9	13.2	1.0	425	2.6	392	14.8	19
Oglethorpe, GA	15.8	45.2	24.4	0.4	. . .	5.2	184	12.6	28
Paulding, GA	12.1	24.9	19.3	0.7	819	7.7	1 402	15.5	61
Peach, GA	12.4	64.6	60.5	2.7	. . .	15.4	282	14.4	31
Pickens, GA	12.9	39.9	4.2	0.9	204	6.0	286	14.7	14
Pierce, GA	15.4	55.2	15.6	3.8	161	6.4	212	16.1	16
Pike, GA	12.2	31.8	14.5	0.0	151	7.2	181	16.6	12
Polk, GA	16.8	47.2	28.4	5.2	323	10.0	493	14.4	11
Pulaski, GA	14.1	58.0	44.3	0.9	86	9.2	123	13.8	11
Putnam, GA	15.5	70.7	55.5	3.1	118	10.5	206	12.9	15
Quitman, GA	14.8	97.7	80.5	0.0	. . .	. . .	25	12.4	3
Rabun, GA	15.3	51.2	10.3	5.0	110	9.6	163	13.8	11
Randolph, GA	11.1	87.0	89.9	0.5	82	7.9	116	13.7	16
Richmond, GA	11.7	68.8	76.5	0.3	1 664	5.0	2 372	14.4	112
Rockdale, GA	10.1	40.5	52.4	3.1	796	4.2	956	15.3	38
Schley, GA	8.4	46.5	24.3	0.3	. . .	10.4	81	15.4	18
Screven, GA	17.5	78.9	55.9	0.3	184	7.3	203	14.9	10
Seminole, GA	14.2	72.7	55.3	0.6	92	29.1	121	14.4	9
Spalding, GA	15.1	58.8	48.8	0.6	. . .	13.2	771	14.0	62
Stephens, GA	14.1	46.6	18.7	0.8	239	9.2	301	14.4	12
Stewart, GA	13.6	93.5	95.9	0.0	24	17.9	54	13.0	8
Sumter, GA	10.6	74.3	79.2	1.2	255	14.0	384	14.7	19
Talbot, GA	14.0	88.8	94.6	0.1	38	6.8	58	13.4	6
Taliaferro, GA	10.2	93.8	89.2	0.4	19	9.0	25	10.9	3
Tattnall, GA	12.8	68.0	45.9	3.4	133	8.1	221	15.3	11
Taylor, GA	10.7	71.9	51.2	0.0	59	12.5	110	14.6	11
Telfair, GA	15.7	72.2	49.4	1.9	82	8.2	128	13.2	8
Terrell, GA	11.4	70.1	97.2	0.4	61	6.4	125	13.2	8
Thomas, GA	14.6	62.1	51.0	0.3	476	4.3	567	15.2	37
Tift, GA	12.5	56.6	49.7	4.7	350	9.4	505	15.3	21
Toombs, GA	12.0	64.5	45.9	4.0	250	6.4	370	14.6	20
Towns, GA	9.0	40.6	1.4	0.2	126	75.3	166	9.7	6
Treutlen, GA	16.4	69.2	41.9	0.0	63	6.6	83	14.9	6

[2]IEP = Individual Education Program. See notes and definitions at the end of this section.
. . . = Not available.

Table C-1. Population, School, and Student Characteristics by County—Continued

STATE County	Revenue, 2003–2004 Total revenue (thousands of dollars)	Percent of revenue from: Federal government	State government	Local government	Current expenditures, 2003–2004 Total expenditures (thousands of dollars)	Amount per student (dollars)	Percent for instruction	Resident population, 16 to 19 years, 2000 Total	Percent in armed forces	Percent high school graduates	Percent not enrolled, not employed, not in armed forces, not high school graduate
	19	20	21	22	23	24	25	26	27	28	29
Gilmer, GA	41 456	8.9	44.8	46.2	33 274	8 244	70.6	1 144	0.0	7.2	13.0
Glascock, GA	5 100	17.8	58.8	23.4	4 755	7 925	62.0	140	0.0	9.3	12.1
Glynn, GA	112 624	10.1	35.8	54.2	99 251	8 259	70.9	3 714	0.0	13.8	7.5
Gordon, GA	80 007	6.9	56.7	36.4	65 083	7 093	69.1	2 497	0.0	14.3	5.8
Grady, GA	35 382	14.3	60.8	24.9	33 069	7 380	70.8	1 473	0.0	12.5	9.0
Greene, GA	25 217	17.1	32.4	50.6	22 445	9 918	66.8	821	0.0	13.0	14.1
Gwinnett, GA	1 527 152	3.7	33.6	62.7	996 161	7 587	68.5	31 269	0.0	9.8	5.0
Habersham, GA	56 133	8.1	49.4	42.5	44 718	7 400	69.8	2 244	0.4	11.8	16.5
Hall, GA	228 791	8.6	48.0	43.4	197 207	7 235	68.9	8 005	0.0	8.5	12.8
Hancock, GA	13 184	25.6	48.4	26.0	15 249	9 591	58.4	587	0.0	11.6	8.9
Haralson, GA	43 739	9.2	57.3	33.6	37 742	6 952	71.2	1 523	0.0	10.2	7.6
Harris, GA	34 282	6.7	49.4	44.0	31 411	7 123	66.0	1 150	0.0	5.9	2.1
Hart, GA	30 629	9.4	45.4	45.3	27 057	7 596	68.7	1 096	0.3	12.9	7.8
Heard, GA	17 878	8.4	49.3	42.3	15 063	7 016	69.1	534	0.0	9.2	14.2
Henry, GA	247 484	3.9	42.4	53.7	198 399	6 648	70.7	6 124	0.0	11.9	4.6
Houston, GA	220 899	7.8	55.9	36.3	177 877	7 603	70.6	6 690	5.7	15.1	4.7
Irwin, GA	17 877	18.7	57.8	23.5	14 620	8 024	67.7	743	0.0	10.5	5.2
Jackson, GA	78 767	6.9	49.3	43.9	65 147	7 428	67.9	2 284	0.0	11.9	10.2
Jasper, GA	17 565	15.2	47.4	37.4	15 175	7 247	65.5	680	0.0	19.1	6.5
Jeff Davis, GA	19 594	15.9	65.7	18.4	19 548	7 539	70.3	739	0.0	17.3	6.0
Jefferson, GA	28 663	20.2	55.5	24.3	25 723	7 561	64.0	1 085	0.0	10.2	7.6
Jenkins, GA	14 377	23.0	59.0	18.0	13 185	7 661	69.0	516	0.0	8.9	10.1
Johnson, GA	11 811	23.4	62.4	14.2	11 349	8 578	65.7	731	0.0	5.6	25.2
Jones, GA	34 274	8.0	62.6	29.4	29 992	5 782	70.7	1 553	0.0	13.8	1.9
Lamar, GA	21 991	9.1	56.9	34.0	16 818	6 488	67.3	1 065	0.0	7.0	6.6
Lanier, GA	13 899	23.8	61.5	14.7	11 828	7 912	64.9	424	0.0	12.3	7.1
Laurens, GA	74 925	11.6	56.3	32.2	66 851	7 192	69.9	2 591	0.3	10.7	6.8
Lee, GA	39 288	6.4	61.3	32.3	34 814	6 389	70.3	1 666	0.0	6.7	2.1
Liberty, GA	92 510	18.9	61.0	20.1	79 777	6 868	69.4	4 433	26.0	35.6	5.8
Lincoln, GA	12 488	15.3	59.3	25.4	11 629	8 087	68.5	450	4.0	4.7	9.3
Long, GA	14 696	15.2	66.3	18.5	12 013	5 806	67.9	617	2.4	8.6	11.3
Lowndes, GA	134 539	11.0	52.9	36.1	114 172	6 979	69.5	6 030	2.5	9.9	6.0
Lumpkin, GA	29 627	8.0	44.2	47.7	26 304	7 412	66.0	1 663	1.1	10.8	4.8
McDuffie, GA	38 328	12.2	57.8	30.0	33 550	7 784	70.3	1 224	0.0	10.5	9.6
McIntosh, GA	15 915	11.9	55.7	32.4	13 689	7 082	64.2	641	0.0	11.4	8.9
Macon, GA	18 476	15.0	53.6	31.4	16 977	7 860	67.1	929	0.0	9.3	11.9
Madison, GA	36 858	8.1	61.5	30.5	33 882	7 308	70.3	1 342	0.0	15.9	7.0
Marion, GA	15 627	29.8	51.4	18.8	13 073	7 623	61.1	386	0.0	17.4	4.4
Meriwether, GA	34 987	14.2	59.4	26.4	32 766	8 475	66.5	1 359	0.0	17.3	9.8
Miller, GA	9 306	11.3	65.8	22.9	9 274	8 057	69.8	413	0.0	16.0	4.8
Mitchell, GA	38 982	16.0	56.4	27.6	35 048	7 876	68.2	1 467	0.0	11.4	11.7
Monroe, GA	37 087	6.9	48.2	44.9	31 069	8 133	67.9	1 241	0.0	15.0	5.6
Montgomery, GA	10 334	12.7	63.7	23.5	9 727	7 540	66.1	526	0.0	5.3	6.1
Morgan, GA	30 047	7.3	49.3	43.4	23 180	7 235	72.1	820	0.0	11.5	11.1
Murray, GA	59 424	8.8	62.2	29.0	49 768	6 659	72.3	1 995	0.3	13.3	12.5
Muscogee, GA	266 774	11.4	57.8	30.8	255 594	7 732	68.1	12 458	14.4	23.2	6.9
Newton, GA	114 486	8.2	50.6	41.2	100 602	6 838	71.8	3 508	0.0	10.2	8.2
Oconee, GA	51 330	4.2	53.4	42.4	39 498	6 849	71.8	1 493	0.0	10.6	2.5
Oglethorpe, GA	26 200	11.3	49.6	39.1	24 346	10 811	63.9	671	0.0	13.6	8.5
Paulding, GA	159 718	4.2	54.6	41.1	135 893	6 642	72.7	3 607	0.0	13.4	6.2
Peach, GA	34 057	17.1	56.2	26.8	32 220	8 045	65.3	1 796	0.0	6.5	9.6
Pickens, GA	37 064	8.3	40.6	51.0	31 073	7 531	67.4	1 029	0.0	10.2	10.0
Pierce, GA	25 731	11.3	62.1	26.6	22 457	6 840	69.6	760	0.0	18.7	11.2
Pike, GA	19 697	8.0	59.8	32.1	17 679	5 883	69.5	717	0.0	6.4	9.2
Polk, GA	54 822	10.6	61.4	28.0	49 302	6 978	71.9	2 229	0.0	9.2	15.2
Pulaski, GA	12 926	10.2	62.0	27.8	12 420	7 419	66.9	587	0.0	9.5	10.6
Putnam, GA	30 558	13.0	31.0	56.0	23 023	8 781	63.8	952	0.0	9.7	10.5
Quitman, GA	4 044	23.6	51.3	25.1	3 520	11 932	58.9	144	0.0	6.9	11.1
Rabun, GA	25 689	7.8	26.0	66.2	19 710	8 992	69.7	715	0.0	15.0	4.8
Randolph, GA	16 363	30.0	53.8	16.2	15 523	9 642	63.1	653	0.0	2.3	11.3
Richmond, GA	299 903	12.3	48.5	39.3	260 100	7 561	67.1	13 139	12.5	20.5	5.7
Rockdale, GA	120 654	6.1	43.0	50.8	101 670	7 127	68.5	4 315	0.0	12.4	5.8
Schley, GA	10 750	10.0	63.7	26.2	9 859	8 209	63.9	203	0.0	2.5	5.4
Screven, GA	24 696	15.2	63.5	21.3	21 966	7 204	65.3	899	0.0	9.8	2.3
Seminole, GA	15 837	22.0	54.4	23.6	13 744	7 818	67.9	525	6.1	14.7	8.2
Spalding, GA	97 470	10.1	50.4	39.5	83 940	7 850	67.7	3 477	0.0	8.9	15.4
Stephens, GA	36 501	11.2	51.6	37.2	32 784	7 601	71.0	1 448	0.0	11.3	6.8
Stewart, GA	7 399	17.4	58.5	24.0	7 258	10 208	63.9	335	0.0	10.4	14.9
Sumter, GA	46 073	18.3	54.7	27.0	42 357	7 426	70.0	2 313	0.0	8.6	8.6
Talbot, GA	8 889	18.1	46.1	35.8	7 533	9 834	63.2	310	0.0	17.1	4.5
Taliaferro, GA	3 013	18.0	51.9	30.1	2 692	9 347	65.9	109	0.0	14.7	18.3
Tattnall, GA	26 948	17.5	61.3	21.2	23 842	7 203	66.1	1 224	0.4	13.0	15.5
Taylor, GA	15 868	12.6	65.5	21.8	12 679	7 476	64.0	538	0.0	5.2	20.3
Telfair, GA	15 216	13.8	57.2	29.0	13 518	7 942	69.5	654	0.0	7.0	12.5
Terrell, GA	20 309	16.1	65.8	18.1	14 260	8 508	67.1	719	0.0	2.4	13.4
Thomas, GA	71 995	12.2	56.3	31.4	66 832	7 785	65.3	2 440	0.0	11.7	6.9
Tift, GA	58 332	12.8	56.0	31.2	51 622	6 738	72.2	2 630	0.0	7.6	9.4
Toombs, GA	42 382	12.2	60.7	27.1	35 857	6 831	69.2	1 484	0.0	9.7	10.8
Towns, GA	14 026	6.8	50.0	43.2	11 080	6 938	69.3	557	0.0	5.9	2.3
Treutlen, GA	8 731	17.7	71.3	11.0	8 823	7 421	67.7	489	0.0	9.0	19.8

Table C-1. Population, School, and Student Characteristics by County—*Continued*

STATE County	High school graduates, 2000			College enrollment, 2000		College graduates, 2000 (percent)						
	Population 25 years and over	High school graduate or less (percent)	High school graduate or more (percent)	Number	Percent public	Bachelor's degree or more	+/- U.S. percentage with bachelor's degree or more	Non-Hispanic White	Black	American Indian and Alaska Native	Asian or Pacific Islander	Hispanic[3]
	30	31	32	33	34	35	36	37	38	39	40	41
Gilmer, GA	15 718	67.3	66.0	471	76.9	12.9	-11.5	13.2	0.0	0.0	16.9	7.6
Glascock, GA	1 764	74.2	66.1	71	74.6	6.5	-17.9	7.2	0.0	0.0	. . .	0.0
Glynn, GA	44 806	47.0	82.2	2 300	88.0	23.8	-0.6	28.5	8.2	25.6	21.0	20.6
Gordon, GA	28 490	68.2	65.9	1 266	86.7	10.6	-13.8	11.1	3.5	12.3	30.1	4.5
Grady, GA	14 988	70.3	69.4	764	91.6	10.6	-13.8	13.3	3.7	16.9	84.6	6.0
Greene, GA	9 508	63.2	70.1	330	74.2	17.6	-6.8	26.8	3.0	0.0	27.7	6.0
Gwinnett, GA	372 628	34.7	87.3	27 694	75.5	34.1	9.7	36.2	31.4	17.1	42.2	14.7
Habersham, GA	23 501	62.9	70.9	1 506	51.7	15.8	-8.6	16.8	11.7	23.7	9.0	3.7
Hall, GA	86 821	59.1	70.5	4 668	76.6	18.7	-5.7	22.3	11.1	3.8	14.8	3.3
Hancock, GA	6 618	72.2	62.2	330	88.5	9.8	-14.6	12.1	8.6	38.1	. . .	0.0
Haralson, GA	16 814	73.1	63.0	635	92.9	9.0	-15.4	9.3	3.9	0.0	0.0	25.0
Harris, GA	16 231	50.5	79.0	879	92.2	21.1	-3.3	24.5	6.1	0.0	37.8	50.0
Hart, GA	15 838	65.8	71.1	613	71.3	13.5	-10.9	15.0	2.8	31.8	30.9	28.1
Heard, GA	7 020	75.7	66.0	252	91.7	7.3	-17.1	7.8	3.2	0.0	12.8	2.9
Henry, GA	75 501	50.1	84.2	4 652	78.5	19.5	-4.9	18.0	24.5	22.2	42.9	26.3
Houston, GA	69 038	48.1	84.3	5 898	86.2	19.8	-4.6	21.2	13.9	9.6	31.1	17.6
Irwin, GA	6 196	70.8	67.7	268	98.1	9.9	-14.5	10.8	5.8	0.0	71.4	15.6
Jackson, GA	26 849	67.5	68.1	1 032	85.3	11.7	-12.7	12.4	5.3	14.6	18.3	4.8
Jasper, GA	7 531	67.4	69.7	236	90.3	11.5	-12.9	13.4	6.0	0.0	16.3	17.7
Jeff Davis, GA	8 036	72.1	63.3	289	73.0	9.4	-15.0	9.7	4.9	0.0	69.4	1.6
Jefferson, GA	10 799	75.4	58.5	366	81.7	9.1	-15.3	13.8	4.9	0.0	0.0	10.7
Jenkins, GA	5 335	70.8	62.0	267	87.6	10.8	-13.6	15.2	2.5	0.0	100.0	0.0
Johnson, GA	5 206	77.0	62.4	287	93.4	7.8	-16.6	9.3	3.5	. . .	100.0	12.7
Jones, GA	15 383	63.2	77.9	824	80.0	15.0	-9.4	15.1	14.1	0.0	35.1	37.6
Lamar, GA	10 227	65.7	71.3	1 151	91.6	11.3	-13.1	12.6	8.2	5.6	36.4	0.0
Lanier, GA	4 487	67.2	67.0	208	96.2	8.8	-15.6	10.4	4.2	14.0	0.0	0.0
Laurens, GA	28 875	66.8	70.3	1 517	91.0	14.4	-10.0	17.6	6.7	28.0	53.3	9.4
Lee, GA	15 036	54.6	81.3	1 136	88.5	17.0	-7.4	18.1	9.2	38.1	56.4	9.8
Liberty, GA	30 797	47.5	86.8	2 604	81.5	14.5	-9.9	18.2	10.4	10.2	19.5	12.1
Lincoln, GA	5 701	65.3	71.0	191	84.8	10.1	-14.3	13.2	3.6	0.0	0.0	8.0
Long, GA	5 527	67.3	74.3	286	83.9	5.8	-18.6	6.5	4.1	16.7	12.9	3.6
Lowndes, GA	54 237	52.9	77.7	9 466	94.5	19.7	-4.7	24.2	10.3	12.4	16.9	17.3
Lumpkin, GA	12 665	58.4	72.0	2 321	93.4	17.6	-6.8	18.4	13.8	10.2	0.0	7.5
McDuffie, GA	13 442	68.5	66.7	614	87.8	11.7	-12.7	15.2	4.3	36.1	35.7	2.1
McIntosh, GA	6 978	66.7	71.2	231	82.7	11.1	-13.3	13.9	5.8	0.0	25.0	0.0
Macon, GA	8 844	72.0	63.2	542	90.6	10.0	-14.4	14.0	6.9	10.3	33.0	9.2
Madison, GA	16 881	70.0	70.8	669	83.0	10.9	-13.5	11.3	6.3	8.3	18.7	8.2
Marion, GA	4 437	70.7	65.4	166	89.8	8.9	-15.5	11.6	3.9	47.1	0.0	0.0
Meriwether, GA	14 434	69.9	65.8	473	79.9	10.8	-13.6	14.4	5.2	0.0	35.0	15.8
Miller, GA	4 281	66.9	69.0	195	88.2	11.3	-13.1	14.4	1.3	. . .	54.5	0.0
Mitchell, GA	14 972	70.1	65.3	825	89.2	9.1	-15.3	12.6	4.5	0.0	41.9	13.9
Monroe, GA	14 185	61.0	77.7	1 012	82.5	17.1	-7.3	20.9	6.4	39.4	71.2	0.0
Montgomery, GA	5 108	68.0	71.4	729	36.4	13.5	-10.9	16.2	5.4	. . .	48.8	0.0
Morgan, GA	10 125	63.1	74.0	397	67.5	18.7	-5.7	22.8	6.9	39.1	66.7	33.3
Murray, GA	22 803	74.3	61.1	779	85.0	7.2	-17.2	7.4	4.8	34.0	0.0	1.0
Muscogee, GA	114 045	49.3	78.9	10 058	90.7	20.3	-4.1	26.4	12.0	21.4	33.7	15.8
Newton, GA	39 144	60.0	74.7	2 259	61.8	14.5	-9.9	16.0	8.5	5.2	45.3	11.5
Oconee, GA	16 470	36.7	86.7	1 045	78.1	30.8	15.4	42.0	12.0	9.8	63.1	17.7
Oglethorpe, GA	8 436	65.4	72.1	441	83.7	15.6	-8.8	19.0	1.4	9.1	0.0	19.1
Paulding, GA	50 422	58.3	80.8	2 407	75.9	15.2	-9.2	14.3	24.4	13.9	27.9	26.2
Peach, GA	14 055	59.8	73.4	2 274	71.7	16.8	-7.6	18.0	15.7	32.0	38.5	3.9
Pickens, GA	15 868	62.9	70.2	504	82.5	15.6	-8.8	15.8	4.8	0.0	62.5	6.8
Pierce, GA	10 131	71.4	69.8	593	95.8	10.1	-14.3	10.5	4.0	0.0	. . .	22.2
Pike, GA	8 833	64.8	75.3	501	82.4	14.0	-10.4	15.5	6.2	25.0	0.0	4.8
Polk, GA	24 703	71.8	63.3	1 270	84.0	8.0	-16.4	8.3	8.4	0.0	0.0	1.5
Pulaski, GA	6 445	62.8	73.4	311	88.4	12.9	-11.5	16.0	5.4	0.0	86.4	8.6
Putnam, GA	12 931	65.1	75.5	549	79.8	14.4	-10.0	18.8	2.5	0.0	0.0	6.6
Quitman, GA	1 773	76.3	57.8	34	97.1	6.1	-18.3	9.0	2.1	0.0	. . .	0.0
Rabun, GA	10 675	59.6	75.4	270	63.7	17.6	-6.8	18.3	7.4	2.9	0.0	4.2
Randolph, GA	4 783	70.1	62.4	428	51.2	9.5	-14.9	15.7	4.2	. . .	. . .	21.9
Richmond, GA	122 592	51.7	78.0	11 630	81.8	18.7	-5.7	24.2	12.5	8.9	27.8	16.6
Rockdale, GA	44 794	47.0	82.4	2 578	81.8	23.4	-1.0	24.0	21.9	0.0	41.8	12.1
Schley, GA	2 364	70.1	70.0	102	93.1	13.7	-10.7	16.2	8.1	0.0	. . .	11.1
Screven, GA	9 685	71.7	66.9	580	91.4	10.2	-14.2	15.4	2.2	30.0	22.9	20.7
Seminole, GA	6 114	68.9	67.9	387	83.5	8.6	-15.8	9.9	6.1	0.0	50.0	0.0
Spalding, GA	37 110	67.0	67.8	1 678	85.3	12.5	-11.9	14.9	5.3	12.0	44.0	7.5
Stephens, GA	16 771	64.7	71.1	1 500	30.3	14.1	-10.3	15.0	6.3	29.6	12.9	0.0
Stewart, GA	3 495	73.9	63.2	152	91.4	9.3	-15.1	15.4	4.2	0.0	65.5	0.0
Sumter, GA	20 040	60.3	69.9	2 219	92.0	19.3	-5.1	28.1	8.4	39.5	55.6	5.6
Talbot, GA	4 403	75.5	64.8	178	80.3	7.9	-16.5	15.6	2.4	0.0	. . .	0.0
Taliaferro, GA	1 434	76.4	56.2	46	41.3	8.4	-16.0	13.0	5.1	. . .	. . .	0.0
Tattnall, GA	14 688	72.9	66.3	568	70.8	7.9	-16.5	11.0	2.7	0.0	20.0	0.0
Taylor, GA	5 594	75.4	63.6	256	92.2	8.5	-15.9	10.5	5.0	0.0	100.0	0.0
Telfair, GA	7 906	76.5	63.6	247	81.8	8.3	-16.1	11.0	4.0	. . .	. . .	0.0
Terrell, GA	6 741	68.3	64.5	336	97.6	10.7	-13.7	16.3	5.7	0.0	0.0	25.7
Thomas, GA	27 697	60.0	73.5	1 646	65.4	16.8	-7.6	22.0	7.1	11.7	33.3	8.4
Tift, GA	23 433	62.4	67.9	2 390	96.2	15.6	-8.8	19.8	5.6	13.1	37.6	5.2
Toombs, GA	16 212	67.6	67.3	731	88.1	12.7	-11.7	15.8	4.8	0.0	17.0	2.8
Towns, GA	6 935	58.3	75.1	582	34.2	17.4	-7.0	17.5	. . .	0.0	16.7	14.3
Treutlen, GA	4 292	77.8	61.8	216	72.2	8.5	-15.9	9.7	5.3	0.0	8.2	0.0

[3]May be of any race.
. . . = Not available.

Table C-1. Population, School, and Student Characteristics by County—*Continued*

STATE County	State/ county code	County type[1]	Population, 2005 Total	Population, 2005 Percent 5 to 17 years	Number of schools and students, 2004–2005 School districts	Number of schools and students, 2004–2005 Schools	Number of schools and students, 2004–2005 Students	Resident enrollment, 2000 Total	Resident enrollment, 2000 Percent public	Resident enrollment, 2000 K–12	Resident enrollment, 2000 Percent public
			1	2	3	4	5	6	7	8	9
Troup, GA	13285	4	62 015	19.3	1	22	12 099	15 898	86.2	12 477	92.0
Turner, GA	13287	6	9 474	20.4	1	6	1 890	2 621	96.5	2 117	97.5
Twiggs, GA	13289	3	10 299	18.4	1	5	1 383	2 644	81.7	2 237	81.6
Union, GA	13291	9	19 782	14.2	1	8	2 582	3 414	90.2	2 681	94.9
Upson, GA	13293	6	27 679	18.3	1	6	4 983	6 844	90.6	5 366	92.5
Walker, GA	13295	2	63 890	17.4	2	20	10 291	13 598	89.7	11 006	92.2
Walton, GA	13297	1	75 647	19.2	2	22	12 811	15 459	86.1	12 393	90.1
Ware, GA	13299	4	34 492	18.0	2	13	6 393	8 641	94.4	6 982	96.0
Warren, GA	13301	8	6 101	18.4	1	3	864	1 645	91.6	1 329	94.1
Washington, GA	13303	7	20 118	19.0	2	8	3 671	5 802	89.5	4 679	90.9
Wayne, GA	13305	6	28 390	17.8	1	10	5 400	6 292	93.4	5 194	95.0
Webster, GA	13307	8	2 289	17.5	1	1	410	549	85.8	469	86.8
Wheeler, GA	13309	9	6 706	14.0	1	3	1 120	1 358	94.6	1 071	97.6
White, GA	13311	8	24 055	16.2	2	8	3 836	4 506	83.9	3 284	95.4
Whitfield, GA	13313	3	90 889	19.5	2	33	18 667	19 439	92.5	16 101	95.1
Wilcox, GA	13315	9	8 721	15.3	1	3	1 452	1 855	91.8	1 519	91.6
Wilkes, GA	13317	6	10 457	16.3	1	7	1 823	2 461	93.3	1 976	95.4
Wilkinson, GA	13319	8	10 143	18.2	1	4	1 688	2 710	84.5	2 089	86.3
Worth, GA	13321	3	21 996	19.5	1	6	4 099	6 158	91.6	5 000	93.8
HAWAII	15000		1 275 194	16.4	1	285	183 185	320 842	79.5	223 185	84.5
Hawaii, HI	15001	5	167 293	18.5	(5)	(5)	(5)	40 194	87.7	30 747	91.3
Honolulu, HI	15003	2	905 266	15.8	5(1)	5(285)	5(183 185)	234 038	76.7	155 556	81.8
Kalawao, HI	15005	9	111	0.9	(5)	(5)	(5)	0	X	0	X
Kauai, HI	15007	5	62 640	17.8	(5)	(5)	(5)	14 881	89.8	12 272	92.4
Maui, HI	15009	5	139 884	17.2	(5)	(5)	(5)	31 729	85.0	24 610	89.6
IDAHO	16000		1 429 096	18.8	123	707	256 084	368 579	87.8	270 423	93.0
Ada, ID	16001	2	344 727	18.2	8	107	60 528	81 730	87.7	58 736	91.6
Adams, ID	16003	8	3 591	15.1	2	3	497	774	90.6	688	91.4
Bannock, ID	16005	3	78 155	18.3	2	37	13 330	25 491	92.5	15 052	94.0
Bear Lake, ID	16007	7	6 176	20.8	1	7	1 305	1 933	97.1	1 724	99.7
Benewah, ID	16009	6	9 218	17.5	2	8	1 616	2 139	89.4	1 868	89.9
Bingham, ID	16011	6	43 739	22.5	5	33	10 039	13 297	95.5	11 100	98.7
Blaine, ID	16013	7	21 166	15.8	1	8	3 188	4 341	82.8	3 440	86.5
Boise, ID	16015	2	7 535	17.6	3	6	1 062	1 611	89.3	1 327	89.4
Bonner, ID	16017	6	40 908	16.8	2	19	5 646	8 413	81.5	7 188	84.0
Bonneville, ID	16019	3	91 856	20.5	3	38	18 599	24 784	92.8	19 682	97.5
Boundary, ID	16021	7	10 619	18.6	1	7	1 573	2 237	81.7	1 996	83.7
Butte, ID	16023	8	2 808	19.8	1	4	521	758	95.9	651	96.5
Camas, ID	16025	9	1 050	14.7	1	2	174	250	94.8	210	98.1
Canyon, ID	16027	2	164 593	20.5	10	65	29 884	35 560	85.4	28 095	91.9
Caribou, ID	16029	6	7 131	20.1	3	11	1 676	2 190	96.5	1 795	98.4
Cassia, ID	16031	7	21 324	22.6	1	17	4 947	6 560	93.5	5 641	95.0
Clark, ID	16033	8	943	20.9	1	3	239	289	96.9	243	97.1
Clearwater, ID	16035	6	8 373	14.3	1	8	1 377	2 056	89.0	1 720	90.1
Custer, ID	16037	9	4 077	16.6	2	7	689	1 018	97.2	909	98.2
Elmore, ID	16039	4	28 634	18.6	4	18	4 887	7 773	91.3	5 757	96.2
Franklin, ID	16041	3	12 371	24.4	2	8	3 031	3 506	95.9	3 142	98.6
Fremont, ID	16043	6	12 242	21.3	1	10	2 395	3 534	93.0	3 039	98.4
Gem, ID	16045	2	16 273	18.5	1	8	3 042	3 788	91.1	3 180	94.8
Gooding, ID	16047	7	14 461	19.4	5	10	3 100	3 470	93.7	2 944	95.0
Idaho, ID	16049	6	15 697	16.0	2	13	1 826	3 608	86.8	3 080	87.9
Jefferson, ID	16051	3	21 580	22.9	3	15	5 364	6 224	93.4	5 235	98.5
Jerome, ID	16053	7	19 638	21.0	2	8	3 957	5 187	89.9	4 311	92.7
Kootenai, ID	16055	3	127 668	18.2	4	42	19 772	28 610	86.9	21 760	88.8
Latah, ID	16057	4	34 714	12.7	6	18	4 956	14 797	91.5	5 153	85.6
Lemhi, ID	16059	7	7 909	16.8	2	9	1 171	1 763	89.6	1 580	93.7
Lewis, ID	16061	8	3 750	16.5	3	5	932	885	92.8	753	93.1
Lincoln, ID	16063	9	4 545	20.5	3	5	880	1 127	97.6	946	99.2
Madison, ID	16065	6	30 975	16.8	2	17	5 599	15 041	42.0	13 204	98.1
Minidoka, ID	16067	7	19 014	20.5	1	11	4 123	5 884	92.9	4 896	96.2
Nez Perce, ID	16069	3	37 931	15.9	3	18	5 776	9 620	90.5	6 565	91.5
Oneida, ID	16071	8	4 209	20.0	1	5	902	1 245	97.0	1 053	98.7
Owyhee, ID	16073	2	11 073	20.5	4	14	2 598	2 883	92.3	2 532	94.2
Payette, ID	16075	6	22 197	20.3	3	11	4 301	5 547	94.0	4 757	94.7
Power, ID	16077	3	7 753	21.8	3	7	1 768	2 319	95.2	1 898	97.0
Shoshone, ID	16079	6	13 157	15.6	4	12	2 134	2 907	95.7	2 463	97.8
Teton, ID	16081	9	7 467	20.6	1	6	1 420	1 655	85.2	1 375	90.5
Twin Falls, ID	16083	5	69 419	18.4	8	31	11 928	17 741	90.5	13 204	92.0
Valley, ID	16085	8	8 332	14.8	2	9	1 371	1 634	94.6	1 474	96.8
Washington, ID	16087	6	10 098	18.3	3	7	1 961	2 400	94.4	2 052	97.9

[1]County type codes are from the Economic Research Service of the United States Department of Agriculture. See notes and definitions at the end of this section.
[5]Hawaii County, Kalawao County, Kauai County, and Maui County are included with Honolulu County.
X = Not applicable.

Table C-1. Population, School, and Student Characteristics by County—*Continued*

STATE County	Characteristics of students, 2004–2005				Outcomes		Staff and students, 2004–2005		
	Percent with IEP[2]	Percent eligible for free or reduced-price lunch	Percent minority	Percent English-language learners	Number of graduates, 2003–2004	Percent dropouts, grades 9–12, 2001–2002	Number of teachers	Student-teacher ratio	Central administration staff
	10	11	12	13	14	15	16	17	18
Troup, GA	11.7	55.8	44.3	0.5	519	6.9	790	15.3	42
Turner, GA	15.0	69.0	57.7	0.0	105	6.7	138	13.7	10
Twiggs, GA	15.0	81.2	64.1	0.1	78	6.9	109	12.7	10
Union, GA	18.1	41.2	2.4	1.0	142	2.6	195	13.2	15
Upson, GA	16.2	57.8	39.3	0.4	286	8.3	325	15.4	11
Walker, GA	14.3	49.6	6.1	0.6	443	9.5	676	15.2	22
Walton, GA	12.8	40.2	24.7	1.1	545	4.0	878	14.6	41
Ware, GA	14.4	60.0	40.9	1.0	. . .	9.5	498	12.8	34
Warren, GA	7.3	99.0	94.5	0.0	41	3.6	54	15.9	7
Washington, GA	11.3	67.5	69.4	0.4	. . .	5.6	251	14.7	22
Wayne, GA	14.1	55.9	26.9	1.3	282	10.9	344	15.7	18
Webster, GA	8.0	67.8	56.9	0.0	. . .	. . .	29	14.0	3
Wheeler, GA	13.3	71.1	38.5	0.2	73	6.1	79	14.2	5
White, GA	14.0	39.5	5.1	1.1	. . .	5.2	281	13.6	39
Whitfield, GA	11.1	56.0	44.1	15.1	815	8.4	1 225	15.2	55
Wilcox, GA	11.3	65.3	46.6	0.0	67	7.8	99	14.7	10
Wilkes, GA	13.8	64.3	55.3	0.6	92	9.3	130	14.1	7
Wilkinson, GA	15.0	72.9	61.5	0.2	103	8.0	120	14.1	7
Worth, GA	7.6	62.8	42.5	0.1	214	9.5	279	14.7	13
HAWAII	12.4	41.6	79.9	9.3	. . .	5.1	11 146	16.4	. . .
Hawaii, HI	(5)	53.4	78.8	(5)	(5)	(5)	(5)	(5)	(5)
Honolulu, HI	[5]12.4	40.3	80.7	[5]9.3	[5]10 501	[5]5.1	[5]11 146	[5]16.4	[5]1 016
Kalawao, HI	(5)	X	X	(5)	(5)	(5)	(5)	(5)	(5)
Kauai, HI	(5)	39.3	77.8	(5)	(5)	(5)	(5)	(5)	(5)
Maui, HI	(5)	36.1	77.4	(5)	(5)	(5)	(5)	(5)	(5)
IDAHO	11.2	39.5	16.5	8.2	. . .	3.9	14 269	17.9	. . .
Ada, ID	10.9	25.7	10.9	5.3	. . .	3.9	3 166	19.1	. . .
Adams, ID	13.9	47.3	4.8	0.2	42	3.4	40	12.3	3
Bannock, ID	11.4	42.3	14.4	0.8	894	4.1	699	19.1	51
Bear Lake, ID	9.3	40.6	3.5	0.2	92	1.2	79	16.6	4
Benewah, ID	15.0	49.2	18.6	0.0	91	6.9	106	15.3	10
Bingham, ID	11.4	48.2	26.0	20.2	686	2.9	548	18.3	33
Blaine, ID	11.7	25.4	22.9	15.3	201	5.0	233	13.7	18
Boise, ID	12.1	42.7	0.9	0.1	09	2.5	70	13.7	7
Bonner, ID	11.7	48.0	4.0	0.1	393	5.1	338	16.7	25
Bonneville, ID	10.4	31.6	13.8	6.2	. . .	3.9	961	19.3	50
Boundary, ID	12.7	48.5	7.9	7.2	117	9.0	97	16.3	8
Butte, ID	18.6	. . .	5.2	1.2	40	3.0	34	15.3	4
Camas, ID	10.3	35.1	1.7	0.0	14	. . .	15	11.4	1
Canyon, ID	12.4	51.1	31.2	17.0	. . .	4.8	1 611	18.6	. . .
Caribou, ID	11.4	36.5	5.5	1.7	134	0.3	103	16.2	8
Cassia, ID	10.2	52.8	27.5	15.2	326	3.0	284	17.4	12
Clark, ID	10.5	53.1	50.2	29.7	12	. . .	18	13.4	2
Clearwater, ID	13.9	52.0	7.9	0.1	78	3.4	84	16.5	8
Custer, ID	7.5	37.2	8.2	1.5	64	1.9	56	12.4	6
Elmore, ID	14.0	39.0	25.1	12.5	. . .	3.8	285	17.1	20
Franklin, ID	11.4	55.2	7.8	4.5	213	0.3	155	19.5	7
Fremont, ID	12.0	48.3	18.8	14.3	137	1.9	135	17.7	8
Gem, ID	13.6	44.1	14.6	5.9	214	7.3	164	18.5	9
Gooding, ID	12.5	51.7	30.3	21.0	. . .	4.6	235	13.2	27
Idaho, ID	13.3	49.9	5.9	0.0	152	3.6	126	14.5	8
Jefferson, ID	9.3	44.9	13.8	8.8	380	1.4	292	18.4	16
Jerome, ID	9.5	53.8	33.1	23.2	212	7.0	216	18.3	15
Kootenai, ID	10.0	37.8	5.8	0.2	1 142	3.4	1 034	19.1	55
Latah, ID	11.6	26.6	7.1	0.7	305	2.3	295	16.8	28
Lemhi, ID	11.2	47.6	4.2	0.0	68	4.4	77	15.2	6
Lewis, ID	12.7	49.5	16.4	0.0	70	4.3	69	13.6	7
Lincoln, ID	11.3	60.3	26.9	14.9	56	0.7	67	13.2	6
Madison, ID	10.2	37.7	8.4	4.3	424	2.5	290	19.3	11
Minidoka, ID	10.9	58.3	41.2	17.0	240	5.3	241	17.1	13
Nez Perce, ID	12.3	32.6	14.8	3.9	394	6.3	339	17.1	30
Oneida, ID	11.3	43.2	8.8	2.1	72	0.3	54	16.8	3
Owyhee, ID	10.5	60.9	37.4	20.4	. . .	6.3	160	16.2	15
Payette, ID	11.1	46.6	21.3	11.9	277	3.4	241	17.9	12
Power, ID	10.8	58.2	38.1	30.5	. . .	3.3	112	15.7	9
Shoshone, ID	13.0	38.5	5.7	0.0	. . .	5.3	148	14.4	17
Teton, ID	11.9	37.7	23.2	14.5	80	1.3	78	18.3	5
Twin Falls, ID	10.5	44.5	17.8	9.3	. . .	3.4	700	17.0	44
Valley, ID	11.5	25.9	4.7	1.6	89	2.6	88	15.5	9
Washington, ID	10.0	50.4	22.8	16.7	119	4.5	121	16.2	9

2IEP = Individual Education Program. See notes and definitions at the end of this section.
5Hawaii County, Kalawao County, Kauai County, and Maui County are included with Honolulu County.
X = Not applicable.
. . . = Not available.

Table C-1. Population, School, and Student Characteristics by County—*Continued*

STATE County	Revenue, 2003–2004				Current expenditures, 2003–2004			Resident population, 16 to 19 years, 2000			
	Total revenue (thousands of dollars)	Percent of revenue from:			Total expenditures (thousands of dollars)	Amount per student (dollars)	Percent for instruction	Total	Percent in armed forces	Percent high school graduates	Percent not enrolled, not employed, not in armed forces, not high school graduate
		Federal government	State government	Local government							
	19	20	21	22	23	24	25	26	27	28	29
Troup, GA	103 667	5.9	51.9	42.2	86 123	7 181	68.4	3 493	0.0	8.7	8.4
Turner, GA	16 920	21.8	59.7	18.6	15 758	8 302	67.8	605	0.0	15.5	4.5
Twiggs, GA	15 086	26.4	43.7	29.9	14 095	9 933	62.5	624	0.0	14.6	14.6
Union, GA	23 069	8.7	49.4	41.9	20 578	7 836	66.3	737	0.0	20.1	4.1
Upson, GA	37 411	11.7	60.0	28.3	35 422	7 096	67.8	1 272	0.0	14.9	6.0
Walker, GA	79 232	9.8	58.4	31.8	72 436	7 134	67.8	3 095	0.3	10.7	11.7
Walton, GA	115 043	7.8	50.6	41.6	90 273	7 402	67.9	3 385	0.0	12.8	7.8
Ware, GA	57 725	12.0	60.7	27.3	52 241	8 236	68.1	1 782	0.0	14.3	7.2
Warren, GA	9 075	22.0	46.4	31.6	7 812	9 180	59.3	401	0.0	10.7	16.2
Washington, GA	32 890	13.1	51.3	35.6	31 443	8 473	62.4	1 209	0.0	8.4	9.1
Wayne, GA	38 386	11.7	60.3	28.0	36 978	6 961	68.9	1 463	0.0	8.5	6.4
Webster, GA	4 579	15.4	58.7	26.0	3 954	9 551	61.7	110	0.0	12.7	4.5
Wheeler, GA	10 289	20.5	61.2	18.3	9 555	8 426	58.2	334	0.0	2.7	16.8
White, GA	41 031	15.5	43.6	40.9	36 542	9 459	67.2	1 070	0.0	9.9	5.6
Whitfield, GA	166 205	8.1	48.2	43.7	144 249	7 938	70.1	4 452	0.0	11.2	15.7
Wilcox, GA	11 872	19.6	64.5	15.9	10 677	7 420	69.2	449	0.0	10.0	6.7
Wilkes, GA	15 039	12.2	49.4	38.3	13 935	7 520	64.2	628	0.0	10.2	7.5
Wilkinson, GA	15 266	12.1	47.8	40.1	14 022	8 186	66.5	603	0.0	7.3	6.3
Worth, GA	31 639	14.7	61.9	23.4	29 590	7 207	67.7	1 355	0.0	7.3	2.4
HAWAII	2 138 137	11.1	86.6	2.4	1 566 793	8 533	65.6	64 343	4.1	17.1	3.6
Hawaii, HI	(5)	(5)	(5)	(5)	(5)	(5)	(5)	8 798	0.0	13.6	5.0
Honolulu, HI	5 2 138 137	5 11.1	5 86.6	5 2.4	5 1 566 793	5 8 533	5 65.6	45 427	5.9	17.8	3.2
Kalawao, HI	(5)	(5)	(5)	(5)	(5)	(5)	(5)	0	X	X	X
Kauai, HI	(5)	(5)	(5)	(5)	(5)	(5)	(5)	3 275	0.0	16.1	2.5
Maui, HI	(5)	(5)	(5)	(5)	(5)	(5)	(5)	6 843	0.0	17.5	5.1
IDAHO	1 733 838	10.2	58.1	31.6	1 519 374	6 028	66.1	87 734	0.3	14.0	4.0
Ada, ID	397 177	6.0	49.4	44.6	343 477	6 046	65.3	17 019	0.1	17.3	2.5
Adams, ID	4 925	12.6	63.3	24.1	4 275	8 237	67.1	207	0.0	13.0	3.9
Bannock, ID	88 565	11.8	62.6	25.6	79 983	5 936	67.2	5 556	0.2	15.8	3.2
Bear Lake, ID	8 758	8.1	71.5	20.4	7 954	5 861	60.4	510	0.0	15.3	1.0
Benewah, ID	13 508	21.2	52.8	25.9	12 191	7 424	59.4	524	0.0	10.7	7.1
Bingham, ID	65 283	13.2	69.4	17.4	57 978	5 795	66.5	3 155	0.4	12.3	4.3
Blaine, ID	41 610	3.4	24.6	72.0	32 292	10 235	69.2	889	0.0	8.3	4.0
Boise, ID	8 823	12.0	58.1	29.9	7 803	7 159	56.2	332	0.0	11.7	4.8
Bonner, ID	37 324	12.6	48.3	39.1	33 788	5 974	60.3	2 159	0.4	14.8	6.3
Bonneville, ID	114 079	8.2	65.8	26.0	98 553	5 344	66.5	5 848	0.0	13.8	3.3
Boundary, ID	12 493	15.1	51.5	33.4	10 689	6 813	66.9	595	0.0	19.0	8.6
Butte, ID	13 269	8.3	82.1	9.6	12 291	5 102	70.3	183	0.0	14.2	0.0
Camas, ID	1 989	9.5	52.0	38.5	1 554	9 534	62.4	59	0.0	5.1	8.5
Canyon, ID	183 942	11.2	63.5	25.3	158 930	5 476	67.9	8 576	0.0	13.7	8.4
Caribou, ID	13 711	8.5	61.0	30.5	12 102	7 073	65.7	542	0.0	6.8	2.6
Cassia, ID	32 539	12.6	66.8	20.5	27 960	5 590	65.2	1 547	0.0	13.8	5.6
Clark, ID	2 311	9.7	62.4	27.9	1 878	8 422	64.5	86	0.0	14.0	5.8
Clearwater, ID	10 844	15.6	60.0	24.4	10 275	7 392	66.6	453	0.0	15.7	2.4
Custer, ID	6 371	8.3	60.5	31.2	5 783	7 922	62.1	202	0.0	13.4	5.0
Elmore, ID	33 450	21.2	62.1	16.7	29 470	5 844	65.6	1 564	9.2	30.0	4.2
Franklin, ID	17 397	10.5	74.9	14.6	15 511	5 160	67.8	834	0.0	14.0	1.8
Fremont, ID	16 156	11.6	58.0	30.5	14 018	5 865	67.1	1 036	0.2	11.6	5.2
Gem, ID	18 255	9.8	70.1	20.1	16 053	5 358	70.4	950	0.0	19.6	6.4
Gooding, ID	21 629	13.7	65.7	20.7	18 761	6 229	64.4	1 005	0.0	12.3	7.1
Idaho, ID	17 461	19.9	55.2	24.9	15 619	8 221	65.0	1 023	0.0	10.7	7.1
Jefferson, ID	33 097	10.0	73.8	16.3	29 575	5 563	65.2	1 528	0.1	15.6	5.4
Jerome, ID	24 452	12.2	62.3	25.5	21 491	5 807	68.4	1 189	0.0	10.9	7.1
Kootenai, ID	124 875	8.5	53.1	38.5	106 621	5 553	67.2	6 362	0.1	16.1	3.6
Latah, ID	40 333	11.8	49.0	39.2	35 314	8 055	63.8	3 480	0.5	7.4	0.2
Lemhi, ID	8 333	13.0	66.8	20.2	7 944	6 609	64.3	473	0.0	16.9	3.2
Lewis, ID	8 725	16.2	61.0	22.8	7 809	8 488	63.2	208	0.0	8.7	1.9
Lincoln, ID	7 528	11.5	67.9	20.6	6 750	7 644	64.3	244	0.0	9.8	5.7
Madison, ID	32 795	13.6	70.1	16.3	30 102	5 547	69.7	6 308	0.0	4.0	0.4
Minidoka, ID	27 945	14.5	66.9	18.6	24 992	5 885	66.0	1 525	0.0	15.7	7.3
Nez Perce, ID	45 150	12.2	48.9	38.9	42 017	7 283	66.2	2 165	0.0	15.5	3.0
Oneida, ID	6 462	10.9	68.3	20.8	5 592	6 355	67.3	287	0.0	17.1	3.8
Owyhee, ID	18 918	14.2	68.1	17.6	16 793	6 522	65.7	698	0.0	12.3	9.3
Payette, ID	27 979	11.9	68.2	20.0	24 545	5 617	68.0	1 340	0.0	12.1	4.1
Power, ID	14 876	10.6	55.3	34.0	13 278	7 502	63.3	508	0.0	13.4	1.8
Shoshone, ID	20 019	15.6	55.1	29.3	18 156	8 336	60.4	678	0.0	12.8	4.9
Teton, ID	9 237	12.4	48.8	38.8	7 974	5 812	66.2	366	0.0	15.6	4.4
Twin Falls, ID	74 014	11.3	66.8	21.9	67 417	5 664	66.1	4 434	0.0	13.5	4.4
Valley, ID	13 377	12.4	35.4	52.2	11 278	8 616	66.0	447	1.1	13.0	1.1
Washington, ID	13 854	12.3	67.5	20.3	12 538	6 551	66.0	640	0.0	14.2	6.9

5Hawaii County, Kalawao County, Kauai County, and Maui County are included with Honolulu County.
X = Not applicable.

Table C-1. Population, School, and Student Characteristics by County—*Continued*

STATE County	Population 25 years and over	High school graduate or less (percent)	High school graduate or more (percent)	College enrollment, 2000 Number	Percent public	Bachelor's degree or more	+/- U.S. percentage with bachelor's degree or more	Non-Hispanic White	Black	American Indian and Alaska Native	Asian or Pacific Islander	Hispanic[3]
	30	31	32	33	34	35	36	37	38	39	40	41
Troup, GA	36 815	60.7	73.0	2 079	62.2	18.0	-6.4	22.5	6.5	5.7	37.8	15.5
Turner, GA	5 707	71.0	67.7	299	95.0	10.5	-13.9	14.5	3.5	0.0	9.1	1.5
Twiggs, GA	6 702	77.6	63.2	243	82.3	5.4	-19.0	6.9	2.5	0.0	34.0	19.6
Union, GA	12 730	60.9	74.2	552	73.7	12.5	-11.9	12.7	0.0	26.2	0.0	0.0
Upson, GA	18 325	70.5	66.7	952	90.7	11.5	-12.9	14.7	2.1	7.0	15.0	0.0
Walker, GA	40 837	68.2	66.8	1 683	82.8	10.2	-14.2	10.3	4.1	0.0	46.1	12.0
Walton, GA	38 527	62.1	73.5	1 606	80.5	13.0	-11.4	14.1	5.2	8.5	36.0	11.2
Ware, GA	23 380	68.4	70.3	1 061	86.8	11.4	-13.0	13.0	6.6	31.0	13.6	4.6
Warren, GA	4 061	77.6	57.1	165	86.1	8.0	-16.4	13.7	2.9	0.0	71.4	20.0
Washington, GA	13 626	70.5	68.3	615	89.8	10.5	-13.9	16.7	4.3	0.0	0.0	0.0
Wayne, GA	17 531	66.9	70.1	711	86.5	11.6	-12.8	13.1	7.2	0.0	1.3	3.4
Webster, GA	1 588	72.7	61.3	47	97.9	9.1	-15.3	15.0	2.7	. . .	. . .	0.0
Wheeler, GA	4 144	74.0	67.9	146	69.9	7.1	-17.3	9.2	3.2	0.0	0.0	2.6
White, GA	13 473	59.2	76.0	970	48.4	15.4	-9.0	15.5	2.0	11.8	29.8	15.5
Whitfield, GA	52 570	66.0	63.0	2 007	89.4	12.8	-11.6	15.1	6.5	5.8	29.8	2.2
Wilcox, GA	5 761	75.5	68.2	200	93.0	7.0	-17.4	8.4	4.1	33.3	25.0	4.2
Wilkes, GA	7 265	70.9	65.0	289	92.4	12.0	-12.4	17.4	5.1	16.0	0.0	0.0
Wilkinson, GA	6 509	71.0	70.4	391	79.8	9.6	-14.8	12.5	4.9	0.0	0.0	4.7
Worth, GA	13 979	69.8	68.3	692	93.6	8.6	-15.8	8.7	8.6	0.0	0.0	0.0
HAWAII	802 477	43.9	84.6	79 748	74.0	26.2	1.8	37.3	21.0	21.5	24.5	13.3
Hawaii, HI	97 708	46.8	84.6	7 220	84.9	22.1	-2.3	32.4	14.3	17.4	19.4	9.4
Honolulu, HI	579 998	43.0	84.8	65 507	71.8	27.9	3.5	40.4	20.9	22.8	26.3	15.1
Kalawao, HI	147	80.3	39.5	0	X	10.2	-14.2	0.0	0.0	0.0	12.7	0.0
Kauai, HI	38 872	46.4	83.3	1 736	88.5	19.4	-5.0	30.9	23.0	19.3	14.9	7.7
Maui, HI	85 752	46.1	83.4	5 285	80.7	22.4	-2.0	33.1	31.8	24.0	17.8	11.2
IDAHO	787 505	43.8	84.7	77 392	79.2	21.7	-2.7	22.6	22.4	9.5	36.8	6.6
Ada, ID	188 662	32.3	90.8	17 989	88.2	31.2	6.8	31.7	27.3	16.0	41.0	16.2
Adams, ID	2 468	56.6	80.8	57	86.0	14.9	-9.5	14.6	0.0	18.9	0.0	6.7
Bannock, ID	43 285	38.4	87.5	9 013	97.0	24.9	0.5	25.5	23.1	8.8	41.8	14.3
Bear Lake, ID	3 837	56.7	85.5	101	91.1	11.7	-12.7	11.9	0.0	0.0	100.0	2.6
Benewah, ID	6 051	61.3	79.8	156	94.2	11.4	-13.0	11.9	0.0	6.1	0.0	3.5
Bingham, ID	23 155	50.5	80.6	1 423	85.2	14.4	-10.0	16.7	0.0	4.2	20.3	1.8
Blaine, ID	13 021	25.7	90.2	648	77.2	43.1	18.7	46.3	11.1	25.0	29.7	8.1
Boise, ID	4 547	46.2	86.3	165	89.7	18.9	-4.5	20.2	. . .	0.8	22.2	12.5
Bonner, ID	25 043	47.9	85.6	761	82.5	16.9	-7.5	17.1	0.0	13.1	29.8	9.1
Bonneville, ID	48 502	38.7	87.8	3 547	86.3	26.1	1.7	27.1	40.7	6.6	35.1	10.4
Boundary, ID	6 314	55.9	80.0	151	82.1	14.7	-9.7	15.0	. . .	15.8	20.0	4.8
Butte, ID	1 873	50.4	82.6	74	89.2	13.0	-11.4	13.8	0.0	0.0	0.0	4.0
Camas, ID	675	43.0	88.4	34	91.2	22.2	-2.2	22.7	0.0	0.0	. . .	0.0
Canyon, ID	76 619	54.3	76.0	5 511	62.9	14.9	-9.5	16.6	21.0	5.5	20.4	4.4
Caribou, ID	4 391	47.6	86.6	214	93.5	15.9	-8.5	16.2	0.0	18.2	0.0	7.8
Cassia, ID	12 206	52.9	76.9	596	95.8	13.9	-10.5	15.9	0.0	16.0	15.1	1.1
Clark, ID	580	60.5	64.0	6	100.0	12.6	-11.8	16.0	100.0	66.7	. . .	1.2
Clearwater, ID	6 352	57.2	80.1	244	88.9	13.4	-11.0	13.5	. . .	4.6	50.0	11.0
Custer, ID	3 012	53.0	84.5	69	89.9	17.4	-7.0	17.6	. . .	28.6	. . .	12.4
Elmore, ID	17 034	37.8	87.2	1 494	84.5	17.3	-7.1	18.6	13.2	2.4	26.7	8.5
Franklin, ID	6 069	51.8	88.2	187	90.9	13.6	-10.8	14.0	. . .	12.5	33.3	0.0
Fremont, ID	6 790	54.2	80.4	327	66.4	12.0	-12.4	13.1	. . .	0.0	0.0	0.8
Gem, ID	9 663	55.6	79.4	417	80.8	11.4	-13.0	11.6	. . .	5.7	32.2	3.5
Gooding, ID	8 761	62.1	72.6	363	93.1	12.0	-12.4	13.7	. . .	0.0	6.7	0.6
Idaho, ID	10 638	55.4	82.9	284	91.2	14.4	-10.0	14.7	. . .	6.7	27.3	13.4
Jefferson, ID	10 335	45.0	84.4	602	79.2	15.2	-9.2	16.3	0.0	6.8	50.0	1.2
Jerome, ID	10 946	51.7	75.1	570	92.1	14.0	-10.4	15.7	0.0	14.3	29.1	3.5
Kootenai, ID	69 872	43.0	87.3	5 072	89.5	19.1	-5.3	19.3	10.8	8.1	33.2	13.3
Latah, ID	19 493	31.6	91.0	9 171	96.9	41.0	16.6	40.1	48.3	37.1	78.8	32.0
Lemhi, ID	5 373	48.8	82.5	66	75.8	17.9	-6.5	17.9	. . .	0.0	100.0	11.6
Lewis, ID	2 596	50.5	84.2	92	87.0	14.8	-9.6	14.7	22.2	7.4	20.0	7.4
Lincoln, ID	2 458	55.5	77.4	120	90.0	13.0	-11.4	14.2	0.0	7.1	14.3	1.3
Madison, ID	9 320	33.8	88.5	9 416	11.2	24.4	0.0	25.3	. . .	12.5	33.7	4.1
Minidoka, ID	11 940	59.1	73.7	670	85.7	10.1	-14.3	12.2	0.0	0.0	20.0	1.8
Nez Perce, ID	24 759	46.3	85.5	2 459	94.8	18.9	-5.5	19.2	20.0	11.7	37.4	5.8
Oneida, ID	2 493	45.3	86.4	113	86.7	15.0	-9.4	15.1	. . .	0.0	100.0	0.0
Owyhee, ID	6 372	67.0	67.6	207	76.8	10.2	-14.2	12.1	28.6	4.5	22.8	1.6
Payette, ID	12 761	57.5	74.5	536	89.6	10.6	-13.8	11.6	0.0	14.8	20.5	0.2
Power, ID	4 344	58.1	74.7	275	93.1	14.3	-10.1	17.4	. . .	2.7	0.0	0.9
Shoshone, ID	9 670	62.4	77.9	285	91.6	10.2	-14.2	10.3	62.5	5.1	23.8	9.0
Teton, ID	3 614	35.3	87.3	170	66.5	28.1	3.7	30.4	0.0	0.0	100.0	2.8
Twin Falls, ID	39 544	49.1	81.3	3 482	94.6	16.0	-8.4	16.9	0.0	8.7	9.8	4.7
Valley, ID	5 525	40.2	88.9	91	86.8	26.3	1.9	26.8	. . .	0.0	23.8	16.1
Washington, ID	6 542	58.9	76.6	164	80.5	12.7	-11.7	13.7	0.0	28.6	44.4	0.0

[3]May be of any race.
X = Not applicable.
. . . = Not available.

Table C-1. Population, School, and Student Characteristics by County—*Continued*

STATE County	State/ county code	County type[1]	Population, 2005 Total	Population, 2005 Percent 5 to 17 years	Number of schools and students, 2004–2005 School districts	Number of schools and students, 2004–2005 Schools	Number of schools and students, 2004–2005 Students	Resident enrollment, 2000 Total	Resident enrollment, 2000 Percent public	Resident enrollment, 2000 K–12	Resident enrollment, 2000 Percent public
			1	2	3	4	5	6	7	8	9
ILLINOIS	17000		12 763 371	18.4	1 118	4 405	2 113 483	3 450 604	80.8	2 387 464	86.9
Adams, IL	17001	5	67 040	17.6	9	30	10 225	17 661	76.2	13 042	81.7
Alexander, IL	17003	7	8 927	17.6	4	14	1 363	2 413	94.0	1 937	94.5
Bond, IL	17005	1	18 027	15.1	2	8	2 318	4 596	74.4	2 917	95.7
Boone, IL	17007	2	50 483	20.2	3	16	9 568	11 539	82.7	9 317	85.6
Brown, IL	17009	7	6 835	11.7	1	3	749	1 306	90.7	1 086	91.0
Bureau, IL	17011	6	35 330	17.1	15	28	5 828	8 576	89.4	6 738	91.9
Calhoun, IL	17013	1	5 163	15.8	2	4	725	1 192	82.8	919	83.4
Carroll, IL	17015	7	16 086	16.7	6	14	2 866	4 020	95.3	3 177	97.2
Cass, IL	17017	6	13 898	17.6	4	10	2 347	3 273	89.2	2 571	92.4
Champaign, IL	17019	3	184 905	14.1	19	60	24 018	73 433	92.7	27 413	89.4
Christian, IL	17021	6	35 176	17.2	8	27	6 864	8 254	88.2	6 481	90.3
Clark, IL	17023	6	16 976	17.8	3	10	3 027	4 100	96.3	3 248	98.4
Clay, IL	17025	7	14 122	16.8	4	11	2 593	3 331	98.9	2 665	99.1
Clinton, IL	17027	1	36 095	17.2	15	35	7 349	9 052	84.0	6 852	84.7
Coles, IL	17029	5	51 065	13.4	6	30	7 255	19 136	95.0	7 503	95.5
Cook, IL	17031	1	5 303 683	18.3	173	1 385	866 919	1 491 276	76.2	1 025 425	84.2
Crawford, IL	17033	6	19 898	15.9	7	12	3 278	5 498	94.9	4 035	96.3
Cumberland, IL	17035	9	10 973	18.4	2	7	1 885	2 845	92.5	2 274	93.7
DeKalb, IL	17037	1	97 665	15.5	14	45	16 567	35 173	93.4	14 995	93.1
De Witt, IL	17039	6	16 617	17.2	2	10	3 042	4 046	92.8	3 168	94.7
Douglas, IL	17041	6	19 950	18.3	4	11	2 877	4 859	87.3	3 988	86.9
DuPage, IL	17043	1	929 113	19.0	51	228	143 268	254 238	77.4	175 369	86.8
Edgar, IL	17045	6	19 157	16.7	5	15	3 421	4 346	92.8	3 580	94.9
Edwards, IL	17047	9	6 784	15.8	1	3	992	1 626	94.7	1 220	97.4
Effingham, IL	17049	7	34 581	19.6	5	21	6 291	9 514	84.7	7 337	85.2
Fayette, IL	17051	6	21 713	16.6	7	16	3 341	4 939	92.8	3 925	94.2
Ford, IL	17053	3	14 157	18.0	3	6	1 745	3 420	92.5	2 677	93.9
Franklin, IL	17055	5	39 723	16.2	13	22	6 542	9 032	94.8	6 783	96.7
Fulton, IL	17057	6	37 708	15.5	10	29	7 069	8 460	94.8	6 491	97.4
Gallatin, IL	17059	8	6 152	15.9	1	3	906	1 474	96.3	1 113	97.3
Greene, IL	17061	6	14 581	17.6	3	8	2 393	3 569	90.2	2 830	93.3
Grundy, IL	17063	1	43 838	17.9	15	28	10 004	10 016	89.8	7 686	94.9
Hamilton, IL	17065	7	8 301	16.8	1	4	1 307	1 983	92.4	1 530	92.3
Hancock, IL	17067	7	19 153	17.1	7	19	3 603	4 985	93.3	3 940	94.7
Hardin, IL	17069	9	4 718	14.1	1	3	703	953	95.9	708	95.8
Henderson, IL	17071	9	7 972	16.2	3	5	1 113	1 882	92.3	1 461	94.8
Henry, IL	17073	2	50 591	17.6	12	32	9 141	12 859	91.2	9 918	94.3
Iroquois, IL	17075	6	30 677	17.8	13	36	6 631	7 606	91.0	6 120	93.6
Jackson, IL	17077	5	57 954	12.4	11	24	7 618	26 116	95.2	8 336	92.1
Jasper, IL	17079	7	10 020	17.4	1	7	1 545	2 708	91.7	2 078	92.2
Jefferson, IL	17081	7	40 434	16.9	21	27	6 388	9 817	93.1	7 349	94.5
Jersey, IL	17083	1	22 456	17.2	2	8	2 983	5 988	79.6	4 232	86.8
Jo Daviess, IL	17085	6	22 580	16.0	9	23	3 494	5 104	86.0	3 967	88.3
Johnson, IL	17087	7	13 169	13.3	6	7	1 889	2 829	95.3	2 159	96.2
Kane, IL	17089	1	482 113	20.7	14	106	74 133	114 833	82.1	85 895	88.0
Kankakee, IL	17091	3	107 972	18.9	16	47	19 161	28 166	81.7	20 874	87.8
Kendall, IL	17093	1	79 514	19.3	7	39	26 749	15 369	83.7	11 607	90.1
Knox, IL	17095	4	53 309	15.9	8	28	7 977	13 125	82.0	9 142	92.8
Lake, IL	17097	1	702 682	20.8	51	193	127 629	185 035	81.0	135 526	89.4
La Salle, IL	17099	4	112 604	17.7	30	50	17 082	27 018	86.3	21 364	87.8
Lawrence, IL	17101	7	15 930	15.3	2	7	2 441	3 396	95.0	2 703	95.9
Lee, IL	17103	4	35 669	17.0	8	17	5 175	9 047	85.7	6 980	87.7
Livingston, IL	17105	4	39 186	17.2	14	25	6 993	9 388	90.3	7 786	92.1
Logan, IL	17107	6	30 603	15.1	10	17	3 741	7 826	74.7	5 382	89.0
McDonough, IL	17109	5	31 966	11.2	7	21	3 821	13 645	95.9	4 459	95.6
McHenry, IL	17111	1	303 990	20.7	22	80	51 121	76 811	85.8	57 221	91.0
McLean, IL	17113	3	159 013	15.9	17	54	24 278	52 781	87.1	25 605	89.0
Macon, IL	17115	3	110 167	17.6	12	52	17 658	29 235	80.1	20 713	88.7
Macoupin, IL	17117	1	49 111	16.9	11	36	9 491	12 504	89.7	9 305	95.0
Madison, IL	17119	1	264 309	17.3	22	78	36 695	70 430	84.6	48 026	86.6
Marion, IL	17121	4	40 144	18.0	14	24	6 057	10 286	91.0	8 022	92.3
Marshall, IL	17123	2	13 217	17.0	4	7	1 954	3 090	93.1	2 381	95.3
Mason, IL	17125	6	15 741	17.1	4	10	3 399	3 734	95.6	2 923	99.2
Massac, IL	17127	7	15 348	16.4	2	11	2 656	3 373	97.4	2 595	98.4
Menard, IL	17129	3	12 738	18.4	3	11	2 652	3 307	91.7	2 558	94.3
Mercer, IL	17131	2	16 912	17.0	3	12	3 269	4 186	93.7	3 312	98.0
Monroe, IL	17133	1	31 040	17.7	5	13	4 967	7 520	79.5	5 685	82.2
Montgomery, IL	17135	6	30 396	16.6	5	18	5 009	7 203	93.0	5 680	93.7
Morgan, IL	17137	4	35 722	15.8	7	25	5 431	9 652	75.6	6 607	88.3
Moultrie, IL	17139	6	14 510	17.7	3	9	2 032	3 304	88.3	2 739	89.2
Ogle, IL	17141	4	54 290	19.1	11	29	10 558	13 620	93.3	10 898	95.8
Peoria, IL	17143	2	182 328	17.9	21	80	27 967	49 942	74.4	33 553	83.9
Perry, IL	17145	7	22 815	15.6	5	8	2 865	5 382	90.4	4 020	91.5
Piatt, IL	17147	3	16 680	17.5	5	16	3 306	4 303	93.6	3 156	98.1
Pike, IL	17149	7	17 099	16.6	5	15	2 925	4 152	92.4	3 443	95.8
Pope, IL	17151	9	4 211	14.9	1	2	581	959	94.4	731	97.5
Pulaski, IL	17153	9	6 794	19.4	4	13	1 300	2 064	96.9	1 572	96.3
Putnam, IL	17155	8	6 094	17.4	2	4	963	1 497	90.0	1 164	92.4
Randolph, IL	17157	6	33 122	15.4	8	15	4 425	7 438	83.6	5 795	84.4
Richland, IL	17159	7	15 798	17.2	3	13	2 550	4 095	91.3	2 941	91.6

[1]County type codes are from the Economic Research Service of the United States Department of Agriculture. See notes and definitions at the end of this section.

Table C-1. Population, School, and Student Characteristics by County—*Continued*

STATE County	Characteristics of students, 2004–2005				Outcomes		Staff and students, 2004–2005		
	Percent with IEP[2]	Percent eligible for free or reduced-price lunch	Percent minority	Percent English-language learners	Number of graduates, 2003–2004	Percent dropouts, grades 9–12, 2001–2002	Number of teachers	Student-teacher ratio	Central administration staff
	10	11	12	13	14	15	16	17	18
ILLINOIS	15.3	39.5	43.0	...	...	6.4	131 047	16.1	...
Adams, IL	16.5	41.7	8.4	...	...	4.4	635	16.1	...
Alexander, IL	22.3	76.0	57.7	...	...	4.3	114	12.0	...
Bond, IL	18.3	30.4	6.2	...	...	2.0	145	16.0	...
Boone, IL	12.5	28.4	26.6	...	...	1.2	543	17.6	...
Brown, IL	20.7	36.7	7.3	...	...	96.2	55	13.6	...
Bureau, IL	18.0	29.7	11.2	...	...	3.7	435	13.4	...
Calhoun, IL	22.9	36.1	0.6	...	...	1.4	55	13.1	...
Carroll, IL	17.4	31.0	4.8	...	...	27.8	224	12.8	...
Cass, IL	18.2	47.5	23.5	...	...	4.1	166	14.2	...
Champaign, IL	18.3	35.5	33.2	...	...	4.6	1 668	14.4	...
Christian, IL	17.3	36.2	2.4	...	...	10.5	552	12.4	...
Clark, IL	20.2	34.4	1.5	...	...	2.1	196	15.4	...
Clay, IL	21.8	37.1	2.5	...	...	6.2	188	13.8	...
Clinton, IL	19.5	24.4	5.5	...	...	29.0	478	15.4	...
Coles, IL	21.4	34.9	5.9	...	...	11.0	554	13.1	...
Cook, IL	13.8	56.5	70.5	...	...	9.9	52 949	16.4	...
Crawford, IL	21.3	36.4	3.9	...	...	3.5	248	13.2	...
Cumberland, IL	19.4	27.7	0.1	...	...	1.9	131	14.4	...
DeKalb, IL	13.0	17.0	15.8	...	...	2.9	1 103	15.0	...
De Witt, IL	18.0	30.1	4.7	...	...	6.2	196	15.5	...
Douglas, IL	22.0	22.9	10.0	...	...	2.5	219	13.2	...
DuPage, IL	14.1	9.0	29.1	...	...	1.8	8 904	16.1	...
Edgar, IL	22.4	36.5	2.0	...	...	4.1	255	13.4	...
Edwards, IL	20.3	31.9	3.1	...	...	1.6	73	13.5	...
Effingham, IL	16.6	24.5	2.1	...	...	2.2	398	15.8	...
Fayette, IL	16.7	39.3	2.7	...	...	6.2	218	15.4	...
Ford, IL	15.1	26.6	2.4	...	...	4.1	127	13.8	...
Franklin, IL	22.1	48.7	1.2	...	...	3.2	424	15.4	...
Fulton, IL	18.7	45.7	2.6	...	...	3.9	505	14.0	...
Gallatin, IL	20.8	45.8	1.1	...	...	7.5	57	15.9	...
Greene, IL	18.8	36.6	1.0	...	...	2.9	165	14.5	...
Grundy, IL	15.1	13.9	9.1	...	...	4.9	653	15.3	...
Hamilton, IL	23.6	44.1	1.0	...	...	4.8	79	16.5	...
Hancock, IL	18.4	37.5	1.0	...	...	1.4	275	13.1	...
Hardin, IL	20.1	56.8	2.8	...	...	9.0	46	15.2	...
Henderson, IL	21.2	42.7	1.2	...	...	3.0	89	12.5	...
Henry, IL	15.3	29.2	7.8	...	...	16.6	614	14.9	...
Iroquois, IL	18.9	32.6	9.9	...	...	3.4	487	13.6	...
Jackson, IL	20.4	46.6	27.9	...	...	3.9	552	13.8	...
Jasper, IL	18.0	37.4	1.4	...	...	2.8	108	14.3	...
Jefferson, IL	24.1	45.0	15.9	...	...	4.8	467	13.7	...
Jersey, IL	13.4	33.0	1.2	...	...	2.3	184	16.2	...
Jo Daviess, IL	16.0	25.4	1.7	...	...	3.1	286	12.2	...
Johnson, IL	18.9	41.4	5.5	...	...	1.7	118	16.0	...
Kane, IL	14.0	33.3	44.0	...	...	3.8	4 206	17.6	...
Kankakee, IL	16.5	42.5	35.5	...	...	4.9	1 173	16.3	...
Kendall, IL	13.7	5.8	23.3	...	...	3.6	1 581	16.9	...
Knox, IL	16.1	46.6	15.5	...	...	9.2	599	13.3	...
Lake, IL	16.2	22.7	36.0	...	...	3.5	8 219	15.5	...
La Salle, IL	17.7	27.8	12.4	...	...	4.8	1 162	14.7	...
Lawrence, IL	16.5	37.2	3.5	...	...	5.5	170	14.4	...
Lee, IL	14.0	30.0	8.1	...	...	5.0	350	14.8	...
Livingston, IL	18.2	27.3	6.1	...	...	2.5	500	14.0	...
Logan, IL	18.3	32.1	4.8	...	...	2.8	305	12.3	...
McDonough, IL	21.5	40.0	7.6	...	...	12.0	341	11.2	...
McHenry, IL	15.6	12.0	14.4	...	...	2.8	2 920	17.5	...
McLean, IL	15.7	23.9	21.0	...	...	4.5	1 545	15.7	...
Macon, IL	15.0	42.1	28.6	...	...	6.3	1 111	15.9	...
Macoupin, IL	18.5	29.8	1.7	...	...	3.3	580	16.4	...
Madison, IL	18.6	35.6	16.8	...	...	5.4	2 185	16.8	...
Marion, IL	19.9	47.8	7.5	...	...	5.4	398	15.2	...
Marshall, IL	20.4	28.0	3.7	...	...	3.3	156	12.6	...
Mason, IL	20.2	39.0	1.1	...	...	3.6	227	14.9	...
Massac, IL	17.3	48.3	9.3	...	...	2.9	166	16.0	...
Menard, IL	17.1	19.5	2.0	...	...	2.4	164	16.1	...
Mercer, IL	14.3	26.0	2.5	...	...	1.0	240	13.6	...
Monroe, IL	13.3	10.1	1.5	...	...	4.3	316	15.7	...
Montgomery, IL	16.6	35.8	2.3	...	...	2.8	284	17.6	...
Morgan, IL	19.1	42.3	11.4	...	...	3.2	411	13.2	...
Moultrie, IL	18.0	27.4	2.4	...	...	2.7	142	14.3	...
Ogle, IL	15.2	19.8	11.2	...	...	2.3	679	15.6	...
Peoria, IL	19.8	43.3	39.3	...	...	7.2	1 925	14.5	...
Perry, IL	19.3	34.3	7.2	...	...	4.3	188	15.3	...
Piatt, IL	13.9	20.4	1.8	...	...	2.4	225	14.7	...
Pike, IL	21.4	34.8	0.6	...	...	5.6	216	13.5	...
Pope, IL	12.9	48.5	2.4	...	...	6.3	40	14.5	...
Pulaski, IL	17.1	79.1	54.5	...	...	16.9	121	10.7	...
Putnam, IL	15.0	23.5	6.4	...	...	0.7	65	14.7	...
Randolph, IL	18.3	37.9	9.1	...	...	1.6	316	14.0	...
Richland, IL	16.9	40.3	2.3	...	...	3.6	185	13.8	...

[2]IEP = Individual Education Program. See notes and definitions at the end of this section.
. . . = Not available.

Table C-1. Population, School, and Student Characteristics by County—Continued

STATE County	Revenue, 2003–2004				Current expenditures, 2003–2004			Resident population, 16 to 19 years, 2000			
	Total revenue (thousands of dollars)	Percent of revenue from:			Total expenditures (thousands of dollars)	Amount per student (dollars)	Percent for instruction	Total	Percent in armed forces	Percent high school graduates	Percent not enrolled, not employed, not in armed forces, not high school graduate
		Federal government	State government	Local government							
	19	20	21	22	23	24	25	26	27	28	29
ILLINOIS	21 084 488	8.3	32.3	59.3	18 043 671	8 679	64.0	704 632	0.8	10.6	5.7
Adams, IL	81 021	13.0	42.9	44.1	73 237	7 199	62.3	4 153	0.0	10.8	2.9
Alexander, IL	14 914	20.7	62.3	17.1	13 221	9 018	59.2	490	0.0	9.6	2.9
Bond, IL	17 216	6.2	58.7	35.1	15 867	6 495	61.8	1 053	0.0	7.6	5.0
Boone, IL	74 389	4.2	33.8	61.9	57 664	6 384	63.8	2 341	0.0	11.0	4.6
Brown, IL	6 292	5.5	55.6	38.9	5 486	7 454	55.9	329	0.6	8.8	16.7
Bureau, IL	51 204	5.2	42.1	52.8	46 184	7 907	63.2	2 049	0.0	9.3	4.3
Calhoun, IL	5 592	6.8	54.6	38.6	5 190	7 033	63.5	269	0.0	6.7	4.8
Carroll, IL	26 070	8.2	39.3	52.6	22 318	7 576	65.1	915	0.0	12.9	3.0
Cass, IL	26 759	6.1	69.5	24.5	16 542	7 262	65.7	772	0.0	9.1	8.2
Champaign, IL	207 825	8.8	34.5	56.7	193 064	8 149	65.4	17 484	0.1	5.6	1.4
Christian, IL	57 557	11.0	39.6	49.4	48 799	8 434	65.1	1 722	0.5	13.1	7.5
Clark, IL	21 809	8.4	59.5	32.1	19 319	6 410	59.5	928	0.0	5.6	4.0
Clay, IL	19 768	7.7	63.3	29.0	18 175	6 924	63.2	773	0.0	10.6	4.3
Clinton, IL	40 237	5.2	52.1	42.7	36 306	6 505	67.1	2 018	0.0	12.0	4.5
Coles, IL	72 784	17.3	38.3	44.4	65 762	9 901	61.6	4 817	0.0	7.2	2.0
Cook, IL	8 764 997	10.7	30.4	59.0	7 657 613	9 362	64.9	287 976	0.1	10.3	7.4
Crawford, IL	36 461	12.4	48.7	38.9	29 525	8 756	54.3	1 127	0.0	11.1	1.8
Cumberland, IL	14 910	7.7	57.8	34.5	12 285	6 388	63.1	682	0.0	11.6	3.2
DeKalb, IL	178 725	5.6	27.0	67.4	139 665	8 636	60.9	8 241	0.0	6.8	1.4
De Witt, IL	25 413	6.3	23.2	70.4	24 874	8 169	66.0	915	0.0	7.4	3.5
Douglas, IL	24 032	6.6	39.8	53.5	20 913	7 169	64.0	1 293	0.0	10.2	4.1
DuPage, IL	1 753 198	3.3	17.9	78.8	1 544 791	9 578	66.1	47 205	0.0	7.7	2.8
Edgar, IL	29 410	9.5	44.0	46.5	25 962	7 519	60.2	1 068	0.0	13.7	7.2
Edwards, IL	7 581	6.0	62.4	31.7	6 834	6 861	64.9	398	0.0	11.6	0.8
Effingham, IL	48 160	7.3	50.8	41.9	40 901	6 492	61.8	1 943	0.0	13.6	2.2
Fayette, IL	26 812	6.6	60.5	32.9	20 974	6 418	60.9	1 268	0.0	16.4	8.3
Ford, IL	22 917	6.6	42.4	51.0	19 065	7 706	64.6	666	0.3	7.8	5.7
Franklin, IL	50 826	10.0	67.1	22.9	48 829	7 589	65.9	1 948	0.2	10.0	6.1
Fulton, IL	47 469	7.5	50.0	42.5	42 838	7 546	65.9	1 980	0.1	11.6	7.1
Gallatin, IL	7 759	8.4	59.1	32.5	7 024	7 433	64.2	393	0.0	10.7	3.6
Greene, IL	17 644	7.0	59.4	33.6	16 246	6 772	65.0	854	0.0	14.8	7.3
Grundy, IL	107 371	2.8	15.4	81.8	82 169	8 796	58.7	2 354	0.0	13.3	3.2
Hamilton, IL	10 458	7.7	61.3	31.0	10 098	7 638	58.9	490	0.0	9.8	3.3
Hancock, IL	29 796	7.2	54.3	38.4	26 336	7 176	62.7	1 156	0.6	9.9	3.3
Hardin, IL	5 452	12.7	73.3	14.0	5 307	7 759	62.4	297	0.0	12.8	8.1
Henderson, IL	9 147	8.1	48.6	43.3	8 412	7 340	62.2	470	0.0	10.9	3.4
Henry, IL	79 285	6.6	44.3	49.1	68 806	7 454	65.2	2 885	0.0	12.8	2.0
Iroquois, IL	48 955	8.1	43.1	48.8	42 930	8 467	59.6	1 832	0.0	10.9	5.9
Jackson, IL	75 707	14.3	45.7	40.0	70 849	9 301	62.6	5 741	0.1	6.8	4.1
Jasper, IL	14 088	7.2	37.9	54.9	12 962	8 056	63.9	752	0.0	12.4	1.3
Jefferson, IL	60 126	14.9	51.7	33.4	54 038	8 420	60.2	2 131	0.0	12.3	7.0
Jersey, IL	25 403	8.2	55.4	36.5	22 120	7 310	63.2	1 480	0.0	10.9	4.0
Jo Daviess, IL	39 373	4.5	38.0	57.5	29 522	8 620	65.0	1 150	0.0	9.7	2.7
Johnson, IL	14 702	10.4	55.0	34.6	12 812	6 955	62.5	705	0.0	7.8	14.6
Kane, IL	1 045 953	4.7	34.7	60.6	856 563	7 765	63.6	23 853	0.1	10.3	7.7
Kankakee, IL	180 438	10.2	45.2	44.6	148 606	7 865	63.2	6 115	0.0	14.0	5.7
Kendall, IL	141 647	2.9	28.7	68.4	106 659	7 349	58.7	3 225	0.0	6.8	3.6
Knox, IL	61 788	10.5	45.5	44.0	62 357	7 807	68.2	3 154	0.0	9.2	7.4
Lake, IL	1 661 810	4.6	21.6	73.8	1 302 296	9 708	61.5	38 104	12.6	20.6	3.7
La Salle, IL	180 105	6.5	36.0	57.5	147 283	8 634	63.5	6 275	0.1	13.0	5.1
Lawrence, IL	21 330	8.0	71.5	20.5	16 907	6 923	63.9	721	0.0	12.9	4.7
Lee, IL	46 187	6.0	37.2	56.8	40 266	7 699	63.1	1 955	0.0	12.0	4.3
Livingston, IL	66 230	6.7	39.3	54.0	60 882	8 362	64.7	2 204	0.0	11.7	9.8
Logan, IL	33 348	6.5	36.8	56.7	30 237	8 113	64.2	2 055	0.6	9.2	4.1
McDonough, IL	43 315	14.5	34.0	51.4	38 767	10 210	61.1	3 482	0.0	3.0	1.9
McHenry, IL	449 127	3.8	26.7	69.5	400 467	8 084	62.9	13 662	0.1	8.8	2.5
McLean, IL	219 712	5.4	27.5	67.2	193 324	8 177	63.3	11 738	0.0	6.8	2.1
Macon, IL	167 512	9.2	47.3	43.5	131 629	7 571	60.6	6 574	0.0	11.9	7.5
Macoupin, IL	71 938	7.4	60.0	32.5	58 119	6 207	63.2	2 969	0.1	11.2	4.2
Madison, IL	363 180	8.6	45.6	45.8	316 694	7 384	61.5	14 923	0.0	10.1	4.7
Marion, IL	71 259	12.4	57.4	30.2	60 429	7 925	62.8	2 234	0.2	13.8	6.8
Marshall, IL	17 663	11.8	30.7	57.6	13 730	8 870	58.1	715	0.0	11.7	4.1
Mason, IL	27 994	7.0	49.7	43.3	24 814	7 292	66.3	914	0.0	9.2	7.8
Massac, IL	21 310	5.5	59.9	34.5	18 033	6 795	56.1	817	0.0	12.4	6.6
Menard, IL	25 596	5.4	51.0	43.7	16 134	5 921	61.7	717	0.0	8.5	1.4
Mercer, IL	11 742	8.7	49.9	41.4	11 252	7 037	67.2	1 074	0.0	14.9	2.0
Monroe, IL	37 468	3.7	39.6	56.7	34 681	7 269	61.7	1 704	0.0	13.0	1.3
Montgomery, IL	39 048	7.9	47.4	44.7	34 063	6 783	61.2	1 646	0.2	11.8	5.7
Morgan, IL	47 479	13.8	36.8	49.4	45 912	8 554	61.9	2 557	0.3	8.7	5.5
Moultrie, IL	16 281	7.1	42.6	50.3	13 414	6 785	61.4	816	0.0	11.9	4.4
Ogle, IL	98 070	4.4	34.2	61.4	84 297	8 078	64.5	2 985	0.0	11.3	2.8
Peoria, IL	279 045	10.5	39.0	50.5	249 428	8 436	61.8	10 361	0.1	9.4	5.0
Perry, IL	23 643	8.0	57.1	34.9	20 685	7 155	64.2	1 378	0.0	10.4	12.0
Piatt, IL	28 960	3.1	34.7	62.2	23 596	7 176	59.3	972	0.0	11.9	0.5
Pike, IL	23 333	6.9	56.2	36.9	20 837	6 988	63.7	922	0.0	10.5	6.7
Pope, IL	4 964	10.1	66.6	23.3	4 042	6 945	63.1	264	0.0	18.9	17.8
Pulaski, IL	21 005	22.5	60.1	17.4	14 850	11 565	63.2	472	0.0	8.7	16.3
Putnam, IL	6 814	5.3	21.4	73.3	6 705	6 685	62.6	334	0.0	8.1	1.8
Randolph, IL	41 383	11.0	47.9	41.1	35 507	7 929	60.9	1 757	0.0	14.3	9.0
Richland, IL	19 723	9.9	51.8	38.2	17 620	6 902	61.0	938	0.0	9.3	6.8

Table C-1. Population, School, and Student Characteristics by County—*Continued*

STATE County	High school graduates, 2000			College enrollment, 2000		College graduates, 2000 (percent)						
	Population 25 years and over	High school graduate or less (percent)	High school graduate or more (percent)	Number	Percent public	Bachelor's degree or more	+/- U.S. percentage with bachelor's degree or more	Non-Hispanic White	Black	American Indian and Alaska Native	Asian or Pacific Islander	Hispanic[3]
	30	31	32	33	34	35	36	37	38	39	40	41
ILLINOIS	7 973 671	46.3	81.4	810 038	69.4	26.1	1.7	28.8	14.7	13.3	57.4	9.1
Adams, IL	45 101	53.8	83.7	3 338	57.8	17.6	-6.8	17.8	6.3	0.0	45.5	24.4
Alexander, IL	6 395	67.7	67.0	275	89.5	6.9	-17.5	8.6	3.6	0.0	8.3	0.0
Bond, IL	11 731	61.4	72.8	1 371	30.4	15.0	-9.4	16.4	2.1	4.2	23.1	9.6
Boone, IL	26 061	57.5	80.8	1 392	80.0	14.5	-9.9	15.4	15.4	1.6	42.0	4.6
Brown, IL	4 844	65.6	63.3	142	87.3	9.2	-15.2	11.7	0.0	0.0	10.0	5.5
Bureau, IL	24 085	54.9	84.1	1 147	86.1	15.7	-8.7	15.8	24.0	9.1	52.2	6.1
Calhoun, IL	3 528	64.7	79.9	179	86.6	9.4	-15.0	9.3	. . .	27.8	0.0	14.3
Carroll, IL	11 516	60.7	83.3	503	89.1	13.1	-11.3	13.1	7.1	0.0	57.1	1.7
Cass, IL	9 056	64.3	80.0	410	81.0	12.6	-11.8	13.1	0.0	13.3	77.3	2.1
Champaign, IL	100 559	33.3	91.0	42 713	97.6	38.0	13.6	37.7	16.6	11.1	79.4	41.4
Christian, IL	24 202	62.6	81.0	1 063	87.5	10.5	-13.9	10.7	2.0	9.8	23.0	7.0
Clark, IL	11 569	59.3	80.0	554	93.1	13.6	-10.8	13.6	0.0	0.0	0.0	35.0
Clay, IL	9 898	62.3	75.9	452	96.9	9.7	-14.7	9.7	. . .	0.0	23.9	0.0
Clinton, IL	23 463	57.6	77.4	1 666	82.2	13.0	-11.4	13.6	1.2	0.0	11.9	10.6
Coles, IL	30 326	49.7	82.9	10 787	97.9	20.8	-3.6	20.3	21.5	7.7	66.4	31.4
Cook, IL	3 454 738	46.5	77.7	359 786	58.3	28.0	3.6	36.7	15.0	15.3	54.5	8.8
Crawford, IL	13 995	57.6	79.3	1 063	98.1	10.3	-14.1	10.7	1.7	0.0	32.0	8.0
Cumberland, IL	7 352	62.8	80.2	436	92.4	10.1	-14.3	10.1	0.0	15.4	66.7	3.7
DeKalb, IL	48 912	42.4	87.5	18 467	96.3	26.8	2.4	26.8	30.4	23.3	58.6	14.6
De Witt, IL	11 354	60.1	83.5	542	90.0	13.4	-11.0	13.3	0.0	0.0	89.3	0.0
Douglas, IL	12 923	60.3	79.3	581	96.6	13.8	-10.6	13.9	0.0	0.0	48.8	3.8
DuPage, IL	589 120	30.6	90.0	57 695	59.4	41.7	17.3	41.8	33.5	14.3	66.4	14.8
Edgar, IL	13 395	60.5	81.4	477	81.3	13.3	-11.1	13.5	0.0	2.4	100.0	8.2
Edwards, IL	4 815	56.6	82.3	297	88.9	9.8	-14.6	9.5	0.0	36.4	45.5	. . .
Effingham, IL	21 635	54.7	83.4	1 366	91.5	15.1	-9.3	15.1	45.5	14.3	33.8	12.7
Fayette, IL	14 611	68.7	72.2	646	85.0	9.0	-15.4	9.7	0.0	0.0	0.0	0.0
Ford, IL	9 557	56.0	86.0	456	97.4	13.9	-10.5	13.8	15.8	100.0	55.6	4.7
Franklin, IL	26 965	57.7	76.7	1 697	93.0	11.3	-13.1	11.2	0.0	33.8	50.0	2.8
Fulton, IL	26 529	59.7	78.3	1 358	88.1	11.4	-13.0	11.8	2.0	0.0	13.9	1.7
Gallatin, IL	4 481	63.3	73.6	294	95.2	7.7	-16.7	7.7	37.5	0.0	40.0	4.3
Greene, IL	9 688	64.9	78.9	436	78.9	10.1	-14.3	10.2	0.0	0.0	23.1	14.8
Grundy, IL	24 297	52.0	86.9	1 710	77.9	15.2	-9.2	15.3	0.0	0.0	55.8	12.5
Hamilton, IL	5 866	57.6	74.3	324	92.6	10.5	-13.9	10.4	0.0	0.0	100.0	0.0
Hancock, IL	13 724	55.8	85.7	731	93.0	15.6	-8.8	15.7	0.0	0.0	0.0	16.4
Hardin, IL	0 442	00.9	68.1	214	95.8	9.6	-14.8	9.7	0.0	. . .	61.1	0.0
Henderson, IL	5 680	63.9	82.4	278	84.2	10.0	-14.4	10.1	0.0	0.0	100.0	0.0
Henry, IL	34 183	52.7	84.5	2 008	86.1	15.7	-8.7	16.0	14.0	16.7	34.9	3.0
Iroquois, IL	21 111	60.3	80.3	1 007	86.2	11.8	-12.6	11.8	8.7	31.6	78.2	5.0
Jackson, IL	32 659	39.7	85.2	16 882	97.9	32.0	7.6	30.9	24.9	30.6	77.8	27.1
Jasper, IL	6 579	58.0	82.6	459	96.5	11.2	-13.2	11.1	. . .	0.0	0.0	0.0
Jefferson, IL	26 841	56.0	77.0	1 631	92.7	13.7	-10.7	14.2	7.0	10.9	44.1	5.1
Jersey, IL	13 982	56.8	82.5	1 427	61.3	12.6	-11.8	12.4	28.0	14.6	29.5	53.1
Jo Daviess, IL	15 625	58.0	83.6	725	72.3	15.2	-9.2	15.4	0.0	9.4	20.0	1.6
Johnson, IL	9 057	60.7	67.1	501	94.6	11.7	-12.7	13.9	0.0	0.0	53.8	4.1
Kane, IL	245 486	44.8	80.2	19 754	69.9	27.7	3.3	33.6	15.2	4.5	46.6	4.9
Kankakee, IL	65 844	56.0	79.8	5 437	62.2	15.0	-9.4	16.3	7.1	17.7	38.6	7.2
Kendall, IL	34 362	40.2	89.9	2 555	73.3	25.3	0.9	26.1	24.0	30.8	41.4	8.5
Knox, IL	38 049	54.9	81.8	3 207	53.4	14.6	-9.8	15.2	4.7	0.0	47.0	6.0
Lake, IL	398 265	34.8	86.6	32 659	64.8	38.6	14.2	43.1	17.3	14.1	64.6	8.4
La Salle, IL	74 431	57.2	81.4	3 807	88.8	13.3	-11.1	13.5	3.0	5.7	57.2	6.7
Lawrence, IL	10 752	60.6	81.3	537	94.6	9.7	-14.7	9.7	14.3	0.0	0.0	0.0
Lee, IL	24 540	56.5	80.2	1 434	87.2	13.2	-11.2	13.9	2.0	0.0	32.0	4.0
Livingston, IL	26 496	63.2	78.1	1 009	84.4	12.6	-11.8	13.5	0.4	28.3	13.0	0.8
Logan, IL	20 714	60.0	80.4	1 933	37.2	14.2	-10.2	15.2	1.7	0.0	46.6	4.5
McDonough, IL	17 944	46.5	86.9	8 722	96.3	26.9	2.5	25.6	33.1	0.0	85.1	44.9
McHenry, IL	163 780	39.1	89.2	12 583	81.6	27.7	3.3	28.4	46.6	17.4	55.4	9.3
McLean, IL	87 220	37.5	90.7	24 570	88.4	36.2	11.8	35.8	30.7	7.3	73.1	23.9
Macon, IL	75 195	54.9	83.2	6 495	56.2	16.9	-7.5	18.3	5.2	14.5	53.6	11.0
Macoupin, IL	32 878	59.5	82.1	2 312	71.3	11.8	-12.6	11.8	5.2	12.5	35.9	18.0
Madison, IL	170 432	49.7	84.3	17 380	87.5	19.2	-5.2	19.6	11.1	16.4	48.9	18.3
Marion, IL	27 710	56.8	79.1	1 491	93.0	12.1	-12.3	12.1	7.6	16.7	55.2	20.3
Marshall, IL	9 135	55.2	85.0	468	84.8	14.5	-9.9	14.7	0.0	0.0	0.0	0.0
Mason, IL	10 890	62.2	79.9	476	89.5	11.2	-13.2	11.3	0.0	0.0	0.0	0.0
Massac, IL	10 471	58.3	76.5	597	92.6	10.7	-13.7	10.9	6.7	0.0	33.3	4.1
Menard, IL	8 298	50.0	88.3	445	81.3	20.5	-3.9	20.7	7.1	10.5	7.1	34.1
Mercer, IL	11 529	58.7	84.9	605	84.8	12.6	-11.8	12.6	0.0	0.0	35.5	30.6
Monroe, IL	18 277	45.4	87.2	1 344	79.5	20.4	-4.0	20.3	0.0	26.5	60.4	10.4
Montgomery, IL	20 874	63.9	77.1	899	90.8	11.2	-13.2	11.7	1.0	13.3	13.2	6.1
Morgan, IL	24 276	57.2	79.9	2 407	42.9	19.9	-4.5	20.8	4.0	11.9	63.5	6.7
Moultrie, IL	9 515	59.1	78.8	357	80.7	14.7	-9.7	14.6	0.0	0.0	53.8	33.8
Ogle, IL	33 317	53.3	83.1	1 842	88.0	17.0	-7.4	17.5	18.5	9.7	64.9	4.5
Peoria, IL	118 498	45.6	83.8	12 443	52.1	23.3	-1.1	24.4	10.1	6.0	68.7	19.3
Perry, IL	15 727	61.9	72.3	977	94.6	10.1	-14.3	10.9	1.1	0.0	28.6	5.5
Piatt, IL	11 118	48.5	88.7	728	94.0	21.0	-3.4	21.0	0.0	0.0	57.1	5.0
Pike, IL	11 864	64.2	79.6	473	73.8	9.9	-14.5	9.7	0.0	0.0	55.6	31.1
Pope, IL	2 989	57.3	75.8	186	80.6	10.5	-13.9	10.6	6.1	0.0	. . .	. . .
Pulaski, IL	4 704	60.9	70.7	326	98.2	7.1	-17.3	6.7	8.8	0.0	0.0	0.0
Putnam, IL	4 136	54.2	83.8	210	83.3	12.1	-12.3	12.2	0.0	25.0	0.0	4.1
Randolph, IL	23 141	65.9	71.3	1 095	85.5	8.6	-15.8	9.3	2.9	0.0	21.4	2.4
Richland, IL	10 827	49.4	83.4	898	94.3	15.2	-9.2	15.2	. . .	0.0	61.8	0.0

[3]May be of any race.
. . . = Not available.

Table C-1. Population, School, and Student Characteristics by County—*Continued*

STATE County	State/ county code	County type[1]	Population, 2005 Total	Percent 5 to 17 years	Number of schools and students, 2004–2005 School districts	Schools	Students	Resident enrollment, 2000 Total	Percent public	K–12	Percent public
			1	2	3	4	5	6	7	8	9
Rock Island, IL	17161	2	147 808	16.7	14	60	22 241	37 839	82.5	26 365	88.9
St. Clair, IL	17163	1	260 067	19.2	36	119	51 988	73 803	84.9	54 017	87.8
Saline, IL	17165	7	26 072	17.6	5	15	4 320	6 262	97.4	4 663	97.5
Sangamon, IL	17167	3	192 789	17.5	19	116	31 365	48 266	82.1	34 965	82.8
Schuyler, IL	17169	7	7 073	16.0	1	4	1 165	1 580	94.6	1 282	98.4
Scott, IL	17171	9	5 412	17.6	2	5	1 014	1 315	88.3	1 031	92.6
Shelby, IL	17173	6	22 322	17.8	4	11	2 663	5 454	92.6	4 273	94.2
Stark, IL	17175	2	6 169	17.5	2	6	1 117	1 457	89.2	1 200	91.3
Stephenson, IL	17177	4	47 965	17.7	7	23	7 433	12 693	85.9	9 402	88.3
Tazewell, IL	17179	2	129 999	16.9	21	53	19 653	31 754	87.6	23 416	91.2
Union, IL	17181	7	18 202	16.2	7	16	3 282	4 290	94.8	3 292	95.2
Vermilion, IL	17183	3	82 344	17.8	16	44	14 253	19 917	90.8	15 297	92.0
Wabash, IL	17185	6	12 570	16.9	2	5	1 995	3 334	91.6	2 379	91.6
Warren, IL	17187	7	17 558	16.0	9	16	2 918	5 142	77.1	3 344	94.6
Washington, IL	17189	6	14 922	17.6	7	10	2 137	3 895	86.6	2 962	86.7
Wayne, IL	17191	7	16 796	16.7	8	14	2 760	3 981	96.9	3 053	98.0
White, IL	17193	6	15 284	14.7	5	12	2 563	3 321	96.0	2 567	97.7
Whiteside, IL	17195	4	59 863	17.6	14	31	9 923	14 998	88.7	11 644	91.4
Will, IL	17197	1	642 813	20.6	36	172	107 084	147 354	82.1	107 495	89.1
Williamson, IL	17199	5	63 617	16.0	7	21	9 623	14 961	90.8	10 550	91.6
Winnebago, IL	17201	2	288 695	18.8	14	96	47 311	72 350	78.6	54 037	81.9
Woodford, IL	17203	2	37 448	18.5	11	25	7 634	9 879	85.8	7 307	91.0
INDIANA	18000		6 271 973	18.7	361	2 005	1 021 403	1 603 554	83.4	1 142 156	88.7
Adams, IN	18001	6	33 849	22.1	3	11	4 921	9 020	80.5	7 246	81.3
Allen, IN	18003	2	344 006	20.2	6	92	53 801	91 489	75.3	65 971	79.1
Bartholomew, IN	18005	3	73 540	19.4	2	19	11 801	17 865	84.4	13 359	88.7
Benton, IN	18007	3	9 039	20.2	1	5	1 978	2 424	85.6	1 963	89.5
Blackford, IN	18009	6	13 849	17.9	1	5	2 284	3 178	90.2	2 579	93.4
Boone, IN	18011	1	52 061	20.1	4	20	10 884	11 649	87.8	9 369	93.0
Brown, IN	18013	1	15 154	16.6	1	6	2 523	3 303	90.9	2 724	94.5
Carroll, IN	18015	3	20 426	19.0	2	6	2 865	4 612	89.4	3 813	92.3
Cass, IN	18017	4	40 130	19.1	3	14	6 922	9 488	90.3	7 749	93.5
Clark, IN	18019	1	101 592	17.7	4	31	15 365	21 962	85.5	16 552	88.2
Clay, IN	18021	3	27 142	18.8	1	10	4 730	6 549	90.5	5 323	93.3
Clinton, IN	18023	6	34 091	19.6	4	13	6 364	7 947	91.8	6 832	95.2
Crawford, IN	18025	8	11 216	18.6	1	6	1 738	2 346	90.8	2 049	92.4
Daviess, IN	18027	7	30 466	20.8	5	12	4 352	7 094	81.5	5 947	82.9
Dearborn, IN	18029	1	49 082	19.5	2	10	4 561	11 922	83.2	9 685	87.8
Decatur, IN	18031	6	25 184	19.1	2	7	4 327	5 684	88.3	4 608	92.9
De Kalb, IN	18033	4	41 659	20.2	3	14	7 412	10 316	89.6	8 065	93.5
Delaware, IN	18035	3	116 362	15.6	9	40	17 156	37 225	94.1	19 279	95.4
Dubois, IN	18037	7	40 858	19.5	5	18	7 415	10 124	88.8	8 012	92.2
Elkhart, IN	18039	3	195 362	20.6	7	55	34 655	44 933	85.4	36 607	90.5
Fayette, IN	18041	7	24 885	17.7	2	12	3 946	5 544	89.8	4 439	91.6
Floyd, IN	18043	1	71 997	18.9	2	20	11 625	18 474	82.8	13 808	84.5
Fountain, IN	18045	6	17 462	19.1	3	7	3 249	4 260	92.1	3 520	95.7
Franklin, IN	18047	1	23 085	20.1	2	9	5 004	5 644	78.2	4 611	82.1
Fulton, IN	18049	7	20 665	18.9	3	10	5 020	4 904	91.8	4 084	95.5
Gibson, IN	18051	2	33 408	17.9	4	14	5 016	7 933	81.5	6 100	88.5
Grant, IN	18053	4	70 557	17.3	5	34	12 359	19 117	73.4	12 773	93.1
Greene, IN	18055	3	33 479	18.1	6	13	5 779	7 678	92.3	5 980	95.3
Hamilton, IN	18057	1	240 685	21.6	6	53	41 833	51 209	79.2	38 339	86.9
Hancock, IN	18059	1	63 138	18.8	4	21	11 776	14 151	85.2	10 799	91.7
Harrison, IN	18061	1	36 827	18.1	3	16	6 142	8 341	85.3	6 637	87.6
Hendricks, IN	18063	1	127 483	19.8	6	35	22 769	27 181	86.2	21 421	92.0
Henry, IN	18065	4	47 244	17.8	5	24	8 233	10 911	91.6	8 779	94.8
Howard, IN	18067	3	84 977	18.6	5	31	13 973	20 385	87.3	15 619	91.6
Huntington, IN	18069	6	38 236	18.7	2	11	6 345	9 918	81.5	7 419	91.1
Jackson, IN	18071	4	42 237	18.3	4	17	6 460	9 233	84.7	7 554	87.5
Jasper, IN	18073	1	31 876	19.4	2	9	5 026	8 012	78.8	6 113	87.5
Jay, IN	18075	6	21 606	20.2	1	10	3 866	5 006	92.7	4 202	95.1
Jefferson, IN	18077	6	32 430	17.8	3	11	4 920	8 115	76.6	5 619	90.4
Jennings, IN	18079	6	28 427	20.3	1	10	5 240	6 562	86.2	5 392	89.1
Johnson, IN	18081	1	128 436	19.5	8	37	22 454	29 119	81.9	22 205	89.2
Knox, IN	18083	4	38 366	16.6	3	14	5 563	11 067	93.0	6 828	93.3
Kosciusko, IN	18085	4	76 072	19.7	3	21	12 002	18 081	85.2	14 606	90.2
Lagrange, IN	18087	6	36 875	23.4	3	14	6 196	7 998	77.9	7 099	78.0
Lake, IN	18089	1	493 297	19.5	25	151	85 084	130 977	84.7	96 754	88.8
La Porte, IN	18091	3	110 512	17.9	7	18	8 368	27 395	85.7	20 758	88.9
Lawrence, IN	18093	4	46 403	17.7	2	20	7 633	9 850	91.5	8 125	94.9
Madison, IN	18095	3	130 412	17.5	5	39	19 938	31 151	83.5	23 306	92.4
Marion, IN	18097	1	863 133	18.8	30	252	137 474	218 164	77.9	156 431	83.7
Marshall, IN	18099	6	46 945	19.8	7	18	9 203	11 369	85.5	9 285	89.7
Martin, IN	18101	6	10 386	17.6	2	5	1 829	2 269	89.5	1 942	90.8
Miami, IN	18103	6	35 620	18.6	3	12	5 918	8 768	90.3	6 949	92.2
Monroe, IN	18105	3	121 407	12.2	3	29	13 495	52 065	93.0	15 547	90.6
Montgomery, IN	18107	6	38 239	18.8	3	19	6 567	9 352	85.2	7 207	95.9
Morgan, IN	18109	1	69 778	19.4	4	25	11 791	15 760	89.3	13 108	93.8
Newton, IN	18111	1	14 456	18.5	2	7	2 648	3 438	91.9	2 961	93.5
Noble, IN	18113	6	47 448	20.8	3	16	7 863	11 357	87.3	9 512	91.1
Ohio, IN	18115	1	5 874	16.9	1	2	980	1 310	92.5	1 082	96.5
Orange, IN	18117	6	19 770	18.5	4	7	3 472	4 377	91.9	3 605	93.7
Owen, IN	18119	3	22 823	18.6	1	6	3 116	5 037	91.0	4 296	94.2

[1]County type codes are from the Economic Research Service of the United States Department of Agriculture. See notes and definitions at the end of this section.

Table C-1. Population, School, and Student Characteristics by County—*Continued*

STATE County	Characteristics of students, 2004–2005				Outcomes		Staff and students, 2004–2005		
	Percent with IEP[2]	Percent eligible for free or reduced-price lunch	Percent minority	Percent English-language learners	Number of graduates, 2003–2004	Percent dropouts, grades 9–12, 2001–2002	Number of teachers	Student-teacher ratio	Central administration staff
	10	11	12	13	14	15	16	17	18
Rock Island, IL	17.4	42.5	30.1	...	...	4.3	1 376	16.2	...
St. Clair, IL	17.4	40.9	46.8	...	...	5.0	3 080	16.9	...
Saline, IL	17.9	49.9	10.9	...	...	5.9	278	15.5	...
Sangamon, IL	19.8	38.2	22.6	...	...	2.8	2 316	13.5	...
Schuyler, IL	20.2	43.4	1.6	...	...	4.0	71	16.3	...
Scott, IL	19.6	28.8	1.7	...	...	3.6	78	13.1	...
Shelby, IL	20.5	31.4	1.5	...	...	3.5	205	13.0	...
Stark, IL	18.4	30.5	1.5	...	...	2.5	86	13.0	...
Stephenson, IL	14.2	38.1	20.0	...	...	5.1	516	14.4	...
Tazewell, IL	17.4	26.4	3.3	...	...	3.6	1 253	15.7	...
Union, IL	18.4	47.3	7.8	...	...	8.2	218	15.1	...
Vermilion, IL	20.1	48.4	23.1	...	...	7.3	931	15.3	...
Wabash, IL	17.8	31.9	1.7	...	...	6.1	128	16.6	...
Warren, IL	15.3	40.7	10.5	...	...	4.8	206	14.2	...
Washington, IL	16.9	21.4	2.0	...	...	1.0	142	15.1	...
Wayne, IL	18.8	37.1	1.5	...	...	3.7	198	13.9	...
White, IL	...	39.2	1.4	...	...	4.8	219	11.7	...
Whiteside, IL	18.4	34.4	14.2	...	...	3.6	638	15.6	...
Will, IL	14.9	20.1	32.9	...	...	3.7	5 933	18.0	...
Williamson, IL	19.8	38.8	7.5	...	...	3.3	631	15.2	...
Winnebago, IL	14.6	48.6	36.9	...	...	6.6	2 699	17.5	...
Woodford, IL	15.5	16.5	2.4	...	...	2.4	498	15.3	...
INDIANA	17.1	36.3	19.0	5.0	...	2.3	60 562	16.9	...
Adams, IN	13.4	23.2	6.1	3.3	374	2.2	287	17.1	28
Allen, IN	17.2	39.7	29.3	7.3	...	2.0	3 030	17.8	...
Bartholomew, IN	15.6	33.5	7.2	5.3	712	1.5	660	17.9	28
Benton, IN	26.9	33.2	5.4	1.4	146	...	129	15.3	4
Blackford, IN	20.4	38.9	1.4	0.4	142	3.0	145	15.8	9
Boone, IN	17.4	18.1	3.5	1.6	...	1.1	612	17.8	47
Brown, IN	15.7	27.0	1.7	0.0	147	0.5	148	17.0	11
Carroll, IN	15.2	30.1	4.9	4.4	182	4.1	153	18.7	8
Cass, IN	14.0	37.5	15.6	11.4	394	0.4	473	14.6	37
Clark, IN	19.5	38.4	13.5	1.7	...	2.7	929	16.5	...
Clay, IN	21.2	40.7	1.4	0.4	312	0.2	280	16.9	10
Clinton, IN	15.4	40.4	13.9	10.7	387	2.7	384	16.6	29
Crawford, IN	17.8	51.9	0.4	0.5	...	1.7	98	17.7	4
Daviess, IN	19.8	37.9	4.6	7.5	...	2.6	292	14.9	15
Dearborn, IN	19.4	17.6	1.2	0.2	288	2.7	275	16.6	12
Decatur, IN	17.1	29.9	1.6	1.0	...	1.8	254	17.0	12
De Kalb, IN	16.0	29.2	2.7	1.2	456	3.3	437	17.0	29
Delaware, IN	20.6	39.4	11.4	0.8	...	3.3	1 141	15.0	78
Dubois, IN	12.0	17.6	5.6	5.2	...	1.0	412	18.0	...
Elkhart, IN	16.1	38.9	24.4	17.7	...	2.5	2 048	16.9	89
Fayette, IN	20.8	46.9	2.8	0.4	...	1.8	261	15.1	...
Floyd, IN	17.9	33.1	9.7	1.9	...	2.8	657	17.7	20
Fountain, IN	14.9	31.7	1.6	0.8	202	2.5	204	15.9	13
Franklin, IN	16.4	29.4	0.6	0.6	321	2.4	272	18.4	19
Fulton, IN	14.1	31.0	3.4	2.7	321	1.1	263	19.1	21
Gibson, IN	18.7	25.8	2.4	0.3	...	3.1	357	14.1	19
Grant, IN	16.4	42.7	14.4	2.0	...	3.4	801	15.4	43
Greene, IN	18.3	35.1	1.2	0.1	...	0.1	353	16.4	31
Hamilton, IN	14.9	9.6	9.2	5.7	2 092	0.9	2 190	19.1	91
Hancock, IN	19.1	14.9	3.2	0.6	...	1.3	696	16.9	35
Harrison, IN	17.7	29.6	1.4	0.7	398	1.1	358	17.2	19
Hendricks, IN	14.7	14.8	6.6	2.3	...	0.4	1 208	18.8	54
Henry, IN	23.6	33.4	1.9	0.1	...	2.2	514	16.0	66
Howard, IN	21.3	33.3	13.4	2.0	...	0.9	923	15.1	49
Huntington, IN	16.2	27.9	1.7	0.3	...	...	382	16.6	...
Jackson, IN	18.7	33.4	5.0	4.3	...	3.4	373	17.3	24
Jasper, IN	18.6	28.5	5.7	3.8	332	2.5	277	18.2	13
Jay, IN	18.0	40.1	2.6	2.6	204	2.2	230	16.8	9
Jefferson, IN	23.3	40.9	2.2	0.5	...	0.7	337	14.6	43
Jennings, IN	21.9	45.4	2.1	0.7	251	3.2	283	18.5	9
Johnson, IN	14.7	21.3	3.8	1.7	...	1.2	1 257	17.9	95
Knox, IN	16.3	40.0	2.9	0.4	...	1.1	350	15.9	18
Kosciusko, IN	13.5	30.7	9.9	7.6	673	3.3	668	18.0	47
Lagrange, IN	13.4	27.3	5.6	21.1	350	0.6	367	16.9	16
Lake, IN	14.5	45.2	50.2	8.5	...	1.3	4 663	18.2	...
La Porte, IN	12.8	38.5	18.3	3.7	...	0.7	516	16.2	...
Lawrence, IN	18.6	42.9	1.5	0.3	437	1.9	444	17.2	14
Madison, IN	19.3	41.5	14.1	1.3	...	0.8	1 196	16.7	64
Marion, IN	16.5	52.5	47.6	7.9	...	2.0	8 482	16.2	...
Marshall, IN	13.4	34.3	10.0	7.3	...	1.1	590	15.6	40
Martin, IN	19.9	35.8	0.3	0.7	128	2.1	107	17.0	11
Miami, IN	16.2	36.1	5.0	1.4	...	2.2	357	16.6	23
Monroe, IN	17.3	28.8	8.9	5.2	...	2.4	807	16.7	41
Montgomery, IN	17.6	33.6	3.7	2.4	...	1.6	408	16.1	32
Morgan, IN	14.3	25.4	1.1	0.3	...	1.8	674	17.5	28
Newton, IN	17.4	31.6	5.6	3.4	170	2.2	168	15.8	9
Noble, IN	15.1	37.3	14.7	11.7	465	0.6	454	17.3	25
Ohio, IN	16.7	21.2	1.3	0.4	61	4.7	56	17.7	3
Orange, IN	18.1	42.6	1.8	0.1	...	3.2	197	17.6	16
Owen, IN	21.2	36.5	1.4	0.0	161	5.8	188	16.6	11

[2]IEP = Individual Education Program. See notes and definitions at the end of this section.
. . . = Not available.

Table C-1. Population, School, and Student Characteristics by County—*Continued*

STATE County	Revenue, 2003–2004				Current expenditures, 2003–2004			Resident population, 16 to 19 years, 2000			
	Total revenue (thousands of dollars)	Percent of revenue from:			Total expenditures (thousands of dollars)	Amount per student (dollars)	Percent for instruction	Total	Percent in armed forces	Percent high school graduates	Percent not enrolled, not employed, not in armed forces, not high school graduate
		Federal government	State government	Local government							
	19	20	21	22	23	24	25	26	27	28	29
Rock Island, IL	225 222	11.4	35.7	52.9	190 673	7 855	66.3	9 001	0.1	10.2	5.0
St. Clair, IL	434 779	12.0	53.8	34.3	365 417	8 009	61.5	15 449	1.1	12.4	6.0
Saline, IL	32 806	9.7	63.1	27.2	30 403	6 933	69.5	1 971	0.0	7.6	24.6
Sangamon, IL	284 704	10.1	31.3	58.6	224 980	7 728	61.2	9 836	0.3	12.6	4.5
Schuyler, IL	9 356	5.5	60.3	34.3	8 224	7 195	59.2	353	1.4	4.2	2.8
Scott, IL	8 030	5.9	57.2	36.9	6 984	6 807	66.1	323	0.0	17.3	2.5
Shelby, IL	28 947	6.7	55.8	37.6	25 342	6 945	63.8	1 271	1.1	10.4	4.9
Stark, IL	10 382	4.8	35.1	60.1	8 594	7 467	63.3	352	0.0	6.0	6.8
Stephenson, IL	70 747	7.5	40.9	51.5	58 791	7 787	62.6	2 799	0.0	11.4	5.0
Tazewell, IL	177 399	7.9	37.1	55.0	145 322	7 485	63.6	6 903	0.0	12.6	2.4
Union, IL	27 336	10.5	58.9	30.6	24 526	7 348	65.1	1 033	0.0	12.6	4.2
Vermilion, IL	119 782	12.1	50.8	37.1	113 973	8 017	63.7	4 512	0.2	13.6	7.9
Wabash, IL	14 490	6.9	56.3	36.8	13 424	6 695	66.0	840	0.0	11.5	2.0
Warren, IL	24 037	8.4	48.9	42.7	21 277	7 411	63.8	1 374	0.0	7.2	4.7
Washington, IL	19 304	4.9	52.0	43.0	16 123	7 195	64.1	854	0.0	10.8	4.1
Wayne, IL	23 986	6.8	66.0	27.1	20 129	7 312	62.8	904	0.0	14.6	6.1
White, IL	30 422	20.8	46.2	32.9	27 951	10 763	62.3	811	0.0	14.1	9.4
Whiteside, IL	97 966	6.6	34.8	58.5	76 171	7 603	64.9	3 411	0.0	12.7	4.6
Will, IL	933 172	4.8	30.8	64.3	744 893	7 618	63.0	28 159	0.0	10.7	5.3
Williamson, IL	89 990	9.0	50.9	40.1	69 776	7 374	66.2	3 199	0.0	12.3	5.7
Winnebago, IL	439 628	9.5	35.2	55.3	390 644	8 367	64.3	14 919	0.2	10.5	6.6
Woodford, IL	65 989	5.3	37.5	57.2	57 135	7 391	62.4	2 259	0.0	9.1	1.1
INDIANA	10 446 055	6.3	48.4	45.3	8 347 290	8 276	63.5	360 606	0.0	10.6	5.1
Adams, IN	47 253	5.8	50.4	43.8	35 239	7 125	61.6	2 229	0.0	7.9	7.9
Allen, IN	506 008	7.1	46.6	46.3	483 195	9 040	66.9	19 231	0.1	10.4	4.1
Bartholomew, IN	119 710	6.8	43.2	50.0	92 568	7 877	64.8	3 330	0.0	9.8	4.4
Benton, IN	21 528	1.7	48.8	49.5	16 019	8 152	62.0	557	0.0	16.5	4.8
Blackford, IN	25 690	4.9	50.4	44.7	19 376	8 432	64.2	702	0.0	11.3	4.1
Boone, IN	90 398	1.5	50.0	48.5	75 825	8 060	62.9	2 357	0.0	12.6	4.2
Brown, IN	23 366	5.3	44.6	50.1	19 512	8 626	57.1	772	0.0	14.2	4.3
Carroll, IN	25 102	3.7	52.4	43.9	18 578	6 473	59.8	1 051	0.0	14.5	5.9
Cass, IN	75 442	9.7	49.3	41.0	60 334	8 690	63.4	2 406	0.0	11.4	7.8
Clark, IN	115 422	8.5	63.5	28.0	123 786	8 247	67.5	5 178	0.1	13.4	6.1
Clay, IN	38 743	7.6	60.2	32.2	34 999	7 582	68.2	1 574	0.3	10.3	7.4
Clinton, IN	55 433	10.3	55.7	34.0	45 883	7 171	64.2	2 077	0.0	11.0	5.7
Crawford, IN	14 896	7.6	67.5	24.8	14 396	7 777	67.3	582	0.0	17.0	4.0
Daviess, IN	45 651	9.1	48.8	42.2	36 666	8 443	66.6	1 704	0.0	9.5	9.7
Dearborn, IN	65 533	6.3	58.6	35.1	68 662	7 852	62.8	2 819	0.0	11.2	6.1
Decatur, IN	37 395	3.8	50.1	46.2	31 844	7 575	64.0	1 235	0.0	17.3	3.1
De Kalb, IN	72 890	10.0	43.5	46.5	63 930	8 753	63.2	2 225	0.0	12.5	2.5
Delaware, IN	192 074	8.2	47.5	44.3	146 702	8 831	60.2	8 631	0.1	6.1	2.4
Dubois, IN	73 474	8.3	41.6	50.1	66 417	8 839	67.9	2 132	0.0	13.2	2.0
Elkhart, IN	346 641	6.8	47.5	45.7	264 985	7 804	64.2	10 334	0.1	12.1	7.8
Fayette, IN	45 529	11.6	49.2	39.2	35 494	9 020	59.0	1 192	0.0	17.4	8.6
Floyd, IN	115 006	6.7	48.7	44.6	88 680	7 795	66.4	3 882	0.0	8.8	5.1
Fountain, IN	32 031	4.7	50.9	44.4	23 174	7 144	63.8	1 060	0.0	13.0	2.8
Franklin, IN	25 840	4.1	58.8	37.1	21 177	6 948	63.3	1 322	0.4	13.5	6.5
Fulton, IN	23 883	3.3	53.5	43.2	19 558	6 901	61.9	1 120	0.0	12.1	1.8
Gibson, IN	52 151	8.9	40.5	50.6	45 720	9 183	59.4	1 772	0.0	9.3	3.5
Grant, IN	98 730	10.0	60.3	29.7	92 100	8 176	62.9	4 635	0.1	10.8	4.1
Greene, IN	52 095	8.9	59.2	31.9	45 841	7 997	68.2	1 729	0.0	11.6	7.6
Hamilton, IN	509 294	2.1	33.6	64.3	319 878	7 892	62.8	8 025	0.1	6.3	1.7
Hancock, IN	118 188	3.7	44.4	51.9	90 764	8 079	63.9	2 726	0.0	9.2	1.0
Harrison, IN	61 236	6.7	48.4	44.9	45 977	7 522	62.6	2 153	0.0	17.7	2.8
Hendricks, IN	196 048	2.3	49.6	48.0	167 601	7 700	60.4	5 661	0.0	9.7	4.1
Henry, IN	86 391	6.0	53.2	40.7	66 284	7 951	64.7	2 528	0.0	10.5	7.6
Howard, IN	169 191	6.6	39.5	54.0	122 137	8 819	62.0	4 479	0.5	11.9	5.4
Huntington, IN	55 238	6.1	55.4	38.5	47 888	7 557	65.9	2 324	0.0	11.0	3.1
Jackson, IN	55 083	6.2	48.2	45.5	40 385	6 272	60.3	2 036	0.0	16.6	3.2
Jasper, IN	41 426	3.7	49.0	47.3	35 472	7 084	63.3	2 000	0.0	14.0	1.7
Jay, IN	43 001	5.3	46.7	48.1	31 302	8 051	66.5	1 169	0.0	15.0	2.5
Jefferson, IN	56 810	10.1	44.0	45.9	54 402	10 955	68.1	2 024	0.3	13.4	5.9
Jennings, IN	49 080	4.3	58.2	37.5	36 109	6 794	61.6	1 389	0.2	19.7	7.5
Johnson, IN	254 164	3.2	41.2	55.7	173 822	7 923	62.0	6 470	0.2	11.0	4.2
Knox, IN	53 178	9.3	55.1	35.6	45 941	8 167	64.7	3 422	0.0	6.3	4.4
Kosciusko, IN	128 053	6.1	46.9	47.0	108 809	7 755	60.8	4 018	0.0	11.4	5.2
Lagrange, IN	50 228	4.9	56.5	38.6	51 201	8 178	62.6	2 399	0.2	5.4	13.3
Lake, IN	798 769	7.5	61.8	30.7	716 620	8 493	60.8	28 733	0.1	11.5	5.1
La Porte, IN	172 695	6.6	49.7	43.7	146 603	8 394	57.6	5 774	0.0	11.5	6.6
Lawrence, IN	58 588	7.0	61.2	31.8	59 862	7 975	62.3	2 320	0.0	12.3	6.6
Madison, IN	194 053	7.1	55.0	37.9	167 912	8 484	66.7	7 413	0.0	13.0	4.8
Marion, IN	1 748 785	6.7	43.9	49.4	1 205 998	9 018	64.3	45 632	0.0	12.6	8.0
Marshall, IN	80 050	7.9	45.4	46.7	67 023	8 623	64.3	2 884	0.0	13.1	4.3
Martin, IN	14 752	5.7	65.4	28.9	13 933	7 479	62.8	598	0.0	9.2	2.3
Miami, IN	67 884	4.9	61.8	33.3	57 013	7 670	63.7	2 034	0.0	12.2	7.8
Monroe, IN	134 913	5.7	41.8	52.5	109 360	8 131	61.8	12 966	0.0	5.5	1.7
Montgomery, IN	86 711	9.3	34.6	56.1	53 322	8 162	59.1	2 146	0.0	11.5	5.0
Morgan, IN	112 420	4.2	50.7	45.2	81 701	7 069	62.0	3 889	0.0	10.7	5.6
Newton, IN	26 017	3.1	51.9	45.0	20 371	7 693	60.4	924	0.0	15.8	8.9
Noble, IN	66 390	4.8	57.1	38.1	61 882	7 945	62.1	2 693	0.0	10.7	8.6
Ohio, IN	9 210	1.6	47.6	50.8	6 694	6 866	66.2	294	0.0	16.3	3.1
Orange, IN	31 411	6.6	58.2	35.2	26 756	7 642	65.5	985	0.0	15.9	7.2
Owen, IN	33 854	5.8	55.3	38.9	27 472	8 749	65.6	1 327	0.0	16.4	6.5

Table C-1. Population, School, and Student Characteristics by County—*Continued*

STATE County	High school graduates, 2000 Population 25 years and over	High school graduate or less (percent)	High school graduate or more (percent)	College enrollment, 2000 Number	Percent public	College graduates, 2000 (percent) Bachelor's degree or more	+/- U.S. percentage with bachelor's degree or more	Non-Hispanic White	Black	American Indian and Alaska Native	Asian or Pacific Islander	Hispanic[3]
	30	31	32	33	34	35	36	37	38	39	40	41
Rock Island, IL	98 865	51.5	82.6	8 734	68.0	17.1	-7.3	18.0	7.7	4.8	56.0	7.3
St. Clair, IL	162 715	48.2	80.9	14 400	80.6	19.3	-5.1	21.8	11.4	16.0	32.1	17.3
Saline, IL	18 111	54.1	76.1	1 248	97.0	12.1	-12.3	12.2	11.4	16.3	21.6	0.0
Sangamon, IL	126 620	43.0	88.1	9 460	87.1	28.6	4.2	29.3	15.8	24.4	63.6	29.9
Schuyler, IL	5 022	62.6	83.6	186	79.0	11.7	-12.7	11.7	66.7	0.0	0.0	0.0
Scott, IL	3 718	63.5	83.1	165	72.7	12.1	-12.3	12.1	100.0	0.0	0.0	0.0
Shelby, IL	15 448	61.0	82.9	772	90.7	11.5	-12.9	11.4	0.0	18.2	45.1	0.0
Stark, IL	4 312	55.7	83.4	151	73.5	13.4	-11.0	13.5	0.0	0.0	0.0	0.0
Stephenson, IL	32 851	54.2	84.1	2 375	86.4	15.6	-8.8	16.1	7.0	22.9	70.5	10.7
Tazewell, IL	86 666	49.4	85.0	5 906	84.1	18.1	-6.3	18.4	0.5	7.5	30.6	14.2
Union, IL	12 695	56.2	74.8	717	95.7	15.8	-8.6	16.0	2.2	19.6	55.2	4.5
Vermilion, IL	55 778	59.6	78.7	3 097	91.1	12.5	-11.9	12.8	5.9	12.1	58.9	7.6
Wabash, IL	8 627	48.7	82.2	730	96.7	12.6	-11.9	12.3	70.6	0.0	57.1	26.0
Warren, IL	12 131	57.3	82.3	1 492	37.2	15.8	-8.6	15.8	15.6	10.0	73.8	3.7
Washington, IL	10 168	55.8	79.1	689	89.1	13.4	-11.0	13.3	0.0	0.0	29.4	39.3
Wayne, IL	11 723	59.5	75.2	676	93.9	10.0	-14.4	9.8	0.0	0.0	38.0	7.8
White, IL	10 863	61.0	74.6	499	91.8	10.4	-14.0	10.3	18.2	13.3	0.0	20.0
Whiteside, IL	40 585	58.0	79.8	2 286	81.5	11.3	-13.1	11.8	15.1	19.8	30.4	3.9
Will, IL	310 918	42.2	86.9	26 437	69.2	25.5	1.1	26.7	19.1	9.5	58.2	9.5
Williamson, IL	41 973	52.6	79.8	3 462	94.5	17.2	-7.2	17.2	9.6	27.1	50.9	10.6
Winnebago, IL	181 803	51.4	81.4	12 464	74.5	19.4	-5.0	20.8	9.0	3.9	36.4	7.6
Woodford, IL	22 945	47.5	87.8	1 945	70.7	21.1	-3.3	21.1	0.0	0.0	42.7	14.2
INDIANA	3 893 278	55.1	82.1	352 687	76.4	19.4	-5.0	19.9	12.1	10.3	57.0	11.3
Adams, IN	20 158	65.1	80.0	1 145	85.8	10.7	-13.7	10.7	0.0	40.0	89.1	1.4
Allen, IN	208 769	46.3	85.7	18 136	73.8	22.7	-1.7	24.4	9.6	8.0	39.1	7.8
Bartholomew, IN	47 109	52.4	83.8	2 882	84.5	22.0	-2.4	21.4	16.3	11.4	72.4	12.8
Benton, IN	6 158	61.9	86.3	247	87.9	13.0	-11.4	13.4	0.0	50.0	11.1	0.0
Blackford, IN	9 550	68.2	81.3	369	83.5	10.3	-14.1	10.1	...	44.4	55.6	11.4
Boone, IN	30 048	49.6	88.3	1 276	80.5	27.6	3.2	27.7	0.0	0.0	51.1	4.4
Brown, IN	10 530	55.2	83.6	496	76.8	18.5	-5.9	18.5	19.6	29.0	100.0	0.0
Carroll, IN	13 299	64.5	83.2	485	83.3	12.9	-11.5	13.1	0.0	0.0	100.0	6.8
Cass, IN	26 747	63.7	81.8	1 161	87.5	12.0	-12.4	12.3	0.0	10.4	46.9	7.4
Clark, IN	64 389	56.6	79.9	3 884	85.5	14.3	-10.1	14.5	10.0	4.6	45.7	13.5
Clay, IN	17 304	63.3	82.3	872	88.1	12.8	-11.6	12.8	15.4	0.0	40.6	13.2
Clinton, IN	21 744	70.2	80.1	726	75.2	10.1	-14.3	10.2	0.0	0.0	37.9	5.0
Crawford, IN	7 088	74.5	70.6	224	79.9	8.4	-16.0	8.3	0.0	31.6	0.0	10.0
Daviess, IN	18 655	68.1	71.8	653	91.3	9.7	-14.7	9.6	0.0	14.1	65.8	0.7
Dearborn, IN	29 712	59.2	82.0	1 518	73.6	15.4	-9.0	15.3	13.4	56.0	16.9	25.3
Decatur, IN	15 948	68.4	79.1	647	83.2	11.5	-12.9	11.1	0.0	0.0	51.8	6.7
De Kalb, IN	25 500	61.2	84.7	1 537	80.1	12.4	-12.0	12.3	14.3	0.0	12.1	18.0
Delaware, IN	72 444	55.6	81.6	16 227	96.4	20.4	-4.0	20.7	11.1	3.3	68.8	26.1
Dubois, IN	25 733	64.3	80.2	1 112	85.3	14.5	-9.9	14.6	0.0	0.0	78.6	9.4
Elkhart, IN	112 908	61.3	75.7	5 271	70.4	15.5	-8.9	16.6	5.9	1.6	36.3	5.4
Fayette, IN	17 125	72.8	73.7	734	91.3	7.8	-16.6	7.9	0.0	18.2	0.0	9.8
Floyd, IN	46 609	50.7	82.4	3 412	88.1	20.4	-4.0	20.6	13.4	2.9	53.0	13.0
Fountain, IN	11 914	66.8	80.7	415	80.5	10.1	-14.3	10.2	0.0	9.1	0.0	0.0
Franklin, IN	14 218	68.1	76.1	684	67.7	12.5	-11.9	12.6	0.0	0.0	10.3	13.9
Fulton, IN	13 613	69.0	80.2	503	83.1	10.3	-14.1	10.5	0.0	30.2	30.9	0.0
Gibson, IN	21 694	60.1	80.9	1 215	64.6	12.4	-12.0	12.3	2.2	0.0	63.2	11.9
Grant, IN	47 408	62.7	79.2	5 296	27.9	14.1	-10.3	14.4	7.4	22.7	53.2	5.7
Greene, IN	22 396	64.3	79.2	1 162	89.7	10.5	-13.9	10.5	0.0	0.0	31.3	8.9
Hamilton, IN	116 457	25.6	94.2	7 048	77.2	48.9	24.5	48.6	48.8	13.7	69.5	43.9
Hancock, IN	37 073	49.7	87.8	2 262	70.7	22.2	-2.2	22.1	29.2	20.9	38.6	39.0
Harrison, IN	22 457	60.8	80.3	1 159	82.0	13.1	-11.3	13.1	0.0	2.1	42.5	7.7
Hendricks, IN	67 683	48.7	88.5	3 655	75.6	23.1	-1.3	23.1	13.5	11.2	55.0	19.8
Henry, IN	33 198	64.8	79.6	1 428	84.1	11.7	-12.7	11.7	8.1	0.0	40.4	4.0
Howard, IN	56 222	54.7	83.3	2 932	85.7	18.1	-6.3	18.0	13.3	41.8	57.5	14.2
Huntington, IN	24 386	61.7	85.0	1 885	51.9	14.2	-10.2	14.1	74.1	6.6	39.1	16.6
Jackson, IN	27 131	66.9	79.8	1 091	86.5	11.5	-12.9	11.3	7.8	16.3	35.2	11.1
Jasper, IN	18 751	64.0	82.4	1 392	46.3	13.0	-11.4	13.2	47.6	0.0	27.8	4.4
Jay, IN	14 280	71.0	78.5	526	88.0	9.9	-14.5	9.8	0.0	25.0	22.2	5.3
Jefferson, IN	20 605	59.1	81.0	2 077	44.1	16.4	-8.0	16.5	7.8	0.0	42.9	20.9
Jennings, IN	17 709	70.8	76.2	734	79.0	8.4	-16.0	8.0	17.1	16.9	73.3	9.3
Johnson, IN	73 966	50.5	85.7	4 952	66.3	23.1	-1.3	22.9	22.1	1.5	56.3	17.5
Knox, IN	24 865	55.6	81.7	3 756	95.1	14.4	-10.0	14.2	26.9	0.0	27.7	25.5
Kosciusko, IN	47 103	60.5	81.6	2 247	69.4	14.9	-9.5	15.1	15.0	13.1	18.4	8.1
Lagrange, IN	19 519	73.7	60.2	568	78.9	8.9	-15.5	8.9	0.0	0.0	35.9	3.2
Lake, IN	310 220	56.6	80.7	24 644	78.0	16.2	-8.2	18.7	10.8	3.2	58.6	8.5
La Porte, IN	73 723	60.4	80.6	4 525	83.9	14.0	-10.4	14.9	6.3	13.0	30.1	7.3
Lawrence, IN	31 175	69.0	77.4	979	85.8	10.7	-13.7	10.6	10.5	0.0	61.3	20.2
Madison, IN	89 458	59.9	80.1	5 680	59.2	14.4	-10.0	15.0	8.4	4.9	13.9	11.7
Marion, IN	553 459	48.0	81.6	45 864	69.8	25.4	1.0	28.7	13.6	12.2	55.8	14.2
Marshall, IN	28 555	61.3	79.8	1 346	75.2	14.9	-9.5	15.4	40.9	15.4	16.9	4.8
Martin, IN	7 066	68.1	74.2	199	80.4	8.8	-15.6	8.9	0.0	0.0	0.0	0.0
Miami, IN	23 741	64.3	81.9	1 208	89.2	10.4	-14.0	10.7	5.2	3.4	60.0	0.6
Monroe, IN	65 489	37.7	88.5	34 916	96.7	39.6	15.2	38.0	36.8	37.4	81.4	59.7
Montgomery, IN	24 501	61.2	85.7	1 508	45.8	14.7	-9.7	14.5	25.4	30.3	0.0	18.1
Morgan, IN	43 397	64.3	80.7	1 800	72.6	12.6	-11.8	12.4	72.0	1.6	30.5	30.9
Newton, IN	9 576	71.1	78.7	243	84.4	9.6	-14.8	9.7	0.0	0.0	28.6	3.5
Noble, IN	28 554	66.3	77.3	1 061	74.0	11.1	-13.3	11.4	17.0	0.0	7.5	4.6
Ohio, IN	3 780	66.3	78.4	169	71.0	11.6	-12.8	11.7	0.0	...	...	23.5
Orange, IN	12 818	71.4	73.8	471	91.1	10.2	-14.2	10.2	0.0	0.0	0.0	32.6
Owen, IN	14 384	68.6	74.9	495	85.5	9.2	-15.2	9.0	0.0	0.0	29.2	14.5

[3]May be of any race.
. . . = Not available.

Table C-1. Population, School, and Student Characteristics by County—*Continued*

STATE County	State/ county code	County type[1]	Population, 2005 Total	Percent 5 to 17 years	Number of schools and students, 2004–2005 School districts	Schools	Students	Resident enrollment, 2000 Total	Percent public	K–12	Percent public
			1	2	3	4	5	6	7	8	9
Parke, IN	18121	6	17 362	17.1	3	7	2 515	4 019	90.2	3 225	94.1
Perry, IN	18123	6	19 032	15.5	3	6	3 096	4 257	93.0	3 477	97.1
Pike, IN	18125	6	12 766	17.6	1	5	2 084	2 792	94.1	2 279	97.5
Porter, IN	18127	1	157 772	18.0	9	63	33 106	39 988	81.0	28 392	92.8
Posey, IN	18129	2	26 852	19.7	3	11	4 396	7 225	82.4	5 659	84.6
Pulaski, IN	18131	6	13 783	18.8	2	6	2 309	3 478	92.8	2 877	96.6
Putnam, IN	18133	1	36 957	16.9	6	18	6 704	9 600	73.8	6 440	97.1
Randolph, IN	18135	6	26 684	18.5	6	14	4 779	6 095	94.9	5 132	97.0
Ripley, IN	18137	6	27 710	20.0	5	15	7 897	6 526	85.1	5 318	89.1
Rush, IN	18139	6	17 823	19.8	1	6	2 651	4 229	86.4	3 477	91.0
St. Joseph, IN	18141	2	266 160	18.8	7	74	41 945	76 955	67.2	49 543	81.2
Scott, IN	18143	6	23 820	18.9	2	9	4 378	5 152	91.3	4 284	94.1
Shelby, IN	18145	1	43 766	18.9	6	17	7 642	10 554	90.3	8 496	94.7
Spencer, IN	18147	8	20 528	18.8	2	10	3 706	5 109	90.0	4 199	93.6
Starke, IN	18149	6	22 933	19.5	3	8	4 186	5 722	90.2	4 739	93.7
Steuben, IN	18151	7	33 773	18.4	4	11	4 880	8 611	82.3	6 285	96.2
Sullivan, IN	18153	3	21 763	16.1	3	11	3 442	5 101	92.9	4 013	96.3
Switzerland, IN	18155	8	9 718	18.5	1	4	1 640	2 017	94.0	1 752	95.3
Tippecanoe, IN	18157	3	153 875	14.5	5	36	19 756	60 819	92.2	22 061	90.8
Tipton, IN	18159	3	16 385	17.8	2	5	2 880	3 883	88.7	3 108	93.1
Union, IN	18161	8	7 208	19.8	1	4	1 698	1 818	93.8	1 492	96.2
Vanderburgh, IN	18163	2	173 187	16.8	3	44	22 608	44 775	77.5	29 035	81.2
Vermillion, IN	18165	3	16 562	17.4	2	7	2 896	3 892	93.3	3 044	95.7
Vigo, IN	18167	3	102 592	16.8	2	30	16 355	31 055	87.2	17 768	93.5
Wabash, IN	18169	6	33 843	17.4	4	17	5 637	8 948	81.3	6 638	95.4
Warren, IN	18171	8	8 785	19.1	1	4	1 380	2 032	92.2	1 663	96.3
Warrick, IN	18173	2	56 362	19.0	1	16	9 268	13 756	84.5	10 431	89.8
Washington, IN	18175	1	27 885	18.9	4	10	4 928	6 407	91.0	5 241	93.8
Wayne, IN	18177	5	69 192	17.6	6	28	11 204	17 570	87.4	12 838	94.8
Wells, IN	18179	2	28 085	19.2	4	9	4 962	7 028	88.6	5 604	93.7
White, IN	18181	6	24 463	18.2	4	16	5 286	5 855	94.8	4 895	98.3
Whitley, IN	18183	2	32 323	18.7	2	11	4 960	7 674	89.1	6 205	91.9
IOWA	19000		2 966 334	16.5	384	1 541	478 319	792 057	84.6	552 637	90.3
Adair, IA	19001	8	7 859	15.4	2	6	1 123	1 856	94.4	1 524	98.2
Adams, IA	19003	9	4 264	16.2	2	4	613	1 039	96.6	802	96.8
Allamakee, IA	19005	6	14 709	16.8	3	11	2 480	3 436	87.7	2 922	89.6
Appanoose, IA	19007	7	13 666	15.7	3	14	2 197	3 296	92.3	2 593	95.7
Audubon, IA	19009	8	6 457	17.5	2	5	993	1 616	97.0	1 384	99.0
Benton, IA	19011	3	27 000	17.6	3	15	4 063	6 744	91.0	5 344	96.2
Black Hawk, IA	19013	3	125 891	14.8	6	41	17 416	40 461	87.0	22 272	84.1
Boone, IA	19015	6	26 602	16.5	6	20	4 957	6 393	91.4	4 980	94.4
Bremer, IA	19017	3	23 677	15.4	5	18	4 021	6 970	75.3	4 434	95.2
Buchanan, IA	19019	6	21 019	18.7	4	22	3 508	5 468	88.0	4 565	90.0
Buena Vista, IA	19021	7	20 151	17.7	6	20	3 699	5 960	72.1	4 165	87.9
Butler, IA	19023	8	15 072	15.9	5	10	1 843	3 667	95.0	2 989	97.4
Calhoun, IA	19025	9	10 443	14.9	4	12	2 111	2 485	95.2	2 081	96.7
Carroll, IA	19027	7	21 034	17.2	4	11	3 197	5 715	69.9	4 556	69.7
Cass, IA	19029	6	14 219	15.5	4	12	2 620	3 431	93.1	2 815	98.6
Cedar, IA	19031	6	18 254	16.5	5	15	3 421	4 574	94.1	3 549	98.5
Cerro Gordo, IA	19033	5	44 645	15.9	5	21	6 502	11 271	86.8	8 435	88.7
Cherokee, IA	19035	6	12 237	16.3	3	11	1 977	2 998	94.9	2 556	98.2
Chickasaw, IA	19037	6	12 563	17.2	3	8	2 287	3 365	86.4	2 675	87.7
Clarke, IA	19039	6	9 161	17.1	2	6	1 739	2 192	94.2	1 843	99.1
Clay, IA	19041	7	16 897	16.0	3	11	2 593	4 161	91.5	3 230	93.2
Clayton, IA	19043	8	18 337	16.4	7	14	3 558	4 406	90.9	3 812	94.0
Clinton, IA	19045	4	49 717	17.1	6	23	8 230	12 977	86.9	9 837	93.2
Crawford, IA	19047	6	16 889	17.6	5	15	3 337	4 224	88.0	3 525	90.4
Dallas, IA	19049	2	51 762	17.9	5	23	9 522	10 346	86.7	8 120	93.4
Davis, IA	19051	9	8 659	17.4	1	4	1 223	2 038	83.8	1 670	84.7
Decatur, IA	19053	9	8 605	14.5	2	6	1 056	2 733	64.7	1 531	92.7
Delaware, IA	19055	6	18 025	18.5	2	9	2 501	5 181	83.6	4 200	86.2
Des Moines, IA	19057	5	40 810	16.6	5	19	6 466	10 167	85.5	7 642	89.6
Dickinson, IA	19059	7	16 687	14.5	4	10	2 688	3 611	94.2	2 760	98.6
Dubuque, IA	19061	3	91 631	16.9	2	27	13 079	24 497	60.9	17 029	71.7
Emmet, IA	19063	7	10 534	15.9	2	7	1 723	2 916	93.8	2 159	95.0
Fayette, IA	19065	6	21 298	16.4	4	15	3 215	5 850	86.1	4 351	95.2
Floyd, IA	19067	7	16 443	16.7	3	10	2 656	4 072	87.7	3 255	91.4
Franklin, IA	19069	7	10 732	16.4	3	10	1 801	2 506	94.7	2 067	97.2
Fremont, IA	19071	8	7 759	16.7	4	8	1 493	1 936	96.2	1 588	98.7
Greene, IA	19073	6	9 963	16.8	3	10	1 737	2 518	92.6	2 143	95.2
Grundy, IA	19075	3	12 329	16.5	4	14	2 873	3 156	93.9	2 530	96.5
Guthrie, IA	19077	2	11 547	15.3	4	13	2 627	2 510	94.6	2 110	98.2
Hamilton, IA	19079	6	16 209	17.1	4	12	2 929	4 022	90.3	3 100	93.2
Hancock, IA	19081	7	11 786	17.2	4	12	1 867	3 128	90.9	2 584	95.8
Hardin, IA	19083	6	18 003	16.5	6	15	3 115	4 772	95.0	3 602	98.1
Harrison, IA	19085	2	15 884	17.3	5	11	3 145	3 914	92.1	3 208	96.7
Henry, IA	19087	7	20 246	16.2	4	13	3 613	5 245	83.1	3 950	93.3
Howard, IA	19089	7	9 700	17.5	2	9	1 819	2 395	84.1	1 961	86.4
Humboldt, IA	19091	7	9 973	15.8	3	8	1 613	2 621	88.0	2 040	90.5
Ida, IA	19093	8	7 379	16.4	2	8	1 280	1 914	96.0	1 640	97.6
Iowa, IA	19095	8	16 055	17.7	5	10	2 791	3 952	89.1	3 199	90.9
Jackson, IA	19097	6	20 335	16.9	5	15	3 421	5 091	85.0	4 218	87.2
Jasper, IA	19099	6	37 674	16.4	5	20	5 999	8 568	90.2	6 798	94.7

[1]County type codes are from the Economic Research Service of the United States Department of Agriculture. See notes and definitions at the end of this section.

Table C-1. Population, School, and Student Characteristics by County—*Continued*

STATE County	Characteristics of students, 2004–2005				Outcomes		Staff and students, 2004–2005		
	Percent with IEP[2]	Percent eligible for free or reduced-price lunch	Percent minority	Percent English-language learners	Number of graduates, 2003–2004	Percent dropouts, grades 9–12, 2001–2002	Number of teachers	Student-teacher ratio	Central administration staff
	10	11	12	13	14	15	16	17	18
Parke, IN	19.7	41.6	0.6	0.3	...	1.1	171	14.7	12
Perry, IN	13.4	33.3	1.3	0.6	197	5.2	168	18.5	14
Pike, IN	19.1	...	1.1	0.4	...	2.6	123	17.0	5
Porter, IN	16.3	24.3	9.4	1.8	...	1.1	1 912	17.3	105
Posey, IN	24.1	22.2	1.9	0.3	...	2.3	286	15.4	12
Pulaski, IN	18.9	37.3	2.4	0.2	164	1.5	145	15.9	8
Putnam, IN	21.7	32.0	1.9	0.4	...	2.3	431	15.6	...
Randolph, IN	21.7	38.3	2.0	0.9	...	2.5	318	15.1	22
Ripley, IN	18.2	25.9	0.9	0.3	...	1.8	455	17.4	27
Rush, IN	13.6	30.4	3.0	1.0	159	1.2	169	15.6	6
St. Joseph, IN	19.4	46.3	31.2	9.1	...	1.5	2 421	17.3	...
Scott, IN	16.2	48.6	1.4	0.4	...	1.7	240	18.3	11
Shelby, IN	18.8	24.5	4.3	3.0	...	0.7	493	15.5	27
Spencer, IN	13.0	25.3	2.9	2.1	...	0.7	216	17.1	8
Starke, IN	15.2	41.8	3.4	0.4	...	1.4	239	17.6	21
Steuben, IN	13.9	30.0	4.0	2.8	...	1.0	280	17.4	...
Sullivan, IN	24.0	42.4	1.0	0.2	...	2.1	216	16.0	8
Switzerland, IN	17.7	37.8	1.3	0.2	81	...	88	18.6	7
Tippecanoe, IN	17.9	32.0	16.9	10.9	...	3.2	1 245	15.9	...
Tipton, IN	17.5	20.4	2.6	0.7	207	2.5	173	16.6	10
Union, IN	19.9	30.5	0.4	0.1	89	1.1	106	16.1	11
Vanderburgh, IN	20.7	48.5	18.4	1.4	...	1.0	1 443	15.7	52
Vermillion, IN	17.1	39.5	0.6	0.5	164	2.2	183	15.8	6
Vigo, IN	20.6	44.8	8.5	1.7	...	3.8	1 061	15.4	39
Wabash, IN	17.4	29.5	2.2	1.1	...	1.1	379	14.9	28
Warren, IN	22.5	27.4	1.1	0.4	...	2.1	89	15.4	6
Warrick, IN	19.7	19.5	3.2	1.6	597	1.2	485	19.1	16
Washington, IN	16.2	36.4	0.9	0.4	...	2.3	301	16.4	23
Wayne, IN	21.3	45.0	8.5	1.3	...	3.8	701	16.0	...
Wells, IN	14.8	20.9	3.2	1.1	...	1.2	346	14.3	25
White, IN	17.2	36.3	7.9	6.7	...	2.1	324	16.3	30
Whitley, IN	14.6	21.0	1.7	0.1	...	84.1	287	17.3	15
IOWA	15.2	31.1	12.6	3.1	...	2.4	34 693	13.8	...
Adair, IA	15.1	26.0	2.7	0.1	87	...	96	11.8	8
Adams, IA	15.8	37.4	3.1	0.7	...	0.9	52	11.8	7
Allamakee, IA	13.3	38.1	8.6	5.2	222	1.8	173	14.4	13
Appanoose, IA	18.4	46.2	3.5	0.0	173	0.4	190	11.6	11
Audubon, IA	10.2	27.7	1.5	0.2	98	0.5	79	12.6	8
Benton, IA	16.4	24.4	2.3	0.0	310	0.5	306	13.3	13
Black Hawk, IA	15.6	35.2	24.4	4.7	...	5.7	1 438	12.1	72
Boone, IA	15.3	26.8	3.6	0.6	...	1.8	342	14.5	26
Bremer, IA	15.0	17.0	1.9	0.1	368	0.3	258	15.6	21
Buchanan, IA	17.2	25.4	2.8	2.1	273	1.4	247	14.2	19
Buena Vista, IA	14.0	42.5	36.4	28.7	...	1.9	279	13.3	...
Butler, IA	14.8	25.4	2.4	0.0	...	0.8	139	13.3	...
Calhoun, IA	14.4	30.8	2.0	0.0	176	1.3	187	11.3	15
Carroll, IA	13.4	26.6	3.6	1.3	236	0.3	235	13.6	20
Cass, IA	16.1	35.1	1.8	0.0	...	1.3	203	12.9	17
Cedar, IA	12.8	17.6	3.4	0.2	265	1.6	270	12.7	23
Cerro Gordo, IA	18.3	29.6	9.7	0.2	...	2.7	474	13.7	25
Cherokee, IA	17.5	28.3	6.4	1.5	167	1.3	161	12.3	13
Chickasaw, IA	10.8	23.4	2.2	0.3	...	1.4	152	15.0	13
Clarke, IA	16.0	41.2	10.3	7.1	131	2.6	132	13.2	7
Clay, IA	14.0	28.2	5.7	0.7	...	1.1	195	13.3	12
Clayton, IA	14.9	30.2	2.0	0.2	...	1.2	278	12.8	41
Clinton, IA	16.4	34.7	8.1	0.0	...	2.6	608	13.5	28
Crawford, IA	12.7	46.7	25.8	14.9	...	2.2	237	14.1	16
Dallas, IA	11.1	20.0	11.4	3.3	567	1.1	660	14.4	35
Davis, IA	15.1	35.6	3.5	0.0	103	2.9	98	12.5	6
Decatur, IA	22.7	45.1	4.6	1.4	73	1.3	90	11.8	7
Delaware, IA	10.8	26.5	2.0	0.1	241	2.8	174	14.4	11
Des Moines, IA	17.4	35.6	13.9	0.8	...	4.9	477	13.6	33
Dickinson, IA	11.6	21.4	2.7	0.0	...	1.0	201	13.4	17
Dubuque, IA	18.8	33.3	6.5	0.4	992	2.6	901	14.5	26
Emmet, IA	18.2	38.0	12.8	4.5	138	1.7	138	12.5	10
Fayette, IA	17.2	36.9	3.8	0.2	262	0.4	244	13.2	20
Floyd, IA	16.2	33.1	5.0	1.2	244	1.7	199	13.3	16
Franklin, IA	15.5	33.5	14.6	5.3	186	1.5	149	12.1	9
Fremont, IA	15.3	39.5	2.7	1.0	104	0.8	125	11.9	14
Greene, IA	15.0	36.3	4.6	0.1	143	1.4	141	12.4	9
Grundy, IA	13.6	22.1	3.2	0.2	212	1.4	197	14.6	19
Guthrie, IA	13.7	30.5	2.7	0.2	183	1.9	209	12.6	17
Hamilton, IA	13.3	26.7	7.6	2.7	...	3.5	209	14.0	14
Hancock, IA	12.4	28.3	7.5	0.0	182	0.9	156	12.0	15
Hardin, IA	17.0	33.9	6.2	2.2	...	1.0	258	12.1	...
Harrison, IA	15.1	32.8	2.2	0.2	245	0.6	241	13.0	20
Henry, IA	15.4	29.0	8.6	1.6	287	0.8	277	13.0	21
Howard, IA	16.3	31.3	2.9	0.1	184	1.7	150	12.2	7
Humboldt, IA	10.4	29.4	3.5	0.4	...	0.4	119	13.6	10
Ida, IA	13.6	30.2	1.7	0.0	120	0.2	98	13.1	10
Iowa, IA	14.9	19.3	4.2	0.1	...	0.3	216	12.9	17
Jackson, IA	18.1	30.6	3.0	0.0	268	1.8	269	12.7	26
Jasper, IA	14.8	25.7	3.1	0.3	415	2.7	451	13.3	25

[2]IEP = Individual Education Program. See notes and definitions at the end of this section.
. . . = Not available.

Table C-1. Population, School, and Student Characteristics by County—Continued

STATE County	Total revenue (thousands of dollars)	Federal government	State government	Local government	Total expenditures (thousands of dollars)	Amount per student (dollars)	Percent for instruction	Total	Percent in armed forces	Percent high school graduates	Percent not enrolled, not employed, not in armed forces, not high school graduate
		Revenue, 2003–2004	Percent of revenue from:		Current expenditures, 2003–2004			Resident population, 16 to 19 years, 2000			
	19	20	21	22	23	24	25	26	27	28	29
Parke, IN	27 456	5.1	50.0	44.9	19 578	7 606	62.2	909	0.0	8.3	5.3
Perry, IN	27 539	5.1	59.7	35.1	24 009	7 617	63.0	1 074	0.0	13.9	11.1
Pike, IN	21 120	4.0	42.7	53.3	13 538	6 314	53.9	693	0.0	8.7	3.9
Porter, IN	259 573	4.0	47.1	49.0	211 505	8 236	63.1	9 342	0.0	9.8	2.6
Posey, IN	50 385	5.5	35.3	59.2	42 953	9 700	63.7	1 495	0.0	10.1	3.0
Pulaski, IN	25 008	14.1	46.2	39.7	19 692	8 408	59.6	821	0.6	10.2	2.4
Putnam, IN	74 819	5.5	47.7	46.8	54 302	8 019	60.6	2 567	0.0	6.7	7.3
Randolph, IN	44 482	8.3	57.4	34.3	37 331	7 826	64.2	1 419	0.0	13.3	4.2
Ripley, IN	52 811	3.6	53.5	42.9	44 071	7 703	62.0	1 414	0.0	15.8	3.7
Rush, IN	25 245	4.8	49.6	45.6	19 352	7 159	64.0	965	0.0	8.4	8.2
St. Joseph, IN	434 127	6.5	49.0	44.5	355 904	8 760	65.2	17 831	0.1	8.2	4.6
Scott, IN	37 035	8.1	60.5	31.4	30 060	7 056	63.3	1 222	0.0	12.5	9.1
Shelby, IN	66 865	5.5	53.1	41.4	66 819	8 691	64.3	2 308	0.0	16.2	5.6
Spencer, IN	35 369	3.0	40.6	56.4	30 760	8 105	66.6	1 102	0.0	12.3	1.8
Starke, IN	43 854	5.8	55.3	38.9	35 563	8 413	60.8	1 364	0.0	10.8	9.7
Steuben, IN	45 778	5.7	44.7	49.6	43 131	8 682	62.1	2 035	0.4	9.9	1.4
Sullivan, IN	40 474	3.5	46.4	50.2	26 802	7 764	63.5	1 130	0.0	12.7	3.1
Switzerland, IN	16 072	2.5	57.3	40.2	12 280	7 857	61.2	517	0.0	14.1	5.8
Tippecanoe, IN	214 263	5.2	39.8	55.0	155 807	7 944	64.2	14 890	0.0	5.0	2.0
Tipton, IN	29 656	2.6	46.8	50.6	20 789	7 226	60.7	887	0.0	10.5	1.9
Union, IN	19 944	9.6	43.7	46.7	15 017	9 327	63.4	361	0.0	17.2	4.2
Vanderburgh, IN	223 604	10.2	48.1	41.7	186 535	8 237	65.2	10 788	0.0	8.9	6.2
Vermillion, IN	25 375	7.4	47.4	45.2	20 961	7 462	60.2	967	0.0	11.3	4.4
Vigo, IN	149 528	9.5	54.3	36.2	125 557	7 667	65.8	7 380	0.0	7.5	3.7
Wabash, IN	67 809	4.8	45.8	49.5	50 896	8 906	64.0	2 283	0.0	8.7	2.5
Warren, IN	12 879	7.0	51.7	41.3	11 072	8 052	62.5	422	0.0	6.4	2.8
Warrick, IN	82 129	2.4	46.6	51.0	74 278	8 014	67.6	2 868	0.0	12.5	3.8
Washington, IN	46 782	8.1	54.8	37.1	39 269	7 993	64.3	1 488	0.0	14.9	4.9
Wayne, IN	109 439	6.8	58.1	35.0	89 751	8 048	65.6	4 143	0.0	11.7	7.9
Wells, IN	43 575	6.2	54.6	39.2	40 151	8 066	62.3	1 633	0.0	12.2	2.8
White, IN	49 203	5.0	46.9	48.2	39 200	7 333	61.5	1 331	0.0	11.8	3.8
Whitley, IN	42 832	1.8	55.7	42.5	39 203	7 823	61.0	1 684	0.2	16.9	2.1
IOWA	4 396 136	8.0	44.4	47.5	3 672 044	7 631	66.0	178 931	0.1	9.2	2.8
Adair, IA	9 760	5.4	45.5	49.1	7 682	6 611	66.6	427	0.0	6.3	3.3
Adams, IA	6 341	7.9	48.0	44.0	4 597	6 653	64.3	202	0.0	7.9	2.0
Allamakee, IA	21 565	8.8	47.3	44.0	17 850	7 033	67.0	797	0.0	8.4	1.0
Appanoose, IA	18 950	8.9	54.8	36.2	16 777	7 490	69.2	786	0.0	9.0	4.6
Audubon, IA	8 155	5.4	47.6	47.0	7 143	6 777	67.2	338	0.0	9.8	0.6
Benton, IA	32 584	3.7	53.7	42.6	27 792	6 854	67.5	1 402	0.0	12.6	1.2
Black Hawk, IA	176 240	13.8	43.9	42.3	159 680	9 197	60.5	8 922	0.2	7.8	2.3
Boone, IA	37 631	3.8	44.6	51.6	29 098	6 998	67.8	1 533	0.0	10.2	1.5
Bremer, IA	38 273	4.1	48.3	47.6	28 442	5 820	65.3	1 796	0.2	7.2	0.4
Buchanan, IA	25 743	10.9	46.5	42.7	20 540	7 139	68.2	1 202	0.0	6.7	7.8
Buena Vista, IA	34 026	8.9	43.7	47.4	29 177	7 620	68.6	1 487	0.3	5.0	4.2
Butler, IA	17 702	7.6	40.6	51.8	13 547	7 252	63.6	854	0.0	7.1	0.5
Calhoun, IA	19 691	5.0	39.1	55.9	16 978	7 978	66.9	604	0.0	7.1	1.2
Carroll, IA	26 705	6.3	44.2	49.4	22 113	6 891	68.2	1 344	0.0	8.5	1.1
Cass, IA	22 649	5.5	46.8	47.7	18 515	6 940	67.0	821	0.0	12.4	3.0
Cedar, IA	28 118	4.1	45.4	50.5	23 632	6 762	66.8	1 128	0.3	11.1	0.8
Cerro Gordo, IA	61 426	5.7	44.7	49.7	47 395	7 134	70.9	2 655	0.0	8.4	1.7
Cherokee, IA	17 664	5.5	43.1	51.4	14 413	7 083	67.3	796	0.0	9.2	0.9
Chickasaw, IA	19 560	7.7	42.7	49.6	15 304	6 537	67.2	726	0.0	7.9	2.5
Clarke, IA	14 552	7.9	50.5	41.6	11 868	6 728	66.7	464	0.0	14.2	5.8
Clay, IA	22 213	4.5	44.7	50.8	18 931	7 096	71.6	993	0.0	11.5	1.2
Clayton, IA	34 712	23.4	37.0	39.5	39 293	12 745	53.1	1 085	0.0	9.2	1.4
Clinton, IA	73 049	5.7	49.6	44.7	59 770	7 154	68.8	2 828	0.0	7.8	4.4
Crawford, IA	23 062	8.9	48.9	42.2	19 725	7 236	67.4	1 054	0.0	5.9	7.6
Dallas, IA	82 976	4.3	42.0	53.8	63 580	6 626	68.0	2 066	0.0	8.5	3.1
Davis, IA	9 647	8.6	53.7	37.8	8 862	6 972	67.8	511	0.0	4.5	5.9
Decatur, IA	14 042	12.9	47.7	39.4	10 980	7 843	64.1	735	0.0	9.9	3.4
Delaware, IA	26 494	5.4	45.9	48.6	22 166	6 875	67.8	1 122	0.0	7.3	2.2
Des Moines, IA	61 774	10.5	45.8	43.7	54 756	8 322	65.5	2 397	0.0	11.3	3.3
Dickinson, IA	27 345	3.1	30.8	66.1	19 752	7 392	69.6	772	0.3	5.1	1.8
Dubuque, IA	111 227	5.2	45.6	49.2	92 030	7 161	69.0	5 357	0.1	8.3	1.2
Emmet, IA	20 942	11.5	35.7	52.8	14 611	8 436	69.4	834	0.0	6.5	0.8
Fayette, IA	35 091	7.9	48.5	43.7	28 832	7 336	68.7	1 379	0.0	5.7	2.2
Floyd, IA	24 188	6.4	47.1	46.5	19 781	7 164	68.0	920	0.0	12.7	3.8
Franklin, IA	16 167	8.9	44.6	46.4	12 828	7 044	69.0	643	0.0	5.3	2.5
Fremont, IA	13 298	6.5	41.8	51.7	11 052	7 442	64.2	430	1.2	10.0	4.0
Greene, IA	16 283	5.6	43.1	51.2	13 929	7 687	67.9	585	0.0	3.8	5.0
Grundy, IA	18 042	3.2	41.5	55.4	13 825	6 436	63.8	661	0.0	8.3	1.1
Guthrie, IA	21 124	5.7	44.8	49.5	18 086	6 914	64.0	568	0.0	10.2	1.1
Hamilton, IA	24 993	4.9	44.5	50.6	19 742	6 917	66.1	859	0.0	7.2	0.8
Hancock, IA	17 431	3.9	41.4	54.8	14 386	7 497	65.6	746	0.0	8.2	0.4
Hardin, IA	29 230	5.2	43.3	51.5	24 551	7 603	68.1	1 236	0.0	9.0	1.9
Harrison, IA	30 380	12.3	42.4	45.3	22 942	7 169	65.4	902	0.0	9.9	2.4
Henry, IA	29 938	5.2	48.1	46.8	25 040	7 038	69.6	1 126	0.0	8.1	2.6
Howard, IA	16 794	7.7	42.1	50.2	14 315	7 390	62.1	546	0.0	9.5	5.3
Humboldt, IA	15 168	3.4	39.6	57.0	12 031	7 144	65.6	603	0.0	7.1	0.0
Ida, IA	10 800	5.0	46.7	48.3	9 004	6 750	67.5	456	0.0	10.1	0.4
Iowa, IA	24 201	3.1	47.1	49.9	20 689	7 151	66.7	840	0.0	10.6	0.8
Jackson, IA	31 170	8.0	45.9	46.1	24 848	7 280	69.4	1 134	0.0	8.6	1.7
Jasper, IA	51 440	3.5	49.2	47.2	42 081	6 945	66.0	1 872	0.0	10.7	1.2

Table C-1. Population, School, and Student Characteristics by County—*Continued*

STATE County	High school graduates, 2000			College enrollment, 2000		College graduates, 2000 (percent)						
	Population 25 years and over	High school graduate or less (percent)	High school graduate or more (percent)	Number	Percent public	Bachelor's degree or more	+/- U.S. percentage with bachelor's degree or more	Non-Hispanic White	Black	American Indian and Alaska Native	Asian or Pacific Islander	Hispanic[3]
	30	31	32	33	34	35	36	37	38	39	40	41
Parke, IN	11 891	65.1	80.5	488	87.9	11.6	-12.8	11.7	4.2	24.6	22.7	9.4
Perry, IN	12 734	70.7	74.8	608	72.5	9.6	-14.8	9.5	7.2	0.0	0.0	24.4
Pike, IN	8 753	69.9	75.6	333	82.3	8.4	-16.0	8.5	0.0	0.0	0.0	13.2
Porter, IN	94 462	49.8	88.3	8 959	53.7	22.6	-1.8	22.7	38.1	20.7	45.7	12.7
Posey, IN	17 671	57.4	84.4	1 022	90.5	14.8	-9.6	14.9	9.7	7.3	33.3	14.1
Pulaski, IN	9 038	65.3	79.8	403	71.0	10.3	-14.1	10.4	10.6	0.0	0.0	5.1
Putnam, IN	22 740	67.0	81.2	2 674	18.6	13.1	-11.3	13.4	2.3	0.0	42.7	8.9
Randolph, IN	18 310	67.9	79.6	660	89.8	9.9	-14.5	9.9	0.0	48.3	57.7	0.0
Ripley, IN	17 027	67.9	78.9	770	73.8	11.5	-12.9	11.3	. . .	36.5	51.4	14.3
Rush, IN	12 020	71.3	79.6	450	83.6	10.3	-14.1	10.1	0.0	0.0	100.0	26.1
St. Joseph, IN	166 060	50.1	82.4	22 170	40.3	23.6	-0.8	25.0	10.8	8.6	59.0	12.1
Scott, IN	14 760	71.1	71.4	582	86.8	8.8	-15.6	8.7	0.0	21.7	100.0	14.3
Shelby, IN	20 351	64.9	79.8	1 443	78.5	12.7	-11.7	12.6	13.3	72.1	28.2	0.0
Spencer, IN	13 491	61.6	81.2	573	79.6	13.0	-11.4	13.0	4.6	0.0	91.7	1.9
Starke, IN	15 290	71.5	72.0	616	77.6	8.4	-16.0	8.2	0.0	0.0	58.1	1.8
Steuben, IN	21 170	58.7	84.3	1 935	40.7	15.5	-8.9	15.5	10.7	0.0	63.2	19.4
Sullivan, IN	14 782	63.6	80.8	825	84.2	9.4	-15.0	10.0	0.0	0.0	0.0	7.6
Switzerland, IN	5 889	73.1	71.4	184	83.2	7.6	-16.8	7.3	. . .	0.0	90.5	0.0
Tippecanoe, IN	79 911	42.7	87.8	36 162	96.3	33.2	8.8	31.6	29.4	12.4	81.7	18.8
Tipton, IN	11 247	64.7	83.7	490	80.4	12.4	-12.0	12.4	. . .	0.0	5.1	1.3
Union, IN	4 784	65.7	79.9	227	88.1	11.1	-13.3	11.0	0.0	0.0	63.6	. . .
Vanderburgh, IN	112 178	52.6	83.1	12 739	76.6	19.3	-5.6	19.9	7.0	7.1	54.8	16.6
Vermillion, IN	11 410	64.0	81.2	618	88.8	11.2	-13.2	11.3	0.0	0.0	26.9	9.5
Vigo, IN	66 714	53.8	81.0	11 618	82.5	21.4	-3.0	21.4	15.2	8.0	66.0	15.0
Wabash, IN	22 744	64.3	81.7	1 794	37.7	13.7	-10.7	13.8	23.5	5.1	32.8	0.0
Warren, IN	5 648	61.7	85.0	239	86.2	14.0	-10.4	14.2	. . .	0.0	0.0	0.0
Warrick, IN	34 571	47.3	86.3	2 181	85.7	21.8	-2.6	21.6	30.0	22.7	54.9	10.7
Washington, IN	17 648	68.9	75.2	809	91.1	10.2	-14.2	10.1	0.0	0.0	25.0	21.0
Wayne, IN	47 322	61.4	78.1	3 686	67.5	13.7	-10.7	13.9	8.4	0.0	33.5	13.1
Wells, IN	17 767	59.2	87.3	904	73.5	14.3	-10.1	14.4	13.3	15.0	47.6	2.9
White, IN	16 829	65.6	82.1	511	89.0	10.5	-13.9	10.5	55.6	12.1	56.2	4.7
Whitley, IN	19 995	59.2	86.2	905	82.1	13.3	-11.1	13.2	21.4	26.3	5.3	13.5
IOWA	1 895 856	50.0	86.1	187 306	74.0	21.2	-3.2	21.3	14.7	9.9	42.4	11.0
Adair, IA	5 695	60.6	87.8	206	78.2	11.2	-13.2	11.2	0.0	0.0	100.0	6.3
Adams, IA	3 131	56.9	84.5	132	97.7	12.0	-12.4	12.1	. . .	0.0	0.0	0.0
Allamakee, IA	9 946	62.8	81.4	334	79.9	14.4	-10.0	14.6	0.0	9.1	31.3	0.0
Appanoose, IA	9 401	59.7	81.4	527	81.2	12.2	-12.2	12.1	13.8	0.0	52.9	3.9
Audubon, IA	4 704	62.2	82.5	121	81.0	12.3	-12.1	12.3	0.0	0.0	100.0	0.0
Benton, IA	16 567	55.5	87.8	868	76.5	13.9	-10.5	14.0	0.0	0.0	0.0	0.0
Black Hawk, IA	78 401	48.7	86.5	15 933	95.1	23.0	-1.4	23.7	9.9	22.7	60.0	15.4
Boone, IA	17 529	49.2	89.0	994	87.2	18.8	-5.6	18.8	6.1	15.2	42.9	17.5
Bremer, IA	14 835	50.0	87.7	2 064	36.8	21.5	-2.9	21.4	0.0	0.0	34.5	38.5
Buchanan, IA	13 383	59.0	84.6	546	82.1	12.7	-11.7	12.5	17.6	0.0	30.6	22.9
Buena Vista, IA	12 736	54.8	81.3	1 449	24.3	18.7	-5.7	21.1	0.0	33.3	14.3	1.1
Butler, IA	10 563	59.3	82.2	420	80.5	12.4	-12.0	12.4	. . .	0.0	33.3	6.7
Calhoun, IA	7 877	52.7	85.4	284	88.0	15.4	-9.0	15.5	13.3	0.0	0.0	6.1
Carroll, IA	14 074	56.1	83.7	772	81.9	16.0	-8.4	16.0	33.3	. . .	5.7	5.8
Cass, IA	10 296	54.5	85.9	381	78.2	16.6	-7.8	16.6	0.0	0.0	54.3	12.3
Cedar, IA	12 291	54.2	87.7	686	84.3	16.3	-8.1	16.2	0.0	0.0	33.3	20.0
Cerro Gordo, IA	31 215	46.0	87.3	2 055	88.1	20.3	-4.1	20.7	0.0	0.0	17.8	7.8
Cherokee, IA	8 918	55.2	87.5	209	75.6	15.2	-9.2	15.3	0.0	. . .	7.7	0.0
Chickasaw, IA	8 797	61.8	83.4	446	84.3	12.2	-12.2	12.2	0.0	0.0	0.0	35.3
Clarke, IA	6 070	58.6	84.4	179	59.2	12.1	-12.3	12.3	. . .	0.0	16.7	8.7
Clay, IA	11 692	48.8	88.0	502	86.1	16.3	-8.1	16.3	29.4	0.0	7.3	14.6
Clayton, IA	12 743	63.0	82.6	382	69.1	12.8	-11.6	12.7	19.2	0.0	38.9	16.0
Clinton, IA	33 158	55.9	85.6	2 145	67.1	14.4	-10.0	14.4	7.1	4.5	44.6	11.8
Crawford, IA	11 068	64.3	78.5	422	79.6	12.4	-12.0	13.1	0.0	0.0	36.4	2.5
Dallas, IA	26 483	43.2	89.5	1 400	64.4	26.8	2.4	27.5	14.9	0.0	45.8	10.2
Davis, IA	5 578	62.5	78.9	263	81.0	11.4	-13.0	11.6	0.0	0.0	. . .	0.0
Decatur, IA	5 283	59.8	81.7	1 075	22.3	15.1	-9.3	15.0	0.0	0.0	45.5	20.4
Delaware, IA	11 784	62.1	85.1	557	74.0	13.0	-11.4	12.9	. . .	0.0	61.5	10.8
Des Moines, IA	28 425	53.5	85.8	1 820	82.1	16.0	-8.4	16.4	5.2	10.4	31.8	6.6
Dickinson, IA	11 730	46.1	89.2	599	78.6	21.3	-3.1	21.4	0.0	0.0	21.4	7.5
Dubuque, IA	57 236	55.0	85.2	5 714	34.3	21.3	-3.1	21.3	22.7	24.4	50.4	17.3
Emmet, IA	7 265	53.8	82.2	613	92.7	13.0	-11.4	13.3	0.0	0.0	100.0	2.1
Fayette, IA	14 632	59.0	84.8	1 055	50.7	13.8	-10.6	13.8	40.6	0.0	23.2	8.6
Floyd, IA	11 451	55.0	85.9	515	82.5	14.8	-9.6	14.8	0.0	0.0	75.0	0.0
Franklin, IA	7 362	54.6	84.0	303	82.5	14.5	-9.9	15.0	. . .	37.5	5.0	1.7
Fremont, IA	5 557	57.4	85.0	213	87.8	14.0	-10.4	14.1	100.0	36.4	0.0	2.5
Greene, IA	7 048	56.7	85.6	235	75.7	14.6	-9.8	14.9	0.0	0.0	0.0	0.0
Grundy, IA	8 465	51.7	86.5	441	82.1	17.2	-7.2	17.1	100.0	0.0	31.3	25.0
Guthrie, IA	7 976	59.5	85.4	239	73.2	14.9	-9.5	15.0	0.0	0.0	100.0	8.1
Hamilton, IA	11 094	53.1	87.3	539	80.7	17.5	-6.9	17.6	0.0	0.0	20.4	16.1
Hancock, IA	8 084	52.8	85.8	342	66.1	15.6	-9.0	15.6	. . .	33.3	77.8	4.0
Hardin, IA	12 615	51.3	85.7	877	93.2	17.1	-7.3	17.4	0.0	. . .	22.2	0.6
Harrison, IA	10 487	59.1	85.0	459	80.0	12.7	-11.7	12.5	61.5	33.3	40.0	7.7
Henry, IA	13 509	53.5	86.1	974	47.8	16.2	-8.2	16.5	3.0	5.9	19.3	8.8
Howard, IA	6 645	63.7	79.3	234	78.2	12.6	-11.8	12.6	100.0	. . .	66.7	0.0
Humboldt, IA	7 078	52.0	86.3	325	93.8	15.4	-9.0	15.3	0.0	0.0	50.0	14.7
Ida, IA	5 349	58.3	85.0	157	84.1	13.6	-10.8	13.6	. . .	0.0	50.0	25.0
Iowa, IA	10 565	55.1	87.0	490	85.1	15.8	-8.6	15.6	25.0	0.0	23.5	35.2
Jackson, IA	13 596	63.2	81.5	523	79.3	12.1	-12.3	11.9	0.0	28.6	66.7	28.6
Jasper, IA	25 291	58.0	86.8	1 015	74.4	15.9	-8.5	15.9	4.8	8.2	40.2	7.2

[3]May be of any race.
. . . = Not available.

Table C-1. Population, School, and Student Characteristics by County—*Continued*

STATE County	State/ county code	County type[1]	Population, 2005		Number of schools and students, 2004–2005			Resident enrollment, 2000			
			Total	Percent 5 to 17 years	School districts	Schools	Students	Total	Percent public	K–12	Percent public
			1	2	3	4	5	6	7	8	9
Jefferson, IA	19101	7	15 972	15.1	2	9	2 711	4 260	71.0	3 191	79.9
Johnson, IA	19103	3	117 067	12.4	4	32	13 634	45 029	91.6	16 189	89.9
Jones, IA	19105	3	20 509	15.6	4	13	3 142	4 977	88.9	3 906	93.7
Keokuk, IA	19107	8	11 157	17.2	3	8	1 359	2 751	97.3	2 307	99.2
Kossuth, IA	19109	7	16 142	16.8	5	14	2 083	4 259	80.0	3 502	80.2
Lee, IA	19111	5	36 705	16.4	3	18	5 593	8 838	84.6	7 169	86.1
Linn, IA	19113	3	198 903	17.2	12	74	33 451	51 126	80.5	35 536	88.6
Louisa, IA	19115	8	11 842	18.7	4	10	2 924	3 131	96.0	2 529	98.6
Lucas, IA	19117	6	9 672	17.1	2	7	1 649	2 236	90.7	1 852	94.7
Lyon, IA	19119	8	11 750	18.9	3	10	1 850	3 024	85.7	2 574	88.3
Madison, IA	19121	2	15 158	17.7	3	12	3 096	3 444	92.3	2 823	98.0
Mahaska, IA	19123	7	22 364	16.9	3	13	3 027	5 587	82.0	4 223	88.4
Marion, IA	19125	6	32 984	16.5	5	18	5 759	8 619	74.7	6 153	90.1
Marshall, IA	19127	4	39 418	16.7	3	16	6 562	9 625	90.8	7 783	93.4
Mills, IA	19129	2	15 284	18.1	3	11	2 717	3 900	90.5	3 041	95.7
Mitchell, IA	19131	7	10 919	17.8	2	7	1 757	2 586	88.7	2 183	89.5
Monona, IA	19133	6	9 520	15.7	4	8	1 408	2 215	94.4	1 850	97.7
Monroe, IA	19135	7	7 835	17.3	1	5	1 201	1 956	93.9	1 540	96.2
Montgomery, IA	19137	6	11 313	17.2	3	10	1 977	2 706	93.2	2 186	97.8
Muscatine, IA	19139	4	42 756	17.7	3	17	7 484	10 777	92.2	8 391	95.8
O'Brien, IA	19141	7	14 414	15.8	3	8	2 513	3 545	83.1	2 939	84.5
Osceola, IA	19143	7	6 694	17.1	1	4	887	1 719	88.7	1 466	90.9
Page, IA	19145	7	16 253	16.1	4	13	2 736	3 956	91.7	3 201	94.1
Palo Alto, IA	19147	7	9 697	15.5	4	11	1 604	2 695	87.6	1 937	88.8
Plymouth, IA	19149	6	24 958	18.4	5	20	4 361	6 856	80.1	5 590	82.1
Pocahontas, IA	19151	9	7 930	16.7	2	8	1 101	2 189	89.6	1 826	91.7
Polk, IA	19153	2	401 006	17.1	10	131	63 914	96 530	80.2	68 002	90.5
Pottawattamie, IA	19155	2	89 738	17.2	9	43	16 092	21 969	89.5	16 929	92.7
Poweshiek, IA	19157	7	18 925	14.6	3	10	3 001	5 335	73.5	3 304	98.2
Ringgold, IA	19159	9	5 273	15.3	2	4	789	1 271	90.4	996	91.8
Sac, IA	19161	9	10 621	16.4	4	11	1 854	2 717	94.6	2 218	96.9
Scott, IA	19163	2	160 998	17.5	5	55	26 597	44 556	80.1	30 835	89.7
Shelby, IA	19165	6	12 634	17.3	2	7	1 918	3 210	88.6	2 779	91.1
Sioux, IA	19167	6	32 277	17.2	6	15	4 171	10 299	51.4	6 808	67.0
Story, IA	19169	3	79 952	10.8	7	30	10 400	35 450	95.3	11 147	95.6
Tama, IA	19171	6	17 919	18.1	3	10	2 744	4 440	93.6	3 602	95.5
Taylor, IA	19173	9	6 614	16.0	4	7	1 041	1 605	96.9	1 332	97.9
Union, IA	19175	6	11 972	15.8	3	11	1 867	3 013	91.5	2 186	94.6
Van Buren, IA	19177	9	7 786	16.3	3	7	1 141	1 753	87.3	1 477	89.4
Wapello, IA	19179	5	35 965	16.0	4	18	6 217	8 657	92.1	6 430	95.0
Warren, IA	19181	2	42 981	17.4	5	18	8 029	11 429	83.1	8 312	96.8
Washington, IA	19183	3	21 457	17.0	3	14	3 542	4 958	88.1	4 083	90.7
Wayne, IA	19185	9	6 601	15.6	4	9	1 244	1 566	94.1	1 276	96.8
Webster, IA	19187	5	39 003	16.6	4	17	5 284	10 158	86.0	7 580	86.2
Winnebago, IA	19189	7	11 351	16.2	3	11	2 686	3 008	86.1	2 287	97.2
Winneshiek, IA	19191	7	21 234	14.3	4	11	3 024	7 105	56.2	3 900	83.0
Woodbury, IA	19193	3	102 605	18.8	8	45	17 663	27 592	81.3	20 752	88.6
Worth, IA	19195	9	7 768	16.1	2	4	1 036	1 848	96.4	1 493	99.3
Wright, IA	19197	7	13 647	16.3	4	14	2 742	3 218	96.1	2 679	98.0
KANSAS	20000		2 744 687	17.7	309	1 400	469 136	756 960	86.5	529 202	89.6
Allen, KS	20001	7	13 787	16.7	3	11	2 457	3 682	95.9	2 790	97.1
Anderson, KS	20003	6	8 182	17.9	2	9	1 372	1 952	90.0	1 660	89.8
Atchison, KS	20005	6	16 804	17.8	3	8	2 485	4 863	66.1	3 549	78.8
Barber, KS	20007	9	4 958	16.3	2	5	897	1 355	92.4	1 108	94.9
Barton, KS	20009	7	28 105	17.5	4	16	4 835	7 446	88.7	5 651	92.9
Bourbon, KS	20011	6	14 997	17.1	2	6	2 491	4 181	87.1	3 162	87.8
Brown, KS	20013	6	10 239	17.1	2	6	1 616	2 732	94.0	2 160	96.2
Butler, KS	20015	2	62 354	19.1	9	44	14 117	16 975	88.0	12 933	90.4
Chase, KS	20017	8	3 081	16.0	1	3	477	709	94.1	599	95.5
Chautauqua, KS	20019	9	4 109	16.2	2	4	630	1 055	93.2	874	94.1
Cherokee, KS	20021	6	21 555	18.1	4	19	3 835	5 494	94.2	4 460	95.6
Cheyenne, KS	20023	9	2 946	15.9	2	4	496	734	97.0	619	98.4
Clark, KS	20025	9	2 283	17.7	2	5	503	582	97.8	499	98.6
Clay, KS	20027	7	8 629	16.2	1	8	1 435	2 148	97.7	1 746	98.5
Cloud, KS	20029	7	9 759	14.8	2	8	1 347	2 741	94.9	1 847	96.5
Coffey, KS	20031	6	8 683	17.1	3	11	1 770	2 325	94.8	1 880	98.2
Comanche, KS	20033	9	1 935	16.2	1	3	327	393	97.7	337	98.5
Cowley, KS	20035	4	35 298	17.8	5	24	6 676	10 397	83.8	7 205	93.0
Crawford, KS	20037	4	38 222	14.9	5	17	5 998	11 944	92.3	6 338	90.0
Decatur, KS	20039	9	3 191	15.7	2	4	486	833	97.7	675	98.2
Dickinson, KS	20041	7	19 209	17.0	5	20	3 854	4 917	93.1	3 963	95.9
Doniphan, KS	20043	3	7 816	17.5	5	10	1 543	2 377	96.0	1 599	96.6
Douglas, KS	20045	3	102 914	12.7	3	32	12 876	42 645	90.7	15 063	92.0
Edwards, KS	20047	9	3 292	16.5	2	4	504	836	89.7	676	90.4
Elk, KS	20049	8	3 075	14.4	2	5	672	730	96.6	603	97.3
Ellis, KS	20051	5	26 767	13.5	3	13	3 862	9 329	90.6	4 663	87.5
Ellsworth, KS	20053	7	6 343	14.0	2	7	1 076	1 343	95.7	1 085	98.5
Finney, KS	20055	5	38 988	23.6	2	20	8 545	12 187	93.6	9 588	95.0
Ford, KS	20057	5	33 751	21.3	3	15	6 635	8 955	92.8	7 038	93.4
Franklin, KS	20059	1	26 247	18.0	4	18	4 860	6 652	86.1	5 217	93.3

[1]County type codes are from the Economic Research Service of the United States Department of Agriculture. See notes and definitions at the end of this section.

Table C-1. Population, School, and Student Characteristics by County—*Continued*

STATE County	Characteristics of students, 2004–2005				Outcomes		Staff and students, 2004–2005		
	Percent with IEP[2]	Percent eligible for free or reduced-price lunch	Percent minority	Percent English-language learners	Number of graduates, 2003–2004	Percent dropouts, grades 9–12, 2001–2002	Number of teachers	Student-teacher ratio	Central administration staff
	10	11	12	13	14	15	16	17	18
Jefferson, IA	14.2	31.3	5.9	1.1	199	2.5	191	14.2	12
Johnson, IA	14.9	21.1	21.8	1.5	921	1.9	920	14.8	39
Jones, IA	15.8	29.5	2.9	0.0	267	1.3	254	12.4	19
Keokuk, IA	19.1	27.2	2.1	0.0	104	1.6	131	10.4	12
Kossuth, IA	20.3	34.9	3.6	0.0	. . .	. . .	182	11.4	18
Lee, IA	18.4	41.3	10.0	0.1	411	3.8	397	14.1	17
Linn, IA	17.8	26.9	12.5	0.5	. . .	1.8	2 167	15.4	134
Louisa, IA	12.2	44.5	25.8	7.0	. . .	2.3	231	12.7	21
Lucas, IA	17.3	39.8	1.8	2.0	117	1.9	125	13.2	6
Lyon, IA	14.6	22.9	2.0	0.2	139	1.0	150	12.3	12
Madison, IA	13.5	20.9	2.1	0.0	215	0.9	225	13.8	15
Mahaska, IA	14.2	33.9	3.6	0.3	. . .	2.2	216	14.0	13
Marion, IA	14.4	23.7	4.5	0.6	444	1.2	303	14.7	23
Marshall, IA	16.2	46.2	28.0	18.4	444	4.0	434	15.1	20
Mills, IA	16.5	28.9	3.1	0.1	199	2.2	202	13.5	14
Mitchell, IA	10.6	21.9	1.9	0.0	157	0.7	119	14.8	10
Monona, IA	15.8	41.1	4.6	0.4	. . .	1.7	118	12.0	. . .
Monroe, IA	15.7	30.4	3.2	0.3	96	0.3	92	13.1	4
Montgomery, IA	14.2	36.6	3.6	1.2	136	1.9	152	13.0	14
Muscatine, IA	14.0	35.8	26.1	8.0	438	3.4	536	14.0	17
O'Brien, IA	16.4	28.1	4.4	0.8	230	1.9	181	13.9	12
Osceola, IA	17.8	24.7	9.7	1.6	77	0.6	59	15.2	4
Page, IA	15.9	36.1	8.0	0.1	193	1.2	222	12.3	19
Palo Alto, IA	16.1	33.4	1.9	0.1	169	0.4	138	11.6	13
Plymouth, IA	9.6	19.3	5.3	0.5	322	1.1	313	13.9	23
Pocahontas, IA	16.1	29.6	4.2	0.0	116	1.2	102	10.8	7
Polk, IA	15.1	32.9	21.3	6.6	. . .	2.7	4 334	14.7	196
Pottawattamie, IA	16.2	38.4	9.6	3.9	. . .	3.6	1 110	14.5	61
Poweshiek, IA	15.0	26.8	4.7	1.1	228	1.4	215	14.0	12
Ringgold, IA	19.4	42.2	0.9	0.0	84	0.9	78	10.1	7
Sac, IA	9.0	31.9	4.3	0.9	140	0.6	143	13.0	14
Scott, IA	12.4	32.5	21.7	1.4	. . .	3.3	1 823	14.6	66
Shelby, IA	11.1	26.4	3.0	0.4	164	0.5	134	14.4	8
Sioux, IA	15.3	27.5	12.4	6.2	. . .	0.5	327	12.8	30
Story, IA	12.5	17.1	11.2	1.3	847	1.7	734	14.2	40
Tama, IA	16.8	33.9	20.4	5.1	184	2.1	198	13.9	14
Taylor, IA	18.4	41.9	8.3	4.4	. . .	2.2	108	9.6	13
Union, IA	16.7	42.8	3.1	1.0	. . .	2.6	159	11.7	34
Van Buren, IA	16.1	34.9	2.3	0.0	. . .	2.0	96	11.9	. . .
Wapello, IA	17.8	47.0	13.1	4.9	. . .	5.4	474	13.1	32
Warren, IA	13.2	15.5	3.6	0.2	557	1.7	540	14.9	32
Washington, IA	17.5	27.9	9.3	2.9	231	2.0	275	12.9	18
Wayne, IA	17.0	51.4	1.0	0.8	123	1.3	130	9.6	14
Webster, IA	17.7	39.9	12.0	0.5	. . .	3.0	423	12.5	35
Winnebago, IA	15.5	25.8	4.8	0.3	223	1.6	209	12.9	15
Winneshiek, IA	17.2	21.3	2.4	0.1	. . .	0.5	236	12.8	15
Woodbury, IA	15.1	38.1	28.3	9.9	. . .	6.2	1 249	14.1	63
Worth, IA	14.1	28.6	2.0	0.0	91	2.5	78	13.4	8
Wright, IA	13.4	36.0	10.3	4.0	. . .	1.7	211	13.0	19
KANSAS	13.9	38.6	24.2	5.6	. . .	3.1	32 932	14.2	. . .
Allen, KS	18.9	48.4	6.5	0.2	. . .	2.5	174	14.2	12
Anderson, KS	16.0	44.0	2.5	0.0	. . .	3.6	107	12.8	9
Atchison, KS	18.4	49.7	13.3	0.1	. . .	2.6	186	13.3	13
Barber, KS	13.9	36.3	6.1	0.0	. . .	1.2	69	13.1	6
Barton, KS	13.5	48.9	21.7	8.0	. . .	2.2	354	13.7	26
Bourbon, KS	10.6	51.4	7.5	0.6	. . .	4.1	185	13.4	22
Brown, KS	22.2	46.0	20.7	2.5	. . .	2.7	124	13.0	8
Butler, KS	12.5	23.7	7.1	0.3	. . .	1.8	958	14.7	67
Chase, KS	12.6	41.9	4.9	0.0	. . .	1.9	40	12.0	4
Chautauqua, KS	18.7	51.1	10.3	0.0	. . .	5.3	51	12.3	4
Cherokee, KS	12.4	52.1	9.3	0.4	. . .	3.5	279	13.7	25
Cheyenne, KS	14.5	42.3	4.7	0.0	. . .	0.5	53	9.4	4
Clark, KS	14.7	41.1	9.8	3.0	. . .	2.3	40	12.5	5
Clay, KS	15.3	34.4	3.2	0.0	. . .	4.8	136	10.6	6
Cloud, KS	21.3	47.4	2.3	0.7	. . .	1.1	144	9.4	10
Coffey, KS	15.9	33.7	4.6	0.0	. . .	1.1	158	11.2	18
Comanche, KS	21.1	34.3	4.0	2.4	. . .	. . .	28	11.8	4
Cowley, KS	18.1	48.3	18.6	5.3	. . .	2.8	499	13.4	41
Crawford, KS	12.2	46.7	10.0	2.3	. . .	2.9	370	16.2	22
Decatur, KS	17.1	38.1	1.6	0.0	. . .	1.4	50	9.8	4
Dickinson, KS	14.5	39.1	5.7	0.1	. . .	1.2	282	13.7	22
Doniphan, KS	16.5	36.8	5.8	0.0	. . .	2.8	129	11.9	13
Douglas, KS	15.0	28.5	19.1	3.8	. . .	2.2	913	14.1	74
Edwards, KS	14.7	48.6	22.8	10.3	. . .	3.2	46	10.9	5
Elk, KS	27.5	57.4	6.9	0.3	. . .	2.8	67	10.0	7
Ellis, KS	15.8	31.4	8.8	1.3	. . .	2.1	320	12.1	21
Ellsworth, KS	17.8	32.1	6.1	0.0	. . .	2.1	91	11.9	10
Finney, KS	12.2	55.8	62.7	22.7	. . .	3.6	564	15.2	34
Ford, KS	12.7	65.9	64.6	37.5	. . .	1.8	399	16.6	32
Franklin, KS	14.9	33.7	5.9	0.5	. . .	1.1	346	14.1	21

[2]IEP = Individual Education Program. See notes and definitions at the end of this section.
. . . = Not available.

Table C-1. Population, School, and Student Characteristics by County—Continued

STATE County	Revenue, 2003–2004				Current expenditures, 2003–2004			Resident population, 16 to 19 years, 2000			
	Total revenue (thousands of dollars)	Percent of revenue from:			Total expenditures (thousands of dollars)	Amount per student (dollars)	Percent for instruction	Total	Percent in armed forces	Percent high school graduates	Percent not enrolled, not in armed forces, not high school graduate
		Federal government	State government	Local government							
	19	20	21	22	23	24	25	26	27	28	29
Jefferson, IA	15 871	6.0	49.7	44.3	13 627	6 924	65.1	942	0.0	6.8	4.8
Johnson, IA	114 613	3.5	42.3	54.2	97 872	7 226	71.1	9 749	0.2	5.4	0.9
Jones, IA	30 564	7.2	43.9	48.9	22 746	7 071	64.2	1 058	0.0	8.4	3.0
Keokuk, IA	19 063	5.4	43.4	51.2	16 073	7 131	67.6	596	0.0	12.2	1.8
Kossuth, IA	22 778	5.0	37.1	57.9	18 839	8 575	70.3	1 072	0.9	8.1	1.7
Lee, IA	49 936	9.0	48.8	42.1	40 337	7 045	69.7	1 967	0.0	10.8	2.7
Linn, IA	304 402	8.0	43.6	48.4	264 978	7 989	65.2	11 277	0.0	10.4	2.2
Louisa, IA	26 327	7.7	46.4	45.9	20 975	6 978	69.3	704	0.0	6.3	8.7
Lucas, IA	12 622	8.6	53.8	37.7	11 612	7 172	67.0	591	0.0	9.5	7.4
Lyon, IA	16 763	9.1	44.1	46.7	13 193	7 127	67.6	763	0.0	10.6	1.0
Madison, IA	24 328	3.6	49.4	47.0	19 550	6 506	64.5	758	0.7	13.5	3.4
Mahaska, IA	29 114	5.3	44.7	50.0	22 131	7 188	67.0	1 416	0.0	10.2	4.7
Marion, IA	45 289	4.5	51.6	44.0	37 313	6 372	67.0	2 152	0.0	7.6	0.4
Marshall, IA	55 094	9.9	52.8	37.3	48 033	7 258	65.7	2 313	0.0	10.1	5.5
Mills, IA	23 803	6.8	44.8	48.4	18 899	6 971	65.9	778	0.0	8.6	1.8
Mitchell, IA	13 991	3.7	44.3	52.0	12 164	6 841	69.3	563	0.0	8.5	2.0
Monona, IA	16 142	9.1	41.4	49.5	10 916	7 570	62.8	534	0.0	8.6	4.9
Monroe, IA	10 098	6.1	55.1	38.8	8 330	6 734	67.8	477	0.0	13.0	1.0
Montgomery, IA	16 984	7.2	48.1	44.7	13 994	7 195	67.1	664	0.0	5.6	6.5
Muscatine, IA	63 695	6.4	50.1	43.5	51 829	7 069	73.1	2 300	0.0	9.7	6.5
O'Brien, IA	24 990	12.9	40.9	46.2	22 482	8 792	57.5	933	0.0	8.9	2.6
Osceola, IA	7 260	4.8	47.6	47.7	6 098	6 679	66.7	366	0.0	7.1	4.4
Page, IA	23 997	7.6	42.4	50.0	18 288	6 607	69.4	939	0.4	13.5	3.4
Palo Alto, IA	15 816	6.2	39.4	54.5	13 034	7 880	66.2	707	0.0	5.4	1.3
Plymouth, IA	33 827	4.6	46.8	48.6	28 472	6 472	68.2	1 610	0.0	9.2	0.9
Pocahontas, IA	10 445	5.2	42.0	52.7	9 055	7 706	68.5	473	0.0	7.4	0.8
Polk, IA	645 133	8.2	41.2	50.6	520 359	8 333	63.3	19 619	0.1	12.6	3.9
Pottawattamie, IA	148 254	11.4	46.2	42.4	130 501	7 869	64.6	5 187	0.0	11.7	5.0
Poweshiek, IA	27 513	8.0	41.6	50.4	21 203	7 063	67.2	1 369	0.0	8.0	0.7
Ringgold, IA	8 897	12.4	44.3	43.4	7 668	9 843	70.7	340	0.0	5.6	8.2
Sac, IA	16 195	6.0	44.9	49.0	13 472	6 846	66.6	618	0.0	6.3	0.6
Scott, IA	257 501	10.2	42.2	47.6	222 821	8 288	66.7	8 960	0.0	11.8	4.0
Shelby, IA	20 811	5.9	45.7	48.5	15 675	6 575	66.8	762	0.0	9.7	2.0
Sioux, IA	36 103	5.3	42.7	52.0	27 761	6 733	69.4	2 865	0.0	7.2	0.6
Story, IA	100 247	3.3	37.7	59.0	76 743	7 288	70.4	8 266	0.0	4.3	4.3
Tama, IA	27 139	7.9	49.1	43.0	22 798	6 482	65.0	941	0.0	9.6	4.3
Taylor, IA	11 282	7.9	46.9	45.3	8 771	7 634	66.4	402	0.0	10.0	3.2
Union, IA	21 907	23.4	39.7	36.9	20 115	10 411	56.8	809	0.0	9.6	3.3
Van Buren, IA	14 165	23.6	39.4	37.0	10 603	8 476	67.6	418	0.0	13.2	7.9
Wapello, IA	55 304	16.1	51.3	32.6	53 859	8 392	61.0	2 061	0.0	10.8	6.0
Warren, IA	65 075	4.9	51.9	43.2	52 439	6 615	65.7	2 609	0.0	11.2	2.3
Washington, IA	30 071	8.0	48.1	43.9	25 700	7 244	66.6	1 020	0.0	10.7	2.8
Wayne, IA	10 093	11.4	46.0	42.6	8 216	7 817	67.5	355	0.0	8.5	3.4
Webster, IA	57 239	20.0	40.5	39.4	57 602	10 392	57.2	2 648	0.0	11.6	4.8
Winnebago, IA	22 554	3.5	48.6	47.8	19 008	6 847	67.8	938	0.0	6.4	2.9
Winneshiek, IA	23 728	3.5	41.2	55.3	18 783	7 349	71.5	1 974	0.0	4.1	1.4
Woodbury, IA	165 465	10.3	47.8	42.0	144 103	7 948	68.2	6 334	0.1	11.1	4.6
Worth, IA	9 094	5.1	42.3	52.6	7 311	6 923	66.3	412	0.0	7.0	0.5
Wright, IA	23 998	5.7	44.3	50.0	20 732	7 313	66.9	778	0.0	16.3	4.9
KANSAS	4 377 709	7.8	51.4	40.8	3 531 344	7 516	64.6	166 014	0.7	10.0	4.0
Allen, KS	23 713	9.1	67.4	23.4	20 000	8 183	66.1	1 114	0.0	11.1	3.5
Anderson, KS	12 883	6.8	62.5	30.8	11 143	8 104	63.4	496	0.0	2.4	1.8
Atchison, KS	22 845	11.0	58.9	30.1	19 867	8 159	61.9	1 171	0.0	9.3	0.1
Barber, KS	8 901	5.0	59.4	35.6	7 810	8 489	62.9	332	0.0	3.6	1.8
Barton, KS	44 877	8.4	57.8	33.9	34 395	6 960	67.4	1 968	0.6	5.9	4.4
Bourbon, KS	20 094	7.9	68.4	23.7	16 414	6 506	65.8	991	0.0	11.2	1.5
Brown, KS	16 590	8.2	64.1	27.7	14 117	8 520	67.4	648	0.0	10.2	6.2
Butler, KS	117 873	3.1	60.1	36.8	93 368	6 756	64.2	3 806	0.3	11.0	4.1
Chase, KS	5 169	4.6	51.0	44.4	4 458	9 307	59.8	186	0.0	5.9	5.9
Chautauqua, KS	6 126	7.8	76.2	16.1	5 531	8 615	64.8	262	0.0	4.6	2.3
Cherokee, KS	34 793	7.2	69.5	23.2	31 488	8 107	63.4	1 334	0.0	10.6	7.3
Cheyenne, KS	5 546	5.1	59.9	35.1	4 969	9 447	66.9	177	0.0	9.6	0.0
Clark, KS	5 591	4.4	54.4	41.1	4 893	9 557	62.4	157	0.0	8.3	1.9
Clay, KS	13 804	4.4	58.4	37.2	10 106	6 751	63.5	416	0.0	12.5	7.0
Cloud, KS	13 106	5.7	63.4	30.9	11 429	8 111	65.0	805	0.0	6.2	1.0
Coffey, KS	24 747	4.1	26.8	69.2	15 583	8 562	65.9	489	0.0	6.1	2.9
Comanche, KS	3 475	4.0	39.8	56.2	2 868	9 282	56.6	71	0.0	5.6	0.0
Cowley, KS	54 967	9.0	67.1	24.0	47 388	7 055	64.2	2 626	0.0	8.7	4.5
Crawford, KS	50 647	7.7	64.9	27.4	43 736	7 389	65.3	2 708	1.0	9.7	2.4
Decatur, KS	5 901	6.4	56.7	36.9	5 329	10 131	66.9	190	0.0	10.5	0.0
Dickinson, KS	34 245	5.5	65.9	28.6	29 661	7 637	64.3	1 057	0.6	7.4	4.4
Doniphan, KS	14 707	4.8	76.1	19.1	13 580	8 205	64.9	711	0.0	5.9	1.3
Douglas, KS	128 054	9.0	37.7	53.2	98 996	7 813	65.7	9 344	0.1	5.4	1.3
Edwards, KS	5 306	6.8	58.6	34.6	4 932	9 709	61.1	196	0.0	9.7	3.1
Elk, KS	6 780	7.2	73.7	19.1	6 303	9 201	64.1	137	0.0	12.4	2.9
Ellis, KS	35 955	8.9	50.0	41.1	31 066	7 873	68.7	2 324	0.0	10.5	1.9
Ellsworth, KS	11 818	3.7	56.2	40.1	9 383	8 124	62.1	349	0.6	10.9	0.9
Finney, KS	78 834	11.2	50.4	38.4	63 011	7 293	64.0	2 803	0.0	7.3	10.0
Ford, KS	62 418	14.0	60.4	25.6	51 323	7 783	65.8	2 167	0.0	9.6	8.8
Franklin, KS	42 942	5.9	64.0	30.1	35 620	7 284	66.6	1 428	0.0	8.3	2.5

Table C-1. Population, School, and Student Characteristics by County—*Continued*

STATE County	High school graduates, 2000			College enrollment, 2000		College graduates, 2000 (percent)						
	Population 25 years and over	High school graduate or less (percent)	High school graduate or more (percent)	Number	Percent public	Bachelor's degree or more	+/- U.S. percentage with bachelor's degree or more	Non-Hispanic White	Black	American Indian and Alaska Native	Asian or Pacific Islander	Hispanic[3]
	30	31	32	33	34	35	36	37	38	39	40	41
Jefferson, IA	10 893	43.3	88.1	875	42.2	31.2	6.8	31.0	31.0	31.4	50.0	52.4
Johnson, IA	62 859	26.1	93.7	26 885	96.3	47.6	23.2	47.0	34.9	41.1	76.5	34.5
Jones, IA	13 776	57.0	85.3	736	79.5	12.7	-11.7	13.0	3.1	16.1	17.2	3.7
Keokuk, IA	7 667	62.3	84.0	298	86.6	11.6	-12.8	11.5	0.0	0.0	64.7	11.8
Kossuth, IA	11 694	53.4	85.6	475	79.4	13.6	-10.8	13.6	0.0	0.0	7.7	2.5
Lee, IA	25 828	59.1	83.6	1 153	87.3	12.5	-11.9	12.6	4.7	0.0	42.1	10.2
Linn, IA	123 896	39.8	90.6	11 547	65.6	27.7	3.3	27.7	13.2	20.3	55.1	22.7
Louisa, IA	7 828	61.3	79.7	405	81.5	12.7	-11.7	13.5	27.3	0.0	32.5	2.8
Lucas, IA	6 336	65.4	79.1	225	70.2	11.1	-13.3	11.0	0.0	0.0	33.3	60.0
Lyon, IA	7 539	59.6	78.7	298	70.1	14.2	-10.2	14.1	20.0	0.0	100.0	52.6
Madison, IA	9 254	53.4	87.6	408	69.6	14.4	-10.0	14.4	0.0	0.0	35.3	12.5
Mahaska, IA	14 504	58.6	82.6	1 000	56.9	16.5	-7.9	16.5	0.0	0.0	29.9	4.8
Marion, IA	20 684	56.6	84.0	1 856	27.4	18.9	-5.5	18.9	19.1	12.9	18.4	9.8
Marshall, IA	26 179	54.9	82.3	1 316	83.9	17.0	-7.4	18.1	8.1	0.0	15.3	1.7
Mills, IA	9 662	53.5	83.2	541	72.5	16.3	-8.1	16.4	0.0	32.1	9.7	12.5
Mitchell, IA	7 320	60.0	84.4	268	85.8	12.8	-11.6	12.9	0.0	0.0	. . .	0.0
Monona, IA	7 072	61.2	81.7	197	72.1	13.4	-11.0	13.6	0.0	12.5	0.0	0.0
Monroe, IA	5 400	62.1	82.2	263	89.0	12.6	-11.8	12.7	0.0	0.0	. . .	0.0
Montgomery, IA	8 124	58.8	81.8	278	68.0	12.9	-11.5	13.0	. . .	. . .	27.3	0.0
Muscatine, IA	26 877	54.2	80.3	1 688	83.1	17.2	-7.2	18.0	10.8	4.7	27.6	7.9
O'Brien, IA	10 174	58.3	80.7	385	83.6	14.7	-9.7	14.8	25.0	0.0	25.0	1.6
Osceola, IA	4 647	56.5	81.1	172	77.9	13.4	-11.0	13.5	0.0	33.3	0.0	8.7
Page, IA	11 655	53.8	85.5	502	79.3	16.6	-7.8	17.0	0.0	6.8	20.0	5.2
Palo Alto, IA	6 692	51.3	83.7	591	88.7	13.9	-10.5	14.0	. . .	0.0	0.0	0.0
Plymouth, IA	15 994	51.7	87.4	816	74.6	19.3	-5.1	19.4	57.9	0.0	8.7	5.2
Pocahontas, IA	6 002	53.2	86.6	209	77.5	15.0	-9.4	15.1	0.0	0.0	0.0	0.0
Polk, IA	243 458	41.1	88.3	21 022	56.1	29.7	5.3	31.2	16.3	13.3	28.0	11.6
Pottawattamie, IA	57 013	55.3	84.0	3 618	82.1	15.0	-9.4	15.1	5.5	15.0	35.3	12.1
Poweshiek, IA	12 176	55.8	86.7	1 742	27.7	18.5	-5.9	18.3	46.2	20.0	34.4	17.1
Ringgold, IA	3 781	61.6	82.8	196	79.6	13.4	-11.0	13.3	. . .	0.0	88.9	66.7
Sac, IA	7 946	58.8	84.2	295	80.3	13.6	-10.8	13.6	0.0	0.0	16.7	13.3
Scott, IA	102 149	44.4	86.3	10 824	60.9	24.9	0.5	25.8	12.2	10.3	35.9	14.2
Shelby, IA	8 957	59.3	86.6	252	81.7	15.3	-9.1	15.1	0.0	0.0	72.0	8.6
Sioux, IA	18 172	53.3	80.4	2 920	14.0	19.8	-4.6	19.9	4.9	0.0	47.4	7.3
Story, IA	42 148	27.8	93.5	23 057	97.5	44.5	20.1	42.5	62.9	7.3	80.0	43.4
Tama, IA	12 011	56.6	84.2	661	80.7	12.0	11.6	13.3	0.0	5.2	40.2	0.1
Taylor, IA	4 766	63.3	83.3	194	92.8	12.0	-12.4	12.2	. . .	18.2	0.0	2.9
Union, IA	8 342	55.9	87.3	597	88.4	14.7	-9.7	14.7	. . .	0.0	0.0	41.2
Van Buren, IA	5 322	63.5	82.7	171	77.2	11.8	-12.6	11.9	. . .	33.3	0.0	8.3
Wapello, IA	24 120	58.4	81.5	1 607	85.6	14.6	-9.8	14.6	24.6	33.3	23.0	10.6
Warren, IA	25 756	47.8	90.0	2 431	41.0	21.2	-3.2	21.3	20.3	0.0	26.4	20.2
Washington, IA	13 876	56.6	82.5	584	81.3	16.4	-8.0	16.5	10.9	13.3	100.0	9.7
Wayne, IA	4 722	62.0	83.9	191	80.6	12.1	-12.3	12.1	0.0	0.0	58.8	0.0
Webster, IA	25 981	52.6	84.2	1 918	91.5	16.9	-7.5	17.1	8.5	14.8	38.3	5.6
Winnebago, IA	7 772	50.8	87.3	567	40.9	16.5	-7.9	16.5	0.0	0.0	0.0	20.8
Winneshiek, IA	12 864	53.2	84.1	2 830	20.0	20.5	-3.9	20.7	15.4	0.0	2.4	0.0
Woodbury, IA	64 932	53.6	81.4	4 797	57.6	18.9	-5.5	20.6	10.9	2.1	11.8	3.0
Worth, IA	5 476	53.6	86.0	241	86.7	12.7	-11.7	13.0	0.0	0.0	0.0	0.0
Wright, IA	9 882	54.7	84.4	270	75.9	13.5	-10.9	13.9	0.0	0.0	0.0	3.9
KANSAS	1 701 207	43.8	86.0	176 453	85.3	25.8	1.4	27.2	14.9	14.9	40.0	9.7
Allen, KS	9 292	52.7	83.1	647	97.1	15.2	-9.2	15.5	10.8	8.6	22.2	5.9
Anderson, KS	5 459	60.4	81.9	173	89.6	11.7	-12.7	11.7	0.0	0.0	0.0	11.8
Atchison, KS	10 375	56.9	84.7	1 058	26.5	18.0	-6.4	17.8	19.5	0.0	44.4	29.6
Barber, KS	3 646	47.0	85.8	112	88.4	21.0	-3.4	21.2	0.0	0.0	0.0	22.2
Barton, KS	18 265	49.1	82.3	1 206	78.4	16.6	-7.8	17.5	4.4	26.8	53.5	1.3
Bourbon, KS	9 965	47.5	84.2	684	93.1	17.8	-6.6	18.2	6.7	23.5	. . .	15.6
Brown, KS	7 080	54.5	84.6	349	87.7	19.0	-5.4	18.8	39.8	15.0	54.8	15.2
Butler, KS	37 560	45.0	87.3	3 044	87.7	20.4	-4.0	20.8	7.6	13.3	33.6	8.5
Chase, KS	2 081	52.6	87.1	86	94.2	19.6	-4.8	20.1	17.6	0.0	0.0	0.0
Chautauqua, KS	3 058	59.7	81.0	124	87.1	12.3	-12.1	12.1	. . .	18.2	37.5	13.6
Cherokee, KS	14 704	58.5	80.3	781	94.0	11.3	-13.1	11.2	5.4	17.9	19.4	5.4
Cheyenne, KS	2 257	50.2	85.5	71	91.5	16.0	-8.4	16.1	. . .	0.0	0.0	0.0
Clark, KS	1 640	40.1	87.4	56	94.6	22.1	-2.3	22.3	0.0	27.3	0.0	15.2
Clay, KS	6 026	52.5	87.0	244	97.1	16.5	-7.9	16.6	15.4	0.0	36.4	5.0
Cloud, KS	6 909	52.6	85.5	710	94.1	18.0	-6.4	17.8	0.0	29.4	46.2	50.0
Coffey, KS	5 932	53.7	86.9	280	84.6	20.1	-4.3	19.9	0.0	21.6	66.7	20.8
Comanche, KS	1 440	45.8	91.3	31	87.1	15.1	-9.3	15.0	. . .	. . .	100.0	18.2
Cowley, KS	22 982	45.6	85.4	2 584	61.3	18.3	-6.1	19.1	17.2	10.8	3.1	8.4
Crawford, KS	23 395	46.2	84.5	5 069	97.7	23.9	-0.5	24.2	9.5	16.5	53.5	11.3
Decatur, KS	2 479	53.6	86.4	106	93.4	15.4	-9.0	15.2	0.0	0.0	50.0	25.0
Dickinson, KS	13 156	52.9	86.4	663	85.7	15.2	-9.2	15.3	0.0	7.1	33.3	6.4
Doniphan, KS	5 176	56.6	80.2	643	97.0	14.8	-9.6	15.0	9.1	0.0	23.1	10.5
Douglas, KS	53 257	29.9	92.4	25 640	93.2	42.7	18.3	42.8	33.2	25.9	71.3	33.0
Edwards, KS	2 378	51.1	81.2	118	95.8	16.3	-8.1	17.3	37.5	33.3	54.5	0.0
Elk, KS	2 354	61.6	80.0	92	90.2	10.6	-13.8	10.8	. . .	0.0	. . .	0.0
Ellis, KS	16 278	42.7	87.2	4 298	96.9	29.2	4.8	29.2	60.0	0.0	56.9	12.1
Ellsworth, KS	4 660	50.7	84.8	177	83.1	16.4	-8.0	17.6	0.0	13.0	0.0	2.4
Finney, KS	22 196	57.5	67.4	1 747	90.7	14.3	-10.1	20.9	0.0	14.2	18.0	2.8
Ford, KS	18 632	53.2	69.9	1 285	94.5	16.4	-8.0	22.7	9.4	5.3	0.0	3.7
Franklin, KS	15 753	54.2	85.3	1 069	56.8	16.5	-7.9	16.8	12.7	8.6	46.5	6.3

[3]May be of any race.
. . . = Not available.

Table C-1. Population, School, and Student Characteristics by County—*Continued*

STATE County	State/ county code	County type[1]	Population, 2005		Number of schools and students, 2004–2005			Resident enrollment, 2000			
			Total	Percent 5 to 17 years	School districts	Schools	Students	Total	Percent public	K–12	Percent public
			1	2	3	4	5	6	7	8	9
Geary, KS	20061	5	24 585	19.2	1	16	6 678	8 115	91.0	5 664	93.2
Gove, KS	20063	9	2 763	17.6	3	7	656	753	95.5	640	98.0
Graham, KS	20065	9	2 721	14.2	1	3	435	685	95.9	560	98.2
Grant, KS	20067	7	7 530	21.1	1	4	1 824	2 281	93.2	1 954	95.1
Gray, KS	20069	9	5 861	21.1	4	8	1 460	1 565	82.5	1 343	83.2
Greeley, KS	20071	9	1 349	19.3	1	3	281	395	95.2	359	94.7
Greenwood, KS	20073	6	7 338	15.9	3	6	1 093	1 640	97.6	1 418	99.2
Hamilton, KS	20075	9	2 604	17.9	1	2	493	711	90.6	584	93.3
Harper, KS	20077	8	6 081	16.1	2	5	1 093	1 554	94.7	1 337	96.1
Harvey, KS	20079	2	33 843	17.3	5	20	6 082	8 739	79.9	6 503	88.9
Haskell, KS	20081	9	4 232	21.9	2	5	934	1 258	90.4	1 071	90.8
Hodgeman, KS	20083	9	2 110	17.7	2	4	399	615	95.4	519	98.1
Jackson, KS	20085	3	13 535	18.4	3	9	2 553	3 284	91.2	2 712	94.2
Jefferson, KS	20087	3	19 106	17.6	6	20	4 206	4 722	92.8	3 942	96.2
Jewell, KS	20089	9	3 352	14.7	3	8	525	773	95.9	656	98.5
Johnson, KS	20091	1	506 562	18.1	7	141	82 336	124 515	78.8	88 153	84.8
Kearny, KS	20093	9	4 516	22.7	2	6	1 053	1 379	92.8	1 147	95.8
Kingman, KS	20095	6	8 165	18.4	2	7	1 439	2 284	90.8	1 916	92.6
Kiowa, KS	20097	9	2 984	15.7	3	8	671	826	83.9	621	91.6
Labette, KS	20099	7	22 169	17.6	4	17	4 135	5 956	95.9	4 570	96.9
Lane, KS	20101	9	1 894	16.5	2	4	375	514	96.5	440	98.9
Leavenworth, KS	20103	1	73 113	18.1	6	29	12 513	18 935	84.1	13 771	89.6
Lincoln, KS	20105	9	3 411	15.7	2	4	561	803	94.8	657	96.8
Linn, KS	20107	1	9 914	16.7	3	11	2 101	2 094	89.1	1 788	91.3
Logan, KS	20109	9	2 794	16.7	2	5	589	723	89.5	576	93.2
Lyon, KS	20111	5	35 609	16.4	3	18	6 181	11 701	95.8	6 992	95.8
McPherson, KS	20113	6	29 523	16.3	5	18	4 809	8 098	85.6	5 809	89.4
Marion, KS	20115	6	12 952	16.7	5	12	2 359	3 472	81.0	2 604	92.7
Marshall, KS	20117	7	10 405	15.8	4	13	2 184	2 606	87.0	2 317	87.9
Meade, KS	20119	9	4 625	20.3	2	4	683	1 272	90.6	1 027	92.7
Miami, KS	20121	1	30 496	18.2	3	13	4 806	7 575	88.0	6 086	91.2
Mitchell, KS	20123	7	6 420	16.8	3	7	1 226	1 866	85.6	1 424	83.6
Montgomery, KS	20125	5	34 570	16.7	4	12	5 442	9 206	90.1	7 003	91.3
Morris, KS	20127	9	6 049	16.8	1	4	899	1 419	96.3	1 202	97.5
Morton, KS	20129	9	3 196	20.1	2	6	1 029	1 005	95.7	812	97.3
Nemaha, KS	20131	8	10 443	19.3	3	9	1 740	2 698	91.9	2 303	92.7
Neosho, KS	20133	7	16 529	16.8	2	13	2 967	4 518	91.4	3 440	93.1
Ness, KS	20135	9	3 009	14.2	5	6	534	769	91.2	625	92.2
Norton, KS	20137	7	5 664	14.8	3	7	956	1 349	90.3	1 120	92.2
Osage, KS	20139	3	17 150	18.1	5	13	3 142	4 279	94.9	3 378	97.4
Osborne, KS	20141	9	4 050	16.0	2	4	557	1 033	95.2	925	96.0
Ottawa, KS	20143	9	6 123	16.5	2	6	1 224	1 514	90.8	1 244	94.5
Pawnee, KS	20145	7	6 739	17.0	3	7	1 299	1 676	91.9	1 420	93.0
Phillips, KS	20147	7	5 504	16.7	3	7	973	1 384	98.0	1 170	99.7
Pottawatomie, KS	20149	6	19 129	19.4	4	15	3 622	5 159	87.3	4 131	87.7
Pratt, KS	20151	7	9 496	15.8	2	7	1 634	2 533	90.5	1 874	91.0
Rawlins, KS	20153	9	2 672	15.0	1	2	361	666	95.3	593	97.6
Reno, KS	20155	4	63 558	16.3	6	36	10 299	15 601	88.4	11 953	89.4
Republic, KS	20157	9	5 164	14.3	3	8	867	1 306	96.0	1 109	99.3
Rice, KS	20159	7	10 452	16.1	4	13	1 900	3 243	88.3	2 089	97.1
Riley, KS	20161	5	62 826	11.1	3	16	6 176	28 110	94.9	8 195	92.5
Rooks, KS	20163	9	5 351	16.7	3	7	935	1 330	91.7	1 122	92.8
Rush, KS	20165	9	3 406	14.7	2	6	536	790	95.1	644	96.7
Russell, KS	20167	7	6 845	14.7	1	6	1 031	1 627	93.5	1 340	97.5
Saline, KS	20169	5	53 919	17.7	3	17	8 666	14 039	84.4	10 731	89.8
Scott, KS	20171	7	4 600	18.2	1	3	952	1 229	93.1	1 033	95.1
Sedgwick, KS	20173	2	466 061	19.2	10	147	78 813	129 180	82.4	92 478	85.8
Seward, KS	20175	7	23 274	21.3	2	15	5 353	6 348	95.3	5 207	97.5
Shawnee, KS	20177	3	172 365	17.1	6	60	26 950	43 314	83.1	31 221	87.2
Sheridan, KS	20179	9	2 591	16.7	2	5	579	757	99.2	630	99.2
Sherman, KS	20181	7	6 153	16.4	1	5	1 014	1 793	95.3	1 203	98.1
Smith, KS	20183	9	4 121	14.3	2	4	662	979	96.3	817	100.0
Stafford, KS	20185	9	4 488	18.1	3	7	1 068	1 201	96.8	1 020	97.7
Stanton, KS	20187	9	2 245	20.1	1	3	500	644	92.2	538	95.9
Stevens, KS	20189	7	5 412	21.0	2	5	1 366	1 570	96.5	1 292	97.1
Sumner, KS	20191	2	24 797	19.0	7	21	4 452	7 299	91.7	5 745	94.6
Thomas, KS	20193	7	7 639	17.7	2	5	1 224	2 545	91.5	1 622	90.8
Trego, KS	20195	9	3 050	15.6	1	2	393	807	94.1	631	99.0
Wabaunsee, KS	20197	3	6 919	16.8	2	7	1 016	1 699	94.4	1 407	95.5
Wallace, KS	20199	9	1 573	18.6	2	4	367	470	90.9	415	89.6
Washington, KS	20201	9	6 009	16.6	4	11	1 295	1 403	88.0	1 161	88.5
Wichita, KS	20203	9	2 309	19.8	1	3	522	617	91.2	546	93.6
Wilson, KS	20205	7	9 834	17.3	3	9	1 820	2 434	96.9	2 047	98.8
Woodson, KS	20207	9	3 572	13.7	1	2	535	862	96.2	680	99.0
Wyandotte, KS	20209	1	155 750	19.4	5	59	28 056	42 334	86.9	32 339	89.1

[1]County type codes are from the Economic Research Service of the United States Department of Agriculture. See notes and definitions at the end of this section.

Table C-1. Population, School, and Student Characteristics by County—*Continued*

STATE County	Characteristics of students, 2004–2005				Outcomes		Staff and students, 2004–2005		
	Percent with IEP[2]	Percent eligible for free or reduced-price lunch	Percent minority	Percent English-language learners	Number of graduates, 2003–2004	Percent dropouts, grades 9–12, 2001–2002	Number of teachers	Student-teacher ratio	Central administration staff
	10	11	12	13	14	15	16	17	18
Geary, KS	13.9	55.6	43.3	5.3	. . .	4.6	452	14.8	40
Gove, KS	17.2	34.1	3.2	0.3	. . .	0.8	71	9.3	8
Graham, KS	18.4	38.6	6.3	0.0	. . .	0.6	37	11.8	3
Grant, KS	12.7	48.8	53.1	12.7	. . .	2.0	114	16.0	8
Gray, KS	10.5	38.9	22.1	22.7	. . .	1.1	103	14.1	10
Greeley, KS	13.5	41.3	16.0	16.0	. . .	1.8	26	10.9	3
Greenwood, KS	17.0	48.2	2.9	0.5	. . .	1.3	99	11.1	8
Hamilton, KS	15.4	53.8	30.8	22.5	. . .	1.1	39	12.7	4
Harper, KS	17.6	50.9	7.5	0.0	. . .	5.8	87	12.5	8
Harvey, KS	14.9	38.0	18.6	3.7	. . .	2.6	427	14.3	35
Haskell, KS	10.0	47.7	38.8	22.1	. . .	2.5	74	12.6	9
Hodgeman, KS	12.0	35.6	8.7	3.5	. . .	2.4	38	10.6	3
Jackson, KS	13.0	34.0	17.2	0.0	. . .	2.8	198	12.9	17
Jefferson, KS	13.4	26.3	3.5	0.2	. . .	1.0	285	14.8	30
Jewell, KS	12.8	43.8	3.0	0.0	. . .	0.5	60	8.8	7
Johnson, KS	11.3	12.4	15.6	3.6	. . .	1.6	5 459	15.1	269
Kearny, KS	14.0	43.2	38.3	19.5	. . .	2.6	82	12.8	7
Kingman, KS	17.9	38.0	3.9	0.3	. . .	0.5	105	13.8	6
Kiowa, KS	15.2	43.0	10.3	2.4	. . .	1.7	52	12.8	6
Labette, KS	12.6	51.8	19.9	0.0	. . .	2.2	280	14.8	22
Lane, KS	17.6	45.6	5.3	4.3	. . .	1.4	35	10.8	5
Leavenworth, KS	14.4	23.6	17.8	1.1	. . .	3.3	852	14.7	50
Lincoln, KS	13.5	41.1	2.3	0.2	. . .	1.6	47	11.8	7
Linn, KS	15.4	38.8	2.7	0.4	. . .	2.5	147	14.3	16
Logan, KS	17.5	38.7	4.5	0.0	. . .	0.8	50	11.7	6
Lyon, KS	11.4	52.6	39.4	18.8	. . .	2.7	471	13.1	30
McPherson, KS	14.7	24.1	5.0	0.4	. . .	2.5	379	12.7	38
Marion, KS	19.4	35.3	4.9	0.2	. . .	1.4	173	13.7	12
Marshall, KS	15.7	30.7	3.1	0.0	. . .	1.1	174	12.6	13
Meade, KS	17.1	43.8	16.6	5.0	. . .	0.5	53	12.8	5
Miami, KS	13.6	27.2	5.3	0.1	. . .	3.1	367	13.1	22
Mitchell, KS	17.5	34.4	1.8	0.1	. . .	1.8	108	11.3	9
Montgomery, KS	12.8	51.8	24.6	0.4	. . .	2.7	340	16.0	26
Morris, KS	14.7	41.4	3.6	1.2	. . .	1.4	68	13.1	4
Morton, KS	8.7	33.6	26.5	17.7	. . .	2.1	74	13.9	10
Nemaha, KS	14.5	26.1	2.4	0.0	. . .	0.6	141	12.3	14
Neosho, KS	17.3	44.8	6.4	0.9	. . .	2.4	208	14.2	13
Ness, KS	14.6	29.0	8.5	1.5	. . .	3.1	44	12.1	. . .
Norton, KS	19.4	42.5	2.7	0.0	. . .	1.5	84	11.4	6
Osage, KS	19.7	36.6	4.8	0.0	. . .	3.0	225	13.9	18
Osborne, KS	18.7	45.1	4.4	0.0	. . .	. . .	50	11.2	8
Ottawa, KS	13.2	33.7	2.8	0.3	. . .	0.8	93	13.2	8
Pawnee, KS	22.4	43.8	10.3	0.0	. . .	2.0	113	11.5	13
Phillips, KS	18.0	43.6	4.3	0.0	. . .	0.3	92	10.6	11
Pottawatomie, KS	16.6	28.4	3.9	0.0	. . .	1.4	297	12.2	21
Pratt, KS	14.0	40.4	7.8	2.4	. . .	2.4	112	14.6	10
Rawlins, KS	17.2	45.0	3.6	0.0	. . .	. . .	35	10.4	2
Reno, KS	15.1	45.1	14.4	1.3	. . .	4.1	712	14.5	53
Republic, KS	23.4	43.7	2.0	0.0	. . .	0.8	80	10.8	8
Rice, KS	17.1	51.6	14.8	4.6	. . .	1.4	175	10.9	19
Riley, KS	14.8	30.4	17.7	2.0	. . .	2.8	442	14.0	40
Rooks, KS	20.6	43.1	1.6	0.0	. . .	1.1	86	10.9	7
Rush, KS	17.2	41.3	3.0	0.0	. . .	2.5	50	10.8	5
Russell, KS	16.7	38.7	5.5	0.0	. . .	3.2	88	11.7	8
Saline, KS	14.6	43.1	18.9	3.2	. . .	2.6	662	13.1	47
Scott, KS	15.1	42.3	13.4	13.0	. . .	1.7	72	13.2	6
Sedgwick, KS	13.8	49.4	36.6	7.3	. . .	6.3	4 858	16.2	204
Seward, KS	9.7	61.6	70.2	30.4	. . .	7.1	347	15.4	22
Shawnee, KS	15.6	42.5	28.3	2.0	. . .	3.5	2 020	13.3	109
Sheridan, KS	18.3	28.8	4.1	0.7	. . .	1.4	44	13.2	5
Sherman, KS	17.3	39.2	17.4	8.6	. . .	0.8	75	13.5	5
Smith, KS	17.7	41.2	3.8	0.0	. . .	0.4	65	10.2	6
Stafford, KS	19.9	49.1	18.5	7.8	. . .	1.6	86	12.4	9
Stanton, KS	10.6	52.6	41.0	28.6	. . .	. . .	39	12.8	4
Stevens, KS	9.5	48.8	41.2	17.8	. . .	2.4	106	12.9	11
Sumner, KS	16.2	40.1	8.1	0.1	. . .	2.6	323	13.8	33
Thomas, KS	16.5	37.2	5.7	0.6	. . .	1.2	93	13.2	9
Trego, KS	21.4	34.4	3.6	0.0	. . .	1.0	36	10.9	6
Wabaunsee, KS	17.2	28.9	1.7	0.0	. . .	1.3	79	12.8	5
Wallace, KS	13.6	43.4	6.7	3.0	. . .	. . .	40	9.2	4
Washington, KS	14.0	37.4	1.1	0.0	. . .	1.4	117	11.1	16
Wichita, KS	13.2	39.3	30.8	23.6	. . .	2.1	40	13.1	2
Wilson, KS	14.5	47.1	2.9	0.1	. . .	2.5	135	13.5	11
Woodson, KS	18.1	49.0	5.7	0.0	. . .	0.8	39	13.7	4
Wyandotte, KS	13.0	63.3	66.4	15.0	. . .	4.6	1 948	14.4	141

[2]IEP = Individual Education Program. See notes and definitions at the end of this section.
. . . = Not available.

Table C-1. Population, School, and Student Characteristics by County—Continued

STATE County	Revenue, 2003–2004				Current expenditures, 2003–2004			Resident population, 16 to 19 years, 2000			
	Total revenue (thousands of dollars)	Percent of revenue from:			Total expenditures (thousands of dollars)	Amount per student (dollars)	Percent for instruction	Total	Percent in armed forces	Percent high school graduates	Percent not enrolled, not employed, not in armed forces, not high school graduate
		Federal government	State government	Local government							
	19	20	21	22	23	24	25	26	27	28	29
Geary, KS	55 643	33.2	51.7	15.1	51 626	7 769	61.1	1 724	9.2	22.4	3.8
Gove, KS	7 703	4.1	68.8	27.2	7 008	9 898	65.6	179	0.0	6.1	2.2
Graham, KS	4 722	4.9	70.4	24.7	4 210	9 294	65.7	168	0.0	4.8	2.4
Grant, KS	16 686	7.6	13.6	78.8	12 736	6 948	64.6	510	0.0	11.8	6.7
Gray, KS	13 606	4.5	61.9	33.6	11 540	8 387	61.9	371	0.0	7.8	10.2
Greeley, KS	3 116	5.7	48.1	46.2	2 625	8 838	63.0	98	0.0	7.1	5.1
Greenwood, KS	11 984	5.4	50.3	44.2	9 570	8 307	64.1	455	0.0	11.0	11.4
Hamilton, KS	6 035	8.1	34.1	57.8	4 219	8 067	62.7	158	0.0	4.4	3.8
Harper, KS	11 225	7.7	64.3	27.9	10 056	8 837	63.2	378	0.0	9.0	1.9
Harvey, KS	51 382	5.1	63.8	31.1	42 068	6 865	64.0	2 099	0.0	8.9	2.0
Haskell, KS	10 750	4.9	21.9	73.3	8 112	8 808	64.2	288	0.0	11.1	3.1
Hodgeman, KS	4 638	5.2	68.0	26.8	4 052	9 956	64.1	143	0.0	9.1	1.4
Jackson, KS	23 380	8.0	71.7	20.3	19 456	7 672	65.7	743	0.0	12.5	2.4
Jefferson, KS	39 316	3.9	69.9	26.2	34 167	8 060	64.1	1 081	0.0	11.3	2.1
Jewell, KS	6 319	4.6	66.1	29.2	5 743	10 518	57.6	175	0.0	5.7	1.7
Johnson, KS	813 027	3.3	32.2	64.5	581 785	7 190	67.1	23 106	0.0	8.0	1.7
Kearny, KS	12 246	5.9	15.5	78.6	9 476	8 607	61.2	309	0.0	8.7	7.1
Kingman, KS	14 133	5.6	56.2	38.3	11 672	7 594	55.9	516	0.0	4.3	0.8
Kiowa, KS	7 213	4.3	53.6	42.1	6 233	9 458	61.2	217	0.0	8.3	0.9
Labette, KS	35 552	8.7	70.5	20.9	31 440	7 511	65.7	1 454	0.0	10.6	2.6
Lane, KS	4 455	4.4	58.0	37.7	3 840	10 213	61.1	112	0.0	1.8	2.7
Leavenworth, KS	103 230	12.8	57.4	29.8	83 800	6 625	63.4	3 602	1.1	12.5	3.1
Lincoln, KS	5 855	5.0	62.1	32.9	4 858	8 817	63.6	178	0.0	9.0	3.9
Linn, KS	21 281	4.8	47.3	47.9	18 289	8 726	61.5	531	0.0	18.3	3.8
Logan, KS	5 510	5.2	58.5	36.3	5 196	8 222	62.2	184	0.0	14.7	0.5
Lyon, KS	57 801	10.0	59.7	30.3	44 407	7 075	67.7	2 942	0.0	10.5	3.9
McPherson, KS	45 274	2.8	52.8	44.4	35 286	7 284	66.6	2 018	0.1	6.4	2.6
Marion, KS	24 772	4.6	66.0	29.3	20 147	8 562	65.1	823	0.0	6.0	2.9
Marshall, KS	22 373	5.9	62.2	31.8	19 200	8 897	64.0	685	0.0	7.7	1.9
Meade, KS	6 871	4.0	50.2	45.8	6 157	8 709	64.0	270	0.0	7.8	2.2
Miami, KS	44 062	3.9	52.2	43.9	34 677	7 135	62.4	1 588	0.2	8.8	2.3
Mitchell, KS	12 951	4.0	59.5	36.6	11 062	9 343	63.4	579	0.0	2.1	2.1
Montgomery, KS	45 324	8.3	64.6	27.0	40 397	7 227	63.8	2 291	0.0	7.4	3.9
Morris, KS	8 578	9.7	63.8	26.5	7 158	7 503	59.6	352	0.0	15.6	2.6
Morton, KS	12 271	8.7	25.6	65.7	8 837	9 472	65.2	233	0.0	5.6	2.6
Nemaha, KS	15 797	4.5	66.9	28.7	13 546	7 741	66.5	620	0.0	9.5	1.3
Neosho, KS	26 725	10.8	66.7	22.4	23 317	7 739	69.0	1 126	0.0	7.4	2.2
Ness, KS	6 158	4.0	56.6	39.3	5 223	9 690	60.4	164	0.0	4.3	0.0
Norton, KS	9 270	4.5	70.8	24.7	8 363	8 371	63.0	278	0.0	10.4	6.1
Osage, KS	28 115	4.2	72.8	23.0	23 369	7 377	63.3	944	1.0	13.2	2.0
Osborne, KS	4 391	5.7	68.3	26.0	3 620	8 744	66.2	240	0.0	5.0	0.8
Ottawa, KS	11 364	4.1	69.8	26.1	10 052	8 042	64.8	387	0.0	4.4	2.6
Pawnee, KS	12 092	4.4	62.8	32.7	10 138	8 893	60.4	594	0.0	11.1	15.0
Phillips, KS	10 604	4.0	69.2	26.8	9 250	9 325	65.3	316	0.0	7.0	2.2
Pottawatomie, KS	36 331	4.7	46.9	48.4	28 901	7 970	65.1	1 181	0.0	11.7	1.5
Pratt, KS	14 562	7.6	64.2	28.2	12 620	7 363	65.9	697	0.0	9.3	0.9
Rawlins, KS	4 856	4.0	63.0	33.0	4 302	10 649	65.6	187	0.0	7.2	1.7
Reno, KS	92 658	9.5	53.4	37.1	73 875	7 110	62.8	3 815	0.0	10.5	4.0
Republic, KS	9 515	4.8	65.3	30.0	8 550	9 542	62.4	275	0.0	4.4	0.0
Rice, KS	18 694	5.4	63.4	31.3	16 329	8 496	67.0	894	0.0	4.0	2.9
Riley, KS	60 524	12.1	44.6	43.3	52 958	8 368	64.2	6 991	9.5	15.9	1.9
Rooks, KS	9 536	4.6	64.9	30.5	8 849	9 151	63.2	314	0.0	13.4	3.2
Rush, KS	6 264	5.1	62.0	33.0	5 516	9 255	60.7	145	0.0	13.1	0.0
Russell, KS	11 051	8.7	59.5	31.9	10 052	8 497	62.1	431	0.0	6.5	0.2
Saline, KS	94 456	9.6	44.5	45.9	70 243	8 021	68.1	3 217	0.0	8.4	3.9
Scott, KS	10 125	3.4	44.5	52.0	7 697	8 051	66.8	297	0.0	6.1	5.7
Sedgwick, KS	698 178	9.8	54.7	35.5	565 228	7 188	62.6	25 400	0.6	11.2	5.4
Seward, KS	44 257	11.4	55.9	32.7	34 771	6 461	67.7	1 483	0.0	6.3	12.1
Shawnee, KS	240 004	11.0	50.2	38.7	205 893	7 661	64.3	9 610	0.0	13.8	5.9
Sheridan, KS	3 725	4.8	57.9	37.3	3 107	8 375	62.9	175	0.0	1.7	0.0
Sherman, KS	8 652	5.8	62.3	31.9	7 932	7 769	65.8	548	0.0	12.4	9.9
Smith, KS	6 979	5.0	67.7	27.3	6 467	9 318	68.2	253	0.0	2.8	3.2
Stafford, KS	11 742	5.2	59.2	35.7	9 616	8 742	62.0	272	0.0	6.6	7.4
Stanton, KS	5 399	6.5	24.8	68.7	4 730	8 891	59.0	138	0.0	8.0	8.0
Stevens, KS	12 686	6.2	12.6	81.2	10 877	7 649	63.4	420	0.0	6.2	2.4
Sumner, KS	43 008	6.0	68.2	25.9	34 413	7 607	67.1	1 637	0.0	11.6	2.1
Thomas, KS	13 164	4.3	63.5	32.3	11 762	8 112	64.0	632	0.0	4.1	0.9
Trego, KS	4 454	4.4	53.3	42.3	3 881	9 420	63.9	181	0.0	0.0	3.9
Wabaunsee, KS	11 541	5.3	56.6	38.2	8 877	8 931	61.1	374	0.0	8.3	3.7
Wallace, KS	4 371	6.9	59.0	34.1	3 725	9 987	61.9	133	0.0	12.8	1.5
Washington, KS	13 063	4.7	62.1	33.2	11 397	8 727	64.9	329	0.0	8.8	0.9
Wichita, KS	4 832	6.3	53.3	40.4	4 206	8 329	59.7	149	0.0	4.7	4.0
Wilson, KS	17 813	7.0	71.1	22.0	15 725	8 355	63.1	554	0.0	12.5	4.5
Woodson, KS	5 189	5.7	72.6	21.8	4 862	8 792	57.0	212	0.0	6.6	0.0
Wyandotte, KS	253 573	10.1	56.0	33.8	217 233	7 664	64.5	9 384	0.0	14.5	10.6

Table C-1. Population, School, and Student Characteristics by County—*Continued*

STATE County	High school graduates, 2000			College enrollment, 2000		College graduates, 2000 (percent)						
	Population 25 years and over	High school graduate or less (percent)	High school graduate or more (percent)	Number	Percent public	Bachelor's degree or more	+/- U.S. percentage with bachelor's degree or more	Non-Hispanic White	Black	American Indian and Alaska Native	Asian or Pacific Islander	Hispanic[3]
	30	31	32	33	34	35	36	37	38	39	40	41
Geary, KS	15 744	44.0	86.0	1 899	90.2	17.1	-7.3	19.4	10.3	21.3	14.6	12.8
Gove, KS	2 120	50.7	84.5	61	95.1	18.4	-6.0	18.7	0.0	0.0	...	0.0
Graham, KS	2 125	50.4	83.6	81	91.4	17.4	-7.0	17.0	20.6	22.2	66.7	37.5
Grant, KS	4 712	56.5	71.5	199	75.4	15.2	-9.2	19.6	...	18.2	...	3.7
Gray, KS	3 536	52.1	73.6	133	93.2	16.3	-8.1	17.2	0.0	0.0	...	5.8
Greeley, KS	983	45.6	83.7	19	100.0	17.4	-7.0	18.6	...	0.0	...	1.5
Greenwood, KS	5 343	57.7	80.9	168	88.1	14.5	-9.9	14.8	...	5.7	6.9	0.0
Hamilton, KS	1 727	53.7	76.7	63	92.1	17.4	-7.0	20.0	0.0	0.0	25.0	2.2
Harper, KS	4 462	55.3	83.8	144	89.6	14.0	-10.4	13.9	44.0	0.0	33.3	11.8
Harvey, KS	21 278	44.9	85.3	1 711	49.6	23.0	-1.4	24.3	19.8	2.1	12.7	5.3
Haskell, KS	2 505	50.6	74.8	128	94.5	17.5	-6.9	20.7	0.0	0.0	70.4	0.9
Hodgeman, KS	1 376	43.8	86.9	64	78.1	19.7	-4.7	20.3	0.0	0.0	...	0.0
Jackson, KS	8 228	58.2	87.7	305	70.5	15.4	-9.0	15.8	11.4	11.9	63.6	10.2
Jefferson, KS	12 127	53.7	88.9	491	77.8	17.9	-6.5	17.9	17.4	30.4	20.0	19.8
Jewell, KS	2 798	51.9	87.6	73	95.9	13.8	-10.6	13.4	0.0	0.0	100.0	18.8
Johnson, KS	295 829	22.6	94.9	24 951	76.2	47.7	23.3	48.5	41.1	26.6	59.4	25.3
Kearny, KS	2 592	51.9	75.8	134	82.8	15.0	-9.4	17.8	0.0	25.0	100.0	3.7
Kingman, KS	5 809	49.0	84.7	248	89.1	17.8	-6.6	17.5	100.0	40.0	85.7	20.0
Kiowa, KS	2 227	44.8	85.2	150	48.7	18.9	-5.5	19.2	...	0.0	33.3	0.0
Labette, KS	15 007	48.9	83.0	1 066	98.1	15.9	-8.5	16.1	5.1	11.4	80.0	19.3
Lane, KS	1 491	45.6	88.5	28	92.9	18.5	-5.9	18.7	0.0	...	50.0	16.7
Leavenworth, KS	44 792	47.4	86.5	3 720	73.8	23.1	-1.3	24.1	16.4	11.1	22.6	15.1
Lincoln, KS	2 548	50.6	85.0	101	85.1	17.4	-7.0	17.6	0.0	0.0	33.3	17.6
Linn, KS	6 538	58.6	80.9	183	84.2	12.7	-11.7	12.7	7.7	0.0	100.0	12.5
Logan, KS	2 058	52.0	86.7	86	83.7	17.5	-6.9	17.5	0.0	100.0	100.0	6.9
Lyon, KS	20 559	50.0	81.8	4 142	97.9	23.0	-1.4	25.9	9.9	11.7	14.2	5.3
McPherson, KS	19 078	46.2	85.9	1 897	80.3	22.2	-2.2	22.0	20.6	30.8	42.9	18.4
Marion, KS	9 000	54.2	84.4	680	39.7	17.9	-6.5	18.3	0.0	0.0	0.0	6.8
Marshall, KS	7 460	60.6	85.1	153	88.9	13.2	-11.2	13.4	0.0	0.0	3.3	0.0
Meade, KS	2 946	48.2	80.3	146	93.2	19.6	-4.8	20.8	0.0	20.0	11.1	5.3
Miami, KS	18 444	49.2	87.5	838	88.1	19.4	-5.0	19.7	7.1	17.9	06.2	4.7
Mitchell, KS	4 645	48.1	88.1	374	97.3	16.9	-7.5	16.8	...	0.0	77.8	0.0
Montgomery, KS	24 090	49.0	81.2	1 733	93.4	16.0	-8.4	17.1	5.1	8.9	20.2	6.0
Morris, KS	4 224	56.1	84.7	133	97.7	16.0	-8.4	16.2	0.0	0.0	0.0	13.7
Morton, KS	2 165	52.7	81.9	108	89.8	17.6	-6.8	18.1	0.0	14.7	70.2	1.0
Nemaha, KS	7 039	63.5	87.7	224	95.5	14.6	-9.8	14.7	10.5	0.0	67.5	0.0
Neosho, KS	11 113	51.7	83.5	751	97.5	15.0	-9.4	15.1	12.9	29.9	0.0	2.7
Ness, KS	2 498	52.1	84.4	92	92.4	17.9	-6.5	18.1	0.0	...	50.0	0.0
Norton, KS	4 178	52.8	84.8	138	71.7	15.4	-9.0	16.5	0.0	0.0	58.3	0.0
Osage, KS	11 117	56.8	85.5	581	87.4	14.3	-10.1	14.5	0.0	10.0	29.7	7.6
Osborne, KS	3 115	55.5	84.8	72	97.2	15.5	-8.9	15.4	...	60.0	30.0	0.0
Ottawa, KS	4 228	51.7	86.2	149	83.2	16.3	-8.1	16.5	0.0	0.0	37.5	13.3
Pawnee, KS	4 875	45.0	84.8	177	91.0	21.8	-2.6	22.2	15.3	7.0	100.0	4.9
Phillips, KS	4 182	52.5	84.4	124	96.8	16.1	-8.3	16.2	0.0	0.0	30.8	11.1
Pottawatomie, KS	11 441	48.2	89.2	822	88.7	22.7	-1.7	22.8	3.2	16.0	0.0	21.7
Pratt, KS	6 365	41.4	86.3	533	92.7	21.0	-3.4	21.5	29.3	0.0	0.0	5.1
Rawlins, KS	2 152	49.9	84.7	36	88.9	15.9	-8.5	16.1	0.0	0.0	0.0	0.0
Reno, KS	43 082	47.8	82.7	2 673	90.8	17.3	-7.1	18.1	8.6	7.4	23.6	6.0
Republic, KS	4 256	52.7	88.6	110	83.6	14.9	-9.5	14.9	0.0	18.2	0.0	0.0
Rice, KS	6 701	50.2	83.4	989	73.0	17.5	-6.9	18.1	8.3	18.2	33.3	4.9
Riley, KS	29 358	28.6	93.8	19 026	97.4	40.5	16.1	41.5	18.8	36.7	69.1	23.1
Rooks, KS	3 901	54.3	87.1	100	98.0	15.4	-9.0	15.8	0.0	28.6	0.0	0.0
Rush, KS	2 568	49.6	82.8	104	96.2	16.4	-8.0	16.4	...	0.0	50.0	0.0
Russell, KS	5 323	52.7	83.1	135	88.1	16.7	-7.7	17.0	...	0.0	0.0	0.0
Saline, KS	34 680	47.5	87.0	2 260	72.4	20.4	-4.0	21.2	17.0	15.0	12.6	8.5
Scott, KS	3 376	44.3	84.5	130	91.5	23.0	-1.4	23.5	100.0	100.0	0.0	0.0
Sedgwick, KS	282 585	44.2	85.1	27 503	81.1	25.4	1.0	28.0	13.1	13.9	23.8	10.0
Seward, KS	12 690	63.1	63.7	766	91.5	13.6	-10.8	19.8	9.3	7.4	22.6	2.5
Shawnee, KS	111 709	45.5	88.1	8 815	77.4	26.0	1.6	28.0	12.2	15.5	48.7	13.9
Sheridan, KS	1 905	48.8	87.8	63	98.4	15.9	-8.5	15.6	...	0.0	100.0	33.3
Sherman, KS	4 319	49.3	86.6	484	95.5	15.0	-9.4	16.2	0.0	0.0	...	0.0
Smith, KS	3 338	53.4	84.6	69	76.8	16.7	-7.7	16.6	0.0	0.0	45.0	0.0
Stafford, KS	3 254	46.2	82.9	108	89.8	18.4	-6.0	19.1	0.0	9.5	17.6	1.7
Stanton, KS	1 468	53.0	78.0	50	76.0	16.9	-7.5	19.6	0.0	12.5	100.0	4.6
Stevens, KS	3 287	51.5	80.5	184	92.4	17.5	-6.9	19.7	...	26.5	50.0	3.3
Sumner, KS	16 662	51.4	86.3	997	81.1	15.7	-8.7	16.1	12.6	4.9	22.7	3.6
Thomas, KS	4 978	37.5	92.7	745	94.4	25.0	0.6	25.0	0.0	...	56.0	7.1
Trego, KS	2 342	53.3	84.3	131	81.7	14.0	-10.4	14.1	...	0.0	0.0	0.0
Wabaunsee, KS	4 623	55.6	89.9	195	91.3	17.3	-7.1	17.4	0.0	0.0	55.6	28.2
Wallace, KS	1 133	52.7	84.0	31	100.0	17.2	-7.2	17.9	0.0	0.0	...	4.2
Washington, KS	4 572	56.9	81.2	139	90.6	15.2	-9.2	15.3	0.0	16.7	...	0.0
Wichita, KS	1 625	55.1	77.7	37	81.1	15.5	-8.9	17.2	...	33.3	0.0	5.1
Wilson, KS	6 944	56.1	81.1	264	92.4	10.9	-13.5	10.7	0.0	2.2	27.8	22.2
Woodson, KS	2 667	56.8	83.4	120	100.0	11.4	-13.0	11.1	0.0	0.0	55.0	20.0
Wyandotte, KS	96 608	60.3	74.0	6 959	84.1	12.0	-12.4	13.8	10.6	3.7	21.0	5.6

[3]May be of any race.
... = Not available.

Table C-1. Population, School, and Student Characteristics by County—*Continued*

STATE County	State/ county code	County type[1]	Population, 2005		Number of schools and students, 2004–2005			Resident enrollment, 2000			
			Total	Percent 5 to 17 years	School districts	Schools	Students	Total	Percent public	K–12	Percent public
			1	2	3	4	5	6	7	8	9
KENTUCKY	21000		4 173 405	17.0	196	1 457	674 796	1 007 452	85.3	738 747	88.3
Adair, KY	21001	7	17 573	16.2	1	8	2 794	4 198	77.2	2 934	92.0
Allen, KY	21003	6	18 706	17.7	1	4	3 080	3 983	91.1	3 357	92.9
Anderson, KY	21005	6	20 394	18.9	1	6	4 054	4 641	93.2	3 715	95.4
Ballard, KY	21007	9	8 277	16.0	1	4	1 516	1 785	96.0	1 417	96.8
Barren, KY	21009	6	40 073	16.8	3	21	7 231	8 256	90.5	6 748	92.9
Bath, KY	21011	8	11 626	17.0	1	5	2 086	2 341	94.9	1 962	95.5
Bell, KY	21013	7	29 665	16.6	3	15	5 632	6 872	91.7	5 616	94.2
Boone, KY	21015	1	106 272	19.4	2	21	17 612	23 160	77.5	17 525	81.0
Bourbon, KY	21017	2	19 833	17.8	2	10	3 777	4 539	91.9	3 554	93.1
Boyd, KY	21019	2	49 594	15.3	5	20	7 743	11 748	89.7	8 720	92.0
Boyle, KY	21021	7	28 363	16.1	3	13	4 783	7 043	79.4	4 994	95.0
Bracken, KY	21023	1	8 670	17.3	2	4	1 589	1 978	93.1	1 606	93.0
Breathitt, KY	21025	7	15 957	17.5	2	10	2 951	4 131	90.3	3 269	92.6
Breckinridge, KY	21027	8	19 293	17.1	2	9	3 108	4 228	88.6	3 621	89.1
Bullitt, KY	21029	1	68 474	18.6	1	23	11 849	14 974	85.7	12 247	88.8
Butler, KY	21031	8	13 414	17.2	1	8	2 273	2 925	96.3	2 482	97.2
Caldwell, KY	21033	6	12 973	15.9	1	4	2 110	2 797	93.2	2 182	96.2
Calloway, KY	21035	7	35 122	12.4	4	10	4 831	11 875	95.1	5 013	96.5
Campbell, KY	21037	1	87 251	17.8	8	31	12 073	23 663	76.0	16 747	74.8
Carlisle, KY	21039	9	5 329	15.6	1	3	883	1 185	89.8	956	91.2
Carroll, KY	21041	6	10 454	17.2	1	5	1 984	2 243	90.6	1 768	92.2
Carter, KY	21043	6	27 306	17.0	1	11	5 232	6 517	87.5	4 789	95.8
Casey, KY	21045	9	16 290	16.9	2	9	2 534	3 103	90.7	2 740	91.4
Christian, KY	21047	3	70 145	20.6	1	20	9 542	18 278	88.3	13 514	89.4
Clark, KY	21049	2	34 887	17.1	1	12	5 598	7 482	86.2	6 084	89.5
Clay, KY	21051	7	24 146	17.3	1	11	4 180	5 678	89.9	4 815	89.5
Clinton, KY	21053	9	9 559	15.4	1	3	1 746	2 011	95.3	1 570	96.6
Crittenden, KY	21055	6	8 984	16.0	1	3	1 389	2 030	89.5	1 663	90.7
Cumberland, KY	21057	9	7 147	16.1	1	3	1 168	1 566	95.8	1 375	98.5
Daviess, KY	21059	3	93 060	17.6	3	35	16 281	23 030	78.9	17 533	82.8
Edmonson, KY	21061	3	12 030	16.2	1	6	2 127	2 541	98.4	2 170	98.9
Elliott, KY	21063	9	6 902	17.4	1	4	1 240	1 524	97.8	1 251	98.5
Estill, KY	21065	6	15 089	16.7	1	5	2 608	3 394	95.9	2 847	97.6
Fayette, KY	21067	2	268 080	14.6	3	64	35 004	76 330	84.6	40 156	85.6
Fleming, KY	21069	7	14 610	17.6	1	6	2 652	3 295	91.8	2 635	94.7
Floyd, KY	21071	7	42 218	15.8	1	17	6 925	9 447	91.7	7 480	94.5
Franklin, KY	21073	4	48 207	15.5	2	16	7 021	11 593	84.0	8 273	84.9
Fulton, KY	21075	7	7 217	17.1	2	5	1 211	1 835	94.0	1 546	96.2
Gallatin, KY	21077	1	8 134	20.1	1	5	1 586	1 911	92.0	1 630	94.3
Garrard, KY	21079	6	16 579	17.0	1	5	2 651	3 317	92.6	2 688	93.9
Grant, KY	21081	1	24 610	19.6	2	8	4 829	5 436	91.7	4 684	94.3
Graves, KY	21083	7	37 625	17.4	2	19	6 349	8 421	88.9	6 694	90.3
Grayson, KY	21085	6	25 189	16.7	1	7	4 395	5 375	94.0	4 304	96.1
Green, KY	21087	8	11 588	15.6	1	5	1 716	2 523	91.8	2 001	96.1
Greenup, KY	21089	2	37 184	16.3	3	16	6 501	8 244	91.8	6 591	95.5
Hancock, KY	21091	3	8 613	18.8	1	6	1 644	1 977	91.0	1 641	95.4
Hardin, KY	21093	3	96 947	18.7	3	30	16 392	25 768	89.6	19 560	92.6
Harlan, KY	21095	7	31 614	17.3	2	14	6 038	7 775	94.0	6 320	95.3
Harrison, KY	21097	6	18 527	17.0	1	7	3 365	4 119	92.9	3 420	94.6
Hart, KY	21099	8	18 319	17.6	1	6	2 563	3 765	91.8	3 178	92.2
Henderson, KY	21101	2	45 573	16.8	1	12	7 183	10 565	88.2	8 367	90.0
Henry, KY	21103	1	15 903	17.6	2	7	2 860	3 368	88.9	2 770	92.2
Hickman, KY	21105	9	5 075	15.6	1	2	842	1 077	97.2	923	98.8
Hopkins, KY	21107	4	46 705	16.8	3	17	8 187	10 750	90.9	8 418	92.9
Jackson, KY	21109	9	13 618	17.6	1	6	2 422	2 999	93.8	2 680	95.1
Jefferson, KY	21111	1	699 827	17.1	4	173	98 421	175 028	75.3	123 874	78.0
Jessamine, KY	21113	2	43 463	18.2	1	11	7 154	11 132	71.7	7 372	87.9
Johnson, KY	21115	7	24 001	16.2	2	12	4 705	5 335	95.9	4 333	97.0
Kenton, KY	21117	1	153 665	18.4	5	43	21 822	38 232	71.7	28 640	73.4
Knott, KY	21119	9	17 561	16.4	1	10	2 975	4 684	88.9	3 352	94.6
Knox, KY	21121	7	32 069	18.1	3	22	8 242	7 599	90.0	6 176	96.8
Larue, KY	21123	3	13 699	17.0	1	6	2 445	3 123	91.3	2 527	92.7
Laurel, KY	21125	7	56 338	17.5	2	18	9 597	11 653	91.1	9 704	93.7
Lawrence, KY	21127	6	16 166	17.2	1	5	2 686	3 631	96.7	3 083	97.2
Lee, KY	21129	9	7 709	15.2	1	5	1 290	1 738	86.0	1 513	87.0
Leslie, KY	21131	9	11 994	16.5	1	7	2 283	2 862	93.5	2 347	95.2
Letcher, KY	21133	9	24 434	15.8	2	16	4 502	5 801	94.8	4 656	95.8
Lewis, KY	21135	8	13 872	17.3	1	7	2 662	3 393	95.0	2 737	96.6
Lincoln, KY	21137	7	25 122	17.7	1	10	4 637	5 338	94.4	4 377	96.6
Livingston, KY	21139	9	9 760	15.4	1	7	1 418	2 160	94.4	1 758	95.4
Logan, KY	21141	6	27 169	17.9	2	9	4 847	5 915	92.2	4 992	92.3
Lyon, KY	21143	8	8 160	11.3	1	3	1 045	1 466	84.0	1 240	83.0
McCracken, KY	21145	5	64 698	16.4	2	21	10 153	15 279	86.2	11 690	89.5
McCreary, KY	21147	9	17 233	18.9	1	14	3 390	4 288	93.9	3 653	93.9
McLean, KY	21149	3	9 926	16.6	1	5	1 697	2 167	92.2	1 740	96.3
Madison, KY	21151	2	77 749	15.3	3	21	11 457	22 171	87.8	11 078	91.8
Magoffin, KY	21153	9	13 472	17.5	1	8	2 517	3 284	96.8	2 717	97.6
Marion, KY	21155	6	18 939	17.2	1	7	3 274	4 229	86.3	3 538	89.9
Marshall, KY	21157	7	30 967	15.0	1	11	4 812	6 568	90.5	5 122	93.5
Martin, KY	21159	8	12 215	18.7	1	7	3 038	3 166	97.8	2 630	99.5

[1]County type codes are from the Economic Research Service of the United States Department of Agriculture. See notes and definitions at the end of this section.

Table C-1. Population, School, and Student Characteristics by County—*Continued*

STATE County	Characteristics of students, 2004–2005				Outcomes		Staff and students, 2004–2005		
	Percent with IEP[2]	Percent eligible for free or reduced-price lunch	Percent minority	Percent English-language learners	Number of graduates, 2003–2004	Percent dropouts, grades 9–12, 2001–2002	Number of teachers	Student-teacher ratio	Central administration staff
	10	11	12	13	14	15	16	17	18
KENTUCKY	15.8	...	13.4	1.6	...	4.0	41 463	16.3	...
Adair, KY	17.3	...	5.0	1.1	185	5.0	197	14.2	20
Allen, KY	13.0	...	1.4	0.0	187	4.2	174	17.7	22
Anderson, KY	19.7	...	3.4	0.3	231	4.0	211	19.2	21
Ballard, KY	21.9	...	4.9	0.0	95	2.3	90	16.8	10
Barren, KY	16.2	...	6.8	0.6	428	4.1	448	16.1	44
Bath, KY	12.1	...	2.6	0.4	99	5.8	123	17.0	18
Bell, KY	17.3	...	2.9	0.1	342	6.0	399	14.1	39
Boone, KY	13.8	...	6.4	1.9	888	1.9	1 003	17.6	56
Bourbon, KY	13.4	...	12.7	1.1	200	2.3	225	16.8	27
Boyd, KY	17.7	...	4.0	0.1	...	2.6	508	15.2	60
Boyle, KY	20.4	...	12.3	1.3	277	2.4	309	15.5	46
Bracken, KY	15.8	...	1.7	0.0	105	1.5	100	15.9	18
Breathitt, KY	20.0	...	1.6	0.1	149	4.7	195	15.1	28
Breckinridge, KY	18.0	...	3.9	0.3	204	2.4	169	18.4	34
Bullitt, KY	14.1	...	1.5	0.2	634	4.2	657	18.0	47
Butler, KY	15.9	...	1.9	0.1	136	2.1	140	16.2	11
Caldwell, KY	14.7	...	8.0	0.1	135	2.5	140	15.1	20
Calloway, KY	17.6	...	7.2	1.1	...	1.6	317	15.2	47
Campbell, KY	17.3	...	4.1	0.8	...	2.4	750	16.1	90
Carlisle, KY	17.3	...	2.9	0.0	51	2.0	56	15.8	7
Carroll, KY	15.7	...	7.0	2.8	88	4.8	117	17.0	17
Carter, KY	17.8	...	0.9	0.1	235	3.0	345	15.2	25
Casey, KY	16.4	...	2.7	0.2	...	5.0	154	16.5	18
Christian, KY	15.8	...	38.9	1.1	540	4.5	544	17.5	55
Clark, KY	14.5	...	8.5	0.7	268	6.5	339	16.5	27
Clay, KY	21.6	...	1.1	0.0	180	8.8	312	13.4	23
Clinton, KY	21.0	...	1.9	0.9	87	4.8	107	16.3	20
Crittenden, KY	19.2	...	1.9	0.0	96	1.8	87	16.0	18
Cumberland, KY	18.5	...	2.7	0.0	56	4.8	75	15.6	11
Daviess, KY	16.9	...	8.6	0.7	...	2.1	977	16.7	113
Edmonson, KY	20.8	...	1.7	0.0	111	4.6	145	14.7	15
Elliott, KY	22.7	...	0.7	0.0	61	4.6	84	14.8	10
Estill, KY	19.1	...	1.0	0.1	158	4.8	172	15.2	12
Fayette, KY	10.5	...	32.6	4.7	...	5.0	2 502	14.0	164
Fleming, KY	14.1	...	3.5	0.5	139	4.6	164	16.2	15
Floyd, KY	18.9	...	1.8	0.1	383	6.1	443	15.6	55
Franklin, KY	14.9	...	13.6	1.0	441	2.9	435	16.1	44
Fulton, KY	21.4	...	37.9	0.0	68	3.4	95	12.7	15
Gallatin, KY	18.7	...	3.8	2.6	72	2.8	92	17.2	12
Garrard, KY	15.9	...	5.0	2.5	147	4.5	167	15.9	16
Grant, KY	13.5	...	1.8	0.6	208	3.4	265	18.2	28
Graves, KY	15.2	...	13.3	3.7	363	2.4	381	16.7	34
Grayson, KY	13.9	...	1.2	0.1	251	4.5	269	16.3	15
Green, KY	15.9	...	3.4	0.1	118	1.6	113	15.2	9
Greenup, KY	14.3	...	1.7	0.0	381	2.6	383	17.0	46
Hancock, KY	15.1	...	2.2	0.7	87	...	97	16.9	16
Hardin, KY	16.0	...	20.8	0.9	...	3.4	1 016	16.1	86
Harlan, KY	16.5	...	3.2	0.0	341	6.5	383	15.8	43
Harrison, KY	16.0	...	4.5	0.6	206	2.9	179	18.8	30
Hart, KY	18.8	...	7.3	0.1	156	4.8	163	15.7	13
Henderson, KY	16.4	...	11.3	0.4	449	4.8	438	16.4	36
Henry, KY	12.8	...	7.5	2.2	161	3.6	166	17.2	26
Hickman, KY	21.6	...	14.0	0.0	46	2.8	56	15.0	7
Hopkins, KY	21.2	...	11.4	0.2	...	4.3	536	15.3	50
Jackson, KY	21.9	...	0.5	0.0	144	4.7	163	14.9	26
Jefferson, KY	14.1	...	40.6	4.1	...	5.9	5 742	17.1	458
Jessamine, KY	17.0	...	5.1	1.0	381	5.3	441	16.2	39
Johnson, KY	15.7	...	0.4	0.0	272	3.1	301	15.6	30
Kenton, KY	15.7	...	9.0	1.1	1 206	2.0	1 312	16.6	134
Knott, KY	17.4	...	1.2	0.0	179	4.5	179	16.6	16
Knox, KY	15.3	...	1.5	0.0	476	4.8	507	16.3	55
Larue, KY	18.5	...	6.2	0.9	138	4.1	152	16.1	15
Laurel, KY	17.2	...	2.0	0.4	...	5.7	536	17.9	48
Lawrence, KY	18.1	...	0.5	0.0	145	3.4	181	14.8	17
Lee, KY	16.9	...	0.7	0.0	74	3.1	80	16.1	13
Leslie, KY	17.7	...	0.2	0.0	134	3.0	130	17.6	17
Letcher, KY	20.2	...	1.7	0.0	242	4.6	271	16.6	35
Lewis, KY	15.8	...	0.5	0.0	134	4.0	168	15.8	16
Lincoln, KY	22.3	...	3.6	0.4	289	6.8	305	15.2	30
Livingston, KY	17.6	...	0.9	1.7	60	5.9	96	14.8	8
Logan, KY	18.3	...	10.7	0.7	274	2.6	297	16.3	30
Lyon, KY	17.0	...	3.8	0.3	67	0.7	62	16.9	7
McCracken, KY	14.1	...	20.5	0.7	598	3.0	617	16.5	54
McCreary, KY	18.0	...	2.1	0.0	223	4.3	227	14.9	29
McLean, KY	15.1	...	0.8	0.1	110	2.2	107	15.9	11
Madison, KY	19.6	...	8.0	0.4	...	1.7	671	17.1	49
Magoffin, KY	17.3	...	0.3	0.0	132	5.3	169	14.9	25
Marion, KY	17.3	...	10.1	1.2	184	4.1	206	15.9	19
Marshall, KY	13.0	...	0.6	0.0	293	2.5	310	15.5	33
Martin, KY	17.9	...	0.6	0.0	136	5.7	158	19.2	16

[2]IEP = Individual Education Program. See notes and definitions at the end of this section.
... = Not available.

Table C-1. Population, School, and Student Characteristics by County—*Continued*

STATE County	Revenue, 2003–2004				Current expenditures, 2003–2004			Resident population, 16 to 19 years, 2000			
	Total revenue (thousands of dollars)	Percent of revenue from:			Total expenditures (thousands of dollars)	Amount per student (dollars)	Percent for instruction	Total	Percent in armed forces	Percent high school graduates	Percent not enrolled, not employed, not in armed forces, not high school graduate
		Federal government	State government	Local government							
	19	20	21	22	23	24	25	26	27	28	29
KENTUCKY	5 135 262	11.8	57.8	30.4	4 573 150	6 888	64.7	228 979	0.8	11.9	7.1
Adair, KY	21 322	14.4	69.8	15.7	19 024	6 935	67.4	1 172	0.0	8.2	9.4
Allen, KY	21 119	10.0	71.6	18.4	18 141	5 919	66.1	1 015	0.0	15.5	9.4
Anderson, KY	26 015	8.1	61.6	30.3	22 250	5 581	68.1	900	0.0	11.7	4.2
Ballard, KY	11 482	12.5	65.3	22.2	9 915	6 451	61.4	380	0.0	9.2	3.7
Barren, KY	52 891	11.0	61.2	27.8	47 343	6 678	65.7	2 012	0.0	14.4	7.9
Bath, KY	14 723	12.7	71.3	15.9	12 561	6 228	63.9	621	0.8	8.2	11.4
Bell, KY	44 850	18.8	67.6	13.6	39 867	7 024	65.4	1 676	0.0	10.1	10.6
Boone, KY	123 224	5.1	40.4	54.5	99 380	5 994	63.7	4 691	0.0	13.2	6.0
Bourbon, KY	28 330	16.3	58.5	25.2	24 624	6 657	67.0	932	0.0	7.9	7.1
Boyd, KY	61 150	15.9	60.7	23.4	54 154	6 992	67.8	2 790	0.0	10.4	4.5
Boyle, KY	38 643	11.0	58.9	30.1	34 887	7 373	68.5	1 635	0.0	10.9	7.3
Bracken, KY	11 590	12.5	70.8	16.7	9 836	6 257	66.9	410	0.0	7.3	4.6
Breathitt, KY	24 724	18.4	71.1	10.5	21 842	7 404	64.0	1 033	0.0	13.7	8.9
Breckinridge, KY	24 778	16.2	62.5	21.3	21 498	6 939	60.1	1 038	0.0	10.0	4.1
Bullitt, KY	77 939	8.0	60.9	31.1	65 856	5 708	69.5	3 475	0.4	12.5	3.2
Butler, KY	16 532	11.4	72.4	16.2	14 332	6 356	64.2	824	0.0	12.6	3.2
Caldwell, KY	15 901	11.7	69.9	18.4	13 978	6 682	64.2	722	0.0	10.2	4.3
Calloway, KY	36 299	11.3	62.1	26.6	32 627	6 738	66.4	2 686	0.0	9.1	1.7
Campbell, KY	94 663	9.2	51.9	38.9	84 723	6 955	64.9	5 010	0.0	11.0	5.9
Carlisle, KY	6 234	11.9	72.5	15.6	5 713	6 390	65.1	275	0.0	12.0	6.2
Carroll, KY	16 607	13.9	48.8	37.3	13 681	7 074	63.4	532	0.0	15.0	11.8
Carter, KY	38 885	13.9	73.8	12.3	34 397	6 743	64.0	1 586	0.0	12.2	5.9
Casey, KY	18 998	16.0	69.3	14.7	16 872	6 779	65.8	807	0.0	13.8	12.4
Christian, KY	68 315	13.8	66.0	20.2	59 030	6 231	63.4	4 276	21.3	31.5	8.2
Clark, KY	36 630	10.4	58.5	31.1	33 994	6 173	63.6	1 844	0.0	11.9	10.5
Clay, KY	34 273	18.5	71.1	10.5	32 208	7 614	63.4	1 504	0.0	13.3	16.8
Clinton, KY	14 660	21.3	62.3	16.4	12 619	7 388	66.0	470	0.0	14.0	11.1
Crittenden, KY	10 419	12.4	68.3	19.3	9 352	6 690	61.3	534	0.9	12.7	20.0
Cumberland, KY	9 296	17.1	67.3	15.6	8 345	6 983	64.8	372	0.0	6.7	9.9
Daviess, KY	118 164	10.7	60.0	29.3	107 121	6 981	65.3	5 545	0.0	10.5	3.1
Edmonson, KY	16 957	14.8	69.1	16.1	14 649	6 795	64.8	675	0.0	11.6	5.9
Elliott, KY	11 108	14.7	75.8	9.5	9 930	8 100	59.7	400	0.0	17.3	11.3
Estill, KY	19 797	14.4	73.0	12.6	17 839	6 882	65.6	873	0.0	7.3	14.4
Fayette, KY	286 988	7.6	39.2	53.2	261 805	7 642	64.8	15 177	0.2	8.0	4.9
Fleming, KY	18 642	14.2	70.3	15.5	16 457	6 125	66.3	806	0.0	10.8	10.5
Floyd, KY	57 902	18.5	65.9	15.5	49 996	7 062	61.1	2 405	0.0	11.2	13.7
Franklin, KY	53 389	7.9	54.2	37.9	44 511	6 382	63.7	2 671	0.0	10.1	6.4
Fulton, KY	12 485	21.1	60.9	17.9	11 426	8 810	66.9	443	0.0	17.6	7.0
Gallatin, KY	11 811	11.6	63.0	25.4	10 303	6 356	57.8	445	0.0	12.8	13.5
Garrard, KY	19 983	10.7	65.5	23.9	17 318	6 733	65.6	836	0.0	19.1	8.5
Grant, KY	33 636	10.8	67.0	22.3	28 887	6 088	64.1	1 275	0.0	17.5	5.3
Graves, KY	44 106	11.7	66.2	22.1	38 855	6 213	63.6	1 907	0.0	12.0	8.5
Grayson, KY	29 667	11.9	69.3	18.9	26 016	5 945	66.4	1 296	0.0	14.4	8.2
Green, KY	12 833	12.2	71.6	16.1	11 442	6 606	63.5	557	0.0	9.3	3.1
Greenup, KY	47 949	10.2	67.6	22.2	41 922	6 521	62.9	1 879	0.0	11.4	4.5
Hancock, KY	12 313	8.5	56.7	34.8	11 693	7 205	59.3	434	0.0	6.2	2.8
Hardin, KY	117 057	9.2	65.3	25.5	103 893	6 514	65.7	6 193	12.9	25.3	3.3
Harlan, KY	44 826	16.7	69.3	14.0	40 904	6 860	66.6	1 960	0.0	9.3	15.5
Harrison, KY	21 275	10.7	67.0	22.3	17 869	5 453	63.1	978	0.0	8.4	2.6
Hart, KY	19 032	12.5	70.9	16.5	16 300	6 471	60.9	847	0.0	16.9	9.8
Henderson, KY	52 544	9.7	62.5	27.7	47 630	6 769	63.4	2 613	0.0	14.8	6.9
Henry, KY	20 274	11.3	65.8	22.9	18 233	6 456	63.2	774	0.0	15.8	7.8
Hickman, KY	6 774	15.2	63.5	21.2	5 832	6 918	61.8	261	0.0	4.2	6.1
Hopkins, KY	60 870	10.4	69.7	19.9	54 059	6 644	65.8	2 442	0.0	14.4	8.1
Jackson, KY	20 675	17.8	73.1	9.1	18 744	7 669	64.0	768	0.0	15.2	16.0
Jefferson, KY	847 508	12.0	41.5	46.5	807 167	8 405	63.8	35 085	0.1	10.6	6.7
Jessamine, KY	53 491	8.9	57.6	33.5	45 560	6 372	66.7	2 362	0.0	9.7	3.9
Johnson, KY	36 023	14.5	67.8	17.7	30 355	6 471	68.0	1 332	0.0	8.2	9.9
Kenton, KY	166 378	9.9	48.8	41.3	142 387	6 597	63.1	7 870	0.0	12.7	5.4
Knott, KY	23 734	19.2	64.0	16.8	21 740	7 208	67.3	1 250	0.0	6.0	11.1
Knox, KY	43 856	17.6	69.4	13.0	38 761	6 616	63.9	1 734	0.0	10.0	16.5
Larue, KY	18 254	10.9	70.5	18.6	15 295	6 344	66.9	663	0.0	8.6	2.7
Laurel, KY	66 715	13.2	67.2	19.6	57 572	6 031	66.0	2 800	0.0	16.6	10.4
Lawrence, KY	21 553	16.5	70.1	13.5	18 733	6 925	68.1	978	0.0	8.0	10.7
Lee, KY	10 822	19.9	69.0	11.1	10 235	7 570	63.5	431	0.0	16.9	16.0
Leslie, KY	19 685	16.1	68.1	15.8	17 220	7 653	59.7	682	0.0	8.7	7.5
Letcher, KY	34 231	16.3	67.5	16.2	31 509	7 182	62.0	1 577	0.0	11.0	10.3
Lewis, KY	20 038	16.9	70.5	12.6	18 004	6 781	61.7	838	0.0	19.1	6.4
Lincoln, KY	34 203	16.0	71.1	13.0	31 977	7 048	70.3	1 166	0.0	14.9	6.4
Livingston, KY	11 459	9.8	63.6	26.7	10 295	7 364	66.3	527	0.0	13.7	2.8
Logan, KY	36 179	11.1	66.8	22.1	30 912	6 396	65.3	1 479	0.0	12.6	5.3
Lyon, KY	7 610	8.9	51.6	39.5	6 650	6 545	63.9	214	0.0	24.3	0.0
McCracken, KY	76 026	13.1	54.2	32.6	70 129	6 941	64.5	3 145	0.2	8.5	5.7
McCreary, KY	27 674	17.5	73.6	8.9	25 143	7 369	64.1	1 091	0.0	9.0	20.2
McLean, KY	12 646	10.8	69.3	19.9	10 945	6 546	58.7	501	0.0	12.4	7.8
Madison, KY	81 338	10.5	61.9	27.6	70 134	6 277	66.6	5 219	0.0	9.1	4.1
Magoffin, KY	21 800	18.3	68.7	13.0	18 491	7 274	62.4	852	0.0	14.1	13.6
Marion, KY	24 299	11.0	65.8	23.2	21 302	6 695	65.9	1 008	0.0	13.7	9.3
Marshall, KY	32 623	8.6	59.9	31.5	30 482	6 374	65.5	1 377	0.0	12.6	4.1
Martin, KY	20 761	16.2	68.8	15.0	18 510	7 422	62.8	828	0.0	14.9	15.2

Table C-1. Population, School, and Student Characteristics by County—*Continued*

STATE County	High school graduates, 2000			College enrollment, 2000		College graduates, 2000 (percent)						
	Population 25 years and over	High school graduate or less (percent)	High school graduate or more (percent)	Number	Percent public	Bachelor's degree or more	+/- U.S. percentage with bachelor's degree or more	Non-Hispanic White	Black	American Indian and Alaska Native	Asian or Pacific Islander	Hispanic[3]
	30	31	32	33	34	35	36	37	38	39	40	41
KENTUCKY	2 646 397	59.4	74.1	206 367	81.2	17.1	-7.3	17.4	10.7	13.9	52.0	13.0
Adair, KY	11 270	71.1	60.1	1 122	37.9	10.9	-13.5	10.9	12.7	0.0	27.8	0.0
Allen, KY	11 643	74.7	64.5	430	80.9	9.1	-15.3	8.9	5.5	0.0	28.6	12.4
Anderson, KY	12 600	62.6	80.4	539	79.2	12.0	-12.4	12.3	3.8	0.0	0.0	12.3
Ballard, KY	5 766	64.1	76.3	222	95.9	10.6	-13.8	10.8	0.0	100.0	70.0	0.0
Barren, KY	25 751	70.9	69.5	983	89.6	11.1	-13.3	11.1	8.1	0.0	43.9	7.0
Bath, KY	7 451	75.5	59.0	232	86.2	10.1	-14.3	10.0	0.0	0.0	46.7	47.6
Bell, KY	20 042	76.5	56.6	912	80.8	9.0	-15.4	8.9	13.2	22.2	30.4	0.0
Boone, KY	54 166	47.7	85.1	3 592	80.8	22.8	-1.6	22.5	20.2	16.1	61.8	14.6
Bourbon, KY	13 015	63.3	75.4	558	86.2	13.5	-10.9	14.0	5.8	0.0	0.0	6.5
Boyd, KY	34 697	57.3	78.0	2 318	87.7	14.1	-10.3	14.3	9.8	29.8	38.5	2.3
Boyle, KY	18 491	57.7	76.6	1 614	34.4	19.3	-5.1	20.6	8.0	0.0	63.7	5.7
Bracken, KY	5 460	71.0	69.6	263	95.4	9.5	-14.9	9.4	17.1	0.0	. . .	. . .
Breathitt, KY	10 393	73.6	57.5	677	77.0	10.0	-14.4	9.8	. . .	0.0	90.5	0.0
Breckinridge, KY	12 501	75.3	68.9	364	88.5	7.4	-17.0	7.4	4.4	0.0	60.0	11.6
Bullitt, KY	39 307	65.1	76.0	1 964	78.2	9.2	-15.2	9.2	16.9	6.1	34.6	11.8
Butler, KY	8 489	79.7	60.7	324	90.1	6.4	-18.0	6.2	0.0	. . .	9.8	15.3
Caldwell, KY	9 265	68.1	73.1	456	88.8	10.0	-14.4	10.4	3.0	0.0	31.3	10.2
Calloway, KY	21 032	52.4	77.9	6 520	95.5	24.0	-0.4	23.6	23.7	12.5	60.4	23.1
Campbell, KY	57 184	53.9	80.8	5 232	87.5	20.5	-3.9	20.5	10.2	0.0	55.0	23.4
Carlisle, KY	3 690	66.1	73.4	180	81.7	10.6	-13.8	10.6	9.5	0.0	. . .	0.0
Carroll, KY	6 690	69.4	68.1	281	80.8	8.3	-16.1	7.9	0.0	34.1	55.6	0.0
Carter, KY	17 394	72.9	64.4	1 317	56.1	8.9	-15.5	8.9	0.0	0.0	18.0	13.6
Casey, KY	10 423	79.3	57.4	259	86.1	7.4	-17.0	7.4	0.0	0.0	0.0	0.0
Christian, KY	40 344	56.1	77.2	3 364	90.3	12.5	-11.9	14.3	5.6	6.9	33.7	11.3
Clark, KY	22 187	61.2	75.0	951	83.3	15.6	-8.8	16.0	7.5	0.0	29.7	5.0
Clay, KY	16 083	79.5	49.4	518	87.3	8.0	-16.4	8.2	5.5	12.5	46.7	7.9
Clinton, KY	6 594	78.1	53.5	293	86.0	8.0	-16.4	8.1	0.0	. . .	0.0	7.4
Crittenden, KY	6 460	73.2	67.0	266	85.7	7.3	-17.1	7.2	0.0	0.0	100.0	17.2
Cumberland, KY	4 972	80.4	56.0	140	68.6	7.1	-17.3	7.1	8.5	0.0	20.0	0.0
Daviess, KY	59 745	56.9	80.7	3 889	67.5	17.0	-7.4	17.2	7.6	17.6	63.5	17.6
Edmonson, KY	7 865	78.4	61.7	282	94.3	4.9	-19.5	4.9	0.0	33.3	0.0	0.0
Elliott, KY	4 422	78.5	52.6	176	100.0	7.8	-16.6	7.8	. . .	. . .	. . .	. . .
Estill, KY	10 189	78.8	58.5	385	83.4	6.9	-17.5	6.7	0.0	0.0	35.7	41.2
Fayette, KY	167 235	36.6	85.8	31 508	89.4	35.6	11.2	38.7	14.5	17.7	67.3	14.6
Fleming, KY	9 154	71.5	66.5	412	86.7	8.8	-15.6	9.0	5.0	0.0	. . .	0.0
Floyd, KY	28 370	68.6	61.3	1 534	85.0	9.7	-14.7	9.6	2.5	0.0	76.9	6.1
Franklin, KY	32 388	52.6	78.8	2 644	87.1	23.8	-0.6	23.7	24.9	20.0	74.2	14.3
Fulton, KY	5 111	69.4	69.5	133	81.2	11.5	-12.9	13.9	1.1	. . .	. . .	0.0
Gallatin, KY	5 007	76.4	68.0	155	78.1	6.9	-17.5	6.7	12.5	0.0	0.0	11.5
Garrard, KY	9 951	66.3	69.4	476	90.1	10.5	-13.9	10.5	0.0	100.0	36.8	17.9
Grant, KY	13 861	71.8	72.4	503	82.5	9.4	-15.0	9.3	0.0	65.5	13.4	0.0
Graves, KY	24 932	65.5	73.4	1 251	84.1	12.6	-11.8	12.7	7.7	20.0	56.9	1.5
Grayson, KY	15 940	74.3	62.8	684	88.0	7.7	-16.7	7.7	7.1	13.3	0.0	8.3
Green, KY	7 983	74.8	61.4	377	69.5	9.1	-15.3	8.9	6.1	0.0	40.0	0.0
Greenup, KY	25 323	62.6	75.1	1 152	88.5	11.5	-12.9	11.2	14.2	0.0	65.7	26.4
Hancock, KY	5 427	68.5	77.2	253	72.3	8.1	-16.3	8.3	0.0	0.0	0.0	0.0
Hardin, KY	58 358	52.0	82.3	4 879	84.1	15.4	-9.0	15.7	11.5	13.1	30.9	10.8
Harlan, KY	22 041	75.6	58.7	1 004	90.1	8.9	-15.5	8.7	5.6	13.0	51.3	19.4
Harrison, KY	12 009	68.5	74.2	518	89.8	10.6	-13.8	10.6	5.7	7.9	0.0	9.4
Hart, KY	11 474	76.9	58.2	420	87.6	7.0	-17.4	7.3	0.9	34.0	100.0	2.4
Henderson, KY	29 960	59.5	78.3	1 374	92.1	13.8	-10.6	13.9	6.7	15.8	63.2	32.4
Henry, KY	10 032	71.1	73.4	331	68.3	9.8	-14.6	9.8	9.3	0.0	35.0	9.4
Hickman, KY	3 734	74.7	64.4	113	83.2	8.8	-15.6	9.3	0.9	0.0	85.7	18.2
Hopkins, KY	31 464	67.0	71.3	1 433	92.3	10.6	-13.8	10.7	8.2	9.4	45.2	8.1
Jackson, KY	8 611	80.5	52.9	189	77.2	6.8	-17.6	6.8	. . .	0.0	0.0	0.0
Jefferson, KY	464 284	47.2	81.8	37 969	75.5	24.8	0.4	27.2	11.9	19.1	50.6	18.4
Jessamine, KY	24 182	53.3	79.1	3 131	36.0	21.5	-2.9	21.4	14.6	14.3	62.8	24.4
Johnson, KY	15 735	71.4	63.8	778	92.4	9.3	-15.1	9.0	22.2	0.0	61.7	9.1
Kenton, KY	97 727	50.4	82.1	6 815	75.5	22.9	-1.5	23.4	9.4	18.9	43.0	13.5
Knott, KY	11 427	72.1	58.7	1 107	71.2	10.2	-14.2	10.2	0.0	70.6	7.7	0.0
Knox, KY	20 401	78.5	54.1	987	49.4	8.8	-15.6	8.8	5.7	15.0	44.4	11.4
Larue, KY	9 017	69.2	71.0	400	90.0	10.9	-13.5	10.7	6.1	32.1	0.0	49.1
Laurel, KY	34 431	71.0	63.9	1 465	83.5	10.6	-13.8	10.6	5.6	13.5	50.5	13.8
Lawrence, KY	10 256	74.8	58.2	401	95.0	6.6	-17.8	6.5	0.0	50.0	. . .	0.0
Lee, KY	5 381	79.9	50.9	163	71.2	6.3	-18.1	6.5	0.0	0.0	0.0	0.0
Leslie, KY	8 214	77.6	52.5	342	82.2	6.3	-18.1	6.2	0.0	0.0	100.0	15.4
Letcher, KY	16 930	74.4	58.5	858	91.5	7.7	-16.7	7.5	11.7	0.0	68.0	0.0
Lewis, KY	9 256	77.3	57.4	374	83.2	6.4	-18.0	6.4	0.0	6.5	. . .	0.0
Lincoln, KY	15 440	76.1	64.6	603	81.9	8.4	-16.0	8.3	3.6	0.0	91.7	23.6
Livingston, KY	6 851	66.4	74.3	306	89.9	8.4	-16.0	8.3	0.0	8.7	0.0	0.0
Logan, KY	17 471	71.0	68.5	521	95.8	9.6	-14.8	9.9	4.8	0.0	69.7	5.7
Lyon, KY	6 185	68.5	68.0	160	90.6	10.1	-14.3	10.5	0.0	0.0	76.7	6.5
McCracken, KY	45 038	53.1	80.3	2 443	84.2	18.1	-6.3	19.2	6.9	9.7	46.4	16.9
McCreary, KY	10 668	78.4	52.6	433	91.5	6.7	-17.7	6.4	0.0	0.0	52.2	49.1
McLean, KY	6 737	67.8	70.8	327	78.3	8.7	-15.7	8.9	0.0	0.0	0.0	0.0
Madison, KY	42 125	54.5	75.2	10 200	86.2	21.8	-2.6	22.0	10.5	16.2	67.4	13.0
Magoffin, KY	8 410	78.1	50.1	410	91.0	6.3	-18.1	6.3	0.0	0.0	20.0	0.0
Marion, KY	11 772	73.4	70.5	462	60.4	9.1	-15.3	9.2	3.7	0.0	47.2	19.7
Marshall, KY	21 278	61.1	76.9	1 056	85.7	13.7	-10.7	13.8	0.0	11.8	27.0	13.2
Martin, KY	7 835	75.6	54.0	435	89.2	9.0	-15.4	9.2	0.0	0.0	. . .	0.0

[3]May be of any race.
. . . = Not available.

Table C-1.Population, School, and Student Characteristics by Count—*Continued*

STATE County	State/ county code	County type[1]	Population, 2005		Number of schools and students, 2004–2005			Resident enrollment, 2000			
			Total	Percent 5 to 17 years	School districts	Schools	Students	Total	Percent public	K–12	Percent public
			1	2	3	4	5	6	7	8	9
Mason, KY	21161	6	17 140	16.8	1	5	2 940	3 816	90.0	3 002	92.5
Meade, KY	21163	1	28 447	20.7	1	10	4 944	6 800	92.6	5 499	94.8
Menifee, KY	21165	9	6 809	16.6	1	6	1 233	1 478	96.5	1 264	96.3
Mercer, KY	21167	6	21 610	17.4	3	10	3 844	4 555	91.5	3 691	96.2
Metcalfe, KY	21169	9	10 197	17.3	1	5	1 709	2 146	91.6	1 807	91.8
Monroe, KY	21171	9	11 660	16.6	1	5	2 069	2 660	95.9	2 077	99.1
Montgomery, KY	21173	6	24 256	17.3	1	9	4 434	4 925	92.4	4 032	94.1
Morgan, KY	21175	7	14 334	15.1	1	8	2 385	3 092	90.6	2 506	90.9
Muhlenberg, KY	21177	6	31 548	15.8	1	13	5 397	6 747	92.9	5 522	94.3
Nelson, KY	21179	1	41 088	18.8	2	15	7 151	9 404	81.7	7 711	83.7
Nicholas, KY	21181	8	7 027	16.2	1	2	1 261	1 392	99.4	1 178	99.4
Ohio, KY	21183	6	23 676	16.8	1	8	4 206	5 308	95.1	4 398	95.7
Oldham, KY	21185	1	53 533	18.5	1	19	10 579	13 104	79.2	10 171	84.6
Owen, KY	21187	8	11 374	17.6	1	4	1 973	2 396	93.9	2 076	95.2
Owsley, KY	21189	9	4 746	15.8	1	2	897	1 167	92.4	936	92.2
Pendleton, KY	21191	1	15 125	19.5	1	4	2 910	3 590	93.8	3 053	95.5
Perry, KY	21193	7	29 452	16.4	3	17	5 709	6 979	95.6	5 444	96.5
Pike, KY	21195	7	66 922	16.3	2	28	11 719	15 519	92.3	12 398	96.9
Powell, KY	21197	6	13 687	17.2	1	5	2 686	3 021	95.8	2 704	97.3
Pulaski, KY	21199	5	59 200	16.1	3	19	10 253	12 531	92.7	10 027	93.8
Robertson, KY	21201	8	2 279	17.4	1	2	452	519	94.8	425	96.7
Rockcastle, KY	21203	7	16 712	16.5	1	6	3 084	3 509	97.3	2 971	98.4
Rowan, KY	21205	7	22 226	13.7	1	8	3 152	8 071	93.8	3 346	90.6
Russell, KY	21207	9	17 020	15.7	1	6	2 993	3 471	94.6	2 771	97.3
Scott, KY	21209	2	39 380	18.2	1	12	6 941	9 002	76.7	6 358	90.1
Shelby, KY	21211	1	38 205	17.2	3	10	5 755	7 538	83.8	6 228	86.8
Simpson, KY	21213	6	17 021	18.6	1	6	3 171	3 705	91.2	3 074	91.8
Spencer, KY	21215	1	15 651	18.4	1	6	2 555	2 845	86.4	2 321	90.1
Taylor, KY	21217	7	23 754	15.8	2	7	3 976	5 780	77.5	4 009	94.4
Todd, KY	21219	8	11 944	18.6	1	4	2 186	2 687	90.0	2 208	90.6
Trigg, KY	21221	3	13 349	16.2	1	3	2 149	2 654	96.2	2 101	97.7
Trimble, KY	21223	1	9 023	18.3	1	4	1 674	2 007	92.5	1 683	94.8
Union, KY	21225	6	15 592	17.9	1	9	2 565	3 952	87.3	3 197	89.6
Warren, KY	21227	3	98 960	15.8	4	34	15 760	28 046	92.7	15 725	93.4
Washington, KY	21229	8	11 399	17.3	1	6	1 941	2 699	80.5	2 182	84.8
Wayne, KY	21231	7	20 352	17.4	2	12	3 694	4 496	97.7	3 808	98.7
Webster, KY	21233	2	14 161	16.5	2	8	2 426	3 296	92.1	2 617	93.3
Whitley, KY	21235	7	38 029	17.6	3	13	5 776	9 292	85.0	6 860	97.9
Wolfe, KY	21237	9	7 070	17.5	1	5	1 377	1 649	93.8	1 333	93.6
Woodford, KY	21239	2	24 246	17.3	1	8	3 861	5 753	76.3	4 442	83.3
LOUISIANA	22000		4 523 628	18.2	91	1 541	724 281	1 271 299	81.1	923 702	83.1
Acadia, LA	22001	4	59 552	20.1	1	27	9 499	16 063	79.1	12 993	77.6
Allen, LA	22003	6	25 270	17.0	1	12	4 299	6 125	89.2	5 056	89.5
Ascension, LA	22005	2	90 501	19.6	1	23	16 363	21 867	82.9	17 104	86.7
Assumption, LA	22007	6	23 196	18.9	1	10	4 331	6 255	88.8	5 203	89.2
Avoyelles, LA	22009	6	42 098	17.7	2	15	7 047	10 352	87.9	8 525	88.2
Beauregard, LA	22011	6	34 562	18.9	1	14	6 153	8 255	89.3	6 966	91.3
Bienville, LA	22013	6	15 176	18.0	1	8	2 422	4 152	89.4	3 377	89.5
Bossier, LA	22015	2	105 541	18.9	1	35	18 868	27 569	90.6	20 323	94.4
Caddo, LA	22017	2	251 309	18.0	1	74	43 524	68 792	88.8	50 825	91.9
Calcasieu, LA	22019	3	185 419	18.2	1	60	32 449	50 285	86.2	37 247	88.0
Caldwell, LA	22021	8	10 563	16.7	1	6	1 871	2 531	96.1	2 067	97.4
Cameron, LA	22023	3	9 558	18.7	1	6	1 797	2 578	92.8	2 165	95.2
Catahoula, LA	22025	9	10 447	17.0	1	10	1 754	2 633	93.4	2 161	94.4
Claiborne, LA	22027	7	16 309	17.3	1	9	2 736	4 244	86.5	3 463	85.4
Concordia, LA	22029	7	19 273	18.8	1	11	3 865	5 092	89.8	4 294	91.7
De Soto, LA	22031	2	26 383	18.8	1	13	5 012	6 702	92.5	5 510	94.5
East Baton Rouge, LA	22033	2	411 417	17.5	12	139	54 701	134 817	78.3	79 781	74.4
East Carroll, LA	22035	7	8 756	20.5	1	5	1 597	2 997	87.8	2 518	87.3
East Feliciana, LA	22037	2	20 823	16.9	1	8	2 343	5 150	75.3	4 186	74.7
Evangeline, LA	22039	6	35 540	20.2	1	12	6 050	9 554	89.9	7 763	89.4
Franklin, LA	22041	7	20 380	18.6	1	8	3 585	5 329	86.2	4 430	86.6
Grant, LA	22043	3	19 503	19.2	1	9	3 629	4 695	93.0	3 868	94.3
Iberia, LA	22045	4	74 388	20.1	1	32	14 064	20 021	87.4	16 481	87.8
Iberville, LA	22047	2	32 386	17.2	1	9	4 286	8 553	79.2	6 794	79.4
Jackson, LA	22049	6	15 135	16.6	1	7	2 296	3 746	92.0	2 916	92.3
Jefferson, LA	22051	1	452 824	17.2	1	86	51 403	121 830	62.7	86 794	63.9
Jefferson Davis, LA	22053	6	31 272	19.8	1	14	5 840	8 365	86.9	6 879	88.4
Lafayette, LA	22055	3	197 390	18.0	1	44	29 816	56 319	80.0	38 737	78.9
Lafourche, LA	22057	3	92 179	18.3	1	29	14 653	24 776	84.3	18 800	84.5
La Salle, LA	22059	6	14 040	17.8	1	10	2 675	3 312	95.3	2 811	96.1
Lincoln, LA	22061	4	42 108	14.3	1	19	6 632	17 955	90.9	7 049	85.6
Livingston, LA	22063	2	109 206	18.9	1	40	21 397	25 283	91.1	20 338	95.0
Madison, LA	22065	7	12 457	21.4	1	7	2 306	4 076	87.9	3 448	88.3
Morehouse, LA	22067	6	29 989	18.5	1	16	5 109	7 885	86.5	6 574	85.8
Natchitoches, LA	22069	6	38 541	17.2	2	16	7 230	13 663	91.2	7 674	89.3
Orleans, LA	22071	1	454 863	17.7	8	131	65 943	150 096	73.0	99 998	81.9
Ouachita, LA	22073	3	148 237	18.8	3	57	27 995	44 054	89.0	30 577	90.2
Plaquemines, LA	22075	1	28 995	19.3	2	10	5 942	7 807	81.5	6 134	85.5
Pointe Coupee, LA	22077	2	22 377	17.6	1	9	3 009	5 974	72.8	4 852	71.9
Rapides, LA	22079	3	128 462	18.2	2	53	22 893	33 345	86.4	26 221	89.8

[1]County type codes are from the Economic Research Service of the United States Department of Agriculture. See notes and definitions at the end of this section.

Table C-1. Population, School, and Student Characteristics by County—*Continued*

STATE County	Characteristics of students, 2004–2005				Outcomes		Staff and students, 2004–2005		
	Percent with IEP[2]	Percent eligible for free or reduced-price lunch	Percent minority	Percent English-language learners	Number of graduates, 2003–2004	Percent dropouts, grades 9–12, 2001–2002	Number of teachers	Student-teacher ratio	Central administration staff
	10	11	12	13	14	15	16	17	18
Mason, KY	14.8	...	10.3	0.4	173	2.8	179	16.4	19
Meade, KY	16.9	...	4.0	0.2	333	3.2	276	17.9	17
Menifee, KY	21.9	...	3.4	0.0	100	5.6	91	13.5	13
Mercer, KY	18.9	...	5.9	0.6	192	1.7	236	16.3	32
Metcalfe, KY	16.4	...	1.7	0.2	99	3.0	125	13.7	15
Monroe, KY	15.2	...	7.2	1.3	129	2.6	139	14.9	20
Montgomery, KY	13.9	...	4.6	1.3	236	3.4	267	16.6	41
Morgan, KY	18.2	...	0.8	0.1	136	4.6	166	14.4	20
Muhlenberg, KY	18.3	...	4.8	0.3	394	3.5	361	15.0	35
Nelson, KY	15.5	...	9.4	0.3	443	2.5	411	17.4	37
Nicholas, KY	14.4	...	1.4	0.2	85	3.4	73	17.3	14
Ohio, KY	16.7	...	2.6	1.1	265	2.6	260	16.2	22
Oldham, KY	15.1	...	5.9	2.6	665	1.1	600	17.6	67
Owen, KY	11.6	...	2.6	0.9	109	6.9	107	18.4	8
Owsley, KY	15.1	...	0.8	0.0	55	4.1	81	11.1	9
Pendleton, KY	15.1	...	1.3	0.4	197	1.9	174	16.7	20
Perry, KY	20.2	...	3.0	0.1	...	3.9	369	15.5	40
Pike, KY	13.9	...	1.0	0.0	689	4.0	757	15.5	66
Powell, KY	18.5	...	1.2	0.2	131	6.5	181	14.8	21
Pulaski, KY	15.3	...	3.6	0.5	...	3.8	611	16.8	74
Robertson, KY	17.7	...	0.0	0.0	29	4.3	28	16.1	4
Rockcastle, KY	17.8	...	0.3	0.0	191	4.5	201	15.3	19
Rowan, KY	19.0	...	2.8	0.4	175	3.4	204	15.5	19
Russell, KY	19.0	...	1.4	0.9	158	5.7	211	14.2	35
Scott, KY	14.4	...	8.1	0.8	310	3.4	413	16.8	32
Shelby, KY	14.9	...	20.2	5.9	...	3.9	342	16.8	57
Simpson, KY	11.8	...	13.4	0.1	148	3.4	182	17.4	27
Spencer, KY	18.7	...	2.5	0.2	155	3.2	134	19.1	14
Taylor, KY	17.4	...	7.3	0.8	235	3.6	248	16.0	33
Todd, KY	19.3	...	12.8	1.1	97	4.1	119	18.4	14
Trigg, KY	16.7	...	15.2	0.0	112	7.7	144	14.9	24
Trimble, KY	14.3	...	2.7	1.2	85	3.0	105	15.9	11
Union, KY	21.7	...	16.0	0.1	168	3.6	160	16.0	19
Warren, KY	12.6	...	18.6	6.0	...	2.6	928	17.0	67
Washington, KY	19.9	...	14.7	1.7	134	3.7	124	15.7	14
Wayne, KY	18.2	...	4.6	1.3	196	4.1	225	16.4	39
Webster, KY	10.0	...	0.0	4.0	158	2.0	146	16.6	17
Whitley, KY	18.3	...	0.8	0.1	...	4.1	375	15.4	45
Wolfe, KY	20.0	...	0.9	0.0	87	6.4	96	14.3	12
Woodford, KY	11.4	...	10.6	3.4	257	2.5	214	18.0	14
LOUISIANA	14.1	61.6	51.7	1.8	...	7.0	49 191	14.7	...
Acadia, LA	18.1	66.5	29.5	0.6	493	7.1	626	15.2	51
Allen, LA	12.4	60.7	26.1	0.0	204	2.2	331	13.0	18
Ascension, LA	15.3	44.2	32.5	2.1	788	4.7	1 063	15.4	77
Assumption, LA	14.5	58.9	45.4	1.3	216	7.3	305	14.2	40
Avoyelles, LA	10.9	78.9	43.9	0.5	...	6.7	409	17.2	27
Beauregard, LA	13.7	46.3	18.0	0.3	348	2.0	408	15.1	32
Bienville, LA	13.0	72.0	60.0	0.0	148	7.7	193	12.6	19
Bossier, LA	12.0	41.7	35.9	3.8	1 090	4.6	1 198	15.7	98
Caddo, LA	13.1	58.6	64.7	1.2	2 588	10.0	2 885	15.1	319
Calcasieu, LA	15.4	51.7	36.0	0.1	1 789	4.8	2 231	14.5	203
Caldwell, LA	14.1	58.6	20.1	0.0	107	4.8	137	13.7	12
Cameron, LA	18.9	46.1	8.5	1.6	122	2.1	164	11.0	12
Catahoula, LA	11.1	67.7	38.7	0.0	103	6.3	133	13.2	15
Claiborne, LA	18.2	74.3	68.5	0.0	153	2.5	228	12.0	14
Concordia, LA	10.4	74.1	51.2	0.2	178	6.2	284	13.6	35
De Soto, LA	14.9	66.2	56.5	1.4	290	4.5	356	14.1	35
East Baton Rouge, LA	13.6	67.8	77.4	3.0	...	9.2	3 757	14.6	...
East Carroll, LA	14.4	93.4	92.1	0.0	73	7.6	124	12.8	17
East Feliciana, LA	15.7	84.7	79.6	0.0	127	5.4	148	15.8	21
Evangeline, LA	17.3	75.1	40.9	0.3	269	6.6	408	14.8	37
Franklin, LA	13.0	76.1	50.3	0.0	164	7.2	243	14.8	23
Grant, LA	15.1	61.6	16.0	0.0	176	6.0	256	14.2	19
Iberia, LA	17.0	66.7	48.6	1.8	760	5.9	991	14.2	85
Iberville, LA	14.4	82.8	76.8	0.4	238	7.5	337	12.7	23
Jackson, LA	11.2	58.7	37.9	0.0	131	6.0	161	14.3	16
Jefferson, LA	14.2	64.6	66.3	7.1	2 144	9.7	3 405	15.1	288
Jefferson Davis, LA	17.7	55.1	26.0	0.2	350	3.6	374	15.6	33
Lafayette, LA	11.8	50.7	44.5	1.9	1 660	7.8	2 126	14.0	157
Lafourche, LA	14.1	57.8	28.9	2.3	935	5.8	1 111	13.2	121
La Salle, LA	8.5	57.4	13.8	0.0	183	3.9	181	14.8	20
Lincoln, LA	12.9	55.7	52.1	0.4	339	6.4	506	13.1	29
Livingston, LA	12.4	44.5	6.5	0.6	1 081	1.2	1 351	15.8	69
Madison, LA	12.6	84.4	90.9	0.0	92	10.9	149	15.5	20
Morehouse, LA	15.6	75.6	64.3	0.5	203	9.2	377	13.5	32
Natchitoches, LA	12.1	66.3	55.4	0.6	448	6.3	514	14.1	37
Orleans, LA	10.9	77.3	96.5	1.9	...	9.1	3 883	17.0	...
Ouachita, LA	13.8	58.6	51.3	0.6	...	8.9	1 869	15.0	190
Plaquemines, LA	11.8	62.1	43.4	1.8	...	5.9	397	15.0	45
Pointe Coupee, LA	21.5	78.9	64.4	0.1	158	11.6	216	13.9	27
Rapides, LA	14.8	64.3	46.5	1.7	...	8.7	1 579	14.5	111

[2]IEP = Individual Education Program. See notes and definitions at the end of this section.
. . . = Not available.

Table C-1. Population, School, and Student Characteristics by County—*Continued*

STATE County	Revenue, 2003–2004				Current expenditures, 2003–2004			Resident population, 16 to 19 years, 2000			
	Total revenue (thousands of dollars)	Percent of revenue from:			Total expenditures (thousands of dollars)	Amount per student (dollars)	Percent for instruction	Total	Percent in armed forces	Percent high school graduates	Percent not enrolled, not employed, not in armed forces, not high school graduate
		Federal government	State government	Local government							
	19	20	21	22	23	24	25	26	27	28	29
Mason, KY	21 017	12.6	60.2	27.2	18 227	6 168	69.0	958	0.3	17.0	3.1
Meade, KY	31 950	8.8	71.8	19.4	27 924	5 807	67.0	1 551	0.6	17.4	7.6
Menifee, KY	9 474	13.4	74.9	11.7	8 340	6 814	63.6	496	0.0	11.3	20.0
Mercer, KY	27 240	9.4	66.1	24.5	24 279	6 406	65.2	949	0.0	14.9	7.4
Metcalfe, KY	13 572	18.2	65.7	16.1	12 638	7 395	62.1	540	0.0	13.3	13.1
Monroe, KY	17 909	16.1	67.9	15.9	15 197	7 271	64.5	701	0.0	10.4	8.0
Montgomery, KY	31 012	13.8	62.4	23.8	27 094	6 404	66.6	1 145	0.0	14.5	10.3
Morgan, KY	18 553	16.2	71.9	11.9	15 915	6 520	61.6	809	0.0	17.3	11.6
Muhlenberg, KY	42 034	9.3	62.0	28.6	36 749	6 836	67.7	1 809	0.0	12.5	13.7
Nelson, KY	48 846	9.7	58.7	31.6	43 272	6 183	65.2	2 121	0.0	11.3	5.6
Nicholas, KY	8 254	12.8	69.3	17.9	7 251	6 022	64.7	364	0.0	18.7	4.4
Ohio, KY	31 430	12.0	70.4	17.6	27 916	6 666	59.9	1 317	0.0	9.3	5.4
Oldham, KY	73 287	4.8	53.3	41.9	59 664	5 847	67.5	2 389	0.0	6.4	3.9
Owen, KY	13 872	12.4	66.2	21.5	11 535	5 791	59.0	622	0.0	15.0	6.3
Owsley, KY	9 398	37.1	54.2	8.7	8 559	9 144	65.1	292	0.0	12.0	18.8
Pendleton, KY	21 706	9.4	70.0	20.7	18 122	6 098	63.7	885	0.0	12.5	5.2
Perry, KY	44 738	13.4	69.0	17.6	40 173	7 021	64.9	1 843	0.0	10.1	12.6
Pike, KY	93 598	13.6	63.1	23.2	81 890	6 929	64.3	3 840	0.0	10.6	9.0
Powell, KY	19 656	14.0	73.7	12.3	17 778	6 666	66.2	871	0.0	11.7	6.4
Pulaski, KY	68 722	14.2	62.5	23.2	61 187	6 114	66.6	3 108	0.0	9.7	6.7
Robertson, KY	3 419	17.5	69.3	13.1	2 983	6 780	63.6	130	0.0	13.8	6.2
Rockcastle, KY	23 623	13.9	73.4	12.7	21 225	6 989	65.7	832	0.0	13.6	8.2
Rowan, KY	23 401	11.0	65.0	24.0	21 010	6 749	65.0	2 245	0.0	5.1	2.6
Russell, KY	22 781	15.8	65.4	18.8	21 003	7 156	63.8	867	0.0	11.0	11.3
Scott, KY	48 573	6.8	52.8	40.5	40 401	5 642	66.8	2 233	0.0	7.5	3.0
Shelby, KY	43 613	7.6	51.6	40.8	35 914	6 486	63.3	1 923	1.0	9.6	8.4
Simpson, KY	20 432	9.6	62.5	27.9	18 705	6 014	66.7	708	0.0	18.9	3.2
Spencer, KY	17 708	7.9	63.5	28.6	15 124	6 126	63.4	631	0.0	11.7	4.3
Taylor, KY	29 162	12.4	65.6	22.0	26 262	6 727	66.4	1 385	0.0	12.9	7.1
Todd, KY	15 681	11.8	70.6	17.6	13 316	6 314	60.3	623	0.0	17.2	3.2
Trigg, KY	15 814	8.9	62.1	29.0	14 230	6 665	61.9	492	0.0	11.2	5.7
Trimble, KY	11 650	14.0	62.5	23.4	10 205	6 245	66.0	407	0.0	17.9	4.7
Union, KY	20 980	12.4	65.1	22.5	17 783	7 232	64.2	1 607	0.0	13.8	16.9
Warren, KY	112 377	10.5	56.2	33.4	93 981	6 113	65.8	6 961	0.0	8.4	4.6
Washington, KY	14 435	12.5	67.1	20.3	12 343	6 412	63.1	684	0.0	14.0	8.0
Wayne, KY	28 021	16.1	69.6	14.3	25 195	6 943	66.9	1 151	0.0	13.7	12.4
Webster, KY	18 049	12.5	67.3	20.2	15 838	6 454	63.7	853	0.0	9.4	7.9
Whitley, KY	61 395	16.2	68.6	15.2	53 938	6 883	67.4	2 382	0.0	9.4	9.2
Wolfe, KY	11 616	19.0	71.9	9.1	10 303	7 439	59.2	413	0.0	10.4	19.6
Woodford, KY	25 809	7.1	50.3	42.5	23 490	6 128	67.5	1 151	0.0	14.5	5.2
LOUISIANA	5 713 792	13.8	48.0	38.3	5 200 332	7 209	65.1	289 111	0.4	10.4	8.0
Acadia, LA	65 268	19.2	60.2	20.6	62 443	6 471	65.7	3 945	0.2	10.3	10.3
Allen, LA	32 260	9.9	62.1	28.0	31 586	7 378	59.6	1 453	0.2	13.8	11.2
Ascension, LA	121 184	8.9	45.5	45.6	113 373	7 171	68.3	4 719	0.2	10.8	4.9
Assumption, LA	37 093	18.0	58.3	23.7	36 001	8 125	65.4	1 438	0.0	5.6	12.7
Avoyelles, LA	45 510	21.4	61.6	17.0	41 841	6 354	63.9	2 560	0.0	10.2	18.3
Beauregard, LA	44 155	8.7	58.2	33.1	40 627	6 631	62.5	2 068	0.2	13.9	8.0
Bienville, LA	24 877	13.4	39.9	46.7	21 721	8 695	62.7	979	0.3	11.5	6.8
Bossier, LA	134 807	9.6	51.6	38.8	124 539	6 635	64.1	5 796	4.4	13.7	6.1
Caddo, LA	366 072	12.9	50.1	37.0	329 823	7 416	66.5	15 746	0.3	11.3	9.5
Calcasieu, LA	250 048	11.2	43.2	45.6	216 131	6 723	64.2	11 513	0.1	12.7	5.8
Caldwell, LA	15 133	21.1	59.6	19.3	13 166	7 152	65.1	512	0.0	11.3	18.8
Cameron, LA	20 055	6.4	38.3	55.3	17 147	9 427	62.1	612	0.0	12.6	7.4
Catahoula, LA	15 402	21.0	60.1	18.9	13 316	7 398	62.1	843	0.0	14.9	16.6
Claiborne, LA	22 960	12.6	60.3	27.1	21 618	7 631	67.5	1 032	0.0	11.2	12.8
Concordia, LA	31 516	19.3	54.0	26.6	27 642	7 278	65.4	1 161	0.6	9.8	14.3
De Soto, LA	45 770	15.1	43.7	41.2	41 442	8 416	65.6	1 533	0.0	14.6	10.8
East Baton Rouge, LA	446 326	12.8	34.5	52.6	413 300	7 926	58.4	30 936	0.0	8.2	6.0
East Carroll, LA	14 019	24.9	59.7	15.4	13 430	8 018	64.1	622	0.0	10.6	10.3
East Feliciana, LA	20 256	16.8	59.7	23.6	18 932	7 992	65.2	1 273	0.0	11.9	8.4
Evangeline, LA	45 415	16.9	63.3	19.8	41 914	6 665	67.2	2 313	0.0	8.7	13.7
Franklin, LA	27 215	25.5	60.0	14.5	26 199	6 803	66.8	1 346	0.0	15.1	13.4
Grant, LA	27 012	22.4	65.6	11.9	23 896	6 599	62.2	1 052	0.0	13.4	9.2
Iberia, LA	107 869	14.1	56.8	29.2	98 244	6 918	65.4	4 571	0.0	11.5	10.2
Iberville, LA	40 368	15.2	27.7	57.1	35 953	8 180	57.1	2 182	0.0	12.6	14.5
Jackson, LA	22 650	13.6	46.9	39.5	21 817	9 132	64.3	961	0.0	13.2	11.9
Jefferson, LA	423 917	13.4	36.6	50.0	358 343	6 964	66.3	25 239	0.1	9.7	6.5
Jefferson Davis, LA	48 043	12.0	56.9	31.1	42 928	7 468	64.2	2 076	0.0	16.3	9.7
Lafayette, LA	221 576	13.2	39.7	47.1	206 332	6 921	70.1	12 509	0.1	9.9	6.7
Lafourche, LA	113 458	11.9	52.0	36.1	107 095	7 201	66.4	6 126	0.0	12.7	5.4
La Salle, LA	19 248	11.6	60.9	27.5	19 607	7 265	65.1	1 078	0.0	9.1	18.8
Lincoln, LA	54 249	10.7	47.3	42.0	47 902	7 262	67.7	4 912	0.0	4.2	2.5
Livingston, LA	135 642	8.6	67.0	24.4	125 122	6 032	66.4	5 829	0.0	12.0	6.2
Madison, LA	18 917	20.7	66.2	13.0	16 945	7 307	64.5	1 402	0.0	6.8	20.3
Morehouse, LA	41 769	18.4	51.2	30.4	39 959	7 755	65.9	2 109	0.0	12.5	14.2
Natchitoches, LA	50 755	19.4	52.8	27.8	48 874	7 019	64.2	3 932	0.0	6.3	5.7
Orleans, LA	538 644	15.7	44.0	40.3	494 182	7 276	64.7	30 841	0.3	9.6	8.0
Ouachita, LA	226 375	12.0	49.9	38.2	196 742	7 059	66.8	10 101	0.1	10.9	8.8
Plaquemines, LA	44 698	11.8	27.9	60.3	39 502	7 953	60.4	1 648	0.0	12.0	4.3
Pointe Coupee, LA	26 513	19.6	42.9	37.6	27 061	8 504	64.2	1 517	0.5	12.3	8.0
Rapides, LA	172 423	15.1	52.2	32.7	161 520	7 132	64.3	8 535	0.2	11.7	9.8

Table C-1. Population, School, and Student Characteristics by County—*Continued*

STATE County	High school graduates, 2000			College enrollment, 2000		College graduates, 2000 (percent)						
	Population 25 years and over	High school graduate or less (percent)	High school graduate or more (percent)	Number	Percent public	Bachelor's degree or more	+/- U.S. percentage with bachelor's degree or more	Non-Hispanic White	Black	American Indian and Alaska Native	Asian or Pacific Islander	Hispanic[3]
	30	31	32	33	34	35	36	37	38	39	40	41
Mason, KY	11 372	62.5	73.3	598	82.8	14.4	-10.0	15.0	6.6	0.0	27.3	0.0
Meade, KY	16 131	62.0	77.9	976	84.7	11.3	-13.1	11.0	16.6	0.0	33.0	14.8
Menifee, KY	4 213	81.7	57.6	177	97.7	8.4	-16.0	8.6	0.0	0.0	. . .	0.0
Mercer, KY	14 158	65.8	75.8	529	78.6	13.5	-10.9	13.9	8.3	0.0	19.1	0.0
Metcalfe, KY	6 729	79.6	58.0	258	93.0	6.6	-17.8	6.7	13.0	0.0	. . .	0.0
Monroe, KY	7 896	76.8	57.8	438	82.2	8.4	-16.0	8.6	0.0	0.0	100.0	0.0
Montgomery, KY	15 033	68.8	70.5	574	94.9	13.4	-11.0	13.5	9.3	0.0	85.7	18.9
Morgan, KY	9 321	76.4	56.4	420	89.5	7.7	-16.7	7.9	2.5	0.0	15.4	2.0
Muhlenberg, KY	21 676	74.9	65.8	919	89.2	8.1	-16.3	8.3	5.2	0.0	0.0	0.0
Nelson, KY	23 785	64.1	79.0	1 030	76.8	13.4	-11.0	13.4	9.4	0.0	52.5	15.6
Nicholas, KY	4 636	74.7	62.9	158	98.7	7.5	-16.9	7.2	21.7	0.0	. . .	0.0
Ohio, KY	15 237	74.5	67.0	646	91.0	7.4	-17.0	7.4	15.0	0.0	100.0	0.0
Oldham, KY	30 366	40.0	86.5	1 972	73.9	30.6	6.2	31.7	0.8	50.8	43.7	16.1
Owen, KY	6 999	73.3	67.9	227	86.3	9.1	-15.3	9.0	18.4	0.0	28.6	3.5
Owsley, KY	3 242	78.7	49.2	154	89.6	7.7	-16.7	7.8	. . .	0.0	. . .	0.0
Pendleton, KY	9 081	74.1	72.8	345	83.5	9.7	-14.7	9.8	6.9	0.0	33.3	0.0
Perry, KY	19 596	73.0	58.3	1 179	91.2	8.9	-15.5	8.6	7.4	0.0	78.6	0.0
Pike, KY	46 153	72.6	61.8	2 322	66.5	9.9	-14.5	9.9	0.0	0.0	35.2	13.0
Powell, KY	8 485	80.4	56.1	196	71.9	6.5	-17.9	6.5	0.0	13.3	. . .	10.4
Pulaski, KY	38 430	69.2	65.6	1 781	93.9	10.5	-13.9	10.4	5.7	8.6	40.2	0.7
Robertson, KY	1 566	75.5	60.9	81	84.0	8.7	-15.7	8.8	0.0	. . .	0.0	0.0
Rockcastle, KY	11 109	79.3	57.7	366	87.4	8.3	-16.1	8.3	0.0	0.0	. . .	2.9
Rowan, KY	12 455	58.1	70.9	4 503	98.0	21.9	-2.5	21.7	47.3	0.0	92.4	0.0
Russell, KY	11 437	72.6	61.8	541	78.9	9.6	-14.8	9.6	5.3	33.3	12.1	0.0
Scott, KY	20 459	52.8	80.5	2 150	40.1	20.3	-4.1	20.6	11.8	0.0	66.1	19.5
Shelby, KY	22 096	55.4	79.1	820	74.3	18.7	-5.7	20.4	7.5	0.0	0.0	5.7
Simpson, KY	10 680	67.4	73.6	394	93.4	11.9	-12.5	12.9	3.6	0.0	22.2	0.0
Spencer, KY	7 672	65.0	75.4	307	70.7	11.1	-13.3	11.2	0.0	0.0	0.0	0.0
Taylor, KY	15 253	68.1	68.0	1 403	32.3	12.2	-12.2	12.4	11.7	0.0	0.0	0.0
Todd, KY	7 758	73.2	63.5	237	92.8	9.2	-15.2	10.2	0.6	0.0	0.0	5.6
Trigg, KY	8 897	64.6	72.1	399	90.0	12.0	-12.4	12.7	4.6	0.0	41.7	5.0
Trimble, KY	5 340	70.2	70.7	215	81.4	7.6	-16.8	7.7	18.2	0.0	. . .	0.0
Union, KY	9 524	66.0	76.9	530	77.5	10.9	-13.5	11.4	6.0	0.0	21.6	0.0
Warren, KY	56 069	51.0	80.3	10 926	95.6	24.7	0.3	25.8	10.6	17.1	50.1	9.5
Washington, KY	7 144	69.7	68.8	369	48.0	13.3	-11.1	14.1	2.7	39.1	18.2	0.0
Wayne, KY	13 153	78.0	57.8	423	87.5	7.2	-17.2	7.4	0.0	13.5	0.0	0.0
Webster, KY	9 424	72.6	70.9	543	92.4	7.1	-17.3	7.3	4.5	. . .	0.0	0.0
Whitley, KY	22 708	70.1	61.3	1 972	38.1	13.4	-11.0	13.3	0.0	28.0	53.2	13.0
Wolfe, KY	4 571	77.1	53.6	217	91.7	10.6	-13.8	10.2	0.0	. . .	84.6	61.5
Woodford, KY	15 546	46.9	82.6	960	59.8	25.9	1.5	27.1	11.8	100.0	90.0	3.7
LOUISIANA	2 775 468	57.6	74.8	258 000	81.7	18.7	-5.7	21.7	10.9	9.2	35.2	19.5
Acadia, LA	35 573	73.4	64.7	1 884	89.0	9.4	-15.0	10.2	5.0	0.0	19.0	14.5
Allen, LA	16 817	74.8	63.2	646	87.2	9.3	-15.1	11.3	4.2	0.7	6.4	10.3
Ascension, LA	46 258	62.1	79.6	3 105	83.8	14.5	-9.9	15.9	7.8	6.6	26.1	15.0
Assumption, LA	14 411	77.5	59.4	666	89.2	7.4	-17.0	7.9	6.4	0.0	8.8	0.0
Avoyelles, LA	26 606	77.3	59.8	1 013	86.8	8.3	-16.1	9.4	4.4	4.8	28.7	17.2
Beauregard, LA	21 036	64.5	75.0	853	88.2	13.8	-10.6	14.2	8.6	20.2	14.3	28.4
Bienville, LA	10 172	69.4	71.9	514	91.6	11.5	-12.9	13.6	8.5	7.7	0.0	8.3
Bossier, LA	61 237	49.5	83.0	5 161	87.3	18.1	-6.3	20.5	8.5	12.7	23.8	13.1
Caddo, LA	159 011	53.5	78.7	13 004	84.7	20.6	-3.8	27.1	10.6	11.6	43.8	17.8
Calcasieu, LA	114 563	57.5	77.0	9 274	90.3	16.9	-7.5	19.0	8.3	6.3	37.0	19.5
Caldwell, LA	6 922	73.2	65.4	311	90.4	8.8	-15.6	9.8	4.2	0.0	22.2	6.3
Cameron, LA	6 257	74.7	68.1	230	95.2	7.9	-16.5	8.3	4.2	0.0	0.0	6.8
Catahoula, LA	6 904	75.3	61.4	325	92.3	9.4	-15.0	10.4	6.0	0.0	. . .	12.5
Claiborne, LA	11 169	69.5	65.7	455	93.0	12.4	-12.0	17.4	6.0	25.0	0.0	14.9
Concordia, LA	12 814	69.9	64.6	406	85.0	9.6	-14.8	10.9	6.6	3.8	41.9	7.4
De Soto, LA	16 118	70.3	70.3	782	85.5	10.2	-14.2	12.6	6.7	0.8	40.0	7.3
East Baton Rouge, LA	245 296	42.5	83.9	45 355	91.7	30.8	6.4	37.4	17.8	27.3	51.6	35.8
East Carroll, LA	5 542	73.3	57.9	218	93.6	12.3	-12.1	18.1	8.4	100.0	70.6	0.0
East Feliciana, LA	13 877	68.8	70.7	530	84.2	11.3	-13.1	16.4	4.8	0.0	18.6	8.5
Evangeline, LA	21 511	75.2	55.5	1 127	94.9	9.5	-14.9	11.4	3.6	0.0	22.1	2.0
Franklin, LA	13 423	75.1	61.4	464	89.9	9.8	-14.6	10.6	7.1	0.0	25.0	0.0
Grant, LA	11 921	68.5	73.1	436	90.8	9.8	-14.6	10.1	5.6	18.3	22.9	15.4
Iberia, LA	43 965	71.6	66.9	2 222	89.9	11.2	-13.2	13.1	6.4	20.5	7.9	12.0
Iberville, LA	21 101	73.2	65.7	1 124	88.6	9.6	-14.8	11.9	6.6	0.0	11.1	13.1
Jackson, LA	10 062	66.1	73.6	541	94.6	12.9	-11.5	12.9	13.1	0.0	29.4	0.0
Jefferson, LA	298 761	50.7	79.3	25 389	68.5	21.5	-2.9	23.6	12.2	10.9	35.4	18.6
Jefferson Davis, LA	19 352	71.8	69.4	903	90.7	9.9	-14.5	10.8	6.2	4.5	15.2	0.0
Lafayette, LA	116 183	49.2	79.8	13 951	91.8	25.5	1.1	29.1	11.1	17.5	46.2	20.5
Lafourche, LA	55 891	71.7	66.3	4 683	90.6	12.4	-12.0	13.1	5.1	3.7	42.4	13.9
La Salle, LA	9 219	70.0	68.5	371	91.4	11.2	-13.2	12.2	4.3	0.0	3.4	3.1
Lincoln, LA	22 059	44.3	80.4	10 157	96.7	31.8	7.4	35.1	22.9	27.1	84.5	22.0
Livingston, LA	56 528	66.0	77.2	3 235	89.4	11.4	-13.0	11.6	6.5	9.6	26.5	11.7
Madison, LA	7 670	70.3	63.4	325	87.7	11.0	-13.4	14.8	8.0	0.0	28.6	6.9
Morehouse, LA	19 446	72.2	66.6	810	97.5	9.7	-14.7	11.6	6.7	14.7	0.0	6.8
Natchitoches, LA	22 033	59.4	72.7	5 204	95.8	18.4	-6.0	23.8	8.6	12.3	50.7	26.7
Orleans, LA	300 568	48.8	74.7	39 625	53.9	25.8	1.4	47.6	13.4	17.1	31.5	27.1
Ouachita, LA	88 430	51.4	78.6	10 363	92.5	22.7	-1.7	26.6	13.1	9.1	48.0	12.2
Plaquemines, LA	16 448	65.5	68.7	1 234	70.9	10.8	-13.6	13.4	3.3	1.6	10.3	7.7
Pointe Coupee, LA	14 577	70.0	69.1	683	85.9	12.8	-11.6	14.7	9.0	0.0	3.0	12.3
Rapides, LA	79 811	59.1	74.6	4 620	75.2	16.5	-7.9	19.5	8.5	9.0	37.3	14.9

[3] May be of any race.

. . . = Not available.

Table C-1. Population, School, and Student Characteristics by County—*Continued*

STATE County	State/county code	County type[1]	Population, 2005		Number of schools and students, 2004–2005			Resident enrollment, 2000			
			Total	Percent 5 to 17 years	School districts	Schools	Students	Total	Percent public	K–12	Percent public
			1	2	3	4	5	6	7	8	9
Red River, LA	22081	6	9 465	20.2	1	5	1 603	2 747	89.7	2 257	89.5
Richland, LA	22083	6	20 526	18.4	2	13	3 829	5 489	86.4	4 427	87.2
Sabine, LA	22085	6	23 786	17.8	1	14	4 198	5 663	94.7	4 685	95.4
St. Bernard, LA	22087	1	65 364	17.3	1	14	8 802	17 654	70.1	12 950	71.5
St. Charles, LA	22089	1	50 633	19.8	1	20	9 719	14 720	82.5	11 466	85.9
St. Helena, LA	22091	2	10 259	19.9	1	3	1 364	2 993	81.6	2 370	82.0
St. James, LA	22093	6	21 150	19.3	1	10	4 022	6 103	81.0	4 953	80.3
St. John the Baptist, LA	22095	1	46 393	20.8	1	12	6 466	13 204	67.3	10 116	67.5
St. Landry, LA	22097	4	89 937	19.6	1	39	15 162	24 609	86.7	19 809	86.9
St. Martin, LA	22099	3	50 434	19.5	1	18	8 535	13 235	84.2	10 914	84.6
St. Mary, LA	22101	4	51 416	19.8	2	28	10 477	14 750	86.8	12 006	88.5
St. Tammany, LA	22103	1	220 295	18.9	1	52	35 620	54 129	76.5	41 459	80.5
Tangipahoa, LA	22105	4	106 502	18.3	1	38	18 563	30 230	86.5	20 980	86.6
Tensas, LA	22107	9	6 125	17.5	1	4	894	1 750	82.3	1 428	84.8
Terrebonne, LA	22109	3	107 491	18.9	1	41	19 135	28 789	83.7	23 114	85.7
Union, LA	22111	3	22 901	17.2	1	10	3 371	5 345	91.2	4 340	92.5
Vermilion, LA	22113	4	55 195	18.6	1	20	8 995	14 156	87.8	11 657	89.3
Vernon, LA	22115	4	48 745	21.4	1	20	9 889	14 157	93.8	10 708	95.6
Washington, LA	22117	6	44 623	18.0	2	23	7 664	10 968	90.6	9 038	92.1
Webster, LA	22119	6	41 356	17.3	1	22	7 605	10 694	92.9	8 397	94.2
West Baton Rouge, LA	22121	2	21 634	18.5	1	11	3 405	5 967	82.2	4 728	84.0
West Carroll, LA	22123	9	11 806	17.1	1	8	2 346	2 913	96.7	2 498	97.8
West Feliciana, LA	22125	2	15 199	13.0	1	5	2 448	3 830	80.6	3 181	81.9
Winn, LA	22127	6	15 968	16.7	1	8	2 785	4 107	95.7	3 319	97.3
MAINE	23000		1 321 505	15.9	331	684	198 820	321 041	85.7	236 267	92.2
Androscoggin, ME	23001	3	108 039	16.2	14	43	16 130	25 970	80.3	18 993	89.2
Aroostook, ME	23003	7	73 240	15.2	35	54	11 653	17 892	95.5	13 414	96.9
Cumberland, ME	23005	2	274 950	16.0	20	95	39 514	68 515	82.4	47 766	91.4
Franklin, ME	23007	6	29 704	15.5	10	18	4 607	8 413	92.4	5 706	94.5
Hancock, ME	23009	6	53 660	14.8	39	37	7 116	12 336	86.0	9 173	92.8
Kennebec, ME	23011	4	120 986	15.8	24	52	17 191	30 287	83.7	22 240	93.4
Knox, ME	23013	7	41 219	14.8	13	28	6 688	8 546	85.7	6 908	90.1
Lincoln, ME	23015	8	35 240	15.0	22	16	3 296	7 510	82.4	6 137	86.9
Oxford, ME	23017	6	56 628	16.1	15	42	10 266	12 792	87.9	10 674	91.4
Penobscot, ME	23019	3	147 068	15.2	38	89	23 589	40 435	88.0	26 268	92.8
Piscataquis, ME	23021	8	17 674	14.8	12	14	2 723	3 892	89.8	3 221	93.5
Sagadahoc, ME	23023	2	36 962	17.0	9	21	6 314	8 939	88.0	7 054	94.2
Somerset, ME	23025	6	51 667	16.5	13	37	8 818	11 942	90.2	9 920	93.6
Waldo, ME	23027	6	38 705	16.2	8	25	4 819	8 692	88.5	6 873	95.6
Washington, ME	23029	7	33 448	15.3	43	42	4 634	8 044	92.2	6 122	94.0
York, ME	23031	2	202 315	16.7	16	71	31 462	46 836	84.1	35 798	91.4
MARYLAND	24000		5 600 388	18.2	26	1 421	865 561	1 475 484	79.6	1 024 955	85.1
Allegany, MD	24001	3	73 639	14.6	1	27	9 840	18 070	91.9	11 666	92.6
Anne Arundel, MD	24003	1	510 878	18.1	1	119	73 991	131 201	79.4	93 322	83.5
Baltimore, MD	24005	1	786 113	17.1	1	168	107 701	201 904	76.6	135 001	80.3
Calvert, MD	24009	1	87 925	20.0	1	27	17 451	21 773	87.6	17 349	91.4
Caroline, MD	24011	6	31 822	18.6	1	10	5 412	7 456	90.4	6 178	91.3
Carroll, MD	24013	1	168 541	19.3	1	45	28 792	41 776	81.6	31 629	90.2
Cecil, MD	24015	1	97 796	19.1	1	31	16 535	22 438	85.5	17 589	89.5
Charles, MD	24017	1	138 822	20.2	1	34	26 026	35 134	82.5	26 224	85.9
Dorchester, MD	24019	6	31 401	16.6	1	13	4 788	7 043	88.6	5 525	90.6
Frederick, MD	24021	1	220 701	19.4	1	61	39 489	54 005	84.0	39 734	92.6
Garrett, MD	24023	6	29 909	17.8	1	18	4 737	6 978	91.6	5 660	93.9
Harford, MD	24025	1	239 259	19.8	1	51	40 294	61 532	82.3	45 281	87.5
Howard, MD	24027	1	269 457	20.0	1	70	48 219	73 343	80.2	51 631	87.8
Kent, MD	24029	6	19 899	14.4	1	8	2 514	4 940	68.5	3 114	90.1
Montgomery, MD	24031	1	927 583	18.0	1	197	139 393	240 098	74.9	164 578	81.9
Prince George's, MD	24033	1	846 123	19.0	1	205	136 095	249 844	80.3	162 830	84.6
Queen Anne's, MD	24035	1	45 612	18.2	1	13	7 713	9 899	87.0	7 714	89.9
St. Mary's, MD	24037	4	96 518	19.2	1	27	16 567	25 031	82.0	17 963	84.1
Somerset, MD	24039	3	25 845	13.1	1	10	2 952	7 036	89.1	3 949	92.8
Talbot, MD	24041	6	35 683	15.1	1	8	4 505	7 292	76.9	5 584	80.7
Washington, MD	24043	3	141 895	16.7	1	46	20 807	29 792	86.4	23 374	90.7
Wicomico, MD	24045	3	90 402	17.1	1	27	14 387	24 554	88.3	16 004	90.0
Worcester, MD	24047	4	48 750	14.4	1	14	6 676	9 832	89.5	7 510	92.3
Baltimore city, MD	24510	1	635 815	17.9	3	192	90 677	184 513	76.9	125 546	84.7
MASSACHUSETTS	25000		6 398 743	16.6	493	1 878	975 574	1 726 111	74.0	1 129 778	88.4
Barnstable, MA	25001	3	226 514	14.1	23	60	30 728	47 762	85.2	35 283	93.5
Berkshire, MA	25003	3	131 868	15.6	40	51	19 448	34 081	81.2	23 446	90.9
Bristol, MA	25005	1	546 331	17.4	29	168	91 320	137 870	82.2	99 120	90.3
Dukes, MA	25007	7	15 592	15.0	10	8	2 448	3 307	89.4	2 622	97.0
Essex, MA	25009	1	738 301	17.8	49	212	116 398	194 443	78.6	138 179	87.6
Franklin, MA	25011	2	72 334	15.7	35	41	10 314	18 575	87.9	13 222	89.7
Hampden, MA	25013	2	461 591	18.4	29	147	77 745	127 601	81.9	90 633	89.9
Hampshire, MA	25015	2	153 339	12.9	27	53	20 799	55 111	77.6	23 193	89.2
Middlesex, MA	25017	1	1 459 011	15.9	75	378	213 451	391 638	67.9	239 751	88.1
Nantucket, MA	25019	7	10 168	12.4	1	3	1 223	1 800	76.3	1 412	87.6

[1]County type codes are from the Economic Research Service of the United States Department of Agriculture. See notes and definitions at the end of this section.

Table C-1. Population, School, and Student Characteristics by County—*Continued*

STATE County	Characteristics of students, 2004–2005				Outcomes		Staff and students, 2004–2005		
	Percent with IEP[2]	Percent eligible for free or reduced-price lunch	Percent minority	Percent English-language learners	Number of graduates, 2003–2004	Percent dropouts, grades 9–12, 2001–2002	Number of teachers	Student-teacher ratio	Central administration staff
	10	11	12	13	14	15	16	17	18
Red River, LA	13.6	82.8	68.7	0.0	78	20.5	118	13.6	14
Richland, LA	13.8	70.9	52.4	0.0	...	7.3	270	14.2	29
Sabine, LA	16.7	65.4	48.4	0.9	277	5.0	309	13.6	38
St. Bernard, LA	14.2	57.2	25.4	0.6	464	6.3	627	14.0	48
St. Charles, LA	12.0	47.7	40.5	1.5	609	3.4	786	12.4	71
St. Helena, LA	19.2	85.0	93.1	0.2	70	2.2	82	16.6	15
St. James, LA	13.7	72.7	68.4	0.1	199	7.0	309	13.0	34
St. John the Baptist, LA	19.4	82.4	78.3	1.5	262	8.5	474	13.7	45
St. Landry, LA	15.2	75.9	56.9	0.6	771	5.0	1 049	14.4	99
St. Martin, LA	14.6	70.0	49.0	0.9	485	6.4	547	15.6	55
St. Mary, LA	15.9	65.8	49.6	3.7	...	4.9	753	13.9	60
St. Tammany, LA	17.4	36.4	21.8	1.7	2 013	4.0	2 560	13.9	163
Tangipahoa, LA	14.4	68.7	47.4	0.6	994	7.0	1 070	17.3	122
Tensas, LA	20.1	79.3	90.4	0.0	44	6.8	73	12.3	19
Terrebonne, LA	16.2	60.5	39.1	2.0	1 031	8.3	1 353	14.1	109
Union, LA	14.2	66.7	45.2	3.1	177	4.1	208	16.2	18
Vermilion, LA	15.7	56.5	25.0	1.8	542	4.0	623	14.4	49
Vernon, LA	14.1	48.4	28.4	1.0	453	4.1	702	14.1	48
Washington, LA	19.8	83.7	45.0	0.7	440	4.0	554	13.8	99
Webster, LA	14.5	54.3	45.0	0.1	413	3.8	490	15.5	30
West Baton Rouge, LA	14.5	66.5	50.9	0.0	205	6.8	257	13.3	22
West Carroll, LA	12.5	72.5	22.3	0.4	119	5.6	179	13.1	16
West Feliciana, LA	14.7	49.4	43.8	0.4	135	3.4	195	12.6	27
Winn, LA	11.5	67.1	37.3	0.0	165	5.5	194	14.4	19
MAINE	16.8	33.5	4.5	1.4	...	2.8	16 656	11.9	...
Androscoggin, ME	17.7	40.7	6.9	3.5	...	3.3	1 335	12.1	...
Aroostook, ME	15.0	45.9	4.6	2.7	...	1.3	978	11.9	...
Cumberland, ME	14.1	21.6	7.9	3.4	...	2.7	3 249	12.2	328
Franklin, ME	14.8	43.3	2.9	0.2	...	3.9	422	10.9	...
Hancock, ME	19.9	30.7	3.1	0.3	...	6.0	699	10.2	...
Kennebec, ME	18.8	33.5	2.7	0.7	...	2.3	1 435	12.0	...
Knox, ME	16.5	31.9	2.0	0.2	...	1.8	615	10.9	...
Lincoln, ME	23.8	33.2	1.9	0.3	...	4.3	323	10.2	...
Oxford, ME	16.9	43.4	2.5	0.2	...	3.4	864	11.9	95
Penobscot, ME	15.9	36.2	3.9	0.3	...	2.8	1 948	12.1	...
Piscataquis, ME	17.0	53.5	2.4	0.1	...	4.7	200	13.6	...
Sagadahoc, ME	19.4	28.1	4.5	0.6	...	2.8	551	11.5	...
Somerset, ME	19.5	46.7	1.9	0.1	...	2.9	733	12.0	...
Waldo, ME	20.6	46.8	2.2	0.2	...	2.8	452	10.7	41
Washington, ME	17.9	52.1	6.2	0.5	...	3.6	468	9.9	...
York, ME	17.1	25.8	3.2	0.9	...	2.5	2 385	13.2	...
MARYLAND	12.9	32.1	50.5	3.0	...	3.9	55 101	15.7	...
Allegany, MD	15.8	46.5	5.9	0.1	697	4.1	702	14.0	46
Anne Arundel, MD	13.6	18.2	29.1	1.5	4 774	4.4	4 603	16.1	184
Baltimore, MD	13.0	30.7	46.0	2.1	7 485	3.0	7 368	14.6	342
Calvert, MD	10.4	13.4	10.4	0.6	1 131	3.3	1 059	16.5	67
Caroline, MD	13.0	46.0	23.9	1.6	325	5.8	350	15.4	25
Carroll, MD	12.8	9.6	6.4	0.4	2 070	2.0	1 769	16.3	112
Cecil, MD	15.2	26.1	12.0	0.7	956	3.0	1 054	15.7	63
Charles, MD	9.3	22.6	50.0	0.6	1 723	3.3	1 506	17.3	109
Dorchester, MD	11.3	50.4	45.1	1.5	304	5.8	319	15.0	25
Frederick, MD	12.4	15.0	19.1	1.6	2 610	1.8	2 475	16.0	144
Garrett, MD	14.6	42.5	0.6	0.0	281	4.8	365	13.0	26
Harford, MD	15.1	18.9	23.2	0.8	2 707	3.4	2 378	16.9	320
Howard, MD	10.4	10.9	36.1	3.0	3 184	2.0	3 361	14.3	226
Kent, MD	14.3	39.3	31.0	2.3	166	6.3	159	15.8	18
Montgomery, MD	12.7	23.2	56.7	9.2	9 108	1.9	9 135	15.3	621
Prince George's, MD	10.9	45.9	92.9	...	7 663	3.1	8 174	16.7	204
Queen Anne's, MD	13.2	15.2	11.8	0.9	458	3.3	456	16.9	45
St. Mary's, MD	13.6	23.0	24.1	0.7	893	3.1	1 010	16.4	76
Somerset, MD	12.5	60.1	50.7	2.2	163	5.3	205	14.4	21
Talbot, MD	10.5	28.1	27.3	2.8	285	3.3	297	15.2	33
Washington, MD	12.8	34.4	14.1	1.0	1 409	3.1	1 331	15.6	77
Wicomico, MD	11.6	43.4	42.1	2.1	887	6.2	1 027	14.0	85
Worcester, MD	10.8	33.6	28.8	2.4	478	3.2	538	12.4	47
Baltimore city, MD	16.6	72.8	91.5	1.5	...	11.5	5 463	16.6	...
MASSACHUSETTS	16.6	27.7	25.8	5.1	...	...	73 397	13.3	...
Barnstable, MA	15.6	16.9	8.4	1.6	...	...	2 477	12.4	192
Berkshire, MA	15.8	27.3	9.7	1.8	...	...	1 604	12.1	166
Bristol, MA	16.4	30.0	15.1	2.1	...	...	6 314	14.5	595
Dukes, MA	21.7	10.8	15.0	4.1	...	...	256	9.6	23
Essex, MA	16.1	30.2	27.6	6.1	...	...	8 582	13.6	746
Franklin, MA	18.7	32.4	7.3	1.3	...	...	905	11.4	116
Hampden, MA	18.3	46.4	41.6	8.4	...	...	6 244	12.5	604
Hampshire, MA	17.0	19.8	12.9	1.6	...	...	1 585	13.1	181
Middlesex, MA	16.7	18.2	22.3	5.2	...	...	16 247	13.1	1 722
Nantucket, MA	15.0	11.7	16.5	2.8	82	...	120	10.2	13

[2]IEP = Individual Education Program. See notes and definitions at the end of this section.
... = Not available.

Table C-1. Population, School, and Student Characteristics by County—Continued

STATE County	Revenue, 2003–2004				Current expenditures, 2003–2004			Resident population, 16 to 19 years, 2000			
	Total revenue (thousands of dollars)	Percent of revenue from:			Total expenditures (thousands of dollars)	Amount per student (dollars)	Percent for instruction	Total	Percent in armed forces	Percent high school graduates	Percent not enrolled, not employed, not in armed forces, not high school graduate
		Federal government	State government	Local government							
	19	20	21	22	23	24	25	26	27	28	29
Red River, LA	16 429	18.7	57.3	24.0	13 875	8 507	66.2	689	0.0	8.9	10.2
Richland, LA	27 245	16.9	62.0	21.1	26 473	7 614	66.3	1 283	0.0	12.2	13.4
Sabine, LA	33 345	18.9	58.0	23.1	29 507	6 912	64.5	1 334	0.0	8.5	8.0
St. Bernard, LA	70 377	13.2	45.2	41.6	62 142	7 007	66.7	3 813	0.2	11.6	5.8
St. Charles, LA	109 786	7.8	24.9	67.3	89 040	9 194	64.4	3 070	0.0	7.0	6.6
St. Helena, LA	11 067	20.3	63.4	16.3	10 510	7 873	59.6	740	0.0	13.4	9.3
St. James, LA	37 903	11.9	33.8	54.2	35 000	8 616	60.2	1 450	0.0	10.8	9.2
St. John the Baptist, LA	57 638	13.6	49.2	37.3	52 723	8 319	66.0	2 839	0.3	7.2	9.5
St. Landry, LA	113 353	16.2	57.8	26.0	107 176	7 037	68.0	5 787	0.0	9.0	9.8
St. Martin, LA	61 573	17.0	60.8	22.2	58 456	6 768	63.5	3 133	0.0	9.2	10.2
St. Mary, LA	74 610	14.4	50.7	34.9	72 460	7 109	64.6	3 311	0.0	10.9	9.5
St. Tammany, LA	297 150	8.8	49.7	41.6	266 410	7 666	67.6	10 690	0.1	8.3	5.1
Tangipahoa, LA	127 084	16.9	58.9	24.3	111 798	6 055	67.9	7 310	0.1	9.8	10.0
Tensas, LA	11 540	39.3	42.3	18.4	9 199	10 406	64.5	456	0.0	9.6	14.5
Terrebonne, LA	135 071	14.3	54.6	31.1	130 117	6 757	68.5	7 026	0.0	8.5	8.6
Union, LA	21 648	18.7	59.9	21.5	22 620	6 732	64.2	1 297	0.0	8.9	7.2
Vermilion, LA	61 644	15.6	52.1	32.3	57 351	6 435	65.2	3 486	0.3	8.8	10.4
Vernon, LA	76 173	22.5	58.7	18.8	70 154	7 105	64.8	3 387	18.1	30.5	4.2
Washington, LA	66 165	18.4	61.1	20.5	61 935	8 036	64.5	2 637	0.3	13.7	11.4
Webster, LA	54 802	14.1	57.2	28.7	50 613	6 592	65.6	2 383	0.0	9.9	9.7
West Baton Rouge, LA	26 888	11.9	39.7	48.4	25 682	7 257	62.3	1 482	0.0	14.2	6.3
West Carroll, LA	15 334	15.1	67.5	17.3	14 574	6 147	63.0	773	0.0	14.4	7.6
West Feliciana, LA	24 955	12.5	41.8	45.7	22 942	9 426	62.5	749	0.0	11.3	8.9
Winn, LA	22 545	15.2	58.1	26.7	21 360	7 678	63.2	966	0.0	6.3	10.1
MAINE	2 228 749	8.5	39.0	52.4	1 960 145	9 723	69.8	69 770	0.3	10.0	3.4
Androscoggin, ME	173 329	9.0	50.2	40.9	151 205	9 266	69.8	5 914	0.1	12.6	3.9
Aroostook, ME	120 658	11.0	53.7	35.3	110 044	9 385	66.3	4 324	0.0	9.4	4.5
Cumberland, ME	433 648	6.4	28.2	65.5	387 774	9 785	70.6	13 901	0.6	8.9	2.2
Franklin, ME	54 292	11.8	37.7	50.6	48 152	10 002	69.4	2 046	0.0	5.5	4.3
Hancock, ME	99 413	8.0	22.7	69.3	82 589	11 194	69.8	2 771	0.8	8.8	4.8
Kennebec, ME	199 829	11.5	47.3	41.2	174 340	9 745	68.5	6 528	0.0	8.6	3.2
Knox, ME	82 207	6.4	30.4	63.1	71 191	10 407	69.3	1 781	0.4	14.6	4.0
Lincoln, ME	53 238	5.8	23.8	70.4	44 720	12 985	72.4	1 605	0.2	12.3	5.1
Oxford, ME	116 746	8.6	42.7	48.7	100 120	9 667	67.1	2 969	0.1	12.4	3.9
Penobscot, ME	252 623	9.1	44.6	46.3	216 628	9 151	69.9	9 564	0.1	8.9	2.8
Piscataquis, ME	29 489	12.0	48.1	39.9	26 398	9 705	72.1	971	0.0	12.3	5.0
Sagadahoc, ME	75 004	6.9	39.8	53.3	65 027	9 926	70.6	1 848	0.6	10.3	3.2
Somerset, ME	94 832	10.4	46.9	42.7	86 563	9 604	72.1	2 737	0.1	9.7	4.4
Waldo, ME	58 665	11.2	42.6	46.1	52 508	10 714	69.3	1 860	0.3	10.1	3.2
Washington, ME	63 027	15.0	38.0	47.1	54 779	11 880	66.4	1 912	0.8	11.7	6.0
York, ME	321 749	6.4	37.7	55.8	288 107	9 081	71.2	9 039	0.5	11.4	3.2
MARYLAND	9 123 493	6.4	37.7	56.0	8 006 635	9 212	68.3	277 834	0.7	11.6	4.8
Allegany, MD	100 840	11.8	52.8	35.3	94 543	9 525	67.1	4 583	0.0	13.3	3.9
Anne Arundel, MD	721 559	5.5	32.0	62.5	645 296	8 661	67.2	24 457	5.6	15.8	4.1
Baltimore, MD	1 074 341	6.3	35.1	58.6	983 521	9 063	66.3	39 091	0.0	11.5	3.9
Calvert, MD	168 336	5.2	37.3	57.5	150 322	8 628	68.5	4 209	0.0	14.0	1.8
Caroline, MD	50 668	10.2	62.0	27.8	46 991	8 702	66.2	1 692	0.1	17.8	5.3
Carroll, MD	277 788	4.8	38.3	56.9	238 032	8 256	65.1	8 043	0.0	12.4	2.5
Cecil, MD	152 789	6.5	44.2	49.3	135 318	8 214	66.1	4 586	0.2	19.6	6.0
Charles, MD	251 729	5.4	44.0	50.6	211 535	8 260	63.4	6 551	0.3	15.2	3.7
Dorchester, MD	53 858	11.0	45.6	43.5	44 159	9 194	66.7	1 435	0.0	16.6	7.6
Frederick, MD	407 770	3.9	36.3	59.8	329 456	8 458	67.7	10 177	0.1	11.5	1.9
Garrett, MD	48 175	10.8	45.2	44.0	44 993	9 354	65.1	1 783	0.0	11.0	6.1
Harford, MD	359 900	5.5	42.0	52.5	324 614	8 075	66.4	10 922	0.5	13.0	2.2
Howard, MD	537 507	3.3	27.4	69.3	478 322	10 000	69.3	11 305	0.1	8.4	1.8
Kent, MD	28 016	9.9	34.7	55.4	26 088	10 171	62.9	1 140	0.0	11.8	2.5
Montgomery, MD	1 812 254	4.1	18.9	77.0	1 553 788	11 162	72.6	38 934	0.2	7.1	3.3
Prince George's, MD	1 397 924	6.8	45.3	47.9	1 187 040	8 647	61.7	46 313	0.4	10.0	4.1
Queen Anne's, MD	82 431	5.4	31.1	63.5	64 284	8 542	66.5	1 952	0.6	11.6	5.1
St. Mary's, MD	160 704	8.1	46.4	45.5	134 539	8 274	64.0	5 076	2.5	14.8	4.7
Somerset, MD	30 660	14.4	53.2	32.4	29 911	10 136	63.1	1 704	0.2	12.3	2.1
Talbot, MD	46 224	8.2	22.7	69.1	41 870	9 390	68.4	1 267	0.0	13.5	9.2
Washington, MD	184 505	7.2	45.7	47.1	171 908	8 453	67.6	6 116	0.1	16.4	8.0
Wicomico, MD	130 420	9.8	50.6	39.6	128 408	8 916	66.4	5 618	0.0	11.5	4.5
Worcester, MD	79 804	8.5	21.0	70.5	73 334	10 811	68.2	1 930	0.0	14.4	4.1
Baltimore city, MD	965 291	12.0	64.8	23.2	868 363	9 233	77.5	38 950	0.0	12.0	11.6
MASSACHUSETTS	11 979 937	6.5	39.5	54.1	10 756 272	11 175	70.3	330 827	0.1	8.2	3.7
Barnstable, MA	390 200	5.0	24.3	70.7	340 726	11 364	69.6	8 984	0.5	10.1	2.9
Berkshire, MA	255 193	7.0	43.8	49.1	225 358	11 375	70.1	7 721	0.0	10.2	3.0
Bristol, MA	1 017 076	7.2	53.9	38.9	938 986	10 041	69.3	28 560	0.1	9.7	5.0
Dukes, MA	48 188	3.3	23.9	72.8	41 880	18 185	72.0	693	0.0	11.8	6.3
Essex, MA	1 378 113	6.8	42.8	50.4	1 239 372	10 681	70.6	35 775	0.1	7.8	3.4
Franklin, MA	150 414	6.5	44.7	48.7	125 398	11 878	66.8	3 862	0.1	7.8	5.7
Hampden, MA	947 694	9.6	57.5	32.9	848 414	11 153	70.6	26 293	0.1	8.2	6.8
Hampshire, MA	256 546	5.8	39.8	54.4	218 263	10 721	67.6	14 283	0.0	4.0	1.0
Middlesex, MA	2 730 665	4.8	29.4	65.8	2 479 391	11 807	70.7	70 607	0.0	7.8	2.5
Nantucket, MA	23 149	1.3	12.8	85.9	20 340	17 414	67.5	263	0.0	11.8	1.9

Table C-1. Population, School, and Student Characteristics by County—*Continued*

STATE County	High school graduates, 2000			College enrollment, 2000		College graduates, 2000 (percent)						
	Population 25 years and over	High school graduate or less (percent)	High school graduate or more (percent)	Number	Percent public	Bachelor's degree or more	+/- U.S. percentage with bachelor's degree or more	Non-Hispanic White	Black	American Indian and Alaska Native	Asian or Pacific Islander	Hispanic[3]
	30	31	32	33	34	35	36	37	38	39	40	41
Red River, LA	5 792	74.4	67.4	285	93.7	8.7	-15.7	11.0	4.7	0.0	0.0	0.0
Richland, LA	13 060	70.3	61.9	647	87.0	12.8	-11.6	16.9	3.9	0.0	100.0	19.0
Sabine, LA	15 388	70.1	70.8	705	89.9	11.1	-13.3	12.6	4.7	7.2	39.1	6.0
St. Bernard, LA	44 127	64.8	73.1	3 378	78.1	8.9	-15.5	9.1	5.6	7.9	20.3	7.4
St. Charles, LA	29 551	56.1	80.0	2 134	81.6	17.5	-6.9	19.5	9.7	0.0	42.3	19.3
St. Helena, LA	6 489	72.0	67.5	453	77.5	11.2	-13.2	13.6	8.9	0.0	0.0	14.6
St. James, LA	12 840	71.2	73.9	712	84.7	10.1	-14.3	11.1	8.7	0.0	13.3	18.4
St. John the Baptist, LA	25 377	62.1	76.9	1 978	77.5	12.9	-11.5	14.5	10.0	9.6	44.5	13.5
St. Landry, LA	53 592	71.2	62.0	3 169	89.9	10.7	-13.7	12.7	7.4	4.7	24.6	9.7
St. Martin, LA	29 617	74.9	62.9	1 475	85.3	8.5	-15.9	10.6	3.4	9.6	5.5	14.4
St. Mary, LA	33 158	72.3	65.9	1 563	83.9	9.4	-15.0	10.8	6.1	3.9	9.5	11.5
St. Tammany, LA	122 959	42.6	83.9	8 143	79.8	28.3	3.9	29.7	15.0	20.7	38.0	28.9
Tangipahoa, LA	59 909	62.8	71.5	7 455	92.1	16.3	-8.1	19.2	7.2	11.1	30.4	17.9
Tensas, LA	4 208	68.3	63.2	179	92.2	14.8	-9.6	23.3	6.7	0.0	0.0	9.6
Terrebonne, LA	63 271	68.7	67.1	3 785	86.9	12.3	-12.1	13.6	7.0	2.0	32.0	15.7
Union, LA	14 819	68.4	71.7	670	91.5	11.8	-12.6	13.5	6.5	17.0	0.0	10.5
Vermilion, LA	33 616	72.4	65.6	1 667	88.9	10.7	-13.7	11.4	6.9	14.6	4.0	5.9
Vernon, LA	29 329	56.3	80.1	2 577	91.3	13.5	-10.9	14.3	8.9	9.1	22.7	15.2
Washington, LA	27 954	71.9	68.2	1 262	85.1	10.9	-13.5	12.7	6.6	10.6	0.0	10.2
Webster, LA	27 687	65.1	70.8	1 480	90.8	12.6	-11.8	14.3	8.4	8.1	27.7	4.7
West Baton Rouge, LA	13 347	67.2	73.4	838	86.0	11.1	-13.3	12.2	9.2	17.6	0.0	15.5
West Carroll, LA	7 994	75.3	59.5	305	95.4	9.5	-14.9	10.9	2.8	0.0	0.0	0.0
West Feliciana, LA	10 749	70.8	53.3	447	74.0	10.6	-13.8	19.1	2.7	0.0	11.8	8.8
Winn, LA	11 093	74.6	65.4	494	89.7	9.4	-15.0	11.8	4.1	0.0	11.8	0.0
MAINE	869 893	50.8	85.4	67 216	71.0	22.9	-1.5	22.9	22.5	12.1	31.7	21.6
Androscoggin, ME	69 560	60.3	79.8	5 688	54.1	14.4	-10.0	14.3	14.9	19.8	29.7	14.5
Aroostook, ME	51 439	61.6	76.9	3 541	91.4	14.6	-9.8	14.6	33.9	2.5	41.1	12.1
Cumberland, ME	181 276	38.1	90.1	16 414	67.6	34.2	9.8	34.6	26.3	16.4	28.0	30.3
Franklin, ME	19 260	55.8	85.2	2 382	90.1	20.9	-3.5	20.8	0.0	27.3	25.6	46.3
Hancock, ME	36 416	46.7	87.8	2 559	69.1	27.1	2.7	27.1	41.7	10.9	42.6	10.6
Kennebec, ME	79 362	52.4	85.2	6 428	58.0	20.7	-3.7	20.7	20.4	6.2	28.8	16.4
Knox, ME	28 303	48.9	87.5	1 146	73.9	26.2	1.8	26.3	0.0	30.4	36.5	18.6
Lincoln, ME	24 094	47.2	87.9	976	70.4	26.6	2.2	26.6	0.0	17.0	57.8	19.6
Oxford, ME	37 929	60.7	82.4	1 405	77.3	15.7	-8.7	15.8	37.9	6.2	29.4	9.4
Penobscot, ME	95 505	52.7	85.7	12 276	82.8	20.3	-4.1	20.2	15.0	11.0	47.8	26.1
Piscataquis, ME	12 240	63.4	80.3	432	79.2	13.3	-11.1	13.5	16.7	3.3	0.0	8.3
Sagadahoc, ME	23 862	47.8	88.0	1 396	69.7	25.0	0.6	25.0	26.0	50.0	36.2	26.4
Somerset, ME	34 750	64.5	80.8	1 445	76.3	11.8	-12.6	11.9	16.7	8.6	2.6	9.6
Waldo, ME	24 818	54.2	84.6	1 306	59.1	22.3	-2.1	22.4	21.4	11.1	35.6	24.7
Washington, ME	23 488	62.0	79.9	1 543	87.8	14.7	-9.7	14.6	12.1	6.5	38.2	20.0
York, ME	127 591	48.5	86.5	8 279	64.8	22.9	-1.5	22.9	22.6	20.2	25.1	17.3
MARYLAND	3 495 595	42.9	83.8	354 477	72.9	31.4	7.0	34.9	20.3	21.2	54.7	21.4
Allegany, MD	51 205	62.5	79.9	5 521	94.3	14.1	-10.3	14.0	9.3	7.9	58.7	17.3
Anne Arundel, MD	326 999	41.5	86.4	29 356	78.2	30.6	6.2	32.1	19.4	22.8	40.7	28.2
Baltimore, MD	511 434	43.2	84.3	53 162	75.0	30.6	6.2	30.9	24.6	17.9	54.8	29.1
Calvert, MD	47 768	47.5	86.9	3 148	81.4	22.5	-1.9	24.4	8.4	9.9	50.1	20.2
Caroline, MD	19 550	67.0	75.0	836	90.3	12.1	-12.3	13.3	4.2	35.9	50.0	3.4
Carroll, MD	98 684	48.0	85.3	7 232	61.6	24.8	0.4	24.8	16.4	38.2	39.9	28.3
Cecil, MD	55 809	56.7	81.2	3 383	74.0	16.4	-8.0	16.3	11.1	29.9	50.1	22.9
Charles, MD	76 987	47.5	85.8	6 299	80.7	20.0	-4.4	21.2	15.9	7.6	31.5	26.4
Dorchester, MD	21 435	67.8	74.2	1 012	85.5	12.0	-12.4	14.0	5.6	0.0	37.0	11.9
Frederick, MD	127 256	43.0	87.1	10 587	66.2	30.0	5.6	30.8	11.5	20.9	54.4	27.1
Garrett, MD	20 004	64.4	79.2	1 015	84.3	13.8	-10.6	13.8	0.0	25.0	100.0	15.8
Harford, MD	143 056	41.5	86.7	11 837	75.8	27.3	2.9	27.8	20.3	38.7	36.6	23.3
Howard, MD	163 308	23.1	93.1	16 025	73.7	52.9	28.5	54.5	42.9	35.1	62.0	37.5
Kent, MD	13 103	57.1	78.8	1 568	25.9	21.7	-2.7	25.3	5.6	21.4	96.3	5.9
Montgomery, MD	594 034	24.2	90.3	57 291	68.7	54.6	30.2	62.1	39.6	32.2	59.7	22.1
Prince George's, MD	503 698	42.4	84.9	72 662	77.7	27.2	2.8	34.4	23.9	17.6	46.6	12.8
Queen Anne's, MD	28 018	46.0	84.2	1 540	83.5	25.4	1.0	27.2	6.7	23.5	25.9	27.2
St. Mary's, MD	54 552	49.6	85.3	5 548	82.0	22.6	-1.8	23.9	8.6	11.7	50.6	31.5
Somerset, MD	16 321	67.2	69.5	2 785	83.9	11.6	-12.8	13.7	7.3	0.0	52.7	6.5
Talbot, MD	24 809	46.3	84.4	1 167	75.5	27.8	3.4	31.4	6.6	22.2	34.5	22.3
Washington, MD	90 371	61.1	77.8	4 852	74.6	14.6	-9.8	15.2	4.1	8.5	32.3	15.3
Wicomico, MD	53 521	53.7	80.7	7 234	89.4	21.9	-2.5	24.9	9.9	22.9	32.5	25.7
Worcester, MD	34 092	52.5	81.7	1 681	86.6	21.6	-2.8	24.1	6.9	0.0	35.4	10.4
Baltimore city, MD	419 581	59.8	68.4	48 736	58.6	19.1	-5.3	32.9	10.0	16.7	51.8	24.6
MASSACHUSETTS	4 273 275	42.5	84.8	473 403	46.7	33.2	8.8	34.6	19.7	19.2	49.6	14.1
Barnstable, MA	165 115	35.4	91.8	8 492	70.8	33.6	9.2	34.4	20.0	15.5	42.4	21.3
Berkshire, MA	93 339	49.1	85.1	8 313	59.4	26.0	1.6	26.2	12.3	4.3	53.4	19.9
Bristol, MA	357 829	56.4	73.2	28 891	64.3	19.9	-4.5	20.1	16.9	16.6	39.6	9.5
Dukes, MA	10 693	32.8	90.4	409	64.1	38.4	14.0	39.4	32.0	14.7	42.6	40.6
Essex, MA	487 103	43.5	84.6	41 131	61.0	31.3	6.9	33.4	16.6	20.1	40.3	9.1
Franklin, MA	49 121	43.3	88.0	4 171	86.8	29.1	4.7	29.2	31.5	14.5	43.3	17.2
Hampden, MA	295 837	53.4	79.2	28 292	62.5	20.5	-3.9	22.7	14.4	10.2	31.5	6.2
Hampshire, MA	93 193	36.4	89.4	29 423	70.9	37.9	13.5	37.0	55.6	49.4	67.8	36.7
Middlesex, MA	1 006 497	34.9	88.5	121 081	35.7	43.6	19.2	43.9	30.3	34.1	61.2	24.1
Nantucket, MA	6 976	36.1	91.6	250	44.0	38.4	14.0	42.4	7.5	. . .	43.1	7.1

[3]May be of any race.
. . . = Not available.

Table C-1. Population, School, and Student Characteristics by County—*Continued*

STATE County	State/ county code	County type[1]	Population, 2005		Number of schools and students, 2004–2005			Resident enrollment, 2000			
			Total	Percent 5 to 17 years	School districts	Schools	Students	Total	Percent public	K–12	Percent public
			1	2	3	4	5	6	7	8	9
Norfolk, MA	25021	1	653 595	16.9	35	186	99 854	169 601	69.6	112 513	85.9
Plymouth, MA	25023	1	492 409	18.7	36	143	82 485	128 952	83.2	95 640	91.8
Suffolk, MA	25025	1	654 428	13.3	22	176	75 915	209 914	57.7	110 369	82.7
Worcester, MA	25027	2	783 262	18.0	82	252	133 446	205 456	78.7	144 395	89.5
MICHIGAN	26000		10 120 860	18.5	835	4 067	1 750 451	2 780 378	86.2	1 971 459	89.4
Alcona, MI	26001	9	11 653	13.5	1	4	1 051	2 113	94.6	1 764	95.7
Alger, MI	26003	9	9 662	14.1	4	5	1 369	2 015	94.5	1 715	96.5
Allegan, MI	26005	4	113 174	19.7	15	72	27 021	28 058	85.3	23 175	87.7
Alpena, MI	26007	7	30 428	16.4	3	15	5 159	7 992	89.4	5 933	91.4
Antrim, MI	26009	9	24 422	16.9	7	14	4 477	5 301	95.0	4 437	96.2
Arenac, MI	26011	8	17 154	16.0	3	8	2 849	4 010	94.8	3 230	97.3
Baraga, MI	26013	9	8 746	15.4	3	7	1 403	2 051	93.4	1 668	93.6
Barry, MI	26015	2	59 892	18.8	5	25	10 895	14 796	89.3	11 597	91.4
Bay, MI	26017	3	109 029	17.3	7	41	17 009	27 880	83.7	20 593	85.3
Benzie, MI	26019	9	17 644	16.1	2	8	2 651	3 445	90.0	2 795	92.2
Berrien, MI	26021	3	162 611	18.4	19	73	24 625	42 978	79.6	32 070	86.6
Branch, MI	26023	6	46 460	17.5	6	24	8 325	11 468	90.1	9 109	92.1
Calhoun, MI	26025	3	139 191	18.4	16	78	27 297	36 415	86.1	27 015	92.2
Cass, MI	26027	2	51 996	18.0	6	34	11 845	12 592	91.2	10 025	92.7
Charlevoix, MI	26029	7	26 722	18.1	8	18	4 847	6 278	91.1	5 162	94.1
Cheboygan, MI	26031	7	27 463	16.6	4	14	3 863	5 790	89.2	4 839	90.0
Chippewa, MI	26033	5	38 780	14.5	9	23	5 866	10 308	93.6	6 715	94.1
Clare, MI	26035	7	31 653	17.0	4	16	5 270	7 307	93.6	5 985	94.8
Clinton, MI	26037	2	69 329	19.3	7	68	26 533	18 094	87.5	13 925	89.6
Crawford, MI	26039	7	15 074	17.0	1	5	2 056	3 404	94.6	2 843	95.9
Delta, MI	26041	5	38 347	16.3	6	18	5 819	9 845	91.8	7 366	92.8
Dickinson, MI	26043	5	28 032	17.1	5	14	4 766	6 743	93.9	5 563	94.8
Eaton, MI	26045	2	107 394	17.8	12	48	20 485	28 631	87.0	21 041	91.3
Emmet, MI	26047	7	33 580	17.4	6	17	5 966	7 935	90.2	6 103	91.4
Genesee, MI	26049	2	443 883	19.5	33	177	86 914	120 255	88.8	90 051	91.8
Gladwin, MI	26051	6	27 209	16.2	3	10	3 664	5 597	90.4	4 696	91.4
Gogebic, MI	26053	7	16 861	14.2	5	8	2 206	3 902	88.9	2 933	89.9
Grand Traverse, MI	26055	5	83 971	17.0	5	16	3 721	19 918	84.3	15 076	85.4
Gratiot, MI	26057	6	42 345	16.4	7	26	7 979	11 080	82.3	7 956	93.5
Hillsdale, MI	26059	6	47 066	18.2	11	31	7 643	12 176	84.2	9 235	93.3
Houghton, MI	26061	5	35 705	14.4	10	21	5 681	12 652	94.3	6 172	96.1
Huron, MI	26063	7	34 640	16.8	17	31	6 678	8 425	87.9	6 984	90.1
Ingham, MI	26065	2	278 592	16.1	24	73	29 657	102 939	91.2	49 177	91.5
Ionia, MI	26067	2	64 608	18.2	10	33	10 264	15 973	88.1	13 143	90.3
Iosco, MI	26069	7	26 992	15.6	6	19	5 472	5 740	93.0	4 899	93.9
Iron, MI	26071	7	12 299	14.9	2	6	1 783	2 727	97.4	2 246	97.9
Isabella, MI	26073	5	65 618	13.2	5	21	6 938	28 337	93.7	9 886	88.7
Jackson, MI	26075	3	163 629	18.2	15	62	24 981	41 089	84.6	31 331	88.8
Kalamazoo, MI	26077	2	240 536	17.0	14	83	35 703	78 268	87.1	42 746	88.4
Kalkaska, MI	26079	7	17 239	17.8	2	7	1 829	3 785	94.0	3 169	95.4
Kent, MI	26081	2	596 666	19.8	39	279	112 601	165 304	78.8	120 383	84.0
Keweenaw, MI	26083	9	2 195	14.5	1	1	3	501	86.8	423	89.1
Lake, MI	26085	8	12 069	15.5	1	4	763	2 313	92.1	1 939	92.8
Lapeer, MI	26087	1	93 361	19.1	7	35	15 580	24 153	88.2	19 201	90.2
Leelanau, MI	26089	9	22 157	16.7	5	30	13 653	5 224	85.0	4 165	87.4
Lenawee, MI	26091	4	102 033	18.0	13	49	18 763	26 304	84.1	20 161	91.7
Livingston, MI	26093	1	181 517	19.6	9	60	37 328	44 359	87.8	34 074	92.0
Luce, MI	26095	7	6 789	15.0	1	4	1 108	1 638	89.6	1 391	88.4
Mackinac, MI	26097	7	11 331	15.6	6	11	1 684	2 544	96.2	2 148	96.9
Macomb, MI	26099	1	829 453	17.5	33	269	142 598	200 126	86.4	141 959	89.0
Manistee, MI	26101	7	25 226	15.5	6	16	3 607	5 638	87.8	4 633	89.6
Marquette, MI	26103	5	64 760	14.3	10	27	9 326	18 785	94.2	11 017	94.3
Mason, MI	26105	7	28 986	16.8	5	18	4 929	6 780	90.6	5 450	93.0
Mecosta, MI	26107	6	42 391	15.2	5	27	7 430	14 409	94.0	6 865	91.7
Menominee, MI	26109	7	24 996	16.8	7	18	4 503	5 896	92.6	4 709	94.2
Midland, MI	26111	4	84 064	18.9	7	35	15 417	23 890	84.9	17 269	92.8
Missaukee, MI	26113	9	15 299	18.3	2	7	2 263	3 629	87.0	3 056	89.4
Monroe, MI	26115	3	153 935	19.1	13	59	28 585	39 786	86.3	30 708	88.3
Montcalm, MI	26117	6	63 893	18.6	7	29	7 604	15 656	90.9	12 865	92.3
Montmorency, MI	26119	9	10 445	14.0	2	4	1 022	1 978	93.8	1 700	95.2
Muskegon, MI	26121	3	175 554	19.3	17	79	34 207	46 749	90.3	36 265	93.7
Newaygo, MI	26123	2	50 019	20.2	7	26	10 264	12 809	90.6	10 726	92.2
Oakland, MI	26125	1	1 214 361	18.2	52	397	205 221	326 864	82.5	225 089	87.2
Oceana, MI	26127	8	28 473	18.9	6	20	4 263	7 065	92.4	5 974	94.4
Ogemaw, MI	26129	9	21 905	16.2	1	5	2 609	5 004	91.3	4 137	92.2
Ontonagon, MI	26131	9	7 363	13.9	4	7	1 078	1 534	97.3	1 281	99.0
Osceola, MI	26133	7	23 750	18.5	4	17	5 251	5 867	90.9	4 933	92.7
Oscoda, MI	26135	9	9 298	16.2	2	4	1 156	2 015	89.6	1 704	91.3
Otsego, MI	26137	7	24 665	18.2	3	11	4 524	5 748	83.6	4 899	85.4
Ottawa, MI	26139	3	255 406	19.6	14	76	38 571	73 944	77.8	51 323	81.8

[1]County type codes are from the Economic Research Service of the United States Department of Agriculture. See notes and definitions at the end of this section.

Table C-1. Population, School, and Student Characteristics by County—*Continued*

STATE County	Characteristics of students, 2004–2005				Outcomes		Staff and students, 2004–2005		
	Percent with IEP[2]	Percent eligible for free or reduced-price lunch	Percent minority	Percent English-language learners	Number of graduates, 2003–2004	Percent dropouts, grades 9–12, 2001–2002	Number of teachers	Student-teacher ratio	Central administration staff
	10	11	12	13	14	15	16	17	18
Norfolk, MA	16.9	11.1	16.0	2.5	...	...	7 474	13.4	719
Plymouth, MA	14.6	20.2	15.8	1.9	...	...	5 714	14.4	513
Suffolk, MA	18.5	70.6	80.6	15.0	...	...	6 370	11.9	716
Worcester, MA	15.9	25.3	20.3	4.7	...	...	9 505	14.0	817
MICHIGAN	14.0	36.0	27.2	3.6	...	...	99 288	17.6	...
Alcona, MI	14.4	...	1.0	0.0	65	...	57	18.3	5
Alger, MI	15.9	41.1	14.1	0.0	...	...	88	15.5	12
Allegan, MI	13.2	28.1	9.6	6.0	...	...	1 489	18.1	129
Alpena, MI	12.3	38.0	2.0	0.0	...	...	294	17.5	25
Antrim, MI	12.1	38.9	4.9	0.0	202	...	246	18.2	23
Arenac, MI	13.2	55.7	3.3	0.0	...	...	154	18.5	14
Baraga, MI	12.9	...	32.9	23.2	...	...	85	16.4	5
Barry, MI	12.9	25.9	4.2	0.0	...	...	568	19.2	42
Bay, MI	14.6	38.4	11.4	3.3	...	...	925	18.4	97
Benzie, MI	13.3	47.3	8.5	0.0	160	...	144	18.4	9
Berrien, MI	15.1	45.8	32.6	1.5	...	...	1 506	16.4	135
Branch, MI	14.2	42.3	6.5	2.6	526	...	489	17.0	53
Calhoun, MI	14.0	38.3	24.8	1.0	...	...	1 701	16.0	134
Cass, MI	14.6	42.2	16.7	0.0	585	...	664	17.8	61
Charlevoix, MI	14.9	32.8	7.6	0.0	...	...	318	15.2	31
Cheboygan, MI	16.1	45.4	4.2	0.0	...	...	241	16.0	24
Chippewa, MI	14.0	45.7	35.2	0.0	...	...	372	15.8	49
Clare, MI	18.6	50.6	3.5	0.0	322	...	314	16.8	38
Clinton, MI	17.9	19.3	7.2	4.8	...	...	1 633	16.2	123
Crawford, MI	16.4	...	3.2	0.0	118	...	118	17.4	6
Delta, MI	15.1	38.4	6.9	0.0	479	...	336	17.3	37
Dickinson, MI	15.4	29.8	2.1	0.0	...	...	296	16.1	35
Eaton, MI	16.0	26.2	11.3	0.3	...	...	1 199	17.1	121
Emmet, MI	11.6	28.2	8.5	0.0	451	...	351	17.0	20
Genesee, MI	12.8	39.9	30.7	1.0	...	...	4 592	18.9	389
Gladwin, MI	17.6	42.5	3.3	0.0	...	...	212	17.3	15
Gogebic, MI	14.4	51.9	7.1	0.0	...	...	146	15.1	...
Grand Traverse, MI	20.9	30.6	5.8	6.7	...	...	319	11.7	29
Gratiot, MI	17.9	39.8	5.1	0.0	461	...	493	16.2	43
Hillsdale, MI	15.5	42.5	3.6	0.0	...	...	452	16.9	47
Houghton, MI	10.1	46.2	2.6	0.0	...	...	359	15.8	34
Huron, MI	14.8	44.6	3.4	0.0	...	...	391	17.1	47
Ingham, MI	14.6	35.7	34.3	0.8	...	...	1 689	17.6	...
Ionia, MI	17.9	35.1	6.0	3.0	...	...	621	16.5	58
Iosco, MI	16.1	...	3.7	0.0	...	...	329	16.6	38
Iron, MI	17.4	52.5	4.3	0.0	123	...	108	16.5	9
Isabella, MI	14.6	35.1	11.8	0.0	...	...	395	17.6	29
Jackson, MI	15.3	39.3	16.3	0.3	...	...	1 435	17.4	110
Kalamazoo, MI	11.9	36.0	25.4	2.8	...	...	2 126	16.8	...
Kalkaska, MI	15.8	54.8	3.7	0.0	...	...	103	17.8	15
Kent, MI	15.2	37.3	30.3	6.5	...	...	6 649	16.9	432
Keweenaw, MI	0.0	0.0	0.0	0.0	...	...	1	3.0	...
Lake, MI	19.0	81.8	36.6	0.0	53	...	49	15.7	3
Lapeer, MI	11.6	25.9	6.1	1.4	...	...	794	19.6	80
Leelanau, MI	13.7	31.0	16.7	0.9	1 069	...	722	18.9	63
Lenawee, MI	16.7	28.3	12.5	2.5	...	...	1 097	17.1	124
Livingston, MI	14.6	9.3	4.4	0.0	...	...	1 938	19.3	140
Luce, MI	18.7	...	10.2	0.0	81	...	70	15.9	10
Mackinac, MI	10.1	47.0	42.2	0.0	...	...	110	15.4	11
Macomb, MI	13.4	22.3	13.9	3.8	...	...	7 505	19.0	523
Manistee, MI	12.1	46.7	8.8	0.0	...	...	226	16.0	18
Marquette, MI	16.5	32.5	5.5	0.0	...	...	548	17.0	55
Mason, MI	15.5	43.5	5.2	0.0	400	...	310	15.9	39
Mecosta, MI	17.1	48.7	9.1	0.0	...	...	466	16.0	48
Menominee, MI	15.8	39.8	7.0	2.4	...	...	271	16.6	22
Midland, MI	15.8	23.9	6.2	0.0	...	...	810	19.0	58
Missaukee, MI	10.6	...	3.1	0.0	169	...	138	16.4	6
Monroe, MI	16.5	24.7	7.7	0.6	...	...	1 587	18.0	119
Montcalm, MI	18.8	41.0	4.7	0.0	...	...	462	16.5	42
Montmorency, MI	12.7	53.8	1.5	0.0	62	...	64	16.0	9
Muskegon, MI	15.9	48.5	26.9	0.9	...	...	1 866	18.3	195
Newaygo, MI	15.8	43.0	10.2	2.1	...	...	573	17.9	53
Oakland, MI	11.9	18.9	27.0	6.1	...	...	11 770	17.4	970
Oceana, MI	15.9	54.4	30.8	12.1	249	...	269	15.9	33
Ogemaw, MI	14.6	47.1	2.1	0.0	176	...	159	16.4	4
Ontonagon, MI	20.0	35.2	3.4	0.0	105	...	82	13.2	13
Osceola, MI	15.2	51.4	4.4	0.0	383	...	300	17.5	34
Oscoda, MI	22.0	...	1.6	0.0	72	...	72	16.1	6
Otsego, MI	12.7	36.7	2.8	0.0	285	...	260	17.4	12
Ottawa, MI	13.2	23.1	18.6	2.7	...	...	2 174	17.7	160

[2]IEP = Individual Education Program. See notes and definitions at the end of this section.
. . . = Not available.

Table C-1. Population, School, and Student Characteristics by County—*Continued*

STATE County	Revenue, 2003–2004				Current expenditures, 2003–2004			Resident population, 16 to 19 years, 2000			
	Total revenue (thousands of dollars)	Percent of revenue from:			Total expenditures (thousands of dollars)	Amount per student (dollars)	Percent for instruction	Total	Percent in armed forces	Percent high school graduates	Percent not enrolled, not employed, not in armed forces, not high school graduate
		Federal government	State government	Local government							
	19	20	21	22	23	24	25	26	27	28	29
Norfolk, MA	1 146 535	4.1	26.5	69.4	1 046 304	10 664	70.0	28 590	0.0	6.7	1.9
Plymouth, MA	877 842	5.6	42.5	51.9	786 396	9 903	69.4	24 590	0.0	9.3	3.3
Suffolk, MA	1 237 228	9.9	33.8	56.3	1 107 912	15 036	71.5	41 057	0.1	7.4	4.9
Worcester, MA	1 521 094	6.7	49.6	43.7	1 337 532	10 172	70.3	39 549	0.1	10.2	4.2
MICHIGAN	18 684 930	7.6	59.7	32.7	15 942 960	9 155	62.0	566 976	0.0	9.1	4.9
Alcona, MI	9 209	8.0	33.5	58.5	8 014	7 788	63.9	516	0.6	8.7	5.0
Alger, MI	13 197	5.5	62.9	31.5	11 594	8 068	63.0	488	0.0	13.9	4.1
Allegan, MI	179 422	6.6	62.9	30.5	156 577	8 403	61.3	6 337	0.0	12.4	4.8
Alpena, MI	50 772	10.3	59.6	30.1	44 385	8 664	59.5	1 803	0.0	7.0	3.8
Antrim, MI	40 299	4.2	45.3	50.5	34 527	7 707	64.2	1 093	0.0	9.0	3.8
Arenac, MI	25 689	7.7	66.1	26.3	22 676	7 844	64.7	927	0.0	13.1	6.8
Baraga, MI	13 961	12.8	60.1	27.0	11 848	8 561	64.2	449	0.0	11.1	4.7
Barry, MI	74 300	5.2	69.9	24.9	63 510	7 632	66.2	3 145	0.1	9.9	4.4
Bay, MI	166 950	8.7	61.7	29.5	148 508	8 825	62.4	5 860	0.3	7.9	4.3
Benzie, MI	21 929	4.8	49.5	45.7	20 143	7 786	63.3	767	0.0	14.1	2.9
Berrien, MI	283 027	10.6	61.9	27.5	254 956	8 905	61.8	9 364	0.0	7.8	6.8
Branch, MI	69 105	9.5	59.3	31.2	61 260	9 501	67.2	2 534	0.0	9.6	5.4
Calhoun, MI	290 576	10.7	59.2	30.1	237 792	9 421	62.5	7 887	0.0	9.3	7.7
Cass, MI	76 731	17.2	60.6	22.2	61 095	8 236	58.4	2 834	0.0	9.1	7.2
Charlevoix, MI	65 795	7.0	37.1	55.9	53 285	11 201	58.2	1 357	0.0	12.7	3.2
Cheboygan, MI	52 128	7.8	42.1	50.1	39 022	9 864	63.5	1 358	0.0	10.7	4.1
Chippewa, MI	65 940	20.3	55.9	23.8	57 098	9 834	61.4	2 214	0.0	11.2	4.0
Clare, MI	55 548	14.5	58.4	27.1	50 322	9 409	65.2	1 582	0.0	12.4	5.5
Clinton, MI	104 093	7.1	64.8	28.0	85 445	8 467	62.9	3 817	0.0	7.2	2.0
Crawford, MI	18 369	7.1	56.4	36.6	16 509	7 850	61.6	745	0.0	10.5	3.6
Delta, MI	66 911	9.5	60.1	30.4	59 426	9 113	64.1	2 386	0.0	12.0	1.8
Dickinson, MI	51 178	9.2	58.3	32.4	43 046	8 987	66.3	1 513	0.0	11.0	3.7
Eaton, MI	168 419	7.1	65.0	27.9	140 860	8 301	63.6	6 355	0.0	11.8	4.0
Emmet, MI	55 322	3.2	32.4	64.4	45 519	7 948	67.9	1 778	0.0	9.4	2.6
Genesee, MI	870 319	10.2	66.1	23.7	754 828	8 893	62.7	24 358	0.0	10.6	6.8
Gladwin, MI	31 139	6.5	69.0	24.5	28 838	7 577	63.3	1 282	0.2	9.5	8.1
Gogebic, MI	22 239	11.3	58.1	30.5	20 503	8 922	65.8	1 080	0.0	10.5	6.4
Grand Traverse, MI	165 145	9.9	48.5	41.6	133 419	9 717	59.1	4 385	0.0	8.1	2.2
Gratiot, MI	86 430	10.5	65.9	23.7	72 347	9 252	61.8	2 718	0.0	9.4	4.7
Hillsdale, MI	70 474	6.7	69.6	23.7	65 412	8 919	63.7	3 098	0.0	8.5	6.9
Houghton, MI	58 300	9.4	66.0	24.7	50 291	8 973	62.1	3 162	0.3	5.7	2.9
Huron, MI	60 668	8.0	55.2	36.8	52 545	9 497	62.8	1 908	0.6	9.6	3.0
Ingham, MI	572 881	7.1	57.8	35.1	485 049	9 942	60.1	22 172	0.0	5.2	3.2
Ionia, MI	121 691	7.1	66.6	26.3	103 123	8 545	60.5	3 880	0.0	12.9	9.8
Iosco, MI	52 838	9.7	55.0	35.3	47 288	8 309	63.9	1 337	0.3	10.9	8.4
Iron, MI	17 072	7.3	57.3	35.4	15 305	8 465	67.6	629	0.2	7.8	2.1
Isabella, MI	68 196	7.0	61.7	31.3	59 053	8 440	62.9	7 903	0.0	3.5	1.7
Jackson, MI	279 989	6.4	63.4	30.2	243 702	8 869	61.4	8 107	0.0	8.6	7.0
Kalamazoo, MI	367 177	8.4	57.8	33.8	305 764	8 670	64.2	16 967	0.1	6.9	2.9
Kalkaska, MI	23 395	6.3	58.7	35.0	21 220	7 822	63.1	868	0.0	14.9	7.4
Kent, MI	1 127 231	6.7	57.7	35.7	929 534	8 756	62.4	34 941	0.0	9.8	5.2
Keweenaw, MI	90	0.0	0.0	100.0	94	31 333	55.3	171	0.0	4.1	5.3
Lake, MI	11 069	12.6	41.9	45.5	7 388	9 632	61.0	824	0.0	16.5	23.1
Lapeer, MI	137 387	4.9	71.6	23.4	117 858	7 668	65.4	5 230	0.0	10.4	3.4
Leelanau, MI	26 637	5.1	35.9	58.9	22 003	8 275	64.5	1 082	0.0	6.7	1.2
Lenawee, MI	186 825	6.7	64.7	28.7	166 942	9 057	62.9	5 962	0.0	10.0	2.9
Livingston, MI	296 639	3.7	60.7	35.6	238 561	8 036	61.2	8 764	0.0	8.1	4.5
Luce, MI	10 109	7.6	60.5	31.8	9 453	8 192	68.1	377	0.0	8.5	16.7
Mackinac, MI	16 712	8.3	39.7	52.0	15 361	9 270	62.7	592	0.5	9.6	7.6
Macomb, MI	1 482 610	5.4	60.9	33.7	1 237 223	8 974	61.4	37 980	0.1	9.5	3.5
Manistee, MI	39 359	9.9	52.0	38.1	33 965	8 952	59.9	1 350	0.0	9.2	5.9
Marquette, MI	90 061	9.6	61.8	28.6	79 045	8 445	64.0	4 651	0.0	8.8	2.0
Mason, MI	53 436	7.6	49.5	42.9	48 937	9 745	64.0	1 587	0.3	8.1	4.2
Mecosta, MI	78 707	8.8	58.9	32.2	67 961	9 618	60.2	3 794	0.2	5.3	2.7
Menominee, MI	36 892	8.8	66.7	24.5	34 497	8 850	60.5	1 422	0.1	12.1	3.0
Midland, MI	147 774	4.9	56.1	39.0	133 573	9 110	66.9	4 905	0.0	7.7	2.4
Missaukee, MI	19 669	6.5	68.3	25.2	17 151	7 342	65.7	866	0.0	9.4	3.6
Monroe, MI	255 756	4.9	57.6	37.5	221 771	8 721	61.6	8 547	0.0	10.3	4.0
Montcalm, MI	129 629	7.3	69.7	23.0	114 439	8 316	63.2	3 461	0.0	8.4	7.7
Montmorency, MI	10 303	8.5	46.6	44.9	8 790	8 348	64.4	491	0.0	11.4	3.9
Muskegon, MI	369 618	10.8	62.0	27.2	299 942	8 734	61.3	9 731	0.0	9.6	5.5
Newaygo, MI	103 662	7.7	65.8	26.5	87 155	8 502	64.7	2 708	0.0	13.0	5.6
Oakland, MI	2 559 617	4.1	49.3	46.6	2 045 719	9 950	61.9	57 371	0.0	7.1	2.6
Oceana, MI	41 436	13.4	59.9	26.7	36 409	8 648	63.3	1 736	1.2	9.6	7.0
Ogemaw, MI	22 759	7.5	58.3	34.2	21 521	8 081	65.9	1 151	0.0	7.5	5.2
Ontonagon, MI	15 359	14.4	45.4	40.3	13 283	12 368	59.2	347	0.3	5.2	4.3
Osceola, MI	44 860	8.0	70.1	21.8	42 110	7 797	65.4	1 443	0.0	12.8	4.3
Oscoda, MI	11 110	9.3	51.1	39.6	10 070	8 484	69.6	485	0.0	5.2	6.8
Otsego, MI	41 153	4.6	47.2	48.2	35 332	7 708	67.9	1 223	0.0	8.9	1.6
Ottawa, MI	450 179	5.0	55.7	39.3	362 863	8 489	65.1	16 429	0.0	8.9	1.9

Table C-1. Population, School, and Student Characteristics by County—*Continued*

STATE County	Population 25 years and over	High school graduate or less (percent)	High school graduate or more (percent)	College enrollment 2000 Number	College enrollment 2000 Percent public	Bachelor's degree or more	+/- U.S. percentage with bachelor's degree or more	Non-Hispanic White	Black	American Indian and Alaska Native	Asian or Pacific Islander	Hispanic[3]
	30	31	32	33	34	35	36	37	38	39	40	41
Norfolk, MA	452 517	33.0	91.3	42 232	38.0	42.9	18.5	42.8	37.3	19.4	52.0	37.3
Plymouth, MA	312 683	43.1	87.6	23 274	65.0	27.8	3.4	29.1	16.0	12.6	36.4	14.3
Suffolk, MA	446 504	47.6	78.1	91 260	27.6	32.5	8.1	42.7	15.7	12.9	35.7	13.2
Worcester, MA	495 868	46.7	83.5	46 184	52.9	26.9	2.5	27.6	19.3	17.3	42.7	11.5
MICHIGAN	6 415 941	47.9	83.4	635 836	82.5	21.8	-2.6	22.7	12.8	10.3	60.5	12.9
Alcona, MI	8 958	62.1	79.7	211	86.3	10.9	-13.5	10.8	0.0	0.0	46.7	0.0
Alger, MI	7 169	60.8	81.5	190	92.1	14.7	-9.7	15.8	0.0	9.3	33.3	13.6
Allegan, MI	66 925	56.8	82.3	3 319	79.7	15.8	-8.6	16.3	7.8	8.5	31.6	6.2
Alpena, MI	21 399	52.6	83.1	1 635	87.1	13.2	-11.2	13.1	24.1	1.5	48.7	14.0
Antrim, MI	16 025	52.5	84.6	565	90.1	19.4	-5.0	19.5	20.8	4.3	50.0	23.7
Arenac, MI	11 868	65.4	76.8	567	84.8	9.1	-15.3	9.1	3.9	7.7	57.5	1.9
Baraga, MI	6 097	58.4	80.6	224	87.1	10.9	-13.5	12.1	0.0	6.7	30.8	0.0
Barry, MI	37 132	62.5	86.8	2 195	87.2	14.7	0.7	14.7	13.6	12.0	47.6	19.7
Bay, MI	74 146	54.5	82.4	5 444	89.5	14.2	-10.2	14.3	7.0	8.8	42.0	6.3
Benzie, MI	11 283	51.0	85.4	435	89.0	20.0	-4.4	20.4	0.0	5.5	28.6	11.1
Berrien, MI	106 690	49.9	81.9	8 218	59.4	19.6	-4.8	20.5	10.9	11.1	61.0	18.2
Branch, MI	30 300	60.8	80.0	1 547	86.2	10.6	-13.8	11.0	2.8	1.5	49.2	4.0
Calhoun, MI	90 137	52.4	83.2	7 216	68.8	16.0	-8.4	16.6	9.7	7.7	41.7	11.2
Cass, MI	34 286	57.2	80.4	1 816	87.7	12.1	-12.3	12.6	7.2	6.2	24.2	5.2
Charlevoix, MI	17 528	49.1	86.0	761	83.4	19.8	-4.6	20.1	29.2	10.8	34.4	11.4
Cheboygan, MI	18 562	58.7	81.9	587	88.9	13.9	-10.5	14.3	0.0	4.4	31.5	0.0
Chippewa, MI	25 683	53.6	82.4	3 124	93.6	15.0	-9.4	16.7	4.2	10.4	25.4	10.5
Clare, MI	21 333	64.3	76.1	953	90.6	8.8	-15.6	8.8	0.0	5.9	36.4	8.8
Clinton, MI	41 864	43.7	89.2	3 148	89.6	21.2	-3.2	21.3	34.1	14.2	38.3	12.8
Crawford, MI	9 871	56.8	80.8	400	88.8	12.9	-11.5	13.2	0.0	3.2	29.2	27.7
Delta, MI	26 362	49.7	86.1	1 968	91.4	17.1	-7.3	17.3	46.2	4.1	36.2	10.3
Dickinson, MI	18 831	55.6	88.8	775	89.7	16.7	-7.7	16.5	53.1	1.6	42.3	14.5
Eaton, MI	67 044	40.8	89.5	5 893	76.9	21.7	-2.7	21.2	29.1	18.9	48.2	14.8
Emmet, MI	21 258	42.4	89.0	1 372	92.0	26.2	1.8	26.9	0.0	8.2	41.7	11.0
Genesee, MI	277 660	50.2	83.1	22 250	80.8	16.2	-8.2	17.3	10.3	9.1	58.1	10.1
Gladwin, MI	18 308	63.3	78.3	660	89.1	9.2	-15.2	9.1	8.3	7.3	32.4	16.2
Gogebic, MI	12 311	53.0	85.5	725	92.1	15.8	-8.6	16.2	0.0	0.0	33.3	4.0
Grand Traverse, MI	51 801	38.6	89.3	3 729	89.2	26.1	1.7	26.5	12.9	15.2	31.1	6.2
Gratiot, MI	27 322	58.6	83.5	2 560	48.3	12.9	-11.5	13.5	4.2	3.5	49.1	6.5
Hillsdale, MI	29 595	59.8	83.1	2 261	49.5	12.0	-12.4	12.0	31.0	2.4	43.7	1.0
Houghton, MI	21 233	51.4	84.6	6 142	92.3	23.0	-1.4	22.4	21.1	16.2	71.3	9.3
Huron, MI	24 954	64.7	78.3	888	85.6	10.9	-13.5	10.8	12.5	5.3	56.6	3.2
Ingham, MI	162 909	35.3	88.1	49 242	93.2	33.0	8.6	34.0	22.8	16.8	63.3	15.4
Ionia, MI	37 835	57.0	83.4	1 877	82.0	10.8	-13.6	11.1	3.9	11.2	25.2	6.5
Iosco, MI	19 764	62.3	77.9	569	88.0	11.3	-13.1	11.3	0.0	18.2	38.5	6.1
Iron, MI	9 670	60.8	84.8	253	90.9	13.7	-10.7	13.9	0.0	13.5	23.8	9.3
Isabella, MI	31 677	47.8	86.1	17 635	97.3	23.9	-0.5	23.9	21.9	6.3	70.9	12.8
Jackson, MI	104 880	48.6	84.2	7 379	72.2	16.3	-8.1	17.2	5.2	7.6	56.1	9.2
Kalamazoo, MI	144 995	37.2	88.8	31 709	89.4	31.2	6.8	32.1	16.3	19.1	69.9	18.0
Kalkaska, MI	11 073	64.7	80.0	399	87.2	9.7	-14.7	9.8	8.0	7.1	33.3	0.0
Kent, MI	351 875	43.6	84.6	34 031	66.8	25.8	1.4	28.1	11.7	8.2	32.9	9.1
Keweenaw, MI	1 634	53.5	83.7	57	64.9	19.1	-5.3	18.9	. . .	. . .	0.0	50.0
Lake, MI	7 964	67.5	72.2	237	84.4	7.8	-16.6	8.1	7.5	0.0	0.0	5.8
Lapeer, MI	56 454	54.0	84.5	3 526	84.7	12.7	-11.7	12.9	2.8	9.4	42.1	6.5
Leelanau, MI	14 785	35.7	90.7	769	83.9	31.4	7.0	32.5	0.0	7.3	33.3	10.9
Lenawee, MI	64 311	55.1	83.4	4 573	59.3	16.3	-8.1	16.6	13.1	5.2	59.7	8.0
Livingston, MI	101 381	36.9	91.4	7 127	82.3	28.2	3.8	28.2	15.1	10.8	52.4	26.5
Luce, MI	4 927	61.9	75.5	147	99.3	11.8	-12.6	13.4	0.0	10.4	100.0	0.0
Mackinac, MI	8 588	58.8	82.5	246	93.9	14.9	-9.5	16.9	0.0	3.6	33.3	9.5
Macomb, MI	535 836	49.8	82.9	45 059	83.4	17.6	-6.8	17.1	15.2	11.5	44.2	17.9
Manistee, MI	17 298	58.0	81.4	651	80.6	14.2	-10.2	14.7	0.0	2.8	8.7	6.1
Marquette, MI	41 934	46.9	88.5	6 988	97.0	23.7	-0.7	24.2	6.3	8.3	21.0	14.7
Mason, MI	19 449	52.8	82.7	965	89.7	15.9	-8.5	16.4	5.0	5.3	30.6	3.2
Mecosta, MI	23 314	52.7	83.8	7 024	97.7	19.1	-5.3	19.0	14.3	11.2	82.4	15.5
Menominee, MI	17 342	62.9	83.5	831	87.2	11.0	-13.4	11.1	0.0	6.3	0.0	16.7
Midland, MI	53 497	41.0	89.0	5 050	69.7	29.3	4.9	28.4	54.5	6.0	75.1	41.7
Missaukee, MI	9 466	64.0	78.6	369	80.5	10.2	-14.2	10.2	0.0	0.0	30.8	5.4
Monroe, MI	94 281	54.2	83.1	6 669	85.5	14.3	-10.1	14.4	6.6	3.9	40.2	11.1
Montcalm, MI	39 560	58.8	81.2	1 937	85.1	10.8	-13.6	11.0	6.3	4.0	23.6	4.6
Montmorency, MI	7 604	66.9	74.8	186	87.1	8.2	-16.2	8.3	0.0	9.5	0.0	5.7
Muskegon, MI	108 661	52.4	83.1	7 581	79.0	13.9	-10.5	15.5	5.5	8.2	26.9	5.4
Newaygo, MI	30 329	61.7	78.7	1 354	81.6	11.4	-13.0	11.7	7.2	4.2	28.9	3.5
Oakland, MI	807 910	32.8	89.3	76 393	78.5	38.2	13.8	37.9	30.2	17.2	72.6	25.8
Oceana, MI	17 134	59.6	79.8	734	82.0	12.6	-11.8	13.5	6.5	11.1	27.3	1.5
Ogemaw, MI	15 191	64.9	75.0	611	89.4	9.6	-14.8	9.5	0.0	4.3	60.7	3.4
Ontonagon, MI	5 899	59.7	83.8	186	84.9	13.0	-11.4	12.9	. . .	3.2	33.3	38.2
Osceola, MI	15 033	63.3	80.5	652	79.4	11.3	-13.1	11.2	14.3	17.9	36.0	7.9
Oscoda, MI	6 716	66.8	73.7	221	87.3	8.0	-16.4	8.0	42.9	0.0	100.0	0.0
Otsego, MI	15 468	50.9	85.5	534	80.1	17.4	-7.0	17.5	0.0	9.6	31.6	14.0
Ottawa, MI	141 870	44.5	86.6	18 166	71.9	26.0	1.6	27.1	12.2	18.1	26.5	8.3

[3]May be of any race.
. . . = Not available.

Table C-1. Population, School, and Student Characteristics by County—*Continued*

STATE County	State/ county code	County type[1]	Population, 2005		Number of schools and students, 2004–2005			Resident enrollment, 2000			
			Total	Percent 5 to 17 years	School districts	Schools	Students	Total	Percent public	K–12	Percent public
			1	2	3	4	5	6	7	8	9
Presque Isle, MI	26141	7	14 330	14.6	4	11	1 868	3 000	87.3	2 388	88.4
Roscommon, MI	26143	7	26 079	14.5	3	13	4 042	5 232	90.7	4 212	92.9
Saginaw, MI	26145	3	208 356	19.0	20	95	37 587	58 489	88.1	43 311	88.6
St. Clair, MI	26147	1	171 426	18.7	11	60	27 540	42 822	89.1	33 310	92.4
St. Joseph, MI	26149	4	62 984	19.3	10	38	11 978	15 335	90.1	12 532	91.4
Sanilac, MI	26151	6	44 752	18.6	8	25	8 562	11 139	92.8	9 257	95.1
Schoolcraft, MI	26153	7	8 819	16.1	1	5	1 132	1 881	89.3	1 618	88.9
Shiawassee, MI	26155	4	72 945	18.7	9	40	14 931	19 093	89.1	14 847	92.6
Tuscola, MI	26157	6	58 428	18.5	9	33	11 177	15 594	87.9	12 490	89.9
Van Buren, MI	26159	2	78 812	19.5	12	39	15 830	20 117	91.1	16 500	93.5
Washtenaw, MI	26161	2	341 847	15.5	19	99	47 124	117 309	89.4	51 410	90.0
Wayne, MI	26163	1	1 998 217	20.5	107	692	354 171	587 853	85.7	438 464	89.3
Wexford, MI	26165	7	31 876	18.2	5	20	6 038	7 690	89.8	6 305	93.2
MINNESOTA	27000		5 132 799	17.4	561	2 646	838 503	1 362 507	84.2	975 733	89.6
Aitkin, MN	27001	8	16 174	13.7	3	9	2 180	3 142	96.6	2 584	97.8
Anoka, MN	27003	1	323 996	19.6	12	127	72 947	83 625	87.7	64 379	92.6
Becker, MN	27005	6	31 868	17.0	5	20	4 565	7 526	95.1	6 313	96.2
Beltrami, MN	27007	7	42 871	18.2	9	37	7 848	13 148	92.9	8 628	92.6
Benton, MN	27009	3	38 505	17.0	4	9	5 331	9 595	88.1	7 027	87.3
Big Stone, MN	27011	9	5 481	16.1	2	7	1 040	1 443	95.4	1 200	96.1
Blue Earth, MN	27013	5	58 030	13.3	9	34	10 408	20 028	88.9	9 039	87.9
Brown, MN	27015	7	26 534	16.1	7	17	3 902	7 413	62.9	5 538	69.2
Carlton, MN	27017	2	34 026	16.2	8	23	6 236	8 607	91.4	6 397	94.5
Carver, MN	27019	1	84 864	20.4	5	39	11 267	21 079	74.9	16 043	82.4
Cass, MN	27021	9	28 910	16.0	7	26	4 444	6 556	95.3	5 583	96.4
Chippewa, MN	27023	7	12 802	17.1	3	13	2 414	3 082	94.7	2 643	95.6
Chisago, MN	27025	1	49 400	18.9	6	20	8 540	11 266	90.6	9 221	94.7
Clay, MN	27027	3	53 838	16.2	6	28	8 705	17 797	80.3	9 873	92.7
Clearwater, MN	27029	8	8 476	16.7	2	4	1 565	2 066	95.9	1 734	96.4
Cook, MN	27031	9	5 367	13.5	3	7	697	962	93.6	826	95.6
Cottonwood, MN	27033	7	11 834	17.2	5	9	2 029	2 897	90.2	2 391	91.9
Crow Wing, MN	27035	5	59 917	16.4	5	27	10 173	13 331	93.3	10 486	94.9
Dakota, MN	27037	1	383 592	19.8	16	157	76 639	101 596	84.1	76 682	90.3
Dodge, MN	27039	3	19 595	19.5	4	11	3 981	4 988	93.9	4 102	96.1
Douglas, MN	27041	7	35 138	15.4	7	27	5 546	8 170	90.0	6 271	91.8
Faribault, MN	27043	7	15 506	16.2	3	11	2 312	3 880	92.3	3 224	93.2
Fillmore, MN	27045	8	21 368	17.1	7	19	3 847	5 095	91.7	4 306	92.0
Freeborn, MN	27047	7	31 946	15.9	3	15	4 391	7 375	93.1	6 153	94.2
Goodhue, MN	27049	4	45 585	17.1	7	23	7 115	11 305	91.1	9 219	93.9
Grant, MN	27051	9	6 114	15.5	5	7	1 254	1 476	96.1	1 215	97.5
Hennepin, MN	27053	1	1 119 364	16.3	64	548	156 523	297 966	82.1	197 828	88.2
Houston, MN	27055	3	19 941	17.8	6	17	3 843	5 283	85.9	4 268	86.7
Hubbard, MN	27057	7	18 861	15.8	3	9	2 553	4 254	94.0	3 538	95.6
Isanti, MN	27059	1	37 664	17.5	4	18	6 285	8 631	91.9	7 169	93.9
Itasca, MN	27061	6	44 384	16.0	7	30	6 961	10 950	92.7	8 676	93.8
Jackson, MN	27063	7	11 182	16.2	2	6	1 530	2 795	91.7	2 261	91.9
Kanabec, MN	27065	6	16 215	17.4	2	6	2 583	3 844	94.6	3 324	97.5
Kandiyohi, MN	27067	4	41 199	17.4	4	23	5 919	10 814	91.3	8 630	92.9
Kittson, MN	27069	9	4 792	17.9	3	7	874	1 288	91.5	1 093	90.9
Koochiching, MN	27071	7	13 907	16.0	3	11	2 132	3 451	90.1	2 770	91.4
Lac qui Parle, MN	27073	9	7 604	16.2	3	8	1 698	1 860	94.7	1 588	96.4
Lake, MN	27075	6	11 156	14.5	1	6	1 635	2 402	93.0	1 956	93.7
Lake of the Woods, MN	27077	9	4 421	15.9	1	2	677	1 073	97.1	940	97.9
Le Sueur, MN	27079	6	27 490	17.5	5	17	4 435	6 677	88.7	5 495	91.6
Lincoln, MN	27081	9	6 050	16.2	4	5	741	1 465	94.0	1 187	95.7
Lyon, MN	27083	7	24 472	17.2	10	20	4 511	7 659	86.7	5 024	85.1
McLeod, MN	27085	6	36 636	18.1	7	21	5 854	9 193	84.1	7 328	86.6
Mahnomen, MN	27087	8	5 113	19.6	2	8	1 339	1 414	94.3	1 161	94.4
Marshall, MN	27089	8	9 965	16.3	6	10	1 495	2 429	96.0	2 029	96.2
Martin, MN	27091	7	21 002	16.4	5	17	3 543	5 316	86.9	4 421	88.9
Meeker, MN	27093	6	23 371	17.3	3	12	3 603	5 764	95.1	4 762	96.7
Mille Lacs, MN	27095	6	25 680	17.0	4	18	6 794	5 643	89.3	4 771	91.0
Morrison, MN	27097	6	32 788	18.1	6	18	5 360	8 143	90.5	6 879	91.9
Mower, MN	27099	4	38 799	17.2	6	26	5 829	9 295	89.0	7 306	90.1
Murray, MN	27101	9	8 852	16.3	2	6	1 272	2 144	88.3	1 812	90.2
Nicollet, MN	27103	5	30 848	15.7	4	14	2 405	9 887	65.3	5 666	84.1
Nobles, MN	27105	7	20 508	17.8	6	16	3 472	5 134	90.8	4 207	93.0
Norman, MN	27107	8	7 003	17.6	3	8	1 251	1 769	96.7	1 479	97.9
Olmsted, MN	27109	3	135 189	17.7	8	56	20 976	34 049	82.9	25 301	87.4
Otter Tail, MN	27111	6	57 658	16.4	10	28	8 319	14 133	90.9	11 462	92.6
Pennington, MN	27113	6	13 608	16.1	4	6	2 209	3 589	93.4	2 556	93.5
Pine, MN	27115	6	28 485	16.3	4	15	4 146	6 412	91.4	5 447	93.8
Pipestone, MN	27117	6	9 421	16.7	3	9	1 797	2 509	87.8	2 079	88.3
Polk, MN	27119	3	31 133	17.0	9	22	5 437	8 889	91.8	6 352	91.6

[1]County type codes are from the Economic Research Service of the United States Department of Agriculture. See notes and definitions at the end of this section.

Table C-1. Population, School, and Student Characteristics by County—*Continued*

STATE County	Characteristics of students, 2004–2005				Outcomes		Staff and students, 2004–2005		
	Percent with IEP[2]	Percent eligible for free or reduced-price lunch	Percent minority	Percent English-language learners	Number of graduates, 2003–2004	Percent dropouts, grades 9–12, 2001–2002	Number of teachers	Student-teacher ratio	Central administration staff
	10	11	12	13	14	15	16	17	18
Presque Isle, MI	10.8	...	2.6	0.0	...	...	114	16.4	10
Roscommon, MI	15.5	51.0	3.9	0.0	225	...	255	15.9	37
Saginaw, MI	16.5	49.2	42.0	1.9	...	...	2 171	17.3	173
St. Clair, MI	13.6	29.0	8.6	0.5	...	...	1 591	17.3	147
St. Joseph, MI	13.5	42.8	13.2	2.7	...	...	709	16.9	78
Sanilac, MI	12.5	39.5	4.3	0.0	627	...	454	18.9	55
Schoolcraft, MI	15.2	50.0	18.9	0.0	80	...	66	17.3	10
Shiawassee, MI	13.5	26.7	3.7	0.0	1 001	...	819	18.2	87
Tuscola, MI	16.6	38.9	6.6	0.0	...	...	645	17.3	59
Van Buren, MI	11.9	43.2	19.0	9.1	...	...	969	16.3	112
Washtenaw, MI	14.2	21.9	28.7	3.7	...	...	2 724	17.3	238
Wayne, MI	13.3	51.2	57.2	6.3	...	...	19 720	18.0	...
Wexford, MI	14.4	...	3.6	0.0	379	...	357	16.9	34
MINNESOTA	13.7	29.5	20.7	6.8	...	3.8	52 104	16.1	...
Aitkin, MN	14.7	47.3	6.6	0.1	...	2.9	156	13.9	20
Anoka, MN	12.8	22.4	13.9	4.8	...	4.4	4 102	17.8	...
Becker, MN	16.9	39.3	15.1	0.3	...	3.7	328	13.9	37
Beltrami, MN	16.6	53.6	34.4	7.0	...	5.2	610	12.9	76
Benton, MN	14.0	27.0	4.9	0.4	...	1.3	310	17.2	35
Big Stone, MN	12.9	44.8	2.7	0.3	...	2.4	83	12.5	8
Blue Earth, MN	16.1	29.4	9.7	2.4	...	3.5	661	15.7	77
Brown, MN	13.5	25.1	9.5	4.9	...	2.3	271	14.4	...
Carlton, MN	12.6	27.5	9.8	0.0	...	2.8	379	16.4	50
Carver, MN	11.4	12.0	9.7	4.9	...	2.5	705	16.0	87
Cass, MN	19.2	55.7	29.3	0.1	...	9.4	364	12.2	37
Chippewa, MN	15.8	35.3	6.5	2.4	...	4.1	168	14.4	18
Chisago, MN	10.7	18.9	4.7	1.6	...	2.1	453	18.9	61
Clay, MN	15.0	26.0	12.3	4.8	...	2.5	545	16.0	48
Clearwater, MN	15.3	50.9	22.3	0.6	...	4.0	116	13.5	9
Cook, MN	12.2	29.2	20.5	0.7	...	4.1	46	15.2	...
Cottonwood, MN	17.0	37.9	16.3	11.9	...	1.3	159	12.8	20
Crow Wing, MN	15.2	35.0	3.4	0.0	...	5.6	602	16.9	50
Dakota, MN	13.9	14.5	15.9	4.3	...	2.8	4 544	16.9	...
Dodge, MN	10.6	18.3	6.9	2.6	...	1.9	243	16.4	21
Douglas, MN	15.5	26.4	3.0	0.2	...	3.4	360	15.4	41
Faribault, MN	14.7	40.2	9.6	3.2	...	2.4	156	14.8	16
Fillmore, MN	13.4	27.1	1.7	0.2	...	1.6	273	14.1	21
Freeborn, MN	17.6	36.4	13.9	4.3	...	2.5	283	15.5	28
Goodhue, MN	11.7	18.6	7.4	1.3	...	3.1	424	16.8	43
Grant, MN	13.1	31.6	3.1	0.0	...	0.2	101	12.4	...
Hennepin, MN	12.6	34.1	38.6	11.5	...	5.3	9 506	16.5	...
Houston, MN	12.1	18.1	3.0	0.0	...	1.4	242	15.9	26
Hubbard, MN	19.8	45.0	9.8	0.0	...	5.0	168	15.2	18
Isanti, MN	10.4	25.0	5.1	1.3	...	3.9	362	17.4	41
Itasca, MN	15.3	40.0	12.0	0.0	...	5.7	423	16.5	...
Jackson, MN	15.0	33.2	7.6	3.3	...	2.8	109	14.0	10
Kanabec, MN	12.1	33.9	4.8	0.0	...	3.9	166	15.5	14
Kandiyohi, MN	13.5	38.1	20.6	10.1	...	4.5	420	14.1	26
Kittson, MN	17.4	46.0	5.8	0.0	...	0.3	76	11.6	7
Koochiching, MN	13.3	35.8	9.8	0.1	...	3.8	141	15.1	18
Lac qui Parle, MN	15.7	34.6	4.4	1.9	...	1.0	123	13.8	11
Lake, MN	14.3	25.2	4.4	0.0	...	3.2	109	14.9	7
Lake of the Woods, MN	11.4	34.4	3.7	0.0	...	2.0	44	15.5	5
Le Sueur, MN	15.3	26.5	10.6	5.5	...	2.8	287	15.5	27
Lincoln, MN	13.4	36.2	1.3	0.1	...	1.1	69	10.7	6
Lyon, MN	12.7	31.1	14.6	7.0	...	3.0	335	13.5	65
McLeod, MN	12.2	23.8	9.1	3.7	...	3.3	377	15.5	37
Mahnomen, MN	17.4	60.7	65.4	0.0	...	3.6	111	12.1	7
Marshall, MN	15.3	44.0	7.0	2.3	...	0.9	127	11.8	15
Martin, MN	16.5	37.8	6.8	2.4	...	3.1	229	15.5	30
Meeker, MN	15.2	30.8	5.7	1.2	...	2.4	249	14.4	19
Mille Lacs, MN	13.4	28.3	6.6	0.3	...	2.8	412	16.5	31
Morrison, MN	14.8	38.8	3.0	0.3	...	2.0	339	15.8	37
Mower, MN	14.0	36.7	14.8	7.0	...	4.2	385	15.1	44
Murray, MN	15.4	31.7	4.7	1.6	...	0.8	90	14.1	9
Nicollet, MN	19.0	25.6	9.7	4.1	...	1.5	167	14.4	20
Nobles, MN	14.6	43.6	29.5	10.9	...	6.9	255	13.6	22
Norman, MN	14.4	43.0	14.2	2.8	...	1.1	109	11.5	5
Olmsted, MN	11.8	24.8	19.3	10.5	...	2.7	1 236	17.0	141
Otter Tail, MN	13.6	33.1	7.6	3.7	...	4.6	568	14.6	52
Pennington, MN	13.5	31.0	6.8	1.4	...	1.8	149	14.8	21
Pine, MN	10.8	41.6	7.8	0.4	...	6.3	304	13.6	22
Pipestone, MN	12.9	36.4	5.1	2.4	...	1.9	132	13.6	11
Polk, MN	14.4	37.0	13.1	3.7	...	3.7	375	14.5	...

[2]IEP = Individual Education Program. See notes and definitions at the end of this section.
. . . = Not available.

Table C-1. Population, School, and Student Characteristics by County—*Continued*

STATE County	Revenue, 2003–2004				Current expenditures, 2003–2004			Resident population, 16 to 19 years, 2000			
	Total revenue (thousands of dollars)	Percent of revenue from:			Total expenditures (thousands of dollars)	Amount per student (dollars)	Percent for instruction	Total	Percent in armed forces	Percent high school graduates	Percent not enrolled, not employed, not in armed forces, not high school graduate
		Federal government	State government	Local government							
	19	20	21	22	23	24	25	26	27	28	29
Presque Isle, MI	16 336	6.9	58.0	35.1	15 522	8 097	66.4	806	0.0	8.8	4.7
Roscommon, MI	42 891	15.4	44.2	40.4	41 637	10 491	63.1	1 180	0.0	9.2	4.2
Saginaw, MI	357 720	10.3	69.1	20.6	320 717	8 779	62.7	11 932	0.1	7.7	6.4
St. Clair, MI	276 283	6.2	62.2	31.6	247 949	8 165	64.3	9 089	0.0	10.4	5.2
St. Joseph, MI	117 082	6.9	63.9	29.2	99 685	8 396	63.1	3 779	0.4	9.9	7.2
Sanilac, MI	79 448	7.9	69.5	22.7	69 718	8 118	63.6	2 566	0.2	9.4	3.4
Schoolcraft, MI	9 958	9.8	61.1	29.1	10 885	9 548	51.0	386	0.0	13.2	7.8
Shiawassee, MI	137 572	6.8	72.4	20.8	121 295	8 212	64.3	4 146	0.0	8.9	3.6
Tuscola, MI	116 297	7.9	72.5	19.6	106 961	9 162	63.3	3 616	0.0	6.4	5.8
Van Buren, MI	186 136	7.9	63.9	28.2	163 748	9 197	63.1	4 696	0.0	9.5	5.8
Washtenaw, MI	584 169	4.3	51.1	44.6	469 817	9 820	59.9	23 697	0.0	5.2	2.0
Wayne, MI	3 997 007	10.4	64.3	25.3	3 577 459	9 710	60.5	108 591	0.0	11.4	7.6
Wexford, MI	60 560	8.3	57.7	34.0	52 513	9 770	60.5	1 908	0.1	10.5	5.6
MINNESOTA	8 839 523	5.9	69.5	24.6	7 038 212	8 414	69.6	293 223	0.1	8.5	2.8
Aitkin, MN	21 468	6.5	77.2	16.3	18 622	8 453	66.2	789	0.0	8.7	2.2
Anoka, MN	618 037	4.3	72.4	23.3	493 932	7 628	71.1	16 477	0.0	9.6	3.4
Becker, MN	43 946	8.3	76.3	15.4	38 114	8 075	69.0	1 887	0.0	9.2	4.9
Beltrami, MN	96 073	18.1	66.1	15.8	80 114	10 280	71.5	3 157	0.0	5.9	5.8
Benton, MN	49 638	3.8	74.4	21.8	38 318	7 254	67.9	2 105	0.8	15.5	1.3
Big Stone, MN	11 312	5.1	73.5	21.4	9 555	8 631	65.3	364	0.0	1.6	9.3
Blue Earth, MN	88 974	5.6	77.2	17.2	73 845	7 434	71.5	5 277	0.0	5.7	0.7
Brown, MN	35 939	4.3	78.3	17.5	30 833	7 890	68.9	1 820	0.0	7.3	0.4
Carlton, MN	60 959	8.7	73.5	17.8	48 865	7 779	68.9	1 856	0.0	8.6	2.5
Carver, MN	148 836	3.2	63.1	33.7	106 668	8 163	69.7	3 635	0.0	9.3	0.6
Cass, MN	54 750	13.0	68.8	18.2	42 284	9 180	67.6	1 495	0.0	9.7	3.9
Chippewa, MN	26 380	6.8	69.3	23.9	22 865	10 007	69.2	777	0.0	9.1	3.0
Chisago, MN	77 674	4.3	72.2	23.5	60 119	6 961	68.0	2 258	0.0	8.4	3.7
Clay, MN	86 300	5.8	79.9	14.3	65 060	7 491	72.3	4 649	0.0	5.2	2.0
Clearwater, MN	16 256	7.9	76.4	15.7	13 065	8 259	66.1	565	0.0	10.4	4.6
Cook, MN	7 806	6.2	66.5	27.3	5 844	8 519	65.8	210	0.0	14.8	0.0
Cottonwood, MN	21 501	5.3	76.0	18.7	17 020	8 144	68.6	686	0.0	8.6	2.8
Crow Wing, MN	101 764	6.1	70.4	23.5	81 664	7 979	71.4	3 131	0.0	11.3	3.6
Dakota, MN	723 459	3.5	68.8	27.6	581 186	7 887	71.3	19 283	0.2	8.8	1.8
Dodge, MN	33 061	2.7	78.1	19.2	26 296	6 703	68.4	1 207	0.0	7.7	2.9
Douglas, MN	50 997	6.0	74.4	19.6	41 472	7 654	71.2	2 089	0.0	7.5	1.5
Faribault, MN	22 105	6.3	78.4	15.3	19 148	8 045	69.8	973	0.0	7.6	2.0
Fillmore, MN	27 566	4.7	77.5	17.8	22 655	7 620	68.0	1 294	0.0	6.6	4.7
Freeborn, MN	42 950	6.4	76.6	17.0	35 638	8 003	68.6	1 850	0.0	9.0	5.9
Goodhue, MN	70 998	4.3	68.2	27.5	55 177	7 648	67.9	2 867	0.0	10.6	2.8
Grant, MN	13 027	4.1	75.0	20.8	10 426	8 242	66.0	376	0.0	8.5	3.2
Hennepin, MN	1 927 938	6.1	62.9	30.9	1 467 054	9 493	69.2	56 930	0.0	8.6	3.7
Houston, MN	34 158	3.7	78.4	17.9	27 144	7 173	65.9	1 148	0.0	12.5	1.7
Hubbard, MN	27 403	6.9	71.9	21.2	21 884	8 264	67.6	1 044	0.0	10.5	5.7
Isanti, MN	50 231	5.4	75.5	19.1	38 639	6 582	71.5	2 105	0.0	9.4	3.9
Itasca, MN	73 187	8.4	69.7	21.9	59 762	8 526	69.7	2 789	0.0	8.1	3.4
Jackson, MN	16 235	4.0	73.9	22.1	11 971	7 577	68.7	679	0.0	4.6	1.3
Kanabec, MN	21 687	5.2	79.8	15.0	18 512	7 071	71.1	940	0.0	10.0	4.3
Kandiyohi, MN	59 211	6.3	74.8	18.9	48 259	8 028	71.4	2 842	0.0	10.2	2.7
Kittson, MN	10 788	4.8	73.5	21.7	8 738	9 602	65.0	252	0.0	7.5	0.0
Koochiching, MN	23 578	5.2	73.7	21.1	18 985	8 765	67.1	829	0.0	10.5	3.4
Lac qui Parle, MN	17 854	6.3	78.9	14.8	14 883	8 375	68.4	466	0.0	8.6	3.0
Lake, MN	18 931	3.9	64.5	31.6	13 979	8 602	65.4	573	0.0	18.8	1.7
Lake of the Woods, MN	7 439	3.0	73.9	23.1	5 595	7 981	62.4	195	0.0	8.2	0.5
Le Sueur, MN	39 986	4.5	78.5	17.0	31 971	7 056	68.2	1 640	0.0	8.4	2.3
Lincoln, MN	8 608	8.8	76.8	14.4	7 309	8 946	67.4	318	0.0	3.1	0.0
Lyon, MN	59 704	15.3	53.2	31.5	47 514	10 828	67.7	1 885	0.0	7.6	2.3
McLeod, MN	52 007	5.3	76.0	18.7	43 772	7 384	67.3	1 949	0.0	8.4	1.4
Mahnomen, MN	17 223	21.5	68.6	9.9	14 560	10 858	66.0	370	0.0	7.3	5.9
Marshall, MN	18 903	11.4	68.8	19.8	16 041	10 471	63.9	600	0.0	5.7	3.0
Martin, MN	37 828	6.8	67.7	25.5	30 611	9 070	69.1	1 363	0.0	10.8	0.2
Meeker, MN	51 806	4.4	79.1	16.5	44 084	7 379	68.7	1 431	0.0	10.6	3.7
Mille Lacs, MN	57 418	5.7	77.3	17.0	47 623	7 004	67.7	1 375	0.0	9.3	4.9
Morrison, MN	52 429	7.1	75.3	17.5	42 565	7 783	70.0	2 052	0.1	13.0	1.7
Mower, MN	54 278	6.1	78.8	15.0	45 684	7 878	68.4	2 263	0.0	9.1	6.5
Murray, MN	12 772	4.8	77.4	17.9	10 746	8 007	65.4	523	0.0	8.0	3.6
Nicollet, MN	32 111	8.8	51.4	39.8	26 004	11 476	68.4	2 757	0.0	5.1	1.6
Nobles, MN	33 949	7.0	78.1	14.9	27 879	8 032	70.4	1 283	0.0	5.0	3.1
Norman, MN	13 122	5.1	79.6	15.3	11 561	8 053	66.7	418	0.0	6.9	1.0
Olmsted, MN	215 964	4.8	70.7	24.4	167 239	7 575	68.5	6 769	0.0	7.5	1.9
Otter Tail, MN	84 141	5.9	70.5	23.7	70 703	8 495	67.9	3 746	0.0	8.2	2.3
Pennington, MN	23 041	6.0	75.6	18.4	19 470	8 607	63.3	949	0.0	7.2	1.8
Pine, MN	39 497	5.7	74.6	19.6	33 514	7 882	69.6	1 564	0.0	10.5	6.2
Pipestone, MN	19 278	6.1	70.9	22.9	14 459	7 687	66.7	599	0.0	8.0	0.8
Polk, MN	54 320	8.8	76.3	15.0	46 584	8 381	68.5	2 145	0.4	9.0	2.7

Table C-1. Population, School, and Student Characteristics by County—*Continued*

STATE County	High school graduates, 2000			College enrollment, 2000		College graduates, 2000 (percent)						
	Population 25 years and over	High school graduate or less (percent)	High school graduate or more (percent)	Number	Percent public	Bachelor's degree or more	+/- U.S. percentage with bachelor's degree or more	Non-Hispanic White	Black	American Indian and Alaska Native	Asian or Pacific Islander	Hispanic3
	30	31	32	33	34	35	36	37	38	39	40	41
Presque Isle, MI	10 463	61.3	77.0	443	87.1	11.5	-12.9	11.6	33.3	0.0	0.0	6.5
Roscommon, MI	18 930	59.8	79.5	763	87.4	10.9	-13.5	10.9	20.0	9.9	25.4	7.1
Saginaw, MI	135 198	54.6	81.6	11 612	91.6	15.9	-8.5	17.5	8.5	10.5	57.4	7.7
St. Clair, MI	107 583	54.4	82.8	6 578	82.5	12.6	-11.8	12.7	8.3	8.6	39.1	5.3
St. Joseph, MI	39 807	59.7	78.6	1 819	87.4	12.7	-11.7	13.1	2.6	3.8	30.7	6.4
Sanilac, MI	29 197	64.2	79.7	1 231	82.0	10.0	-14.4	10.0	0.0	9.3	42.6	1.5
Schoolcraft, MI	6 272	64.5	79.4	144	91.0	11.3	-13.1	12.1	0.0	1.9	18.2	4.8
Shiawassee, MI	46 557	54.1	84.4	2 940	75.6	13.7	-10.7	13.8	22.6	5.2	51.4	8.2
Tuscola, MI	37 898	60.6	81.2	2 369	83.4	10.6	-13.8	10.7	8.9	0.6	43.0	3.3
Van Buren, MI	48 920	57.0	78.9	2 430	86.5	14.3	-10.1	15.6	4.3	5.8	26.2	4.1
Washtenaw, MI	197 414	25.6	91.5	60 032	93.3	48.1	23.7	49.1	25.0	27.2	82.3	44.1
Wayne, MI	1 305 288	53.7	77.0	110 846	77.8	17.2	-7.2	21.4	10.3	12.9	57.3	10.6
Wexford, MI	19 965	56.7	82.0	914	78.4	15.3	-9.1	15.2	25.0	18.2	52.8	14.2
MINNESOTA	3 164 345	40.9	87.9	296 258	72.9	27.4	3.0	28.0	18.7	8.8	36.1	14.0
Aitkin, MN	11 263	59.2	80.4	349	89.7	11.3	-13.1	11.5	37.5	3.6	0.0	0.0
Anoka, MN	187 122	41.4	91.0	13 340	74.1	21.3	-3.1	21.3	20.4	8.8	31.3	13.3
Becker, MN	19 834	51.7	82.9	784	89.8	16.7	-7.7	17.5	29.2	4.6	17.5	19.2
Beltrami, MN	22 748	45.2	83.4	3 916	94.7	23.5	-0.9	26.4	45.6	4.5	31.4	11.5
Benton, MN	20 789	49.9	84.9	2 068	91.1	17.2	-7.2	17.2	27.1	23.7	14.0	11.0
Big Stone, MN	4 050	61.1	79.0	113	87.6	11.4	-13.0	11.3	0.0	18.2	. . .	0.0
Blue Earth, MN	31 684	40.4	87.7	10 105	92.1	26.6	2.2	26.6	26.0	15.1	44.1	20.1
Brown, MN	17 485	56.8	81.7	1 418	38.8	16.5	-7.9	16.7	0.0	3.7	43.5	4.6
Carlton, MN	21 238	53.1	84.3	1 582	82.1	14.9	-9.5	15.3	1.0	12.4	11.9	7.6
Carver, MN	43 218	35.3	91.4	2 867	57.2	34.3	9.9	34.8	37.0	14.1	40.1	9.7
Cass, MN	18 721	52.5	83.9	582	89.2	16.6	-7.8	17.4	100.0	6.4	14.0	11.3
Chippewa, MN	8 819	56.0	81.6	263	89.0	13.7	-10.7	13.8	50.0	3.2	14.3	11.0
Chisago, MN	25 859	48.4	88.7	1 228	78.1	15.3	-9.1	15.4	7.8	9.4	19.8	11.3
Clay, MN	29 580	41.5	86.7	7 152	64.3	24.7	0.3	25.5	29.3	4.4	23.3	6.6
Clearwater, MN	5 576	59.0	76.4	202	92.1	14.7	-9.7	15.4	. . .	6.5	38.5	0.0
Cook, MN	3 864	39.9	88.7	71	81.7	28.8	4.4	30.8	0.0	6.4	0.0	66.7
Cottonwood, MN	8 344	56.8	80.4	287	83.3	14.2	-10.2	14.1	0.0	100.0	32.9	7.7
Crow Wing, MN	37 092	47.2	86.3	1 951	89.2	18.4	-6.0	18.4	13.9	10.2	54.5	24.8
Dakota, MN	224 313	30.3	93.2	17 197	70.0	34.9	10.5	35.4	30.9	11.2	42.0	13.7
Dodge, MN	10 989	49.2	86.7	525	85.1	17.1	-7.3	17.2	0.0	20.0	38.1	7.1
Douglas, MN	21 961	47.5	85.6	1 249	90.6	17.2	7.1	17.4	0.0	28.1	17.5	20.6
Faribault, MN	11 128	57.2	83.6	369	85.4	13.8	-10.6	14.0	66.7	0.0	3.6	4.8
Fillmore, MN	14 116	55.2	81.7	493	86.4	15.1	-9.3	15.0	0.0	0.0	42.1	17.4
Freeborn, MN	22 363	56.5	81.2	789	88.7	12.8	-11.6	13.2	4.9	0.0	23.9	3.7
Goodhue, MN	29 127	49.8	86.7	1 302	79.8	19.1	-5.3	19.3	19.4	5.6	22.5	7.7
Grant, MN	4 370	51.8	83.5	165	84.8	15.7	-8.7	15.8	. . .	0.0	0.0	0.0
Hennepin, MN	740 444	30.5	90.6	78 624	74.9	39.1	14.7	42.0	17.8	10.1	38.6	18.0
Houston, MN	13 063	49.2	85.5	645	88.2	20.5	3.0	20.2	55.6	0.0	49.2	33.8
Hubbard, MN	12 694	48.3	86.1	467	86.9	20.2	-4.2	20.5	0.0	9.3	27.6	0.0
Isanti, MN	19 915	51.8	86.6	959	87.0	14.5	-9.9	14.5	19.7	17.7	32.6	11.4
Itasca, MN	29 931	47.7	85.6	1 681	90.5	17.6	-6.8	18.0	27.0	8.0	4.5	5.1
Jackson, MN	7 768	53.9	84.1	350	95.7	14.2	-10.2	14.2	0.0	13.3	20.7	9.7
Kanabec, MN	9 797	61.6	80.6	209	80.7	10.5	-13.9	10.4	22.2	4.7	25.9	4.3
Kandiyohi, MN	26 419	47.7	83.5	1 628	88.9	18.3	-6.1	19.1	3.4	6.7	61.3	2.3
Kittson, MN	3 661	54.8	79.7	101	95.0	14.8	-9.6	14.7	42.9	0.0	0.0	6.7
Koochiching, MN	9 999	55.5	81.9	475	88.8	15.1	-9.3	15.4	0.0	4.4	40.0	0.0
Lac qui Parle, MN	5 644	56.9	80.8	128	79.7	13.0	-11.4	12.8	0.0	50.0	38.9	14.3
Lake, MN	7 847	51.1	86.4	322	87.0	19.5	-4.9	19.5	0.0	28.1	. . .	6.3
Lake of the Woods, MN	3 155	52.8	84.6	85	87.1	17.2	-7.2	17.3	0.0	0.0	0.0	60.0
Le Sueur, MN	16 499	53.7	84.6	729	77.1	16.9	-7.5	17.2	3.6	5.2	25.0	3.6
Lincoln, MN	4 516	58.7	79.8	169	85.8	14.1	-10.3	14.0	. . .	. . .	100.0	0.0
Lyon, MN	15 355	49.8	82.6	2 194	94.4	21.4	-3.0	21.7	20.0	26.8	44.1	3.2
McLeod, MN	22 495	52.6	84.7	1 188	83.8	15.4	-9.0	15.5	3.6	20.0	44.6	3.4
Mahnomen, MN	3 292	59.0	75.0	149	93.3	12.4	-12.0	14.8	0.0	6.8	17.1	0.0
Marshall, MN	6 914	57.9	79.1	248	95.6	12.0	-12.4	12.1	40.0	8.3	20.0	1.8
Martin, MN	14 935	54.2	83.7	492	85.2	16.1	-8.3	16.2	0.0	0.0	25.8	2.6
Meeker, MN	14 841	56.8	81.5	570	87.2	13.9	-10.5	14.0	0.0	4.4	0.0	5.8
Mille Lacs, MN	14 622	59.0	81.3	536	80.8	12.2	-12.2	12.3	20.0	3.8	53.1	7.4
Morrison, MN	20 347	59.0	79.7	850	80.4	12.6	-11.8	12.6	37.5	10.0	36.6	6.1
Mower, MN	25 749	53.0	82.3	1 309	88.2	14.7	-9.7	15.0	7.4	8.1	30.6	3.6
Murray, MN	6 320	58.7	79.1	211	87.2	11.9	-12.5	11.9	28.6	18.2	13.3	1.5
Nicollet, MN	17 496	37.6	90.1	3 662	36.3	29.3	4.9	29.9	7.8	50.0	22.8	7.0
Nobles, MN	13 654	58.5	75.8	593	89.2	13.5	-10.9	14.3	12.5	12.9	13.2	4.7
Norman, MN	5 105	54.8	80.0	147	89.8	13.1	-11.3	13.4	0.0	0.0	54.5	3.8
Olmsted, MN	80 277	32.9	91.1	6 285	77.2	34.7	10.3	34.7	16.8	21.2	54.1	14.5
Otter Tail, MN	38 739	51.7	81.4	1 858	91.8	17.2	-7.2	17.4	10.5	2.9	23.8	4.7
Pennington, MN	8 848	49.8	81.3	795	93.7	14.9	-9.5	14.8	33.3	0.0	35.8	9.5
Pine, MN	17 714	61.9	79.0	690	75.5	10.3	-14.1	10.7	2.2	5.8	20.4	3.7
Pipestone, MN	6 671	58.5	77.6	256	91.8	13.9	-10.5	14.2	0.0	3.0	0.0	11.5
Polk, MN	20 203	49.8	82.0	2 029	94.0	17.6	-6.8	18.0	15.4	7.8	27.8	6.6

3May be of any race.
. . . = Not available.

Table C-1. Population, School, and Student Characteristics by County—*Continued*

STATE County	State/ county code	County type[1]	Population, 2005 Total	Population, 2005 Percent 5 to 17 years	Number of schools and students, 2004–2005 School districts	Number of schools and students, 2004–2005 Schools	Number of schools and students, 2004–2005 Students	Resident enrollment, 2000 Total	Resident enrollment, 2000 Percent public	Resident enrollment, 2000 K–12	Resident enrollment, 2000 Percent public
			1	2	3	4	5	6	7	8	9
Pope, MN	27121	8	11 252	15.7	2	7	1 420	2 750	94.0	2 357	95.2
Ramsey, MN	27123	1	494 920	17.4	42	264	84 424	148 722	74.7	98 122	85.2
Red Lake, MN	27125	8	4 317	15.6	4	7	762	1 072	91.4	871	91.7
Redwood, MN	27127	7	16 022	17.3	7	16	2 865	4 054	88.4	3 504	89.0
Renville, MN	27129	9	16 764	17.8	3	8	2 230	4 278	89.9	3 651	90.4
Rice, MN	27131	4	60 949	16.3	7	27	8 517	18 631	62.2	11 284	86.7
Rock, MN	27133	6	9 520	17.0	2	7	1 617	2 525	90.3	2 019	93.5
Roseau, MN	27135	7	16 495	19.8	5	15	3 402	4 373	96.5	3 729	97.2
St. Louis, MN	27137	2	197 179	14.7	21	102	27 524	54 961	89.1	35 402	92.2
Scott, MN	27139	1	119 825	20.2	6	47	17 596	25 390	82.6	19 902	87.7
Sherburne, MN	27141	1	81 752	19.3	5	54	26 470	19 430	88.3	14 644	92.0
Sibley, MN	27143	8	15 237	18.6	5	8	2 267	3 952	86.8	3 274	87.8
Stearns, MN	27145	3	142 654	16.4	17	51	13 417	43 624	80.0	26 236	85.1
Steele, MN	27147	5	35 755	18.2	3	20	6 459	8 991	86.4	7 229	90.4
Stevens, MN	27149	7	9 826	13.0	4	7	1 434	3 536	95.2	1 680	94.0
Swift, MN	27151	7	11 324	15.0	2	7	1 685	2 722	94.7	2 212	95.6
Todd, MN	27153	6	24 603	17.7	7	17	4 277	6 472	88.7	5 498	89.0
Traverse, MN	27155	9	3 810	16.9	2	4	594	1 000	97.6	825	98.2
Wabasha, MN	27157	3	22 200	17.5	5	12	4 932	5 671	91.3	4 651	91.9
Wadena, MN	27159	7	13 650	17.4	4	8	3 047	3 538	93.9	2 792	94.9
Waseca, MN	27161	7	19 330	17.1	3	13	3 057	4 864	88.2	3 883	90.6
Washington, MN	27163	1	220 426	19.8	10	73	30 141	58 157	83.6	44 185	89.6
Watonwan, MN	27165	7	11 234	19.0	3	7	2 009	3 074	89.5	2 536	91.3
Wilkin, MN	27167	6	6 802	18.7	3	7	1 254	1 839	87.4	1 530	88.6
Winona, MN	27169	4	49 276	14.3	7	26	6 120	17 104	79.6	8 791	82.1
Wright, MN	27171	1	110 730	19.6	11	55	21 738	25 341	89.4	20 802	92.2
Yellow Medicine, MN	27173	9	10 449	17.4	4	8	1 868	2 864	95.4	2 282	95.8
MISSISSIPPI	28000		2 921 088	18.4	163	1 049	495 376	789 903	87.2	582 848	89.5
Adams, MS	28001	5	32 099	18.2	1	8	4 526	9 809	80.4	7 561	79.0
Alcorn, MS	28003	7	35 306	16.5	2	17	5 678	7 421	92.2	5 928	95.7
Amite, MS	28005	8	13 435	16.8	1	4	1 338	3 261	76.9	2 407	77.2
Attala, MS	28007	6	19 552	17.5	2	11	3 411	5 044	88.4	4 109	90.4
Benton, MS	28009	8	7 852	18.0	1	4	1 339	2 002	90.5	1 627	93.0
Bolivar, MS	28011	5	38 641	19.2	6	24	7 315	14 277	92.7	9 559	91.5
Calhoun, MS	28013	7	14 652	16.7	1	7	2 591	3 470	88.6	2 950	91.3
Carroll, MS	28015	9	10 397	16.0	1	3	1 067	2 647	75.0	2 175	74.8
Chickasaw, MS	28017	7	19 184	19.4	3	9	3 340	4 950	91.3	4 121	92.9
Choctaw, MS	28019	9	9 572	18.9	1	5	1 820	2 513	88.2	2 091	87.8
Claiborne, MS	28021	6	11 492	17.6	1	4	1 864	4 792	95.1	2 350	92.1
Clarke, MS	28023	9	17 670	17.9	2	9	3 234	4 411	93.3	3 627	94.8
Clay, MS	28025	7	21 223	19.2	2	10	3 797	6 257	84.6	4 843	85.1
Coahoma, MS	28027	5	29 002	22.2	3	18	5 751	9 446	89.1	7 404	89.1
Copiah, MS	28029	2	29 164	17.6	2	6	4 741	8 378	82.8	6 183	83.9
Covington, MS	28031	8	20 273	19.1	1	8	3 468	5 285	92.8	4 337	93.2
DeSoto, MS	28033	1	137 004	19.4	1	27	25 298	27 677	83.6	21 613	88.0
Forrest, MS	28035	3	75 095	16.1	4	21	11 388	24 754	88.3	12 986	91.2
Franklin, MS	28037	9	8 411	17.3	1	5	1 554	2 176	93.4	1 809	94.1
George, MS	28039	3	21 259	19.5	1	8	4 132	4 817	94.9	4 096	97.1
Greene, MS	28041	8	13 183	16.3	1	6	2 025	2 768	94.1	2 292	96.6
Grenada, MS	28043	7	22 861	18.9	1	6	4 685	6 164	88.2	4 888	90.3
Hancock, MS	28045	3	46 711	17.3	2	12	6 707	10 116	82.8	8 068	84.2
Harrison, MS	28047	3	193 810	18.0	6	54	30 892	48 256	85.4	35 754	89.0
Hinds, MS	28049	2	249 345	19.0	7	85	43 238	78 720	80.5	53 035	86.7
Holmes, MS	28051	6	21 099	21.0	2	9	4 189	7 369	90.9	5 799	91.3
Humphreys, MS	28053	7	10 527	21.0	1	5	1 885	3 643	86.5	3 076	86.3
Issaquena, MS	28055	9	1 909	17.8	. . .	. . .	. . .	658	90.9	560	90.7
Itawamba, MS	28057	7	23 359	16.9	1	8	3 789	5 744	96.5	4 215	98.5
Jackson, MS	28059	3	135 940	18.9	4	51	25 270	34 736	91.7	27 188	94.4
Jasper, MS	28061	9	18 162	18.3	2	7	2 946	4 891	90.7	3 964	90.8
Jefferson, MS	28063	7	9 432	18.6	1	5	1 516	2 748	93.8	2 133	92.9
Jefferson Davis, MS	28065	8	13 158	18.7	1	5	2 178	3 815	86.2	2 991	85.6
Jones, MS	28067	4	66 160	17.2	3	23	11 001	16 331	91.8	12 363	95.1
Kemper, MS	28069	9	10 246	16.6	1	4	1 333	2 955	86.3	2 011	82.7
Lafayette, MS	28071	6	40 842	12.2	3	12	5 428	16 076	94.0	5 569	95.0
Lamar, MS	28073	3	44 616	18.7	2	15	8 037	11 465	88.3	8 107	90.8
Lauderdale, MS	28075	5	77 218	18.4	3	25	13 204	20 890	90.1	15 416	92.7
Lawrence, MS	28077	8	13 502	18.2	1	6	2 346	3 493	92.5	2 808	93.4
Leake, MS	28079	6	22 453	20.6	1	8	3 268	5 007	80.3	4 251	80.0
Lee, MS	28081	5	78 793	18.7	4	34	15 926	19 509	91.7	15 438	94.8
Leflore, MS	28083	5	36 431	19.9	2	16	6 254	11 798	87.3	8 537	86.5
Lincoln, MS	28085	6	33 906	17.9	3	12	6 104	8 437	88.9	6 673	90.3
Lowndes, MS	28087	5	59 895	19.5	3	22	10 526	18 414	85.2	13 298	86.6
Madison, MS	28089	2	84 286	19.3	2	24	13 642	21 716	72.7	15 931	79.0
Marion, MS	28091	6	25 235	19.0	2	13	4 421	6 517	89.1	5 432	90.4
Marshall, MS	28093	1	35 659	18.0	2	11	5 299	8 919	78.3	7 008	83.0
Monroe, MS	28095	7	37 704	18.1	3	17	6 059	9 518	92.2	7 890	93.9
Montgomery, MS	28097	7	11 829	18.1	2	5	1 909	3 213	91.0	2 600	92.7
Neshoba, MS	28099	7	29 905	19.3	2	6	4 166	7 642	82.0	6 084	82.1

[1]County type codes are from the Economic Research Service of the United States Department of Agriculture. See notes and definitions at the end of this section.
. . . = Not available.

Table C-1. Population, School, and Student Characteristics by County—*Continued*

STATE County	Characteristics of students, 2004–2005				Outcomes		Staff and students, 2004–2005		
	Percent with IEP[2]	Percent eligible for free or reduced-price lunch	Percent minority	Percent English-language learners	Number of graduates, 2003–2004	Percent dropouts, grades 9–12, 2001–2002	Number of teachers	Student-teacher ratio	Central administration staff
	10	11	12	13	14	15	16	17	18
Pope, MN	18.9	39.0	2.2	0.1	...	...	97	14.7	8
Ramsey, MN	15.2	49.1	50.5	21.6	...	4.7	5 316	15.9	...
Red Lake, MN	15.5	50.1	4.6	0.5	...	1.4	70	10.8	10
Redwood, MN	14.3	36.7	16.4	1.0	...	1.8	207	13.8	...
Renville, MN	14.0	39.6	16.4	6.3	...	3.6	153	14.6	13
Rice, MN	15.4	26.8	15.0	8.5	...	4.5	565	15.1	69
Rock, MN	15.0	32.2	6.1	2.4	...	0.4	112	14.4	6
Roseau, MN	14.6	29.9	7.9	0.7	...	1.2	218	15.6	22
St. Louis, MN	14.1	34.0	9.4	0.3	...	5.2	1 700	16.2	186
Scott, MN	11.3	14.9	13.2	5.6	...	1.7	1 038	17.0	102
Sherburne, MN	14.7	16.4	6.5	3.5	...	4.0	1 536	17.2	126
Sibley, MN	11.5	29.9	16.0	8.4	...	6.1	152	14.9	...
Stearns, MN	13.1	25.0	8.3	2.2	...	2.9	831	16.2	...
Steele, MN	12.4	26.1	13.3	5.1	...	3.3	377	17.1	41
Stevens, MN	16.7	24.9	4.2	0.5	...	0.6	107	13.4	14
Swift, MN	17.1	34.7	7.0	1.2	...	1.3	112	15.0	11
Todd, MN	14.9	50.1	9.7	4.8	...	3.4	313	13.6	52
Traverse, MN	14.6	41.9	14.1	0.2	...	...	50	11.8	7
Wabasha, MN	13.5	18.7	5.1	1.4	...	1.6	316	15.6	24
Wadena, MN	15.0	51.1	2.9	0.0	...	1.0	220	13.8	28
Waseca, MN	17.1	24.9	7.8	4.2	...	3.8	209	14.6	25
Washington, MN	12.8	12.3	12.4	1.3	...	2.3	1 728	17.4	166
Watonwan, MN	12.6	44.7	34.8	15.5	...	2.8	146	13.8	7
Wilkin, MN	15.3	31.1	7.3	1.6	...	1.1	98	12.8	10
Winona, MN	14.7	31.3	9.4	2.9	...	3.9	412	14.9	26
Wright, MN	12.8	18.6	4.4	1.2	...	1.7	1 255	17.3	...
Yellow Medicine, MN	17.9	45.6	10.5	2.5	...	3.1	131	14.2	11
MISSISSIPPI	13.8	64.6	53.0	0.7	...	3.9	31 322	15.8	...
Adams, MS	12.4	92.1	88.6	0.2	275	3.6	268	16.9	41
Alcorn, MS	15.8	50.4	18.1	1.4	311	3.7	411	13.8	29
Amite, MS	11.5	99.3	83.0	0.2	76	4.8	100	13.3	15
Attala, MS	15.7	69.5	55.9	0.2	179	0.9	231	14.8	20
Benton, MS	19.7	92.5	59.0	1.6	75	3.6	85	15.8	13
Bolivar, MS	14.6	85.8	84.0	0.0	394	2.0	492	14.9	82
Calhoun, MS	17.4	70.9	47.5	3.6	139	2.9	159	16.3	13
Carroll, MS	14.8	85.8	72.3	0.2	64	6.2	76	14.0	14
Chickasaw, MS	16.0	74.9	61.3	2.7	163	4.3	250	13.4	20
Choctaw, MS	12.7	71.0	39.7	0.0	100	4.0	120	15.1	18
Claiborne, MS	10.4	99.5	99.6	0.0	118	3.4	53	35.1	21
Clarke, MS	16.8	67.3	44.4	0.0	180	5.9	213	15.2	31
Clay, MS	11.9	82.8	80.3	0.2	...	4.7	221	17.2	31
Coahoma, MS	14.0	95.4	94.5	0.7	260	5.3	367	15.7	57
Copiah, MS	9.2	82.9	74.0	0.7	224	8.9	296	16.0	31
Covington, MS	19.0	80.5	51.2	0.0	184	3.9	210	16.5	21
DeSoto, MS	12.4	33.3	26.9	1.4	1 116	0.9	1 381	18.3	66
Forrest, MS	17.2	67.5	51.8	0.4	574	4.6	793	14.4	105
Franklin, MS	18.6	71.3	49.0	0.0	88	2.1	111	14.0	12
George, MS	15.6	51.4	11.8	0.0	178	0.5	245	16.9	20
Greene, MS	14.9	75.2	19.8	0.0	120	6.0	139	14.6	16
Grenada, MS	14.2	59.0	53.5	0.0	179	3.8	248	18.9	32
Hancock, MS	16.1	63.2	12.2	0.4	347	4.9	425	15.8	49
Harrison, MS	14.1	59.4	38.5	1.1	...	3.9	1 950	15.8	200
Hinds, MS	11.5	59.6	86.4	0.4	...	6.2	2 484	17.4	286
Holmes, MS	10.6	98.1	99.2	0.0	217	3.2	222	18.9	37
Humphreys, MS	11.0	96.6	98.2	0.0	101	5.8	111	17.0	22
Issaquena, MS	...	...	...	...	...	...	...	...	...
Itawamba, MS	14.5	55.8	8.8	0.2	225	4.9	250	15.2	15
Jackson, MS	13.3	53.1	33.1	1.2	1 413	3.2	1 596	15.8	173
Jasper, MS	15.2	84.8	76.6	0.1	154	1.4	194	15.2	32
Jefferson, MS	14.4	99.4	99.9	0.0	95	0.4	100	15.1	24
Jefferson Davis, MS	20.6	99.4	87.8	0.0	116	4.8	154	14.2	17
Jones, MS	15.3	67.4	42.8	1.4	...	2.7	758	14.5	81
Kemper, MS	9.8	99.0	97.4	0.0	60	4.1	91	14.6	13
Lafayette, MS	14.8	50.7	42.9	0.7	...	2.4	378	14.3	42
Lamar, MS	16.8	43.2	21.7	0.7	454	3.1	512	15.7	47
Lauderdale, MS	14.7	61.8	57.1	0.2	...	4.4	829	15.9	99
Lawrence, MS	12.6	64.7	40.5	0.0	143	5.4	163	14.4	20
Leake, MS	14.5	72.9	62.4	2.0	173	5.1	189	17.3	25
Lee, MS	15.8	52.7	38.3	0.7	806	4.8	1 060	15.0	104
Leflore, MS	15.7	99.3	94.2	0.8	290	6.9	423	14.8	54
Lincoln, MS	11.1	60.7	38.7	0.1	...	3.4	359	17.0	36
Lowndes, MS	13.0	62.3	61.0	0.3	674	4.4	708	14.9	69
Madison, MS	8.7	47.3	56.5	0.8	710	2.6	851	16.0	89
Marion, MS	18.3	78.1	47.8	0.0	258	3.4	271	16.3	35
Marshall, MS	14.8	86.7	74.8	1.1	264	3.8	291	18.2	40
Monroe, MS	15.8	62.8	41.4	0.1	373	4.3	420	14.4	42
Montgomery, MS	13.7	70.8	62.1	0.1	85	4.9	119	16.1	20
Neshoba, MS	13.2	62.2	39.4	0.0	216	5.5	253	16.4	28

[2]IEP = Individual Education Program. See notes and definitions at the end of this section.
. . . = Not available.

Table C-1. Population, School, and Student Characteristics by County—*Continued*

STATE County	Revenue, 2003–2004 — Total revenue (thousands of dollars)	Percent of revenue from: Federal government	State government	Local government	Current expenditures, 2003–2004 — Total expenditures (thousands of dollars)	Amount per student (dollars)	Percent for instruction	Resident population, 16 to 19 years, 2000 — Total	Percent in armed forces	Percent high school graduates	Percent not enrolled, not employed, not in armed forces, not high school graduate
	19	20	21	22	23	24	25	26	27	28	29
Pope, MN	14 163	4.7	76.9	18.4	11 989	7 914	68.8	707	0.0	3.4	1.8
Ramsey, MN	1 009 589	7.8	71.4	20.8	816 565	9 517	71.2	30 219	0.1	9.0	3.9
Red Lake, MN	8 630	8.0	75.0	17.0	7 587	10 143	64.4	311	0.0	10.6	1.9
Redwood, MN	27 226	5.4	78.3	16.3	22 579	7 772	67.4	1 004	0.0	6.7	2.4
Renville, MN	20 405	7.5	79.9	12.6	18 128	7 784	68.2	1 024	0.0	7.2	2.8
Rice, MN	81 306	5.0	74.5	20.5	66 227	8 035	70.2	4 870	0.0	6.6	1.6
Rock, MN	14 564	4.9	76.9	18.2	12 167	7 501	69.2	583	0.0	4.8	1.4
Roseau, MN	32 400	4.9	80.0	15.1	26 977	7 748	67.3	1 001	0.0	8.9	2.1
St. Louis, MN	284 804	8.4	73.1	18.5	242 707	8 593	69.2	13 530	0.1	8.4	2.4
Scott, MN	159 158	4.2	67.8	27.9	119 664	7 403	71.0	4 375	0.0	10.9	1.9
Sherburne, MN	148 875	2.1	72.3	25.7	110 474	6 848	68.0	3 971	0.1	13.2	2.9
Sibley, MN	24 458	9.5	68.7	21.8	20 129	8 887	72.4	888	0.0	9.5	0.5
Stearns, MN	233 118	6.7	73.0	20.3	189 354	8 196	72.8	11 213	0.0	6.5	1.3
Steele, MN	58 836	4.3	74.9	20.9	46 082	7 189	68.0	2 056	0.0	6.9	1.3
Stevens, MN	15 644	6.4	66.6	27.0	12 591	8 707	70.0	1 126	0.0	3.5	1.1
Swift, MN	15 336	3.9	80.3	15.8	12 865	7 484	68.1	617	0.0	4.2	0.6
Todd, MN	51 526	10.7	65.1	24.2	68 088	16 043	43.5	1 777	0.0	7.3	3.9
Traverse, MN	6 855	8.6	69.4	22.0	5 873	9 565	70.4	243	0.0	5.3	1.8
Wabasha, MN	41 938	2.8	80.5	16.7	35 541	7 031	68.3	1 296	0.0	9.4	1.8
Wadena, MN	28 715	7.6	82.4	10.0	22 891	7 358	69.5	757	0.0	6.6	1.8
Waseca, MN	36 134	5.9	72.4	21.7	29 120	7 736	68.7	1 133	0.0	7.4	3.3
Washington, MN	391 440	2.6	61.1	36.2	300 461	8 165	71.3	10 958	0.0	7.6	1.7
Watonwan, MN	20 296	7.1	79.0	14.0	16 500	7 895	65.5	706	0.0	6.5	1.6
Wilkin, MN	11 520	6.0	82.4	11.6	9 845	7 703	67.8	417	0.0	2.6	2.6
Winona, MN	64 402	7.4	71.4	21.2	52 498	8 540	69.0	4 572	0.0	6.7	1.0
Wright, MN	196 893	4.4	69.1	26.5	148 852	7 345	71.1	5 251	0.0	9.8	2.2
Yellow Medicine, MN	19 964	7.2	71.6	21.1	16 355	8 572	67.8	750	0.0	6.5	1.3
MISSISSIPPI	3 481 643	14.8	54.8	30.4	3 072 009	6 237	64.3	184 029	1.2	9.9	7.8
Adams, MS	33 932	19.3	49.3	31.4	31 638	6 799	64.0	2 125	0.0	8.3	6.4
Alcorn, MS	39 911	11.7	60.3	28.0	36 021	6 447	69.0	1 759	0.0	13.5	6.9
Amite, MS	13 065	21.0	44.3	34.7	11 216	7 811	63.2	854	0.0	11.6	8.3
Attala, MS	23 811	13.6	59.0	27.3	21 239	6 274	65.2	1 173	0.0	6.5	8.1
Benton, MS	8 626	20.1	64.7	15.3	8 197	6 262	62.2	483	0.0	8.3	10.6
Bolivar, MS	56 301	22.6	56.3	21.1	52 369	6 979	63.2	3 414	0.1	7.2	6.6
Calhoun, MS	17 300	14.9	62.0	23.0	15 321	6 018	64.0	935	0.0	14.1	6.3
Carroll, MS	8 960	16.4	58.5	25.1	7 522	6 783	64.0	633	0.0	5.7	13.6
Chickasaw, MS	24 070	16.7	63.5	19.9	21 445	6 390	64.9	1 159	0.0	8.6	7.9
Choctaw, MS	12 853	15.6	58.5	25.9	11 568	6 473	67.4	670	0.0	7.3	6.6
Claiborne, MS	14 692	18.7	47.3	34.0	13 613	8 508	65.8	1 275	0.0	7.1	6.4
Clarke, MS	21 522	14.1	59.7	26.1	19 700	6 086	63.9	1 063	0.5	9.0	7.8
Clay, MS	28 388	18.2	55.4	26.4	22 404	5 682	61.8	1 445	0.3	7.1	12.6
Coahoma, MS	42 417	22.5	55.4	22.1	38 669	6 529	64.5	2 163	0.0	8.2	14.2
Copiah, MS	31 474	19.4	57.4	23.2	28 058	5 869	61.6	2 235	7.7	10.6	2.1
Covington, MS	22 961	18.4	60.4	21.2	21 291	6 059	64.9	1 244	0.0	9.6	8.1
DeSoto, MS	137 420	6.2	59.0	34.8	112 053	4 734	65.0	5 314	0.0	9.7	8.8
Forrest, MS	88 070	14.3	52.2	33.5	77 826	6 771	65.1	5 766	1.6	9.4	6.4
Franklin, MS	12 819	20.7	52.8	26.5	11 700	7 462	63.5	562	0.0	7.4	12.4
George, MS	24 193	14.9	66.2	18.9	21 643	5 323	67.7	1 128	0.0	12.2	6.1
Greene, MS	14 892	24.0	56.4	19.5	13 813	7 087	61.8	813	0.2	14.1	17.7
Grenada, MS	29 577	14.4	59.0	26.6	25 800	5 472	65.0	1 257	0.0	9.1	14.4
Hancock, MS	47 428	11.8	49.2	39.0	41 518	6 249	61.7	2 214	0.0	8.4	5.2
Harrison, MS	231 118	13.4	47.7	38.9	208 772	6 779	62.6	11 619	11.9	22.2	7.4
Hinds, MS	309 025	13.4	48.2	38.5	271 070	6 360	63.0	17 271	0.1	6.8	6.5
Holmes, MS	29 946	26.6	58.7	14.7	25 493	6 065	60.5	1 697	0.0	7.0	7.7
Humphreys, MS	13 961	25.7	58.0	16.3	11 575	6 035	60.7	904	0.0	2.9	8.5
Issaquena, MS	. . .	. . .	. . .	. . .	. . .	. . .	. . .	158	0.0	3.2	11.4
Itawamba, MS	24 167	11.5	64.5	24.0	21 151	5 533	68.1	1 538	0.0	7.0	5.9
Jackson, MS	179 732	11.6	51.8	36.6	156 017	6 176	63.6	7 461	1.4	12.4	6.4
Jasper, MS	23 614	17.5	53.1	29.4	18 622	6 191	61.3	1 226	0.0	10.9	6.5
Jefferson, MS	11 954	22.6	57.8	19.6	11 041	6 931	66.7	705	0.0	11.6	9.6
Jefferson Davis, MS	18 289	23.9	51.6	24.5	16 130	7 096	63.2	951	0.0	10.3	10.3
Jones, MS	77 712	14.7	55.9	29.4	68 867	6 290	65.5	4 375	0.0	6.8	6.4
Kemper, MS	9 526	24.2	58.6	17.2	9 245	6 910	63.9	832	0.0	8.7	4.1
Lafayette, MS	40 981	10.7	51.5	37.8	36 120	6 801	65.9	3 715	0.1	3.5	2.8
Lamar, MS	51 882	10.4	58.8	30.8	46 113	5 810	66.9	2 298	0.3	11.7	5.0
Lauderdale, MS	90 458	14.2	56.8	29.0	83 761	6 280	66.4	5 091	4.3	12.9	6.1
Lawrence, MS	16 688	18.0	55.0	27.0	15 455	6 440	64.9	898	0.0	8.7	7.5
Leake, MS	20 871	16.6	61.3	22.1	18 255	5 457	62.3	1 227	0.0	9.0	10.4
Lee, MS	109 918	9.9	52.4	37.7	93 843	6 298	66.5	4 086	0.0	10.2	7.2
Leflore, MS	44 373	22.3	58.0	19.7	41 039	6 394	63.5	2 781	0.0	6.9	12.8
Lincoln, MS	40 351	11.8	55.2	33.0	34 745	5 956	62.5	1 912	0.0	14.6	4.6
Lowndes, MS	75 526	14.1	52.9	33.0	65 451	6 319	64.3	3 766	1.1	8.4	5.9
Madison, MS	98 463	10.0	46.5	43.5	76 046	5 725	64.7	4 043	0.3	7.6	5.8
Marion, MS	32 145	16.2	60.4	23.4	28 394	6 459	63.8	1 605	0.0	10.6	9.3
Marshall, MS	34 670	18.2	62.6	19.2	28 726	5 442	64.6	2 362	0.0	9.1	13.9
Monroe, MS	42 113	13.8	60.7	25.4	37 519	6 150	65.7	2 347	0.0	9.6	6.1
Montgomery, MS	14 652	20.1	58.8	21.2	13 480	7 518	65.1	779	0.0	7.2	7.6
Neshoba, MS	26 760	19.8	59.4	20.8	23 733	5 731	68.6	1 808	0.0	13.4	8.8

. . . = Not available.

Table C-1. Population, School, and Student Characteristics by County—*Continued*

STATE County	High school graduates, 2000			College enrollment, 2000		College graduates, 2000 (percent)						
	Population 25 years and over	High school graduate or less (percent)	High school graduate or more (percent)	Number	Percent public	Bachelor's degree or more	+/- U.S. percentage with bachelor's degree or more	Non-Hispanic White	Black	American Indian and Alaska Native	Asian or Pacific Islander	Hispanic[3]
	30	31	32	33	34	35	36	37	38	39	40	41
Pope, MN	7 719	51.7	81.8	247	87.0	14.7	-9.7	14.7	50.0	0.0	0.0	0.0
Ramsey, MN	323 214	37.7	87.6	41 484	54.3	34.3	9.9	37.0	18.6	16.2	29.6	16.1
Red Lake, MN	2 879	59.4	78.8	122	91.8	10.7	-13.7	10.9	...	0.0	50.0	0.0
Redwood, MN	11 269	56.8	80.2	303	85.8	13.4	-11.0	13.8	0.0	1.7	6.7	11.9
Renville, MN	11 464	57.1	80.9	367	86.1	12.6	-11.8	13.0	0.0	0.0	20.0	2.6
Rice, MN	33 400	47.8	85.2	6 359	21.2	22.4	-2.0	23.2	11.8	3.4	27.7	8.0
Rock, MN	6 485	54.2	81.5	276	83.7	15.4	-9.0	15.2	27.5	58.3	38.9	6.1
Roseau, MN	10 366	55.3	82.5	303	91.7	14.9	-9.5	15.1	44.4	0.0	14.5	0.0
St. Louis, MN	132 801	44.6	87.2	16 743	85.8	21.9	-2.5	22.1	21.0	9.0	28.8	13.8
Scott, MN	55 564	37.4	91.0	3 500	70.4	29.4	5.0	30.1	15.7	7.5	30.6	7.6
Sherburne, MN	38 349	42.6	89.9	3 410	81.6	19.4	-5.0	19.5	12.5	10.2	33.1	16.7
Sibley, MN	9 970	60.9	79.2	370	78.9	11.6	-12.8	11.8	0.0	0.0	56.3	2.9
Stearns, MN	77 519	47.1	86.2	15 315	73.1	22.0	-2.4	21.9	13.9	8.7	31.1	18.7
Steele, MN	21 550	49.4	86.6	1 184	73.0	20.1	-4.3	20.4	3.4	0.0	28.8	9.7
Stevens, MN	5 790	49.7	84.4	1 713	97.6	20.6	-3.8	20.2	42.1	0.0	55.6	47.2
Swift, MN	8 336	54.8	80.4	347	87.0	14.0	-10.4	15.0	0.6	7.7	9.3	2.3
Todd, MN	15 758	62.0	79.3	663	91.3	10.0	-14.4	10.1	0.0	2.9	4.4	6.4
Traverse, MN	2 850	57.4	82.2	122	92.6	10.7	-13.7	10.8	...	0.0	20.0	20.0
Wabasha, MN	14 189	51.8	85.6	654	87.6	16.9	-7.5	16.9	40.0	52.6	19.7	15.0
Wadena, MN	9 047	57.4	79.5	569	95.1	13.4	-11.0	13.2	6.5	7.5	82.9	0.0
Waseca, MN	12 818	53.7	84.8	582	88.1	16.2	-8.2	16.8	0.3	2.0	93.3	8.9
Washington, MN	128 215	32.0	94.0	9 321	71.4	33.9	9.5	33.9	28.9	11.3	52.2	26.0
Watonwan, MN	7 745	63.1	75.9	261	80.1	13.7	-10.7	15.1	0.0	26.7	17.0	2.2
Wilkin, MN	4 673	48.0	84.5	175	86.9	14.0	-10.4	14.3	0.0	0.0	42.9	0.0
Winona, MN	29 165	46.2	84.0	7 565	79.4	23.2	-1.2	23.3	5.8	13.5	39.1	11.9
Wright, MN	55 234	48.7	88.1	2 738	77.5	17.9	-6.5	18.0	12.4	9.0	36.4	3.6
Yellow Medicine, MN	7 394	53.4	81.9	405	93.8	14.4	-10.0	14.4	0.0	14.7	71.4	0.0
MISSISSIPPI	1 757 517	56.5	72.9	152 997	86.7	16.9	-7.5	20.1	10.1	9.1	35.2	12.1
Adams, MS	22 211	58.3	73.4	1 538	92.6	17.5	-6.9	24.0	10.7	14.3	9.4	16.6
Alcorn, MS	23 159	66.8	68.1	1 016	88.3	11.7	-12.7	12.1	7.5	21.7	43.6	9.9
Amite, MS	8 981	68.4	67.2	392	80.1	9.4	-15.0	11.7	6.0	0.0	0.0	9.8
Attala, MS	12 674	66.4	63.4	576	84.2	11.6	-12.8	14.9	5.9	0.0	0.0	14.0
Benton, MS	5 073	73.3	58.8	210	66.2	7.8	-16.6	7.7	8.2	0.0	...	0.0
Bolivar, MS	22 956	59.1	65.3	3 752	96.2	18.8	-5.6	33.3	9.4	6.9	50.6	9.0
Calhoun, MS	10 021	70.2	64.4	338	91.4	10.2	-14.2	11.8	4.7	0.0	50.0	21.9
Carroll, MS	7 121	68.1	66.6	336	70.7	10.0	13.6	12.6	6.7	...	11.1	5.7
Chickasaw, MS	12 159	71.0	59.4	487	88.9	9.5	-14.9	11.1	7.1	0.0	0.0	0.6
Choctaw, MS	6 171	67.6	65.1	276	86.6	11.2	-13.2	14.1	3.6	27.3	...	0.0
Claiborne, MS	5 954	53.7	71.6	2 118	98.6	18.9	-5.5	28.6	15.9	0.0	...	16.7
Clarke, MS	11 541	68.0	68.8	488	91.6	9.6	-14.8	12.1	4.0	0.0	52.4	7.0
Clay, MS	13 441	63.1	68.6	1 013	86.3	14.6	-9.8	19.8	9.3	21.9	31.8	8.1
Coahoma, MS	17 403	50.3	62.2	1 000	95.7	16.2	-8.2	25.1	10.5	0.0	61.8	6.6
Copiah, MS	17 405	60.9	69.3	1 605	84.0	11.6	-12.8	15.0	7.6	31.3	24.0	0.0
Covington, MS	11 923	64.7	67.2	648	97.8	11.4	-13.0	13.7	6.4	0.0	0.0	12.5
DeSoto, MS	68 302	52.5	81.6	4 155	79.2	14.3	-10.1	14.9	9.0	10.4	27.2	9.3
Forrest, MS	41 526	48.6	79.3	10 506	88.3	22.8	-1.6	28.2	10.2	0.0	39.0	12.5
Franklin, MS	5 377	66.3	67.5	235	95.3	10.5	-13.9	12.4	6.8	3.0	0.0	0.0
George, MS	11 838	68.9	69.8	452	87.4	9.1	-15.3	9.8	2.9	0.0	0.0	6.8
Greene, MS	8 352	70.6	67.4	311	87.8	8.0	-16.4	9.2	4.0	0.0	60.0	13.1
Grenada, MS	14 675	63.8	63.8	740	91.5	13.5	-10.9	17.0	7.1	24.1	23.2	8.8
Hancock, MS	28 840	51.4	77.9	1 463	86.5	17.3	-7.1	17.9	8.7	13.9	37.5	16.3
Harrison, MS	119 169	48.1	80.3	8 867	84.4	18.4	-6.0	20.3	10.8	12.9	16.7	15.8
Hinds, MS	150 287	41.5	80.4	19 813	70.5	27.2	2.8	37.7	18.5	13.9	58.0	24.5
Holmes, MS	12 071	67.0	59.7	1 087	89.6	11.2	-13.2	20.0	7.9	50.0	22.2	8.6
Humphreys, MS	6 379	67.9	53.7	337	91.7	11.6	-12.8	16.9	8.9	12.5	0.0	14.5
Issaquena, MS	1 380	72.4	58.8	63	90.5	7.1	-17.3	10.6	4.6	...	...	0.0
Itawamba, MS	14 833	65.6	65.9	1 268	91.6	8.8	-15.6	8.8	6.5	0.0	38.5	16.5
Jackson, MS	82 818	51.1	81.0	5 397	92.3	16.5	-7.9	18.1	9.1	12.0	21.4	11.8
Jasper, MS	11 263	67.8	66.7	576	90.3	9.8	-14.6	13.8	5.3	0.0	25.0	5.7
Jefferson, MS	5 785	68.5	59.7	419	95.5	10.6	-13.8	16.9	9.4	0.0	100.0	0.0
Jefferson Davis, MS	8 613	68.4	66.4	445	87.2	10.4	-14.0	13.6	7.6	0.0	0.0	0.0
Jones, MS	41 403	58.4	73.9	3 040	89.1	14.0	-10.4	16.1	6.9	7.4	44.9	7.4
Kemper, MS	6 498	67.8	60.5	729	97.1	10.3	-14.1	16.1	5.5	0.0	0.0	0.0
Lafayette, MS	20 628	44.2	78.5	9 856	96.1	31.1	6.7	36.8	11.9	8.6	70.7	30.5
Lamar, MS	23 855	44.0	83.0	2 681	91.1	26.8	2.4	28.1	15.7	15.0	49.5	33.1
Lauderdale, MS	49 511	53.2	74.9	3 921	91.6	16.2	-8.2	19.7	8.7	3.6	51.1	16.7
Lawrence, MS	8 394	61.2	72.9	458	93.9	12.0	-12.4	12.2	11.1	77.8	9.1	12.0
Leake, MS	13 160	67.7	64.1	436	88.3	11.6	-12.8	14.2	6.9	7.6	20.8	12.7
Lee, MS	48 382	53.5	74.7	2 574	92.4	18.1	-6.3	20.7	8.8	16.7	47.5	4.5
Leflore, MS	21 581	63.7	61.9	2 418	92.4	15.9	-8.5	23.2	10.9	28.6	52.0	13.2
Lincoln, MS	21 074	59.6	72.0	1 149	90.1	12.4	-12.0	13.5	9.3	0.0	57.8	0.0
Lowndes, MS	37 520	54.3	75.5	3 480	91.6	20.5	-3.9	27.2	9.2	31.0	32.2	12.1
Madison, MS	46 773	35.3	83.0	3 713	64.2	37.9	13.5	48.7	16.3	0.0	48.1	16.6
Marion, MS	16 025	66.9	66.5	726	93.1	11.5	-12.9	12.7	8.1	0.0	18.2	15.2
Marshall, MS	21 519	71.5	61.0	1 444	58.0	9.0	-15.4	8.1	10.0	0.0	30.8	2.5
Monroe, MS	24 288	66.9	65.5	889	90.7	10.9	-13.5	12.6	6.1	15.0	50.0	4.3
Montgomery, MS	7 830	69.9	62.1	363	95.3	11.0	-13.4	15.1	4.9	0.0	0.0	4.5
Neshoba, MS	17 780	64.0	67.7	891	92.9	11.4	-13.0	13.0	8.7	3.3	20.0	0.0

[3]May be of any race.
... = Not available.

Table C-1. Population, School, and Student Characteristics by County—*Continued*

STATE County	State/county code	County type[1]	Population, 2005 Total	Percent 5 to 17 years	School districts	Schools	Students	Resident enrollment, 2000 Total	Percent public	K–12	Percent public
			1	2	3	4	5	6	7	8	9
Newton, MS	28101	7	22 366	18.0	3	9	3 710	6 028	89.4	4 247	88.4
Noxubee, MS	28103	7	12 202	20.3	1	6	2 170	3 505	82.6	2 955	80.5
Oktibbeha, MS	28105	5	41 247	12.6	2	13	4 850	19 744	90.9	6 653	83.2
Panola, MS	28107	6	35 331	19.5	2	14	6 556	9 472	90.9	7 843	91.4
Pearl River, MS	28109	6	52 659	18.3	3	20	8 715	12 637	90.0	9 827	92.4
Perry, MS	28111	3	12 160	19.5	2	8	2 115	2 986	93.6	2 470	95.6
Pike, MS	28113	7	39 426	18.8	3	17	6 688	10 215	87.7	7 868	88.8
Pontotoc, MS	28115	7	28 208	18.8	2	11	5 406	6 412	93.6	5 267	96.6
Prentiss, MS	28117	7	25 593	17.4	2	11	3 581	6 548	97.1	4 658	97.5
Quitman, MS	28119	6	9 512	21.9	1	4	1 586	2 901	87.0	2 433	86.4
Rankin, MS	28121	2	131 841	17.2	4	31	20 195	28 701	85.8	21 903	92.0
Scott, MS	28123	6	28 739	19.1	2	11	5 527	7 148	91.2	6 012	93.2
Sharkey, MS	28125	9	5 967	21.4	1	4	1 348	2 026	88.5	1 716	88.2
Simpson, MS	28127	2	27 944	19.4	1	9	4 266	6 941	88.4	5 802	90.0
Smith, MS	28129	8	16 058	18.8	1	6	3 091	4 070	91.1	3 404	95.3
Stone, MS	28131	1	14 862	17.6	1	4	2 639	3 916	93.5	2 687	97.2
Sunflower, MS	28133	5	32 311	18.6	3	16	5 227	10 048	86.8	7 690	87.0
Tallahatchie, MS	28135	7	14 191	20.2	2	7	2 764	4 489	91.8	3 664	91.4
Tate, MS	28137	1	26 548	18.0	2	10	4 629	7 177	87.7	5 059	87.7
Tippah, MS	28139	7	21 212	16.5	2	10	4 079	4 775	91.2	3 900	95.6
Tishomingo, MS	28141	8	19 202	16.2	1	8	3 270	3 842	95.8	3 228	98.2
Tunica, MS	28143	1	10 321	20.5	1	7	2 307	2 471	90.1	2 166	89.6
Union, MS	28145	7	26 784	18.1	2	9	4 771	5 916	95.0	4 833	95.9
Walthall, MS	28147	9	15 460	18.8	1	7	2 703	4 094	95.1	3 329	96.7
Warren, MS	28149	4	49 131	19.4	1	15	8 898	13 651	85.1	10 568	88.9
Washington, MS	28151	5	59 220	21.3	4	29	11 457	19 083	86.3	15 260	86.2
Wayne, MS	28153	7	21 291	19.3	1	8	3 924	5 535	91.7	4 731	93.5
Webster, MS	28155	9	10 092	17.2	1	5	1 846	2 474	89.7	1 992	92.8
Wilkinson, MS	28157	8	10 269	16.5	1	5	1 524	2 669	78.7	2 241	77.4
Winston, MS	28159	7	19 870	17.8	1	7	2 911	5 032	83.9	4 234	84.8
Yalobusha, MS	28161	7	13 417	17.4	2	4	2 018	3 267	90.3	2 646	92.8
Yazoo, MS	28163	6	28 195	18.8	2	10	4 710	7 155	80.7	6 117	82.0
MISSOURI	29000		5 800 310	17.3	532	2 363	919 051	1 479 573	81.5	1 057 556	86.8
Adair, MO	29001	7	24 509	12.1	3	9	3 074	10 082	90.1	3 520	90.4
Andrew, MO	29003	3	16 899	17.7	3	10	2 864	4 144	90.3	3 290	94.0
Atchison, MO	29005	9	6 246	16.8	3	7	931	1 417	94.6	1 144	97.8
Audrain, MO	29007	6	25 759	16.4	3	10	3 389	5 632	86.0	4 572	89.4
Barry, MO	29009	6	35 599	17.9	6	15	4 694	7 860	94.4	6 700	95.9
Barton, MO	29011	6	13 057	18.7	3	10	2 163	2 959	92.9	2 446	95.4
Bates, MO	29013	1	17 027	17.4	7	13	2 816	3 883	90.3	3 379	92.1
Benton, MO	29015	9	18 854	13.9	3	10	2 916	3 197	92.4	2 727	95.0
Bollinger, MO	29017	9	12 325	17.5	4	8	1 945	2 686	90.2	2 402	90.6
Boone, MO	29019	3	143 326	15.1	6	46	21 681	49 784	89.3	22 625	93.1
Buchanan, MO	29021	3	84 904	16.6	3	32	12 829	21 945	87.5	15 543	89.5
Butler, MO	29023	7	41 338	16.4	3	16	6 644	9 296	91.3	7 334	94.0
Caldwell, MO	29025	1	9 307	18.2	8	14	1 814	2 186	94.9	1 840	97.0
Callaway, MO	29027	3	42 541	17.3	6	60	6 274	10 500	80.2	7 820	92.3
Camden, MO	29029	7	39 432	14.0	4	14	5 153	6 943	91.5	5 598	96.0
Cape Girardeau, MO	29031	5	71 161	15.6	5	24	9 624	19 596	85.5	12 000	82.9
Carroll, MO	29033	6	10 193	17.6	5	13	1 841	2 272	94.1	1 921	97.0
Carter, MO	29035	9	5 910	17.4	2	4	1 351	1 441	96.7	1 168	97.7
Cass, MO	29037	1	94 232	19.0	10	40	17 857	21 176	85.1	16 705	90.7
Cedar, MO	29039	6	14 160	17.0	2	6	2 323	3 058	88.2	2 529	95.5
Chariton, MO	29041	9	8 124	15.1	4	9	1 261	1 908	89.4	1 604	90.8
Christian, MO	29043	2	67 266	18.2	7	27	11 799	14 178	87.5	10 704	93.6
Clark, MO	29045	9	7 323	17.4	4	7	1 249	1 778	92.1	1 383	96.2
Clay, MO	29047	1	202 078	17.7	5	57	30 901	47 240	82.8	33 951	90.5
Clinton, MO	29049	1	20 715	17.4	5	14	4 181	4 790	92.5	3 836	95.5
Cole, MO	29051	3	72 757	16.4	5	60	11 463	18 439	73.1	12 875	71.8
Cooper, MO	29053	6	17 294	15.7	6	15	2 606	4 281	84.2	3 264	88.7
Crawford, MO	29055	6	23 932	17.5	3	9	3 601	5 230	90.3	4 525	92.4
Dade, MO	29057	8	7 830	16.3	4	8	1 244	1 758	90.3	1 528	92.3
Dallas, MO	29059	2	16 437	18.5	1	5	1 919	3 824	89.9	3 218	91.5
Daviess, MO	29061	8	8 121	18.3	5	10	1 365	1 830	90.6	1 560	90.9
DeKalb, MO	29063	3	12 342	13.0	4	8	1 247	2 508	90.0	2 096	92.4
Dent, MO	29065	7	15 083	17.1	5	8	2 362	3 282	91.6	2 739	96.1
Douglas, MO	29067	6	13 594	17.4	3	5	1 829	3 163	89.5	2 584	93.5
Dunklin, MO	29069	7	32 545	18.2	7	21	6 246	7 596	95.5	6 185	97.2
Franklin, MO	29071	1	99 090	18.2	10	42	17 027	23 737	83.6	19 146	85.5
Gasconade, MO	29073	6	15 745	16.6	2	8	3 098	3 449	90.0	2 906	91.8
Gentry, MO	29075	8	6 555	17.6	3	7	1 286	1 682	93.2	1 402	93.5
Greene, MO	29077	2	250 784	15.0	8	80	34 526	67 577	82.9	38 501	91.5
Grundy, MO	29079	7	10 327	16.0	5	8	1 703	2 421	94.4	1 766	98.9
Harrison, MO	29081	7	8 876	16.0	5	12	1 591	1 871	92.5	1 565	94.1
Henry, MO	29083	6	22 577	15.9	7	14	3 202	4 848	93.4	4 055	95.1
Hickory, MO	29085	8	9 271	13.8	4	10	1 907	1 551	95.5	1 371	97.0
Holt, MO	29087	8	5 081	15.4	3	6	780	1 239	96.0	1 062	96.9
Howard, MO	29089	3	9 957	15.8	3	7	1 435	3 018	66.7	1 894	89.5
Howell, MO	29091	7	38 400	17.6	8	18	6 956	9 017	92.9	7 057	95.3
Iron, MO	29093	6	10 273	17.0	4	9	2 288	2 522	96.4	2 038	97.8
Jackson, MO	29095	1	662 959	17.7	12	228	112 507	171 287	82.2	123 402	87.4
Jasper, MO	29097	3	110 624	17.6	6	30	12 020	26 027	88.0	19 008	92.8
Jefferson, MO	29099	1	213 669	18.6	12	59	34 877	52 378	85.3	40 986	90.0

[1]County type codes are from the Economic Research Service of the United States Department of Agriculture. See notes and definitions at the end of this section.

Table C-1. Population, School, and Student Characteristics by County—*Continued*

STATE County	Characteristics of students, 2004–2005				Outcomes		Staff and students, 2004–2005		
	Percent with IEP[2]	Percent eligible for free or reduced-price lunch	Percent minority	Percent English-language learners	Number of graduates, 2003–2004	Percent dropouts, grades 9–12, 2001–2002	Number of teachers	Student-teacher ratio	Central administration staff
	10	11	12	13	14	15	16	17	18
Newton, MS	15.1	61.9	45.7	0.2	154	3.8	246	15.1	32
Noxubee, MS	14.7	99.3	99.7	0.0	132	4.8	147	14.7	18
Oktibbeha, MS	16.7	68.9	72.2	0.2	269	4.9	348	13.9	49
Panola, MS	12.9	75.8	68.0	0.0	320	4.6	450	14.6	46
Pearl River, MS	12.6	59.7	19.7	0.1	463	3.0	536	16.2	62
Perry, MS	16.7	71.6	33.2	0.0	107	4.4	155	13.7	18
Pike, MS	12.7	84.4	68.0	0.0	346	4.9	419	16.0	69
Pontotoc, MS	14.1	50.0	21.4	2.5	299	0.9	336	16.1	33
Prentiss, MS	21.4	58.0	17.7	0.0	194	1.6	266	13.5	27
Quitman, MS	17.1	99.4	97.9	0.0	84	2.0	105	15.0	18
Rankin, MS	11.8	37.6	25.0	1.4	. . .	1.6	1 345	15.0	124
Scott, MS	14.9	74.5	54.9	3.7	260	5.1	327	16.9	35
Sharkey, MS	10.5	99.3	96.2	0.0	67	6.2	82	16.4	16
Simpson, MS	12.7	77.8	53.2	0.3	245	5.4	266	16.0	30
Smith, MS	17.0	61.4	32.7	0.2	176	2.2	219	14.1	19
Stone, MS	14.3	54.9	25.8	0.0	140	0.4	163	16.2	21
Sunflower, MS	12.6	92.9	95.9	0.9	286	2.6	307	17.0	54
Tallahatchie, MS	13.5	90.5	81.4	0.2	104	5.5	182	15.2	22
Tate, MS	14.2	61.0	44.8	0.2	237	3.8	282	16.4	32
Tippah, MS	16.0	60.0	24.2	1.6	228	3.8	273	14.9	16
Tishomingo, MS	14.1	54.8	4.7	1.3	189	2.0	211	15.5	15
Tunica, MS	9.2	95.6	97.9	0.2	89	5.0	158	14.6	28
Union, MS	14.9	53.7	22.8	1.5	274	1.6	316	15.1	30
Walthall, MS	15.0	58.5	64.2	0.0	152	5.1	168	16.1	18
Warren, MS	13.4	67.0	62.5	0.3	403	5.8	551	16.1	76
Washington, MS	14.4	91.8	88.7	0.1	594	6.1	743	15.4	105
Wayne, MS	14.8	77.7	54.0	0.0	220	4.6	254	15.5	25
Webster, MS	13.9	59.9	29.0	1.2	110	3.2	121	15.3	12
Wilkinson, MS	16.7	99.0	99.5	0.0	78	4.1	105	14.6	19
Winston, MS	13.4	77.9	64.7	1.9	151	2.6	190	15.3	20
Yalobusha, MS	14.6	73.8	59.8	0.0	81	3.8	144	14.1	27
Yazoo, MS	13.2	87.9	81.5	0.1	231	5.2	277	17.0	45
MISSOURI	. . .	39.1	22.6	2.0	. . .	3.6	65 465	14.0	. . .
Adair, MO	. . .	36.8	4.6	0.4	. . .	2.7	244	12.6	49
Andrew, MO	. . .	01.0	3.1	0.0	. . .	2.6	209	13.7	25
Atchison, MO	. . .	49.2	2.3	0.0	. . .	6.8	106	8.8	13
Audrain, MO	. . .	43.3	10.6	0.6	. . .	3.1	256	13.3	42
Barry, MO	. . .	50.6	13.0	4.4	. . .	2.5	312	15.0	48
Barton, MO	. . .	47.0	3.2	0.0	. . .	4.0	159	13.6	24
Bates, MO	. . .	43.4	4.2	0.4	. . .	3.0	229	12.3	38
Benton, MO	. . .	52.4	2.7	0.5	. . .	2.6	188	15.5	26
Bollinger, MO	. . .	45.9	1.0	0.1	. . .	2.8	139	14.0	25
Boone, MO	. . .	29.3	23.8	1.6	. . .	4.1	1 579	13.7	213
Buchanan, MO	. . .	48.6	10.9	0.5	. . .	3.2	898	14.3	102
Butler, MO	. . .	53.0	10.6	0.0	. . .	4.5	426	15.6	68
Caldwell, MO	. . .	40.7	1.4	0.0	. . .	2.1	165	11.0	26
Callaway, MO	. . .	39.1	8.4	0.0	. . .	4.0	543	11.6	90
Camden, MO	. . .	45.4	3.0	0.5	. . .	2.1	377	13.7	69
Cape Girardeau, MO	. . .	36.1	13.7	0.5	. . .	2.0	665	14.5	106
Carroll, MO	. . .	47.8	4.3	0.1	. . .	2.0	161	11.4	29
Carter, MO	. . .	71.4	0.4	0.0	. . .	4.1	102	13.3	21
Cass, MO	. . .	24.7	8.1	0.6	. . .	3.0	1 118	16.0	186
Cedar, MO	. . .	48.0	2.2	0.0	. . .	2.1	173	13.4	22
Chariton, MO	. . .	39.9	4.1	0.4	. . .	1.2	113	11.2	16
Christian, MO	. . .	29.3	3.6	0.1	. . .	2.7	784	15.0	108
Clark, MO	. . .	40.9	1.2	0.0	. . .	4.7	103	12.1	14
Clay, MO	. . .	24.2	15.1	1.9	. . .	4.6	2 028	15.2	352
Clinton, MO	. . .	27.3	5.7	0.0	. . .	2.4	304	13.8	51
Cole, MO	. . .	33.0	18.4	2.0	. . .	4.1	952	12.0	214
Cooper, MO	. . .	39.5	9.7	0.1	. . .	2.6	218	12.0	33
Crawford, MO	. . .	48.7	1.3	0.2	. . .	5.9	245	14.7	34
Dade, MO	. . .	53.1	2.3	0.2	. . .	2.2	107	11.7	21
Dallas, MO	. . .	51.7	2.6	0.0	. . .	5.9	149	12.8	24
Daviess, MO	. . .	47.7	2.4	0.0	. . .	2.3	137	10.0	22
DeKalb, MO	. . .	40.7	2.0	0.0	. . .	2.4	117	10.6	15
Dent, MO	. . .	44.6	3.1	0.0	. . .	7.9	171	13.8	27
Douglas, MO	. . .	60.1	1.8	0.1	. . .	1.0	136	13.4	16
Dunklin, MO	. . .	63.9	23.2	4.0	. . .	4.6	466	15.4	65
Franklin, MO	. . .	30.4	3.1	0.4	. . .	3.2	1 107	15.4	178
Gasconade, MO	. . .	35.3	2.3	0.0	. . .	2.9	210	14.8	35
Gentry, MO	. . .	37.4	2.2	0.0	. . .	2.5	114	11.3	16
Greene, MO	. . .	37.5	9.2	0.6	. . .	4.2	2 160	16.0	291
Grundy, MO	. . .	47.8	3.3	0.6	. . .	3.5	133	12.8	24
Harrison, MO	. . .	43.3	1.3	0.0	. . .	2.6	147	10.9	23
Henry, MO	. . .	40.9	4.7	0.0	. . .	3.3	270	11.9	42
Hickory, MO	. . .	61.4	3.9	0.0	. . .	2.1	153	12.5	20
Holt, MO	. . .	46.1	1.6	0.0	. . .	1.1	76	10.2	9
Howard, MO	. . .	39.1	10.1	0.0	. . .	4.1	130	11.0	20
Howell, MO	. . .	52.5	3.4	1.4	. . .	3.5	491	14.2	269
Iron, MO	. . .	55.9	4.4	0.0	. . .	2.4	173	13.3	33
Jackson, MO	. . .	44.3	47.4	5.5	. . .	4.3	7 486	15.0	1 189
Jasper, MO	. . .	48.1	11.8	2.7	. . .	5.4	775	15.5	113
Jefferson, MO	. . .	27.8	3.1	0.4	. . .	3.5	2 222	15.7	299

[2]IEP = Individual Education Program. See notes and definitions at the end of this section.
. . . = Not available.

Table C-1. Population, School, and Student Characteristics by County—*Continued*

STATE County	Revenue, 2003–2004				Current expenditures, 2003–2004			Resident population, 16 to 19 years, 2000			
	Total revenue (thousands of dollars)	Percent of revenue from:			Total expenditures (thousands of dollars)	Amount per student (dollars)	Percent for instruction	Total	Percent in armed forces	Percent high school graduates	Percent not enrolled, not employed, not in armed forces, not high school graduate
		Federal government	State government	Local government							
	19	20	21	22	23	24	25	26	27	28	29
Newton, MS	26 781	14.9	60.1	25.0	23 514	6 469	62.4	1 523	0.3	7.4	2.9
Noxubee, MS	18 796	20.5	49.6	29.9	14 853	6 691	59.2	881	0.2	9.1	7.9
Oktibbeha, MS	42 958	15.6	49.6	34.8	37 861	7 875	63.7	4 337	0.1	4.0	2.8
Panola, MS	45 334	17.4	60.6	22.0	39 758	6 197	65.5	2 449	0.0	8.3	10.1
Pearl River, MS	58 853	13.7	58.2	28.1	52 974	6 127	64.5	2 788	0.0	8.1	6.2
Perry, MS	15 594	19.4	58.9	21.7	14 508	7 022	65.2	878	0.8	9.8	8.9
Pike, MS	49 400	19.2	55.5	25.3	44 129	6 549	62.6	2 711	0.3	15.0	8.3
Pontotoc, MS	33 907	10.3	65.9	23.8	30 732	5 691	69.0	1 509	0.0	13.3	11.2
Prentiss, MS	33 465	11.9	62.4	25.7	30 342	6 545	65.0	1 819	0.3	6.1	5.9
Quitman, MS	11 986	27.6	55.7	16.6	10 538	6 570	63.4	655	0.0	11.5	13.9
Rankin, MS	135 191	8.1	50.2	41.7	112 663	5 730	66.6	6 799	0.0	11.3	9.6
Scott, MS	34 194	17.1	64.9	18.0	30 747	5 584	66.7	1 756	0.2	9.5	10.0
Sharkey, MS	11 405	24.2	50.9	24.9	9 996	7 521	58.3	500	0.0	2.8	16.8
Simpson, MS	28 869	17.9	61.5	20.6	25 600	6 025	63.7	1 566	0.6	7.1	11.2
Smith, MS	19 703	15.7	64.0	20.4	17 323	5 583	64.0	883	0.0	11.3	5.4
Stone, MS	17 704	15.1	59.6	25.3	16 400	6 217	67.7	1 060	0.0	7.4	4.2
Sunflower, MS	37 369	24.3	58.2	17.5	34 313	6 345	65.5	2 833	0.1	9.5	18.1
Tallahatchie, MS	19 905	20.0	60.0	20.0	19 012	6 751	63.3	975	0.0	5.5	13.5
Tate, MS	29 400	13.7	66.6	19.7	25 709	5 588	65.3	1 923	0.0	10.5	6.8
Tippah, MS	26 674	12.5	68.6	18.9	23 345	5 742	66.4	1 213	0.0	11.8	8.4
Tishomingo, MS	22 024	13.4	60.7	25.9	19 249	5 980	64.6	901	0.0	11.3	6.7
Tunica, MS	20 661	13.9	37.0	49.1	21 307	9 499	59.2	591	1.0	10.0	14.2
Union, MS	31 881	11.8	62.6	25.6	28 656	6 005	65.0	1 405	0.0	4.3	10.5
Walthall, MS	18 143	16.5	61.7	21.8	16 453	6 128	68.2	1 099	0.0	17.0	6.8
Warren, MS	61 886	13.3	48.8	38.0	57 626	6 446	61.9	3 021	0.0	9.6	9.5
Washington, MS	87 563	25.9	52.9	21.1	81 842	7 049	60.9	4 186	0.0	6.7	8.9
Wayne, MS	26 504	17.7	60.3	22.1	23 445	5 907	65.9	1 424	0.0	12.3	7.4
Webster, MS	12 087	12.6	64.1	23.3	11 381	6 054	67.9	677	0.0	8.1	10.3
Wilkinson, MS	11 453	21.1	56.0	22.9	10 288	6 582	62.5	683	0.0	17.0	10.8
Winston, MS	20 825	17.5	60.9	21.6	19 607	6 613	65.9	1 230	0.0	8.3	13.9
Yalobusha, MS	14 850	20.0	60.1	19.9	13 460	6 720	65.5	828	0.0	8.8	8.9
Yazoo, MS	32 701	20.5	55.9	23.6	29 091	6 104	63.2	1 783	0.0	8.9	11.8
MISSOURI	7 893 957	7.9	33.9	58.3	6 715 590	7 347	65.0	323 992	0.7	11.2	5.6
Adair, MO	25 136	8.5	39.0	52.4	21 252	6 991	67.1	2 820	0.0	4.7	0.6
Andrew, MO	20 741	6.3	47.5	46.2	18 172	6 294	65.1	925	0.0	10.7	1.8
Atchison, MO	9 771	9.5	31.9	58.6	8 264	7 533	65.9	376	0.0	8.0	13.3
Audrain, MO	27 020	9.0	37.9	53.1	22 600	6 610	66.5	1 323	0.0	12.9	9.8
Barry, MO	47 642	10.5	44.2	45.3	41 179	6 184	68.3	1 877	0.0	12.3	7.7
Barton, MO	14 950	5.2	44.1	50.7	13 384	6 168	65.9	701	0.0	8.7	6.0
Bates, MO	21 213	8.1	45.3	46.6	18 793	6 525	66.1	967	0.0	15.0	5.4
Benton, MO	18 114	12.2	38.2	49.6	16 093	5 504	65.5	790	0.0	10.9	2.7
Bollinger, MO	13 405	10.6	51.3	38.1	12 415	6 251	62.3	699	0.0	14.6	8.0
Boone, MO	184 044	6.8	33.9	59.3	151 431	7 045	66.8	11 018	0.0	7.0	2.1
Buchanan, MO	103 662	9.8	39.4	50.8	88 242	6 392	67.9	5 210	0.0	11.5	7.3
Butler, MO	44 390	15.6	42.7	41.8	38 240	5 837	65.5	2 111	0.0	10.7	10.5
Caldwell, MO	14 583	8.0	48.1	43.9	12 686	6 824	62.2	488	0.4	15.6	3.1
Callaway, MO	42 446	7.4	37.4	55.2	35 327	6 686	63.4	2 679	0.0	14.6	7.4
Camden, MO	43 282	7.6	23.7	68.7	37 418	7 295	66.1	1 571	0.0	13.7	3.9
Cape Girardeau, MO	70 225	8.0	28.3	63.7	59 498	6 140	65.2	4 820	0.1	9.4	4.9
Carroll, MO	14 431	8.3	43.8	47.9	13 136	7 282	67.2	527	0.0	14.8	10.6
Carter, MO	9 594	15.9	54.8	29.3	8 832	6 405	68.1	317	3.2	7.6	5.0
Cass, MO	139 264	4.5	42.0	53.5	109 635	6 286	63.7	4 374	0.2	13.3	4.8
Cedar, MO	16 555	9.6	47.2	43.2	14 312	6 095	67.9	737	0.0	9.4	13.3
Chariton, MO	10 002	9.4	33.0	57.7	9 142	7 493	66.7	509	0.0	10.4	3.5
Christian, MO	77 190	6.3	46.9	46.8	61 326	5 538	68.2	3 004	0.0	12.3	4.7
Clark, MO	9 080	9.1	40.9	50.0	8 146	6 501	66.6	438	0.0	13.0	4.1
Clay, MO	292 763	4.2	27.3	68.5	232 509	6 950	67.3	9 711	0.2	10.0	4.1
Clinton, MO	25 792	6.0	45.2	48.8	23 128	6 751	69.8	1 150	0.0	11.0	4.2
Cole, MO	81 844	7.1	23.6	69.3	70 362	6 766	71.2	3 815	0.0	11.2	3.3
Cooper, MO	21 547	7.3	40.6	52.1	18 252	7 102	64.9	1 103	0.0	14.1	9.4
Crawford, MO	24 293	10.1	45.8	44.1	20 998	5 849	69.7	1 325	0.0	11.0	6.9
Dade, MO	9 272	7.6	43.9	48.5	8 249	6 756	65.7	467	0.0	13.5	4.7
Dallas, MO	15 771	9.7	52.1	38.2	13 045	6 464	67.5	859	0.0	7.2	6.5
Daviess, MO	12 557	9.9	48.2	41.9	10 619	7 607	66.9	419	0.0	11.5	8.8
DeKalb, MO	10 165	7.4	51.2	41.4	9 942	7 695	65.6	569	0.0	13.5	6.7
Dent, MO	17 854	9.8	42.9	47.4	14 406	6 089	67.0	776	0.0	12.9	9.0
Douglas, MO	14 248	12.6	52.4	35.0	11 152	6 178	65.4	736	0.0	19.6	5.3
Dunklin, MO	44 978	14.8	47.1	38.1	38 412	6 115	68.8	1 923	0.0	10.3	10.5
Franklin, MO	128 409	6.6	31.2	62.2	103 356	6 077	64.8	5 360	0.1	13.0	4.5
Gasconade, MO	24 320	6.5	37.2	56.3	19 319	6 202	65.8	833	0.0	12.5	5.9
Gentry, MO	10 751	7.9	48.4	43.7	10 202	8 103	67.6	404	0.0	8.4	3.2
Greene, MO	251 050	8.1	29.6	62.3	221 950	6 097	66.4	15 093	0.1	10.9	4.3
Grundy, MO	13 070	7.6	41.4	51.0	10 803	6 673	66.4	639	0.0	6.6	10.2
Harrison, MO	12 734	8.1	43.4	48.5	11 616	7 929	64.9	458	0.0	18.8	3.7
Henry, MO	24 424	10.0	38.3	51.7	20 787	6 252	68.1	1 033	0.0	15.5	9.0
Hickory, MO	15 209	13.3	46.0	40.7	12 353	6 505	62.8	379	0.0	12.1	6.6
Holt, MO	6 591	6.9	28.7	64.4	5 981	7 339	64.3	272	0.0	7.7	2.2
Howard, MO	12 024	9.2	44.6	46.2	10 817	7 255	66.1	813	0.0	6.2	1.2
Howell, MO	52 893	11.9	47.8	40.3	46 060	6 650	68.8	2 134	0.0	12.2	6.1
Iron, MO	17 049	13.5	37.5	49.0	14 839	6 427	66.9	638	0.0	13.5	5.2
Jackson, MO	1 077 449	7.4	36.8	55.8	879 205	7 828	63.2	34 885	0.0	12.5	7.1
Jasper, MO	133 277	10.1	36.2	53.7	110 880	5 786	68.3	6 416	0.2	12.4	7.3
Jefferson, MO	254 447	6.3	42.5	51.2	226 093	6 449	65.8	11 789	0.0	11.5	6.0

Table C-1. Population, School, and Student Characteristics by County—*Continued*

STATE County	Population 25 years and over	High school graduate or less (percent)	High school graduate or more (percent)	College enrollment 2000 Number	Percent public	Bachelor's degree or more	+/- U.S. percentage with bachelor's degree or more	Non-Hispanic White	Black	American Indian and Alaska Native	Asian or Pacific Islander	Hispanic[3]
	30	31	32	33	34	35	36	37	38	39	40	41
Newton, MS	13 663	60.5	72.9	1 443	97.8	12.1	-12.3	15.8	3.0	0.0	21.4	5.5
Noxubee, MS	7 456	72.2	58.4	387	91.2	10.9	-13.5	19.8	6.2	0.0	0.0	5.3
Oktibbeha, MS	21 250	41.8	80.0	12 335	96.7	34.8	10.4	45.9	12.6	65.9	80.7	39.5
Panola, MS	20 668	66.1	63.5	1 070	91.7	10.8	-13.6	15.7	3.7	0.0	35.7	1.1
Pearl River, MS	30 940	56.6	74.6	2 015	90.1	13.9	-10.5	14.6	7.7	6.3	26.8	18.8
Perry, MS	7 400	66.1	72.0	326	78.8	7.7	-16.7	8.0	6.5	12.5	3.4	0.0
Pike, MS	24 139	61.7	70.3	1 453	93.8	12.5	-11.9	17.1	5.8	20.8	34.8	5.9
Pontotoc, MS	17 082	67.1	66.7	787	88.9	11.4	-13.0	11.8	8.1	6.1	31.8	8.3
Prentiss, MS	16 114	66.4	64.9	1 586	96.8	9.9	-14.5	10.8	2.9	44.4	0.0	11.2
Quitman, MS	5 906	69.9	55.1	237	88.2	10.6	-13.8	15.8	7.2	28.6	58.3	0.0
Rankin, MS	74 885	45.6	81.8	4 647	74.2	23.8	-0.6	26.0	11.7	23.0	42.3	16.0
Scott, MS	17 496	70.0	62.0	669	81.9	8.6	-15.8	11.4	4.1	0.0	90.9	2.8
Sharkey, MS	3 704	68.2	60.6	156	93.6	12.6	-11.8	21.5	7.4	. . .	29.4	0.0
Simpson, MS	17 269	66.5	68.8	777	90.1	10.9	-13.5	12.7	5.9	0.0	68.3	7.6
Smith, MS	10 274	67.5	70.8	444	87.4	9.1	-15.3	11.0	1.8	0.0	0.0	0.0
Stone, MS	8 258	55.4	74.8	970	94.3	12.4	-12.0	13.5	4.3	0.0	0.0	26.5
Sunflower, MS	19 976	66.3	59.3	1 673	90.1	12.0	-12.4	18.8	8.3	18.2	21.1	9.9
Tallahatchie, MS	8 979	69.8	54.4	519	94.0	10.9	-13.5	16.3	5.8	100.0	31.8	0.0
Tate, MS	15 460	60.8	71.7	1 708	92.7	12.3	-12.1	14.6	6.2	0.0	33.3	0.0
Tippah, MS	13 557	70.3	65.5	607	65.1	9.0	-15.4	10.1	2.9	0.0	0.0	11.5
Tishomingo, MS	13 276	71.3	64.6	375	95.5	8.7	-15.7	8.9	3.5	6.1	18.2	6.5
Tunica, MS	5 263	69.6	60.5	132	95.5	9.1	-15.3	19.2	3.5	14.3	0.0	5.2
Union, MS	16 499	65.3	68.5	819	91.2	13.2	-11.2	13.8	8.5	0.0	67.2	5.4
Walthall, MS	9 366	67.1	67.0	493	96.1	10.4	-14.0	12.8	5.9	0.0	74.3	12.2
Warren, MS	30 955	49.5	77.0	1 814	85.4	20.8	-3.6	26.8	10.5	14.3	53.0	26.8
Washington, MS	36 852	62.2	66.5	2 144	90.8	16.4	-8.0	23.8	10.7	17.6	46.3	13.4
Wayne, MS	12 933	70.1	64.7	453	91.2	9.5	-14.9	10.9	5.9	0.0	100.0	0.0
Webster, MS	6 717	66.3	67.7	309	76.7	13.0	-11.4	13.8	8.1	0.0	0.0	32.5
Wilkinson, MS	6 515	75.0	58.1	251	89.2	10.0	-14.4	15.9	6.8	0.0	. . .	23.7
Winston, MS	12 896	65.1	68.2	534	88.8	13.8	-10.6	18.4	6.8	0.0	46.2	6.3
Yalobusha, MS	8 539	68.6	69.0	453	87.2	9.6	-14.8	12.4	3.5	23.3	0.0	21.4
Yazoo, MS	17 308	66.0	65.0	618	67.8	11.8	-12.6	16.8	7.4	0.0	31.7	5.3
MISSOURI	3 634 906	51.4	81.3	319 515	71.8	21.6	-2.8	22.3	13.2	12.9	50.1	16.1
Adair, MO	13 316	48.9	84.6	6 226	91.7	28.5	4.1	28.0	32.6	7.7	79.8	11.9
Andrew, MO	10 847	56.8	84.7	597	80.4	10.0	-5.0	10.7	10.4	10.0	61.0	14.0
Atchison, MO	4 500	59.2	80.0	163	83.4	16.6	-7.8	16.8	0.0	0.0	30.8	11.1
Audrain, MO	17 476	67.8	75.1	636	74.8	12.7	-11.7	13.4	2.7	11.3	30.0	5.0
Barry, MO	22 381	65.4	75.7	710	86.2	10.7	-13.7	10.9	13.8	0.0	52.3	4.5
Barton, MO	8 070	65.7	77.3	289	94.5	10.6	-13.8	10.6	12.5	22.7	3.1	10.2
Bates, MO	10 977	68.4	76.9	323	85.8	10.1	-14.3	10.1	0.0	8.3	31.8	0.0
Benton, MO	12 669	66.8	71.8	293	90.4	8.8	-15.6	8.7	0.0	9.5	0.0	6.1
Bollinger, MO	7 956	75.8	70.7	220	87.3	6.9	-17.5	7.0	0.0	4.7	0.0	9.1
Boone, MO	77 919	34.1	89.2	24 827	89.7	41.7	17.3	42.6	22.3	28.7	71.2	38.9
Buchanan, MO	55 583	56.5	81.5	4 905	91.7	16.9	-7.5	17.2	9.6	28.7	35.3	8.9
Butler, MO	27 596	63.8	70.5	1 257	86.2	11.6	-12.8	11.5	3.5	5.1	47.7	32.2
Caldwell, MO	5 890	64.7	81.5	199	91.5	11.7	-12.7	11.8	28.6	18.2	22.2	0.0
Callaway, MO	25 848	58.2	78.9	2 025	38.5	16.5	-7.9	17.1	7.6	1.4	42.0	12.6
Camden, MO	27 303	54.4	82.9	952	72.9	17.7	-6.7	17.8	42.2	8.6	46.7	3.2
Cape Girardeau, MO	43 440	52.2	81.1	6 607	96.1	21.2	-0.2	24.4	17.2	14.6	61.6	14.5
Carroll, MO	6 945	67.3	79.1	173	82.7	14.0	-10.4	14.3	5.6	12.8	0.0	5.6
Carter, MO	3 959	68.7	66.6	186	93.0	10.8	-13.6	10.4	. . .	0.0	0.0	16.7
Cass, MO	52 767	51.0	86.7	2 813	71.8	17.7	-6.7	17.7	22.9	14.6	26.7	17.3
Cedar, MO	9 473	69.8	74.0	376	55.9	10.0	-14.4	9.9	0.0	4.8	23.9	16.7
Chariton, MO	5 900	68.6	79.6	179	84.4	11.4	-13.0	11.6	4.9	0.0	0.0	25.0
Christian, MO	34 790	48.3	85.9	2 318	75.8	20.9	-3.5	21.1	57.4	9.8	22.6	8.1
Clark, MO	4 976	65.7	79.6	284	75.0	10.7	-13.7	10.6	. . .	100.0	100.0	0.0
Clay, MO	120 500	43.3	88.7	9 442	68.2	24.9	0.5	25.2	21.4	15.9	39.2	15.8
Clinton, MO	12 496	56.4	86.1	582	87.1	14.5	-9.9	14.7	9.1	11.0	8.1	14.0
Cole, MO	47 339	46.7	85.3	4 429	86.2	27.4	3.0	28.1	18.2	11.5	65.0	24.5
Cooper, MO	10 545	63.5	80.3	738	69.2	13.7	-10.7	14.5	2.3	0.0	11.1	35.9
Crawford, MO	15 057	69.8	69.4	480	79.2	8.4	-16.0	8.5	0.0	2.0	13.3	0.9
Dade, MO	5 451	66.9	78.5	134	82.8	9.9	-14.5	9.7	0.0	19.4	0.0	32.0
Dallas, MO	10 251	68.7	72.8	446	80.7	9.5	-14.9	9.6	0.0	10.2	21.4	0.0
Daviess, MO	5 213	63.2	79.1	179	86.0	12.0	-12.4	12.0	50.0	0.0	0.0	0.0
DeKalb, MO	8 252	64.2	77.0	280	86.1	10.7	-13.7	11.6	2.5	6.7	67.6	0.0
Dent, MO	10 098	69.5	66.3	402	66.2	10.1	-14.3	10.1	0.0	6.7	0.0	21.6
Douglas, MO	8 774	69.1	69.7	387	74.2	9.9	-14.5	10.0	. . .	4.9	50.0	1.8
Dunklin, MO	21 890	73.7	63.7	817	88.5	9.1	-15.3	9.6	2.1	5.7	49.3	1.0
Franklin, MO	60 467	57.9	77.7	3 167	79.7	12.8	-11.6	12.9	8.0	3.2	19.9	12.2
Gasconade, MO	10 530	66.2	74.0	322	94.4	10.4	-14.0	10.4	20.0	0.0	0.0	17.1
Gentry, MO	4 599	63.8	81.8	129	88.4	14.5	-9.9	14.6	0.0	0.0	66.7	0.0
Greene, MO	153 930	46.1	84.7	25 481	73.2	24.2	-0.2	24.5	14.0	11.3	41.6	17.3
Grundy, MO	7 149	60.4	79.0	450	86.7	12.5	-11.9	12.6	0.0	23.1	21.7	5.0
Harrison, MO	6 101	67.8	80.1	171	80.7	9.3	-15.1	9.2	0.0	0.0	63.6	7.7
Henry, MO	15 050	66.6	77.3	486	88.5	11.7	-12.7	11.6	8.2	11.1	25.6	12.1
Hickory, MO	6 712	68.8	73.4	107	82.2	7.7	-16.7	7.6	0.0	0.0	28.6	22.0
Holt, MO	3 736	67.6	81.9	128	95.3	11.7	-12.7	11.7	. . .	0.0	0.0	0.0
Howard, MO	6 420	61.7	81.3	974	22.1	17.9	-6.5	18.6	7.0	64.0	0.0	3.8
Howell, MO	24 600	65.5	73.4	1 369	87.4	10.9	-13.5	10.9	5.6	4.7	33.8	2.9
Iron, MO	7 204	69.9	65.2	293	91.1	8.4	-16.0	8.2	6.6	2.3	30.0	10.7
Jackson, MO	427 077	46.6	83.4	34 768	73.0	23.4	-1.0	26.9	13.2	15.3	34.9	11.0
Jasper, MO	66 206	55.9	79.5	5 495	79.5	16.5	-7.9	16.7	12.9	11.5	34.2	7.9
Jefferson, MO	125 956	57.0	79.4	7 775	76.4	12.1	-12.3	12.1	8.2	10.1	34.5	14.8

[3]May be of any race.
. . . = Not available.

Table C-1. Population, School, and Student Characteristics by County—*Continued*

STATE County	State/ county code	County type[1]	Population, 2005		Number of schools and students, 2004–2005			Resident enrollment, 2000			
			Total	Percent 5 to 17 years	School districts	Schools	Students	Total	Percent public	K–12	Percent public
			1	2	3	4	5	6	7	8	9
Johnson, MO	29101	4	50 784	16.3	7	27	7 882	17 035	93.8	8 573	95.6
Knox, MO	29103	9	4 171	17.2	1	2	582	900	87.1	780	89.4
Laclede, MO	29105	6	34 492	17.7	4	13	6 135	7 953	92.0	6 408	95.8
Lafayette, MO	29107	1	33 108	17.5	6	18	5 905	8 064	88.5	6 574	91.2
Lawrence, MO	29109	6	37 127	18.8	7	22	8 203	8 171	89.1	6 744	91.3
Lewis, MO	29111	9	10 186	17.5	2	5	1 685	2 870	70.7	1 904	90.9
Lincoln, MO	29113	1	47 727	19.5	5	20	9 642	10 611	84.1	8 749	89.3
Linn, MO	29115	7	13 133	17.4	5	13	2 671	3 150	94.2	2 630	94.9
Livingston, MO	29117	6	14 291	16.3	3	10	2 394	3 413	91.2	2 700	94.4
McDonald, MO	29119	2	22 844	19.6	1	7	3 640	5 135	92.1	4 447	93.3
Macon, MO	29121	7	15 600	16.6	6	14	2 418	3 393	91.5	2 833	93.5
Madison, MO	29123	7	12 151	16.3	2	6	2 153	2 620	95.5	2 177	97.7
Maries, MO	29125	8	8 989	17.6	2	5	1 352	2 034	85.2	1 704	86.8
Marion, MO	29127	5	28 375	17.6	3	13	5 061	6 983	80.2	5 474	89.1
Mercer, MO	29129	9	3 595	15.5	2	4	590	809	93.9	671	93.9
Miller, MO	29131	6	24 712	17.5	5	15	5 034	5 473	91.5	4 555	95.7
Mississippi, MO	29133	7	13 599	16.8	2	8	2 420	3 143	96.1	2 592	97.8
Moniteau, MO	29135	3	15 084	17.5	6	10	2 412	3 474	84.1	2 923	86.9
Monroe, MO	29137	9	9 379	17.5	5	10	1 747	2 126	88.5	1 817	90.6
Montgomery, MO	29139	8	12 166	16.9	2	7	1 868	2 798	89.9	2 364	93.7
Morgan, MO	29141	8	20 436	16.3	2	7	2 258	3 916	86.1	3 290	87.5
New Madrid, MO	29143	7	18 566	17.6	4	13	3 302	4 677	96.6	3 895	96.6
Newton, MO	29145	3	55 554	17.9	7	38	16 310	12 541	87.7	9 905	89.5
Nodaway, MO	29147	6	21 710	11.8	7	17	2 923	8 420	92.5	3 338	91.4
Oregon, MO	29149	9	10 403	16.7	4	8	2 001	2 232	95.1	1 838	96.0
Osage, MO	29151	3	13 485	17.6	3	6	1 755	3 316	76.6	2 661	74.4
Ozark, MO	29153	9	9 490	14.6	5	9	1 723	1 902	92.7	1 584	92.7
Pemiscot, MO	29155	7	19 412	20.7	8	19	4 514	5 262	98.0	4 356	99.1
Perry, MO	29157	7	18 511	17.3	2	6	2 449	4 250	72.9	3 386	72.6
Pettis, MO	29159	4	40 121	18.1	7	18	6 503	9 733	86.6	7 583	89.3
Phelps, MO	29161	5	42 125	15.5	4	14	6 595	12 582	89.6	7 081	90.3
Pike, MO	29163	6	18 762	15.7	4	11	2 946	4 039	87.6	3 415	90.1
Platte, MO	29165	1	82 085	17.3	4	29	13 442	19 324	84.3	14 016	92.3
Polk, MO	29167	2	28 892	17.4	6	18	5 284	7 619	71.3	4 889	94.6
Pulaski, MO	29169	5	44 187	18.4	6	23	8 532	11 608	89.6	8 183	95.4
Putnam, MO	29171	9	5 168	16.8	1	3	835	1 139	94.6	924	96.4
Ralls, MO	29173	9	9 761	16.8	1	4	814	2 197	90.4	1 817	96.6
Randolph, MO	29175	6	25 336	16.4	5	15	3 994	5 935	87.4	4 618	91.6
Ray, MO	29177	1	24 101	18.5	6	20	7 149	5 815	91.5	4 916	96.1
Reynolds, MO	29179	9	6 585	16.5	4	8	1 148	1 519	95.5	1 250	96.2
Ripley, MO	29181	9	13 851	16.9	4	8	2 355	2 972	92.4	2 501	93.1
St. Charles, MO	29183	1	329 940	19.1	5	70	52 660	82 278	76.8	60 232	83.1
St. Clair, MO	29185	8	9 686	15.7	4	7	1 484	1 941	94.8	1 738	97.1
Ste. Genevieve, MO	29186	6	18 198	17.6	1	4	2 083	4 398	76.2	3 636	77.3
St. Francois, MO	29187	4	61 661	15.5	5	26	10 580	13 139	91.6	10 223	93.3
St. Louis, MO	29189	1	1 004 666	17.3	23	252	146 148	281 608	68.5	193 194	75.2
Saline, MO	29195	6	23 075	16.6	8	17	3 699	6 338	78.7	4 267	95.8
Schuyler, MO	29197	9	4 308	16.9	1	3	731	919	95.0	783	97.3
Scotland, MO	29199	9	4 928	19.6	2	3	703	1 129	81.8	976	82.5
Scott, MO	29201	5	41 143	18.6	7	23	7 306	10 018	89.4	8 074	91.0
Shannon, MO	29203	9	8 367	17.8	2	4	903	2 042	95.5	1 680	97.5
Shelby, MO	29205	9	6 744	17.3	2	5	1 138	1 592	89.6	1 324	94.3
Stoddard, MO	29207	7	29 714	16.3	7	18	5 591	6 629	95.4	5 455	96.9
Stone, MO	29209	5	30 931	15.0	5	18	4 405	5 502	93.3	4 560	95.0
Sullivan, MO	29211	8	6 907	17.4	3	6	1 105	1 520	95.4	1 302	98.4
Taney, MO	29213	7	42 985	15.3	7	18	6 582	8 973	80.4	6 354	95.2
Texas, MO	29215	6	24 614	15.9	7	15	4 140	5 405	90.6	4 354	94.1
Vernon, MO	29217	7	20 441	18.5	4	13	3 212	5 081	85.5	4 047	91.6
Warren, MO	29219	1	28 764	17.8	1	4	2 772	5 978	81.2	4 928	84.6
Washington, MO	29221	1	24 032	17.4	4	12	4 085	5 577	92.7	4 737	93.7
Wayne, MO	29223	9	13 097	15.7	2	7	2 076	2 743	94.6	2 401	96.3
Webster, MO	29225	2	34 745	19.3	5	17	6 796	7 879	89.0	6 524	92.1
Worth, MO	29227	9	2 174	17.2	1	2	378	565	98.2	469	99.1
Wright, MO	29229	6	18 306	18.2	5	14	3 540	4 349	92.4	3 515	94.6
St. Louis city, MO	29510	1	344 362	17.6	3	120	45 649	98 331	72.6	67 241	80.7
MONTANA	30000		935 670	16.2	533	856	146 758	241 754	89.8	176 805	92.7
Beaverhead, MT	30001	7	8 773	15.8	10	13	1 284	2 812	92.2	1 587	97.0
Big Horn, MT	30003	6	13 149	22.1	10	15	2 335	4 140	89.0	3 455	89.8
Blaine, MT	30005	9	6 629	20.9	14	17	1 376	2 097	92.9	1 724	93.3
Broadwater, MT	30007	9	4 517	15.5	2	3	710	1 046	90.5	869	93.0
Carbon, MT	30009	3	9 902	15.4	13	22	1 525	2 219	91.4	1 854	95.4
Carter, MT	30011	9	1 320	15.6	9	6	166	335	88.1	306	91.5
Cascade, MT	30013	3	79 569	16.9	16	43	12 493	20 212	86.0	15 730	92.4
Chouteau, MT	30015	8	5 463	19.2	15	16	760	1 675	94.7	1 369	96.4
Custer, MT	30017	7	11 267	16.3	14	17	1 937	2 903	91.5	2 237	93.2
Daniels, MT	30019	9	1 836	13.7	4	9	286	405	97.3	365	100.0

[1]County type codes are from the Economic Research Service of the United States Department of Agriculture. See notes and definitions at the end of this section.

Table C-1. Population, School, and Student Characteristics by County—*Continued*

STATE County	Characteristics of students, 2004–2005				Outcomes		Staff and students, 2004–2005		
	Percent with IEP[2]	Percent eligible for free or reduced-price lunch	Percent minority	Percent English-language learners	Number of graduates, 2003–2004	Percent dropouts, grades 9–12, 2001–2002	Number of teachers	Student-teacher ratio	Central administration staff
	10	11	12	13	14	15	16	17	18
Johnson, MO	. . .	33.7	11.1	1.4	. . .	3.2	587	13.4	73
Knox, MO	. . .	53.6	1.5	0.0	. . .	3.5	51	11.5	9
Laclede, MO	. . .	46.8	3.1	0.2	. . .	3.2	380	16.1	62
Lafayette, MO	. . .	31.7	6.7	1.6	. . .	2.8	445	13.3	68
Lawrence, MO	. . .	49.8	7.0	5.3	. . .	2.8	598	13.7	86
Lewis, MO	. . .	39.1	5.6	0.0	. . .	1.4	130	13.0	21
Lincoln, MO	. . .	33.4	5.8	0.5	. . .	3.9	553	17.4	81
Linn, MO	. . .	38.4	3.1	0.1	. . .	2.1	232	11.5	39
Livingston, MO	. . .	40.7	3.0	0.0	. . .	3.2	182	13.2	25
McDonald, MO	. . .	62.4	18.2	12.3	. . .	5.0	244	14.9	24
Macon, MO	. . .	43.5	5.3	0.0	. . .	3.7	207	11.7	37
Madison, MO	. . .	47.1	1.5	0.7	. . .	2.9	142	15.2	25
Maries, MO	. . .	37.6	1.3	0.0	. . .	3.7	103	13.1	17
Marion, MO	. . .	41.0	8.9	0.2	. . .	3.5	387	13.1	85
Mercer, MO	. . .	44.3	0.9	0.0	. . .	0.5	62	9.6	11
Miller, MO	. . .	45.3	2.4	0.0	. . .	3.3	365	13.8	58
Mississippi, MO	. . .	64.7	30.8	0.0	. . .	3.0	172	14.1	22
Moniteau, MO	. . .	35.4	6.6	3.3	. . .	4.8	189	12.7	25
Monroe, MO	. . .	40.6	7.8	0.3	. . .	2.9	146	12.0	20
Montgomery, MO	. . .	43.3	6.0	0.2	. . .	2.2	144	13.0	26
Morgan, MO	. . .	58.6	2.5	0.2	. . .	4.5	173	13.0	26
New Madrid, MO	. . .	62.1	27.0	0.0	. . .	3.7	251	13.2	45
Newton, MO	. . .	49.0	11.5	1.8	. . .	3.7	1 060	15.4	154
Nodaway, MO	. . .	32.6	2.1	0.1	. . .	1.7	272	10.8	48
Oregon, MO	. . .	59.6	3.2	0.0	. . .	0.6	172	11.6	21
Osage, MO	. . .	30.5	0.7	0.1	. . .	1.8	139	12.7	21
Ozark, MO	. . .	61.0	1.1	0.6	. . .	1.5	151	11.4	31
Pemiscot, MO	. . .	68.2	42.4	0.4	. . .	3.7	365	12.4	64
Perry, MO	. . .	36.7	0.9	0.4	. . .	2.2	179	13.7	33
Pettis, MO	. . .	46.9	14.2	5.2	. . .	5.2	461	14.1	65
Phelps, MO	. . .	42.7	6.8	0.3	. . .	3.7	429	15.4	82
Pike, MO	. . .	40.6	8.9	0.2	. . .	2.0	222	13.3	39
Platte, MO	. . .	18.4	14.5	2.7	. . .	2.5	922	14.6	162
Polk, MO	. . .	51.6	2.6	0.5	. . .	3.2	398	13.3	57
Pulaski, MO	. . .	38.6	26.3	0.6	. . .	2.7	591	14.4	91
Putnam, MO	. . .	43.3	1.7	0.0	. . .	1.5	65	12.8	8
Ralls, MO	. . .	38.0	1.7	0.0	. . .	2.5	63	12.9	8
Randolph, MO	. . .	47.5	7.5	0.1	. . .	5.0	300	13.3	50
Ray, MO	. . .	28.8	3.7	0.1	. . .	1.5	487	14.7	71
Reynolds, MO	. . .	64.5	5.4	0.0	. . .	1.3	109	10.6	21
Ripley, MO	. . .	65.9	0.9	0.0	. . .	4.2	175	13.5	25
St. Charles, MO	. . .	13.3	8.9	0.8	. . .	3.1	3 349	15.7	553
St. Clair, MO	. . .	52.0	2.8	0.3	. . .	5.6	122	12.2	20
Ste. Genevieve, MO	. . .	40.5	1.8	0.0	. . .	2.6	135	15.5	19
St. Francois, MO	. . .	47.6	2.7	0.2	. . .	3.0	704	15.0	119
St. Louis, MO	. . .	28.9	43.5	2.3	. . .	2.8	11 221	13.0	2 293
Saline, MO	. . .	47.2	17.5	4.2	. . .	4.2	306	12.1	45
Schuyler, MO	. . .	52.9	1.4	0.0	. . .	1.4	59	12.5	11
Scotland, MO	. . .	44.6	0.0	0.0	. . .	1.4	60	11.7	10
Scott, MO	. . .	51.5	21.8	0.2	. . .	2.8	512	14.3	97
Shannon, MO	. . .	73.6	1.8	0.3	. . .	0.7	68	13.3	12
Shelby, MO	. . .	40.2	1.1	0.0	. . .	1.1	92	12.3	13
Stoddard, MO	. . .	51.3	3.5	0.0	. . .	9.7	392	14.3	54
Stone, MO	. . .	52.8	3.1	0.2	. . .	3.5	337	13.1	53
Sullivan, MO	. . .	63.4	17.8	18.1	. . .	2.2	101	11.0	16
Taney, MO	. . .	48.9	8.6	2.1	. . .	3.8	454	14.5	78
Texas, MO	. . .	51.4	1.7	0.0	. . .	2.6	316	13.1	44
Vernon, MO	. . .	52.5	2.9	0.2	. . .	3.3	252	12.7	44
Warren, MO	. . .	31.6	6.7	0.5	. . .	3.6	170	16.3	22
Washington, MO	. . .	52.4	1.7	0.1	. . .	3.7	265	15.4	43
Wayne, MO	. . .	62.5	1.5	0.0	. . .	5.0	152	13.6	25
Webster, MO	. . .	41.6	3.1	0.1	. . .	3.2	459	14.8	66
Worth, MO	. . .	47.1	1.3	0.0	. . .	3.2	34	11.2	4
Wright, MO	. . .	60.5	2.3	0.0	. . .	4.1	283	12.5	46
St. Louis city, MO	. . .	83.7	85.0	6.4	. . .	8.2	3 598	12.7	524
MONTANA	13.2	34.3	15.5	4.6	. . .	3.9	10 232	14.3	. . .
Beaverhead, MT	13.3	25.8	5.9	1.9	. . .	3.0	83	15.5	. . .
Big Horn, MT	13.5	72.4	79.9	57.3	. . .	9.6	207	11.3	. . .
Blaine, MT	14.0	64.6	63.4	25.6	. . .	7.0	126	10.9	. . .
Broadwater, MT	12.7	31.7	5.1	0.0	. . .	1.3	52	13.7	. . .
Carbon, MT	14.9	24.5	4.1	0.1	. . .	2.2	138	11.0	. . .
Carter, MT	7.8	35.9	3.6	0.6	. . .	1.5	19	8.8	. . .
Cascade, MT	12.2	33.0	15.4	0.8	. . .	2.8	860	14.5	. . .
Chouteau, MT	10.7	41.0	2.1	2.0	. . .	0.7	77	9.8	. . .
Custer, MT	17.4	. . .	7.0	0.0	. . .	4.4	142	13.6	. . .
Daniels, MT	23.1	30.2	10.5	0.0	. . .	0.7	35	8.2	. . .

[2]IEP = Individual Education Program. See notes and definitions at the end of this section.
. . . = Not available.

Table C-1. Population, School, and Student Characteristics by County—*Continued*

STATE County	Revenue, 2003–2004				Current expenditures, 2003–2004			Resident population, 16 to 19 years, 2000			
	Total revenue (thousands of dollars)	Percent of revenue from:			Total expenditures (thousands of dollars)	Amount per student (dollars)	Percent for instruction	Total	Percent in armed forces	Percent high school graduates	Percent not enrolled, not employed, not in armed forces, not high school graduate
		Federal government	State government	Local government							
	19	20	21	22	23	24	25	26	27	28	29
Johnson, MO	63 141	16.4	41.3	42.4	50 212	6 459	65.1	4 128	4.6	14.2	3.3
Knox, MO	5 149	10.8	34.3	54.9	4 278	7 118	65.5	202	0.0	23.3	0.0
Laclede, MO	40 324	10.4	45.9	43.7	34 282	5 604	67.8	1 948	0.0	13.7	7.0
Lafayette, MO	48 615	6.9	44.1	49.0	41 047	6 867	68.9	1 906	0.0	11.9	3.9
Lawrence, MO	42 348	9.8	48.6	41.5	37 789	6 214	67.6	1 799	0.0	13.6	9.9
Lewis, MO	12 565	8.9	44.6	46.5	10 759	6 670	69.0	702	0.0	7.4	3.7
Lincoln, MO	51 983	7.0	41.9	51.2	42 456	5 340	65.3	2 353	0.0	12.0	5.4
Linn, MO	21 976	8.7	50.3	41.0	19 109	7 080	68.1	776	0.0	8.9	4.3
Livingston, MO	19 786	7.9	43.6	48.5	16 653	7 006	70.3	856	0.0	8.5	5.1
McDonald, MO	23 981	13.7	51.9	34.4	21 684	6 101	70.5	1 275	0.0	13.6	6.3
Macon, MO	19 113	8.3	45.8	45.9	17 226	7 034	66.7	913	0.8	13.9	5.4
Madison, MO	14 691	10.1	50.8	39.1	12 964	5 887	68.5	635	0.0	16.4	4.7
Maries, MO	9 924	8.2	43.2	48.6	8 864	6 287	63.2	470	0.0	12.3	7.4
Marion, MO	36 819	9.6	38.6	51.8	31 748	6 297	68.8	1 823	0.4	11.2	6.1
Mercer, MO	6 176	6.2	38.0	55.8	5 360	8 645	61.5	209	0.0	14.8	1.4
Miller, MO	37 316	9.2	31.9	58.8	33 246	6 643	68.3	1 341	0.0	11.9	8.2
Mississippi, MO	16 252	16.1	44.8	39.0	15 216	6 356	66.0	824	0.0	9.5	13.8
Moniteau, MO	17 552	8.0	39.8	52.2	15 159	6 322	66.1	768	0.0	12.0	3.6
Monroe, MO	14 536	8.5	40.3	51.2	11 649	6 691	65.3	565	0.0	18.2	2.7
Montgomery, MO	13 864	8.5	38.6	52.9	12 282	6 568	64.4	730	0.0	14.1	8.5
Morgan, MO	16 025	11.5	27.8	60.8	13 911	6 009	67.6	898	0.0	9.4	5.3
New Madrid, MO	25 964	12.9	33.8	53.3	24 251	7 327	63.6	1 160	0.0	11.6	8.9
Newton, MO	53 977	10.6	47.2	42.2	47 270	5 407	67.1	3 040	0.1	12.9	8.3
Nodaway, MO	27 605	6.4	35.3	58.3	23 050	7 814	64.3	2 357	0.2	4.0	1.7
Oregon, MO	14 775	12.3	50.6	37.1	13 059	6 530	70.3	574	0.0	13.1	10.6
Osage, MO	12 918	7.0	38.6	54.4	10 955	6 127	62.5	770	0.0	9.1	2.6
Ozark, MO	13 580	14.1	46.1	39.8	11 407	6 434	65.7	505	0.4	18.2	6.7
Pemiscot, MO	36 878	14.4	54.6	30.9	33 643	7 207	68.4	1 248	0.0	11.7	12.8
Perry, MO	17 738	8.1	29.0	62.9	16 167	6 580	60.4	992	0.0	14.6	4.6
Pettis, MO	44 604	10.1	38.5	51.4	36 248	5 573	64.3	2 403	0.0	11.3	8.9
Phelps, MO	58 526	8.9	46.9	44.3	43 174	6 525	68.1	2 892	0.3	9.4	4.2
Pike, MO	23 349	9.1	39.4	51.6	19 714	6 744	66.0	1 082	0.0	9.3	14.1
Platte, MO	129 330	3.5	20.0	76.5	102 264	7 407	65.2	3 765	0.0	12.3	1.1
Polk, MO	37 299	12.3	48.3	39.4	33 166	6 328	64.1	1 976	0.1	10.3	2.0
Pulaski, MO	68 444	31.3	42.6	26.0	56 016	6 555	66.3	3 777	48.4	55.2	1.9
Putnam, MO	6 667	8.6	41.8	49.6	5 976	7 461	69.2	265	0.0	3.0	5.7
Ralls, MO	6 180	7.7	39.4	52.9	5 224	6 060	66.0	524	0.0	13.2	4.4
Randolph, MO	30 956	8.7	38.0	53.4	25 637	6 459	67.4	1 322	0.0	12.2	6.7
Ray, MO	28 175	6.1	45.5	48.4	23 677	6 112	65.0	1 424	0.0	16.3	3.9
Reynolds, MO	10 103	15.6	38.4	46.0	9 081	7 586	62.2	379	0.0	6.1	7.9
Ripley, MO	16 150	13.6	55.6	30.8	14 213	6 185	68.3	718	0.0	18.1	11.0
St. Charles, MO	423 996	3.7	25.4	70.8	358 827	6 980	64.3	15 689	0.0	8.6	3.0
St. Clair, MO	11 679	10.6	46.1	43.2	10 672	6 925	63.4	426	0.0	11.0	7.0
Ste. Genevieve, MO	15 225	6.3	21.1	72.6	12 935	6 078	65.9	1 046	0.0	10.3	4.3
St. Francois, MO	78 101	10.3	47.1	42.7	65 755	6 215	68.9	3 248	0.0	10.3	12.4
St. Louis, MO	1 681 950	5.3	20.4	74.4	1 465 491	9 696	64.7	55 360	0.1	7.7	3.2
Saline, MO	30 029	10.3	44.5	45.2	26 247	7 163	70.3	1 637	0.0	10.8	5.1
Schuyler, MO	5 445	10.5	48.1	41.3	4 580	6 335	61.8	231	0.0	6.1	1.3
Scotland, MO	5 867	10.3	41.2	48.4	5 475	7 777	69.4	269	0.0	12.6	9.7
Scott, MO	51 102	11.0	45.5	43.5	43 945	5 982	66.4	2 275	0.0	10.4	9.5
Shannon, MO	7 219	14.1	51.8	34.1	6 084	6 570	63.8	483	0.0	20.1	14.5
Shelby, MO	9 380	7.9	42.1	50.1	8 497	7 369	67.8	406	0.0	16.5	6.9
Stoddard, MO	37 751	11.1	44.1	44.8	32 537	5 781	67.2	1 820	0.0	11.8	8.0
Stone, MO	35 948	9.6	36.5	53.9	29 087	6 694	64.4	1 443	0.0	15.5	7.6
Sullivan, MO	9 664	10.2	47.0	42.8	8 405	7 141	66.2	317	0.0	16.7	1.9
Taney, MO	52 885	7.7	27.5	64.8	40 505	6 294	64.5	2 329	0.0	13.1	4.6
Texas, MO	29 486	12.2	51.1	36.7	25 779	6 249	68.8	1 358	0.0	12.6	9.6
Vernon, MO	26 432	10.1	44.7	45.2	21 302	6 665	67.1	1 402	0.1	8.2	4.5
Warren, MO	28 079	7.8	32.5	59.7	22 861	5 547	65.5	1 369	0.0	12.3	6.4
Washington, MO	28 352	12.5	52.9	34.6	24 455	6 074	65.1	1 522	0.0	18.7	12.1
Wayne, MO	14 366	14.7	48.1	37.2	13 144	6 238	66.4	727	0.0	10.3	8.1
Webster, MO	32 017	10.0	51.9	38.1	28 030	5 749	69.1	1 745	0.0	11.6	8.9
Worth, MO	3 068	10.6	45.0	44.5	2 899	7 452	68.2	152	0.0	4.6	2.6
Wright, MO	27 511	12.3	52.5	35.3	24 772	6 912	67.5	1 128	0.0	15.4	9.1
St. Louis city, MO	471 530	12.7	39.5	47.8	428 362	10 492	56.9	19 036	0.0	10.4	10.3
MONTANA	1 270 790	15.1	44.1	40.8	1 149 729	7 760	65.1	55 369	0.6	11.0	4.4
Beaverhead, MT	11 170	7.2	45.6	47.2	10 509	7 967	71.7	835	0.0	4.6	1.6
Big Horn, MT	28 174	42.5	33.0	24.6	26 719	11 448	57.2	908	0.0	8.9	12.4
Blaine, MT	19 860	46.6	36.1	17.3	16 031	11 508	61.8	506	0.0	9.9	8.5
Broadwater, MT	5 335	10.2	47.3	42.5	4 427	5 942	70.8	226	0.0	10.6	8.8
Carbon, MT	14 452	7.3	46.7	46.0	12 738	8 150	66.5	520	0.0	8.3	5.2
Carter, MT	2 318	10.0	39.1	50.9	2 183	11 612	64.4	86	0.0	0.0	0.0
Cascade, MT	91 667	12.4	47.6	40.0	85 722	6 768	67.5	4 335	7.0	21.6	3.9
Chouteau, MT	9 319	8.8	39.2	52.0	8 505	10 918	61.2	369	0.0	5.1	7.9
Custer, MT	13 239	12.6	50.5	36.9	12 553	6 785	68.2	756	0.0	11.9	0.7
Daniels, MT	3 980	5.5	46.3	48.2	3 440	11 862	60.1	114	0.0	2.6	0.0

Table C-1. Population, School, and Student Characteristics by County—*Continued*

STATE County	High school graduates, 2000			College enrollment, 2000		College graduates, 2000 (percent)						
	Population 25 years and over	High school graduate or less (percent)	High school graduate or more (percent)	Number	Percent public	Bachelor's degree or more	+/- U.S. percentage with bachelor's degree or more	Non-Hispanic White	Black	American Indian and Alaska Native	Asian or Pacific Islander	Hispanic[3]
	30	31	32	33	34	35	36	37	38	39	40	41
Johnson, MO	26 558	46.5	86.0	7 687	95.2	23.2	-1.2	23.3	18.5	24.2	39.4	13.1
Knox, MO	2 990	66.6	80.0	90	73.3	12.8	-11.6	13.0	...	0.0	0.0	0.0
Laclede, MO	21 120	68.2	72.9	1 016	72.9	11.3	-13.1	11.5	4.9	0.0	7.0	5.3
Lafayette, MO	21 863	62.3	79.9	947	84.5	13.8	-10.6	13.8	12.1	2.3	29.7	26.1
Lawrence, MO	22 882	64.1	77.4	852	87.3	12.1	-12.3	12.2	0.0	10.0	14.3	13.4
Lewis, MO	6 533	65.0	79.5	776	19.7	13.0	-11.4	13.1	3.7	55.6	...	0.0
Lincoln, MO	24 092	66.5	76.4	1 230	64.9	9.7	-14.7	9.5	10.7	7.1	22.2	24.9
Linn, MO	9 279	69.0	80.0	298	87.9	10.8	-13.6	10.8	0.0	30.0	0.0	13.5
Livingston, MO	9 954	65.1	80.6	452	87.4	13.1	-11.3	13.3	8.8	8.0	13.3	35.1
McDonald, MO	13 418	69.1	69.4	382	80.9	7.0	-17.4	7.4	18.2	10.0	3.8	1.9
Macon, MO	10 718	67.0	77.8	339	92.6	13.0	-11.4	13.2	4.3	25.6	0.0	0.0
Madison, MO	7 964	70.4	68.6	261	87.4	7.8	-16.6	7.3	0.0	15.8	69.6	0.0
Maries, MO	5 969	67.7	74.5	212	79.2	11.0	-13.4	10.9	0.0	0.0	0.0	45.5
Marion, MO	18 322	61.4	79.4	1 080	41.5	15.6	-8.8	16.1	7.4	0.0	25.0	5.8
Mercer, MO	2 647	64.0	82.5	83	90.4	12.2	-12.2	12.3	...	0.0	0.0	0.0
Miller, MO	15 369	66.3	73.9	659	75.3	11.4	-13.0	11.6	0.0	0.0	11.9	0.0
Mississippi, MO	8 702	76.6	61.1	311	85.2	9.6	-14.8	9.9	8.0	0.0	18.8	0.0
Moniteau, MO	9 751	66.3	77.6	406	78.6	13.0	-11.4	13.9	3.9	0.0	24.5	0.0
Monroe, MO	6 212	67.9	78.7	170	78.2	9.5	-14.9	9.7	3.5	8.6	0.0	20.0
Montgomery, MO	8 182	70.4	71.1	269	70.6	9.9	-14.5	9.8	0.0	0.0	41.7	0.0
Morgan, MO	13 466	66.1	74.5	385	79.2	10.7	-13.7	10.8	4.5	9.4	57.1	6.6
New Madrid, MO	12 868	76.0	63.6	499	95.4	9.6	-14.8	10.5	2.8	31.8	100.0	0.0
Newton, MO	34 211	54.6	79.8	1 910	82.5	16.1	-8.3	16.4	4.8	17.2	22.3	12.1
Nodaway, MO	12 169	54.1	87.1	4 747	95.8	23.6	-0.8	23.4	12.5	0.0	75.8	0.0
Oregon, MO	7 134	72.3	72.0	240	92.5	9.1	-15.3	9.0	0.0	2.2	43.8	28.6
Osage, MO	8 375	68.9	75.2	531	93.8	10.4	-14.0	10.3	...	6.9	85.7	0.0
Ozark, MO	6 795	70.0	73.0	196	87.8	8.3	-16.1	8.2	0.0	35.0	13.3	17.2
Pemiscot, MO	12 228	75.6	58.2	499	96.8	8.4	-16.0	9.8	2.8	0.0	57.1	0.0
Perry, MO	11 865	73.2	71.2	497	88.1	9.9	-14.5	10.0	0.0	0.0	13.0	0.0
Pettis, MO	25 355	55.5	78.3	1 572	89.6	15.0	-9.4	15.0	12.3	10.8	71.3	4.0
Phelps, MO	24 665	53.9	79.0	4 814	94.5	21.1	-3.3	19.9	15.2	7.3	74.9	22.0
Pike, MO	12 242	68.2	76.0	429	69.5	10.2	-14.2	10.6	5.4	41.4	41.9	2.2
Platte, MO	48 721	34.8	91.8	3 735	71.9	33.3	8.9	33.7	26.9	22.6	45.7	19.6
Polk, MO	16 645	62.2	77.5	2 320	21.8	14.6	-9.8	14.3	40.5	28.9	70.3	27.4
Pulaski, MO	23 062	48.5	85.1	2 825	74.9	18.8	-5.6	18.5	21.2	12.9	26.8	16.0
Putnam, MO	3 649	64.8	80.0	174	89.7	11.2	-13.2	11.2	0.0	0.0	100.0	0.0
Ralls, MO	6 506	67.8	78.7	221	63.8	12.3	-12.1	12.3	4.9	0.0	53.3	34.8
Randolph, MO	16 452	61.2	77.1	944	78.6	11.7	-12.7	12.3	3.5	10.8	47.7	16.2
Ray, MO	15 165	66.6	79.3	554	67.9	10.8	-13.6	11.0	0.0	0.0	23.8	3.7
Reynolds, MO	4 639	74.5	65.2	175	89.7	7.5	-16.9	7.7	0.0	0.0	55.6	0.0
Ripley, MO	9 092	71.0	62.1	272	91.5	7.8	-16.6	7.8	0.0	4.3	36.2	0.0
St. Charles, MO	178 498	40.5	89.1	15 745	65.4	26.3	1.9	26.3	22.7	16.4	51.9	26.7
St. Clair, MO	6 876	72.6	73.1	140	82.1	9.0	-15.4	8.9	0.0	3.3	70.8	11.4
Ste. Genevieve, MO	11 743	69.0	73.8	496	83.3	8.1	-16.3	8.0	25.5	0.0	100.0	11.4
St. Francois, MO	37 236	62.3	72.4	1 941	89.1	10.2	-14.2	10.2	4.3	23.6	24.8	19.6
St. Louis, MO	677 027	36.0	88.0	64 556	58.5	35.4	11.0	38.4	17.4	16.4	65.7	32.7
Saline, MO	15 185	64.2	74.0	1 643	36.3	15.8	-8.6	16.0	12.3	6.0	38.2	11.6
Schuyler, MO	2 870	65.2	81.4	76	94.7	11.6	-12.8	11.7	...	0.0	0.0	0.0
Scotland, MO	3 172	67.8	76.8	79	75.9	11.2	-13.2	11.3	...	0.0	0.0	6.7
Scott, MO	25 749	69.8	72.9	1 166	90.1	10.6	-13.8	11.3	2.6	14.3	28.6	2.9
Shannon, MO	5 552	75.6	67.6	220	77.7	7.6	-16.8	7.5	0.0	11.5	0.0	3.4
Shelby, MO	4 589	66.4	81.0	185	69.7	12.5	-11.9	12.6	0.0	0.0	0.0	27.8
Stoddard, MO	20 121	72.0	66.9	811	89.9	10.1	-14.3	10.0	0.6	8.3	48.2	18.4
Stone, MO	20 799	58.5	80.4	517	85.9	14.2	-10.2	14.1	0.0	14.6	0.0	37.0
Sullivan, MO	4 870	72.4	72.4	107	80.4	8.4	-16.0	8.8	0.0	0.0	0.0	3.2
Taney, MO	26 814	56.4	81.4	2 123	37.9	14.9	-9.5	15.1	19.3	8.1	11.0	16.8
Texas, MO	15 641	68.3	71.4	712	77.0	10.8	-13.6	10.8	22.2	4.3	23.1	9.6
Vernon, MO	13 169	63.3	76.6	704	59.9	14.2	-10.2	14.1	7.1	18.2	33.3	0.0
Warren, MO	16 137	60.8	79.5	664	70.9	11.1	-13.3	11.3	5.5	0.0	0.0	19.2
Washington, MO	14 796	72.9	62.5	634	92.7	7.5	-16.9	7.6	0.0	15.2	47.6	4.1
Wayne, MO	9 301	74.6	59.7	222	77.9	6.8	-17.6	6.7	0.0	3.1	53.8	28.6
Webster, MO	19 515	65.0	74.8	825	85.5	11.0	-13.4	11.2	1.5	9.3	43.1	2.1
Worth, MO	1 644	65.5	80.2	42	90.5	11.3	-13.1	11.3	...	18.2	...	0.0
Wright, MO	11 638	69.6	71.1	549	81.6	9.8	-14.6	10.0	14.8	15.5	0.0	3.0
St. Louis city, MO	221 951	56.2	71.3	24 410	51.8	19.1	-5.3	28.2	8.8	11.3	33.0	16.6
MONTANA	586 621	44.1	87.2	51 255	88.0	24.4	0.0	25.2	33.2	10.5	38.9	15.4
Beaverhead, MT	5 825	39.8	89.3	1 117	89.3	26.4	2.0	27.0	0.0	3.4	...	5.2
Big Horn, MT	7 051	53.8	76.4	420	84.0	14.3	-10.1	20.3	...	9.3	36.7	0.0
Blaine, MT	4 144	49.3	78.7	213	89.2	17.4	-7.0	22.1	0.0	9.6	0.0	10.3
Broadwater, MT	3 061	54.5	85.2	112	85.7	15.0	-9.4	15.3	0.0	0.0	100.0	0.0
Carbon, MT	6 701	48.0	88.1	215	87.9	23.3	-1.1	23.4	66.7	21.4	14.3	15.6
Carter, MT	946	52.5	83.3	15	53.3	13.6	-10.8	13.9	0.0	0.0	0.0	...
Cascade, MT	52 333	46.2	87.1	3 154	69.8	21.5	-2.9	22.1	27.2	7.2	25.4	17.1
Chouteau, MT	3 837	43.3	87.1	174	87.9	20.5	-3.9	21.6	0.0	9.7	55.6	23.5
Custer, MT	7 819	44.9	84.9	514	93.8	18.8	-5.6	19.2	...	3.5	37.0	1.1
Daniels, MT	1 467	51.0	85.3	30	70.0	14.1	-10.3	14.3	...	0.0	33.3	0.0

[3]May be of any race.
... = Not available.

Table C-1. Population, School, and Student Characteristics by County—*Continued*

STATE County	State/ county code	County type[1]	Population, 2005		Number of schools and students, 2004–2005			Resident enrollment, 2000			
			Total	Percent 5 to 17 years	School districts	Schools	Students	Total	Percent public	K–12	Percent public
			1	2	3	4	5	6	7	8	9
Dawson, MT	30021	7	8 688	14.5	9	10	1 339	2 206	93.6	1 678	93.9
Deer Lodge, MT	30023	7	8 948	14.5	3	5	1 325	2 218	94.6	1 811	97.0
Fallon, MT	30025	9	2 717	15.2	3	7	469	653	97.2	608	99.3
Fergus, MT	30027	7	11 551	15.3	16	24	1 881	2 689	95.0	2 340	97.9
Flathead, MT	30029	5	83 172	16.3	25	50	13 361	17 987	88.4	14 879	91.0
Gallatin, MT	30031	5	78 210	13.9	23	42	10 123	22 806	90.9	10 879	89.6
Garfield, MT	30033	9	1 199	15.8	11	10	211	277	93.5	250	94.0
Glacier, MT	30035	7	13 552	21.0	7	15	2 803	4 330	95.6	3 548	96.8
Golden Valley, MT	30037	8	1 159	14.8	3	6	195	242	90.5	227	90.7
Granite, MT	30039	8	2 965	14.9	5	7	452	622	90.8	556	91.4
Hill, MT	30041	7	16 304	17.8	15	20	3 036	5 291	92.0	3 528	93.1
Jefferson, MT	30043	9	11 170	17.4	9	12	1 721	2 611	91.6	2 312	94.4
Judith Basin, MT	30045	8	2 198	17.2	6	11	382	556	91.2	487	94.9
Lake, MT	30047	6	28 297	17.6	13	21	4 371	7 008	92.6	5 485	95.6
Lewis and Clark, MT	30049	5	58 449	16.1	12	28	9 409	14 412	84.3	10 836	95.1
Liberty, MT	30051	9	2 003	14.2	8	10	341	512	93.8	456	93.9
Lincoln, MT	30053	7	19 193	15.9	11	14	2 926	4 528	92.7	3 918	93.6
McCone, MT	30055	9	1 805	16.3	5	5	267	435	96.6	397	99.5
Madison, MT	30057	9	7 274	14.2	7	13	944	1 480	95.4	1 251	97.4
Meagher, MT	30059	9	1 999	15.9	5	5	288	428	94.2	384	96.6
Mineral, MT	30061	8	4 014	15.0	4	9	771	888	92.3	784	94.6
Missoula, MT	30063	3	100 086	14.4	16	40	13 348	30 019	91.5	16 769	92.2
Musselshell, MT	30065	8	4 497	14.1	5	6	623	1 008	92.9	847	94.1
Park, MT	30067	7	15 968	15.1	12	16	2 179	3 349	86.3	2 678	89.2
Petroleum, MT	30069	9	470	17.4	2	3	95	113	100.0	97	100.0
Phillips, MT	30071	9	4 179	16.8	8	16	834	1 174	94.4	1 043	97.4
Pondera, MT	30073	7	6 087	18.0	11	16	1 112	1 825	91.3	1 534	95.3
Powder River, MT	30075	9	1 705	17.7	6	5	370	437	93.1	388	97.7
Powell, MT	30077	7	6 999	14.0	10	9	977	1 483	86.7	1 245	92.1
Prairie, MT	30079	9	1 105	11.1	2	3	164	215	97.2	187	97.3
Ravalli, MT	30081	6	39 940	16.4	10	23	6 112	8 361	85.9	7 168	87.3
Richland, MT	30083	7	9 096	17.4	13	16	1 802	2 399	95.7	2 129	98.1
Roosevelt, MT	30085	7	10 524	22.1	14	22	2 518	3 651	95.2	2 891	97.3
Rosebud, MT	30087	9	9 212	20.6	11	15	1 779	2 924	89.7	2 426	91.1
Sanders, MT	30089	8	11 057	14.4	14	18	1 810	2 280	90.3	1 967	93.3
Sheridan, MT	30091	9	3 524	13.9	6	12	569	852	92.3	750	96.8
Silver Bow, MT	30093	5	32 982	15.6	6	12	4 873	9 439	86.7	6 390	87.0
Stillwater, MT	30095	8	8 493	15.9	15	18	1 448	1 888	93.5	1 657	96.0
Sweet Grass, MT	30097	9	3 672	17.4	6	6	618	808	91.5	713	96.2
Teton, MT	30099	8	6 240	17.2	12	17	1 274	1 586	90.0	1 398	92.9
Toole, MT	30101	7	5 031	16.3	5	10	898	1 297	90.0	1 135	94.5
Treasure, MT	30103	8	689	17.3	2	3	131	212	97.6	199	97.5
Valley, MT	30105	7	7 143	16.0	9	17	1 238	1 808	93.9	1 596	95.2
Wheatland, MT	30107	9	2 037	18.6	7	7	432	478	93.3	393	98.0
Wibaux, MT	30109	9	951	15.6	2	3	168	249	98.8	228	99.1
Yellowstone, MT	30111	3	136 691	16.6	22	58	21 899	33 876	88.4	24 867	92.4
NEBRASKA	31000		1 758 787	17.5	567	1 256	285 769	480 705	82.8	338 004	86.5
Adams, NE	31001	5	33 070	16.5	12	28	4 816	8 746	73.1	5 519	83.7
Antelope, NE	31003	9	7 004	18.1	8	15	1 209	1 892	88.2	1 636	88.8
Arthur, NE	31005	9	378	13.5	2	3	84	116	97.4	105	100.0
Banner, NE	31007	9	733	19.1	1	2	159	205	95.6	187	97.9
Blaine, NE	31009	9	484	15.3	1	2	135	136	99.3	125	100.0
Boone, NE	31011	9	5 772	19.4	5	9	1 040	1 676	88.2	1 459	90.1
Box Butte, NE	31013	7	11 374	18.5	6	11	2 168	3 384	92.1	2 779	96.9
Boyd, NE	31015	9	2 261	15.7	5	6	411	568	97.9	509	99.2
Brown, NE	31017	9	3 328	16.1	7	7	572	810	92.2	699	97.7
Buffalo, NE	31019	5	43 572	16.2	18	35	7 183	14 318	91.4	7 775	91.8
Burt, NE	31021	8	7 455	17.2	4	10	1 419	1 891	95.9	1 632	96.7
Butler, NE	31023	6	8 720	18.1	7	11	1 228	2 263	71.3	1 942	70.7
Cass, NE	31025	2	25 734	18.7	7	17	3 865	6 664	87.6	5 203	91.4
Cedar, NE	31027	9	9 066	19.7	5	11	1 421	2 646	73.7	2 293	73.9
Chase, NE	31029	9	3 866	15.8	5	7	847	969	94.2	822	97.1
Cherry, NE	31031	7	6 098	18.0	24	26	1 039	1 524	90.4	1 291	94.7
Cheyenne, NE	31033	7	9 993	16.9	7	12	1 699	2 414	95.7	2 060	98.6
Clay, NE	31035	9	6 733	17.2	5	13	2 046	1 891	92.2	1 568	93.4
Colfax, NE	31037	7	10 433	18.3	9	13	2 148	2 799	90.9	2 336	91.6
Cuming, NE	31039	7	9 688	17.9	5	10	1 581	2 552	66.3	2 182	65.7
Custer, NE	31041	7	11 410	18.2	13	22	1 986	2 835	92.8	2 520	95.1
Dakota, NE	31043	3	20 349	20.9	4	14	3 908	5 524	88.5	4 479	90.5
Dawes, NE	31045	7	8 636	13.7	14	18	1 468	3 367	96.2	1 535	95.5
Dawson, NE	31047	7	24 617	20.1	16	28	5 142	6 269	96.0	5 288	98.1
Deuel, NE	31049	9	2 004	14.3	3	5	437	466	92.5	421	94.3
Dixon, NE	31051	3	6 155	18.1	5	8	1 137	1 670	94.2	1 411	96.5
Dodge, NE	31053	4	36 078	16.4	7	24	6 083	9 093	80.1	6 752	89.5
Douglas, NE	31055	2	486 929	17.9	14	75	34 400	132 512	75.8	89 728	80.2
Dundy, NE	31057	9	2 133	15.0	1	3	322	530	94.7	421	99.3
Fillmore, NE	31059	9	6 385	17.8	5	11	1 123	1 609	92.3	1 361	94.4

[1]County type codes are from the Economic Research Service of the United States Department of Agriculture. See notes and definitions at the end of this section.

Table C-1. Population, School, and Student Characteristics by County—*Continued*

STATE County	Characteristics of students, 2004–2005				Outcomes		Staff and students, 2004–2005		
	Percent with IEP[2]	Percent eligible for free or reduced-price lunch	Percent minority	Percent English-language learners	Number of graduates, 2003–2004	Percent dropouts, grades 9–12, 2001–2002	Number of teachers	Student-teacher ratio	Central administration staff
	10	11	12	13	14	15	16	17	18
Dawson, MT	16.1	30.8	4.0	0.1	. . .	2.6	103	13.0	. . .
Deer Lodge, MT	16.2	49.3	8.8	0.2	. . .	4.5	85	15.6	. . .
Fallon, MT	7.5	23.0	2.6	0.0	. . .	. . .	52	9.0	. . .
Fergus, MT	14.9	35.2	4.1	0.3	. . .	2.7	152	12.4	. . .
Flathead, MT	10.1	30.2	5.5	0.5	. . .	4.6	801	16.7	. . .
Gallatin, MT	9.2	19.3	6.0	1.2	. . .	2.7	622	16.3	. . .
Garfield, MT	9.5	38.0	3.8	0.0	. . .	1.5	23	9.1	. . .
Glacier, MT	15.1	53.6	78.1	43.5	. . .	6.5	224	12.5	. . .
Golden Valley, MT	18.5	52.8	0.5	15.4	. . .	. . .	23	8.5	. . .
Granite, MT	18.6	38.7	2.2	0.2	. . .	4.7	40	11.4	. . .
Hill, MT	14.3	47.6	42.3	11.3	. . .	6.0	217	14.0	. . .
Jefferson, MT	12.3	25.4	7.0	0.1	. . .	1.7	121	14.2	. . .
Judith Basin, MT	11.8	44.0	2.1	7.1	. . .	. . .	46	8.3	. . .
Lake, MT	12.7	51.4	46.2	14.0	. . .	7.1	307	14.2	. . .
Lewis and Clark, MT	12.5	24.4	9.4	0.2	. . .	4.6	570	16.5	. . .
Liberty, MT	14.4	29.3	1.9	0.0	. . .	. . .	38	9.0	. . .
Lincoln, MT	12.3	47.0	6.1	0.0	. . .	2.8	193	15.2	. . .
McCone, MT	15.7	24.9	7.5	0.0	. . .	2.4	24	11.4	. . .
Madison, MT	9.9	31.6	2.4	1.2	. . .	0.5	83	11.4	. . .
Meagher, MT	18.1	52.3	1.4	11.8	. . .	9.0	26	11.2	. . .
Mineral, MT	17.1	54.9	5.8	0.5	. . .	1.1	63	12.2	. . .
Missoula, MT	15.2	30.4	8.5	4.2	. . .	3.2	814	16.4	. . .
Musselshell, MT	18.3	40.3	5.9	0.2	. . .	4.8	52	12.1	. . .
Park, MT	12.7	29.6	4.2	0.0	. . .	3.6	160	13.6	. . .
Petroleum, MT	10.5	71.6	3.2	0.0	. . .	. . .	12	8.3	. . .
Phillips, MT	16.3	51.8	21.1	3.0	. . .	. . .	86	9.7	. . .
Pondera, MT	13.7	43.5	24.2	10.4	. . .	6.6	93	12.0	. . .
Powder River, MT	8.6	24.7	4.1	0.0	. . .	. . .	30	12.5	. . .
Powell, MT	20.8	38.5	3.5	0.9	. . .	8.3	75	13.1	. . .
Prairie, MT	13.4	44.5	7.3	0.0	. . .	4.5	17	9.5	. . .
Ravalli, MT	12.8	34.9	4.5	0.0	. . .	3.4	396	15.4	. . .
Richland, MT	14.1	30.7	6.9	0.4	. . .	1.7	136	13.2	. . .
Roosevelt, MT	15.8	62.9	76.1	32.6	. . .	5.6	251	10.0	. . .
Rosebud, MT	18.5	51.2	47.2	24.2	. . .	6.7	161	11.1	. . .
Sanders, MT	9.8	49.3	13.4	0.9	. . .	3.1	131	13.8	. . .
Sheridan, MT	17.4	36.5	13.4	0.4	. . .	1.2	63	9.1	. . .
Silver Bow, MT	12.9	32.7	8.7	0.1	. . .	8.5	293	16.6	. . .
Stillwater, MT	10.7	16.7	4.6	0.6	. . .	0.8	119	12.1	. . .
Sweet Grass, MT	9.9	23.3	1.9	0.3	. . .	2.6	45	13.9	. . .
Teton, MT	11.1	31.9	6.8	3.1	. . .	0.7	105	12.1	. . .
Toole, MT	15.1	31.2	8.1	2.8	. . .	8.2	67	13.3	. . .
Treasure, MT	9.2	37.4	10.7	0.0	. . .	. . .	15	8.9	. . .
Valley, MT	15.7	42.5	18.8	0.6	. . .	2.4	120	10.3	. . .
Wheatland, MT	15.0	60.6	4.2	21.5	. . .	1.4	43	10.1	. . .
Wibaux, MT	13.1	45.8	3.6	0.0	. . .	. . .	18	9.2	. . .
Yellowstone, MT	14.7	29.1	14.0	1.0	. . .	3.5	1 382	15.9	. . .
NEBRASKA	16.5	34.8	21.5	5.6	. . .	4.2	20 956	13.6	. . .
Adams, NE	19.5	36.2	15.3	5.7	. . .	4.3	367	13.1	55
Antelope, NE	15.2	46.5	2.1	1.2	. . .	1.6	122	10.0	22
Arthur, NE	17.9	0.0	0.0	0.0	. . .	. . .	12	7.2	2
Banner, NE	6.9	35.8	6.3	1.3	15	. . .	18	8.7	3
Blaine, NE	17.8	53.3	0.0	0.0	14	1.9	19	7.0	3
Boone, NE	15.7	40.0	2.1	0.0	. . .	1.1	90	11.6	13
Box Butte, NE	16.8	33.3	22.7	3.0	. . .	1.3	175	12.4	25
Boyd, NE	19.0	48.9	2.4	0.0	. . .	0.8	49	8.3	. . .
Brown, NE	15.6	33.9	2.6	0.0	. . .	1.3	55	10.4	. . .
Buffalo, NE	15.4	32.3	13.3	3.1	. . .	1.4	527	13.6	71
Burt, NE	17.8	30.7	6.6	0.0	. . .	2.1	117	12.1	15
Butler, NE	16.6	33.4	5.0	1.1	. . .	2.1	101	12.2	. . .
Cass, NE	19.0	25.6	5.2	0.5	. . .	2.9	288	13.4	41
Cedar, NE	16.0	34.7	1.9	0.0	140	0.4	127	11.2	20
Chase, NE	12.5	31.1	11.3	4.5	. . .	1.8	76	11.1	. . .
Cherry, NE	12.4	41.5	11.5	1.4	. . .	2.8	103	10.1	8
Cheyenne, NE	15.4	36.3	9.5	0.0	. . .	3.5	138	12.3	. . .
Clay, NE	25.2	38.1	9.7	3.3	. . .	0.6	173	11.8	21
Colfax, NE	11.8	53.9	42.5	17.7	. . .	4.2	169	12.7	20
Cuming, NE	17.4	43.2	19.6	12.5	. . .	1.7	121	13.1	13
Custer, NE	15.6	38.5	3.8	0.1	. . .	1.3	177	11.2	22
Dakota, NE	16.2	41.9	52.7	20.7	. . .	4.8	294	13.3	39
Dawes, NE	16.8	34.1	18.5	0.3	. . .	15.3	115	12.8	21
Dawson, NE	16.3	58.5	46.1	13.7	. . .	3.9	369	13.9	. . .
Deuel, NE	14.6	46.5	7.6	0.0	. . .	2.9	42	10.5	. . .
Dixon, NE	15.0	29.0	4.1	0.7	. . .	0.4	94	12.1	. . .
Dodge, NE	19.1	36.2	13.1	4.8	. . .	4.1	410	14.8	51
Douglas, NE	14.7	36.5	34.8	1.5	2 405	6.7	2 290	15.0	263
Dundy, NE	17.1	37.9	8.1	3.1	27	. . .	30	10.7	4
Fillmore, NE	23.0	28.4	7.3	0.0	. . .	1.7	95	11.9	16

[2]IEP = Individual Education Program. See notes and definitions at the end of this section.
. . . = Not available.

Table C-1. Population, School, and Student Characteristics by County—*Continued*

STATE County	Revenue, 2003–2004				Current expenditures, 2003–2004			Resident population, 16 to 19 years, 2000			
	Total revenue (thousands of dollars)	Percent of revenue from:			Total expenditures (thousands of dollars)	Amount per student (dollars)	Percent for instruction	Total	Percent in armed forces	Percent high school graduates	Percent not enrolled, not employed, not in armed forces, not high school graduate
		Federal government	State government	Local government							
	19	20	21	22	23	24	25	26	27	28	29
Dawson, MT	12 937	11.5	45.1	43.4	11 807	8 568	61.8	605	0.0	9.6	0.2
Deer Lodge, MT	10 132	13.8	53.5	32.7	10 009	7 149	61.9	591	0.0	17.4	5.9
Fallon, MT	8 030	3.3	81.4	15.4	5 943	11 792	63.5	166	0.0	4.8	0.0
Fergus, MT	18 230	10.7	47.4	42.0	17 171	8 659	61.0	680	0.0	9.6	4.3
Flathead, MT	97 833	8.8	45.1	46.2	88 276	6 675	67.4	4 238	0.0	10.1	4.8
Gallatin, MT	74 794	7.6	41.8	50.6	67 109	6 805	65.4	5 008	0.0	8.2	1.5
Garfield, MT	2 188	10.6	44.9	44.5	2 003	9 771	61.9	81	0.0	13.6	3.7
Glacier, MT	35 497	43.1	33.4	23.5	30 206	10 550	60.3	913	0.0	11.1	9.2
Golden Valley, MT	2 494	5.9	42.0	52.0	1 950	11 538	62.8	50	0.0	4.0	6.0
Granite, MT	4 335	7.5	41.5	51.1	3 972	8 258	63.6	129	0.0	11.6	9.3
Hill, MT	33 726	34.6	39.2	26.1	30 027	9 587	56.7	1 207	0.0	8.8	5.0
Jefferson, MT	13 063	6.9	50.1	43.1	11 824	6 866	66.5	658	0.0	9.7	4.1
Judith Basin, MT	4 772	6.8	39.9	53.3	4 161	10 300	65.5	140	0.0	8.6	9.3
Lake, MT	39 923	29.9	41.0	29.1	34 733	7 921	69.7	1 805	0.0	9.4	14.0
Lewis and Clark, MT	72 870	11.2	45.9	42.9	67 241	7 059	66.9	3 520	0.4	11.3	1.2
Liberty, MT	4 506	11.9	42.8	45.3	4 164	11 631	62.8	149	0.0	2.7	14.8
Lincoln, MT	25 995	13.9	47.8	38.3	22 428	7 446	67.6	1 144	0.0	11.8	3.5
McCone, MT	2 634	7.7	42.6	49.7	2 398	8 414	60.3	114	0.0	5.3	7.9
Madison, MT	11 166	5.2	36.2	58.5	8 986	9 580	63.2	355	0.0	9.0	3.1
Meagher, MT	2 705	8.3	41.4	50.3	2 545	8 899	62.8	123	0.0	10.6	13.0
Mineral, MT	7 528	15.6	44.1	40.3	6 756	8 831	67.5	221	0.0	9.5	5.0
Missoula, MT	110 030	9.7	41.7	48.6	98 791	7 293	65.3	6 412	0.1	10.4	2.2
Musselshell, MT	5 986	10.0	48.9	41.1	5 608	8 433	64.1	274	0.0	6.6	4.4
Park, MT	19 664	14.7	41.1	44.2	17 758	8 191	65.3	742	0.0	20.1	4.0
Petroleum, MT	1 199	10.8	44.5	44.8	1 090	10 583	58.1	22	0.0	0.0	0.0
Phillips, MT	10 561	10.3	53.3	36.4	9 354	10 678	65.1	291	0.0	10.3	1.0
Pondera, MT	13 879	26.1	39.8	34.2	11 972	10 285	60.8	409	0.0	5.9	7.8
Powder River, MT	3 185	8.4	56.1	35.5	3 106	8 239	60.0	101	0.0	15.8	0.0
Powell, MT	10 148	18.9	40.6	40.5	8 732	8 723	67.0	336	1.5	5.1	12.5
Prairie, MT	2 100	21.2	36.6	42.2	1 958	11 253	60.9	47	0.0	0.0	4.3
Ravalli, MT	45 620	12.9	50.6	36.5	40 520	6 510	64.8	2 087	0.1	12.2	8.2
Richland, MT	16 148	7.4	57.5	35.1	14 900	8 223	66.3	587	0.0	11.2	2.7
Roosevelt, MT	34 105	39.7	34.2	26.1	31 937	12 519	62.7	766	0.4	7.3	12.4
Rosebud, MT	26 601	24.1	36.1	39.8	23 592	12 243	60.9	661	0.0	7.9	9.4
Sanders, MT	15 981	15.5	44.7	39.8	14 741	8 226	62.6	628	0.0	7.6	4.6
Sheridan, MT	7 935	8.3	52.1	39.6	7 136	12 497	61.6	212	0.0	6.1	0.0
Silver Bow, MT	36 357	11.7	47.3	41.0	34 271	6 839	60.9	1 981	0.0	9.7	4.0
Stillwater, MT	14 054	8.3	39.7	52.0	11 951	7 925	64.9	423	0.0	8.5	0.5
Sweet Grass, MT	5 203	7.6	39.7	52.6	4 689	7 674	70.6	175	0.0	8.0	1.1
Teton, MT	11 995	11.3	45.4	43.3	10 699	8 464	68.4	368	0.5	13.9	5.2
Toole, MT	9 294	10.9	42.8	46.3	7 423	8 454	68.9	348	0.0	7.5	8.3
Treasure, MT	1 484	7.2	41.1	51.7	1 469	10 418	60.3	53	0.0	11.3	1.9
Valley, MT	13 081	17.1	38.6	44.3	12 220	9 652	64.0	460	0.0	7.4	4.3
Wheatland, MT	4 138	10.8	44.4	44.9	3 927	8 650	70.0	124	0.0	9.7	4.8
Wibaux, MT	2 053	6.7	57.4	35.8	1 857	11 606	66.7	64	0.0	3.1	3.1
Yellowstone, MT	165 117	10.0	46.6	43.5	153 492	7 004	67.2	7 246	0.1	12.2	3.4
NEBRASKA	2 734 724	8.8	32.0	59.2	2 289 490	8 057	67.8	107 180	0.3	9.0	3.4
Adams, NE	51 143	9.6	32.7	57.6	43 286	9 257	72.4	2 035	0.6	5.7	1.7
Antelope, NE	17 965	7.6	26.9	65.5	15 030	12 846	70.0	496	0.0	9.3	0.2
Arthur, NE	1 385	4.5	26.6	68.9	1 151	14 388	67.9	26	0.0	0.0	0.0
Banner, NE	2 233	5.2	32.9	62.0	2 000	11 561	62.6	51	0.0	11.8	3.9
Blaine, NE	1 838	11.3	9.6	79.1	1 668	10 974	64.8	38	0.0	15.8	0.0
Boone, NE	10 808	4.9	21.5	73.6	9 142	8 560	71.3	362	0.0	7.2	0.8
Box Butte, NE	19 056	10.2	45.0	44.9	17 108	7 734	70.2	824	0.0	13.2	1.9
Boyd, NE	7 939	12.8	45.1	42.1	6 992	11 692	68.6	166	0.0	3.0	3.0
Brown, NE	8 539	5.7	29.9	64.3	7 050	12 093	67.8	179	0.0	7.8	0.0
Buffalo, NE	68 656	9.6	32.4	58.1	58 018	8 303	69.6	3 642	0.0	6.7	2.5
Burt, NE	12 312	6.2	27.0	66.8	11 501	7 883	68.5	443	0.0	4.7	2.3
Butler, NE	11 198	6.5	13.3	80.2	9 740	7 767	65.8	499	0.0	5.4	1.6
Cass, NE	35 199	9.5	29.6	61.0	28 719	7 618	65.1	1 461	0.0	9.7	3.7
Cedar, NE	14 667	7.7	25.8	66.4	12 647	8 534	70.3	615	0.0	7.3	0.7
Chase, NE	9 432	5.9	17.6	76.5	8 057	9 293	67.4	241	0.0	3.7	5.0
Cherry, NE	12 378	7.2	27.7	65.1	10 058	9 746	72.0	326	0.0	8.9	3.1
Cheyenne, NE	19 107	10.6	32.8	56.6	16 768	9 223	67.5	608	0.0	15.8	0.3
Clay, NE	9 202	11.4	25.7	63.0	7 548	8 187	67.9	468	0.0	6.2	1.9
Colfax, NE	18 829	5.7	34.3	60.0	15 473	7 078	68.7	720	0.0	9.7	9.3
Cuming, NE	14 964	8.4	20.1	71.6	12 458	7 748	66.6	598	0.0	8.0	3.7
Custer, NE	21 580	6.9	30.9	62.2	18 105	8 879	68.6	599	0.5	4.8	0.7
Dakota, NE	33 730	10.0	52.1	37.9	27 364	6 970	68.3	1 218	0.0	11.2	5.5
Dawes, NE	12 327	12.6	46.9	40.5	9 573	7 461	65.9	1 088	1.6	7.4	4.6
Dawson, NE	45 600	10.5	43.0	46.5	35 852	6 782	67.7	1 522	0.0	6.2	8.3
Deuel, NE	4 440	6.3	14.1	79.6	4 074	10 314	66.5	132	0.0	8.3	2.3
Dixon, NE	7 137	6.3	36.4	57.3	6 207	7 927	70.8	368	0.0	6.5	4.1
Dodge, NE	54 615	8.1	31.2	60.7	48 418	7 844	68.2	2 296	0.0	8.4	3.3
Douglas, NE	738 109	8.9	32.5	58.6	610 298	7 668	64.2	26 622	0.0	9.2	5.4
Dundy, NE	3 616	5.4	20.9	73.6	3 458	10 384	63.9	118	0.0	5.1	2.5
Fillmore, NE	11 456	4.9	14.5	80.5	10 110	9 413	66.0	399	0.0	10.0	2.8

Table C-1. Population, School, and Student Characteristics by County—*Continued*

STATE County	High school graduates, 2000			College enrollment, 2000		College graduates, 2000 (percent)						
	Population 25 years and over	High school graduate or less (percent)	High school graduate or more (percent)	Number	Percent public	Bachelor's degree or more	+/- U.S. percentage with bachelor's degree or more	Non-Hispanic White	Black	American Indian and Alaska Native	Asian or Pacific Islander	Hispanic[3]
	30	31	32	33	34	35	36	37	38	39	40	41
Dawson, MT	6 161	47.8	82.7	445	94.4	15.1	-9.3	15.2	0.0	0.0	0.0	25.7
Deer Lodge, MT	6 584	58.4	84.5	330	82.1	14.7	-9.7	14.9	...	5.5	44.0	0.0
Fallon, MT	1 935	57.7	85.7	16	75.0	14.4	-10.0	14.3	50.0	0.0	100.0	20.0
Fergus, MT	8 290	50.4	86.3	187	85.0	19.1	-5.3	19.4	100.0	6.6	50.0	0.0
Flathead, MT	49 648	43.2	87.4	2 223	85.6	22.4	-2.0	22.5	64.0	15.5	31.9	20.8
Gallatin, MT	40 461	27.9	93.3	10 816	96.8	41.0	16.6	41.1	45.9	29.4	64.6	25.7
Garfield, MT	871	54.1	84.7	14	78.6	16.8	-7.6	16.8	...	...	...	0.0
Glacier, MT	7 383	48.7	78.6	469	88.1	16.5	-7.9	26.0	0.0	8.6	0.0	0.0
Golden Valley, MT	704	58.4	70.5	13	100.0	16.2	-8.2	16.4	...	0.0	...	0.0
Granite, MT	1 988	47.1	87.8	39	87.2	22.1	-2.3	22.5	...	0.0	0.0	13.3
Hill, MT	10 031	45.3	86.8	1 378	97.0	20.0	-4.4	20.9	0.0	12.3	32.1	22.4
Jefferson, MT	6 717	41.0	90.2	210	75.7	27.7	3.3	28.0	0.0	10.5	23.5	18.8
Judith Basin, MT	1 595	42.8	87.6	23	65.2	23.6	-0.8	23.9	...	0.0	0.0	0.0
Lake, MT	16 971	47.5	84.2	1 057	86.7	22.2	-2.2	24.6	8.3	11.1	35.5	24.9
Lewis and Clark, MT	36 690	37.9	91.4	2 691	52.5	31.6	7.2	32.1	34.8	11.4	52.3	25.8
Liberty, MT	1 470	50.0	75.0	34	94.1	17.6	-6.8	17.5	...	...	0.0	100.0
Lincoln, MT	13 008	57.8	80.2	428	89.5	13.7	-10.7	13.8	100.0	6.9	0.0	0.0
McCone, MT	1 374	52.1	86.1	24	79.2	16.4	-8.0	16.4	0.0	0.0	100.0	25.0
Madison, MT	4 945	42.8	89.8	138	92.0	25.5	1.1	25.8	...	12.5	0.0	22.9
Meagher, MT	1 334	53.8	83.4	10	40.0	18.7	-5.7	18.9	...	27.3	...	0.0
Mineral, MT	2 691	60.5	83.2	68	88.2	12.3	-12.1	12.5	...	6.7	20.0	21.4
Missoula, MT	59 298	35.5	91.0	11 985	94.4	32.8	8.4	33.1	50.7	19.3	39.9	29.4
Musselshell, MT	3 181	55.5	82.6	120	90.8	16.7	-7.7	16.8	...	0.0	50.0	3.0
Park, MT	11 013	44.7	87.6	376	84.8	23.1	-1.3	23.4	0.0	21.6	42.4	15.5
Petroleum, MT	333	52.9	82.9	12	100.0	17.4	-7.0	17.7	...	...	...	0.0
Phillips, MT	3 102	53.1	82.4	55	92.7	17.1	-7.3	17.6	...	11.9	22.6	0.0
Pondera, MT	4 108	53.4	81.6	159	81.1	19.8	-4.6	21.1	0.0	9.8	12.5	0.0
Powder River, MT	1 272	48.0	83.4	14	100.0	16.0	-8.4	16.0	...	16.7	0.0	0.0
Powell, MT	5 098	56.9	81.9	155	68.4	13.1	-11.3	13.3	68.2	1.1	44.0	0.0
Prairie, MT	913	53.6	78.8	25	100.0	14.8	-9.6	14.8	...	22.2	0.0	0.0
Ravalli, MT	24 565	44.1	87.4	798	87.3	22.5	-1.9	22.7	87.5	13.8	33.3	17.4
Richland, MT	6 398	51.9	83.5	162	82.1	17.2	-7.2	17.8	...	0.0	...	2.4
Roosevelt, MT	6 107	51.8	80.6	492	82.3	15.6	-8.8	20.9	...	8.9	29.8	38.2
Rosebud, MT	5 543	51.5	84.4	291	88.0	17.6	-6.8	20.2	...	10.2	23.1	8.9
Sanders, MT	7 242	56.0	81.2	229	78.6	15.5	-8.9	16.0	0.0	7.3	15.6	25.6
Sheridan, MT	2 931	50.3	81.2	70	67.1	18.4	-6.0	18.8	...	0.0	25.0	10.5
Silver Bow, MT	23 097	49.2	85.1	2 458	91.6	21.7	-2.7	22.2	18.2	8.4	45.6	9.8
Stillwater, MT	5 632	51.6	87.5	138	86.2	17.8	-6.6	17.8	50.0	28.6	42.9	18.3
Sweet Grass, MT	2 487	46.5	88.9	53	69.8	23.6	-0.8	24.1	...	0.0	0.0	0.0
Teton, MT	4 295	48.4	83.4	106	73.6	20.8	-3.6	21.3	...	9.6	42.9	17.2
Toole, MT	3 570	54.1	81.0	104	50.0	16.8	-7.6	17.7	0.0	3.4	0.0	0.0
Treasure, MT	577	54.8	86.3	9	100.0	18.2	-6.2	18.1	...	0.0	100.0	0.0
Valley, MT	5 345	55.8	83.9	129	87.6	15.7	-8.7	16.8	40.0	4.6	0.0	0.0
Wheatland, MT	1 508	61.8	69.0	40	77.5	13.5	-10.9	13.7	...	15.4	...	0.0
Wibaux, MT	738	58.0	76.8	17	100.0	16.0	-8.4	16.0	...	0.0	...	0.0
Yellowstone, MT	84 233	42.6	88.5	6 681	85.7	26.4	2.0	27.0	38.9	15.4	48.1	10.3
NEBRASKA	1 087 241	44.7	86.6	112 315	79.0	23.7	-0.7	24.6	14.1	8.8	41.6	8.5
Adams, NE	19 814	46.8	86.3	2 565	54.2	19.9	-4.5	20.3	21.6	14.8	18.2	5.6
Antelope, NE	4 939	54.3	85.5	163	92.0	14.3	-10.1	14.3	0.0	11.1	...	40.0
Arthur, NE	306	42.5	89.5	11	72.7	15.7	-8.7	16.1	...	0.0	...	0.0
Banner, NE	551	38.8	94.2	13	92.3	19.6	-4.8	19.7	0.0	...	...	28.6
Blaine, NE	407	45.2	93.4	10	100.0	12.3	-12.1	11.9	...	...	...	...
Boone, NE	4 134	57.4	84.4	131	85.5	13.1	-11.3	13.1	...	0.0	50.0	0.0
Box Butte, NE	7 864	49.4	88.1	394	81.2	15.3	-9.1	16.4	0.0	6.7	0.0	4.1
Boyd, NE	1 698	59.9	83.0	33	93.9	12.8	-11.6	12.8	...	...	33.3	...
Brown, NE	2 478	54.0	83.3	44	88.6	17.2	-7.2	17.0	...	0.0	0.0	50.0
Buffalo, NE	24 177	37.5	89.2	5 852	94.9	30.2	5.8	30.8	52.9	9.0	61.3	11.0
Burt, NE	5 382	56.5	84.1	172	90.7	14.2	10.2	14.4	0.0	0.0	0.0	4.0
Butler, NE	5 741	58.2	83.4	195	79.0	13.6	-10.8	13.6	0.0	0.0	71.4	0.0
Cass, NE	15 887	47.6	89.4	1 018	79.8	18.7	-5.7	18.8	33.3	11.8	20.0	6.7
Cedar, NE	6 208	56.7	83.5	215	81.4	13.0	-11.4	13.0	0.0	0.0	0.0	0.0
Chase, NE	2 791	53.2	86.4	57	93.0	16.6	-7.8	16.8	...	0.0	0.0	0.0
Cherry, NE	4 115	46.1	85.2	127	74.8	19.4	-5.0	19.7	...	11.5	0.0	22.2
Cheyenne, NE	6 543	48.5	86.7	256	82.4	16.8	-7.6	17.2	...	2.5	52.6	0.0
Clay, NE	4 685	50.7	86.7	193	85.5	16.2	-8.2	16.2	66.7	20.0	42.9	2.2
Colfax, NE	6 562	65.0	72.0	296	90.9	11.5	-12.9	13.2	...	0.0	0.0	3.8
Cuming, NE	6 755	61.8	78.7	200	90.0	12.3	-12.1	12.7	...	0.0	100.0	0.0
Custer, NE	8 026	51.3	87.5	168	85.7	16.1	-8.3	16.2	...	0.0	0.0	8.6
Dakota, NE	12 103	62.8	73.5	647	83.9	12.4	-12.0	14.1	32.7	8.0	8.6	4.8
Dawes, NE	5 018	39.2	86.9	1 769	97.9	28.4	4.0	29.0	0.0	21.1	0.0	6.6
Dawson, NE	15 175	61.9	73.6	530	87.0	14.4	-10.0	17.4	0.0	6.9	8.0	2.1
Deuel, NE	1 515	50.6	85.3	22	90.9	17.4	-7.0	17.1	...	0.0	81.8	0.0
Dixon, NE	4 147	57.4	82.1	179	86.6	14.1	-10.3	14.5	...	22.7	0.0	2.4
Dodge, NE	23 787	56.7	83.5	1 741	49.3	15.0	-9.4	15.4	32.6	0.0	22.5	4.7
Douglas, NE	293 076	38.9	87.3	33 759	70.9	30.6	6.2	33.6	12.0	7.6	57.0	11.1
Dundy, NE	1 630	48.5	82.4	59	86.4	16.7	-7.7	17.1	...	0.0	25.0	0.0
Fillmore, NE	4 561	54.5	88.2	133	86.5	15.7	-8.7	15.8	0.0	0.0	25.0	0.0

[3]May be of any race.
... = Not available.

Table C-1. Population, School, and Student Characteristics by County—*Continued*

STATE County	State/ county code	County type[1]	Population, 2005		Number of schools and students, 2004–2005			Resident enrollment, 2000			
			Total	Percent 5 to 17 years	School districts	Schools	Students	Total	Percent public	K–12	Percent public
			1	2	3	4	5	6	7	8	9
Franklin, NE	31061	9	3 421	16.5	1	2	347	829	96.3	689	99.3
Frontier, NE	31063	9	2 795	16.3	3	7	658	947	96.6	664	98.3
Furnas, NE	31065	9	5 019	16.4	3	8	1 147	1 226	94.2	1 020	97.5
Gage, NE	31067	6	23 306	15.8	5	13	3 432	5 467	89.0	4 267	92.3
Garden, NE	31069	9	1 997	13.1	5	5	316	492	94.3	427	97.4
Garfield, NE	31071	9	1 816	16.1	5	4	351	437	95.0	385	98.4
Gosper, NE	31073	9	2 020	15.1	1	2	277	501	95.8	427	98.1
Grant, NE	31075	9	670	14.9	5	5	142	210	92.4	193	96.9
Greeley, NE	31077	9	2 512	18.2	5	8	497	725	82.6	593	80.1
Hall, NE	31079	5	55 104	18.4	11	34	10 911	12 912	89.4	10 391	92.0
Hamilton, NE	31081	7	9 568	19.1	3	7	1 691	2 594	91.8	2 143	94.4
Harlan, NE	31083	9	3 462	16.3	1	2	340	924	91.2	782	93.6
Hayes, NE	31085	9	1 027	18.6	1	2	191	289	97.2	259	97.7
Hitchcock, NE	31087	9	2 970	14.9	5	5	280	764	95.3	628	98.6
Holt, NE	31089	7	10 784	18.0	21	25	1 747	2 924	86.8	2 558	86.9
Hooker, NE	31091	9	744	15.2	1	2	175	181	94.5	160	100.0
Howard, NE	31093	9	6 708	18.2	4	6	897	1 723	95.0	1 495	96.1
Jefferson, NE	31095	7	7 925	15.4	3	7	1 584	1 844	87.6	1 528	89.1
Johnson, NE	31097	8	4 695	15.5	4	7	869	1 028	92.6	878	94.0
Kearney, NE	31099	7	6 774	17.7	3	10	1 420	1 779	94.7	1 467	96.4
Keith, NE	31101	7	8 330	16.4	5	9	1 360	2 090	92.9	1 814	95.5
Keya Paha, NE	31103	9	902	16.5	6	4	124	196	96.4	182	98.4
Kimball, NE	31105	6	3 782	16.6	1	3	608	913	95.1	778	98.2
Knox, NE	31107	9	8 916	17.0	7	12	1 561	2 258	91.1	1 957	93.0
Lancaster, NE	31109	2	264 814	15.6	16	90	36 917	76 553	83.1	42 543	84.1
Lincoln, NE	31111	5	35 636	17.5	12	29	5 644	8 777	89.8	6 868	92.2
Logan, NE	31113	9	740	14.5	1	2	158	201	98.0	171	98.8
Loup, NE	31115	9	686	17.8	1	2	118	168	89.3	150	89.3
McPherson, NE	31117	9	507	18.7	4	4	79	132	90.9	117	90.6
Madison, NE	31119	5	35 488	17.8	16	22	1 861	9 710	78.4	7 256	78.4
Merrick, NE	31121	7	8 066	18.2	3	6	1 159	2 058	86.5	1 682	88.5
Morrill, NE	31123	9	5 165	17.4	5	7	1 001	1 378	95.5	1 161	97.2
Nance, NE	31125	9	3 666	18.6	4	9	893	1 026	94.2	865	97.2
Nemaha, NE	31127	7	6 965	15.3	5	10	1 158	2 268	94.9	1 481	97.2
Nuckolls, NE	31129	9	4 739	14.8	3	0	0	1 187	92.2	981	93.1
Otoe, NE	31131	6	15 509	17.7	8	11	2 578	3 963	85.6	3 134	88.6
Pawnee, NE	31133	9	2 878	15.9	2	4	505	672	96.3	579	98.3
Perkins, NE	31135	9	3 057	17.1	3	4	443	779	88.1	694	89.6
Phelps, NE	31137	7	9 449	17.8	8	16	1 672	2 387	93.5	1 987	96.5
Pierce, NE	31139	9	7 600	19.3	4	7	1 405	2 264	86.4	1 865	88.3
Platte, NE	31141	5	31 262	19.7	6	17	4 530	8 809	70.8	6 970	70.4
Polk, NE	31143	9	5 421	16.6	4	12	1 284	1 408	95.2	1 140	97.3
Red Willow, NE	31145	7	11 060	16.9	4	12	1 912	2 925	93.5	2 257	95.6
Richardson, NE	31147	7	8 732	17.0	5	10	1 484	2 298	90.9	1 927	93.0
Rock, NE	31149	9	1 567	14.3	7	7	193	363	92.0	333	93.7
Saline, NE	31151	6	14 195	17.2	8	13	2 676	3 929	77.5	2 680	95.7
Sarpy, NE	31153	2	139 371	19.9	8	143	67 393	38 813	83.3	27 289	88.2
Saunders, NE	31155	2	20 458	18.6	15	24	3 020	5 208	79.9	4 334	80.9
Scotts Bluff, NE	31157	5	36 752	17.4	13	26	6 272	9 375	88.4	7 191	92.6
Seward, NE	31159	2	16 739	16.2	5	9	2 649	5 376	67.2	3 218	80.5
Sheridan, NE	31161	9	5 668	16.6	17	20	929	1 549	95.1	1 254	97.7
Sherman, NE	31163	9	3 112	15.8	3	5	485	770	97.3	676	98.7
Sioux, NE	31165	9	1 458	15.9	7	7	97	360	90.8	306	92.5
Stanton, NE	31167	9	6 534	19.7	3	18	4 568	1 832	83.2	1 498	89.3
Thayer, NE	31169	9	5 436	16.6	6	11	865	1 356	90.0	1 178	91.5
Thomas, NE	31171	9	623	12.5	2	3	116	166	98.2	141	100.0
Thurston, NE	31173	8	7 365	24.4	4	9	1 453	2 352	91.7	1 970	93.7
Valley, NE	31175	9	4 402	16.6	6	8	679	1 095	90.0	898	92.7
Washington, NE	31177	2	19 772	17.8	3	10	3 419	5 340	81.6	3 954	90.7
Wayne, NE	31179	6	9 211	13.2	4	8	1 618	4 077	95.6	1 673	93.7
Webster, NE	31181	9	3 762	16.5	3	4	642	953	91.3	795	93.8
Wheeler, NE	31183	9	820	19.6	1	2	134	236	94.9	205	94.1
York, NE	31185	7	14 397	16.6	4	10	1 759	4 000	76.6	2 860	89.7
NEVADA	32000		2 414 807	18.5	18	572	400 083	492 885	90.9	366 909	94.7
Churchill, NV	32001	6	24 556	20.4	1	10	4 553	6 660	95.4	5 258	98.1
Clark, NV	32003	1	1 710 551	18.7	1	308	283 221	329 929	90.7	246 960	94.7
Douglas, NV	32005	4	47 017	15.7	1	16	7 190	10 499	90.3	7 885	94.7
Elko, NV	32007	5	45 570	22.9	2	25	9 548	13 237	93.6	10 760	96.7
Esmeralda, NV	32009	9	787	12.7	1	3	66	235	90.2	185	94.1
Eureka, NV	32011	9	1 428	19.0	1	3	236	440	96.1	379	96.6
Humboldt, NV	32013	7	17 129	22.2	1	16	3 461	4 563	95.7	3 824	99.1
Lander, NV	32015	7	5 114	23.2	1	7	1 226	1 755	96.4	1 456	99.0
Lincoln, NV	32017	8	4 391	21.1	1	9	1 006	1 192	98.0	1 007	98.3
Lyon, NV	32019	6	47 515	18.5	1	17	8 172	8 802	91.1	7 280	93.4
Mineral, NV	32021	7	4 910	17.8	1	5	734	1 176	93.5	973	92.8
Nye, NV	32023	6	40 477	16.9	1	24	5 827	6 644	91.6	5 747	94.0
Pershing, NV	32027	8	6 360	18.3	1	4	797	1 830	94.2	1 537	95.3
Storey, NV	32029	2	4 074	14.2	1	4	479	665	92.6	513	93.0
Washoe, NV	32031	2	389 872	17.9	1	100	63 322	89 970	90.4	62 229	93.8
White Pine, NV	32033	7	8 994	16.6	1	8	1 371	2 290	93.1	1 810	98.3
Carson City city, NV	32510	3	56 062	16.7	1	13	8 874	12 998	91.3	9 106	94.6

[1]County type codes are from the Economic Research Service of the United States Department of Agriculture. See notes and definitions at the end of this section.

Table C-1. Population, School, and Student Characteristics by County—*Continued*

STATE County	Characteristics of students, 2004–2005				Outcomes		Staff and students, 2004–2005		
	Percent with IEP[2]	Percent eligible for free or reduced-price lunch	Percent minority	Percent English-language learners	Number of graduates, 2003–2004	Percent dropouts, grades 9–12, 2001–2002	Number of teachers	Student-teacher ratio	Central administration staff
	10	11	12	13	14	15	16	17	18
Franklin, NE	13.5	40.0	0.9	0.0	25	...	32	10.9	3
Frontier, NE	17.6	38.8	3.2	0.0	71	0.7	66	10.0	9
Furnas, NE	19.2	43.1	4.3	0.0	121	2.8	98	11.7	14
Gage, NE	18.7	32.3	5.7	0.0	265	2.3	257	13.3	39
Garden, NE	11.4	48.2	7.6	0.0	...	1.4	30	10.6	8
Garfield, NE	15.7	41.9	2.8	0.0	...	...	34	10.5	...
Gosper, NE	24.9	33.0	6.3	0.0	25	0.9	21	13.2	3
Grant, NE	10.6	26.8	2.1	0.0	...	...	20	7.2	3
Greeley, NE	18.3	60.8	2.7	0.0	...	1.4	60	8.2	...
Hall, NE	15.2	44.5	29.7	15.5	...	3.6	743	14.7	90
Hamilton, NE	17.7	26.3	3.8	0.0	153	1.4	122	13.9	17
Harlan, NE	16.8	35.3	3.5	0.0	30	0.8	27	12.4	4
Hayes, NE	10.5	45.0	3.7	2.6	13	1.6	20	9.5	4
Hitchcock, NE	20.0	43.1	8.7	0.0	...	2.0	38	7.4	9
Holt, NE	17.4	43.8	3.9	0.9	...	1.0	170	10.3	...
Hooker, NE	12.6	48.6	0.0	0.0	17	...	21	8.5	4
Howard, NE	17.6	43.5	2.3	0.0	...	1.1	73	12.3	9
Jefferson, NE	21.0	35.7	3.7	0.6	140	1.2	115	13.7	17
Johnson, NE	15.2	32.3	14.4	10.9	...	1.3	76	11.4	9
Kearney, NE	21.1	23.1	4.2	0.5	128	0.5	107	13.2	12
Keith, NE	15.1	30.7	9.4	0.0	...	3.7	103	13.2	28
Keya Paha, NE	8.1	55.6	0.0	0.0	...	2.3	17	7.2	...
Kimball, NE	14.3	36.4	8.8	1.2	49	3.0	48	12.7	9
Knox, NE	15.4	48.1	13.5	0.0	...	2.2	142	11.0	20
Lancaster, NE	17.3	28.1	17.3	6.5	...	5.4	2 610	14.1	449
Lincoln, NE	19.7	35.0	12.1	0.7	...	2.8	401	14.1	57
Logan, NE	16.5	32.5	12.3	0.0	12	...	18	8.9	2
Loup, NE	15.3	68.6	3.4	0.0	13	...	14	8.7	2
McPherson, NE	12.7	0.0	1.3	0.0	...	...	12	6.5	2
Madison, NE	15.3	44.0	27.4	5.6	...	2.0	165	11.3	21
Merrick, NE	16.7	39.2	4.6	0.5	...	0.6	88	13.2	12
Morrill, NE	13.2	53.8	18.0	3.8	...	2.0	83	12.1	9
Nance, NE	10.4	35.8	1.9	0.1	...	0.9	73	12.2	10
Nemaha, NE	12.2	29.2	4.5	0.0	...	1.7	94	12.3	...
Nuckolls, NE	...	31.4	2.1	...	...	0.8	...	...	...
Otoe, NE	17.9	28.4	6.9	1.7	...	2.2	186	13.8	...
Pawnee, NE	18.0	47.7	1.8	0.4	36	...	49	10.4	6
Perkins, NE	17.4	34.8	5.4	0.0	...	2.0	45	9.8	...
Phelps, NE	20.2	29.0	5.0	1.9	...	2.2	153	10.9	27
Pierce, NE	17.5	31.3	2.7	0.5	...	1.7	114	12.4	13
Platte, NE	17.4	38.8	21.7	14.1	...	4.1	309	14.7	53
Polk, NE	13.5	34.4	2.7	0.7	121	0.2	108	11.9	17
Red Willow, NE	22.2	39.7	6.5	1.5	...	1.6	150	12.7	23
Richardson, NE	16.9	48.2	7.6	0.0	...	2.0	133	11.1	...
Rock, NE	21.8	35.1	3.1	0.0	...	...	28	6.8	4
Saline, NE	15.5	31.8	22.4	15.4	...	1.9	190	14.1	24
Sarpy, NE	15.8	22.0	19.3	8.8	4 006	2.6	4 513	14.9	778
Saunders, NE	16.9	27.0	3.2	0.4	...	1.7	232	13.0	28
Scotts Bluff, NE	12.0	43.9	33.2	2.7	...	6.4	451	13.9	71
Seward, NE	14.9	21.3	4.2	0.2	...	0.6	184	14.4	32
Sheridan, NE	13.3	46.8	22.5	0.0	...	1.6	95	9.8	14
Sherman, NE	15.9	52.0	5.4	0.0	...	1.5	46	10.5	5
Sioux, NE	8.2	12.4	1.1	0.0	...	...	20	4.9	2
Stanton, NE	19.2	40.0	9.4	7.0	...	4.7	324	14.1	51
Thayer, NE	16.9	32.9	5.8	0.0	...	44.8	77	11.2	12
Thomas, NE	12.1	51.4	2.7	0.0	...	2.0	14	8.6	2
Thurston, NE	28.2	71.9	76.7	17.0	83	4.6	139	10.5	21
Valley, NE	15.6	40.6	6.1	2.2	...	1.1	65	10.5	9
Washington, NE	16.1	14.5	3.3	0.4	266	1.7	223	15.3	23
Wayne, NE	15.8	32.3	14.3	6.9	...	0.9	127	12.8	21
Webster, NE	23.1	36.7	2.7	0.0	...	0.5	49	13.0	7
Wheeler, NE	11.2	60.4	0.0	0.0	9	...	16	8.2	3
York, NE	22.2	32.1	7.7	2.7	186	2.7	158	11.1	26
NEVADA	11.3	28.7	0.0	17.9	...	6.4	20 950	19.1	...
Churchill, NV	15.7	52.3	0.0	4.3	252	1.8	267	17.1	...
Clark, NV	10.7	27.8	0.0	20.9	11 389	8.1	14 222	19.9	...
Douglas, NV	11.4	28.7	0.0	5.5	408	0.5	424	17.0	...
Elko, NV	11.5	26.0	0.0	6.3	...	3.1	591	16.1	...
Esmeralda, NV	12.1	62.1	0.0	3.0	...	...	9	7.3	...
Eureka, NV	11.4	37.3	0.0	0.4	39	2.1	23	10.3	...
Humboldt, NV	12.1	97.8	0.0	7.7	203	5.1	215	16.1	...
Lander, NV	12.2	100.0	0.0	2.2	94	1.1	69	17.9	...
Lincoln, NV	7.8	97.1	0.0	0.4	50	2.6	82	12.3	...
Lyon, NV	12.5	72.1	0.0	4.7	443	1.6	474	17.2	...
Mineral, NV	18.5	43.3	0.0	0.0	41	1.8	59	12.4	...
Nye, NV	17.8	15.2	0.0	5.3	297	3.6	410	14.2	...
Pershing, NV	21.8	104.0	0.0	12.3	55	1.1	68	11.8	...
Storey, NV	11.5	88.1	0.0	0.0	24	13.0	37	13.1	...
Washoe, NV	12.6	20.6	0.0	13.6	2 940	3.4	3 496	18.1	...
White Pine, NV	14.1	38.7	0.0	0.0	75	8.0	82	16.7	...
Carson City city, NV	12.2	19.3	0.0	18.0	451	1.8	425	20.9	...

[2]IEP = Individual Education Program. See notes and definitions at the end of this section.
... = Not available.

Table C-1. Population, School, and Student Characteristics by County—*Continued*

STATE County	Revenue, 2003–2004				Current expenditures, 2003–2004			Resident population, 16 to 19 years, 2000			
	Total revenue (thousands of dollars)	Percent of revenue from:			Total expenditures (thousands of dollars)	Amount per student (dollars)	Percent for instruction	Total	Percent in armed forces	Percent high school graduates	Percent not enrolled, not employed, not in armed forces, not high school graduate
		Federal government	State government	Local government							
	19	20	21	22	23	24	25	26	27	28	29
Franklin, NE	3 564	5.8	37.2	57.0	3 043	8 950	68.6	170	0.0	6.5	1.8
Frontier, NE	7 820	5.5	31.1	63.4	6 950	9 720	61.5	290	0.0	4.5	0.7
Furnas, NE	13 404	7.9	35.1	57.0	10 442	8 948	66.8	317	0.0	5.7	1.3
Gage, NE	37 059	14.2	34.6	51.3	29 952	8 930	70.0	1 333	0.0	9.8	3.4
Garden, NE	4 989	6.2	21.4	72.4	4 086	11 913	66.3	118	0.0	12.7	3.4
Garfield, NE	3 503	7.1	46.3	46.6	3 220	9 148	70.1	100	0.0	4.0	0.0
Gosper, NE	2 645	4.9	10.9	84.2	2 101	7 220	66.8	112	0.0	1.8	2.7
Grant, NE	2 240	4.7	8.3	87.0	2 135	13 261	61.4	55	0.0	0.0	0.0
Greeley, NE	6 068	9.2	30.4	60.4	5 787	10 408	66.2	184	0.0	0.0	0.0
Hall, NE	97 137	7.7	38.2	54.2	83 536	8 151	76.0	3 014	0.0	13.7	6.4
Hamilton, NE	14 115	6.7	22.6	70.6	12 553	7 298	68.5	581	0.0	6.0	2.8
Harlan, NE	3 384	16.8	29.2	54.0	2 668	8 012	69.3	224	0.0	6.7	0.0
Hayes, NE	2 060	6.4	27.6	66.0	2 082	11 567	56.4	62	0.0	9.7	4.8
Hitchcock, NE	6 911	6.0	37.2	56.8	6 792	19 079	62.4	206	0.0	5.8	0.5
Holt, NE	19 403	8.1	29.9	62.0	16 415	9 274	68.8	722	0.0	5.0	0.7
Hooker, NE	2 065	4.5	4.8	90.7	2 008	11 882	66.9	52	0.0	5.8	0.0
Howard, NE	12 634	8.3	35.5	56.2	10 833	7 222	63.0	331	0.0	9.4	2.1
Jefferson, NE	16 075	6.2	24.0	69.7	13 248	8 015	67.4	464	0.0	12.1	5.6
Johnson, NE	8 041	5.7	28.2	66.1	7 154	7 984	65.3	240	0.0	7.5	2.1
Kearney, NE	14 394	5.6	17.8	76.6	11 819	8 145	64.5	413	0.0	2.9	3.4
Keith, NE	17 085	11.8	26.0	62.2	15 012	11 195	72.7	549	0.0	9.8	1.5
Keya Paha, NE	1 816	5.4	11.1	83.5	1 434	11 291	71.1	54	0.0	13.0	0.0
Kimball, NE	6 007	5.7	33.9	60.4	5 468	8 920	70.6	193	0.0	4.7	2.1
Knox, NE	15 496	17.3	31.7	50.9	13 010	9 266	63.6	490	0.0	5.1	1.2
Lancaster, NE	350 331	7.8	25.4	66.8	288 592	7 849	69.1	17 077	0.0	9.0	2.0
Lincoln, NE	49 605	7.1	36.6	56.3	41 787	7 490	69.1	2 168	0.0	11.5	3.6
Logan, NE	2 027	5.8	32.0	62.2	1 748	10 857	63.0	44	0.0	0.0	0.0
Loup, NE	1 527	9.0	25.1	65.9	1 198	9 740	62.8	28	0.0	17.9	7.1
McPherson, NE	1 280	3.0	13.0	84.0	1 102	11 245	74.3	30	0.0	0.0	0.0
Madison, NE	55 270	6.8	34.8	58.4	44 903	7 311	69.6	2 661	0.1	10.0	2.1
Merrick, NE	11 099	5.9	23.3	70.8	8 488	7 261	67.0	456	0.0	15.6	3.1
Morrill, NE	9 953	10.0	44.5	45.6	8 949	8 869	66.5	344	0.0	7.3	6.7
Nance, NE	8 801	5.4	28.2	66.4	7 875	8 819	68.1	228	0.0	8.8	2.2
Nemaha, NE	15 240	8.6	34.0	57.4	13 236	11 797	58.0	607	0.0	8.9	0.0
Nuckolls, NE	13 656	9.1	40.8	50.1	11 185	9 535	67.9	296	0.0	7.4	0.0
Otoe, NE	22 774	4.8	27.9	67.3	19 500	7 677	70.4	840	0.2	6.4	3.3
Pawnee, NE	4 760	6.4	31.6	61.9	4 514	8 697	67.2	160	0.0	6.9	2.5
Perkins, NE	5 011	4.9	11.9	83.3	4 718	10 124	70.0	211	0.0	7.6	1.4
Phelps, NE	19 693	5.9	22.9	71.2	18 164	10 704	74.1	544	0.0	8.3	1.7
Pierce, NE	13 381	6.6	34.9	58.5	11 424	7 967	68.6	548	0.0	5.3	3.8
Platte, NE	45 024	11.0	29.0	60.0	39 383	8 748	67.8	2 076	0.0	7.9	2.2
Polk, NE	12 690	4.5	13.8	81.8	11 213	8 740	65.6	333	0.0	5.4	4.8
Red Willow, NE	18 883	7.0	34.8	58.2	15 665	8 262	67.9	737	0.0	9.5	1.4
Richardson, NE	15 434	6.7	36.7	56.5	13 361	8 366	67.5	600	0.0	14.7	3.5
Rock, NE	2 852	8.1	9.7	82.2	2 761	12 437	73.7	109	0.0	3.7	1.8
Saline, NE	24 176	9.2	32.5	58.3	19 493	7 290	66.9	1 086	0.7	9.2	3.1
Sarpy, NE	179 173	12.3	41.1	46.6	145 658	7 255	70.6	7 065	3.6	13.9	1.6
Saunders, NE	27 299	5.8	26.4	67.7	22 464	7 584	69.9	1 094	0.0	7.9	4.7
Scotts Bluff, NE	56 663	10.8	44.1	45.1	48 710	7 802	70.4	2 264	0.3	10.7	6.8
Seward, NE	29 947	6.5	20.8	72.7	24 871	9 507	70.1	1 521	0.0	6.5	1.0
Sheridan, NE	10 374	8.9	42.6	48.5	8 587	8 889	70.5	378	0.0	5.6	2.1
Sherman, NE	5 552	6.6	29.7	63.7	4 674	9 819	70.4	194	0.0	7.7	0.0
Sioux, NE	1 964	2.7	7.8	89.5	1 622	13 630	70.4	86	0.0	3.5	2.3
Stanton, NE	4 489	7.5	38.6	53.9	3 562	7 436	65.8	418	0.0	4.5	3.3
Thayer, NE	10 331	4.2	18.8	77.1	9 268	10 437	67.5	327	0.0	4.0	0.6
Thomas, NE	1 405	5.8	15.3	78.9	1 194	9 787	59.9	45	0.0	0.0	0.0
Thurston, NE	23 351	22.9	47.6	29.5	18 674	10 610	64.2	465	0.0	9.9	15.7
Valley, NE	7 231	6.8	43.8	49.4	6 437	9 079	66.7	207	0.0	6.3	2.9
Washington, NE	27 960	4.1	28.1	67.8	23 758	6 884	66.2	1 189	0.0	6.9	0.4
Wayne, NE	21 540	15.2	26.0	58.8	18 131	11 318	73.6	1 133	0.0	5.5	1.1
Webster, NE	6 082	9.8	38.0	52.3	5 382	8 556	64.9	201	0.0	6.0	0.0
Wheeler, NE	2 220	6.7	4.6	88.7	1 584	11 396	60.6	57	0.0	7.0	3.5
York, NE	18 301	5.3	23.6	71.1	16 034	8 714	70.4	919	0.0	6.0	1.6
NEVADA	3 069 531	7.2	29.6	63.2	2 466 131	6 399	66.4	98 513	0.3	12.7	8.3
Churchill, NV	41 683	12.0	55.5	32.6	36 345	7 983	68.3	1 249	1.8	15.1	3.0
Clark, NV	2 132 656	6.8	26.1	67.1	1 652 435	6 108	66.4	65 482	0.5	13.6	9.5
Douglas, NV	62 397	6.4	25.9	67.7	54 728	7 612	60.0	2 027	0.0	9.5	4.2
Elko, NV	83 850	8.1	45.2	46.7	73 906	7 713	68.8	3 053	0.0	8.1	6.8
Esmeralda, NV	1 738	9.7	45.8	44.5	1 466	21 246	41.1	68	0.0	8.8	0.0
Eureka, NV	4 165	8.7	2.9	88.4	4 547	20 668	57.8	93	0.0	5.4	8.6
Humboldt, NV	29 941	9.4	45.7	44.9	27 761	7 880	69.1	1 059	0.0	11.7	5.9
Lander, NV	10 416	7.4	49.9	42.7	9 789	7 800	64.7	327	0.0	5.2	0.0
Lincoln, NV	11 813	11.1	70.6	18.3	10 652	10 526	61.3	328	0.0	11.6	2.1
Lyon, NV	63 352	7.0	61.2	31.7	54 951	7 157	63.0	2 086	0.0	12.7	4.5
Mineral, NV	8 571	19.2	54.2	26.6	7 859	10 577	62.7	269	0.0	9.7	3.7
Nye, NV	52 613	10.6	45.1	44.3	44 465	8 127	58.8	1 235	0.0	11.2	5.9
Pershing, NV	10 722	9.4	60.1	30.5	9 175	10 900	66.2	355	0.0	8.5	6.8
Storey, NV	6 078	5.2	49.2	45.6	5 222	11 182	63.1	161	0.0	34.2	0.0
Washoe, NV	463 123	7.7	29.0	63.2	399 325	6 430	68.7	17 960	0.1	11.1	6.6
White Pine, NV	14 701	6.6	62.2	31.2	12 331	8 936	55.8	471	0.0	9.3	2.5
Carson City city, NV	71 712	7.2	36.9	55.9	61 174	6 953	67.4	2 290	0.0	10.5	7.0

Table C-1. Population, School, and Student Characteristics by County—*Continued*

STATE County	High school graduates, 2000			College enrollment, 2000		College graduates, 2000 (percent)						
	Population 25 years and over	High school graduate or less (percent)	High school graduate or more (percent)	Number	Percent public	Bachelor's degree or more	+/- U.S. percentage with bachelor's degree or more	Non-Hispanic White	Black	American Indian and Alaska Native	Asian or Pacific Islander	Hispanic[3]
	30	31	32	33	34	35	36	37	38	39	40	41
Franklin, NE	2 533	53.6	85.7	83	100.0	15.8	-8.6	15.9	...	0.0	0.0	0.0
Frontier, NE	1 941	46.4	88.3	240	99.2	17.9	-6.5	18.1	66.7	0.0	0.0	21.1
Furnas, NE	3 764	55.6	84.2	104	81.7	16.1	-8.3	16.3	...	0.0	0.0	9.5
Gage, NE	15 689	56.9	82.0	800	88.3	15.4	-9.0	15.4	11.1	0.0	81.6	10.6
Garden, NE	1 685	55.1	85.2	23	73.9	14.2	-10.2	14.5	...	0.0	0.0	0.0
Garfield, NE	1 374	55.5	81.1	31	93.5	13.4	-11.0	13.3	...	...	0.0	28.6
Gosper, NE	1 517	50.1	88.9	42	81.0	17.6	-6.8	17.6	...	...	100.0	10.0
Grant, NE	493	41.0	90.3	12	25.0	24.7	0.3	24.9	...	...	...	0.0
Greeley, NE	1 813	56.1	83.2	101	97.0	13.5	-10.9	13.5	0.0	...	...	0.0
Hall, NE	34 369	53.3	82.2	1 645	86.7	15.9	-8.5	17.4	4.7	10.3	24.7	2.9
Hamilton, NE	6 126	45.5	89.6	264	92.4	18.6	-5.8	18.6	0.0	...	...	29.0
Harlan, NE	2 675	52.1	85.8	62	95.2	15.3	-9.1	15.4	25.0	0.0	...	0.0
Hayes, NE	727	51.4	89.1	27	92.6	11.6	-12.8	11.8	...	...	...	0.0
Hitchcock, NE	2 180	52.0	85.6	101	94.1	13.8	-10.6	13.8	0.0	0.0	100.0	0.0
Holt, NE	7 748	56.6	84.5	216	92.1	14.5	-9.9	14.6	...	0.0	28.6	0.0
Hooker, NE	562	51.4	89.7	7	100.0	15.7	-8.7	15.4	...	0.0	...	40.0
Howard, NE	4 327	56.0	87.2	161	91.9	14.2	-10.2	14.4	0.0	0.0	0.0	0.0
Jefferson, NE	5 878	56.4	84.2	184	94.0	14.4	-10.0	14.0	0.0	64.7	0.0	22.2
Johnson, NE	3 143	63.0	80.4	95	85.3	14.7	-9.7	15.0	...	0.0	19.7	3.2
Kearney, NE	4 594	47.0	88.5	205	95.1	21.3	-3.1	21.4	100.0	0.0	0.0	19.0
Keith, NE	6 103	50.3	86.6	145	80.7	16.8	-7.6	17.0	...	19.0	14.7	6.2
Keya Paha, NE	681	53.9	82.2	12	83.3	15.7	-8.7	16.0	...	...	...	0.0
Kimball, NE	2 849	52.5	84.6	84	82.1	13.5	-10.9	13.6	0.0	12.0	60.0	5.7
Knox, NE	6 462	57.6	82.0	197	82.7	14.4	-10.0	14.8	0.0	5.1	26.7	0.0
Lancaster, NE	152 747	34.7	90.5	29 849	86.5	32.6	8.2	33.4	17.7	17.6	36.3	19.3
Lincoln, NE	22 736	47.0	86.3	1 332	90.4	16.2	-8.2	16.6	28.6	12.2	38.7	3.8
Logan, NE	524	47.1	90.8	13	100.0	10.5	-13.9	10.8	...	0.0	...	0.0
Loup, NE	487	50.9	91.8	8	75.0	13.3	-11.1	13.0	...	...	...	66.7
McPherson, NE	360	51.1	88.6	14	100.0	22.2	-2.2	22.5	...	0.0	...	...
Madison, NE	21 724	51.2	82.6	1 964	86.9	17.0	-7.4	18.1	5.0	6.0	29.8	2.8
Merrick, NE	5 432	56.3	85.3	197	79.2	14.9	-9.5	15.1	0.0	0.0	0.0	7.9
Morrill, NE	3 575	55.7	79.4	114	99.1	14.3	-10.1	15.2	0.0	22.2	0.0	3.7
Nance, NE	2 651	58.2	80.6	83	90.4	11.4	-13.0	11.4	...	0.0	33.3	0.0
Nemaha, NE	4 907	47.6	85.5	679	91.5	22.9	-1.5	23.0	0.0	0.0	43.6	8.0
Nuckolls, NE	3 567	55.5	84.5	119	94.1	13.1	-11.3	12.8	100.0	0.0	100.0	6.7
Otoe, NE	10 373	53.9	85.6	496	86.9	18.1	-6.3	18.2	30.8	13.3	26.5	11.3
Pawnee, NE	2 228	61.4	83.7	40	70.6	14.4	+10.0	14.4	...	12.5	0.0	40.0
Perkins, NE	2 159	47.7	87.1	53	90.6	17.6	-6.8	17.8	...	...	0.0	0.0
Phelps, NE	6 565	46.8	89.1	227	88.1	20.4	-4.0	20.8	...	9.1	100.0	0.0
Pierce, NE	5 019	57.6	84.6	282	87.9	13.3	-11.1	13.3	100.0	0.0	15.4	0.0
Platte, NE	19 988	51.5	84.7	1 155	85.4	17.2	-7.2	17.8	0.0	11.4	53.0	2.0
Polk, NE	3 886	53.4	86.6	152	88.8	13.5	-10.9	13.4	...	0.0	...	21.1
Red Willow, NE	7 490	47.0	87.9	454	93.4	15.2	-9.2	15.3	...	45.5	...	5.8
Richardson, NE	6 543	60.1	81.8	209	90.4	13.6	-10.8	13.6	0.0	13.3	26.4	0.0
Rock, NE	1 242	54.6	87.4	22	77.3	12.2	-12.2	12.2	...	0.0	40.0	0.0
Saline, NE	8 691	58.2	81.2	1 012	29.1	14.0	-10.4	15.1	0.0	0.0	12.0	0.0
Sarpy, NE	73 804	31.4	93.3	8 803	78.3	30.2	5.8	30.9	28.2	13.6	33.6	14.8
Saunders, NE	13 047	51.6	86.8	585	83.9	16.9	-7.5	16.9	0.0	0.0	44.4	15.9
Scotts Bluff, NE	24 314	50.0	79.6	1 541	84.8	17.3	-7.1	19.2	0.0	0.8	50.9	5.2
Seward, NE	10 009	44.4	87.5	1 915	47.7	22.6	-1.8	22.4	0.0	10.5	56.8	28.0
Sheridan, NE	4 232	50.3	86.1	186	88.2	17.2	-7.2	17.9	0.0	5.2	10.0	21.6
Sherman, NE	2 355	58.8	82.0	67	85.1	10.8	-13.6	11.0	0.0	...	0.0	0.0
Sioux, NE	1 009	45.5	86.4	36	80.6	21.5	-2.9	22.0	...	50.0	0.0	0.0
Stanton, NE	4 065	51.8	86.2	193	80.3	13.7	-10.7	14.0	...	0.0	0.0	8.3
Thayer, NE	4 301	56.4	80.9	99	89.9	15.0	-9.4	15.0	...	0.0	...	16.0
Thomas, NE	528	48.5	83.7	19	100.0	17.2	-7.2	17.9	...	0.0	...	0.0
Thurston, NE	3 953	56.7	80.4	217	81.1	12.0	-12.4	14.9	14.3	6.7	33.3	0.0
Valley, NE	3 285	53.4	84.7	100	84.0	16.4	-8.0	16.5	...	0.0	0.0	0.0
Washington, NE	11 956	45.9	89.7	993	56.6	22.7	-1.7	22.7	45.2	34.2	24.2	10.0
Wayne, NE	5 115	44.1	87.0	2 296	98.6	28.0	3.6	28.2	100.0	0.0	35.7	3.3
Webster, NE	2 910	55.9	83.6	82	89.0	13.7	-10.7	13.7	0.0	0.0	24.0	0.0
Wheeler, NE	577	46.4	90.8	17	100.0	14.9	-9.5	15.1	...	...	...	0.0
York, NE	9 579	50.4	87.2	890	38.4	17.0	-7.4	17.3	0.0	12.5	100.0	3.5
NEVADA	1 310 176	48.7	80.7	98 631	86.5	18.2	-6.2	20.7	12.0	8.6	27.1	6.4
Churchill, NV	15 167	45.4	85.1	1 101	87.1	16.7	-7.7	17.6	21.4	7.1	21.8	7.4
Clark, NV	900 400	50.4	79.5	64 457	85.0	17.3	-7.1	20.0	11.9	10.1	26.2	6.4
Douglas, NV	29 279	35.0	91.6	1 924	88.8	23.2	-1.2	24.0	35.1	6.8	25.7	12.2
Elko, NV	26 798	51.3	79.1	1 917	85.2	14.8	-9.6	17.4	8.4	6.1	19.7	4.0
Esmeralda, NV	711	65.4	78.9	39	79.5	9.6	-14.8	9.9	...	0.0	0.0	0.0
Eureka, NV	1 104	55.0	76.7	39	89.7	13.6	-10.8	14.4	0.0	0.0	30.0	0.0
Humboldt, NV	9 846	53.0	78.3	432	88.7	14.2	-10.2	17.1	0.0	0.5	12.5	4.2
Lander, NV	3 581	57.6	79.2	210	83.3	10.8	-13.6	11.9	...	6.6	0.0	4.9
Lincoln, NV	2 654	54.7	83.0	116	94.0	15.1	-9.3	15.1	0.0	0.0	93.8	3.4
Lyon, NV	22 863	51.4	81.5	1 086	88.6	11.3	-13.1	12.0	24.6	5.0	17.8	3.3
Mineral, NV	3 527	59.1	77.1	142	95.1	10.1	-14.3	11.9	0.0	6.8	64.3	3.4
Nye, NV	23 234	62.0	79.2	601	83.5	10.1	-14.3	10.5	7.2	2.9	7.2	6.9
Pershing, NV	4 498	60.7	75.9	230	91.7	8.7	-15.7	11.1	0.8	4.2	4.3	3.1
Storey, NV	2 540	43.0	86.7	144	96.5	18.0	-6.4	16.8	...	30.5	36.7	32.5
Washoe, NV	221 837	41.2	83.9	22 839	89.9	23.7	-0.7	26.4	16.7	8.8	32.4	6.9
White Pine, NV	6 184	52.8	82.0	359	78.8	11.8	-12.6	13.5	2.1	6.0	9.5	4.8
Carson City city, NV	35 953	45.4	82.5	2 995	92.5	18.5	-5.9	20.1	3.6	13.4	40.3	4.8

[3]May be of any race.
. . . = Not available.

Table C-1. Population, School, and Student Characteristics by County—*Continued*

STATE County	State/ county code	County type[1]	Population, 2005		Number of schools and students, 2004–2005			Resident enrollment, 2000			
			Total	Percent 5 to 17 years	School districts	Schools	Students	Total	Percent public	K–12	Percent public
			1	2	3	4	5	6	7	8	9
NEW HAMPSHIRE	33000		1 309 940	17.6	265	481	207 423	332 888	79.4	237 188	89.1
Belknap, NH	33001	4	61 547	16.3	17	25	10 443	13 322	85.3	10 516	91.1
Carroll, NH	33003	8	47 439	15.5	18	23	6 995	9 809	87.8	8 026	92.9
Cheshire, NH	33005	4	77 287	15.9	15	33	10 197	21 073	81.0	13 485	90.1
Coos, NH	33007	7	33 655	15.7	24	28	5 351	7 435	92.0	6 106	94.3
Grafton, NH	33009	5	84 708	14.9	40	55	13 288	24 139	71.5	13 924	93.1
Hillsborough, NH	33011	2	401 291	18.8	39	111	67 168	103 468	76.1	75 632	87.4
Merrimack, NH	33013	4	146 881	17.4	27	53	21 137	36 957	78.0	26 380	89.7
Rockingham, NH	33015	1	295 076	18.8	51	88	49 509	73 404	79.2	55 638	87.7
Strafford, NH	33017	1	119 015	16.3	16	33	16 372	34 333	86.3	20 046	88.8
Sullivan, NH	33019	7	43 041	16.6	18	32	6 963	8 948	88.8	7 435	93.3
NEW JERSEY	34000		8 717 925	18.1	676	2 469	1 389 185	2 217 832	78.2	1 566 107	86.3
Atlantic, NJ	34001	2	271 015	18.3	34	102	57 179	66 098	85.1	48 899	89.1
Bergen, NJ	34003	1	902 561	17.3	81	283	134 530	220 538	73.2	150 192	83.5
Burlington, NJ	34005	1	450 743	18.1	41	141	75 829	111 053	81.2	82 014	88.2
Camden, NJ	34007	1	518 249	19.3	48	166	89 330	141 671	81.8	104 979	86.8
Cape May, NJ	34009	3	99 286	16.3	19	32	13 980	23 063	83.3	18 054	88.5
Cumberland, NJ	34011	3	153 252	18.0	15	34	16 760	37 622	87.0	29 889	89.4
Essex, NJ	34013	1	791 057	19.1	34	232	124 098	221 424	77.2	155 379	84.8
Gloucester, NJ	34015	1	276 910	18.5	30	84	48 484	73 630	82.0	51 446	87.9
Hudson, NJ	34017	1	603 521	16.2	24	122	82 284	157 624	74.4	106 450	82.1
Hunterdon, NJ	34019	1	130 404	18.7	31	52	23 183	31 562	82.8	23 496	92.0
Mercer, NJ	34021	2	366 256	17.6	18	101	60 058	99 649	73.5	62 905	86.1
Middlesex, NJ	34023	1	789 516	17.2	27	183	117 162	200 431	81.3	130 731	87.9
Monmouth, NJ	34025	1	635 952	19.1	60	187	109 305	165 915	77.4	120 378	86.7
Morris, NJ	34027	1	490 593	18.4	42	154	79 191	122 655	74.7	84 319	87.1
Ocean, NJ	34029	1	558 341	16.9	30	109	78 468	118 859	77.6	88 689	85.9
Passaic, NJ	34031	1	499 060	19.1	25	135	80 268	129 731	77.9	94 172	84.1
Salem, NJ	34033	1	66 346	18.2	15	31	12 173	16 618	86.9	13 039	90.5
Somerset, NJ	34035	1	319 900	19.0	22	77	53 014	76 743	76.9	54 020	86.6
Sussex, NJ	34037	1	153 130	20.0	28	47	28 271	40 610	83.6	30 665	91.6
Union, NJ	34039	1	531 457	18.6	26	154	86 690	136 230	78.3	96 772	85.9
Warren, NJ	34041	2	110 376	19.0	26	43	18 928	26 106	83.3	19 619	91.5
NEW MEXICO	35000		1 928 384	18.4	89	842	326 102	533 786	89.2	384 924	91.7
Bernalillo, NM	35001	2	603 562	17.1	1	157	93 341	156 057	85.3	102 911	87.6
Catron, NM	35003	9	3 409	13.3	2	6	358	714	89.8	583	92.1
Chaves, NM	35005	5	61 860	19.0	4	31	11 172	18 132	91.0	13 835	93.3
Cibola, NM	35006	6	27 620	19.4	1	12	3 670	7 644	86.3	5 833	86.7
Colfax, NM	35007	7	13 755	16.6	4	18	2 330	3 353	93.2	2 885	94.6
Curry, NM	35009	5	45 846	20.4	4	28	9 301	14 012	94.5	9 807	96.3
DeBaca, NM	35011	9	2 016	14.3	1	3	333	532	99.6	439	99.5
Dona Ana, NM	35013	3	189 444	19.4	3	70	39 352	60 034	93.9	39 730	95.7
Eddy, NM	35015	5	51 437	19.1	3	30	10 109	14 292	91.9	11 526	94.5
Grant, NM	35017	7	29 747	16.7	2	16	4 722	8 657	92.3	6 107	94.1
Guadalupe, NM	35019	7	4 369	14.7	2	7	768	1 279	92.0	1 017	93.9
Harding, NM	35021	9	740	12.3	2	4	137	174	89.7	151	91.4
Hidalgo, NM	35023	7	5 139	20.6	2	8	1 040	1 699	97.4	1 499	98.7
Lea, NM	35025	5	56 719	19.6	5	38	11 747	16 534	93.0	13 004	96.2
Lincoln, NM	35027	7	21 007	15.1	5	17	3 446	4 483	91.9	3 497	92.5
Los Alamos, NM	35028	6	18 822	17.0	1	7	3 624	5 057	87.5	3 656	94.1
Luna, NM	35029	6	26 498	20.1	1	14	5 443	6 401	97.3	5 600	98.7
McKinley, NM	35031	4	71 918	25.3	2	44	14 889	28 043	90.7	22 597	92.2
Mora, NM	35033	8	5 107	17.0	2	7	801	1 418	90.1	1 112	89.1
Otero, NM	35035	4	63 538	19.4	3	23	8 269	18 135	92.6	13 944	94.9
Quay, NM	35037	7	9 259	16.1	4	13	1 687	2 619	97.9	2 062	98.5
Rio Arriba, NM	35039	6	40 828	18.2	5	35	6 715	11 581	87.8	8 918	89.7
Roosevelt, NM	35041	7	18 238	18.3	4	15	3 577	6 636	94.3	3 739	95.8
Sandoval, NM	35043	2	107 460	19.3	4	32	17 144	26 442	87.1	20 360	89.8
San Juan, NM	35045	3	126 208	21.3	4	53	23 569	36 608	93.6	28 682	95.4
San Miguel, NM	35047	6	29 530	17.7	3	23	4 933	9 583	90.9	6 438	95.0
Santa Fe, NM	35049	3	140 855	15.7	2	41	15 667	33 486	79.4	23 538	85.6
Sierra, NM	35051	6	12 815	14.0	1	6	1 574	2 595	90.1	2 156	93.0
Socorro, NM	35053	6	18 148	18.2	2	11	2 489	5 817	94.3	3 840	97.1
Taos, NM	35055	7	31 722	15.3	3	20	4 365	7 505	87.0	5 752	87.8
Torrance, NM	35057	2	17 501	19.3	3	16	5 391	4 660	93.5	3 946	94.2
Union, NM	35059	9	3 850	17.4	2	7	679	1 084	91.6	977	92.5
Valencia, NM	35061	2	69 417	19.7	2	30	13 460	18 520	90.7	14 783	92.7
NEW YORK	36000		19 254 630	17.1	835	4 624	2 882 157	5 217 030	76.4	3 584 279	85.9
Albany, NY	36001	2	297 414	15.6	17	69	42 896	83 713	77.0	50 548	87.1
Allegany, NY	36003	7	50 602	15.9	12	22	8 124	16 263	76.6	9 624	93.7
Bronx, NY	36005	1	1 357 589	20.8	[6]16	[6]55	[6]5 759	419 114	78.5	310 307	85.0
Broome, NY	36007	2	196 947	15.9	11	51	27 555	56 153	89.7	35 644	91.1
Cattaraugus, NY	36009	4	82 502	17.6	12	35	12 065	22 211	82.6	16 729	93.4
Cayuga, NY	36011	4	81 454	17.1	8	28	11 957	20 377	88.5	15 927	93.1
Chautauqua, NY	36013	4	136 409	16.8	18	58	23 437	37 459	92.0	26 607	94.8
Chemung, NY	36015	3	89 512	16.9	4	27	13 458	22 739	79.9	17 140	88.2
Chenango, NY	36017	6	51 755	17.8	9	25	9 908	13 094	93.3	10 767	95.8
Clinton, NY	36019	5	82 047	15.3	9	35	13 671	22 184	90.3	14 676	90.5

[1]County type codes are from the Economic Research Service of the United States Department of Agriculture. See notes and definitions at the end of this section.
[6]Public schools in Bronx County, New York County, Queens County, and Richmond County are included with Kings County. A small number of charter schools are separately included for the other boroughs in columns 3 through 5.

Table C-1. Population, School, and Student Characteristics by County—*Continued*

STATE County	Characteristics of students, 2004–2005				Outcomes		Staff and students, 2004–2005		
	Percent with IEP2	Percent eligible for free or reduced-price lunch	Percent minority	Percent English- language learners	Number of graduates, 2003–2004	Percent dropouts, grades 9–12, 2001–2002	Number of teachers	Student- teacher ratio	Central administration staff
	10	11	12	13	14	15	16	17	18
NEW HAMPSHIRE	14.7	16.6	6.2	1.2	. . .	4.0	15 354	13.5	. . .
Belknap, NH	13.7	21.1	3.4	0.8	. . .	3.9	802	13.0	. . .
Carroll, NH	14.3	22.1	2.0	0.2	. . .	4.2	567	12.3	. . .
Cheshire, NH	15.4	20.1	3.1	0.4	. . .	2.9	785	13.0	. . .
Coos, NH	14.1	31.3	2.7	0.1	. . .	3.3	446	12.0	. . .
Grafton, NH	14.5	20.1	4.6	0.4	. . .	3.8	1 180	11.3	. . .
Hillsborough, NH	14.5	17.0	11.0	2.7	. . .	4.3	4 634	14.5	. . .
Merrimack, NH	14.4	14.9	4.2	0.9	. . .	4.7	1 525	13.9	. . .
Rockingham, NH	14.3	9.3	4.1	0.4	. . .	3.2	3 669	13.5	. . .
Strafford, NH	16.8	21.5	5.5	1.1	. . .	5.3	1 171	14.0	. . .
Sullivan, NH	15.7	24.0	2.2	0.1	. . .	3.8	574	12.1	. . .
NEW JERSEY	. . .	. . .	42.9	. . .	. . .	2.5	114 786	12.1	. . .
Atlantic, NJ	. . .	. . .	47.9	. . .	. . .	5.0	5 018	11.4	. . .
Bergen, NJ	. . .	. . .	36.2	. . .	. . .	1.2	10 921	12.3	. . .
Burlington, NJ	. . .	. . .	30.5	. . .	. . .	1.4	6 213	12.2	556
Camden, NJ	. . .	. . .	46.5	. . .	. . .	4.0	7 336	12.2	. . .
Cape May, NJ	. . .	. . .	16.7	. . .	. . .	1.9	1 362	10.3	. . .
Cumberland, NJ	. . .	. . .	57.0	. . .	. . .	4.8	1 550	10.8	177
Essex, NJ	. . .	. . .	71.3	. . .	. . .	2.8	10 587	11.7	. . .
Gloucester, NJ	. . .	. . .	19.0	. . .	. . .	2.1	3 818	12.7	. . .
Hudson, NJ	. . .	. . .	81.2	. . .	. . .	4.1	7 060	11.7	755
Hunterdon, NJ	. . .	. . .	7.3	. . .	. . .	0.8	1 976	11.7	. . .
Mercer, NJ	. . .	. . .	50.0	. . .	. . .	4.5	4 883	12.3	. . .
Middlesex, NJ	. . .	. . .	52.4	. . .	. . .	1.5	9 286	12.6	. . .
Monmouth, NJ	. . .	. . .	23.9	. . .	. . .	1.2	8 830	12.4	. . .
Morris, NJ	. . .	. . .	22.2	. . .	. . .	0.8	6 480	12.2	. . .
Ocean, NJ	. . .	. . .	15.5	. . .	. . .	2.3	5 912	13.3	. . .
Passaic, NJ	. . .	. . .	62.2	. . .	. . .	4.5	6 875	11.7	. . .
Salem, NJ	. . .	. . .	29.6	. . .	. . .	2.4	1 054	11.5	112
Somerset, NJ	. . .	. . .	34.9	. . .	. . .	0.8	4 370	12.1	. . .
Sussex, NJ	. . .	. . .	8.0	. . .	. . .	1.4	2 214	12.8	. . .
Union, NJ	. . .	. . .	58.8	. . .	. . .	3.2	7 420	11.7	. . .
Warren, NJ	. . .	. . .	10.9	. . .	. . .	3.1	1 621	11.7	. . .
NEW MEXICO	19.0	50.1	68.1	19.1	. . .	5.2	21 730	15.0	. . .
Bernalillo, NM	19.3	49.3	65.0	14.9	4 577	7.1	6 199	15.1	1 204
Catron, NM	20.9	56.1	39.1	0.0	27	. . .	37	9.7	4
Chaves, NM	23.7	68.7	65.5	10.6	593	8.0	688	16.2	82
Cibola, NM	16.6	77.4	80.5	13.8	228	8.0	256	14.4	30
Colfax, NM	21.9	69.5	55.5	4.0	168	3.4	188	12.4	9
Curry, NM	19.2	62.8	54.4	7.4	419	5.7	599	15.5	70
DeBaca, NM	25.5	55.3	42.6	0.9	23	0.9	30	11.0	3
Dona Ana, NM	20.8	67.2	82.1	29.7	2 662	4.8	2 535	15.5	304
Eddy, NM	24.2	55.4	54.3	7.6	644	1.4	657	15.4	50
Grant, NM	19.6	62.8	65.7	20.0	356	3.8	339	13.9	17
Guadalupe, NM	18.2	64.6	95.6	44.0	60	0.7	64	12.1	8
Harding, NM	20.4	55.5	46.0	0.0	11	. . .	19	7.2	3
Hidalgo, NM	19.2	75.2	73.3	8.4	60	3.3	79	13.1	15
Lea, NM	17.7	60.9	61.8	15.6	721	3.2	752	15.6	72
Lincoln, NM	17.2	62.5	51.3	13.9	193	4.0	241	14.3	27
Los Alamos, NM	31.9	0.0	24.4	1.4	274	2.5	253	14.3	47
Luna, NM	11.4	80.2	81.0	24.2	286	1.4	315	17.3	35
McKinley, NM	15.0	78.3	93.7	40.4	1 009	3.5	1 012	14.7	200
Mora, NM	25.5	79.2	89.5	26.8	52	1.7	71	11.3	15
Otero, NM	19.1	47.8	46.2	2.8	497	1.6	553	14.9	92
Quay, NM	21.2	69.4	54.5	2.0	107	7.7	139	12.1	14
Rio Arriba, NM	14.2	74.2	95.9	47.9	336	10.1	447	15.0	69
Roosevelt, NM	19.8	68.5	51.4	6.7	220	2.0	242	14.8	32
Sandoval, NM	18.1	45.3	58.1	18.2	988	3.6	1 151	14.9	171
San Juan, NM	19.6	57.0	64.2	30.9	1 347	6.0	1 558	15.1	190
San Miguel, NM	18.8	68.3	91.9	49.8	303	1.6	364	13.5	59
Santa Fe, NM	18.0	51.7	76.4	19.7	652	6.5	1 051	14.9	111
Sierra, NM	23.0	71.8	47.5	20.6	89	2.6	105	14.9	9
Socorro, NM	21.7	61.4	73.6	6.5	132	2.2	181	13.8	26
Taos, NM	20.8	58.0	82.4	15.9	274	4.4	316	13.8	36
Torrance, NM	20.8	65.3	43.1	4.9	284	1.2	367	14.7	36
Union, NM	17.4	60.8	46.8	0.0	66	4.2	63	10.8	6
Valencia, NM	23.0	64.1	71.4	8.5	648	4.7	857	15.7	84
NEW YORK	. . .	18.2	46.9	. . .	. . .	7.1	. . .	. . .	. . .
Albany, NY	. . .	30.6	28.6	. . .	. . .	2.1	. . .	. . .	. . .
Allegany, NY	. . .	45.8	2.2	. . .	. . .	3.8	. . .	. . .	. . .
Bronx, NY	. . .	0.9	95.8	. . .	. . .	(6)	. . .	. . .	. . .
Broome, NY	. . .	36.2	12.9	. . .	. . .	1.8	. . .	. . .	. . .
Cattaraugus, NY	. . .	41.1	10.0	. . .	. . .	4.4	. . .	. . .	. . .
Cayuga, NY	. . .	27.9	6.5	. . .	. . .	5.5	. . .	. . .	. . .
Chautauqua, NY	. . .	40.4	12.0	. . .	. . .	4.5	. . .	. . .	. . .
Chemung, NY	. . .	40.1	12.8	. . .	. . .	5.2	. . .	. . .	. . .
Chenango, NY	. . .	42.8	3.2	. . .	. . .	2.5	. . .	. . .	. . .
Clinton, NY	. . .	30.8	3.9	. . .	. . .	3.9	. . .	. . .	. . .

2IEP = Individual Education Program. See notes and definitions at the end of this section.
6Public schools in Bronx County, New York County, Queens County, and Richmond County are included with Kings County. A small number of charter schools are separately included for the other boroughs in columns 3 through 5.
. . . = Not available.

Table C-1. Population, School, and Student Characteristics by County—*Continued*

STATE County	Revenue, 2003–2004				Current expenditures, 2003–2004			Resident population, 16 to 19 years, 2000			
	Total revenue (thousands of dollars)	Percent of revenue from:			Total expenditures (thousands of dollars)	Amount per student (dollars)	Percent for instruction	Total	Percent in armed forces	Percent high school graduates	Percent not enrolled, not employed, not in armed forces, not high school graduate
		Federal government	State government	Local government							
	19	20	21	22	23	24	25	26	27	28	29
NEW HAMPSHIRE	2 202 560	5.4	44.0	50.6	1 867 599	9 158	67.3	67 668	0.0	8.9	3.1
Belknap, NH	123 620	5.5	39.8	54.7	97 591	9 484	65.9	2 705	0.0	9.9	4.1
Carroll, NH	90 309	6.0	39.4	54.6	74 121	10 273	68.1	2 073	0.0	11.4	2.3
Cheshire, NH	130 244	5.9	41.8	52.3	112 418	10 901	66.2	5 241	0.0	6.8	3.1
Coos, NH	60 705	8.8	45.1	46.1	50 305	9 401	63.8	1 721	0.0	8.7	5.1
Grafton, NH	171 072	4.8	36.8	58.4	150 562	11 035	68.3	6 267	0.0	6.7	2.9
Hillsborough, NH	639 282	5.9	47.4	46.8	557 238	8 302	68.1	19 010	0.1	9.0	3.3
Merrimack, NH	221 309	5.0	44.5	50.5	187 364	8 850	65.9	7 363	0.0	8.7	3.1
Rockingham, NH	509 127	3.6	43.4	53.1	423 008	9 346	67.0	13 218	0.1	9.2	2.8
Strafford, NH	174 997	7.3	45.7	47.0	144 775	8 718	67.6	8 166	0.0	9.9	2.6
Sullivan, NH	81 895	8.4	45.2	46.4	70 217	10 099	70.0	1 904	0.0	11.1	3.2
NEW JERSEY	21 547 880	4.2	41.1	54.6	18 481 945	13 443	62.8	408 187	0.2	8.9	4.3
Atlantic, NJ	703 985	5.5	40.4	54.1	588 280	12 674	62.4	12 559	0.0	10.2	5.5
Bergen, NJ	2 101 808	2.8	19.3	78.0	1 774 801	13 648	63.5	37 929	0.0	6.7	1.7
Burlington, NJ	1 153 884	4.3	39.5	56.2	946 233	12 498	62.1	21 045	1.2	9.8	3.9
Camden, NJ	1 313 866	5.8	52.5	41.6	1 157 873	12 993	64.0	27 751	0.0	8.2	6.2
Cape May, NJ	259 672	5.1	30.3	64.6	212 208	14 248	61.7	4 563	3.3	11.6	4.0
Cumberland, NJ	402 576	7.7	74.4	17.9	377 991	14 526	63.3	7 976	0.0	11.4	6.0
Essex, NJ	2 338 312	5.2	57.8	37.0	2 006 458	15 766	61.5	41 257	0.1	10.3	6.9
Gloucester, NJ	657 218	4.1	45.0	50.9	557 628	11 751	60.9	14 528	0.0	9.4	2.8
Hudson, NJ	1 349 389	7.2	66.4	26.5	1 225 670	15 045	65.9	29 361	0.1	10.0	7.7
Hunterdon, NJ	372 541	1.7	18.5	79.9	316 473	14 006	58.7	5 282	0.0	5.9	2.2
Mercer, NJ	1 078 159	3.1	43.6	53.3	855 392	14 528	62.2	19 442	0.1	7.0	4.0
Middlesex, NJ	1 641 788	3.6	33.5	62.9	1 467 757	12 777	63.5	37 947	0.0	8.1	3.6
Monmouth, NJ	1 649 502	3.3	34.8	61.9	1 389 171	12 809	62.4	29 062	1.0	8.1	2.6
Morris, NJ	1 212 534	2.0	21.2	76.8	1 048 184	13 404	61.6	20 713	0.0	6.3	1.8
Ocean, NJ	1 026 207	4.0	37.6	58.4	878 541	11 175	63.9	21 495	0.2	10.7	2.8
Passaic, NJ	1 331 472	5.8	56.4	37.8	1 134 156	14 286	64.2	25 693	0.0	10.8	7.1
Salem, NJ	165 703	6.2	49.2	44.6	143 982	12 206	62.7	3 614	0.0	10.2	3.7
Somerset, NJ	790 349	2.2	21.5	76.3	651 334	12 677	62.3	11 724	0.0	7.4	2.0
Sussex, NJ	392 213	2.8	34.8	62.4	353 705	12 447	61.1	7 179	0.0	8.9	1.5
Union, NJ	1 330 897	4.2	41.3	54.5	1 161 980	13 645	62.3	24 207	0.0	9.8	3.9
Warren, NJ	275 805	3.5	39.4	57.1	234 128	12 484	61.8	4 860	0.0	11.6	2.3
NEW MEXICO	2 855 893	17.2	69.7	13.1	2 368 418	7 331	61.2	113 028	0.4	11.2	7.5
Bernalillo, NM	720 897	12.9	72.1	15.0	616 905	6 814	63.9	31 866	0.5	12.3	7.0
Catron, NM	7 340	10.4	83.6	6.1	4 646	12 489	56.1	188	0.0	8.5	13.3
Chaves, NM	92 550	14.7	75.9	9.4	80 188	7 172	60.8	4 460	0.3	10.1	8.2
Cibola, NM	36 475	28.8	63.1	8.1	29 355	7 912	62.2	1 603	0.1	17.2	7.4
Colfax, NM	26 603	10.0	80.7	9.3	20 850	8 983	59.8	952	0.2	10.8	10.5
Curry, NM	70 363	14.4	76.9	8.8	61 223	6 673	60.8	2 839	7.6	19.2	5.5
DeBaca, NM	4 203	8.4	77.7	13.9	3 641	11 169	58.7	131	0.0	7.6	3.8
Dona Ana, NM	319 882	14.2	75.4	10.3	271 031	7 050	61.1	12 338	0.1	8.2	6.6
Eddy, NM	95 242	10.1	72.9	17.0	79 941	7 734	62.5	3 339	0.0	11.7	7.7
Grant, NM	48 333	12.9	75.0	12.1	41 135	8 524	59.7	1 799	0.0	13.3	7.1
Guadalupe, NM	13 103	11.2	79.2	9.6	8 743	10 929	55.8	279	0.0	20.1	5.0
Harding, NM	4 126	5.4	86.5	8.1	2 487	16 362	48.1	44	0.0	0.0	6.8
Hidalgo, NM	13 596	12.4	76.4	11.1	10 477	10 074	55.6	389	0.0	10.5	6.4
Lea, NM	92 564	12.3	71.1	16.6	78 904	6 705	61.0	4 063	0.1	9.1	7.1
Lincoln, NM	34 322	10.7	77.6	11.7	29 451	8 566	59.6	950	0.8	13.5	3.9
Los Alamos, NM	34 885	23.9	61.1	15.0	31 804	8 721	61.2	963	0.0	5.1	3.0
Luna, NM	41 588	18.0	74.8	7.2	35 353	6 462	62.9	1 570	0.0	10.3	13.1
McKinley, NM	157 069	51.6	42.6	5.9	124 891	8 146	59.9	5 677	0.0	9.0	9.0
Mora, NM	13 394	21.8	73.5	4.7	10 355	12 690	55.2	348	0.0	12.4	5.7
Otero, NM	69 621	17.4	72.8	9.8	60 120	7 167	61.0	3 602	2.3	14.4	8.9
Quay, NM	22 140	10.6	78.3	11.1	15 702	9 242	61.4	600	0.0	4.5	9.3
Rio Arriba, NM	76 229	20.4	61.8	17.8	56 365	8 694	55.9	2 409	0.0	8.2	11.7
Roosevelt, NM	35 030	11.0	78.1	10.9	26 883	7 642	58.4	1 397	0.0	9.6	6.2
Sandoval, NM	141 027	17.7	68.8	13.5	118 847	7 223	61.5	5 178	0.0	13.1	7.3
San Juan, NM	215 014	26.6	57.3	16.1	173 087	7 394	61.4	8 335	0.0	10.9	7.7
San Miguel, NM	60 705	19.5	71.3	9.3	47 364	9 324	56.0	2 274	0.0	5.0	3.8
Santa Fe, NM	143 331	11.7	64.6	23.7	104 526	6 713	60.6	6 863	0.0	11.6	8.3
Sierra, NM	14 800	15.2	72.8	12.0	12 898	7 879	58.4	602	0.0	5.6	8.8
Socorro, NM	25 621	24.5	67.8	7.7	22 284	9 029	59.5	1 361	0.5	11.1	8.1
Taos, NM	51 124	16.9	73.9	9.1	45 136	9 033	57.3	1 664	0.0	17.3	8.2
Torrance, NM	48 251	10.7	77.4	11.9	39 846	7 284	57.5	968	0.0	10.5	12.1
Union, NM	9 539	10.9	77.5	11.6	8 488	11 470	54.5	230	0.0	6.1	0.0
Valencia, NM	116 974	11.7	76.4	11.9	95 492	7 093	58.7	3 747	0.0	10.3	9.3
NEW YORK	40 932 652	7.5	43.3	49.2	37 419 525	13 150	71.7	1 017 375	0.3	8.1	5.6
Albany, NY	553 256	6.5	37.1	56.5	520 867	12 681	67.6	17 925	0.0	6.4	3.0
Allegany, NY	122 697	7.8	70.6	21.6	108 403	13 344	62.8	4 482	0.0	5.5	2.3
Bronx, NY	(6)	(6)	(6)	(6)	(6)	(6)	(6)	80 832	0.0	7.7	11.1
Broome, NY	401 911	6.5	56.1	37.4	367 708	11 472	70.4	12 657	0.0	7.7	3.0
Cattaraugus, NY	214 026	7.9	67.2	24.9	189 255	11 751	69.8	5 430	0.0	10.3	6.4
Cayuga, NY	139 526	6.4	61.8	31.8	124 245	10 618	71.7	4 806	0.0	10.7	6.1
Chautauqua, NY	308 411	7.9	63.0	29.1	269 541	11 501	71.9	9 278	2.4	8.2	5.8
Chemung, NY	164 684	8.3	62.6	29.1	147 306	11 245	67.8	5 057	0.0	10.2	7.3
Chenango, NY	130 777	7.6	70.4	22.0	111 772	11 607	67.9	2 771	0.0	9.7	5.2
Clinton, NY	178 315	6.1	60.1	33.8	159 316	11 998	69.8	5 362	0.0	7.4	5.4

6Public schools in Bronx County, New York County, Queens County, and Richmond County are included with Kings County. A small number of charter schools are separately included for the other boroughs in columns 3 through 5.

Table C-1. Population, School, and Student Characteristics by County—*Continued*

STATE County	High school graduates, 2000 — Population 25 years and over	High school graduate or less (percent)	High school graduate or more (percent)	College enrollment, 2000 — Number	Percent public	College graduates, 2000 (percent) — Bachelor's degree or more	+/- U.S. percentage with bachelor's degree or more	Non-Hispanic White	Black	American Indian and Alaska Native	Asian or Pacific Islander	Hispanic[3]
	30	31	32	33	34	35	36	37	38	39	40	41
NEW HAMPSHIRE	823 987	42.7	87.4	74 832	60.2	28.7	4.3	28.5	27.8	17.0	54.2	22.7
Belknap, NH	39 260	46.9	85.7	2 006	72.5	23.3	-1.1	23.4	37.0	10.4	24.9	26.9
Carroll, NH	31 534	44.0	88.2	1 231	71.3	26.5	2.1	26.5	31.0	17.8	25.6	31.9
Cheshire, NH	48 032	48.2	86.2	6 717	66.8	26.6	2.2	26.5	36.0	17.3	46.2	28.0
Coos, NH	23 490	64.7	76.9	932	82.3	11.9	-12.5	11.9	11.1	3.8	20.4	23.9
Grafton, NH	52 795	43.3	87.7	9 172	41.2	32.7	8.3	32.4	40.7	16.8	68.4	42.7
Hillsborough, NH	251 908	40.5	87.0	20 594	48.9	30.1	5.7	29.9	24.3	21.0	58.1	18.3
Merrimack, NH	91 278	41.5	88.2	8 216	50.1	29.1	4.7	29.0	26.4	1.5	59.1	28.7
Rockingham, NH	187 172	38.1	90.5	12 255	61.9	31.7	7.3	31.5	32.3	26.0	52.3	26.0
Strafford, NH	70 319	44.1	86.4	12 656	88.2	26.4	2.0	26.2	29.3	19.5	43.9	29.7
Sullivan, NH	28 199	55.5	83.0	1 053	71.4	19.7	-4.7	19.6	64.9	4.8	26.1	24.0
NEW JERSEY	5 657 799	47.3	82.1	470 302	65.4	29.8	5.4	32.3	16.2	16.4	61.9	12.5
Atlantic, NJ	168 546	56.5	78.2	12 659	80.6	18.7	-5.7	21.0	10.8	21.1	30.7	7.2
Bergen, NJ	623 469	39.6	86.6	50 740	58.0	38.2	13.8	38.1	27.3	19.3	60.8	20.8
Burlington, NJ	285 553	44.0	87.2	20 140	71.3	28.4	4.0	29.7	19.8	22.5	48.0	18.8
Camden, NJ	331 765	51.9	80.3	25 699	72.9	24.0	-0.4	26.5	13.9	12.0	47.6	8.6
Cape May, NJ	72 878	54.5	81.9	3 466	72.4	22.0	-2.4	22.6	7.8	28.0	54.3	13.5
Cumberland, NJ	96 899	67.8	68.5	5 087	81.1	11.7	-12.7	14.4	6.0	7.5	46.4	5.6
Essex, NJ	513 570	51.6	75.6	47 684	62.1	27.5	3.1	41.5	14.6	12.7	62.9	10.7
Gloucester, NJ	164 801	52.6	84.3	17 149	76.0	22.0	-2.4	21.9	17.1	17.7	54.2	19.0
Hudson, NJ	408 799	56.3	70.5	41 431	58.0	25.3	0.9	31.8	16.5	19.2	56.4	12.1
Hunterdon, NJ	83 548	34.0	91.5	4 876	68.7	41.8	17.4	42.0	14.4	30.3	70.9	29.6
Mercer, NJ	231 139	43.8	81.8	28 687	54.5	34.0	9.6	39.5	12.8	17.3	71.1	11.6
Middlesex, NJ	501 552	44.7	84.4	54 877	77.1	33.0	8.6	29.7	26.1	22.5	70.4	11.4
Monmouth, NJ	413 058	39.5	87.9	30 358	61.6	34.6	10.2	36.0	14.8	18.1	63.5	16.6
Morris, NJ	323 881	33.4	90.6	25 292	56.0	44.1	19.7	44.8	26.8	27.9	69.9	18.5
Ocean, NJ	358 354	54.7	83.0	20 490	60.2	19.5	-4.9	19.5	15.3	11.3	47.1	12.2
Passaic, NJ	316 401	57.9	73.3	25 785	68.2	21.2	-3.2	27.9	8.7	4.7	48.1	7.8
Salem, NJ	42 789	59.8	79.4	2 436	79.6	15.2	-9.2	16.5	7.2	3.2	48.6	8.9
Somerset, NJ	204 343	31.9	89.6	14 627	65.9	46.5	22.1	47.4	31.5	29.9	76.0	18.5
Sussex, NJ	95 094	43.6	89.8	6 368	72.2	27.2	2.8	27.1	24.5	18.8	56.8	22.5
Union, NJ	351 903	50.4	79.3	28 216	65.1	28.5	4.1	35.0	16.6	16.9	61.0	12.7
Warren, NJ	69 457	50.5	84.9	4 235	64.1	24.4	0.0	24.4	24.7	12.5	51.9	18.5
NEW MEXICO	1 134 801	47.7	78.9	120 265	96.9	23.5	0.0	34.0	10.0	7.7	43.0	10.8
Bernalillo, NM	358 680	40.3	84.4	44 365	87.1	30.5	6.1	42.2	22.9	15.0	38.8	13.8
Catron, NM	2 657	50.6	78.4	92	81.5	18.4	-6.0	20.7	100.0	9.4	100.0	8.3
Chaves, NM	37 811	53.9	72.6	3 290	86.4	16.2	-8.2	22.6	5.9	10.6	54.9	5.1
Cibola, NM	15 273	61.5	75.0	1 259	83.2	12.0	-12.4	23.4	11.8	7.4	29.7	6.0
Colfax, NM	9 518	53.4	80.8	324	81.2	18.5	-5.9	28.4	0.0	7.2	0.0	5.4
Curry, NM	26 403	49.5	78.4	3 355	94.7	15.3	0.1	19.6	11.0	5.9	27.7	4.2
DeBaca, NM	1 584	57.6	72.3	42	100.0	16.2	-8.2	23.2	...	0.0	0.0	2.2
Dona Ana, NM	99 893	52.4	70.0	17 779	93.3	22.3	-2.1	39.3	25.0	14.7	64.2	9.6
Eddy, NM	32 572	59.4	75.0	1 944	83.2	13.5	-10.9	17.3	13.7	8.4	51.4	4.8
Grant, NM	20 350	49.7	79.4	2 049	93.1	20.5	-3.9	28.5	40.0	10.0	28.2	9.8
Guadalupe, NM	3 000	60.2	68.3	218	83.9	10.3	-14.1	18.5	6.4	11.3	100.0	8.5
Harding, NM	609	59.6	72.2	20	75.0	18.1	-6.3	26.2	...	0.0	...	9.0
Hidalgo, NM	3 596	68.1	68.8	116	80.2	9.9	-14.5	17.4	0.0	3.6	0.0	2.9
Lea, NM	33 291	60.8	67.1	2 754	84.4	11.6	-12.8	15.7	5.3	4.4	37.5	4.1
Lincoln, NM	13 849	43.6	84.5	746	93.3	22.8	-1.6	26.5	12.5	16.5	29.1	8.8
Los Alamos, NM	12 822	15.7	96.3	997	88.3	60.5	36.1	63.4	0.0	61.7	76.1	31.7
Luna, NM	15 777	70.1	59.8	539	93.1	10.4	-14.0	15.6	8.1	21.3	26.1	3.7
McKinley, NM	38 988	62.7	65.2	3 502	87.1	12.0	-12.4	42.9	17.0	4.6	58.3	7.2
Mora, NM	3 348	61.9	69.8	212	96.7	15.5	-8.9	34.0	...	6.9	...	10.7
Otero, NM	38 061	48.1	81.0	3 323	90.3	15.4	-9.0	20.2	11.5	8.3	25.2	5.2
Quay, NM	6 970	62.9	73.8	413	94.2	13.7	-10.7	17.1	21.3	0.0	31.9	6.6
Rio Arriba, NM	25 930	58.3	73.0	2 050	81.4	15.4	-9.0	34.6	7.2	9.7	32.5	11.1
Roosevelt, NM	10 245	48.5	75.2	2 589	95.0	22.6	-1.8	28.0	7.6	25.8	77.4	9.2
Sandoval, NM	56 479	42.6	86.0	4 415	81.7	24.8	0.4	33.4	23.2	5.8	37.6	14.2
San Juan, NM	65 262	53.7	76.8	6 004	89.8	13.5	-10.9	19.8	27.5	5.4	25.2	6.5
San Miguel, NM	18 531	51.1	74.5	2 723	80.9	21.2	-3.2	37.5	10.4	25.7	68.1	15.4
Santa Fe, NM	87 870	35.2	84.5	8 294	67.7	36.9	12.5	56.2	30.2	16.8	56.6	14.0
Sierra, NM	9 906	55.3	76.1	352	77.0	13.1	-11.3	14.6	27.8	18.9	44.4	6.7
Socorro, NM	10 642	56.9	72.1	1 715	90.4	19.4	-5.0	31.6	13.5	11.2	73.3	7.6
Taos, NM	20 526	47.5	79.1	1 330	85.0	25.9	1.5	46.7	50.5	10.9	42.4	11.1
Torrance, NM	10 556	55.9	77.1	569	91.0	14.4	-10.0	19.1	1.1	18.1	31.7	4.9
Union, NM	2 786	64.0	79.9	50	82.0	13.0	-11.4	17.2	...	50.0	100.0	2.2
Valencia, NM	40 917	56.2	76.1	2 835	83.6	14.8	-9.6	20.6	15.7	9.4	27.3	8.9
NEW YORK	12 542 536	48.7	79.1	1 301 375	57.0	27.4	3.0	31.8	15.8	14.4	41.2	11.5
Albany, NY	195 381	40.7	86.3	28 317	64.6	33.3	8.9	34.3	15.7	27.8	66.5	30.6
Allegany, NY	30 010	56.4	83.2	6 015	49.4	17.2	-7.2	16.8	8.8	21.5	67.7	20.2
Bronx, NY	794 792	63.5	62.3	86 014	57.5	14.6	-9.8	26.0	14.1	9.4	35.4	8.2
Broome, NY	132 541	49.8	83.8	17 211	92.1	22.7	-1.7	22.3	20.5	2.7	50.4	26.6
Cattaraugus, NY	54 154	60.0	81.2	4 328	44.1	14.9	-9.5	14.9	9.3	10.3	48.5	15.6
Cayuga, NY	54 649	56.9	79.1	3 240	74.6	15.5	-8.9	16.2	3.0	13.7	16.8	7.9
Chautauqua, NY	91 261	55.3	81.2	8 752	89.9	16.9	-7.5	17.5	5.7	6.6	47.0	5.2
Chemung, NY	60 796	54.0	82.1	4 239	55.3	18.6	-5.8	19.0	9.9	3.2	51.7	10.4
Chenango, NY	34 363	59.3	80.6	1 583	86.9	14.4	-10.0	14.4	4.9	11.7	51.9	19.6
Clinton, NY	51 598	57.1	76.4	6 653	95.8	17.8	-6.6	18.5	3.1	10.4	36.4	6.6

[3]May be of any race.
. . . = Not available.

Table C-1. Population, School, and Student Characteristics by County—*Continued*

STATE County	State/county code	County type[1]	Population, 2005		Number of schools and students, 2004–2005			Resident enrollment, 2000			
			Total	Percent 5 to 17 years	School districts	Schools	Students	Total	Percent public	K–12	Percent public
			1	2	3	4	5	6	7	8	9
Columbia, NY	36021	6	63 622	17.0	7	22	9 650	15 183	85.1	12 255	89.8
Cortland, NY	36023	4	48 622	15.8	5	18	7 576	15 221	92.8	8 751	93.4
Delaware, NY	36025	6	47 534	15.9	14	28	7 987	11 874	93.4	8 884	97.2
Dutchess, NY	36027	2	294 849	17.6	14	86	48 022	78 962	77.2	53 680	89.2
Erie, NY	36029	1	930 703	17.1	47	245	147 361	256 351	78.9	176 728	85.1
Essex, NY	36031	6	38 676	15.2	11	16	4 856	8 857	89.2	7 210	92.4
Franklin, NY	36033	5	51 033	15.3	8	27	9 189	12 024	87.7	9 270	96.0
Fulton, NY	36035	4	55 625	17.1	8	26	10 240	13 249	93.7	10 748	96.9
Genesee, NY	36037	4	59 257	17.9	9	23	10 798	16 129	87.5	12 183	90.8
Greene, NY	36039	6	49 682	16.3	6	19	8 546	10 810	88.9	8 504	93.9
Hamilton, NY	36041	8	5 228	13.3	7	7	623	1 059	92.0	868	94.2
Herkimer, NY	36043	2	63 780	16.7	12	25	11 137	16 600	92.9	12 567	97.5
Jefferson, NY	36045	4	116 384	17.7	12	40	18 574	28 331	89.9	21 771	92.0
Kings, NY	36047	1	2 486 235	18.4	[6]19	[6]1 261	[6]1 029 143	731 672	73.8	512 325	79.7
Lewis, NY	36049	6	26 571	18.2	5	13	4 597	6 915	92.4	6 031	95.0
Livingston, NY	36051	1	64 205	15.4	8	25	9 659	19 552	88.4	11 944	92.1
Madison, NY	36053	2	70 337	16.7	9	21	9 333	20 630	79.0	13 451	95.8
Monroe, NY	36055	1	733 366	17.9	24	191	123 747	214 378	76.3	145 226	89.3
Montgomery, NY	36057	4	48 968	17.0	5	17	7 952	11 609	89.2	9 532	92.9
Nassau, NY	36059	1	1 333 137	17.8	57	310	207 338	357 675	73.7	246 184	86.3
New York, NY	36061	1	1 593 200	10.8	[6]19	[6]73	[6]7 456	358 066	60.2	195 948	78.0
Niagara, NY	36063	1	217 008	17.2	10	59	34 891	57 484	82.9	41 852	88.9
Oneida, NY	36065	2	234 105	16.8	18	92	40 786	60 218	84.4	44 252	92.7
Onondaga, NY	36067	2	458 053	17.9	23	130	80 669	132 420	76.0	89 450	91.3
Ontario, NY	36069	1	104 461	17.2	8	27	16 398	26 901	81.4	19 305	92.7
Orange, NY	36071	2	372 893	20.3	18	90	65 179	101 077	79.1	75 204	86.4
Orleans, NY	36073	1	43 387	18.2	6	17	8 142	10 701	92.0	8 851	95.3
Oswego, NY	36075	2	123 373	18.0	9	38	23 276	35 840	93.8	25 412	96.5
Otsego, NY	36077	6	62 746	14.7	12	23	9 251	19 248	90.9	11 317	95.1
Putnam, NY	36079	1	100 507	18.7	6	22	16 948	25 652	78.7	18 867	89.6
Queens, NY	36081	1	2 241 600	15.7	[6]11	[6]22	[6]5 693	586 090	75.1	389 860	82.8
Rensselaer, NY	36083	2	155 251	16.7	14	46	23 472	42 526	73.1	27 840	88.2
Richmond, NY	36085	1	464 573	18.0	[6]1	[6]1	[6]650	122 303	69.2	85 662	75.4
Rockland, NY	36087	1	292 916	19.6	10	70	43 185	84 629	62.3	60 015	69.8
St. Lawrence, NY	36089	5	111 380	15.5	18	46	17 446	32 990	80.4	20 580	94.6
Saratoga, NY	36091	2	214 859	16.9	11	49	31 790	51 400	82.0	37 384	93.5
Schenectady, NY	36093	2	149 078	17.2	8	46	26 678	37 662	81.0	26 871	92.1
Schoharie, NY	36095	2	32 277	16.1	6	15	5 479	8 606	89.5	5 836	95.9
Schuyler, NY	36097	6	19 342	17.3	2	8	2 417	4 643	90.4	3 770	93.8
Seneca, NY	36099	6	34 855	16.2	4	15	5 214	8 433	83.2	6 410	89.8
Steuben, NY	36101	4	98 632	17.8	16	44	18 997	24 686	90.3	19 977	93.6
Suffolk, NY	36103	1	1 474 927	18.5	77	357	272 746	387 491	82.8	273 741	92.7
Sullivan, NY	36105	4	76 539	17.4	9	26	11 663	18 389	86.8	14 622	91.8
Tioga, NY	36107	2	51 475	18.2	7	28	13 300	13 238	89.8	10 850	93.5
Tompkins, NY	36109	3	100 018	11.5	8	34	13 082	42 942	47.7	14 395	94.5
Ulster, NY	36111	3	182 693	16.3	11	56	31 233	46 266	87.5	32 223	92.1
Warren, NY	36113	3	65 548	16.2	9	21	11 107	15 874	88.8	11 896	96.7
Washington, NY	36115	3	63 024	16.7	12	25	11 439	14 653	92.8	12 040	96.9
Wayne, NY	36117	1	93 609	19.0	12	40	18 369	24 533	90.1	19 792	94.2
Westchester, NY	36119	1	940 807	18.1	49	257	149 900	244 926	71.3	170 768	84.4
Wyoming, NY	36121	6	42 693	16.1	5	15	5 552	10 379	90.0	8 372	94.0
Yates, NY	36123	6	24 756	18.6	3	9	4 591	6 376	74.7	4 836	85.5
NORTH CAROLINA	37000		8 683 242	17.7	216	2 289	1 385 650	2 043 225	86.2	1 445 635	92.0
Alamance, NC	37001	3	140 533	17.5	5	37	22 798	32 488	79.8	23 114	92.3
Alexander, NC	37003	2	35 492	17.5	1	10	5 680	7 232	92.4	5 825	96.4
Alleghany, NC	37005	9	10 900	14.5	1	4	1 573	2 029	93.6	1 524	98.4
Anson, NC	37007	1	25 499	17.7	1	9	4 414	6 464	94.1	5 003	96.1
Ashe, NC	37009	9	25 347	14.4	1	5	3 288	4 610	94.8	3 566	95.8
Avery, NC	37011	8	17 641	13.6	3	11	2 528	3 841	81.1	2 609	92.2
Beaufort, NC	37013	6	46 018	16.7	2	15	7 657	10 641	91.0	8 251	93.0
Bertie, NC	37015	9	19 480	18.3	1	10	3 421	4 939	88.9	4 164	89.8
Bladen, NC	37017	6	32 938	18.0	1	14	5 937	7 732	92.5	5 739	94.0
Brunswick, NC	37019	2	89 162	15.4	2	17	11 631	14 593	88.9	11 662	91.4
Buncombe, NC	37021	2	218 876	15.9	5	52	29 898	47 002	85.1	33 328	90.9
Burke, NC	37023	2	89 399	17.8	2	27	14 965	20 594	91.6	16 382	96.3
Cabarrus, NC	37025	1	150 244	18.7	2	29	22 806	32 182	87.2	24 893	92.8
Caldwell, NC	37027	2	79 122	17.3	1	25	13 041	16 808	91.5	13 418	95.0
Camden, NC	37029	8	8 967	17.0	1	3	1 691	1 720	93.3	1 353	97.4
Carteret, NC	37031	4	62 525	14.9	3	18	8 611	12 345	86.8	9 458	90.1
Caswell, NC	37033	8	23 608	17.0	1	6	3 430	5 432	91.7	4 358	93.9
Catawba, NC	37035	2	151 641	17.6	4	42	24 534	32 637	88.3	25 244	95.3
Chatham, NC	37037	2	58 002	16.4	3	17	7 881	10 643	88.9	8 127	92.9
Cherokee, NC	37039	9	25 796	15.0	2	14	3 867	4 813	94.5	3 761	95.6

[1]County type codes are from the Economic Research Service of the United States Department of Agriculture. See notes and definitions at the end of this section.
[6]Public schools in Bronx County, New York County, Queens County, and Richmond County are included with Kings County. A small number of charter schools are separately included for the other boroughs in columns 3 through 5.

PART C—COUNTY EDUCATION STATISTICS 417

Table C-1. Population, School, and Student Characteristics by County—*Continued*

STATE County	Characteristics of students, 2004–2005				Outcomes		Staff and students, 2004–2005		
	Percent with IEP2	Percent eligible for free or reduced-price lunch	Percent minority	Percent English-language learners	Number of graduates, 2003–2004	Percent dropouts, grades 9–12, 2001–2002	Number of teachers	Student-teacher ratio	Central administration staff
	10	11	12	13	14	15	16	17	18
Columbia, NY	...	32.2	13.4	...	...	2.3	...	...	...
Cortland, NY	...	33.4	4.1	...	...	3.6	...	...	...
Delaware, NY	...	42.1	4.8	...	...	1.7	...	...	...
Dutchess, NY	...	20.4	24.8	...	...	4.2	...	...	...
Erie, NY	...	38.2	28.5	...	...	4.3	...	...	...
Essex, NY	...	40.0	2.1	...	...	2.7	...	...	...
Franklin, NY	...	40.8	13.3	...	...	1.9	...	...	...
Fulton, NY	...	34.0	4.5	...	...	2.6	...	...	...
Genesee, NY	...	29.6	7.7	...	...	3.3	...	...	...
Greene, NY	...	34.6	7.8	...	...	3.8	...	...	...
Hamilton, NY	...	26.4	1.4	...	...	3.9	...	...	...
Herkimer, NY	...	38.2	2.8	...	...	4.0	...	...	...
Jefferson, NY	...	43.5	12.9	...	...	3.5	...	...	...
Kings, NY	...	...	85.6	...	...	6]14.2	...	...	...
Lewis, NY	...	46.1	2.8	...	...	2.7	...	...	...
Livingston, NY	...	26.0	4.8	...	...	2.5	...	...	...
Madison, NY	...	29.4	3.1	...	...	3.2	...	...	...
Monroe, NY	...	34.8	34.8	...	...	4.3	...	...	...
Montgomery, NY	...	39.5	15.4	...	...	4.1	...	...	...
Nassau, NY	...	15.0	35.1	...	...	2.0	...	...	...
New York, NY	...	...	88.8	...	...	(6)	...	...	...
Niagara, NY	...	33.1	16.6	...	...	5.2	...	...	...
Oneida, NY	...	41.5	15.3	...	...	3.3	...	...	...
Onondaga, NY	...	32.3	24.6	...	...	3.3	...	...	...
Ontario, NY	...	23.8	8.3	...	...	2.9	...	...	...
Orange, NY	...	28.3	32.5	...	...	2.3	...	...	...
Orleans, NY	...	34.4	10.9	...	...	4.4	...	...	...
Oswego, NY	...	37.6	3.3	...	...	5.3	...	...	...
Otsego, NY	...	33.9	5.4	...	...	2.0	...	...	...
Putnam, NY	...	6.8	11.8	...	...	1.4	...	...	...
Queens, NY	...	...	85.4	...	...	(6)	...	...	...
Rensselaer, NY	...	29.8	14.0	...	...	3.5	...	...	...
Richmond, NY	...	...	43.1	...	...	(6)	...	...	...
Rockland, NY	...	22.2	41.8	...	...	3.3	...	...	...
St. Lawrence, NY	...	45.1	4.6	...	...	3.7	...	...	...
Saratoga, NY	...	15.2	4.9	...	...	1.1	...	...	...
Schenectady, NY	...	32.2	25.8	...	...	0.4	...	...	...
Schoharie, NY	...	34.6	2.9	...	...	2.9	...	...	...
Schuyler, NY	...	34.3	3.5	...	...	4.7	...	...	...
Seneca, NY	...	37.3	6.0	...	...	3.7	...	...	...
Steuben, NY	...	42.7	4.1	...	...	4.8	...	...	...
Suffolk, NY	...	19.6	26.7	...	...	2.2	...	...	...
Sullivan, NY	...	39.9	28.4	...	...	3.8	...	...	...
Tioga, NY	...	35.3	3.2	...	...	2.8	...	...	...
Tompkins, NY	...	29.4	15.5	...	...	2.0	...	...	...
Ulster, NY	...	26.3	18.2	...	...	5.0	...	...	...
Warren, NY	...	24.7	4.1	...	...	2.5	...	...	...
Washington, NY	...	32.4	2.1	...	...	2.8	...	...	...
Wayne, NY	...	31.6	9.9	...	...	3.1	...	...	...
Westchester, NY	...	28.3	44.7	...	...	3.0	...	...	...
Wyoming, NY	...	28.7	1.7	...	...	2.6	...	...	...
Yates, NY	...	41.9	2.6	...	...	2.8	...	...	...
NORTH CAROLINA	13.9	46.2	42.6	4.9	...	5.7	92 542	15.0	...
Alamance, NC	14.7	41.0	40.2	10.3	...	5.6	1 554	14.7	...
Alexander, NC	14.2	40.7	15.1	7.1	302	8.1	347	16.4	25
Alleghany, NC	19.2	56.4	10.6	6.2	98	3.6	138	11.4	19
Anson, NC	18.7	70.4	65.6	1.2	206	6.5	303	14.6	25
Ashe, NC	15.6	52.0	5.7	3.2	195	6.6	248	13.3	19
Avery, NC	16.4	52.2	6.0	3.2	...	4.1	204	12.4	...
Beaufort, NC	17.0	61.3	48.1	5.1	...	6.9	562	13.6	38
Bertie, NC	14.1	84.9	86.8	0.4	193	5.7	231	14.8	29
Bladen, NC	12.5	66.5	57.2	5.0	303	4.1	405	14.7	33
Brunswick, NC	14.6	50.6	28.9	2.8	...	9.1	753	15.4	...
Buncombe, NC	13.1	40.4	20.3	4.2	...	6.1	2 037	14.7	...
Burke, NC	16.2	50.4	23.1	9.1	...	5.0	1 039	14.4	...
Cabarrus, NC	14.9	35.8	30.4	5.6	...	5.0	1 537	14.8	...
Caldwell, NC	11.6	44.2	14.0	3.1	624	5.1	881	14.8	56
Camden, NC	14.4	28.1	17.5	0.1	96	5.6	113	15.0	12
Carteret, NC	16.9	38.2	15.0	1.4	...	4.9	659	13.1	...
Caswell, NC	14.0	52.0	47.4	1.7	226	4.0	242	14.2	23
Catawba, NC	13.4	40.0	30.4	10.7	...	4.9	1 617	15.2	88
Chatham, NC	12.1	41.3	40.3	12.7	...	7.6	516	15.3	...
Cherokee, NC	15.6	55.2	7.0	0.4	...	3.4	286	13.5	17

2IEP = Individual Education Program. See notes and definitions at the end of this section.
6Public schools in Bronx County, New York County, Queens County, and Richmond County are included with Kings County. A small number of charter schools are separately included for the other boroughs in columns 3 through 5.
... = Not available.

THE ALMANAC OF AMERICAN EDUCATION (BERNAN PRESS)

Table C-1. Population, School, and Student Characteristics by County—Continued

STATE County	Total revenue (thousands of dollars)	Percent of revenue from: Federal government	State government	Local government	Total expenditures (thousands of dollars)	Amount per student (dollars)	Percent for instruction	Total	Percent in armed forces	Percent high school graduates	Percent not enrolled, not employed, not in armed forces, not high school graduate
	19	20	21	22	23	24	25	26	27	28	29
Columbia, NY	136 262	6.2	40.9	52.9	122 861	12 732	68.7	3 355	0.1	6.4	3.6
Cortland, NY	92 093	8.3	65.4	26.3	84 903	11 207	70.2	3 836	0.1	6.6	2.8
Delaware, NY	109 347	5.9	53.5	40.6	93 730	13 155	68.3	3 127	0.0	7.8	3.1
Dutchess, NY	594 778	3.9	41.7	54.5	549 457	11 541	69.5	16 633	0.1	7.0	5.3
Erie, NY	1 816 399	8.2	54.2	37.6	1 628 364	11 798	69.7	50 513	0.0	8.3	4.4
Essex, NY	74 222	6.4	39.6	54.0	65 883	13 567	69.5	1 895	0.0	9.8	4.2
Franklin, NY	120 367	7.9	65.7	26.4	109 560	12 538	69.4	2 877	0.0	8.9	5.0
Fulton, NY	112 982	7.3	63.2	29.5	102 245	10 260	71.4	2 993	0.2	7.4	6.3
Genesee, NY	136 734	5.6	62.9	31.6	122 343	11 764	69.9	3 500	1.0	11.7	3.2
Greene, NY	102 762	5.2	43.7	51.1	90 855	10 631	67.4	2 717	0.0	10.8	27.3
Hamilton, NY	16 569	3.2	14.1	82.7	14 077	22 596	65.8	272	0.0	9.9	5.5
Herkimer, NY	141 550	6.9	65.7	27.5	122 300	10 981	71.1	3 633	0.0	7.0	3.6
Jefferson, NY	224 575	12.5	64.6	22.9	196 010	10 816	69.4	6 514	12.1	21.0	4.7
Kings, NY	[6]14 723 474	[6]11.6	[6]41.8	[6]46.5	[6]13 682 193	[6]13 131	[6]75.6	140 351	0.1	8.9	8.0
Lewis, NY	62 117	6.4	70.9	22.8	53 455	11 628	68.5	1 663	0.5	12.7	2.4
Livingston, NY	130 452	4.7	65.0	30.3	108 859	11 270	69.2	5 183	0.0	6.0	3.1
Madison, NY	149 462	5.2	61.0	33.9	129 316	10 882	68.9	5 586	0.0	4.9	2.6
Monroe, NY	1 661 061	6.9	48.5	44.5	1 448 134	12 094	68.3	41 721	0.0	7.5	3.8
Montgomery, NY	102 072	7.3	64.1	28.7	92 013	11 571	69.9	2 523	0.0	9.0	5.9
Nassau, NY	3 673 710	2.6	24.9	72.5	3 412 492	16 137	69.0	64 413	0.0	6.0	2.3
New York, NY	(6)	(6)	(6)	(6)	(6)	(6)	(6)	61 349	0.0	6.1	7.0
Niagara, NY	459 615	6.5	60.0	33.4	404 723	11 600	70.1	12 334	0.1	10.3	3.9
Oneida, NY	454 483	7.5	62.5	30.1	422 584	11 243	70.2	13 254	0.0	7.6	3.4
Onondaga, NY	972 560	7.3	54.0	38.7	881 617	11 367	70.3	26 156	0.0	7.7	4.5
Ontario, NY	243 741	5.4	51.3	43.3	205 086	11 397	71.2	5 640	0.3	7.8	3.5
Orange, NY	894 735	5.4	46.4	48.2	823 573	12 341	69.1	19 867	5.0	12.9	4.7
Orleans, NY	96 058	6.9	67.2	25.9	85 063	10 656	71.9	2 641	0.2	13.3	12.4
Oswego, NY	302 399	7.8	59.6	32.6	276 685	11 276	70.3	7 967	0.0	10.2	5.4
Otsego, NY	122 333	6.6	59.5	33.9	107 219	11 590	69.9	5 220	0.1	5.8	5.1
Putnam, NY	269 909	1.9	31.3	66.8	246 681	14 555	70.6	4 536	0.0	7.5	2.5
Queens, NY	(6)	(6)	(6)	(6)	(6)	(6)	(6)	108 616	0.0	9.0	6.2
Rensselaer, NY	317 071	6.4	54.6	39.0	277 090	12 011	67.5	9 232	0.0	6.9	5.3
Richmond, NY	(6)	(6)	(6)	(6)	(6)	(6)	(6)	22 953	0.1	7.9	4.2
Rockland, NY	732 779	4.9	28.1	67.0	679 078	15 944	69.0	15 172	0.1	5.2	3.9
St. Lawrence, NY	232 196	6.9	68.0	25.0	209 532	12 384	70.2	8 623	0.0	5.3	4.0
Saratoga, NY	440 490	4.5	46.1	49.5	387 533	10 998	69.4	10 398	1.2	7.9	3.0
Schenectady, NY	285 803	7.1	50.1	42.8	255 163	11 182	71.0	7 012	0.0	7.7	4.1
Schoharie, NY	79 102	5.7	61.5	32.8	69 964	12 769	69.4	2 544	0.1	6.8	3.7
Schuyler, NY	32 347	7.3	66.9	25.8	27 522	11 387	68.0	1 235	0.0	11.7	14.5
Seneca, NY	65 900	7.0	62.0	30.9	57 803	11 086	70.0	1 580	0.0	6.5	7.3
Steuben, NY	241 150	7.2	65.6	27.2	214 435	11 441	68.6	5 585	0.0	10.2	6.4
Suffolk, NY	4 097 454	3.1	39.3	57.7	3 753 114	14 275	69.6	68 844	0.0	8.9	3.3
Sullivan, NY	186 956	6.1	43.4	50.6	167 548	14 702	69.6	4 092	0.0	9.8	7.1
Tioga, NY	108 452	6.1	67.8	26.1	97 945	11 176	68.1	2 719	0.0	12.1	4.4
Tompkins, NY	175 517	5.7	43.9	50.4	159 789	12 409	68.8	10 977	0.2	3.9	1.3
Ulster, NY	421 153	4.5	40.3	55.2	383 445	13 421	71.5	9 585	0.3	9.0	5.1
Warren, NY	145 102	5.8	41.5	52.8	128 971	11 612	71.0	3 419	0.3	6.8	4.7
Washington, NY	134 055	6.2	61.3	32.6	120 527	11 032	70.9	3 197	0.0	7.5	11.5
Wayne, NY	238 927	6.0	60.0	33.9	206 695	11 622	68.6	4 896	0.0	10.8	5.0
Westchester, NY	2 679 682	3.9	29.8	66.3	2 448 900	16 477	69.1	41 585	0.0	6.7	4.9
Wyoming, NY	72 187	5.8	67.4	26.7	60 428	10 884	68.8	2 444	0.2	10.4	4.3
Yates, NY	35 905	9.1	50.4	40.5	33 349	11 139	70.2	1 798	0.0	12.8	5.3
NORTH CAROLINA	10 724 729	9.6	57.9	32.5	9 109 578	6 760	65.5	428 384	1.8	11.8	6.4
Alamance, NC	146 151	11.0	65.3	23.7	139 988	6 300	66.9	7 316	0.0	10.1	7.3
Alexander, NC	38 139	11.3	65.8	22.9	34 501	6 163	64.3	1 582	0.0	11.2	4.9
Alleghany, NC	14 589	11.6	66.1	22.3	12 551	8 486	64.0	526	0.0	17.7	9.7
Anson, NC	34 659	17.3	64.7	18.0	31 191	7 074	62.0	1 194	0.0	14.2	6.2
Ashe, NC	33 646	10.1	55.0	34.9	24 441	7 696	63.8	1 108	0.0	16.8	4.9
Avery, NC	24 733	13.9	58.2	27.9	21 186	8 729	63.3	825	0.0	12.2	4.8
Beaufort, NC	56 529	14.4	64.2	21.4	51 553	6 938	65.0	2 219	0.0	14.8	6.4
Bertie, NC	28 251	17.3	70.4	12.4	25 569	7 496	57.1	1 092	0.0	4.6	9.3
Bladen, NC	47 240	16.7	62.7	20.6	39 321	6 840	61.1	1 877	0.0	11.7	12.7
Brunswick, NC	95 932	8.9	52.2	39.0	80 317	7 242	62.3	3 253	5.6	18.1	5.6
Buncombe, NC	243 707	9.3	56.1	34.6	204 886	6 972	65.8	9 782	0.1	13.1	6.7
Burke, NC	105 946	11.3	64.3	24.4	91 768	6 263	65.3	4 896	0.0	12.6	17.4
Cabarrus, NC	247 131	5.9	45.3	48.8	165 030	6 273	65.3	6 202	0.1	9.2	6.0
Caldwell, NC	87 735	8.9	67.0	24.1	79 234	6 154	67.7	3 415	0.0	13.1	8.0
Camden, NC	17 445	4.7	55.3	40.0	11 035	6 984	62.6	404	0.0	4.0	5.2
Carteret, NC	65 879	9.2	60.1	30.8	63 008	7 453	66.8	2 592	0.7	8.9	6.4
Caswell, NC	26 161	10.3	73.3	16.4	24 265	7 081	66.7	1 071	0.0	13.4	6.8
Catawba, NC	180 377	7.9	60.2	31.9	152 879	6 358	69.3	6 953	0.0	13.2	7.1
Chatham, NC	61 425	8.1	58.2	33.7	56 554	7 342	65.4	2 021	0.0	12.3	5.8
Cherokee, NC	35 127	22.2	57.5	20.3	26 506	7 055	67.9	1 110	0.0	6.2	6.9

[6]Public schools in Bronx County, New York County, Queens County, and Richmond County are included with Kings County. A small number of charter schools are separately included for the other boroughs in columns 3 through 5.

Table C-1. Population, School, and Student Characteristics by County—*Continued*

STATE County	High school graduates, 2000			College enrollment, 2000		College graduates, 2000 (percent)						
	Population 25 years and over	High school graduate or less (percent)	High school graduate or more (percent)	Number	Percent public	Bachelor's degree or more	+/- U.S. percentage with bachelor's degree or more	Non-Hispanic White	Black	American Indian and Alaska Native	Asian or Pacific Islander	Hispanic[3]
	30	31	32	33	34	35	36	37	38	39	40	41
Columbia, NY	43 990	51.7	81.0	2 000	70.1	22.6	-1.8	23.3	6.4	13.2	34.7	13.1
Cortland, NY	29 527	53.0	82.8	5 898	94.6	18.8	-5.6	18.8	14.0	9.4	88.5	13.1
Delaware, NY	33 070	57.5	79.9	2 388	85.4	16.6	-7.8	16.5	23.2	13.9	65.9	10.7
Dutchess, NY	183 725	44.1	84.0	20 086	53.2	27.6	3.2	28.9	12.2	16.2	62.4	16.7
Erie, NY	637 676	47.0	82.9	63 289	68.4	24.5	0.1	26.0	11.5	13.1	64.0	15.3
Essex, NY	27 337	57.7	80.4	1 200	81.7	18.3	-6.1	19.0	2.3	17.2	28.0	4.0
Franklin, NY	34 482	64.1	69.7	2 202	58.9	13.0	-11.4	14.8	1.8	7.3	38.5	1.7
Fulton, NY	37 483	60.8	77.8	1 822	82.0	13.5	-10.9	13.6	6.9	0.0	46.0	8.7
Genesee, NY	40 125	53.7	84.4	2 893	82.3	16.3	-8.1	16.6	2.8	7.8	39.3	8.6
Greene, NY	32 570	57.9	78.6	1 577	78.7	16.4	-8.0	17.1	5.7	1.9	27.8	5.0
Hamilton, NY	4 022	53.9	83.4	131	80.9	18.4	-6.0	18.7	0.0	10.0	0.0	0.0
Herkimer, NY	43 455	56.0	79.4	3 133	80.5	15.7	-8.7	15.5	7.7	11.9	48.6	23.2
Jefferson, NY	68 965	53.4	82.9	4 962	89.3	16.0	-8.4	16.5	6.5	9.1	23.9	13.0
Kings, NY	1 552 870	57.9	68.8	174 210	60.1	21.8	-2.6	33.7	14.4	13.5	23.5	8.5
Lewis, NY	17 367	67.1	81.0	617	79.6	11.7	-12.7	11.7	10.6	11.7	35.3	11.1
Livingston, NY	40 081	51.5	82.3	6 866	87.2	19.2	-5.2	20.0	3.8	12.9	36.0	4.7
Madison, NY	43 762	49.8	83.3	6 099	46.9	21.6	-2.8	21.7	9.9	10.0	46.5	18.2
Monroe, NY	477 957	41.3	84.9	56 430	49.5	31.2	6.8	34.2	11.4	15.7	53.7	13.3
Montgomery, NY	33 900	61.1	78.1	1 456	79.7	13.6	-10.8	13.8	4.1	26.9	52.8	4.4
Nassau, NY	908 693	40.1	86.7	81 375	49.0	35.4	11.0	37.7	23.7	13.9	57.4	15.4
New York, NY	1 125 987	34.8	78.7	141 083	37.5	49.4	25.0	73.9	18.9	19.2	45.3	14.0
Niagara, NY	147 153	53.7	83.3	12 165	69.7	17.4	-7.0	17.8	8.0	14.7	46.7	19.2
Oneida, NY	158 846	53.5	79.0	12 772	61.8	18.3	-6.1	19.3	5.9	4.3	27.9	6.5
Onondaga, NY	296 914	43.4	85.7	35 188	40.9	28.5	4.1	29.5	10.5	19.7	55.8	23.3
Ontario, NY	66 539	44.2	87.4	5 865	52.2	24.7	0.3	25.0	10.5	13.1	51.7	13.3
Orange, NY	228 16	49.2	81.8	18 607	64.3	22.5	-1.9	24.1	13.4	11.2	50.3	11.6
Orleans, NY	29 043	63.2	76.4	1 208	84.4	13.0	-11.4	14.1	2.5	4.6	20.7	5.5
Oswego, NY	76 165	60.8	80.4	8 876	90.2	14.4	-10.0	14.2	28.3	18.9	46.5	14.0
Otsego, NY	38 808	51.7	83.0	7 215	86.6	22.0	-2.4	21.8	30.0	23.3	57.2	22.5
Putnam, NY	64 624	37.9	90.2	4 700	55.3	33.9	9.5	34.3	33.1	36.9	64.3	22.6
Queens, NY	1 509 502	53.4	74.4	164 114	61.2	24.3	-0.1	29.2	17.8	14.1	37.6	11.6
Rensselaer, NY	100 233	47.6	84.9	12 107	43.8	23.7	-0.7	23.5	17.1	24.6	71.3	21.2
Richmond, NY	293 795	51.1	82.6	28 243	57.9	23.2	-1.2	23.2	18.7	8.9	46.8	13.0
Rockland, NY	184 012	37.2	85.3	17 843	48.2	37.5	13.1	40.5	22.2	18.2	58.5	16.8
St. Lawrence, NY	70 201	58.5	79.2	11 180	55.1	16.4	-8.0	16.7	4.2	15.5	60.6	4.5
Saratoga, NY	135 015	40.8	88.2	10 297	53.9	30.9	6.5	30.6	20.9	16.4	63.0	38.8
Schenectady, NY	99 568	46.1	84.8	8 381	53.6	26.3	1.9	26.8	12.8	16.4	62.0	13.2
Schoharie, NY	20 695	56.4	81.7	2 354	76.6	17.3	-7.1	17.5	8.5	0.0	20.0	21.2
Schuyler, NY	12 842	57.5	82.4	610	76.4	15.5	-8.9	15.5	9.6	28.3	29.4	19.1
Seneca, NY	22 585	56.6	79.1	1 543	61.6	17.5	-6.9	17.8	7.5	23.4	31.6	6.7
Steuben, NY	65 765	54.5	82.8	3 253	81.1	17.9	-6.5	17.3	28.2	11.7	67.0	29.8
Suffolk, NY	942 401	45.1	86.2	82 092	65.5	27.5	3.1	29.1	16.5	23.0	56.7	12.0
Sullivan, NY	50 228	57.7	76.2	2 730	73.9	16.7	-7.7	18.1	6.6	4.1	38.1	8.7
Tioga, NY	34 223	52.6	84.8	1 571	78.7	19.7	-4.7	19.5	26.7	19.3	42.6	21.6
Tompkins, NY	53 075	30.9	91.4	27 205	22.6	47.5	23.1	45.0	37.7	45.4	87.9	61.2
Ulster, NY	120 670	48.3	81.7	11 682	83.4	25.0	0.6	26.3	11.5	16.7	51.6	12.1
Warren, NY	43 364	49.0	84.6	2 944	65.6	23.2	-1.2	23.2	26.3	8.8	45.2	17.4
Washington, NY	40 957	61.1	79.2	1 750	73.1	14.3	-10.1	14.8	2.0	22.3	14.5	3.5
Wayne, NY	61 731	53.9	82.3	3 271	76.6	17.0	-7.4	17.7	3.1	7.4	20.0	5.7
Westchester, NY	628 941	38.5	83.6	52 847	43.4	40.9	16.5	47.5	22.6	17.1	65.7	16.3
Wyoming, NY	29 522	63.4	75.6	1 414	81.1	11.5	-12.9	12.6	0.3	24.4	43.8	1.9
Yates, NY	15 714	56.2	80.0	1 279	37.3	18.2	-6.2	18.4	3.4	36.7	60.0	1.3
NORTH CAROLINA	5 282 994	50.3	78.1	462 275	78.5	22.5	-1.9	25.2	13.1	10.4	43.0	10.5
Alamance, NC	86 635	54.6	76.5	7 545	49.3	19.2	-5.2	22.1	9.3	24.7	37.6	5.0
Alexander, NC	22 729	66.9	68.7	979	80.4	9.3	-15.1	9.6	2.9	0.0	14.1	2.2
Alleghany, NC	7 829	63.8	68.0	392	85.5	11.7	-12.7	12.0	0.0	27.3	26.7	2.3
Anson, NC	16 824	68.2	70.2	1 107	89.3	9.2	-15.2	12.7	4.9	0.0	52.6	22.6
Ashe, NC	17 722	64.7	68.6	795	92.0	12.1	-12.3	12.3	2.3	7.7	11.8	7.4
Avery, NC	12 058	61.2	70.6	1 024	51.5	14.5	-9.9	14.7	5.1	7.7	44.9	17.2
Beaufort, NC	30 868	58.7	75.0	1 728	91.1	16.0	-8.4	20.2	5.1	0.0	0.0	10.2
Bertie, NC	13 135	72.9	63.8	481	84.4	8.8	-15.6	11.4	6.7	44.1	45.8	15.2
Bladen, NC	21 409	63.2	70.6	1 484	94.1	11.3	-13.1	14.1	6.8	6.0	66.7	11.2
Brunswick, NC	52 605	55.0	78.3	2 062	89.9	16.1	-8.3	17.3	9.2	5.8	29.2	6.6
Buncombe, NC	143 649	46.4	81.9	10 777	78.6	25.3	0.9	26.5	9.9	14.3	41.3	13.7
Burke, NC	59 922	62.8	67.6	3 109	83.7	12.8	-11.6	13.6	6.6	12.0	7.9	3.0
Cabarrus, NC	86 732	51.9	78.2	5 028	78.8	19.1	-5.3	20.4	12.7	15.7	34.0	3.6
Caldwell, NC	53 539	65.9	66.2	2 403	87.8	10.4	-14.0	10.7	6.3	7.6	22.5	1.6
Camden, NC	4 770	51.9	82.1	264	85.6	16.2	-8.2	16.1	15.4	0.0	0.0	51.0
Carteret, NC	43 457	47.6	82.1	2 223	85.4	19.8	-4.6	20.7	6.4	14.8	5.5	26.9
Caswell, NC	16 212	67.5	69.2	786	89.1	8.3	-16.1	10.4	4.2	4.2	42.4	10.1
Catawba, NC	94 747	56.5	74.8	5 405	69.1	17.0	-7.4	18.6	7.8	3.9	13.5	4.3
Chatham, NC	34 920	48.8	77.9	1 797	86.0	27.6	3.2	33.2	10.8	30.8	62.0	3.7
Cherokee, NC	17 709	61.5	73.3	835	89.5	11.0	-13.4	11.1	12.6	7.0	0.0	12.1

[3]May be of any race.

Table C-1. Population, School, and Student Characteristics by County—*Continued*

STATE County	State/ county code	County type[1]	Population, 2005 Total	Percent 5 to 17 years	Number of schools and students, 2004–2005 School districts	Schools	Students	Resident enrollment, 2000 Total	Percent public	K–12	Percent public
			1	2	3	4	5	6	7	8	9
Chowan, NC	37041	7	14 528	17.7	1	4	2 498	3 709	81.9	2 579	95.9
Clay, NC	37043	9	9 765	13.4	1	3	1 304	1 774	95.7	1 279	98.8
Cleveland, NC	37045	4	98 288	18.7	3	28	17 480	23 444	87.2	17 800	95.4
Columbus, NC	37047	6	54 746	18.2	2	24	9 826	13 690	93.6	10 826	95.4
Craven, NC	37049	5	90 795	17.8	1	22	14 697	22 182	87.8	15 939	92.6
Cumberland, NC	37051	2	304 520	20.5	2	87	53 436	88 163	87.3	61 841	93.0
Currituck, NC	37053	1	23 112	17.9	1	8	3 867	4 264	88.2	3 441	92.9
Dare, NC	37055	5	33 903	15.4	1	10	4 892	6 006	88.7	4 960	94.2
Davidson, NC	37057	4	154 623	17.9	3	40	25 339	32 736	89.2	26 183	94.0
Davie, NC	37059	2	39 136	17.6	1	9	6 246	8 108	87.6	6 395	93.4
Duplin, NC	37061	6	51 985	18.8	1	15	8 989	11 574	93.7	9 674	95.6
Durham, NC	37063	2	242 582	16.2	10	54	33 415	63 107	71.0	36 078	87.3
Edgecombe, NC	37065	3	54 129	19.5	1	15	7 826	14 634	93.6	11 844	96.4
Forsyth, NC	37067	2	325 967	17.5	7	77	50 496	78 172	78.5	53 625	89.2
Franklin, NC	37069	2	54 429	18.1	2	15	8 314	11 252	84.8	8 663	91.6
Gaston, NC	37071	1	196 137	18.1	3	55	32 778	44 264	85.7	34 448	90.6
Gates, NC	37073	8	11 224	19.0	1	5	1 949	2 709	94.2	2 281	97.3
Graham, NC	37075	9	8 085	15.8	1	3	1 266	1 474	93.6	1 173	94.1
Granville, NC	37077	6	53 674	17.6	1	14	8 674	11 186	89.5	8 670	94.4
Greene, NC	37079	3	20 026	17.9	1	4	3 250	4 652	89.8	3 749	93.5
Guilford, NC	37081	2	443 519	17.4	5	110	69 688	114 435	84.0	74 078	89.8
Halifax, NC	37083	4	56 023	18.7	3	22	9 445	14 896	91.5	11 856	92.5
Harnett, NC	37085	1	103 692	19.4	1	26	17 011	25 203	84.0	17 716	95.5
Haywood, NC	37087	2	56 482	15.4	1	15	7 935	11 291	90.7	8 354	95.0
Henderson, NC	37089	2	97 217	15.4	2	22	12 738	17 967	87.2	13 934	90.7
Hertford, NC	37091	7	23 574	16.9	1	5	3 686	5 716	87.8	4 586	90.8
Hoke, NC	37093	2	41 016	21.2	1	11	6 954	9 385	91.2	7 050	94.9
Hyde, NC	37095	9	5 413	14.4	1	4	662	1 255	88.4	1 124	87.6
Iredell, NC	37097	4	140 924	18.5	5	41	24 526	28 540	89.4	22 667	93.4
Jackson, NC	37099	6	35 368	13.2	2	8	3 823	10 089	94.0	4 647	95.5
Johnston, NC	37101	2	146 437	19.0	1	35	26 168	28 470	91.0	22 380	96.0
Jones, NC	37103	8	10 311	18.6	1	6	1 448	2 635	86.7	2 091	87.6
Lee, NC	37105	4	55 704	18.6	2	13	9 306	11 864	89.0	9 442	91.4
Lenoir, NC	37107	4	57 961	18.5	3	21	10 360	14 821	90.2	11 328	93.2
Lincoln, NC	37109	4	69 851	18.3	2	22	12 109	14 743	90.1	11 777	94.1
McDowell, NC	37111	6	43 201	16.7	1	11	6 503	9 182	93.7	7 313	95.0
Macon, NC	37113	7	32 148	14.7	1	10	4 194	6 010	90.1	4 626	93.4
Madison, NC	37115	2	20 256	15.5	1	6	2 629	4 542	74.5	3 000	91.3
Martin, NC	37117	6	24 643	18.1	1	12	4 528	6 555	93.3	5 229	95.1
Mecklenburg, NC	37119	1	796 372	18.2	9	146	121 430	183 309	79.6	125 015	85.8
Mitchell, NC	37121	9	15 784	15.1	1	8	2 296	3 102	91.2	2 508	94.2
Montgomery, NC	37123	6	27 322	18.3	1	10	4 688	6 120	93.2	4 965	96.0
Moore, NC	37125	4	81 685	16.3	3	24	12 204	16 320	91.4	12 571	94.5
Nash, NC	37127	3	91 378	18.5	2	30	19 454	22 221	86.3	16 862	91.1
New Hanover, NC	37129	2	179 553	15.1	2	35	23 579	42 293	87.8	24 410	90.4
Northampton, NC	37131	9	21 483	17.6	2	11	3 567	5 438	90.1	4 343	90.7
Onslow, NC	37133	3	152 440	17.7	1	33	22 230	37 631	91.2	26 211	96.0
Orange, NC	37135	2	118 386	14.3	5	29	17 719	44 716	90.1	18 131	88.5
Pamlico, NC	37137	9	12 735	14.8	2	5	2 044	2 810	92.8	2 171	95.8
Pasquotank, NC	37139	7	38 270	17.7	1	12	6 139	10 325	89.6	6 789	95.0
Pender, NC	37141	2	46 429	16.7	1	15	7 162	9 203	91.6	7 385	95.1
Perquimans, NC	37143	9	12 080	16.0	1	4	1 779	2 592	90.9	2 100	93.1
Person, NC	37145	2	37 217	17.8	2	11	6 166	8 423	90.6	6 460	93.8
Pitt, NC	37147	3	142 570	16.6	1	33	21 833	45 735	91.7	23 462	91.2
Polk, NC	37149	8	19 134	15.3	1	6	2 436	3 529	85.3	2 662	87.3
Randolph, NC	37151	2	138 367	18.3	2	36	22 921	29 217	89.6	23 613	93.5
Richmond, NC	37153	4	46 781	19.5	1	18	8 305	11 419	93.4	9 150	96.2
Robeson, NC	37155	4	127 586	20.5	2	42	24 668	34 487	94.0	26 723	95.9
Rockingham, NC	37157	2	92 614	17.2	1	25	14 826	19 909	90.7	15 761	93.7
Rowan, NC	37159	4	135 099	18.1	3	38	25 617	31 855	84.4	24 024	92.1
Rutherford, NC	37161	4	63 771	17.6	2	19	10 351	14 178	90.5	11 037	93.7
Sampson, NC	37163	6	63 063	18.8	2	20	11 162	14 305	93.7	11 235	97.2
Scotland, NC	37165	6	37 180	19.7	3	17	7 223	10 267	90.1	7 652	96.5
Stanly, NC	37167	6	58 964	18.1	2	23	10 014	14 133	87.9	11 004	95.0
Stokes, NC	37169	2	45 858	17.9	1	18	7 407	9 914	88.7	8 106	92.5
Surry, NC	37171	4	72 601	17.8	4	23	12 161	15 791	93.7	12 328	97.0
Swain, NC	37173	8	13 167	17.7	2	6	1 910	3 071	92.9	2 409	96.7
Transylvania, NC	37175	6	29 626	14.8	2	10	4 002	6 292	81.9	4 469	93.1
Tyrrell, NC	37177	9	4 157	14.6	1	3	673	994	93.9	803	94.3
Union, NC	37179	1	162 929	19.7	2	37	29 416	32 693	82.2	24 979	90.5
Vance, NC	37181	4	43 771	20.1	2	16	8 826	10 894	92.4	8 523	94.7
Wake, NC	37183	2	748 815	18.0	16	149	119 437	178 475	82.0	112 881	89.4
Warren, NC	37185	8	19 729	16.7	2	7	3 230	4 667	87.6	3 818	87.8
Washington, NC	37187	7	13 282	18.5	1	5	2 285	3 423	91.8	2 797	92.6
Watauga, NC	37189	6	42 472	10.6	1	9	4 604	16 832	91.9	5 355	92.7
Wayne, NC	37191	3	114 448	18.7	2	32	19 555	29 896	86.7	22 655	91.8
Wilkes, NC	37193	6	67 390	16.4	2	23	10 466	13 770	93.2	10 722	97.6
Wilson, NC	37195	4	76 281	18.4	2	24	13 323	18 243	86.3	13 997	93.2
Yadkin, NC	37197	2	37 668	17.9	1	11	6 099	7 982	90.0	6 360	93.6
Yancey, NC	37199	8	18 201	15.6	1	9	2 537	3 307	91.1	2 764	95.0

[1]County type codes are from the Economic Research Service of the United States Department of Agriculture. See notes and definitions at the end of this section.

Table C-1. Population, School, and Student Characteristics by County—*Continued*

STATE County	Characteristics of students, 2004–2005				Outcomes		Staff and students, 2004–2005		
	Percent with IEP[2]	Percent eligible for free or reduced-price lunch	Percent minority	Percent English-language learners	Number of graduates, 2003–2004	Percent dropouts, grades 9–12, 2001–2002	Number of teachers	Student-teacher ratio	Central administration staff
	10	11	12	13	14	15	16	17	18
Chowan, NC	14.1	56.8	50.3	0.8	157	5.2	188	13.3	21
Clay, NC	13.6	46.0	2.4	0.1	89	2.8	102	12.8	9
Cleveland, NC	13.9	45.6	33.4	1.1	...	5.3	1 257	13.9	...
Columbus, NC	13.1	67.2	50.3	2.4	581	6.8	700	14.0	51
Craven, NC	12.1	49.2	41.8	2.1	833	6.6	1 025	14.3	71
Cumberland, NC	13.7	54.4	60.5	1.9	...	4.3	3 302	16.2	250
Currituck, NC	14.8	24.4	12.9	0.4	225	6.2	256	15.1	28
Dare, NC	12.0	21.6	10.8	2.9	278	5.7	364	13.4	29
Davidson, NC	12.3	41.1	21.5	3.2	1 364	6.1	1 630	15.5	107
Davie, NC	14.5	31.6	17.5	4.1	284	7.0	417	15.0	28
Duplin, NC	11.1	65.3	56.7	16.1	431	6.2	626	14.4	34
Durham, NC	12.7	44.7	73.2	9.0	...	6.6	1 974	16.9	...
Edgecombe, NC	11.6	70.4	70.0	4.2	382	5.8	520	15.1	58
Forsyth, NC	14.7	45.1	52.4	7.4	...	6.3	3 401	14.8	...
Franklin, NC	9.9	54.1	47.4	3.5	...	6.6	533	15.6	...
Gaston, NC	11.8	44.1	28.3	4.5	...	6.4	2 015	16.3	...
Gates, NC	18.2	54.1	42.7	0.8	132	6.9	165	11.8	20
Graham, NC	12.3	50.9	12.5	0.2	69	8.0	94	13.5	11
Granville, NC	11.8	47.8	46.2	5.2	...	8.5	563	15.4	46
Greene, NC	14.3	66.4	66.4	11.0	165	6.4	229	14.2	18
Guilford, NC	15.0	45.3	55.3	6.9	...	3.9	4 547	15.3	...
Halifax, NC	14.6	70.8	73.3	0.8	...	6.8	675	14.0	70
Harnett, NC	15.0	50.5	43.0	5.9	852	7.9	1 112	15.3	58
Haywood, NC	13.5	41.3	6.0	1.6	...	7.5	551	14.4	38
Henderson, NC	12.4	38.7	20.3	8.5	...	5.9	821	15.5	50
Hertford, NC	15.3	69.7	83.0	1.2	220	7.2	256	14.4	19
Hoke, NC	14.9	64.0	70.5	4.9	252	9.1	421	16.5	43
Hyde, NC	21.5	71.0	51.2	4.1	...	3.6	79	8.4	11
Iredell, NC	13.1	35.8	26.5	4.0	...	5.9	1 610	15.2	...
Jackson, NC	15.6	37.4	16.3	2.2	...	5.2	267	14.3	...
Johnston, NC	16.0	40.1	35.0	9.5	1 177	6.5	1 869	14.0	95
Jones, NC	16.0	78.4	58.6	2.6	71	6.9	121	12.0	11
Lee, NC	12.2	50.6	49.4	11.9	458	8.5	592	15.7	41
Lenoir, NC	14.2	56.4	58.6	3.1	...	6.9	709	14.6	...
Lincoln, NC	14.7	39.7	18.2	6.1	...	5.5	827	14.6	...
McDowell, NC	15.4	48.9	12.7	6.0	337	4.0	425	15.3	31
Macon, NC	16.8	46.6	7.6	2.7	...	6.1	302	13.9	25
Madison, NC	16.1	54.8	3.3	1.2	140	4.1	191	13.8	15
Martin, NC	13.8	62.6	57.5	0.7	256	5.3	342	13.2	24
Mecklenburg, NC	12.0	48.1	59.7	1.3	...	5.8	7 930	15.3	...
Mitchell, NC	15.5	51.4	5.6	3.6	151	7.1	170	13.5	17
Montgomery, NC	12.5	60.8	51.7	20.0	241	6.1	332	14.1	25
Moore, NC	12.9	42.4	33.5	3.8	...	3.1	825	14.8	...
Nash, NC	13.7	51.8	58.5	4.7	...	6.2	1 235	15.8	...
New Hanover, NC	13.7	41.3	34.7	3.1	...	5.5	1 560	15.1	108
Northampton, NC	12.0	83.5	83.0	1.1	...	5.7	253	14.1	...
Onslow, NC	13.3	40.5	37.2	2.0	1 222	6.0	1 404	15.8	96
Orange, NC	14.1	25.1	35.6	6.5	...	2.9	1 362	13.0	...
Pamlico, NC	19.9	52.1	31.0	1.9	...	4.8	180	11.4	18
Pasquotank, NC	14.1	56.0	53.6	1.1	342	6.8	425	14.4	27
Pender, NC	12.4	54.5	34.9	5.2	368	7.1	516	13.9	33
Perquimans, NC	15.0	60.5	37.0	0.4	105	5.7	133	13.4	21
Person, NC	15.3	43.2	41.4	1.7	...	6.2	415	14.9	26
Pitt, NC	14.0	50.1	58.4	3.6	1 005	6.7	1 513	14.4	79
Polk, NC	17.0	45.0	17.6	5.0	141	4.6	198	12.3	17
Randolph, NC	12.0	41.0	22.3	8.0	...	6.4	1 470	15.6	107
Richmond, NC	12.9	68.3	50.4	2.6	...	6.0	565	14.7	34
Robeson, NC	17.5	79.2	80.2	5.0	...	9.1	1 444	17.1	86
Rockingham, NC	15.2	48.6	32.8	4.1	807	6.0	959	15.5	57
Rowan, NC	13.7	46.1	32.3	7.5	...	5.6	1 707	15.0	96
Rutherford, NC	14.0	53.7	21.3	2.7	609	8.1	694	14.9	53
Sampson, NC	12.1	63.2	55.7	11.3	592	5.3	775	14.4	50
Scotland, NC	15.2	67.8	62.9	0.9	...	7.0	570	12.7	34
Stanly, NC	18.3	42.9	24.4	5.2	...	3.4	686	14.6	...
Stokes, NC	14.2	33.5	8.8	0.7	444	5.6	533	13.9	45
Surry, NC	15.9	45.5	19.3	8.1	...	5.4	849	14.3	63
Swain, NC	19.3	...	25.5	0.8	...	3.1	150	12.7	...
Transylvania, NC	11.9	48.7	12.1	1.0	...	5.1	250	16.0	...
Tyrrell, NC	14.9	61.4	52.3	10.5	...	4.2	60	11.2	8
Union, NC	12.5	31.3	27.4	4.2	...	4.7	1 875	15.7	128
Vance, NC	12.1	75.5	70.5	4.1	...	8.7	629	14.0	49
Wake, NC	15.2	28.1	43.0	5.7	...	3.8	7 972	15.0	...
Warren, NC	15.7	70.1	81.5	1.7	...	8.1	211	15.3	...
Washington, NC	18.4	79.7	77.7	1.5	116	6.7	189	12.1	20
Watauga, NC	16.4	26.6	6.0	1.5	...	5.2	361	12.8	29
Wayne, NC	15.2	51.7	53.1	5.4	...	4.8	1 254	15.6	...
Wilkes, NC	13.1	49.7	13.4	5.2	...	8.3	703	14.9	...
Wilson, NC	10.9	57.4	63.2	5.3	...	6.8	881	15.1	54
Yadkin, NC	17.0	38.2	18.5	6.8	351	6.3	387	15.8	26
Yancey, NC	15.8	49.9	7.3	4.5	...	6.0	167	15.2	19

[2]IEP = Individual Education Program. See notes and definitions at the end of this section.
. . . = Not available.

Table C-1. Population, School, and Student Characteristics by County—*Continued*

STATE County	Revenue, 2003–2004				Current expenditures, 2003–2004			Resident population, 16 to 19 years, 2000			
	Total revenue (thousands of dollars)	Percent of revenue from:			Total expenditures (thousands of dollars)	Amount per student (dollars)	Percent for instruction	Total	Percent in armed forces	Percent high school graduates	Percent not enrolled, not employed, not in armed forces, not high school graduate
		Federal government	State government	Local government							
	19	20	21	22	23	24	25	26	27	28	29
Chowan, NC	22 555	10.6	63.3	26.1	19 418	7 736	64.9	940	0.0	12.2	1.3
Clay, NC	11 910	7.8	74.3	17.9	10 970	8 679	67.3	340	0.0	12.1	7.6
Cleveland, NC	131 814	11.7	63.5	24.8	120 281	6 819	69.0	4 941	0.0	11.2	8.0
Columbus, NC	75 706	14.0	66.4	19.6	64 567	6 638	64.2	3 173	0.2	10.6	7.8
Craven, NC	100 830	15.1	66.8	18.1	94 747	6 518	65.6	4 794	11.5	22.9	6.3
Cumberland, NC	368 995	13.8	61.9	24.3	335 745	6 352	65.5	18 240	13.2	21.5	4.6
Currituck, NC	28 799	6.7	63.2	30.1	26 857	7 332	61.4	831	1.0	15.8	5.4
Dare, NC	75 543	2.8	29.3	67.9	38 733	8 068	65.6	1 337	1.0	19.4	2.5
Davidson, NC	173 245	9.7	64.5	25.8	155 493	6 168	66.2	6 866	0.0	10.4	7.7
Davie, NC	42 010	6.7	65.9	27.4	38 658	6 400	67.1	1 620	0.0	9.3	6.2
Duplin, NC	63 721	17.1	66.3	16.5	56 986	6 489	67.6	2 630	0.1	10.0	9.8
Durham, NC	285 482	7.9	51.7	40.4	245 970	7 598	62.7	12 343	0.1	6.5	7.0
Edgecombe, NC	56 080	15.6	67.7	16.8	51 674	6 780	64.5	3 223	0.0	10.8	9.3
Forsyth, NC	424 290	7.8	51.9	40.3	344 074	7 020	68.8	15 448	0.0	9.7	6.1
Franklin, NC	58 795	10.9	63.9	25.2	52 557	6 538	63.3	2 375	0.0	10.9	6.8
Gaston, NC	232 059	10.3	58.6	31.1	191 722	6 087	68.1	9 162	0.0	11.1	9.2
Gates, NC	17 694	8.5	69.9	21.6	16 006	8 133	61.3	526	0.0	5.7	8.2
Graham, NC	11 215	17.5	71.4	11.1	10 383	8 696	64.2	368	0.0	13.9	12.2
Granville, NC	58 421	9.2	67.6	23.2	54 367	6 263	64.7	2 273	0.0	9.6	20.1
Greene, NC	25 347	15.5	71.2	13.3	24 041	7 536	63.2	982	0.0	5.6	5.3
Guilford, NC	524 659	9.1	56.0	34.9	478 345	7 118	63.5	24 144	0.0	8.4	3.3
Halifax, NC	79 723	19.8	62.2	18.1	70 998	7 461	62.3	2 911	0.0	15.5	7.9
Harnett, NC	117 882	10.5	64.8	24.7	101 153	5 990	69.3	4 959	1.1	12.7	8.8
Haywood, NC	60 531	10.0	60.1	29.9	55 736	7 044	61.2	2 318	0.0	14.7	4.2
Henderson, NC	92 501	9.8	59.8	30.4	80 339	6 482	67.7	3 764	0.0	12.1	7.1
Hertford, NC	30 419	14.9	70.5	14.7	26 878	7 485	60.2	1 408	0.0	7.7	7.0
Hoke, NC	44 918	15.3	70.9	13.8	40 493	6 336	66.4	1 896	0.5	19.6	10.4
Hyde, NC	11 229	8.0	57.2	34.8	8 559	12 813	56.7	265	0.0	7.5	17.4
Iredell, NC	181 171	6.5	57.1	36.4	148 692	6 228	65.6	5 937	0.0	13.7	7.9
Jackson, NC	33 355	10.4	57.7	31.9	29 141	7 677	63.5	2 707	0.1	6.1	2.5
Johnston, NC	192 065	8.0	58.9	33.1	163 171	6 546	69.3	5 837	0.0	12.0	7.7
Jones, NC	14 759	15.8	72.8	11.4	13 155	9 540	63.7	593	0.0	7.9	5.9
Lee, NC	63 672	11.4	64.8	23.8	57 924	6 369	68.2	2 655	0.0	8.7	9.6
Lenoir, NC	72 182	14.3	68.5	17.2	69 610	6 715	65.1	3 200	0.5	8.1	12.2
Lincoln, NC	82 354	7.1	63.8	29.1	73 379	6 250	68.4	2 958	0.0	9.4	5.5
McDowell, NC	49 369	12.6	70.8	16.6	43 462	6 715	69.6	1 966	0.0	13.7	7.3
Macon, NC	48 436	7.4	41.5	51.0	28 242	6 848	64.6	1 421	0.7	17.9	8.2
Madison, NC	22 974	11.8	68.2	20.0	20 225	7 839	62.3	1 162	0.3	11.5	5.0
Martin, NC	36 752	14.1	66.3	19.6	33 518	7 463	66.6	1 359	0.0	9.6	4.2
Mecklenburg, NC	1 083 895	7.2	47.1	45.7	829 260	7 144	63.5	34 198	0.0	8.6	5.7
Mitchell, NC	18 152	10.9	74.4	14.7	16 964	7 265	62.2	740	0.0	21.4	5.7
Montgomery, NC	35 802	13.7	64.4	21.9	32 688	7 318	67.3	1 425	0.1	8.8	11.8
Moore, NC	90 048	9.1	60.3	30.6	81 780	6 830	66.6	3 374	0.0	13.6	6.0
Nash, NC	138 288	11.0	67.3	21.7	123 147	6 462	66.2	4 745	0.0	11.9	6.8
New Hanover, NC	182 260	10.0	56.1	33.8	164 990	7 302	60.9	8 624	0.6	8.5	3.6
Northampton, NC	31 858	17.3	65.9	16.8	27 975	7 928	61.3	1 148	0.0	12.8	9.1
Onslow, NC	151 084	12.8	64.5	22.7	132 566	6 099	66.2	11 465	36.1	48.3	3.4
Orange, NC	175 360	5.6	46.0	48.4	149 663	8 583	67.4	10 630	0.0	4.0	1.8
Pamlico, NC	19 372	10.2	68.7	21.1	16 818	8 043	65.2	615	0.0	15.0	11.4
Pasquotank, NC	47 007	10.3	61.5	28.3	39 773	6 733	63.4	2 189	0.0	6.4	2.0
Pender, NC	50 052	12.6	64.5	22.9	46 743	6 693	62.6	2 057	0.0	10.7	8.5
Perquimans, NC	16 221	16.0	67.8	16.2	14 937	8 624	61.8	622	0.0	8.4	13.0
Person, NC	45 647	10.6	60.7	28.7	39 134	6 429	68.3	1 605	0.0	12.1	4.6
Pitt, NC	158 037	10.8	62.0	27.2	139 764	6 584	67.7	10 156	0.1	6.0	4.2
Polk, NC	23 641	7.8	61.8	30.4	19 044	7 958	67.5	637	0.0	10.4	6.6
Randolph, NC	142 901	8.3	70.8	21.0	135 239	5 998	67.8	6 383	0.0	10.3	8.9
Richmond, NC	58 591	13.9	70.9	15.2	54 095	6 526	66.0	2 850	2.7	15.5	13.4
Robeson, NC	162 567	14.4	71.3	14.3	152 504	6 311	65.8	7 841	0.0	10.3	11.6
Rockingham, NC	113 213	10.0	67.9	22.1	99 372	6 723	65.7	4 393	0.3	13.7	8.4
Rowan, NC	144 121	10.3	63.5	26.2	130 648	6 258	67.1	6 535	0.0	12.3	6.2
Rutherford, NC	93 899	10.1	52.2	37.7	65 678	6 390	67.2	3 047	0.3	11.9	10.1
Sampson, NC	77 829	13.6	67.4	19.0	72 195	6 588	66.4	3 314	0.1	10.6	9.8
Scotland, NC	59 455	17.1	60.5	22.4	53 350	7 492	66.0	2 083	0.0	10.6	5.8
Stanly, NC	68 900	9.4	66.4	24.2	64 294	6 420	68.8	3 090	0.2	10.9	6.6
Stokes, NC	57 216	9.5	65.2	25.2	51 802	6 969	63.9	2 042	0.0	13.4	6.2
Surry, NC	89 454	9.9	63.8	26.3	79 369	6 708	66.3	3 178	0.0	11.4	6.6
Swain, NC	17 375	24.9	64.0	11.1	15 470	8 220	64.4	813	0.0	24.8	7.3
Transylvania, NC	35 068	8.2	57.8	34.0	28 667	7 192	67.7	1 557	0.0	11.1	6.5
Tyrrell, NC	7 770	10.3	77.4	12.3	7 186	11 246	57.9	198	0.0	7.6	3.5
Union, NC	208 291	6.1	55.6	38.2	169 773	6 227	68.1	6 438	0.0	12.3	4.6
Vance, NC	63 179	15.5	63.7	20.8	56 060	6 570	66.5	2 354	0.1	14.1	18.8
Wake, NC	997 148	5.5	48.3	46.1	763 064	6 754	64.2	32 322	0.0	7.9	3.9
Warren, NC	27 214	15.4	65.5	19.1	24 093	7 413	62.7	1 056	0.0	11.0	10.4
Washington, NC	20 901	20.2	66.9	12.8	18 731	8 700	68.5	796	0.0	9.3	8.3
Watauga, NC	36 337	7.4	63.2	29.4	33 853	7 251	68.2	4 685	0.0	3.6	0.8
Wayne, NC	129 288	12.4	68.8	18.8	118 760	6 135	68.9	6 104	1.8	10.8	6.9
Wilkes, NC	75 196	10.8	63.4	25.7	68 750	6 738	64.2	3 082	0.0	10.3	6.0
Wilson, NC	94 669	11.6	61.9	26.5	84 075	6 430	64.9	4 250	0.0	8.7	11.3
Yadkin, NC	41 261	8.0	67.3	24.7	37 386	6 200	63.7	1 581	0.0	8.9	5.8
Yancey, NC	21 958	10.4	64.9	24.7	18 466	7 247	61.5	852	0.0	21.4	8.7

Table C-1. Population, School, and Student Characteristics by County—*Continued*

STATE County	High school graduates, 2000			College enrollment, 2000		College graduates, 2000 (percent)						
	Population 25 years and over	High school graduate or less (percent)	High school graduate or more (percent)	Number	Percent public	Bachelor's degree or more	+/- U.S. percentage with bachelor's degree or more	Non-Hispanic White	Black	American Indian and Alaska Native	Asian or Pacific Islander	Hispanic[3]
	30	31	32	33	34	35	36	37	38	39	40	41
Chowan, NC	9 583	60.5	73.1	899	50.3	16.4	-8.0	19.7	10.0	0.0	0.0	20.7
Clay, NC	6 578	57.3	76.5	426	89.4	15.4	-9.0	15.5	0.0	15.8	0.0	0.0
Cleveland, NC	63 396	61.9	72.2	4 276	59.9	13.3	-11.1	14.9	6.3	6.2	30.4	10.4
Columbus, NC	35 921	65.1	68.6	2 284	90.4	10.1	-14.3	12.0	6.1	5.8	36.6	3.5
Craven, NC	57 027	47.9	82.1	4 413	85.9	19.3	-5.1	23.4	7.0	16.7	23.2	10.6
Cumberland, NC	176 714	43.4	85.0	20 830	76.4	19.1	-5.3	22.5	14.6	10.9	19.6	13.6
Currituck, NC	12 361	56.9	77.6	555	79.1	13.3	-11.1	13.4	8.9	8.5	32.3	14.5
Dare, NC	21 713	39.0	88.6	682	83.6	27.7	3.3	28.2	6.6	19.4	28.6	18.0
Davidson, NC	100 128	61.2	72.0	4 371	82.5	12.8	-11.6	13.3	7.9	7.4	18.5	4.8
Davie, NC	23 840	56.6	78.1	1 180	77.4	17.6	-6.8	18.6	9.2	0.0	100.0	2.5
Duplin, NC	31 700	65.8	65.8	1 402	84.7	10.5	-13.9	12.9	7.4	0.0	12.9	5.1
Durham, NC	143 804	36.2	83.0	23 187	50.6	40.1	15.7	49.5	26.6	35.3	77.8	14.5
Edgecombe, NC	35 748	71.3	65.6	1 822	83.0	8.5	-15.9	12.0	5.8	0.0	8.6	4.3
Forsyth, NC	204 081	45.0	82.0	18 750	58.0	28.7	4.3	32.8	18.0	20.0	52.8	8.9
Franklin, NC	31 467	60.9	73.6	1 802	62.3	13.2	-11.2	16.1	6.4	5.7	48.1	6.0
Gaston, NC	127 748	58.2	71.4	7 020	75.9	14.2	-10.2	14.8	9.8	7.4	22.5	10.4
Gates, NC	7 095	63.9	71.4	324	86.4	10.5	-13.9	10.3	9.7	32.4	46.8	0.0
Graham, NC	5 622	67.6	68.4	220	88.2	11.2	-13.2	11.8	. . .	0.0	0.0	0.0
Granville, NC	32 641	61.1	73.0	1 852	84.2	13.0	-11.4	16.8	6.3	4.1	26.7	7.9
Greene, NC	12 380	69.3	65.4	628	85.0	8.2	-16.2	11.4	3.9	0.0	0.0	4.8
Guilford, NC	275 494	42.2	83.0	32 524	79.6	30.3	5.9	35.1	19.7	12.3	30.8	13.3
Halifax, NC	37 719	67.7	65.4	1 959	90.3	11.1	-13.3	15.6	7.0	2.8	32.7	10.1
Harnett, NC	57 138	57.6	75.0	6 071	56.8	12.8	-11.6	14.9	6.4	8.0	20.9	6.2
Haywood, NC	39 552	54.4	77.7	2 173	85.2	16.0	-8.4	16.0	7.0	27.3	64.7	5.9
Henderson, NC	65 039	46.0	83.2	2 843	88.0	24.1	-0.3	25.4	8.2	3.0	26.3	5.6
Hertford, NC	14 976	65.3	65.6	781	77.0	11.1	-13.3	14.2	8.8	12.1	17.0	7.3
Hoke, NC	19 934	58.9	73.5	1 723	81.3	10.9	-13.5	16.3	4.6	7.1	23.0	9.8
Hyde, NC	4 190	67.9	68.4	72	91.7	10.6	-13.8	12.7	6.4	0.0	. . .	0.0
Iredell, NC	82 036	53.7	78.4	4 050	83.5	17.4	-7.0	19.4	5.4	11.8	26.8	7.9
Jackson, NC	20 881	46.9	78.8	5 086	94.9	25.5	1.1	27.2	36.7	8.9	19.5	14.9
Johnston, NC	80 268	55.9	75.9	4 186	82.6	15.9	-8.5	17.5	9.5	20.7	25.8	6.9
Jones, NC	6 998	64.2	72.2	379	85.8	9.5	-14.9	10.8	7.1	0.0	37.5	1.6
Lee, NC	32 043	53.6	76.3	1 780	86.2	17.2	-7.2	21.2	6.7	13.0	40.8	5.6
Lenoir, NC	39 833	59.4	71.9	2 379	89.1	13.3	-11.1	17.1	7.4	8.1	39.7	0.9
Lincoln, NC	43 259	60.1	71.7	2 024	83.2	13.0	-11.4	13.6	4.8	12.8	15.2	11.1
McDowell, NC	29 157	65.9	70.2	1 318	85.5	9.0	-15.4	9.0	5.4	10.1	20.5	1.3
Macon, NC	21 908	54.9	77.3	1 062	88.2	16.2	-8.2	16.2	12.4	0.0	34.7	5.3
Madison, NC	13 409	62.5	69.3	1 267	35.8	16.1	-8.3	16.1	5.0	66.7	10.5	18.9
Martin, NC	17 014	63.9	70.7	930	89.0	11.6	-12.8	15.9	6.0	0.0	35.7	3.3
Mecklenburg, NC	455 163	33.7	86.2	42 462	74.5	37.1	12.7	45.2	20.3	20.7	39.7	14.3
Mitchell, NC	11 315	64.3	68.6	452	79.2	12.2	-12.2	12.0	0.0	0.0	56.7	13.0
Montgomery, NC	17 713	67.9	64.2	844	86.1	10.0	-14.4	12.3	4.6	8.1	14.4	1.7
Moore, NC	53 347	43.3	82.6	2 803	92.3	26.8	2.4	30.7	6.7	11.0	38.5	8.3
Nash, NC	57 522	58.3	75.6	3 925	78.3	17.2	-7.2	21.6	8.3	19.9	45.6	7.7
New Hanover, NC	107 671	38.2	86.3	14 962	91.5	31.0	6.6	34.4	13.2	21.5	49.9	17.0
Northampton, NC	15 199	69.0	62.5	733	89.9	10.8	-13.6	15.2	7.3	24.2	20.0	6.4
Onslow, NC	75 286	48.5	84.3	8 820	84.0	14.8	-9.6	16.1	10.0	14.3	11.6	12.7
Orange, NC	69 530	28.3	87.6	24 674	95.4	51.5	27.1	57.2	19.5	15.7	80.6	27.6
Pamlico, NC	9 332	56.1	75.2	457	89.3	14.7	-9.7	18.1	4.8	0.0	3.8	1.7
Pasquotank, NC	22 223	53.5	76.8	2 936	83.3	16.4	-8.0	16.1	16.2	32.5	29.3	20.8
Pender, NC	28 566	56.7	76.8	1 339	82.4	13.6	-10.8	15.8	6.8	0.0	27.5	6.3
Perquimans, NC	7 970	61.1	71.9	343	91.8	12.3	-12.1	13.3	9.6	0.0	. . .	19.1
Person, NC	24 473	63.2	74.9	1 268	88.9	10.3	-14.1	11.4	7.3	0.0	30.1	18.5
Pitt, NC	79 040	45.3	79.9	20 154	95.8	26.4	2.0	34.0	11.0	30.6	53.7	13.6
Polk, NC	13 653	47.6	80.6	582	83.5	25.7	1.3	26.7	6.4	49.1	74.1	14.0
Randolph, NC	87 450	65.7	70.0	3 898	84.9	11.1	-13.3	11.5	6.9	6.7	25.4	5.6
Richmond, NC	29 870	66.5	69.2	1 641	89.2	10.1	-14.3	11.6	6.6	7.6	14.0	6.1
Robeson, NC	74 458	65.8	64.9	5 683	91.7	11.4	-13.0	16.4	8.3	8.5	27.7	5.0
Rockingham, NC	63 470	64.4	68.9	2 722	85.3	10.8	-13.6	12.0	6.5	8.2	17.7	2.6
Rowan, NC	86 345	59.3	74.2	5 618	64.4	14.2	-10.2	14.8	12.2	10.6	15.9	4.4
Rutherford, NC	42 889	62.9	70.4	2 368	86.7	12.5	-11.9	13.3	5.0	4.8	29.5	11.8
Sampson, NC	38 796	66.1	69.1	2 078	86.3	11.1	-13.3	13.5	6.9	9.8	10.4	6.6
Scotland, NC	22 563	58.1	71.4	1 881	72.7	15.9	-8.5	20.7	10.3	2.8	48.9	42.0
Stanly, NC	38 702	62.5	73.4	2 196	65.7	12.7	-11.7	13.4	6.5	4.9	30.0	9.2
Stokes, NC	30 598	66.9	73.2	1 163	77.2	9.3	-15.1	9.6	4.8	0.0	32.5	6.2
Surry, NC	49 018	62.5	67.0	2 652	84.5	12.0	-12.4	12.8	6.7	4.6	15.1	1.3
Swain, NC	8 739	59.6	70.5	438	81.3	13.9	-10.5	14.8	24.4	9.8	59.1	9.3
Transylvania, NC	20 973	47.5	82.5	1 462	57.2	23.7	-0.7	24.0	14.3	19.7	50.0	16.1
Tyrrell, NC	2 828	67.5	66.3	156	96.8	10.6	-13.8	13.9	5.0	0.0	0.0	15.7
Union, NC	78 878	50.6	80.2	4 781	66.7	21.3	-3.1	23.6	9.1	23.8	41.8	6.6
Vance, NC	27 360	66.2	68.1	1 332	87.4	10.7	-13.7	14.0	6.6	11.1	68.5	5.4
Wake, NC	403 481	28.4	89.3	51 713	78.9	43.9	19.5	49.2	24.3	29.8	65.6	17.8
Warren, NC	13 599	64.5	67.5	618	88.7	11.6	-12.8	16.8	7.2	2.0	17.0	20.5
Washington, NC	9 091	67.5	69.9	377	88.1	11.6	-12.8	15.9	5.9	. . .	63.3	3.9
Watauga, NC	23 939	42.2	81.6	10 952	93.2	33.2	8.8	33.5	27.0	28.3	56.1	33.6
Wayne, NC	72 894	55.3	77.2	5 211	78.5	15.0	-9.4	17.9	9.5	2.5	31.9	6.1
Wilkes, NC	45 498	65.5	66.0	2 024	87.8	11.3	-13.1	11.7	4.7	0.0	20.1	4.1
Wilson, NC	48 061	62.3	69.4	3 210	66.0	15.1	-9.3	21.4	5.5	31.0	38.9	3.1
Yadkin, NC	24 916	64.8	72.0	1 149	77.0	10.3	-14.1	10.5	4.4	0.0	82.9	6.5
Yancey, NC	12 709	65.7	71.1	444	70.3	13.1	-11.3	13.2	0.0	19.2	8.3	6.6

[3]May be of any race.
. . . = Not available.

Table C-1. Population, School, and Student Characteristics by County

STATE County	State/ county code	County type[1]	Population, 2005		Number of schools and students, 2004–2005			Resident enrollment, 2000			
			Total	Percent 5 to 17 years	School districts	Schools	Students	Total	Percent public	K–12	Percent public
			1	2	3	4	5	6	7	8	9
NORTH DAKOTA	38 000		636 677	15.7	253	549	100 460	179 667	91.1	123 939	93.3
Adams, ND	38 001	9	2 433	14.0	1	2	350	577	96.7	526	99.6
Barnes, ND	38 003	6	11 075	14.4	6	12	1 661	3 096	94.8	2 060	95.1
Benson, ND	38 005	9	6 999	23.5	7	11	998	2 216	98.1	1 927	98.0
Billings, ND	38 007	9	813	12.5	1	2	56	210	96.7	183	97.8
Bottineau, ND	38 009	9	6 741	13.9	5	7	990	1 786	98.4	1 324	99.8
Bowman, ND	38 011	9	3 048	14.7	3	6	660	752	97.7	665	98.6
Burke, ND	38 013	9	2 032	13.2	3	6	277	438	94.3	408	94.6
Burleigh, ND	38 015	3	73 818	15.2	11	33	10 776	18 617	79.3	12 849	86.6
Cass, ND	38 017	3	131 019	14.5	11	48	19 252	37 145	91.8	20 881	93.2
Cavalier, ND	38 019	9	4 330	15.6	3	7	625	1 094	91.2	1 031	91.3
Dickey, ND	38 021	9	5 487	15.5	3	6	908	1 531	78.7	1 047	94.7
Divide, ND	38 023	9	2 149	12.5	1	2	281	436	99.5	407	99.5
Dunn, ND	38 025	9	3 442	17.2	4	6	500	972	95.8	862	96.2
Eddy, ND	38 027	9	2 626	14.7	3	5	504	597	97.5	522	98.7
Emmons, ND	38 029	8	3 845	16.2	6	8	679	923	96.1	840	98.3
Foster, ND	38 031	9	3 580	17.0	1	2	623	982	95.0	816	98.2
Golden Valley, ND	38 033	9	1 739	19.8	2	3	371	505	94.7	445	96.2
Grand Forks, ND	38 035	3	65 940	14.3	10	33	9 490	23 794	95.1	11 757	94.6
Grant, ND	38 037	8	2 615	13.6	2	3	320	629	96.8	552	98.9
Griggs, ND	38 039	9	2 497	14.1	2	4	490	609	98.0	545	99.8
Hettinger, ND	38 041	9	2 486	14.3	3	6	467	596	98.0	540	99.6
Kidder, ND	38 043	8	2 481	14.0	5	7	454	539	97.4	507	99.0
LaMoure, ND	38 045	9	4 384	14.6	5	11	735	1 074	94.3	977	96.5
Logan, ND	38 047	9	2 059	14.9	3	5	361	483	93.4	421	96.0
McHenry, ND	38 049	9	5 511	14.7	4	10	1 046	1 351	99.0	1 183	99.8
McIntosh, ND	38 051	9	3 013	12.8	3	6	459	654	94.3	569	96.8
McKenzie, ND	38 053	9	5 594	19.4	5	9	830	1 675	94.0	1 454	95.0
McLean, ND	38 055	8	8 604	14.9	7	14	1 577	2 082	98.1	1 858	99.3
Mercer, ND	38 057	6	8 364	17.1	5	8	1 567	2 442	95.1	2 188	97.0
Morton, ND	38 059	3	25 528	17.3	10	21	4 392	6 330	89.1	5 190	91.3
Mountrail, ND	38 061	9	6 513	17.7	4	8	1 368	1 796	95.2	1 464	96.7
Nelson, ND	38 063	8	3 424	12.9	2	4	565	823	93.2	730	95.2
Oliver, ND	38 065	8	1 813	16.2	2	3	282	549	90.9	500	92.8
Pembina, ND	38 067	9	8 038	14.8	7	14	1 397	1 954	97.5	1 734	99.0
Pierce, ND	38 069	7	4 291	15.4	2	4	609	1 028	93.6	894	93.4
Ramsey, ND	38 071	7	11 429	16.5	6	13	2 105	3 016	91.1	2 346	92.7
Ransom, ND	38 073	8	5 810	15.9	5	10	1 288	1 311	95.7	1 181	97.1
Renville, ND	38 075	9	2 422	14.1	4	7	633	596	95.3	521	99.0
Richland, ND	38 077	6	17 340	16.1	10	17	2 675	5 726	93.6	3 497	93.8
Rolette, ND	38 079	9	13 864	22.3	6	12	2 941	4 863	97.1	3 857	97.4
Sargent, ND	38 081	9	4 150	17.5	2	4	511	988	96.4	874	97.8
Sheridan, ND	38 083	9	1 430	12.6	2	4	148	339	98.5	322	100.0
Sioux, ND	38 085	8	4 182	24.7	3	5	467	1 566	91.3	1 258	93.4
Slope, ND	38 087	9	709	14.4	3	3	16	180	96.1	157	100.0
Stark, ND	38 089	7	22 073	15.9	6	17	3 424	6 347	81.6	4 586	78.6
Steele, ND	38 091	8	2 007	17.9	2	3	326	585	97.8	500	99.6
Stutsman, ND	38 093	7	20 835	14.5	8	19	2 967	5 399	76.4	3 983	93.2
Towner, ND	38 095	9	2 544	14.5	3	6	375	679	97.3	595	99.5
Traill, ND	38 097	8	8 321	15.8	5	10	1 544	2 369	98.6	1 606	98.7
Walsh, ND	38 099	6	11 607	15.7	11	18	2 161	2 811	95.5	2 438	97.1
Ward, ND	38 101	5	55 767	17.1	12	36	9 103	16 316	91.5	11 203	91.8
Wells, ND	38 103	9	4 574	14.1	5	8	721	1 158	95.3	998	97.4
Williams, ND	38 105	7	19 282	16.4	8	21	3 135	5 133	91.4	4 161	91.7
OHIO	39 000		11 464 042	17.7	1 138	3 999	1 840 032	3 014 460	82.1	2 157 981	86.6
Adams, OH	39 001	6	28 454	17.9	3	12	5 031	6 202	93.6	5 423	94.0
Allen, OH	39 003	3	106 234	18.2	16	39	15 678	28 722	80.7	21 705	85.9
Ashland, OH	39 005	4	54 123	17.5	8	25	10 311	14 026	77.1	10 029	90.3
Ashtabula, OH	39 007	4	103 221	18.1	9	41	17 301	24 547	90.2	20 225	93.1
Athens, OH	39 009	4	62 062	11.6	7	21	8 449	28 058	96.2	8 535	95.6
Auglaize, OH	39 011	4	47 242	18.9	8	21	8 579	12 239	90.0	9 877	93.5
Belmont, OH	39 013	3	69 228	15.0	9	26	9 042	15 628	85.4	12 369	87.1
Brown, OH	39 015	1	44 398	18.8	7	17	8 504	10 406	92.9	8 815	94.7
Butler, OH	39 017	1	350 412	17.8	17	92	57 542	95 720	85.6	63 221	87.7
Carroll, OH	39 019	2	29 388	17.1	5	15	4 330	6 740	91.2	5 595	94.0
Champaign, OH	39 021	6	39 698	18.0	7	17	6 641	9 309	87.3	7 597	93.6
Clark, OH	39 023	3	142 376	17.6	15	57	25 013	36 734	84.1	27 318	91.4
Clermont, OH	39 025	1	190 589	19.0	12	53	33 163	46 454	82.1	36 411	85.9
Clinton, OH	39 027	6	42 570	18.0	5	15	8 352	10 521	84.1	7 852	94.8
Columbiana, OH	39 029	4	110 928	16.7	14	42	16 780	26 376	90.9	21 122	94.6
Coshocton, OH	39 031	6	36 945	17.8	5	17	5 974	8 641	88.2	7 235	90.9
Crawford, OH	39 033	4	45 774	17.3	6	26	7 883	10 769	87.0	8 889	90.6
Cuyahoga, OH	39 035	1	1 335 317	17.8	89	374	197 872	365 498	75.7	263 086	81.1
Darke, OH	39 037	6	52 983	18.1	8	23	8 951	13 068	89.9	10 595	92.2
Defiance, OH	39 039	4	39 112	17.7	5	19	6 833	10 009	85.6	7 970	91.8

[1]County type codes are from the Economic Research Service of the United States Department of Agriculture. See notes and definitions at the end of this section.

Table C-1. Population, School, and Student Characteristics by County—*Continued*

STATE County	Characteristics of students, 2004–2005				Outcomes		Staff and students, 2004–2005		
	Percent with IEP2	Percent eligible for free or reduced-price lunch	Percent minority	Percent English-language learners	Number of graduates, 2003–2004	Percent dropouts, grades 9–12, 2001–2002	Number of teachers	Student-teacher ratio	Central administration staff
	10	11	12	13	14	15	16	17	18
NORTH DAKOTA	14.6	29.1	12.8	2.0	...	2.0	8 061	12.5	...
Adams, ND	14.0	34.0	1.1	0.0	...	...	30	11.5	4
Barnes, ND	15.8	29.9	2.0	0.1	...	0.7	155	10.7	16
Benson, ND	21.6	57.9	52.8	0.0	...	7.6	105	9.5	13
Billings, ND	17.9	30.4	0.0	0.0	...	...	10	5.5	3
Bottineau, ND	15.5	30.3	4.5	0.0	...	0.6	91	10.9	...
Bowman, ND	11.1	30.9	1.8	0.0	...	1.1	59	11.1	5
Burke, ND	14.4	25.6	1.4	0.0	...	...	41	6.7	5
Burleigh, ND	13.4	21.0	7.6	2.6	...	1.3	707	15.2	48
Cass, ND	12.2	18.2	8.3	4.6	...	3.2	1 261	15.3	100
Cavalier, ND	14.4	26.9	3.0	0.0	...	0.3	60	10.4	6
Dickey, ND	11.5	28.4	5.8	5.4	...	0.4	74	12.2	9
Divide, ND	10.0	41.6	1.1	0.0	...	0.8	26	10.8	2
Dunn, ND	11.8	35.0	12.0	0.0	...	...	62	8.0	8
Eddy, ND	10.3	37.5	14.7	0.0	...	0.5	44	11.4	6
Emmons, ND	12.8	39.5	1.6	0.0	...	...	60	11.3	...
Foster, ND	11.7	21.0	2.7	0.0	...	...	46	13.5	2
Golden Valley, ND	12.1	47.4	9.7	0.0	...	...	37	10.0	4
Grand Forks, ND	15.6	30.5	10.9	1.4	...	1.3	765	12.4	...
Grant, ND	15.9	49.7	7.5	0.0	...	...	32	10.1	5
Griggs, ND	15.1	49.6	1.2	0.0	...	0.5	40	12.4	6
Hettinger, ND	11.1	35.5	1.5	0.0	...	1.5	41	11.4	4
Kidder, ND	11.9	37.9	5.3	0.0	...	2.3	49	9.2	8
LaMoure, ND	13.9	39.7	4.2	6.0	...	0.6	81	9.1	11
Logan, ND	14.4	34.6	1.9	0.0	...	...	38	9.5	6
McHenry, ND	17.0	38.2	2.8	1.1	...	1.3	94	11.2	10
McIntosh, ND	15.0	38.1	1.1	0.0	...	...	49	9.3	5
McKenzie, ND	15.4	40.9	29.5	0.0	...	2.6	101	8.2	12
McLean, ND	14.6	34.4	12.8	0.0	...	0.9	151	10.5	15
Mercer, ND	14.7	14.5	7.9	0.0	...	0.7	115	13.6	...
Morton, ND	16.2	29.9	7.5	0.0	...	1.9	329	13.3	25
Mountrail, ND	18.4	49.6	63.5	0.0	...	2.4	114	12.0	13
Nelson, ND	17.2	31.0	4.1	0.5	...	0.8	46	12.2	4
Oliver, ND	14.9	17.3	5.5	0.0	...	4.3	26	11.0	...
Pembina, ND	18.3	30.5	11.7	4.4	...	0.9	119	11.8	13
Pierce, ND	15.3	27.6	3.4	0.0	...	...	60	10.2	3
Ramsey, ND	18.4	38.8	27.0	0.0	...	2.9	175	12.0	30
Ransom, ND	14.8	25.5	3.1	2.4	...	1.4	98	13.2	8
Renville, ND	19.9	39.2	7.5	0.0	...	1.1	66	9.6	...
Richland, ND	14.3	25.2	7.0	0.7	...	1.6	234	11.4	...
Rolette, ND	9.9	68.6	80.0	12.6	...	9.9	301	9.8	36
Sargent, ND	16.4	22.9	2.1	0.0	...	0.4	43	11.9	3
Sheridan, ND	18.9	44.6	2.7	0.0	...	1.4	21	7.1	2
Sioux, ND	25.1	72.4	97.4	0.0	...	...	66	7.1	9
Slope, ND	50.0	0.0	0.0	0.0	...	...	4	3.7	1
Stark, ND	14.6	31.2	4.0	0.0	...	2.0	250	13.7	18
Steele, ND	14.1	27.9	2.8	0.0	...	...	33	9.8	2
Stutsman, ND	16.1	31.0	4.9	0.5	...	1.4	261	11.4	25
Towner, ND	14.9	36.0	10.7	0.0	...	...	44	8.6	5
Traill, ND	13.5	22.6	5.6	0.0	...	2.1	117	13.2	12
Walsh, ND	16.5	37.2	17.1	5.6	...	1.3	201	10.7	19
Ward, ND	16.2	26.6	16.5	0.0	...	2.0	675	13.5	...
Wells, ND	13.3	33.1	2.5	0.0	...	0.6	71	10.1	11
Williams, ND	16.7	32.6	12.7	0.0	...	2.3	281	11.2	21
OHIO	14.2	31.3	20.9	1.5	...	3.1	118 060	15.6	...
Adams, OH	15.4	55.6	0.8	0.0	...	3.2	344	14.6	...
Allen, OH	13.3	37.4	19.4	0.2	...	4.1	1 018	15.4	...
Ashland, OH	14.3	27.3	2.5	0.1	...	2.0	645	16.0	...
Ashtabula, OH	13.9	43.4	8.0	1.0	...	2.7	1 070	16.2	161
Athens, OH	18.3	40.3	4.3	0.9	...	2.5	647	13.1	166
Auglaize, OH	14.7	18.7	1.1	0.2	...	0.9	566	15.2	78
Belmont, OH	16.0	39.7	3.7	0.0	...	1.5	650	13.9	98
Brown, OH	10.5	32.6	1.1	0.0	...	2.3	537	15.8	81
Butler, OH	13.3	21.7	12.8	2.0	...	2.6	3 518	16.4	...
Carroll, OH	14.9	37.5	1.5	0.0	...	1.2	247	17.6	...
Champaign, OH	15.8	20.9	3.4	0.1	...	2.4	521	12.8	85
Clark, OH	12.4	32.8	14.2	0.7	...	3.6	1 563	16.0	217
Clermont, OH	11.6	20.2	2.5	0.4	...	4.1	1 917	17.3	261
Clinton, OH	11.6	26.1	3.3	0.0	...	2.0	518	16.1	114
Columbiana, OH	15.1	38.8	2.5	0.0	...	1.6	1 141	14.7	164
Coshocton, OH	18.3	33.7	1.7	0.0	...	1.7	377	15.8	...
Crawford, OH	18.3	32.5	1.6	0.2	...	3.2	496	15.9	86
Cuyahoga, OH	15.3	44.3	49.9	2.9	...	5.8	12 303	16.1	...
Darke, OH	12.2	21.7	1.6	0.2	...	2.2	576	15.5	86
Defiance, OH	16.2	21.5	11.0	0.3	...	2.8	436	15.7	55

2IEP = Individual Education Program. See notes and definitions at the end of this section.
. . . = Not available.

Table C-1. Population, School, and Student Characteristics by County—*Continued*

STATE County	Revenue, 2003–2004				Current expenditures, 2003–2004			Resident population, 16 to 19 years, 2000			
	Total revenue (thousands of dollars)	Percent of revenue from:			Total expenditures (thousands of dollars)	Amount per student (dollars)	Percent for instruction	Total	Percent in armed forces	Percent high school graduates	Percent not enrolled, not employed, not in armed forces, not high school graduate
		Federal government	State government	Local government							
	19	20	21	22	23	24	25	26	27	28	29
NORTH DAKOTA	925 393	14.6	36.4	49.1	786 860	7 723	64.1	43 073	1.0	8.6	2.6
Adams, ND	3 290	6.9	36.4	56.7	2 880	7 978	59.9	142	0.0	6.3	1.4
Barnes, ND	17 011	9.2	42.9	47.9	13 771	8 044	68.0	860	0.1	6.9	2.9
Benson, ND	12 066	41.2	34.0	24.8	10 514	10 168	68.4	490	0.0	5.3	10.2
Billings, ND	1 802	27.5	2.3	70.3	1 559	20 513	48.4	59	0.0	6.8	0.0
Bottineau, ND	10 317	14.8	34.5	50.7	9 406	9 053	59.5	538	0.0	3.7	0.4
Bowman, ND	6 165	5.5	38.4	56.1	5 551	8 335	63.7	165	0.0	2.4	0.0
Burke, ND	3 387	8.1	35.3	56.7	3 146	10 701	64.1	120	0.0	2.5	1.7
Burleigh, ND	86 864	11.6	38.3	50.1	75 498	7 053	67.6	4 638	0.0	7.7	1.6
Cass, ND	169 847	6.7	32.4	60.8	141 683	7 405	66.3	7 786	0.1	8.6	2.1
Cavalier, ND	5 953	7.0	31.6	61.4	5 628	8 739	59.5	246	0.0	1.6	0.0
Dickey, ND	7 541	6.6	39.4	54.1	6 012	6 687	57.5	355	0.0	8.5	0.8
Divide, ND	2 841	9.4	35.0	55.6	2 645	8 817	58.5	122	0.0	2.5	4.1
Dunn, ND	6 778	30.9	30.4	38.7	6 668	12 605	52.8	203	0.0	8.4	2.5
Eddy, ND	4 965	18.3	33.5	48.2	4 594	9 531	60.4	140	0.0	7.1	2.1
Emmons, ND	6 338	11.9	41.0	47.1	5 691	7 839	58.9	215	0.0	2.8	0.0
Foster, ND	4 454	6.8	43.1	50.1	3 919	6 057	63.8	208	0.0	5.8	0.0
Golden Valley, ND	3 835	11.3	34.9	53.8	3 575	9 383	56.7	155	0.0	7.1	2.6
Grand Forks, ND	84 557	16.6	35.7	47.7	68 757	7 021	67.0	5 458	2.0	8.7	1.7
Grant, ND	3 635	12.1	39.8	48.1	3 104	8 744	53.1	175	0.0	5.7	2.3
Griggs, ND	5 949	7.7	42.9	49.3	4 491	9 260	56.1	171	0.0	2.3	0.6
Hettinger, ND	5 493	11.5	37.5	51.0	4 371	9 125	55.7	145	0.0	7.6	1.4
Kidder, ND	4 563	9.7	34.3	56.0	4 136	9 110	58.6	178	0.0	10.7	7.9
LaMoure, ND	7 953	14.0	34.0	52.0	7 007	9 018	61.3	319	0.0	3.1	2.8
Logan, ND	4 036	13.1	43.0	43.9	3 420	9 421	56.8	98	0.0	5.1	2.0
McHenry, ND	8 908	10.7	39.6	49.6	7 965	7 629	63.1	355	0.0	6.8	0.8
McIntosh, ND	4 241	7.9	40.4	51.8	3 945	7 986	59.7	166	0.0	3.0	0.0
McKenzie, ND	12 077	33.5	26.7	39.7	11 547	12 578	56.9	400	0.0	5.0	2.3
McLean, ND	14 204	8.8	41.7	49.5	13 487	8 274	57.3	570	0.2	7.0	1.4
Mercer, ND	14 429	6.7	39.6	53.7	13 134	7 726	58.4	597	0.0	6.9	0.8
Morton, ND	32 590	11.6	44.9	43.5	28 953	6 650	62.8	1 511	0.2	9.7	5.6
Mountrail, ND	12 406	34.3	39.3	26.4	11 149	7 615	62.4	400	0.3	4.8	5.3
Nelson, ND	5 354	7.8	34.4	57.8	4 648	7 986	58.3	205	0.0	1.0	0.0
Oliver, ND	2 348	5.6	35.8	58.6	2 117	8 468	57.3	135	0.0	1.5	1.5
Pembina, ND	15 132	8.0	34.8	57.2	13 257	8 553	63.7	555	0.0	8.5	3.6
Pierce, ND	5 256	8.7	40.8	50.5	4 984	7 691	64.8	249	0.0	8.0	0.0
Ramsey, ND	19 528	15.3	41.0	43.7	16 773	8 130	62.7	844	0.0	11.7	6.0
Ransom, ND	8 359	4.9	36.1	59.0	6 856	6 580	59.7	329	0.0	4.6	2.7
Renville, ND	6 017	11.5	38.2	50.3	5 469	8 586	61.3	165	1.2	11.5	0.0
Richland, ND	24 338	8.5	37.5	54.0	21 208	7 695	65.0	1 655	0.0	5.5	0.3
Rolette, ND	32 410	53.4	34.6	12.1	28 451	9 443	65.6	1 027	0.0	6.3	11.9
Sargent, ND	6 136	6.4	40.6	52.9	5 267	6 486	61.9	194	0.0	7.2	0.0
Sheridan, ND	1 885	9.0	36.5	54.5	1 892	11 679	59.9	75	0.0	4.0	5.3
Sioux, ND	6 979	45.5	31.8	22.7	6 357	14 350	64.6	348	0.0	6.6	12.9
Slope, ND	427	19.4	18.5	62.1	290	10 357	65.9	52	0.0	7.7	0.0
Stark, ND	27 246	14.9	43.3	41.8	23 946	6 875	64.1	1 687	0.2	10.8	3.2
Steele, ND	3 150	4.5	33.1	62.4	2 626	8 105	55.9	139	0.0	2.9	2.2
Stutsman, ND	26 266	10.2	38.5	51.3	22 292	7 506	63.3	1 471	0.2	9.2	3.3
Towner, ND	4 336	15.2	31.9	52.9	3 606	8 668	61.6	165	0.0	2.4	2.4
Traill, ND	14 467	7.9	35.1	57.0	12 389	7 906	60.0	544	0.0	4.2	1.3
Walsh, ND	20 159	16.4	37.2	46.5	16 609	8 601	64.6	789	0.0	11.9	2.4
Ward, ND	88 167	20.2	34.8	45.0	66 986	7 231	65.2	3 782	7.7	17.8	2.7
Wells, ND	7 918	11.7	36.6	51.7	7 026	8 663	59.3	278	0.0	4.0	4.0
Williams, ND	31 020	15.1	37.2	47.7	25 605	8 004	65.2	1 400	0.1	6.6	2.0
OHIO	19 238 482	6.8	43.9	49.2	16 668 698	9 043	63.5	639 825	0.1	10.5	4.6
Adams, OH	45 106	9.9	55.8	34.3	38 418	7 536	65.6	1 538	0.0	16.2	6.2
Allen, OH	185 899	6.9	51.2	41.9	148 141	8 340	62.2	6 965	0.1	9.2	4.9
Ashland, OH	66 902	5.5	46.0	48.4	60 295	8 201	65.7	3 732	0.0	10.5	5.6
Ashtabula, OH	201 133	7.4	59.0	33.6	147 355	8 364	64.9	5 742	0.2	16.9	5.9
Athens, OH	99 239	12.3	51.5	36.2	84 034	9 913	62.7	7 591	0.0	4.0	1.1
Auglaize, OH	75 281	4.8	46.5	48.7	67 029	7 648	66.2	2 790	0.0	9.7	0.2
Belmont, OH	86 516	9.6	55.8	34.6	79 979	8 752	64.0	3 577	0.0	10.2	3.2
Brown, OH	87 628	5.0	68.5	26.4	64 531	7 538	62.9	2 323	0.2	12.6	4.4
Butler, OH	529 055	5.7	44.2	50.1	473 244	8 358	62.8	21 825	0.1	10.6	3.1
Carroll, OH	26 519	8.0	58.0	34.0	26 809	7 002	63.0	1 449	0.0	13.8	2.1
Champaign, OH	74 527	4.5	46.8	48.8	66 314	8 666	63.5	2 230	0.0	14.4	3.5
Clark, OH	260 354	6.9	58.6	34.5	203 945	8 371	63.5	8 403	0.2	9.6	6.8
Clermont, OH	259 290	4.8	46.4	48.9	233 631	8 219	62.3	9 787	0.0	11.1	5.1
Clinton, OH	73 965	6.6	46.8	46.7	65 046	7 826	62.8	2 584	0.0	12.9	1.2
Columbiana, OH	162 290	7.8	57.0	35.2	143 488	8 434	63.9	6 022	0.0	12.4	3.5
Coshocton, OH	51 478	6.9	53.2	39.9	48 717	8 032	64.7	2 168	0.0	10.7	5.2
Crawford, OH	68 038	6.9	46.6	46.6	61 695	7 778	64.5	2 618	0.0	14.2	3.3
Cuyahoga, OH	2 437 682	8.1	37.6	54.3	2 132 695	10 514	62.3	70 120	0.1	9.6	5.9
Darke, OH	74 709	6.6	49.8	43.6	68 671	7 639	67.5	2 868	0.0	10.5	2.8
Defiance, OH	55 934	4.6	45.4	50.0	50 348	7 316	65.0	2 452	0.0	10.6	3.4

Table C-1. Population, School, and Student Characteristics by County—*Continued*

STATE County	High school graduates, 2000			College enrollment, 2000		College graduates, 2000 (percent)						
	Population 25 years and over	High school graduate or less (percent)	High school graduate or more (percent)	Number	Percent public	Bachelor's degree or more	+/- U.S. percentage with bachelor's degree or more	Non-Hispanic White	Black	American Indian and Alaska Native	Asian or Pacific Islander	Hispanic[3]
	30	31	32	33	34	35	36	37	38	39	40	41
NORTH DAKOTA	408 585	44.0	83.9	47 003	89.2	22.0	-2.4	22.4	20.5	9.7	47.4	16.3
Adams, ND	1 885	52.3	83.1	35	80.0	16.6	-7.8	16.5	11.1	8.7	...	60.0
Barnes, ND	7 792	47.5	85.0	912	96.3	22.1	-2.3	22.1	13.3	14.9	38.9	56.3
Benson, ND	3 902	56.4	73.8	169	97.0	10.9	-13.5	14.1	...	4.4	0.0	8.0
Billings, ND	644	54.2	77.8	23	87.0	18.8	-5.6	18.9	...	...	...	...
Bottineau, ND	4 973	48.4	81.3	406	97.5	14.9	-9.5	14.8	...	20.0	100.0	0.0
Bowman, ND	2 290	49.9	82.2	61	93.4	17.9	-6.5	17.8	0.0	50.0	...	100.0
Burke, ND	1 687	56.1	78.8	21	100.0	12.0	-12.4	11.8	100.0	0.0	0.0	...
Burleigh, ND	44 636	35.8	87.9	4 801	63.5	28.7	4.3	29.2	6.7	6.8	38.1	26.6
Cass, ND	74 668	32.0	90.9	14 297	94.2	31.3	6.9	31.5	22.6	8.5	59.8	16.6
Cavalier, ND	3 462	51.6	78.8	28	78.6	13.1	-11.3	13.1	...	25.0	0.0	0.0
Dickey, ND	3 815	52.3	79.6	418	37.3	16.6	-7.8	16.4	0.0	26.3	100.0	15.6
Divide, ND	1 741	54.5	80.4	24	100.0	13.3	-11.1	13.2	...	0.0	50.0	0.0
Dunn, ND	2 393	54.7	77.5	71	94.4	16.3	-8.1	16.5	0.0	13.1	66.7	0.0
Eddy, ND	1 933	52.5	75.5	48	91.7	15.9	-8.5	15.8	...	17.4	100.0	0.0
Emmons, ND	3 125	64.1	65.9	60	90.0	12.3	-12.1	12.2	0.0	50.0	0.0	10.0
Foster, ND	2 569	51.9	78.0	77	64.9	19.8	-4.6	19.9	...	...	60.0	0.0
Golden Valley, ND	1 278	46.6	87.4	49	83.7	19.8	-4.6	19.9	...	...	...	0.0
Grand Forks, ND	37 366	35.2	89.2	11 022	97.4	27.8	3.4	28.3	16.6	17.0	40.2	16.9
Grant, ND	2 044	59.7	73.4	41	70.7	11.2	-13.2	10.9	...	18.2	100.0	0.0
Griggs, ND	1 993	53.9	78.7	40	82.5	15.7	-8.7	15.6	...	50.0	0.0	...
Hettinger, ND	1 978	57.8	74.8	37	81.1	14.4	-10.0	14.3	...	22.2	0.0	0.0
Kidder, ND	1 982	63.0	72.0	26	65.4	11.0	-13.4	11.1	...	0.0	...	0.0
LaMoure, ND	3 297	58.5	75.3	65	73.8	13.9	-10.5	13.8	...	22.2	...	18.2
Logan, ND	1 693	63.7	66.0	42	88.1	12.9	-11.5	12.7	...	...	25.0	54.5
McHenry, ND	4 192	57.9	76.9	108	96.3	13.2	-11.2	13.1	33.3	25.0	60.0	20.0
McIntosh, ND	2 580	66.6	59.3	63	74.6	9.9	-14.5	9.6	...	0.0	60.0	16.7
McKenzie, ND	3 644	53.5	79.1	116	92.2	15.7	-8.7	16.4	33.3	10.5	31.6	12.5
McLean, ND	6 620	51.8	79.0	159	87.4	15.1	-9.3	15.2	...	12.4	60.0	11.8
Mercer, ND	5 780	52.0	79.0	151	81.5	14.4	-10.0	14.1	...	15.7	84.6	42.9
Morton, ND	16 520	51.7	80.2	716	76.5	17.0	-7.4	17.0	75.0	11.1	0.0	11.3
Mountrail, ND	4 309	51.7	77.9	235	85.5	15.6	-8.8	16.0	...	10.6	78.1	0.0
Nelson, ND	2 753	49.5	81.4	61	83.6	17.5	-6.9	17.2	100.0	12.5	88.9	...
Oliver, ND	1 402	55.4	79.9	39	64.1	12.0	-12.4	12.2	...	0.0	...	50.0
Pembina, ND	5 908	52.1	79.8	101	86.1	16.4	-8.0	16.7	50.0	5.6	80.0	9.4
Pierce, ND	3 300	53.3	76.7	101	99.0	14.7	0.7	14.0	...	21.1	0.0	...
Ramsey, ND	8 123	45.1	80.1	518	97.1	18.8	-5.6	19.4	...	7.6	66.7	28.9
Ransom, ND	4 065	54.4	81.3	75	92.0	15.8	-8.6	15.7	0.0	0.0	80.0	23.5
Renville, ND	1 872	48.8	84.1	50	88.0	16.1	-8.3	15.6	...	18.2	57.1	0.0
Richland, ND	10 991	44.2	83.2	2 039	95.3	15.2	-9.2	15.3	...	5.1	23.3	3.5
Rolette, ND	7 406	52.9	73.7	719	95.5	14.7	-9.7	21.8	0.0	10.3	73.4	0.0
Sargent, ND	2 989	54.0	81.1	56	87.5	12.7	-11.7	12.6	100.0	28.6	...	0.0
Sheridan, ND	1 280	63.4	67.8	11	72.7	9.7	-14.7	9.8	...	0.0	...	0.0
Sioux, ND	1 919	53.5	78.5	196	74.5	11.2	-13.2	17.5	...	8.5	12.5	9.1
Slope, ND	538	53.9	82.5	8	100.0	16.0	-8.4	16.0	...	...	...	...
Stark, ND	14 252	47.9	79.9	1 509	95.4	22.3	-2.1	22.2	84.6	31.0	74.1	2.4
Steele, ND	1 529	42.2	86.1	59	88.1	19.8	-4.6	19.8	0.0	16.7	...	66.7
Stutsman, ND	14 618	52.9	81.1	1 215	23.7	19.7	-4.7	19.6	0.0	13.0	64.7	31.6
Towner, ND	2 057	51.9	81.9	49	91.8	16.1	-8.3	16.6	0.0	0.0	...	0.0
Traill, ND	5 542	42.2	83.7	670	98.5	21.8	-2.6	22.2	0.0	5.3	0.0	0.0
Walsh, ND	8 530	55.5	76.6	194	88.7	13.3	-11.1	13.8	0.0	0.0	0.0	0.7
Ward, ND	35 957	41.6	87.4	4 170	96.2	22.1	-2.3	22.4	21.1	8.5	20.0	25.6
Wells, ND	3 715	58.3	72.6	95	89.5	13.7	-10.7	13.8	0.0	0.0	...	0.0
Williams, ND	13 048	49.2	82.5	747	94.9	16.5	-7.9	17.1	...	8.5	23.8	2.4
OHIO	7 411 740	53.1	83.0	652 393	75.1	21.1	-3.3	21.8	11.9	12.4	58.0	15.2
Adams, OH	17 775	75.8	68.6	550	91.3	7.2	-17.2	7.2	...	15.2	22.2	0.0
Allen, OH	69 669	60.1	82.5	5 414	65.1	13.4	-11.0	14.1	7.4	14.3	46.4	9.1
Ashland, OH	33 339	63.7	83.3	3 166	38.1	15.9	-8.5	15.7	12.3	0.0	56.3	11.8
Ashtabula, OH	67 994	65.9	79.9	2 903	82.2	11.1	-13.3	11.3	6.6	2.4	25.6	4.1
Athens, OH	31 563	51.2	82.9	18 795	97.2	25.7	1.3	24.3	31.5	19.1	76.6	49.4
Auglaize, OH	30 093	61.9	85.7	1 549	82.1	13.4	-11.0	13.4	8.7	0.0	53.6	11.9
Belmont, OH	49 616	65.5	80.9	2 477	85.2	11.1	-13.3	11.2	1.9	10.2	69.1	27.1
Brown, OH	27 209	70.5	74.8	1 164	79.0	8.8	-15.6	8.8	11.0	0.0	22.4	23.8
Butler, OH	207 213	50.3	83.3	26 012	89.4	23.5	-0.9	23.3	18.2	17.8	56.4	22.2
Carroll, OH	19 460	72.9	80.1	679	79.2	9.1	-15.3	9.1	11.8	24.4	27.8	13.7
Champaign, OH	25 644	65.8	82.3	1 085	55.4	10.6	-13.8	10.4	12.2	17.3	26.0	6.9
Clark, OH	95 298	58.4	81.2	7 419	64.6	14.9	-9.5	15.2	10.5	10.0	50.8	12.5
Clermont, OH	113 513	53.3	82.0	6 609	79.0	20.8	-3.6	20.4	28.7	16.9	55.4	22.9
Clinton, OH	25 720	59.0	83.1	2 142	47.5	14.1	-10.3	14.1	12.0	10.9	68.2	7.9
Columbiana, OH	76 022	67.1	80.6	3 521	81.5	10.8	-13.6	11.0	3.8	13.6	40.7	2.9
Coshocton, OH	24 172	72.4	78.7	758	77.4	9.8	-14.6	9.8	3.3	0.0	21.2	0.0
Crawford, OH	31 379	69.2	80.2	1 143	72.9	9.7	-14.7	9.5	9.0	10.1	57.1	6.9
Cuyahoga, OH	936 148	48.4	81.6	75 981	63.7	25.1	0.7	29.5	10.9	14.3	60.1	13.8
Darke, OH	35 206	67.6	82.8	1 540	88.4	10.1	-14.3	10.0	7.9	0.0	40.2	13.0
Defiance, OH	25 426	61.1	84.7	1 478	61.8	14.3	-10.1	14.9	10.2	0.0	8.3	6.9

[3]May be of any race.
... = Not available.

Table C-1. Population, School, and Student Characteristics by County—*Continued*

STATE County	State/ county code	County type[1]	Population, 2005		Number of schools and students, 2004–2005			Resident enrollment, 2000			
			Total	Percent 5 to 17 years	School districts	Schools	Students	Total	Percent public	K–12	Percent public
			1	2	3	4	5	6	7	8	9
Delaware, OH	39 041	1	150 268	18.6	10	75	45 662	30 948	74.6	22 024	86.2
Erie, OH	39 043	3	78 665	16.9	9	32	13 747	19 104	85.8	15 363	89.6
Fairfield, OH	39 045	1	138 423	18.4	16	47	23 794	31 818	85.4	24 594	90.4
Fayette, OH	39 047	6	28 199	17.7	2	16	5 063	6 481	94.5	5 355	96.8
Franklin, OH	39 049	1	1 090 771	17.6	78	328	154 129	307 823	83.0	191 642	88.0
Fulton, OH	39 051	2	42 955	19.4	8	24	9 086	11 406	89.0	8 815	94.1
Gallia, OH	39 053	6	31 362	16.9	4	14	4 873	7 742	84.0	5 887	91.8
Geauga, OH	39 055	1	95 218	19.3	9	32	15 269	24 286	73.7	19 058	77.2
Greene, OH	39 057	2	151 996	16.3	10	36	22 752	46 402	78.3	26 857	85.9
Guernsey, OH	39 059	6	41 123	18.1	4	14	6 155	9 866	90.1	8 153	93.5
Hamilton, OH	39 061	1	806 652	17.9	51	235	115 452	233 939	73.5	163 773	75.8
Hancock, OH	39 063	4	73 503	17.7	11	38	12 641	19 271	78.5	13 404	92.4
Hardin, OH	39 065	6	32 032	16.4	6	16	4 919	9 275	68.1	5 458	96.3
Harrison, OH	39 067	6	15 920	16.3	1	6	2 047	3 343	91.6	2 750	94.0
Henry, OH	39 069	6	29 453	18.8	5	16	5 158	7 621	85.8	6 173	88.5
Highland, OH	39 071	6	42 818	18.7	5	20	8 175	9 963	92.9	8 190	96.3
Hocking, OH	39 073	6	29 009	17.4	1	8	4 097	6 737	91.0	5 370	92.8
Holmes, OH	39 075	7	41 567	24.0	3	17	4 647	8 965	65.2	8 145	64.2
Huron, OH	39 077	4	60 385	19.4	6	22	9 533	15 240	82.8	12 304	85.4
Jackson, OH	39 079	7	33 526	17.6	3	12	5 861	7 870	90.4	6 429	94.0
Jefferson, OH	39 081	3	70 599	15.3	7	33	10 944	17 543	79.2	12 315	86.7
Knox, OH	39 083	4	58 398	16.8	10	21	8 496	14 679	74.1	10 108	90.6
Lake, OH	39 085	1	232 466	17.0	12	61	34 731	56 308	81.0	41 818	84.4
Lawrence, OH	39 087	2	63 112	17.1	9	26	10 787	15 147	94.2	11 614	95.8
Licking, OH	39 089	1	154 806	17.9	17	69	32 835	37 916	82.2	28 214	90.2
Logan, OH	39 091	4	46 580	18.5	9	18	8 778	10 951	91.3	9 184	95.1
Lorain, OH	39 093	1	296 307	18.4	28	101	47 548	75 017	79.6	55 489	85.9
Lucas, OH	39 095	2	448 229	18.4	49	150	73 388	129 500	79.7	88 948	80.3
Madison, OH	39 097	1	41 295	17.1	7	19	6 842	9 790	83.0	7 663	88.2
Mahoning, OH	39 099	2	254 274	16.4	25	88	38 293	64 677	84.7	47 024	86.9
Marion, OH	39 101	4	65 932	17.1	13	29	12 619	16 180	89.6	12 999	93.1
Medina, OH	39 103	1	167 010	18.7	8	44	28 384	40 364	83.3	31 234	88.1
Meigs, OH	39 105	6	23 232	16.1	3	8	3 606	5 161	94.0	4 275	96.6
Mercer, OH	39 107	7	41 202	20.2	7	21	8 841	11 195	92.8	9 147	95.9
Miami, OH	39 109	2	101 619	17.7	11	40	17 325	24 416	87.0	19 342	90.3
Monroe, OH	39 111	8	14 698	16.2	1	10	2 719	3 438	88.5	2 778	88.3
Montgomery, OH	39 113	2	547 435	17.3	57	172	82 739	150 213	78.3	101 609	85.8
Morgan, OH	39 115	6	14 958	17.5	2	5	2 249	3 555	93.2	2 863	96.2
Morrow, OH	39 117	1	34 322	18.3	8	17	5 779	7 830	89.9	6 556	93.0
Muskingum, OH	39 119	4	85 579	18.1	14	45	16 120	21 558	83.9	16 340	91.6
Noble, OH	39 121	6	14 156	14.7	2	4	2 219	3 540	89.7	2 613	93.3
Ottawa, OH	39 123	2	41 583	15.5	7	21	6 325	9 895	90.6	7 672	94.0
Paulding, OH	39 125	6	19 537	18.3	4	10	3 598	5 172	90.3	4 243	94.3
Perry, OH	39 127	6	35 246	19.5	6	15	6 520	8 928	91.4	7 113	92.6
Pickaway, OH	39 129	1	52 989	17.4	8	20	9 824	12 644	89.8	9 880	95.8
Pike, OH	39 131	7	28 146	18.6	5	14	5 703	6 897	92.9	5 690	95.1
Portage, OH	39 133	2	155 631	16.1	15	54	24 180	46 475	89.5	26 926	91.8
Preble, OH	39 135	2	42 527	17.6	7	18	7 435	10 416	91.7	8 465	94.8
Putnam, OH	39 137	6	34 928	20.0	10	25	6 841	9 685	87.8	7 856	90.3
Richland, OH	39 139	3	127 949	17.3	14	49	19 701	31 084	86.6	24 217	90.0
Ross, OH	39 141	4	75 197	16.6	9	25	11 830	17 385	92.1	13 531	95.3
Sandusky, OH	39 143	4	61 676	17.9	7	29	11 697	16 006	86.0	12 286	88.6
Scioto, OH	39 145	4	76 561	17.0	13	34	12 986	18 990	92.8	14 844	94.7
Seneca, OH	39 147	4	57 483	17.7	9	22	6 183	16 006	77.3	11 688	88.2
Shelby, OH	39 149	4	48 736	19.8	9	24	9 037	12 315	88.6	10 196	90.9
Stark, OH	39 151	2	380 608	17.5	46	136	62 221	94 779	82.2	71 024	89.2
Summit, OH	39 153	2	546 604	17.7	61	173	85 248	142 049	84.2	101 486	86.5
Trumbull, OH	39 155	2	219 296	17.0	26	84	34 944	53 297	86.5	41 257	89.2
Tuscarawas, OH	39 157	4	91 944	17.2	16	46	16 553	21 272	89.4	17 119	91.6
Union, OH	39 159	1	45 751	19.1	4	15	7 389	10 216	87.1	8 259	91.7
Van Wert, OH	39 161	6	29 154	18.2	6	22	6 350	7 501	86.7	5 933	91.3
Vinton, OH	39 163	9	13 429	18.5	1	7	2 659	3 146	95.5	2 646	97.6
Warren, OH	39 165	1	196 622	18.9	11	46	32 329	41 655	81.4	32 241	86.7
Washington, OH	39 167	3	62 210	16.2	8	30	9 991	15 573	83.7	11 269	91.3
Wayne, OH	39 169	4	113 697	18.7	15	50	17 597	29 064	80.3	22 085	86.8
Williams, OH	39 171	7	38 688	17.9	7	19	6 863	9 356	91.3	7 807	93.8
Wood, OH	39 173	2	123 929	15.6	14	59	21 730	42 352	90.4	22 026	90.0
Wyandot, OH	39 175	7	22 813	17.4	4	11	3 767	5 557	85.0	4 476	88.0
OKLAHOMA	40 000		3 547 884	17.2	603	1 787	629 477	930 865	89.4	667 503	93.4
Adair, OK	40 001	6	21 988	20.0	13	18	4 908	5 702	94.1	4 761	95.0
Alfalfa, OK	40 003	9	5 725	12.8	4	8	955	1 228	95.7	982	97.4
Atoka, OK	40 005	7	14 456	15.8	9	12	2 265	3 231	96.0	2 646	96.5
Beaver, OK	40 007	9	5 379	18.2	4	8	1 116	1 434	97.6	1 254	98.6
Beckham, OK	40 009	7	18 880	16.9	6	17	4 142	4 648	95.5	3 766	98.5
Blaine, OK	40 011	6	12 859	14.5	4	11	2 086	2 801	96.6	2 336	97.6
Bryan, OK	40 013	6	37 815	16.7	11	24	7 016	9 959	94.3	6 831	97.2
Caddo, OK	40 015	6	30 229	18.8	12	30	6 069	8 304	95.5	6 832	96.7
Canadian, OK	40 017	1	98 701	18.0	11	40	19 252	24 386	89.8	18 887	94.2
Carter, OK	40 019	5	47 125	17.4	11	30	8 967	11 129	93.9	9 131	95.3

[1]County type codes are from the Economic Research Service of the United States Department of Agriculture. See notes and definitions at the end of this section.

Table C-1. Population, School, and Student Characteristics by County—*Continued*

STATE County	Characteristics of students, 2004–2005				Outcomes		Staff and students, 2004–2005		
	Percent with IEP[2]	Percent eligible for free or reduced-price lunch	Percent minority	Percent English-language learners	Number of graduates, 2003–2004	Percent dropouts, grades 9–12, 2001–2002	Number of teachers	Student-teacher ratio	Central administration staff
	10	11	12	13	14	15	16	17	18
Delaware, OH	11.2	10.8	8.5	3.8	...	1.5	2 762	16.5	...
Erie, OH	16.4	32.4	14.2	0.3	...	1.8	974	14.1	186
Fairfield, OH	10.9	20.0	7.8	0.8	...	2.0	1 424	16.7	...
Fayette, OH	13.7	27.5	3.6	0.2	...	3.4	305	16.6	34
Franklin, OH	14.0	31.3	37.7	5.3	...	4.4	9 434	16.3	...
Fulton, OH	13.8	21.7	8.8	1.5	...	1.6	635	14.3	171
Gallia, OH	20.5	39.5	4.7	0.0	...	2.5	374	13.0	46
Geauga, OH	12.1	10.0	2.7	0.3	...	1.0	949	16.1	183
Greene, OH	13.4	19.3	10.6	0.4	...	2.9	1 348	16.9	206
Guernsey, OH	15.5	41.7	3.6	0.1	...	3.6	422	14.6	84
Hamilton, OH	15.4	35.8	43.4	1.4	...	3.9	7 493	15.4	...
Hancock, OH	15.9	21.8	6.0	0.5	...	2.5	854	14.8	...
Hardin, OH	14.6	27.2	2.0	0.0	...	2.1	327	15.0	53
Harrison, OH	28.9	43.1	3.9	0.0	...	2.9	139	14.8	12
Henry, OH	17.4	22.7	8.5	1.1	...	1.4	390	13.2	57
Highland, OH	12.0	30.0	2.1	0.2	...	3.0	465	17.6	65
Hocking, OH	16.5	38.6	1.0	0.0	...	6.2	228	18.0	67
Holmes, OH	14.4	31.6	1.2	20.6	...	1.5	302	15.4	...
Huron, OH	14.2	27.1	7.6	0.7	...	2.8	564	16.9	60
Jackson, OH	15.9	39.4	0.9	0.0	...	2.5	338	17.3	44
Jefferson, OH	15.6	43.5	9.3	0.0	...	1.9	726	15.1	108
Knox, OH	17.9	24.1	1.9	0.1	...	1.5	610	13.9	...
Lake, OH	12.6	20.9	7.5	3.0	...	2.2	2 058	16.9	...
Lawrence, OH	16.7	46.3	3.0	0.0	...	2.5	714	15.1	100
Licking, OH	13.4	21.7	5.3	1.0	...	3.5	2 148	15.3	...
Logan, OH	16.5	22.1	3.6	0.3	...	2.3	612	14.3	...
Lorain, OH	13.2	33.9	21.8	0.7	...	3.0	3 183	14.9	...
Lucas, OH	14.6	36.3	35.3	1.2	...	4.8	4 396	16.7	...
Madison, OH	13.0	19.6	4.3	0.9	...	2.2	483	14.2	...
Mahoning, OH	14.7	40.1	27.7	0.5	...	2.4	2 672	14.3	...
Marion, OH	15.6	33.8	7.5	0.4	...	3.1	1 051	12.0	...
Medina, OH	11.8	11.0	2.8	0.2	...	1.1	1 676	16.9	224
Meigs, OH	20.1	50.3	1.4	0.0	...	1.7	267	13.5	26
Mercer, OH	14.8	15.4	1.3	0.0	...	1.2	572	15.5	119
Miami, OH	12.3	21.4	4.7	0.8	...	1.6	1 110	15.6	166
Monroe, OH	17.1	39.8	0.5	0.0	...	2.7	207	13.2	26
Montgomery, OH	14.9	38.2	34.3	1.2	...	0.0	5 177	16.0	...
Morgan, OH	14.0	45.5	4.8	0.0	...	5.0	164	13.7	...
Morrow, OH	16.8	23.9	1.1	0.0	...	1.5	338	17.1	...
Muskingum, OH	15.8	37.1	5.9	0.0	...	2.9	1 068	15.1	...
Noble, OH	15.5	30.2	0.3	0.0	...	1.4	138	16.0	30
Ottawa, OH	14.4	22.7	5.1	0.0	...	2.1	396	16.0	61
Paulding, OH	16.9	23.9	4.0	0.0	...	0.9	244	14.8	56
Perry, OH	15.5	38.6	0.8	0.0	...	3.4	444	14.7	...
Pickaway, OH	13.6	24.8	2.3	0.0	...	2.9	588	16.7	...
Pike, OH	14.8	42.5	1.6	0.0	...	3.6	371	15.4	54
Portage, OH	13.9	22.5	5.5	0.3	...	2.4	1 673	14.5	...
Preble, OH	11.8	20.9	0.9	0.2	...	3.3	471	15.8	85
Putnam, OH	12.9	15.4	6.2	0.7	...	1.0	445	15.4	79
Richland, OH	15.1	36.3	13.7	0.1	...	2.8	1 447	13.6	...
Ross, OH	13.6	28.2	4.4	0.0	...	1.8	793	14.9	140
Sandusky, OH	15.7	32.6	14.5	3.5	...	1.6	819	14.3	123
Scioto, OH	12.6	49.1	3.1	0.0	...	2.8	874	14.9	151
Seneca, OH	15.0	29.3	6.8	0.4	...	3.5	436	14.2	...
Shelby, OH	15.2	21.5	3.6	1.0	...	1.7	540	16.7	105
Stark, OH	13.7	33.9	12.9	0.5	...	3.8	4 151	15.0	...
Summit, OH	13.6	32.0	25.0	1.3	...	2.5	5 693	15.0	...
Trumbull, OH	13.6	33.5	13.2	0.2	...	1.7	2 228	15.7	...
Tuscarawas, OH	15.8	25.4	1.6	0.2	...	1.3	1 224	13.5	...
Union, OH	14.6	11.9	3.1	0.2	...	0.8	499	14.8	67
Van Wert, OH	13.9	21.9	3.1	0.0	...	1.4	441	14.4	53
Vinton, OH	17.4	58.7	0.3	0.0	...	5.0	168	15.8	27
Warren, OH	10.8	9.3	6.0	0.9	...	1.7	1 823	17.7	317
Washington, OH	15.6	29.6	1.7	0.0	...	1.8	653	15.3	99
Wayne, OH	12.8	26.5	3.7	0.2	...	1.6	1 205	14.6	...
Williams, OH	13.0	19.0	3.4	0.4	...	2.1	420	16.4	59
Wood, OH	13.4	18.3	7.1	0.5	...	1.2	1 584	13.7	250
Wyandot, OH	15.3	18.2	2.5	0.0	...	1.7	248	15.2	...
OKLAHOMA	15.1	53.9	39.4	7.1	...	4.4	40 415	15.6	...
Adair, OK	18.4	73.4	73.5	33.4	...	3.8	366	13.4	...
Alfalfa, OK	18.1	48.5	8.9	0.1	...	...	88	10.8	10
Atoka, OK	19.8	72.6	43.0	0.6	...	6.4	172	13.1	...
Beaver, OK	10.3	46.4	25.1	19.6	...	1.1	100	11.1	12
Beckham, OK	13.5	50.9	22.8	3.2	...	3.4	297	13.9	...
Blaine, OK	16.3	65.3	33.0	6.6	...	0.3	176	11.9	13
Bryan, OK	17.9	66.2	42.3	3.4	...	6.2	470	14.9	...
Caddo, OK	17.4	72.3	49.5	7.5	...	2.3	468	13.0	...
Canadian, OK	11.9	29.8	20.8	4.3	...	3.8	1 154	16.7	...
Carter, OK	18.5	60.7	35.4	2.0	...	2.9	579	15.5	...

[2]IEP = Individual Education Program. See notes and definitions at the end of this section.
... = Not available.

Table C-1. Population, School, and Student Characteristics by County—*Continued*

STATE County	Total revenue (thousands of dollars)	Percent of revenue from: Federal government	State government	Local government	Total expenditures (thousands of dollars)	Amount per student (dollars)	Percent for instruction	Total	Percent in armed forces	Percent high school graduates	Percent not enrolled, not employed, not in armed forces, not high school graduate
	19	20	21	22	23	24	25	26	27	28	29
Delaware, OH	189 155	3.0	23.6	73.3	164 985	9 203	62.1	5 872	0.0	9.6	2.3
Erie, OH	164 727	5.6	35.2	59.2	150 444	10 705	63.2	3 995	0.0	10.0	3.1
Fairfield, OH	206 247	3.9	49.2	47.0	184 491	7 906	64.6	6 316	0.2	10.5	3.6
Fayette, OH	40 979	6.5	51.1	42.4	36 550	7 261	63.1	1 575	0.0	16.1	4.5
Franklin, OH	1 933 115	6.7	36.8	56.4	1 760 184	9 483	64.1	59 036	0.0	10.1	4.6
Fulton, OH	100 994	6.6	37.1	56.4	87 419	9 496	64.9	2 467	0.0	11.2	1.9
Gallia, OH	53 390	11.4	53.6	35.0	45 968	9 362	65.0	2 026	0.4	10.6	6.5
Geauga, OH	125 389	3.9	28.7	67.4	113 242	8 538	59.3	5 057	0.0	7.5	7.8
Greene, OH	231 564	5.6	38.5	55.8	203 145	8 586	63.5	11 371	0.9	6.1	2.9
Guernsey, OH	70 772	7.9	61.5	30.7	53 513	8 620	63.1	2 326	0.0	11.3	4.5
Hamilton, OH	1 362 879	8.0	35.4	56.6	1 259 902	10 432	63.6	48 268	0.0	9.0	6.0
Hancock, OH	103 525	5.3	39.9	54.8	97 461	8 152	66.8	4 131	0.3	9.6	2.5
Hardin, OH	55 030	7.4	49.2	43.4	49 003	8 108	63.5	2 406	0.0	8.1	4.5
Harrison, OH	21 403	8.3	57.4	34.3	19 385	7 274	62.2	808	0.0	12.0	3.7
Henry, OH	64 610	4.1	49.5	46.5	51 204	9 858	59.3	1 818	0.0	8.9	9.5
Highland, OH	64 923	6.4	61.2	32.4	57 018	6 947	62.7	2 293	0.0	13.4	6.3
Hocking, OH	35 134	7.7	54.6	37.7	28 121	6 981	60.5	1 598	0.0	13.7	1.9
Holmes, OH	38 796	9.3	43.2	47.5	34 169	7 329	64.3	2 701	0.0	7.7	19.7
Huron, OH	96 530	6.9	48.8	44.3	83 170	6 889	65.3	3 327	0.0	12.5	6.2
Jackson, OH	65 482	6.0	67.8	26.2	41 010	6 998	63.7	1 734	0.0	16.4	3.4
Jefferson, OH	101 802	11.9	48.0	40.1	90 234	8 333	62.4	4 010	0.0	12.0	2.9
Knox, OH	83 204	6.8	46.5	46.8	71 501	8 480	65.4	3 711	0.0	7.8	2.7
Lake, OH	348 464	4.7	33.2	62.1	324 906	9 316	61.8	11 692	0.0	11.0	2.6
Lawrence, OH	107 614	9.8	65.8	24.4	89 059	8 248	59.3	3 417	0.1	10.1	7.2
Licking, OH	239 183	5.1	41.9	53.0	207 739	8 085	62.8	8 478	0.0	11.5	4.1
Logan, OH	78 062	5.7	42.4	51.9	66 043	8 719	64.4	2 484	0.0	11.3	3.1
Lorain, OH	500 734	7.1	46.9	46.0	414 870	8 668	64.7	15 543	0.0	11.5	4.5
Lucas, OH	816 139	7.6	47.7	44.7	709 847	9 834	63.7	25 237	0.0	10.1	5.9
Madison, OH	63 201	5.2	43.2	51.6	56 637	8 239	62.1	2 427	0.0	14.3	6.3
Mahoning, OH	423 841	8.6	52.7	38.7	370 776	9 481	63.6	13 145	0.0	10.7	4.5
Marion, OH	123 453	5.4	56.5	38.1	102 041	8 107	65.8	3 280	0.0	11.3	6.0
Medina, OH	269 458	3.3	39.6	57.1	244 561	8 222	64.2	7 814	0.0	9.6	2.0
Meigs, OH	34 112	11.2	65.4	23.4	29 947	8 160	60.9	1 308	0.0	13.9	7.6
Mercer, OH	97 573	5.5	59.9	34.6	76 142	8 191	68.2	2 664	0.0	12.0	2.1
Miami, OH	168 637	5.4	40.4	54.3	145 866	8 417	64.9	5 406	0.0	12.9	3.4
Monroe, OH	23 907	10.2	50.2	39.6	22 370	8 093	66.1	841	0.0	13.4	6.9
Montgomery, OH	1 006 476	7.3	49.0	43.7	788 577	9 498	62.9	30 764	0.2	11.2	6.0
Morgan, OH	21 773	12.8	63.0	24.2	18 917	8 352	64.5	873	0.0	12.0	4.7
Morrow, OH	56 408	6.4	61.9	31.7	42 603	7 396	66.4	1 811	0.0	15.0	2.9
Muskingum, OH	159 757	8.8	53.1	38.1	140 710	8 738	65.5	4 856	0.1	12.8	4.4
Noble, OH	17 438	7.0	59.8	33.1	16 908	7 348	62.4	762	0.0	16.0	3.3
Ottawa, OH	61 819	3.8	38.2	58.0	56 902	8 848	63.1	2 130	0.7	12.4	1.4
Paulding, OH	37 754	4.1	60.0	35.9	28 071	7 603	65.6	1 258	0.0	11.8	2.0
Perry, OH	60 125	7.2	64.8	27.9	53 683	8 103	61.5	2 012	0.0	13.0	5.7
Pickaway, OH	80 850	6.9	49.5	43.6	76 952	7 932	64.8	2 688	0.0	14.2	8.1
Pike, OH	78 469	8.4	70.6	20.9	49 869	8 880	55.8	1 664	0.0	14.2	7.4
Portage, OH	240 415	4.7	44.4	50.9	212 895	8 602	63.6	10 892	0.1	8.2	1.8
Preble, OH	66 860	4.6	45.9	49.6	59 267	7 935	62.7	2 336	0.0	12.8	2.5
Putnam, OH	64 971	5.6	49.2	45.2	54 638	7 901	67.9	2 204	0.0	8.7	1.9
Richland, OH	235 509	6.9	48.5	44.6	203 999	9 676	64.4	6 751	0.3	11.3	4.0
Ross, OH	118 903	8.2	54.1	37.7	104 966	8 635	65.6	3 851	0.1	12.0	4.7
Sandusky, OH	103 583	6.9	48.5	44.5	93 077	8 877	66.3	3 570	0.1	10.9	4.3
Scioto, OH	159 618	12.4	63.4	24.2	118 299	9 066	61.1	4 630	0.0	13.6	6.2
Seneca, OH	80 319	6.0	44.8	49.2	71 024	8 227	64.7	3 819	0.0	11.4	2.4
Shelby, OH	78 741	5.4	38.9	55.7	69 238	7 694	61.5	2 734	0.3	9.3	2.4
Stark, OH	648 372	7.1	49.3	43.6	532 355	8 270	63.5	20 471	0.0	10.3	4.0
Summit, OH	949 766	6.2	37.1	56.8	775 581	9 079	64.7	28 072	0.1	11.6	3.3
Trumbull, OH	352 343	6.6	51.9	41.5	301 870	8 566	63.4	11 881	0.0	12.0	5.6
Tuscarawas, OH	135 928	7.6	46.4	46.0	121 771	8 023	64.2	4 984	0.0	13.9	2.9
Union, OH	66 032	3.7	37.2	59.1	58 173	8 165	65.4	2 015	0.0	14.0	4.6
Van Wert, OH	52 617	5.7	45.4	48.8	44 879	10 466	63.4	1 888	0.0	12.6	4.3
Vinton, OH	24 383	13.7	66.1	20.2	21 041	7 991	63.2	662	0.0	8.6	4.7
Warren, OH	281 348	3.0	38.1	58.9	248 465	7 995	61.1	7 779	0.1	11.5	2.9
Washington, OH	88 995	6.8	46.1	47.1	80 814	8 005	63.9	3 646	0.0	11.4	3.3
Wayne, OH	177 849	7.5	42.3	50.2	160 065	8 974	65.4	7 222	0.0	10.0	4.8
Williams, OH	68 836	3.7	53.7	42.6	50 814	7 336	66.5	2 325	0.0	15.4	6.2
Wood, OH	205 090	5.1	34.2	60.7	177 106	9 682	65.3	10 651	0.1	6.3	1.7
Wyandot, OH	31 562	4.5	48.5	46.9	27 861	7 307	63.8	1 258	0.0	12.7	2.8
OKLAHOMA	4 622 080	12.8	51.1	36.1	3 865 005	6 176	59.6	213 273	1.1	11.3	5.6
Adair, OK	55 287	25.6	48.4	25.9	45 162	9 411	60.8	1 263	0.0	13.9	6.5
Alfalfa, OK	7 017	8.3	52.2	39.6	6 411	7 542	60.6	276	0.0	7.6	1.1
Atoka, OK	38 199	11.0	48.5	40.5	22 231	9 885	60.7	751	0.0	9.9	3.3
Beaver, OK	10 980	5.1	45.5	49.3	9 962	8 648	55.2	365	0.8	11.8	4.7
Beckham, OK	32 137	12.4	50.9	36.7	24 548	6 874	60.7	1 033	0.0	5.1	5.4
Blaine, OK	17 762	17.8	54.1	28.1	16 380	7 654	60.4	684	0.0	7.5	7.3
Bryan, OK	49 093	18.8	60.3	20.9	44 824	6 597	58.6	2 337	0.0	10.0	6.2
Caddo, OK	57 566	21.9	54.0	24.1	46 210	7 341	59.7	2 150	0.0	11.7	8.5
Canadian, OK	129 871	7.5	50.7	41.9	103 881	5 569	60.2	5 547	0.1	8.0	2.6
Carter, OK	65 646	12.0	55.6	32.4	55 016	6 146	59.9	2 472	0.2	10.2	5.6

Table C-1. Population, School, and Student Characteristics by County—*Continued*

STATE County	High school graduates, 2000			College enrollment, 2000		College graduates, 2000 (percent)						
	Population 25 years and over	High school graduate or less (percent)	High school graduate or more (percent)	Number	Percent public	Bachelor's degree or more	+/- U.S. percentage with bachelor's degree or more	Non-Hispanic White	Black	American Indian and Alaska Native	Asian or Pacific Islander	Hispanic[3]
	30	31	32	33	34	35	36	37	38	39	40	41
Delaware, OH	70 617	32.1	92.9	6 126	50.6	41.0	16.6	40.7	36.5	33.3	71.1	38.5
Erie, OH	54 232	57.0	84.0	2 641	75.8	16.6	-7.8	17.6	6.5	0.0	40.1	8.0
Fairfield, OH	79 948	50.8	87.6	4 719	78.6	20.8	-3.6	20.5	29.8	7.3	44.6	21.2
Fayette, OH	18 954	68.9	78.7	718	89.0	10.7	-13.7	10.8	10.1	0.0	22.6	0.0
Franklin, OH	676 318	41.4	85.7	95 799	79.6	31.8	7.4	34.5	15.2	15.7	59.8	21.1
Fulton, OH	26 887	58.8	85.3	1 611	80.6	13.2	-11.2	13.6	4.0	0.0	25.7	4.4
Gallia, OH	20 207	67.9	73.7	1 494	55.5	11.6	-12.8	11.5	8.0	0.0	67.8	5.1
Geauga, OH	59 216	41.8	86.3	3 361	68.2	31.7	7.3	31.8	16.0	17.4	59.1	35.6
Greene, OH	92 414	41.1	87.8	16 907	70.3	31.1	6.7	30.2	35.9	27.2	56.0	40.4
Guernsey, OH	26 839	67.8	78.4	1 105	76.0	10.0	-14.4	9.9	6.6	0.0	50.0	22.0
Hamilton, OH	546 048	45.0	82.7	53 200	74.7	29.2	4.8	32.9	12.4	14.9	66.7	36.2
Hancock, OH	45 871	52.2	88.4	4 538	44.4	21.7	-2.7	21.5	17.5	19.5	62.7	10.7
Hardin, OH	19 220	69.9	80.6	3 395	22.2	11.4	-13.0	11.3	10.1	16.0	8.4	19.3
Harrison, OH	11 097	70.1	79.6	392	83.4	9.0	-15.4	9.1	0.0	0.0	. . .	30.0
Henry, OH	18 833	66.4	83.5	852	80.0	11.1	-13.3	11.3	0.0	14.1	52.8	0.9
Highland, OH	26 372	68.5	76.3	1 221	79.6	9.7	-14.7	9.6	0.0	18.0	68.5	8.1
Hocking, OH	18 720	68.2	78.0	979	85.6	9.8	-14.6	9.9	3.7	0.0	55.0	29.3
Holmes, OH	21 016	80.6	51.5	372	80.9	8.3	-16.1	8.3	0.0	0.0	21.6	1.9
Huron, OH	37 576	67.7	81.0	1 801	76.6	10.9	-13.5	11.1	7.6	7.7	24.1	6.9
Jackson, OH	21 306	69.6	73.5	917	75.5	11.0	-13.4	11.0	9.0	0.0	23.4	27.5
Jefferson, OH	51 819	64.8	81.7	4 123	56.6	11.8	-12.6	11.8	9.8	26.3	41.7	24.4
Knox, OH	34 485	60.3	81.8	3 824	30.9	16.7	-7.7	16.6	25.2	7.3	52.4	3.6
Lake, OH	156 177	48.0	86.4	10 082	76.5	21.5	-2.9	21.5	13.3	13.3	54.7	14.2
Lawrence, OH	41 685	67.8	75.6	2 743	91.4	10.3	-14.1	10.0	10.3	26.8	66.0	28.8
Licking, OH	95 009	56.0	84.7	7 135	59.0	18.4	-6.0	18.3	21.4	8.7	38.1	21.0
Logan, OH	29 962	68.2	83.6	1 230	73.5	11.5	-12.9	11.5	12.4	12.7	24.9	2.3
Lorain, OH	185 491	54.0	82.8	13 711	64.3	16.6	-7.8	17.8	7.7	10.6	48.9	6.2
Lucas, OH	291 022	49.4	82.9	31 806	85.7	21.3	-3.1	23.2	10.2	13.0	60.8	10.1
Madison, OH	26 615	62.7	79.0	1 584	64.3	13.0	-11.4	13.3	4.8	36.6	45.3	16.0
Mahoning, OH	174 803	57.7	82.4	12 736	86.6	17.5	-6.9	19.3	6.8	7.2	45.2	11.8
Marion, OH	44 466	64.7	80.3	2 291	80.2	11.1	-13.3	11.3	6.4	9.7	34.8	6.0
Medina, OH	99 005	47.6	88.8	5 804	77.7	24.8	0.4	24.7	13.5	13.8	55.1	27.4
Meigs, OH	15 602	73.4	73.2	688	82.0	7.4	-17.0	7.4	14.9	0.0	26.7	0.0
Mercer, OH	25 614	65.8	84.0	1 275	86.0	12.7	-11.7	12.5	0.0	0.0	62.0	21.6
Miami, OH	65 765	57.1	82.7	3 450	79.5	16.3	-8.1	16.2	6.3	0.0	43.3	14.9
Monroe, OH	10 544	71.3	78.8	493	90.5	8.4	-16.0	8.4	0.0	0.0	45.0	0.0
Montgomery, OH	367 099	46.9	83.5	38 583	63.4	22.9	-1.6	24.0	14.9	17.2	53.6	29.1
Morgan, OH	9 804	69.9	80.6	504	80.4	9.1	-15.3	9.4	0.9	0.0	73.9	0.0
Morrow, OH	20 591	68.7	78.6	871	79.0	9.5	-14.9	9.4	10.3	6.7	0.0	2.2
Muskingum, OH	54 616	63.7	80.6	3 766	57.0	12.6	-12.8	12.6	13.3	14.3	29.8	28.8
Noble, OH	9 210	69.3	78.6	798	78.4	8.1	-16.3	8.2	3.8	14.6	68.2	1.3
Ottawa, OH	28 829	56.3	84.2	1 503	84.8	16.0	-8.4	16.5	0.0	9.9	17.9	4.7
Paulding, OH	13 108	70.9	81.6	601	68.7	7.8	-16.6	7.9	7.5	7.4	40.0	3.7
Perry, OH	21 626	72.2	78.9	1 068	88.3	6.9	-17.5	6.8	1.6	0.0	44.6	12.5
Pickaway, OH	35 258	65.5	77.2	1 905	67.3	11.4	-13.0	12.2	2.2	0.0	27.1	14.8
Pike, OH	17 710	71.4	70.1	774	80.9	9.7	-14.7	9.5	4.3	5.2	79.7	9.3
Portage, OH	94 073	54.0	85.9	17 050	90.0	21.0	-3.4	20.7	16.2	6.8	76.1	20.1
Preble, OH	28 079	67.8	81.7	1 356	83.2	10.1	-14.3	10.0	3.7	3.8	44.6	16.3
Putnam, OH	21 524	61.6	86.1	1 215	75.0	12.9	-11.5	13.3	35.0	11.9	8.3	2.8
Richland, OH	86 184	62.8	80.2	4 997	79.1	12.6	-11.8	13.2	6.5	7.3	32.5	4.6
Ross, OH	49 443	66.1	76.1	2 809	83.9	11.3	-13.1	11.6	6.7	2.2	39.8	9.3
Sandusky, OH	40 565	61.6	82.1	2 609	84.2	11.9	-12.5	12.5	6.4	5.0	16.3	2.4
Scioto, OH	52 236	65.8	74.1	3 208	89.6	10.1	-14.3	10.2	4.5	6.5	50.3	2.0
Seneca, OH	37 271	63.2	83.1	3 270	43.7	12.5	-11.9	12.6	7.3	5.1	27.3	6.3
Shelby, OH	30 280	63.8	81.5	1 321	83.4	12.8	-11.6	12.4	16.2	15.6	49.0	17.1
Stark, OH	252 971	57.8	83.4	16 696	63.2	17.9	-6.5	18.6	7.0	11.6	48.0	19.4
Summit, OH	362 645	47.9	85.7	29 977	87.7	25.1	0.7	26.5	10.6	10.9	61.1	26.7
Trumbull, OH	153 044	61.8	82.5	8 496	85.1	14.5	-9.9	14.9	6.9	8.1	48.3	12.3
Tuscarawas, OH	60 653	67.9	80.3	2 663	86.7	12.2	-12.2	12.1	5.2	14.1	41.3	15.1
Union, OH	26 534	57.9	86.0	1 275	78.4	15.9	-8.5	16.2	2.5	0.0	53.0	18.6
Van Wert, OH	19 453	65.0	86.6	875	65.1	12.0	-12.4	12.0	20.0	0.0	15.2	4.3
Vinton, OH	8 223	76.9	70.7	296	75.3	6.0	-18.4	6.0	0.0	11.4	. . .	9.1
Warren, OH	103 306	45.0	86.2	5 886	76.4	28.4	4.0	28.3	13.9	12.3	66.1	29.3
Washington, OH	42 770	58.5	84.5	3 317	65.3	15.0	-9.4	15.0	14.7	0.0	57.7	10.2
Wayne, OH	69 953	62.0	80.0	5 283	58.6	17.2	-7.2	17.0	17.9	7.8	53.5	23.9
Williams, OH	25 690	65.6	83.1	983	82.8	10.7	-13.7	10.8	0.0	14.9	0.0	8.2
Wood, OH	71 551	46.2	88.6	18 158	95.0	26.2	1.8	26.1	34.6	28.3	59.3	11.0
Wyandot, OH	15 097	66.5	82.5	772	76.0	9.8	-14.6	9.8	0.0	0.0	25.9	7.5
OKLAHOMA	2 203 173	50.9	80.6	203 262	82.3	20.3	-4.1	21.7	13.7	13.2	36.7	9.6
Adair, OK	12 764	71.4	66.7	511	83.4	9.8	-14.6	11.3	0.0	7.1	27.3	3.9
Alfalfa, OK	4 543	59.4	81.4	170	88.2	14.9	-9.5	16.5	4.5	2.0	. . .	2.6
Atoka, OK	9 377	70.5	69.4	383	95.0	10.1	-14.3	10.7	1.6	10.3	0.0	0.0
Beaver, OK	3 898	55.1	81.2	119	98.3	17.6	-6.8	18.6	0.0	22.0	71.4	6.4
Beckham, OK	12 968	58.8	75.9	566	80.2	15.5	-8.9	16.8	0.0	15.7	76.7	5.4
Blaine, OK	8 118	65.7	75.5	266	96.2	14.0	-10.4	16.7	10.9	3.2	11.4	3.3
Bryan, OK	23 175	56.9	74.9	2 495	88.6	17.9	-6.5	17.6	13.9	16.9	53.5	11.7
Caddo, OK	19 020	64.6	75.9	1 024	90.5	14.2	-10.2	15.2	5.9	13.2	7.7	5.0
Canadian, OK	56 207	44.7	87.3	3 883	85.4	20.9	-3.5	21.4	13.5	16.2	32.1	9.8
Carter, OK	30 195	59.8	77.0	1 212	89.5	15.1	-9.3	15.8	9.7	8.6	53.1	18.8

[3]May be of any race.
. . . = Not available.

Table C-1. Population, School, and Student Characteristics by County—*Continued*

STATE County	State/ county code	County type[1]	Population, 2005		Number of schools and students, 2004–2005			Resident enrollment, 2000			
			Total	Percent 5 to 17 years	School districts	Schools	Students	Total	Percent public	K–12	Percent public
			1	2	3	4	5	6	7	8	9
Cherokee, OK	40 021	6	44 671	17.0	14	20	7 388	13 564	94.0	8 375	95.3
Choctaw, OK	40 023	7	15 297	17.2	8	14	2 715	3 715	96.9	2 962	98.0
Cimarron, OK	40 025	9	2 833	18.8	3	6	474	780	95.4	685	97.1
Cleveland, OK	40 027	1	224 898	16.0	7	63	37 687	67 969	90.8	37 689	92.8
Coal, OK	40 029	9	5 743	18.1	4	8	1 233	1 519	95.8	1 241	95.8
Comanche, OK	40 031	3	112 429	19.4	11	55	21 909	32 582	93.0	23 102	95.8
Cotton, OK	40 033	6	6 589	17.6	3	7	1 229	1 557	97.4	1 301	99.4
Craig, OK	40 035	6	15 078	16.2	5	15	3 206	3 336	96.4	2 777	97.3
Creek, OK	40 037	2	68 708	18.1	16	40	13 530	17 579	91.9	14 067	94.9
Custer, OK	40 039	7	25 208	14.8	5	14	3 909	8 868	96.5	5 064	96.7
Delaware, OK	40 041	6	39 146	16.6	9	17	6 641	7 983	94.4	6 721	96.2
Dewey, OK	40 043	9	4 568	14.6	3	7	760	1 121	96.8	956	98.3
Ellis, OK	40 045	9	3 963	14.5	4	8	734	848	96.0	729	96.2
Garfield, OK	40 047	5	56 958	17.0	11	32	9 729	14 040	89.8	10 951	92.1
Garvin, OK	40 049	6	27 228	16.5	8	21	5 333	6 197	96.6	5 211	97.4
Grady, OK	40 051	1	49 369	17.6	13	34	8 879	12 198	93.7	9 242	95.8
Grant, OK	40 053	9	4 779	16.9	4	8	915	1 322	95.6	1 115	96.7
Greer, OK	40 055	7	5 901	12.4	3	7	1 016	1 265	94.9	971	96.0
Harmon, OK	40 057	9	3 030	17.5	1	3	565	793	97.7	728	98.4
Harper, OK	40 059	9	3 313	14.8	2	6	692	829	97.6	713	99.7
Haskell, OK	40 061	6	12 183	17.3	6	10	2 320	2 759	98.8	2 301	99.3
Hughes, OK	40 063	7	13 835	15.6	7	14	2 506	3 242	94.2	2 591	94.4
Jackson, OK	40 065	5	26 518	20.3	7	19	5 490	8 036	96.0	5 965	98.4
Jefferson, OK	40 067	8	6 461	16.5	4	9	1 318	1 494	97.9	1 255	98.6
Johnston, OK	40 069	7	10 259	17.2	7	13	1 888	2 768	96.2	2 038	96.8
Kay, OK	40 071	5	46 480	17.8	9	26	8 890	12 077	91.8	9 483	93.3
Kingfisher, OK	40 073	6	14 302	17.2	7	15	3 159	3 504	91.3	3 003	92.6
Kiowa, OK	40 075	6	9 848	16.1	4	10	1 853	2 390	98.1	1 934	98.5
Latimer, OK	40 077	7	10 635	17.3	5	9	1 751	2 953	97.2	2 020	97.3
Le Flore, OK	40 079	2	49 528	17.3	18	37	9 806	11 821	96.1	9 487	97.0
Lincoln, OK	40 081	1	32 311	18.3	9	23	5 742	8 108	92.5	6 765	94.5
Logan, OK	40 083	1	36 894	16.4	4	12	4 496	10 009	89.7	6 700	90.5
Love, OK	40 085	9	9 126	17.0	4	8	1 605	2 124	95.0	1 740	96.6
McClain, OK	40 087	1	30 096	17.1	8	19	6 240	7 367	91.8	5 761	94.0
McCurtain, OK	40 089	7	33 992	19.0	17	32	7 414	8 723	97.5	7 167	98.4
McIntosh, OK	40 091	6	19 965	15.1	6	13	3 209	4 197	94.3	3 409	95.1
Major, OK	40 093	9	7 364	15.7	3	5	1 060	1 762	90.4	1 470	91.6
Marshall, OK	40 095	6	14 461	15.8	2	6	2 765	2 820	96.8	2 290	98.0
Mayes, OK	40 097	6	39 471	17.8	9	23	7 360	9 429	94.8	7 797	97.3
Murray, OK	40 099	7	12 880	16.0	3	9	2 453	2 765	97.5	2 273	98.4
Muskogee, OK	40 101	4	70 607	17.2	13	40	13 654	17 289	95.1	13 298	97.3
Noble, OK	40 103	6	11 211	16.8	4	9	2 179	2 796	96.2	2 256	99.1
Nowata, OK	40 105	6	10 864	17.5	3	8	2 067	2 578	96.4	2 114	98.2
Okfuskee, OK	40 107	6	11 434	15.8	7	15	2 283	2 678	95.0	2 224	96.9
Oklahoma, OK	40 109	1	684 543	17.0	20	206	111 274	177 872	84.6	122 501	90.4
Okmulgee, OK	40 111	2	39 732	18.0	11	23	7 122	10 580	95.4	8 238	97.1
Osage, OK	40 113	2	45 416	17.4	15	113	48 265	11 443	92.2	9 312	94.4
Ottawa, OK	40 115	6	32 866	17.8	10	26	6 432	8 325	95.7	6 198	97.7
Pawnee, OK	40 117	2	16 860	17.6	3	8	2 770	4 117	96.2	3 437	97.4
Payne, OK	40 119	4	69 151	11.6	10	28	9 957	28 426	96.6	9 937	96.5
Pittsburg, OK	40 121	5	44 641	15.7	15	34	7 881	10 214	95.1	8 296	97.2
Pontotoc, OK	40 123	7	35 346	16.4	10	24	6 652	10 199	95.8	6 720	96.0
Pottawatomie, OK	40 125	4	68 272	17.2	15	36	12 848	17 776	85.1	12 422	95.3
Pushmataha, OK	40 127	9	11 693	17.4	7	14	2 288	2 777	98.0	2 361	99.1
Roger Mills, OK	40 129	9	3 311	14.5	5	10	791	758	96.8	641	96.6
Rogers, OK	40 131	2	80 757	18.7	11	45	22 135	19 354	90.4	15 430	93.5
Seminole, OK	40 133	7	24 770	17.4	12	24	5 046	6 499	95.5	5 073	97.7
Sequoyah, OK	40 135	2	40 868	18.5	13	25	8 852	9 537	96.5	7 874	97.6
Stephens, OK	40 137	4	42 946	16.5	9	25	8 090	10 155	94.5	8 339	96.5
Texas, OK	40 139	7	20 112	19.0	10	23	3 897	5 517	93.5	4 143	98.1
Tillman, OK	40 141	6	8 513	18.4	5	10	1 770	2 304	96.8	2 032	97.4
Tulsa, OK	40 143	2	572 059	17.6	12	56	40 189	152 977	79.7	107 559	87.9
Wagoner, OK	40 145	2	64 183	18.6	5	38	21 402	15 269	89.5	12 342	93.9
Washington, OK	40 147	4	49 149	16.5	5	19	8 250	12 166	88.3	9 627	93.8
Washita, OK	40 149	7	11 471	16.8	6	11	2 015	3 007	94.8	2 476	94.8
Woods, OK	40 151	7	8 546	12.5	4	9	1 314	2 625	97.9	1 454	98.8
Woodward, OK	40 153	7	19 088	16.1	5	13	3 409	4 392	95.6	3 724	97.8
OREGON	41 000		3 641 056	17.1	223	1 289	552 015	876 492	86.0	621 408	90.6
Baker, OR	41 001	7	16 287	16.2	4	13	2 426	3 629	93.2	3 141	95.9
Benton, OR	41 003	3	78 640	14.0	5	44	17 815	30 859	92.7	12 857	90.7
Clackamas, OR	41 005	1	368 470	18.1	11	105	57 140	87 642	83.9	66 117	89.2
Clatsop, OR	41 007	4	36 798	16.1	5	15	5 365	8 478	89.4	6 425	93.0
Columbia, OR	41 009	1	48 065	18.5	5	25	8 521	10 694	91.2	8 920	94.8
Coos, OR	41 011	5	64 711	14.9	7	26	8 738	14 249	93.6	10 859	96.6
Crook, OR	41 013	6	22 067	17.9	1	7	3 166	4 562	91.1	3 743	95.6
Curry, OR	41 015	7	22 427	13.5	3	10	2 927	3 801	93.4	3 197	96.5
Deschutes, OR	41 017	3	141 382	16.6	5	40	22 044	27 802	87.9	21 359	91.3
Douglas, OR	41 019	4	104 202	16.3	15	50	15 989	22 732	89.9	18 784	91.6

[1]County type codes are from the Economic Research Service of the United States Department of Agriculture. See notes and definitions at the end of this section.

Table C-1. Population, School, and Student Characteristics by County—*Continued*

STATE County	Characteristics of students, 2004–2005				Outcomes		Staff and students, 2004–2005		
	Percent with IEP[2]	Percent eligible for free or reduced-price lunch	Percent minority	Percent English-language learners	Number of graduates, 2003–2004	Percent dropouts, grades 9–12, 2001–2002	Number of teachers	Student-teacher ratio	Central administration staff
	10	11	12	13	14	15	16	17	18
Cherokee, OK	16.7	75.2	68.9	12.5	...	3.5	522	14.2	...
Choctaw, OK	15.4	70.7	49.4	0.5	...	4.6	200	13.6	...
Cimarron, OK	15.0	63.9	27.8	20.9	...	1.1	54	8.7	9
Cleveland, OK	13.7	34.5	26.5	3.6	...	4.3	2 241	16.8	...
Coal, OK	28.1	75.5	49.6	1.4	...	2.6	92	13.4	11
Comanche, OK	15.7	48.9	45.8	7.6	...	4.2	1 429	15.3	...
Cotton, OK	15.9	47.8	23.3	0.0	...	1.7	88	14.0	12
Craig, OK	20.0	62.8	54.4	0.6	...	4.2	226	14.2	24
Creek, OK	13.5	58.1	30.8	0.8	...	3.4	836	16.2	...
Custer, OK	13.3	60.0	33.8	12.6	...	3.6	284	13.7	...
Delaware, OK	17.2	64.7	52.7	10.6	...	5.4	448	14.8	...
Dewey, OK	18.6	52.5	15.1	4.3	...	1.5	75	10.1	10
Ellis, OK	14.7	57.8	11.2	4.1	...	1.4	70	10.5	10
Garfield, OK	13.5	49.7	23.3	7.6	...	4.7	692	14.1	...
Garvin, OK	19.8	60.1	33.4	4.4	...	2.7	372	14.4	28
Grady, OK	13.8	45.5	17.1	1.4	...	3.4	566	15.7	...
Grant, OK	19.0	53.7	9.3	0.0	...	0.3	85	10.8	9
Greer, OK	14.1	63.0	24.3	5.2	...	13.5	79	12.9	...
Harmon, OK	18.9	66.9	46.2	19.1	...	5.1	48	11.9	4
Harper, OK	16.9	47.1	22.3	17.5	...	0.4	52	13.3	5
Haskell, OK	18.0	73.5	37.7	0.3	...	3.5	160	14.5	...
Hughes, OK	18.2	73.0	42.4	3.7	...	7.2	183	13.7	...
Jackson, OK	11.3	53.8	38.4	15.0	...	4.5	374	14.7	...
Jefferson, OK	18.5	65.2	23.3	6.3	...	4.1	102	12.9	11
Johnston, OK	17.3	69.5	39.6	1.3	...	2.9	145	13.0	14
Kay, OK	15.4	61.1	30.7	4.7	...	5.9	586	15.2	...
Kingfisher, OK	14.8	54.8	22.2	10.1	...	0.9	232	13.6	...
Kiowa, OK	14.6	65.8	29.3	2.1	...	3.3	131	14.1	11
Latimer, OK	17.8	70.0	39.4	2.1	...	0.2	124	14.2	...
Le Flore, OK	16.0	67.2	39.2	4.9	...	5.1	686	14.3	...
Lincoln, OK	13.9	53.6	20.4	0.3	...	3.0	365	15.7	27
Logan, OK	16.5	57.1	22.0	0.7	...	3.5	303	14.8	31
Love, OK	16.6	65.4	34.9	12.3	...	1.5	110	14.6	11
McClain, OK	13.0	37.9	26.8	5.2	...	3.8	384	16.3	...
McCurtain, OK	14.4	75.0	44.2	4.0	...	1.4	542	13.7	...
McIntosh, OK	18.1	76.7	45.5	2.8	...	3.9	212	15.2	22
Major, OK	21.5	47.3	12.0	10.1	...	2.4	80	13.2	...
Marshall, OK	12.0	65.2	50.5	15.9	...	1.2	166	16.7	14
Mayes, OK	15.1	59.5	51.4	3.9	...	4.6	477	15.4	...
Murray, OK	15.4	60.0	33.8	4.0	...	2.0	146	16.9	...
Muskogee, OK	14.9	61.3	55.5	4.8	...	2.6	858	15.9	...
Noble, OK	16.5	50.8	27.4	0.7	...	3.5	167	13.0	16
Nowata, OK	16.2	57.5	42.9	0.0	...	1.7	139	14.9	11
Okfuskee, OK	17.0	77.5	47.0	2.4	...	3.2	159	14.4	16
Oklahoma, OK	14.1	55.4	49.0	14.0	...	6.3	6 509	17.1	...
Okmulgee, OK	18.3	67.0	46.7	0.9	...	3.3	482	14.8	...
Osage, OK	16.9	63.7	52.2	10.2	...	3.3	3 069	15.7	392
Ottawa, OK	15.2	66.5	48.1	3.6	...	5.0	418	15.4	...
Pawnee, OK	14.3	50.6	26.5	0.0	...	5.1	181	15.3	10
Payne, OK	17.7	43.9	23.8	2.5	...	4.1	672	14.8	...
Pittsburg, OK	19.2	64.4	43.7	1.0	...	5.5	552	14.3	...
Pontotoc, OK	18.1	63.9	41.6	1.8	...	3.3	486	13.7	...
Pottawatomie, OK	15.2	56.8	33.1	3.8	...	5.1	846	15.2	...
Pushmataha, OK	16.7	71.8	41.3	0.3	...	6.3	171	13.4	36
Roger Mills, OK	11.5	43.7	15.2	0.0	...	1.9	95	8.3	13
Rogers, OK	14.0	38.2	37.8	2.0	...	2.6	1 319	16.8	89
Seminole, OK	15.3	72.6	45.8	2.7	...	4.4	371	13.6	37
Sequoyah, OK	20.0	69.1	51.5	7.0	...	3.6	577	15.3	...
Stephens, OK	12.6	49.5	20.7	4.0	...	3.7	520	15.6	...
Texas, OK	10.6	59.6	49.1	35.6	...	4.4	315	12.4	26
Tillman, OK	18.7	72.3	48.7	23.6	...	3.2	126	14.1	...
Tulsa, OK	12.8	48.2	40.9	7.0	...	4.5	2 226	18.1	...
Wagoner, OK	15.9	50.7	40.1	2.5	...	5.3	1 295	16.5	106
Washington, OK	12.7	40.3	26.2	2.5	...	3.3	517	16.0	...
Washita, OK	11.7	60.0	15.5	2.5	...	0.9	157	12.9	...
Woods, OK	15.7	45.2	8.6	1.8	...	2.8	117	11.3	...
Woodward, OK	13.6	39.3	13.5	4.2	...	5.4	242	14.1	...
OREGON	14.2	41.9	24.4	11.7	...	4.9	27 432	20.1	...
Baker, OR	16.1	50.7	7.9	0.9	189	0.8	144	16.9	17
Benton, OR	13.7	27.0	15.7	5.0	1 308	2.7	787	22.6	77
Clackamas, OR	13.2	27.6	15.0	8.4	3 852	2.9	2 710	21.1	226
Clatsop, OR	15.8	36.8	12.0	15.6	375	3.5	287	18.7	27
Columbia, OR	14.7	32.1	9.1	0.9	609	2.3	401	21.2	38
Coos, OR	17.4	51.9	20.9	6.3	646	3.9	431	20.3	42
Crook, OR	14.0	48.5	12.9	5.4	200	5.2	160	19.8	9
Curry, OR	14.8	55.6	14.5	0.1	191	3.2	153	19.1	9
Deschutes, OR	14.7	35.2	10.3	4.1	...	3.0	1 006	21.9	86
Douglas, OR	15.2	46.8	9.1	0.6	1 079	4.9	820	19.5	99

[2]IEP = Individual Education Program. See notes and definitions at the end of this section.
. . . = Not available.

Table C-1. Population, School, and Student Characteristics by County—*Continued*

STATE County	Revenue, 2003–2004				Current expenditures, 2003–2004			Resident population, 16 to 19 years, 2000			
	Total revenue (thousands of dollars)	Percent of revenue from:			Total expenditures (thousands of dollars)	Amount per student (dollars)	Percent for instruction	Total	Percent in armed forces	Percent high school graduates	Percent not enrolled, not employed, not in armed forces, not high school graduate
		Federal government	State government	Local government							
	19	20	21	22	23	24	25	26	27	28	29
Cherokee, OK	56 705	24.1	58.9	17.1	51 191	6 828	61.4	3 278	0.1	9.0	6.3
Choctaw, OK	20 629	23.9	59.9	16.3	18 773	6 899	59.3	847	0.0	9.7	11.6
Cimarron, OK	5 476	10.1	51.0	38.8	5 447	10 162	59.5	165	0.0	3.0	4.2
Cleveland, OK	248 186	7.7	51.2	41.1	200 212	5 409	62.8	14 804	0.3	7.6	2.8
Coal, OK	11 227	24.1	54.0	21.9	9 665	7 794	58.6	341	0.0	12.0	8.2
Comanche, OK	145 939	17.8	58.0	24.2	129 814	5 920	58.8	8 397	21.3	32.6	5.7
Cotton, OK	8 225	13.6	60.9	25.4	7 647	6 147	62.1	397	0.8	12.3	4.0
Craig, OK	22 269	15.7	54.2	30.1	20 205	6 283	62.7	862	0.0	8.7	5.3
Creek, OK	99 233	11.8	56.8	31.4	81 139	6 009	59.5	4 151	0.0	11.3	3.7
Custer, OK	32 901	11.9	56.8	31.3	28 865	6 539	59.5	2 358	0.0	6.2	3.4
Delaware, OK	62 067	16.6	45.4	38.0	48 353	7 076	59.4	1 901	0.0	13.5	7.8
Dewey, OK	7 282	8.2	53.6	38.2	6 852	8 980	56.2	329	0.0	7.3	1.5
Ellis, OK	6 501	8.7	51.6	39.6	6 079	8 362	56.3	236	0.0	4.2	5.5
Garfield, OK	69 222	9.2	52.9	37.9	58 623	6 213	61.5	3 212	0.0	8.3	6.4
Garvin, OK	37 223	15.7	56.6	27.7	32 945	6 176	60.9	1 646	0.0	10.9	5.0
Grady, OK	53 223	10.4	60.5	29.1	47 490	5 468	60.8	3 000	0.0	10.4	4.4
Grant, OK	8 818	7.8	40.8	51.4	8 227	8 952	59.1	301	0.0	8.3	0.7
Greer, OK	7 412	16.9	60.4	22.7	6 915	7 325	58.5	344	0.0	14.5	2.9
Harmon, OK	4 481	13.5	64.2	22.2	4 263	7 350	69.6	219	0.0	8.7	7.8
Harper, OK	6 312	9.8	44.9	45.2	5 879	8 447	57.4	212	0.0	7.1	2.4
Haskell, OK	16 313	16.5	63.9	19.7	15 852	6 910	60.9	710	0.0	18.5	3.7
Hughes, OK	21 783	20.1	53.2	26.6	17 504	6 908	58.1	643	0.0	10.6	6.8
Jackson, OK	38 403	17.2	60.7	22.1	33 556	5 992	62.6	1 801	6.6	16.0	6.9
Jefferson, OK	9 626	12.7	65.8	21.5	9 279	7 255	62.0	334	0.0	9.9	4.5
Johnston, OK	13 811	18.3	59.2	22.5	12 738	6 662	61.6	743	0.0	9.0	6.7
Kay, OK	66 834	11.4	49.2	39.4	56 254	6 232	59.6	2 970	0.0	9.6	6.7
Kingfisher, OK	25 912	13.4	43.0	43.6	21 755	6 939	60.1	877	0.0	8.9	2.9
Kiowa, OK	13 771	17.2	58.0	24.8	12 433	6 753	60.1	623	0.0	13.6	7.2
Latimer, OK	13 678	19.6	59.1	21.3	11 930	6 710	59.6	810	0.0	3.7	7.8
Le Flore, OK	69 990	22.4	59.1	18.5	64 064	6 676	62.3	3 001	0.0	13.9	6.4
Lincoln, OK	37 156	14.2	59.1	26.7	31 826	5 455	60.4	1 954	0.0	11.7	4.1
Logan, OK	28 358	11.2	59.4	29.4	26 810	6 084	60.6	2 637	0.0	8.6	4.1
Love, OK	12 271	13.1	59.9	27.0	10 297	6 356	59.2	521	0.0	5.2	6.1
McClain, OK	43 011	8.0	53.0	39.0	32 993	5 680	62.7	1 782	0.0	13.0	3.3
McCurtain, OK	53 912	19.9	60.0	20.1	50 269	6 766	60.1	2 022	0.0	12.6	8.5
McIntosh, OK	22 956	20.6	59.3	20.1	21 130	6 444	57.8	1 016	0.0	11.6	10.1
Major, OK	16 104	9.0	49.0	42.0	11 753	7 867	59.9	421	0.0	2.4	5.2
Marshall, OK	18 636	20.0	55.0	25.0	16 295	5 973	62.0	729	0.0	10.3	8.2
Mayes, OK	47 657	15.7	58.8	25.5	44 631	6 131	59.4	2 327	0.0	10.4	6.1
Murray, OK	14 405	12.4	63.4	24.2	12 297	5 436	62.9	765	0.0	14.2	0.4
Muskogee, OK	92 111	16.8	52.1	31.1	82 258	6 048	59.2	4 261	0.0	10.9	6.7
Noble, OK	17 915	14.7	39.2	46.1	16 078	7 178	59.1	622	0.0	9.0	2.1
Nowata, OK	14 472	14.6	61.9	23.5	12 541	6 076	60.6	576	0.0	10.2	3.8
Okfuskee, OK	17 027	24.6	55.0	20.4	15 424	6 913	60.3	703	0.0	13.1	10.8
Oklahoma, OK	794 422	10.7	46.1	43.2	654 481	5 925	59.2	38 506	0.7	11.9	6.7
Okmulgee, OK	51 414	16.7	61.3	22.0	45 804	6 247	58.9	2 682	0.1	9.3	8.7
Osage, OK	33 857	20.2	56.2	23.6	30 908	7 170	57.3	2 643	0.1	11.3	3.7
Ottawa, OK	41 347	19.3	60.5	20.2	38 381	6 242	62.1	2 180	0.0	8.5	6.8
Pawnee, OK	17 482	15.6	59.6	24.9	15 380	5 743	61.9	986	0.0	13.4	4.9
Payne, OK	78 589	9.0	50.1	40.9	62 611	6 320	59.1	6 044	0.5	6.9	1.9
Pittsburg, OK	62 483	17.2	53.1	29.7	51 590	6 590	60.1	2 398	0.0	11.0	5.6
Pontotoc, OK	52 091	17.3	57.9	24.8	44 542	6 603	59.7	2 380	0.0	9.6	4.3
Pottawatomie, OK	92 180	15.3	58.0	26.7	77 721	6 169	60.7	4 293	0.0	13.3	6.7
Pushmataha, OK	18 703	21.4	63.6	15.0	17 174	7 246	61.0	665	0.0	12.5	6.9
Roger Mills, OK	12 229	11.9	45.9	42.2	10 210	13 208	54.7	218	0.0	5.5	0.9
Rogers, OK	85 895	9.9	54.4	35.8	74 981	5 373	58.7	4 198	0.0	12.5	4.4
Seminole, OK	37 955	23.6	54.7	21.8	34 355	6 885	59.4	1 728	0.0	6.9	9.0
Sequoyah, OK	57 908	20.3	63.6	16.1	52 495	6 096	60.1	2 354	0.0	15.2	8.4
Stephens, OK	57 476	10.8	56.5	32.7	46 302	5 688	58.3	2 537	0.0	8.2	3.1
Texas, OK	29 756	10.7	53.9	35.4	27 412	6 950	59.4	1 478	0.0	7.2	7.8
Tillman, OK	28 573	11.8	48.6	39.7	16 355	9 041	59.3	542	0.9	8.1	2.0
Tulsa, OK	814 107	9.3	41.5	49.2	640 824	5 991	57.6	31 914	0.0	10.4	6.3
Wagoner, OK	38 387	12.9	62.6	24.4	34 448	5 623	61.3	3 573	0.0	9.7	5.1
Washington, OK	61 485	9.8	51.9	38.3	51 022	6 136	60.9	2 723	0.1	11.6	4.9
Washita, OK	14 699	10.5	58.4	31.1	13 512	6 585	59.5	729	0.0	6.4	1.5
Woods, OK	11 027	7.2	46.8	46.0	10 110	7 326	56.4	623	0.0	3.4	1.8
Woodward, OK	27 014	9.2	55.1	35.7	21 211	6 215	60.9	1 153	0.0	12.1	7.6
OREGON	5 086 083	9.1	52.3	38.7	4 207 059	7 660	63.1	191 546	0.1	12.3	5.4
Baker, OR	23 077	9.6	62.9	27.5	20 962	8 298	59.7	875	0.0	12.1	7.7
Benton, OR	83 507	5.6	47.7	46.7	66 160	6 967	60.1	6 792	0.1	5.5	0.7
Clackamas, OR	487 232	5.7	51.0	43.3	399 161	7 055	61.3	18 703	0.0	11.9	4.4
Clatsop, OR	50 366	8.1	41.3	50.6	41 170	7 456	64.1	2 291	1.0	12.7	8.7
Columbia, OR	64 438	6.3	55.7	38.0	54 459	6 406	61.7	2 267	1.0	15.1	4.1
Coos, OR	83 971	10.1	54.7	35.2	78 525	8 976	58.8	3 549	0.7	13.2	5.8
Crook, OR	25 760	10.7	52.5	36.8	21 483	6 699	62.9	1 073	0.0	14.7	10.1
Curry, OR	26 044	15.5	47.8	36.6	22 706	7 702	62.6	884	0.0	10.9	4.6
Deschutes, OR	197 607	8.3	44.5	47.2	155 721	7 300	62.0	5 855	0.0	14.4	2.8
Douglas, OR	139 282	13.6	60.8	25.6	125 264	7 709	62.4	5 456	0.2	12.0	5.6

Table C-1. Population, School, and Student Characteristics by County—*Continued*

STATE County	High school graduates, 2000			College enrollment, 2000		College graduates, 2000 (percent)						
	Population 25 years and over	High school graduate or less (percent)	High school graduate or more (percent)	Number	Percent public	Bachelor's degree or more	+/- U.S. percentage with bachelor's degree or more	Non-Hispanic White	Black	American Indian and Alaska Native	Asian or Pacific Islander	Hispanic[3]
	30	31	32	33	34	35	36	37	38	39	40	41
Cherokee, OK	25 237	53.5	76.7	4 448	94.5	22.1	-2.3	23.8	26.2	18.1	22.7	9.9
Choctaw, OK	10 210	67.7	69.0	495	93.5	9.9	-14.5	9.6	5.2	13.2	22.7	28.2
Cimarron, OK	2 077	55.0	76.6	66	84.8	17.7	-6.7	19.7	0.0	16.7	0.0	1.3
Cleveland, OK	126 569	38.6	88.1	26 884	92.9	28.0	3.6	28.1	27.1	21.8	48.6	17.9
Coal, OK	3 964	68.4	68.6	172	93.6	12.4	-12.0	12.2	0.0	14.8	35.7	10.6
Comanche, OK	67 220	46.3	85.2	7 129	89.4	19.1	-5.3	21.8	11.6	13.0	21.5	11.2
Cotton, OK	4 436	62.2	77.0	155	92.9	14.0	-10.4	14.8	1.4	11.8	33.3	7.5
Craig, OK	10 197	63.8	76.9	386	94.6	10.5	-13.9	10.5	8.8	9.5	0.0	21.6
Creek, OK	43 523	62.4	77.6	2 269	83.4	11.7	-12.7	12.1	9.8	8.0	20.5	7.6
Custer, OK	15 156	50.2	81.2	3 431	97.8	22.8	-1.6	25.2	3.1	12.0	29.0	4.6
Delaware, OK	25 549	61.7	75.4	796	84.9	13.3	-11.1	14.0	15.4	11.2	24.0	5.8
Dewey, OK	3 310	61.0	79.8	107	90.7	16.6	-7.8	17.3	0.0	3.7	100.0	1.6
Ellis, OK	2 918	57.1	81.2	63	90.5	19.2	-5.2	19.5	. . .	16.7	. . .	8.9
Garfield, OK	38 067	53.4	82.2	2 079	87.8	19.6	-4.8	20.2	5.6	10.5	25.9	12.6
Garvin, OK	18 263	67.4	73.0	572	90.2	12.0	-12.4	12.2	14.7	9.3	26.0	5.6
Grady, OK	29 172	58.8	79.5	2 073	92.6	14.4	-10.0	14.7	7.0	17.4	29.9	4.3
Grant, OK	3 500	53.3	85.7	113	89.4	16.2	-8.2	16.0	0.0	22.9	22.2	34.5
Greer, OK	4 302	59.6	76.7	261	92.3	12.6	-11.8	14.6	4.1	2.7	58.8	0.0
Harmon, OK	2 192	69.0	63.2	43	86.0	12.1	-12.3	15.6	0.0	0.0	50.0	1.7
Harper, OK	2 507	54.2	82.1	74	81.1	19.2	-5.2	19.3	. . .	22.7	0.0	14.5
Haskell, OK	7 762	65.7	66.9	281	98.2	10.3	-14.1	10.6	10.5	8.1	0.0	2.5
Hughes, OK	9 762	68.3	70.8	434	92.6	9.7	-14.7	10.8	2.2	5.4	0.0	6.5
Jackson, OK	17 270	47.8	79.1	1 543	93.6	18.5	-5.9	20.5	10.6	21.3	35.1	5.6
Jefferson, OK	4 710	68.1	69.3	149	96.0	10.6	-13.8	10.8	0.0	13.3	5.9	8.5
Johnston, OK	6 759	61.4	69.1	536	97.4	13.3	-11.1	13.8	0.0	11.1	36.8	15.3
Kay, OK	31 106	52.3	80.9	1 774	92.8	18.3	-6.1	19.4	4.2	8.7	35.3	8.9
Kingfisher, OK	8 984	57.6	81.2	316	88.6	16.1	-8.3	17.5	4.8	11.3	0.0	1.8
Kiowa, OK	6 963	58.9	77.4	314	95.5	14.8	-9.6	16.1	2.0	5.3	. . .	11.1
Latimer, OK	6 716	61.1	73.8	754	96.4	12.0	-12.4	11.6	25.0	14.4	25.0	26.7
Le Flore, OK	30 966	64.7	70.4	1 658	95.4	11.3	-13.1	11.7	10.4	10.4	29.1	4.1
Lincoln, OK	20 746	64.5	77.5	883	83.5	11.1	-13.3	11.4	11.4	8.6	11.4	2.4
Logan, OK	21 195	53.1	81.5	2 817	93.2	19.1	-5.3	18.9	23.1	15.2	43.4	17.1
Love, OK	5 931	67.8	73.6	248	91.5	10.8	-13.6	11.1	1.8	19.7	0.0	3.2
McClain, OK	18 069	57.4	79.3	1 154	88.8	15.7	-8.7	16.1	8.8	18.8	28.6	4.6
McCurtain, OK	21 875	66.9	69.2	908	92.4	10.8	-13.6	11.7	7.3	9.0	8.0	1.9
McIntosh, OK	13 787	62.6	71.6	557	91.7	13.1	-11.3	12.5	9.1	16.1	20.0	15.1
Major, OK	5 191	61.8	78.6	129	00.4	14.4	+10.0	14.9	14.3	6.4	. . .	0.0
Marshall, OK	9 078	63.3	71.0	332	91.0	11.4	-13.0	12.1	0.7	10.8	0.0	4.1
Mayes, OK	24 849	62.0	76.1	1 062	83.1	12.1	-12.3	12.8	3.0	9.2	50.9	6.5
Murray, OK	8 566	61.5	74.3	325	90.2	14.9	-9.5	15.1	30.4	12.0	18.2	6.7
Muskogee, OK	44 890	56.8	75.1	2 819	87.0	15.4	-9.0	16.5	12.3	12.0	40.4	11.9
Noble, OK	7 635	58.6	81.5	371	89.2	15.8	-8.6	16.3	3.9	10.9	36.5	0.0
Nowata, OK	7 092	66.5	76.2	270	03.0	9.5	-14.9	9.9	11.6	10.6	. . .	12.7
Okfuskee, OK	7 904	70.2	69.4	288	84.7	9.2	-15.2	9.8	7.9	7.9	0.0	10.4
Oklahoma, OK	420 823	43.5	82.5	43 237	74.4	25.4	1.0	28.8	14.8	14.6	34.4	8.5
Okmulgee, OK	25 225	60.5	74.7	1 790	90.2	11.4	-13.0	11.8	9.3	11.1	9.7	13.5
Osage, OK	29 417	56.2	80.2	1 282	83.6	14.6	-9.8	14.1	22.3	11.5	35.9	9.6
Ottawa, OK	21 510	58.9	75.7	1 586	93.1	12.2	-12.2	12.5	13.3	11.9	19.7	2.7
Pawnee, OK	10 997	61.4	78.8	460	88.9	12.1	-12.3	12.5	8.6	10.4	18.2	2.7
Payne, OK	37 237	40.0	86.7	17 412	98.1	34.2	9.8	33.8	22.5	23.8	80.6	36.6
Pittsburg, OK	30 162	60.3	76.2	1 301	89.7	12.9	-11.5	13.3	7.7	12.4	35.7	7.0
Pontotoc, OK	22 031	53.5	78.2	2 957	96.0	21.8	-2.6	22.6	11.9	18.0	77.8	10.3
Pottawatomie, OK	41 142	56.4	79.3	4 315	59.4	15.5	-8.9	16.3	9.2	10.3	24.0	7.6
Pushmataha, OK	7 861	66.3	69.0	277	89.5	12.4	-12.0	12.1	4.4	11.5	64.7	14.5
Roger Mills, OK	2 396	59.3	79.3	59	100.0	15.8	-8.6	16.6	. . .	3.7	0.0	10.3
Rogers, OK	45 152	49.4	83.4	2 378	85.4	16.9	-7.5	17.4	12.8	13.1	30.9	23.2
Seminole, OK	15 988	61.6	73.2	1 022	84.5	12.1	-12.3	12.9	10.9	6.9	50.0	4.4
Sequoyah, OK	24 980	64.7	70.2	1 007	90.4	10.9	-13.5	10.3	12.9	13.6	42.9	6.3
Stephens, OK	29 111	60.3	77.0	1 230	88.6	16.6	-7.8	16.9	8.9	13.2	65.6	10.1
Texas, OK	11 776	56.7	71.9	1 065	83.5	17.7	-6.7	21.9	0.0	17.8	43.9	3.6
Tillman, OK	6 141	67.0	67.4	160	90.0	12.5	-11.9	15.4	5.0	2.8	27.6	1.3
Tulsa, OK	359 386	41.5	85.1	34 049	62.5	26.9	2.5	29.7	14.3	17.8	38.6	11.8
Wagoner, OK	36 895	54.5	81.3	1 948	75.7	15.4	-9.0	16.0	16.0	11.9	13.6	6.6
Washington, OK	32 905	46.9	85.2	1 783	65.8	25.8	1.4	28.0	12.1	10.2	19.4	16.8
Washita, OK	7 613	59.3	79.7	378	95.0	15.1	-9.3	15.5	0.0	10.3	0.0	8.3
Woods, OK	5 993	49.2	82.7	995	98.9	23.7	-0.7	24.9	8.0	27.6	84.6	13.9
Woodward, OK	11 992	58.2	79.9	397	95.7	15.2	-9.2	15.8	7.6	11.6	26.3	5.0
OREGON	2 250 998	41.1	85.1	204 811	81.7	25.1	0.7	26.0	17.8	12.2	37.2	9.6
Baker, OR	11 712	51.0	80.3	284	76.1	16.4	-8.0	16.8	0.0	0.0	2.7	7.7
Benton, OR	45 758	22.2	93.1	16 823	97.4	47.4	23.0	47.6	49.0	30.7	67.2	28.0
Clackamas, OR	223 211	35.2	88.9	15 812	80.0	28.4	4.0	28.5	27.4	20.5	44.2	14.5
Clatsop, OR	24 069	43.5	85.6	1 633	84.1	19.1	-5.3	19.6	16.3	9.1	22.7	7.0
Columbia, OR	28 725	49.6	85.6	1 210	83.6	14.0	-10.4	14.1	20.0	9.3	32.1	11.1
Coos, OR	44 667	49.2	81.6	2 558	92.0	15.0	-9.4	15.3	23.5	8.5	26.9	10.9
Crook, OR	12 692	58.4	80.5	485	79.2	12.6	-11.8	13.1	. . .	12.1	14.7	1.6
Curry, OR	16 168	50.4	81.7	463	82.9	16.4	-8.0	17.1	28.0	6.4	2.4	7.4
Deschutes, OR	77 981	38.8	88.4	4 761	89.2	25.0	0.6	25.6	0.0	13.2	31.3	8.2
Douglas, OR	68 783	53.7	81.0	3 038	89.8	13.3	-11.1	13.3	8.9	9.9	22.6	13.8

[3]May be of any race.
. . . = Not available.

Table C-1. Population, School, and Student Characteristics by County—*Continued*

STATE County	State/ county code	County type[1]	Population, 2005 Total	Percent 5 to 17 years	Number of schools and students, 2004–2005 School districts	Schools	Students	Resident enrollment, 2000 Total	Percent public	K–12	Percent public
			1	2	3	4	5	6	7	8	9
Gilliam, OR	41 021	9	1 794	14.7	3	4	286	438	95.9	381	99.2
Grant, OR	41 023	9	7 297	17.2	6	8	1 098	1 888	88.1	1 612	90.1
Harney, OR	41 025	7	6 898	18.5	11	14	1 231	1 713	94.5	1 535	95.0
Hood River, OR	41 027	6	21 284	18.9	1	9	3 907	5 124	88.1	4 269	90.3
Jackson, OR	41 029	3	195 322	16.8	10	57	28 950	44 630	89.4	32 724	91.0
Jefferson, OR	41 031	6	20 100	20.2	5	12	3 643	4 882	94.4	4 137	97.8
Josephine, OR	41 033	4	80 761	16.2	2	25	11 705	16 787	86.6	13 426	88.8
Klamath, OR	41 035	5	66 192	18.0	2	32	10 589	16 355	90.6	12 484	92.7
Lake, OR	41 037	7	7 313	16.5	6	8	1 109	1 669	95.0	1 497	96.3
Lane, OR	41 039	2	335 180	15.6	17	129	47 498	90 503	90.6	54 942	92.1
Lincoln, OR	41 041	4	45 994	15.0	1	21	5 890	9 074	91.5	7 409	94.6
Linn, OR	41 043	4	108 914	18.0	7	29	9 606	25 835	86.3	19 774	88.6
Malheur, OR	41 045	6	31 330	19.2	11	23	5 328	8 244	90.9	6 489	92.6
Marion, OR	41 047	2	305 265	19.2	13	64	18 825	73 702	85.2	55 606	91.0
Morrow, OR	41 049	6	11 666	21.7	2	9	2 301	2 868	96.4	2 526	97.9
Multnomah, OR	41 051	1	672 906	15.9	8	77	43 465	162 670	80.7	104 972	88.3
Polk, OR	41 053	2	70 295	17.0	5	85	44 586	17 391	87.6	11 511	89.4
Sherman, OR	41 055	9	1 749	16.4	1	3	281	465	94.0	411	94.6
Tillamook, OR	41 057	6	25 277	15.3	3	11	3 444	5 039	91.0	4 214	92.4
Umatilla, OR	41 059	5	73 878	19.3	11	35	13 226	18 290	92.0	14 484	94.9
Union, OR	41 061	7	24 540	16.5	7	17	3 867	7 032	93.6	4 662	94.1
Wallowa, OR	41 063	9	7 014	15.4	5	9	956	1 677	89.2	1 450	91.9
Wasco, OR	41 065	6	23 593	17.7	6	12	3 463	5 507	87.8	4 426	89.5
Washington, OR	41 067	1	499 794	18.6	9	224	126 537	116 491	82.5	83 868	88.7
Wheeler, OR	41 069	9	1 455	14.2	3	4	215	358	86.0	296	84.5
Yamhill, OR	41 071	1	92 196	18.1	7	33	15 878	23 412	77.3	16 901	90.8
PENNSYLVANIA	42 000		12 429 616	16.8	730	3 260	1 812 109	3 135 934	76.5	2 228 837	84.6
Adams, PA	42 001	4	99 749	17.2	7	26	14 754	23 246	77.6	17 333	88.3
Allegheny, PA	42 003	1	1 235 841	15.8	59	322	166 856	322 016	75.7	212 715	85.1
Armstrong, PA	42 005	1	70 586	16.0	5	25	11 216	15 812	91.9	12 826	95.5
Beaver, PA	42 007	1	177 377	16.2	18	57	29 287	41 572	84.1	31 636	91.7
Bedford, PA	42 009	6	50 091	16.6	6	21	8 138	10 487	91.5	8 761	94.2
Berks, PA	42 011	2	396 314	17.4	20	104	65 866	94 301	82.7	69 719	88.9
Blair, PA	42 013	3	126 795	15.9	9	37	18 956	29 585	85.9	22 369	90.2
Bradford, PA	42 015	6	62 537	17.8	8	30	10 848	14 740	88.0	12 501	91.4
Bucks, PA	42 017	1	621 342	18.0	21	142	92 274	157 810	72.4	115 596	80.6
Butler, PA	42 019	1	182 087	17.3	8	43	27 778	45 627	87.6	32 159	92.1
Cambria, PA	42 021	3	148 073	14.8	17	43	19 948	34 592	81.5	24 953	86.4
Cameron, PA	42 023	7	5 639	16.6	1	2	938	1 384	91.0	1 192	93.3
Carbon, PA	42 025	2	61 959	15.4	6	20	9 069	12 781	86.3	10 303	90.0
Centre, PA	42 027	3	140 561	11.2	9	37	16 247	56 564	92.9	18 306	92.4
Chester, PA	42 029	1	474 027	18.2	24	104	73 719	119 787	73.0	84 718	80.4
Clarion, PA	42 031	6	40 589	14.9	8	16	6 364	12 036	92.3	6 868	92.2
Clearfield, PA	42 033	4	82 783	15.8	8	27	11 416	18 092	89.3	14 719	92.3
Clinton, PA	42 035	6	37 439	14.7	3	15	4 968	9 857	90.2	6 141	91.3
Columbia, PA	42 037	4	64 939	14.1	6	16	7 559	17 963	92.2	10 468	93.7
Crawford, PA	42 039	4	89 442	17.0	6	32	14 011	22 134	80.6	16 917	90.0
Cumberland, PA	42 041	2	223 089	15.4	11	67	34 162	54 249	77.8	35 816	87.0
Dauphin, PA	42 043	2	253 995	17.3	16	74	55 163	60 052	82.9	46 556	87.7
Delaware, PA	42 045	1	555 648	18.0	20	109	73 400	154 448	62.9	103 230	74.2
Elk, PA	42 047	7	33 577	16.8	3	10	4 356	7 993	76.4	6 516	79.8
Erie, PA	42 049	2	280 446	17.6	20	83	41 851	77 763	74.2	53 964	80.9
Fayette, PA	42 051	1	146 142	16.0	9	50	22 951	32 185	88.4	25 608	91.8
Forest, PA	42 053	9	5 739	15.6	2	6	1 373	1 101	76.0	993	74.8
Franklin, PA	42 055	4	137 409	16.9	9	47	22 101	28 494	84.3	22 600	88.2
Fulton, PA	42 057	8	14 673	17.2	4	8	2 416	2 996	94.1	2 580	96.1
Greene, PA	42 059	6	39 808	15.5	6	16	5 984	9 468	86.9	7 221	95.6
Huntingdon, PA	42 061	6	45 947	15.0	5	15	4 607	10 515	83.4	8 043	95.4
Indiana, PA	42 063	4	88 703	13.9	9	24	11 481	27 443	92.8	14 434	93.1
Jefferson, PA	42 065	7	45 759	16.1	4	16	6 090	10 163	89.7	8 348	92.0
Juniata, PA	42 067	6	23 507	17.2	1	12	3 215	4 798	86.6	4 117	88.8
Lackawanna, PA	42 069	2	209 525	15.6	14	51	27 730	52 278	68.5	36 314	81.2
Lancaster, PA	42 071	2	490 562	18.6	20	125	69 313	115 931	76.3	89 947	81.2
Lawrence, PA	42 073	4	92 809	16.4	10	31	15 045	21 804	86.3	16 641	94.6
Lebanon, PA	42 075	3	125 578	16.6	7	35	18 701	26 552	80.4	21 104	87.6
Lehigh, PA	42 077	2	330 433	17.3	15	94	64 181	77 729	76.8	57 231	86.4
Luzerne, PA	42 079	2	312 861	15.2	18	75	44 927	73 449	74.2	53 178	81.7
Lycoming, PA	42 081	3	118 395	16.2	10	38	17 600	29 073	84.5	21 522	92.6
McKean, PA	42 083	7	44 370	16.8	7	15	7 234	10 674	88.1	8 417	92.3
Mercer, PA	42 085	2	119 598	16.7	16	41	17 924	29 378	78.8	21 881	90.5
Mifflin, PA	42 087	4	46 235	17.3	5	19	7 726	9 564	82.1	8 244	85.4
Monroe, PA	42 089	1	163 234	19.0	7	38	32 660	39 478	87.1	28 869	91.9
Montgomery, PA	42 091	1	775 883	17.3	33	162	107 505	194 722	66.6	134 756	77.7
Montour, PA	42 093	6	18 032	17.2	3	8	2 696	4 244	83.3	3 479	88.3
Northampton, PA	42 095	2	287 767	16.5	13	41	29 988	70 501	71.5	48 206	86.0
Northumberland, PA	42 097	4	92 610	15.1	8	26	13 120	19 600	84.6	16 362	88.1
Perry, PA	42 099	2	44 728	17.6	5	15	7 296	9 718	90.0	8 317	92.2

[1]County type codes are from the Economic Research Service of the United States Department of Agriculture. See notes and definitions at the end of this section.

Table C-1. Population, School, and Student Characteristics by County—*Continued*

STATE County	Characteristics of students, 2004–2005				Outcomes		Staff and students, 2004–2005		
	Percent with IEP[2]	Percent eligible for free or reduced-price lunch	Percent minority	Percent English-language learners	Number of graduates, 2003–2004	Percent dropouts, grades 9–12, 2001–2002	Number of teachers	Student-teacher ratio	Central administration staff
	10	11	12	13	14	15	16	17	18
Gilliam, OR	13.6	32.3	5.0	0.0	38	. . .	27	10.6	3
Grant, OR	15.3	43.5	5.0	11.1	. . .	0.4	90	12.2	8
Harney, OR	16.4	55.3	10.5	2.0	. . .	0.9	88	14.0	18
Hood River, OR	14.6	36.2	43.8	39.1	272	2.0	207	18.9	20
Jackson, OR	12.9	41.7	17.7	7.9	. . .	6.9	1 287	22.5	114
Jefferson, OR	15.6	75.4	56.9	44.1	. . .	4.1	221	16.5	27
Josephine, OR	11.3	52.3	11.9	1.4	762	5.1	510	23.0	33
Klamath, OR	15.4	52.5	25.1	9.4	643	3.4	534	19.8	41
Lake, OR	13.3	50.9	13.6	5.4	. . .	2.8	71	15.7	11
Lane, OR	17.2	41.1	17.0	3.4	3 476	3.8	2 222	21.4	221
Lincoln, OR	18.1	60.8	21.3	5.8	457	5.9	280	21.0	25
Linn, OR	14.6	49.4	11.7	2.3	619	6.1	434	22.1	53
Malheur, OR	13.9	66.3	46.3	30.2	. . .	3.2	338	15.8	31
Marion, OR	14.9	50.4	34.8	26.7	. . .	0.0	1 071	17.6	. . .
Morrow, OR	13.9	65.6	39.9	31.3	146	2.6	148	15.5	8
Multnomah, OR	13.8	49.9	36.2	20.8	2 632	8.0	2 240	19.4	219
Polk, OR	13.6	37.5	22.1	14.8	2 830	4.6	2 094	21.3	225
Sherman, OR	17.8	42.7	9.9	5.0	35	. . .	22	12.7	3
Tillamook, OR	16.6	50.2	19.7	10.3	279	4.6	198	17.4	21
Umatilla, OR	14.1	52.5	35.5	20.8	745	4.3	724	18.3	64
Union, OR	17.0	40.3	7.6	1.1	312	2.5	244	15.8	24
Wallowa, OR	16.1	41.8	4.0	0.0	. . .	. . .	64	14.9	3
Wasco, OR	16.1	54.2	17.5	14.3	. . .	3.4	156	22.2	. . .
Washington, OR	13.3	29.9	31.0	14.9	8 118	4.1	6 475	19.5	679
Wheeler, OR	10.2	62.1	8.5	0.0	30	. . .	26	8.4	3
Yamhill, OR	14.2	40.8	21.4	11.6	1 136	5.2	764	20.8	70
PENNSYLVANIA	14.5	28.5	24.4	. . .	. . .	3.3	121 152	15.0	. . .
Adams, PA	12.9	21.9	10.8	. . .	. . .	2.5	1 325	11.1	231
Allegheny, PA	14.8	27.5	25.9	. . .	. . .	2.4	12 208	13.7	. . .
Armstrong, PA	15.6	31.1	1.7	. . .	. . .	2.0	768	14.6	59
Beaver, PA	12.4	23.3	11.6	. . .	. . .	3.2	1 870	15.7	146
Bedford, PA	16.3	35.3	1.5	. . .	. . .	2.8	530	15.4	48
Berks, PA	13.6	24.3	27.2	. . .	. . .	3.3	4 169	15.8	465
Blair, PA	16.7	37.7	3.4	. . .	. . .	3.0	1 264	15.0	150
Bradford, PA	15.1	30.9	3.0	. . .	. . .	3.2	746	14.5	61
Bucks, PA	15.1	11.3	11.2	. . .	. . .	1.4	6 026	15.3	. . .
Butler, PA	12.0	10.0	2.6	. . .	. . .	2.3	1 735	16.0	98
Cambria, PA	14.6	41.3	6.1	. . .	. . .	1.9	1 531	13.0	160
Cameron, PA	16.7	42.6	2.1	. . .	. . .	1.1	57	16.5	4
Carbon, PA	15.2	27.5	5.4	. . .	. . .	1.6	600	15.1	56
Centre, PA	14.0	20.4	6.0	. . .	. . .	1.5	1 185	13.7	101
Chester, PA	14.4	10.4	18.1	. . .	. . .	1.5	5 095	14.5	. . .
Clarion, PA	14.2	35.1	1.9	. . .	. . .	2.6	548	11.6	55
Clearfield, PA	15.5	41.8	1.6	. . .	. . .	2.1	827	13.8	86
Clinton, PA	17.7	39.1	2.4	. . .	. . .	2.5	406	12.2	26
Columbia, PA	14.8	26.8	3.9	. . .	. . .	3.3	531	14.2	46
Crawford, PA	16.1	34.2	4.7	. . .	. . .	2.7	956	14.7	65
Cumberland, PA	14.2	11.2	8.8	. . .	. . .	2.2	2 473	13.8	256
Dauphin, PA	15.6	. . .	34.6	. . .	. . .	2.8	2 753	20.0	194
Delaware, PA	17.6	21.9	32.9	. . .	. . .	2.1	5 068	14.5	. . .
Elk, PA	14.0	26.6	2.4	. . .	. . .	2.5	280	15.6	27
Erie, PA	14.4	39.9	17.2	. . .	. . .	2.7	2 854	14.7	229
Fayette, PA	16.6	48.9	8.1	. . .	. . .	4.1	1 445	15.9	105
Forest, PA	19.2	38.3	1.4	. . .	. . .	3.3	107	12.8	7
Franklin, PA	15.4	23.9	11.7	. . .	. . .	2.5	1 316	16.8	136
Fulton, PA	11.4	26.0	2.2	. . .	. . .	2.6	180	13.4	19
Greene, PA	21.3	40.6	1.9	. . .	. . .	3.4	458	13.1	39
Huntingdon, PA	16.8	37.6	3.9	. . .	. . .	2.4	350	13.2	32
Indiana, PA	15.5	36.4	3.5	. . .	. . .	2.2	894	12.8	84
Jefferson, PA	17.2	31.9	1.4	. . .	. . .	2.4	426	14.3	35
Juniata, PA	10.5	25.4	4.5	. . .	. . .	2.0	205	15.7	16
Lackawanna, PA	15.4	28.6	10.2	. . .	. . .	2.0	1 923	14.4	125
Lancaster, PA	16.3	21.4	20.5	. . .	. . .	3.4	4 760	14.6	490
Lawrence, PA	13.8	30.2	9.5	. . .	. . .	2.5	940	16.0	72
Lebanon, PA	13.8	20.7	16.5	. . .	. . .	3.1	1 161	16.1	83
Lehigh, PA	12.8	27.6	34.4	. . .	. . .	3.9	3 923	16.4	332
Luzerne, PA	14.2	24.9	10.2	. . .	. . .	2.7	2 834	15.9	230
Lycoming, PA	17.1	31.2	10.4	. . .	. . .	3.9	1 312	13.4	149
McKean, PA	14.5	37.1	2.5	. . .	. . .	3.4	594	12.2	78
Mercer, PA	15.1	30.6	12.2	. . .	. . .	2.7	1 380	13.0	117
Mifflin, PA	16.0	24.6	4.6	. . .	. . .	4.3	609	12.7	46
Monroe, PA	13.7	21.3	30.4	. . .	. . .	2.4	2 121	15.4	. . .
Montgomery, PA	13.9	10.3	22.4	. . .	. . .	1.6	7 382	14.6	735
Montour, PA	13.3	25.9	8.3	. . .	. . .	1.3	185	14.6	11
Northampton, PA	12.9	19.0	21.2	. . .	. . .	3.6	2 206	13.6	185
Northumberland, PA	11.8	34.4	4.3	. . .	. . .	3.3	884	14.8	84
Perry, PA	18.0	22.2	3.4	. . .	. . .	3.6	524	13.9	42

[2]IEP = Individual Education Program. See notes and definitions at the end of this section.
. . . = Not available.

Table C-1. Population, School, and Student Characteristics by County—*Continued*

STATE County	Revenue, 2003–2004 Total revenue (thousands of dollars)	Percent of revenue from: Federal government	State government	Local government	Current expenditures, 2003–2004 Total expenditures (thousands of dollars)	Amount per student (dollars)	Percent for instruction	Resident population, 16 to 19 years, 2000 Total	Percent in armed forces	Percent high school graduates	Percent not enrolled, not employed, not in armed forces, not high school graduate
	19	20	21	22	23	24	25	26	27	28	29
Gilliam, OR	8 666	10.0	55.0	35.0	6 448	20 405	61.3	94	0.0	5.3	2.1
Grant, OR	20 192	32.8	40.6	26.6	13 763	11 673	55.9	466	0.0	9.7	3.0
Harney, OR	14 892	16.2	60.8	23.0	13 944	10 461	51.6	453	0.0	14.3	8.6
Hood River, OR	37 075	11.5	55.2	33.3	30 744	7 793	66.3	1 147	0.0	12.3	6.8
Jackson, OR	249 145	9.7	56.6	33.7	212 570	7 267	64.3	10 013	0.1	12.6	5.8
Jefferson, OR	42 527	20.8	54.6	24.6	32 066	8 620	59.2	921	0.0	11.2	9.6
Josephine, OR	92 188	10.7	58.3	30.9	83 575	7 197	64.2	3 650	0.0	14.5	7.6
Klamath, OR	88 432	14.9	63.3	21.8	84 381	8 004	62.1	3 556	0.0	13.4	4.3
Lake, OR	12 531	19.4	53.9	26.7	10 438	9 140	57.6	365	0.0	11.5	2.5
Lane, OR	442 703	10.5	51.7	37.7	366 786	7 682	64.3	19 632	0.0	12.9	3.6
Lincoln, OR	52 059	12.8	31.9	55.2	47 165	7 908	62.5	2 274	1.0	18.1	7.7
Linn, OR	161 672	10.1	58.8	31.1	131 897	7 313	59.2	6 161	0.0	12.1	6.9
Malheur, OR	54 548	14.7	70.6	14.7	46 686	8 712	63.1	1 807	0.0	11.8	5.9
Marion, OR	511 751	10.4	61.8	27.8	432 373	7 774	66.8	17 704	0.0	13.9	8.5
Morrow, OR	24 983	5.4	52.2	42.3	17 722	7 557	62.1	710	0.0	9.3	7.2
Multnomah, OR	954 480	8.4	43.4	48.1	786 292	8 634	63.6	33 149	0.0	12.7	5.7
Polk, OR	53 062	8.1	61.5	30.3	41 912	6 595	65.5	4 256	0.0	10.7	3.4
Sherman, OR	3 837	5.1	63.3	31.6	3 097	10 498	57.3	103	0.0	13.6	5.8
Tillamook, OR	32 782	9.7	41.9	48.5	26 953	7 750	60.2	1 322	0.7	14.7	4.8
Umatilla, OR	122 725	9.8	62.2	27.9	107 278	8 196	62.1	4 001	0.0	8.8	6.8
Union, OR	48 979	10.3	57.4	32.3	42 585	10 765	64.0	1 748	0.5	7.9	2.7
Wallowa, OR	15 516	7.6	51.2	41.2	12 058	12 653	64.0	341	0.0	10.3	2.1
Wasco, OR	37 936	11.4	53.8	34.8	32 281	9 335	59.6	1 182	0.0	8.6	5.6
Washington, OR	684 600	5.9	50.3	43.7	529 299	6 863	63.5	23 102	0.0	12.1	5.3
Wheeler, OR	4 233	10.3	68.7	21.0	3 538	14 266	57.6	99	0.0	12.1	0.0
Yamhill, OR	133 285	8.2	58.9	32.8	105 597	6 625	62.8	5 545	0.0	10.2	5.0
PENNSYLVANIA	21 449 890	7.7	33.6	58.7	17 931 284	9 988	64.3	672 849	0.1	9.3	4.0
Adams, PA	217 498	12.6	32.2	55.2	197 410	13 410	61.0	5 427	0.1	11.0	3.2
Allegheny, PA	2 323 156	7.2	27.8	65.0	1 937 381	11 540	65.2	64 811	0.0	8.6	3.1
Armstrong, PA	125 325	4.3	45.3	50.4	107 693	9 877	64.5	3 837	0.0	11.6	4.1
Beaver, PA	301 758	6.6	44.8	48.6	257 723	9 009	64.2	9 127	0.0	10.2	3.6
Bedford, PA	77 534	8.4	53.5	38.1	66 613	8 179	63.4	2 431	0.0	14.7	4.2
Berks, PA	742 042	8.3	29.5	62.2	608 079	9 021	64.4	20 694	0.0	10.0	4.9
Blair, PA	185 751	8.1	51.8	40.2	158 268	8 269	64.6	7 576	0.1	13.1	3.4
Bradford, PA	110 558	6.2	55.6	38.1	98 522	8 931	65.3	3 428	0.0	12.0	5.1
Bucks, PA	1 228 927	3.5	21.0	75.5	1 036 681	11 437	67.6	29 976	0.1	9.1	2.2
Butler, PA	253 687	3.3	40.8	55.9	213 191	7 668	66.5	9 699	0.0	8.2	2.1
Cambria, PA	237 432	10.5	50.9	38.6	207 010	10 771	63.3	8 601	0.1	10.1	3.8
Cameron, PA	10 172	3.9	61.8	34.3	7 819	8 053	62.4	313	0.0	8.9	3.2
Carbon, PA	98 681	4.7	33.0	62.3	77 791	9 157	65.2	2 820	0.0	12.1	5.2
Centre, PA	181 520	8.0	27.0	65.0	152 598	10 748	63.5	11 929	0.1	4.8	1.6
Chester, PA	983 920	4.2	18.9	76.8	790 814	11 545	62.3	23 454	0.0	6.7	2.9
Clarion, PA	92 384	15.0	56.4	28.6	84 305	11 796	59.1	3 245	0.0	5.7	2.6
Clearfield, PA	144 812	7.9	53.1	38.9	124 336	8 401	67.1	4 163	0.2	11.4	7.4
Clinton, PA	56 952	9.9	46.4	43.7	47 805	9 665	66.6	2 646	0.4	7.6	5.3
Columbia, PA	107 631	4.6	42.9	52.4	92 725	8 923	67.2	4 862	0.2	5.7	2.8
Crawford, PA	116 696	7.6	49.6	42.8	96 466	8 785	62.8	5 741	0.1	9.7	4.8
Cumberland, PA	330 991	7.5	28.9	63.6	285 216	9 954	62.9	13 107	0.1	7.2	2.7
Dauphin, PA	431 370	6.2	31.7	62.0	359 208	9 475	64.5	12 418	0.0	10.4	4.6
Delaware, PA	930 857	6.0	24.5	69.5	807 053	11 228	65.4	32 263	0.0	6.7	3.2
Elk, PA	40 924	3.4	47.9	48.7	36 479	8 192	64.4	1 785	0.0	14.8	2.2
Erie, PA	473 834	10.1	41.8	48.1	385 696	9 247	62.7	18 122	0.0	8.2	3.5
Fayette, PA	199 298	9.7	59.5	30.8	174 728	8 661	62.8	7 221	0.1	13.3	5.1
Forest, PA	9 433	12.7	37.6	49.7	8 126	11 760	61.3	322	0.0	11.5	1.9
Franklin, PA	170 577	5.1	37.0	57.9	142 733	7 921	67.0	6 695	0.0	12.7	4.4
Fulton, PA	27 874	7.5	56.1	36.4	21 407	8 777	63.3	681	0.0	19.1	4.0
Greene, PA	73 163	8.6	45.4	46.0	61 936	10 194	63.5	2 254	0.2	12.7	3.3
Huntingdon, PA	57 510	7.7	57.1	35.2	49 629	8 028	64.0	2 532	0.0	9.9	4.7
Indiana, PA	151 576	9.0	49.6	41.4	130 820	11 183	64.7	7 091	0.0	6.4	3.2
Jefferson, PA	68 420	5.9	54.7	39.4	56 599	9 698	65.0	2 512	0.0	10.7	4.1
Juniata, PA	25 154	5.9	50.7	43.4	23 812	7 497	64.4	1 166	0.0	17.2	5.7
Lackawanna, PA	308 068	7.5	35.9	56.5	266 849	9 701	65.9	11 494	0.0	8.0	2.9
Lancaster, PA	818 550	9.1	26.9	64.0	663 790	9 654	65.2	26 608	0.1	10.2	5.3
Lawrence, PA	143 005	4.7	54.6	40.7	119 676	8 206	68.1	4 946	0.3	9.8	5.6
Lebanon, PA	171 327	4.3	35.8	59.9	140 514	7 623	66.2	6 325	0.0	11.1	4.6
Lehigh, PA	539 805	6.2	27.3	66.5	445 880	9 286	63.3	15 872	0.1	10.3	5.1
Luzerne, PA	421 088	8.0	39.0	53.0	371 330	9 165	65.4	16 639	0.0	8.5	3.9
Lycoming, PA	196 408	9.4	44.1	46.5	176 982	9 910	66.3	7 224	0.2	10.3	3.8
McKean, PA	98 355	11.8	50.1	38.1	83 229	11 364	67.9	2 437	0.0	9.2	3.2
Mercer, PA	244 908	14.0	42.3	43.6	210 052	11 174	65.9	7 085	0.0	7.1	3.7
Mifflin, PA	78 012	16.9	46.2	36.9	71 893	11 701	66.2	2 298	0.1	14.8	8.6
Monroe, PA	342 792	3.1	22.9	74.0	278 321	8 843	62.5	8 287	0.2	9.4	2.8
Montgomery, PA	1 488 548	3.8	16.8	79.4	1 272 770	12 002	64.5	35 196	0.1	8.0	1.7
Montour, PA	26 685	7.0	36.6	56.4	21 852	8 325	68.3	1 002	0.0	11.8	3.9
Northampton, PA	518 302	5.3	23.9	70.7	405 475	9 206	62.9	15 697	0.0	7.1	3.0
Northumberland, PA	121 730	6.3	51.5	42.2	105 536	7 904	67.4	4 801	0.0	11.4	4.5
Perry, PA	69 172	3.7	48.7	47.6	57 881	7 992	61.8	2 341	0.1	12.9	6.8

Table C-1. Population, School, and Student Characteristics by County—*Continued*

STATE County	High school graduates, 2000			College enrollment, 2000		College graduates, 2000 (percent)						
	Population 25 years and over	High school graduate or less (percent)	High school graduate or more (percent)	Number	Percent public	Bachelor's degree or more	+/- U.S. percentage with bachelor's degree or more	Non-Hispanic White	Black	American Indian and Alaska Native	Asian or Pacific Islander	Hispanic[3]
	30	31	32	33	34	35	36	37	38	39	40	41
Gilliam, OR	1 368	45.8	89.3	37	67.6	13.4	-11.0	13.5	0.0	20.0	0.0	0.0
Grant, OR	5 428	52.8	84.5	145	86.9	15.7	-8.7	16.0	. . .	9.1	85.7	4.5
Harney, OR	5 130	57.1	81.2	72	97.2	11.9	-12.5	11.9	. . .	15.1	19.3	9.7
Hood River, OR	12 972	48.5	78.2	562	86.8	23.1	-1.3	26.7	20.7	1.0	34.6	5.2
Jackson, OR	121 155	45.1	85.0	9 304	92.4	22.3	-2.1	23.0	16.1	14.2	26.0	10.4
Jefferson, OR	11 972	55.2	76.5	388	80.7	13.7	-10.7	17.1	30.0	4.4	14.4	1.6
Josephine, OR	53 427	49.3	81.8	2 498	89.2	14.1	-10.3	14.5	32.1	6.5	18.9	4.6
Klamath, OR	41 833	52.6	81.5	2 970	91.5	15.9	-8.5	16.8	15.5	10.2	24.5	5.3
Lake, OR	5 199	53.7	79.6	101	81.2	15.5	-8.9	16.0	. . .	10.0	16.7	7.8
Lane, OR	210 601	38.3	87.5	30 647	94.3	25.5	1.1	25.7	29.2	15.6	47.0	15.8
Lincoln, OR	32 000	44.1	84.9	1 053	91.3	20.8	-3.6	21.3	3.5	11.2	40.3	6.0
Linn, OR	67 605	51.1	81.9	4 574	86.9	13.4	-11.0	13.8	9.0	3.4	16.2	5.4
Malheur, OR	19 587	59.5	71.0	1 349	86.7	11.1	-13.3	13.2	3.0	3.9	22.2	1.7
Marion, OR	177 683	47.0	79.3	14 424	72.2	19.8	-4.6	22.1	10.9	10.2	24.8	5.0
Morrow, OR	6 627	57.9	74.1	209	92.8	11.0	-13.4	12.9	14.3	2.2	34.1	1.9
Multnomah, OR	446 322	37.4	85.6	47 924	71.1	30.7	6.3	33.3	15.2	13.5	27.2	12.7
Polk, OR	39 357	40.4	85.5	5 087	89.1	25.3	0.9	26.9	6.3	10.3	25.2	8.5
Sherman, OR	1 316	48.6	84.3	16	87.5	19.0	-5.4	18.9	100.0	31.6	0.0	20.0
Tillamook, OR	17 145	52.9	84.1	547	94.0	17.6	-6.8	18.1	0.0	2.8	14.5	6.6
Umatilla, OR	44 515	51.9	77.8	2 743	88.8	16.0	-8.4	17.6	15.4	9.9	17.2	5.9
Union, OR	15 562	45.3	85.6	2 077	96.2	21.8	-2.6	22.1	14.3	21.1	15.6	14.1
Wallowa, OR	5 099	49.2	87.5	161	83.2	20.3	-4.1	20.6	. . .	0.0	0.0	13.0
Wasco, OR	16 023	51.9	82.1	777	83.1	15.7	-8.7	16.5	15.9	5.6	34.8	6.3
Washington, OR	285 518	31.2	88.9	24 771	75.9	34.5	10.1	35.7	32.0	21.0	50.2	11.3
Wheeler, OR	1 143	57.8	79.4	31	90.3	14.3	-10.1	13.9	0.0	0.0	. . .	26.9
Yamhill, OR	52 645	48.1	82.8	5 277	40.0	20.6	-3.8	22.1	9.8	15.8	22.6	6.6
PENNSYLVANIA	8 266 284	56.2	81.9	703 163	59.7	22.4	-2.0	23.2	12.0	13.2	48.8	12.0
Adams, PA	60 173	64.1	79.7	4 694	43.3	16.7	-7.7	16.7	15.4	21.3	55.5	6.7
Allegheny, PA	891 171	47.5	86.3	87 059	60.5	28.3	3.9	29.3	13.4	19.1	72.5	37.9
Armstrong, PA	50 638	71.1	80.0	2 012	83.0	10.4	-14.0	10.5	3.9	4.8	15.4	24.2
Beaver, PA	126 933	58.8	83.6	6 954	60.6	15.8	-8.6	16.2	7.1	3.1	48.1	18.1
Bedford, PA	34 582	72.4	78.3	1 066	82.3	10.2	-14.2	10.2	10.3	19.2	8.5	12.9
Berks, PA	248 864	61.3	78.0	18 185	71.2	18.5	-5.9	19.6	8.4	9.0	38.6	4.7
Blair, PA	88 366	66.2	83.8	5 251	79.0	13.9	-10.5	13.8	9.9	3.6	55.1	14.1
Bradford, PA	42 428	65.4	81.7	1 436	75.8	14.8	-9.6	14.7	6.7	15.4	67.8	24.1
Bucks, PA	402 575	43.6	88.6	28 682	59.4	31.2	6.8	31.1	22.4	26.2	57.0	16.2
Butler, PA	116 070	52.2	86.8	10 254	85.6	23.5	-0.9	23.2	23.6	3.7	65.4	28.7
Cambria, PA	106 780	67.3	80.0	7 614	71.3	13.7	-10.7	13.9	5.1	5.4	41.4	8.7
Cameron, PA	4 150	70.2	79.8	95	78.9	12.1	-12.3	12.1	0.0	. . .	100.0	0.0
Carbon, PA	41 690	68.9	79.0	1 770	76.2	11.0	-13.4	10.9	31.5	62.9	19.0	8.6
Centre, PA	74 785	45.6	88.2	36 356	96.1	36.3	11.9	34.5	20.0	24.8	84.4	48.8
Chester, PA	285 816	36.7	89.3	25 130	64.9	42.5	18.1	44.2	17.5	21.0	70.0	16.6
Clarion, PA	26 334	68.7	81.8	4 650	96.1	15.3	-9.1	15.0	60.5	0.0	44.2	18.5
Clearfield, PA	58 138	71.9	79.1	2 156	81.9	11.1	-13.3	11.1	2.3	7.7	66.2	7.7
Clinton, PA	24 701	67.6	80.4	3 407	90.6	13.4	-11.0	13.4	2.4	5.9	27.0	7.0
Columbia, PA	41 658	65.8	80.6	6 640	95.2	15.8	-8.6	15.5	41.1	0.0	49.8	11.7
Crawford, PA	59 684	66.6	81.6	4 041	44.6	14.7	-9.7	14.7	8.3	9.3	37.7	8.0
Cumberland, PA	144 215	49.7	86.1	15 608	63.3	27.9	3.5	28.0	13.3	26.5	46.4	15.9
Dauphin, PA	171 783	54.0	83.4	9 782	76.3	23.5	-0.9	25.6	12.8	18.8	39.3	9.0
Delaware, PA	365 174	46.5	86.5	39 670	41.9	30.0	5.6	31.4	15.4	12.9	50.9	30.0
Elk, PA	24 337	66.8	82.7	882	78.9	12.3	-12.1	12.2	0.0	0.0	40.5	30.0
Erie, PA	180 106	57.1	84.6	18 832	62.3	20.9	-3.5	21.5	8.7	10.8	51.0	11.0
Fayette, PA	103 227	71.8	76.0	4 864	79.1	11.5	-12.9	11.5	10.1	0.0	27.0	7.1
Forest, PA	3 540	73.8	79.4	61	77.0	8.9	-15.5	9.0	0.0	6.3	50.0	0.0
Franklin, PA	87 959	66.0	78.9	4 467	74.0	14.8	-9.6	14.7	8.5	5.3	52.8	12.7
Fulton, PA	9 687	75.1	73.2	285	76.8	9.3	-15.1	9.3	0.0	33.3	30.0	0.0
Greene, PA	27 758	71.8	75.7	1 857	58.4	12.2	-12.2	12.7	2.2	0.0	46.9	2.7
Huntingdon, PA	31 152	72.7	74.6	2 034	40.4	11.9	-12.5	12.5	1.2	38.9	19.4	2.7
Indiana, PA	55 995	65.4	81.0	11 991	94.6	17.0	-7.4	16.6	27.3	8.5	60.5	21.4
Jefferson, PA	31 583	70.4	81.0	1 283	84.6	11.7	-12.7	11.5	9.5	0.0	58.5	24.4
Juniata, PA	15 225	77.2	74.5	433	78.1	8.8	-15.6	8.7	33.3	0.0	12.5	11.9
Lackawanna, PA	148 116	58.5	82.0	12 508	37.8	19.6	-4.8	19.6	8.6	8.4	46.6	11.0
Lancaster, PA	302 503	61.5	77.4	18 811	64.3	20.5	-3.9	21.2	11.8	9.6	24.6	7.4
Lawrence, PA	64 767	64.1	81.6	3 916	59.5	15.1	-9.3	15.3	3.8	2.5	54.0	29.9
Lebanon, PA	82 008	68.0	78.6	4 081	50.7	15.4	-9.0	15.7	12.7	31.4	35.1	3.8
Lehigh, PA	212 665	53.8	81.1	15 378	52.4	23.3	-1.1	24.3	10.4	5.4	52.8	7.0
Luzerne, PA	226 374	60.4	81.1	15 918	56.1	16.4	-8.0	16.4	5.8	10.3	50.3	10.4
Lycoming, PA	80 500	61.3	80.6	6 190	64.9	15.1	-9.3	15.2	6.9	12.1	38.6	13.8
McKean, PA	31 529	65.7	82.2	1 656	80.4	14.0	-10.4	14.5	1.3	10.0	29.8	3.5
Mercer, PA	81 499	62.2	82.9	5 921	41.5	17.3	-7.1	17.7	6.2	12.5	44.9	21.1
Mifflin, PA	31 722	74.8	77.2	722	68.3	10.9	-13.5	10.8	35.6	0.0	35.2	7.8
Monroe, PA	89 793	54.8	83.8	8 213	81.1	20.5	-3.9	20.6	21.5	27.2	47.1	13.9
Montgomery, PA	515 871	38.8	88.5	43 540	46.3	38.7	14.3	39.4	22.4	21.6	57.4	28.6
Montour, PA	12 573	59.8	82.3	498	65.3	22.1	-2.3	21.3	23.3	78.9	86.0	30.3
Northampton, PA	180 018	55.8	80.7	17 800	39.2	21.2	-3.2	21.5	15.7	16.3	55.7	10.1
Northumberland, PA	67 112	72.3	77.8	2 148	71.9	11.1	-13.3	11.0	9.3	8.2	35.2	17.6
Perry, PA	29 250	69.7	79.9	982	84.0	11.3	-13.1	11.2	6.3	14.3	53.6	21.1

[3]May be of any race.
. . . = Not available.

Table C-1. Population, School, and Student Characteristics by County—*Continued*

STATE County	State/county code	County type[1]	Population, 2005		Number of schools and students, 2004–2005			Resident enrollment, 2000			
			Total	Percent 5 to 17 years	School districts	Schools	Students	Total	Percent public	K–12	Percent public
			1	2	3	4	5	6	7	8	9
Philadelphia, PA	42 101	1	1 463 281	18.0	52	320	211 996	440 307	66.9	298 504	77.0
Pike, PA	42 103	1	56 337	19.0	1	7	5 616	11 944	88.2	9 714	95.9
Potter, PA	42 105	9	17 834	18.2	5	10	2 965	4 194	92.1	3 590	94.8
Schuylkill, PA	42 107	4	147 447	14.6	14	39	19 260	30 760	84.3	24 600	88.8
Snyder, PA	42 109	7	38 207	16.3	2	11	5 260	9 512	70.1	6 727	87.4
Somerset, PA	42 111	4	78 907	15.3	12	35	11 404	16 927	90.7	14 074	92.9
Sullivan, PA	42 113	8	6 391	15.2	1	3	793	1 347	91.1	1 140	93.7
Susquehanna, PA	42 115	6	42 124	17.6	7	15	7 938	10 047	89.8	8 458	93.5
Tioga, PA	42 117	6	41 649	16.1	3	16	6 390	10 811	91.6	7 667	93.0
Union, PA	42 119	4	43 131	13.3	4	11	4 303	10 801	62.4	6 646	88.6
Venango, PA	42 121	4	55 928	17.1	5	25	7 137	13 090	88.1	11 097	90.1
Warren, PA	42 123	6	42 033	16.9	2	19	5 889	10 028	88.9	8 301	91.6
Washington, PA	42 125	1	206 406	15.7	18	58	30 395	46 477	84.7	34 487	92.4
Wayne, PA	42 127	6	50 113	16.7	3	17	9 795	10 913	88.3	8 953	93.4
Westmoreland, PA	42 129	1	367 635	15.6	22	97	51 944	84 043	83.5	63 187	90.1
Wyoming, PA	42 131	2	28 160	17.5	2	8	4 456	7 072	84.9	5 615	94.4
York, PA	42 133	2	408 801	17.2	19	101	59 540	90 912	82.1	71 383	90.5
RHODE ISLAND	44 000		1 076 189	16.8	49	342	156 498	290 605	75.6	190 389	87.1
Bristol, RI	44 001	1	52 743	15.8	2	15	7 041	14 156	64.5	9 004	81.6
Kent, RI	44 003	1	171 590	16.6	5	53	26 074	40 874	80.0	29 276	86.4
Newport, RI	44 005	1	83 740	16.3	6	27	11 262	22 211	74.0	14 785	85.4
Providence, RI	44 007	1	639 653	17.2	28	207	93 818	176 038	73.4	115 371	87.4
Washington, RI	44 009	1	128 463	16.1	8	40	18 303	37 326	86.2	21 953	90.2
SOUTH CAROLINA	45 000		4 255 083	17.5	102	1 172	703 736	1 053 152	85.9	767 586	90.4
Abbeville, SC	45 001	6	26 133	17.8	1	11	3 777	6 687	81.8	5 041	89.8
Aiken, SC	45 003	2	150 181	18.2	1	40	25 299	37 855	86.9	28 650	89.6
Allendale, SC	45 005	6	10 917	18.0	1	4	1 747	3 132	94.3	2 505	94.5
Anderson, SC	45 007	3	175 514	17.6	6	48	29 764	39 271	86.3	29 839	92.7
Bamberg, SC	45 009	7	15 880	17.4	2	7	2 744	4 940	84.5	3 485	91.9
Barnwell, SC	45 011	6	23 345	19.2	4	11	4 721	6 391	93.1	5 287	95.3
Beaufort, SC	45 013	5	137 849	16.4	2	30	19 113	27 897	82.8	20 802	85.2
Berkeley, SC	45 015	2	151 673	19.3	1	35	28 387	39 541	87.1	30 440	91.1
Calhoun, SC	45 017	2	15 100	17.3	1	4	1 861	3 652	83.9	2 971	84.3
Charleston, SC	45 019	2	330 368	16.4	1	81	43 812	87 355	80.1	55 508	84.3
Cherokee, SC	45 021	4	53 844	18.5	1	19	9 364	12 165	89.9	9 811	96.4
Chester, SC	45 023	6	33 228	18.8	1	12	6 110	8 226	93.0	6 922	95.3
Chesterfield, SC	45 025	6	43 435	18.8	1	16	8 077	10 526	90.0	8 840	92.8
Clarendon, SC	45 027	6	33 363	17.3	4	12	5 899	8 452	89.9	7 083	91.9
Colleton, SC	45 029	6	39 605	18.9	1	12	6 592	9 704	87.9	7 878	89.2
Darlington, SC	45 031	3	67 346	18.9	1	22	11 826	17 661	86.3	14 074	90.7
Dillon, SC	45 033	6	30 974	19.9	4	14	6 207	8 481	91.8	6 996	93.1
Dorchester, SC	45 035	2	112 858	19.6	3	24	21 318	28 267	84.3	21 791	88.1
Edgefield, SC	45 037	2	25 528	16.6	1	9	4 118	6 110	89.7	4 936	91.6
Fairfield, SC	45 039	2	24 047	18.0	1	9	3 775	5 873	89.0	4 946	90.1
Florence, SC	45 041	3	131 097	17.7	5	37	22 867	33 873	86.7	25 584	89.0
Georgetown, SC	45 043	4	60 983	16.8	1	17	10 479	13 450	92.5	10 912	95.7
Greenville, SC	45 045	2	407 383	17.4	1	94	65 265	96 798	76.2	69 888	86.0
Greenwood, SC	45 047	4	67 979	18.0	4	22	12 351	17 843	88.9	12 478	90.5
Hampton, SC	45 049	6	21 329	18.8	2	10	4 305	5 899	88.9	4 917	91.7
Horry, SC	45 051	3	226 992	15.0	1	45	33 566	42 752	89.2	31 435	93.0
Jasper, SC	45 053	6	21 398	18.5	1	4	3 192	5 407	78.9	4 429	81.3
Kershaw, SC	45 055	2	56 486	18.1	1	19	10 377	12 532	90.5	10 443	94.7
Lancaster, SC	45 057	4	63 113	18.1	1	20	11 415	14 891	92.2	12 038	94.9
Laurens, SC	45 059	2	70 293	18.1	2	19	9 566	17 251	84.8	13 504	91.2
Lee, SC	45 061	6	20 638	17.1	1	8	2 721	5 138	84.0	4 312	84.6
Lexington, SC	45 063	2	235 272	18.2	5	66	51 276	55 402	89.8	41 574	94.3
McCormick, SC	45 065	8	10 108	13.2	1	5	1 001	2 139	88.3	1 737	88.5
Marion, SC	45 067	6	34 904	18.6	4	12	6 287	9 764	93.1	7 824	94.4
Marlboro, SC	45 069	6	28 021	17.9	1	9	4 988	7 049	91.6	5 872	93.1
Newberry, SC	45 071	6	37 250	16.8	1	14	5 948	8 802	83.0	6 688	93.7
Oconee, SC	45 073	6	69 577	16.2	1	21	10 949	14 546	90.0	11 032	93.2
Orangeburg, SC	45 075	4	92 167	17.3	5	30	15 449	27 308	85.3	18 826	88.1
Pickens, SC	45 077	2	113 575	15.3	1	25	16 425	34 574	90.7	17 757	91.6
Richland, SC	45 079	2	340 078	17.0	4	93	50 159	97 237	85.6	59 220	90.2
Saluda, SC	45 081	2	18 895	17.3	1	5	2 149	4 394	94.2	3 701	94.9
Spartanburg, SC	45 083	2	266 809	17.7	11	78	45 123	61 998	86.2	46 790	93.2
Sumter, SC	45 085	3	105 517	19.4	3	27	18 451	30 345	85.0	22 355	88.1
Union, SC	45 087	6	28 539	17.5	1	9	4 959	6 799	94.1	5 463	97.2
Williamsburg, SC	45 089	6	35 395	19.3	1	14	6 019	10 681	92.4	8 584	92.9
York, SC	45 091	1	190 097	18.3	4	49	33 938	44 094	89.0	32 418	92.4

[1]County type codes are from the Economic Research Service of the United States Department of Agriculture. See notes and definitions at the end of this section.

Table C-1. Population, School, and Student Characteristics by County—*Continued*

STATE County	Characteristics of students, 2004–2005				Outcomes		Staff and students, 2004–2005		
	Percent with IEP[2]	Percent eligible for free or reduced-price lunch	Percent minority	Percent English-language learners	Number of graduates, 2003–2004	Percent dropouts, grades 9–12, 2001–2002	Number of teachers	Student-teacher ratio	Central administration staff
	10	11	12	13	14	15	16	17	18
Philadelphia, PA	12.4	63.3	85.5	...	...	9.4	11 273	18.8	...
Pike, PA	10.3	18.6	19.4	...	...	1.2	338	16.6	11
Potter, PA	13.4	37.2	2.9	...	...	2.1	220	13.5	26
Schuylkill, PA	16.8	30.2	3.8	...	...	3.0	1 441	13.4	140
Snyder, PA	13.4	21.3	4.2	...	...	2.2	344	15.3	21
Somerset, PA	15.1	34.1	1.4	...	...	1.7	808	14.1	65
Sullivan, PA	16.4	35.3	1.8	...	...	3.4	60	13.2	5
Susquehanna, PA	19.1	32.6	2.3	...	...	2.6	574	13.8	43
Tioga, PA	12.8	40.3	5.7	...	...	2.7	473	13.5	29
Union, PA	10.1	19.7	5.2	...	...	1.9	454	9.5	70
Venango, PA	21.2	36.8	4.1	...	...	4.0	503	14.2	42
Warren, PA	18.1	30.8	1.8	...	...	2.8	410	14.4	40
Washington, PA	13.9	22.1	7.1	...	...	2.9	2 212	13.7	153
Wayne, PA	15.1	34.9	5.0	...	...	2.7	651	15.1	28
Westmoreland, PA	12.4	23.7	5.9	...	...	2.0	3 368	15.4	252
Wyoming, PA	14.4	31.9	2.2	...	...	2.1	319	14.0	24
York, PA	15.7	19.8	15.3	...	...	3.3	3 787	15.7	275
RHODE ISLAND	18.1	32.4	29.1	5.8	...	4.3	11 794	13.3	...
Bristol, RI	15.4	12.3	4.0	2.2	...	3.9	610	11.5	...
Kent, RI	18.2	17.8	7.4	1.0	...	2.5	1 864	14.0	...
Newport, RI	19.6	19.8	14.7	1.5	...	2.6	945	11.9	...
Providence, RI	18.3	43.5	43.2	8.8	...	5.6	6 932	13.5	...
Washington, RI	17.0	12.1	6.6	0.9	...	2.1	1 443	12.7	...
SOUTH CAROLINA	14.3	52.3	46.0	1.8	...	3.3	46 903	15.0	...
Abbeville, SC	16.5	62.0	42.6	1.6	208	4.5	269	14.1	...
Aiken, SC	13.7	52.4	40.5	1.7	1 272	3.2	1 580	16.0	...
Allendale, SC	19.7	86.1	96.8	0.7	104	1.9	137	12.7	...
Anderson, SC	17.3	44.4	26.1	1.2	...	4.0	1 906	15.6	...
Bamberg, SC	20.6	73.1	73.9	0.3	141	3.9	195	14.1	...
Barnwell, SC	21.3	65.2	54.8	0.1	...	2.7	327	14.4	...
Beaufort, SC	12.4	48.0	53.5	4.6	...	1.7	1 360	14.1	...
Berkeley, SC	16.4	52.8	42.5	2.3	1 490	4.3	1 661	17.1	...
Calhoun, SC	17.9	86.9	80.0	1.5	87	...	131	14.2	...
Charleston, SC	13.8	51.4	59.7	0.2	2 067	3.2	3 144	13.9	...
Cherokee, SC	11.5	57.5	31.6	3.1	404	3.5	668	14.0	...
Chester, SC	14.6	58.6	51.9	0.4	301	6.7	431	14.2	...
Chesterfield, SC	17.2	63.1	44.3	1.2	441	4.2	520	15.5	...
Clarendon, SC	18.7	74.4	68.1	1.1	...	1.4	355	16.6	...
Colleton, SC	15.9	73.8	60.5	0.5	299	6.8	448	14.7	...
Darlington, SC	19.0	66.8	60.0	0.3	562	2.7	781	15.1	...
Dillon, SC	14.9	76.5	63.5	1.4	...	4.6	382	16.2	...
Dorchester, SC	13.2	36.7	38.6	0.9	...	3.9	1 362	15.7	...
Edgefield, SC	18.7	60.0	51.3	0.7	187	5.6	290	14.2	...
Fairfield, SC	19.0	79.6	86.5	0.5	192	1.6	301	12.6	...
Florence, SC	17.9	61.1	57.1	0.9	1 185	5.4	1 523	15.0	...
Georgetown, SC	17.7	63.6	54.8	1.7	605	2.7	735	14.3	...
Greenville, SC	1.5	39.8	36.9	0.7	3 345	2.6	4 023	16.2	...
Greenwood, SC	17.3	50.9	44.5	4.2	...	2.0	826	15.0	...
Hampton, SC	13.2	72.5	70.2	0.3	205	4.4	290	14.9	...
Horry, SC	17.8	56.3	31.4	2.7	1 721	2.1	2 207	15.2	...
Jasper, SC	14.6	84.9	87.0	7.0	149	3.1	208	15.4	...
Kershaw, SC	12.4	52.9	35.3	1.2	573	5.1	656	15.8	...
Lancaster, SC	13.9	50.5	37.6	1.7	616	5.4	753	15.2	...
Laurens, SC	19.4	61.0	39.7	2.8	410	2.1	579	16.5	...
Lee, SC	19.0	86.8	95.7	0.7	138	4.6	202	13.5	...
Lexington, SC	15.2	36.0	26.3	1.9	2 745	2.8	3 477	14.7	...
McCormick, SC	56.6	78.6	85.4	0.0	65	3.0	78	12.8	...
Marion, SC	23.6	78.9	76.3	0.5	...	1.7	420	15.0	...
Marlboro, SC	2.9	82.9	68.1	0.0	243	7.1	342	14.6	...
Newberry, SC	18.9	59.6	53.3	5.4	294	5.8	440	13.5	...
Oconee, SC	19.1	49.7	19.3	2.6	556	4.0	810	13.5	...
Orangeburg, SC	19.4	78.8	80.7	0.4	...	4.6	1 093	14.1	...
Pickens, SC	14.0	40.5	12.7	1.9	794	6.3	1 030	15.9	...
Richland, SC	12.9	51.8	72.9	2.4	...	2.9	3 561	14.1	...
Saluda, SC	17.6	60.4	50.3	7.4	114	1.4	147	14.6	...
Spartanburg, SC	14.8	48.5	36.0	4.0	...	2.6	3 198	14.1	...
Sumter, SC	15.3	66.5	65.2	0.7	...	1.8	1 151	16.0	...
Union, SC	20.0	61.5	40.7	0.0	251	3.5	353	14.1	...
Williamsburg, SC	21.5	90.4	92.3	0.2	323	1.9	351	17.1	...
York, SC	13.1	35.0	30.6	2.0	1 796	2.2	2 206	15.4	...

[2]IEP = Individual Education Program. See notes and definitions at the end of this section.
... = Not available.

Table C-1. Population, School, and Student Characteristics by County—*Continued*

STATE County	Revenue, 2003–2004				Current expenditures, 2003–2004			Resident population, 16 to 19 years, 2000			
	Total revenue (thousands of dollars)	Percent of revenue from:			Total expenditures (thousands of dollars)	Amount per student (dollars)	Percent for instruction	Total	Percent in armed forces	Percent high school graduates	Percent not enrolled, not employed, not in armed forces, not high school graduate
		Federal government	State government	Local government							
	19	20	21	22	23	24	25	26	27	28	29
Philadelphia, PA	2 637 240	15.0	43.4	41.6	2 138 087	10 114	61.6	88 916	0.0	10.1	7.4
Pike, PA	49 820	4.0	27.4	68.6	41 513	7 719	68.7	2 212	0.0	9.2	2.3
Potter, PA	32 606	4.3	53.6	42.1	26 752	8 838	62.9	947	0.0	17.7	3.7
Schuylkill, PA	225 145	6.9	43.3	49.8	180 880	9 353	63.9	6 825	0.1	11.1	5.2
Snyder, PA	50 780	4.6	41.3	54.1	42 797	7 961	68.1	2 487	0.0	9.2	3.7
Somerset, PA	114 343	6.7	56.0	37.3	96 412	8 325	64.6	4 227	0.0	11.8	3.5
Sullivan, PA	9 829	3.8	36.1	60.2	9 111	11 276	62.4	535	0.0	11.0	11.8
Susquehanna, PA	83 905	5.9	51.4	42.7	72 074	9 019	64.9	2 370	0.0	10.8	4.6
Tioga, PA	62 710	7.4	52.7	39.9	56 136	8 715	66.4	2 805	0.0	9.6	1.8
Union, PA	98 481	28.0	29.9	42.1	89 248	20 578	47.0	3 014	0.0	6.7	3.8
Venango, PA	107 418	5.4	55.7	38.8	85 792	8 737	64.5	3 341	0.0	9.2	3.6
Warren, PA	57 480	7.3	53.8	39.0	53 364	8 720	65.4	2 277	0.1	11.0	4.7
Washington, PA	360 267	8.5	39.7	51.9	303 798	9 965	63.9	10 346	0.0	9.2	3.1
Wayne, PA	110 014	6.5	27.1	66.3	92 024	9 420	66.5	2 409	0.0	12.5	4.3
Westmoreland, PA	569 764	5.8	39.5	54.7	474 048	8 532	64.4	17 603	0.1	9.3	2.4
Wyoming, PA	48 149	5.7	46.0	48.3	43 416	9 523	65.4	1 662	0.0	9.3	1.6
York, PA	657 767	3.8	31.3	64.9	527 130	8 016	66.6	19 672	0.1	12.0	4.0
RHODE ISLAND	1 846 125	7.2	40.3	52.4	1 647 051	10 447	67.5	61 409	0.3	8.7	4.6
Bristol, RI	86 293	4.2	30.9	64.9	77 060	10 820	68.4	3 024	0.0	6.8	2.2
Kent, RI	310 652	4.3	32.1	63.6	283 069	10 737	68.4	7 752	0.0	11.1	3.3
Newport, RI	142 269	8.3	27.9	63.8	122 891	10 453	69.1	4 400	3.6	11.1	3.9
Providence, RI	1 076 796	8.9	49.7	41.5	956 909	10 173	67.2	38 449	0.0	8.9	5.9
Washington, RI	230 115	3.9	19.2	76.9	207 122	11 289	66.8	7 784	0.0	4.6	0.8
SOUTH CAROLINA	5 961 494	10.3	46.0	43.7	5 022 976	7 213	65.5	235 984	3.0	13.2	6.4
Abbeville, SC	29 759	10.8	50.3	39.0	26 701	7 004	66.6	1 566	0.0	8.0	4.9
Aiken, SC	189 148	10.5	49.9	39.6	163 480	6 453	67.8	8 068	0.1	10.1	5.9
Allendale, SC	22 169	19.3	54.5	26.2	18 642	9 953	62.0	699	0.0	8.0	14.6
Anderson, SC	244 325	9.2	47.3	43.5	202 527	6 824	64.7	8 498	0.0	13.2	8.0
Bamberg, SC	28 690	22.6	51.8	25.6	23 544	8 439	63.2	1 424	1.3	12.8	3.4
Barnwell, SC	43 748	11.8	60.9	27.3	35 724	7 508	65.1	1 439	0.0	11.0	5.0
Beaufort, SC	183 994	8.3	25.7	66.0	156 782	8 554	63.4	7 076	30.5	39.5	3.0
Berkeley, SC	214 720	12.2	49.6	38.2	182 096	6 527	62.8	10 369	18.0	31.1	4.1
Calhoun, SC	19 289	12.4	47.3	40.3	16 908	8 420	66.4	791	0.0	9.9	5.9
Charleston, SC	394 804	12.2	36.1	51.7	353 960	8 025	66.1	18 939	1.1	9.1	4.9
Cherokee, SC	83 040	9.0	47.6	43.4	68 735	7 377	66.4	2 788	0.0	15.7	10.5
Chester, SC	56 679	10.6	56.4	33.0	46 130	6 757	64.3	1 880	0.0	15.3	13.1
Chesterfield, SC	62 719	11.2	54.2	34.6	57 483	6 974	67.1	2 324	0.1	11.8	9.5
Clarendon, SC	48 921	22.1	52.3	25.6	39 390	6 494	64.2	2 077	0.0	10.2	9.1
Colleton, SC	49 530	15.3	51.8	32.9	46 766	6 960	63.5	2 146	0.0	10.1	11.4
Darlington, SC	100 320	12.8	52.5	34.7	87 217	7 244	65.9	3 497	0.0	9.7	7.1
Dillon, SC	50 302	22.1	53.6	24.3	43 638	6 879	63.3	1 941	0.3	11.3	9.6
Dorchester, SC	154 018	8.2	54.0	37.8	134 890	6 525	66.1	5 397	0.0	11.3	5.0
Edgefield, SC	34 859	12.7	54.2	33.1	29 423	7 358	65.4	1 542	0.0	10.6	14.7
Fairfield, SC	42 307	11.6	40.2	48.2	35 564	9 446	62.2	1 271	0.0	14.1	4.1
Florence, SC	190 878	13.4	49.6	37.1	154 999	6 872	67.9	7 754	0.1	10.5	6.1
Georgetown, SC	95 290	11.5	40.2	48.3	84 757	8 018	64.6	2 997	0.0	11.2	6.5
Greenville, SC	557 680	7.5	41.1	51.4	410 169	6 384	66.4	20 669	0.0	9.5	5.4
Greenwood, SC	101 112	10.6	46.5	42.8	83 538	6 668	68.2	3 786	0.3	9.6	10.7
Hampton, SC	39 695	17.5	57.3	25.2	32 388	7 476	63.7	1 292	0.2	11.7	5.7
Horry, SC	275 978	8.5	36.7	54.8	235 293	7 435	64.6	10 024	0.0	12.3	7.6
Jasper, SC	30 803	14.9	50.2	34.9	23 799	7 321	65.3	1 233	0.0	11.4	10.0
Kershaw, SC	76 557	10.0	54.3	35.7	69 686	6 785	64.1	2 747	0.0	15.4	6.6
Lancaster, SC	85 876	11.1	53.7	35.3	74 532	6 554	67.2	3 320	0.0	13.1	10.1
Laurens, SC	72 425	12.9	55.9	31.2	65 111	6 796	64.7	4 189	0.0	10.9	8.1
Lee, SC	28 608	16.6	60.1	23.2	22 888	7 890	63.3	1 109	0.0	14.4	7.6
Lexington, SC	423 511	6.7	48.4	44.9	374 108	7 457	65.2	10 975	0.2	12.6	3.8
McCormick, SC	14 212	22.7	45.2	32.1	9 644	9 345	62.9	521	0.0	9.0	13.8
Marion, SC	55 038	23.1	53.2	23.7	46 193	7 209	67.5	2 204	0.2	10.8	5.9
Marlboro, SC	41 605	15.2	53.8	31.0	37 351	7 218	64.9	1 682	0.0	12.5	11.4
Newberry, SC	59 991	10.2	54.5	35.3	46 601	7 866	65.2	2 200	0.0	8.5	9.5
Oconee, SC	97 423	8.0	40.1	51.9	87 990	8 035	64.8	3 211	0.4	13.9	6.7
Orangeburg, SC	149 790	12.0	50.3	37.7	128 437	8 193	63.0	6 474	0.0	9.2	5.8
Pickens, SC	122 547	8.3	55.9	35.8	103 152	6 343	66.7	8 600	0.0	6.3	4.4
Richland, SC	472 826	8.1	40.3	51.6	391 289	8 351	66.3	23 297	11.5	17.6	5.6
Saluda, SC	18 497	12.3	53.9	33.8	16 242	7 379	57.9	1 109	0.0	9.0	9.7
Spartanburg, SC	375 280	7.9	46.8	45.2	322 076	7 238	67.6	13 520	0.1	11.4	7.6
Sumter, SC	142 405	15.6	53.6	30.9	120 133	6 356	63.9	6 376	2.5	13.2	6.6
Union, SC	38 811	14.0	59.1	27.0	36 162	7 075	66.9	1 531	0.0	11.7	9.6
Williamsburg, SC	54 965	25.8	53.8	20.4	43 502	7 149	63.8	2 407	0.5	9.5	6.6
York, SC	286 350	6.5	43.2	50.4	233 336	7 009	65.5	9 025	0.0	10.5	5.8

Table C-1. Population, School, and Student Characteristics by County—*Continued*

STATE County	High school graduates, 2000			College enrollment, 2000		College graduates, 2000 (percent)						
	Population 25 years and over	High school graduate or less (percent)	High school graduate or more (percent)	Number	Percent public	Bachelor's degree or more	+/- U.S. percentage with bachelor's degree or more	Non-Hispanic White	Black	American Indian and Alaska Native	Asian or Pacific Islander	Hispanic[3]
	30	31	32	33	34	35	36	37	38	39	40	41
Philadelphia, PA	966 197	62.1	71.2	115 671	43.2	17.9	-6.5	24.1	10.3	9.9	32.6	9.2
Pike, PA	31 525	54.5	86.8	1 412	59.3	19.0	-5.4	18.8	29.0	6.9	31.4	18.0
Potter, PA	12 144	66.7	80.6	301	78.1	12.3	-12.1	12.2	0.0	0.0	41.1	12.8
Schuylkill, PA	108 010	71.1	77.2	4 303	70.4	10.7	-13.7	10.9	1.8	1.5	41.1	3.7
Snyder, PA	24 217	73.2	73.2	2 379	22.4	12.5	-11.9	12.6	4.6	0.0	0.0	6.2
Somerset, PA	55 956	72.9	77.5	1 978	84.9	10.8	-13.6	11.0	1.6	0.0	6.7	5.2
Sullivan, PA	4 659	67.6	78.0	165	74.5	12.8	-11.6	12.9	0.0	0.0	0.0	0.0
Susquehanna, PA	28 581	64.7	82.5	1 028	70.0	13.2	-11.2	13.2	8.1	11.1	36.6	25.8
Tioga, PA	27 176	64.2	80.5	2 767	92.7	14.2	-10.2	14.1	23.9	9.8	51.0	23.3
Union, PA	27 521	65.9	73.1	3 717	14.8	18.0	-6.4	20.5	1.8	8.0	18.0	2.9
Venango, PA	39 366	68.4	81.0	1 398	81.5	13.1	-11.3	13.2	7.2	0.0	14.7	4.9
Warren, PA	30 535	63.7	84.8	1 060	79.1	14.2	-10.2	14.2	17.2	20.4	41.0	13.8
Washington, PA	142 118	60.0	82.6	8 902	69.5	18.8	-5.6	19.0	10.2	6.1	45.2	13.2
Wayne, PA	33 326	62.8	80.7	1 318	63.0	14.6	-9.8	14.7	6.8	10.5	24.0	9.1
Westmoreland, PA	263 593	55.6	85.6	14 834	69.7	20.2	-4.2	20.2	12.3	13.2	59.9	20.1
Wyoming, PA	18 741	61.6	83.7	1 011	43.5	15.4	-9.0	15.3	16.0	27.6	26.0	45.1
York, PA	259 040	60.9	80.7	13 146	54.2	18.4	-6.0	18.7	9.8	7.3	36.3	10.8
RHODE ISLAND	694 573	49.8	78.0	84 009	55.0	25.6	1.2	27.3	16.7	14.1	35.9	8.6
Bristol, RI	34 218	42.7	80.7	4 188	35.7	34.3	9.9	34.1	32.4	32.3	75.8	37.3
Kent, RI	116 628	47.2	83.9	8 945	70.9	24.8	0.4	24.5	34.0	7.0	46.8	23.8
Newport, RI	59 084	36.4	87.7	6 086	52.6	38.3	13.9	39.3	17.8	22.3	48.3	26.1
Providence, RI	403 779	55.6	72.5	51 819	46.1	21.3	-3.1	23.4	15.6	12.4	31.2	7.0
Washington, RI	80 864	37.4	88.6	12 971	87.3	35.5	11.1	35.7	20.6	17.5	49.3	31.2
SOUTH CAROLINA	2 596 010	53.6	76.3	216 839	79.4	20.4	-4.0	24.3	9.9	11.2	39.8	14.1
Abbeville, SC	17 068	65.8	70.1	1 241	57.9	12.8	-11.6	15.9	4.2	0.0	46.5	37.3
Aiken, SC	92 922	54.0	77.7	6 691	88.3	19.9	-4.5	23.4	9.0	12.1	40.7	10.0
Allendale, SC	7 094	71.3	60.0	439	97.7	9.3	-15.1	19.2	4.7	0.0	0.0	0.0
Anderson, SC	111 037	59.3	73.4	6 724	73.5	15.9	-8.5	17.3	7.4	8.1	42.8	17.9
Bamberg, SC	10 213	63.6	64.7	1 135	59.2	15.4	-9.0	19.7	11.6	100.0	0.0	37.5
Barnwell, SC	14 770	67.2	67.5	669	90.6	11.6	-12.8	14.8	6.4	6.7	65.2	13.2
Beaufort, SC	78 502	36.3	87.8	4 807	83.9	33.2	8.8	40.7	10.8	10.7	31.9	13.1
Berkeley, SC	86 015	54.1	80.2	6 897	80.1	14.4	-10.0	15.4	10.0	12.8	28.4	14.8
Calhoun, SC	10 266	62.5	72.8	462	84.0	14.2	-10.2	20.4	6.5	22.6	9.4	0.0
Charleston, SC	199 361	41.4	81.5	25 683	78.4	30.7	6.3	40.4	10.7	19.6	41.2	19.0
Cherokee, SC	34 283	69.9	66.7	1 664	63.9	11.8	-12.6	13.1	6.0	0.0	28.6	14.5
Chester, SC	22 043	69.0	67.1	800	87.8	9.6	-14.8	11.9	5.0	0.0	22.7	21.2
Chesterfield, SC	27 769	69.4	65.2	1 026	81.2	9.7	-14.7	11.7	4.2	12.8	52.7	20.0
Clarendon, SC	20 698	69.2	65.3	883	81.3	11.4	-13.0	17.7	5.0	36.5	0.0	5.9
Colleton, SC	24 716	67.3	69.6	1 129	88.8	11.5	-12.9	14.7	6.6	0.0	33.3	7.7
Darlington, SC	43 512	63.2	69.3	2 538	71.8	13.5	-10.9	17.4	6.7	10.2	30.1	18.4
Dillon, SC	18 867	72.9	60.7	835	93.4	9.2	-15.2	12.1	5.1	2.7	8.9	5.7
Dorchester, SC	61 334	47.5	82.2	4 471	79.8	21.4	-3.0	24.4	11.7	14.3	46.9	9.6
Edgefield, SC	16 227	64.0	71.4	829	87.8	12.5	-12.1	17.7	5.0	17.2	34.2	0.0
Fairfield, SC	15 244	68.7	67.0	646	85.3	11.7	-12.7	20.5	4.5	0.0	100.0	2.1
Florence, SC	80 904	57.8	73.1	6 166	88.9	18.7	-5.7	23.6	9.0	17.3	58.6	13.2
Georgetown, SC	37 340	55.0	75.2	1 500	83.2	20.0	-4.4	26.0	7.7	47.6	53.8	10.5
Greenville, SC	250 258	46.0	79.5	20 732	54.4	26.2	-1.8	29.6	11.1	7.4	43.5	14.6
Greenwood, SC	42 412	56.6	73.1	4 024	93.2	18.9	-5.5	24.0	7.1	9.0	37.6	5.0
Hampton, SC	13 668	70.8	66.9	603	67.8	10.1	-14.3	14.5	6.3	18.4	22.5	2.9
Horry, SC	136 551	51.0	81.1	8 531	87.3	18.7	-5.7	20.4	8.0	12.4	28.4	10.8
Jasper, SC	13 112	70.8	65.2	578	67.6	8.7	-15.7	11.5	5.9	6.0	32.2	6.3
Kershaw, SC	34 863	60.1	75.4	1 348	82.6	16.3	-8.1	18.5	9.9	7.0	8.3	11.8
Lancaster, SC	40 520	65.8	69.8	1 936	85.8	10.2	-14.2	11.6	5.5	10.5	26.5	14.4
Laurens, SC	45 470	67.3	67.7	2 822	55.7	11.7	-12.7	13.7	5.2	14.2	39.6	7.2
Lee, SC	12 918	73.7	61.4	465	78.3	9.2	-15.2	14.3	5.7	0.0	0.0	5.8
Lexington, SC	142 083	46.5	83.0	10 063	87.6	24.6	0.2	26.0	13.2	8.6	46.9	17.8
McCormick, SC	7 192	64.4	66.1	255	88.6	16.0	-8.4	26.9	4.3	. . .	100.0	6.9
Marion, SC	22 224	70.5	68.0	1 234	87.9	10.2	-14.2	14.2	6.5	0.0	73.7	0.3
Marlboro, SC	18 482	74.1	60.9	698	89.4	8.3	-16.1	10.4	5.8	5.6	58.0	19.8
Newberry, SC	23 881	64.4	69.1	1 525	45.4	14.8	-9.6	19.8	4.2	27.5	52.6	5.2
Oconee, SC	45 896	59.3	73.9	2 461	86.1	18.2	-6.2	18.9	7.3	14.4	67.4	12.5
Orangeburg, SC	57 037	60.1	71.5	6 858	81.3	16.3	-8.1	18.1	15.0	7.8	25.6	4.1
Pickens, SC	66 787	57.1	73.7	15 364	93.5	19.1	-5.3	19.2	9.5	5.6	68.6	12.8
Richland, SC	198 703	37.7	85.2	31 645	83.4	32.5	8.1	43.5	18.0	21.9	50.1	23.0
Saluda, SC	12 654	69.3	69.3	509	96.7	11.9	-12.5	15.6	3.9	0.0	25.7	1.3
Spartanburg, SC	167 802	56.8	73.1	11 226	67.4	18.2	-6.2	20.6	8.0	10.0	26.1	14.2
Sumter, SC	64 144	55.4	74.3	5 724	77.8	15.8	-8.6	19.9	10.5	13.8	22.4	14.1
Union, SC	20 222	69.5	66.9	967	86.9	9.8	-14.6	11.3	5.8	0.0	26.8	0.0
Williamsburg, SC	23 189	69.6	65.5	1 289	92.4	11.5	-12.9	15.1	9.2	12.8	46.2	2.4
York, SC	105 757	51.2	77.2	8 717	90.1	20.9	-3.5	23.7	8.8	5.6	28.6	16.0

[3]May be of any race.
. . . = Not available.

Table C-1. Population, School, and Student Characteristics by County—*Continued*

STATE County	State/county code	County type[1]	Population, 2005 Total	Percent 5 to 17 years	Number of schools and students, 2004–2005 School districts	Schools	Students	Resident enrollment, 2000 Total	Percent public	K–12	Percent public
			1	2	3	4	5	6	7	8	9
SOUTH DAKOTA	46 000		775 933	17.5	194	722	125 253	208 229	88.6	152 642	92.6
Aurora, SD	46 003	9	2 901	20.3	3	9	506	759	94.5	664	97.6
Beadle, SD	46 005	7	15 896	16.4	4	12	2 359	4 139	81.1	3 358	90.6
Bennett, SD	46 007	9	3 585	23.5	1	5	542	1 257	94.9	983	97.3
Bon Homme, SD	46 009	9	7 087	15.3	4	13	1 239	1 529	92.9	1 341	95.4
Brookings, SD	46 011	7	28 121	12.3	5	19	3 954	11 458	96.8	4 361	96.8
Brown, SD	46 013	5	34 706	15.5	8	22	4 899	9 554	85.5	6 207	86.5
Brule, SD	46 015	9	5 187	21.2	2	7	1 215	1 475	93.8	1 315	97.0
Buffalo, SD	46 017	9	2 100	24.9	...	...	...	779	89.7	662	89.1
Butte, SD	46 019	6	9 326	18.3	2	7	1 797	2 361	89.2	2 000	92.8
Campbell, SD	46 021	9	1 565	18.3	2	6	228	410	96.6	380	98.7
Charles Mix, SD	46 023	9	9 194	21.5	5	15	1 736	2 522	87.5	2 178	88.7
Clark, SD	46 025	9	3 799	17.3	2	10	662	974	97.1	880	98.0
Clay, SD	46 027	6	12 995	10.7	2	7	1 513	6 399	96.7	1 853	96.6
Codington, SD	46 029	7	26 010	17.8	6	21	4 549	6 730	87.3	5 198	91.0
Corson, SD	46 031	9	4 366	25.1	3	8	898	1 410	96.7	1 181	97.6
Custer, SD	46 033	8	7 904	17.0	2	8	1 209	1 731	89.1	1 476	92.5
Davison, SD	46 035	7	18 777	16.9	3	7	466	5 217	77.9	3 642	88.4
Day, SD	46 037	9	5 757	16.7	5	9	932	1 449	96.0	1 284	97.9
Deuel, SD	46 039	9	4 296	16.8	1	3	530	1 079	95.7	922	97.8
Dewey, SD	46 041	9	6 161	24.7	3	11	668	2 154	97.1	1 745	98.2
Douglas, SD	46 043	9	3 309	17.3	2	6	412	842	76.6	761	79.0
Edmunds, SD	46 045	9	4 112	18.3	3	13	712	1 050	88.8	919	89.1
Fall River, SD	46 047	7	7 355	15.4	4	11	1 268	1 418	90.2	1 209	93.2
Faulk, SD	46 049	9	2 386	17.2	2	7	372	606	85.6	539	86.6
Grant, SD	46 051	7	7 384	17.1	3	8	1 335	1 871	90.4	1 591	94.2
Gregory, SD	46 053	9	4 290	15.4	3	10	787	1 051	97.8	957	97.8
Haakon, SD	46 055	9	1 912	15.1	2	10	367	517	97.5	461	98.7
Hamlin, SD	46 057	9	5 707	18.5	4	11	1 220	1 477	92.3	1 267	93.3
Hand, SD	46 059	9	3 307	16.1	2	5	541	825	96.2	723	99.7
Hanson, SD	46 061	8	3 747	18.4	3	15	3 034	763	95.7	685	96.8
Harding, SD	46 063	9	1 218	17.2	1	6	243	395	91.9	365	92.6
Hughes, SD	46 065	7	16 875	18.7	2	10	2 711	4 081	91.2	3 589	94.3
Hutchinson, SD	46 067	8	7 581	16.9	4	22	1 704	1 797	89.3	1 538	92.3
Hyde, SD	46 069	9	1 614	17.3	1	3	261	357	94.1	305	97.7
Jackson, SD	46 071	8	2 858	22.5	1	4	347	964	97.9	803	99.8
Jerauld, SD	46 073	9	2 136	13.0	1	4	332	473	96.6	402	98.5
Jones, SD	46 075	9	1 033	15.7	2	3	183	303	98.0	281	99.3
Kingsbury, SD	46 077	9	5 532	16.3	4	13	1 081	1 360	94.5	1 177	96.1
Lake, SD	46 079	6	11 039	14.4	4	12	1 461	3 471	94.1	2 085	94.8
Lawrence, SD	46 081	6	22 395	14.5	3	10	3 147	6 595	93.3	4 091	95.1
Lincoln, SD	46 083	3	33 381	18.2	4	15	3 889	6 784	86.8	5 286	92.7
Lyman, SD	46 085	9	3 919	21.7	1	4	407	1 128	96.5	934	98.0
McCook, SD	46 087	3	5 930	19.0	4	13	1 090	1 493	89.4	1 281	90.6
McPherson, SD	46 089	9	2 617	16.4	2	9	488	546	94.1	497	96.2
Marshall, SD	46 091	9	4 418	17.7	2	8	776	1 110	94.6	925	97.3
Meade, SD	46 093	3	24 623	18.7	2	17	3 023	6 506	89.0	5 047	91.9
Mellette, SD	46 095	9	2 088	24.4	2	7	444	647	96.0	533	98.1
Miner, SD	46 097	8	2 584	16.3	2	5	406	678	96.9	611	98.4
Minnehaha, SD	46 099	3	160 087	17.2	10	73	26 975	38 766	79.6	27 965	88.9
Moody, SD	46 101	8	6 637	18.6	2	7	975	1 788	94.7	1 535	96.1
Pennington, SD	46 103	3	93 580	17.3	5	41	16 914	24 276	88.3	17 352	92.2
Perkins, SD	46 105	9	3 023	16.1	4	7	501	732	95.9	652	97.1
Potter, SD	46 107	9	2 351	14.3	2	6	453	583	91.9	535	93.6
Roberts, SD	46 109	9	10 044	20.1	4	15	1 736	2 692	97.8	2 294	98.4
Sanborn, SD	46 111	9	2 541	16.7	2	6	427	653	95.4	570	98.9
Shannon, SD	46 113	7	13 657	28.0	1	4	1 000	4 956	94.2	4 036	94.7
Spink, SD	46 115	7	6 899	16.8	6	20	1 463	1 700	92.6	1 483	95.4
Stanley, SD	46 117	9	2 829	16.7	1	6	576	698	93.3	603	97.2
Sully, SD	46 119	9	1 430	17.2	1	4	312	358	96.6	330	97.6
Todd, SD	46 121	9	9 882	28.2	1	12	2 049	3 548	98.6	2 824	99.8
Tripp, SD	46 123	7	6 065	18.3	2	9	1 118	1 609	95.3	1 421	96.7
Turner, SD	46 125	3	8 520	17.3	6	15	1 380	2 149	91.9	1 860	94.7
Union, SD	46 127	3	13 462	18.2	7	15	2 741	3 301	87.3	2 602	90.1
Walworth, SD	46 129	7	5 494	16.6	3	7	857	1 323	92.4	1 134	94.2
Yankton, SD	46 135	7	21 718	17.0	3	12	3 566	5 720	82.3	4 219	92.2
Ziebach, SD	46 137	9	2 631	26.3	1	3	267	883	92.6	735	92.7
TENNESSEE	47 000		5 962 959	16.8	136	1 710	941 091	1 415 105	85.1	1 037 539	90.1
Anderson, TN	47 001	2	72 430	16.0	3	28	12 275	16 224	92.3	12 729	95.5
Bedford, TN	47 003	6	42 204	17.4	1	12	7 117	8 678	90.2	7 088	93.7
Benton, TN	47 005	7	16 467	15.4	1	8	2 485	3 320	91.5	2 861	94.5
Bledsoe, TN	47 007	8	12 928	16.3	1	6	1 969	2 571	91.8	2 178	92.3
Blount, TN	47 009	2	115 535	15.7	3	29	17 387	23 856	87.5	18 075	94.8
Bradley, TN	47 011	3	92 092	16.2	2	25	13 905	22 171	79.1	15 197	93.2
Campbell, TN	47 013	6	40 686	15.6	1	16	6 370	7 939	95.1	6 799	96.7
Cannon, TN	47 015	1	13 337	17.4	1	7	2 170	2 831	90.2	2 358	91.3
Carroll, TN	47 017	6	29 121	15.8	6	14	5 232	6 547	89.7	5 136	97.1
Carter, TN	47 019	3	58 865	14.3	2	23	8 244	12 454	91.3	9 100	97.9

[1]County type codes are from the Economic Research Service of the United States Department of Agriculture. See notes and definitions at the end of this section.
. . . = Not available.

Table C-1. Population, School, and Student Characteristics by County—*Continued*

STATE County	Characteristics of students, 2004–2005				Outcomes		Staff and students, 2004–2005		
	Percent with IEP[2]	Percent eligible for free or reduced-price lunch	Percent minority	Percent English-language learners	Number of graduates, 2003–2004	Percent dropouts, grades 9–12, 2001–2002	Number of teachers	Student-teacher ratio	Central administration staff
	10	11	12	13	14	15	16	17	18
SOUTH DAKOTA	14.0	30.0	15.4	3.3	...	2.8	9 063	13.8	...
Aurora, SD	10.3	27.3	4.9	0.4	...	0.6	51	9.9	11
Beadle, SD	13.5	32.6	7.9	2.2	...	2.6	155	15.3	...
Bennett, SD	14.0	48.4	58.9	1.7	...	12.7	56	9.7	5
Bon Homme, SD	13.6	33.4	4.2	1.7	...	1.5	90	13.8	16
Brookings, SD	12.6	19.2	7.5	0.5	...	1.5	282	14.0	26
Brown, SD	15.5	21.6	9.0	0.2	...	3.4	324	15.1	...
Brule, SD	13.9	40.0	26.9	1.6	...	2.2	99	12.2	10
Buffalo, SD	...	...	...	...	...	...	...	...	...
Butte, SD	14.0	40.3	6.2	0.0	...	3.8	124	14.4	13
Campbell, SD	13.6	31.6	2.7	0.0	...	...	24	9.4	4
Charles Mix, SD	16.9	49.4	40.2	9.0	...	6.3	155	11.2	27
Clark, SD	12.4	40.7	2.9	5.3	...	...	57	11.6	8
Clay, SD	14.0	17.2	14.0	0.8	...	2.4	106	14.2	12
Codington, SD	12.9	21.2	5.5	0.6	...	2.3	310	14.7	35
Corson, SD	21.2	91.5	81.6	13.5	...	14.5	90	9.9	17
Custer, SD	15.1	37.5	17.5	0.9	...	1.7	94	12.9	8
Davison, SD	13.7	25.4	7.7	0.0	...	1.3	40	11.5	8
Day, SD	12.1	48.8	13.5	0.4	...	2.0	72	12.9	...
Deuel, SD	12.3	28.3	2.4	0.0	...	2.1	36	14.8	4
Dewey, SD	45.2	68.6	66.9	4.6	...	5.8	92	7.3	15
Douglas, SD	12.1	25.2	4.3	0.0	...	0.5	36	11.3	5
Edmunds, SD	10.3	39.6	2.8	9.3	...	0.8	63	11.4	6
Fall River, SD	14.5	5.9	21.8	2.3	...	3.1	97	13.0	14
Faulk, SD	11.0	31.3	0.3	8.6	...	1.4	31	11.9	...
Grant, SD	12.4	22.4	2.6	0.4	...	1.7	98	13.6	10
Gregory, SD	13.9	55.9	15.0	0.6	...	1.4	75	10.4	11
Haakon, SD	9.0	18.6	5.3	0.0	...	...	36	10.1	5
Hamlin, SD	12.4	36.7	3.3	1.2	...	1.0	96	12.7	13
Hand, SD	12.0	37.2	0.0	5.0	...	1.7	45	12.1	4
Hanson, SD	14.5	28.8	1.0	2.4	...	0.7	224	13.6	22
Harding, SD	7.8	11.9	0.8	0.0	...	...	25	9.8	3
Hughes, SD	12.0	21.6	16.3	0.7	...	1.2	173	15.7	14
Hutchinson, SD	12.0	29.5	3.3	6.0	...	1.2	137	12.5	13
Hyde, SD	10.3	34.1	6.1	0.8	...	...	22	11.8	2
Jackson, SD	20.5	0.0	44.1	0.3	...	1.9	37	9.4	5
Jerauld, SD	10.8	39.3	0.9	4.5	...	0.8	30	11.3	5
Jones, SD	9.3	13.0	5.6	0.5	...	1.1	17	10.6	4
Kingsbury, SD	14.1	28.3	2.3	0.1	...	1.8	93	11.7	14
Lake, SD	11.2	25.9	4.9	2.1	...	1.7	119	12.3	15
Lawrence, SD	14.1	20.6	9.5	0.7	...	3.6	222	14.2	51
Lincoln, SD	14.6	15.0	3.4	0.2	...	2.4	249	15.6	26
Lyman, SD	12.0	45.2	31.0	0.0	...	0.8	38	10.8	3
McCook, SD	18.5	29.0	2.5	3.1	...	0.3	86	12.6	14
McPherson, SD	9.0	37.4	2.1	13.7	...	2.0	46	10.6	5
Marshall, SD	10.6	35.7	1.2	2.6	...	...	59	13.2	7
Meade, SD	10.9	24.6	7.7	0.1	...	2.1	210	14.4	14
Mellette, SD	20.5	91.3	76.3	2.5	...	8.9	49	9.1	7
Miner, SD	15.8	32.8	2.7	0.5	...	0.5	36	11.4	8
Minnehaha, SD	13.3	25.4	13.2	3.4	...	3.2	1 714	15.7	150
Moody, SD	12.5	23.7	27.7	10.2	...	2.2	81	12.1	8
Pennington, SD	13.6	29.9	20.0	1.2	...	3.4	1 070	15.8	137
Perkins, SD	10.8	45.0	3.2	0.2	...	...	53	9.5	7
Potter, SD	10.8	25.5	2.9	0.0	...	1.2	44	10.3	5
Roberts, SD	19.6	44.8	40.3	0.9	...	1.6	163	10.6	16
Sanborn, SD	11.9	42.2	2.3	5.2	...	1.8	41	10.4	6
Shannon, SD	22.6	93.8	98.8	36.2	...	...	98	10.2	14
Spink, SD	16.1	29.3	2.5	4.8	...	1.0	123	11.9	...
Stanley, SD	12.2	29.3	19.1	0.2	...	1.7	38	15.4	6
Sully, SD	14.7	23.0	4.0	0.0	...	...	30	10.3	6
Todd, SD	15.8	98.2	96.2	65.0	...	18.3	186	11.0	35
Tripp, SD	11.8	41.9	19.0	0.3	...	3.2	95	11.7	10
Turner, SD	16.1	14.5	3.1	0.0	...	1.3	111	12.5	19
Union, SD	13.0	21.7	5.8	0.7	...	1.5	195	14.1	20
Walworth, SD	18.6	33.4	20.9	0.4	...	4.1	65	13.2	9
Yankton, SD	15.3	27.2	6.9	0.4	...	3.4	217	16.5	17
Ziebach, SD	16.1	59.4	73.3	2.2	...	10.7	33	8.2	5
TENNESSEE	17.8	...	...	...	...	3.8	60 019	15.7	...
Anderson, TN	26.2	...	...	...	...	3.0	869	14.1	...
Bedford, TN	15.4	...	...	...	334	2.2	437	16.3	...
Benton, TN	20.8	...	...	...	122	1.2	172	14.4	...
Bledsoe, TN	27.4	...	...	...	94	4.9	123	16.0	...
Blount, TN	18.9	...	...	...	1 038	2.7	1 053	16.5	...
Bradley, TN	15.3	...	...	...	763	2.7	873	15.9	...
Campbell, TN	16.4	...	...	...	301	2.2	393	16.2	...
Cannon, TN	19.8	...	...	...	115	2.4	147	14.8	...
Carroll, TN	17.3	...	...	...	...	1.7	331	15.8	...
Carter, TN	17.1	...	...	...	426	2.1	588	14.0	...

[2]IEP = Individual Education Program. See notes and definitions at the end of this section.
... = Not available.

Table C-1. Population, School, and Student Characteristics by County—Continued

STATE County	Revenue, 2003–2004 Total revenue (thousands of dollars)	Percent of revenue from: Federal government	State government	Local government	Current expenditures, 2003–2004 Total expenditures (thousands of dollars)	Amount per student (dollars)	Percent for instruction	Resident population, 16 to 19 years, 2000 Total	Percent in armed forces	Percent high school graduates	Percent not enrolled, not employed, not in armed forces, not high school graduate
	19	20	21	22	23	24	25	26	27	28	29
SOUTH DAKOTA	1 007 135	15.5	34.1	50.4	869 863	6 950	64.7	49 305	0.3	10.2	4.7
Aurora, SD	4 684	11.6	34.5	53.8	4 137	7 577	62.8	230	0.0	4.8	11.7
Beadle, SD	21 699	10.3	36.2	53.5	18 436	6 910	62.3	987	0.0	14.1	2.8
Bennett, SD	6 700	49.0	31.3	19.7	5 511	9 930	71.8	245	0.0	6.5	15.1
Bon Homme, SD	9 918	14.2	42.3	43.5	8 686	7 028	59.1	432	0.0	12.5	5.1
Brookings, SD	30 014	6.7	35.0	58.3	25 441	6 365	66.6	2 817	0.1	6.1	0.2
Brown, SD	36 713	8.2	31.6	60.2	30 433	6 178	64.8	2 384	0.0	9.2	1.4
Brule, SD	10 573	20.7	34.3	45.0	8 808	7 365	68.5	372	0.0	5.1	7.5
Buffalo, SD	...	...	...	...	...	...	...	200	1.5	10.5	14.5
Butte, SD	12 827	14.2	47.1	38.7	10 942	6 238	65.3	583	0.0	16.8	1.5
Campbell, SD	2 360	7.9	47.4	44.7	2 227	9 053	63.7	96	0.0	5.2	0.0
Charles Mix, SD	18 706	42.1	31.1	26.9	14 217	8 417	65.4	580	0.0	5.9	13.8
Clark, SD	5 435	12.6	32.9	54.5	4 795	7 178	63.9	268	0.0	9.0	4.9
Clay, SD	11 191	10.1	35.3	54.7	10 123	6 799	60.1	1 472	0.0	2.4	0.7
Codington, SD	33 186	8.3	42.5	49.2	27 082	6 013	68.5	1 741	0.0	12.2	2.3
Corson, SD	11 136	56.5	31.8	11.7	10 161	11 178	63.3	290	0.0	6.9	13.1
Custer, SD	8 872	14.2	15.6	70.2	7 329	7 054	65.7	609	0.0	9.4	1.8
Davison, SD	23 306	11.2	39.8	49.0	19 771	6 459	65.9	1 338	0.0	6.7	3.3
Day, SD	8 603	13.0	38.2	48.9	7 345	7 360	59.8	351	0.0	10.3	2.8
Deuel, SD	4 219	7.3	38.5	54.2	3 561	6 150	62.6	248	0.0	9.3	2.0
Dewey, SD	10 500	51.8	34.8	13.4	9 072	11 797	69.2	467	0.0	13.3	13.7
Douglas, SD	3 460	11.3	42.5	46.2	2 852	7 294	60.4	208	0.0	7.2	2.4
Edmunds, SD	5 257	11.0	33.2	55.8	5 225	7 422	60.1	239	0.0	3.8	7.1
Fall River, SD	9 240	17.6	34.6	47.8	8 760	7 532	62.6	347	0.0	7.8	2.6
Faulk, SD	3 277	11.3	43.9	44.8	3 840	8 930	63.9	167	0.0	4.2	10.8
Grant, SD	10 813	7.9	28.2	63.9	8 803	6 609	60.5	442	0.0	9.5	6.1
Gregory, SD	7 881	24.9	41.3	33.8	7 022	8 330	63.6	257	0.0	8.9	1.2
Haakon, SD	3 221	10.4	31.5	58.1	3 217	8 165	65.8	156	0.0	8.3	0.0
Hamlin, SD	9 612	8.6	37.6	53.8	7 802	6 464	61.4	380	0.0	8.4	5.3
Hand, SD	4 432	10.3	28.1	61.5	3 628	6 706	64.3	222	0.0	2.7	0.9
Hanson, SD	4 754	14.0	44.6	41.4	3 976	7 349	62.9	188	0.0	8.5	6.9
Harding, SD	2 491	11.7	23.7	64.6	1 991	8 331	61.1	128	0.0	0.0	16.4
Hughes, SD	20 048	9.8	39.6	50.6	17 286	6 279	65.3	992	0.0	13.0	3.9
Hutchinson, SD	13 639	10.9	39.2	49.9	11 792	6 852	63.3	453	0.0	2.9	10.2
Hyde, SD	2 456	12.2	26.9	60.9	1 835	7 282	64.0	86	0.0	5.8	0.0
Jackson, SD	3 396	28.9	37.6	33.6	3 296	9 311	65.3	211	0.0	15.6	2.4
Jerauld, SD	2 900	12.6	29.9	57.5	2 589	7 798	64.0	122	0.0	2.5	2.5
Jones, SD	1 554	7.1	26.8	66.1	1 658	9 263	69.3	83	0.0	0.0	0.0
Kingsbury, SD	7 656	6.9	38.0	55.1	6 143	7 176	59.2	351	0.0	6.6	2.3
Lake, SD	14 252	10.1	34.3	55.6	12 425	6 756	64.5	1 055	0.4	6.9	2.7
Lawrence, SD	23 199	8.8	24.6	66.6	19 913	6 411	65.2	1 900	0.0	11.9	4.6
Lincoln, SD	26 834	6.0	35.4	58.6	22 131	5 938	62.5	1 421	0.5	7.4	0.6
Lyman, SD	4 200	29.2	23.7	47.0	3 535	9 064	55.9	213	0.0	4.7	4.7
McCook, SD	9 375	8.1	37.4	54.5	7 665	6 994	63.3	326	0.0	9.2	4.9
McPherson, SD	3 823	12.4	28.0	59.6	3 687	7 778	63.4	118	0.0	6.8	12.7
Marshall, SD	6 190	9.9	36.3	53.8	5 030	6 524	64.3	271	0.0	7.4	14.0
Meade, SD	20 982	11.5	38.7	49.8	18 365	6 390	65.1	1 376	8.0	21.7	4.8
Mellette, SD	4 773	43.6	36.3	20.0	4 658	10 260	63.9	136	0.0	14.7	5.9
Miner, SD	3 635	8.5	37.4	54.0	3 084	7 222	61.3	175	0.0	5.1	1.1
Minnehaha, SD	200 014	9.0	30.8	60.2	168 926	6 368	65.5	8 653	0.0	12.3	3.7
Moody, SD	8 964	17.1	38.5	44.4	7 754	7 880	61.8	466	0.0	5.4	5.6
Pennington, SD	126 384	16.6	31.4	52.0	115 768	6 886	65.8	5 548	0.3	13.7	4.5
Perkins, SD	4 524	13.1	33.9	53.0	4 244	8 371	62.4	186	0.0	10.2	3.8
Potter, SD	3 659	9.9	30.5	59.6	3 629	7 317	69.7	137	0.0	2.2	0.0
Roberts, SD	16 766	26.6	41.2	32.2	14 704	8 092	64.9	627	0.0	6.9	10.7
Sanborn, SD	3 848	14.2	39.8	46.0	3 234	7 452	61.8	174	0.0	7.5	6.9
Shannon, SD	16 693	64.5	31.2	4.3	13 346	12 686	62.7	1 015	0.0	12.2	27.6
Spink, SD	11 381	10.7	37.6	51.7	9 823	7 202	63.2	462	0.6	5.6	8.9
Stanley, SD	4 025	20.0	31.0	49.0	3 623	6 204	61.7	178	0.0	6.2	2.2
Sully, SD	3 053	7.3	22.2	70.6	2 692	8 546	63.3	92	0.0	13.0	0.0
Todd, SD	25 328	56.6	35.9	7.6	24 423	11 499	65.1	754	0.0	10.1	12.9
Tripp, SD	9 034	17.5	39.1	43.4	7 766	6 879	66.6	391	0.0	8.4	9.7
Turner, SD	11 293	8.4	44.4	47.2	9 635	6 809	60.5	490	0.4	9.6	1.0
Union, SD	21 668	6.8	25.8	67.4	18 109	6 780	63.5	721	0.0	11.0	1.4
Walworth, SD	6 617	13.4	40.3	46.3	6 035	7 167	67.5	320	0.0	10.0	9.7
Yankton, SD	26 491	9.0	39.6	51.4	22 658	6 278	63.4	1 157	0.0	7.8	3.0
Ziebach, SD	3 401	53.6	36.8	9.6	3 209	12 535	62.8	201	0.0	9.5	23.4
TENNESSEE	6 349 101	10.9	43.2	45.9	5 929 523	6 504	69.9	312 760	0.2	12.4	5.2
Anderson, TN	101 753	12.1	40.6	47.3	90 945	7 514	69.1	3 567	0.0	15.7	2.1
Bedford, TN	38 424	10.4	57.3	32.3	35 351	5 285	69.5	2 189	0.0	9.5	8.3
Benton, TN	17 500	13.6	49.8	36.6	15 483	6 351	72.1	759	0.0	14.2	5.1
Bledsoe, TN	12 573	15.4	64.8	19.9	11 339	6 321	67.2	615	0.0	13.5	10.1
Blount, TN	119 563	8.5	42.6	49.0	113 605	6 718	71.0	5 248	0.1	12.1	3.3
Bradley, TN	85 423	10.6	45.6	43.7	80 276	5 913	71.5	5 067	0.0	14.6	3.7
Campbell, TN	37 586	17.9	60.1	21.9	34 626	5 727	70.4	1 994	0.3	15.9	11.7
Cannon, TN	13 936	13.0	63.1	23.9	12 732	5 961	71.1	641	0.0	14.0	5.5
Carroll, TN	34 543	11.2	56.1	32.8	29 053	5 984	69.0	1 578	0.0	15.2	4.6
Carter, TN	55 899	14.1	54.9	31.1	52 618	6 523	71.7	2 857	0.0	14.9	4.3

... = Not available.

Table C-1. Population, School, and Student Characteristics by County—*Continued*

STATE County	High school graduates, 2000			College enrollment, 2000		College graduates, 2000 (percent)						
	Population 25 years and over	High school graduate or less (percent)	High school graduate or more (percent)	Number	Percent public	Bachelor's degree or more	+/- U.S. percentage with bachelor's degree or more	Non-Hispanic White	Black	American Indian and Alaska Native	Asian or Pacific Islander	Hispanic[3]
	30	31	32	33	34	35	36	37	38	39	40	41
SOUTH DAKOTA	474 359	48.3	84.6	42 894	82.0	21.5	-2.9	22.3	19.3	8.5	39.2	11.7
Aurora, SD	2 020	56.5	79.5	75	68.0	12.7	-11.7	12.9	...	0.0	0.0	8.0
Beadle, SD	11 368	51.9	83.0	517	36.9	18.3	-6.1	18.0	13.8	46.9	9.3	0.0
Bennett, SD	1 972	56.4	71.3	170	81.2	12.7	-11.7	16.4	23.1	5.9	...	14.3
Bon Homme, SD	5 026	57.1	79.0	96	80.2	15.3	-9.1	15.7	0.0	4.0	...	14.3
Brookings, SD	14 819	38.0	90.2	6 622	98.8	32.2	7.8	31.8	78.1	5.2	68.7	20.6
Brown, SD	22 959	45.8	85.8	2 787	88.6	23.6	-0.8	23.8	37.9	14.0	63.0	16.4
Brule, SD	3 371	50.5	81.1	78	92.3	20.6	-3.8	20.7	...	21.5	0.0	30.8
Buffalo, SD	948	69.7	63.9	49	91.8	5.4	-19.0	13.8	0.0	2.9	0.0	0.0
Butte, SD	5 859	57.2	79.8	258	87.6	12.2	-12.2	12.3	...	2.9	0.0	13.3
Campbell, SD	1 251	54.1	79.2	16	87.5	14.8	-9.6	14.9	...	0.0	...	...
Charles Mix, SD	5 676	59.9	74.7	160	73.1	14.1	-10.3	16.2	0.0	6.1	25.0	8.2
Clark, SD	2 781	63.3	76.6	53	81.1	11.4	-13.0	11.3	...	0.0	33.3	0.0
Clay, SD	6 719	33.6	89.5	4 397	97.5	38.7	14.3	38.0	59.5	23.8	77.5	53.6
Codington, SD	16 377	52.8	85.3	1 100	87.0	18.8	-5.6	19.1	0.0	1.5	7.5	15.7
Corson, SD	2 238	61.9	76.0	116	84.5	11.3	-13.1	15.4	0.0	7.1	50.0	0.0
Custer, SD	5 099	44.4	88.9	185	73.0	24.4	0.0	24.7	...	19.4	0.0	36.0
Davison, SD	11 719	50.0	83.9	1 283	54.3	20.2	-4.2	20.2	56.4	6.0	37.0	0.0
Day, SD	4 354	58.3	80.0	102	79.4	15.4	-9.0	15.7	...	6.9	30.8	0.0
Deuel, SD	3 094	60.3	81.9	89	78.7	13.3	-11.1	13.3	0.0	0.0	...	22.2
Dewey, SD	3 107	54.8	77.4	262	90.8	12.2	-12.2	20.4	100.0	7.5	14.8	28.6
Douglas, SD	2 332	59.8	68.8	41	78.0	14.5	-9.9	14.5	...	14.3	...	0.0
Edmunds, SD	2 975	59.7	73.6	59	78.0	15.5	-8.9	15.6	...	...	0.0	0.0
Fall River, SD	5 313	51.9	82.5	125	64.0	19.2	-5.2	19.9	0.0	6.2	25.0	24.1
Faulk, SD	1 803	60.4	73.7	27	74.1	13.1	-11.3	13.3	...	0.0	0.0	0.0
Grant, SD	5 303	63.1	79.5	119	71.4	14.8	-9.6	14.8	...	0.0	0.0	80.0
Gregory, SD	3 367	61.3	77.7	43	95.3	12.0	-12.4	12.4	0.0	0.7	0.0	0.0
Haakon, SD	1 477	54.4	86.3	32	87.5	15.4	-9.0	15.1	...	14.8	0.0	100.0
Hamlin, SD	3 507	62.9	79.9	123	95.1	12.8	-11.6	12.7	0.0	26.3	50.0	18.8
Hand, SD	2 627	58.1	80.1	33	63.6	15.6	-8.8	15.6	0.0	0.0	0.0	0.0
Hanson, SD	1 962	61.1	75.1	61	85.2	14.0	-10.4	13.8	...	...	60.0	50.0
Harding, SD	850	46.6	87.8	28	82.1	17.8	-6.6	17.5	...	50.0	...	...
Hughes, SD	10 853	38.1	89.5	183	84.7	32.0	7.6	33.3	13.0	8.4	72.7	12.2
Hutchinson, SD	5 629	57.6	71.7	139	82.7	14.1	-10.3	14.1	100.0	18.8	...	25.0
Hyde, SD	1 147	56.2	80.5	20	95.0	16.0	-8.4	16.0	...	12.1	...	...
Jackson, SD	1 002	31.0	82.7	137	86.9	16.2	-8.2	21.7	...	5.9	0.0	100.0
Jerauld, SD	1 661	61.0	79.6	49	81.6	12.3	-12.1	12.2	...	50.0	...	0.0
Jones, SD	811	53.3	86.2	12	83.3	17.8	-6.6	18.2	...	12.5	...	...
Kingsbury, SD	4 015	59.6	82.3	97	89.7	16.2	-8.2	16.2	...	12.5	25.0	0.0
Lake, SD	6 917	50.9	85.7	1 213	97.4	21.1	-3.3	20.6	0.0	19.0	86.5	22.0
Lawrence, SD	13 746	44.2	87.5	2 245	95.7	24.0	-0.4	24.1	0.0	18.4	44.8	15.1
Lincoln, SD	15 093	41.4	89.4	994	75.8	25.5	1.1	25.5	27.3	17.1	36.5	25.6
Lyman, SD	2 344	59.7	81.1	101	94.1	15.9	-8.5	17.9	0.0	8.7	37.5	0.0
McCook, SD	3 827	55.8	82.9	140	86.4	16.3	-8.1	16.3	...	0.0	100.0	8.7
McPherson, SD	2 128	68.7	58.8	23	78.3	10.7	-13.7	10.7	...	...	...	0.0
Marshall, SD	3 111	57.8	75.6	99	93.9	16.2	-8.2	16.7	...	8.3	...	0.0
Meade, SD	14 816	46.1	87.7	1 061	82.2	16.8	-7.6	17.0	19.7	5.8	23.5	20.6
Mellette, SD	1 199	56.3	78.1	66	95.5	16.6	-7.8	25.3	...	4.6	66.7	0.0
Miner, SD	1 982	60.8	79.6	40	95.0	13.5	-10.9	13.4	0.0	40.0	0.0	0.0
Minnehaha, SD	93 400	42.3	88.5	7 981	50.9	20.0	1.6	26.8	20.0	7.7	28.7	7.6
Moody, SD	4 193	51.8	84.7	191	91.1	17.4	-7.0	17.9	23.1	9.5	37.1	33.3
Pennington, SD	55 535	41.5	87.8	5 409	84.0	25.0	0.6	26.5	10.5	9.7	29.9	8.8
Perkins, SD	2 367	56.9	80.3	27	59.3	14.6	-9.8	14.9	0.0	0.0	33.3	0.0
Potter, SD	1 969	56.6	80.8	26	76.9	16.2	-8.2	16.1	...	22.2	50.0	...
Roberts, SD	6 301	61.4	75.8	210	93.8	13.4	-11.0	14.4	0.0	8.4	77.8	0.0
Sanborn, SD	1 788	56.2	82.7	67	70.1	14.8	-9.6	15.1	...	0.0	0.0	5.6
Shannon, SD	5 524	56.4	70.0	537	89.4	12.1	-12.3	41.3	0.0	9.3	64.0	9.5
Spink, SD	5 024	57.5	81.4	90	78.9	14.4	-10.0	14.4	0.0	17.7	0.0	0.0
Stanley, SD	1 823	47.3	87.7	42	52.4	22.1	-2.3	22.3	0.0	11.3	100.0	0.0
Sully, SD	1 065	53.2	84.9	13	84.6	16.4	-8.0	16.6	...	0.0	...	0.0
Todd, SD	4 173	57.2	74.1	504	93.3	12.1	-12.3	22.2	...	8.4	73.3	0.0
Tripp, SD	4 218	58.7	80.2	65	92.3	13.5	-10.9	14.0	...	2.6	0.0	9.1
Turner, SD	6 019	54.1	83.2	203	77.3	17.0	-7.4	17.0	0.0	0.0	0.0	0.0
Union, SD	8 262	45.6	87.2	477	85.5	26.3	1.9	25.5	19.0	24.3	74.6	30.8
Walworth, SD	4 083	58.7	78.1	113	77.0	15.8	-8.6	15.8	...	9.6	0.0	0.0
Yankton, SD	14 178	47.9	86.1	1 130	54.0	23.0	-1.4	23.9	9.4	2.5	0.0	10.5
Ziebach, SD	1 223	64.3	71.4	84	95.2	12.0	-12.4	17.1	...	8.4	22.2	...
TENNESSEE	3 744 928	55.7	75.9	287 550	75.9	19.6	-4.8	20.5	12.9	14.8	46.7	14.1
Anderson, TN	49 499	54.0	78.9	2 453	87.0	20.8	-3.6	20.7	14.6	19.4	67.8	20.8
Bedford, TN	24 232	69.3	69.7	966	88.6	11.1	-13.3	12.3	4.3	0.0	16.4	4.5
Benton, TN	11 798	76.6	65.8	246	77.2	6.3	-18.1	6.1	12.7	14.6	30.2	0.0
Bledsoe, TN	8 455	75.1	66.0	228	87.7	7.1	-17.3	7.5	0.0	0.0	0.0	3.3
Blount, TN	72 938	56.0	78.4	4 291	67.1	17.9	-6.5	18.1	9.6	7.0	47.7	19.4
Bradley, TN	57 163	56.0	73.3	5 736	48.4	15.9	-8.5	15.8	10.3	11.2	39.0	28.4
Campbell, TN	27 359	76.8	58.7	809	81.5	7.0	-17.4	6.9	7.5	0.0	40.4	19.5
Cannon, TN	8 486	76.0	67.2	323	88.9	8.4	-16.0	8.4	12.5	0.0	0.0	0.0
Carroll, TN	20 238	70.5	67.9	1 042	60.6	11.1	-13.3	11.6	7.2	22.2	17.4	11.7
Carter, TN	39 450	64.4	69.1	2 710	71.3	12.8	-11.6	12.8	11.7	16.7	14.7	10.6

[3]May be of any race.
... = Not available.

Table C-1. Population, School, and Student Characteristics by County—*Continued*

STATE County	State/ county code	County type[1]	Population, 2005		Number of schools and students, 2004–2005			Resident enrollment, 2000			
			Total	Percent 5 to 17 years	School districts	Schools	Students	Total	Percent public	K–12	Percent public
			1	2	3	4	5	6	7	8	9
Cheatham, TN	47 021	1	38 603	18.5	1	13	6 731	8 906	87.4	7 369	92.0
Chester, TN	47 023	3	15 941	16.6	1	6	2 546	4 531	67.8	2 770	93.3
Claiborne, TN	47 025	6	31 033	16.2	1	14	4 956	6 863	88.1	5 431	94.5
Clay, TN	47 027	8	7 992	15.2	1	5	1 087	1 712	99.1	1 388	100.0
Cocke, TN	47 029	6	34 929	15.5	2	13	5 500	6 849	95.1	5 823	97.3
Coffee, TN	47 031	4	50 869	17.2	3	18	9 390	11 485	91.2	8 906	95.4
Crockett, TN	47 033	8	14 595	17.1	3	7	2 816	3 233	91.1	2 787	94.1
Cumberland, TN	47 035	7	51 346	14.6	1	10	7 089	9 432	92.3	7 599	93.9
Davidson, TN	47 037	1	575 261	15.3	1	130	72 807	141 200	70.8	90 547	82.3
Decatur, TN	47 039	9	11 686	15.0	1	4	1 562	2 284	94.2	1 897	96.5
DeKalb, TN	47 041	6	18 254	15.7	1	5	2 752	3 693	92.3	3 071	95.3
Dickson, TN	47 043	1	45 894	18.0	1	15	8 181	10 311	89.9	8 621	93.0
Dyer, TN	47 045	5	37 829	17.7	2	12	6 999	8 964	91.3	7 032	94.7
Fayette, TN	47 047	1	34 458	17.1	1	10	3 640	6 736	73.9	5 551	73.8
Fentress, TN	47 049	9	17 159	16.5	1	6	2 352	3 601	95.6	3 084	96.4
Franklin, TN	47 051	6	41 003	15.5	2	21	10 058	9 706	78.1	6 782	93.9
Gibson, TN	47 053	4	48 148	16.5	5	19	8 514	10 813	92.8	8 732	95.7
Giles, TN	47 055	6	29 297	16.9	1	8	4 512	6 974	88.0	5 637	94.2
Grainger, TN	47 057	3	22 283	15.7	1	7	3 239	4 193	95.4	3 564	97.3
Greene, TN	47 059	6	65 318	15.4	2	23	9 782	13 201	88.6	10 392	94.9
Grundy, TN	47 061	8	14 608	16.8	1	7	2 390	3 040	94.1	2 654	95.8
Hamblen, TN	47 063	3	59 898	16.0	1	18	9 484	11 928	92.6	9 572	96.0
Hamilton, TN	47 065	2	310 935	15.9	1	80	40 805	77 307	78.1	53 191	81.5
Hancock, TN	47 067	8	6 704	15.0	1	2	1 017	1 401	94.1	1 218	93.7
Hardeman, TN	47 069	6	28 170	16.1	1	9	4 464	6 246	89.2	5 433	92.1
Hardin, TN	47 071	6	25 930	16.3	1	10	3 809	5 325	89.2	4 457	92.0
Hawkins, TN	47 073	3	56 196	16.0	3	29	14 671	11 234	92.0	9 175	94.6
Haywood, TN	47 075	6	19 656	18.4	1	7	3 693	4 975	93.8	4 095	95.7
Henderson, TN	47 077	6	26 425	16.7	2	12	4 607	5 456	91.1	4 547	93.8
Henry, TN	47 079	7	31 511	15.3	2	9	4 700	6 506	93.8	5 384	96.8
Hickman, TN	47 081	1	23 793	17.1	1	7	3 886	4 976	85.2	4 174	89.9
Houston, TN	47 083	8	7 988	16.8	1	5	1 445	1 742	93.9	1 490	95.8
Humphreys, TN	47 085	6	18 212	16.5	1	7	3 069	3 901	90.0	3 242	93.9
Jackson, TN	47 087	8	11 072	15.8	1	5	2 024	2 188	94.6	1 807	96.1
Jefferson, TN	47 089	3	48 394	15.8	1	10	7 261	10 701	80.7	7 627	95.1
Johnson, TN	47 091	6	18 116	13.3	1	7	2 340	3 316	93.5	2 768	95.3
Knox, TN	47 093	2	404 972	15.4	1	88	54 247	102 622	85.6	62 407	86.8
Lake, TN	47 095	9	7 583	12.1	1	3	916	1 424	93.8	1 167	95.9
Lauderdale, TN	47 097	6	26 795	16.8	1	7	4 557	6 156	91.3	5 096	93.6
Lawrence, TN	47 099	6	41 101	17.7	1	13	6 999	9 223	90.9	7 663	93.7
Lewis, TN	47 101	6	11 435	17.3	1	4	1 964	2 649	86.5	2 176	90.2
Lincoln, TN	47 103	6	32 392	16.3	1	3	1 007	7 089	92.7	5 671	95.9
Loudon, TN	47 105	2	43 387	15.1	2	12	7 210	7 829	92.3	6 232	95.2
McMinn, TN	47 107	4	51 327	16.6	3	15	7 943	10 614	89.7	8 587	95.6
McNairy, TN	47 109	6	25 285	16.6	1	8	4 271	5 328	89.6	4 393	92.3
Macon, TN	47 111	1	21 549	17.7	1	7	3 697	4 610	96.6	3 926	97.9
Madison, TN	47 113	3	94 916	17.7	1	29	14 334	24 814	72.1	17 759	82.5
Marion, TN	47 115	2	27 757	16.1	2	10	4 522	6 125	92.9	5 111	94.8
Marshall, TN	47 117	6	28 372	17.2	1	9	4 811	6 342	94.3	5 294	96.4
Maury, TN	47 119	4	76 292	17.6	1	18	11 518	16 743	83.1	13 184	86.8
Meigs, TN	47 121	8	11 657	17.1	1	4	1 871	2 335	88.4	2 017	90.1
Monroe, TN	47 123	6	43 185	16.9	2	16	6 871	8 665	89.7	7 117	95.3
Montgomery, TN	47 125	3	147 202	19.9	1	30	25 899	38 242	90.2	27 284	94.1
Moore, TN	47 127	9	6 024	16.5	1	2	958	1 312	92.8	1 015	95.5
Morgan, TN	47 129	6	20 157	15.7	1	8	3 265	4 260	94.8	3 480	95.5
Obion, TN	47 131	7	32 213	16.2	2	11	5 674	7 182	95.0	5 636	98.5
Overton, TN	47 133	7	20 523	15.7	1	9	3 369	4 459	95.6	3 473	97.1
Perry, TN	47 135	8	7 574	16.8	1	4	1 160	1 594	93.7	1 392	93.9
Pickett, TN	47 137	9	4 821	14.7	1	2	692	1 021	96.0	825	97.0
Polk, TN	47 139	3	15 944	16.0	1	8	2 660	3 089	91.4	2 577	92.9
Putnam, TN	47 141	4	66 580	15.1	1	18	10 275	17 803	92.9	9 895	94.5
Rhea, TN	47 143	6	29 918	16.2	2	7	4 730	6 583	91.1	5 023	94.6
Roane, TN	47 145	4	52 889	15.3	1	18	7 449	10 736	91.7	8 612	93.6
Robertson, TN	47 147	1	60 379	17.8	1	17	10 043	12 851	87.3	10 877	90.0
Rutherford, TN	47 149	1	218 292	17.8	2	50	37 627	53 906	90.4	34 723	92.4
Scott, TN	47 151	6	21 868	17.6	2	10	4 145	4 995	97.3	4 182	98.7
Sequatchie, TN	47 153	2	12 691	16.9	1	3	2 059	2 422	88.6	1 943	92.6
Sevier, TN	47 155	4	79 282	15.6	1	25	13 787	15 086	90.7	12 154	94.0
Shelby, TN	47 157	1	909 035	19.3	2	245	166 015	259 171	83.5	189 061	87.7
Smith, TN	47 159	1	18 647	17.3	1	12	3 208	3 995	94.2	3 366	97.4
Stewart, TN	47 161	3	12 969	16.6	1	6	2 176	2 710	94.5	2 300	96.5
Sullivan, TN	47 163	3	152 716	15.2	2	37	16 486	32 281	88.3	25 279	93.6
Sumner, TN	47 165	1	145 009	17.6	1	42	24 707	32 250	85.4	25 901	89.2
Tipton, TN	47 167	1	55 998	19.4	1	13	11 338	14 163	89.9	11 411	94.2
Trousdale, TN	47 169	1	7 677	16.6	1	3	1 302	1 609	90.9	1 398	93.2
Unicoi, TN	47 171	3	17 572	14.4	1	6	2 569	3 316	95.9	2 692	97.6
Union, TN	47 173	2	19 076	17.3	1	7	3 118	3 890	95.8	3 345	97.3
Van Buren, TN	47 175	9	5 470	15.8	1	2	791	1 203	96.1	1 016	96.5
Warren, TN	47 177	6	39 753	16.2	1	11	6 176	7 910	93.9	6 653	95.8
Washington, TN	47 179	3	112 507	14.7	2	24	15 933	26 774	91.7	16 544	93.5
Wayne, TN	47 181	8	16 909	14.6	1	8	2 652	3 539	95.1	2 826	98.0
Weakley, TN	47 183	7	33 732	15.0	1	11	4 885	10 280	95.3	5 595	97.0
White, TN	47 185	7	24 253	16.2	1	9	4 006	4 904	94.4	4 215	95.7
Williamson, TN	47 187	1	153 595	19.3	2	44	27 705	35 558	77.1	28 159	83.5
Wilson, TN	47 189	1	100 508	17.7	2	24	16 162	21 923	80.8	17 549	85.5

[1]County type codes are from the Economic Research Service of the United States Department of Agriculture. See notes and definitions at the end of this section.

Table C-1. Population, School, and Student Characteristics by County—*Continued*

STATE County	Characteristics of students, 2004–2005				Outcomes		Staff and students, 2004–2005		
	Percent with IEP[2]	Percent eligible for free or reduced-price lunch	Percent minority	Percent English-language learners	Number of graduates, 2003–2004	Percent dropouts, grades 9–12, 2001–2002	Number of teachers	Student-teacher ratio	Central administration staff
	10	11	12	13	14	15	16	17	18
Cheatham, TN	14.5	...	...	...	432	0.7	438	15.4	...
Chester, TN	9.4	...	...	...	113	2.7	144	17.7	...
Claiborne, TN	21.6	...	...	...	223	1.1	363	13.7	...
Clay, TN	22.5	...	...	...	105	...	91	12.0	...
Cocke, TN	20.4	...	...	...	...	0.8	366	15.0	...
Coffee, TN	20.8	...	...	...	...	1.3	575	16.3	...
Crockett, TN	13.5	...	...	...	...	1.7	173	16.3	...
Cumberland, TN	17.9	...	...	...	335	3.2	415	17.1	...
Davidson, TN	17.9	...	...	...	3 667	7.6	4 839	15.0	...
Decatur, TN	29.9	...	...	...	97	1.6	111	14.1	...
DeKalb, TN	22.6	...	...	...	125	2.7	177	15.6	...
Dickson, TN	19.7	...	...	...	492	5.5	535	15.3	...
Dyer, TN	18.9	...	...	...	374	3.5	432	16.2	...
Fayette, TN	18.6	...	...	...	179	9.7	258	14.1	...
Fentress, TN	19.4	...	...	...	52	2.9	164	14.4	...
Franklin, TN	17.6	...	...	...	637	5.2	643	15.6	...
Gibson, TN	16.0	...	...	...	507	1.8	527	16.2	...
Giles, TN	17.7	...	...	...	253	4.2	293	15.4	...
Grainger, TN	17.6	...	...	...	183	1.3	212	15.3	...
Greene, TN	22.7	...	...	...	554	1.8	647	15.1	...
Grundy, TN	28.1	...	...	...	125	1.7	173	13.8	...
Hamblen, TN	15.6	...	...	...	498	1.8	584	16.2	...
Hamilton, TN	20.3	...	...	...	2 108	5.8	2 646	15.4	...
Hancock, TN	21.8	...	...	...	87	2.8	80	12.6	...
Hardeman, TN	21.6	...	...	...	237	6.6	323	13.8	...
Hardin, TN	18.8	...	...	...	204	3.5	272	14.0	...
Hawkins, TN	20.6	...	...	...	...	5.1	1 003	14.6	...
Haywood, TN	17.5	...	...	...	169	4.1	237	15.6	...
Henderson, TN	17.3	...	...	...	...	3.2	302	15.2	...
Henry, TN	16.5	...	...	...	...	2.8	300	15.7	...
Hickman, TN	21.9	...	...	...	226	1.3	237	16.4	...
Houston, TN	15.8	...	...	...	96	2.1	94	15.4	...
Humphreys, TN	21.2	...	...	...	201	1.5	205	15.0	...
Jackson, TN	15.5	...	...	...	90	1.6	126	16.1	...
Jefferson, TN	18.2	...	...	...	389	0.4	447	16.3	...
Johnson, TN	18.6	...	...	...	159	3.2	157	14.9	...
Knox, TN	16.0	...	...	...	0 129	0.0	3 594	15.1	...
Lake, TN	20.9	...	...	...	54	3.6	71	12.9	...
Lauderdale, TN	22.6	...	...	...	247	3.9	308	14.8	...
Lawrence, TN	19.8	...	...	...	437	6.1	463	15.1	...
Lewis, TN	15.0	...	...	...	130	2.6	128	15.3	...
Lincoln, TN	10.3	...	...	...	0	5.2	67	15.1	...
Loudon, TN	13.4	...	...	...	320	2.7	410	17.3	...
McMinn, TN	19.7	...	...	...	...	2.0	485	16.4	...
McNairy, TN	14.1	...	...	...	223	1.4	291	14.7	...
Macon, TN	15.4	...	...	...	199	4.2	221	16.7	...
Madison, TN	23.1	...	...	...	748	4.8	986	14.5	...
Marion, TN	18.6	...	...	...	...	2.6	290	15.6	...
Marshall, TN	15.9	...	...	...	276	2.4	294	16.4	...
Maury, TN	21.6	...	...	...	620	2.7	779	14.8	...
Meigs, TN	21.2	...	...	...	104	1.2	117	16.0	...
Monroe, TN	17.0	...	...	...	...	2.4	398	17.3	...
Montgomery, TN	16.2	...	...	...	1 276	3.3	1 623	16.0	...
Moore, TN	17.2	...	...	...	57	6.0	65	14.7	...
Morgan, TN	18.7	...	...	...	229	2.6	230	14.2	...
Obion, TN	16.7	...	...	...	300	3.5	354	16.1	...
Overton, TN	21.0	...	...	...	172	1.1	213	15.8	...
Perry, TN	28.4	...	...	...	80	2.9	86	13.5	...
Pickett, TN	15.5	...	...	...	49	...	57	12.1	...
Polk, TN	12.0	...	...	...	126	5.2	167	16.0	...
Putnam, TN	18.9	...	...	...	538	1.7	608	16.9	...
Rhea, TN	12.3	...	...	...	...	2.6	301	15.7	...
Roane, TN	21.3	...	...	...	418	3.6	485	15.3	...
Robertson, TN	19.8	...	...	...	501	3.9	632	15.9	...
Rutherford, TN	16.3	...	...	...	...	2.2	2 277	16.5	...
Scott, TN	12.6	...	...	...	213	3.9	284	14.6	...
Sequatchie, TN	20.6	...	...	...	98	2.8	135	15.3	...
Sevier, TN	18.6	...	...	...	730	2.4	865	15.9	...
Shelby, TN	16.0	...	...	...	7 839	6.6	10 029	16.6	...
Smith, TN	21.7	...	...	...	259	1.2	208	15.5	...
Stewart, TN	18.5	...	...	...	118	2.2	131	16.7	...
Sullivan, TN	21.2	...	...	...	971	2.7	1 082	15.2	...
Sumner, TN	18.5	...	...	...	1 521	1.4	1 625	15.2	...
Tipton, TN	17.4	...	...	...	645	3.6	665	17.1	...
Trousdale, TN	29.4	...	...	...	82	4.0	81	16.1	...
Unicoi, TN	29.4	...	...	...	177	1.4	155	16.5	...
Union, TN	22.9	...	...	...	171	0.6	226	13.8	...
Van Buren, TN	11.6	...	...	...	45	0.9	59	13.4	...
Warren, TN	24.4	...	...	...	390	0.8	409	15.1	...
Washington, TN	16.6	...	...	...	952	2.0	1 003	15.9	...
Wayne, TN	17.6	...	...	...	177	2.2	203	13.1	...
Weakley, TN	17.2	...	...	...	257	1.0	310	15.7	...
White, TN	19.8	...	...	...	237	1.2	252	15.9	...
Williamson, TN	16.2	...	...	...	...	1.7	1 723	16.1	...
Wilson, TN	14.4	...	...	...	...	2.3	997	16.2	...

[2]IEP = Individual Education Program. See notes and definitions at the end of this section.
. . . = Not available.

Table C-1. Population, School, and Student Characteristics by County—*Continued*

STATE County	Revenue, 2003–2004				Current expenditures, 2003–2004			Resident population, 16 to 19 years, 2000			
	Total revenue (thousands of dollars)	Percent of revenue from:			Total expenditures (thousands of dollars)	Amount per student (dollars)	Percent for instruction	Total	Percent in armed forces	Percent high school graduates	Percent not enrolled, not employed, not in armed forces, not high school graduate
		Federal government	State government	Local government							
	19	20	21	22	23	24	25	26	27	28	29
Cheatham, TN	41 058	7.8	58.5	33.7	39 131	5 646	71.5	1 771	0.0	12.6	3.6
Chester, TN	13 507	12.3	67.7	20.0	12 213	4 839	67.2	1 147	0.0	8.7	4.4
Claiborne, TN	36 124	21.0	52.4	26.7	28 040	6 033	74.0	1 589	0.0	15.1	6.2
Clay, TN	8 981	14.3	60.7	25.1	7 709	6 698	72.4	419	2.1	27.9	2.9
Cocke, TN	35 613	16.5	54.8	28.6	32 301	5 953	69.1	1 631	0.0	12.4	7.4
Coffee, TN	61 654	10.7	43.7	45.6	56 600	6 318	70.8	2 636	0.3	10.5	4.7
Crockett, TN	16 941	14.8	63.5	21.7	15 174	5 717	67.7	794	0.0	10.7	7.6
Cumberland, TN	41 629	14.4	51.0	34.6	37 532	5 440	71.0	2 124	0.0	18.3	3.2
Davidson, TN	593 685	9.4	27.2	63.4	570 110	8 304	67.8	32 378	0.0	10.0	6.6
Decatur, TN	10 347	12.1	58.8	29.1	8 889	5 946	75.7	572	0.0	16.4	2.8
DeKalb, TN	16 688	15.9	58.3	25.7	15 418	5 967	70.2	940	0.0	17.6	5.3
Dickson, TN	51 649	8.9	47.4	43.7	48 564	5 987	68.2	2 410	0.0	13.4	4.1
Dyer, TN	49 809	11.1	43.8	45.1	46 560	6 888	63.7	1 898	0.0	14.3	7.1
Fayette, TN	25 886	23.1	49.3	27.6	24 765	7 708	67.3	1 663	0.0	15.6	4.9
Fentress, TN	15 492	15.6	61.9	22.5	13 930	6 186	73.0	818	0.0	10.6	6.5
Franklin, TN	38 265	10.8	53.7	35.5	34 092	5 902	70.1	2 411	0.0	10.0	4.8
Gibson, TN	52 257	11.7	54.0	34.3	46 199	5 613	69.7	2 453	0.0	16.3	4.6
Giles, TN	27 341	10.4	53.3	36.2	26 794	6 046	69.5	1 705	0.0	18.2	2.9
Grainger, TN	21 696	18.3	62.4	19.3	19 469	5 836	75.1	985	0.0	13.2	5.2
Greene, TN	69 674	10.9	45.6	43.5	60 132	6 230	70.1	2 947	0.5	19.2	3.8
Grundy, TN	16 395	20.3	61.9	17.8	14 203	6 298	71.7	802	0.0	12.5	10.8
Hamblen, TN	58 940	10.4	42.2	47.4	55 168	6 033	71.2	3 083	0.2	20.1	4.4
Hamilton, TN	283 449	13.4	32.5	54.1	282 176	7 037	69.0	16 060	0.0	10.6	5.2
Hancock, TN	8 239	20.6	65.1	14.3	6 990	6 793	66.9	428	0.0	13.3	4.4
Hardeman, TN	29 949	14.1	59.2	26.8	26 365	5 905	77.8	1 500	0.0	9.0	9.4
Hardin, TN	25 027	13.7	51.8	34.5	23 097	6 154	71.1	1 275	0.0	14.7	5.8
Hawkins, TN	51 659	11.9	56.9	31.2	48 042	6 104	71.5	2 464	0.0	15.7	5.7
Haywood, TN	23 646	17.2	54.5	28.2	22 258	6 340	68.9	1 174	0.0	14.1	7.3
Henderson, TN	27 181	12.2	58.4	29.5	25 206	5 742	76.5	1 211	0.0	18.8	7.2
Henry, TN	32 752	12.9	48.4	38.7	27 152	5 868	66.8	1 608	0.0	15.5	7.0
Hickman, TN	24 059	10.5	66.4	23.1	21 083	5 529	72.7	1 114	0.0	20.6	5.2
Houston, TN	9 103	10.9	67.2	21.9	8 471	5 887	67.5	366	1.1	21.3	0.5
Humphreys, TN	19 059	11.0	54.3	34.7	18 411	6 137	69.6	956	0.0	15.6	2.6
Jackson, TN	12 001	12.1	63.2	24.7	10 229	6 132	68.7	604	0.0	12.3	4.6
Jefferson, TN	42 981	11.2	57.0	31.8	41 559	5 907	70.2	2 513	0.0	10.3	5.1
Johnson, TN	17 968	19.9	55.0	25.0	16 012	7 007	67.2	747	0.0	7.1	9.9
Knox, TN	363 394	6.4	32.3	61.3	341 801	6 491	70.0	22 203	0.0	9.8	3.7
Lake, TN	6 598	17.6	58.4	24.0	5 823	6 470	74.7	429	0.0	6.5	20.3
Lauderdale, TN	29 020	15.5	59.9	24.6	26 456	5 822	69.6	1 509	0.0	15.4	8.0
Lawrence, TN	41 235	13.1	56.5	30.4	39 624	5 905	71.2	2 081	0.0	10.3	6.6
Lewis, TN	11 646	14.7	65.7	19.7	10 365	5 264	70.4	708	0.0	13.3	8.8
Lincoln, TN	30 457	10.5	56.2	33.3	27 500	5 522	74.4	1 543	0.0	14.4	5.3
Loudon, TN	45 880	9.9	48.9	41.2	40 962	5 952	76.8	1 748	0.0	14.7	3.4
McMinn, TN	51 715	11.2	49.4	39.4	46 299	5 861	70.9	2 446	0.0	14.6	6.5
McNairy, TN	26 920	16.6	56.2	27.2	23 763	5 614	74.2	1 289	0.0	16.4	3.1
Macon, TN	22 436	10.9	61.1	27.9	18 701	5 272	75.3	1 135	0.1	13.4	4.3
Madison, TN	105 290	10.4	34.6	55.0	94 248	6 925	70.1	5 751	0.0	10.9	4.3
Marion, TN	27 612	11.9	55.2	32.9	25 171	5 654	69.1	1 481	0.0	11.3	7.6
Marshall, TN	29 623	8.8	49.4	41.8	29 514	6 112	66.2	1 554	0.0	13.4	6.4
Maury, TN	74 876	9.3	47.5	43.2	71 437	6 412	71.5	4 198	0.0	16.7	4.7
Meigs, TN	11 467	14.7	62.8	22.5	10 156	5 517	70.8	520	0.0	12.7	7.7
Monroe, TN	40 784	12.4	57.8	29.9	38 621	5 839	70.2	2 095	0.0	15.6	7.0
Montgomery, TN	149 386	11.4	48.9	39.8	144 966	5 816	67.5	7 580	7.2	19.2	3.0
Moore, TN	6 604	8.0	55.1	36.9	6 353	6 687	65.0	254	0.0	6.3	5.1
Morgan, TN	20 612	13.5	66.6	19.9	19 665	6 051	70.1	1 042	0.0	17.6	3.4
Obion, TN	36 102	12.2	47.3	40.5	32 846	6 150	70.2	1 554	0.0	14.7	4.2
Overton, TN	21 111	14.5	61.3	24.2	18 817	5 718	68.1	1 142	0.0	14.3	3.1
Perry, TN	7 821	13.1	61.5	25.4	7 332	6 506	68.2	350	0.0	13.1	2.6
Pickett, TN	5 317	15.3	59.4	25.3	4 741	6 792	70.5	261	0.0	17.2	4.6
Polk, TN	16 439	14.5	58.2	27.3	14 712	5 810	69.9	660	0.0	16.1	8.0
Putnam, TN	59 822	10.7	46.0	43.3	58 105	5 886	68.8	4 098	0.0	12.6	4.1
Rhea, TN	28 244	12.6	60.4	27.0	26 079	5 739	69.1	1 649	0.0	15.3	2.9
Roane, TN	49 091	11.2	50.8	38.0	46 173	6 242	72.0	2 421	0.0	15.1	4.7
Robertson, TN	57 442	8.8	54.0	37.2	54 378	5 610	76.6	3 183	0.0	20.7	3.7
Rutherford, TN	219 856	7.5	45.2	47.2	200 100	5 638	74.5	11 646	0.0	11.3	3.0
Scott, TN	26 201	13.9	59.2	26.8	24 580	6 342	72.8	1 185	0.0	13.2	6.6
Sequatchie, TN	13 917	14.9	53.5	31.6	11 224	5 864	72.0	490	0.0	22.2	1.2
Sevier, TN	90 200	8.8	34.3	56.9	82 904	6 351	68.1	3 433	0.0	14.3	4.2
Shelby, TN	1 213 807	12.6	37.5	49.9	1 151 309	7 062	69.2	51 491	0.1	9.5	7.1
Smith, TN	18 159	9.1	61.6	29.3	16 759	5 330	70.3	1 003	0.0	14.6	5.3
Stewart, TN	13 989	11.6	70.5	17.8	12 402	5 889	65.0	672	0.0	25.9	1.5
Sullivan, TN	172 703	8.7	36.5	54.8	156 342	6 786	69.9	7 230	0.1	12.0	5.3
Sumner, TN	150 259	8.0	48.7	43.3	143 960	5 998	70.9	7 587	0.0	13.4	4.0
Tipton, TN	64 518	11.7	61.4	26.9	61 000	5 469	71.4	3 060	0.0	15.0	5.8
Trousdale, TN	8 142	9.6	69.0	21.3	6 798	5 332	72.9	436	0.0	16.1	5.7
Unicoi, TN	15 916	15.1	57.6	27.3	14 576	5 739	69.8	824	1.6	19.2	5.3
Union, TN	20 500	13.6	66.9	19.5	19 083	6 249	70.7	1 041	0.0	25.8	4.3
Van Buren, TN	5 905	11.1	62.8	26.1	4 993	6 369	66.9	287	0.0	17.8	5.9
Warren, TN	39 155	12.0	50.2	37.8	35 450	5 909	69.9	1 748	0.0	18.1	3.1
Washington, TN	103 576	9.0	40.8	50.2	93 299	5 972	73.0	5 817	0.1	10.0	3.3
Wayne, TN	17 562	16.1	62.4	21.6	15 784	6 180	77.9	758	0.0	12.9	7.5
Weakley, TN	28 772	11.5	57.7	30.8	26 638	5 597	72.4	2 710	0.0	10.8	2.8
White, TN	22 675	12.2	63.5	24.2	20 623	5 291	72.4	1 244	0.0	16.9	5.3
Williamson, TN	195 757	3.8	35.3	60.8	184 413	7 187	69.1	6 880	0.0	7.4	1.5
Wilson, TN	102 710	6.7	43.8	49.5	96 606	6 213	63.5	4 623	0.0	14.1	2.8

Table C-1. Population, School, and Student Characteristics by County—*Continued*

STATE County	High school graduates, 2000			College enrollment, 2000		College graduates, 2000 (percent)						
	Population 25 years and over	High school graduate or less (percent)	High school graduate or more (percent)	Number	Percent public	Bachelor's degree or more	+/- U.S. percentage with bachelor's degree or more	Non-Hispanic White	Black	American Indian and Alaska Native	Asian or Pacific Islander	Hispanic[3]
	30	31	32	33	34	35	36	37	38	39	40	41
Cheatham, TN	23 341	61.7	75.4	989	73.7	15.1	-9.3	15.1	10.0	22.5	32.7	20.4
Chester, TN	9 531	65.3	67.8	1 525	22.3	11.2	-13.2	11.6	7.1	. . .	85.7	0.0
Claiborne, TN	20 200	74.2	60.3	1 005	55.5	8.9	-15.5	9.0	3.8	0.0	68.8	0.0
Clay, TN	5 623	80.2	58.4	245	94.7	6.8	-17.6	6.4	0.0	0.0	72.7	0.0
Cocke, TN	23 070	76.9	61.2	713	84.9	6.2	-18.2	6.2	1.8	0.0	35.5	0.0
Coffee, TN	32 079	59.2	73.7	1 738	82.3	17.5	-6.9	17.3	13.3	19.8	46.7	15.6
Crockett, TN	9 690	72.1	65.1	302	70.9	9.1	-15.3	10.3	2.8	0.0	60.0	3.4
Cumberland, TN	33 595	63.1	72.5	1 259	88.6	13.7	-10.7	13.6	37.7	13.6	25.5	13.4
Davidson, TN	377 734	43.1	81.5	41 321	50.5	30.5	6.1	34.1	20.2	15.9	50.0	14.4
Decatur, TN	8 247	76.3	63.6	280	85.7	7.3	-17.1	7.4	2.7	0.0	50.0	0.0
DeKalb, TN	11 870	72.9	64.6	389	90.5	11.3	-13.1	11.0	21.1	88.9	45.5	6.7
Dickson, TN	28 108	67.1	72.6	1 006	78.7	11.3	-13.1	11.6	4.0	13.5	31.0	15.1
Dyer, TN	24 356	67.3	66.3	1 232	85.1	12.0	-12.4	12.6	5.7	0.0	37.0	10.2
Fayette, TN	18 991	64.3	70.6	775	86.8	12.8	-11.6	15.4	7.5	8.6	33.3	5.1
Fentress, TN	11 275	79.9	57.3	341	92.4	8.3	-16.1	8.3	0.0	. . .	0.0	19.6
Franklin, TN	25 963	61.7	73.8	2 292	36.3	15.3	-9.1	15.8	6.6	3.4	31.8	15.4
Gibson, TN	32 751	68.4	70.9	1 395	85.2	10.1	-14.3	10.8	6.8	0.0	13.0	10.7
Giles, TN	19 829	70.1	72.5	1 011	65.3	10.6	-13.8	11.2	4.1	39.6	51.3	3.4
Grainger, TN	14 210	77.1	60.1	523	83.6	7.8	-16.6	7.8	0.0	47.4	0.0	1.3
Greene, TN	43 752	67.8	69.6	2 118	68.1	12.8	-11.6	12.8	8.7	0.0	40.4	6.9
Grundy, TN	9 441	80.3	55.2	244	81.1	7.1	-17.3	7.1	0.0	10.5	50.0	6.6
Hamblen, TN	39 340	63.7	69.3	1 719	86.0	13.3	-11.1	13.5	8.6	5.8	35.7	9.8
Hamilton, TN	207 180	46.5	80.7	18 563	77.6	23.9	-0.5	26.6	10.6	22.1	48.9	19.4
Hancock, TN	4 617	76.0	55.9	116	94.8	10.2	-14.2	10.1	0.0	0.0	46.2	16.7
Hardeman, TN	18 595	71.3	66.7	607	66.7	7.8	-16.6	9.4	5.1	2.7	16.2	0.0
Hardin, TN	17 644	72.1	66.9	588	80.6	9.8	-14.6	10.0	4.4	0.0	17.0	7.6
Hawkins, TN	37 146	69.3	70.4	1 552	82.5	10.0	-14.4	9.7	13.4	0.0	60.6	19.4
Haywood, TN	12 421	71.8	65.6	451	80.9	11.1	-13.3	15.9	5.7	25.0	52.2	0.0
Henderson, TN	17 140	70.5	69.3	577	78.0	9.3	-15.1	9.3	8.8	15.9	0.0	16.4
Henry, TN	21 791	69.6	70.5	716	90.6	12.1	-12.3	12.5	7.4	0.0	61.1	11.5
Hickman, TN	14 899	73.1	64.3	457	72.0	6.7	-17.7	6.9	2.4	0.0	0.0	5.9
Houston, TN	5 539	71.0	70.1	138	91.3	10.3	-14.1	10.0	2.4	0.0	87.5	19.6
Humphreys, TN	12 270	71.2	72.0	424	80.0	9.3	-15.1	9.1	2.7	4.8	47.8	8.3
Jackson, TN	7 671	77.2	61.6	212	88.2	8.4	-16.0	7.8	0.0	21.9	71.4	0.0
Jefferson, TN	29 455	64.6	71.0	2 593	41.0	12.8	-11.6	12.8	14.5	0.0	50.8	6.3
Johnson, TN	12 755	76.1	58.4	392	92.9	6.9	-17.5	6.9	2.1	0.0	40.7	6.4
Knox, TN	252 530	44.6	82.5	33 984	90.2	29.0	4.6	30.7	16.1	10.4	00.0	00.0
Lake, TN	5 492	79.3	56.0	205	90.7	5.4	-19.0	7.3	0.9	0.0	. . .	0.0
Lauderdale, TN	17 507	75.9	62.3	702	88.3	7.7	-16.7	9.3	4.1	24.4	6.0	18.1
Lawrence, TN	26 145	72.8	65.5	1 058	84.2	8.7	-15.7	8.8	9.7	0.0	13.8	4.8
Lewis, TN	7 466	70.7	69.5	346	83.2	8.5	-15.9	8.3	7.7	46.2	50.0	0.0
Lincoln, TN	21 361	67.1	69.6	943	86.4	11.9	-12.5	12.5	4.3	0.0	0.0	13.2
Loudon, TN	27 899	57.6	75.6	1 118	87.8	17.0	-7.4	17.3	4.1	42.4	31.8	8.4
McMinn, TN	33 110	66.9	69.3	1 433	63.2	10.8	-13.6	10.7	10.4	5.1	69.7	6.5
McNairy, TN	16 787	71.7	68.5	592	80.6	8.8	-15.6	8.8	6.2	0.0	67.9	0.0
Macon, TN	13 331	78.8	60.2	378	96.8	5.6	-18.8	5.6	0.0	0.0	51.9	1.3
Madison, TN	58 038	52.1	78.8	5 342	43.3	21.5	-2.9	25.6	11.4	16.8	50.8	15.1
Marion, TN	18 815	69.8	64.6	763	89.8	9.5	-14.9	9.8	3.7	0.0	16.7	8.3
Marshall, TN	17 615	67.6	73.6	784	87.6	10.6	-13.8	11.2	4.7	0.0	50.0	6.3
Maury, TN	45 288	58.4	77.9	2 338	83.0	13.6	-10.8	14.9	6.0	4.3	65.5	7.1
Meigs, TN	7 405	73.2	63.5	223	79.4	7.0	-17.4	7.1	0.0	0.0	100.0	0.0
Monroe, TN	25 955	70.5	66.7	1 196	64.9	10.1	-14.3	10.1	7.3	8.2	24.5	9.4
Montgomery, TN	79 823	46.1	84.3	8 526	88.2	19.3	-5.1	21.6	10.6	6.5	18.1	16.0
Moore, TN	3 939	63.4	76.6	245	82.9	11.8	-12.6	12.1	6.6	0.0	0.0	. . .
Morgan, TN	13 371	77.1	63.8	556	91.4	6.0	-18.4	6.2	0.0	61.1	0.0	0.0
Obion, TN	22 119	70.3	71.0	980	90.8	10.3	-14.1	10.8	3.7	0.0	60.0	11.5
Overton, TN	13 751	78.9	59.0	661	94.1	8.3	-16.1	8.2	0.0	14.0	57.1	10.1
Perry, TN	5 209	74.6	63.8	146	93.2	7.1	-17.3	7.2	3.8	0.0	. . .	0.0
Pickett, TN	3 466	76.5	62.9	162	95.1	9.1	-15.3	8.7	0.0	37.5	. . .	68.8
Polk, TN	11 113	75.4	62.2	304	82.2	7.5	-16.9	7.5	100.0	0.0	0.0	10.0
Putnam, TN	39 403	59.5	72.6	6 958	95.5	20.2	-4.2	20.1	25.1	6.5	60.1	9.7
Rhea, TN	18 894	68.9	65.3	1 202	85.3	9.1	-15.3	9.3	1.4	8.0	21.9	4.9
Roane, TN	36 455	61.3	74.8	1 573	91.7	14.8	-9.6	14.7	6.9	22.6	53.9	10.2
Robertson, TN	35 252	64.2	74.8	1 227	81.0	11.9	-12.5	12.7	4.4	4.9	17.6	3.3
Rutherford, TN	109 913	50.0	81.8	16 117	92.4	22.9	-1.5	23.5	18.8	17.5	31.1	11.8
Scott, TN	13 480	77.4	60.7	608	91.8	7.5	-16.9	7.5	0.0	14.3	0.0	0.0
Sequatchie, TN	7 610	71.8	66.7	316	87.0	10.2	-14.2	9.6	0.0	. . .	63.8	20.8
Sevier, TN	48 843	61.8	74.6	2 101	84.0	13.5	-10.9	13.4	16.5	24.2	35.5	8.4
Shelby, TN	558 056	45.4	80.8	50 931	77.9	25.3	0.9	35.1	12.8	16.2	48.6	15.2
Smith, TN	11 798	73.0	67.5	391	77.2	9.3	-15.1	9.1	6.9	23.2	58.5	1.2
Stewart, TN	8 486	67.7	74.3	329	90.9	10.2	-14.2	9.9	8.0	0.0	31.4	82.6
Sullivan, TN	108 605	57.2	75.8	4 970	76.9	18.1	-6.3	18.2	13.2	2.4	41.7	12.2
Sumner, TN	85 651	52.4	79.7	4 410	79.6	18.6	-5.8	18.8	11.8	17.3	38.2	13.2
Tipton, TN	31 856	62.1	74.6	1 769	79.4	10.8	-13.6	11.5	6.7	14.0	37.1	6.9
Trousdale, TN	4 852	73.8	61.4	154	76.6	8.9	-15.5	9.5	5.3	36.4	0.0	0.0
Unicoi, TN	12 744	68.3	67.7	495	92.1	10.6	-13.8	10.6	. . .	0.0	100.0	4.1
Union, TN	11 632	79.2	56.3	379	88.7	5.8	-18.6	5.8	0.0	0.0	0.0	0.0
Van Buren, TN	3 738	80.4	62.0	149	98.0	7.8	-16.6	7.9	0.0	0.0	. . .	0.0
Warren, TN	25 691	72.0	67.2	864	95.1	9.1	-15.3	9.4	1.8	0.0	60.4	5.5
Washington, TN	72 947	51.8	77.2	8 627	93.0	22.9	-1.5	22.7	17.2	46.6	71.1	21.3
Wayne, TN	11 733	76.7	61.3	553	88.1	8.0	-16.4	7.5	14.1	0.0	23.1	0.0
Weakley, TN	21 908	65.6	70.3	4 274	94.6	15.3	-9.1	15.0	12.3	0.0	58.8	19.1
White, TN	15 806	74.3	64.8	477	91.2	7.9	-16.5	8.0	2.8	0.0	33.3	0.0
Williamson, TN	81 620	29.8	90.1	4 118	69.3	44.4	20.0	46.2	20.9	26.7	56.5	17.6
Wilson, TN	58 683	53.0	80.9	2 961	71.5	19.6	-4.8	20.1	10.9	38.3	41.1	20.5

[3]May be of any race.
. . . = Not available.

452 THE ALMANAC OF AMERICAN EDUCATION (BERNAN PRESS)

Table C-1. Population, School, and Student Characteristics by County—*Continued*

STATE County	State/ county code	County type[1]	Population, 2005 Total	Percent 5 to 17 years	Number of schools and students, 2004–2005 School districts	Schools	Students	Resident enrollment, 2000 Total	Percent public	K–12	Percent public
			1	2	3	4	5	6	7	8	9
TEXAS	48 000		22 859 968	19.5	1 279	8 746	4 405 215	5 948 260	88.6	4 355 276	93.1
Anderson, TX	48 001	5	56 408	14.4	7	24	8 419	11 231	92.4	9 247	93.9
Andrews, TX	48 003	6	12 748	20.6	1	7	2 861	3 864	95.8	3 345	98.1
Angelina, TX	48 005	5	81 557	19.4	7	43	16 819	21 101	92.6	16 317	94.6
Aransas, TX	48 007	2	24 640	16.4	1	5	3 350	5 072	90.5	4 278	93.1
Archer, TX	48 009	3	9 095	19.6	4	8	1 982	2 406	93.5	1 914	98.2
Armstrong, TX	48 011	3	2 173	17.3	1	2	373	546	95.6	441	98.2
Atascosa, TX	48 013	1	43 226	21.3	5	30	8 569	11 272	94.5	9 568	95.8
Austin, TX	48 015	1	26 123	18.3	3	13	5 546	5 952	91.2	4 954	94.0
Bailey, TX	48 017	7	6 726	20.3	1	5	1 538	1 775	96.3	1 520	98.9
Bandera, TX	48 019	1	19 988	17.3	2	6	2 991	4 107	90.7	3 514	94.3
Bastrop, TX	48 021	1	69 932	19.3	3	20	9 881	14 375	91.1	12 022	94.0
Baylor, TX	48 023	6	3 843	16.4	1	3	620	878	96.8	725	97.5
Bee, TX	48 025	4	32 873	15.6	5	15	5 192	7 807	92.1	6 038	92.8
Bell, TX	48 027	2	256 057	20.2	13	122	54 254	65 774	88.3	47 400	94.6
Bexar, TX	48 029	1	1 518 370	19.8	41	487	285 329	407 384	85.9	293 733	91.0
Blanco, TX	48 031	8	9 110	17.7	2	6	1 669	1 847	91.6	1 529	93.5
Borden, TX	48 033	9	648	16.5	1	2	168	201	94.5	169	97.6
Bosque, TX	48 035	6	18 053	17.2	8	19	3 340	3 846	95.6	3 183	98.2
Bowie, TX	48 037	3	90 643	17.6	14	44	16 966	22 200	93.7	17 634	96.3
Brazoria, TX	48 039	1	278 484	19.7	8	89	52 598	68 391	88.6	51 867	92.2
Brazos, TX	48 041	3	156 305	14.3	4	43	22 861	73 264	94.2	23 599	93.2
Brewster, TX	48 043	7	9 079	14.8	4	7	1 307	2 971	95.1	1 557	97.3
Briscoe, TX	48 045	9	1 644	19.5	1	1	208	436	94.5	391	95.9
Brooks, TX	48 047	6	7 687	21.4	2	5	1 706	2 428	97.9	1 946	99.2
Brown, TX	48 049	5	38 664	18.1	9	35	7 397	9 963	85.6	7 533	96.7
Burleson, TX	48 051	3	17 238	18.2	3	12	3 117	3 971	91.2	3 357	94.7
Burnet, TX	48 053	6	41 676	16.0	2	13	6 903	7 243	91.2	6 182	94.2
Caldwell, TX	48 055	1	36 523	19.5	3	15	6 284	8 294	91.5	6 758	96.2
Calhoun, TX	48 057	3	20 606	20.1	1	9	4 260	5 469	90.7	4 555	94.2
Callahan, TX	48 059	3	13 516	17.6	4	11	2 679	3 130	95.8	2 652	99.0
Cameron, TX	48 061	2	378 311	22.8	11	142	92 249	109 790	93.9	85 966	95.3
Camp, TX	48 063	6	12 238	19.5	1	5	2 404	3 000	90.2	2 441	93.3
Carson, TX	48 065	3	6 586	19.5	4	8	1 267	1 779	95.0	1 445	97.9
Cass, TX	48 067	6	30 155	17.1	4	22	5 776	7 138	93.6	5 920	96.3
Castro, TX	48 069	6	7 640	22.9	3	6	1 753	2 425	94.6	2 104	99.0
Chambers, TX	48 071	1	28 411	19.7	3	20	5 932	7 139	93.6	5 800	96.6
Cherokee, TX	48 073	6	48 464	18.5	5	19	8 300	11 603	88.8	9 174	94.7
Childress, TX	48 075	7	7 676	15.6	1	3	1 115	1 691	91.4	1 356	98.7
Clay, TX	48 077	3	11 287	17.7	5	9	1 976	2 661	95.2	2 156	97.9
Cochran, TX	48 079	9	3 289	21.4	2	8	905	1 081	98.4	945	98.7
Coke, TX	48 081	8	3 612	18.2	2	17	803	937	97.2	803	98.4
Coleman, TX	48 083	6	8 665	16.9	4	15	1 590	2 018	94.3	1 748	98.2
Collin, TX	48 085	1	659 457	19.8	14	199	107 968	136 630	82.7	96 997	90.6
Collingsworth, TX	48 087	9	2 968	19.4	2	4	669	797	95.6	671	98.7
Colorado, TX	48 089	6	20 736	17.5	3	12	3 578	5 113	86.6	4 002	92.2
Comal, TX	48 091	1	96 018	17.3	4	35	19 297	19 006	87.4	15 339	90.6
Comanche, TX	48 093	7	13 709	18.4	4	9	2 398	3 192	96.0	2 762	98.6
Concho, TX	48 095	8	3 735	10.7	2	20	452	740	92.2	544	95.2
Cooke, TX	48 097	6	38 847	19.1	9	21	6 677	9 620	88.5	7 465	90.8
Coryell, TX	48 099	2	75 802	19.4	4	20	10 476	19 217	90.1	13 801	96.0
Cottle, TX	48 101	9	1 746	15.5	1	1	245	399	98.5	365	99.5
Crane, TX	48 103	6	3 837	21.6	1	3	958	1 256	97.3	1 055	96.8
Crockett, TX	48 105	7	3 934	18.6	1	4	808	1 129	98.8	1 026	100.0
Crosby, TX	48 107	3	6 686	21.2	3	11	1 400	1 992	96.4	1 671	98.4
Culberson, TX	48 109	9	2 627	21.8	1	3	622	888	96.4	741	97.2
Dallam, TX	48 111	7	6 174	22.9	1	1	147	1 650	93.0	1 394	93.8
Dallas, TX	48 113	1	2 305 454	19.4	46	652	407 793	591 553	84.7	441 372	90.6
Dawson, TX	48 115	6	14 256	17.7	4	7	2 622	3 867	94.6	3 057	97.6
Deaf Smith, TX	48 117	6	18 538	23.5	2	9	4 219	5 645	92.4	4 821	94.0
Delta, TX	48 119	1	5 480	17.3	1	3	904	1 344	93.8	1 091	94.8
Denton, TX	48 121	1	554 642	19.1	14	233	128 926	130 034	87.2	82 738	92.5
DeWitt, TX	48 123	6	20 507	16.4	6	22	4 551	4 753	92.9	3 894	94.2
Dickens, TX	48 125	8	2 646	12.9	2	2	417	545	96.0	443	97.1
Dimmit, TX	48 127	6	10 395	22.6	1	6	2 416	3 249	95.8	2 679	97.3
Donley, TX	48 129	8	3 889	15.8	2	4	677	1 031	96.9	716	98.0
Duval, TX	48 131	7	12 578	20.0	4	11	2 939	3 856	96.7	2 972	97.9
Eastland, TX	48 133	6	18 393	16.5	5	14	3 146	4 568	94.5	3 255	97.1
Ector, TX	48 135	3	125 339	20.8	2	42	26 327	36 067	94.1	27 951	96.3
Edwards, TX	48 137	9	1 987	21.1	2	5	694	598	97.8	510	98.4
Ellis, TX	48 139	1	133 474	20.1	11	54	27 802	32 112	88.6	25 302	92.2
El Paso, TX	48 141	2	721 598	21.7	14	264	167 885	226 320	91.9	167 423	94.2
Erath, TX	48 143	7	34 076	16.7	9	18	5 631	11 111	93.0	5 998	95.4
Falls, TX	48 145	6	17 646	20.6	5	16	3 237	5 024	91.7	4 202	94.4
Fannin, TX	48 147	6	33 142	16.5	9	25	5 642	7 106	91.7	5 730	93.9
Fayette, TX	48 149	6	22 537	16.2	5	12	3 701	4 935	86.7	4 067	89.1
Fisher, TX	48 151	8	4 089	17.2	2	7	694	971	97.6	832	99.5
Floyd, TX	48 153	6	7 174	22.3	2	11	1 674	2 161	95.5	1 888	99.0
Foard, TX	48 155	9	1 518	18.9	1	2	280	402	98.3	336	98.8
Fort Bend, TX	48 157	1	463 650	21.0	7	173	136 542	114 365	85.7	87 855	91.4
Franklin, TX	48 159	8	10 200	16.6	1	4	1 517	2 230	95.4	1 781	97.2

[1]County type codes are from the Economic Research Service of the United States Department of Agriculture. See notes and definitions at the end of this section.

Table C-1. Population, School, and Student Characteristics by County—*Continued*

STATE County	Characteristics of students, 2004–2005				Outcomes		Staff and students, 2004–2005		
	Percent with IEP[2]	Percent eligible for free or reduced-price lunch	Percent minority	Percent English-language learners	Number of graduates, 2003–2004	Percent dropouts, grades 9–12, 2001–2002	Number of teachers	Student-teacher ratio	Central administration staff
	10	11	12	13	14	15	16	17	18
TEXAS	11.8	47.7	62.3	15.5	. . .	3.8	294 545	15.0	. . .
Anderson, TX	14.6	53.4	36.0	4.0	. . .	2.1	644	13.1	72
Andrews, TX	18.4	36.6	59.8	9.3	. . .	2.5	209	13.7	12
Angelina, TX	14.5	57.5	44.1	10.2	. . .	5.8	1 189	14.1	61
Aransas, TX	15.9	58.1	40.2	4.6	. . .	2.5	232	14.4	13
Archer, TX	10.0	32.7	9.7	3.3	. . .	1.2	164	12.1	. . .
Armstrong, TX	16.6	48.5	9.7	1.6	. . .	0.9	39	9.6	3
Atascosa, TX	13.4	66.1	71.1	4.7	. . .	3.5	612	14.0	55
Austin, TX	14.7	40.4	42.5	8.6	. . .	1.3	416	13.3	19
Bailey, TX	13.8	73.2	70.4	14.3	. . .	3.9	120	12.8	8
Bandera, TX	17.0	44.4	22.8	3.3	. . .	3.8	234	12.8	11
Bastrop, TX	12.8	53.6	47.8	8.7	. . .	3.4	670	14.7	52
Baylor, TX	18.5	41.0	21.1	1.8	. . .	2.9	59	10.6	2
Bee, TX	11.7	69.5	75.6	2.5	. . .	3.3	362	14.4	19
Bell, TX	14.3	48.2	56.3	6.1	. . .	3.5	3 958	13.7	. . .
Bexar, TX	13.5	41.5	76.7	9.6	. . .	4.6	18 377	15.5	. . .
Blanco, TX	14.5	37.9	25.9	5.4	. . .	1.0	148	11.3	10
Borden, TX	10.1	11.9	24.4	1.2	. . .	. . .	19	8.8	3
Bosque, TX	14.7	51.9	27.1	6.5	. . .	3.9	264	12.7	. . .
Bowie, TX	16.8	50.0	37.1	1.3	. . .	2.9	1 257	13.5	. . .
Brazoria, TX	12.3	39.4	47.0	7.4	. . .	3.5	3 297	16.0	. . .
Brazos, TX	9.4	46.2	54.3	10.3	. . .	2.2	1 514	15.1	. . .
Brewster, TX	14.2	58.0	68.7	14.2	. . .	1.6	124	10.5	22
Briscoe, TX	11.1	46.6	29.8	8.2	. . .	. . .	22	9.6	2
Brooks, TX	14.9	83.4	95.1	4.7	. . .	4.5	132	12.9	. . .
Brown, TX	17.3	49.8	33.3	2.4	. . .	3.3	549	13.5	. . .
Burleson, TX	15.5	51.0	41.8	5.5	. . .	3.2	251	12.4	39
Burnet, TX	13.5	46.2	29.1	7.4	. . .	2.4	478	14.4	27
Caldwell, TX	13.9	57.7	61.5	5.7	. . .	3.1	444	14.2	15
Calhoun, TX	13.0	57.0	61.8	7.2	. . .	3.6	270	15.8	3
Callahan, TX	17.1	43.9	11.8	0.9	. . .	2.4	245	11.0	8
Cameron, TX	12.2	25.2	95.7	36.0	. . .	4.2	5 766	16.0	. . .
Camp, TX	16.1	63.6	49.8	13.3	. . .	2.9	171	14.1	8
Carson, TX	15.1	31.5	10.3	0.7	. . .	1.2	111	11.5	10
Cass, TX	18.1	53.7	26.8	0.9	. . .	1.2	487	11.9	39
Castro, TX	9.6	70.7	74.2	12.0	. . .	4.6	160	11.0	12
Chambers, TX	9.9	31.6	26.6	5.4	. . .	1.5	402	14.8	18
Cherokee, TX	12.3	66.9	49.3	15.4	. . .	2.5	622	13.3	41
Childress, TX	16.2	51.7	42.8	2.9	. . .	1.1	95	11.8	3
Clay, TX	15.0	35.4	7.2	0.5	. . .	1.9	173	11.4	. . .
Cochran, TX	15.0	69.0	60.0	11.5	. . .	2.6	95	9.5	6
Coke, TX	18.2	59.7	38.7	3.6	. . .	5.3	74	10.9	4
Coleman, TX	15.3	60.1	26.7	1.8	. . .	3.7	153	10.4	8
Collin, TX	11.7	17.5	34.3	9.1	. . .	1.4	7 508	14.4	349
Collingsworth, TX	13.0	61.6	41.7	7.6	. . .	2.2	68	9.9	4
Colorado, TX	14.9	51.3	49.5	7.3	. . .	2.7	288	12.4	18
Comal, TX	13.3	33.9	34.1	4.5	. . .	3.0	1 233	15.6	. . .
Comanche, TX	13.1	57.8	39.4	9.0	. . .	3.2	196	12.2	22
Concho, TX	12.6	55.5	43.2	2.4	. . .	. . .	43	10.5	3
Cooke, TX	16.4	45.4	27.4	7.4	. . .	3.1	491	13.6	. . .
Coryell, TX	14.5	40.8	38.6	1.3	. . .	2.9	756	13.9	38
Cottle, TX	15.1	66.5	52.7	1.6	. . .	. . .	26	9.6	1
Crane, TX	13.7	39.1	61.2	11.2	. . .	1.3	96	10.0	6
Crockett, TX	12.5	53.8	66.7	13.6	. . .	0.7	74	10.9	3
Crosby, TX	23.5	65.9	73.4	7.1	. . .	3.5	144	9.7	38
Culberson, TX	11.9	82.0	83.4	11.7	. . .	2.6	54	11.5	3
Dallam, TX	10.2	58.1	38.0	17.0	. . .	4.6	16	9.1	2
Dallas, TX	10.3	59.0	77.7	22.5	. . .	3.9	26 448	15.4	. . .
Dawson, TX	13.1	60.8	70.7	8.9	. . .	2.2	213	12.3	17
Deaf Smith, TX	13.1	71.2	80.8	13.1	. . .	3.4	292	14.4	15
Delta, TX	17.0	52.2	21.0	1.2	. . .	1.5	74	12.2	4
Denton, TX	11.4	25.2	34.8	11.8	. . .	2.0	9 029	14.3	299
DeWitt, TX	14.5	54.7	49.3	3.3	. . .	3.0	347	13.1	20
Dickens, TX	10.6	42.0	35.7	0.5	. . .	4.1	49	8.5	5
Dimmit, TX	9.6	79.6	92.7	9.8	. . .	6.8	175	13.8	10
Donley, TX	18.8	59.4	21.6	2.5	. . .	1.4	73	9.3	5
Duval, TX	11.1	75.1	93.5	9.2	. . .	2.8	235	12.5	. . .
Eastland, TX	17.9	58.2	21.7	4.1	. . .	1.7	270	11.7	26
Ector, TX	11.8	60.7	66.0	12.9	. . .	9.0	1 692	15.6	. . .
Edwards, TX	17.4	58.2	59.5	8.2	. . .	1.8	67	10.4	6
Ellis, TX	15.9	38.5	38.0	7.1	. . .	2.1	1 862	14.9	108
El Paso, TX	10.0	65.9	91.9	30.3	. . .	4.5	10 994	15.3	. . .
Erath, TX	11.7	46.8	31.0	9.4	. . .	2.1	412	13.7	31
Falls, TX	17.8	69.6	67.0	8.1	. . .	2.2	224	14.4	. . .
Fannin, TX	16.3	48.3	17.7	2.8	. . .	2.3	448	12.6	40
Fayette, TX	12.0	42.9	37.4	7.7	. . .	2.0	279	13.2	12
Fisher, TX	20.9	65.0	44.3	2.7	. . .	2.3	70	9.9	4
Floyd, TX	12.8	65.0	72.5	9.2	. . .	1.8	151	11.1	13
Foard, TX	18.9	76.4	26.1	2.1	. . .	. . .	26	10.8	2
Fort Bend, TX	10.4	29.9	63.9	10.7	. . .	2.4	8 494	16.1	358
Franklin, TX	14.6	43.8	24.6	7.9	. . .	2.8	113	13.5	3

[2]IEP = Individual Education Program. See notes and definitions at the end of this section.
. . . = Not available.

Table C-1. Population, School, and Student Characteristics by County—*Continued*

STATE County	Total revenue (thousands of dollars)	Federal government	State government	Local government	Total expenditures (thousands of dollars)	Amount per student (dollars)	Percent for instruction	Total	Percent in armed forces	Percent high school graduates	Percent not enrolled, not employed, not in armed forces, not high school graduate
	Revenue, 2003–2004				Current expenditures, 2003–2004			Resident population, 16 to 19 years, 2000			
	19	20	21	22	23	24	25	26	27	28	29
TEXAS	36 474 488	10.5	37.1	52.3	30 700 152	7 094	65.8	1 289 185	0.9	11.0	7.1
Anderson, TX	64 924	10.0	45.9	44.1	56 905	6 841	66.4	2 368	0.0	18.1	7.3
Andrews, TX	35 404	5.7	7.2	87.1	23 420	7 896	64.5	1 054	0.0	8.8	8.9
Angelina, TX	123 508	10.8	52.7	36.6	109 617	6 627	64.6	4 890	0.0	11.5	5.4
Aransas, TX	31 192	11.8	14.1	74.1	24 704	7 390	61.1	1 352	0.4	16.3	4.7
Archer, TX	16 385	8.6	56.4	35.1	14 990	7 767	66.6	542	0.0	12.5	1.8
Armstrong, TX	3 700	5.7	54.4	39.9	2 932	7 840	70.5	120	0.0	9.2	5.0
Atascosa, TX	71 247	13.4	61.6	25.0	65 865	7 742	65.6	2 596	0.0	13.4	5.3
Austin, TX	41 289	7.2	41.6	51.1	37 959	7 050	67.1	1 567	0.0	9.3	2.9
Bailey, TX	12 581	12.4	62.5	25.1	10 885	7 330	66.3	412	0.5	6.6	2.2
Bandera, TX	27 783	6.6	40.1	53.3	22 158	7 366	65.9	907	0.0	6.5	2.0
Bastrop, TX	104 094	9.0	40.4	50.6	89 461	6 994	64.5	3 217	0.0	16.1	6.6
Baylor, TX	7 180	6.6	60.8	32.6	5 770	8 850	66.9	182	0.0	8.8	8.8
Bee, TX	44 234	14.8	54.3	30.9	38 757	7 412	63.8	2 204	0.0	6.9	12.6
Bell, TX	456 185	18.4	53.5	28.1	393 433	7 343	66.6	14 633	8.5	21.9	5.4
Bexar, TX	2 427 055	12.0	45.9	42.1	2 028 515	7 235	66.0	87 106	4.4	14.3	6.8
Blanco, TX	14 421	6.7	29.5	63.9	13 004	8 052	66.3	427	0.0	8.9	7.3
Borden, TX	4 841	3.5	4.8	91.7	3 448	21 550	52.3	48	0.0	0.0	8.3
Bosque, TX	28 607	10.9	40.3	48.8	25 273	7 772	63.5	938	0.0	10.8	4.4
Bowie, TX	128 939	12.1	49.4	38.5	111 408	6 708	66.4	4 819	0.0	13.7	4.8
Brazoria, TX	417 424	6.7	29.3	64.0	338 536	6 632	64.3	13 901	0.1	10.6	6.3
Brazos, TX	188 526	9.8	30.5	59.7	152 248	6 813	67.0	17 536	0.1	5.0	1.8
Brewster, TX	14 110	13.1	43.8	43.1	11 528	8 124	65.6	601	0.0	9.2	2.5
Briscoe, TX	2 192	9.3	53.5	37.2	1 968	8 410	68.2	110	0.0	5.5	6.4
Brooks, TX	15 284	16.2	26.5	57.2	14 225	8 368	63.8	597	0.0	9.2	16.2
Brown, TX	57 465	11.6	52.0	36.4	50 850	7 308	67.1	2 771	0.0	12.6	7.1
Burleson, TX	26 209	12.0	46.0	42.0	24 471	7 891	62.9	980	0.0	12.0	5.1
Burnet, TX	59 949	7.5	20.3	72.2	50 783	7 483	62.8	1 721	0.0	16.8	4.6
Caldwell, TX	50 276	12.5	51.7	35.8	44 931	7 108	65.8	1 963	0.0	16.1	7.5
Calhoun, TX	56 427	5.7	6.6	87.7	30 680	7 138	61.6	1 206	0.0	12.7	6.6
Callahan, TX	23 668	5.6	63.1	31.3	20 841	7 499	64.5	731	0.0	11.9	3.4
Cameron, TX	792 323	15.7	64.7	19.6	666 212	7 236	65.8	23 139	0.1	8.2	8.1
Camp, TX	18 728	13.1	46.7	40.2	16 102	6 902	72.0	723	0.0	16.5	3.7
Carson, TX	12 070	4.3	15.8	80.0	10 408	8 820	64.3	394	0.0	13.5	1.0
Cass, TX	49 171	12.6	54.0	33.4	45 078	7 649	67.9	1 700	0.0	14.1	6.1
Castro, TX	16 721	16.7	53.2	30.1	14 926	8 698	67.1	561	0.0	8.9	6.2
Chambers, TX	62 227	4.4	22.9	72.6	42 675	7 549	64.6	1 623	0.0	9.1	5.5
Cherokee, TX	63 545	12.6	56.0	31.4	55 776	6 778	65.1	2 826	0.0	14.6	6.0
Childress, TX	10 426	10.7	63.3	26.0	8 822	7 665	67.3	424	0.0	9.4	18.2
Clay, TX	18 182	9.6	55.0	35.5	16 136	8 056	64.2	607	0.0	9.1	7.4
Cochran, TX	12 223	9.7	35.7	54.6	10 856	12 143	61.5	310	0.0	9.7	3.5
Coke, TX	8 978	7.5	60.0	32.5	7 618	9 511	65.7	411	0.0	5.4	21.7
Coleman, TX	16 278	9.0	57.7	33.3	13 441	8 395	61.9	473	0.0	14.0	2.3
Collin, TX	1 115 396	3.4	13.9	82.7	805 010	7 083	68.2	23 575	0.0	10.8	3.5
Collingsworth, TX	6 456	7.0	71.1	21.9	6 048	8 894	69.3	203	0.0	10.3	3.9
Colorado, TX	30 234	9.9	34.3	55.8	27 593	7 402	64.2	1 417	0.0	10.3	4.0
Comal, TX	151 613	7.0	19.3	73.7	120 118	6 515	62.7	4 523	0.0	15.8	5.1
Comanche, TX	18 914	13.1	59.2	27.7	16 918	7 111	67.1	814	0.0	5.7	4.5
Concho, TX	4 535	8.0	35.3	56.6	4 167	8 923	56.8	210	0.0	7.1	18.1
Cooke, TX	51 693	9.8	46.7	43.5	46 557	7 394	65.2	2 350	0.1	10.3	5.8
Coryell, TX	85 658	18.5	56.3	25.2	74 137	6 898	67.2	4 827	31.6	41.0	4.3
Cottle, TX	2 995	9.9	38.5	51.6	2 320	8 722	68.0	92	0.0	6.5	5.4
Crane, TX	14 140	4.4	7.3	88.3	10 790	10 704	65.9	341	0.0	10.3	6.5
Crockett, TX	17 057	3.4	5.5	91.1	8 706	10 553	63.0	203	0.0	0.0	0.0
Crosby, TX	16 630	20.6	56.7	22.6	14 972	10 603	65.1	456	0.0	11.2	6.8
Culberson, TX	6 476	11.6	33.8	54.6	5 987	9 003	62.8	257	0.0	9.3	5.1
Dallam, TX	13 608	13.2	36.5	50.2	12 788	7 221	66.9	397	0.0	14.6	7.8
Dallas, TX	3 661 632	9.5	25.4	65.1	2 984 893	6 917	66.5	126 851	0.0	10.6	9.6
Dawson, TX	24 582	14.1	40.6	45.2	21 024	7 827	64.4	880	0.0	11.8	9.5
Deaf Smith, TX	32 062	16.7	55.8	27.5	28 153	6 862	66.4	1 254	0.0	16.8	6.4
Delta, TX	10 611	10.4	67.9	21.8	8 984	7 772	65.4	317	0.0	12.0	7.9
Denton, TX	741 628	4.9	16.4	78.7	582 971	7 074	66.7	24 095	0.1	10.6	3.0
DeWitt, TX	38 857	10.6	55.8	33.6	34 976	7 738	67.2	1 062	0.0	9.8	9.2
Dickens, TX	5 839	19.7	42.8	37.5	5 527	12 648	65.9	120	0.0	8.3	10.8
Dimmit, TX	21 424	17.6	61.3	21.1	18 855	7 588	64.6	637	0.0	7.5	6.8
Donley, TX	7 113	6.4	64.4	29.2	6 363	8 777	65.8	300	0.0	6.3	0.7
Duval, TX	28 164	13.7	56.7	29.6	25 082	8 369	63.7	867	0.0	11.3	4.0
Eastland, TX	27 215	12.0	58.4	29.6	24 622	7 902	66.0	1 262	0.0	5.5	5.9
Ector, TX	183 272	13.0	46.6	40.4	163 363	6 229	65.9	8 435	0.1	10.4	5.9
Edwards, TX	7 508	10.6	27.9	61.5	6 726	9 636	60.3	120	0.0	1.7	0.0
Ellis, TX	216 215	6.7	41.8	51.6	189 824	6 987	66.0	7 342	0.0	11.7	4.2
El Paso, TX	1 314 768	16.9	59.5	23.6	1 199 010	7 247	66.2	45 857	1.3	9.9	6.6
Erath, TX	44 292	9.2	45.4	45.4	36 613	6 526	66.9	2 435	0.0	7.2	3.8
Falls, TX	29 608	14.6	53.8	31.5	24 474	8 501	66.7	1 445	0.1	11.7	12.5
Fannin, TX	45 693	10.9	58.4	30.7	39 796	7 469	65.2	1 694	0.0	17.0	9.4
Fayette, TX	32 547	6.0	22.9	71.1	26 850	7 231	65.0	1 245	0.0	7.9	5.4
Fisher, TX	7 580	7.5	66.8	25.6	6 859	9 999	64.6	269	0.0	13.0	1.9
Floyd, TX	15 972	13.7	60.9	25.4	14 574	8 573	66.0	509	0.0	3.7	15.3
Foard, TX	3 002	10.5	52.9	36.5	2 821	9 435	60.5	90	0.0	4.4	0.0
Fort Bend, TX	651 653	5.8	37.9	56.3	566 834	6 706	66.6	22 536	0.0	8.0	4.6
Franklin, TX	11 042	9.9	18.0	72.1	10 058	6 898	69.0	545	0.0	10.6	5.0

Table C-1. Population, School, and Student Characteristics by County—*Continued*

STATE County	High school graduates, 2000			College enrollment, 2000		College graduates, 2000 (percent)						
	Population 25 years and over	High school graduate or less (percent)	High school graduate or more (percent)	Number	Percent public	Bachelor's degree or more	+/- U.S. percentage with bachelor's degree or more	Non-Hispanic White	Black	American Indian and Alaska Native	Asian or Pacific Islander	Hispanic[3]
	30	31	32	33	34	35	36	37	38	39	40	41
TEXAS	12 790 893	49.2	75.7	1 202 890	82.6	23.2	-1.2	30.0	15.3	15.7	47.2	8.9
Anderson, TX	38 506	63.8	64.4	1 438	88.0	11.1	-13.3	14.9	4.3	17.9	27.3	2.3
Andrews, TX	7 815	64.6	68.0	334	83.8	12.4	-12.0	16.9	6.3	16.3	0.0	3.8
Angelina, TX	50 290	58.1	71.2	3 308	92.4	14.7	-9.7	17.5	5.9	7.3	26.0	5.0
Aransas, TX	15 728	54.5	74.6	498	86.1	16.7	-7.7	19.7	1.8	1.1	7.1	4.9
Archer, TX	5 729	54.9	81.1	316	90.2	15.9	-8.5	15.9	0.0	32.1	85.7	7.9
Armstrong, TX	1 458	45.4	82.4	81	95.1	20.5	-3.9	20.9	. . .	50.0	. . .	0.0
Atascosa, TX	22 751	66.8	65.2	1 183	89.9	10.5	-13.9	17.3	0.0	19.2	28.1	4.3
Austin, TX	15 280	57.8	74.5	647	91.5	17.3	-7.1	21.0	3.5	20.0	72.0	3.0
Bailey, TX	3 960	70.0	61.5	139	92.1	9.3	-15.1	14.5	0.0	0.0	. . .	1.3
Bandera, TX	12 287	47.1	84.8	423	71.4	19.4	-5.0	20.8	0.0	14.7	8.3	9.0
Bastrop, TX	37 249	54.8	76.9	1 514	83.0	17.0	-7.4	21.0	6.6	4.4	14.6	6.5
Baylor, TX	2 939	62.6	70.1	99	89.9	12.1	-12.3	13.4	0.0	15.8	0.0	2.8
Bee, TX	20 568	61.1	73.7	1 373	91.5	12.2	-12.2	20.4	3.7	0.0	25.9	7.5
Bell, TX	137 430	42.8	84.7	13 867	75.4	19.8	-4.6	24.5	11.1	17.0	22.3	9.5
Bexar, TX	849 004	47.4	76.9	88 075	77.0	22.7	-1.7	36.6	17.8	13.3	38.0	10.8
Blanco, TX	5 895	49.9	80.6	196	75.5	22.2	-2.2	24.8	23.2	26.2	0.0	3.0
Borden, TX	490	49.0	83.9	29	75.9	21.4	-3.0	23.2	. . .	0.0	100.0	0.0
Bosque, TX	11 910	56.2	75.9	456	89.5	15.4	-9.0	16.7	5.1	9.0	64.3	2.5
Bowie, TX	58 767	54.6	77.3	3 226	91.1	16.1	-8.3	19.1	7.5	18.2	48.1	3.7
Brazoria, TX	152 244	47.7	79.5	11 894	87.4	19.6	-4.8	22.3	17.2	11.8	51.2	7.6
Brazos, TX	70 708	38.8	81.3	47 039	97.8	37.0	12.6	43.7	10.4	24.4	80.6	14.9
Brewster, TX	5 519	42.5	78.6	1 330	95.6	27.7	3.3	36.9	44.0	0.0	38.1	12.7
Briscoe, TX	1 181	55.6	74.8	26	84.6	17.5	-6.9	20.9	6.7	. . .	. . .	1.1
Brooks, TX	4 717	73.5	49.9	280	96.8	6.8	-17.6	9.7	0.0	21.8	. . .	6.3
Brown, TX	24 016	60.4	74.6	1 805	41.5	15.0	-9.4	16.7	10.1	11.9	35.3	2.6
Burleson, TX	10 787	66.4	71.1	413	85.0	13.2	-11.2	16.4	4.5	19.5	85.7	2.7
Burnet, TX	23 436	54.7	77.8	599	86.5	17.4	-7.0	19.2	2.4	10.8	12.9	3.5
Caldwell, TX	20 337	63.5	71.3	948	82.3	13.3	-11.1	19.9	3.9	7.3	35.2	4.7
Calhoun, TX	13 012	64.1	69.0	541	80.6	12.1	-12.3	15.0	3.0	0.0	65.0	3.1
Callahan, TX	8 658	58.8	79.3	308	78.9	12.3	-12.1	12.8	7.4	4.2	62.5	1.1
Cameron, TX	187 064	64.9	55.2	16 722	91.1	13.4	-11.0	28.9	28.0	10.4	56.6	8.9
Camp, TX	7 474	63.1	69.5	333	93.4	12.2	-12.2	15.2	5.4	0.0	50.9	1.1
Carson, TX	4 305	48.4	82.6	264	85.6	15.5	-8.9	16.1	0.0	0.0	50.0	5.9
Cass, TX	20 546	63.2	75.0	817	85.3	12.0	-12.4	13.6	4.8	8.5	4.3	6.0
Castro, TX	4 871	64.3	65.4	140	00.0	14.7	-9.7	24.7	7.7	0.0	0.0	2.4
Chambers, TX	16 348	55.5	76.9	942	91.8	12.1	-12.3	13.0	8.3	18.0	21.4	6.1
Cherokee, TX	30 008	63.6	68.4	1 712	64.1	11.4	-13.0	13.4	5.7	16.7	43.5	3.3
Childress, TX	5 173	66.0	65.0	237	61.6	8.6	-15.8	10.9	6.0	0.0	50.0	0.0
Clay, TX	7 549	59.2	80.4	372	91.1	13.9	-10.5	14.1	0.0	0.0	0.0	8.0
Cochran, TX	2 236	65.6	62.7	85	94.1	10.2	-14.2	15.1	9.5	0.0	. . .	2.5
Coke, TX	2 620	59.8	74.2	80	07.5	14.7	-9.7	15.7	0.0	40.0	100.0	5.4
Coleman, TX	6 373	67.2	71.0	180	71.1	11.7	-12.7	12.7	2.3	19.6	0.0	4.1
Collin, TX	315 665	23.2	91.8	25 951	82.3	47.3	22.9	48.2	42.9	28.7	72.0	22.4
Collingsworth, TX	2 159	54.2	71.3	81	95.1	15.3	-9.1	18.0	9.7	0.0	100.0	1.9
Colorado, TX	13 383	64.3	69.1	821	72.5	14.4	-10.0	18.6	5.0	38.9	0.0	3.1
Comal, TX	52 549	44.6	83.9	2 441	86.6	26.2	1.8	30.0	26.3	20.7	46.6	0.0
Comanche, TX	9 411	64.4	70.2	291	80.1	13.0	-11.4	14.8	0.0	0.0	9.1	2.6
Concho, TX	2 921	67.9	59.3	144	86.1	14.1	-10.3	19.8	15.2	50.0	0.0	5.9
Cooke, TX	23 148	52.3	79.2	1 538	91.1	15.7	-8.7	16.6	10.8	11.6	57.5	3.5
Coryell, TX	41 764	51.0	81.1	4 134	77.0	12.4	-12.0	14.8	7.4	7.6	17.8	6.6
Cottle, TX	1 342	64.5	66.1	17	82.4	15.3	-9.1	19.0	0.0	. . .	. . .	2.1
Crane, TX	2 394	64.2	68.7	127	100.0	12.8	-11.6	17.6	0.0	0.0	89.5	2.1
Crockett, TX	2 659	66.8	62.1	42	85.7	10.4	-14.0	19.4	0.0	31.8	0.0	1.9
Crosby, TX	4 299	68.8	61.8	184	81.0	10.5	-13.9	17.8	2.9	0.0	0.0	1.4
Culberson, TX	1 781	71.5	56.1	111	90.1	13.9	-10.5	31.0	66.7	0.0	80.0	4.5
Dallam, TX	3 703	67.1	65.0	138	94.2	9.6	-14.8	12.7	0.0	17.3	. . .	0.1
Dallas, TX	1 365 848	46.7	75.0	108 942	72.2	27.0	2.6	38.0	17.0	16.2	45.2	7.0
Dawson, TX	9 949	69.6	65.2	579	85.3	10.5	-13.9	20.2	1.3	54.5	15.4	1.4
Deaf Smith, TX	10 539	65.6	60.9	553	85.2	11.8	-12.6	20.7	2.4	0.0	21.8	2.2
Delta, TX	3 618	60.6	75.5	186	86.0	13.9	-10.5	15.1	3.1	14.8	0.0	0.0
Denton, TX	265 220	30.5	89.4	37 656	88.8	36.6	12.2	38.7	33.8	24.1	47.1	17.9
DeWitt, TX	13 969	65.0	67.9	578	92.6	11.8	-12.6	17.1	2.3	0.0	53.8	2.4
Dickens, TX	1 940	67.9	70.6	63	88.9	8.4	-16.0	10.8	0.0	44.4	25.0	0.8
Dimmit, TX	5 982	72.0	54.3	419	89.7	10.1	-14.3	19.1	27.2	42.1	45.5	7.5
Donley, TX	2 586	48.3	78.2	282	93.6	15.8	-8.6	16.6	0.0	6.4	0.0	7.2
Duval, TX	8 042	70.0	59.7	583	91.3	8.9	-15.5	13.7	0.0	0.0	0.0	8.3
Eastland, TX	12 171	60.9	72.6	1 000	90.8	12.7	-11.7	13.6	18.4	4.5	100.0	2.4
Ector, TX	71 756	58.8	68.0	5 731	93.0	12.0	-12.4	16.2	7.7	8.3	56.4	4.5
Edwards, TX	1 418	62.3	67.1	44	93.2	17.3	-7.1	26.1	0.0	0.0	0.0	3.5
Ellis, TX	67 470	53.0	77.8	4 799	81.8	17.1	-7.3	19.8	11.6	16.0	62.9	4.2
El Paso, TX	391 540	56.8	65.8	46 798	87.3	16.6	-7.8	35.1	21.1	13.6	40.8	10.6
Erath, TX	19 350	49.5	77.1	4 587	94.7	25.0	0.6	27.4	50.9	0.0	50.6	4.2
Falls, TX	12 013	67.9	66.2	539	82.6	9.6	-14.8	12.8	5.3	0.0	37.5	1.8
Fannin, TX	21 120	63.2	72.5	945	85.1	12.6	-11.8	13.9	3.0	10.0	31.7	3.2
Fayette, TX	15 183	64.5	71.3	585	86.8	14.6	-9.8	16.7	1.5	37.9	77.3	2.8
Fisher, TX	3 036	65.1	73.3	77	88.3	12.4	-12.0	15.1	0.0	0.0	100.0	0.8
Floyd, TX	4 773	67.5	63.5	122	72.1	12.3	-12.1	18.9	0.0	0.0	0.0	1.5
Foard, TX	1 116	65.1	70.0	40	92.5	10.5	-13.9	12.1	8.3	0.0	0.0	2.6
Fort Bend, TX	214 461	35.1	84.3	18 037	81.3	36.9	12.5	44.1	30.0	18.0	56.1	11.9
Franklin, TX	6 421	58.2	77.4	308	93.8	16.2	-8.2	17.5	5.0	4.5	16.7	2.1

[3]May be of any race.
. . . = Not available.

Table C-1. Population, School, and Student Characteristics by County—*Continued*

STATE County	State/ county code	County type[1]	Population, 2005		Number of schools and students, 2004–2005			Resident enrollment, 2000			
			Total	Percent 5 to 17 years	School districts	Schools	Students	Total	Percent public	K–12	Percent public
			1	2	3	4	5	6	7	8	9
Freestone, TX	48 161	7	18 800	16.2	4	14	3 445	4 486	92.0	3 443	93.7
Frio, TX	48 163	6	16 387	19.6	2	11	3 177	4 659	96.2	3 752	97.7
Gaines, TX	48 165	7	14 712	23.1	3	11	2 903	4 369	88.8	3 831	89.2
Galveston, TX	48 167	1	277 563	18.6	12	114	72 169	69 639	89.0	50 267	92.4
Garza, TX	48 169	6	5 002	21.3	2	5	1 133	1 384	94.4	1 104	96.9
Gillespie, TX	48 171	7	23 088	14.7	3	10	3 445	4 229	84.5	3 474	88.7
Glasscock, TX	48 173	8	1 327	22.9	1	2	314	458	98.3	389	100.0
Goliad, TX	48 175	3	7 102	17.2	1	4	1 320	1 652	92.4	1 429	93.9
Gonzales, TX	48 177	6	19 587	18.5	3	14	3 830	4 671	95.0	3 989	96.7
Gray, TX	48 179	6	21 479	17.2	3	9	3 685	5 609	91.4	4 460	94.3
Grayson, TX	48 181	3	116 834	17.7	13	67	21 031	27 885	88.0	20 779	95.4
Gregg, TX	48 183	3	115 649	18.5	7	43	17 401	29 686	88.2	22 659	94.4
Grimes, TX	48 185	6	25 192	16.8	4	13	4 135	5 846	94.2	4 727	97.6
Guadalupe, TX	48 187	1	103 032	19.5	4	37	18 066	25 322	85.7	19 460	92.8
Hale, TX	48 189	4	36 233	21.2	5	25	7 959	10 891	88.6	8 463	96.1
Hall, TX	48 191	9	3 700	19.5	2	5	820	880	94.9	767	97.8
Hamilton, TX	48 193	6	8 105	17.1	3	7	1 824	1 863	95.4	1 544	98.8
Hansford, TX	48 195	7	5 230	19.5	3	7	1 278	1 408	95.6	1 193	98.7
Hardeman, TX	48 197	7	4 291	17.3	2	5	808	1 135	97.7	928	100.0
Hardin, TX	48 199	2	50 976	18.7	5	26	10 861	12 456	93.2	10 212	96.6
Harris, TX	48 201	1	3 693 050	20.0	68	947	680 957	973 905	87.8	722 117	92.6
Harrison, TX	48 203	4	63 459	18.6	6	33	12 277	17 187	83.7	12 987	94.2
Hartley, TX	48 205	9	5 450	14.6	3	7	1 888	1 190	79.4	942	84.3
Haskell, TX	48 207	6	5 541	16.1	4	7	930	1 375	97.8	1 172	98.6
Hays, TX	48 209	1	124 432	16.2	6	42	22 514	35 718	92.5	17 740	92.6
Hemphill, TX	48 211	9	3 422	19.8	1	5	625	908	97.2	784	100.0
Henderson, TX	48 213	4	80 017	17.3	8	33	10 657	16 770	92.0	13 310	94.5
Hidalgo, TX	48 215	2	678 275	23.5	26	283	175 953	188 181	96.2	148 929	97.5
Hill, TX	48 217	6	35 424	17.7	12	38	6 261	7 820	93.1	6 183	96.5
Hockley, TX	48 219	6	22 787	19.7	6	21	4 880	6 942	96.0	5 043	97.3
Hood, TX	48 221	4	47 930	16.7	3	15	7 509	9 233	90.7	7 446	94.4
Hopkins, TX	48 223	6	33 381	18.1	7	17	6 548	7 986	92.9	6 452	95.6
Houston, TX	48 225	7	23 218	16.4	6	16	3 778	5 478	87.6	4 723	88.0
Howard, TX	48 227	5	32 522	16.8	3	14	5 235	8 543	93.7	6 459	96.6
Hudspeth, TX	48 229	8	3 295	23.8	3	5	853	1 000	96.0	857	97.9
Hunt, TX	48 231	1	82 543	18.2	11	46	14 696	21 088	91.0	15 431	93.6
Hutchinson, TX	48 233	6	22 484	19.3	4	15	4 407	6 379	93.5	4 939	95.8
Irion, TX	48 235	3	1 756	17.4	1	2	355	474	94.5	392	96.7
Jack, TX	48 237	6	9 064	16.4	3	7	1 652	2 103	89.2	1 705	93.6
Jackson, TX	48 239	6	14 339	18.6	3	10	3 129	3 738	96.3	3 043	98.5
Jasper, TX	48 241	6	35 587	18.4	5	16	7 030	8 698	93.3	7 329	95.2
Jeff Davis, TX	48 243	9	2 306	17.6	2	4	413	555	89.9	486	89.1
Jefferson, TX	48 245	2	247 571	18.3	12	89	43 863	67 831	89.7	51 343	92.3
Jim Hogg, TX	48 247	6	5 029	21.2	1	3	1 135	1 506	96.7	1 255	99.1
Jim Wells, TX	48 249	4	40 951	21.5	5	21	8 932	11 609	95.9	9 350	97.3
Johnson, TX	48 251	1	146 376	19.6	8	55	20 422	34 577	86.7	27 610	92.2
Jones, TX	48 253	3	19 736	15.9	5	14	2 818	5 352	91.2	4 722	92.9
Karnes, TX	48 255	6	15 351	14.9	4	17	2 381	3 494	95.5	2 936	97.0
Kaufman, TX	48 257	1	89 129	19.4	7	46	20 032	19 166	88.7	15 607	92.8
Kendall, TX	48 259	1	28 607	18.4	2	13	6 846	6 471	88.4	5 062	93.5
Kenedy, TX	48 261	9	417	18.5	1	1	83	104	97.1	94	100.0
Kent, TX	48 263	9	782	13.2	1	1	128	179	98.9	165	98.8
Kerr, TX	48 265	4	46 496	16.0	5	21	7 032	9 399	85.1	7 821	93.2
Kimble, TX	48 267	7	4 591	16.5	1	3	723	1 035	95.7	908	99.3
King, TX	48 269	9	307	24.4	1	1	96	84	97.6	82	97.6
Kinney, TX	48 271	9	3 327	17.2	1	4	611	807	98.0	699	98.1
Kleberg, TX	48 273	4	30 757	18.4	4	20	5 699	11 650	92.4	6 437	93.0
Knox, TX	48 275	9	3 781	20.2	3	7	854	1 129	96.5	985	97.9
Lamar, TX	48 277	4	49 644	18.7	5	26	9 292	12 054	91.2	9 355	93.8
Lamb, TX	48 279	6	14 467	19.8	6	19	3 314	3 793	96.1	3 310	98.4
Lampasas, TX	48 281	2	19 669	18.7	3	6	3 634	4 706	93.2	3 831	96.6
La Salle, TX	48 283	6	6 016	19.9	1	7	1 271	1 545	97.7	1 318	99.5
Lavaca, TX	48 285	6	18 925	16.5	6	17	2 118	4 471	83.9	3 668	86.0
Lee, TX	48 287	6	16 526	20.3	4	11	3 373	3 941	88.3	3 331	89.7
Leon, TX	48 289	8	16 344	16.4	5	12	2 968	3 454	94.7	2 957	97.4
Liberty, TX	48 291	1	75 141	19.2	7	41	14 790	17 632	93.0	15 097	95.6
Limestone, TX	48 293	6	22 763	17.9	3	13	4 235	5 437	95.5	4 356	97.1
Lipscomb, TX	48 295	9	3 101	19.2	4	5	722	737	98.4	664	98.9
Live Oak, TX	48 297	6	11 717	15.2	2	8	1 837	2 803	91.8	2 360	94.7
Llano, TX	48 299	7	18 236	11.9	1	4	1 947	2 364	92.4	2 070	95.0
Loving, TX	48 301	9	62	12.9	. . .	. . .	27	85.2	16	100.0	
Lubbock, TX	48 303	3	252 284	17.4	13	158	43 007	80 919	90.8	46 144	94.0
Lynn, TX	48 305	6	6 237	20.9	4	9	1 435	1 884	95.3	1 625	97.0
McCulloch, TX	48 307	7	7 956	18.8	3	7	1 648	1 813	97.1	1 587	98.6
McLennan, TX	48 309	3	224 668	18.6	24	144	41 260	68 392	76.0	41 749	92.7
McMullen, TX	48 311	8	883	14.8	1	1	180	191	94.8	172	97.1
Madison, TX	48 313	6	13 167	14.9	2	6	2 468	2 887	93.2	2 184	98.3
Marion, TX	48 315	8	10 952	16.1	1	3	1 395	2 167	90.8	1 872	92.1
Martin, TX	48 317	6	4 391	23.6	2	4	1 000	1 383	96.2	1 176	98.6
Mason, TX	48 319	9	3 880	15.1	1	3	603	756	95.4	666	96.1

[1]County type codes are from the Economic Research Service of the United States Department of Agriculture. See notes and definitions at the end of this section.
. . . = Not available.

Table C-1. Population, School, and Student Characteristics by County—*Continued*

STATE County	Characteristics of students, 2004–2005				Outcomes		Staff and students, 2004–2005		
	Percent with IEP[2]	Percent eligible for free or reduced-price lunch	Percent minority	Percent English-language learners	Number of graduates, 2003–2004	Percent dropouts, grades 9–12, 2001–2002	Number of teachers	Student-teacher ratio	Central administration staff
	10	11	12	13	14	15	16	17	18
Freestone, TX	14.7	41.0	33.2	5.3	...	1.8	257	13.4	38
Frio, TX	12.6	68.7	88.4	8.4	...	4.2	237	13.4	12
Gaines, TX	15.3	58.1	48.4	11.5	...	1.7	247	11.7	13
Galveston, TX	10.3	40.9	46.8	7.0	...	3.7	4 398	16.4	...
Garza, TX	18.5	62.2	51.7	4.2	...	4.4	104	10.9	3
Gillespie, TX	11.8	42.6	34.9	7.5	...	1.4	254	13.6	...
Glasscock, TX	11.1	47.8	36.9	11.1	...	...	28	11.1	2
Goliad, TX	14.7	45.4	48.9	2.8	...	0.7	112	11.8	42
Gonzales, TX	11.1	67.0	65.3	8.8	...	1.7	284	13.5	26
Gray, TX	11.9	44.0	30.6	4.6	...	3.9	267	13.8	20
Grayson, TX	16.3	41.3	22.0	5.2	...	2.9	1 573	13.4	87
Gregg, TX	12.9	49.3	44.6	7.8	...	3.6	1 221	14.3	...
Grimes, TX	11.1	58.0	49.2	6.0	...	1.8	290	14.3	20
Guadalupe, TX	12.3	40.2	51.6	4.9	...	2.9	1 240	14.6	34
Hale, TX	14.6	63.6	73.2	8.1	...	4.0	582	13.7	32
Hall, TX	14.9	65.6	52.9	13.4	...	0.9	75	11.0	5
Hamilton, TX	12.5	43.6	12.9	4.7	...	2.0	155	11.8	9
Hansford, TX	10.2	53.9	51.5	17.3	...	1.8	128	10.0	9
Hardeman, TX	18.9	57.8	35.4	2.1	...	...	78	10.4	13
Hardin, TX	15.3	34.5	12.7	0.7	...	1.9	770	14.1	40
Harris, TX	10.0	55.5	73.4	21.9	...	4.7	42 610	16.0	...
Harrison, TX	13.4	50.9	39.8	6.4	...	3.5	903	13.6	56
Hartley, TX	15.1	55.1	34.8	6.8	...	...	159	11.9	11
Haskell, TX	17.2	68.8	38.7	3.9	...	1.7	98	9.5	...
Hays, TX	12.1	39.7	52.8	6.9	...	2.9	1 490	15.1	73
Hemphill, TX	12.5	40.8	33.8	10.9	...	1.4	68	9.1	2
Henderson, TX	14.7	54.1	25.9	7.6	...	2.6	755	14.1	60
Hidalgo, TX	8.8	30.3	97.2	36.9	...	5.7	11 248	15.6	...
Hill, TX	14.6	57.3	33.5	6.5	...	4.0	495	12.6	53
Hockley, TX	14.3	57.0	56.8	3.3	...	4.0	416	11.7	42
Hood, TX	12.9	35.8	14.2	5.3	...	3.4	533	14.1	29
Hopkins, TX	15.0	48.2	28.2	8.2	...	1.7	509	12.9	33
Houston, TX	15.6	57.6	46.2	3.9	...	4.0	309	12.2	...
Howard, TX	11.7	53.6	50.5	2.1	...	4.2	379	13.8	13
Hudspeth, TX	9.1	85.2	87.7	36.0	...	3.4	75	11.4	...
Hunt, TX	15.1	45.6	29.4	5.5	...	3.8	1 066	13.8	97
Hutchinson, TX	16.1	45.5	28.5	4.6	...	3.3	358	12.3	31
Irion, TX	10.4	37.7	31.8	1.7	...	...	30	11.9	3
Jack, TX	14.0	46.0	15.0	2.8	...	1.6	139	11.9	8
Jackson, TX	11.3	45.0	41.8	4.6	...	2.1	246	12.7	15
Jasper, TX	14.4	53.4	28.8	2.2	...	2.2	540	13.0	46
Jeff Davis, TX	31.2	8.7	40.4	9.4	...	1.2	53	7.8	6
Jefferson, TX	11.9	58.7	64.5	6.1	...	4.2	2 941	14.9	...
Jim Hogg, TX	13.9	60.3	90.7	15.2	...	3.9	92	12.4	3
Jim Wells, TX	12.0	69.5	85.5	6.0	...	4.1	645	13.8	27
Johnson, TX	13.0	41.3	23.6	8.0	...	2.5	1 423	14.4	85
Jones, TX	19.1	60.9	34.4	3.3	...	1.6	270	10.4	...
Karnes, TX	14.2	58.6	64.4	2.1	...	3.5	220	10.8	13
Kaufman, TX	14.3	39.3	29.2	6.5	...	1.8	1 352	14.8	63
Kendall, TX	13.0	25.8	27.3	6.1	...	0.9	500	13.7	19
Kenedy, TX	14.5	34.9	72.3	2.4	...	...	8	10.4	3
Kent, TX	10.2	28.9	20.3	1.6	...	1.7	17	7.4	3
Kerr, TX	11.8	49.7	39.9	5.3	...	4.4	524	13.4	23
Kimble, TX	14.8	50.1	35.7	4.3	...	1.6	72	10.1	5
King, TX	12.5	30.2	16.7	10.4	...	...	18	5.5	2
Kinney, TX	17.0	65.0	68.7	7.0	...	1.7	46	13.3	4
Kleberg, TX	14.2	66.5	82.3	9.6	...	4.1	415	13.7	33
Knox, TX	14.2	58.0	50.1	4.8	...	0.9	86	10.0	...
Lamar, TX	15.5	51.1	27.2	2.5	...	2.0	714	13.0	39
Lamb, TX	13.9	67.0	65.8	9.9	...	3.0	266	12.5	28
Lampasas, TX	15.9	47.5	28.8	4.0	...	6.1	258	14.1	14
La Salle, TX	11.6	70.3	90.2	24.5	...	4.1	108	11.8	11
Lavaca, TX	14.8	38.0	22.9	1.6	...	1.2	172	12.3	12
Lee, TX	14.1	56.0	49.2	9.1	...	0.6	236	14.3	...
Leon, TX	13.4	43.5	24.6	5.1	...	2.1	246	12.1	25
Liberty, TX	11.9	50.2	29.9	7.4	...	3.1	989	15.0	...
Limestone, TX	16.1	57.4	48.7	7.4	...	3.1	314	13.5	18
Lipscomb, TX	13.4	60.5	37.5	16.3	...	0.8	80	9.1	6
Live Oak, TX	11.4	46.9	51.2	3.3	...	2.5	140	13.1	12
Llano, TX	18.0	46.7	16.1	2.9	...	2.8	141	13.8	5
Loving, TX	...	...	...	...	...	...	...	...	...
Lubbock, TX	14.9	53.0	56.3	2.7	...	3.4	3 067	14.0	...
Lynn, TX	17.1	50.3	59.0	7.3	...	1.1	143	10.1	9
McCulloch, TX	17.4	61.2	41.4	2.1	...	1.2	157	10.5	13
McLennan, TX	15.3	54.8	50.9	6.9	...	4.5	2 903	14.2	...
McMullen, TX	10.0	47.8	46.7	5.6	...	2.9	19	9.3	2
Madison, TX	11.6	60.6	40.4	10.3	...	2.1	182	13.5	12
Marion, TX	18.9	69.3	47.3	0.6	...	4.8	110	12.7	9
Martin, TX	13.8	39.8	52.2	5.7	...	3.1	87	11.6	20
Mason, TX	15.1	53.8	35.8	3.5	...	0.5	52	11.6	3

[2]IEP = Individual Education Program. See notes and definitions at the end of this section.
... = Not available.

Table C-1. Population, School, and Student Characteristics by County—*Continued*

STATE County	Revenue, 2003–2004				Current expenditures, 2003–2004			Resident population, 16 to 19 years, 2000			
	Total revenue (thousands of dollars)	Percent of revenue from:			Total expenditures (thousands of dollars)	Amount per student (dollars)	Percent for instruction	Total	Percent in armed forces	Percent high school graduates	Percent not enrolled, not employed, not in armed forces, not high school graduate
		Federal government	State government	Local government							
	19	20	21	22	23	24	25	26	27	28	29
Freestone, TX	47 946	6.0	10.1	83.9	27 396	8 156	63.4	984	0.7	10.9	6.0
Frio, TX	28 275	16.0	62.0	22.0	25 678	8 191	63.4	978	0.0	11.7	7.5
Gaines, TX	41 405	7.8	13.3	79.0	29 890	10 233	65.2	1 139	0.0	7.1	15.0
Galveston, TX	542 608	7.7	22.8	69.4	461 361	6 560	64.6	14 462	0.1	9.2	5.6
Garza, TX	10 254	9.9	36.8	53.2	9 616	8 311	68.0	294	0.0	18.4	3.7
Gillespie, TX	30 797	7.5	19.1	73.4	25 521	7 575	63.9	936	0.0	13.0	4.3
Glasscock, TX	6 267	3.5	5.2	91.3	3 214	11 199	57.5	124	0.0	1.6	6.5
Goliad, TX	13 325	21.4	15.5	63.2	12 587	9 407	62.1	417	0.0	8.9	5.3
Gonzales, TX	30 745	12.5	56.6	30.9	28 044	7 230	65.2	1 060	0.0	11.1	10.8
Gray, TX	28 402	10.0	35.6	54.4	25 015	6 739	67.0	1 261	0.0	19.2	4.0
Grayson, TX	174 663	9.0	46.2	44.9	155 427	7 370	66.3	6 426	0.0	11.5	7.2
Gregg, TX	193 006	16.4	32.4	51.2	169 456	7 260	66.1	7 360	0.0	10.5	9.5
Grimes, TX	35 307	10.0	32.7	57.4	29 415	7 069	62.2	1 213	0.0	13.7	6.7
Guadalupe, TX	136 310	8.2	40.5	51.3	115 867	6 585	66.3	5 454	0.7	13.0	4.0
Hale, TX	57 103	13.9	55.6	30.5	53 541	6 724	65.5	2 597	0.0	11.4	6.8
Hall, TX	7 770	14.0	60.9	25.1	7 255	9 035	66.2	204	0.0	5.4	6.4
Hamilton, TX	14 514	5.5	58.9	35.5	11 778	7 091	66.9	385	0.0	5.7	4.7
Hansford, TX	11 674	7.3	18.6	74.1	11 009	8 765	64.9	357	0.0	3.9	5.6
Hardeman, TX	8 066	17.6	35.0	47.3	7 677	9 669	62.4	306	0.0	14.1	5.6
Hardin, TX	80 144	7.9	56.0	36.1	73 120	6 786	64.3	3 021	0.0	11.0	3.3
Harris, TX	5 747 939	9.6	31.3	59.1	4 947 193	6 936	65.9	199 589	0.0	9.4	8.4
Harrison, TX	92 951	11.4	27.9	60.7	82 703	6 765	66.3	4 405	0.1	10.6	5.0
Hartley, TX	3 328	6.3	19.5	74.3	2 914	10 955	61.7	179	0.0	6.1	2.2
Haskell, TX	10 906	14.2	57.8	27.9	9 703	9 881	63.6	349	0.0	11.7	2.0
Hays, TX	186 774	8.7	28.4	62.9	152 569	7 092	61.9	8 049	0.1	8.9	5.3
Hemphill, TX	10 405	3.1	9.7	87.2	6 642	9 739	64.7	263	0.0	6.8	3.0
Henderson, TX	84 144	9.6	40.9	49.4	72 018	6 899	64.6	3 964	0.0	12.9	4.8
Hidalgo, TX	1 449 186	18.0	63.5	18.5	1 266 389	7 595	65.4	40 746	0.0	7.2	11.1
Hill, TX	55 818	9.6	54.3	36.1	49 772	7 964	62.2	2 009	0.0	7.5	8.9
Hockley, TX	47 581	10.2	34.9	55.0	42 438	8 515	64.9	1 843	0.0	10.6	4.5
Hood, TX	62 139	5.9	22.7	71.4	50 871	6 788	64.3	2 183	0.0	11.5	4.2
Hopkins, TX	52 898	12.3	46.4	41.3	48 795	7 506	66.8	1 918	0.2	13.7	3.8
Houston, TX	30 759	12.4	49.5	38.2	27 972	7 691	65.6	1 282	0.0	13.4	10.1
Howard, TX	39 941	11.5	43.8	44.7	37 309	6 922	64.3	2 044	0.0	15.0	10.7
Hudspeth, TX	10 126	12.1	48.8	39.1	8 438	10 021	64.4	233	0.0	9.9	6.9
Hunt, TX	118 925	9.7	57.0	33.3	102 161	6 907	62.9	4 650	0.0	12.3	4.9
Hutchinson, TX	41 731	10.5	37.7	51.7	33 719	7 445	67.5	1 654	0.0	11.3	5.0
Irion, TX	4 055	4.9	10.4	84.7	3 680	10 082	57.9	96	0.0	5.2	0.0
Jack, TX	14 085	5.8	50.3	44.0	12 691	7 829	67.5	513	0.0	15.2	7.6
Jackson, TX	31 151	7.8	31.5	60.7	23 494	7 508	65.2	912	0.0	12.8	3.1
Jasper, TX	59 395	12.7	48.8	38.5	52 278	7 432	63.8	2 086	0.4	9.7	5.7
Jeff Davis, TX	6 659	5.2	57.5	37.3	5 191	12 723	64.5	116	0.0	4.3	1.7
Jefferson, TX	359 205	12.3	24.3	63.4	307 622	6 979	63.6	15 411	0.1	10.8	7.1
Jim Hogg, TX	10 296	18.8	27.5	53.7	9 739	8 513	63.8	344	0.0	10.8	1.2
Jim Wells, TX	75 509	12.3	61.8	25.9	65 730	7 316	65.2	2 643	0.0	8.5	9.1
Johnson, TX	217 792	7.2	50.4	42.4	181 715	6 583	66.1	8 065	0.2	12.1	6.7
Jones, TX	27 228	13.1	68.1	18.8	25 092	8 649	65.4	1 529	0.0	8.2	23.9
Karnes, TX	24 598	19.7	56.6	23.7	21 410	8 778	69.1	817	0.0	12.0	8.0
Kaufman, TX	160 363	8.2	47.4	44.4	137 306	7 133	64.3	4 403	0.0	10.2	8.5
Kendall, TX	54 175	4.8	17.9	77.3	47 175	7 157	65.0	1 296	0.0	7.9	3.2
Kenedy, TX	5 040	0.0	1.8	98.2	1 087	13 759	54.1	27	0.0	7.4	11.1
Kent, TX	5 765	1.3	4.4	94.3	2 248	16 652	54.0	42	0.0	0.0	0.0
Kerr, TX	61 381	9.7	31.6	58.7	49 930	7 084	65.7	2 204	0.0	10.7	3.5
Kimble, TX	6 829	6.8	53.0	40.2	5 982	7 892	70.9	249	0.0	10.0	9.2
King, TX	2 302	1.6	8.3	90.1	2 039	19 606	59.0	9	0.0	0.0	0.0
Kinney, TX	6 309	8.8	65.3	25.9	5 192	8 228	62.8	180	0.0	6.7	2.8
Kleberg, TX	50 522	12.5	51.2	36.3	45 082	7 684	64.9	2 384	0.2	6.4	4.5
Knox, TX	9 140	15.7	58.1	26.2	8 054	9 565	63.6	249	0.0	8.0	0.8
Lamar, TX	77 621	10.5	47.7	41.7	62 095	6 659	68.0	2 750	0.0	9.5	5.6
Lamb, TX	35 371	10.7	53.5	35.7	27 765	8 348	66.2	992	0.0	9.2	7.0
Lampasas, TX	29 930	12.9	53.5	33.6	26 014	7 143	63.9	1 187	0.8	7.1	3.4
La Salle, TX	11 793	9.6	57.5	32.9	12 385	9 767	59.4	367	0.0	10.1	16.9
Lavaca, TX	18 775	5.3	26.1	68.6	15 198	7 079	66.1	1 116	0.0	9.8	6.2
Lee, TX	25 315	9.9	43.5	46.6	23 122	7 483	66.6	1 236	0.0	10.4	19.0
Leon, TX	27 270	7.4	39.4	53.2	23 193	7 913	63.4	896	0.0	8.6	3.7
Liberty, TX	114 405	8.9	47.3	43.9	96 583	6 543	63.6	4 116	0.0	12.9	7.9
Limestone, TX	38 157	12.3	41.8	45.9	33 524	7 866	65.3	1 204	0.0	12.1	5.2
Lipscomb, TX	7 761	7.8	23.4	68.8	7 346	10 245	63.2	193	0.0	8.3	2.6
Live Oak, TX	15 749	8.4	28.7	62.9	14 750	8 008	64.0	741	0.0	13.5	5.7
Llano, TX	25 659	5.3	6.4	88.3	13 087	6 830	66.1	527	0.0	16.5	5.1
Loving, TX	. . .	. . .	. . .	. . .	. . .	. . .	. . .	5	0.0	0.0	0.0
Lubbock, TX	350 238	14.2	42.7	43.1	321 409	7 486	67.1	17 939	0.1	10.6	3.8
Lynn, TX	15 711	13.0	60.5	26.5	13 360	9 070	63.6	449	0.0	11.1	5.6
McCulloch, TX	16 705	11.9	60.8	27.3	14 886	8 736	62.6	374	0.0	12.8	8.3
McLennan, TX	345 753	11.9	49.3	38.9	297 636	7 351	63.8	16 641	0.1	8.6	5.5
McMullen, TX	4 163	0.9	8.2	90.9	2 416	15 100	53.4	46	0.0	17.4	0.0
Madison, TX	20 598	10.4	58.5	31.1	17 464	7 036	63.3	496	0.0	11.5	5.4
Marion, TX	11 967	14.2	33.0	52.8	10 308	7 475	63.8	554	0.0	14.1	6.0
Martin, TX	9 548	7.0	40.1	52.9	9 556	9 490	64.8	334	0.0	6.3	9.9
Mason, TX	6 268	6.3	50.3	43.4	5 100	8 320	59.2	182	0.0	7.7	8.8

. . . = Not available.

Table C-1. Population, School, and Student Characteristics by County—*Continued*

STATE County	High school graduates, 2000			College enrollment, 2000		College graduates, 2000 (percent)						
	Population 25 years and over	High school graduate or less (percent)	High school graduate or more (percent)	Number	Percent public	Bachelor's degree or more	+/- U.S. percentage with bachelor's degree or more	Non-Hispanic White	Black	American Indian and Alaska Native	Asian or Pacific Islander	Hispanic[3]
	30	31	32	33	34	35	36	37	38	39	40	41
Freestone, TX	12 085	60.9	76.8	826	94.4	10.9	-13.5	11.6	10.3	22.9	32.0	2.8
Frio, TX	9 807	70.7	57.7	584	87.2	8.4	-16.0	20.8	14.0	14.3	30.0	3.1
Gaines, TX	8 006	70.2	56.2	268	81.0	10.5	-13.9	15.2	0.0	0.0	100.0	2.0
Galveston, TX	161 503	45.5	80.9	14 654	89.1	22.7	-1.7	27.0	10.7	22.4	47.9	10.1
Garza, TX	3 131	68.3	70.1	164	95.7	10.0	-14.4	14.8	4.3	. . .	. . .	1.2
Gillespie, TX	15 255	49.4	80.1	397	73.8	22.9	-1.5	25.3	0.0	22.2	13.0	4.4
Glasscock, TX	836	54.3	69.9	40	92.5	18.7	-5.7	24.7	100.0	0.0	. . .	1.4
Goliad, TX	4 603	57.2	72.4	159	87.4	12.3	-12.1	16.5	10.9	20.0	0.0	3.2
Gonzales, TX	11 797	71.8	62.0	312	85.9	10.7	-13.7	17.1	2.0	6.7	35.3	1.4
Gray, TX	15 420	58.3	75.3	920	86.7	11.9	-12.5	12.9	8.0	9.7	66.0	3.8
Grayson, TX	72 382	49.8	80.2	5 331	70.6	17.2	-7.2	17.9	10.5	12.7	46.6	8.0
Gregg, TX	70 006	48.6	79.1	5 017	72.8	19.5	-4.9	22.8	10.3	17.7	33.9	6.5
Grimes, TX	16 080	65.5	67.3	787	86.9	10.3	-14.1	13.7	3.4	9.8	25.6	2.7
Guadalupe, TX	55 679	52.0	78.1	4 172	65.9	19.1	-5.3	24.2	21.1	28.2	16.9	6.3
Hale, TX	21 498	62.8	65.9	1 730	55.3	14.4	-10.0	21.7	4.2	6.3	78.1	4.3
Hall, TX	2 527	71.1	61.7	54	87.0	10.3	-14.1	13.6	0.0	0.0	0.0	1.3
Hamilton, TX	5 792	59.2	73.8	196	88.3	16.8	-7.6	17.6	. . .	0.0	. . .	2.8
Hansford, TX	3 420	59.9	69.9	94	97.9	18.6	-5.8	24.3	. . .	6.8	. . .	0.5
Hardeman, TX	3 135	62.6	70.7	99	94.9	12.8	-11.6	14.3	2.4	26.7	70.6	1.4
Hardin, TX	30 747	60.8	79.5	1 418	92.8	13.0	-11.4	13.5	5.7	4.5	29.8	10.1
Harris, TX	2 067 399	47.0	74.6	186 214	81.5	26.9	2.5	38.5	17.4	18.1	45.6	8.2
Harrison, TX	39 130	55.8	78.3	3 252	50.4	15.4	-9.0	16.6	11.7	3.0	31.4	10.0
Hartley, TX	4 136	56.6	77.3	174	72.4	17.6	-6.8	21.3	8.3	0.0	0.0	5.5
Haskell, TX	4 314	65.4	71.1	90	84.4	14.4	-10.0	17.4	9.8	0.0	0.0	0.3
Hays, TX	53 635	38.2	84.7	16 274	95.7	31.3	6.9	39.6	11.0	23.3	48.5	10.8
Hemphill, TX	2 190	49.3	79.9	59	84.7	17.9	-6.5	20.0	0.0	0.0	. . .	2.7
Henderson, TX	49 886	58.9	73.5	2 412	88.6	12.1	-12.3	12.7	7.6	27.3	26.5	3.4
Hidalgo, TX	304 670	69.8	50.5	27 046	91.8	12.9	-11.5	27.8	16.7	7.4	65.1	9.6
Hill, TX	21 209	61.5	71.8	1 100	84.9	12.5	-11.9	14.4	3.0	17.8	51.3	1.6
Hockley, TX	13 466	58.0	68.2	1 511	93.4	13.6	-10.8	19.0	3.1	7.4	83.8	2.4
Hood, TX	28 621	46.1	83.5	1 234	87.3	20.5	-3.9	21.1	70.0	23.9	44.6	7.5
Hopkins, TX	21 003	62.1	73.6	1 000	90.7	15.1	-9.3	16.6	5.3	2.7	80.3	4.0
Houston, TX	16 244	64.7	70.0	487	91.6	12.2	-12.2	15.0	7.8	6.1	7.1	1.1
Howard, TX	22 544	60.7	70.6	1 702	86.6	11.1	-13.3	15.7	12.6	0.0	39.6	2.8
Hudspeth, TX	1 910	74.5	46.1	69	68.1	9.7	-14.7	26.5	0.0	25.0	0.0	2.5
Hunt, TX	48 548	57.4	76.9	4 348	90.4	16.8	-7.6	18.1	7.7	12.3	56.6	7.1
Hutchinson, TX	15 282	64.6	70.6	1 034	00.0	14.0	-10.1	15.4	4.8	16.9	58.6	7.1
Irion, TX	1 217	52.2	78.8	54	90.7	21.5	-2.9	26.9	0.0	0.0	. . .	3.8
Jack, TX	5 830	60.8	75.8	315	73.0	12.8	-11.6	13.5	8.6	0.0	58.6	3.5
Jackson, TX	9 278	61.6	72.7	397	97.7	12.8	-11.6	16.9	3.3	0.0	69.2	2.0
Jasper, TX	23 420	66.6	73.0	751	85.4	10.5	-13.9	12.0	3.4	11.6	31.5	5.3
Jeff Davis, TX	1 560	44.3	74.7	54	94.4	35.1	10.7	46.0	. . .	. . .	. . .	12.0
Jefferson, TX	161 261	54.7	78.5	11 506	91.4	16.3	-8.1	21.2	8.2	7.5	32.5	7.9
Jim Hogg, TX	3 203	70.3	58.0	168	86.3	9.5	-14.9	11.8	0.0	0.0	0.0	9.3
Jim Wells, TX	23 525	67.5	64.8	1 531	92.6	10.9	-13.5	17.3	10.6	13.6	64.9	8.2
Johnson, TX	79 417	55.7	77.6	4 806	67.4	13.8	-10.6	14.7	8.9	13.0	27.7	4.6
Jones, TX	13 780	70.3	64.3	438	74.0	8.2	-16.2	11.3	1.3	0.0	5.1	1.1
Karnes, TX	10 352	73.2	59.1	336	87.5	9.4	-15.0	17.2	1.6	6.6	50.0	2.7
Kaufman, TX	44 059	59.3	74.5	2 336	78.6	12.3	-12.1	13.4	8.1	8.5	38.5	4.3
Kendall, TX	15 827	37.6	85.4	820	81.2	31.4	7.0	34.5	0.0	24.3	69.7	11.8
Kenedy, TX	261	64.0	57.9	6	50.0	20.3	-4.1	45.7	0.0	. . .	. . .	14.9
Kent, TX	643	58.9	78.1	12	100.0	15.1	-9.3	16.1	0.0	0.0	. . .	7.5
Kerr, TX	31 006	48.0	81.2	1 142	39.1	23.3	-1.1	26.9	2.6	11.0	19.7	4.9
Kimble, TX	3 146	62.1	72.1	42	61.9	17.3	-7.1	20.3	0.0	0.0	50.0	2.3
King, TX	228	47.8	78.1	2	100.0	24.6	0.2	26.0	. . .	. . .	. . .	0.0
Kinney, TX	2 335	60.4	66.9	57	94.7	17.7	-6.7	28.4	0.0	0.0	63.6	3.7
Kleberg, TX	17 896	54.8	68.2	4 469	94.0	20.4	-4.0	32.8	8.8	21.9	48.5	13.5
Knox, TX	2 819	66.9	66.8	78	84.6	11.8	-12.6	14.6	1.2	33.3	53.3	2.7
Lamar, TX	31 612	56.9	76.3	1 847	92.5	14.5	-9.9	15.9	5.7	13.1	34.2	7.9
Lamb, TX	9 202	64.7	63.7	284	84.5	11.1	-13.3	16.7	2.0	0.0	0.0	2.9
Lampasas, TX	11 491	51.7	78.8	605	78.8	16.2	-8.2	18.0	9.2	0.0	13.1	6.5
La Salle, TX	3 602	75.6	50.1	157	81.5	6.4	-18.0	20.7	0.0	0.0	10.0	2.2
Lavaca, TX	13 214	68.1	68.6	546	86.1	11.4	-13.0	12.6	7.1	4.8	30.8	3.4
Lee, TX	9 804	65.0	71.7	323	85.1	13.1	-11.3	15.5	6.9	0.0	0.0	4.2
Leon, TX	10 652	64.1	73.8	338	87.9	12.1	-12.3	13.6	6.7	0.0	0.0	0.7
Liberty, TX	44 206	66.6	69.6	1 634	85.9	8.1	-16.3	9.3	4.5	11.4	11.3	2.0
Limestone, TX	14 564	62.6	67.4	785	89.8	11.1	-13.3	14.3	3.2	10.7	0.0	1.1
Lipscomb, TX	2 047	54.8	74.5	37	91.9	18.9	-5.5	21.3	37.5	0.0	. . .	5.6
Live Oak, TX	8 399	61.2	67.1	284	81.0	12.0	-12.4	17.3	1.8	9.4	20.0	3.0
Llano, TX	13 571	49.1	83.5	182	75.3	21.0	-3.4	21.9	0.0	0.0	0.0	2.8
Loving, TX	51	51.0	86.3	11	63.6	5.9	-18.5	6.3	. . .	. . .	. . .	0.0
Lubbock, TX	141 363	46.9	78.4	30 844	90.4	24.4	0.0	31.1	10.0	14.6	64.2	7.2
Lynn, TX	4 037	66.1	61.9	168	82.1	13.4	-11.0	21.7	2.7	38.5	33.3	0.4
McCulloch, TX	5 550	64.5	70.5	84	83.3	14.0	-10.4	16.4	15.9	0.0	. . .	5.0
McLennan, TX	125 961	51.3	76.6	22 657	46.9	19.1	-5.3	23.2	9.1	9.0	47.7	6.8
McMullen, TX	613	60.5	74.7	19	73.7	16.2	-8.2	20.8	0.0	100.0	. . .	3.9
Madison, TX	8 907	71.1	72.8	542	87.6	11.5	-12.9	16.2	1.5	27.3	82.8	3.8
Marion, TX	7 792	65.7	67.5	238	81.9	8.5	-15.9	9.4	5.4	9.9	. . .	0.0
Martin, TX	2 785	65.6	65.8	103	83.5	11.8	-12.6	16.4	0.0	0.0	45.5	3.1
Mason, TX	2 701	49.7	78.1	44	79.5	18.7	-5.7	21.4	0.0	35.1	. . .	2.9

[3]May be of any race.
. . . = Not available.

Table C-1. Population, School, and Student Characteristics by County—*Continued*

STATE County	State/ county code	County type[1]	Population, 2005		Number of schools and students, 2004–2005			Resident enrollment, 2000			
			Total	Percent 5 to 17 years	School districts	Schools	Students	Total	Percent public	K–12	Percent public
			1	2	3	4	5	6	7	8	9
Matagorda, TX	48 321	4	37 849	21.0	5	25	7 886	10 524	92.2	8 924	94.3
Maverick, TX	48 323	5	51 181	25.1	1	24	13 532	15 541	96.5	13 100	98.3
Medina, TX	48 325	1	43 027	19.7	5	22	8 593	10 809	92.4	8 698	96.2
Menard, TX	48 327	8	2 201	14.8	1	4	361	544	98.5	482	99.0
Midland, TX	48 329	3	121 371	20.5	6	45	23 347	34 805	86.7	26 914	88.4
Milam, TX	48 331	6	25 354	19.1	6	16	4 887	6 297	93.9	5 256	96.1
Mills, TX	48 333	9	5 237	18.8	4	8	997	1 128	97.3	1 050	98.7
Mitchell, TX	48 335	7	9 413	13.7	3	8	1 332	2 012	95.2	1 662	95.5
Montague, TX	48 337	6	19 677	16.7	7	15	3 378	4 192	95.2	3 510	97.9
Montgomery, TX	48 339	1	378 033	19.9	7	100	70 796	81 114	87.7	63 588	91.9
Moore, TX	48 341	6	20 348	23.3	2	12	4 579	5 772	96.8	4 854	98.5
Morris, TX	48 343	6	12 936	17.9	2	8	2 475	3 217	95.6	2 607	98.1
Motley, TX	48 345	8	1 299	15.4	1	1	164	294	85.0	241	88.0
Nacogdoches, TX	48 347	5	60 468	16.5	9	33	10 284	21 373	93.8	10 692	94.1
Navarro, TX	48 349	4	48 687	19.2	8	26	9 606	12 175	93.4	9 301	95.5
Newton, TX	48 351	8	14 309	18.3	3	10	2 448	3 518	93.3	3 083	93.6
Nolan, TX	48 353	6	14 878	19.2	4	13	2 873	4 262	95.6	3 396	99.1
Nueces, TX	48 355	2	319 704	19.6	18	125	61 588	91 444	91.4	67 291	93.8
Ochiltree, TX	48 357	7	9 385	20.8	1	6	2 059	2 357	94.4	2 020	97.7
Oldham, TX	48 359	8	2 118	27.7	4	7	846	715	96.8	641	96.4
Orange, TX	48 361	2	84 983	19.0	6	28	16 190	22 128	91.4	17 626	94.4
Palo Pinto, TX	48 363	6	27 478	18.5	6	13	4 981	6 254	95.2	5 296	97.4
Panola, TX	48 365	6	22 997	17.4	4	9	3 769	5 765	93.9	4 667	95.6
Parker, TX	48 367	1	102 801	18.7	9	51	23 303	23 189	90.0	18 732	93.6
Parmer, TX	48 369	7	9 754	23.1	4	11	2 411	3 082	96.2	2 689	97.2
Pecos, TX	48 371	7	15 859	18.4	3	11	2 903	4 947	94.9	3 906	95.9
Polk, TX	48 373	6	46 640	15.9	6	17	7 052	9 215	93.4	7 149	95.3
Potter, TX	48 375	3	119 852	19.7	4	9	3 072	31 113	92.1	22 798	93.9
Presidio, TX	48 377	7	7 722	21.5	2	5	2 022	2 151	98.6	1 869	99.6
Rains, TX	48 379	8	11 305	15.8	1	4	1 600	2 022	95.0	1 696	96.2
Randall, TX	48 381	3	110 053	18.4	3	67	37 854	30 922	89.2	19 793	91.2
Reagan, TX	48 383	6	2 995	22.0	1	3	752	1 036	99.1	910	100.0
Real, TX	48 385	9	3 031	16.0	2	2	330	742	96.5	596	98.3
Red River, TX	48 387	6	13 575	16.8	4	12	2 651	3 114	94.7	2 610	96.4
Reeves, TX	48 389	7	11 638	19.5	2	7	2 473	3 606	98.5	3 116	99.5
Refugio, TX	48 391	6	7 639	17.8	3	8	1 486	1 906	96.0	1 640	98.1
Roberts, TX	48 393	9	820	16.8	1	1	161	217	92.6	184	96.7
Robertson, TX	48 395	3	16 192	20.0	5	16	3 431	4 049	94.2	3 339	96.6
Rockwall, TX	48 397	1	62 944	19.6	1	16	10 573	12 565	86.6	9 821	92.9
Runnels, TX	48 399	6	10 974	19.0	4	16	2 277	2 833	95.6	2 481	97.3
Rusk, TX	48 401	3	47 971	17.1	9	30	11 079	11 399	91.2	9 081	95.0
Sabine, TX	48 403	9	10 416	15.4	2	5	1 600	2 043	93.5	1 747	95.9
San Augustine, TX	48 405	9	8 907	16.4	2	7	1 434	1 961	95.8	1 657	97.7
San Jacinto, TX	48 407	1	24 801	17.8	2	8	3 653	5 092	92.8	4 384	94.0
San Patricio, TX	48 409	2	69 209	21.4	7	37	15 586	19 646	94.4	15 739	97.1
San Saba, TX	48 411	7	6 076	20.7	4	8	1 468	1 514	96.7	1 329	98.1
Schleicher, TX	48 413	8	2 742	18.2	1	5	584	798	99.5	669	100.0
Scurry, TX	48 415	7	16 217	17.5	3	10	2 970	4 259	95.6	3 247	99.2
Shackelford, TX	48 417	8	3 167	18.3	2	3	651	882	95.6	732	97.1
Shelby, TX	48 419	6	26 346	18.8	6	17	4 975	6 145	94.0	5 129	96.5
Sherman, TX	48 421	9	3 002	21.8	2	4	1 026	927	93.9	774	94.7
Smith, TX	48 423	3	190 594	18.4	11	75	33 019	46 077	88.1	34 152	90.0
Somervell, TX	48 425	8	7 578	18.7	2	5	1 743	1 907	92.4	1 502	96.9
Starr, TX	48 427	4	60 941	24.5	3	24	16 140	18 163	97.8	14 828	98.7
Stephens, TX	48 429	7	9 561	16.4	1	6	1 617	2 381	93.1	1 944	96.7
Sterling, TX	48 431	8	1 303	18.8	1	8	266	395	94.4	336	93.5
Stonewall, TX	48 433	8	1 372	14.3	1	2	230	363	92.6	312	94.2
Sutton, TX	48 435	7	4 212	19.5	1	3	983	1 085	96.5	937	98.0
Swisher, TX	48 437	6	7 828	19.1	3	8	1 585	2 196	93.9	1 823	96.4
Tarrant, TX	48 439	1	1 620 479	19.6	29	483	302 404	399 208	84.2	291 485	91.1
Taylor, TX	48 441	3	125 039	18.4	7	63	22 478	37 937	75.0	25 143	94.5
Terrell, TX	48 443	9	996	17.0	1	3	142	277	91.0	249	93.6
Terry, TX	48 445	6	12 419	19.3	3	6	2 461	3 351	97.4	2 833	98.9
Throckmorton, TX	48 447	9	1 618	17.6	2	3	316	443	99.1	386	100.0
Titus, TX	48 449	7	29 445	21.6	5	15	6 616	7 916	94.7	6 333	98.0
Tom Green, TX	48 451	3	103 611	17.9	7	72	18 356	29 720	94.2	20 707	95.8
Travis, TX	48 453	1	888 185	16.5	26	229	129 557	235 906	88.5	133 691	92.5
Trinity, TX	48 455	8	14 363	16.2	4	9	2 256	2 836	96.0	2 369	97.7
Tyler, TX	48 457	6	20 617	16.3	5	15	3 683	4 466	93.2	3 784	95.7
Upshur, TX	48 459	3	37 881	18.1	8	29	9 027	8 817	92.0	7 267	95.4
Upton, TX	48 461	8	3 056	18.5	2	5	702	959	99.3	868	99.4
Uvalde, TX	48 463	7	26 955	21.7	5	17	6 342	7 779	93.5	6 142	94.6
Val Verde, TX	48 465	5	47 596	21.7	3	16	10 651	12 850	92.4	10 622	95.6
Van Zandt, TX	48 467	6	52 491	17.7	8	36	9 758	11 226	91.4	9 289	93.2
Victoria, TX	48 469	3	85 648	20.2	5	35	15 370	24 141	87.9	18 552	89.7
Walker, TX	48 471	4	62 735	12.3	4	15	7 741	20 291	90.2	10 092	88.0
Waller, TX	48 473	1	34 821	17.7	2	8	3 103	11 274	94.0	6 445	95.3
Ward, TX	48 475	6	10 237	20.8	3	10	2 338	3 113	94.8	2 640	96.4
Washington, TX	48 477	6	31 521	17.1	2	12	5 298	8 413	86.7	5 844	88.7
Webb, TX	48 479	3	224 695	24.0	6	81	59 525	67 101	93.2	51 488	95.4

[1]County type codes are from the Economic Research Service of the United States Department of Agriculture. See notes and definitions at the end of this section.

Table C-1. Population, School, and Student Characteristics by County—*Continued*

STATE County	Characteristics of students, 2004–2005				Outcomes		Staff and students, 2004–2005		
	Percent with IEP[2]	Percent eligible for free or reduced-price lunch	Percent minority	Percent English-language learners	Number of graduates, 2003–2004	Percent dropouts, grades 9–12, 2001–2002	Number of teachers	Student-teacher ratio	Central administration staff
	10	11	12	13	14	15	16	17	18
Matagorda, TX	12.8	58.6	62.0	7.3	...	1.9	548	14.4	...
Maverick, TX	8.8	79.1	98.9	38.2	...	5.5	794	17.0	19
Medina, TX	12.3	50.2	59.7	5.2	...	2.5	620	13.9	45
Menard, TX	21.3	67.8	60.4	3.9	...	0.7	36	10.1	14
Midland, TX	10.7	49.0	57.0	9.0	...	6.1	1 543	15.1	...
Milam, TX	15.9	55.0	44.3	5.0	...	2.4	375	13.0	21
Mills, TX	24.5	53.6	31.7	6.3	...	1.5	116	8.6	21
Mitchell, TX	13.1	58.1	55.8	3.7	...	2.2	132	10.1	7
Montague, TX	15.0	44.8	13.6	4.1	...	3.5	288	11.7	...
Montgomery, TX	11.3	34.6	28.3	9.3	...	2.1	4 512	15.7	...
Moore, TX	10.3	56.8	67.0	23.4	...	3.3	346	13.2	21
Morris, TX	15.4	59.8	42.7	3.0	...	5.5	205	12.0	11
Motley, TX	13.4	74.4	24.4	3.0	...	3.0	20	8.1	2
Nacogdoches, TX	11.4	59.6	47.9	10.8	...	3.3	742	13.9	63
Navarro, TX	15.4	55.4	46.2	8.8	...	3.8	676	14.2	...
Newton, TX	18.6	61.4	29.8	0.1	...	1.3	213	11.5	11
Nolan, TX	15.8	57.1	45.0	2.2	...	4.9	251	11.5	43
Nueces, TX	13.9	57.9	74.6	7.2	...	4.4	3 877	15.9	...
Ochiltree, TX	9.9	55.7	54.1	20.9	...	2.2	149	13.8	10
Oldham, TX	18.3	30.4	22.8	2.0	...	0.5	115	7.3	10
Orange, TX	16.2	42.9	18.9	1.2	...	2.6	1 133	14.3	...
Palo Pinto, TX	16.2	52.3	28.2	6.6	...	3.3	374	13.3	48
Panola, TX	16.9	42.3	30.8	2.1	...	3.0	262	14.4	13
Parker, TX	12.8	30.6	13.7	2.9	...	2.2	1 609	14.5	90
Parmer, TX	12.4	74.9	70.6	17.3	...	2.3	215	11.2	12
Pecos, TX	11.0	62.6	75.6	11.0	...	4.3	226	12.9	12
Polk, TX	18.4	56.8	32.0	4.8	...	2.8	498	14.2	32
Potter, TX	12.6	65.8	57.5	1.3	...	3.1	232	13.3	19
Presidio, TX	9.3	79.8	96.3	44.3	...	6.2	152	13.3	5
Rains, TX	16.1	51.9	14.5	4.6	...	1.2	126	12.7	3
Randall, TX	12.9	29.5	25.0	7.4	...	1.8	2 573	14.7	...
Reagan, TX	15.6	44.7	69.8	16.0	...	0.3	71	10.5	6
Real, TX	25.2	66.1	28.5	3.3	...	...	37	9.0	6
Red River, TX	16.9	57.4	35.9	4.6	...	3.5	238	11.1	25
Reeves, TX	13.1	70.9	90.7	7.8	...	3.8	180	13.7	11
Refugio, TX	19.3	52.5	61.4	2.6	...	4.3	136	10.9	7
Roberts, TX	8.1	31.1	0.7	0.0	...	...	22	7.4	2
Robertson, TX	12.7	66.3	55.1	6.3	...	2.6	262	13.1	23
Rockwall, TX	10.3	20.4	25.1	5.9	...	2.8	640	16.5	27
Runnels, TX	13.1	56.0	46.5	5.0	...	2.7	193	11.8	14
Rusk, TX	13.9	54.9	40.6	8.8	...	2.5	848	13.1	...
Sabine, TX	16.7	60.2	15.3	0.3	...	3.2	130	12.3	9
San Augustine, TX	15.5	77.5	47.7	3.8	...	2.8	121	11.9	6
San Jacinto, TX	15.0	57.6	26.9	2.8	...	2.8	285	12.8	20
San Patricio, TX	13.4	54.8	63.8	4.2	...	2.8	1 035	15.1	59
San Saba, TX	26.0	70.6	42.8	9.1	...	2.0	103	14.2	...
Schleicher, TX	9.2	43.0	66.3	10.6	...	1.0	60	9.7	1
Scurry, TX	16.3	51.9	50.2	5.0	...	3.1	224	13.2	...
Shackelford, TX	16.1	51.3	15.7	2.9	...	1.7	63	10.4	7
Shelby, TX	12.9	60.5	42.5	11.4	...	2.7	387	12.8	29
Sherman, TX	8.2	47.8	46.3	21.3	...	1.3	70	14.8	5
Smith, TX	12.2	48.7	48.7	10.5	...	3.9	2 364	14.0	...
Somervell, TX	14.2	43.0	22.1	7.2	...	3.0	141	12.3	8
Starr, TX	11.3	52.7	99.8	49.2	...	8.3	1 099	14.7	37
Stephens, TX	14.2	58.5	31.8	8.3	...	4.8	118	13.8	4
Sterling, TX	16.5	42.1	42.5	1.1	...	0.9	28	9.4	2
Stonewall, TX	18.3	38.7	24.8	0.4	...	2.8	24	9.4	1
Sutton, TX	13.9	43.9	66.3	13.3	...	2.1	89	11.1	4
Swisher, TX	12.9	64.2	57.7	5.8	...	3.0	146	10.8	12
Tarrant, TX	10.0	44.0	54.2	14.1	...	3.6	18 842	16.0	...
Taylor, TX	16.8	49.3	38.8	2.0	...	4.6	1 687	13.3	...
Terrell, TX	14.1	40.1	65.5	5.6	...	...	21	6.8	3
Terry, TX	14.4	64.7	66.1	6.4	...	2.8	199	12.4	17
Throckmorton, TX	10.8	50.6	11.7	1.3	...	1.5	34	9.2	4
Titus, TX	14.2	65.6	61.9	30.1	...	2.3	492	13.5	...
Tom Green, TX	13.2	53.1	51.9	4.9	...	3.9	1 230	14.9	...
Travis, TX	13.0	41.0	63.1	18.5	...	5.1	8 729	14.8	...
Trinity, TX	14.8	60.3	24.5	3.3	...	2.6	188	12.0	16
Tyler, TX	15.9	52.9	17.6	0.5	...	2.9	292	12.6	23
Upshur, TX	15.1	48.0	19.8	2.3	...	2.2	696	13.0	49
Upton, TX	19.7	50.6	55.3	6.8	...	2.6	64	11.0	13
Uvalde, TX	11.3	72.0	82.3	8.5	...	5.4	468	13.6	26
Val Verde, TX	12.4	73.6	90.1	18.2	...	5.8	624	17.1	...
Van Zandt, TX	13.3	44.8	15.8	3.9	...	2.7	679	14.4	39
Victoria, TX	12.4	56.7	64.3	3.6	...	4.2	1 057	14.5	...
Walker, TX	11.8	53.4	48.7	6.5	...	2.3	504	15.4	...
Waller, TX	13.8	65.2	68.1	16.2	...	3.0	235	13.2	12
Ward, TX	20.0	52.8	59.6	5.0	...	5.0	154	15.2	...
Washington, TX	13.4	45.7	45.7	6.5	...	3.0	396	13.4	12
Webb, TX	12.5	58.1	98.7	53.4	...	3.5	3 704	16.1	...

[2]IEP = Individual Education Program. See notes and definitions at the end of this section.
... = Not available.

Table C-1. Population, School, and Student Characteristics by County—Continued

STATE County	Total revenue (thousands of dollars)	Federal government	State government	Local government	Total expenditures (thousands of dollars)	Amount per student (dollars)	Percent for instruction	Total	Percent in armed forces	Percent high school graduates	Percent not enrolled, not employed, not in armed forces, not high school graduate
	19	20	21	22	23	24	25	26	27	28	29
Matagorda, TX	72 135	8.8	32.8	58.4	59 967	7 554	63.8	2 573	0.0	12.5	8.0
Maverick, TX	104 126	18.6	66.7	14.7	90 700	6 721	65.0	3 350	0.0	7.0	13.9
Medina, TX	70 332	12.3	59.3	28.4	60 854	7 017	64.7	2 431	0.0	10.8	4.9
Menard, TX	4 782	22.1	47.8	30.1	4 677	12 023	54.2	150	0.0	9.3	4.0
Midland, TX	176 046	13.2	37.4	49.4	161 460	6 915	65.8	7 590	0.0	9.4	5.4
Milam, TX	40 691	8.2	49.9	41.9	35 301	7 325	65.7	1 463	0.0	13.3	2.6
Mills, TX	12 153	14.0	62.2	23.8	11 421	11 175	68.2	284	0.0	8.1	7.4
Mitchell, TX	13 432	12.4	45.1	42.5	12 173	9 044	64.8	723	0.0	15.6	19.4
Montague, TX	28 593	10.3	51.1	38.6	25 845	7 877	67.2	1 067	0.0	15.1	9.0
Montgomery, TX	522 877	6.1	34.6	59.3	442 590	6 491	63.6	17 271	0.1	10.0	6.3
Moore, TX	33 883	11.8	17.5	70.7	30 338	6 454	69.3	1 300	0.0	18.0	6.4
Morris, TX	20 805	11.1	27.7	61.2	18 566	7 520	65.9	741	0.0	14.2	6.2
Motley, TX	2 386	24.9	38.9	36.2	2 438	13 250	71.4	80	0.0	13.8	2.5
Nacogdoches, TX	81 392	11.0	49.8	39.2	69 939	6 749	62.8	5 187	0.0	6.0	3.2
Navarro, TX	74 092	10.2	56.5	33.3	62 665	6 711	66.6	3 172	0.0	6.7	8.0
Newton, TX	28 346	11.9	36.0	52.1	20 825	8 277	63.9	1 053	0.0	16.2	11.5
Nolan, TX	26 321	12.1	45.0	43.0	24 301	8 291	61.7	999	0.0	14.3	3.9
Nueces, TX	507 894	13.0	43.4	43.5	440 281	7 152	65.7	20 381	0.6	10.6	7.3
Ochiltree, TX	14 212	10.4	29.8	59.8	13 295	6 701	68.4	477	0.0	6.7	6.1
Oldham, TX	11 540	8.4	49.3	42.3	10 611	12 831	71.2	195	0.0	5.6	3.6
Orange, TX	142 792	12.5	41.1	46.4	123 061	7 512	64.6	5 240	0.0	12.0	4.4
Palo Pinto, TX	48 036	9.1	45.3	45.6	38 914	7 715	66.1	1 644	0.0	10.0	11.4
Panola, TX	41 430	7.7	10.6	81.6	27 707	7 373	63.3	1 545	0.0	8.9	2.7
Parker, TX	138 478	6.2	42.9	51.0	121 459	7 092	64.6	5 353	0.0	10.8	6.1
Parmer, TX	20 711	12.7	56.6	30.7	19 512	7 780	68.1	677	0.0	9.3	5.5
Pecos, TX	37 426	6.9	8.8	84.3	25 372	8 734	62.4	1 395	0.0	18.6	10.7
Polk, TX	59 356	11.8	43.8	44.4	52 257	7 510	62.8	1 972	0.1	9.8	9.0
Potter, TX	277 460	15.5	40.9	43.5	236 332	7 254	68.0	7 166	0.0	14.0	15.2
Presidio, TX	16 926	16.6	57.8	25.6	13 597	6 864	66.2	512	0.0	8.4	12.1
Rains, TX	11 893	7.1	51.8	41.1	10 755	6 921	64.0	548	0.0	16.4	4.4
Randall, TX	52 551	6.5	32.6	60.9	44 527	5 767	67.1	6 773	0.1	11.7	2.3
Reagan, TX	8 310	7.7	9.5	82.8	8 178	10 274	67.8	251	0.0	5.6	0.0
Real, TX	3 525	7.6	45.0	47.3	3 405	10 984	60.5	172	0.0	11.0	4.1
Red River, TX	24 718	14.9	59.2	25.9	22 151	8 324	65.4	860	0.0	12.3	8.8
Reeves, TX	19 835	15.2	44.5	40.3	19 488	7 666	64.2	825	0.0	9.9	7.0
Refugio, TX	13 836	7.9	27.2	64.9	12 683	8 771	66.1	492	0.0	12.0	4.5
Roberts, TX	5 372	1.4	4.6	94.0	1 960	10 370	61.5	54	0.0	0.0	3.7
Robertson, TX	31 062	11.6	38.7	49.7	27 340	8 308	64.0	925	0.0	16.5	12.3
Rockwall, TX	107 176	4.2	23.3	72.5	81 381	6 363	63.5	2 275	0.0	9.5	3.9
Runnels, TX	21 458	12.3	62.8	24.9	18 526	8 311	66.9	681	0.0	8.4	5.0
Rusk, TX	68 341	9.0	33.5	57.6	53 673	7 187	66.0	2 579	0.0	11.4	6.9
Sabine, TX	14 161	15.3	49.4	35.4	12 278	7 631	67.7	471	0.0	5.5	4.7
San Augustine, TX	13 045	15.7	62.1	22.1	11 390	8 055	63.6	421	1.2	10.7	1.7
San Jacinto, TX	28 883	12.6	49.8	37.5	26 492	7 127	61.6	1 249	0.0	11.4	7.7
San Patricio, TX	129 468	13.2	48.9	37.9	106 979	6 930	63.7	4 600	3.3	15.5	7.7
San Saba, TX	10 805	8.1	61.7	30.2	9 257	8 362	67.5	640	0.0	12.7	28.1
Schleicher, TX	5 497	7.1	36.8	56.1	5 262	8 460	65.5	180	0.0	9.4	3.3
Scurry, TX	25 835	10.0	31.4	58.6	22 513	7 565	65.3	1 306	0.0	10.4	15.0
Shackelford, TX	6 499	8.1	50.1	41.8	5 891	9 063	62.1	182	0.0	9.9	1.1
Shelby, TX	41 600	12.2	59.7	28.0	36 106	7 411	63.9	1 477	0.0	11.0	9.6
Sherman, TX	7 614	8.2	11.5	80.2	6 388	6 876	65.2	193	0.0	8.3	5.7
Smith, TX	247 723	11.1	35.2	53.7	218 025	6 677	67.2	11 093	0.0	11.7	5.8
Somervell, TX	25 026	4.8	9.7	85.5	15 300	8 890	61.1	385	0.0	8.8	2.3
Starr, TX	143 459	21.2	64.6	14.2	127 042	7 939	64.9	4 069	0.0	7.0	13.0
Stephens, TX	10 521	10.6	35.3	54.1	11 423	7 148	66.3	599	0.0	6.3	12.5
Sterling, TX	4 721	3.7	7.4	88.9	3 124	11 443	63.7	84	0.0	11.9	0.0
Stonewall, TX	2 242	8.3	25.3	66.4	2 509	10 631	60.5	115	0.0	13.9	0.0
Sutton, TX	11 100	5.1	9.6	85.3	8 446	9 082	67.5	241	0.0	6.6	3.3
Swisher, TX	14 943	10.8	62.9	26.3	13 537	8 519	63.7	499	0.0	13.4	8.6
Tarrant, TX	2 366 697	7.6	30.4	61.9	1 956 965	6 629	66.5	81 998	0.1	11.4	6.9
Taylor, TX	201 301	22.9	42.4	34.8	174 022	7 708	68.4	9 283	3.0	14.0	4.9
Terrell, TX	5 287	3.1	4.9	92.0	3 135	19 116	57.4	70	0.0	8.6	2.9
Terry, TX	22 873	19.6	42.0	38.4	20 428	8 201	66.5	874	0.0	15.1	5.1
Throckmorton, TX	3 417	6.4	46.3	47.3	3 387	10 584	67.7	122	0.0	6.6	1.6
Titus, TX	66 117	19.6	36.8	43.6	56 938	8 766	65.9	1 766	0.0	10.8	7.2
Tom Green, TX	143 372	14.0	52.2	33.8	130 586	7 148	66.9	7 663	6.7	17.7	4.1
Travis, TX	1 249 168	7.8	12.6	79.6	920 609	7 530	64.6	48 677	0.1	9.7	6.5
Trinity, TX	20 635	13.4	55.7	30.9	17 977	7 843	64.2	721	0.0	15.3	9.0
Tyler, TX	32 431	10.0	56.6	33.4	28 498	7 759	61.0	1 026	0.7	12.8	6.2
Upshur, TX	52 916	8.8	49.4	41.8	49 793	7 417	65.7	2 166	0.0	10.5	6.9
Upton, TX	18 300	4.8	4.7	90.5	9 385	13 237	59.0	274	0.0	5.8	2.6
Uvalde, TX	55 008	16.8	57.3	25.9	47 162	7 335	64.5	1 758	0.0	8.0	7.1
Val Verde, TX	79 460	18.7	61.0	20.3	71 651	6 669	67.5	2 750	1.1	10.0	10.2
Van Zandt, TX	75 996	9.5	54.7	35.8	64 506	6 538	65.9	2 568	0.0	11.3	4.2
Victoria, TX	120 627	15.1	37.1	47.8	112 312	7 171	64.2	5 069	0.0	11.8	4.8
Walker, TX	72 979	17.3	47.2	35.5	59 040	7 562	63.6	5 932	0.2	14.3	13.4
Waller, TX	68 234	9.9	47.5	42.6	57 982	7 303	65.1	3 146	0.0	8.0	3.5
Ward, TX	17 045	9.3	14.8	75.9	15 425	7 441	63.6	873	0.0	13.5	9.3
Washington, TX	40 401	9.6	22.7	67.6	36 705	7 025	66.2	2 541	0.0	7.9	3.6
Webb, TX	478 640	13.9	60.7	25.4	409 546	7 070	66.1	13 908	0.0	8.0	10.3

Table C-1. Population, School, and Student Characteristics by County—*Continued*

STATE County	High school graduates, 2000			College enrollment, 2000		College graduates, 2000 (percent)						
	Population 25 years and over	High school graduate or less (percent)	High school graduate or more (percent)	Number	Percent public	Bachelor's degree or more	+/- U.S. percentage with bachelor's degree or more	Non-Hispanic White	Black	American Indian and Alaska Native	Asian or Pacific Islander	Hispanic[3]
	30	31	32	33	34	35	36	37	38	39	40	41
Matagorda, TX	23 509	60.9	70.3	932	88.6	12.5	-11.9	17.6	8.1	15.4	14.3	2.1
Maverick, TX	25 468	76.7	42.1	1 552	87.8	9.1	-15.3	33.0	17.1	2.9	25.2	8.0
Medina, TX	24 629	61.2	72.2	1 529	84.3	13.3	-11.1	19.5	0.4	23.1	29.6	5.3
Menard, TX	1 660	61.6	69.4	33	90.9	17.2	-7.2	23.0	42.9	0.0	100.0	1.1
Midland, TX	71 008	43.8	79.2	5 824	91.8	24.8	0.4	32.1	10.4	21.9	50.0	6.0
Milam, TX	15 641	66.1	70.9	647	93.0	11.6	-12.8	14.1	3.4	16.5	0.0	2.4
Mills, TX	3 582	59.2	76.7	57	71.9	20.2	-4.2	21.6	50.0	80.0	. . .	2.5
Mitchell, TX	6 634	69.3	71.7	248	97.2	10.4	-14.0	16.6	0.4	5.0	0.0	2.7
Montague, TX	13 208	62.4	73.0	446	92.4	11.3	-13.1	11.4	0.0	4.4	43.5	5.5
Montgomery, TX	183 743	45.8	81.6	11 460	87.7	25.3	0.9	27.1	15.4	14.5	50.0	11.3
Moore, TX	11 460	66.4	62.1	612	95.8	11.0	-13.4	16.7	0.0	0.0	34.8	1.2
Morris, TX	8 776	60.7	73.7	419	88.3	11.2	-13.2	13.6	4.1	11.5	21.7	4.5
Motley, TX	987	60.2	73.5	28	78.6	14.7	-9.7	16.1	0.0	100.0	. . .	3.9
Nacogdoches, TX	33 175	53.6	73.7	9 575	96.7	22.8	-1.6	27.3	8.6	10.5	61.1	5.3
Navarro, TX	28 324	61.0	71.7	2 132	90.0	12.2	-12.2	15.0	4.2	31.3	26.0	3.6
Newton, TX	9 738	76.7	68.7	214	95.3	5.5	-18.9	5.5	4.8	0.0	68.0	5.1
Nolan, TX	10 203	62.2	69.9	559	91.2	13.2	-11.2	17.2	4.8	0.0	10.6	1.7
Nueces, TX	191 848	50.7	74.4	18 244	91.9	18.8	-5.6	29.3	13.8	11.5	43.2	9.4
Ochiltree, TX	5 441	58.2	69.2	178	82.6	16.1	-8.3	19.9	. . .	26.2	0.0	3.7
Oldham, TX	1 250	46.6	80.5	57	100.0	19.4	-5.0	19.4	80.0	0.0	. . .	17.1
Orange, TX	54 229	59.7	79.0	2 925	90.2	11.0	-13.4	11.3	7.3	3.4	19.4	6.4
Palo Pinto, TX	17 764	60.5	71.2	610	88.0	12.1	-12.3	13.4	4.2	2.9	9.0	1.9
Panola, TX	14 848	58.9	75.9	831	90.9	13.4	-11.0	15.7	4.6	0.0	0.0	0.5
Parker, TX	57 072	49.9	80.5	3 105	84.5	18.6	-5.8	19.7	4.9	16.4	18.1	4.9
Parmer, TX	5 868	64.7	60.7	280	92.5	13.4	-11.0	22.0	0.0	15.6	27.3	1.4
Pecos, TX	9 870	66.9	62.5	787	91.7	12.9	-11.5	22.9	9.3	25.0	8.6	6.2
Polk, TX	28 453	66.5	70.0	1 496	91.8	10.4	-14.0	12.1	2.2	2.3	44.8	5.3
Potter, TX	69 427	58.2	71.1	5 877	92.0	13.5	-10.9	17.8	5.6	10.0	16.5	3.6
Presidio, TX	4 303	75.2	44.7	164	87.8	11.7	-12.7	34.5	28.6	60.0	44.0	6.0
Rains, TX	6 298	64.5	73.0	216	90.3	11.5	-12.9	11.7	7.6	12.1	47.6	2.7
Randall, TX	65 628	33.8	89.5	9 190	94.8	28.9	4.5	30.3	14.5	26.5	46.7	12.8
Reagan, TX	1 955	66.9	63.0	40	100.0	9.2	-15.2	15.1	0.0	31.6	0.0	0.5
Real, TX	2 150	55.3	73.0	95	90.5	17.3	-7.1	19.7	0.0	0.0	0.0	6.3
Red River, TX	9 801	68.0	65.7	306	92.2	9.0	-15.4	10.2	4.2	1.5	88.9	0.9
Reeves, TX	7 692	78.2	46.6	297	93.3	8.0	-16.4	22.0	5.6	5.4	68.6	2.2
Refugio, TX	5 178	64.4	68.1	166	95.2	11.6	-12.8	19.1	0.6	0.0	16.7	3.4
Roberts, TX	623	00.5	90.0	25	92.0	25.4	1.0	25.4	. . .	. . .	0.0	0.0
Robertson, TX	10 218	67.8	68.1	368	81.5	12.7	-11.7	16.5	6.4	0.0	0.0	1.7
Rockwall, TX	27 113	36.2	86.7	1 854	77.0	32.7	8.3	34.8	27.4	37.1	41.4	10.0
Runnels, TX	7 723	66.3	68.9	227	86.3	13.1	-11.3	15.9	0.0	25.4	12.5	3.1
Rusk, TX	31 843	58.9	74.1	1 715	81.5	12.8	-11.6	15.8	3.8	28.4	24.3	1.5
Sabine, TX	7 676	65.2	72.5	188	79.8	10.6	-13.8	10.9	7.6	18.8	50.0	4.5
San Augustine, TX	6 221	68.7	69.9	178	96.6	11.8	-12.6	14.0	5.3	27.8	0.0	6.8
San Jacinto, TX	15 040	66.0	72.6	386	84.7	9.6	-14.8	10.4	4.9	50.0	0.0	1.9
San Patricio, TX	39 551	58.4	71.4	2 740	87.4	13.0	-11.4	19.2	13.1	13.0	22.2	5.7
San Saba, TX	3 997	61.2	70.0	136	83.8	15.8	-8.6	18.2	0.0	15.4	33.3	3.4
Schleicher, TX	1 913	60.2	60.4	75	100.0	17.6	-6.8	26.3	0.0	0.0	80.0	2.3
Scurry, TX	10 632	59.6	72.3	704	94.2	11.8	-12.6	15.3	5.6	0.0	43.3	1.6
Shackelford, TX	2 221	53.4	79.2	82	86.6	20.8	-3.6	21.8	0.0	0.0	66.7	5.1
Shelby, TX	16 266	66.6	68.9	653	90.0	12.2	-12.2	14.8	4.2	8.3	24.5	3.7
Sherman, TX	1 968	53.8	73.1	95	96.8	20.4	-4.0	25.6	25.0	0.0	0.0	2.8
Smith, TX	111 020	44.6	80.2	9 012	91.3	22.5	-1.9	26.9	11.2	17.9	47.6	3.4
Somervell, TX	4 372	54.4	78.0	263	82.5	17.2	-7.2	18.9	0.0	28.0	14.3	0.9
Starr, TX	27 716	82.2	34.7	2 009	91.7	6.9	-17.5	26.0	34.6	0.0	79.8	6.2
Stephens, TX	6 471	57.0	72.3	346	84.1	13.4	-11.0	14.2	17.7	0.0	46.9	0.0
Sterling, TX	916	57.5	70.4	42	100.0	17.1	-7.3	23.0	. . .	0.0	. . .	2.0
Stonewall, TX	1 211	66.9	71.0	23	60.9	12.6	-11.8	14.1	5.7	0.0	. . .	2.8
Sutton, TX	2 632	65.4	64.4	63	92.1	13.0	-11.4	21.4	. . .	0.0	82.4	3.0
Swisher, TX	5 200	61.3	69.7	193	80.3	16.2	-8.2	23.6	0.0	13.6	0.0	1.5
Tarrant, TX	898 850	42.2	81.3	78 661	72.2	26.6	2.2	31.7	17.1	18.5	35.9	9.6
Taylor, TX	75 496	47.2	81.2	10 826	32.0	22.5	-1.9	25.9	15.3	13.4	27.2	6.5
Terrell, TX	736	56.5	70.9	17	47.1	19.0	-5.4	31.9	. . .	0.0	. . .	4.7
Terry, TX	8 008	69.3	62.5	304	83.9	9.5	-14.9	15.0	2.1	0.0	100.0	0.6
Throckmorton, TX	1 272	56.1	77.4	38	89.5	18.2	-6.2	19.4	. . .	0.0	. . .	1.4
Titus, TX	16 899	63.9	65.5	929	89.9	13.2	-11.2	16.9	8.8	17.9	40.0	2.1
Tom Green, TX	63 430	52.3	76.2	7 281	95.7	19.5	-4.9	24.7	12.4	17.0	27.3	6.1
Travis, TX	501 361	32.7	84.7	87 661	89.8	40.6	16.2	51.0	20.5	24.9	63.3	15.8
Trinity, TX	9 623	66.4	73.1	256	91.0	9.4	-15.0	9.9	5.7	0.0	50.0	10.4
Tyler, TX	14 433	69.6	71.9	491	82.3	9.7	-14.7	10.9	2.6	3.6	66.7	4.0
Upshur, TX	22 977	60.0	76.3	1 046	82.1	11.1	-13.3	11.6	7.5	8.5	24.6	6.6
Upton, TX	2 165	67.1	67.1	57	96.5	11.8	-12.6	17.6	0.0	17.4	. . .	2.7
Uvalde, TX	15 280	62.8	59.6	1 099	93.4	13.8	-10.6	25.6	0.0	6.0	30.1	5.4
Val Verde, TX	26 281	66.1	58.7	1 443	82.6	14.1	-10.3	27.0	25.2	15.2	42.5	9.0
Van Zandt, TX	32 427	62.4	72.0	1 205	91.4	11.6	-12.8	12.3	3.3	10.3	19.0	2.8
Victoria, TX	51 985	52.8	76.2	3 966	92.7	16.2	-8.2	22.3	9.4	6.8	50.3	6.0
Walker, TX	36 678	58.6	73.1	9 404	95.1	18.3	-6.1	25.3	6.4	7.4	45.5	4.3
Waller, TX	18 395	57.6	73.9	4 267	95.3	16.8	-7.6	18.2	21.4	13.7	19.7	4.9
Ward, TX	6 765	64.4	70.1	253	92.5	12.4	-12.0	17.9	0.0	3.9	100.0	4.5
Washington, TX	19 451	56.5	72.1	1 938	95.4	19.0	-5.4	23.0	5.9	0.0	21.4	2.8
Webb, TX	101 182	65.0	53.0	11 089	89.6	13.9	-10.5	36.7	23.4	6.1	43.9	12.3

[3]May be of any race.
. . . = Not available.

464 THE ALMANAC OF AMERICAN EDUCATION (BERNAN PRESS)

Table C-1. Population, School, and Student Characteristics by County—*Continued*

STATE County	State/ county code	County type[1]	Population, 2005 — Total	Population, 2005 — Percent 5 to 17 years	Number of schools and students, 2004–2005 — School districts	Number of schools and students, 2004–2005 — Schools	Number of schools and students, 2004–2005 — Students	Resident enrollment, 2000 — Total	Resident enrollment, 2000 — Percent public	Resident enrollment, 2000 — K–12	Resident enrollment, 2000 — Percent public
			1	2	3	4	5	6	7	8	9
Wharton, TX	48 481	4	41 554	19.6	5	19	8 340	11 527	92.0	9 347	94.3
Wheeler, TX	48 483	9	4 799	17.3	4	6	924	1 214	94.4	1 098	95.0
Wichita, TX	48 485	3	125 894	18.0	7	55	22 181	35 683	90.5	24 628	94.5
Wilbarger, TX	48 487	6	13 896	19.8	4	9	2 761	3 816	94.2	2 881	95.9
Willacy, TX	48 489	6	20 382	21.1	4	12	4 611	6 058	97.9	5 013	98.9
Williamson, TX	48 491	1	333 457	20.2	11	143	75 754	70 940	85.8	53 372	93.3
Wilson, TX	48 493	1	37 529	20.0	4	27	7 581	7 581	92.5	7 296	95.6
Winkler, TX	48 495	6	6 690	19.2	2	6	1 506	1 938	99.5	1 698	99.6
Wise, TX	48 497	1	56 696	19.3	7	28	8 678	12 621	92.9	10 784	95.1
Wood, TX	48 499	6	40 855	15.2	6	22	6 196	7 855	89.5	6 157	95.1
Yoakum, TX	48 501	7	7 408	21.1	2	7	1 803	2 286	99.0	1 972	100.0
Young, TX	48 503	6	18 000	17.2	3	11	3 349	4 167	93.9	3 556	96.5
Zapata, TX	48 505	6	13 373	22.2	1	7	3 396	3 703	97.1	3 093	97.9
Zavala, TX	48 507	7	11 796	23.4	2	7	2 589	3 883	96.7	3 147	97.2
UTAH	49 000		2 469 585	20.5	84	930	494 574	741 524	87.1	508 724	95.7
Beaver, UT	49 001	9	6 204	22.1	1	6	1 517	1 757	95.5	1 488	99.3
Box Elder, UT	49 003	4	46 440	23.0	1	29	10 541	13 949	95.7	11 538	97.9
Cache, UT	49 005	3	98 055	18.9	6	40	19 766	37 654	95.8	19 663	98.0
Carbon, UT	49 007	7	19 437	18.5	3	13	3 824	6 264	94.8	4 291	98.0
Daggett, UT	49 009	8	943	14.3	1	3	161	192	100.0	165	100.0
Davis, UT	49 011	2	268 187	22.2	4	98	59 686	80 293	92.2	60 679	96.6
Duchesne, UT	49 013	6	15 354	23.1	1	15	3 911	4 687	96.0	4 002	98.2
Emery, UT	49 015	9	10 711	22.5	1	10	2 363	3 518	96.9	3 042	99.0
Garfield, UT	49 017	9	4 470	20.8	1	9	950	1 301	96.8	1 119	99.6
Grand, UT	49 019	7	8 743	17.4	2	5	1 495	2 054	93.1	1 649	94.6
Iron, UT	49 021	4	38 311	19.4	3	15	7 771	13 246	96.2	7 356	98.1
Juab, UT	49 023	2	9 113	24.8	2	10	2 231	2 607	93.2	2 251	95.5
Kane, UT	49 025	6	6 202	18.6	1	9	1 198	1 688	93.8	1 371	95.3
Millard, UT	49 027	7	12 284	24.0	2	11	3 031	4 187	96.5	3 704	97.5
Morgan, UT	49 029	2	7 906	22.6	1	3	1 973	2 628	93.8	2 103	98.6
Piute, UT	49 031	9	1 365	19.5	1	4	321	392	97.4	313	96.8
Rich, UT	49 033	8	2 051	21.6	1	4	431	640	95.3	544	97.8
Salt Lake, UT	49 035	2	948 172	19.6	17	273	176 750	275 773	88.7	193 851	93.9
San Juan, UT	49 037	7	14 104	25.2	1	13	2 964	5 470	98.0	4 410	98.8
Sanpete, UT	49 039	6	24 044	21.8	2	18	5 062	8 638	95.2	5 588	97.5
Sevier, UT	49 041	7	19 386	22.4	2	14	4 415	5 971	94.5	4 876	97.1
Summit, UT	49 043	2	35 001	18.4	3	14	6 575	8 606	87.1	6 661	94.3
Tooele, UT	49 045	2	51 311	22.4	1	24	11 042	12 109	92.5	9 805	96.6
Uintah, UT	49 047	7	26 995	21.1	2	13	5 712	7 936	95.2	6 634	97.7
Utah, UT	49 049	2	443 738	21.7	13	136	92 631	148 809	70.4	83 763	96.7
Wasatch, UT	49 051	2	18 974	20.9	3	8	4 257	4 874	91.5	3 926	96.2
Washington, UT	49 053	3	118 885	19.5	2	41	21 795	26 270	91.4	19 539	94.9
Wayne, UT	49 055	9	2 450	21.7	1	4	517	719	97.8	599	99.0
Weber, UT	49 057	2	210 749	20.0	5	88	41 684	59 292	93.1	43 794	96.2
VERMONT	50 000		623 050	16.2	363	388	97 781	164 156	81.9	114 318	91.6
Addison, VT	50 001	6	36 965	16.8	31	28	5 700	10 568	68.8	6 890	92.0
Bennington, VT	50 003	6	36 999	15.9	24	23	6 448	9 380	77.4	6 897	89.2
Caledonia, VT	50 005	7	30 440	16.4	22	20	4 357	7 986	80.0	5 971	82.3
Chittenden, VT	50 007	3	149 613	15.9	33	62	23 501	45 835	79.4	25 849	89.8
Essex, VT	50 009	9	6 602	17.1	22	10	1 264	1 543	92.5	1 322	93.1
Franklin, VT	50 011	3	47 914	19.1	21	23	8 974	11 338	93.8	9 512	97.3
Grand Isle, VT	50 013	3	7 703	16.2	6	6	803	1 629	89.6	1 327	95.4
Lamoille, VT	50 015	8	24 495	16.2	14	18	3 954	6 279	89.5	4 237	93.1
Orange, VT	50 017	9	29 287	16.8	23	23	4 193	7 349	85.9	5 634	89.9
Orleans, VT	50 019	7	27 640	16.2	25	23	4 238	6 344	89.0	5 214	92.2
Rutland, VT	50 021	5	63 743	15.5	37	37	9 601	16 135	86.4	11 748	94.2
Washington, VT	50 023	4	59 478	15.6	29	33	9 414	15 111	79.1	10 728	93.5
Windham, VT	50 025	6	44 143	15.7	34	36	6 512	10 936	77.0	8 180	88.8
Windsor, VT	50 027	7	58 028	15.5	42	46	8 822	13 723	84.8	10 809	93.9
VIRGINIA	51 000		7 567 465	17.3	228	2 084	1 204 739	1 868 101	83.8	1 291 600	90.4
Accomack, VA	51 001	7	39 424	17.1	1	13	5 385	8 559	89.2	7 110	92.0
Albemarle, VA	51 003	3	90 717	16.4	3	28	12 420	21 699	82.4	14 705	86.2
Alleghany, VA	51 005	6	16 715	16.3	1	7	2 933	3 617	93.4	2 906	96.4
Amelia, VA	51 007	1	12 273	17.0	2	4	1 761	2 734	84.5	2 238	87.3
Amherst, VA	51 009	3	32 134	16.9	2	11	4 738	7 838	74.9	5 609	88.0
Appomattox, VA	51 011	3	13 967	17.4	1	4	2 321	3 174	87.4	2 628	92.2
Arlington, VA	51 013	1	195 965	10.9	1	32	18 802	40 996	66.7	21 548	88.2
Augusta, VA	51 015	4	69 725	16.6	5	25	10 871	14 557	85.5	12 054	90.8
Bath, VA	51 017	9	4 937	14.8	1	3	783	1 034	93.3	836	95.0
Bedford, VA	51 019	3	65 286	17.1	[7]2	[7]22	[7]11 031	13 656	82.2	10 747	89.3
Bland, VA	51 021	8	6 943	13.4	1	4	895	1 436	87.7	1 104	91.5
Botetourt, VA	51 023	2	32 027	16.4	1	12	4 830	6 949	84.9	5 518	91.1
Brunswick, VA	51 025	6	17 920	14.2	2	7	2 322	4 414	81.8	3 224	89.7
Buchanan, VA	51 027	9	24 755	14.9	1	11	3 570	5 598	95.4	4 398	97.1
Buckingham, VA	51 029	8	16 058	16.0	1	6	2 244	3 417	92.7	2 914	93.5
Campbell, VA	51 031	3	52 339	17.1	2	16	8 906	12 058	84.6	9 357	89.8
Caroline, VA	51 033	1	25 563	17.2	1	6	3 928	4 940	92.3	4 191	95.0
Carroll, VA	51 035	6	29 438	15.5	3	12	4 061	5 729	94.4	4 542	95.7
Charles City, VA	51 036	1	7 119	14.4	1	3	857	1 543	84.5	1 216	87.9
Charlotte, VA	51 037	8	12 404	17.3	2	8	2 271	2 876	92.0	2 414	94.6

[1]County type codes are from the Economic Research Service of the United States Department of Agriculture. See notes and definitions at the end of this section.
[7]Bedford city is included in Bedford County.

Table C-1. Population, School, and Student Characteristics by County—*Continued*

STATE County	Characteristics of students, 2004–2005				Outcomes		Staff and students, 2004–2005		
	Percent with IEP[2]	Percent eligible for free or reduced-price lunch	Percent minority	Percent English-language learners	Number of graduates, 2003–2004	Percent dropouts, grades 9–12, 2001–2002	Number of teachers	Student-teacher ratio	Central administration staff
	10	11	12	13	14	15	16	17	18
Wharton, TX	12.6	57.4	61.7	7.0	. . .	1.6	598	13.9	27
Wheeler, TX	9.1	51.5	32.4	7.5	. . .	1.7	101	9.2	25
Wichita, TX	13.5	49.2	36.0	3.3	. . .	2.4	1 635	13.6	. . .
Wilbarger, TX	16.8	60.4	50.1	4.3	. . .	3.3	207	13.4	. . .
Willacy, TX	11.5	27.2	96.1	13.5	. . .	5.1	323	14.3	36
Williamson, TX	10.5	27.7	36.9	6.3	. . .	2.1	5 271	14.4	166
Wilson, TX	13.1	42.2	45.0	3.1	. . .	2.5	531	14.3	35
Winkler, TX	13.9	44.5	60.0	10.8	. . .	1.6	144	10.5	8
Wise, TX	13.6	36.8	22.2	7.7	. . .	1.4	664	13.1	35
Wood, TX	15.3	47.2	19.7	5.3	. . .	2.0	468	13.3	42
Yoakum, TX	12.4	60.3	63.1	14.8	. . .	1.9	144	12.6	9
Young, TX	14.8	44.5	21.3	5.1	. . .	1.2	263	12.8	19
Zapata, TX	10.1	38.6	97.9	38.7	. . .	8.0	241	14.1	7
Zavala, TX	9.9	64.4	98.2	18.2	. . .	7.6	176	14.7	15
UTAH	12.6	32.4	17.3	9.1	. . .	3.7	22 286	22.2	. . .
Beaver, UT	16.0	47.3	12.9	4.0	88	1.9	73	20.8	6
Box Elder, UT	12.5	34.8	10.9	4.0	762	2.0	486	21.7	20
Cache, UT	11.9	30.2	13.4	6.9	. . .	3.8	907	21.8	. . .
Carbon, UT	20.5	43.6	13.8	0.2	. . .	2.0	204	18.7	. . .
Daggett, UT	13.7	24.8	5.6	1.2	21	. . .	14	11.3	4
Davis, UT	11.2	24.1	10.3	4.3	. . .	2.4	2 709	22.0	. . .
Duchesne, UT	16.1	43.2	12.4	1.9	269	5.9	224	17.4	12
Emery, UT	14.9	48.2	7.9	3.3	185	1.2	127	18.6	10
Garfield, UT	17.3	44.6	11.7	3.5	79	0.3	61	15.5	10
Grand, UT	14.0	48.1	17.3	3.0	. . .	0.6	90	16.6	23
Iron, UT	14.1	38.4	11.6	5.9	. . .	1.2	346	22.5	. . .
Juab, UT	12.6	40.8	4.2	0.0	135	0.8	111	20.0	8
Kane, UT	17.4	28.6	4.9	1.2	96	0.7	71	16.8	7
Millard, UT	14.5	46.9	14.3	9.0	260	1.9	167	18.2	9
Morgan, UT	6.9	19.0	2.9	0.3	159	1.1	95	20.8	10
Piute, UT	9.7	70.7	14.3	3.1	23	. . .	25	13.1	3
Rich, UT	10.9	49.9	3.0	2.3	37	. . .	33	13.0	3
Salt Lake, UT	12.6	33.4	23.9	14.0	. . .	5.9	7 723	22.9	. . .
San Juan, UT	11.2	73.1	58.6	41.2	185	2.9	202	14.7	29
Sanpete, UT	14.6	44.2	11.3	7.7	387	2.2	276	18.3	18
Sevier, UT	13.4	43.8	8.2	2.9	. . .	6.4	214	20.6	. . .
Summit, UT	11.4	13.2	11.1	8.1	447	2.6	359	18.3	28
Tooele, UT	13.6	36.4	14.3	4.4	504	2.6	494	22.3	39
Uintah, UT	14.5	40.6	15.7	10.1	380	4.5	285	20.0	28
Utah, UT	11.8	28.2	12.4	6.5	. . .	1.9	3 894	23.8	. . .
Wasatch, UT	13.6	27.1	11.7	8.8	. . .	1.7	199	21.4	. . .
Washington, UT	11.4	32.4	12.9	7.6	1 475	0.9	990	22.0	66
Wayne, UT	12.2	51.1	4.4	0.0	41	. . .	37	14.0	6
Weber, UT	14.5	38.3	22.3	8.1	. . .	3.3	1 869	22.3	. . .
VERMONT	13.1	25.2	4.2	2.0	. . .	4.0	8 664	11.3	. . .
Addison, VT	12.7	21.9	2.2	0.8	. . .	4.6	526	10.8	. . .
Bennington, VT	13.6	26.8	2.4	1.3	. . .	2.8	573	11.3	. . .
Caledonia, VT	11.2	29.9	5.2	1.3	. . .	5.4	427	10.2	. . .
Chittenden, VT	11.4	16.8	6.9	5.0	. . .	3.3	1 797	13.1	. . .
Essex, VT	9.9	37.9	2.0	2.1	. . .	4.8	121	10.4	. . .
Franklin, VT	14.9	26.5	5.7	0.7	. . .	5.3	772	11.6	. . .
Grand Isle, VT	15.6	42.7	0.9	0.5	. . .	. . .	73	11.1	6
Lamoille, VT	10.1	29.4	2.5	0.3	. . .	5.5	338	11.7	. . .
Orange, VT	14.4	31.0	1.6	0.4	. . .	5.1	405	10.4	. . .
Orleans, VT	16.9	45.4	2.7	0.8	. . .	5.8	427	9.9	. . .
Rutland, VT	13.3	29.2	2.3	0.6	. . .	3.9	890	10.8	. . .
Washington, VT	12.0	22.3	3.9	2.2	. . .	2.4	812	11.6	. . .
Windham, VT	16.5	27.1	4.8	1.6	. . .	4.5	663	9.8	. . .
Windsor, VT	14.4	23.4	3.2	1.1	. . .	4.0	841	10.5	. . .
VIRGINIA	14.5	32.6	39.4	5.6	. . .	2.9	93 732	12.9	. . .
Accomack, VA	13.0	60.2	55.8	6.1	339	5.0	445	12.1	33
Albemarle, VA	15.9	19.6	21.1	6.0	. . .	1.2	1 061	11.7	53
Alleghany, VA	17.0	36.7	8.5	0.2	183	4.2	247	11.9	12
Amelia, VA	16.8	40.4	34.9	0.8	. . .	3.7	116	15.2	9
Amherst, VA	12.5	37.9	29.4	0.2	. . .	2.6	364	13.0	27
Appomattox, VA	14.3	37.4	31.0	0.1	162	5.6	197	11.8	12
Arlington, VA	16.6	38.4	56.4	29.2	1 128	3.0	1 770	10.6	269
Augusta, VA	15.0	28.9	5.5	1.6	. . .	2.9	898	12.1	40
Bath, VA	14.6	33.7	2.8	0.3	. . .	0.9	79	9.9	5
Bedford, VA	[7]11.4	25.9	10.0	[7]0.4	. . .	[7]1.8	[7]863	[7]12.8	[7]31
Bland, VA	14.7	35.2	1.6	0.0	64	1.5	82	10.9	5
Botetourt, VA	15.9	14.4	4.8	0.3	359	2.8	380	12.7	23
Brunswick, VA	13.9	70.4	79.9	0.3	. . .	7.4	209	11.1	32
Buchanan, VA	21.8	74.5	0.2	0.0	230	5.1	324	11.0	20
Buckingham, VA	13.7	56.0	47.8	0.0	149	8.3	180	12.5	14
Campbell, VA	11.9	32.4	21.0	0.4	605	1.6	665	13.4	19
Caroline, VA	13.3	39.9	43.5	1.3	. . .	7.9	288	13.6	15
Carroll, VA	17.2	51.1	5.2	2.0	. . .	2.4	376	10.8	24
Charles City, VA	16.1	40.1	77.4	0.0	59	6.5	90	9.5	8
Charlotte, VA	15.3	52.3	40.6	0.3	. . .	2.5	186	12.2	19

[2]IEP = Individual Education Program. See notes and definitions at the end of this section.
[7]Bedford city is included in Bedford County.
. . . = Not available.

Table C-1. Population, School, and Student Characteristics by County—*Continued*

STATE County	Revenue, 2003–2004				Current expenditures, 2003–2004			Resident population, 16 to 19 years, 2000			
	Total revenue (thousands of dollars)	Percent of revenue from:			Total expenditures (thousands of dollars)	Amount per student (dollars)	Percent for instruction	Total	Percent in armed forces	Percent high school graduates	Percent not enrolled, not employed, not in armed forces, not high school graduate
		Federal government	State government	Local government							
	19	20	21	22	23	24	25	26	27	28	29
Wharton, TX	63 346	8.9	49.7	41.4	60 185	7 212	66.7	2 943	0.0	11.1	6.8
Wheeler, TX	13 578	9.0	23.2	67.9	9 380	10 504	64.7	333	0.0	9.6	2.7
Wichita, TX	179 514	15.7	42.1	42.2	161 017	7 194	68.1	10 345	24.1	35.5	5.8
Wilbarger, TX	20 856	11.2	37.6	51.2	18 717	7 050	68.1	1 235	0.0	14.3	14.8
Willacy, TX	44 438	22.8	61.3	16.0	39 220	8 257	62.8	1 527	0.0	11.3	13.2
Williamson, TX	618 606	4.9	15.8	79.3	498 820	6 919	64.4	13 778	0.0	11.0	2.4
Wilson, TX	59 684	10.5	57.1	32.4	53 923	7 209	64.6	1 950	0.0	7.5	7.4
Winkler, TX	18 940	9.5	24.3	66.3	15 635	9 952	62.9	506	0.0	9.9	5.3
Wise, TX	77 734	6.4	37.4	56.2	66 077	7 592	62.7	2 800	0.0	15.1	5.2
Wood, TX	49 635	10.6	41.7	47.8	43 438	7 039	66.2	2 096	0.0	14.7	6.9
Yoakum, TX	32 211	5.1	5.2	89.7	15 540	8 905	60.3	588	0.0	5.8	3.7
Young, TX	27 053	10.4	55.6	34.0	23 129	6 912	69.2	1 041	0.0	7.5	5.3
Zapata, TX	33 419	11.8	15.2	72.9	26 923	8 512	64.5	938	0.0	13.1	13.6
Zavala, TX	25 654	20.0	66.4	13.6	22 224	8 722	63.2	901	0.0	6.7	11.1
UTAH	3 015 796	10.0	55.3	34.7	2 453 331	5 002	68.3	173 747	0.1	13.8	3.9
Beaver, UT	12 121	8.1	52.9	39.0	9 327	6 268	61.4	384	0.5	14.1	1.6
Box Elder, UT	64 477	11.9	60.5	27.7	53 471	5 093	63.9	3 425	0.0	15.0	4.9
Cache, UT	113 810	11.5	61.6	27.0	96 853	5 039	71.0	8 606	0.0	12.9	2.4
Carbon, UT	33 458	12.0	49.4	38.6	26 498	6 722	59.7	1 724	0.0	8.5	3.0
Daggett, UT	3 914	6.9	35.3	57.8	2 160	12 781	56.7	59	0.0	10.2	3.4
Davis, UT	344 281	9.3	60.1	30.6	293 356	4 829	67.0	18 896	0.7	15.9	2.9
Duchesne, UT	28 270	12.8	64.1	23.2	24 260	6 221	65.4	1 158	0.0	15.4	7.8
Emery, UT	20 108	8.4	45.8	45.8	15 779	6 477	67.4	943	0.0	9.1	3.0
Garfield, UT	10 736	8.8	57.6	33.5	8 415	8 684	63.4	344	0.0	17.4	0.9
Grand, UT	11 029	9.5	48.3	42.2	8 701	5 903	66.9	539	0.0	13.5	6.9
Iron, UT	49 209	10.4	51.3	38.3	36 724	4 925	65.1	3 214	0.0	8.3	1.9
Juab, UT	15 654	10.6	62.2	27.2	12 607	5 705	65.8	643	0.0	9.5	1.9
Kane, UT	11 547	7.7	54.0	38.2	8 848	7 229	61.7	425	0.0	9.2	3.5
Millard, UT	26 942	9.2	41.5	49.3	22 134	6 882	64.6	1 107	0.0	8.8	3.6
Morgan, UT	12 124	8.0	54.1	37.9	9 928	4 991	65.5	726	0.0	9.6	1.5
Piute, UT	3 907	14.5	70.4	15.1	3 128	8 861	65.0	105	0.0	12.4	1.9
Rich, UT	5 201	5.8	56.3	37.9	4 057	9 016	63.8	152	0.0	10.5	2.6
Salt Lake, UT	1 072 411	10.0	51.8	38.2	855 603	4 818	69.5	62 241	0.0	13.9	4.6
San Juan, UT	36 365	32.0	47.5	20.5	30 216	10 143	60.9	1 122	0.0	10.8	4.1
Sanpete, UT	36 587	13.5	65.3	21.2	31 002	5 999	70.2	2 615	0.3	6.8	2.3
Sevier, UT	29 112	13.8	61.9	24.3	23 777	5 360	65.4	1 548	0.0	8.6	5.6
Summit, UT	70 092	3.6	21.6	74.8	42 792	6 684	63.9	1 752	0.0	10.4	5.7
Tooele, UT	62 388	8.1	60.1	31.8	48 230	4 590	65.9	3 169	0.1	15.1	9.1
Uintah, UT	42 447	17.0	50.9	32.1	33 618	5 949	64.8	2 151	0.4	15.9	4.9
Utah, UT	506 538	9.4	60.7	29.9	418 163	4 677	70.4	34 454	0.0	14.1	2.5
Wasatch, UT	27 617	7.5	44.2	48.3	20 415	4 994	67.5	1 040	0.0	10.7	2.4
Washington, UT	122 538	7.9	52.5	39.6	94 477	4 574	69.4	6 967	0.0	14.5	3.3
Wayne, UT	4 936	13.9	65.3	20.8	4 231	8 168	66.0	164	0.0	12.8	0.0
Weber, UT	237 977	9.4	62.0	28.6	214 561	5 186	67.8	14 074	0.1	14.7	5.4
VERMONT	1 517 789	6.2	52.8	41.0	1 092 378	11 729	67.3	36 432	0.1	10.2	2.5
Addison, VT	103 380	3.8	42.5	53.7	62 746	11 737	66.1	2 868	0.0	8.7	5.0
Bennington, VT	97 624	6.8	47.8	45.3	63 583	13 244	66.5	2 015	0.0	11.7	1.6
Caledonia, VT	64 647	8.2	64.3	27.5	54 083	14 125	73.4	1 941	0.0	12.1	4.8
Chittenden, VT	323 869	5.4	53.6	41.1	245 040	10 584	67.0	9 953	0.0	5.9	1.5
Essex, VT	13 754	6.2	67.0	26.8	10 615	11 834	67.0	342	0.0	18.1	6.4
Franklin, VT	107 562	8.1	63.6	28.3	85 762	11 240	70.1	2 438	0.1	18.9	3.2
Grand Isle, VT	13 039	5.9	67.4	26.8	9 358	12 802	65.2	321	0.0	5.9	2.2
Lamoille, VT	57 990	8.1	52.3	39.6	42 674	10 998	62.8	1 316	0.0	9.8	2.4
Orange, VT	88 319	5.5	57.0	37.5	63 199	12 921	66.4	1 679	0.0	11.4	1.9
Orleans, VT	72 715	9.8	52.7	37.5	49 402	11 635	65.1	1 408	0.0	14.3	4.3
Rutland, VT	154 484	5.8	51.9	42.3	109 134	11 398	68.9	3 623	0.2	11.5	2.7
Washington, VT	141 876	5.5	51.7	42.8	100 935	10 829	67.1	3 245	0.3	11.0	1.1
Windham, VT	129 639	7.1	46.9	46.0	90 463	14 521	68.3	2 438	0.0	9.1	3.2
Windsor, VT	148 891	5.0	50.8	44.1	105 384	12 241	65.5	2 845	0.0	12.1	2.1
VIRGINIA	11 151 172	6.9	38.0	55.1	9 798 208	8 227	67.6	382 918	2.0	12.2	4.0
Accomack, VA	48 004	12.4	52.9	34.7	42 650	7 913	67.3	1 972	0.0	13.8	8.2
Albemarle, VA	130 416	4.5	25.4	70.1	106 241	8 455	65.1	3 371	0.0	9.1	3.9
Alleghany, VA	25 836	6.6	50.9	42.5	23 241	8 067	63.5	599	0.0	13.2	1.5
Amelia, VA	14 161	10.1	53.4	36.5	12 667	7 347	64.7	533	0.0	10.7	2.1
Amherst, VA	36 236	7.7	56.0	36.3	32 656	7 190	69.2	2 053	0.0	14.7	6.3
Appomattox, VA	17 317	8.2	61.0	30.8	15 659	6 729	68.1	667	0.0	6.9	1.6
Arlington, VA	325 607	4.3	11.5	84.2	273 452	14 274	69.6	5 912	3.9	12.1	3.7
Augusta, VA	90 167	7.9	47.2	44.9	75 759	7 071	70.3	3 215	0.0	15.2	2.9
Bath, VA	9 085	7.5	17.6	74.9	8 811	11 181	62.0	181	0.0	4.4	0.0
Bedford, VA	[7]86 584	[7]5.9	[7]45.6	[7]48.5	[7]69 454	[7]6 388	[7]68.8	2 735	0.0	16.6	3.7
Bland, VA	8 224	7.7	59.8	32.5	6 881	7 487	68.0	325	0.0	7.4	4.9
Botetourt, VA	38 492	4.3	46.3	49.3	35 332	7 421	70.0	1 502	0.0	13.3	1.3
Brunswick, VA	21 127	15.0	58.0	27.0	19 870	8 167	66.6	990	0.7	12.0	9.0
Buchanan, VA	31 966	13.8	58.1	28.1	29 770	8 158	66.2	1 585	0.0	13.3	12.6
Buckingham, VA	19 767	12.8	57.6	29.6	16 904	7 463	65.1	672	0.0	19.2	10.3
Campbell, VA	62 194	7.0	57.7	35.3	58 950	6 687	69.4	2 394	0.0	14.3	1.5
Caroline, VA	29 645	10.8	52.1	37.1	26 940	7 180	68.8	1 117	0.0	19.3	6.4
Carroll, VA	34 261	10.9	55.5	33.6	30 671	7 514	70.8	1 200	0.0	13.8	5.0
Charles City, VA	11 099	7.0	32.4	60.6	9 304	10 135	60.9	353	0.0	14.7	1.1
Charlotte, VA	17 798	11.5	63.0	25.4	16 362	7 154	65.3	671	0.0	15.6	8.5

[7]Bedford city is included in Bedford County.

Table C-1. Population, School, and Student Characteristics by County—*Continued*

STATE County	High school graduates, 2000			College enrollment, 2000		College graduates, 2000 (percent)						
	Population 25 years and over	High school graduate or less (percent)	High school graduate or more (percent)	Number	Percent public	Bachelor's degree or more	+/- U.S. percentage with bachelor's degree or more	Non-Hispanic White	Black	American Indian and Alaska Native	Asian or Pacific Islander	Hispanic[3]
	30	31	32	33	34	35	36	37	38	39	40	41
Wharton, TX	25 567	59.5	69.8	1 417	94.6	14.3	-10.1	20.2	9.2	8.3	47.1	2.6
Wheeler, TX	3 601	58.6	72.0	82	84.1	13.0	-11.4	13.8	0.0	0.0	62.5	7.0
Wichita, TX	80 740	49.9	79.9	8 736	87.6	20.0	-4.4	22.5	10.5	16.1	21.0	8.6
Wilbarger, TX	9 313	57.3	72.2	665	97.1	17.1	-7.3	20.2	4.8	77.1	41.9	2.8
Willacy, TX	11 332	75.6	48.7	620	91.1	7.5	-16.9	23.3	0.7	0.0	0.0	4.7
Williamson, TX	155 565	33.4	88.8	11 436	75.6	33.6	9.2	36.3	29.0	24.1	55.3	16.7
Wilson, TX	20 590	60.3	73.8	1 099	80.9	12.8	-11.6	15.8	7.8	16.2	28.7	6.5
Winkler, TX	4 380	67.0	60.3	135	97.0	10.5	-13.9	16.0	0.0	25.0	0.0	1.6
Wise, TX	31 130	58.7	76.1	1 230	81.7	13.0	-11.4	13.8	5.8	7.7	34.5	4.1
Wood, TX	25 895	56.5	76.3	1 175	68.4	14.5	-9.9	15.4	8.2	6.7	29.0	3.8
Yoakum, TX	4 322	67.1	59.4	182	87.9	10.2	-14.2	14.9	19.4	0.0	100.0	2.3
Young, TX	12 265	60.0	72.1	443	84.0	14.4	-10.0	15.1	20.1	9.8	75.9	4.2
Zapata, TX	6 945	74.6	53.1	359	88.3	8.7	-15.7	12.2	...	...	0.0	7.6
Zavala, TX	6 371	76.9	43.4	460	98.3	7.6	-16.8	26.3	0.0	0.0	100.0	5.4
UTAH	1 197 892	36.9	87.7	186 743	72.3	26.1	1.7	27.7	19.8	9.1	31.1	9.8
Beaver, UT	3 442	55.2	83.2	127	85.0	12.1	-12.3	12.5	0.0	0.0	35.7	1.1
Box Elder, UT	22 766	43.6	87.8	1 685	91.6	19.5	-4.9	20.4	0.0	20.6	22.5	4.0
Cache, UT	42 544	32.2	90.4	16 337	97.7	31.9	7.5	32.9	38.1	6.5	51.7	7.7
Carbon, UT	12 090	50.3	81.1	1 565	93.3	12.3	-12.1	13.4	0.0	3.7	26.1	2.9
Daggett, UT	632	51.6	83.7	11	100.0	11.9	-12.5	13.0	...	...	0.0	0.0
Davis, UT	125 532	31.1	92.2	14 267	88.1	28.8	4.4	29.9	19.2	11.3	24.9	10.9
Duchesne, UT	7 752	56.7	81.0	445	88.3	12.7	-11.7	13.2	...	7.1	30.8	8.4
Emery, UT	5 980	51.1	84.2	283	93.6	11.6	-12.8	12.1	0.0	11.5	0.0	2.3
Garfield, UT	2 829	46.7	85.8	82	86.6	20.3	-4.1	20.8	0.0	0.0	0.0	18.5
Grand, UT	5 486	44.3	82.5	248	91.9	22.9	-1.5	23.7	0.0	0.0	25.0	15.7
Iron, UT	16 318	35.5	88.6	5 249	96.5	23.8	-0.6	24.5	0.0	11.1	39.0	7.2
Juab, UT	4 290	52.4	82.9	186	83.9	12.2	-12.2	12.3	...	0.0	...	0.0
Kane, UT	3 842	39.8	86.4	243	94.2	21.1	-3.3	21.4	0.0	0.0	0.0	12.5
Millard, UT	6 769	43.9	86.7	216	90.3	16.8	-7.6	17.4	...	22.5	17.9	2.6
Morgan, UT	3 805	37.0	92.6	377	93.1	23.3	-1.1	23.6	...	0.0	33.3	4.8
Piute, UT	893	51.1	85.7	35	100.0	14.4	-10.0	14.8	...	0.0	0.0	0.0
Rich, UT	1 144	42.5	91.5	51	100.0	22.0	-2.4	22.4	...	0.0	...	0.0
Salt Lake, UT	509 453	37.2	86.8	63 514	84.2	27.4	3.0	29.5	22.5	11.4	30.0	10.0
San Juan, UT	7 290	54.0	69.6	725	96.7	13.9	-10.5	26.2	0.0	3.5	20.0	5.7
Sanpete, UT	11 522	44.3	84.6	2 563	93.0	17.3	-7.1	17.9	22.6	5.6	14.0	7.3
Sevier, UT	10 480	48.6	85.0	661	94.1	15.2	-9.2	15.7	0.0	0.0	11.1	7.8
Summit, UT	18 366	24.6	92.5	1 350	74.5	45.5	21.1	48.1	22.2	58.5	60.5	9.9
Tooele, UT	21 752	47.4	85.6	1 318	88.2	15.9	-8.5	17.1	8.7	11.0	20.8	5.1
Uintah, UT	13 736	56.2	79.8	773	91.5	13.2	-11.2	13.9	0.0	4.0	41.3	9.1
Utah, UT	166 240	28.3	90.9	57 002	35.6	31.5	7.1	32.5	25.7	20.6	41.6	16.2
Wasatch, UT	8 448	35.7	89.3	620	81.8	26.3	1.9	27.0	...	11.1	47.4	8.1
Washington, UT	51 842	39.1	87.6	5 019	91.4	21.0	-3.4	21.7	17.0	9.1	19.0	5.2
Wayne, UT	1 493	37.8	88.5	76	92.1	20.9	-3.5	20.9	100.0	10.0	0.0	0.0
Weber, UT	111 156	42.6	85.0	11 715	91.6	19.9	-4.5	21.7	10.1	13.7	27.9	5.9
VERMONT	404 223	45.9	86.4	40 318	60.4	29.4	5.0	29.4	34.8	18.1	46.1	36.8
Addison, VT	22 468	47.4	86.4	3 126	20.9	29.8	5.4	29.9	45.5	14.5	57.7	32.6
Bennington, VT	25 311	48.2	84.9	1 816	41.6	27.1	2.7	27.2	34.4	0.0	45.6	25.1
Caledonia, VT	19 596	55.0	82.6	1 584	73.0	22.5	-1.9	22.6	15.4	6.3	42.5	28.7
Chittenden, VT	92 651	32.9	90.6	17 217	69.8	41.2	16.8	41.1	38.3	33.2	46.3	47.1
Essex, VT	4 384	71.0	75.0	121	85.1	10.8	-13.6	10.4	0.0	5.4	18.2	62.5
Franklin, VT	29 485	58.5	82.6	1 223	75.5	16.6	-7.8	16.8	30.0	8.1	36.1	4.9
Grand Isle, VT	4 796	49.6	84.2	192	68.2	25.0	0.6	25.2	50.0	0.0	30.0	20.0
Lamoille, VT	15 281	43.6	87.0	1 637	84.5	31.2	6.8	31.5	31.3	26.6	37.5	42.3
Orange, VT	18 821	53.4	84.1	1 232	77.1	23.9	-0.5	23.8	29.6	10.7	55.0	32.3
Orleans, VT	17 814	62.5	78.2	811	75.2	16.1	-8.3	16.1	38.1	8.7	31.8	17.1
Rutland, VT	43 289	51.5	84.3	3 396	65.6	23.2	-1.2	23.2	12.7	14.4	45.7	37.5
Washington, VT	39 167	43.1	88.4	3 593	40.1	32.2	7.8	32.3	29.7	33.6	39.1	38.0
Windham, VT	30 642	45.4	87.3	2 145	40.4	30.5	6.1	30.3	47.5	14.3	51.1	44.6
Windsor, VT	40 618	44.2	88.1	2 225	51.2	30.2	5.8	30.1	33.3	33.8	53.4	24.5
VIRGINIA	4 666 574	44.5	81.5	450 800	76.3	29.5	5.1	32.4	15.1	19.6	48.5	20.7
Accomack, VA	25 894	66.2	67.9	881	87.6	13.5	-10.9	17.8	4.7	0.0	44.2	2.3
Albemarle, VA	53 847	30.4	87.4	5 379	87.8	47.7	23.3	49.8	20.7	27.7	77.5	32.0
Alleghany, VA	12 278	61.6	76.9	502	89.2	12.6	-11.8	12.4	9.4	0.0	79.3	0.0
Amelia, VA	7 789	67.9	68.3	219	91.8	9.8	-14.6	10.9	7.1	0.0	0.0	100.0
Amherst, VA	21 293	62.8	70.6	1 757	40.4	13.1	-11.3	15.0	4.7	9.8	43.1	9.7
Appomattox, VA	9 421	67.6	70.7	350	73.1	10.5	-13.9	12.4	2.6	0.0	50.0	59.0
Arlington, VA	138 844	23.9	87.8	16 371	43.9	60.2	35.8	73.8	29.9	31.7	59.8	20.6
Augusta, VA	45 609	62.1	78.2	1 580	73.5	15.4	-9.0	15.7	8.2	0.0	32.1	17.3
Bath, VA	3 705	65.1	74.0	135	83.7	11.1	-13.3	11.5	0.0	...	0.0	33.9
Bedford, VA	42 413	52.6	80.1	1 752	69.1	20.9	-3.5	21.8	3.6	27.8	42.7	17.8
Bland, VA	4 989	67.2	70.9	258	84.9	9.2	-15.2	9.3	0.0	...	...	57.1
Botetourt, VA	21 621	52.5	81.4	937	73.0	19.6	-4.8	19.9	12.3	4.0	36.4	25.7
Brunswick, VA	12 777	67.8	63.2	908	54.0	10.8	-13.6	10.9	10.9	22.2	0.0	7.6
Buchanan, VA	18 851	74.7	52.9	905	86.1	10.8	-16.4	7.9	11.7	...	29.8	3.0
Buckingham, VA	10 893	75.3	62.8	336	82.4	8.5	-15.9	10.1	6.1	...	100.0	13.7
Campbell, VA	35 018	59.9	73.4	1 918	70.2	14.6	-9.8	15.9	4.6	7.3	59.4	24.1
Caroline, VA	15 082	66.3	71.3	459	77.6	12.1	-12.3	15.3	5.8	6.0	21.1	14.4
Carroll, VA	21 006	69.6	64.3	935	93.9	9.5	-14.9	9.5	0.0	0.0	20.0	15.9
Charles City, VA	4 845	68.9	65.7	240	82.9	10.5	-13.9	19.1	5.3	1.2	0.0	0.0
Charlotte, VA	8 570	71.6	63.2	284	81.7	10.3	-14.1	12.2	5.9	...	0.0	17.9

[3]May be of any race.
... = Not available.

Table C-1. Population, School, and Student Characteristics by County—*Continued*

STATE County	State/county code	County type[1]	Population, 2005		Number of schools and students, 2004-2005			Resident enrollment, 2000			
			Total	Percent 5 to 17 years	School districts	Schools	Students	Total	Percent public	K–12	Percent public
			1	2	3	4	5	6	7	8	9
Chesterfield, VA	51 041	1	288 876	19.7	1	60	56 242	76 024	86.8	56 777	92.4
Clarke, VA	51 043	1	14 205	16.7	1	5	2 161	2 927	82.6	2 349	88.3
Craig, VA	51 045	2	5 154	17.1	1	2	689	1 057	87.1	883	91.7
Culpeper, VA	51 047	6	42 530	17.6	3	11	6 489	8 160	86.7	6 702	89.7
Cumberland, VA	51 049	1	9 378	17.9	1	3	1 479	2 035	78.7	1 712	81.0
Dickenson, VA	51 051	9	16 243	15.3	1	9	2 538	3 605	97.9	2 829	99.1
Dinwiddie, VA	51 053	1	25 391	17.5	3	9	4 532	5 586	89.1	4 508	93.2
Essex, VA	51 057	8	10 492	16.1	2	4	1 612	2 300	88.2	1 912	89.7
Fairfax, VA	51 059	1	1 006 529	18.2	[8]5	[8]208	[8]164 765	265 920	78.8	181 731	86.8
Fauquier, VA	51 061	1	64 997	18.5	2	19	10 741	14 403	80.3	11 091	84.5
Floyd, VA	51 063	8	14 649	16.0	1	5	2 095	2 800	90.3	2 169	93.5
Fluvanna, VA	51 065	3	24 751	16.9	3	7	3 395	4 657	85.8	3 538	89.7
Franklin, VA	51 067	2	50 345	15.8	1	15	7 347	10 503	84.8	7 814	94.2
Frederick, VA	51 069	3	69 123	18.3	2	18	11 745	14 489	88.7	11 715	94.3
Giles, VA	51 071	3	17 098	16.1	1	6	2 538	3 462	94.1	2 747	95.9
Gloucester, VA	51 073	1	37 787	17.8	1	9	6 144	9 365	89.1	7 144	93.6
Goochland, VA	51 075	1	19 360	15.3	1	5	2 220	3 725	69.6	2 779	73.3
Grayson, VA	51 077	9	16 366	15.1	1	11	2 211	3 280	91.2	2 667	94.4
Greene, VA	51 079	3	17 418	19.6	1	7	2 714	3 751	84.9	3 014	87.2
Greensville, VA	51 081	6	11 088	12.6	[9]2	[9]5	[9]2 647	2 619	86.4	2 063	84.3
Halifax, VA	51 083	6	36 284	16.8	1	15	5 936	8 208	92.8	6 553	94.7
Hanover, VA	51 085	1	97 426	19.0	1	21	18 529	23 954	84.3	17 536	94.8
Henrico, VA	51 087	1	280 581	17.9	2	97	46 711	65 953	83.8	46 900	90.5
Henry, VA	51 089	4	56 501	15.8	4	18	7 815	12 980	90.0	9 981	94.4
Highland, VA	51 091	9	2 475	13.7	1	2	298	483	93.0	412	98.1
Isle of Wight, VA	51 093	1	33 417	17.6	1	9	5 167	7 272	81.0	5 731	84.0
James City, VA	51 095	1	57 525	15.9	[10]3	[10]13	[10]9 404	11 808	85.0	8 630	89.3
King and Queen, VA	51 097	1	6 796	16.0	1	3	828	1 339	88.6	1 132	90.6
King George, VA	51 099	8	20 637	19.2	1	5	3 349	4 551	86.1	3 444	93.2
King William, VA	51 101	1	14 732	18.1	3	8	2 698	3 138	89.6	2 537	93.8
Lancaster, VA	51 103	9	11 593	12.9	1	3	1 475	2 169	86.5	1 805	89.3
Lee, VA	51 105	8	23 686	16.5	1	14	3 680	5 068	93.1	3 985	96.4
Loudoun, VA	51 107	1	255 518	20.1	1	68	43 975	46 444	79.9	33 317	88.9
Louisa, VA	51 109	1	30 020	16.8	1	5	4 408	5 754	89.9	4 854	91.8
Lunenburg, VA	51 111	9	13 194	14.8	1	4	1 774	2 602	90.7	2 160	92.3
Madison, VA	51 113	8	13 398	16.6	1	4	1 844	2 711	79.7	2 212	83.6
Mathews, VA	51 115	1	9 194	13.9	1	3	1 263	1 744	89.5	1 390	95.0
Mecklenburg, VA	51 117	7	32 529	15.2	1	12	4 931	6 732	93.2	5 325	95.2
Middlesex, VA	51 119	8	10 493	13.7	2	4	1 308	1 929	91.0	1 552	92.7
Montgomery, VA	51 121	3	84 303	11.3	2	22	9 504	37 615	94.8	10 341	92.1
Nelson, VA	51 125	3	15 101	14.9	1	4	2 026	2 892	89.2	2 353	93.0
New Kent, VA	51 127	1	16 107	17.1	1	4	2 626	3 026	92.6	2 549	95.4
Northampton, VA	51 131	9	13 548	16.1	2	6	1 999	3 230	87.2	2 566	88.1
Northumberland, VA	51 133	9	12 874	13.0	2	4	1 477	2 114	87.0	1 753	92.1
Nottoway, VA	51 135	6	15 560	16.3	3	9	2 450	3 322	91.5	2 965	93.1
Orange, VA	51 137	6	30 246	15.9	1	8	4 298	5 494	86.3	4 492	90.7
Page, VA	51 139	6	23 831	16.2	1	8	3 626	4 692	92.7	4 080	95.9
Patrick, VA	51 141	8	19 209	15.6	1	7	2 582	3 770	93.4	2 997	97.4
Pittsylvania, VA	51 143	3	61 854	16.2	2	21	9 300	13 858	87.5	11 025	92.3
Powhatan, VA	51 145	1	26 598	16.8	2	7	4 208	5 353	85.6	4 188	90.5
Prince Edward, VA	51 147	6	20 455	14.1	1	3	2 788	7 257	80.7	3 130	86.5
Prince George, VA	51 149	1	36 725	16.6	2	9	6 236	8 720	88.5	6 578	92.3
Prince William, VA	51 153	1	348 588	20.8	3	80	66 298	83 548	83.5	61 279	90.4
Pulaski, VA	51 155	3	35 081	14.8	2	10	4 936	6 831	96.0	5 145	99.6
Rappahannock, VA	51 157	8	7 271	15.4	1	2	1 012	1 453	80.2	1 166	84.0
Richmond, VA	51 159	9	9 114	11.2	3	5	1 202	1 743	89.0	1 374	92.6
Roanoke, VA	51 161	2	88 172	16.2	4	32	14 512	20 624	81.6	15 132	91.7
Rockbridge, VA	51 163	6	21 242	15.5	1	8	2 928	4 498	84.6	3 550	95.5
Rockingham, VA	51 165	3	71 251	17.5	1	20	11 244	16 106	81.9	12 333	89.3
Russell, VA	51 167	6	28 949	15.6	2	15	4 260	6 333	93.7	4 934	95.9
Scott, VA	51 169	3	22 962	14.8	2	15	3 648	4 540	97.0	3 654	99.1
Shenandoah, VA	51 171	6	39 184	15.8	1	10	5 954	7 076	86.5	5 774	89.4
Smyth, VA	51 173	6	32 640	16.0	2	15	5 145	6 761	95.2	5 448	97.7
Southampton, VA	51 175	6	17 585	16.1	1	6	2 805	3 963	85.2	3 189	85.7
Spotsylvania, VA	51 177	1	116 549	20.2	2	31	22 948	25 581	85.7	20 291	90.9
Stafford, VA	51 179	1	117 874	21.4	2	28	25 633	29 156	87.5	22 283	93.0
Surry, VA	51 181	1	7 013	17.2	1	3	1 123	1 750	83.4	1 443	84.8
Sussex, VA	51 183	1	12 071	13.4	1	5	1 348	2 713	83.6	2 200	82.6
Tazewell, VA	51 185	7	44 795	15.1	1	17	6 873	9 714	90.6	7 262	96.0
Warren, VA	51 187	1	35 556	18.0	1	8	5 174	7 320	79.6	5 905	85.7
Washington, VA	51 191	3	52 085	14.8	2	18	7 412	10 974	85.2	7 994	93.8
Westmoreland, VA	51 193	7	17 227	16.1	2	6	2 505	3 622	91.1	3 019	92.7
Wise, VA	51 195	7	41 997	15.5	2	18	6 894	9 569	94.3	7 019	96.8
Wythe, VA	51 197	6	28 421	15.2	2	14	4 197	5 862	92.7	4 471	98.4
York, VA	51 199	1	61 758	19.8	2	20	12 363	17 228	85.1	12 874	91.1
Alexandria city, VA	51 510	1	135 337	10.7	1	16	10 996	26 509	72.1	14 135	83.5
Bedford city, VA	51 515	3	6 211	15.3	([7])	([7])	([7])	1 345	89.0	1 022	94.8
Bristol city, VA	51 520	3	17 335	14.7	2	8	2 319	3 677	80.3	2 616	93.2
Buena Vista city, VA	51 530	6	6 437	15.9	1	4	1 129	1 501	82.2	1 018	98.1
Charlottesville city, VA	51 540	3	40 437	10.7	3	11	4 405	20 969	93.6	4 959	91.9

[1]County type codes are from the Economic Research Service of the United States Department of Agriculture. See notes and definitions at the end of this section.
[7]Bedford city is included in Bedford County.
[8]Fairfax city is included with Fairfax County.
[9]Emporia city is included with Greensville County.
[10]Williamsburg city is included with James City County.

Table C-1. Population, School, and Student Characteristics by County—Continued

STATE County	Characteristics of students, 2004–2005				Outcomes		Staff and students, 2004–2005		
	Percent with IEP[2]	Percent eligible for free or reduced-price lunch	Percent minority	Percent English-language learners	Number of graduates, 2003–2004	Percent dropouts, grades 9–12, 2001–2002	Number of teachers	Student-teacher ratio	Central administration staff
	10	11	12	13	14	15	16	17	18
Chesterfield, VA	14.8	...	34.6	2.5	3 725	4.3	3 922	14.3	252
Clarke, VA	9.5	14.0	9.8	2.0	137	1.9	165	13.1	9
Craig, VA	17.3	27.6	0.6	0.0	61	0.5	68	10.1	5
Culpeper, VA	11.2	...	26.7	2.8	...	6.2	501	13.0	38
Cumberland, VA	14.6	59.4	52.5	0.0	...	5.2	112	13.2	20
Dickenson, VA	17.6	59.8	0.7	0.0	187	3.4	220	11.5	16
Dinwiddie, VA	14.5	38.9	42.9	0.8	...	4.4	341	13.3	22
Essex, VA	18.1	49.2	57.8	1.1	...	3.1	139	11.6	7
Fairfax, VA	[8]14.3	20.0	45.7	[8]17.9	...	[8]2.7	[8]12 627	[8]13.0	[8]1 353
Fauquier, VA	13.3	15.2	16.3	2.2	...	3.0	870	12.3	51
Floyd, VA	18.0	34.3	5.0	2.0	134	2.9	160	13.1	16
Fluvanna, VA	15.2	19.1	21.6	0.0	...	3.1	270	12.6	14
Franklin, VA	18.9	40.3	14.9	0.8	509	4.3	559	13.1	37
Frederick, VA	17.1	18.3	11.1	2.6	...	3.1	933	12.6	84
Giles, VA	13.9	33.8	2.9	0.0	167	2.1	193	13.2	11
Gloucester, VA	12.5	...	13.9	0.1	439	2.4	464	13.2	39
Goochland, VA	17.8	21.1	37.6	0.6	148	3.8	181	12.3	5
Grayson, VA	14.0	52.9	5.0	0.5	154	1.7	196	11.3	17
Greene, VA	19.0	26.8	14.4	2.0	164	4.8	238	11.4	14
Greensville, VA	[9]14.8	66.5	75.7	[9]0.7	...	[9]2.2	[9]209	[9]12.7	[9]19
Halifax, VA	19.8	61.8	50.3	0.3	357	1.4	507	11.7	40
Hanover, VA	15.8	...	13.9	0.9	1 168	0.7	1 462	12.7	101
Henrico, VA	14.8	...	46.8	4.2	...	2.3	3 321	14.1	329
Henry, VA	19.0	47.1	33.2	3.1	...	3.5	670	11.7	14
Highland, VA	20.5	48.3	1.7	0.3	24	...	37	8.1	6
Isle of Wight, VA	13.5	33.2	35.8	0.5	351	3.9	371	13.9	25
James City, VA	[10]14.1	22.9	27.5	[10]2.2	...	[10]1.5	[10]821	[10]11.5	[10]43
King and Queen, VA	23.9	69.2	53.5	0.0	54	0.7	80	10.4	7
King George, VA	12.8	21.8	27.8	0.5	...	2.0	231	14.5	21
King William, VA	16.1	27.2	25.8	0.4	...	0.9	235	11.5	20
Lancaster, VA	13.0	50.4	54.1	0.1	103	2.9	127	11.6	9
Lee, VA	19.7	64.3	1.4	0.0	202	5.7	367	10.0	22
Loudoun, VA	10.5	11.6	29.1	5.5	2 144	1.1	3 233	13.6	170
Louisa, VA	14.6	39.8	28.0	0.7	272	2.9	333	13.2	34
Lunenburg, VA	17.3	62.2	49.8	1.4	108	5.4	139	12.8	13
Madison, VA	11.6	21.9	15.8	0.7	134	2.8	154	12.0	11
Mathews, VA	18.2	23.0	12.9	0.0	98	2.9	104	12.1	11
Mecklenburg, VA	17.5	57.7	50.0	0.9	285	2.5	444	11.1	31
Middlesex, VA	17.0	35.2	28.3	1.4	...	5.7	112	11.7	8
Montgomery, VA	13.7	33.9	11.3	2.4	...	4.0	862	11.0	58
Nelson, VA	18.3	40.2	21.3	2.0	159	1.4	170	11.9	11
New Kent, VA	18.7	14.1	18.5	0.2	179	1.6	207	12.7	9
Northampton, VA	15.4	68.5	60.9	5.5	...	7.0	176	11.4	17
Northumberland, VA	13.7	49.4	48.1	1.5	...	4.8	124	11.9	12
Nottoway, VA	17.2	52.4	49.2	0.8	...	5.1	178	13.8	15
Orange, VA	13.4	29.9	21.5	1.1	283	1.4	339	12.7	20
Page, VA	11.3	39.2	3.8	0.9	200	3.7	276	13.1	15
Patrick, VA	17.0	45.9	12.1	2.6	168	2.4	194	13.3	10
Pittsylvania, VA	14.2	39.5	31.9	1.3	...	3.1	715	13.0	53
Powhatan, VA	15.4	12.5	12.4	0.4	...	2.6	318	13.2	35
Prince Edward, VA	20.0	74.9	62.4	0.1	183	5.1	234	11.9	17
Prince George, VA	11.9	...	44.3	0.5	...	3.1	424	14.7	27
Prince William, VA	11.9	26.0	51.2	12.5	...	4.0	4 417	15.0	670
Pulaski, VA	17.3	38.8	8.8	0.6	...	2.7	402	12.3	28
Rappahannock, VA	16.9	14.3	7.9	0.4	83	1.1	88	11.5	7
Richmond, VA	15.0	38.7	37.0	4.0	...	2.0	103	11.7	10
Roanoke, VA	16.0	15.8	9.6	1.3	...	1.7	1 268	11.4	82
Rockbridge, VA	13.2	31.1	7.9	0.3	261	3.1	260	11.3	19
Rockingham, VA	12.1	28.9	8.6	5.8	713	2.9	906	12.4	50
Russell, VA	17.7	46.5	1.2	0.0	...	2.5	304	14.0	17
Scott, VA	18.8	52.0	2.1	0.5	...	1.4	312	11.7	19
Shenandoah, VA	14.4	26.9	10.0	2.2	392	2.6	472	12.6	29
Smyth, VA	18.2	45.8	3.3	0.7	...	0.8	474	10.9	17
Southampton, VA	17.1	40.4	50.0	0.0	165	3.1	224	12.5	22
Spotsylvania, VA	14.3	20.2	26.2	1.8	...	2.2	1 710	13.4	83
Stafford, VA	10.3	12.8	28.6	1.6	...	2.5	1 783	14.4	110
Surry, VA	15.9	49.2	67.0	0.0	70	1.1	118	9.5	13
Sussex, VA	14.5	74.0	83.1	1.3	77	8.2	116	11.6	11
Tazewell, VA	15.8	50.9	4.3	0.1	471	3.3	582	11.8	29
Warren, VA	15.7	23.9	11.3	2.1	335	2.8	361	14.3	28
Washington, VA	14.1	39.4	3.0	0.3	...	2.4	551	13.5	46
Westmoreland, VA	12.8	50.9	53.8	4.8	146	1.4	201	12.5	17
Wise, VA	14.3	49.2	2.4	0.3	...	2.8	581	11.9	27
Wythe, VA	12.8	40.9	5.3	0.1	...	2.6	344	12.2	18
York, VA	9.6	14.8	24.9	1.3	...	1.1	874	14.1	39
Alexandria city, VA	18.0	47.3	76.1	21.6	540	3.7	1 098	10.0	124
Bedford city, VA	([7])	53.4	23.1	...	([7])	([7])	([7])	([7])	([7])
Bristol city, VA	18.6	52.5	13.0	0.7	...	4.4	208	11.1	16
Buena Vista city, VA	15.0	30.1	7.9	0.4	...	7.1	98	11.5	10
Charlottesville city, VA	17.9	49.2	52.3	5.2	...	2.9	395	11.2	...

[2]IEP = Individual Education Program. See notes and definitions at the end of this section.
[7]Bedford city is included in Bedford County.
[8]Fairfax city is included with Fairfax County.
[9]Emporia city is included with Greensville County.
[10]Williamsburg city is included with James City County.
... = Not available.

Table C-1. Population, School, and Student Characteristics by County—*Continued*

STATE County	Total revenue (thousands of dollars)	Percent of revenue from: Federal government	State government	Local government	Total expenditures (thousands of dollars)	Amount per student (dollars)	Percent for instruction	Total	Percent in armed forces	Percent high school graduates	Percent not enrolled, not employed, not in armed forces, not high school graduate
	19	20	21	22	23	24	25	26	27	28	29
Chesterfield, VA	481 820	4.6	39.4	56.0	377 056	6 807	67.1	15 826	0.2	8.9	3.1
Clarke, VA	19 291	5.5	33.1	61.4	16 879	8 150	66.2	535	0.0	8.6	3.7
Craig, VA	6 335	8.8	52.9	38.3	5 374	7 537	66.1	206	0.0	21.4	11.2
Culpeper, VA	52 602	5.7	43.5	50.9	45 548	7 315	70.1	2 106	0.0	10.6	13.2
Cumberland, VA	13 099	18.5	49.5	32.0	11 981	8 286	58.5	453	0.0	20.5	4.6
Dickenson, VA	23 356	16.1	54.3	29.6	21 219	8 158	63.3	969	0.0	16.1	4.3
Dinwiddie, VA	37 040	7.8	52.1	40.1	32 451	7 261	65.7	1 075	0.0	12.7	4.4
Essex, VA	14 093	10.3	47.2	42.5	12 468	7 330	67.1	421	0.0	9.0	1.0
Fairfax, VA	[8]1 926 352	[8]3.8	[8]17.1	[8]79.1	[8]1 669 139	[8]10 163	[8]66.8	45 985	0.2	7.0	3.3
Fauquier, VA	99 791	3.8	29.1	67.0	88 378	8 558	70.2	2 883	0.5	16.6	1.7
Floyd, VA	16 482	7.6	54.9	37.5	14 748	7 013	69.0	651	0.0	17.5	2.3
Fluvanna, VA	26 739	5.4	49.8	44.8	24 624	7 381	72.0	868	0.0	9.3	0.6
Franklin, VA	58 243	8.1	47.5	44.4	51 028	7 019	66.3	2 227	0.0	14.1	3.1
Frederick, VA	122 803	3.5	34.4	62.0	91 128	8 024	67.1	3 070	0.1	14.4	3.7
Giles, VA	20 746	6.9	52.7	40.4	18 339	7 206	68.1	745	0.0	18.7	2.7
Gloucester, VA	51 339	6.5	50.8	42.8	45 234	7 229	66.8	1 902	0.0	11.5	2.6
Goochland, VA	18 816	5.4	21.3	73.3	17 538	8 292	67.0	691	0.0	10.9	1.3
Grayson, VA	18 346	11.9	61.8	26.3	17 201	7 631	67.9	769	0.0	20.5	5.6
Greene, VA	24 110	7.2	49.7	43.2	20 741	7 682	70.3	805	0.0	15.8	4.8
Greensville, VA	[9]22 357	[9]10.2	[9]59.0	[9]30.8	[9]20 142	[9]7 647	[9]67.3	459	0.0	13.1	3.5
Halifax, VA	50 056	9.3	62.0	28.7	48 566	8 220	63.9	1 799	0.0	18.6	5.1
Hanover, VA	141 335	4.2	38.8	57.0	123 173	6 791	70.6	4 777	0.0	7.4	2.7
Henrico, VA	359 717	4.7	38.6	56.7	308 507	6 802	68.0	11 991	0.1	10.4	3.1
Henry, VA	66 461	9.4	56.6	34.0	58 361	7 135	65.3	2 787	0.5	15.5	6.6
Highland, VA	3 164	9.9	42.3	47.9	2 726	9 241	66.3	113	0.0	20.4	0.0
Isle of Wight, VA	44 781	6.1	44.4	49.5	37 047	7 317	67.7	1 477	0.0	8.3	4.8
James City, VA	[10]83 117	[10]4.4	[10]28.0	[10]67.7	[10]78 373	[10]8 746	[10]67.3	2 111	0.0	12.2	3.8
King and Queen, VA	10 324	11.3	41.2	47.5	8 826	10 634	62.8	337	0.0	20.8	5.0
King George, VA	23 164	5.3	52.4	42.2	21 897	6 836	67.7	940	6.5	24.5	1.1
King William, VA	24 063	4.9	48.5	46.6	21 024	7 961	70.1	567	0.0	10.8	1.2
Lancaster, VA	14 844	8.2	26.6	65.3	11 470	7 927	65.0	437	0.0	10.5	3.4
Lee, VA	32 794	17.0	64.7	18.2	29 991	8 036	71.3	1 185	0.0	12.9	8.8
Loudoun, VA	445 343	2.7	21.2	76.1	403 464	9 901	69.4	6 931	0.1	8.3	3.1
Louisa, VA	36 459	6.4	32.9	60.7	32 337	7 484	66.1	1 131	0.0	14.4	5.0
Lunenburg, VA	14 861	11.2	61.6	27.2	14 162	8 282	68.8	610	0.0	11.8	8.9
Madison, VA	15 302	6.3	50.3	43.5	13 815	7 408	65.2	649	0.0	28.8	4.3
Mathews, VA	11 212	6.9	42.9	50.2	9 052	6 974	66.7	284	1.1	14.8	0.0
Mecklenburg, VA	36 215	10.4	59.5	30.2	34 784	7 269	70.1	1 577	0.0	13.8	3.7
Middlesex, VA	11 553	7.9	38.9	53.3	9 907	7 388	64.1	401	0.0	11.0	6.7
Montgomery, VA	81 664	6.6	45.9	47.5	71 219	7 523	67.4	9 640	0.1	3.9	0.7
Nelson, VA	21 233	7.3	35.1	57.6	17 220	8 546	60.1	714	1.0	15.1	4.8
New Kent, VA	19 290	5.2	49.3	45.5	17 549	6 893	65.5	662	0.0	15.3	5.3
Northampton, VA	17 873	16.5	54.4	29.1	17 290	8 521	70.6	780	0.0	8.2	4.7
Northumberland, VA	13 370	10.0	33.1	56.9	11 259	7 567	67.4	421	0.0	10.9	0.7
Nottoway, VA	20 634	17.1	58.1	24.8	16 674	6 814	68.9	737	0.0	7.6	6.5
Orange, VA	36 585	8.3	41.9	49.8	31 701	7 751	68.0	1 159	0.0	15.0	5.9
Page, VA	27 203	7.9	57.7	34.4	23 781	6 635	71.7	1 196	0.0	16.5	4.3
Patrick, VA	20 300	10.4	58.2	31.4	18 534	7 167	68.5	838	0.0	23.2	4.2
Pittsylvania, VA	63 081	8.7	66.1	25.1	59 474	6 420	64.4	3 202	0.0	10.6	2.7
Powhatan, VA	36 132	3.5	41.8	54.7	29 373	7 251	67.0	1 094	0.0	14.4	4.8
Prince Edward, VA	22 228	11.8	57.1	31.1	20 060	7 034	68.8	2 403	0.0	3.7	4.2
Prince George, VA	47 198	10.3	56.8	32.9	40 770	6 695	64.2	2 557	33.9	42.3	4.0
Prince William, VA	612 178	4.3	39.3	56.4	511 924	8 074	64.3	15 375	1.5	11.9	3.6
Pulaski, VA	39 055	12.2	52.7	35.2	35 220	7 207	60.6	1 341	0.0	24.7	7.8
Rappahannock, VA	9 945	5.2	26.9	67.8	9 016	8 661	67.0	258	0.0	8.1	4.3
Richmond, VA	10 394	8.1	47.6	44.3	9 236	7 509	65.6	359	0.0	9.2	17.5
Roanoke, VA	126 059	4.3	41.2	54.6	107 448	7 391	69.9	4 242	0.0	8.4	1.6
Rockbridge, VA	26 043	8.2	41.9	49.9	23 613	8 059	68.4	1 027	0.0	17.4	4.9
Rockingham, VA	92 877	6.6	46.3	47.1	83 862	7 498	68.0	3 724	0.0	14.6	4.9
Russell, VA	31 274	13.0	62.1	24.9	28 205	6 703	66.8	1 583	0.4	12.6	3.8
Scott, VA	26 764	11.1	70.1	18.8	25 297	6 775	67.6	1 015	0.0	16.1	3.6
Shenandoah, VA	43 616	6.2	50.8	43.0	40 769	6 997	68.2	1 614	0.0	18.4	3.7
Smyth, VA	36 953	9.1	65.6	25.2	34 497	6 785	71.7	1 645	0.4	14.3	3.7
Southampton, VA	25 761	7.9	53.8	38.3	22 444	7 867	62.2	910	0.0	10.2	7.3
Spotsylvania, VA	184 964	4.5	45.4	50.1	158 048	7 160	68.0	4 902	0.0	13.0	2.9
Stafford, VA	201 831	5.0	46.3	48.7	172 516	6 937	69.3	5 363	0.5	12.8	0.9
Surry, VA	14 208	6.0	15.1	78.8	12 836	11 240	61.2	375	0.0	6.4	0.5
Sussex, VA	15 824	7.8	41.4	50.7	14 533	10 757	61.2	451	0.0	16.2	3.8
Tazewell, VA	51 741	11.3	62.6	26.1	46 896	6 713	68.3	2 341	0.0	11.9	5.6
Warren, VA	40 082	6.2	47.8	46.0	35 309	6 956	67.5	1 522	0.0	12.4	3.4
Washington, VA	57 012	9.4	50.8	39.8	52 321	7 155	66.7	2 728	0.2	13.5	3.4
Westmoreland, VA	21 777	15.1	49.2	35.8	18 111	6 921	64.5	768	0.0	13.9	1.6
Wise, VA	58 262	15.4	56.0	28.6	49 734	7 295	70.3	2 621	0.0	11.5	5.5
Wythe, VA	33 703	9.9	55.2	34.9	31 356	7 336	68.4	1 421	0.0	21.5	2.1
York, VA	93 264	12.7	46.7	40.6	86 512	6 967	62.8	3 212	3.1	8.5	3.4
Alexandria city, VA	161 789	5.9	13.6	80.5	149 687	13 730	67.4	3 819	0.2	11.8	5.3
Bedford city, VA	[7]	[7]	[7]	[7]	[7]	[7]	[7]	244	0.0	7.4	11.9
Bristol city, VA	21 603	11.1	49.5	39.4	19 485	8 384	70.4	792	0.0	13.0	4.2
Buena Vista city, VA	9 748	6.6	56.2	37.2	8 556	7 680	68.0	377	0.0	4.5	0.0
Charlottesville city, VA	55 490	8.9	29.3	61.8	49 361	11 163	68.4	5 798	0.2	3.8	1.5

[7]Bedford city is included in Bedford County.
[8]Fairfax city is included with Fairfax County.
[9]Emporia city is included with Greensville County.
[10]Williamsburg city is included with James City County.

Table C-1. Population, School, and Student Characteristics by County—*Continued*

STATE County	High school graduates, 2000			College enrollment, 2000		College graduates, 2000 (percent)						
	Population 25 years and over	High school graduate or less (percent)	High school graduate or more (percent)	Number	Percent public	Bachelor's degree or more	+/- U.S. percentage with bachelor's degree or more	Non-Hispanic White	Black	American Indian and Alaska Native	Asian or Pacific Islander	Hispanic[3]
	30	31	32	33	34	35	36	37	38	39	40	41
Chesterfield, VA	167 037	36.7	88.1	13 958	83.8	32.6	8.2	33.9	26.4	21.0	45.0	20.8
Clarke, VA	9 015	50.8	82.1	385	69.4	23.9	-0.5	24.9	10.5	32.4	37.2	14.9
Craig, VA	3 561	64.2	76.6	110	69.1	10.8	-13.6	10.9	0.0	0.0	18.2	. . .
Culpeper, VA	22 628	62.0	73.7	919	88.6	15.7	-8.7	17.4	5.0	22.9	46.0	18.5
Cumberland, VA	6 183	69.8	63.8	193	67.9	11.8	-12.6	14.0	7.8	0.0	100.0	12.4
Dickenson, VA	11 308	76.0	58.9	668	92.8	6.7	-17.7	6.7	0.0	0.0	15.4	0.0
Dinwiddie, VA	17 199	68.0	70.0	686	90.5	11.0	-13.4	12.5	7.8	9.3	54.0	5.8
Essex, VA	7 052	61.3	73.5	311	87.5	17.4	-7.0	21.4	9.7	75.0	55.9	37.5
Fairfax, VA	653 237	23.1	90.7	62 896	73.1	54.8	30.4	62.0	37.5	38.2	51.6	23.3
Fauquier, VA	36 792	43.4	84.5	2 217	80.6	27.1	2.7	29.1	6.3	26.4	35.0	25.7
Floyd, VA	9 836	68.2	70.1	405	80.0	12.5	-11.9	12.6	9.0	. . .	52.4	0.0
Fluvanna, VA	14 125	52.5	80.0	827	84.8	24.5	0.1	28.1	9.0	0.0	37.8	24.1
Franklin, VA	33 037	60.4	72.2	2 126	54.4	14.8	-9.6	15.3	8.1	25.6	23.5	14.5
Frederick, VA	39 271	57.1	78.6	1 918	79.0	18.6	-5.8	18.6	13.9	28.3	38.4	10.7
Giles, VA	11 856	64.9	75.9	504	91.9	12.4	-12.0	12.3	12.0	100.0	61.1	10.8
Gloucester, VA	23 273	49.9	81.7	1 627	86.8	17.6	-6.8	18.4	11.1	34.9	32.1	8.2
Goochland, VA	12 248	50.6	78.8	587	72.7	29.4	5.0	36.0	8.4	0.0	71.3	35.0
Grayson, VA	13 086	73.6	64.1	439	81.5	8.0	-16.4	8.1	6.9	0.0	11.1	10.6
Greene, VA	10 120	56.3	78.4	492	89.8	19.8	-4.6	21.1	2.5	0.0	32.0	0.0
Greensville, VA	8 610	77.1	62.1	445	93.3	11.0	-13.4	7.9	12.9	0.0	100.0	13.0
Halifax, VA	26 073	69.9	63.9	1 112	85.4	9.5	-14.9	11.6	5.2	5.3	31.8	20.1
Hanover, VA	56 892	42.2	86.6	4 301	63.7	28.7	4.3	29.8	17.5	14.1	41.3	26.4
Henrico, VA	177 191	37.1	86.6	13 581	80.0	34.9	10.5	39.2	20.1	9.1	50.3	21.4
Henry, VA	40 518	67.8	64.9	2 200	84.4	9.4	-15.0	10.4	6.0	10.9	23.1	4.5
Highland, VA	1 929	65.4	72.8	43	48.8	13.2	-11.2	13.3	0.0	0.0	. . .	0.0
Isle of Wight, VA	20 121	54.3	76.2	969	89.2	17.5	-6.9	21.1	6.7	5.9	28.6	37.6
James City, VA	34 042	31.6	89.3	2 277	87.7	41.5	17.1	46.5	10.8	8.7	60.2	32.8
King and Queen, VA	4 663	69.0	68.2	136	80.9	10.3	-14.1	13.4	4.6	25.6	. . .	12.1
King George, VA	10 803	52.0	80.4	735	79.7	23.6	-0.8	26.3	9.5	11.5	50.0	48.2
King William, VA	8 960	59.1	79.1	348	85.9	14.8	-9.6	16.2	9.5	7.1	32.4	8.8
Lancaster, VA	8 841	53.5	74.4	197	88.3	24.5	0.1	31.7	1.6	100.0	68.9	47.8
Lee, VA	16 314	71.2	60.6	833	78.4	9.5	-14.9	9.3	0.0	25.0	67.2	0.0
Loudoun, VA	109 567	25.1	92.5	8 012	73.7	47.2	22.8	49.6	32.0	23.9	53.0	24.7
Louisa, VA	17 697	63.1	71.7	677	82.1	14.0	-10.4	16.0	6.4	8.1	32.2	0.0
Lunenburg, VA	9 305	68.2	63.4	281	84.0	9.2	-15.2	12.7	3.4	0.0	14.3	7.8
Madison, VA	8 644	61.2	75.0	374	74.6	19.4	-5.0	20.7	5.1	0.0	47.4	32.8
Mathews, VA	6 926	53.0	80.8	261	87.7	19.2	-5.2	20.8	5.0	81.5	. . .	19.1
Mecklenburg, VA	22 981	66.3	67.0	1 027	91.4	12.1	-12.3	15.3	5.6	13.3	68.3	18.1
Middlesex, VA	7 436	56.2	73.7	310	89.0	18.9	-5.5	22.1	5.5	0.0	0.0	0.0
Montgomery, VA	43 106	41.0	82.8	26 224	97.7	35.9	11.5	34.2	29.6	7.4	85.6	37.8
Nelson, VA	10 403	57.6	69.0	393	80.7	20.8	-3.6	22.9	7.9	. . .	27.3	24.4
New Kent, VA	9 285	54.1	80.6	319	91.8	16.3	-8.1	18.6	6.9	6.6	40.0	6.5
Northampton, VA	9 133	61.8	67.4	486	87.7	15.7	-8.7	23.3	5.6	0.0	85.7	3.5
Northumberland, VA	9 476	55.0	75.9	211	75.4	21.7	-2.7	25.8	6.4	63.9	55.6	0.0
Nottoway, VA	10 841	67.4	64.4	226	89.4	11.1	-13.3	15.0	5.7	0.0	19.6	0.0
Orange, VA	18 202	58.8	75.2	720	80.8	18.5	-5.9	20.1	6.7	0.0	21.4	28.3
Page, VA	16 085	74.9	64.8	373	81.2	9.8	-14.6	9.8	9.3	0.0	18.4	9.9
Patrick, VA	13 815	72.2	62.2	543	86.2	8.6	-15.8	8.3	3.3	47.4	94.9	19.5
Pittsylvania, VA	43 120	67.9	67.3	1 891	80.7	9.3	-15.1	10.0	4.4	22.6	0.0	20.9
Powhatan, VA	15 411	53.3	78.9	807	82.4	19.1	-5.3	21.2	8.9	38.9	0.0	45.1
Prince Edward, VA	11 089	58.5	69.9	3 885	76.9	19.2	-5.2	27.2	6.0	0.0	60.6	46.2
Prince George, VA	20 272	50.1	81.6	1 738	83.0	19.4	-5.0	21.5	14.6	8.8	30.1	15.5
Prince William, VA	171 058	36.1	88.8	16 310	75.6	31.5	7.1	34.5	24.9	30.8	40.5	15.2
Pulaski, VA	25 362	59.6	74.2	1 296	89.4	12.5	-11.9	12.9	7.2	7.1	0.0	0.0
Rappahannock, VA	5 059	54.1	76.0	216	79.2	22.9	-1.5	23.6	7.0	0.0	46.7	8.3
Richmond, VA	6 552	71.3	60.0	298	80.9	9.9	-14.5	13.5	3.0	0.0	8.3	8.5
Roanoke, VA	60 771	42.1	85.8	3 952	62.7	28.2	3.8	28.1	22.7	9.8	50.8	34.7
Rockbridge, VA	14 556	61.4	71.0	779	45.2	18.7	-5.7	19.2	8.9	0.0	17.9	4.6
Rockingham, VA	45 123	63.0	72.4	2 824	58.1	17.6	-6.8	18.0	7.2	6.9	16.4	7.9
Russell, VA	21 362	69.9	62.5	1 011	88.1	9.4	-15.0	9.7	1.8	0.0	0.0	4.1
Scott, VA	16 846	71.9	64.4	634	91.0	8.3	-16.1	8.3	5.1	62.1	41.2	2.7
Shenandoah, VA	24 926	63.1	75.3	824	81.9	14.7	-9.7	14.9	10.5	0.0	14.9	12.2
Smyth, VA	23 255	66.9	67.5	1 040	85.8	10.6	-13.8	10.5	13.1	0.0	34.4	12.9
Southampton, VA	12 070	63.3	63.2	565	91.3	11.7	-12.7	15.6	6.3	16.7	. . .	0.0
Spotsylvania, VA	56 633	47.8	83.8	3 690	80.9	22.8	-1.6	23.7	15.4	19.1	26.8	23.1
Stafford, VA	56 029	39.3	88.6	4 879	83.1	29.6	5.2	29.9	25.9	29.7	33.5	31.5
Surry, VA	4 569	62.6	70.4	211	72.5	12.8	-11.6	16.0	9.8	16.7	0.0	15.6
Sussex, VA	8 899	75.6	57.6	442	89.6	10.0	-14.4	16.6	6.1	0.0	0.0	0.0
Tazewell, VA	31 291	65.0	67.5	1 954	76.0	11.0	-13.4	10.5	15.2	0.0	71.4	37.9
Warren, VA	21 127	62.2	75.5	1 085	63.8	15.0	-9.4	15.2	8.6	0.0	49.2	5.1
Washington, VA	35 958	58.9	72.3	2 539	61.8	16.1	-8.3	16.1	14.7	0.0	27.0	40.6
Westmoreland, VA	11 808	64.1	69.3	428	85.3	13.3	-11.1	17.3	3.3	33.3	42.9	9.1
Wise, VA	26 731	67.4	62.5	2 059	91.2	10.8	-13.6	10.6	12.1	0.0	65.6	3.5
Wythe, VA	19 528	62.2	70.2	1 024	82.7	12.1	-12.3	12.0	9.2	0.0	65.8	9.8
York, VA	36 168	29.5	91.7	3 066	81.1	37.4	13.0	39.2	23.5	45.4	44.7	41.3
Alexandria city, VA	95 730	25.8	86.8	10 296	63.8	54.3	29.9	70.0	28.3	55.6	55.4	21.3
Bedford city, VA	4 494	61.5	70.9	232	68.5	15.2	-9.2	17.6	5.4	0.0	45.0	52.6
Bristol city, VA	12 366	56.9	72.4	792	44.7	17.0	-7.4	17.3	5.9	21.7	34.1	34.1
Buena Vista city, VA	4 250	65.0	69.0	419	42.5	10.5	-13.9	10.4	7.8	. . .	100.0	. . .
Charlottesville city, VA	22 868	40.6	80.8	15 501	95.7	40.8	16.4	49.1	8.6	41.9	75.2	47.8

[3]May be of any race.
. . . = Not available.

Table C-1. Population, School, and Student Characteristics by County—*Continued*

STATE County	State/ county code	County type[1]	Population, 2005 Total	Percent 5 to 17 years	Number of schools and students, 2004–2005 School districts	Schools	Students	Resident enrollment, 2000 Total	Percent public	K–12	Percent public
			1	2	3	4	5	6	7	8	9
Chesapeake city, VA	51 550	1	218 968	20.0	2	47	40 265	58 385	84.7	43 542	90.6
Colonial Heights city, VA	51 570	1	17 567	16.0	1	5	2 891	3 884	90.2	2 991	95.4
Covington city, VA	51 580	6	6 205	16.1	3	4	841	1 202	94.5	937	99.4
Danville city, VA	51 590	3	46 143	16.5	1	17	7 312	11 141	88.7	8 649	91.8
Emporia city, VA	51 595	6	5 587	18.0	(9)	(9)	(9)	1 282	92.7	1 113	94.2
Fairfax city, VA	51 600	1	21 963	14.1	(8)	(8)	(8)	5 133	80.7	3 157	86.0
Falls Church city, VA	51 610	1	10 781	15.3	1	4	1 898	2 683	72.8	1 828	84.2
Franklin city, VA	51 620	6	8 594	16.9	1	3	1 383	2 175	88.8	1 709	89.4
Fredericksburg city, VA	51 630	1	20 732	12.0	1	5	2 473	6 061	90.1	2 329	90.3
Galax city, VA	51 640	6	6 676	15.8	2	4	1 302	1 446	97.0	1 171	98.5
Hampton city, VA	51 650	1	145 579	17.2	5	42	22 938	42 305	77.6	27 044	90.1
Harrisonburg city, VA	51 660	3	40 438	9.9	2	7	4 150	19 504	90.7	4 247	91.5
Hopewell city, VA	51 670	1	22 690	19.2	1	8	3 908	5 474	91.3	4 204	92.7
Lexington city, VA	51 678	6	6 776	6.3	1	2	473	3 467	53.6	533	97.6
Lynchburg city, VA	51 680	3	66 973	14.9	4	20	8 620	19 578	61.8	10 830	89.3
Manassas city, VA	51 683	1	37 569	20.5	1	8	6 761	9 941	82.1	7 433	87.1
Manassas Park city, VA	51 685	1	11 622	22.1	1	4	2 374	2 862	84.9	2 118	91.7
Martinsville city, VA	51 690	4	14 925	16.0	1	6	2 636	3 540	93.6	2 630	96.7
Newport News city, VA	51 700	1	179 899	20.1	2	51	33 096	50 215	87.2	35 994	91.6
Norfolk city, VA	51 710	1	231 954	17.0	6	62	36 302	63 867	85.5	40 850	90.2
Norton city, VA	51 720	7	3 677	15.9	1	2	736	906	94.7	699	95.1
Petersburg city, VA	51 730	1	32 604	17.4	3	12	5 128	8 191	90.9	6 381	93.8
Poquoson city, VA	51 735	1	11 811	18.1	1	4	2 596	3 260	87.9	2 524	93.3
Portsmouth city, VA	51 740	1	100 169	18.6	1	27	15 843	26 135	86.3	19 171	89.1
Radford city, VA	51 750	3	14 575	7.1	1	4	1 533	8 502	95.8	1 435	94.7
Richmond city, VA	51 760	1	193 777	15.0	7	69	25 954	54 048	80.8	31 524	87.5
Roanoke city, VA	51 770	2	92 631	17.0	2	32	13 655	20 600	88.7	15 292	93.3
Salem city, VA	51 775	2	24 654	14.8	1	6	3 944	6 792	73.2	4 103	98.3
Staunton city, VA	51 790	4	23 337	14.7	5	11	2 710	5 314	70.3	3 528	84.6
Suffolk city, VA	51 800	1	78 994	19.2	2	21	13 722	17 697	84.3	13 372	87.3
Virginia Beach city, VA	51 810	1	438 415	19.4	1	87	75 515	121 415	84.5	86 963	91.2
Waynesboro city, VA	51 820	4	21 269	17.0	1	6	3 087	4 309	90.6	3 412	95.4
Williamsburg city, VA	51 830	1	11 751	5.6	(10)	(10)	(10)	6 365	90.1	832	90.7
Winchester city, VA	51 840	3	25 119	15.2	1	6	3 678	5 762	76.0	3 690	95.7
WASHINGTON	53 000		6 287 759	17.3	306	2 272	1 020 069	1 584 701	86.3	1 127 448	91.1
Adams, WA	53 001	6	16 803	22.4	5	11	3 848	4 945	93.9	4 249	94.6
Asotin, WA	53 003	3	21 178	16.7	2	11	3 357	5 037	93.3	3 900	94.5
Benton, WA	53 005	3	157 950	19.5	6	55	30 006	40 139	89.9	31 831	93.5
Chelan, WA	53 007	3	69 791	18.5	8	35	12 826	18 093	88.7	14 315	92.2
Clallam, WA	53 009	5	69 689	14.7	5	26	9 856	14 410	89.1	11 058	91.0
Clark, WA	53 011	1	403 766	19.3	9	112	70 678	92 185	88.1	70 778	92.0
Columbia, WA	53 013	6	4 129	15.4	2	4	574	918	90.5	759	92.6
Cowlitz, WA	53 015	3	97 325	18.3	6	41	17 911	23 679	90.4	18 394	94.3
Douglas, WA	53 017	3	34 977	19.7	6	20	6 617	8 929	93.8	7 284	96.7
Ferry, WA	53 019	9	7 542	17.3	5	12	1 116	1 875	92.1	1 554	92.2
Franklin, WA	53 021	3	63 011	21.8	5	28	13 163	14 657	93.8	12 379	95.8
Garfield, WA	53 023	8	2 344	15.7	1	2	403	586	97.1	496	98.4
Grant, WA	53 025	4	81 229	21.3	10	54	17 636	21 570	94.8	17 754	96.9
Grays Harbor, WA	53 027	4	70 900	16.8	14	43	12 277	16 737	94.2	13 316	96.0
Island, WA	53 029	4	79 252	16.7	3	24	9 405	17 742	88.0	13 317	92.4
Jefferson, WA	53 031	6	28 666	13.1	5	14	3 319	5 042	87.4	3 934	93.3
King, WA	53 033	1	1 793 583	15.3	19	473	234 842	444 560	81.9	287 823	87.7
Kitsap, WA	53 035	3	240 661	17.9	6	80	40 689	62 794	87.1	46 929	91.8
Kittitas, WA	53 037	6	36 841	12.7	6	16	4 792	12 277	95.5	5 204	94.7
Klickitat, WA	53 039	6	19 839	17.7	10	19	3 365	4 850	90.6	4 081	93.7
Lewis, WA	53 041	4	72 449	17.6	14	39	12 470	17 267	90.7	13 805	92.8
Lincoln, WA	53 043	8	10 381	16.7	8	15	2 088	2 355	89.3	1 980	91.6
Mason, WA	53 045	6	54 359	15.6	7	21	8 266	11 233	92.4	9 123	94.8
Okanogan, WA	53 047	6	39 782	17.9	8	24	6 470	10 277	93.5	8 692	95.5
Pacific, WA	53 049	7	21 579	14.7	5	18	3 106	4 621	93.5	3 735	95.1
Pend Oreille, WA	53 051	8	12 673	16.8	3	8	1 842	2 986	89.1	2 413	90.9
Pierce, WA	53 053	1	753 787	18.6	15	253	128 973	191 320	85.7	142 171	91.3
San Juan, WA	53 055	9	15 274	12.8	4	14	1 765	2 789	83.8	2 184	89.5
Skagit, WA	53 057	3	113 171	17.5	8	52	19 165	26 225	91.1	20 524	94.4
Skamania, WA	53 059	1	10 664	17.5	5	16	4 127	2 385	91.2	1 955	94.0
Snohomish, WA	53 061	1	655 944	18.7	15	235	127 944	163 166	87.5	122 466	92.0
Spokane, WA	53 063	2	440 706	17.4	15	167	72 664	117 842	84.5	80 540	90.5
Stevens, WA	53 065	6	42 013	18.3	12	34	6 281	10 414	90.2	8 901	92.4
Thurston, WA	53 067	3	228 867	16.8	10	76	38 869	56 997	87.4	40 428	92.4
Wahkiakum, WA	53 069	8	3 849	15.9	1	2	501	912	87.4	690	94.9
Walla Walla, WA	53 071	4	57 558	16.3	7	27	8 847	16 905	71.1	10 530	87.9
Whatcom, WA	53 073	3	183 471	16.1	7	70	26 529	51 210	88.7	29 602	88.7
Whitman, WA	53 075	4	40 170	10.8	13	26	4 673	20 964	95.7	5 320	91.6
Yakima, WA	53 077	3	231 586	21.3	16	95	48 809	63 808	91.2	53 034	94.3

[1]County type codes are from the Economic Research Service of the United States Department of Agriculture. See notes and definitions at the end of this section.
[8]Fairfax city is included with Fairfax County.
[9]Emporia city is included with Greensville County.
[10]Williamsburg city is included with James City County.

Table C-1. Population, School, and Student Characteristics by County—*Continued*

STATE County	Characteristics of students, 2004–2005				Outcomes		Staff and students, 2004–2005		
	Percent with IEP[2]	Percent eligible for free or reduced-price lunch	Percent minority	Percent English-language learners	Number of graduates, 2003–2004	Percent dropouts, grades 9–12, 2001–2002	Number of teachers	Student-teacher ratio	Central administration staff
	10	11	12	13	14	15	16	17	18
Chesapeake city, VA	17.6	24.6	40.7	0.8	...	2.8	2 900	13.9	253
Colonial Heights city, VA	14.9	...	16.7	5.1	...	4.7	251	11.5	16
Covington city, VA	23.9	39.5	23.6	0.0	...	3.4	88	9.6	...
Danville city, VA	14.2	56.8	72.9	2.4	448	5.3	590	12.4	72
Emporia city, VA	(9)	50.0	69.9	(9)	...	(9)	(9)	(9)	(9)
Fairfax city, VA	(8)	19.8	47.3	(8)	...	(8)	(8)	(8)	(8)
Falls Church city, VA	13.8	8.2	23.8	8.7	...	0.4	184	10.3	13
Franklin city, VA	18.9	80.6	78.0	0.4	94	6.2	117	11.8	20
Fredericksburg city, VA	14.6	48.7	56.9	6.4	149	2.0	202	12.2	26
Galax city, VA	10.8	53.0	26.4	13.1	...	1.8	111	11.7	9
Hampton city, VA	14.4	46.7	66.2	1.6	...	3.7	1 912	12.0	98
Harrisonburg city, VA	15.4	...	42.1	34.1	...	0.9	405	10.2	32
Hopewell city, VA	18.4	61.0	58.2	1.4	212	9.7	325	12.0	26
Lexington city, VA	17.8	28.7	11.5	2.3	...	...	56	8.4	5
Lynchburg city, VA	16.8	50.7	54.8	1.3	...	3.2	739	11.7	41
Manassas city, VA	11.8	23.1	50.2	24.4	417	1.5	525	12.9	32
Manassas Park city, VA	10.9	32.7	56.8	21.7	118	2.0	183	13.0	15
Martinsville city, VA	13.8	53.5	62.4	3.7	178	1.4	223	11.8	23
Newport News city, VA	13.0	49.1	65.9	1.4	...	3.0	2 530	13.1	86
Norfolk city, VA	14.0	58.4	74.7	0.7	...	4.6	2 835	12.8	260
Norton city, VA	14.5	48.5	11.4	0.0	...	4.7	66	11.2	4
Petersburg city, VA	13.9	70.4	98.4	0.7	...	7.5	444	11.5	63
Poquoson city, VA	11.1	6.9	4.6	0.6	191	1.1	194	13.4	14
Portsmouth city, VA	15.0	49.5	74.3	0.2	731	3.3	1 161	13.6	89
Radford city, VA	16.4	28.5	14.3	0.6	102	2.6	125	12.3	11
Richmond city, VA	20.7	67.6	92.5	2.1	...	2.7	2 202	11.8	205
Roanoke city, VA	15.9	58.8	49.8	3.9	...	7.2	1 206	11.3	83
Salem city, VA	12.3	21.9	12.9	1.1	269	2.0	305	12.9	24
Staunton city, VA	17.3	43.2	26.1	0.7	...	3.9	289	9.4	28
Suffolk city, VA	11.0	38.5	59.7	0.1	...	3.1	977	14.0	59
Virginia Beach city, VA	13.9	28.7	39.9	1.3	4 716	1.2	5 626	13.4	344
Waynesboro city, VA	10.6	46.5	22.7	3.2	159	1.5	238	13.0	22
Williamsburg city, VA	(10)	22.9	31.8	(10)	...	(10)	(10)	(10)	(10)
Winchester city, VA	19.2	33.4	26.9	10.7	209	3.7	320	11.5	9
WASHINGTON	12.2	36.1	29.3	7.4	...	7.1	53 124	19.2	
Adams, WA	10.0	71.4	67.0	35.9	...	6.1	225	17.1	12
Asotin, WA	16.8	41.1	6.6	0.6	241	8.9	180	18.7	7
Benton, WA	11.5	36.2	25.2	7.8	...	5.0	1 524	19.7	77
Chelan, WA	10.4	48.4	38.1	19.0	...	9.8	672	19.1	47
Clallam, WA	13.8	44.8	20.7	3.1	614	3.6	533	18.5	31
Clark, WA	11.6	34.3	17.0	5.9	...	7.4	3 578	19.8	193
Columbia, WA	8.9	47.9	16.0	3.3	...	3.9	38	15.0	3
Cowlitz, WA	12.6	39.8	16.0	3.0	903	7.2	899	19.9	50
Douglas, WA	12.7	49.6	38.8	18.5	...	6.7	364	18.2	17
Ferry, WA	9.9	45.3	28.7	0.0	...	4.5	74	15.2	7
Franklin, WA	11.2	68.1	70.7	37.9	...	5.4	718	18.3	56
Garfield, WA	17.4	40.2	9.4	1.2	43	0.6	24	16.5	2
Grant, WA	11.5	59.9	50.1	22.9	1 109	6.6	973	18.1	43
Grays Harbor, WA	13.4	48.9	21.3	4.3	...	9.9	689	17.8	43
Island, WA	10.6	24.9	20.7	2.3	623	8.7	477	19.7	23
Jefferson, WA	11.8	38.3	11.4	0.5	...	3.8	179	18.5	10
King, WA	11.4	29.1	38.1	9.0	14 324	8.3	12 218	19.2	636
Kitsap, WA	13.2	26.7	18.9	1.3	...	5.7	2 142	19.0	131
Kittitas, WA	11.6	32.5	15.1	3.9	...	5.6	262	18.3	18
Klickitat, WA	14.3	44.8	22.0	7.6	...	8.3	206	16.4	15
Lewis, WA	12.6	40.3	14.3	3.0	...	5.4	673	18.5	39
Lincoln, WA	9.2	37.6	8.2	0.0	...	1.5	155	13.5	14
Mason, WA	14.0	42.4	19.6	2.9	...	7.1	452	18.3	28
Okanogan, WA	13.2	59.9	42.4	9.7	...	8.9	371	17.4	35
Pacific, WA	14.7	46.0	23.9	6.8	229	16.2	198	15.7	12
Pend Oreille, WA	12.5	55.8	10.0	0.0	133	4.0	111	16.6	8
Pierce, WA	12.7	35.3	31.4	3.3	...	6.6	6 611	19.5	336
San Juan, WA	12.1	26.2	11.3	1.7	...	5.3	109	16.2	9
Skagit, WA	13.3	43.4	27.9	12.2	...	8.1	1 024	18.7	61
Skamania, WA	12.2	35.8	10.3	1.1	...	2.6	219	18.9	11
Snohomish, WA	12.4	25.8	22.0	5.3	...	7.1	6 242	20.5	326
Spokane, WA	12.6	38.6	11.5	2.1	...	4.2	3 850	18.9	189
Stevens, WA	12.4	55.8	14.8	1.0	...	4.1	357	17.6	28
Thurston, WA	12.8	29.0	21.8	1.2	...	5.5	1 979	19.6	108
Wahkiakum, WA	15.2	34.9	7.2	0.0	41	5.4	26	19.2	1
Walla Walla, WA	12.5	45.0	33.6	12.0	...	6.6	514	17.2	31
Whatcom, WA	12.3	38.2	20.3	6.4	1 607	5.2	1 411	18.8	73
Whitman, WA	10.1	28.8	12.7	0.9	...	2.7	285	16.4	22
Yakima, WA	12.0	65.9	62.6	22.4	...	11.9	2 563	19.0	158

[2]IEP = Individual Education Program. See notes and definitions at the end of this section.
[8]Fairfax city is included with Fairfax County.
[9]Emporia city is included with Greensville County.
[10]Williamsburg city is included with James City County.
... = Not available.

Table C-1. Population, School, and Student Characteristics by County—*Continued*

STATE County	Revenue, 2003–2004				Current expenditures, 2003–2004			Resident population, 16 to 19 years, 2000			
	Total revenue (thousands of dollars)	Percent of revenue from:			Total expenditures (thousands of dollars)	Amount per student (dollars)	Percent for instruction	Total	Percent in armed forces	Percent high school graduates	Percent not enrolled, not employed, not in armed forces, not high school graduate
		Federal government	State government	Local government							
	19	20	21	22	23	24	25	26	27	28	29
Chesapeake city, VA	324 872	6.8	49.1	44.1	307 495	7 802	70.4	11 484	1.8	12.3	4.0
Colonial Heights city, VA	24 819	4.2	36.4	59.4	23 507	8 407	71.1	841	0.0	14.0	2.1
Covington city, VA	9 853	9.5	40.6	49.9	8 704	9 802	68.3	264	0.0	25.8	3.4
Danville city, VA	65 603	17.0	49.7	33.3	58 100	7 868	70.0	2 475	0.0	11.6	9.5
Emporia city, VA	(9)	(9)	(9)	(9)	(9)	(9)	(9)	265	0.0	19.6	13.6
Fairfax city, VA	(8)	(8)	(8)	(8)	(8)	(8)	(8)	983	0.0	7.8	4.9
Falls Church city, VA	27 993	2.5	12.5	85.0	25 159	13 425	65.6	426	0.0	4.2	0.0
Franklin city, VA	19 212	11.0	35.9	53.1	12 881	9 334	67.7	477	0.0	8.4	6.7
Fredericksburg city, VA	26 066	17.6	22.6	59.8	25 445	10 386	70.8	1 904	0.8	14.4	2.8
Galax city, VA	10 673	10.8	50.6	38.5	9 061	6 813	67.3	302	0.0	14.9	2.0
Hampton city, VA	182 302	9.0	57.1	33.9	177 992	7 736	64.5	9 310	1.3	13.3	3.0
Harrisonburg city, VA	38 821	9.5	33.6	56.8	37 542	9 313	70.3	6 261	0.0	2.8	2.5
Hopewell city, VA	35 033	12.2	52.1	35.7	32 349	8 324	69.8	1 112	0.0	17.0	6.7
Lexington city, VA	5 309	6.2	42.1	51.6	3 655	7 744	69.4	1 238	0.0	1.5	0.6
Lynchburg city, VA	76 175	11.6	47.2	41.3	69 904	7 966	68.7	4 792	0.3	6.9	4.2
Manassas city, VA	67 709	3.7	37.4	58.9	59 034	8 678	69.7	1 923	0.0	8.6	5.6
Manassas Park city, VA	28 409	3.8	36.3	59.9	19 685	8 604	65.2	499	0.0	11.4	5.2
Martinsville city, VA	22 991	13.7	51.7	34.6	22 093	8 462	64.7	703	0.0	7.7	4.6
Newport News city, VA	285 012	10.9	49.2	39.9	246 994	7 509	67.2	10 506	7.7	19.2	4.0
Norfolk city, VA	319 365	12.8	51.7	35.4	292 437	7 963	69.0	16 165	19.0	27.0	5.6
Norton city, VA	5 939	13.8	56.4	29.8	5 382	7 527	71.5	218	0.0	18.8	3.2
Petersburg city, VA	47 353	15.2	57.5	27.2	43 243	8 063	64.4	1 704	0.3	13.3	11.2
Poquoson city, VA	19 048	5.8	50.0	44.3	16 503	6 487	68.0	651	0.0	5.5	3.8
Portsmouth city, VA	134 301	12.3	59.1	28.5	121 960	7 371	66.3	5 791	9.8	19.7	7.4
Radford city, VA	12 699	6.8	50.0	43.2	11 309	7 358	70.6	2 507	0.0	2.4	0.0
Richmond city, VA	283 466	12.8	35.6	51.7	267 655	10 538	65.7	11 559	0.1	9.9	6.2
Roanoke city, VA	131 091	9.4	42.4	48.2	113 173	8 342	70.0	4 030	0.0	18.1	12.8
Salem city, VA	34 938	4.9	38.3	56.8	29 902	7 648	71.4	1 715	0.0	5.4	0.5
Staunton city, VA	27 376	7.7	46.8	45.6	24 305	9 056	72.3	1 364	0.0	9.7	2.3
Suffolk city, VA	126 555	7.0	45.7	47.3	91 702	6 909	67.9	3 204	0.0	8.7	6.6
Virginia Beach city, VA	630 291	8.9	45.9	45.2	589 852	7 730	68.7	23 384	5.4	15.8	3.7
Waynesboro city, VA	24 329	8.8	44.9	46.2	23 148	7 673	67.2	845	0.0	12.3	6.2
Williamsburg city, VA	(10)	(10)	(10)	(10)	(10)	(10)	(10)	2 080	0.0	1.6	0.0
Winchester city, VA	38 050	6.8	30.2	63.0	36 069	9 953	69.7	1 688	0.0	10.5	9.5
WASHINGTON	8 790 531	8.5	61.6	29.9	7 394 646	7 243	64.6	335 082	0.9	11.3	4.6
Adams, WA	33 916	13.2	69.3	17.5	30 255	8 092	66.3	1 110	0.0	6.8	9.8
Asotin, WA	27 151	11.6	68.6	19.8	25 237	7 321	65.2	1 155	0.0	10.8	3.7
Benton, WA	244 659	7.4	69.0	23.6	212 416	6 980	65.5	8 530	0.0	8.6	6.1
Chelan, WA	110 177	11.5	64.2	24.3	90 694	7 008	65.4	4 091	0.0	11.4	8.9
Clallam, WA	80 088	13.2	65.0	21.8	71 516	7 390	65.6	3 460	0.0	12.5	7.1
Clark, WA	594 833	6.1	66.1	27.8	484 804	6 813	64.5	18 895	0.1	11.3	5.9
Columbia, WA	5 635	12.6	65.4	22.0	5 426	8 954	63.2	251	1.6	15.5	6.4
Cowlitz, WA	158 697	9.3	68.1	22.6	129 858	7 246	63.8	5 382	0.3	12.0	6.5
Douglas, WA	55 336	9.4	70.4	20.2	50 542	7 360	67.9	1 883	0.0	7.5	5.1
Ferry, WA	11 849	28.0	63.5	8.4	11 112	9 904	60.0	587	0.0	16.2	11.8
Franklin, WA	100 556	12.3	69.6	18.1	90 787	7 257	63.9	3 692	0.0	8.5	12.5
Garfield, WA	4 062	10.6	66.1	23.3	3 730	9 165	61.4	153	0.0	8.5	1.3
Grant, WA	131 772	11.7	68.5	19.7	121 131	7 289	66.3	5 232	0.0	10.6	7.9
Grays Harbor, WA	109 266	13.6	62.2	24.2	96 038	7 695	64.7	3 943	0.2	8.7	6.0
Island, WA	74 054	13.5	65.0	21.5	65 147	6 710	65.1	3 514	7.8	16.8	3.2
Jefferson, WA	30 365	13.4	54.2	32.4	26 787	7 979	62.4	1 118	0.0	13.8	5.3
King, WA	2 343 270	6.0	54.3	39.7	1 866 498	7 315	64.6	85 185	0.1	10.3	3.2
Kitsap, WA	347 534	12.0	63.3	24.7	295 448	7 164	64.6	13 475	4.6	14.7	4.4
Kittitas, WA	41 275	9.4	62.6	27.8	35 315	7 347	63.5	2 752	0.0	7.9	2.9
Klickitat, WA	32 731	11.6	71.5	16.8	28 673	8 377	64.5	1 038	0.0	13.8	3.9
Lewis, WA	105 012	10.1	69.2	20.6	91 456	7 320	64.0	4 210	0.1	11.0	7.7
Lincoln, WA	25 140	9.2	69.6	21.1	22 768	10 785	57.1	549	0.0	8.7	1.8
Mason, WA	72 358	9.8	66.1	24.1	61 248	7 321	62.8	2 739	0.0	14.2	9.3
Okanogan, WA	67 372	17.7	64.7	17.6	62 952	8 258	64.3	2 277	0.0	9.2	6.0
Pacific, WA	33 809	11.3	64.3	24.4	29 275	8 860	63.5	1 017	0.7	8.8	4.2
Pend Oreille, WA	16 912	17.0	67.6	15.3	16 165	8 640	61.4	715	0.0	11.3	9.2
Pierce, WA	1 124 186	8.6	61.5	30.0	936 617	7 180	63.6	40 956	3.4	13.8	5.2
San Juan, WA	18 166	5.7	56.4	37.8	14 965	8 460	62.3	567	0.0	13.1	4.8
Skagit, WA	176 757	11.1	61.0	27.9	144 341	7 493	65.8	6 523	0.2	12.1	7.3
Skamania, WA	11 895	46.4	43.9	9.7	10 840	8 469	60.9	614	0.0	12.1	5.7
Snohomish, WA	882 984	5.7	61.9	32.3	740 008	6 867	64.9	33 396	1.2	11.8	3.9
Spokane, WA	604 332	9.0	64.4	26.6	535 791	7 387	64.8	26 628	0.7	12.1	3.1
Stevens, WA	53 252	17.5	70.4	12.2	50 869	7 966	63.5	2 621	0.0	12.1	5.3
Thurston, WA	325 334	6.0	63.5	30.6	274 987	7 147	64.9	12 447	0.0	11.4	2.8
Wahkiakum, WA	4 335	6.8	65.5	27.7	3 662	7 398	57.2	202	0.0	6.4	3.5
Walla Walla, WA	76 663	11.2	63.3	25.5	68 574	7 587	66.6	4 044	0.0	3.7	3.3
Whatcom, WA	216 533	8.2	61.5	30.3	189 110	7 173	65.6	11 267	0.1	9.6	2.7
Whitman, WA	47 800	6.1	65.9	27.9	41 964	8 831	60.4	4 413	0.0	2.9	0.8
Yakima, WA	390 465	17.1	68.9	13.9	357 640	7 295	66.9	14 451	0.0	11.8	8.7

[8] Fairfax city is included with Fairfax County.
[9] Emporia city is included with Greensville County.
[10] Williamsburg city is included with James City County.

Table C-1. Population, School, and Student Characteristics by County—*Continued*

STATE County	High school graduates, 2000			College enrollment, 2000		College graduates, 2000 (percent)						
	Population 25 years and over	High school graduate or less (percent)	High school graduate or more (percent)	Number	Percent public	Bachelor's degree or more	+/- U.S. percentage with bachelor's degree or more	Non-Hispanic White	Black	American Indian and Alaska Native	Asian or Pacific Islander	Hispanic[3]
	30	31	32	33	34	35	36	37	38	39	40	41
Chesapeake city, VA	125 498	42.6	85.1	10 785	79.2	24.7	0.3	25.5	20.3	12.3	49.8	32.2
Colonial Heights city, VA	11 675	50.8	83.7	690	84.3	19.0	-5.4	18.5	28.5	0.0	22.4	19.2
Covington city, VA	4 485	68.4	71.4	164	93.3	6.4	-18.0	7.0	3.8	. . .	0.0	0.0
Danville city, VA	33 196	62.2	68.5	1 709	78.8	13.9	-10.5	18.0	6.7	14.6	45.4	27.8
Emporia city, VA	3 775	70.3	58.5	106	78.3	14.2	-10.2	22.1	7.2	. . .	28.6	0.0
Fairfax city, VA	15 222	30.9	88.6	1 693	80.9	45.7	21.3	48.3	34.5	52.1	52.8	24.4
Falls Church city, VA	7 464	16.7	95.9	636	62.3	63.7	39.3	68.0	37.6	40.0	55.5	31.9
Franklin city, VA	5 642	56.6	71.0	356	93.3	16.4	-8.0	25.1	7.3	0.0	. . .	15.6
Fredericksburg city, VA	11 211	47.3	80.2	3 503	92.3	30.5	6.1	37.5	9.9	32.5	8.3	13.7
Galax city, VA	4 782	68.2	60.4	195	95.4	11.1	-13.3	12.4	0.0	0.0	0.0	3.4
Hampton city, VA	92 477	42.5	85.5	12 830	55.5	21.8	-2.6	24.1	18.7	18.3	24.4	17.4
Harrisonburg city, VA	17 448	46.7	76.8	14 822	91.8	31.2	6.8	34.6	18.5	0.0	29.4	7.2
Hopewell city, VA	14 323	64.1	71.8	859	84.6	10.2	-14.2	11.1	7.5	14.0	21.4	6.6
Lexington city, VA	3 285	40.2	77.1	2 876	45.9	42.6	18.2	47.4	15.9	0.0	0.0	78.9
Lynchburg city, VA	40 806	49.7	78.0	7 622	24.9	25.2	0.8	31.3	8.3	10.1	58.0	26.2
Manassas city, VA	21 188	42.7	81.3	1 916	75.0	28.1	3.7	33.7	17.2	0.0	31.2	9.9
Manassas Park city, VA	6 224	51.0	76.4	477	77.6	20.3	-4.1	18.6	26.7	65.4	68.0	6.2
Martinsville city, VA	10 843	60.8	68.5	661	87.9	16.6	-7.8	23.4	5.6	100.0	50.0	10.1
Newport News city, VA	110 083	45.6	84.5	10 611	81.9	19.9	-4.5	25.0	11.7	18.4	25.2	13.7
Norfolk city, VA	135 258	51.2	78.4	19 085	80.3	19.6	-4.8	26.3	9.7	9.3	34.3	16.5
Norton city, VA	2 665	60.3	66.5	180	100.0	14.0	-10.4	15.0	4.2	0.0	0.0	0.0
Petersburg city, VA	22 289	61.7	68.6	1 388	79.6	14.8	-9.6	21.1	12.4	23.9	34.9	17.0
Poquoson city, VA	7 759	38.5	88.5	527	86.9	31.6	7.2	30.7	40.0	0.0	76.6	39.7
Portsmouth city, VA	63 685	54.2	75.2	5 211	83.1	13.8	-10.6	17.0	10.0	18.2	23.1	18.6
Radford city, VA	6 766	36.3	83.4	6 952	96.9	34.1	9.7	35.6	11.0	0.0	90.2	29.4
Richmond city, VA	128 555	48.4	75.2	19 116	72.6	29.5	5.1	51.4	11.2	22.4	49.0	20.3
Roanoke city, VA	65 593	54.4	76.0	3 590	79.4	18.7	-5.7	22.2	7.8	20.9	37.4	19.4
Salem city, VA	16 657	50.2	82.0	2 195	29.7	19.8	-4.6	20.5	6.5	0.0	29.7	15.9
Staunton city, VA	16 703	55.5	75.6	1 387	42.4	20.4	-4.0	22.3	6.2	0.0	0.0	33.3
Suffolk city, VA	41 662	52.8	76.8	3 129	84.5	17.3	-7.1	21.5	10.8	17.0	40.6	17.0
Virginia Beach city, VA	266 627	35.5	90.4	26 275	76.9	28.1	3.7	30.6	18.1	12.7	33.3	19.1
Waynesboro city, VA	13 303	56.0	77.9	488	87.7	20.6	-3.8	22.4	7.2	18.4	42.9	12.5
Williamsburg city, VA	5 360	31.2	89.6	5 403	90.5	45.0	20.6	54.1	10.3	. . .	38.9	23.8
Winchester city, VA	15 316	51.3	75.4	1 688	39.6	23.7	-0.7	26.6	7.4	0.0	34.2	7.4
WASHINGTON	3 827 507	37.8	87.1	358 414	81.7	27.7	3.3	28.9	19.4	12.4	35.5	11 1
Adams, WA	9 242	62.9	63.3	466	93.6	12.2	-12.2	17.3	0.0	8.6	27.9	3.0
Asotin, WA	13 619	46.9	85.8	853	95.2	18.0	-6.4	17.9	62.5	29.2	57.1	11.6
Benton, WA	88 217	38.9	85.1	5 789	89.3	26.3	1.9	27.6	23.7	10.3	50.1	6.9
Chelan, WA	42 425	46.7	79.1	2 623	87.7	21.9	-2.5	24.9	24.6	6.8	19.0	3.7
Clallam, WA	45 711	42.3	86.5	2 425	89.6	20.8	-3.6	21.5	7.7	11.3	24.1	5.3
Clark, WA	217 293	39.2	87.8	15 495	85.7	22.1	-2.3	22.4	22.5	11.1	29.9	10.1
Columbia, WA	2 827	47.8	82.7	96	93.8	17.5	-6.9	18.3	0.0	28.6	35.7	3.8
Cowlitz, WA	60 355	49.6	83.2	3 602	89.8	13.3	-11.1	13.6	17.7	4.7	12.2	8.8
Douglas, WA	20 435	51.0	78.4	1 088	88.9	16.2	-8.2	18.3	19.3	11.4	16.2	3.5
Ferry, WA	4 748	51.7	82.7	230	91.3	13.5	-10.9	15.4	0.0	4.7	7.7	26.8
Franklin, WA	26 779	60.3	63.5	1 654	90.5	13.6	-10.8	19.4	12.2	5.3	23.1	2.9
Garfield, WA	1 655	45.1	84.4	54	90.7	17.0	-7.4	17.1	. . .	0.0	50.0	25.0
Grant, WA	43 309	55.6	72.2	2 622	92.1	13.7	-10.7	16.9	9.5	14.1	28.2	2.5
Grays Harbor, WA	44 588	53.2	81.1	2 347	93.1	12.7	-11.7	12.0	0.0	9.4	24.0	7.0
Island, WA	47 112	32.2	92.1	3 165	86.6	27.0	2.6	28.0	24.2	15.2	21.1	13.2
Jefferson, WA	19 551	35.6	91.6	678	78.5	28.4	4.0	29.5	12.3	9.9	24.9	4.9
King, WA	1 188 740	28.9	90.3	125 584	79.4	40.0	15.6	42.5	21.1	18.2	40.9	20.4
Kitsap, WA	148 704	34.7	90.8	11 528	83.9	25.3	0.9	26.4	17.7	15.9	24.0	14.1
Kittitas, WA	19 303	43.8	87.2	6 679	97.5	26.2	1.8	26.6	23.5	21.8	39.0	12.7
Klickitat, WA	12 806	52.6	81.7	441	78.0	16.4	-8.0	17.4	0.0	2.9	20.0	4.1
Lewis, WA	44 857	52.4	80.5	2 619	86.6	12.9	-11.5	13.2	30.1	8.8	24.7	4.2
Lincoln, WA	7 117	44.7	86.5	227	85.9	18.8	-5.6	19.0	11.1	15.9	31.3	16.4
Mason, WA	33 936	48.7	83.7	1 522	85.7	15.6	-8.8	16.0	4.2	8.2	28.4	8.7
Okanogan, WA	25 826	54.1	76.6	1 047	85.7	15.9	-8.5	17.9	0.0	11.2	25.0	3.9
Pacific, WA	15 298	52.6	78.9	606	91.4	15.2	-9.2	15.7	0.0	13.3	8.1	10.4
Pend Oreille, WA	7 995	52.4	81.0	365	81.6	12.3	-12.1	12.7	27.3	0.0	1.2	6.6
Pierce, WA	442 665	42.9	86.9	37 999	73.0	20.6	-3.8	21.8	15.0	13.0	19.5	11.8
San Juan, WA	10 691	24.3	94.4	348	87.1	40.2	15.8	41.3	. . .	0.0	8.2	7.4
Skagit, WA	66 959	42.4	84.0	4 095	86.6	20.8	-3.6	22.2	20.7	3.7	33.2	3.7
Skamania, WA	6 557	47.6	85.9	283	83.0	16.8	-7.6	17.4	20.0	3.1	51.6	3.6
Snohomish, WA	388 997	36.7	89.2	29 961	83.3	24.4	0.0	24.3	21.1	10.9	36.6	14.6
Spokane, WA	266 829	37.7	89.1	30 682	76.6	25.0	0.6	25.5	14.8	13.3	27.0	17.3
Stevens, WA	25 984	50.1	85.4	955	84.7	15.3	-9.1	15.7	17.8	6.9	19.2	12.3
Thurston, WA	135 686	34.3	89.5	13 181	81.4	29.8	5.4	30.8	28.7	16.4	24.9	18.9
Wahkiakum, WA	2 715	48.0	84.2	127	87.4	14.8	-9.6	14.7	. . .	23.6	100.0	0.0
Walla Walla, WA	34 372	43.0	81.1	5 541	41.6	23.3	-1.1	25.9	19.1	7.7	30.2	4.8
Whatcom, WA	102 787	40.1	87.5	19 135	93.9	27.2	2.8	28.3	26.7	7.1	31.0	12.5
Whitman, WA	20 070	26.4	92.8	15 058	98.2	44.0	19.6	41.5	58.3	10.8	73.0	66.7
Yakima, WA	130 747	58.7	68.7	7 244	82.2	15.3	-9.1	19.8	16.6	11.7	27.2	3.9

[3]May be of any race.
. . . = Not available.

Table C-1. Population, School, and Student Characteristics by County—*Continued*

STATE County	State/ county code	County type[1]	Population, 2005 Total	Population, 2005 Percent 5 to 17 years	Number of schools and students, 2004–2005 School districts	Number of schools and students, 2004–2005 Schools	Number of schools and students, 2004–2005 Students	Resident enrollment, 2000 Total	Resident enrollment, 2000 Percent public	Resident enrollment, 2000 K–12	Resident enrollment, 2000 Percent public
			1	2	3	4	5	6	7	8	9
WEST VIRGINIA	54 000		1 816 856	15.4	57	791	280 129	418 553	91.0	304 216	94.7
Barbour, WV	54 001	7	15 689	15.7	1	9	2 599	3 687	85.1	2 726	98.7
Berkeley, WV	54 003	3	93 394	18.0	1	29	14 983	17 453	90.2	14 127	94.3
Boone, WV	54 005	2	25 703	15.9	1	17	4 572	5 551	95.9	4 458	97.5
Braxton, WV	54 007	8	14 851	15.5	1	8	2 457	3 065	96.6	2 532	98.0
Brooke, WV	54 009	3	24 515	14.4	1	12	3 638	5 883	81.6	3 926	95.1
Cabell, WV	54 011	2	94 031	14.1	1	31	12 249	25 315	91.4	14 222	91.6
Calhoun, WV	54 013	8	7 387	14.0	1	4	1 187	1 642	92.4	1 335	95.3
Clay, WV	54 015	2	10 356	17.2	1	7	2 111	2 430	96.7	2 016	98.5
Doddridge, WV	54 017	9	7 476	16.9	1	3	1 284	1 737	94.5	1 497	95.9
Fayette, WV	54 019	6	46 823	14.7	1	26	6 919	10 243	92.1	7 779	95.6
Gilmer, WV	54 021	9	6 950	12.8	1	5	1 009	2 212	98.5	1 154	99.3
Grant, WV	54 023	6	11 673	15.7	1	6	1 995	2 273	94.3	1 877	96.8
Greenbrier, WV	54 025	7	35 027	15.1	1	14	5 297	7 168	91.7	5 733	94.2
Hampshire, WV	54 027	3	22 025	17.8	2	13	3 785	4 501	93.7	3 862	95.5
Hancock, WV	54 029	3	31 350	14.7	1	10	4 296	6 671	86.4	5 263	89.4
Hardy, WV	54 031	8	13 287	16.8	1	5	2 330	2 840	95.8	2 286	97.6
Harrison, WV	54 033	5	68 369	16.2	1	29	11 355	15 737	89.9	12 116	94.8
Jackson, WV	54 035	6	28 403	16.6	1	13	5 022	6 340	95.0	5 170	97.3
Jefferson, WV	54 037	1	49 206	16.9	1	13	7 672	10 289	88.8	7 404	91.5
Kanawha, WV	54 039	2	193 559	15.0	2	89	28 485	42 554	88.1	31 608	92.7
Lewis, WV	54 041	7	17 199	15.3	1	7	2 789	3 644	90.8	2 923	93.8
Lincoln, WV	54 043	2	22 374	16.0	1	12	3 764	4 652	97.3	3 861	98.1
Logan, WV	54 045	6	36 237	15.1	1	18	6 050	7 911	94.9	6 299	96.6
McDowell, WV	54 047	7	24 273	15.7	1	17	4 112	5 746	96.7	4 949	97.1
Marion, WV	54 049	4	56 509	14.5	1	22	8 183	13 612	93.3	9 024	95.7
Marshall, WV	54 051	3	34 337	16.0	1	15	5 241	7 980	90.8	6 370	93.9
Mason, WV	54 053	6	25 761	15.7	1	13	4 209	5 443	96.2	4 444	98.3
Mercer, WV	54 055	5	61 589	14.8	1	25	9 336	13 744	94.1	9 810	96.9
Mineral, WV	54 057	3	27 028	16.8	1	14	4 583	6 308	94.5	4 814	96.4
Mingo, WV	54 059	6	27 210	16.2	1	15	4 686	6 305	96.1	5 274	97.1
Monongalia, WV	54 061	3	84 386	11.9	1	27	9 960	30 286	93.7	10 864	91.6
Monroe, WV	54 063	8	13 507	15.6	1	5	2 068	2 971	96.0	2 379	98.2
Morgan, WV	54 065	3	16 022	16.2	1	9	2 574	2 831	92.8	2 480	94.8
Nicholas, WV	54 067	6	26 464	15.5	1	16	4 225	5 967	95.1	4 887	96.7
Ohio, WV	54 069	3	45 112	14.9	1	13	5 359	12 425	74.9	7 815	79.2
Pendleton, WV	54 071	8	7 844	15.0	1	4	1 201	1 718	92.4	1 384	94.0
Pleasants, WV	54 073	3	7 376	16.5	1	5	1 360	1 690	94.4	1 379	96.7
Pocahontas, WV	54 075	9	8 851	14.7	1	5	1 353	1 801	91.3	1 457	94.5
Preston, WV	54 077	3	30 115	15.9	1	12	4 702	6 362	95.7	5 368	97.5
Putnam, WV	54 079	2	54 443	17.2	1	22	8 930	12 580	88.3	9 541	92.6
Raleigh, WV	54 081	4	79 167	14.8	1	31	11 684	17 797	86.6	13 215	95.2
Randolph, WV	54 083	7	28 571	15.5	1	16	4 425	6 028	86.9	4 723	97.1
Ritchie, WV	54 085	8	10 540	15.4	1	6	1 561	2 222	95.5	1 804	97.3
Roane, WV	54 087	6	15 407	15.7	1	6	2 581	3 248	96.9	2 820	98.4
Summers, WV	54 089	7	13 740	12.6	1	5	1 616	2 513	91.4	2 026	94.9
Taylor, WV	54 091	6	16 291	15.5	1	7	2 417	3 632	92.7	2 944	96.2
Tucker, WV	54 093	9	6 943	15.0	1	3	1 197	1 449	93.3	1 212	96.5
Tyler, WV	54 095	6	9 340	15.9	1	4	1 561	2 073	95.7	1 721	98.8
Upshur, WV	54 097	7	23 712	15.2	1	12	3 765	6 164	73.7	4 079	97.0
Wayne, WV	54 099	2	42 091	16.4	1	21	7 575	9 488	95.2	7 637	97.2
Webster, WV	54 101	9	9 804	15.6	1	6	1 624	2 084	97.2	1 752	97.6
Wetzel, WV	54 103	6	17 117	16.3	1	9	3 240	3 967	97.2	3 238	99.0
Wirt, WV	54 105	3	5 896	16.8	1	3	1 017	1 473	97.6	1 249	98.5
Wood, WV	54 107	3	87 047	16.1	1	29	13 746	19 616	89.8	14 998	94.5
Wyoming, WV	54 109	7	24 479	15.3	1	14	4 190	5 232	96.7	4 385	98.4
WISCONSIN	55 000		5 536 201	17.3	461	2 283	864 652	1 463 038	82.7	1 049 456	85.8
Adams, WI	55 001	8	20 828	13.4	1	8	2 049	3 616	93.8	3 073	94.4
Ashland, WI	55 003	7	16 627	17.0	5	12	3 001	4 768	78.3	3 243	91.6
Barron, WI	55 005	6	45 834	16.3	8	31	6 921	10 864	91.6	8 961	93.6
Bayfield, WI	55 007	8	15 145	16.3	4	13	1 917	3 665	89.9	2 996	92.6
Brown, WI	55 009	2	238 987	17.8	10	73	40 162	61 176	79.7	43 878	82.9
Buffalo, WI	55 011	8	13 968	16.7	3	7	1 306	3 261	90.5	2 687	92.0
Burnett, WI	55 013	8	16 528	15.1	3	10	2 274	3 169	91.7	2 733	93.5
Calumet, WI	55 015	3	44 137	19.0	7	51	19 101	11 173	82.3	8 975	85.1
Chippewa, WI	55 017	3	59 950	16.9	8	24	8 675	14 029	83.5	11 414	84.3
Clark, WI	55 019	8	34 098	20.0	8	23	5 558	8 564	81.3	7 381	81.4
Columbia, WI	55 021	2	55 364	16.7	10	40	10 579	12 494	88.9	10 054	91.6
Crawford, WI	55 023	7	17 134	17.2	4	11	2 458	4 180	86.4	3 496	86.8
Dane, WI	55 025	2	458 106	15.3	18	173	63 974	132 595	88.9	71 417	91.2
Dodge, WI	55 027	4	88 103	16.3	12	43	14 453	21 011	79.5	16 963	82.2
Door, WI	55 029	6	28 349	14.6	5	18	3 985	5 892	88.8	4 918	90.8
Douglas, WI	55 031	2	44 208	16.1	3	14	6 451	11 211	89.5	7 878	89.5
Dunn, WI	55 033	6	41 708	15.0	4	17	5 946	14 115	92.7	7 115	91.2
Eau Claire, WI	55 035	3	94 089	15.6	5	35	14 394	30 324	88.7	16 477	86.3
Florence, WI	55 037	9	4 974	15.5	1	3	668	1 077	96.4	935	97.3
Fond du Lac, WI	55 039	3	99 337	16.8	6	33	12 810	25 296	78.1	19 140	84.1

[1]County type codes are from the Economic Research Service of the United States Department of Agriculture. See notes and definitions at the end of this section.

Table C-1. Population, School, and Student Characteristics by County—*Continued*

STATE County	Characteristics of students, 2004–2005				Outcomes		Staff and students, 2004–2005		
	Percent with IEP[2]	Percent eligible for free or reduced-price lunch	Percent minority	Percent English-language learners	Number of graduates, 2003–2004	Percent dropouts, grades 9–12, 2001–2002	Number of teachers	Student-teacher ratio	Central administration staff
	10	11	12	13	14	15	16	17	18
WEST VIRGINIA	17.9	50.4	6.1	0.6	...	3.7	19 955	14.0	...
Barbour, WV	18.7	63.3	2.5	0.2	...	4.3	186	14.0	19
Berkeley, WV	17.5	36.0	13.0	1.8	...	5.5	1 057	14.2	105
Boone, WV	20.3	59.8	1.6	0.0	...	5.4	358	12.8	41
Braxton, WV	19.7	59.1	1.1	0.1	...	4.1	187	13.1	25
Brooke, WV	20.0	39.6	2.0	0.0	...	4.1	256	14.2	39
Cabell, WV	17.0	49.9	9.3	0.9	...	4.6	865	14.2	122
Calhoun, WV	16.2	68.0	0.8	0.0	...	6.4	93	12.8	13
Clay, WV	18.5	71.6	0.8	0.0	...	3.8	158	13.4	15
Doddridge, WV	21.0	57.9	1.2	0.0	...	4.0	89	14.5	14
Fayette, WV	15.6	61.9	7.4	0.2	...	4.9	510	13.6	68
Gilmer, WV	16.0	56.9	2.1	0.1	...	3.5	69	14.7	11
Grant, WV	19.8	50.5	1.9	0.3	...	3.3	141	14.1	18
Greenbrier, WV	20.5	55.9	4.6	0.0	...	3.5	372	14.2	38
Hampshire, WV	22.6	53.0	2.6	0.0	...	4.4	309	12.3	41
Hancock, WV	18.3	37.8	5.2	0.0	...	4.1	302	14.2	32
Hardy, WV	17.9	50.0	4.1	1.2	...	0.7	158	14.8	21
Harrison, WV	18.4	50.6	4.0	0.5	...	2.7	754	15.1	93
Jackson, WV	17.8	45.0	1.4	0.3	...	3.7	349	14.4	36
Jefferson, WV	17.0	31.5	14.3	2.6	...	2.7	522	14.7	68
Kanawha, WV	16.8	46.8	13.7	1.3	...	5.0	2 026	14.1	262
Lewis, WV	21.4	55.8	1.3	0.1	...	3.0	192	14.6	26
Lincoln, WV	22.0	61.8	0.4	0.0	...	3.8	285	13.2	36
Logan, WV	15.8	56.1	3.6	0.4	...	5.0	432	14.0	56
McDowell, WV	20.1	83.2	12.2	0.0	...	1.4	314	13.1	43
Marion, WV	16.6	48.3	6.7	0.0	...	2.3	617	13.3	91
Marshall, WV	19.9	50.1	1.5	0.1	...	3.0	346	15.2	36
Mason, WV	20.9	49.2	2.1	0.2	...	3.6	311	13.5	32
Mercer, WV	16.6	58.2	10.1	0.1	...	3.7	690	13.5	65
Mineral, WV	17.1	44.9	4.3	0.1	...	2.3	317	14.4	38
Mingo, WV	19.4	65.1	3.0	0.0	...	3.9	324	14.5	40
Monongalia, WV	15.3	37.0	9.3	4.3	...	2.8	689	14.5	91
Monroe, WV	21.1	56.9	1.6	0.0	...	2.9	147	14.1	21
Morgan, WV	16.0	42.2	2.3	0.5	...	4.1	177	14.6	23
Nicholas, WV	19.3	61.3	0.9	0.3	...	3.5	318	13.3	45
Ohio, WV	17.3	44.3	9.1	0.4	...	3.4	365	14.7	74
Pendleton, WV	19.5	46.2	4.2	0.0	...	0.8	89	13.5	13
Pleasants, WV	22.7	45.4	1.3	0.0	...	1.3	109	12.5	11
Pocahontas, WV	17.4	54.5	0.6	0.0	...	5.0	99	13.7	13
Preston, WV	19.7	54.1	0.9	0.1	...	5.7	330	14.3	32
Putnam, WV	18.2	37.9	3.1	0.4	...	3.0	613	14.6	73
Raleigh, WV	15.5	55.8	12.0	0.3	...	3.2	814	14.4	124
Randolph, WV	16.8	55.1	1.7	0.0	...	3.1	338	13.1	44
Ritchie, WV	20.4	53.3	1.7	0.0	...	3.2	113	13.8	12
Roane, WV	20.1	60.5	1.5	0.1	...	6.3	186	13.9	18
Summers, WV	23.3	64.2	4.7	0.0	...	5.8	110	14.8	14
Taylor, WV	18.5	49.4	1.5	0.0	...	3.8	155	15.6	22
Tucker, WV	16.9	56.4	1.2	0.0	...	...	87	13.8	15
Tyler, WV	21.7	56.1	0.9	0.1	...	2.2	121	12.9	13
Upshur, WV	20.7	56.5	1.6	0.0	...	3.0	286	13.2	29
Wayne, WV	19.0	56.5	1.1	0.1	...	2.6	528	14.3	50
Webster, WV	16.6	71.4	0.5	0.0	...	2.5	127	12.8	17
Wetzel, WV	21.2	47.0	1.4	0.4	...	2.2	229	14.2	25
Wirt, WV	16.4	54.1	0.6	0.0	...	3.4	79	12.9	8
Wood, WV	15.1	41.5	3.0	0.4	...	3.3	931	14.8	132
Wyoming, WV	19.6	65.4	1.7	0.0	...	3.3	334	12.6	32
WISCONSIN	14.9	29.8	21.7	3.1	...	1.9	60 520	14.3	...
Adams, WI	22.0	53.1	6.6	0.0	...	1.0	159	12.9	3
Ashland, WI	14.7	46.7	18.4	0.0	...	1.0	235	12.8	19
Barron, WI	17.3	32.9	5.6	0.9	...	1.0	573	12.1	21
Bayfield, WI	13.7	40.1	22.5	0.0	...	1.2	153	12.5	7
Brown, WI	16.4	27.9	20.0	6.3	...	1.1	2 807	14.3	128
Buffalo, WI	13.9	23.9	2.4	0.0	...	1.4	105	12.5	4
Burnett, WI	17.5	44.9	13.8	0.0	...	4.1	163	13.9	9
Calumet, WI	14.2	18.2	9.3	5.9	...	0.4	1 245	15.3	...
Chippewa, WI	15.4	31.2	3.5	0.0	...	1.6	612	14.2	28
Clark, WI	14.6	37.5	5.6	0.0	...	0.7	417	13.3	13
Columbia, WI	14.2	19.0	6.7	0.0	...	0.7	794	13.3	47
Crawford, WI	17.7	36.4	4.8	0.0	...	0.8	193	12.7	8
Dane, WI	17.0	22.0	23.1	5.9	...	1.6	5 132	12.5	252
Dodge, WI	17.2	20.9	7.2	0.8	...	0.5	1 015	14.2	34
Door, WI	14.9	20.8	5.6	0.0	...	0.4	315	12.7	11
Douglas, WI	13.5	44.2	8.2	0.0	...	2.2	448	14.4	11
Dunn, WI	14.2	31.2	9.3	2.1	...	0.8	412	14.4	15
Eau Claire, WI	13.9	29.4	11.8	2.9	...	0.7	1 033	13.9	39
Florence, WI	12.3	35.9	3.6	0.0	...	0.3	44	15.4	1
Fond du Lac, WI	15.7	23.3	7.9	1.4	...	2.2	903	14.2	21

[2]IEP = Individual Education Program. See notes and definitions at the end of this section.
. . . = Not available.

Table C-1. Population, School, and Student Characteristics by County—*Continued*

STATE County	Total revenue (thousands of dollars)	Percent of revenue from:			Total expenditures (thousands of dollars)	Amount per student (dollars)	Percent for instruction	Total	Percent in armed forces	Percent high school graduates	Percent not enrolled, not employed, not in armed forces, not high school graduate
		Federal government	State government	Local government							
	19	20	21	22	23	24	25	26	27	28	29
WEST VIRGINIA	2 585 084	11.2	59.8	28.9	2 377 687	8 475	64.2	99 445	0.1	11.8	6.4
Barbour, WV	21 988	13.1	70.6	16.3	19 081	7 416	70.3	931	0.0	11.4	9.8
Berkeley, WV	134 453	9.8	59.9	30.3	116 229	8 141	63.9	4 037	0.0	19.3	8.1
Boone, WV	44 074	9.1	50.3	40.7	42 553	9 283	59.3	1 266	0.0	13.1	2.6
Braxton, WV	21 650	17.1	70.4	12.5	20 757	8 124	64.8	683	0.0	12.7	13.5
Brooke, WV	33 804	8.5	57.5	34.0	32 320	8 988	63.1	1 370	0.2	9.6	5.5
Cabell, WV	123 039	7.7	54.7	37.7	105 221	8 613	64.9	6 110	0.2	9.5	4.9
Calhoun, WV	12 175	17.5	67.6	14.9	11 292	9 286	60.0	445	0.0	12.1	11.2
Clay, WV	19 359	18.3	69.9	11.8	18 522	8 824	61.3	631	0.0	14.4	10.3
Doddridge, WV	12 093	11.4	59.3	29.3	10 902	8 598	61.4	519	0.0	15.4	3.3
Fayette, WV	60 942	10.9	66.4	22.7	59 709	8 529	66.4	2 559	0.1	15.4	7.2
Gilmer, WV	9 501	12.4	60.3	27.3	8 768	8 358	58.9	667	0.0	5.5	7.0
Grant, WV	16 286	10.4	62.6	27.0	15 100	7 611	63.5	427	0.0	15.9	4.0
Greenbrier, WV	47 479	14.8	60.5	24.7	45 117	8 385	66.8	1 691	0.0	13.2	5.2
Hampshire, WV	30 934	13.2	63.6	23.2	27 617	7 721	63.0	1 039	0.0	11.1	6.4
Hancock, WV	40 165	11.2	56.0	32.8	36 761	8 555	63.7	1 548	0.0	11.0	7.4
Hardy, WV	19 066	12.4	68.0	19.6	17 014	7 265	62.4	574	0.0	13.9	4.4
Harrison, WV	105 481	9.2	58.9	31.8	93 579	8 079	65.3	3 828	0.0	11.5	6.1
Jackson, WV	45 771	11.3	61.1	27.6	43 683	8 624	62.4	1 353	0.0	8.2	5.6
Jefferson, WV	62 884	7.4	54.9	37.7	59 757	8 060	64.9	2 565	0.4	12.9	4.0
Kanawha, WV	271 669	10.4	52.4	37.2	239 991	8 478	64.1	9 522	0.1	12.3	8.5
Lewis, WV	23 928	10.5	62.7	26.8	22 799	8 145	60.8	843	1.8	10.6	2.0
Lincoln, WV	35 830	15.6	65.6	18.8	32 863	8 589	66.0	1 319	0.0	13.4	11.2
Logan, WV	55 556	13.9	63.2	23.0	46 245	7 610	71.0	2 087	0.0	12.2	9.8
McDowell, WV	43 185	19.2	62.3	18.5	42 188	9 920	65.1	1 595	0.0	15.0	19.7
Marion, WV	79 220	12.5	59.7	27.8	73 765	8 948	65.4	3 165	0.0	11.4	3.8
Marshall, WV	50 461	8.8	57.9	33.3	46 412	8 709	63.2	1 707	0.0	10.3	4.7
Mason, WV	38 222	11.1	59.9	29.0	35 731	8 503	65.6	1 373	0.0	13.6	6.3
Mercer, WV	83 330	11.7	65.6	22.8	78 743	8 381	64.9	3 199	0.1	11.5	6.5
Mineral, WV	41 967	14.0	64.9	21.1	38 542	8 461	61.2	1 576	0.0	11.7	3.4
Mingo, WV	46 324	14.2	58.7	27.1	44 601	9 479	64.7	1 663	0.0	13.1	13.2
Monongalia, WV	95 856	11.1	50.6	38.4	87 412	8 565	63.8	7 414	0.1	6.6	2.7
Monroe, WV	17 748	14.2	69.6	16.1	16 957	8 349	60.8	633	0.0	14.1	7.6
Morgan, WV	21 238	9.1	60.1	30.7	19 319	7 535	61.8	568	0.0	10.7	5.5
Nicholas, WV	42 121	15.3	60.3	24.4	39 103	9 087	59.9	1 397	0.0	13.3	7.9
Ohio, WV	54 276	9.1	54.8	36.1	48 966	8 983	63.2	2 803	0.0	6.0	4.5
Pendleton, WV	10 449	11.5	72.6	15.9	10 851	8 865	62.1	338	2.1	18.3	2.7
Pleasants, WV	15 743	8.6	42.5	49.0	14 688	10 912	62.5	373	0.0	9.7	4.3
Pocahontas, WV	16 052	13.6	66.0	20.4	12 067	8 814	62.3	368	0.0	13.0	2.7
Preston, WV	36 424	10.3	72.6	17.1	36 289	7 576	65.0	1 729	0.0	15.4	4.4
Putnam, WV	76 601	7.9	56.9	35.1	71 435	8 134	65.1	2 514	0.1	10.5	1.7
Raleigh, WV	119 005	11.2	57.9	30.9	103 636	8 723	60.3	4 028	0.5	16.1	5.3
Randolph, WV	36 975	13.8	72.8	13.4	36 528	8 154	66.1	1 367	0.0	13.7	8.6
Ritchie, WV	15 189	14.7	63.0	22.3	14 141	8 570	65.0	601	0.0	15.3	5.7
Roane, WV	21 683	15.7	71.4	12.9	20 553	7 926	63.3	906	1.2	13.2	7.4
Summers, WV	13 712	13.8	73.0	13.2	13 308	8 266	64.0	715	0.0	9.7	16.2
Taylor, WV	21 562	13.5	66.3	20.2	20 444	8 406	61.4	794	0.0	8.9	6.8
Tucker, WV	10 488	15.0	62.9	22.2	10 671	8 848	61.3	393	0.0	14.0	7.6
Tyler, WV	15 873	9.7	63.1	27.2	14 241	9 065	61.2	478	0.0	10.0	4.0
Upshur, WV	33 416	10.9	67.5	21.5	32 635	8 496	63.7	1 641	0.2	7.1	4.5
Wayne, WV	59 135	11.2	65.0	23.8	61 857	8 309	66.4	2 342	0.0	14.1	9.3
Webster, WV	16 686	23.9	64.7	11.4	15 310	9 151	67.6	556	0.0	9.9	5.4
Wetzel, WV	30 265	8.3	63.4	28.3	27 909	8 406	63.4	945	0.0	8.6	5.4
Wirt, WV	8 394	5.4	78.2	16.3	8 476	8 253	62.6	373	0.0	6.7	4.6
Wood, WV	124 426	10.6	59.0	30.5	116 163	8 456	66.5	4 561	0.1	12.1	6.6
Wyoming, WV	40 931	10.3	61.7	28.0	38 866	9 126	66.6	1 316	0.0	11.7	9.3
WISCONSIN	9 183 588	6.0	51.5	42.5	8 069 091	9 230	66.0	319 738	0.0	10.6	3.4
Adams, WI	22 773	9.4	51.4	39.2	20 046	9 736	64.0	805	0.0	16.8	2.6
Ashland, WI	33 708	9.3	61.4	29.3	29 127	9 635	64.7	1 212	0.0	12.0	3.9
Barron, WI	84 647	4.4	57.2	38.4	70 327	8 709	65.7	2 697	0.0	10.8	3.3
Bayfield, WI	24 128	12.8	31.9	55.3	19 840	9 965	63.7	824	0.0	8.6	0.8
Brown, WI	401 972	5.0	55.2	39.8	351 533	8 850	66.9	13 524	0.1	10.3	4.4
Buffalo, WI	25 776	4.7	60.4	34.9	21 161	8 687	64.9	755	0.0	12.7	0.3
Burnett, WI	24 486	5.2	38.8	56.0	20 136	8 740	62.6	812	0.0	13.3	3.9
Calumet, WI	42 519	2.0	55.7	42.3	32 622	7 998	63.7	2 233	0.0	11.2	1.4
Chippewa, WI	94 001	4.8	54.8	40.4	75 665	8 642	62.1	3 310	0.1	13.5	2.4
Clark, WI	60 264	5.3	61.5	33.2	48 645	8 704	63.9	2 251	0.0	10.8	6.8
Columbia, WI	96 927	3.9	52.9	43.1	81 836	8 665	66.5	2 849	0.0	13.2	2.9
Crawford, WI	26 958	5.8	62.3	31.9	22 951	9 118	66.8	1 216	0.0	18.8	5.8
Dane, WI	738 032	4.5	37.3	58.2	656 393	10 079	66.2	27 257	0.0	8.2	2.4
Dodge, WI	91 177	3.3	56.9	39.8	77 447	9 271	67.4	4 863	0.0	12.2	3.4
Door, WI	44 532	4.9	25.7	69.4	40 069	9 852	66.4	1 455	0.0	8.0	2.1
Douglas, WI	69 852	8.1	59.1	32.8	61 835	9 239	61.7	2 480	0.3	9.4	3.3
Dunn, WI	61 736	5.1	59.7	35.2	53 355	8 847	62.9	3 635	0.1	8.8	1.5
Eau Claire, WI	150 843	5.1	53.2	41.7	129 792	9 498	66.0	7 422	0.0	7.0	2.1
Florence, WI	8 200	8.5	39.0	52.5	7 299	9 346	62.6	250	0.0	11.6	4.0
Fond du Lac, WI	160 472	4.0	58.1	37.9	135 301	8 654	66.3	6 311	0.2	13.2	2.8

Table C-1. Population, School, and Student Characteristics by County—*Continued*

STATE County	High school graduates, 2000			College enrollment, 2000		College graduates, 2000 (percent)						
	Population 25 years and over	High school graduate or less (percent)	High school graduate or more (percent)	Number	Percent public	Bachelor's degree or more	+/- U.S. percentage with bachelor's degree or more	Non-Hispanic White	Black	American Indian and Alaska Native	Asian or Pacific Islander	Hispanic[3]
	30	31	32	33	34	35	36	37	38	39	40	41
WEST VIRGINIA	1 233 581	64.2	75.2	92 329	84.6	14.8	-9.6	14.6	11.5	12.8	62.1	19.7
Barbour, WV	10 510	73.4	72.7	827	39.5	11.8	-12.6	11.7	39.3	7.5	20.0	0.0
Berkeley, WV	50 092	62.8	77.6	2 424	81.8	15.1	-9.3	15.2	11.3	4.2	42.3	10.6
Boone, WV	17 282	77.0	64.0	808	87.0	7.2	-17.2	7.0	14.6	20.0	100.0	11.0
Braxton, WV	10 273	75.0	67.3	320	83.8	9.2	-15.2	9.2	0.0	33.3	100.0	0.0
Brooke, WV	17 855	63.9	79.7	1 611	52.2	13.4	-11.0	13.5	13.4	100.0	0.0	21.9
Cabell, WV	64 444	54.0	80.0	9 752	95.4	20.9	-3.5	21.1	10.6	20.3	48.9	16.4
Calhoun, WV	5 283	77.4	62.4	204	77.0	9.3	-15.1	8.9	...	0.0	100.0	41.7
Clay, WV	6 766	80.8	63.7	258	86.0	7.3	-17.1	7.4	0.0	0.0	0.0	0.0
Doddridge, WV	4 897	71.9	69.4	155	82.6	10.2	-14.2	10.3	...	0.0	50.0	0.0
Fayette, WV	32 721	71.2	68.6	2 079	82.6	10.7	-13.7	10.8	4.9	8.7	69.2	20.9
Gilmer, WV	4 515	66.9	70.0	953	98.1	17.1	-7.3	17.1	0.0	50.0	9.5	0.0
Grant, WV	7 859	72.3	70.8	323	82.0	11.4	-13.0	11.4	0.0	0.0	...	23.5
Greenbrier, WV	24 373	67.8	73.4	1 108	85.4	13.6	-10.8	13.9	4.6	10.1	62.5	7.5
Hampshire, WV	13 690	72.9	71.3	474	87.8	11.3	-13.1	11.3	5.8	50.0	42.5	0.0
Hancock, WV	23 502	64.7	82.9	927	85.9	11.5	-12.9	11.6	9.8	0.0	12.2	27.5
Hardy, WV	8 759	74.3	70.3	345	91.6	9.4	-15.0	9.7	3.3	28.6	...	0.0
Harrison, WV	46 870	62.0	78.4	2 738	75.2	16.3	-8.1	16.2	9.5	11.9	52.8	18.4
Jackson, WV	19 074	62.3	77.4	867	89.3	12.4	-12.0	12.1	100.0	20.6	72.7	14.7
Jefferson, WV	27 920	55.6	79.0	2 359	90.8	21.6	-2.8	22.3	9.5	20.5	35.0	9.5
Kanawha, WV	140 588	56.2	80.0	8 345	81.5	20.6	-3.8	20.4	15.5	24.0	70.3	21.9
Lewis, WV	11 872	70.4	73.7	459	87.8	11.2	-13.2	10.9	100.0	0.0	74.2	71.8
Lincoln, WV	14 864	79.5	62.7	541	90.4	5.9	-18.5	5.9	...	0.0	16.7	2.9
Logan, WV	25 824	71.7	63.1	1 181	85.7	8.8	-15.6	8.2	16.2	0.0	81.3	32.6
McDowell, WV	18 802	83.1	50.0	473	92.6	5.6	-18.8	5.1	9.5	0.0	44.0	2.8
Marion, WV	38 957	60.1	79.5	3 891	91.7	16.0	-8.4	16.1	9.6	0.0	55.6	25.5
Marshall, WV	24 707	66.8	79.7	1 228	85.6	10.7	-13.7	10.5	11.1	26.5	70.2	11.7
Mason, WV	17 947	73.8	72.4	752	87.6	8.8	-15.6	8.5	7.5	57.9	80.8	0.0
Mercer, WV	43 673	64.5	72.1	3 223	88.5	13.8	-10.6	13.5	13.4	28.1	72.6	8.5
Mineral, WV	18 443	66.1	80.3	1 189	93.3	11.7	-12.7	11.8	5.9	...	34.3	4.8
Mingo, WV	18 793	76.1	59.6	765	94.1	7.3	-17.1	6.9	12.1	0.0	71.8	4.8
Monongalia, WV	47 943	46.9	83.6	18 429	97.0	32.4	8.0	31.4	23.5	12.6	80.8	36.1
Monroe, WV	10 474	73.1	73.7	482	89.4	8.2	-16.2	8.8	1.1	30.0	25.0	0.0
Morgan, WV	10 591	70.2	75.8	238	81.9	11.2	-13.2	11.2	2.7	23.7	0.0	5.8
Nicholas, WV	18 149	73.6	70.0	797	88.3	9.8	-14.6	9.4	...	23.1	75.0	59.5
Ohio, WV	32 263	53.1	83.0	3 900	71.3	23.1	-1.3	23.2	10.2	0.0	69.0	29.7
Pendleton, WV	5 813	70.6	72.0	177	72.9	10.8	-13.6	10.9	0.7	0.0	100.0	0.0
Pleasants, WV	5 121	69.6	79.4	215	80.0	9.7	-14.7	9.5	12.5	23.8	40.0	46.2
Pocahontas, WV	6 556	71.7	70.9	234	76.9	11.8	-12.6	11.7	6.5	9.1	87.5	40.0
Preston, WV	20 050	73.1	74.0	691	88.4	10.8	-13.6	10.6	19.2	...	68.4	35.4
Putnam, WV	34 854	55.0	83.8	2 105	88.4	19.7	-4.7	19.2	56.3	0.0	48.9	38.0
Raleigh, WV	55 201	64.3	72.0	3 688	59.7	12.7	-11.7	12.6	5.9	0.0	64.5	12.8
Randolph, WV	19 498	69.4	73.5	998	44.9	13.6	-10.8	13.5	16.6	0.0	32.6	43.4
Ritchie, WV	7 177	70.3	73.4	294	94.2	7.1	-17.3	7.1	31.3	31.8	0.0	4.0
Roane, WV	10 442	74.9	66.8	278	81.7	9.0	-15.4	9.0	0.0	0.0	60.0	25.8
Summers, WV	9 302	74.9	65.4	415	74.0	10.1	-14.3	10.2	3.8	0.0	0.0	0.0
Taylor, WV	11 146	69.4	74.7	444	85.6	11.3	-13.1	11.2	15.2	6.5	31.3	11.3
Tucker, WV	5 301	73.0	75.5	192	72.9	10.6	-13.8	10.3	...	0.0	0.0	0.0
Tyler, WV	6 749	69.4	75.4	245	82.9	8.5	-15.9	8.4	100.0	0.0	71.4	0.0
Upshur, WV	15 222	69.8	74.6	1 781	22.5	13.8	-10.6	13.7	0.0	0.0	40.0	33.0
Wayne, WV	29 223	67.0	70.5	1 433	91.4	11.9	-12.5	11.7	37.5	3.6	43.8	35.6
Webster, WV	6 701	78.2	58.2	152	88.8	8.7	-15.7	8.7	...	0.0	100.0	...
Wetzel, WV	12 287	69.9	77.6	464	86.2	10.4	-14.0	10.3	0.0	19.2	100.0	0.0
Wirt, WV	3 944	72.6	72.4	140	97.1	9.9	-14.5	9.9	0.0	0.0	0.0	0.0
Wood, WV	60 697	56.9	81.4	3 348	80.0	15.2	-9.2	15.0	18.6	17.9	51.5	25.4
Wyoming, WV	17 722	77.5	64.3	610	85.2	7.1	-17.3	7.1	18.9	0.0	0.0	0.0
WISCONSIN	3 475 878	49.5	85.1	328 537	79.7	22.4	-2.0	23.1	10.5	10.4	42.5	11.4
Adams, WI	13 730	65.2	76.7	371	88.7	10.0	-14.4	9.9	7.1	3.9	49.1	5.9
Ashland, WI	10 668	56.4	84.1	1 192	45.8	16.5	-7.9	17.1	0.0	9.2	12.9	23.1
Barron, WI	29 942	57.1	82.4	1 371	88.8	14.9	-9.5	14.9	0.0	1.2	50.0	11.9
Bayfield, WI	10 526	47.2	86.9	453	81.5	21.6	-2.8	22.5	0.0	9.5	30.4	0.0
Brown, WI	144 172	48.6	86.3	13 385	77.3	22.5	-1.9	23.3	7.7	11.1	21.3	7.3
Buffalo, WI	9 384	59.7	84.1	374	85.3	14.0	-10.4	13.9	40.0	9.1	18.2	21.9
Burnett, WI	11 273	59.9	82.8	248	82.3	14.0	-10.4	14.4	0.0	3.3	12.5	0.0
Calumet, WI	26 068	53.2	87.3	1 476	79.3	20.8	-3.6	20.5	60.0	12.9	43.2	32.0
Chippewa, WI	36 330	56.7	84.3	1 800	89.2	14.7	-9.7	14.6	10.0	9.8	29.1	29.1
Clark, WI	20 991	67.3	75.4	711	86.9	10.3	-14.1	10.2	5.4	10.3	51.1	11.8
Columbia, WI	35 529	53.5	86.2	1 668	83.8	16.7	-7.7	16.8	7.6	1.6	42.5	12.5
Crawford, WI	11 301	61.2	81.3	432	85.2	13.2	-11.2	13.2	0.0	4.8	22.9	0.0
Dane, WI	269 998	30.1	92.2	53 744	91.4	40.6	16.2	41.1	19.2	23.1	65.0	27.2
Dodge, WI	57 453	61.2	82.3	2 735	75.2	13.2	-11.2	13.5	2.7	10.7	39.1	8.7
Door, WI	20 062	50.8	87.8	636	83.0	21.4	-3.0	21.5	11.8	8.4	38.9	13.0
Douglas, WI	28 653	50.3	85.9	2 719	93.4	18.3	-6.1	18.7	20.9	2.2	38.0	12.0
Dunn, WI	22 644	50.2	86.6	6 457	96.5	21.1	-3.3	21.2	13.6	29.3	16.0	18.1
Eau Claire, WI	55 290	42.2	88.9	12 337	96.6	27.0	2.6	27.1	29.9	8.6	26.5	25.7
Florence, WI	3 641	60.6	83.7	83	89.2	12.4	-12.0	12.6	0.0	0.0	0.0	0.0
Fond du Lac, WI	63 548	55.9	84.2	4 722	60.5	16.9	-7.5	17.0	8.0	10.5	38.8	8.3

[3]May be of any race.
... = Not available.

Table C-1. Population, School, and Student Characteristics by County—*Continued*

STATE County	State/ county code	County type[1]	Population, 2005 Total	Percent 5 to 17 years	Number of schools and students, 2004–2005 School districts	Schools	Students	Resident enrollment, 2000 Total	Percent public	K–12	Percent public
			1	2	3	4	5	6	7	8	9
Forest, WI	55 041	9	9 961	17.3	3	8	1 854	2 407	94.7	2 045	95.5
Grant, WI	55 043	6	49 671	15.3	11	28	7 657	15 315	90.4	9 319	89.3
Green, WI	55 045	6	35 165	17.9	6	21	5 719	8 301	92.6	6 905	95.6
Green Lake, WI	55 047	6	19 168	15.9	4	11	3 277	4 182	84.8	3 554	85.6
Iowa, WI	55 049	2	23 569	18.0	6	15	4 218	5 763	90.9	4 809	92.8
Iron, WI	55 051	9	6 649	13.5	2	4	871	1 365	96.9	1 104	99.0
Jackson, WI	55 053	6	19 758	16.1	3	11	3 228	4 439	93.7	3 728	95.0
Jefferson, WI	55 055	4	79 328	16.5	7	30	9 219	18 482	79.5	13 994	82.4
Juneau, WI	55 057	7	26 725	16.1	5	17	4 139	5 654	87.0	4 840	88.0
Kenosha, WI	55 059	1	160 544	19.0	13	54	28 802	42 684	82.6	30 494	89.1
Kewaunee, WI	55 061	2	20 840	16.9	3	10	3 628	4 977	83.3	4 139	84.2
La Crosse, WI	55 063	3	108 958	15.8	6	40	15 513	33 296	85.1	19 081	85.1
Lafayette, WI	55 065	8	16 310	17.5	6	16	2 490	4 218	93.6	3 525	95.3
Langlade, WI	55 067	6	20 735	16.3	3	14	3 421	4 619	87.2	3 948	88.2
Lincoln, WI	55 069	6	30 319	17.3	3	13	4 844	7 154	88.3	5 830	89.6
Manitowoc, WI	55 071	4	81 949	17.2	6	32	11 750	20 954	77.8	16 665	80.5
Marathon, WI	55 073	3	128 941	18.2	9	45	19 505	32 716	85.7	25 711	87.4
Marinette, WI	55 075	6	43 406	15.7	8	22	6 891	10 876	83.4	8 300	91.0
Marquette, WI	55 077	8	15 237	15.0	2	8	2 128	3 437	87.1	2 782	88.4
Menominee, WI	55 078	8	4 580	24.8	1	3	934	1 645	95.3	1 335	96.0
Milwaukee, WI	55 079	1	921 654	18.3	32	359	147 123	268 828	76.5	190 432	82.1
Monroe, WI	55 081	6	42 644	18.5	4	26	6 880	10 296	84.8	8 652	85.5
Oconto, WI	55 083	2	37 666	17.0	6	18	4 972	8 738	90.8	7 363	93.0
Oneida, WI	55 085	7	36 994	15.1	4	15	5 382	8 435	88.7	6 676	91.3
Outagamie, WI	55 087	3	171 006	18.6	7	31	17 189	44 269	78.8	33 537	81.3
Ozaukee, WI	55 089	1	86 072	18.0	5	26	13 417	23 199	71.1	16 931	80.0
Pepin, WI	55 091	8	7 380	17.2	2	5	1 465	1 844	84.8	1 498	84.1
Pierce, WI	55 093	1	39 102	15.9	6	24	7 306	12 261	89.4	7 033	92.1
Polk, WI	55 095	6	44 329	17.4	8	26	7 829	10 202	94.0	8 586	96.3
Portage, WI	55 097	4	67 585	15.5	5	43	15 328	21 761	91.3	12 280	90.0
Price, WI	55 099	9	15 220	15.8	3	11	2 263	3 685	90.3	3 111	92.9
Racine, WI	55 101	3	195 708	18.6	14	57	29 802	51 249	78.4	38 957	80.6
Richland, WI	55 103	6	18 403	16.8	2	9	1 823	4 510	85.9	3 620	86.1
Rock, WI	55 105	3	157 538	18.3	9	65	27 803	39 380	86.7	30 300	92.0
Rusk, WI	55 107	6	15 198	16.8	4	14	2 513	3 751	86.5	3 078	93.4
St. Croix, WI	55 109	1	77 144	18.3	6	24	12 226	17 324	86.8	13 251	91.0
Sauk, WI	55 111	4	57 746	17.5	5	33	9 852	13 531	87.0	10 922	89.3
Sawyer, WI	55 113	9	16 975	16.1	2	11	2 449	3 740	88.0	3 075	91.3
Shawano, WI	55 115	6	41 335	17.4	5	18	5 987	9 992	87.4	8 151	89.3
Sheboygan, WI	55 117	3	114 610	17.4	9	46	19 394	28 868	78.5	22 043	83.2
Taylor, WI	55 119	6	19 766	17.5	3	11	3 151	5 003	90.1	4 353	91.4
Trempealeau, WI	55 121	8	27 812	17.3	7	24	4 534	6 266	91.6	5 212	93.3
Vernon, WI	55 123	6	29 055	18.3	6	21	3 806	6 831	83.9	5 816	83.8
Vilas, WI	55 125	9	22 330	13.9	5	10	2 895	4 346	92.0	3 520	94.1
Walworth, WI	55 127	4	99 844	16.3	16	40	15 041	28 372	88.3	17 448	88.1
Washburn, WI	55 129	6	16 601	15.6	4	10	2 671	3 591	92.1	3 056	93.8
Washington, WI	55 131	1	126 158	17.9	9	35	19 348	30 427	77.3	23 736	81.2
Waukesha, WI	55 133	1	378 971	17.8	20	108	61 831	97 499	75.3	72 586	80.9
Waupaca, WI	55 135	6	52 563	17.4	7	31	10 048	12 254	86.4	10 414	87.9
Waushara, WI	55 137	8	24 789	15.4	3	10	3 019	4 997	91.2	4 340	93.0
Winnebago, WI	55 139	3	159 482	16.1	6	63	23 061	43 417	86.3	28 544	86.8
Wood, WI	55 141	4	75 234	17.1	5	18	7 474	19 208	84.3	15 093	86.1
WYOMING	56 000		509 294	16.3	62	378	84 733	136 139	92.9	98 562	95.6
Albany, WY	56 001	4	30 890	11.0	2	19	3 661	14 837	90.9	4 311	93.3
Big Horn, WY	56 003	9	11 333	18.5	4	18	2 218	3 028	95.7	2 557	97.3
Campbell, WY	56 005	5	37 405	18.6	3	22	7 235	9 726	94.7	7 977	97.6
Carbon, WY	56 007	7	15 331	14.6	2	20	2 364	3 674	95.9	2 969	97.8
Converse, WY	56 009	6	12 766	17.2	2	13	2 326	3 154	95.0	2 604	98.2
Crook, WY	56 011	9	6 182	15.7	1	10	1 075	1 512	98.3	1 345	98.7
Fremont, WY	56 013	7	36 491	17.1	8	29	6 324	9 531	94.6	7 484	96.7
Goshen, WY	56 015	7	12 243	15.6	2	12	1 943	3 108	90.6	2 279	95.2
Hot Springs, WY	56 017	7	4 537	13.4	2	5	693	1 043	95.0	900	96.2
Johnson, WY	56 019	7	7 721	15.4	1	7	1 221	1 652	95.8	1 456	97.3
Laramie, WY	56 021	3	85 163	16.8	4	40	13 792	21 266	88.9	15 626	93.3
Lincoln, WY	56 023	7	15 999	18.7	2	13	3 104	4 113	95.1	3 620	97.2
Natrona, WY	56 025	3	69 799	16.6	2	35	11 809	18 067	94.1	12 864	96.9
Niobrara, WY	56 027	9	2 286	14.2	1	4	374	522	95.4	428	97.9
Park, WY	56 029	7	26 664	15.2	3	15	3 893	6 815	92.6	5 000	93.3
Platte, WY	56 031	7	8 619	15.6	2	13	1 440	2 147	93.0	1 841	93.9
Sheridan, WY	56 033	7	27 389	15.2	5	24	4 103	6 752	88.1	5 051	88.9
Sublette, WY	56 035	9	6 926	16.4	2	8	1 292	1 392	91.6	1 178	94.3
Sweetwater, WY	56 037	5	37 975	17.6	2	25	6 817	11 129	95.1	8 471	98.2
Teton, WY	56 039	7	19 032	12.8	3	13	2 357	3 101	86.3	2 438	90.6
Uinta, WY	56 041	7	19 939	20.5	4	16	4 186	5 873	94.7	5 003	97.9
Washakie, WY	56 043	7	7 933	17.6	3	9	1 431	2 112	95.3	1 850	97.6
Weston, WY	56 045	7	6 671	14.1	2	8	1 075	1 585	97.6	1 310	98.5

[1]County type codes are from the Economic Research Service of the United States Department of Agriculture. See notes and definitions at the end of this section.

Table C-1. Population, School, and Student Characteristics by County—*Continued*

STATE County	Characteristics of students, 2004–2005				Outcomes		Staff and students, 2004–2005		
	Percent with IEP[2]	Percent eligible for free or reduced-price lunch	Percent minority	Percent English-language learners	Number of graduates, 2003–2004	Percent dropouts, grades 9–12, 2001–2002	Number of teachers	Student-teacher ratio	Central administration staff
	10	11	12	13	14	15	16	17	18
Forest, WI	17.9	44.1	25.4	0.0	...	1.8	133	13.9	6
Grant, WI	16.8	29.1	2.8	0.0	...	0.5	591	13.0	33
Green, WI	16.0	17.5	4.1	0.0	...	0.8	435	13.1	25
Green Lake, WI	13.8	22.6	7.7	0.0	...	0.1	244	13.5	12
Iowa, WI	15.2	19.3	1.8	0.0	...	0.6	328	12.9	10
Iron, WI	15.6	41.1	2.5	0.0	...	0.3	69	12.6	2
Jackson, WI	14.7	33.6	14.9	0.0	...	0.9	245	13.2	9
Jefferson, WI	14.6	21.7	10.4	0.0	...	1.5	663	13.9	27
Juneau, WI	15.2	39.1	5.2	0.0	...	2.9	326	12.7	12
Kenosha, WI	14.0	31.8	25.5	1.9	...	2.8	1 991	14.5	75
Kewaunee, WI	13.8	15.0	3.6	0.0	...	0.4	252	14.4	8
La Crosse, WI	13.0	28.1	13.8	4.8	...	1.2	1 143	13.6	32
Lafayette, WI	15.4	20.5	2.5	0.0	...	0.6	226	11.0	8
Langlade, WI	18.5	41.7	4.6	0.0	...	1.3	269	12.7	14
Lincoln, WI	13.0	25.9	5.4	0.0	...	2.2	331	14.6	22
Manitowoc, WI	14.5	20.7	10.3	3.6	...	1.9	840	14.0	26
Marathon, WI	12.9	26.2	16.6	9.4	...	1.1	1 350	14.5	54
Marinette, WI	15.3	36.8	2.9	0.0	...	0.8	486	14.2	12
Marquette, WI	16.6	35.3	6.3	0.0	...	1.3	163	13.1	7
Menominee, WI	32.8	80.7	99.6	0.0	...	4.0	99	9.4	9
Milwaukee, WI	15.6	56.8	62.4	4.6	...	5.5	9 426	15.6	...
Monroe, WI	13.5	33.0	7.1	0.7	...	0.9	514	13.4	15
Oconto, WI	16.7	24.3	3.8	0.0	...	1.0	383	13.0	23
Oneida, WI	13.4	27.6	8.0	0.0	...	3.4	380	14.2	12
Outagamie, WI	13.3	17.5	12.1	0.6	...	0.7	1 119	15.4	41
Ozaukee, WI	11.8	6.5	6.8	0.0	...	0.4	813	16.5	43
Pepin, WI	15.4	27.3	1.5	0.0	...	0.8	108	13.6	5
Pierce, WI	12.9	15.8	4.5	0.0	...	0.5	517	14.1	15
Polk, WI	14.2	28.2	4.5	0.0	...	0.4	557	14.1	13
Portage, WI	13.6	18.6	10.9	3.8	...	1.7	1 018	15.1	44
Price, WI	12.5	28.7	3.9	0.0	...	0.8	181	12.5	10
Racine, WI	17.1	32.7	34.2	3.1	...	3.9	1 943	15.3	73
Richland, WI	21.1	29.3	2.9	0.0	...	0.8	141	12.9	5
Rock, WI	16.2	29.8	19.2	3.7	...	1.9	1 920	14.5	93
Rusk, WI	15.5	47.7	4.6	0.0	...	0.7	200	12.5	6
St. Croix, WI	13.3	11.8	4.8	0.0	...	0.7	778	15.7	30
Sauk, WI	16.0	22.0	7.0	1.1	...	1.4	713	13.8	20
Sawyer, WI	15.0	44.3	25.7	0.0	...	2.0	187	13.1	10
Shawano, WI	16.6	32.5	16.4	0.0	...	0.8	439	13.6	18
Sheboygan, WI	15.3	23.4	18.9	10.0	...	1.3	1 347	14.4	49
Taylor, WI	13.5	30.9	3.2	0.0	...	1.2	227	13.9	9
Trempealeau, WI	19.0	30.9	3.8	0.0	...	0.5	441	10.3	17
Vernon, WI	15.8	34.7	2.0	0.0	...	0.7	339	11.2	15
Vilas, WI	14.0	37.7	18.4	0.0	...	1.3	249	11.6	10
Walworth, WI	12.9	23.9	17.4	7.3	...	1.7	1 098	13.7	40
Washburn, WI	16.7	37.4	5.5	0.0	...	0.6	217	12.3	10
Washington, WI	12.3	12.4	5.2	0.0	...	1.1	1 264	15.3	40
Waukesha, WI	12.3	9.4	10.7	1.3	...	0.4	4 038	15.3	116
Waupaca, WI	12.8	23.3	4.9	0.6	...	1.1	723	13.9	30
Waushara, WI	12.8	40.5	15.0	4.5	...	0.2	234	12.9	7
Winnebago, WI	15.0	23.7	11.4	4.9	...	1.9	1 551	14.9	76
Wood, WI	13.4	24.7	8.0	0.0	...	0.7	516	14.5	13
WYOMING	13.8	32.1	14.4	4.2	...	5.8	6 656	12.7	...
Albany, WY	16.0	26.3	19.9	1.6	...	6.4	322	11.4	38
Big Horn, WY	14.5	44.2	11.7	2.5	176	4.4	215	10.3	35
Campbell, WY	11.6	24.9	7.2	1.5	...	4.5	564	12.8	...
Carbon, WY	16.9	33.0	20.9	1.3	165	4.9	214	11.1	28
Converse, WY	14.4	28.8	7.4	1.4	168	2.9	190	12.3	24
Crook, WY	15.3	30.8	4.5	0.0	110	3.0	96	11.2	12
Fremont, WY	16.9	48.2	36.7	30.2	...	6.0	507	12.5	79
Goshen, WY	13.4	49.4	15.7	2.0	...	3.9	159	12.2	...
Hot Springs, WY	15.6	43.3	5.8	2.2	...	4.1	63	11.0	17
Johnson, WY	15.2	28.1	5.2	0.0	88	1.9	111	11.0	13
Laramie, WY	12.4	33.0	22.0	2.1	882	7.9	1 010	13.7	...
Lincoln, WY	11.9	31.2	4.4	0.5	222	2.7	223	13.9	24
Natrona, WY	13.7	32.9	9.9	1.0	673	10.0	803	14.7	118
Niobrara, WY	16.3	29.4	5.1	0.0	32	2.0	41	9.2	8
Park, WY	11.5	27.5	6.9	0.2	314	2.5	294	13.2	37
Platte, WY	13.5	30.1	8.9	4.7	109	4.5	148	9.7	14
Sheridan, WY	12.6	32.6	9.0	1.1	...	3.6	388	10.6	34
Sublette, WY	10.4	21.0	5.9	1.0	95	1.9	102	12.6	18
Sweetwater, WY	15.5	24.5	15.3	4.2	503	7.4	483	14.1	59
Teton, WY	9.4	13.8	15.6	11.4	...	2.7	179	13.1	...
Uinta, WY	15.6	36.8	8.2	3.5	297	4.8	328	12.8	49
Washakie, WY	18.2	41.1	19.0	5.9	...	8.5	121	11.8	16
Weston, WY	17.1	28.1	5.4	0.3	88	1.7	94	11.4	19

[2]IEP = Individual Education Program. See notes and definitions at the end of this section.
... = Not available.

Table C-1. Population, School, and Student Characteristics by County—*Continued*

STATE County	Revenue, 2003–2004				Current expenditures, 2003–2004			Resident population, 16 to 19 years, 2000			
	Total revenue (thousands of dollars)	Percent of revenue from:			Total expenditures (thousands of dollars)	Amount per student (dollars)	Percent for instruction	Total	Percent in armed forces	Percent high school graduates	Percent not enrolled, not employed, not in armed forces, not high school graduate
		Federal government	State government	Local government							
	19	20	21	22	23	24	25	26	27	28	29
Forest, WI	20 806	10.0	33.9	56.1	17 697	9 217	61.0	591	0.0	9.3	8.5
Grant, WI	81 587	5.5	65.4	29.1	73 134	9 331	66.9	4 046	0.2	6.9	2.0
Green, WI	62 604	4.1	58.2	37.7	54 244	9 380	67.6	1 822	0.0	10.8	3.0
Green Lake, WI	36 994	3.8	42.5	53.6	29 417	8 665	66.2	1 146	0.3	13.4	2.6
Iowa, WI	40 434	3.5	59.4	37.1	34 179	9 064	66.7	1 298	0.0	11.6	1.8
Iron, WI	15 254	4.6	32.5	62.9	10 464	10 889	59.6	365	0.5	7.4	1.6
Jackson, WI	32 554	6.9	64.1	29.1	28 722	8 890	64.8	1 038	0.0	12.6	6.8
Jefferson, WI	126 803	4.1	51.6	44.3	112 315	9 418	65.7	3 996	0.1	13.8	2.8
Juneau, WI	46 915	4.9	55.4	39.7	37 894	9 055	64.1	1 292	0.0	13.1	3.0
Kenosha, WI	281 421	5.5	57.1	37.4	256 020	8 979	68.3	8 661	0.2	11.5	3.9
Kewaunee, WI	36 662	3.7	57.7	38.5	30 550	8 386	64.8	1 142	0.0	11.5	0.6
La Crosse, WI	167 256	5.8	56.1	38.0	151 325	9 674	67.0	7 770	0.0	10.3	1.0
Lafayette, WI	35 056	3.9	64.6	31.5	29 841	9 156	65.3	1 063	0.4	6.3	0.8
Langlade, WI	41 100	8.0	49.3	42.7	35 194	10 018	63.6	1 131	0.0	14.3	2.7
Lincoln, WI	50 305	6.4	53.0	40.6	43 697	8 829	65.6	1 781	0.0	9.9	7.2
Manitowoc, WI	114 807	4.3	60.0	35.8	98 800	8 335	66.7	4 655	0.0	10.4	3.0
Marathon, WI	198 353	5.8	59.1	35.1	178 328	9 159	65.6	7 652	0.0	12.7	1.7
Marinette, WI	72 435	4.8	51.7	43.5	61 206	8 705	63.6	2 788	0.0	9.3	2.4
Marquette, WI	22 233	7.4	40.4	52.2	18 017	8 219	65.0	764	0.0	12.6	1.8
Menominee, WI	17 009	42.0	45.0	13.1	12 954	13 840	60.9	347	0.0	16.4	11.0
Milwaukee, WI	1 638 915	11.2	56.5	32.3	1 488 008	9 971	65.5	53 378	0.0	9.9	6.7
Monroe, WI	68 543	6.6	66.1	27.4	57 661	8 452	64.4	2 333	0.1	12.9	4.5
Oconto, WI	51 754	4.6	58.9	36.5	42 063	8 243	64.2	1 929	0.0	8.9	2.6
Oneida, WI	61 882	5.4	25.0	69.6	52 792	9 623	62.7	1 779	0.0	13.6	3.0
Outagamie, WI	301 796	4.0	58.8	37.2	261 872	8 148	65.9	9 485	0.1	12.2	2.3
Ozaukee, WI	136 231	2.3	28.6	69.0	122 724	9 302	66.1	4 502	0.0	8.2	1.6
Pepin, WI	16 433	5.2	56.3	38.5	14 236	9 757	61.7	457	0.0	9.4	1.3
Pierce, WI	78 823	4.4	52.7	42.8	64 084	8 653	66.2	3 203	0.3	8.3	1.4
Polk, WI	86 670	4.5	52.7	42.8	70 434	8 642	64.0	2 405	0.3	12.3	2.6
Portage, WI	95 929	5.5	57.9	36.5	85 731	8 817	69.3	5 331	0.0	8.9	1.3
Price, WI	24 468	6.9	48.3	44.8	22 120	9 125	63.3	858	0.0	11.1	1.6
Racine, WI	304 402	6.0	60.6	33.4	281 605	9 253	67.0	10 703	0.1	11.5	4.5
Richland, WI	22 115	5.3	57.9	36.8	18 083	9 598	64.3	1 151	0.0	9.5	2.4
Rock, WI	275 125	5.8	63.3	30.9	246 533	8 926	67.6	8 757	0.0	11.6	4.6
Rusk, WI	33 627	6.8	54.1	39.1	26 580	10 259	62.0	901	0.0	8.5	3.0
St. Croix, WI	118 107	2.9	51.2	45.9	97 302	8 356	65.0	3 525	0.0	10.2	1.8
Sauk, WI	117 349	4.9	47.7	47.4	102 019	8 752	66.6	3 029	0.0	15.1	3.8
Sawyer, WI	26 786	13.5	20.3	66.2	23 112	9 566	62.6	862	0.0	17.1	4.1
Shawano, WI	60 318	6.6	60.1	33.3	52 500	8 639	66.9	2 320	0.1	12.0	2.9
Sheboygan, WI	195 326	4.1	56.9	39.0	172 742	8 913	68.8	6 439	0.0	11.5	2.9
Taylor, WI	34 221	7.9	58.0	34.1	29 126	8 778	66.2	1 175	0.0	12.1	3.3
Trempealeau, WI	61 743	4.6	63.5	32.0	51 839	9 098	64.1	1 467	0.0	12.0	2.6
Vernon, WI	47 558	6.4	61.2	32.3	41 001	9 436	63.7	1 610	0.0	10.6	7.7
Vilas, WI	42 662	12.3	10.4	77.3	35 288	11 846	64.5	902	0.0	8.8	3.1
Walworth, WI	165 379	3.9	37.7	58.5	138 218	8 917	65.5	6 786	0.0	8.4	1.7
Washburn, WI	30 774	6.9	31.6	61.5	27 058	9 382	65.2	881	0.0	10.3	3.4
Washington, WI	192 121	2.9	44.7	52.4	170 850	8 673	67.1	6 175	0.0	14.5	1.5
Waukesha, WI	641 240	2.6	30.5	66.9	568 110	9 352	65.8	19 496	0.0	10.3	1.1
Waupaca, WI	101 954	4.5	59.2	36.2	87 232	8 631	65.3	2 753	0.0	13.4	3.6
Waushara, WI	32 257	7.8	43.8	48.5	27 188	8 539	66.4	1 232	0.0	12.5	2.6
Winnebago, WI	223 431	4.2	57.0	38.8	197 772	8 535	68.1	9 974	0.1	9.8	1.7
Wood, WI	132 058	4.9	60.9	34.2	123 830	9 240	67.8	4 431	0.0	11.7	3.3
WYOMING	974 888	9.8	52.0	38.1	813 909	9 363	64.4	32 130	0.6	11.4	3.8
Albany, WY	38 067	8.7	63.2	28.1	34 367	9 201	64.8	3 357	0.0	6.1	1.4
Big Horn, WY	29 985	10.6	67.6	21.8	25 005	10 595	63.6	757	0.3	9.5	4.5
Campbell, WY	78 000	8.2	5.7	86.1	63 316	8 643	63.3	2 180	0.0	11.1	4.9
Carbon, WY	30 248	7.3	33.6	59.1	25 766	10 164	62.6	933	0.0	11.9	4.1
Converse, WY	24 890	10.0	36.2	53.8	22 895	9 588	67.3	731	0.7	11.4	4.8
Crook, WY	13 627	6.1	62.0	31.9	12 433	11 131	65.3	403	0.0	7.7	1.7
Fremont, WY	110 034	20.2	60.9	19.0	75 601	11 490	63.3	2 261	0.5	8.7	8.7
Goshen, WY	23 040	11.2	70.0	18.8	19 915	10 487	67.0	722	0.0	12.6	3.9
Hot Springs, WY	10 078	7.3	48.4	44.3	7 225	10 021	62.9	274	0.0	11.3	1.5
Johnson, WY	13 995	7.4	57.9	34.7	12 562	10 042	63.5	442	0.0	10.9	0.0
Laramie, WY	129 842	8.5	70.4	21.1	118 583	8 349	65.7	4 423	3.7	15.1	3.9
Lincoln, WY	32 580	7.6	43.4	49.0	29 136	9 131	63.9	1 019	0.5	12.2	3.2
Natrona, WY	114 286	10.2	68.4	21.4	100 182	8 329	68.3	4 204	0.0	12.7	4.5
Niobrara, WY	5 154	7.1	60.0	32.9	4 841	11 836	62.1	140	0.0	28.6	1.4
Park, WY	47 398	11.6	54.8	33.6	35 777	8 886	64.1	1 737	0.0	8.2	2.1
Platte, WY	17 736	9.9	59.3	30.8	15 947	10 423	66.2	477	0.2	3.8	4.0
Sheridan, WY	51 065	8.3	68.5	23.1	39 709	9 659	67.1	1 590	0.0	6.7	3.2
Sublette, WY	20 016	4.0	3.6	92.4	15 227	11 659	62.5	289	0.0	5.5	2.4
Sweetwater, WY	75 969	8.0	32.8	59.2	64 405	9 185	59.5	2 861	0.0	9.8	2.8
Teton, WY	27 217	4.3	5.2	90.6	24 574	10 556	60.9	800	0.0	29.5	6.6
Uinta, WY	45 850	7.6	52.9	39.5	41 016	9 514	63.1	1 567	0.0	13.1	2.8
Washakie, WY	22 631	7.0	74.5	18.6	13 895	9 649	64.5	519	0.0	17.3	3.7
Weston, WY	13 180	6.4	62.0	31.6	11 532	10 324	60.4	444	0.0	17.1	5.6

Table C-1. Population, School, and Student Characteristics by County—*Continued*

STATE County	Population 25 years and over	High school graduate or less (percent)	High school graduate or more (percent)	College enrollment, 2000		College graduates, 2000 (percent)						
				Number	Percent public	Bachelor's degree or more	+/- U.S. percentage with bachelor's degree or more	Non-Hispanic White	Black	American Indian and Alaska Native	Asian or Pacific Islander	Hispanic[3]
	30	31	32	33	34	35	36	37	38	39	40	41
Forest, WI	6 694	64.2	78.5	222	88.3	10.0	-14.4	10.1	0.0	6.0	66.7	5.0
Grant, WI	30 625	56.5	83.5	5 323	94.5	17.2	-7.2	17.1	5.2	6.6	63.3	21.0
Green, WI	22 523	56.2	84.1	933	84.0	16.7	-7.7	16.7	18.9	16.9	57.1	6.9
Green Lake, WI	13 229	60.0	81.9	402	82.8	14.5	-9.9	14.6	12.5	0.0	100.0	4.2
Iowa, WI	15 100	53.3	88.5	642	88.0	18.5	-5.9	18.4	0.0	16.2	15.4	3.0
Iron, WI	5 124	54.4	83.7	189	83.6	13.2	-11.2	13.1	0.0	0.0	16.7	0.0
Jackson, WI	12 779	62.8	79.0	493	84.8	11.3	-13.1	11.8	3.9	7.3	8.9	6.4
Jefferson, WI	49 057	53.8	84.7	3 174	75.2	17.4	-7.0	17.7	10.7	8.1	38.2	5.8
Juneau, WI	16 457	64.5	78.5	554	85.2	10.0	-14.4	10.0	5.6	4.3	30.6	7.6
Kenosha, WI	95 038	49.8	83.5	9 631	70.3	19.2	-5.2	19.7	11.3	16.2	51.1	9.5
Kewaunee, WI	13 336	63.5	84.0	602	80.2	11.4	-13.0	11.4	. . .	0.0	24.1	3.7
La Crosse, WI	65 263	42.2	89.7	12 713	88.0	25.4	1.0	25.6	15.3	11.4	27.6	16.8
Lafayette, WI	10 528	61.1	85.5	479	88.5	13.3	-11.1	13.3	0.0	20.0	33.3	3.3
Langlade, WI	14 372	64.4	80.9	446	83.2	11.7	-12.7	11.7	15.4	4.6	20.9	8.3
Lincoln, WI	20 120	59.8	81.6	855	91.5	13.6	-10.8	13.6	0.0	0.0	12.9	7.0
Manitowoc, WI	55 452	58.5	84.6	3 031	75.1	15.5	-8.9	15.6	12.0	2.5	21.5	6.7
Marathon, WI	81 925	54.2	83.8	4 793	91.0	18.3	-6.1	18.5	39.1	5.7	11.2	10.5
Marinette, WI	29 575	62.2	82.5	1 945	59.2	12.9	-11.5	12.9	0.0	3.8	32.8	4.5
Marquette, WI	11 428	62.6	78.8	509	85.3	10.1	-14.3	10.4	6.3	9.4	23.8	5.3
Menominee, WI	2 399	63.8	78.2	170	87.1	12.9	-11.5	27.8	60.0	8.8	7.9	0.0
Milwaukee, WI	594 387	49.2	80.2	65 887	63.6	23.6	-0.8	28.3	9.9	11.2	39.9	9.6
Monroe, WI	26 323	60.1	81.1	1 027	84.7	13.2	-11.2	13.2	15.6	10.5	39.6	3.5
Oconto, WI	24 186	64.5	80.6	870	85.6	10.6	-13.8	10.6	0.0	10.4	4.3	12.8
Oneida, WI	26 449	51.4	85.1	1 306	86.6	20.0	-4.4	20.2	5.5	0.0	51.1	11.4
Outagamie, WI	102 218	49.6	88.1	7 729	77.3	22.5	-1.9	22.7	21.5	14.3	28.2	12.3
Ozaukee, WI	54 912	32.3	91.9	4 454	54.2	38.6	14.2	38.5	46.1	23.0	72.0	24.9
Pepin, WI	4 733	60.2	82.6	247	91.1	13.3	-11.1	13.5	. . .	0.0	0.0	0.0
Pierce, WI	21 542	45.3	89.6	4 736	90.4	24.6	0.2	24.5	18.2	44.9	34.6	46.6
Polk, WI	27 725	55.2	85.9	1 120	83.6	15.6	-8.8	15.5	36.4	15.2	27.9	27.5
Portage, WI	40 143	50.8	86.5	8 526	97.2	23.4	-1.0	23.6	0.0	5.3	15.2	6.8
Price, WI	11 122	61.1	82.4	388	77.6	13.0	-11.4	13.0	0.0	6.1	9.1	5.7
Racine, WI	122 356	49.6	82.9	8 818	80.3	20.3	-4.1	22.1	7.1	11.2	43.6	8.3
Richland, WI	11 896	58.7	82.1	626	91.2	14.1	-10.3	14.0	0.0	8.3	61.5	6.2
Rock, WI	98 770	55.3	83.9	6 280	72.7	16.7	-7.7	17.3	6.0	16.7	39.0	5.2
Rusk, WI	10 296	64.3	79.1	477	42.1	11.2	-13.2	11.2	15.4	0.0	8.0	10.3
St. Croix, WI	40 357	41.7	91.6	2 913	80.0	26.3	1.9	26.3	25.9	25.4	49.0	20.6
Sauk, WI	36 701	54.3	83.5	1 768	87.1	17.6	-6.8	17.6	12.6	14.0	45.8	8.2
Sawyer, WI	11 343	55.2	84.7	465	72.3	16.5	-7.9	17.6	7.0	7.8	19.6	31.7
Shawano, WI	27 503	64.3	81.5	1 189	82.6	12.6	-11.8	12.7	0.0	11.5	34.3	7.1
Sheboygan, WI	74 561	55.5	84.4	4 720	64.2	17.9	-6.5	18.3	6.8	3.0	15.2	9.2
Taylor, WI	12 872	66.1	78.3	378	79.6	11.0	-13.4	10.9	0.0	15.2	58.8	3.6
Trempealeau, WI	18 317	59.9	80.9	694	87.8	13.3	-11.1	13.2	12.5	13.3	25.0	18.5
Vernon, WI	18 473	59.6	78.9	679	83.8	14.0	-10.4	14.0	7.1	0.0	19.0	8.1
Vilas, WI	15 667	54.3	85.4	547	84.8	17.6	-6.8	18.1	0.0	6.7	34.6	10.4
Walworth, WI	58 153	49.3	84.2	9 549	92.6	21.8	-2.6	22.5	24.0	3.1	42.1	4.3
Washburn, WI	11 248	55.9	83.7	355	90.1	15.2	-9.2	15.5	0.0	9.5	11.8	0.0
Washington, WI	77 709	46.4	88.8	4 500	76.2	21.9	-2.5	22.0	22.1	21.6	30.8	14.5
Waukesha, WI	241 299	35.7	92.0	17 704	67.2	34.1	9.7	34.0	34.5	9.9	67.9	18.5
Waupaca, WI	34 726	61.0	82.7	1 145	85.8	14.8	-9.6	14.9	27.8	12.1	21.0	10.2
Waushara, WI	16 310	64.3	78.8	437	82.4	11.7	-12.7	11.8	0.0	3.7	45.2	5.5
Winnebago, WI	101 095	51.2	86.3	12 191	92.0	22.8	-1.6	22.9	7.8	10.7	00.0	10.3
Wood, WI	50 259	56.9	84.0	2 792	88.0	16.9	-7.5	16.6	31.5	10.8	39.9	19.3
WYOMING	315 663	43.1	87.9	29 697	91.2	21.9	-2.5	23.0	18.6	8.1	34.3	7.8
Albany, WY	17 016	28.4	93.5	10 055	91.5	44.1	19.7	46.2	37.8	30.2	64.2	13.5
Big Horn, WY	7 343	50.9	83.2	302	91.7	15.9	-8.5	16.6	100.0	0.0	18.8	2.8
Campbell, WY	20 107	47.0	88.3	1 160	88.8	15.7	-8.7	15.9	0.0	3.2	44.7	3.2
Carbon, WY	10 508	51.5	83.5	389	89.2	17.2	-7.2	19.0	13.2	7.5	51.5	4.3
Converse, WY	7 818	49.0	86.4	350	86.3	14.7	-9.7	15.4	27.3	5.3	0.0	1.7
Crook, WY	3 888	52.3	85.8	86	97.7	17.5	-6.9	17.4	. . .	10.0	0.0	31.3
Fremont, WY	23 053	48.4	84.8	1 462	90.2	19.7	-4.7	22.7	37.5	6.4	9.1	10.4
Goshen, WY	8 406	48.7	84.7	660	80.0	18.6	-5.8	19.9	60.7	16.9	. . .	1.3
Hot Springs, WY	3 515	51.9	84.2	94	91.5	17.9	-6.5	18.4	100.0	6.1	0.0	0.0
Johnson, WY	4 981	40.8	90.1	134	97.8	22.2	-2.2	22.2	. . .	0.0	. . .	11.6
Laramie, WY	53 041	37.4	89.1	4 235	90.1	23.4	-1.0	25.3	14.2	12.9	24.9	8.0
Lincoln, WY	9 049	46.9	87.9	328	78.0	17.2	-7.2	17.4	0.0	18.0	27.3	4.4
Natrona, WY	42 656	42.3	88.3	3 904	94.1	20.0	-4.4	20.7	23.7	3.7	33.6	7.0
Niobrara, WY	1 731	51.6	87.3	67	89.6	15.3	-9.1	15.5	. . .	22.2	0.0	22.2
Park, WY	17 145	42.8	87.6	1 469	98.0	23.7	-0.7	23.9	0.0	19.6	26.0	18.0
Platte, WY	6 034	53.6	84.9	173	88.4	15.2	-9.2	15.8	. . .	0.0	0.0	2.5
Sheridan, WY	17 980	40.4	88.4	1 371	94.2	22.4	-2.0	22.8	0.0	4.4	14.6	17.6
Sublette, WY	4 044	46.4	89.0	105	78.1	21.6	-2.8	21.8	0.0	7.7	0.0	15.6
Sweetwater, WY	23 053	47.3	87.4	2 004	93.8	17.0	-7.4	18.0	18.5	3.4	29.4	5.9
Teton, WY	12 838	24.2	94.7	465	77.4	45.8	21.4	47.2	100.0	48.2	48.9	17.4
Uinta, WY	11 443	50.8	84.8	580	84.0	15.0	-9.4	15.5	0.0	10.6	56.3	5.7
Washakie, WY	5 460	48.2	85.6	105	89.5	18.7	-5.7	20.1	. . .	0.0	0.0	5.6
Weston, WY	4 554	55.0	85.2	199	92.5	14.5	-9.9	14.6	0.0	21.4	36.8	1.7

[3]May be of any race.
. . . = Not available.

NOTES AND DEFINITIONS:
COUNTY EDUCATION STATISTICS

Part C presents 41 data items for each county, county equivalent, and independent city. The counties are presented in alphabetical order within states, which are also listed in alphabetical order. Independent cities, which are located in Maryland, Missouri, Nevada, and Virginia, are placed in alphabetical order at the end of the list of counties for those states. The District of Columbia is included as both a county and a state.

Common Core of Data
Source: For Items 3 through 5 and 10 through 25 — National Center for Education Statistics. U.S. Department of Education. *Common Core of Data: 2003–2004.* <http://nces.ed.gov/ccd/>.

NCES uses the Common Core of Data (CCD) system to acquire and maintain statistical data from each of the 50 states, the District of Columbia, and the U.S. outlying areas. Information about staff and students is collected annually at the school level, the Local Education Agency (LEA) or school district level, and the state levels. Information about revenues and expenditures is also collected at the state level. In addition, information about revenues and expenditures at the school district level is taken from the Census Bureau's annual surveys of government finances.

Data are collected for a particular school year (July 1 through June 30) via survey instruments sent to the state education agencies during the subsequent school year. States have one year to modify the data originally submitted. This volume uses the data from the 2004–2005 school year; however, the revenue and expenditure data for counties is from the 2003–2004 school year (fiscal year 2004). The high school graduates and dropouts data also come from earlier years.

Since the CCD is a universe survey, the information is not subject to sampling error. However, nonsampling errors could come from two sources — nonreturn and inaccurate reporting. Almost all of the states submit the six CCD survey instruments each year, but submissions are sometimes incomplete or made too late for publication.

Understandably, when 51 education agencies compile and submit data for more than 95,000 public schools and 18,000 local school districts, misreporting can occur. This typically results from varying interpretation of NCES definitions and differences in record-keeping systems. NCES attempts to minimize these errors by working closely with the Council of Chief State School Officers (CCSSO) and its Committee on Evaluation and Information Systems (CEIS).

The state education agencies report data to NCES from data collected and edited during their regular reporting cycles. NCES encourages the agencies to incorporate the NCES items for which they do not already gather data into their own survey systems, so that those items will be available for the subsequent CCD survey. Over time, this has meant fewer missing data cells in each state's response and a reduction in the need to impute data.

Data from the education agencies is subjected to a comprehensive edit by NCES. Where data are determined to be inconsistent, missing, or out of range, NCES contacts the education agencies for verification. NCES-prepared state summary forms are returned to the state education agencies for verification. States are also given an opportunity to revise their state-level aggregates from the previous survey cycle. The county-level data in this volume have not been adjusted.

The CCD data are collected at three levels — the school level, the school district level, and the state level. In Part C, selected school and school district data items have been aggregated to the county level because the county is a widely used statistical area. School districts, and even some schools, can serve populations in different counties. In this volume, schools and school districts are assigned to the county in which the school district office is located, as coded by NCES in their files. Consequently, the numbers do not necessarily represent the population of a given county. NCES has begun to include the county code in the schools data file. A few items thus represent the county of the individual schools rather than the school district office.

The structure of school districts ranges from that of states like West Virginia and Nevada, where most counties have a single school district, to Maricopa County, Arizona, which includes 258 separate school districts. Some counties have no school districts. Hawaii has a single statewide school district whose offices are located in Honolulu County. New York City has a single school system for all five boroughs (counties). A few other counties report no school districts. These are usually counties with very small populations or independent cities in Virginia whose school systems are run by the neighboring or surrounding county.

The CCD data files now include charter schools. Charter schools are often managed independently from the local school district. When this is the case, each charter school is considered to be a single district. This affects the county aggregations and should be considered in interpreting these data. For example, in New York City, the New York City public school system is counted in Kings County (Brooklyn), but the small numbers that appear in some columns for the other boroughs represent charter schools. Additional attention should be given to the fiscal data because some states include revenues and expenditures for charter schools, while others do not.

2000 Census of Population and Housing. Items 6–9 and 26–41 are from the 2000 census. The population totals and age data are from the complete census count, while the education data are from the long-form questionnaire that was answered by a sample of the population. The sample data are estimates of the actual figures that would have been obtained from a complete count. Estimates derived from a sample are expected to be different from the 100-percent figures because they are subject to sampling and nonsampling errors. Sampling error in data arises from the selection of people and housing units included in the sample. Nonsampling error affects both sample and 100-percent data. It is introduced as a result of errors that may have occurred during the data collection and processing phases of the census.

For additional information about the 2000 census, see <http://www.census.gov/main/www/cen2000.html>.

Geographic identification. Data are presented for 3,141 counties and county equivalents. A five-digit state and county code is given for each entity. The first two digits indicate the state; the remaining three identify the county. Within each state, the counties are numbered in alphabetical order,

beginning with 001, with even numbers usually omitted. Independent cities follow the counties and begin with the number 510.

These codes have been established by the U.S. government as Federal Information Processing Standards and are often referred to as "FIPS codes." They are used by U.S. government agencies and many other organizations for data presentation. They are provided in this volume for use in matching its data given here with other data sources in which counties may be identified by FIPS codes.

Independent cities. Independent cities are not included in any county; data are presented separately in this volume where available.

Maryland
    Baltimore (separate from Baltimore County)

Missouri
    St. Louis (separate from St. Louis County)

Nevada
    Carson City

Virginia
    Alexandria
    Bedford
    Bristol
    Buena Vista
    Charlottesville
    Chesapeake
    Colonial Heights
    Covington
    Danville
    Emporia
    Fairfax
    Falls Church
    Franklin
    Fredericksburg
    Galax
    Hampton
    Harrisonburg
    Hopewell
    Lexington
    Lynchburg
    Manassas
    Manassas Park
    Martinsville
    Newport News

Norfolk
Norton
Petersburg
Poquoson
Portsmouth
Radford
Richmond
Roanoke
Salem
Staunton
Suffolk
Virginia Beach
Waynesboro
Williamsburg
Winchester

County type. Table C's third column provides county type codes which identify each county by its metropolitan/nonmetropolitan status and size. These are the "rural-urban continuum codes" developed by the Economic Research Service of the U.S. Department of Agriculture.

The 2003 rural-urban continuum codes form a classification scheme to distinguish metropolitan counties by size and nonmetropolitan counties by degree of urbanization and proximity to metropolitan areas. The standard Office of Management and Budget (OMB) metropolitan and nonmetropolitan categories have been subdivided into three metropolitan and six nonmetropolitan categories, resulting in a nine-part county codification. This scheme was originally developed in 1974. The codes were updated in 1983 and 1993, and were slightly revised in 1988. The 1988 revision was first published in 1990. This scheme allows researchers to break county data into residential groups beyond metropolitan and nonmetropolitan; this is particularly helpful in analyzing trends in nonmetropolitan areas related to population density and metro influence. The 2003 rural-urban continuum codes are not directly comparable with the codes from previous years because of the new methodology used in developing the 2003 metropolitan areas.

Metropolitan counties
1 Counties in metropolitan areas of 1 million people or more.
2 Counties in metropolitan areas of 250,000 to 1 million people.

3 Counties in metropolitan areas of fewer than 250,000 people.

Nonmetropolitan counties
4 Urban population of 20,000 or more, adjacent to a metropolitan area.
5 Urban population of 20,000 or more, not adjacent to a metropolitan area.
6 Urban population of 2,500 to 19,999, adjacent to a metropolitan area.
7 Urban population of 2,500 to 19,999, not adjacent to a metropolitan area.
8 Completely rural or less than 2,500 urban population, adjacent to a metropolitan area.
9 Completely rural or less than 2,500 urban population, not adjacent to a metropolitan area.

Data sources and explanations. The schools and students data in Table C have been developed by Bernan from the CCD's individual school and school district data. In general, the numbers are consistent with those in the tables available on the CCD Web site through the "Build a Table" feature. The files used were:

• Local Education Agency Universe Survey: School Year 2004–2005, version 1a
• Public Elementary/Secondary School Universe Survey: School Year 2004–2005, version 1a
• School District Finance Survey (F-33): School Year 2003–2004 (Fiscal Year 2004), version 1a
• Local Education Agency (School District) Universe Survey Dropout and Completion Data: School Year 2001–2002, version 0d

The population, characteristics, enrollment, and attainment data in Table C have been compiled from the Census Bureau's Summary File 3 on CD-ROM, and can be found on the Census Bureau Web site in the "American FactFinder" section.

TABLE C (COUNTIES)

POPULATION, ITEMS 1–2
Source: U.S. Census Bureau. *Population Estimates Program.* (July 2005). <http://www.census.gov/popest/counties/asrh/CC-EST2005-alldata.html>.

The population data for 2005 are Census Bureau counts for the resident population as of July 1, 2005.

Age is defined as age at last birthday (that is, number of completed years from birth to July 1, 2005).

The Census Bureau's Population Estimates Program (PEP) produces July 1 estimates for all years after the last published decennial census (2000), as well as for past decades. Existing data series, such as births, deaths, federal tax returns, Medicare enrollment, and immigration, are used to update the decennial census base counts.

SCHOOL DISTRICTS, ITEM 3:
Source: U.S. Department of Education. National Center for Education Statistics. *Common Core of Data, 2004–2005.* <http://nces.ed.gov/ccd//>.

A school district or Local Education Agency (LEA) is a local-level education agency that exists primarily to operate public schools or to contract for public school services. A public school is controlled and operated by publicly elected or appointed officials. It derives its primary support from public funds.

The county totals in this volume include 18,041 regular and special school districts. Special districts typically offer research, administrative, or other support services to client agencies. Charter schools are often included as one agency for each school.

NUMBER OF SCHOOLS AND STUDENTS, ITEMS 4–5
Source: U.S. Department of Education. National Center for Education Statistics. *Common Core of Data, 2004–2005.* <http://nces.ed.gov/ccd//>.

The county table shows the number of schools and students as reported by the LEAs in the school district file.

RESIDENT ENROLLMENT AND TYPE OF SCHOOL, ITEMS 6–9 AND 33–34
Source: U.S. Census Bureau. Summary file 3. *2000 Census of Population and Housing.* <http://factfinder.census.gov>.

Data on school enrollment are from the 2000 census. They were derived from answers given by a sample of the population to long-form question-

naire Items 8a and 8b. People were classified as enrolled in school if they reported attending a "regular" public or private school or college at any time between February 1, 2000, and the time of enumeration. The question included instructions to "include only nursery school or preschool, kindergarten, elementary school, and schooling which leads to a high school diploma or a college degree" as regular school or college. Respondents who did not answer the enrollment question were assigned the enrollment status and type of school of a person with the same age, sex, race and Hispanic origin whose residence was in the same or a nearby area. All persons 3 years old and over are included in the data.

Public and private schools. Public and private schools include people who both attended school during the reference period and indicated that they were enrolled by marking one of the questionnaire categories for either "public school, public college" or "private school, private college." Schools primarily supported and controlled by a federal, state, or local government are defined as public schools (including tribal schools). Those primarily supported and controlled by religious organizations or other private groups are considered private schools.

STUDENTS WITH INDIVIDUAL EDUCATION PROGRAMS, ITEM 10
Source: U.S. Department of Education. National Center for Education Statistics. *Common Core of Data, 2004–2005.* <http://nces.ed.gov/ccd//>.

An Individualized Education Program (IEP) is a written instructional plan for students with disabilities who are designated as special education students under IDEA (Individuals with Disabilities Education Act). This includes a statement of the child's present levels of educational performance; a statement of annual goals, including short-term instructional objectives; a statement of the specific educational services to be provided and the extent to which the child will be able to participate in regular educational programs; a projected date for initiation and the anticipated duration of services; appropriate objectives, criteria, and evaluation procedures; and schedules for determining, on at least an annual basis, whether instructional objectives are being achieved.

IEP counts for the counties are from the agency universe. Some agencies did not report this information. If 20 percent or more of a county's student membership was represented by agencies with missing data, the county was considered "missing." Students with IEPs were counted as a percentage of students in agencies who reported this information, not as a percentage of all students in the county.

STUDENTS WHO ARE ELIGIBLE FOR FREE OR REDUCED-PRICE LUNCH, ITEM 11
Source: U.S. Department of Education. National Center for Education Statistics. *Common Core of Data, 2004–2005.* <http://nces.ed.gov/ccd//>.

The Free and Reduced-Price Lunch Program is a program under the National School Lunch Act that provides cash subsidies for free or reduced-price meals to students based on family size and income criteria. Participation in the Free and Reduced-Price Lunch Program depends on income, and eligibility is often used to estimate student needs.

The number of students eligible for free or reduced-price meals was aggregated from the school universe data file for the 2004–2005 school year. If 20 percent or more of a county's student membership was in schools with missing data, the county was considered "missing." Eligible students were counted as a percentage of students in schools reporting this information, not as a percentage of all students in the county.

MINORITY STUDENTS, ITEM 12
Source: U.S. Department of Education. National Center for Education Statistics. *Common Core of Data, 2004–2005.* <http://nces.ed.gov/ccd//>.

The percentage of a county's students belonging to a minority group was tallied from the CCD school universe. Individual schools reported the number of students who were American Indian and Alaskan Native, Asian or Pacific Islander, Hispanic, non-Hispanic Black, and non-Hispanic White. "Minority" includes all categories except non-Hispanic White.

ENGLISH-LANGUAGE LEARNERS, ITEM 13
Source: U.S. Department of Education. National Center for Education Statistics. *Common Core of Data, 2004–2005.* <http://nces.ed.gov/ccd//>.

This category shows the number of students who were in appropriate programs of language assistance (e.g., English as a Second Language, High Intensity Language Training, or bilingual education). The name of this field changed from Limited-English Proficient (LEP) to English-Language Learners (ELL) in the 2001–2002 school year.

ELL counts for counties are from the agency universe. Some agencies did not report this information. If 20 percent or more of a county's student membership was represented by agencies with missing data, the county was considered "missing." ELL students were counted as a percentage of students in agencies who reported this information, not as a percentage of all students in the county.

GRADUATES, ITEM 14
Source: U.S. Department of Education. National Center for Education Statistics. *Common Core of Data, 2004–2005.* <http://nces.ed.gov/ccd//>.

The county data are from the CCD agency universe. The number of graduates includes respondents who received a regular diploma, respondents who received a diploma from a program different from the regular school program, and respondents who received a certificate of attendance or other certificate of completion in lieu of a diploma during the previous school year and subsequent summer school session. Recipients of high school equivalency certificates are not included.

Graduate data are reported for the most recent year available, usually the year preceding the school year referenced for most other items. Because many counties are missing data in this category, the editors have not included state totals.

DROPOUTS, ITEM 15
Source: U.S. Department of Education. National Center for Education Statistics. *Common Core of Data, 2001–2002.* <http://nces.ed.gov/ccd//>.

The county data are from the CCD agency universe dropout file. A dropout is a student who was enrolled in school at some time during the previous school year but who was not enrolled at the beginning of the current school year, who had not graduated from high school or completed a state- or district-approved educational program, and who did not meet any of the following exclusionary conditions: transferal to another public school district, private school, or state- or district-approved educational program; temporarily absent due to suspension or school-approved illness; or death.

Dropout data are reported for the most recent year available.

TEACHERS, ITEMS 16–17
Source: U.S. Department of Education. National Center for Education Statistics. *Common Core of Data, 2004–2005.* <http://nces.ed.gov/ccd//>.

The number of teachers in each county is aggregated from the full-time-equivalent numbers in the CCD agency universe. The student-teacher ratio is calculated from this agency-based number and the total number of students reported by the school districts in the county.

CENTRAL ADMINISTRATION STAFF, ITEM 18
Source: U.S. Department of Education. National Center for Education Statistics. *Common Core of Data, 2004–2005.* <http://nces.ed.gov/ccd//>.

The county data are aggregated from the CCD agency universe. Central administration staff and support include the LEA superintendents, deputies, assistant superintendents, all persons with district-wide responsibilities, and their support staffs, as well as all other staff, such as curriculum coordinators who supervised instructional programs at the district or sub-district level. Because many counties are missing data in this category, the editors have not included state totals.

REVENUES, ITEMS 19–22
Source: U.S. Department of Education. National Center for Education Statistics. *Common Core of Data, Fiscal Year 2004.* <http://nces.ed.gov/ccd//>.

The county data are aggregated from the 16,498 agencies in the Public School District Financial Survey data file for fiscal year 2004 (school year 2003–2004). Some of these school districts have no students in membership. However, these districts have revenues and expenditures, usually because of financial arrangements with neighboring counties or regional agencies. These revenue and expenditure data are obtained by the Census Bureau through its annual surveys of government finances and are supplied to NCES by the Census

Bureau. The state totals in Table C are also aggregated from the agencies in this file and sometimes result in different numbers than shown in the state data for Table B.

Charter school systems' reporting requirements vary from state to state, and data are currently not reported uniformly to the State Education Agencies (SEAs). Note that some charter school data may be missing from this volume, since some charter schools are not required to submit finance data to the SEA. Only those charter schools that submit data to the SEA and whose data are maintained by the SEA are included in the CCD fiscal files.

Revenues from federal sources include direct grants-in-aid from the federal government, federal grants-in-aid through the state or an intermediate agency, and other revenue in lieu of taxes to compensate a school district for nontaxable federal institutions within its boundaries.

State revenues include those that can be used without restriction, those for categorical purposes, and revenues in lieu of taxation. Included are revenues from payments made by a state for the benefit of the LEA or contributions of equipment or supplies. These revenues also include the payments of pension funds by the state on behalf of LEA employees for services rendered as well as contributions of fixed assets (property, plant, and equipment), such as school buses and textbooks.

Revenues from local sources include local property and non-property tax revenues, taxes levied or assessed by an LEA, revenues from a local government to the LEA, tuition received, transportation fees, earnings on investments from LEA holdings, net revenues from food services (gross receipts less gross expenditures), net revenues from student activities (gross receipts less gross expenditures), and other revenues (such as textbook sales, donations, and property rentals). Intermediate revenues are included in local revenue totals; they come from sources that are not local or state education agencies, but operate at an intermediate level between local and state education agencies and possess independent fundraising capability (such as county or municipal agencies).

EXPENDITURES, ITEMS 23–25
Source: U.S. Department of Education. National Center for Education Statistics. *Common Core of Data, Fiscal Year 2004.* <http://nces.ed.gov/ccd//>.

The county data are aggregated from the 16,498 agencies in the Public School District Financial Survey data file for fiscal year 2004 (school year 2003–2004). Some of these school districts have no students in membership but have revenues and expenditures, usually because of financial arrangements with neighboring counties or regional agencies. These revenue and expenditure data are obtained by the Census Bureau through its annual surveys of government finances and are supplied to NCES by the Census Bureau. The state totals in Table C are also aggregated from the agencies in this file and sometimes result in different numbers than shown in state data in Table B.

Current expenditures are defined as expenditures for the categories of instruction, support services, and non-instructional services for salaries, employee benefits, purchased services and supplies, and state-level payments made for or on behalf of school systems. This does not include expenditures for debt service, capital outlay, and property (e.g., equipment), direct costs (e.g., Head Start, adult education, community colleges, and the like), or community services expenditures.

Current expenditures per student for counties are calculated by dividing current expenditures by the number of students in fall membership. Student membership is the count of students enrolled on or about October 1 and is comparable across all counties. However, comparisons should be made with caution because counties vary greatly in types of school districts as well as in contractual arrangements with regional administrative school agencies or neighboring counties. For example, a county with a small population may have a school district that operates an elementary school and pays an intergovernmental fee to a neighboring county's school district for educational services to children in middle and high school. This hypothetical county would have artificially high per student expenditures because only the elementary school children would be included in its membership count.

Current expenditures for instruction are expenditures for activities dealing directly with the inter-

action between students and teachers (salaries, including sabbatical leave; employee benefits; instructional staff support, such as librarians and instructional specialists; and purchased instructional services).

POPULATION 16 TO 19 YEARS BY SCHOOL ENROLLMENT AND EMPLOYMENT STATUS, ITEMS 26–29
Source: U.S. Census Bureau. Summary file 3. *2000 Census of Population and Housing.* <http://factfinder.census.gov>.

2000 census data on school enrollment, educational attainment, and employment status for the population age 16 to 19 years allows for the calculation the proportion of people age 16 to 19 years who are not enrolled in school and not high school graduates ("dropouts"), as well as an unemployment rate for the "dropout" population.

EDUCATIONAL ATTAINMENT, ITEMS 30–32 AND 35–41
Source: U.S. Census Bureau. Summary file 3. *2000 Census of Population and Housing.* <http://factfinder.census.gov>.

Data on educational attainment were derived from answers given by a sample of the population to the long-form questionnaire Item 9 on the 2000 Census. Data on attainment have been tabulated for the population age 25 years and over. People have been classified according to the highest degree or level of school completed. The order in which degrees were listed on the questionnaire suggested that doctorate degrees were "higher" than professional school degrees, which were "higher" than master's degrees. The question included instructions for people currently enrolled in school to report the level of the previous grade attended or the highest degree received. Respondents who did not report educational attainment or enrollment level were assigned (when possible) the attainment of a person of the same age, race, Hispanic origin, occupation, and sex, who resided in the same area or nearby. Respondents who filled in more than one box were edited to the highest level or degree reported. The question included a response category that allowed respondents to report completing the 12th grade without receiving a high school diploma. It allowed people who received either a high school diploma or the equivalent, such as those who passed the Test of General Educational Development (G.E.D.) but did not attend college, to be reported as "high school graduate(s)."

High school diploma or less. This category includes all people who have not received a high school diploma, as well as all high school graduates who never attended college.

High school graduate or more. This category includes people whose highest degree was a high school diploma or its equivalent, people who attended college but did not receive a degree, and people who received a college, university, or professional degree. People who reported completing the 12th grade but not receiving a diploma are not high school graduates.

Bachelor's degree or more. This category includes people whose highest degree was a bachelor's, master's, professional, or doctorate degree. Master's degrees include the traditional M.A. and M.S. degrees and field-specific degrees. Some examples of professional degrees include degrees in medicine, dentistry, chiropractic, optometry, osteopathic medicine, pharmacy, podiatry, veterinary medicine, law, and theology. Vocational and technical training, such as barber school training; degrees from business, trade, technical, and vocational schools; and all other training for a specific trade are specifically excluded.

The Department of Education is the leader in publishing federal government education information on the Internet. This guide includes many of the online resources made available by the Department of Education, but it also includes information on military education activities, federally sponsored scholarships, and some education-related social services programs. Subsections of this chapter are Adult Education, Curriculum, Early Childhood Education, Education Funding, Education Policy, Education Research and Statistics, Educational Technology, Elementary and Secondary Education, Higher Education, International Education, Kids' Pages, and Teaching. Each entry in this guide are organized as follows:

Site Name: Determining the site name of an Internet source is not as easy as finding the title of a book. For the purposes of this work, several sources may have been to identify the site name, including agency press releases referring to the site, the name given to the site in the HTML <title> tag, or the initial heading or graphic.

URL: The Web address or URL indicates the location that should be entered into your Web browser to retrieve the Web site.

Sponsors: This section identifies the lead organizations that produce the site. Sponsors are most often federal government agencies, but commercial, educational, and nonprofit organizations will be listed here as well when they host or sponsor a specific resource.

Description: The resource description explains a site's organization, principal features, menu items, and significant links. For many agencies, a brief description of the agency's mission is included to help explain the site's subject coverage. The description may mention significant publications available on the site or which sections of the site include online documents. If the site content is available in languages other than English, this is noted. The utility of the site, its ease of use, and the potential audience may be evaluated as well, usually in the last paragraph of the description.

ADULT EDUCATION

DANTES—Defense Activity for Non-Traditional Education Support
http://www.dantes.doded.mil/
Sponsor(s): Defense Department
Description: DANTES provides support for the off-duty, voluntary education programs of the Department of Defense. Its Web site has information about certification programs, counselor support, distance learning, and tuition assistance. It also has a section about the Troops-to-Teachers program, which assists military personnel interested in beginning a second career as public school teacher.

Interagency Coordinating Group for Adult Literacy
http://www.ed.gov/about/bdscomm/list/icgae/edlite-index.html
Sponsor(s): Education Department
Description: This interagency group was established in 2006 to improve the investment in and outcomes of adult education. Its Web site includes a database of federal funding sources for adult literacy education and a directory of foundations likely to fund adult literacy projects.

Literacy Information and Communication System (LINCS)
http://www.nifl.gov/lincs/
Sponsor(s): National Institute for Literacy (NIFL)
Description: NIFL and its partners sponsor this Web site, which serves a gateway to adult education and literacy resources on the Internet. The site has information about grants and funding, literacy job openings, events, discussion lists, Web sites, statistics, and resources for teachers and students. The site also features America's Literacy Directory, a database of local adult education programs that can be searched by town or ZIP code.

National Audiovisual Center (NAC)
http://www.ntis.gov/products/nac/
Sponsor(s): Commerce Department — Technology Administration (TA) — National Technical Information Service (NTIS)
Description: NAC manages a catalog of over 9,000 training and education materials on video, audio-

cassette, CD-ROM, and other types of media. These products are available for sale. The Web site features an online "screening room," with clips from the most popular videos available for purchase. Major topics covered by the collection include language training, law enforcement, health, and safety.

National Institute for Literacy (NIFL)
http://www.nifl.gov/
Sponsor(s): National Institute for Literacy (NIFL)
Description: NIFL promotes literacy efforts, coordinates literacy services and policy, and serves as a resource for adult education and literacy programs. The NIFL Web site provides a section on grants and contracts, information on programs and services, and publications about teaching reading. The Facts and Statistics section compiles literacy data from numerous studies.

Office of Vocational and Adult Education, Department of Education
http://www.ed.gov/about/offices/list/ovae/index.html
Sponsor(s): Education Department — Vocational and Adult Education Office
Description: This site provides information about the Office of Vocational and Adult Education programs, grants, events, legislation, and resources in the fields of adult education and vocational education. Key sections are High Schools, Career and Technical Education, Community Colleges, and Adult Literacy and Education.

USDA Graduate School
http://grad.usda.gov/
Sponsor(s): Agriculture Department (USDA) — Graduate School, USDA
Description: The Graduate School, USDA, is a continuing education institution offering career-related courses to federal workers and the public. The Web site has the current course catalog and information on faculty and certification programs.

CURRICULUM

Agriculture in the Classroom
http://www.agclassroom.org/
Sponsor(s): Agriculture Department (USDA) — Cooperative State Research, Education, and Extension Service (CSREES)
Description: The USDA's Agriculture in the Classroom program coordinates state education programs designed to teach children about the role of agriculture in the economy and in society. The site includes a directory of state programs, information from regional consortiums, and teacher resources. It also has Kid's Zone and Teen Scene sections.

ArtsEdge: The National Arts and Education Information Network
http://artsedge.kennedy-center.org/
Sponsor(s): Kennedy Center for the Performing Arts; National Endowment for the Arts (NEA)
Description: ArtsEdge, from the Kennedy Center, is a major arts resource for educators and students. The site includes lesson plans and content standards for grades K–12. ArtsEdge highlights articles, reports, and organizations related to arts education. The site also features an arts education advocacy section.

This well-designed site should be a primary stopping point for people involved in arts education.

BLM Learning Landscapes
http://www.blm.gov/education/
Sponsor(s): Interior Department — Bureau of Land Management (BLM)
Description: This BLM Web site has information and activities for students and teachers. The Teachers' section has information about field programs (mostly in western states), Web sites, resources, and classroom activities. The site's Curriculum Connections correlates BLM classroom activities to National Science Education Standards and National Geography Standards. Online resources for teachers and learners cover such topics as archeology, geology, paleontology, American history, wildlife, and energy.

Census in Schools
http://www.census.gov/dmd/www/teachers.html
Sponsor(s): Commerce Department — Economics and Statistics Administration (ESA) — Census Bureau
Description: The Census in Schools program provides K–12 teaching materials, workshops for educators, and other outreach activities. Its Web site includes teaching kits and reference materials, primarily about the decennial census.

Directorate for Education and Human Resources—NSF
http://www.nsf.gov/dir/index.jsp?org=ehr
Sponsor(s): National Science Foundation (NSF)
Description: The Directorate for Education and Human Resources (EHR) provides leadership in

the effort to improve science, mathematics, engineering, and technology education in the United States. Its Web site includes links to descriptions of the EHR divisions and the types of projects they sponsor: the Division of Graduate Education (DGE); the Division of Undergraduate Education (DUE); the Experimental Program to Stimulate Competitive Research (EPSCoR); and the Division of Elementary, Secondary and Informal Education (ESIE). The Publications category includes selected full-text documents. The Funding Opportunities section has announcements for opportunities sponsored by directorate and interagency groups.

This site will be of assistance to science and engineering students and educators at all levels who are interested in pursuing grants or scholarships.

EDSITEment

http://edsitement.neh.gov/

Sponsor(s): National Endowment for the Humanities (NEH)

Description: The EDSITEment Web site's tag line is "the best of the humanities on the Web." It provides a cataloged selection of lesson plans built around high-quality, freely accessible material available on the Internet. The lesson plans are organized into sections for Art and Culture, Literature and Language Arts, Foreign Language, and History and Social Studies. Each detailed lesson plan is labeled with the appropriate grade level, subject area, time required, and skills taught. The site is sponsored by a partnership between the National Endowment for the Humanities, the MarcoPolo Foundation, and Verizon.

DSITEment provides quality resources on a well-designed and attractive Web site.

GLOBE Program

http://www.globe.gov/

Sponsor(s): National Aeronautics and Space Administration (NASA)

Description: The Global Learning and Observations to Benefit the Environment (GLOBE) program is designed to promote science education at the elementary and secondary school levels. GLOBE is funded by NASA and the National Science Foundation, supported by the Department of State and implemented through a cooperative agreement between NASA; the University Corporation for Atmospheric Research

in Boulder, CO; and Colorado State University in Fort Collins, CO. The GLOBE program's primary objective is to involve students in taking environmental measurements. Schools in more than 95 countries have submitted thousands of data reports based on observations by GLOBE student scientists. The data is accessible to anyone, and there is information on how new schools can register to be included in the program. The site also has a teacher's guide and schedule of teacher workshops. Much of the content is available in Spanish and other non-English languages.

With participating schools from all over the world, this kind of collaborative project demonstrates how the Internet can be used in a K–12 environment. In addition, this Web site is well designed and makes navigation easy even for those not familiar with the program.

Learning Page of the Library of Congress

http://lcweb2.loc.gov/ammem/ndlpedu/

Sponsor(s): Library of Congress

Description: Designed for the educational community, this Web site helps students and teachers find relevant materials within the National Digital Library collection on the Library of Congress Web pages, with particular emphasis on the American Memory project. The site features sections such as Lesson Plans, Features and Activities, and Professional Development.

NASA Education

http://education.nasa.gov/home/

Sponsor(s): National Aeronautics and Space Administration (NASA) — Education Office

Description: The NASA Education Web site provides information about the education programs that NASA offers to K–12 educators and students, as well as to undergraduate and graduate students and faculty at universities. News and resources are divided into sections, including Elementary and Secondary Education, Higher Education, and Informal Education. The section on Elementary and Secondary School programs has information on Educator Astronauts and the NASA Explorer Schools program. Under the NASA Education Offices heading, the site links to the individual Web sites of NASA education programs, NASA Flight and Research Centers, and each of NASA's directorates.

NOAA Education Resources

http://www.education.noaa.gov/

Sponsor(s): Commerce Department — National Oceanic and Atmospheric Administration (NOAA)

Description: The NOAA Education site has materials for teachers covering weather, climate change, oceans and coasts, weather satellites, and space environments. The Primarily for Students section has educational resources and other information color-coded for K–5 grades, 6–12 grades, and higher education students. The Cool Sites for Everyone section highlights NOAA Web sites covering a variety of topics.

NSF Classroom Resources

http://www.nsf.gov/news/classroom/

Sponsor(s): National Science Foundation (NSF)

Description: NSF Classroom Resources provides organized links to classroom resources on the Internet. The Web site describes its intended audience as "classroom teachers, their students, and students' families." Links are organized into science topics, such as biology, computing, environment, mathematics, and physics. The linked sites are from a variety of educational organizations and institutions.

Office of English Language Acquisition

http://www.ed.gov/about/offices/list/oela/

Sponsor(s): Education Department — English Language Acquisition Office

Description: The full title of this office is the Office of English Language Acquisition, Language Enhancement, and Academic Achievement for Limited English Proficient Students (OELA). OELA administers Title III of the No Child Left Behind Act (Public Law 107-110) on Language Instruction for Limited English Proficient and Immigrant Students. It also administers a state formula grant program. The site has program information and technical assistance for those applying for Title III grants. It also links to the National Clearinghouse for English Language Acquisition and Language Instruction Educational Programs (NCELA), which is funded by the Department of Education.

USGS and Science Education

http://www.usgs.gov/education/

Sponsor(s): Interior Department — U.S. Geological Survey (USGS)

Description: The USGS and Science Education Web site covers topics of concern to USGS scientists, including geography, geology, biology, and water resources. Educational resources are organized for grades K–6, grades 7–12, and undergraduate education. One section aligns USGS and other Web resources with an established list of science and social science curriculum standards for California. The site also covers USGS careers, internships, and postdoctoral fellowships.

The USGS site content spans a number of categories, including general information about science education, links to science education Web sites, specific resources developed at USGS, and information on USGS involvement with the promotion of science education.

EARLY CHILDHOOD EDUCATION

Head Start Bureau

http://www.acf.hhs.gov/programs/hsb/

Sponsor(s): Health and Human Services Department — Administration for Children and Families (ACF) — Head Start Bureau

Description: Head Start is a child development program that serves low-income children and their families. The Programs/Services section describes specific programs such as Early Head Start and the American Indian-Alaska Native Program Branch. The site has sections for grant information and a link to the Head Start Information and Publication Center online. A Research/Statistics section has further links to publications and data on the program. The Budget/Policy section covers program reauthorization, administration policy initiatives, and statistical fact sheets.

The site provides quick access to a breadth of information about the program for its clients and partners, as well as convenient links for policy researchers. There is no search engine at the site; those looking for very specific Head Start resources or programs may wish to use the site map.

National Child Care Information Center (NCCIC)

http://nccic.org/

Sponsor(s): Health and Human Services Department — Administration for Children and Families (ACF) — Child Care Bureau

Description: NCCIC is a national clearinghouse and technical assistance center for parents, early education professionals, governments, researchers, and the general public. The site has background information and an extensive section of links on topics such as licensing regulations, childcare as a business, federal policy, child development, literacy, and school readiness. The State Information section has profiles of childcare in each individual state. Some information is also available in Spanish.

EDUCATION FUNDING

Federal Cyber Service: Scholarship for Service

http://www.sfs.opm.gov/

Sponsor(s): Office of Personnel Management (OPM)

Description: OPM's Scholarship for Service program funds the education expenses of graduate and undergraduate students in information assurance fields in exchange for an obligation to work for the federal government for an agreed-upon term. The program is designed to strengthen the federal government's expertise in information assurance (the security of computer and communication networks and the information they carry). This Web site has further details on the program and a list of participating higher education institutions.

Federal School Code Search Page

http://www.fafsa.ed.gov/fotw0607/fslookup.htm

Sponsor(s): Education Department — Postsecondary Education Office

Description: This site provides searchable access to the federal Title IV School Codes required on many financial aid forms.

Free Application for Federal Student Aid (FAFSA)

http://www.fafsa.ed.gov/

Sponsor(s): Education Department — Federal Student Aid Office

Description: FAFSA on the Web makes it possible to apply online for federal financial aid for college.

The FAFSA renewal application may also be completed online. The site provides guidance on applying for aid, the application process, and deadlines. Some instructions are also available in Spanish.

GI Bill Website

http://www.gibill.va.gov/

Sponsor(s): Veterans Affairs Department

Description: The GI Bill site provides information on the range of education benefits for active duty and reserve servicemembers, veterans, survivors, and dependents. Information on the programs is available in the Education Benefits, Information for Benefit Recipients, and Questions and Answers sections. The site also has a section for school officials working with beneficiaries.

The site has a history of the original GI Bill, the Servicemembers' Readjustment Act of 1944, which preceded the current program.

Information for Financial Aid Professionals (IFAP)

http://ifap.ed.gov/

Sponsor(s): Education Department — Federal Student Aid Office

Description: IFAP is an electronic library for financial aid professionals. It contains publications, regulations, and guidance regarding the administration of the Title IV Federal Student Aid (FSA) Programs. This site features technical documentation, online tools, worksheets, and schedules related to the programs.

Student Aid on the Web

http://studentaid.ed.gov/

Sponsor(s): Education Department — Federal Student Aid Office

Description: This site is a portal and service center for federal student aid information and programs. It begins with information about preparing for, choosing, applying to, and attending a college. Other sections contain facts about funding a college education and repaying student loans. The site links to the Free Application for Federal Student Aid (FAFSA) Web site.

Tax Benefits for Education

http://www.irs.gov/publications/p970/

Sponsor(s): Treasury Department — Internal Revenue Service (IRS)

Description: This Web page has the full text of Publication 970, *Tax Benefits for Education*. The publication outlines the tax deductions and benefits available to those saving for or paying education costs. Most benefits concern higher education.

EDUCATION POLICY

ED.gov — U.S. Department of Education

http://www.ed.gov/

Sponsor(s): Education Department

Description: The Department of Education Web site features current news and links to information on the No Child Left Behind program, pandemic flu preparedness, and other high-profile initiatives. The top menu of the site's home page directs users to information by audience, organized into the following sections: Students (financial aid and homework help), Parents (encouraging reading and college planning), Teachers (how to become a teacher and finding teaching jobs), and Administrators (guidance on the No Child Left Behind Act and policy information). The site also organizes its content into several information centers: Grants and Contracts, Financial Aid, Research and Statistics, Policy, and Programs. In addition, it has an A-Z index and a site map.

The About ED section has a directory of offices, budget and appropriations information, and press releases. Publications are available through the linked ED Pubs Web site and the ERIC (Education Resources Information Center) database. Some information is available in Spanish.

No Child Left Behind

http://www.nclb.gov/

Alternate URL(s): http://www.nochildleftbehind.gov/

Sponsor(s): Education Department

Description: This Department of Education Web site is dedicated to information about Public Law 107-110, better known as the No Child Left Behind Act of 2001. The law concerns educational standards and testing, teacher training and recruitment, English language instruction, school safety, and other matters. The site has an A-Z index and includes information aimed at parents and teachers. It also has policy updates and an e-mail newsletter, *Extra Credit*.

Office of Innovation and Improvement (OII)

http://www.ed.gov/about/offices/list/oii/

Sponsor(s): Education Department — Innovation and Improvement Office

Description: OII administers discretionary grant programs, coordinates public school choice and supplemental educational efforts, works with the non-public education community, and develops guidance for the No Child Left Behind initiative. The Web site's Non-Public Education section includes a private school locator and statistics on private education in the United States.

White House Initiative on Educational Excellence for Hispanic Americans

http://www.yic.gov/

Alternate URL(s): http://www.yosipuedo.gov/

Sponsor(s): President's Advisory Commission on Educational Excellence for Hispanic Americans

Description: The White House Initiative on Educational Excellence for Hispanic Americans and the President's Advisory Commission on Educational Excellence for Hispanic Americans were established by executive order in 2001. The Department of Education provides the primary support for the initiative. The Web site has information on the commission and also features a series of toolkits, or online guides, with educational tips relevant to early childhood, elementary and secondary schooling, and postsecondary education. The alternate URL listed above links to a Spanish-language version of the site.

EDUCATION RESEARCH AND STATISTICS

ERIC — Educational Resources Information Center

http://www.eric.ed.gov/

Sponsor(s): Education Department — Institute of Education Sciences

Description: ERIC is a database and information system funded by the Department of Education to provide organized access to a wide array of published and unpublished material about education. It references education literature from 1966 to the present. The Web site describes ERIC as "the world's largest digital library of education literature."

The ERIC search interface has basic and advanced versions. Searchable fields include title, author, ERIC number, identifier, ISBN, ISSN, journal name, source institution, sponsoring agency, thesaurus descriptor, and date range. Searches can be limited by type of material cited (e.g., journal article, non-print media, or dissertation). The ERIC Thesaurus is linked to the search interface;

users can also browse and search the thesaurus separately. An interface called My ERIC allows for some customization once users register for a My ERIC account.

ERIC is a key resource for research in education and related fields. Although the database was previously handled by a network of academic and nonprofit clearinghouses, the Department of Education established centralized control in late 2004. Since then, new features and content have been phased in. ERIC users should check the ERIC online news for regular updates; however, there is no e-mail or RSS feed subscription available.

Institute of Education Sciences (IES)
http://www.ed.gov/about/offices/list/ies/
Sponsor(s): Education Department — Institute of Education Sciences
Description: IES was set up in 2002 to focus on education research. It includes the National Center for Education Research (NCER), the National Center for Education Statistics (NCES), the National Center for Education Evaluation and Regional Assistance (NCEE), and the National Center for Special Education Research (NCSER). The Web site has information on IES and its grants and component programs.

International Comparisons in Education
http://nces.ed.gov/surveys/international/
Sponsor(s): Education Department — Institute of Education Sciences — National Center for Education Statistics (NCES)
Description: NCES provides a central page for linking to the international education statistics collected by the agency. The site links to information on the Trends in International Mathematics and Science Study (TIMSS) and Program for International Student Assessment (PISA) assessments, as well as the Progress in International Reading Literacy Study (PIRLS) and Adult Literacy and Lifeskills (ALL) international comparative studies.

National Center for Education Statistics
http://nces.ed.gov/
Sponsor(s): Education Department — Institute of Education Sciences — National Center for Education Statistics (NCES)
Description: NCES collects and analyzes data concerning education in the United States and other nations. Its Web site is a primary source for educa-

tion statistics for all educational levels and for data on educational assessment, libraries, and international educational outcomes. Most data on the site are drawn from major NCES statistical publications, such as *Education Statistics Quarterly*, *The Condition of Education*, and the *Digest of Education Statistics*. The NCES Fast Facts section highlights frequently requested information, such as data on the effects of reading to children and data on average tuition costs at colleges and universities. The site also includes a searchable directory of private and public schools, colleges, and public libraries.

For users searching for statistics related to any form of education, this site should be the first place to visit.

EDUCATIONAL TECHNOLOGY

Computers for Learning
http://www.computers.fed.gov/School/user.asp
Sponsor(s): General Services Administration (GSA)
Description: The Computers for Learning Web site is designed for public, private, parochial, and home schools serving the K–12 student population, as well as other nonprofit educational organizations. The service allows these groups of students and nonprofit organizations to request donations of surplus federal computer equipment. The site includes program and eligibility information and sections on how to give and receive computers.

Minority University Space Interdisciplinary Network (MU-SPIN)
http://muspin.gsfc.nasa.gov/
Sponsor(s): National Aeronautics and Space Administration (NASA) — Goddard Space Flight Center (GSFC)
Description: MU-SPIN is designed for Historically Black Colleges and Universities (HBCUs), and Other Minority Universities (OMUs). The program focuses on transferring advanced computer networking technologies to HBCUs and OMUs to help support their multidisciplinary research. The Web site has information about the program and its associated events, conferences, and resources.

For minority colleges and universities, this is an important resource for high technology and computer networking information and training.

Office of Educational Technology (OET), Department of Education
http://www.ed.gov/about/offices/list/os/technology/
Sponsor(s): Education Department — Educational Technology Office
Description: OET develops national educational technology policy and works with the educational community and the Department of Education to promote national goals for educational technology. Major sections of the site are Grants Programs, Reports and Research, and Internet Safety. The site also has a directory of state government contacts for educational technology and the online publication *Teacher's Guide to International Collaboration on the Internet*.

ELEMENTARY AND SECONDARY EDUCATION

Education Resource Organizations Directory (EROD)
http://wdcrobcolp01.ed.gov/Programs/EROD/
Sponsor(s): Education Department — Elementary and Secondary Education Office
Description: EROD is a database of state and regional organizations that provide education-related information. It includes organizations such as state literary resource centers and regional education laboratories. Each organization's entry has complete contact information and a description of its services. The database has simple and advanced search forms.

Emergency Planning
http://www.ed.gov/emergencyplan/
Sponsor(s): Education Department — Office of Safe and Drug-Free Schools
Description: The Emergency Planning Web site, launched in March 2003, describes itself as a "one-stop shop that provides school leaders with information they need to plan for any emergency, including natural disasters, violent incidents and terrorist acts" (from the Web site). The site includes crisis planning resources and model emergency response plans. It also links to information on pandemic flu preparedness for schools.

NSF Division of Elementary, Secondary, and Informal Education (ESIE)
http://www.nsf.gov/div/index.jsp?div=ESIE
Sponsor(s): National Science Foundation (NSF)
Description: As part of the National Science Foundation, ESIE focuses on improving pre-K–12 science, technology, engineering, and mathematics (STEM) education in the United States. Its Web site includes descriptions of the programs and funding opportunities offered by this agency. Program area sections include Advanced Technological Education, Informal Science Education, International Polar Year (2007–2008), and Presidential Awards for Excellence in Mathematics and Science Teaching.

Office of Elementary and Secondary Education (OESE)
http://www.ed.gov/about/offices/list/oese/
Sponsor(s): Education Department — Elementary and Secondary Education Office
Description: The OESE Web site has information on its programs, office contacts, and reports. The Laws, Regulations, and Guidance section is largely concerned with the No Child Left Behind Act. Both the Standards, Assessment, and Accountability section and the Flexibility and Waivers section also cover areas of No Child Left Behind. The Consolidated State Info section has information on the No Child Left Behind Consolidated State Performance Report for states reporting accomplishments and data. The site is searchable through an alphabetical index.

The alphabetical index is useful in uncovering all of the information at this site. Much of the site is intended for elementary and secondary education professionals and officials who need to comply with the No Child Left Behind Act or who are interested in its documents.

Office of Safe and Drug-Free Schools
http://www.ed.gov/about/offices/list/osdfs/
Sponsor(s): Education Department — Office of Safe and Drug-Free Schools
Description: OSDFS's major programs come under the categories of Health, Mental Health, Environmental Health, and Physical Education; Drug-Violence Prevention; and Character and

Civic Education. Many of the programs are for the elementary and secondary level, although some programs also apply to higher education. The Web site has information on the grants that fall under these program categories and offers news, publications, and links to related resources on the Internet.

Office of Special Education Programs (OSEP)
http://www.ed.gov/about/offices/list/osers/osep/
Sponsor(s): Education Department — Special Education and Rehabilitative Services Office — Office of Special Education Programs (OSEP)
Description: OSEP has the primary responsibility of administering programs and projects related to the education of all children, youth, and adults with disabilities, from birth through age 21. Sections describe OSEP's Programs and Projects, Grants and Funding, Legislation and Policy, Publications and Products, and Research and Statistics. It includes extensive information on the Individuals with Disabilities Education Act (IDEA), which authorizes OSEP programs.

School District Demographics
http://nces.ed.gov/surveys/sdds/
Sponsor(s): Education Department — Institute of Education Sciences — National Center for Education Statistics (NCES)
Description: This site presents demographic and geographic data for school districts from the 2000 census and 1990 census. The Map Viewer application allows users to view state or individual school district maps. The School District Profiles section can be used to compare Census 2000 demographic information between any of the nation's school districts. Documentation for the data and the system can be found in the Library section.

The data from this special census tabulation can be helpful for studying school districts, as well as for examining general demographics of children and families with children.

The Nation's Report Card
http://nces.ed.gov/nationsreportcard/
Sponsor(s): Education Department — Institute of Education Sciences — National Center for Education Statistics (NCES)
Description: This is the online home of the National Assessment of Educational Progress (NAEP), an ongoing national assessment for student achievement in grades 4, 8, and 12. It provides background information on the history and current operations of the NAEP. Current results are available in the form of state profiles. Users can also construct custom data tables and get reports at the national level or by state, region, or major urban district. The Subject Areas section provides background and reports on assessments in mathematics, reading, science, civics, and other specific subjects.

U.S. Presidential Scholars Program
http://www.ed.gov/programs/psp/
Sponsor(s): Education Department
Description: The U.S. Presidential Scholars Program recognizes up to 141 outstanding high school graduates each year. The Web site has information on eligibility, the application process, and the current year's Presidential Scholars.

HIGHER EDUCATION

Air Force Institute of Technology
http://www.afit.edu/
Sponsor(s): Air Force — Air Force Institute of Technology (AFIT)
Description: A component of Air University, AFIT is the Air Force's graduate school of engineering and management and its institution for technical professional continuing education. The Web site provides information on each of AFIT's schools and centers.

Air University
http://www.au.af.mil/au/
Sponsor(s): Air Force — Air University
Description: Air University (AU), located at Maxwell Air Force Base in Alabama, conducts professional military education, graduate education, and professional continuing education for officers, enlisted personnel, and civilians. This site links to each of the component schools that make up AU. It also provides information on the university's history and mission. The Other AU Links section links to the university's course catalogs and publications, the Air University Press, and the Air University Library.

Army Logistics Management College
http://www.almc.army.mil/
Sponsor(s): Army — Army Logistics Management College (ALMC)
Description: The Army Logistics Management College site features a course catalog, course schedule, and an online version of *Army Logistician*.

Barry M. Goldwater Scholarships

http://www.act.org/goldwater/

Sponsor(s): Goldwater Scholarship and Excellence in Education Foundation

Description: Goldwater Scholarships are awarded for undergraduate education in the fields of mathematics, science, and engineering. The Goldwater Foundation was established by Congress to encourage study in these fields. The Web site has scholarship application information and lists of past awardees.

Carlisle Barracks and the U.S. Army War College

http://carlisle-www.army.mil/

Sponsor(s): Army — Carlisle Barracks

Description: Carlisle Barracks is the home of the U.S. Army War College, the Center for Strategic Leadership, the Strategic Studies Institute, the Peacekeeping and Stability Operations Institute, the Army Physical Fitness Research Institute, the Army Heritage and Education Center, and the Military History Institute. This site features information on the Barracks and the resident institutions. The Web site's home page features summaries of timely studies in national defense. It also carries the quarterly *Parameters*, the Army's senior professional journal; issues are archived online from 1996 onward.

College Opportunities On-Line

http://www.nces.ed.gov/ipeds/cool/

Sponsor(s): Education Department — Institute of Education Sciences — National Center for Education Statistics (NCES)

Description: This database, also known as COOL, has information about roughly 7,000 colleges, universities, community colleges, technical colleges, and similar institutions. The database can be searched by institution name or by location, type of school, programs offered, or other criteria. For each institution, the database typically supplies phone numbers, a URL, average costs, and basic background information. Up to four colleges can also be compared side-by-side for such factors as estimated student expenses and graduation rates.

The COOL database is a useful reference for college-bound students as well as for those simply looking for a college's phone number or URL.

Note that the site states that an institution's inclusion in the database does not constitute a recommendation by the Department of Education.

Command and General Staff College

http://www-cgsc.army.mil/

Sponsor(s): Army — Army Command and General Staff College

Description: The U.S. Army Command and General Staff College is focused on leadership development within the Army. This site offers information on the college, its training programs, and its organizations.

Defense Language Institute Foreign Language Center (DLIFLC)

http://www.dliflc.edu/

Sponsor(s): Defense Department — Defense Language Institute (DLI)

Description: DLIFLIC is the primary foreign language training institution within the Department of Defense. Programs are for U.S. military personnel and select agency staff. The Web site has information on the history of the center and its current language programs. The center's journal, *Applied Language Learning*, is online dating back to 1996.

The site is primarily of interest to those eligible for and interested in DLI language training.

Harry S. Truman Scholarship Foundation

http://www.truman.gov/

Sponsor(s): Truman Scholarship Foundation

Description: Truman Scholarships are awarded to outstanding undergraduate students who wish to pursue graduate study and careers in government or public service. This Web site has information about the Truman Foundation and its scholarship program, with sections for candidates, faculty, and current Truman Scholars.

Marine Corps University

http://www.mcu.usmc.mil/

Sponsor(s): Marine Corps — Training and Education Command

Description: The Marine Corps University's Web site provides information about its schools, including the Expeditionary Warfare School, the Command and Staff College, the School of Advanced Warfighting, and the Marine Corps War College.

NASA Academy

http://academy.nasa.gov/

Sponsor(s): National Aeronautics and Space Administration (NASA) — Goddard Space Flight Center (GSFC)

Description: This is the central page for NASA Academy summer programs for college students in science, math, engineering, or computer science. The site has application forms and detailed program information.

The information on these pages will be of interest to college students interested in careers or further study with NASA and to the advisers of students with pertinent majors.

NASA Office of Higher Education at Goddard Space Flight Center

http://university.gsfc.nasa.gov/

Sponsor(s): National Aeronautics and Space Administration (NASA) — Goddard Space Flight Center (GSFC)

Description: This office manages fellowships, grants, and other higher education programs at NASA's Goddard Space Flight Center in Maryland. The programs target colleges and universities along the eastern seaboard and aerospace-oriented institutions nationwide with programs of mutual interest to Goddard. The site has information about these and other NASA-wide higher education programs.

National Defense University (NDU)

http://www.ndu.edu/

Sponsor(s): Defense Department — National Defense University (NDU)

Description: The NDU Web site provides an online course catalog and links to the University's component colleges and schools: the Joint Forces Staff College, the National War College, the Industrial College of the Armed Forces, the Information Resources Management College, and the School for National Security Executive Education. NDU Research Centers online include the Institute for National Strategic Studies and the Center for the Study of Weapons of Mass Destruction. A Professional Military Reading Lists section presents bibliographies of recommended reading from the chiefs of the armed services and others.

Naval Postgraduate School

http://www.nps.edu/

Sponsor(s): Navy — Naval Postgraduate School (NPS)

Description: NPS emphasizes education and research programs relevant to the Navy, defense, and national and international security interests. The Web site links to information from each of the NPS component schools: Business and Public Policy, Engineering and Applied Sciences, Operational and Information Sciences, and International Graduate Studies. The Research section includes archives of technical reports and thesis abstracts.

Naval War College

http://www.nwc.navy.mil/

Sponsor(s): Navy — Naval War College (NWC)

Description: This site offers information about the history and academics of the NWC. At the time this book went to press, access to this site was not available to the public.

NSF Division of Graduate Education

http://www.nsf.gov/div/index.jsp?div=DGE

Sponsor(s): National Science Foundation (NSF)

Description: The programs of the NSF's Division of Graduate Education promote the early career development of scientists and engineers by offering support at critical junctures of their careers. This Web site describes the division's research and teaching fellowships for graduate students in the sciences. The Publications section includes program guidelines. There is also a page to search for awards.

NSF Division of Undergraduate Education

http://www.nsf.gov/div/index.jsp?div=DUE

Sponsor(s): National Science Foundation (NSF)

Description: The NSF's Division of Undergraduate Education (DUE) focuses on improving undergraduate education in science, technology, mathematics, and engineering. The division awards funds to scholarship programs at educational institutions; they do not award scholarships directly to students. The division also funds programs for teacher education and curriculum development. The Web site has information on the programs, deadlines, and awards.

Office of Postsecondary Education (OPE)

http://www.ed.gov/about/offices/list/ope/

Sponsor(s): Education Department — Postsecondary Education Office

Description: In the Programs/Initiatives section, this Web site provides a guide to the more than 40 postsecondary-related education programs administered by the OPE. Initiatives include programs for improving educational institutions, supporting international education, funding teacher training, and reaching out to students from disadvantaged backgrounds. The Reports and Resources section of the site has data on student aid programs such as Pell Grants, Federal Student Loans, and Federal Family Education Loans. The Accreditation section of the site explains the accreditation of educational institutions and has a directory of the numerous accrediting agencies.

This is a very useful site with a substantial body of information sources of interest to students, educators, and financial aid offices.

Smithsonian Office of Fellowships

http://www.si.edu/ofg/

Sponsor(s): Smithsonian Institution

Description: The Office of Fellowships has applications, lists of fellowship and internship opportunities, and announcements of the current recipients. The publication *Smithsonian Opportunities for Research and Study* is available online in an HTML format.

U.S. Merchant Marine Academy

http://www.usmma.edu/

Sponsor(s): Transportation Department — Maritime Administration (MARAD)

Description: The U.S. Merchant Marine Academy Web site has information about admissions, academics, and other activities. The site also links to the Global Maritime and Transportation School (GMATS) for maritime and transportation industry professionals. Both the academy and GMATS are operated by the Department of Transportation's Maritime Administration.

United States Air Force Academy

http://www.usafa.af.mil/

Sponsor(s): Air Force — Air Force Academy

Description: The United States Air Force Academy Web site provides information for cadets, staff, and faculty. It includes visitor information and sections on admissions, academics, and cadet life. The academy's libraries are listed in the USAFA Organizations section.

United States Military Academy at West Point

http://www.usma.edu/

Sponsor(s): Army — United States Military Academy (USMA)

Description: The West Point Web site has information for prospective and current students, alumni, visitors, and the West Point community. There are sections on Admissions, Cadet Life, Academic Programs, Physical Programs, and Military Programs. A brief section on USMA history, found in the About the Academy section, includes a timeline and list of notable graduates.

United States Naval Academy

http://www.usna.edu

Sponsor(s): Navy — United States Naval Academy (USNA)

Description: This site contains information on the Naval Academy, mainly for students, prospective students, and midshipmen. The About USNA section links to information about the Academy's history and notable graduates.

White House Initiative on Historically Black Colleges and Universities

http://www.ed.gov/about/inits/list/whhbcu/edlite-index.html

Sponsor(s): Education Department — White House Initiative on Historically Black Colleges and Universities

Description: The White House Initiative on Historically Black Colleges and Universities was established by executive order in 1981. This Web site has information on the initiative's work, board of advisors and staff, and budget. It also has a list of Historically Black Colleges and Universities by state and type of institution, with Web addresses provided for each institution.

White House Initiative on Tribal Colleges and Universities

http://www.ed.gov/about/inits/list/whtc/edlite-index.html

Sponsor(s): Education Department — White House Initiative on Tribal Colleges and Universities

Description: The President's Board of Advisors on Tribal Colleges and Universities and the White House Initiative on Tribal Colleges and Universities were established by executive order in 2002. In addition to information on the board, this site has a directory of tribal colleges and universities.

INTERNATIONAL EDUCATION

Bureau of Educational and Cultural Affairs
http://exchanges.state.gov/
Sponsor(s): State Department — Educational and Cultural Affairs Bureau
Description: The Bureau of Educational and Cultural Affairs Web site has information about its many international exchange and education programs. For U.S. citizens, the site has information on Fulbright Scholarships, English-language teaching abroad, study abroad, and other opportunities. For the audience abroad, the site has information about studying in the United States, the Fulbright Program, and a range of programs from the high school level up to the scholar and professional level. The site covers a range of other initiatives, such as the National Security Language Initiative, the Global Cultural Initiative, and the Edward R. Murrow Journalism Initiative.

EducationUSA
http://www.educationusa.state.gov/
Sponsor(s): State Department — Educational and Cultural Affairs Bureau
Description: EducationUSA is a global network of more than 450 advising and information centers in 170 countries supported by the Department of State's Bureau of Educational and Cultural Affairs. The Web site's About Us section provides contact information for individual centers worldwide. Other sections of the site provide information about finding a school, student visas, and living in the United States. Information is available for all levels of higher education and specialized professional study. Booklets from the department's "If You Want to Study in the United States" series are available online in Arabic, Chinese, French, Russian, Spanish, and English.

Fulbright Scholar Program
http://exchanges.state.gov/education/fulbright/
Alternate URL(s): http://www.iie.org/fulbright/
Sponsor(s): State Department — Educational and Cultural Affairs Bureau; Institute of International Education (IIE)

Description: The Fulbright Program, sponsored by the United States, is an international education program that provides grants for graduate students, scholars, professionals, teachers, and administrators from the United States and other countries. This site, geared toward U.S. and non-U.S. applicants, describes the program and links to the Fulbright Commissions around the world.

Much of the program is administered for the Department of State by the Institute of International Education (IIE), an independent nonprofit organization. The alternate URL for this entry leads to the IIE Fulbright Web site. For applicants from the United States, the relevant applications are available online.

Future State
http://www.future.state.gov/
Sponsor(s): State Department
Description: Designed as the student Web site for the Department of State, Future State is largely written for the students at the secondary school level, although it has one section for students in grades K–6. The site explains the work of the department, international education opportunities available to students, and the nature of careers within the Department of State. A section for parents and educators includes lesson plans and online resources.

Future State includes a substantial amount and variety of information relating to diplomacy, U.S. diplomatic history, country information, international exchange programs, and educational outreach activities.

International Affairs Office
http://www.ed.gov/about/inits/ed/internationaled/
Sponsor(s): Education Department
Description: The International Affairs Office coordinates the Department of Education's international programs and works with international agencies such as the United Nations Educational, Scientific, and Cultural Organization (UNESCO). The Web site provides a directory to Education Department programs that have an international aspect. It also describes the office's activities, such as International Education Week and the United States Network for Education Information (USNEI) program.

U.S. Network for Education Information (USNEI)

http://www.ed.gov/about/offices/list/ous/interna-
tional/usnei/edlite-index.html

Sponsor(s): Education Department

Description: USNEI is an interagency and public-
private partnership set up to provide official information to anyone seeking information about U.S.
education. It also provides U.S. citizens with
authoritative information about education in other
countries. The site covers all levels of education,
with topics including visas, accreditation, professional licensure, and teaching abroad (or in the
United States). The site's Foreign Country
Database links to Web sites for individual countries' official education agencies and organizations.

Worldstudy.gov

http://worldstudy.gov/

Sponsor(s): National Security Education Program
Description: Worldstudy.gov was created by the
National Security Education Program (NSEP), a
government program that works to strengthen
national security by helping educate U.S. citizens
about world cultures and languages. NSEP awards
the David L. Boren Scholarships and Fellowships
for study relating to global security at the graduate
and undergraduate levels. The site provides information on the Boren grants and features accounts
of student experiences while studying abroad.

KIDS' PAGES

America's Story from America's Library

http://www.americaslibrary.gov/

Sponsor(s): Library of Congress
Description: This Library of Congress site is
designed for children and their families. It uses dig-
itized images from the library's collection, accom-
panied by text and graphics, to create educational
pages about American history and culture.
Sections include Explore the States, Jump Back in
Time, and Meet Amazing Americans.

BAM! Body and Mind

http://www.bam.gov/

Sponsor(s): Health and Human Services
Department — Centers for Disease Control and
Prevention (CDC)

Description: BAM!, designed for children ages 9 to
13, has tips on fighting stress and adopting healthy
lifestyles. It contains information about fitness,
nutrition, safety, and handling peer pressure.

Ben's Guide to U.S. Government for Kids

http://bensguide.gpo.gov/

Sponsor(s): Government Printing Office (GPO)
— Superintendent of Documents

Description: With a cartoon version of Benjamin
Franklin as a guide, this GPO site for children covers topics such as the U.S. Constitution, how laws
are made, the branches of the federal government,
and citizenship. It features sections for specific age
groups, plus a special section for parents and educators. The major sections are About Ben, K–2,
3–5, 6–8, 9–12, and Parents and Teachers.

Ben's Guide has received numerous accolades. It
is useful as a grade school or high school student's
homework helper, but may also help older students refresh their basic knowledge of U.S. government and history.

BLM's History Mystery

http://www.blm.gov/heritage/HE_Kids/
kid_pg_rev1.htm

Sponsor(s): Interior Department — Bureau of
Land Management (BLM)

Description: BLM presents three history mysteries
to be solved by students in the upper elementary
grades or high school. The mysteries include
"Butch Cassidy and The Sundance Kid," "The
Mystery of the First Americans," and "The Ghost
Town Mysteries."

BLS Career Information

http://www.bls.gov/k12/

Sponsor(s): Labor Department — Bureau of
Labor Statistics (BLS)

Description: The BLS Career Information page
for youth uses a graphical interface to match kids'

interests with potential careers. It also has an alternative text menu. A Teachers' Guide refers teachers to additional information available from BLS.

The site is easy and fun to use. It is most appropriate for upper elementary grades and high school students.

CIA Home Page for Kids
https://www.cia.gov/cia/ciakids/
Alternate URL(s): https://www.cia.gov/cia/ciakids/index_2.shtml
Sponsor(s): Central Intelligence Agency (CIA)
Description: The CIA offers a variety of information targeted towards children. This Web site features sections including Who We Are and What We Do, Operation History, CIA Canine Corps, Aerial Photography Pigeons, Intelligence Book Lists, and Say No to Drugs. The site at the primary URL is for students in grades 6–12. The alternate URL takes users to the corresponding page for students in grades K–5.

CryptoKids™
http://www.nsa.gov/kids/intro.htm
Sponsor(s): Defense Department — National Security Agency (NSA)
Description: This site has games, activities, and background information about NSA's specialty, cryptography. The Student Resources section has NSA career information for high school and college students.

DOI Just For Kids
http://www.doi.gov/kids/
Sponsor(s): Interior Department
Description: This central Department of the Interior Web site for children links to more than a dozen pages from related agencies. Linked sites include Endangered Species, Earthquakes for Kids, Web Rangers, and Careers in Science.

Dr. E's Energy Lab: Energy Efficiency and Renewable Energy Network
http://www.eere.energy.gov/kids/
Sponsor(s): Energy Department — Energy Efficiency and Renewable Energy Office
Description: This Department of Energy page for children features links to the following sections: Energy Efficiency Tips, Wind Energy, Solar Energy, Geothermal Energy, Alternative Fuels, and General Renewable Energy.

The main page uses a simple cartoon interface, but many of the linked resources are text-heavy.

Energy Department - For Students and Kids
http://www.energy.gov/forstudentsandkids.htm
Description: This site centralizes access to Energy Department Web sites for kids and students, including energy glossaries and agency-sponsored contests and competitions. Linked sites cover a range of topics, from the relationship between garbage and energy to the Virtual Frog Dissection Kit.

Energy Kids' Page: What is Energy?
http://www.eia.doe.gov/kids/
Sponsor(s): Energy Department — Energy Information Administration (EIA)
Description: The Department of Energy's Information Administration provides this educational page. Sections include Energy Facts, Fun and Games, Energy History, Classroom Activities, and Glossary.

EPA Student Center
http://www.epa.gov/students/
Sponsor(s): Environmental Protection Agency (EPA)
Description: The EPA Student Center Web site serves as a portal to information at a variety of educational levels and offers links to a Kids' Page, a site for high schoolers, and a site for teachers. Sections include Environmental Club Projects, Environmental Youth Awards, Fun Activities, and Environmental Basics.

FBI Kids' Page
http://www.fbi.gov/fbikids.htm
Sponsor(s): Justice Department — Federal Bureau of Investigation (FBI)
Description: The FBI site provides pages for kids in kindergarten through 5th grade, such as About Our Dogs, and for those in grades 6 through 12, such as How We Investigate.

FDA Kids' Site
http://www.fda.gov/oc/opacom/kids/
Sponsor(s): Health and Human Services Department — Food and Drug Administration (FDA)
Description: The colorful FDA Web site for children presents health and safety information in several sections, including the Food Safety Quiz and All About Animals. The center box links to a page for teens, which addresses such topics as mononucleosis, tattoos, and birth control. The center box also links to the Parents' Corner, which provides information on child health and safety.

Federal Reserve Kids Page

http://www.federalreserve.gov/kids/

Sponsor(s): Federal Reserve

Description: This site has answers to twelve questions, ranging from "What is inflation?" to "What is the FOMC, and what does it do?"

The Federal Reserve has a broader education site with resources for teachers available at <http://www.federalreserveeducation.org/>.

FEMA for Kids

http://www.fema.gov/kids/

Sponsor(s): Federal Emergency Management Agency (FEMA)

Description: This FEMA site provides information and resources to help children prepare for and prevent disasters. The Get Ready, Get Set section has information and activities about preparing for a disaster, and the Disaster Area section gives details about 10 kinds of disasters (including hurricanes and tornadoes). The Disaster Connections section has children's artwork, poems, and letters with their thoughts on disasters such as tornadoes and the 9-11 attacks. A section called For the Little Ones has games and coloring pages. The site also uses audio and video in appropriate places.

FEMA has done an excellent job pulling together a Web site of resources that explains disasters to children without scaring them.

FirstGov for Kids

http://www.kids.gov/

Sponsor(s): General Services Administration (GSA)

Description: This FirstGov for Kids Web site is a portal to Web pages designed for children. Annotated links are arranged by topic, such as Careers, Geography, History, Homework, Safety, and Space. Each topic features government Web pages but also links to Web sites from commercial, educational, and other sources.

FirstGov for Kids is an easy way for children (as well as teachers and parents) to find kid-friendly information on the Web. It is particularly helpful as an index to government Web pages for children. A few commercial sites require login information or are more appropriate for teachers, but many have appropriate content that is low in advertising.

GirlsHealth.gov

http://girlshealth.gov/

Sponsor(s): Health and Human Services Department

Description: GirlsHealth.gov is designed to help adolescent girls (ages 10 to 16) learn about the health issues and social situations that they will encounter during their teenage years. Sections provide information about fitness, nutrition, the mind, relationships, and other related topics. The site also has sections for parents, caregivers, and teachers.

HHS Pages for Kids

http://www.hhs.gov/kids/

Sponsor(s): Health and Human Services Department

Description: This page links to various kids' pages offered by agencies related to the Department of Health and Human Services. They distribute information about health, avoiding cigarettes and drugs, food safety, and more.

Indian Health Service Native American KIDS page

http://www.ihs.gov/PublicInfo/Publications/Kids/

Sponsor(s): Health and Human Services Department — Indian Health Services (IHS)

Description: This site is divided into sections for children's content on health, safety, Native American culture, and Native American stories. Some of the links lead to material developed for the IHS; others lead to kids' pages at other federal agencies. The McGruff link to the left of the page leads to the Department of Justice's McGruff® and Scruff's® Drug and Violence Prevention Story and Activity Book Web site, which features Indian Country themes.

Justice for Kids and Youth

http://www.usdoj.gov/kidspage/

Sponsor(s): Justice Department

Description: The Department of Justice page for youth provides information about the department and its agencies, primarily the FBI. Information is arranged by category, including Kids (grades K–5), Youth (grades 6–12), Teachers and Parents, and Subjects. Links from the home page lead to special subject sections, such as Inside the Courtroom, Get

It Straight (the Facts about Drugs), Civil Rights, and Cyberethics for Kids.

Kidd Safety

http://www.cpsc.gov/kids/kidsafety/

Sponsor(s): Consumer Product Safety Commission (CPSC)

Description: The Kidd Safety page uses a cartoon goat named Kidd to guide users through games and information about safety. The site covers topics such as bicycle helmets, riding a scooter, and safety around the house.

Kids and Families — Social Security

http://www.ssa.gov/kids/

Sponsor(s): Social Security Administration (SSA)

Description: This SSA Web site includes a Kids' Place section and a Parents' Place section. The Kids' Place offers tales about saving for the future and an introduction to the Social Security card. On the main page, there is also a link to information for the families of youth with disabilities.

Kids' Corner, Endangered Species Program

http://endangered.fws.gov/kids/

Sponsor(s): Interior Department — Fish and Wildlife Service (FWS)

Description: This site features a selection of educational activities about endangered species, most designed to be used by a teacher or parent for the benefit of young learners. The "Endangered Means There is Still Time" activity includes slide shows, a quiz, an activity workbook, and teachers' resources. The site also links to related programs from inside and outside the government, such as the Junior Duck Stamp Program and the National Wildlife Federation's Backyard Wildlife Habitats program.

Kids in the House

http://clerkkids.house.gov/

Sponsor(s): Congress — House of Representatives — Office of the Clerk

Description: The House Clerk's Web site for kids includes material (written primarily for upper grade or high school students) that provides information on House procedures and history. It also discusses how bills are made into law. Features include a cartoon field trip to Capitol Hill, games, and resources for parents and teachers.

Kids Next Door

http://www.hud.gov/kids/kids.html

Sponsor(s): Housing and Urban Development (HUD)

Description: HUD's Web site for children is subtitled "Where kids can learn more about being good citizens." The page features sections including Meet Cool People, See Neat Things, and Visit Awesome Places. Within each of these sections are activities and pages such as Help the Homeless, Kids Volunteer, Safe Places to Play, and Build A Community.

Kid's Zone, Pablo's Classroom

http://www.yesicankids.gov

Alternate URL(s): http://www.yosipuedo.gov/kidszone/kidszone3.html

Sponsor(s): President's Advisory Commission on Educational Excellence for Hispanic Americans

Description: Featuring the cartoon character Pablo the Eagle, this kids' page is part of the White House Initiative on Educational Excellence for Hispanic Americans. Reflecting the initiative's emphasis on reading skills, the site has a collection of bedtime stories with color illustrations. The site also has a Spanish-language version, available at the alternate URL above.

MyPyramid for Kids

http://www.fns.usda.gov/tn/kids-pyramid.html

Sponsor(s): Agriculture Department (USDA) — Food and Nutrition Service (FNS)

Description: The MyPyramid for Kids Web site provides nutrition education resources for teachers and parents of elementary school children. Resources include a MyPyramid for Kids poster, coloring page, and worksheet in PDF format. Classroom materials on the site include three lesson plans. The site also has a "Tips for Families" color brochure. The MyPyramid Blast Off game is intended for use by children.

NASA Kids

http://www.nasa.gov/audience/forkids/home/

Alternate URL(s): http://www.nasa.gov/audience/forstudents/

Sponsor(s): National Aeronautics and Space Administration (NASA) — Education Office

Description: The NASA Kids page features games, stories, and activities related to space and science.

The alternate URL above links to the NASA For Students page, which has sections for students in grades K–4, 5–8, 9–12, and postsecondary levels. Both the Kids page and the For Students page are part of a comprehensive NASA Education Web site at <http://education.nasa.gov/home/>.

NCEH Kids' Page
http://www.cdc.gov/nceh/kids/99kidsday/
Sponsor(s): Health and Human Services Department — Centers for Disease Control and Prevention (CDC) — National Center for Environmental Health (NCEH)
Description: Designed for the young reader, the site is based on *Take Your Children to Work Day*, a booklet created by NCEH for its employees' children to introduce them to the work of the agency. Its sections include Asthma, Cruise Ship Inspection, Disabilities, Emergency Response, Global Health, and Lead Poisoning. The booklet is available as a PDF version that may be downloaded and printed. It is also available in Spanish.

NIEHS' Kids Pages
http://www.niehs.nih.gov/kids/home.htm
Sponsor(s): National Institutes of Health (NIH) — National Institute of Environmental Health Sciences (NIEHS)
Description: This Kids Page offering from the NIEHS has both a Spanish-language and a text-only version. It includes sections such as Games and Activities, Color Our World, and Environmental Health Science Education. It also has a page for kids about pandemic flu.

NROjr.GOV
http://www.nrojr.gov/
Sponsor(s): Defense Department — National Reconnaissance Office (NRO)
Description: The NRO kids' page features games and activities with a satellite and space theme. With content offering simple online coloring pages, stories, and music, it is aimed at the younger set.

Patent and Trademark Office Kids' Page
http://www.uspto.gov/go/kids/
Sponsor(s): Commerce Department — Patent and Trademark Office (PTO)
Description: The PTO Web site offers children's contests, games, and puzzles having to do with creativity, invention, and the operations of the PTO. The site has sections designed for students in grades K–6 and 6–12, as well as information for parents, teachers, and coaches.

Peace Corps Kids' World
http://www.peacecorps.gov/kids/
Sponsor(s): Peace Corps
Description: The Peace Corps offers this kids' page, with sections including: What is the Peace Corps?; Make a Difference; Explore the World; Tell Me a Story; and Food, Friends, and Fun. This site mainly provides information about the Peace Corps program. Some resources on foreign countries are listed in the Explore the World and Food, Friends, and Fun sections.

Safety City
http://www.nhtsa.dot.gov/kids/
Sponsor(s): Transportation Department — National Highway Traffic Safety Administration (NHTSA)
Description: Vince and Larry, the NHTSA's crash test dummies, serve as the guides for this children's Web site, which provides information on vehicle safety. The site features sections such as Safety School, Bike Tour, and School Bus Safety.

Sci4Kids
http://www.ars.usda.gov/is/kids/
Alternate URL(s):
http://www.ars.usda.gov/is/espanol/kids/
Sponsor(s): Agriculture Department (USDA) — Agricultural Research Service (ARS)
Description: Sci4Kids is designed for children between the ages of 8 and 13 years. With a colorful all-graphics menu, it shows how scientific research affects many areas of life. The site includes information about careers in science. The alternate URL links to the Spanish-language version of the site.

ScienceLab
http://www.osti.gov/sciencelab/
Sponsor(s): Energy Department — Scientific and Technical Information Office
Description: ScienceLab links to student resources at government and other Web sites. Major sections for students include Elementary Lab, Middle School Lab, High School Lab, and Experiments. The site also has a Teachers' Lab section and sections with information about science careers, competitions, and summer camps.

Smithsonian Education

http://www.smithsonianeducation.org/students/
Sponsor(s): Smithsonian Institution
Description: The Smithsonian Web site for kids and students includes sections called Mr. President, Walking on the Moon, and Amazing Collections. The section called At the Smithsonian links to pages of interest to kids from many Smithsonian Web sites.

Much of the content will be of interest to students in the upper grades through high school and their parents. The site will be particularly helpful for kids preparing to visit Smithsonian museums.

Space Place

http://spaceplace.jpl.nasa.gov/spacepl.htm
Alternate URL(s):http://spaceplace.jpl.nasa.gov/sp/kids/index.shtml
Sponsor(s): National Aeronautics and Space Administration (NASA) — Jet Propulsion Laboratory (JPL)
Description: Space Place is full of games, projects, and animations relating to earth and space science. The Teachers' Corner has classroom activity articles. A Spanish-language version of the Web site can be accessed via a link at the top of the site's home page or from the alternate URL listed above.

Stop Bullying Now

http://www.stopbullyingnow.hrsa.gov/
Sponsor(s): Health and Human Services Department — Health Resources and Services Administration (HRSA)
Description: This site has information and activities for kids about dealing with bullying behavior. The portion of the site for adults and educators is also available in Spanish.

This site makes extensive use of animation, sound, and features such as webcasts and podcasts. There does not appear to be a text-only version available.

Tobacco Information and Prevention Source (TIPS) for Youth

http://www.cdc.gov/tobacco/tips4youth.htm
Sponsor(s): Health and Human Services Department — Centers for Disease Control and Prevention (CDC) — National Center for Chronic Disease Prevention and Health Promotion (NCCDPHP)
Description: TIPS4Youth links to an extensive list of resources providing information to young peo-ple about smoking. The resources include content aimed directly at kids as well as material (such as videos and program guides) for adults organizing anti-smoking campaigns for children. The site also features *SGR 4 Kids*, the Surgeon General's Report for Kids about Smoking.

ToxMystery

http://toxmystery.nlm.nih.gov/
Sponsor(s): National Institutes of Health (NIH) — National Library of Medicine (NLM)
Description: ToxMystery is an interactive game designed to teach kids about dangerous household substances. The site includes sections for parents and teachers.

U.S. Army Corps of Engineers Education Center

http://education.usace.army.mil/
Sponsor(s): Army — Army Corps of Engineers
Description: This site provides educational information and activities about ports, waterway navigation, engineering, and related topics.

United States Mint's Site for Kids

http://www.usmint.gov/kids/
Sponsor(s): Treasury Department — United States Mint
Description: This site is alternatively called H.I.P (History in Your Pocket)/Pocket Change. It features games and activities to teach children about the history of coins, coins around the world, and coin collecting. It includes a section for teachers.

USA Freedom Corps for Kids

http://www.usafreedomcorpskids.gov/
Sponsor(s): USA Freedom Corps
Description: This USA Freedom Corps page has sections for kids, youth, parents, and teachers—all focused on volunteering. The section for teachers has basic information on service-learning.

USFA Kids

http://www.usfa.fema.gov/kids/flash.shtm
Sponsor(s): Homeland Security Department — Federal Emergency Management Agency (FEMA) — U.S. Fire Administration
Description: USFA Kids has information on home fire safety, smoke alarms, and escaping from fire. It includes coloring pages and a Hazard House game.

VA KIDS

http://www.va.gov/kids/

Sponsor(s): Veterans Affairs Department

Description: VA KIDS has sections for grades K–5 and 6–12 and for teachers. The grades 6–12 section includes information about volunteer and scholarship opportunities. The teacher section has resource guides and contacts for finding classroom speakers.

WhiteHouseKids.Gov

http://www.whitehouse.gov/kids/

Sponsor(s): White House

Description: The White House Web site for kids features sections on White House history and traditions, tours of the White House, the First Family's pets, White House sports, and patriotism. It also features quizzes and games relating to the White House. A Parents and Teachers Guide section outlines educational activities using the site.

World Book @ NASA

http://www.nasa.gov/worldbook/

Sponsor(s): National Aeronautics and Space Administration (NASA)

Description: Through a partnership with *World Book*, the NASA Web site is offering a selection of over 40 *World Book* encyclopedia articles concerning space exploration. Entries range from "Armstrong, Neil" to "Weather."

While not strictly a kids' page, World Book @ NASA will certainly be a homework helper.

TEACHING

Federal Resources for Educational Excellence (FREE)

http://www.ed.gov/free/

Alternate URL(s) :http://www.ed.gov/free/constitution/

Sponsor(s): Education Department

Description: FREE is a central finding aid for the hundreds of Web-based teaching and learning resources supported by 50 agencies across the U.S. federal government. The Searches and Subjects section is the main access point. Recently added materials are listed in the New Resources section.

The More for Students page highlights resources particularly appropriate for K–12 students.

This is one of the most comprehensive finding aids for education-related U.S. government Web sites. Its primary focus is on K–12 resources. The special Constitution Resources section (see alternate URL above) will be helpful to educators planning for the annual Constitution Day.

James Madison Graduate Fellowships

http://www.jamesmadison.com/

Sponsor(s): James Madison Memorial Fellowship Foundation

Description: James Madison Graduate Fellowships are for teachers at the secondary school level who wish to enhance their knowledge of the U.S. Constitution. The fellowships are for graduate study leading to a master's degree. This Web site has more about the program and about the James Madison Memorial Fellowship Foundation, an independent agency within the executive branch of the U.S. government.

NCELA — National Clearinghouse for English Language Acquisition

http://www.ncela.gwu.edu/

Sponsor(s): Education Department — English Language Acquisition Office

Description: NCELA, known in full as the National Clearinghouse for English Language Acquisition and Language Instruction Educational Programs and funded by the Department of Education, is concerned with the effective education of linguistically and culturally diverse learners in the United States. The NCELA Web site provides direct access to a wealth of information on research, funding, and technical assistance for teaching English language learners.

What Works Clearinghouse (WWC)

http://www.whatworks.ed.gov/

Sponsor(s): Education Department — Institute of Education Sciences

Description: WWC collects and reviews studies of the effectiveness of educational programs and practices. The studies and reviews are available in the Products section. The site also has information about the review process and offers an open invitation to submit studies or topics.

INDEX